The Thomas Guide®

Y0-ELK-081

SANTA BARBARA AND SAN LUIS OBISPO COUNTIES

OUR MAPS ARE PUBLISHED TO PROVIDE ACCURATE STREET INFORMATION AND TO ASSIST IN RELATING DEMOGRAPHICS AND CULTURAL FEATURES TO STREET GEOGRAPHY. HOWEVER, THIS PRODUCT IS BEING SOLD ON AN "AS-IS" BASIS AND WE ASSUME NO LIABILITY FOR DAMAGES ARISING FROM ERRORS OR OMISSIONS.

Thomas Bros. Maps®
A RAND MᶜNALLY COMPANY

Call Toll Free:
1-800-899-MAPS
1-800-899-6277

Corporate Office & Showroom
17731 Cowan, Irvine, CA 92614 (949) 863-1984 or 1-888-826-6277
Thomas Bros. Maps & Books
550 Jackson St., San Francisco, CA 94133 (415) 981-7520 or 1-800-969-3072
521 W. 6th St., Los Angeles, CA 90014 (213) 627-4018 or 1-888-277-6277
Customer Service: 1-800-899-6277
World Wide Web: www.thomas.com
e-mail: comments@thomas.com
For more information regarding licensing and copyright permission, please contact us at:
licensing@thomas.com

Introduction — INTRO

❖ How to Use	ii	❖ Key Maps	vi-vii
❖ Legend	iii	❖ Downtown Map	viii
❖ Area Maps	iv-v	❖ Cities & Communities Index	ix

Map Pages — MAP

❖ Arterial Maps	324-386
❖ Detail Maps	453-1018

Indexes — INDEX

❖ List of Abbreviations	1019
❖ Street Index	1020-1040
❖ Points of Interest Index	1041-1044

How To Use This Thomas Guide
Modo De Empleo Del Thomas Guide

To Find a City or Community:
Manera de Localizar una Ciudad o Comunidad:

Start with the Key Map to Detail Pages, then turn to the Detail Page indicated.

Empiece con el mapa clave de páginas detalladas, luego pase a la página detallada que se indica.

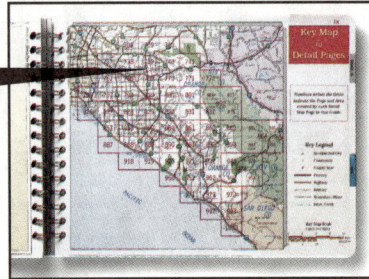

or
o

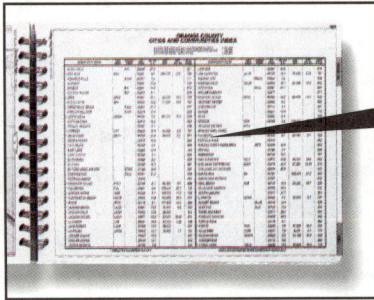

Look up the name in the Cities and Communities Index, then turn to the Detail Page indicated.

Busque el nombre en el Indice de Ciudades y Comunidades, luego pase a la página detallada que se indica.

Thomas Bros. Maps ®

A RAND M^cNALLY COMPANY

www.thomas.com

1-800-899-MAPS
1-800-899-6277

To Find an Address:
Manera de Localizar una Dirección:

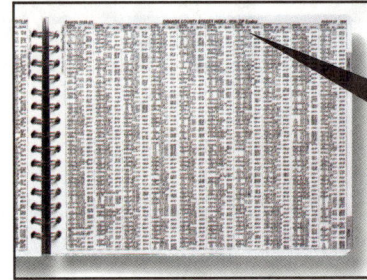

1 Look up the street name in the Street Index. If there are multiple listings, choose the proper city and/or address range. (All city abbreviations are listed in the Cities and Communities Index.)

Localice el nombre de la calle en el Indice de Calles. Si aparecen varias listas, seleccione el área apropiada de la ciudad y/o el domicilio. (Todas las abreviaturas de las ciudades figuran en la lista del Indice de Ciudades y Comunidades).

2 The street name will include a Thomas Bros. Maps Page and Grid™ where the address is located.

El nombre de la calle incluye un cuadro de Thomas Bros. Maps Page and Grid™ con el número de página y de coordenadas que indican la ubicación del domicilio.

	STREET				STREET			
Pg-Grid	Block	City	ZIP	Pg-Grid	Block	City	ZIP	Pg-Grid
	N CARTLEN DR				**CASITAS DE ALIPAZ**			
077 971-G2	1700	PLCN	92670	739-G3	32200	SJCP	92675	972-B2
R	4700	OrCo	92670	739-G3	**CASPE**			
991 892-B7	**CARTWRIGHT RD**				28500	MVJO	92692	892-F6
		IRVN	92714	859-H5	**CASPER ST**			
	CARUSO				12000	GGR	92645	797-D5

3 Turn to the Page indicated.

Pase a la página que se indica.

4 Locate the address by following the indicated Letter column and Number row until the two intersect. The street name is within this Grid area.

Localice el domicilio siguiendo la columna con letras y la hilera con números indicadas hasta que intersecten. El nombre de la calle se encuentra dentro de dicho cuadro.

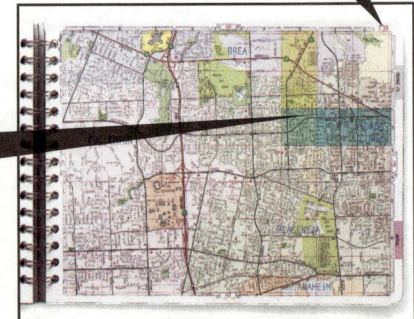

LEGEND OF MAP SYMBOLS

NORTH

Symbol	Description
	Freeway
	Interchange/Ramp
	Highway
	Primary Road
	Secondary Road
	Minor Road
	Restricted Road
	Alley
	Unpaved Road
	Tunnel
	Toll Road
	High Occupancy Veh. Lane
	Stacked Multiple Roadways
	Proposed Road
	Proposed Freeway
	Freeway Under Construction
	One-Way Road
	Two-Way Road
	Trail, Walkway
	Stairs
	Railroad
	Rapid Transit
	Rapid Transit, Underground
	City Boundary
	County Boundary
	State Boundary
	International Boundary
	Military Base, Indian Resv.
	Township, Range, Rancho
	River, Creek, Shoreline
	Ferry
	ZIP Code Boundary

93101

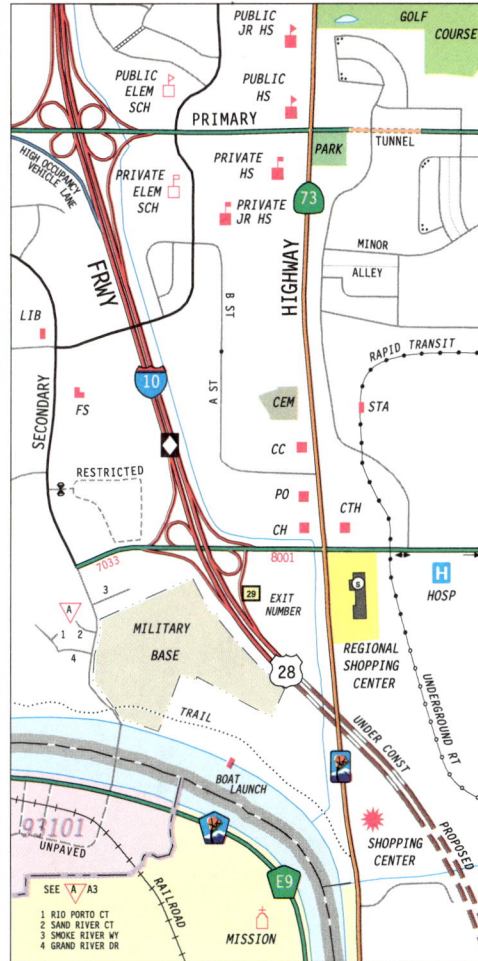

Symbol	Description
5	Interstate
5	Interstate (Business)
3	U.S. Highway
1	State Highway
2	County Highway
	State Scenic Highway
	County Scenic Highway
	Carpool Lane
A	Street List Marker
	Street Name Continuation
•	Street Name Change
	Airport
	Station (Train, Bus)
	Building (see List of Abbr. page)
	Building Footprint
	Public Elementary School
	Public High School
	Private Elementary School
	Private High School
	Shopping Center
	Fire Station
	Library
	Mission
	Winery
	Campground
H	Hospital
	Mountain
	Boat Launch
	Gates, Locks, Barricades
	Lighthouse

Symbol	Description
	County Seat
	County
	Incorporated City
	Incorporated City
	Incorporated City
	Incorporated City
	Incorporated City
	Incorporated City
	City, County, State Park
	National Forest, Park
	Water
	Intermittent Lake, Marsh
	Dry Lake, Beach
	Dam
	Point of Interest
	Golf Course, Country Club
	Cemetery
	Military Base
	Airport
	Parking Lot
	Structure Footprint
	Regional Shopping Center
S	Major Dept. Store (List of Abbr. page)

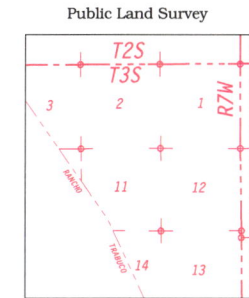

Public Land Survey

T2S
T3S
R7W

3   2   1

11   12

14   13

Detail Map Scale
1 Inch to 2400 Feet

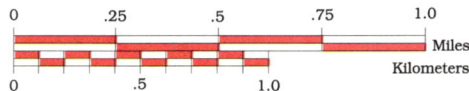

0   .25   .5   .75   1.0   Miles
0   .5   1.0   Kilometers

Detail Grid Equivalents
1 Grid Equals:
.5 x .5 Miles
2640 x 2640 Feet
1.1 x 1.1 Inches

Arterial Map Scale
1 Inch to 5 Miles

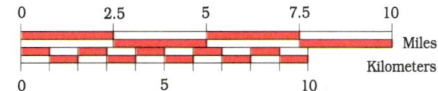

0   2.5   5   7.5   10   Miles
0   5   10   Kilometers

Arterial Grid Equivalents
1 Grid Equals:
1 Detail Page
4.5 x 3.5 Miles
.9 x .7 Inches

326

325

324

PACIFIC

OCEAN

344

346

345

365

366

AREA MAP

- Interstate
- U.S. Highway
- State Highway
- County Highway
- Freeway
- Highway
- Primary Road
- Urbanized Areas
- National Forest
- State Park
- Military Base

1 Inch to 14 Miles

0   7   14   21   28

Miles

0   14   28

Kilometers

PACIFIC OCEAN

SAN LUIS OBISPO

PASO ROBLES

ATASCADERO

MORRO BAY

PISMO BEACH

ARROYO GRANDE

GROVER BEACH

GUADALUPE

SANTA MARIA

LOMPOC

BUELLTON

SOLVANG

SANTA BARBARA

CARPINTERIA

VENTURA

OJAI

SANTA PAULA

BAKERSFIELD

WASCO

SHAFTER

DELANO

TAFT

MARICOPA

LOS PADRES NATIONAL FOREST

VANDENBERG AIR FORCE BASE

KERN NATIONAL WILDLIFE REFUGE

SANTA BARBARA CHANNEL

346

348

345

366

367

368

365

385

386

387

388

PACIFIC

OCEAN

LOS PADRES NATIONAL FOREST

SAN RAFAEL WILDERNESS AREA

LOS PADRES NATIONAL FOREST

ANGELES NATIONAL FOREST

ANGELES NATIONAL FOREST

SESPE CONDOR PRESERVE

HUNGRY VALLEY STATE VEHICULAR REC AREA

CASTAIC LAKE STATE REC AREA

EDWARDS AIR FORCE BASE

DESERT TORTOISE NATURAL AREA

CALIFORNIA CITY

ROGERS LAKE

ROSAMOND LAKE

BUCKHORN LAKE

KERN CO
VENTURA CO

KERN CO
LOS ANGELES CO

LANCASTER

PALMDALE

ROSAMOND

PEARBLOSSOM

SANTA CLARITA

SAN FERNANDO

BURBANK

GLENDALE

MONROVIA

AZUSA

PASADENA

ALHAMBRA

COVINA

POMONA

MONTEBELLO

WHITTIER

DOWNEY

LA MIRADA

FULLERTON

PLACENTIA

ANAHEIM

SANTA ANA

WESTMINSTER

GARDEN GROVE

COSTA MESA

LONG BEACH

CARSON

COMPTON

LAKEWOOD

ARTESIA

BELLFLOWER

LOS ALAMITOS

HUNTINGTON BEACH

TORRANCE

REDONDO BEACH

HERMOSA BEACH

MANHATTAN BEACH

EL SEGUNDO

L A INT AIRPORT

INGLEWOOD

MARINA DEL REY

LOS ANGELES

BEVERLY HILLS

SANTA MONICA

MALIBU

CALABASAS

AGOURA HILLS

WESTLAKE VILLAGE

HIDDEN HILLS

THOUSAND OAKS

SIMI VALLEY

MOORPARK

CAMARILLO

OXNARD

PORT HUENEME

HUENEME

VENTURA

SAN BUENAVENTURA STATE BEACH

SANTA PAULA

FILLMORE

OJAI

CARPINTERIA

SANTA BARBARA

GOLETA

COAL OIL PT

GAVIOTA STATE PARK

REFUGIO STATE BEACH

EL CAPITAN STATE BEACH

BUELLTON

SOLVANG

LAKE CACHUMA

GIBRALTAR RESERVOIR

JAMESON LAKE

LAKE CASITAS

RINCON PT

PT MUGU

POINT MUGU STATE PARK

SANTA MONICA MTNS NAT REC AREA

TOPANGA STATE PARK

PT DUME

RONALD REAGAN FRWY

CHANNEL ISLANDS NATIONAL PARK

SANTA CRUZ ISLAND

SANTA ROSA ISLAND

ANACAPA ISLAND

ANACAPA PASSAGE

SANTA BARBARA CHANNEL

SANTA CRUZ CHANNEL

SANTA BARBARA CHANNEL

PORT HUENEME HARBOR

LOS ANGELES HARBOR

HUNTINGTON HARBOUR

RANCHO PALOS VERDES

TAFT

MARICOPA

PASO

PYRAMID LAKE

CASTAIC LAKE

FRAZIER MTN PARK

SANTA CLARA RIVER

VENTURA RIVER

LOS ANGELES RIVER

SAN GABRIEL RIVER

LOS PADRES NATIONAL FOREST

Key Map to Detail Pages

The Thomas Guide® contains two types of map pages: Arterial and Detail

325 Arterial Page–Small scale area map, shown with a wide border

494 Detail Page–Full scale map page, shown with a solid thin border

Key Legend

- ○ Community
- ▬▬ Freeway
- ▬▬ Highway
- ─── Primary
- ─── Secondary, Minor
- ─── River, Creek

Key Map Scale
1 Inch to 10 Miles

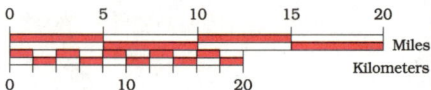

0 5 10 15 20 Miles
0 10 20 Kilometers

COPYRIGHT 2000 Thomas Bros. Maps ®

324   325

344   345

469 470 471 472
469 494
513 514
533 534
528
548
572 573 574
590 591 593
611 612 613
631 632 633
651 652 653 654
673 674
693 694 695
713
734 735 736 737
754 755 756
774 775 776 777
795 796 797
816 817

SEE vii MAP

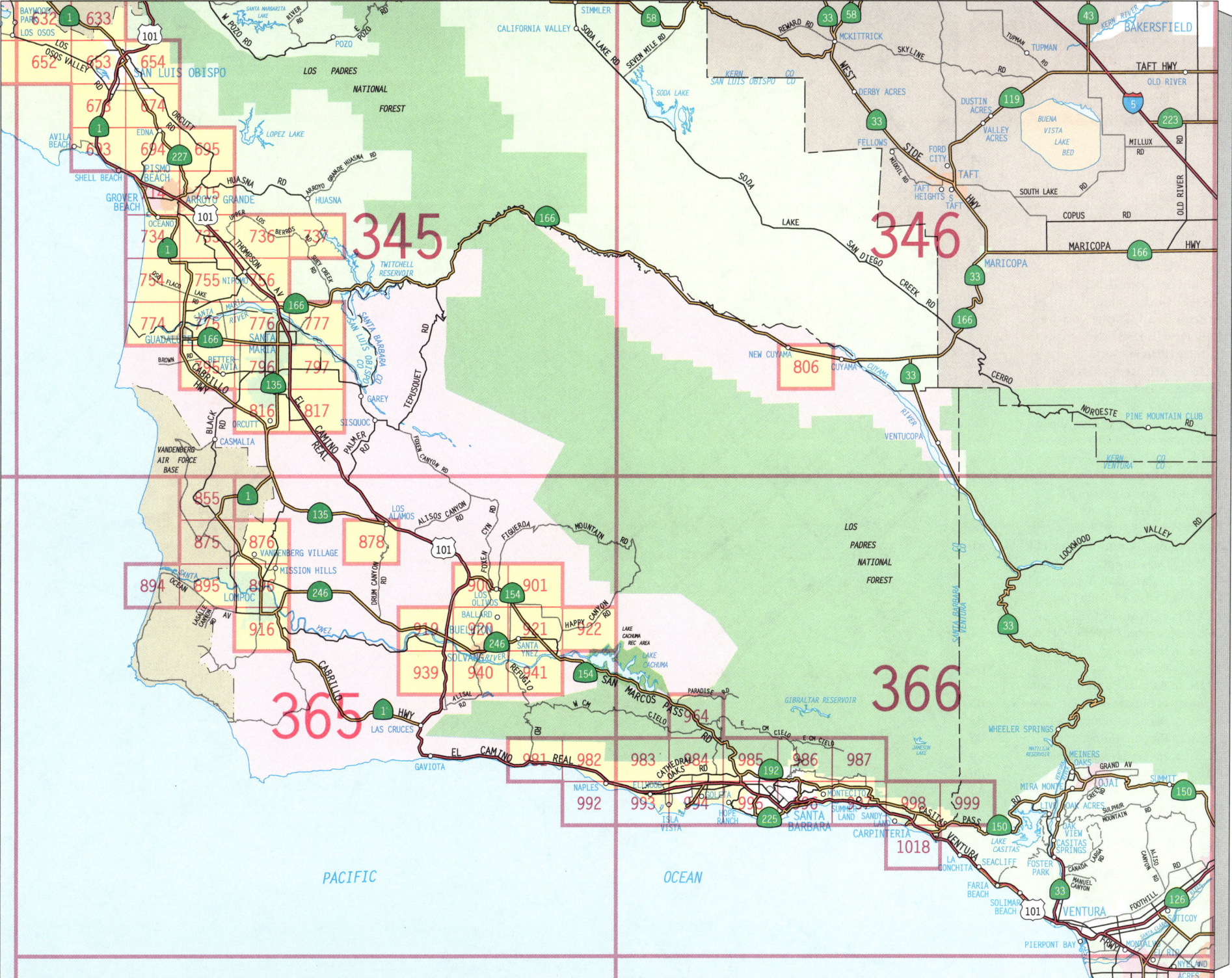

STB & SLO

INTRO

345

346

365

366

BAYWOOD PARK
LOS OSOS
632 633
652 653 654
SAN LUIS OBISPO
673 674
AVILA BEACH
693 694 695
SHELL BEACH
PISMO BEACH
GROVER BEACH
ARROYO GRANDE
OCEANO
734 735 736 737
754 FLACO 755 756
774 775 776 777
GUADALUPE
SANTA MARIA
796 797
816 817
855
875 876 878
LOMPOC
894 895 896
916
VANDENBERG VILLAGE
MISSION HILLS
LOS ALAMOS
901
905 LOS OLIVOS
BALLARD
919 920 921 922
BUELLTON
SOLVANG
SANTA YNEZ
939 940 941
LAS CRUCES
GAVIOTA
EL CAMINO REAL
981 982 983 984 985 986 987
992 993 994 996 998 999
NAPLES
GOLETA
ISLA VISTA
HOPE RANCH
SANTA BARBARA
MONTECITO
SUMMERLAND
CARPINTERIA
LA CONCHITA
1018

LOS PADRES NATIONAL FOREST

SANTA MARGARITA LAKE
POZO
LOPEZ LAKE
TWITCHELL RESERVOIR

PACIFIC OCEAN

CALIFORNIA VALLEY
SIMMLER
SODA LAKE
KERN CO
SAN LUIS OBISPO CO
NEW CUYAMA
806
CUYAMA
VENTUCOPA

BAKERSFIELD
McKITTRICK
DERBY ACRES
TAFT HWY
OLD RIVER
DUSTIN ACRES
VALLEY ACRES
TAFT
TAFT HEIGHTS
SOUTH LAKE
BUENA VISTA LAKE BED
MILLUX
COPUS
MARICOPA

FELLOWS
FORD CITY
WEST SIDE HWY
SAN DIEGO CREEK RD

LOS PADRES NATIONAL FOREST

KERN CO
VENTURA CO

PINE MOUNTAIN CLUB
LOCKWOOD VALLEY

WHEELER SPRINGS
MEINERS OAKS
OJAI
MIRA MONTE
OAK VIEW
CASITAS SPRINGS
FOSTER PARK
LAKE CASITAS
SANTA BARBARA
VENTURA
SEACLIFF
FARIA BEACH
SOLIMAR BEACH
PIERPONT BAY

VANDENBERG AIR FORCE BASE
CAMINO REAL
CABRILLO HWY

SAN MARCOS PASS

GIBRALTAR RESERVOIR
LAKE CACHUMA REC AREA
LAKE CACHUMA
JAMESON LAKE

Downtown Santa Barbara

Points of Interest

1 Amtrak Santa Barbara Station — D5
2 Arlington Theatre — B3
3 Bus Station — B4
4 Casa De Covarrubias & Lugo Adobe — C4
5 Casa De La Guerra — C4
6 City Public Works — D4
7 County Welfare Department — C4
8 De La Guerra Plaza — C4
9 Department of Motor Vehicles — C5
10 El Presidio De Santa Barbara State Historic Park — C4
11 Fernald House & Trussell–Winchester Adobe — C6
12 Granada Theater — B4
13 Guardhouse & Miranda Adobe — C4
14 Harbormasters Office/Police Station — D7
15 Historical Society Museum — C4
16 Lobero Theater — C4
17 Mission Santa Barbara — A1
18 Moreton Bay Fig Tree — D5
19 Museum of Art — B4
20 Museum of Natural History — A1
21 Police Department — C3
22 Saint Francis Medical Center — B2
23 Santa Barbara County Bowl — C2
24 Santa Barbara Central Library — B4
25 Santa Barbara Chamber Of Commerce — B4
26 Santa Barbara City College — C7
27 Santa Barbara City Hall — C4
28 Santa Barbara Co Adminstration & Board of Supervisors — B3
29 Santa Barbara County Courthouse — B3
30 Santa Barbara Harbor — D7
31 Santa Barbara News –Press — C4
32 Stearns Wharf — E6
33 Upham Hotel — A4
34 Victoria Court — B4
35 Visitors & Convention Bureau — C4
36 Visitors Center — D5

Map Scale

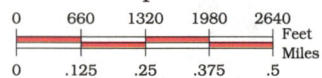

```
0    660   1320  1980  2640
|————|————|————|————|  Feet
0   .125   .25  .375   .5
|————|————|————|————|  Miles
```

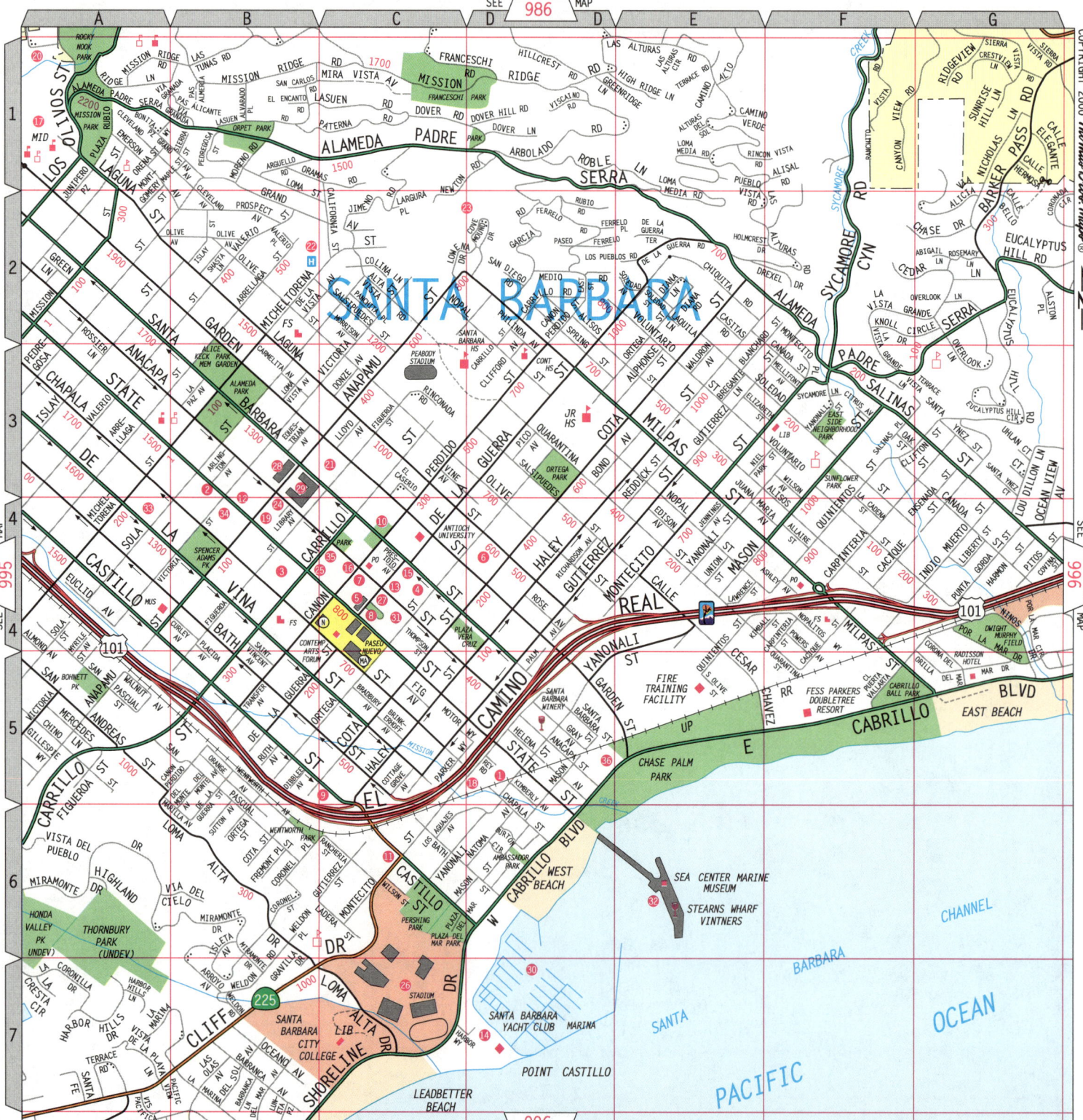

CITIES AND COMMUNITIES
Santa Barbara County

Community Name	Abbr.	ZIP Code	Map Page
BALLARD		93463	920
BETTERAVIA		93455	795
❖ BUELLTON	BLTN	93427	919
❖ CARPINTERIA	CARP	93013	998
CASMALIA		93429	345
CUYAMA		93214	346
ELLWOOD		93117	993
GAREY		93454	345
GAVIOTA		93117	365
GOLETA		93111	994
❖ GUADALUPE	GDLP	93434	775
HOPE RANCH		93110	995
ISLA VISTA		93117	993
LAS CRUCES		93117	365
❖ LOMPOC	LMPC	93436	896
LOS ALAMOS		93440	878
LOS OLIVOS		93441	900
MISSION HILLS		93436	896
MONTECITO		93108	996
NAPLES		93117	992
NEW CUYAMA		93254	806
ORCUTT		93455	816
SANDYLAND		93013	998
❖ SANTA BARBARA	SBAR	93101	996
-- SANTA BARBARA COUNTY	StBC		
❖ SANTA MARIA	SMRA	93454	796
SANTA YNEZ		93460	921
SISQUOC		93454	345
❖ SOLVANG	SLVG	93463	940
SUMMERLAND	Summ	93067	997
VANDENBERG AFB		93437	875
VANDENBERG VILLAGE		93436	876
VENTUCOPA		93252	346

❖ INDICATES INCORPORATED CITY

San Luis Obispo County

Community Name	Abbr.	ZIP Code	Map Page
ADELAIDA		93446	324
❖ ARROYO GRANDE	ARGD	93420	714
❖ ATASCADERO	ATAS	93422	573
AVILA BEACH		93424	693
BAYWOOD PARK		93402	631
BEE ROCK		93426	324
CALIFORNIA VALLEY		93453	345
CAMBRIA	Cmbr	93428	528
CAMP ROBERTS		93451	453
CAYUCOS		93430	590
CHOLAME		93431	325
CRESTON		93432	325
CUESTA BY THE SEA		93402	631
EDNA		93401	694
ESTRELLA		93451	494
GARDEN FARMS		93422	594
❖ GROVER BEACH	GBCH	93433	714
HARMONY		93435	324
HUASNA		93420	345
LOS OSOS		93402	631
❖ MORRO BAY	MOBY	93442	611
NIPOMO	Npmo	93444	756
OCEANO		93445	714
❖ PASO ROBLES	PSRS	93446	513
❖ PISMO BEACH	PBCH	93449	714
POZO		93453	345
❖ SAN LUIS OBISPO	SLO	93401	653
-- SAN LUIS OBISPO CO	SLOC		
SAN MIGUEL		93451	473
SAN SIMEON		93452	324
SANTA MARGARITA		93453	614
SHANDON		93461	325
SHELL BEACH		93449	693
SIMMLER		93453	345
TEMPLETON		93465	553
WELLSONA		93446	493
WHITLEY GARDENS		93451	325

❖ INDICATES INCORPORATED CITY

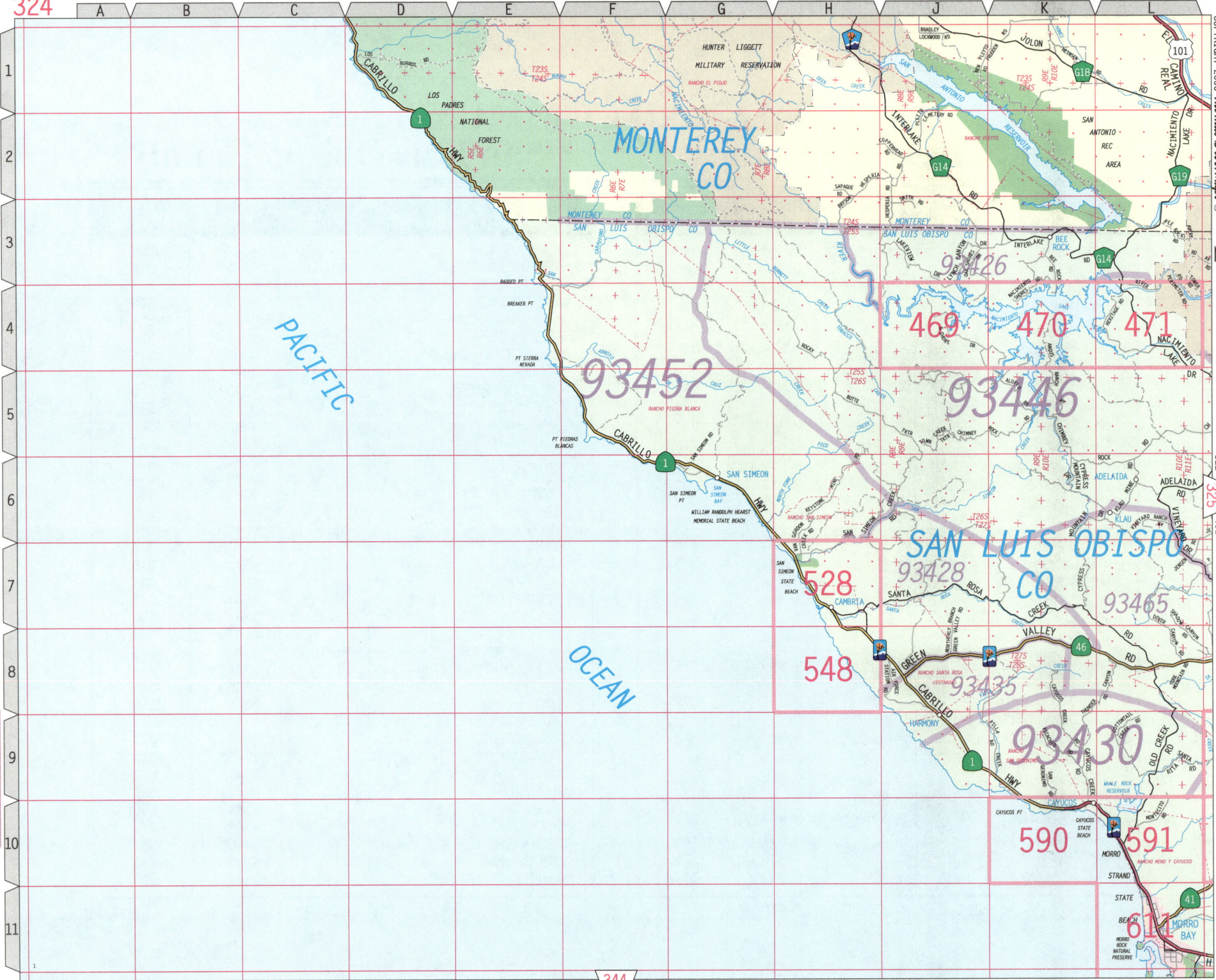

A B C D E F G H J K L

STB & SLO

—N—

101

EL CAMINO REAL

LOS BURROS RD

CABRILLO

LOS PADRES

1

NATIONAL

FOREST

HWY

MONTEREY
CO

HUNTER LIGGETT
MILITARY RESERVATION

RANCHO EL PIOJO

BRADLEY
LOCKWOOD RD

JOLON

G18

SAN ANTONIO LAKE

SAN
ANTONIO
REC
AREA

G14

G19

MONTEREY CO

SAN LUIS OBISPO CO

MONTEREY CO
SAN LUIS OBISPO CO

BEE
ROCK

93426

G14

RAGGED PT

469 470 471

BREAKER PT

NACIMIENTO LAKE

PT SIERRA
NEVADA

PACIFIC

93452

RANCHO PIEDRA BLANCA

93446

PT PIEDRAS
BLANCAS

CABRILLO

SAN SIMEON RD

1

SAN SIMEON

SAN
SIMEON
BAY

ADELAIDA

ADELAIDA RD

SAN SIMEON
PT

WILLIAM RANDOLPH HEARST
MEMORIAL STATE BEACH

RANCHO SAN SIMEON

KLAU

SEE 325 MAP

SAN LUIS OBISPO
CO

SAN SIMEON
STATE
BEACH

528

93428

CAMBRIA

SANTA

ROSA

VALLEY

93465

46

548

OCEAN

GREEN

RANCHO SANTA ROSA
(ESTRADA)

CABRILLO

93435

93430

HARMONY

1

HWY

WHALE ROCK
RESERVOIR

OLD CREEK RD

CAYUCOS

CAYUCOS PT

CAYUCOS
STATE
BEACH

590 591

MORRO

STRAND

STATE

41

611

BEACH

MORRO
BAY

MORRO
ROCK
NATURAL
PRESERVE

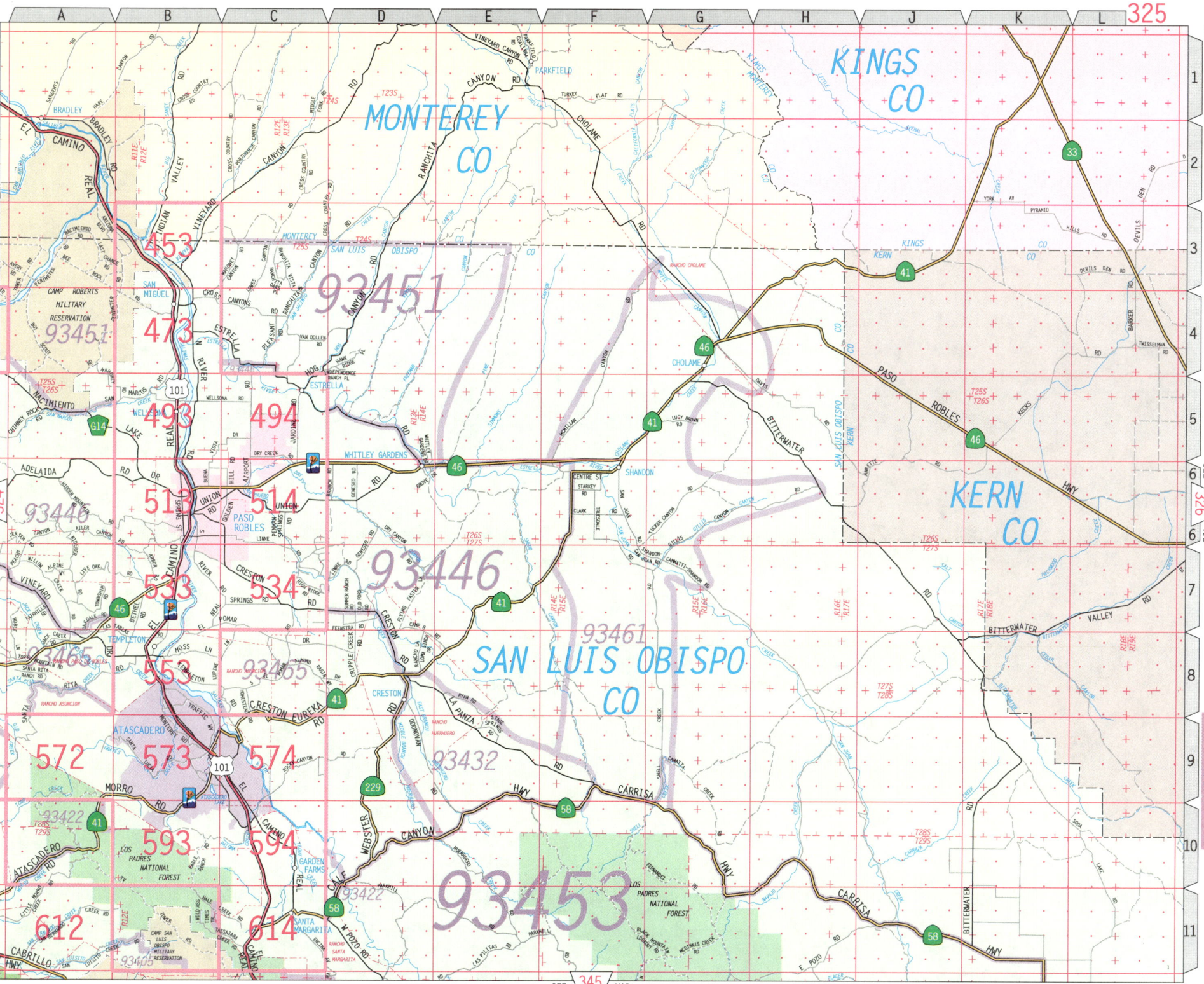

STB & SLO

KINGS CO

MONTEREY CO

KERN CO

SAN LUIS OBISPO CO

93451

93446

93461

93453

93432

93422

93465

93440

453 473 493 494 513 514 533 534 553 572 573 574 593 594 612 614

Thomas Bros. Maps
COPYRIGHT 2000

BRADLEY
EL CAMINO REAL
SAN MIGUEL
CAMP ROBERTS MILITARY RESERVATION
PASO ROBLES
ATASCADERO
TEMPLETON
CRESTON
SANTA MARGARITA
MORRO
GARDEN FARMS
EUREKA
SHANDON
CHOLAME
PARKFIELD
LOS PADRES NATIONAL FOREST
CARRISA
BITTERWATER
CAMP SAN LUIS OBISPO MILITARY RESERVATION

101 41 46 33 58 229 G14

SEE 324 MAP
SEE 326 MAP
SEE 345 MAP

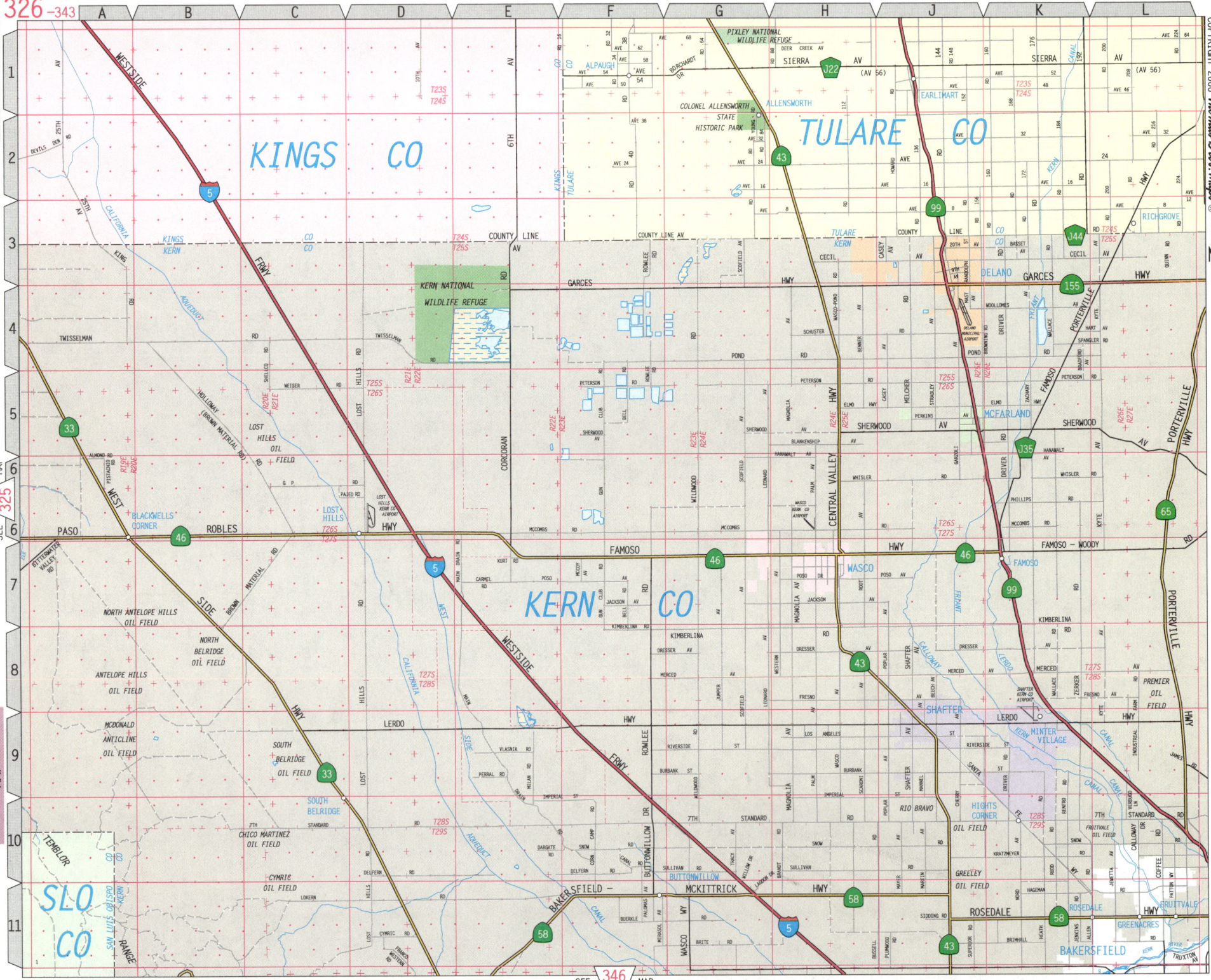

STB & SLO

SEE 325 MAP

MAP

SLO CO

KINGS CO

TULARE CO

KERN CO

PIXLEY NATIONAL WILDLIFE REFUGE

ALPAUGH

SIERRA

ALLENSWORTH

COLONEL ALLENSWORTH STATE HISTORIC PARK

EARLIMART

RICHGROVE

KERN NATIONAL WILDLIFE REFUGE

COUNTY LINE AV

GARCES HWY

DELANO

GARCES

TWISSELMAN

LOST HILLS OIL FIELD

HOLLOWAY (BROWN MATERIAL) RD

WEISER

CORCORAN

PETERSON

SHERWOOD

MCFARLAND

SHERWOOD

CENTRAL VALLEY HWY

WHISLER

PHILLIPS

BLACKWELLS CORNER

PASO ROBLES

LOST HILLS KERN CO AIRPORT

WASCO KERN CO AIRPORT

MCCOMBS

FAMOSO HWY

FAMOSO — WOODY

WASCO

FAMOSO

NORTH ANTELOPE HILLS OIL FIELD

KIMBERLINA

DRESSER

NORTH BELRIDGE OIL FIELD

ANTELOPE HILLS OIL FIELD

SHAFTER

SHAFTER KERN-CO AIRPORT

PREMIER OIL FIELD

MCDONALD ANTICLINE OIL FIELD

LERDO

RIVERSIDE

LOS ANGELES

MINTER VILLAGE

SOUTH BELRIDGE OIL FIELD

VLASNIK

BURBANK ST

RIO BRAVO

HIGHTS CORNER OIL FIELD

FRUITVALE OIL FIELD

CHICO MARTINEZ OIL FIELD

STANDARD

SNOW

SULLIVAN

GREELEY OIL FIELD

CYMRIC OIL FIELD

BUTTONWILLOW

ROSEDALE

ROSEDALE

TEMBLOR

BAKERSFIELD — MCKITTRICK HWY

WASCO

BAKERSFIELD

GREENACRES

FRUITVALE

WESTSIDE FRWY

CALIFORNIA AQUEDUCT

COPYRIGHT 2000 Thomas Bros. Maps

SEE 346 MAP

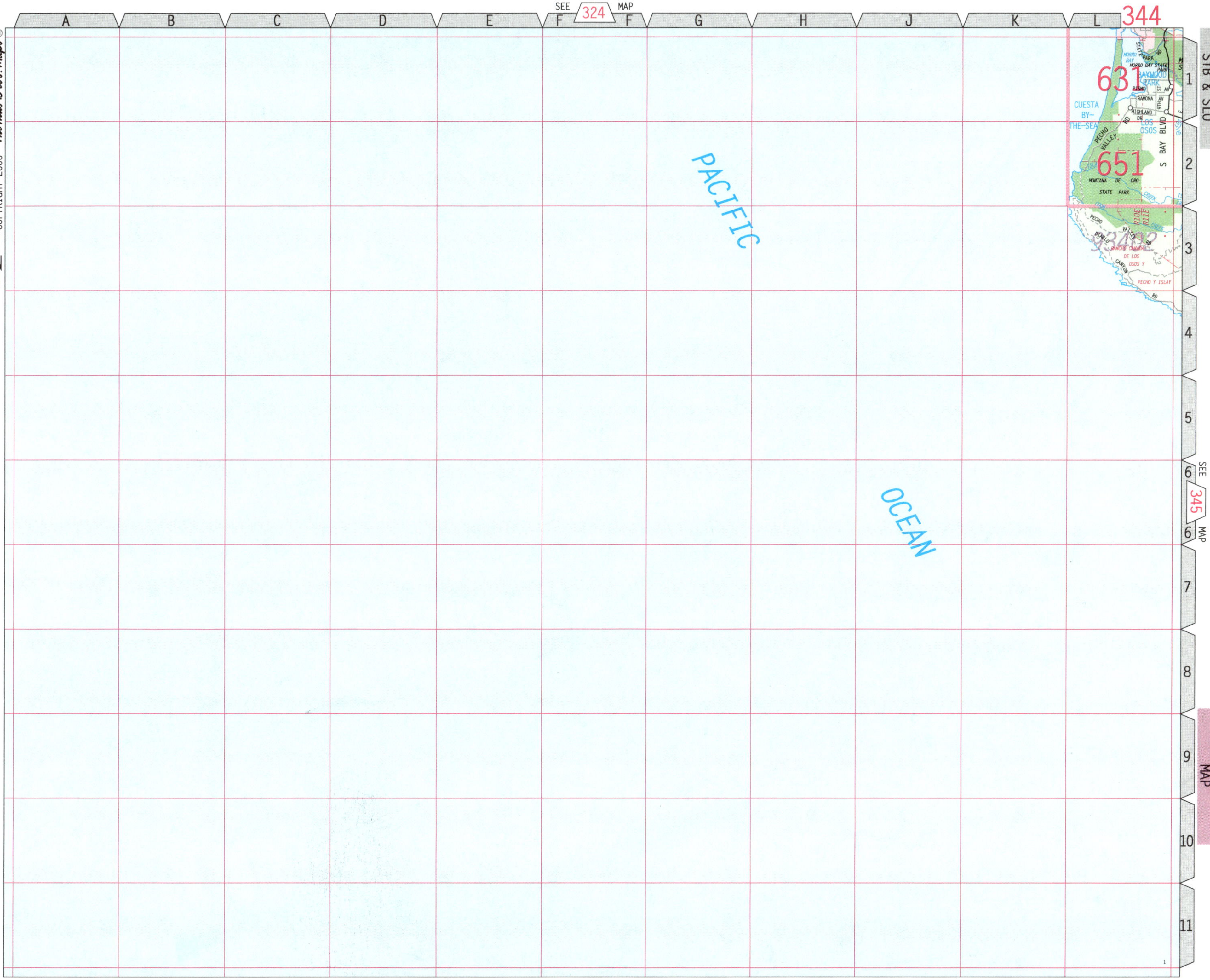

A   B   C   D   E   F   F   G   H   J   K   L

STB & SLO

631

651

3 4 4 3

PACIFIC

OCEAN

SEE 345 MAP

MAP

MORRO
BAY
STATE
PARK
MORRO BAY STATE PARK
BAYWOOD PARK
RAMONA
RAMONA AV
HIGHLAND AV
HIGHLAND
DR

CUESTA
BY-
THE-SEA

LOS
OSOS

S BAY BLVD

PECHO
VALLEY

MONTANA DE ORO
STATE PARK

R3105
R3112

PECHO
RD
PECHO

RANCHO CANADA
DE LOS
OSOS Y
PECHO Y ISLAY
RD

1
2
3
4
5
6
6
7
8
9
10
11

COPYRIGHT 2000

Thomas Bros. Maps

N

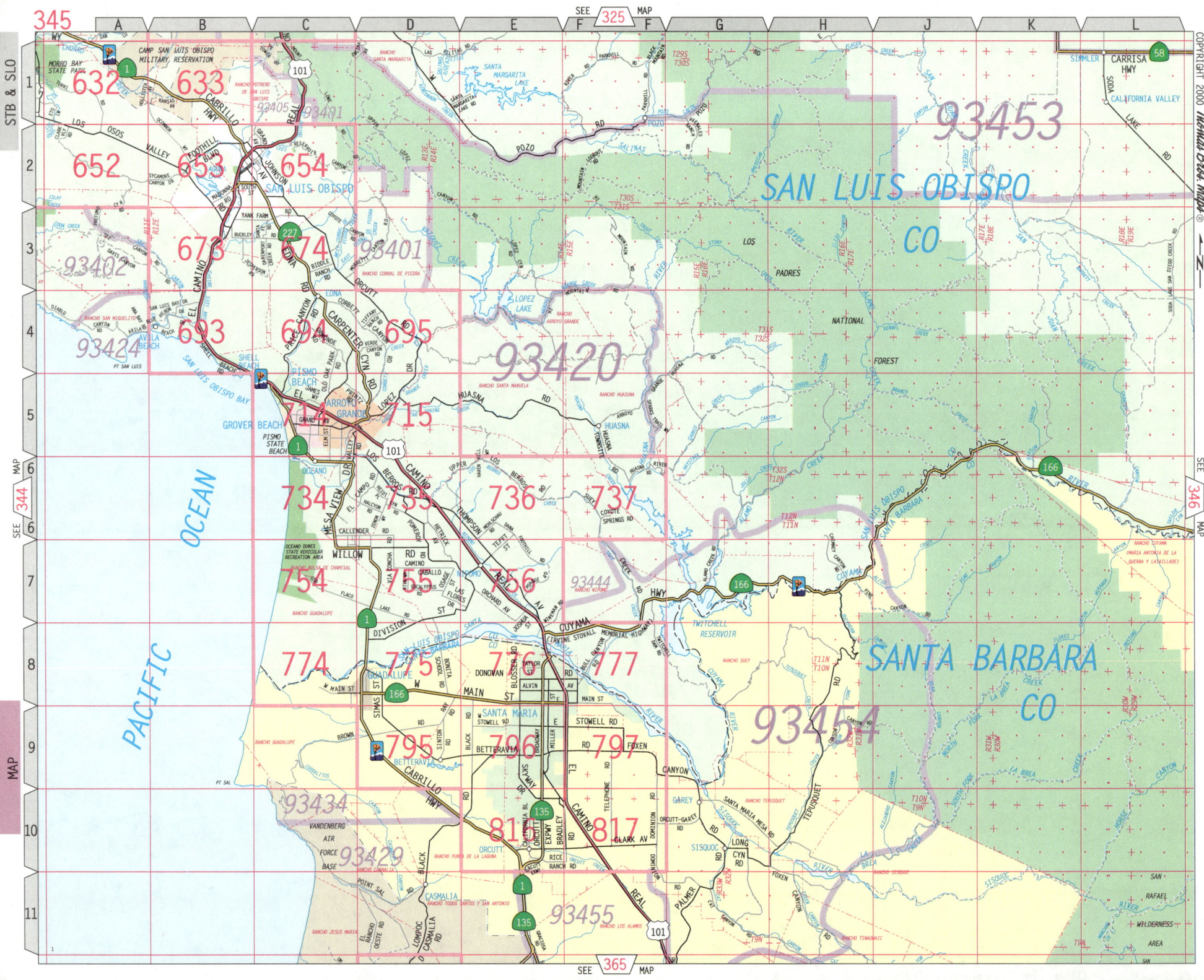

SEE 325 MAP

STB & SLO

MAP

COPYRIGHT 2000 Thomas Bros. Maps® →N

Grid columns: A B C D E F F G H J K L

Grid rows: 1 2 3 4 5 6 6 7 8 9 10 11

632 633

652 653 654

673 674 93401

93402

693 694 695

93424

714 715

734 735 736 737

754 755 756

774 775 776 777

795 706 797

815 817

93434

93429

93455

93453

SAN LUIS OBISPO CO

SANTA BARBARA CO

93420

93444

93454

Place labels:
MORRO BAY STATE PARK
CAMP SAN LUIS OBISPO MILITARY RESERVATION
SAN LUIS OBISPO
PACIFIC OCEAN
PISMO BEACH
GROVER BEACH
PISMO STATE BEACH
ARROYO GRANDE
OCEANO DUNES STATE VEHICULAR RECREATION AREA
WILLOW
AVILA BEACH
SHELL BEACH
GUADALUPE
SANTA MARIA
ORCUTT
BETTERAVIA
VANDENBERG AIR FORCE BASE
LOPEZ LAKE
SANTA MARGARITA LAKE
POZO
HUASNA
TWITCHELL RESERVOIR
CALIFORNIA VALLEY
SIMMLER
CARRISA HWY
LOS PADRES NATIONAL FOREST
PT SAN LUIS
PT SAL
POINT SAL
CASMALIA
LOMPOC
SAN RAFAEL WILDERNESS AREA

Highways: 101, 1, 227, 166, 135, 58

SEE 344 MAP
SEE 346 MAP
SEE 365 MAP

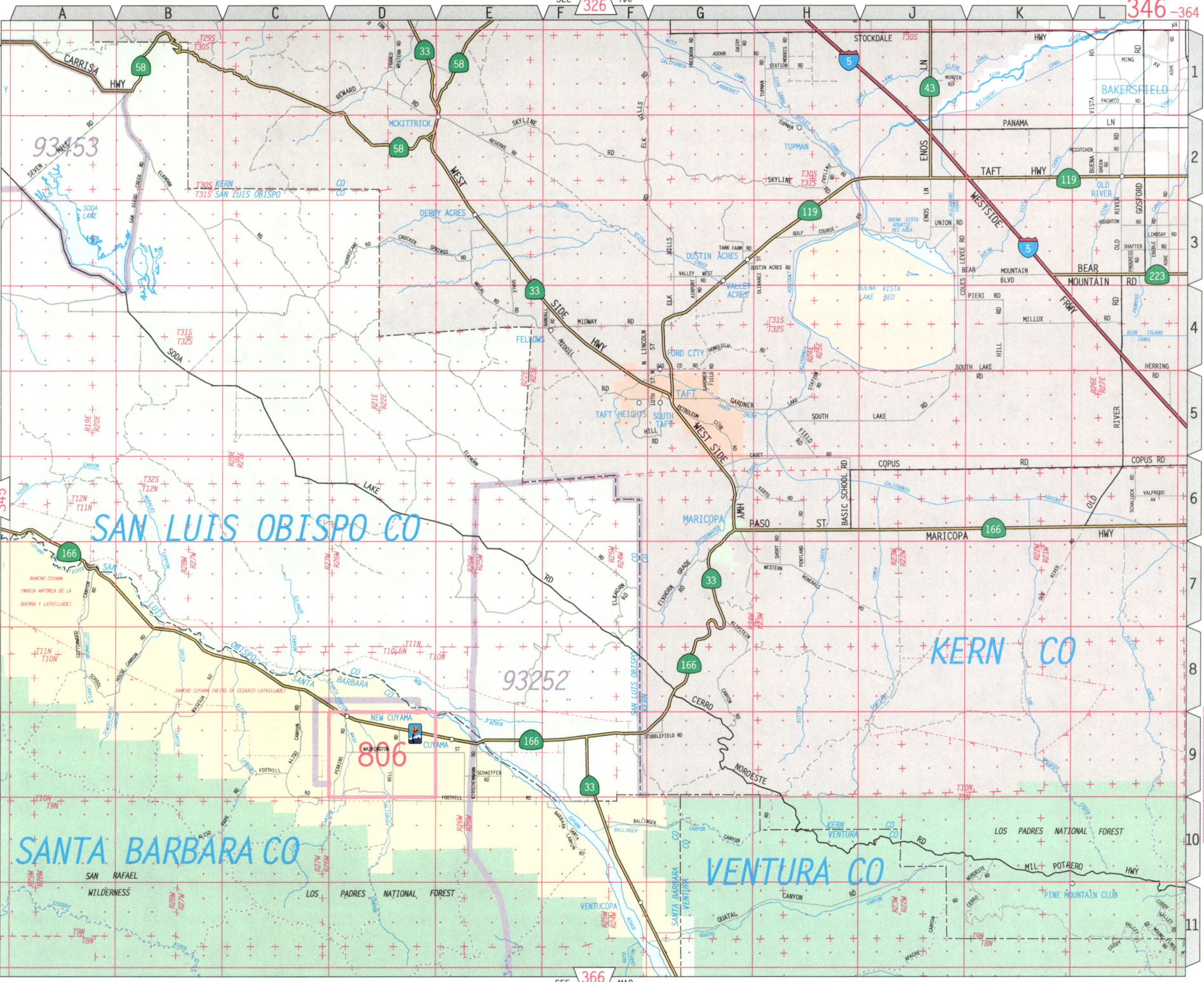

A B C D E F F G H J K L

STB & SLO

1 2 3 4 5 6 7 8 9 10 11

CARRISA HWY

58

93453

SODA LAKE

SAN DIEGO CREEK

T29S T30S

KERN CO
SAN LUIS OBISPO CO

McKITTRICK

58

58

33

WEST SIDE HWY

DERBY ACRES

CROCKER SPRINGS RD

FELLOWS

MIDWAY RD

FORD CITY

TAFT

TAFT HEIGHTS
SOUTH TAFT

SAN LUIS OBISPO CO

SODA

LAKE RD

T31S T32S

T32S T12N

T12N T11N

SAN LUIS OBISPO CO
SANTA BARBARA CO

93252

806

NEW CUYAMA
CUYAMA

SANTA BARBARA CO

SAN RAFAEL
WILDERNESS

LOS PADRES NATIONAL FOREST

STOCKDALE T30S

5

43

BAKERSFIELD

TUPMAN

PANAMA LN

SKYLINE

TAFT HWY

119

OLD RIVER

119

GOLF COURSE

BUENA VISTA AQUATIC REC AREA

DUSTIN ACRES

VALLEY ACRES

BUENA VISTA LAKE BED

5

223

BEAR MOUNTAIN RD

MILLUX

SOUTH LAKE

COPUS RD

COPUS RD

MARICOPA

PASO

166

MARICOPA HWY

33

KERN CO

166

CERRO

NOROESTE

166

33

STUBBLEFIELD RD

VENTURA CO

LOS PADRES NATIONAL FOREST

VENTUCOPA

PINE MOUNTAIN CLUB

POTRERO HWY

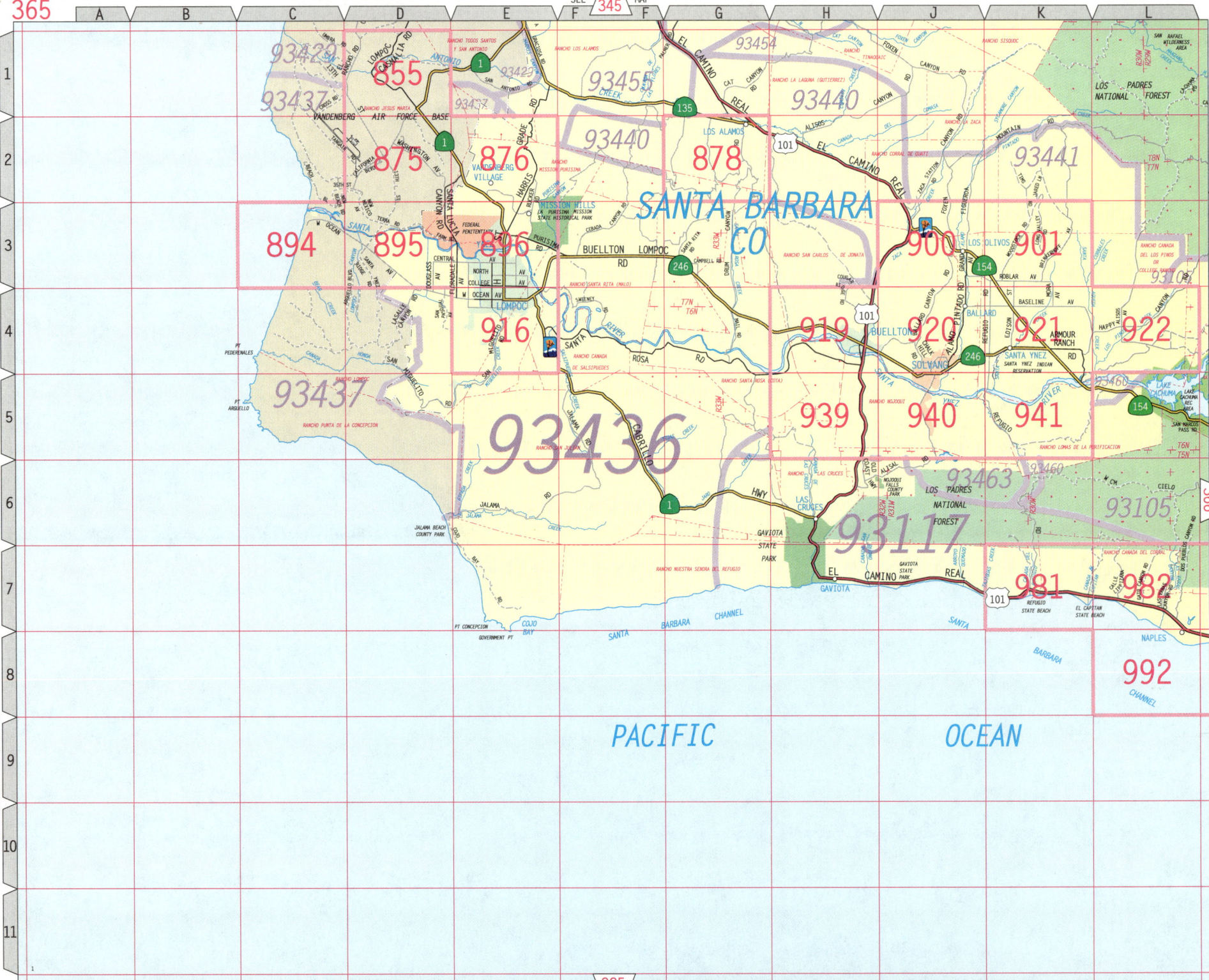

SEE 345 MAP

STB & SLO

A B C D E F F G H J K L

COPYRIGHT 2000 Thomas Bros. Maps ®

1

93429

855

93437

LOMPOC

93437

RANCHO TODOS SANTOS Y SAN ANTONIO

RANCHO LOS ALAMOS

93455

93454

CAT CANYON

RANCHO LA LAGUNA (GUTIERREZ)

LOS PADRES NATIONAL FOREST

2

VANDENBERG AIR FORCE BASE

875

1

876

VANDENBERG VILLAGE

93440

LOS ALAMOS

135

878

101

EL CAMINO REAL

RANCHO CORRAL DE QUATI

93441

T8N T7N

3

894

895

896

MISSION HILLS

LA PURISIMA MISSION STATE HISTORICAL PARK

BUELLTON

LOMPOC

RD

SANTA BARBARA CO

RANCHO SAN CARLOS DE JONATA

246

900

154

901

93105

4

916

919

101

BUELLTON

920

921

922

RANCHO SANTA RITA (MALO)

T7N T6N

SANTA RIVER RD

SOLVANG

246

SANTA YNEZ RD

SANTA YNEZ INDIAN RESERVATION

5

93437

PT PEDERNALES

PT ARGUELLO

RANCHO PUNTA DE LA CONCEPCION

93436

SANTA ROSA RD

RANCHO CANADA DE SALSIPUEDES

RANCHO SANTA ROSA (COTA)

939

RANCHO NOJOQUI

940

941

93460

154

LAKE CACHUMA REC AREA

SAN MARCOS PASS RD

T6N T5N

6

1

CABRILLO HWY

JALAMA

RANCHO SAN JULIAN

LAS CRUCES

RANCHO LAS CRUCES

GAVIOTA STATE PARK

93463

93117

LOS PADRES NATIONAL FOREST

93105

CIELO

7

JALAMA BEACH COUNTY PARK

GAVIOTA STATE PARK

EL CAMINO REAL

GAVIOTA

REFUGIO STATE BEACH

101

981

EL CAPITAN STATE BEACH

982

RANCHO CANADA DEL CORRAL

8

PT CONCEPCION

COJO BAY

GOVERNMENT PT

SANTA BARBARA CHANNEL

NAPLES

BARBARA

992

9

PACIFIC OCEAN

CHANNEL

MAP

10

11

SEE 385 MAP

SEE 366 MAP

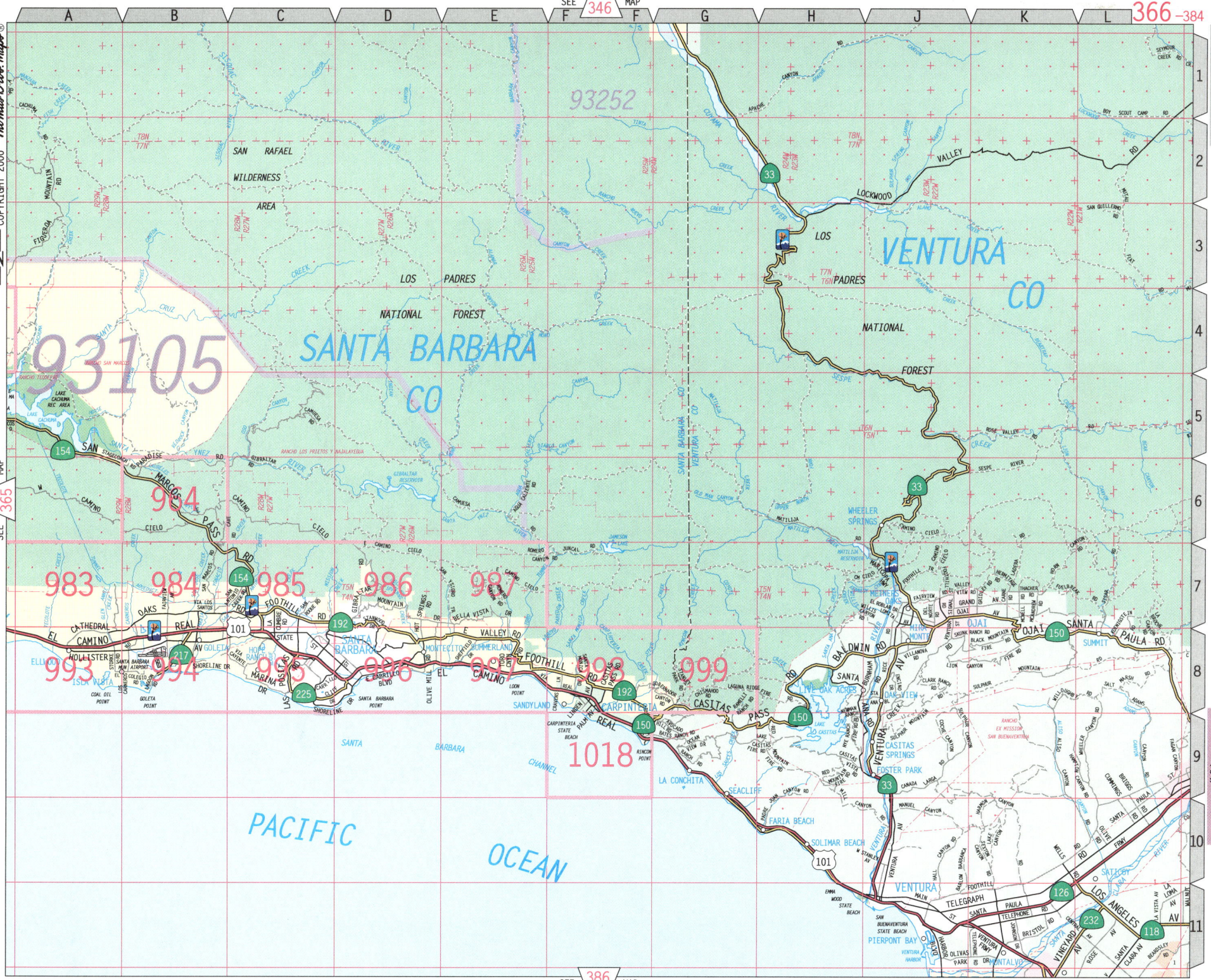

A B C D E F F G H J K L

1 2 3 4 5 6 7 8 9 10 11

Thomas Bros. Maps ®

COPYRIGHT 2000

N

SEE 365 MAP

93252

VENTURA CO

LOS PADRES NATIONAL FOREST

SAN RAFAEL WILDERNESS AREA

LOS PADRES NATIONAL FOREST

93105

SANTA BARBARA CO

LAKE CACHUMA REC AREA

154 SAN MARCOS PASS

964

983 984 985 986 987

993 994 995 996 997 998 999

1018

154
192
225
150
192
150
33
126
232
118

OAKS EL CAMINO REAL

HOLLISTER

CATHEDRAL OAKS

GOLETA SANTA BARBARA

MONTECITO SUMMERLAND

CARPINTERIA

CASITAS PASS

CARPINTERIA STATE BEACH

SANDYLAND

LA CONCHITA SEACLIFF

FARIA BEACH

SOLIMAR BEACH

OJAI

SANTA PAULA RD

BALDWIN RD

SANTA SPRINGS

CASITAS SPRINGS

FOSTER PARK

LAKE CASITAS

WHEELER SPRINGS

33

VENTURA

LOS ANGELES

PIERPONT BAY

SAN BUENAVENTURA STATE BEACH

TELEGRAPH

SANTA CRUZ

PACIFIC OCEAN

SANTA BARBARA CHANNEL

101

SANTA YNEZ RIVER

GIBRALTAR RESERVOIR

MATILIJA RESERVOIR

SESPE RIVER

	A	B	C	D	E	F	F	G	H	J	K	L

STB & SLO

1

2

3

4

CHANNEL ISLANDS NATIONAL PARK

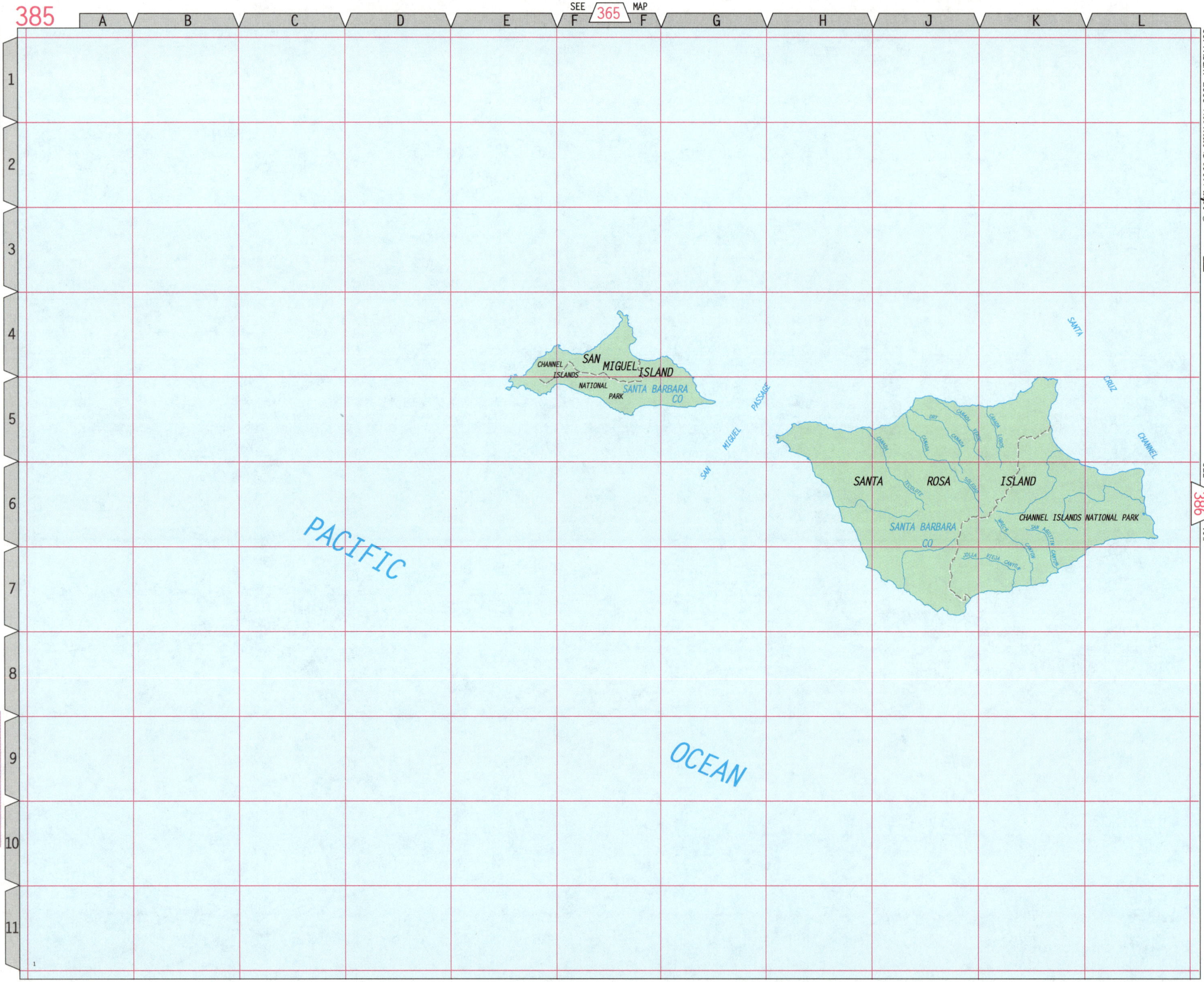

SAN MIGUEL ISLAND

SANTA BARBARA CO

5

SANTA CRUZ CHANNEL

SAN MIGUEL PASSAGE

SANTA ROSA ISLAND

CHANNEL ISLANDS NATIONAL PARK

SEE 386 MAP

6

SANTA BARBARA CO

PACIFIC

7

8

OCEAN

MAP

9

10

11

SEE 385 MAP

	A	B	C	D	E	F	F	G	H	J	K	L		

STB & SLO

MAP

VENTURA CO

VENTURA FRWY

VENTURA
CAMARILLO

OXNARD

PORT HUENEME

HUENEME

GONZALES

HOLLYWOOD BEACH

HOLLYWOOD BY THE SEA

SILVER STRAND

ORMOND BEACH

POINT MUGU NAVAL AIR STATION

SANTA BARBARA CHANNEL

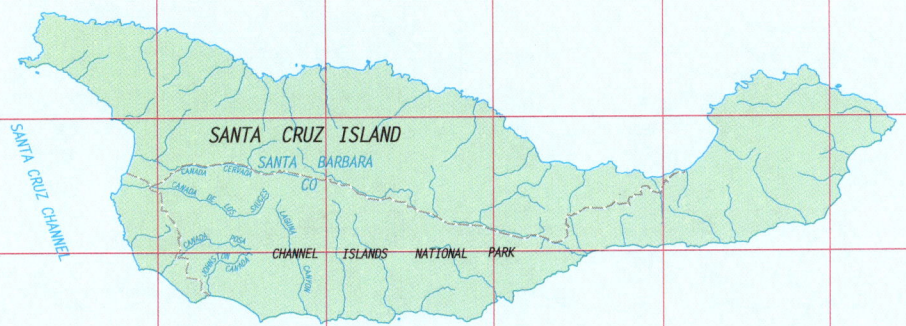

SANTA CRUZ ISLAND

SANTA BARBARA CO

SANTA CRUZ CHANNEL

CHANNEL ISLANDS NATIONAL PARK

ANACAPA PASSAGE

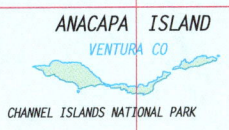

ANACAPA ISLAND

VENTURA CO

CHANNEL ISLANDS NATIONAL PARK

PACIFIC   OCEAN

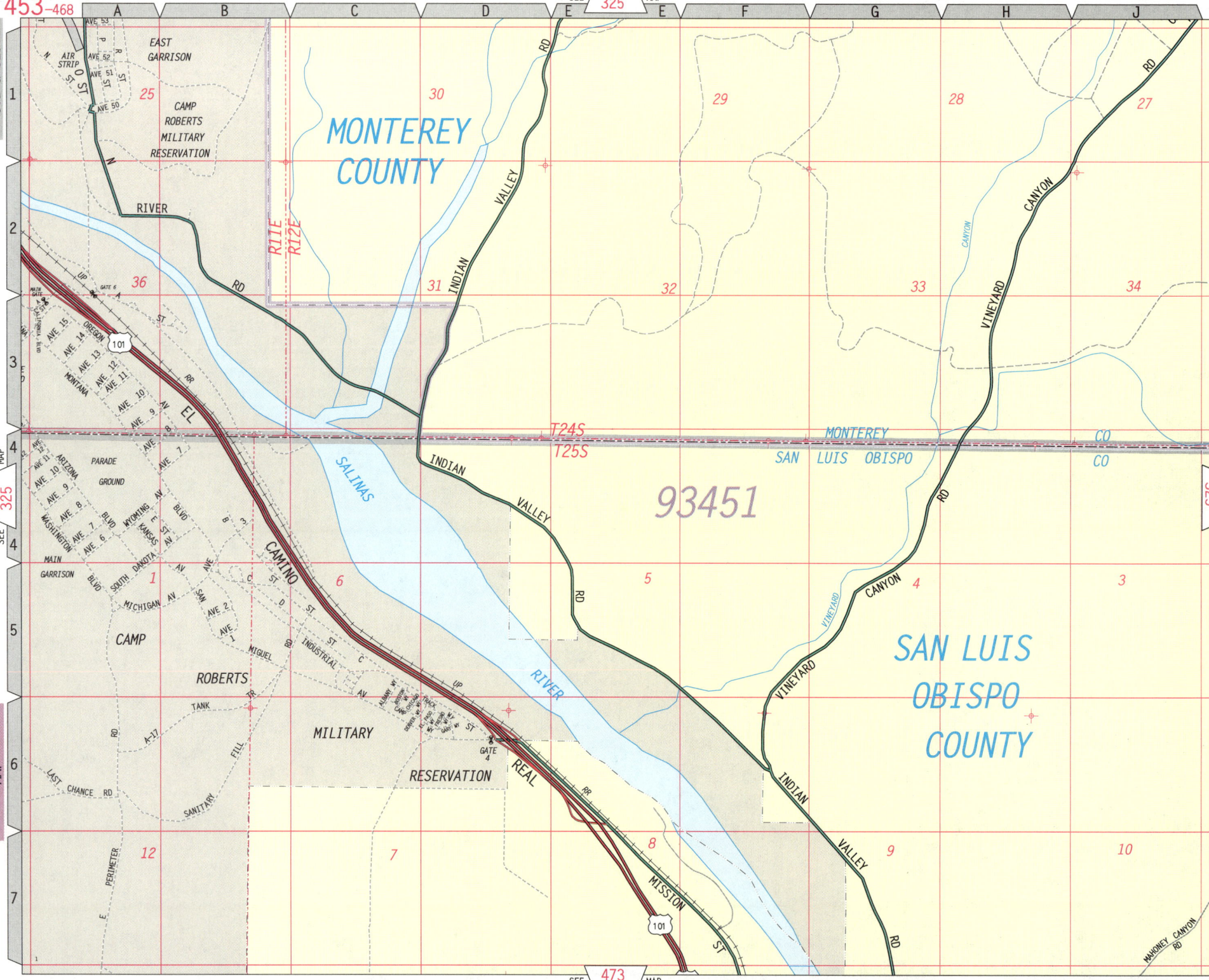

STB & SLO

SEE 325 MAP

COPYRIGHT 2000 *Thomas Bros. Maps*®

—N—

A B C D E E F G H J

1

AIR STRIP
AVE 53
AVE 52
AVE 51
AVE 50
EAST GARRISON
CAMP ROBERTS MILITARY RESERVATION

25

30

MONTEREY COUNTY

29

28

27

RIVER

RD

2

R11E R12E

31

INDIAN VALLEY

32

33

34

VINEYARD CANYON

CANYON

RD

3

UP
GATE 6
101
OREGON
MONTANA
AVE 15
AVE 14
AVE 13
AVE 12
AVE 11
AVE 10
AVE 9
EL
RR
CAMINO

36

SALINAS

4

MAIN GATE
CALIFORNIA BLVD
ARIZONA
WASHINGTON
PARADE GROUND
AVE 12
AVE 10
AVE 9
AVE 8
AVE 7
AVE 6
KANSAS
WYOMING AV
E ST AV
AVE 8
AVE 7
ST
AVE 7

T24S
T25S

INDIAN

VALLEY

MONTEREY
SAN LUIS OBISPO

CO
CO

SEE 325 MAP

MAP

SEE 325 MAP

93451

4

5

MAIN GARRISON
SOUTH DAKOTA BLVD
MICHIGAN AV
CAMP
ROBERTS
SAN AVE
AVE 2
AVE 1
MIGUEL
INDUSTRIAL
B
C
D
C ST
D ST
C ST
B RD
6
UP

RD

5

CANYON

VINEYARD

4

3

SAN LUIS
OBISPO
COUNTY

6

TANK
A-17
FILL
SANITARY
LAST CHANCE RD
RD
MILITARY
RESERVATION
ALBANY WY
BOSTON WK
CAIRO WK
DENVER WK
EL PASO
WY
FRESNO
WY
GARY WY
TRACK
UP
GATE 4
REAL
RR
RIVER

INDIAN
VALLEY

7

PERIMETER
E
12
7
MISSION
ST
101
8
MAHONEY CANYON RD
9
10

SEE 473 MAP

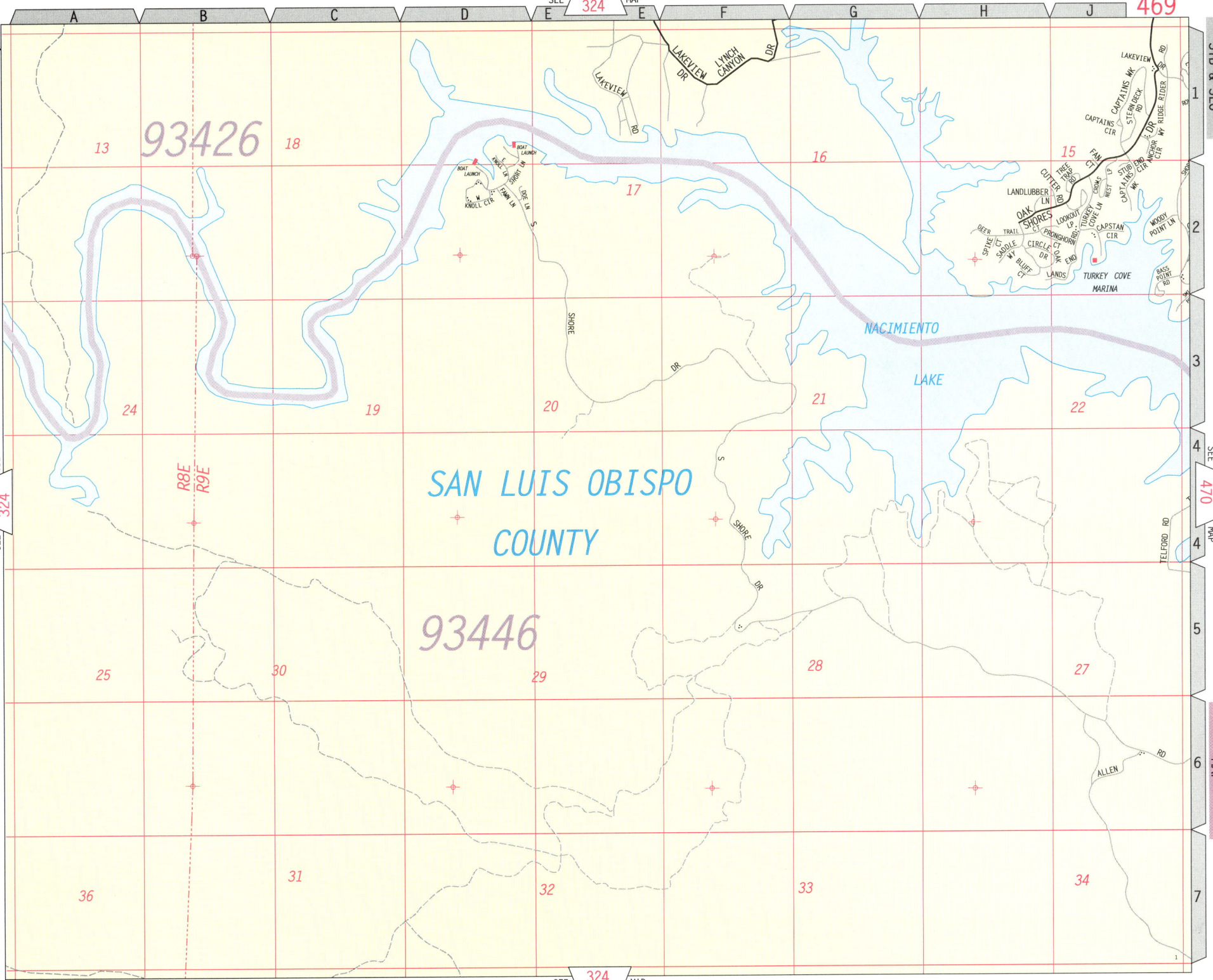

A B C D E E F G H J **469**

—N→

STB & SLO

LAKEVIEW DR
LYNCH CANYON DR

LAKEVIEW DR

LAKEVIEW RD

1

13   **93426**   18

LAKEVIEW
CAPTAINS WK
STEINBECK RD
WY RIDGE RIDER
CAPTAINS CIR
ANCHOR CIR
15
FAM CT
TREE FROG RD
CUTTER RD
STUB END
CROWS
CAPTAINS WK
WK CIR
16

BOAT LAUNCH
BOAT LAUNCH
KNOLL LN
SHORE LN
DOE LN
FAWN LN
KNOLL CIR
M
S

LANDLUBBER LN
OAK SHORES
LOOKOUT CT
TURKEY COVE LN
WEST
WOODY POINT LN

17

DEER TRAIL
SPIKE CT
SADDLE WY
CIRCLE OAK DR
PRONGHORN
CIRCLE OAK END
CAPSTAN CIR
BLUFF CT
LANDS END
BASS POINT RD

TURKEY COVE MARINA

2

SHORE

NACIMIENTO

24   19   20   DR   21   LAKE   22   3

SEE 324 MAP

R8E R9E

SAN LUIS OBISPO

S

SHORE

COUNTY

TELFORD RD

SEE 470 MAP

4

93446

S

SHORE DR

5

25   30   29   28   27

MAP

ALLEN   RD

6

31   32   33   34   36

7

1

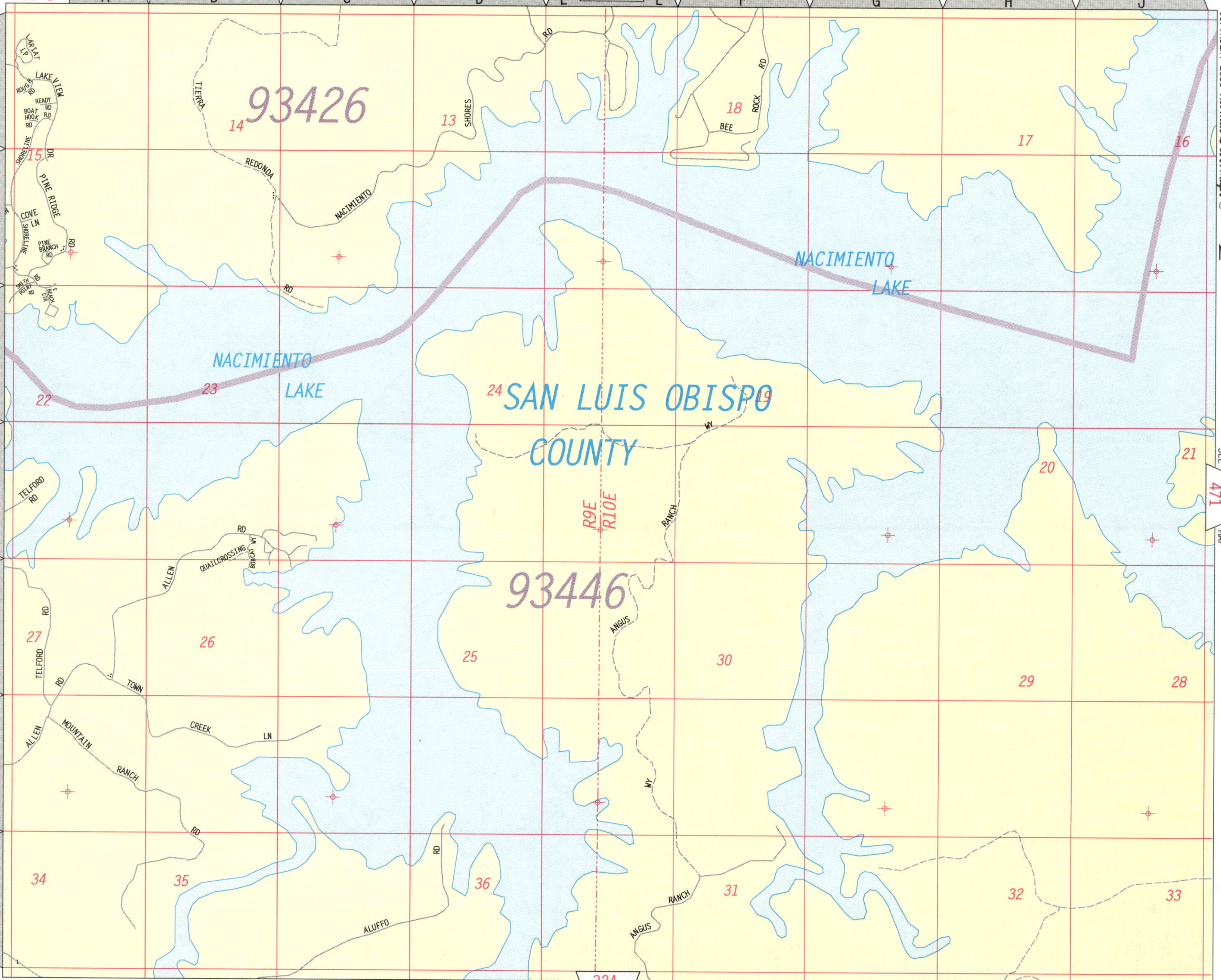

STB & SLO

A B C D E E F G H J

SEE 324 MAP

COPYRIGHT 2000 Thomas Bros. Maps® ← N →

1

LARIAT LP
LAKE VIEW
RD
READY RD
BOAT HOOK RD
SHORELINE
15
COVE LN
PINE RIDGE
PINE BRANCH RD
SHORELINE DR
SMITH POINT RD
BEACH CIR

TIERRA

REDONDA

NACIMIENTO

RD

SHORES

13

93426

14

ROCK RD

BEE

18

17

16

2

3

NACIMIENTO LAKE

22

23

NACIMIENTO LAKE

24 **SAN LUIS OBISPO**

19

COUNTY

4

SEE 469 MAP

TELFORD RD

ALLEN RD

QUAILCROSSING WY

BOBCAT WY

R9E R10E

RANCH

WY

21

20

SEE 471 MAP

93446

5

TELFORD RD

27

26

25

ANGUS

30

29

28

6

ALLEN MOUNTAIN RANCH

TOWN

CREEK LN

RD

WY

31

RANCH

7

34

35

ALUFFO

36

RD

ANGUS RANCH

32

33

MAP

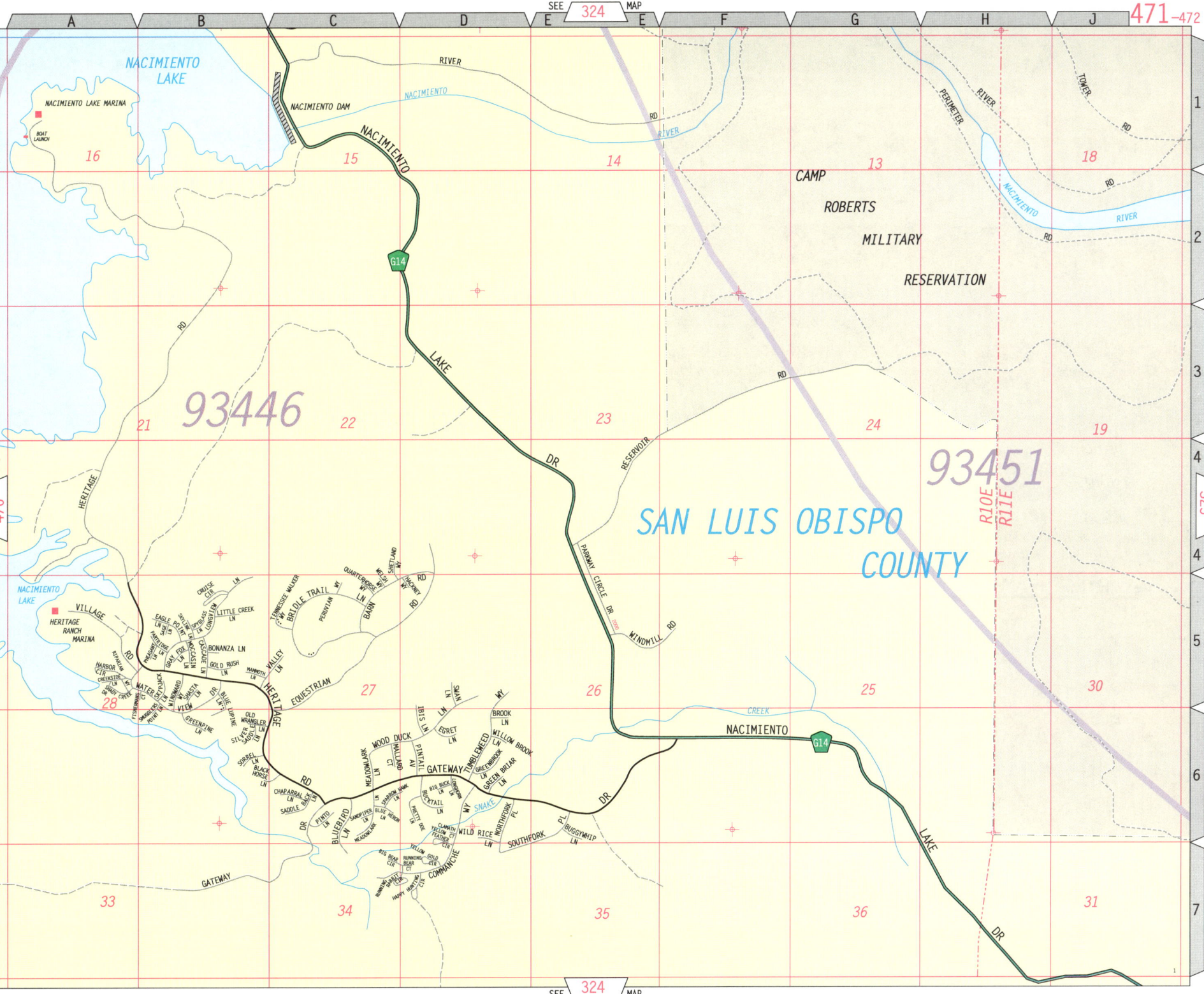

A B C D E E F G H J

Thomas Bros. Maps®

—N→ COPYRIGHT 2000

NACIMIENTO LAKE

RIVER

NACIMIENTO

Nacimiento Lake Marina

NACIMIENTO DAM

BOAT LAUNCH

16

15

RIVER

14

CAMP

ROBERTS

MILITARY

RESERVATION

PERIMETER

RIVER

TOWER

RD

RD

RD

NACIMIENTO

RIVER

13

18

G14

1

2

3

93446

LAKE

RD

21

22

23

24

19

DR

RESERVOIR

93451

SEE 470 MAP

HERITAGE

4

4

SEE 325 MAP

R10E R11E

SAN LUIS OBISPO

COUNTY

NACIMIENTO LAKE

VILLAGE

HERITAGE RANCH MARINA

CRUISE CIR LN

EAGLE POINT LN

SOUTH SPUR

LONGHORN

LITTLE CREEK LN

TENNESSEE WALKER WY

BRIDLE TRAIL

QUARTERHORSE

WEST WY

SHETLAND WY

HACKNEY LN

RD

RD

BARN

PARKWAY CIRCLE DR

WINDMILL RD

PRESSON LN

PAINT LN

GRAY FOX LN

MOCCASIN

CASCADE LN

BONANZA LN

PERUVIAN LN

BLUE LUPINE

VALLEY LN

GOLD RUSH LN

MAMMOTH LN

HERITAGE

EQUESTRIAN

27

26

25

30

5

HARBOR CIR

BETHALIAH WY

CREEKSIDE

WATER

DUCK RD

WINDWARD

SHASTA LN

OLD WRANGLER LN

SILVER SADDLE LN

DR

BLUE LN

FISHERMENS WY

POTTER LN

SMUGGLES

SCOUT CREEK

VIEW

GREENPINE LN

SORREL LN

BLACK HORSE LN

RD

IBIS LN

SWAN LN

EGRET LN

BROOK LN

WILLOW BROOK

CREEK

MEADOWLARK

WOOD DUCK CT

MALLARD AV

PINTAIL LN

GREENBROOK

GREEN BRIAR LN

NACIMIENTO

G14

CHAPARRAL LN

SADDLE BACK LN

PINTO LN

SPARROW HAWK

BLUE HERON

TUMBLEWEED

GATEWAY

BUCK

BIG BUCK

BUCKTAIL LN

LONGHORN

WY

SNAKE

NORTHFORK PL

DR

6

MAP

BLUEBIRD LN

SANDPIPER LN

MEADOWLARK

PRETTY DOE

CLAMATH

YELLOW FEATHER

WILD RICE

GOLD CIR

SOUTHFORK

BUGGYWHIP PL

LAKE

28

33

GATEWAY

BIG BEAR CIR

RUNNING BEAR CT

RUNNING BEAR

YELLOW

HAPPY HUNTING CIR

COMMANCHE

34

35

36

DR

31

7

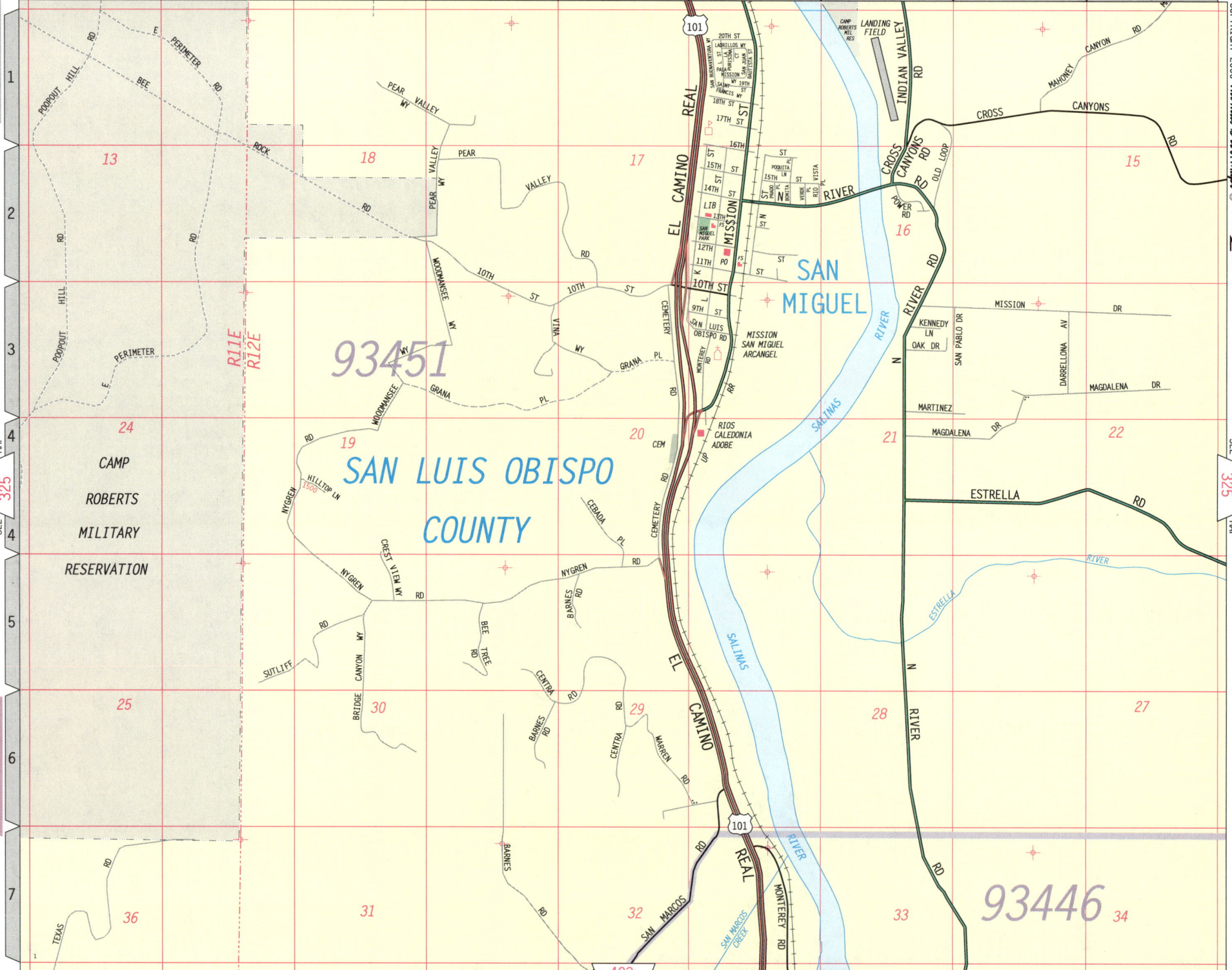

STB & SLO

SEE 453 MAP

A B C D E E F G H J

COPYRIGHT 2000

Thomas Bros. Maps ®

←N→

1

POOPOUT HILL RD
E PERIMETER RD
BEE
ROCK
13
18

20TH ST
LABRILLOS WY
LA PASA CT
SAN BERNAVENTURA WY
PASA E MISSION
SAINT FRANCIS WY
19TH ST
18TH ST
17TH ST
16TH
101
EL CAMINO REAL

CAMP ROBERTS MIL RES
LANDING FIELD

INDIAN VALLEY RD

CROSS CANYONS
MAHONEY CANYON RD

2

RD
RD
PEAR VALLEY WY
PEAR WY VALLEY
PEAR VALLEY WY

17
15TH ST
14TH ST
13TH
LIB FS
SAN MIGUEL PARK
12TH
11TH PO FS

POQUITA LN
RIO VISTA PL
RIO VERDE PL
N ST
ST
ST
ST

RIVER
CROSS CANYONS RD
OLD LOOP
POWER RD
16

CROSS CANYONS

15

POOPOUT HILL E PERIMETER
RD RD

93451
WOODMANSEE WY
VINA WY
10TH ST
10TH ST
RD
GRANA PL
GRANA PL
WOODMANSEE WY

CEMETERY RD
9TH ST
10TH ST
SAN LUIS OBISPO RD
MONTEREY RD
RR
MISSION SAN MIGUEL ARCANGEL

SAN MIGUEL

MISSION DR
KENNEDY LN
OAK DR
SAN PABLO DR
DARRELLONA AV
MAGDALENA DR

3

24
19
RD
HILLTOP LN 1500
NYGREN RD

SAN LUIS OBISPO
COUNTY

20
CEM
RIOS CALEDONIA ADOBE
UP

MARTINEZ
MAGDALENA DR
21
22

SALINAS RIVER

RIVER
N RIVER RD

SEE 325 MAP

4

CAMP ROBERTS MILITARY RESERVATION

CREST VIEW WY
NYGREN WY
RD
BARNES RD
NYGREN RD
RD

CEBADA PL
CEMETERY RD

ESTRELLA RD

SEE 325 MAP

5

SUTLIFF
BRIDGE CANYON WY
RD
BEE TREE RD
BARNES RD
CENTRA RD
EL CAMINO

SALINAS RIVER

ESTRELLA RIVER

6

25
30
31
BARNES RD
CENTRA RD
WARREN RD
29
RD

28
N RIVER RD

27

MAP

7

TEXAS RD
36
31
BARNES RD
32
SAN MARCOS RD
93446
33
34
MONTEREY RD
REAL
101

SAN MARCOS CREEK
RIVER

R11E R12E

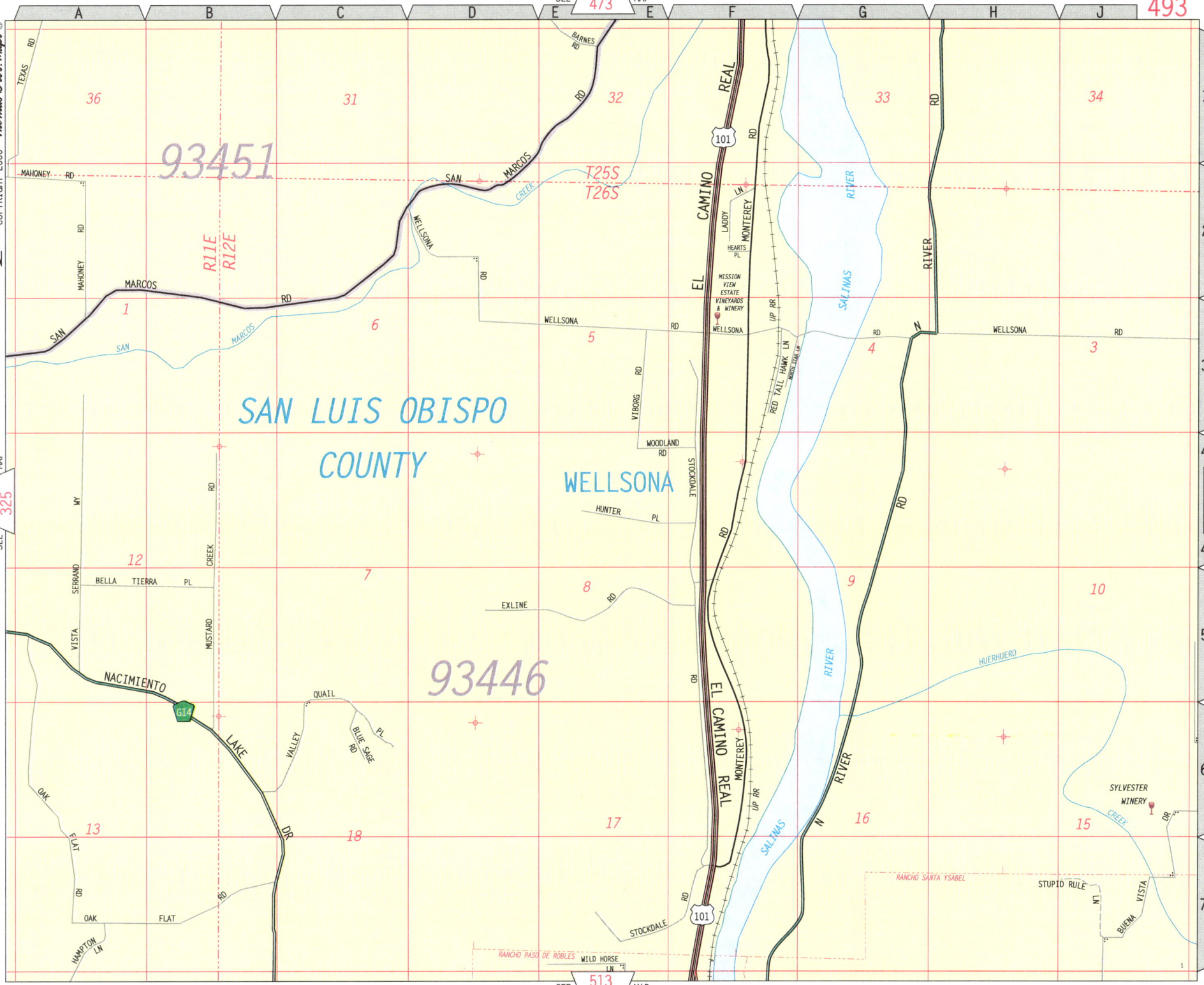

A B C D E E F G H J

STB & SLO

1

TEXAS RD

36

31

BARNES RD

RD

32

33

RD

34

93451

MAHONEY RD

MAHONEY RD

SAN MARCOS CREEK

T25S
T26S

EL CAMINO REAL

101

RD

LADDY LN

MONTEREY

RIVER

SALINAS

RIVER

RIVER

2

R11E
R12E

WELLSONA

RD

SAN

HEARTS PL

MISSION VIEW ESTATE VINEYARDS & WINERY

MARCOS RD

1

6

5

SAN MARCOS

SAN

WELLSONA RD

WELLSONA

UP RR

RED TAIL HAWK LN

MOORE STAR LN

RD

WELLSONA RD

N

4

WELLSONA RD

3

3

SAN LUIS OBISPO

COUNTY

WELLSONA

VIBORG RD

WOODLAND RD

STOCKDALE

RD

4

SEE 325 MAP

SEE 494 MAP

4

12

VISTA WY

SERRANO

BELLA TIERRA PL

CREEK RD

MUSTARD RD

7

HUNTER PL

EXLINE RD

8

9

RD

10

5

93446

NACIMIENTO

G14

LAKE

VALLEY

QUAIL

BLUE SAGE RD

PL

DR

RD

EL CAMINO REAL

MONTEREY

UP RR

SALINAS

RIVER

HUERHUERO

N

SYLVESTER WINERY

CREEK

MAP

6

OAK

FLAT

13

RD

18

17

16

DR

15

RANCHO SANTA YSABEL

STUPID RULE LN

BUENA VISTA

7

HAMPTON LN

OAK FLAT RD

STOCKDALE

101

RANCHO PASO DE ROBLES WILD HORSE LN

STB & SLO

A B C D E E F G H J

Thomas Bros. Maps ®

1

34 35 36 ESTRELLA 31 HOG CANYON RD 32 33

ESTRELLA CIR

T25S
T26S

ESTRELLA

93451

2

3

2

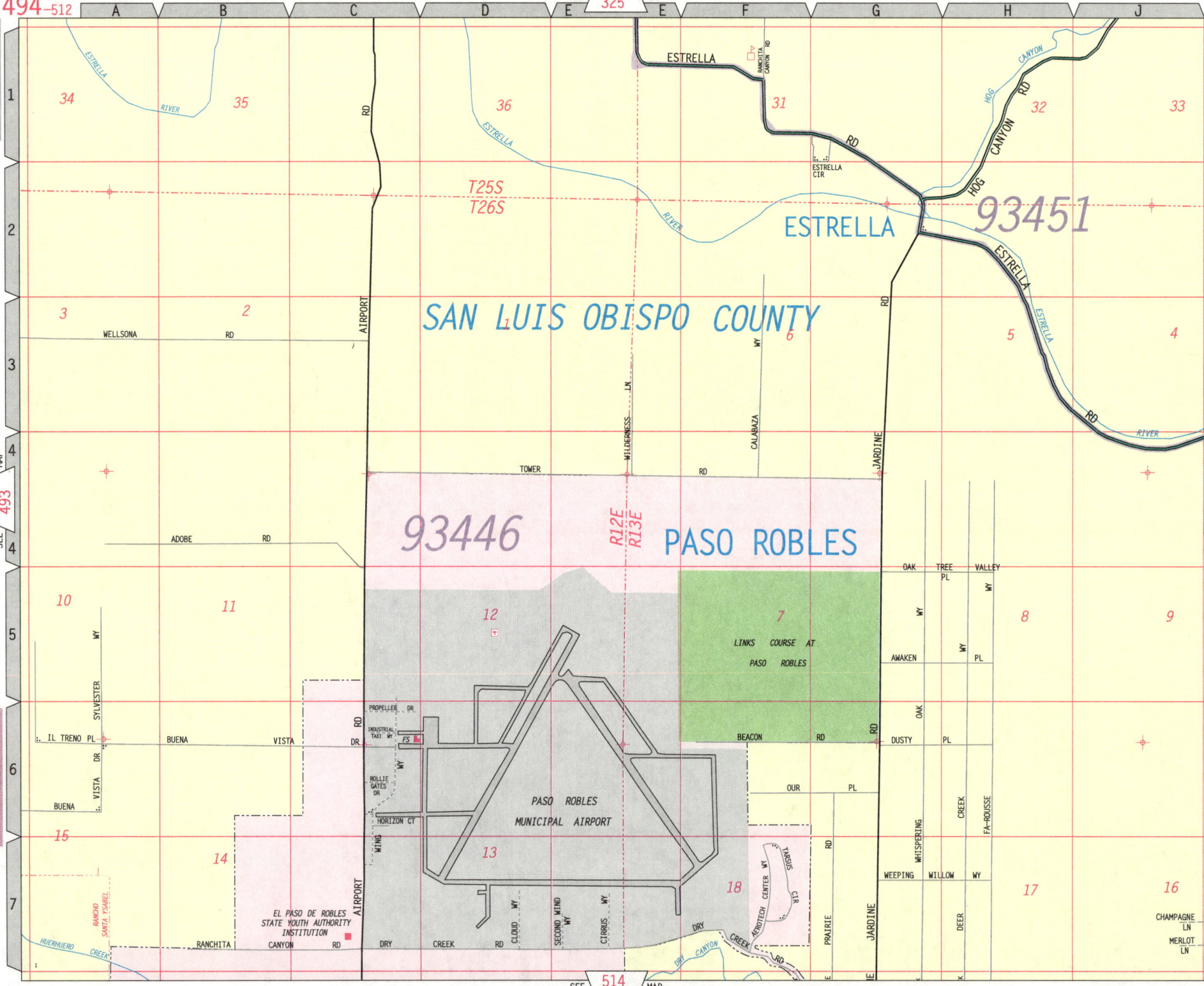

SAN LUIS OBISPO COUNTY

WELLSONA RD

WILDERNESS LN

CALABAZA WY

JARDINE RD

1 6 5 4

3

SEE 493 MAP
SEE 325 MAP

4

TOWER RD

93446

R12E
R13E

PASO ROBLES

ADOBE RD

4

OAK TREE VALLEY
PL WY

10 11 12 7 8 9

LINKS COURSE AT
PASO ROBLES

AWAKEN WY
PL

5

SYLVESTER WY

PROPELLER DR

INDUSTRIAL FS
TAXI WY

IL TRENO PL BUENA VISTA DR RD

VISTA DR

BUENA

ROLLIE
GATES
DR

HORIZON CT

OAK RD
DUSTY PL

BEACON RD

OUR PL

WHISPERING

CREEK

FA-ROUSSE

6

PASO ROBLES
MUNICIPAL AIRPORT

WING

AIRPORT

15

14 13 18 17 16

RANCHO
SANTA YSABEL

EL PASO DE ROBLES
STATE YOUTH AUTHORITY
INSTITUTION

RANCHITA CANYON RD DRY CREEK RD

CLOUD WY

SECOND WIND WY

CITRUS WY

AEROTECH CENTER WY

TARSUS CIR

PRAIRIE RD

JARDINE

WEEPING WILLOW WY

DEER WY

CHAMPAGNE LN

MERLOT LN

7

HUERHUERO CREEK

DRY CANYON RD

SEE 514 MAP

ESTRELLA RIVER

SEE 493 MAP
513
A B C D E F G H J
STB & SLO
SEE 325 MAP
SEE 514 MAP
MAP
SEE 533 MAP

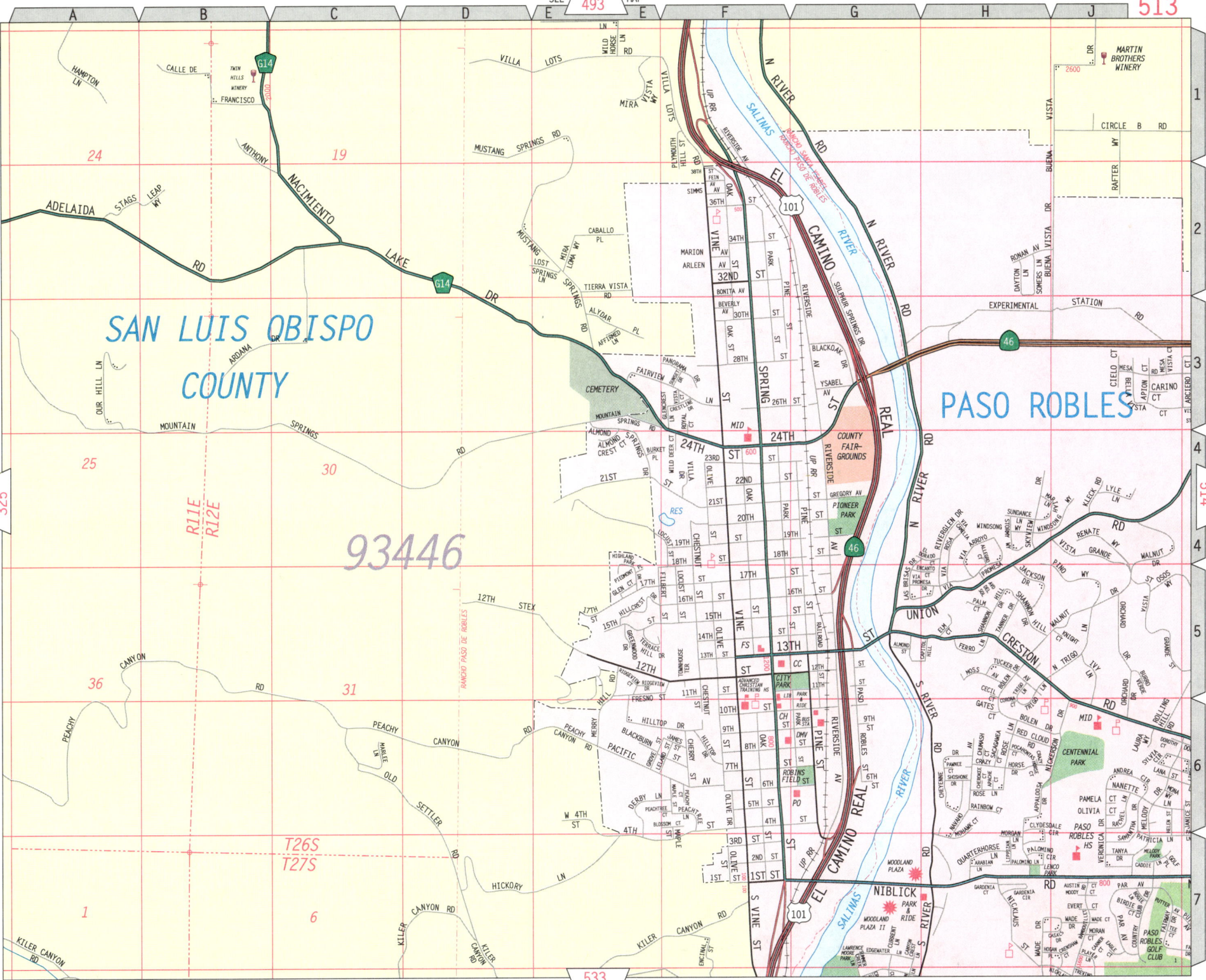

SAN LUIS OBISPO COUNTY

PASO ROBLES

93446

MARTIN BROTHERS WINERY

TWIN HILLS WINERY

HAMPTON LN
CALLE DE FRANCISCO
ADELAIDA
NACIMIENTO LAKE DR
MUSTANG SPRINGS RD
VILLA LOTS
WILD HORSE RD

OUR HILL LN
ARDANA DR
MOUNTAIN SPRINGS RD
PEACHY CANYON RD
KILER CANYON RD
CANYON RD

EL CAMINO REAL
N RIVER RD
SALINAS RIVER
SPRING ST
VINE ST
PINE ST
OAK ST
RIVERSIDE AV
PARK ST
OLIVE ST
CHESTNUT ST
VINE ST
13TH ST
12TH ST
11TH ST
10TH ST
NIBLICK RD

COUNTY FAIRGROUNDS
PIONEER PARK
CITY PARK
ROBINS FIELD
CENTENNIAL PARK
PASO ROBLES HS
PASO ROBLES GOLF CLUB

CEMETERY

UNION RD
CRESTON RD
S RIVER RD
S VINE ST

46
101
G14

WOODLAND PLAZA

EXPERIMENTAL STATION
CIRCLE B RD

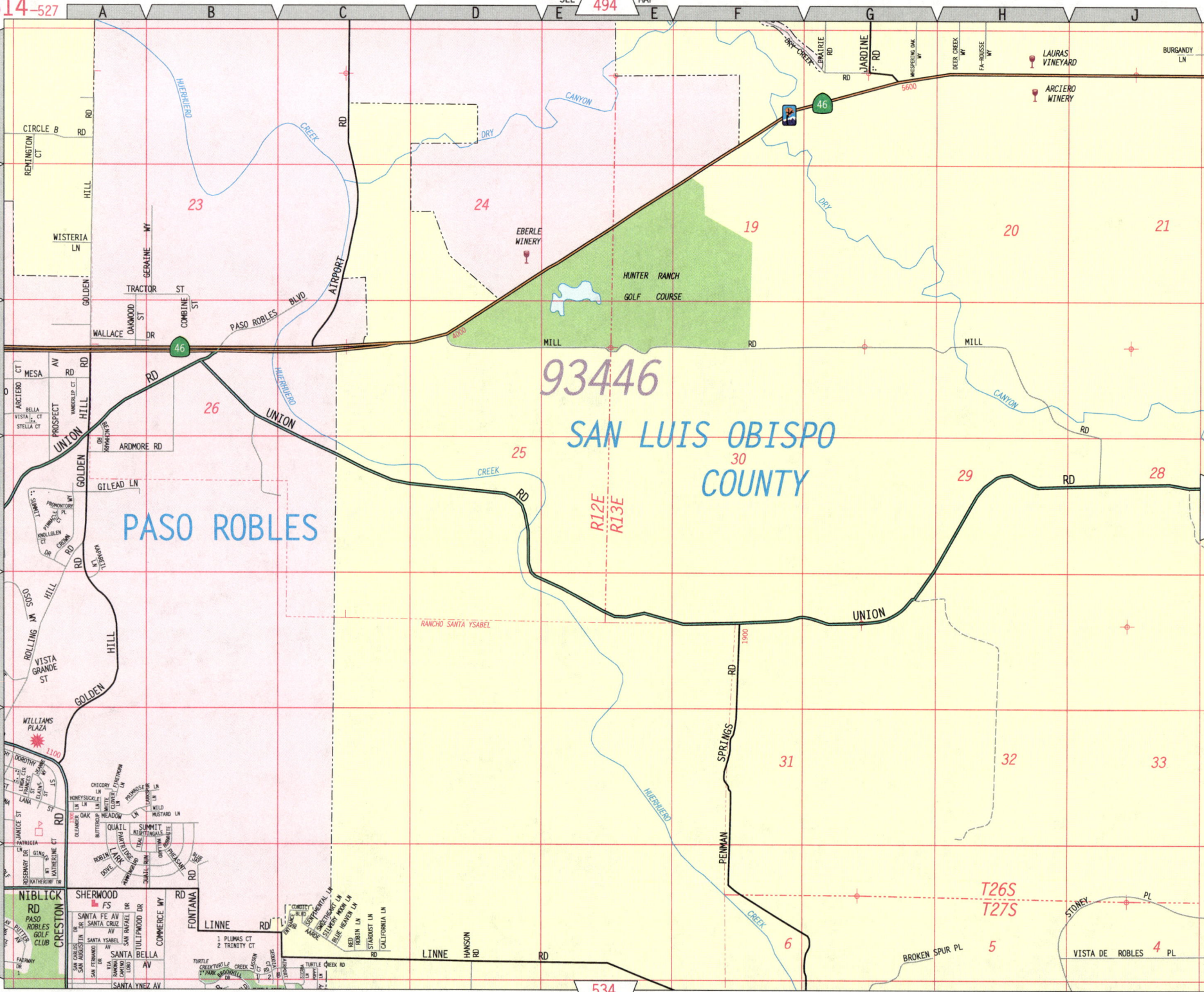

A B C D E E F G H J

SEE 494 MAP

STB & SLO

1

2

3

4

4

5

6

7

SEE 513 MAP

SEE 325 MAP

MAP

SEE 534 MAP

REMINGTON CT
CIRCLE B RD
HILL RD
WISTERIA LN
GOLDEN

HUERHUERO CREEK

23

24

19

20

21

DRY CANYON

DRY CREEK

LOMA PRAIRIE RD
JARDINE RD
WHISPERING OAK WY
DEER CREEK WY
FA-ROUSSE WY
BURGANDY LN

46
5600

LAURAS VINEYARD

ARCIERO WINERY

EBERLE WINERY

HUNTER RANCH GOLF COURSE

TRACTOR ST
COMBINE ST
OAKWOOD ST
GERAINE WY
WALLACE DR
PASO ROBLES BLVD
AIRPORT RD

46

MILL RD
MILL RD

4200

93446

SAN LUIS OBISPO COUNTY

PASO ROBLES

MESA
ARCIERO CT
BELLA VISTA CT
STELLA CT
PROSPECT AV
UNION HILL RD
GOLDEN HILL RD
ARDMORE RD
GILEAD LN
PROMONTORY WY
SUMMIT
PINNACLE PL
PINWOOD
KNOLLGLEN DR
CROWN

26

UNION RD

HUERHUERO

25

30

R12E R13E

CREEK RD

29

UNION RD

28

RANCHO SANTA YSABEL

OSOS ST
ROLLING MW
VISTA GRANDE ST
GOLDEN HILL RD

SPRINGS RD

1900

HUERHUERO

WILLIAMS PLAZA

1100

31

32

33

DOROTHY
LINDA CIR
FRANCIS
ELAINE
CHICORY LN
HONEYSUCKLE LN
OAK
OLEANDER
BUTTERCUP
PRIMROSE LN
WILD MUSTARD LN
CLOVER
PENMAN RD

LARK
ROSEMARY DR
GINA
KATHERINE
QUAIL
PARTRIDGE
NIGHTINGALE
SUMMIT MEADOW
PINECREST
ROBIN
DOVE
QUAIL RUN
BLUE JAY
PINE

NIBLICK RD
PASO ROBLES GOLF CLUB
CRESTON
SHERWOOD FS
SANTA CRUZ
SANTA FE AV
SAN RAFAEL
TULLIPWOOD DR
COMMERCE WY
FONTANA
LINNE RD

JUANICE ST
PATRICIA
SANTA YSABEL
SAN AUGUSTIN
RAMONA CAMINO LOBO

SANTA BELLA AV

T26S T27S

LINNE RD
HANSON RD
LINNE RD

6

STONEY PL

BROKEN SPUR PL

5

VISTA DE ROBLES PL

4

1 PLUMAS CT
2 TRINITY CT

TURTLE CREEK RD
BROOKHILL
PARK

CLAUDE
CRISPYMERLE LN
STARLIGHT LN
INDEPENDENT LN
BLUE HEAVEN LN
ROBIN LN
STARDUST LN
CALIFORNIA LN

SANTA YNEZ AV

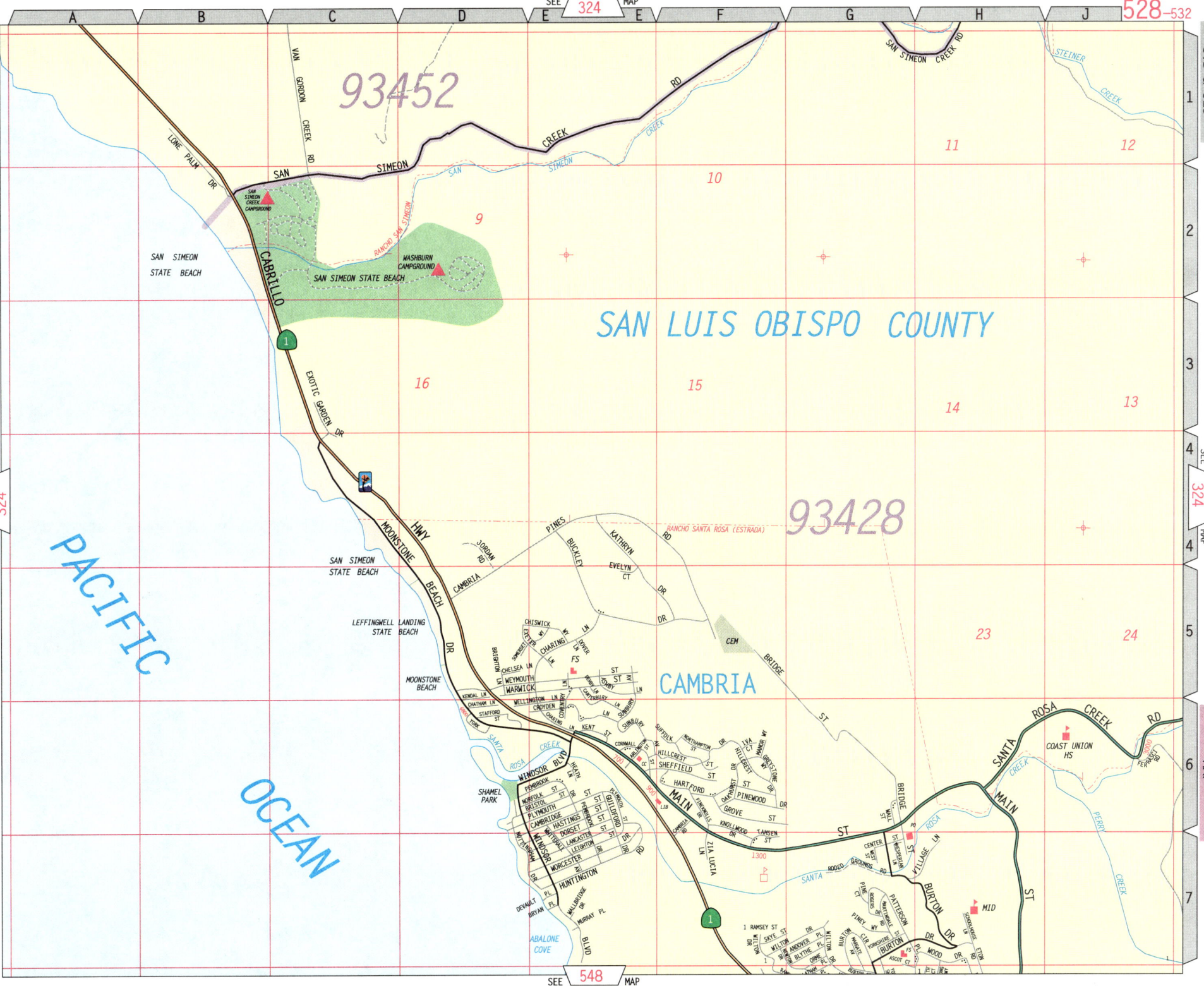

A B C D E E F G H J

93452

Thomas Bros. Maps

COPYRIGHT 2000

N

VAN GORDON CREEK RD

SAN SIMEON CREEK RD

STEINER CREEK

LONE PALM DR

SAN SIMEON CREEK

SAN SIMEON

CREEK

SAN SIMEON

11

12

10

SAN SIMEON CREEK CAMPGROUND

CABRILLO

SAN SIMEON STATE BEACH

RANCHO SAN SIMEON

9

WASHBURN CAMPGROUND

SAN SIMEON STATE BEACH

SAN LUIS OBISPO COUNTY

1

16

15

14

13

SEE 324 MAP
SEE 324 MAP

EXOTIC GARDEN DR

HWY

MOONSTONE BEACH DR

PACIFIC

OCEAN

PINES

RANCHO SANTA ROSA (ESTRADA) RD

93428

JORDAN RD

BUCKLEY

KATHRYN

EVELYN CT

DR

DR

CAMBRIA

SAN SIMEON STATE BEACH

LEFFINGWELL LANDING STATE BEACH

CEM

BRIDGE

23

24

CHISWICK

EXETER

CHARING

DOVER LN

FS

ST

ST

WEYMOUTH

WARWICK

BRIGHTON LN

CHELSEA LN

WELLINGTON LN

CROYDEN

KENDAL LN

CHATHAM LN

STAFFORD

YORK

LN KENT ST

CORNWALL

SUFFOLK

NORTHAMPTON

DR

HILLCREST

SHEFFIELD ST

HARTFORD

PINEWOOD DR

GROVE

KNOLLWOOD DR

TAMSEN

ROSA CREEK RD

COAST UNION HS

SANTA ROSA

MAIN

MOONSTONE BEACH

SANTA ROSA CREEK

WINDSOR BLVD

PEMBROOK

NORFOLK

BRISTOL

PLYMOUTH

CAMBRIDGE

HASTINGS

DORSET

LANCASTER

LEIGHTON

WORCESTER

HUNTINGTON

SHAMEL PARK

HEATH

PEMBROK ST

GUILDFORD ST

ST

MAIN ST

LIB

1300

ZIA LUCIA LN

SANTA

RODEO GROUNDS RD

BRIDGE ST

VILLAGE LN

PERRY

ST

SANTA ROSA LN

CENTER

MID

DEVAULT PL

BRYAN PL

WALLBRIDGE PL

MURRAY PL

ABALONE COVE

BLVD

1

RAMSEY ST

SKYE ST

WILTON DR

WILTON

ANDOVER PL

BLYTHE PL

ORME

PINE CT

ROGERS RD

PINEY WY

PATTERSON DR

BURTON DR

WOOD DR

BURTON

533

A B C D E F G H J

STB & SLO

COPYRIGHT 2000 Thomas Bros. Maps ®

PASO ROBLES

PASO ROBLES GOLF CLUB

LAWRENCE MOORE PARK

KILER CREEK PL

KILER CANYON RD

KILER CANYON RD

CUERNO

EL CORRAL ENCINAL

ALMIRA PARK WY

ARIBA RD

ROBLES ST

101

RIVER

CHAROLAIS LN

HEREFORD LN

CHAROLAIS

R11E R12E

RANCHO PASO DE ROBLES

LARGO

MADRONE ST

MONTE ST

VINE ST

ALMIRA HTS

OAK LN

PUMP HANDLE LN

SPANISH CAMP RD

SAINT ANDREWS CIR

SAN LUIS OBISPO

COUNTY

93446

ARBOR RD

AMBUSH TRAIL PL

CUERNO LARGO WY

EL CAMINO REAL

46

VENDELS CIR

RAMADA DR

SALINAS

BEAVER CREEK LN

SPANISH CAMP RD

CUMBRE

SPANISH CAMP

12

LIVE OAK RD

PAINT HORSE PL

TWELVE OAKS DR

CALLE PROPANO

BARLEY GRAIN RD

RIVER

3

TREANA WINERY

ARBOR RD

GAHAN PL

ALICE PL

FORTINI PL

THEATER DR

RAMADA DR

CONCRETE CT

PROSPECT

SALINAS AV

GILROY AV

1 LAGUNA DEL CAMPO
2 CALLE LOS CHARROS

SEE 325 MAP

CLASSEN RANCH LN

VOLPI

YSABEL RD

RANCHO SANTA YSABEL
RANCHO PASO DE ROBLES

SEE 534 MAP

4

ANDERSON RD

LIVE OAK VINEYARDS

CASTORO CELLARS

DOVER CANYON WINERY

46

COUNTRY BROOK LN

NUTWOOD

CIR

CONCRETE CT

FS

101

MARQUITA WY

CHAUNCEY ST

HANGING TREE LN

5

BETHEL RD

HERDSMAN

WILD OATS WY

GOLDEN MEADOW WY

FIRTREE WY

BIRCHWOOD DR

AMBER CT

OAK KNOLL DR

SPRUCEWOOD CT

BEACHWOOD DR

AMBER DR

LA CRUZ WY

COW

MEADOW PL

PINA SELVA PL

DOESKIN PL

CONCHO RD

6

93465

COBBLE WY

CREEK WY

FRONTIER WY

WRANGLER WY

TEMPLETON CEMETERY RD

THEATER DR

RAMADA DR

CONIFER PL

SALINAS

VAQUERO DR

EL NEAL

7

LOS ROBLES RD

BRAMBLES CT

FOXTAIL LN

CONOVER LN

WINEGRAPE CT

FRONTIER WY

EL CAMINO REAL

N MAIN ST

WATERFALL RD

WHITEWATER RD

REFLECTION PL

CATTAIL PL

GRANITE RD

CREEKSIDE RANCH RD

VAQUERO DR

SPRINGS RD

POMAR DR

MAP

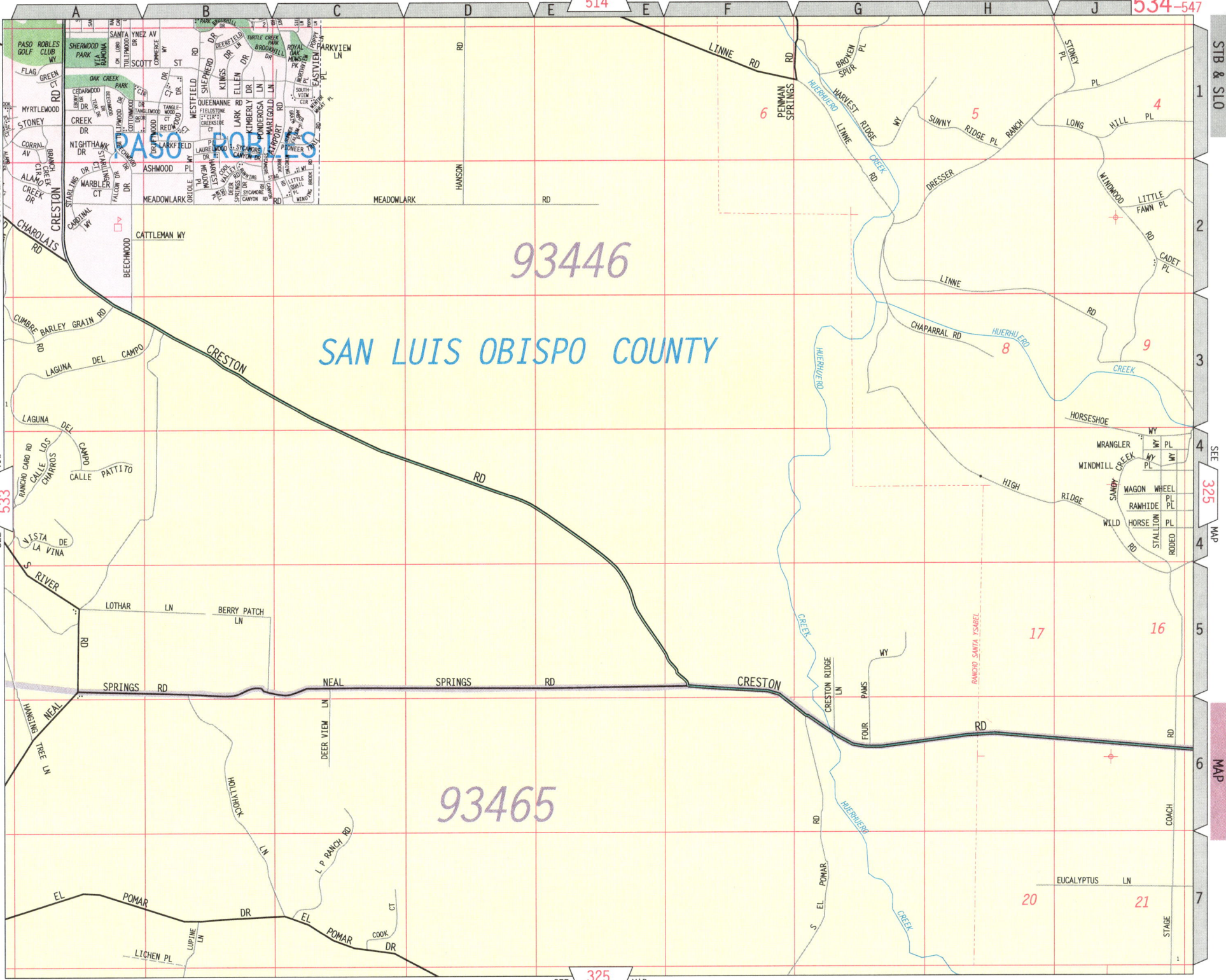

A B C D E E F G H J

Thomas Bros. Maps ®

COPYRIGHT 2000

— N —

SEE 533 MAP

SEE 325 MAP

MAP

PASO ROBLES

PASO ROBLES GOLF CLUB WY
SHERWOOD PARK
VIA RAMONA
SANTA YNEZ AV
SCOTT ST
COMMERCE DR
PARK
DEERFIELD DR
TURTLE CREEK PARK
ROYAL OAK MDWS PK
PARKVIEW LN
POPPY
EASTVIEW

FLAG
GREEN
RD
MYRTLEWOOD
STONEY
CREEK DR
OAK CREEK PARK
CEDARWOOD DR
SHEPHERD
KINGS
WESTFIELD
BROOKHILL
SOUTHVIEW CIR

CORRAL AV
NIGHTHAWK DR
ASHWOOD
WARBLER
STARLING
QUEENANNE RD
LARK
KIMBERLY
MARTIGOLD
PONDEROSA
SYCAMORE CANYON
PIONEER

BRANCH CREEK CIR
ALAMO CREEK DR
CARDINAL WY
FALCON DR
ORIOLE
MEADOWLARK
LAUREL
SPRINGS RD
LITTLE QUAIL
WING

CHAROLAIS RD
CRESTON
BEECHWOOD
CATTLEMAN WY

CUMBRE
BARLEY
GRAIN RD

LAGUNA DEL CAMPO
CRESTON RD

LAGUNA DEL CAMPO
RANCHO CARO RD
CALLE LOS CHARROS
CALLE PATTITO

VISTA DE LA VINA

S RIVER RD

LOTHAR LN
BERRY PATCH LN

SPRINGS RD
NEAL
SPRINGS RD

HANGING TREE LN
NEAL

DEER VIEW LN

HOLLYHOCK LN

L P RANCH RD

EL POMAR DR
EL POMAR DR
COOK DR

LUPINE LN
LICHEN PL

93446

SAN LUIS OBISPO COUNTY

93465

6

PENMAN SPRINGS

LINNE RD
RD
BROKEN SPUR LN
HARVEST RIDGE WY

HUERHUERO CREEK

LINNE RD

HANSON RD

MEADOWLARK RD

STONEY PL
PL

SUNNY RIDGE PL RANCH

5

LONG HILL
PL

4

WINDWOOD
LITTLE FAWN PL

DRESSER

RD

CADET PL

LINNE RD

CHAPARRAL RD
HUERHUERO

8

HUERHUERO RD

CREEK

9

HORSESHOE WY
WRANGLER WY PL
WY
WINDMILL CREEK WY PL
PL
WAGON WHEEL PL
SANDY
RIDGE
RAWHIDE PL
WILD HORSE PL
RD
STALLION
RODEO

HIGH
RIDGE RD

CREEK

CRESTON RIDGE LN

WY

FOUR PAWS

CRESTON RD

RANCHO SANTA YSABEL

17

16

S EL POMAR RD

HUERHUERO RD

CREEK

COACH RD

EUCALYPTUS LN

20

21

STAGE RD

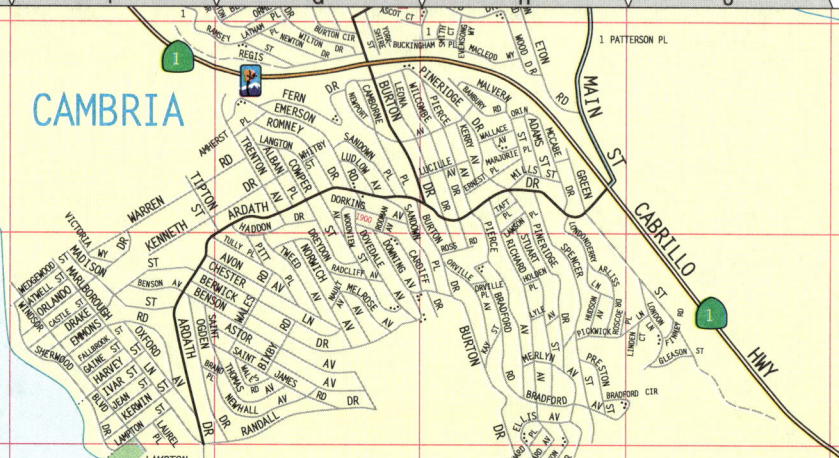

STB & SLO

MAP

PACIFIC

OCEAN

CAMBRIA

SAN LUIS OBISPO
COUNTY

93428

LAMPTON
CLIFFS
COUNTY
PARK

SEE 528 MAP
SEE 324 MAP
SEE 324 MAP

A B C D E E F G H J

1 2 3 4 4 5 6 7

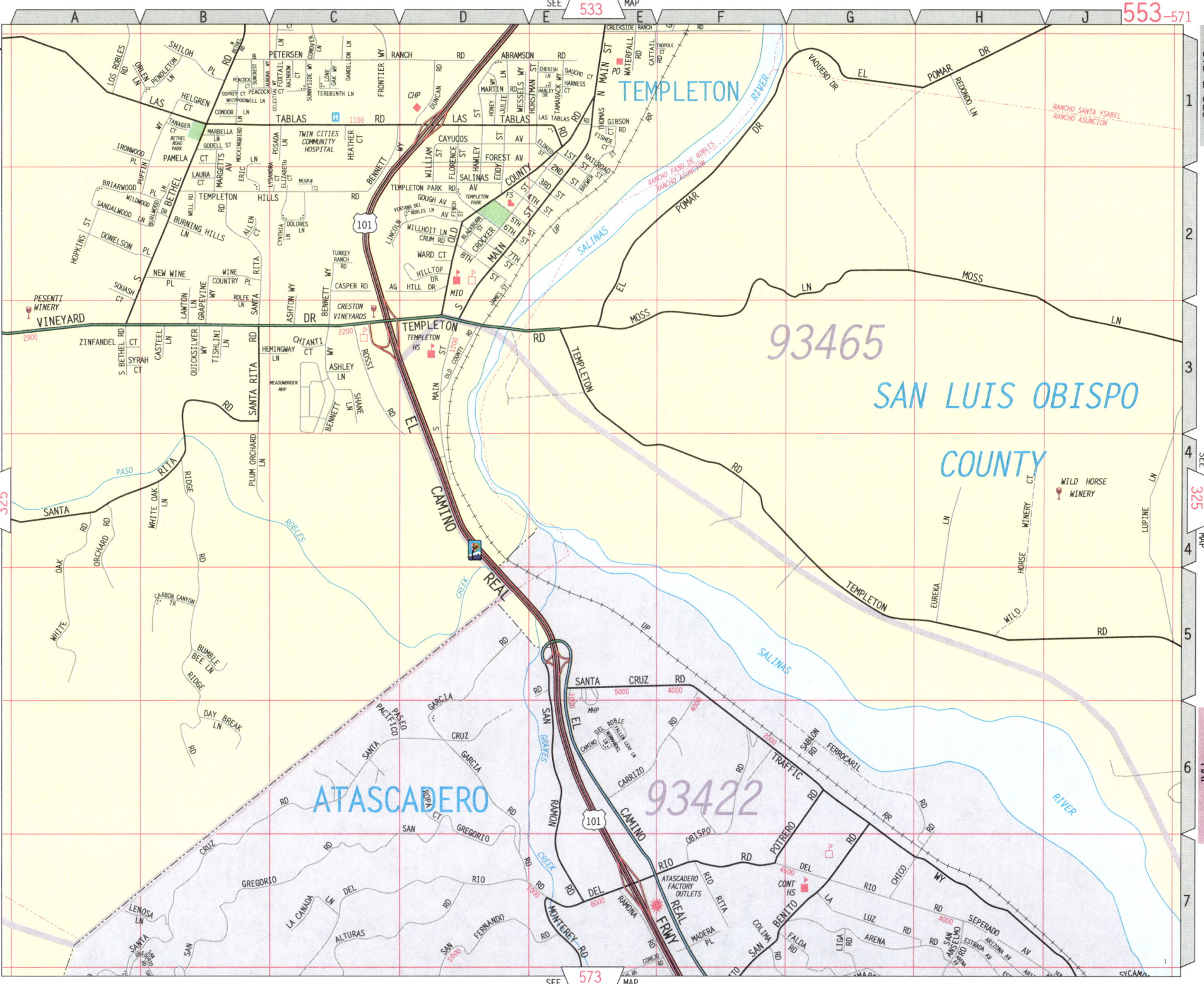

A B C D E E F G H J

ThomasBros.Maps®

COPYRIGHT 2000

N→

TEMPLETON

93465

SAN LUIS OBISPO

COUNTY

ATASCADERO

93422

WILD HORSE WINERY

PESENTI WINERY

CRESTON VINEYARDS

TWIN CITIES COMMUNITY HOSPITAL

TEMPLETON HS

ATASCADERO FACTORY OUTLETS

CONT HS

CHP

Rancho Santa Ysabel
Rancho Asuncion

Rancho Paso de Robles
Rancho Asuncion

SALINAS RIVER

PASO ROBLES CREEK

GRAVES CREEK

VINEYARD DR

EL CAMINO REAL

MONTEREY RD

MONTEREY FRWY

101

US 101

SEE 325 MAP

Street names (partial): LOS ROBLES, ORLEN LN, PENDLETON, SHILOH, HELGREN CT, LAS TABLAS RD, BETHEL, PAMELA, IRONWOOD PL, RUFFIN, HOPKINS ST, SANDALWOOD, WILDWOOD, BRIARWOOD, DONELSON PL, SQUASH CT, NEW WINE PL, WINE COUNTRY PL, GRAPEVINE WY, ZINFANDEL, S BETHEL RD, CASTEEL CT, SYRAH CT, QUICKSILVER WY, TISHLINI, SANTA RITA RD, WHITE OAK LN, RIDGE, PLUM ORCHARD LN, ORCHARD RD, OAK, CARBON CANYON TR, BUMBLE BEE LN, RIDGE, DAY BREAK LN, WHITE, SANTA CRUZ, PASEO PACIFICO, GARCIA, RAMON, LENOSA LN, LA CANADA, ALTURAS, GREGORIO, RIO DEL, SAN FERNANDO, CONEJO, MADERA PL, COLIMA RD, SAN BENITO, POTRERO, OBISPO RD, RIO RITA, RIO CHICO WY, LIGA, ARENA, SEPERADO, SANTA CRUZ RD, DEL RIO RD, TRAFFIC WY, SABLON, FERROCARIL, EUREKA LN, HORSE, WINERY CT, LUPINE LN, WILD, TEMPLETON RD, MOSS LN, EL POMAR DR, VAQUERO DR, REDONDO LN, CREEKSIDE RANCH RD, CATTAIL, TADPOLE, WATERFALL, N MAIN ST, ABRAMSON RD, PETERSEN, FRONTIER WY, RANCH RD, DUNCAN, LAS TABLAS, MARTIN, JULIE, WESSELS ST, HORSTMAN ST, CAYUCOS ST, FLORENCE, HANLEY, FOREST AV, EDDY, 1ST ST, 2ND ST, 3RD ST, 4TH ST, 5TH ST, 6TH ST, 7TH, RAILROAD ST, GIBSON RD, THOMAS, FISHER, BRIDGE ST, EL POMAR, MOSS LN, TEMPLETON, CROCKER, MAIN, JAMES ST, MID, WARD CT, HILLTOP DR, HILL DR, AG, CASPER RD, TURKEY RANCH RD, BENNETT, ASHTON WY, ROLFE LN, LAWTON LN, CHIANTI CT, ROSSI, ASHLEY LN, SHANE LN, HEMINGWAY LN, MEADOWBROOK MHP

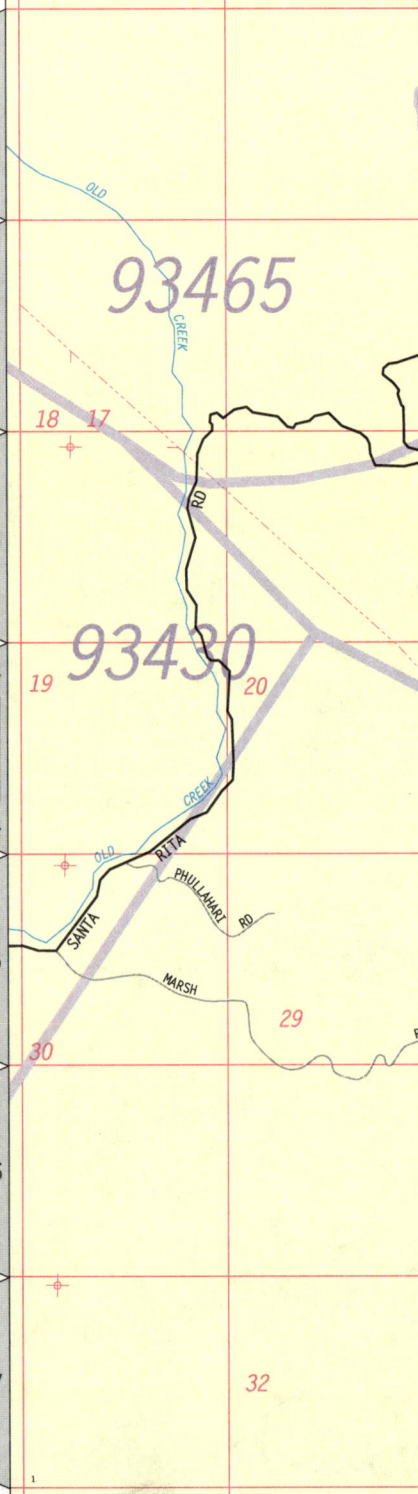

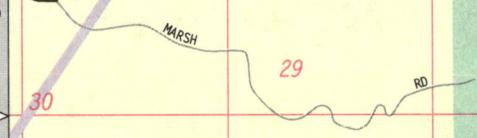
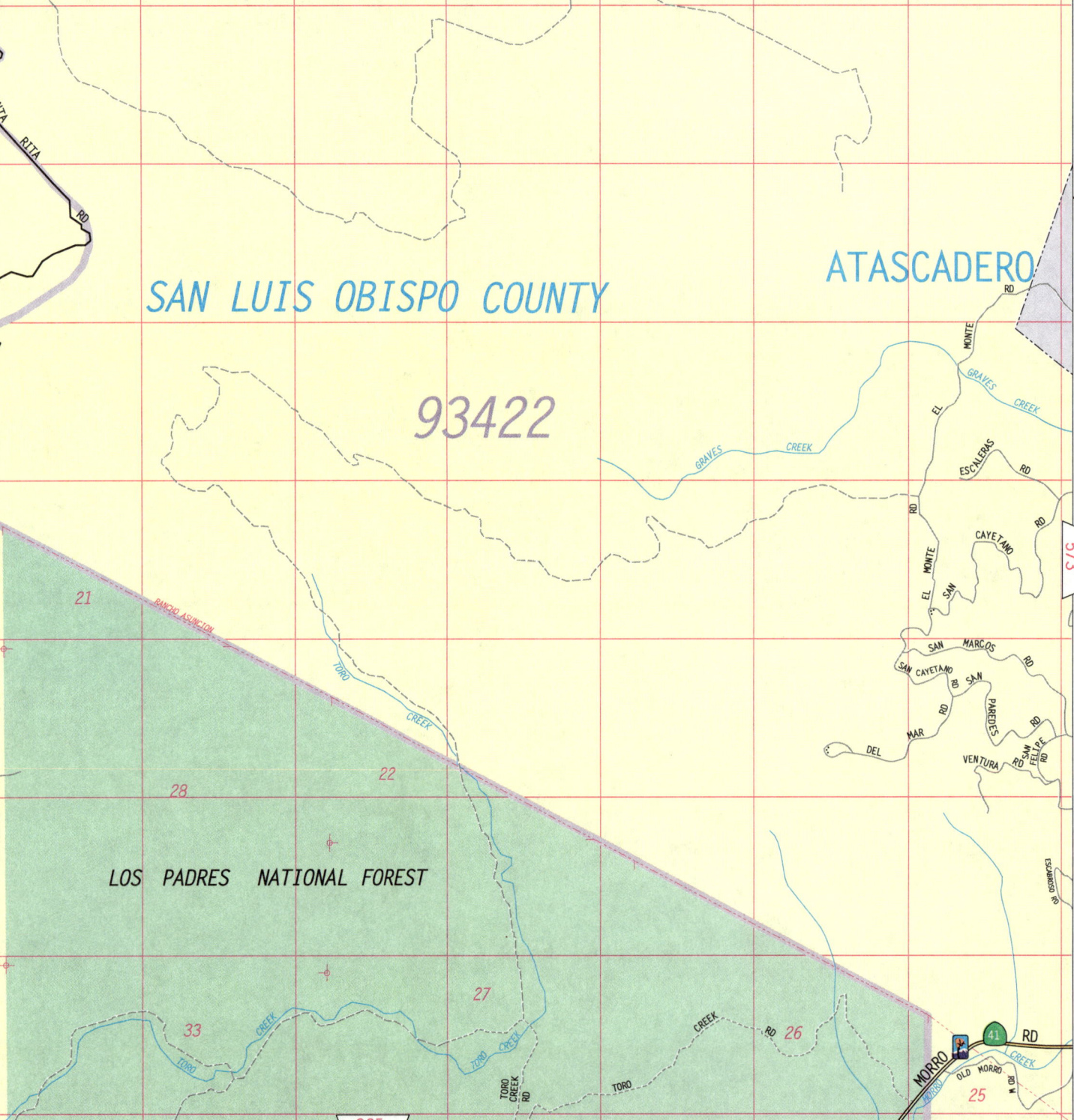
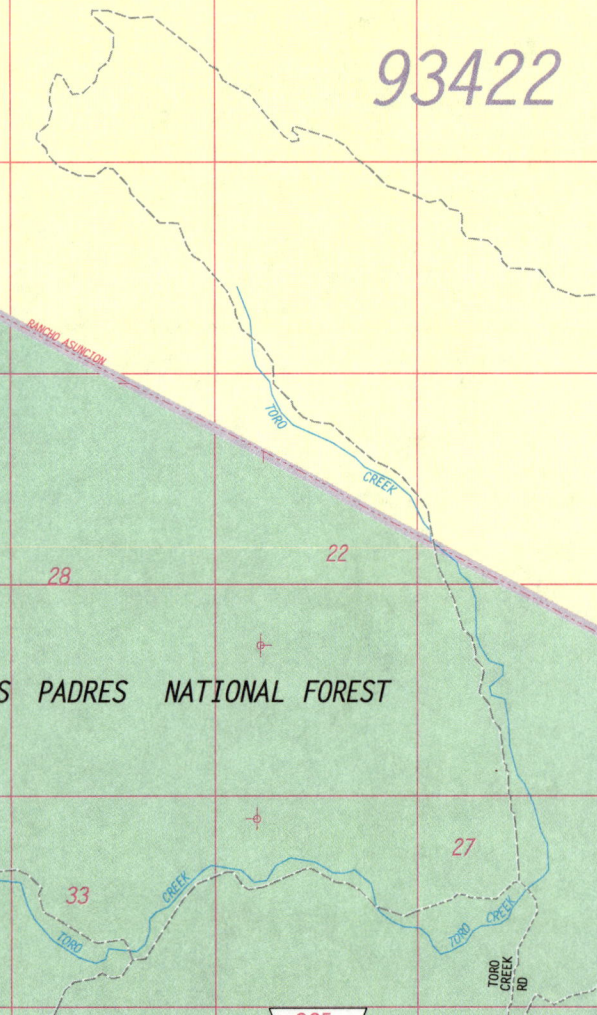
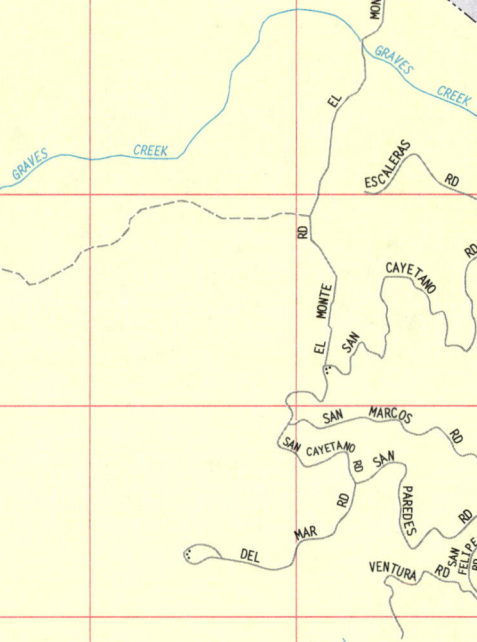

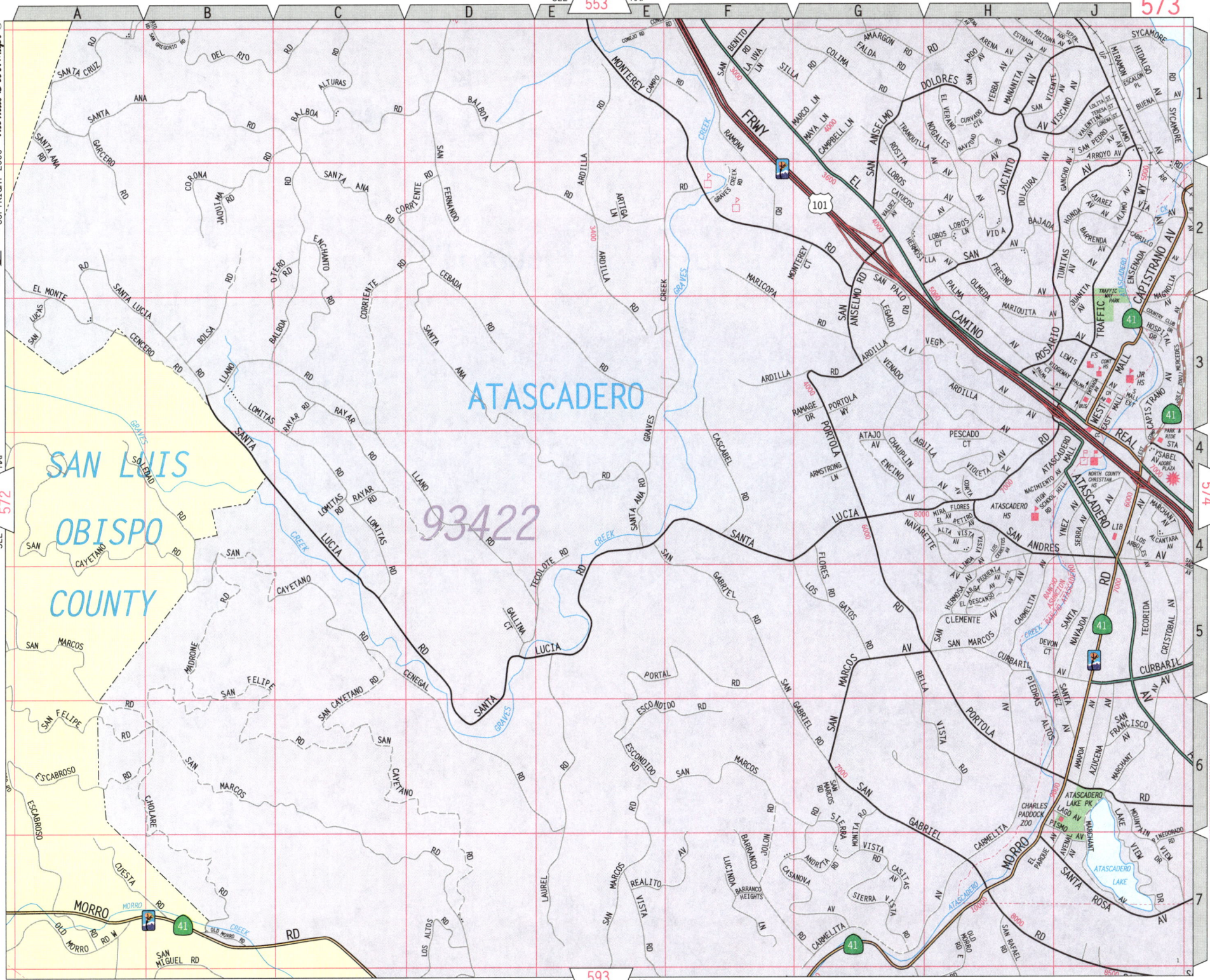

ATASCADERO

93422

SAN LUIS OBISPO COUNTY

SEE 553 MAP
SEE 572 MAP
SEE 574 MAP
SEE 593 MAP

STB & SLO

MAP

Thomas Bros. Maps®
COPYRIGHT 2000

STB & SLO

A B C D E SEE 325 MAP E F G H J

SEE 325 MAP

1

SALINAS

TEMPLETON RD
CRESTON EUREKA RD
ROAD RUNNER LN
CRESTON RD
VIA VISTA WY
EUREKA
TAMARA LN
POCO RD
41
7
8
9

MISTY CANYON WY
KINGSBURY WY

SYCAMORE
MERCEDES AV
MAGNOLIA
CABRILLO
MERCEDES AV
CEM
CEMETERY RD
UP
41
RD

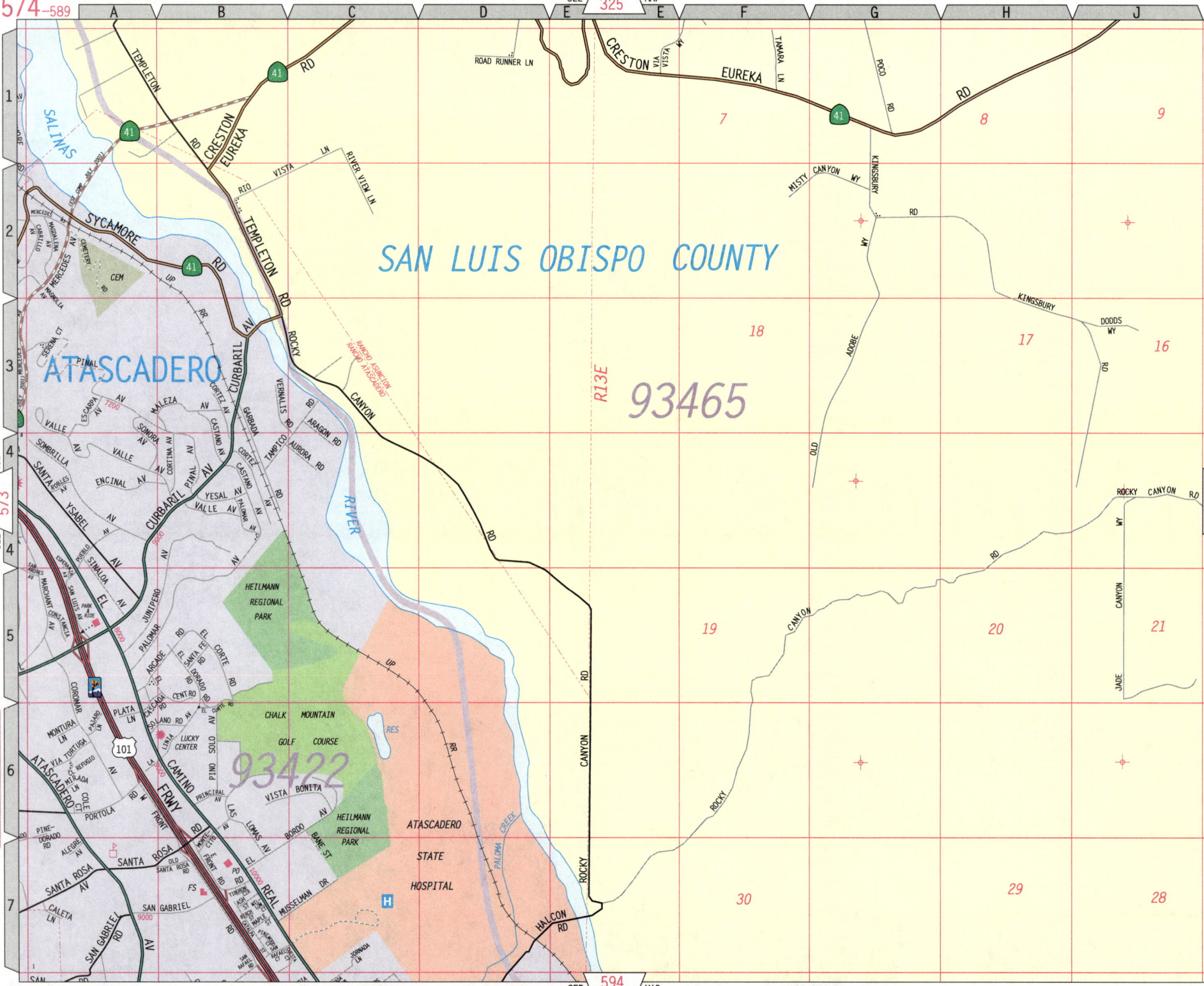

SAN LUIS OBISPO COUNTY

KINGSBURY
DODDS WY

ATASCADERO

PINAL
CURBARIL AV
ESCARPA AV
SEGENA CT
RR
CORTEZ AV
CASTANO AV
ROCKY
VERNALIS RD
ARAGON RD
CANYON
RANCHO ASUNCION RANCHO ATASCADERO

R13E

93465

18
17
16

VALLE
SONORA AV
MALEZA
CORTINA AV
CASTANO AV
TAMPICO
AURORA RD
RD
CANYON

VALLE
ENCINAL AV
YESAL AV
PALOMAR
RIVER
RD
OLD
ADOBE
RD

SOMBRILLA
SANTA ROBLES AV
CURBARIL AV
PINAL AV
CORTEZ AV
VALLE AV

SEE 573 MAP

SANTA YSABEL AV
EL
PUEBLO RD
SINALOA AV
JUNIPERO
RESERVOIR

ROCKY CANYON RD

SEE 325 MAP

SAN SIMONE AV
ESPERANZA
SAN LUIS AV
PARK N RIDE

HEILMANN REGIONAL PARK

RD

WY

4

19
20
21

MARCHANT AV
CONSTANCIA AV
PALOMAR
ARCADE
RD
EL CORTE RD
EL SANTA FE RD
EL DORADO RD
RD

CANYON

ROCKY CANYON WY

JADE CANYON RD

MONTURA LN
COROMAR
VIA TORTUGA
CASCADA
CENTRO
AV
UP
RR

CHALK MOUNTAIN
GOLF COURSE
RES

RD

PLATA LN
PAJARO LN
SOLANO RD AV
EL CUATL RD
SOTO AV
LIMA
LUCKY CENTER

93422

ATASCADERO FRWY
CAMINO
DEL REFUGIO
MIRADA
COLE CT
PORTOLA
101
FRONT RD
PRINCIPAL AV
VISTA BONITA
AV

CANYON
ROCKY

30
29
28

PINE-DORADO RD
ALEGRE AV
SANTA ROSA
OLD SANTA ROSA RD
FS
FRONT RD
EL CAMINO REAL
LAS LOMAS AV
BORDO AV
BANE ST
HEILMANN REGIONAL PARK
MUSSELMAN DR
PALOMA CREEK
ATASCADERO STATE HOSPITAL
H

CALETA LN
SAN GABRIEL RD
SANTA ROSA AV
SAN GABRIEL AV
TIBURON
FLASH
MAPLE
JORNADA LN
HALCON RD

SEE 594 MAP

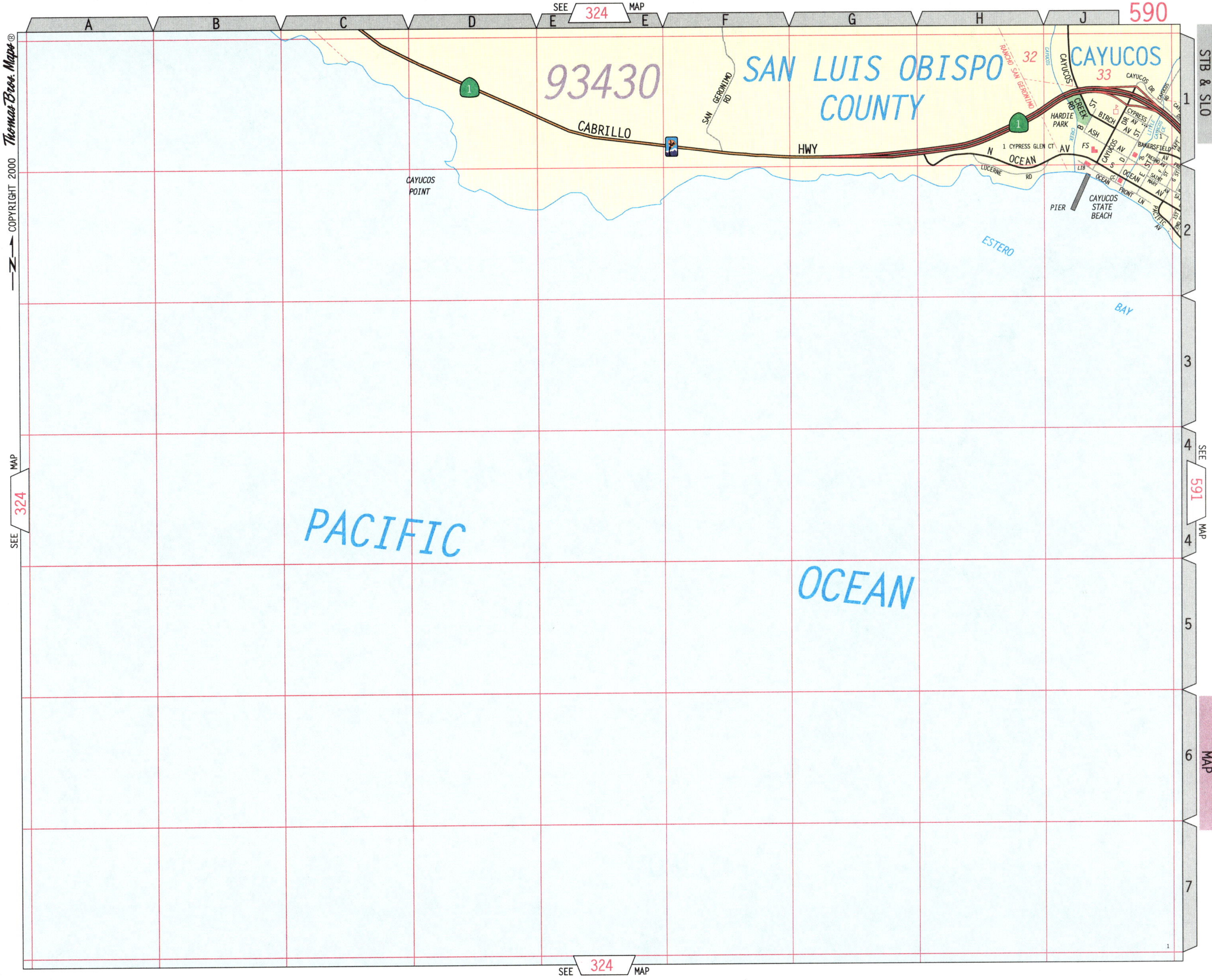

A B C D E E F G H J

93430

SAN LUIS OBISPO COUNTY

RANCHO SAN GERONIMO

32

CABARROS

CAYUCOS

33

CAYUCOS DR

CAYUCOS

CABRILLO

SAN GERONIMO RD

HARDIE PARK

ST BIRCH

CYPRESS

CAYUCOS AV

1

HWY

1 CYPRESS GLEN CT

N OCEAN AV

FS

ASH

BAKERSFIELD

CAYUCOS POINT

LUCERNE RD

1

CAYUCOS AV

OCEAN

FRESNO AV

LIB

OCEAN AV

OCEAN FRONT LN

PACIFIC AV

PIER

CAYUCOS STATE BEACH

ESTERO

BAY

PACIFIC

OCEAN

SEE 591 MAP

SEE 324 MAP

MAP

N

COPYRIGHT 2000

Thomas Bros. Maps®

1 2 3 4 4 5 6 7

591–592

A B C D E E F G H J

SEE 324 MAP

STB & SLO

COPYRIGHT 2000 Thomas Bros. Maps

CAYUCOS

33

34

35

36

31

CYPRESS

HOLLOW

R10E R11E

WHALE ROCK RESERVOIR

1 KENTUCKY AV

MOUNTAIN VIEW

FAIRFAX AV

DAM

ST

RD

1100

RANCHO MORO Y CAYUCOS

BAKERSFIELD

CABRILLO AV

PARK AV

OCEAN

PACIFIC

13TH

OLD CREEK

93430

RD

T28S T29S

CASS

CREEK

MONTECITO

CREEK

WILLOW

OLD

5

1

CIRCLE

CAYUCOS MORRO BAY CEMETERY

SEE 590 MAP

ESTERO

MORRO STRAND STATE BEACH

STUDIO DR

RICHARD

SAN LUIS OBISPO COUNTY

RD

CREEK

NEGRANTI RD

TORO

SEE 325 MAP

PACIFIC

BAY

OCEAN VIEW
GRACIA
FLORES
EL SERENO
DEL MAR
CORONADO
BONITA
ACACIA
THALBERG
MAYER

CHANEY

GILBERT

KEATON

HERBERT

BLVD

TORO

CREEK

TORO

FS (SEASONAL)

CABRILLO

CREEK

RD

CREEK

TORO

MORRO BAY

93442

CABRILLO HWY

1

TORO

ALVA PAUL CREEK

NORTH POINT NATURAL AREA

BLANCA ST
TUSCAN
DAWSON AV
ZANZIBAR ST
YERBA BUENA ST

NORTH POINT

SEE 611 MAP

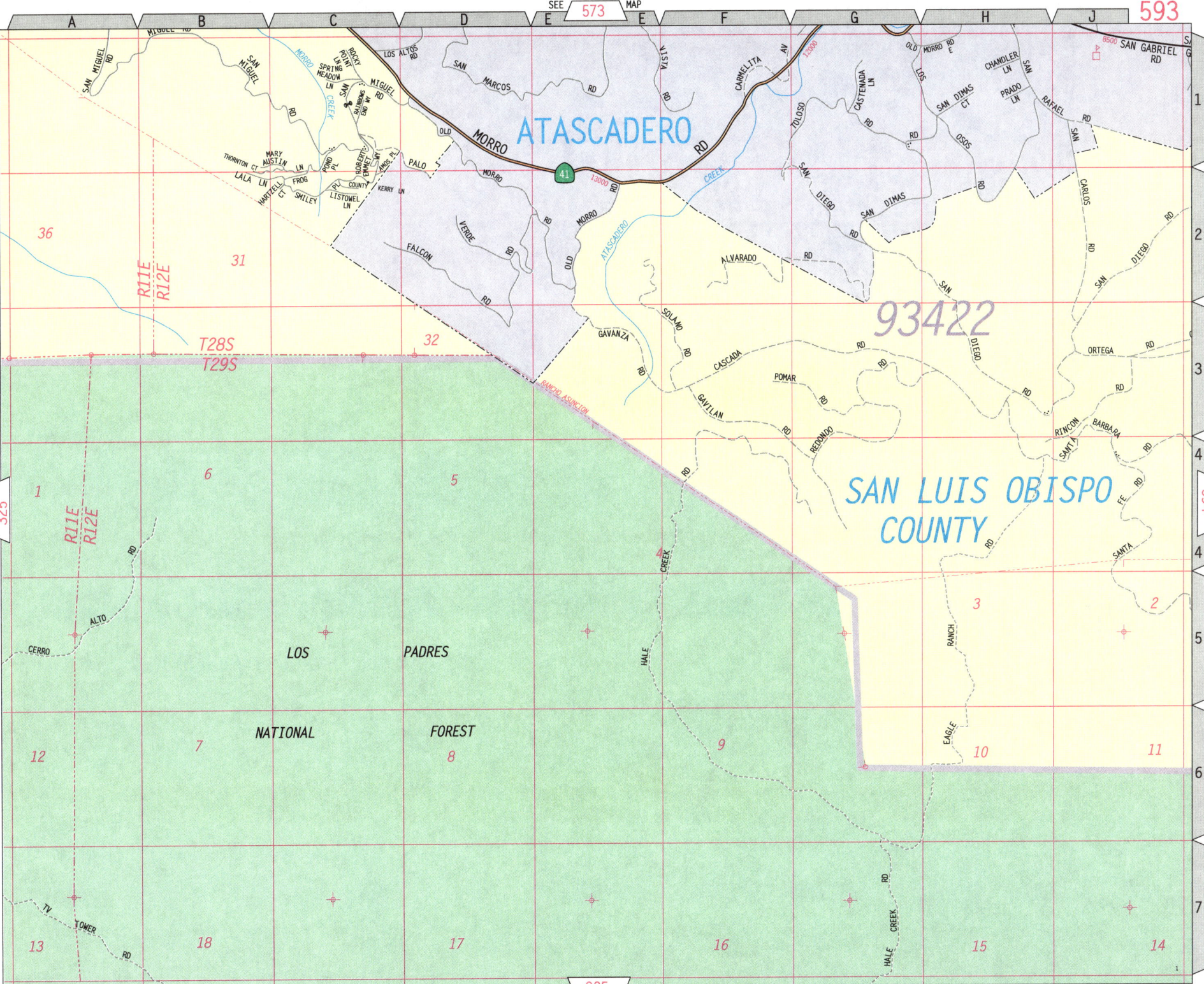

593

STB & SLO

A B C D E E F G H J

ATASCADERO

MIGUEL RD
SAN MIGUEL RD
LOS ALTOS RD
SAN MARCOS RD
VISTA RD
CARMELITA AV
OLD MORRO RD E
SAN GABRIEL RD
8500
SAN G

SPRING MEADOW LN
ROCKY POINT LN
MORRO CREEK
SAN MIGUEL RD
RAINBOWS END WY
CHANDLER LN
SAN DIMAS CT
CASTENADA LN
PRADO LN
SAN RAFAEL RD
1

MARY AUSTIN LN
THORNTON CT
LALA LN
HARTZELL CT
FROG
SMILEY
POND PL
ROBERT EMMENT WY
LISTOWEL LN
ENOS PL
PALO
KERRY LN
OLD MORRO RD
SAN DIEGO RD
SAN DIMAS RD
SAN CARLOS RD

36
31
VERDE RD
FALCON RD
MORRO RD
OLD MORRO RD
ATASCADERO CREEK
ALVARADO RD
SAN DIEGO RD
SAN DIEGO RD
2

41
13000
GAVANZA RD
SOLANO RD
CASCADA RD
POMAR RD
GAVILAN RD
REDONDO RD
SAN DIEGO RD
ORTEGA RD
RINCON
SANTA BARBARA RD
3

93422

RANCHO ASUNCION

SEE 325 MAP
SEE 594 MAP

6
5
CREEK RD
HALE
SANTA FE RD
SANTA RD

SAN LUIS OBISPO COUNTY

R11E R12E
1
ALTO RD
CERRO
4
3
RANCH
2
5

LOS PADRES

12
7
NATIONAL
FOREST
8
9
EAGLE
10
11
6

MAP

TV TOWER RD
HALE CREEK RD
7

13
18
17
16
HALE CREEK RD
15
14

R11E R12E
T28S
T29S
32
4

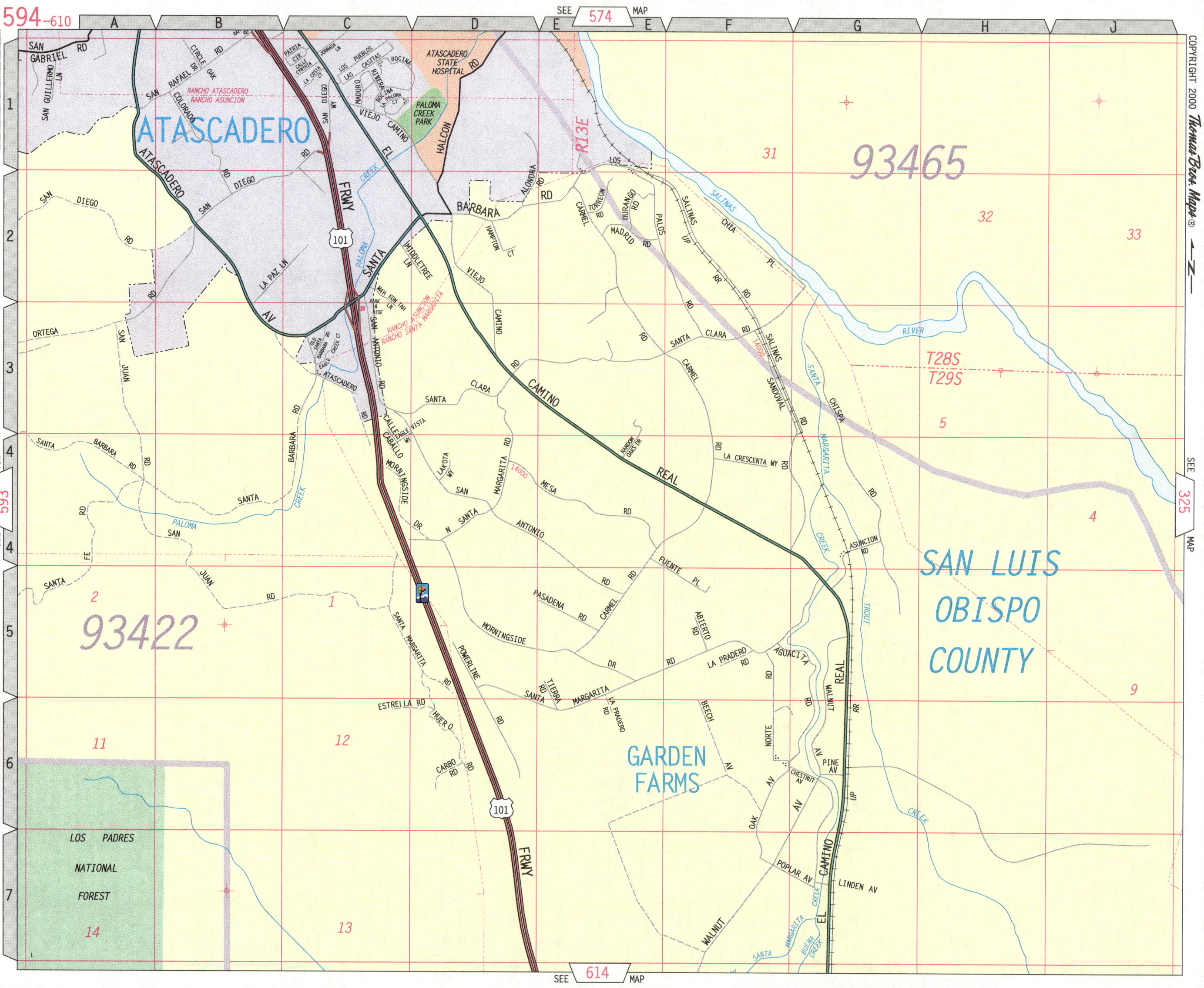

STB & SLO

A B C D E E F G H J

1 2 3 4 5 6 7

ATASCADERO

SAN GABRIEL LN
SAN GUILLERMO LN
SAN RAFAEL RD
CIRCLE OAK RD
SAN DIEGO
COLORADO
RANCHO ATASCADERO
RANCHO ASUNCION
ATASCADERO
SAN DIEGO RD
EL CAMINO REAL
SANTA
PATRIA CIR
CALLE CORTINA
LA CRESTA
JORNADA LN
LOS PUEBLOS
LAS CASITAS
MADURO
RIVERA LN
BOCINA
BOCINA CT
LA PALOMA CT

ATASCADERO STATE HOSPITAL
HALCON RD
PALOMA CREEK PARK

SAN DIEGO RD
SAN JUAN
ORTEGA
LA PAZ LN
PALOMA
SANTA
FRWY
101
MIDDLETREE LN
VIEJO
CAMINO
BARBARA
HAMPTON CT
ALONDRA RD
CARMEL
MADRID
PALOS
TORRECON
DURANGO RD
CHIA
SALINAS
SALINAS RR
RD
SALINAS
SANDOVAL RD
SANTA MARGARITA CREEK
SANTA CHISPA
RIVER

93465

31 32 33

T28S
T29S
5

SEE 574 MAP
R13E
LOS
BARBARA

MAP SEE 593 SEE 325 MAP

SANTA BARBARA RD
SANTA FE RD
SANTA
PALOMA CREEK
SAN JUAN RD
BARBARA RD
MORNINGSIDE DR
CALLE CABALLO
EAGLE VISTA WY
EAGLE CREEK CT
OLD SANTA BARBARA RD
ATASCADERO RD
SAN ANTONIO RD
MAH KON TAH LN
PARK & RIDE
RANCHO ASUNCION
RANCHO SANTA MARGARITA
SANTA CLARA
SANTA CLARA RD
LAKOTA WY
SAN SANTA
MARGARITA RD
14000
MESA RD
CAMINO
REAL
CARMEL RD
LA CRESCENTA WY
RANCHO OAKS DR
ASUNCION RD
TROUT CREEK

SAN LUIS
OBISPO
COUNTY

93422

2 1
11 12 13 14

LOS PADRES
NATIONAL
FOREST

SANTA MARGARITA RD
POWERLINE RD
ESTRELLA RD
HUER O RD
CARBO RD
ANTONIO RD
PASADENA RD
MORNINGSIDE DR
TIERRA RD
SANTA MARGARITA RD
LA PRADERO RD
FUENTE PL
CARMEL
ABIERTO RD
LA PRADERO RD
AGUACITA
BEECH
NORTE AV
OAK AV
CHESTNUT AV
PINE AV
POPLAR AV
WALNUT
EL CAMINO REAL
UP
RR
WALNUT AV
LINDEN AV
SANTA MARGARITA CREEK
BUENA CREEK
CREEK

GARDEN
FARMS

FRWY
101

9
4

SEE 614 MAP

COPYRIGHT 2000 Thomas Bros. Maps

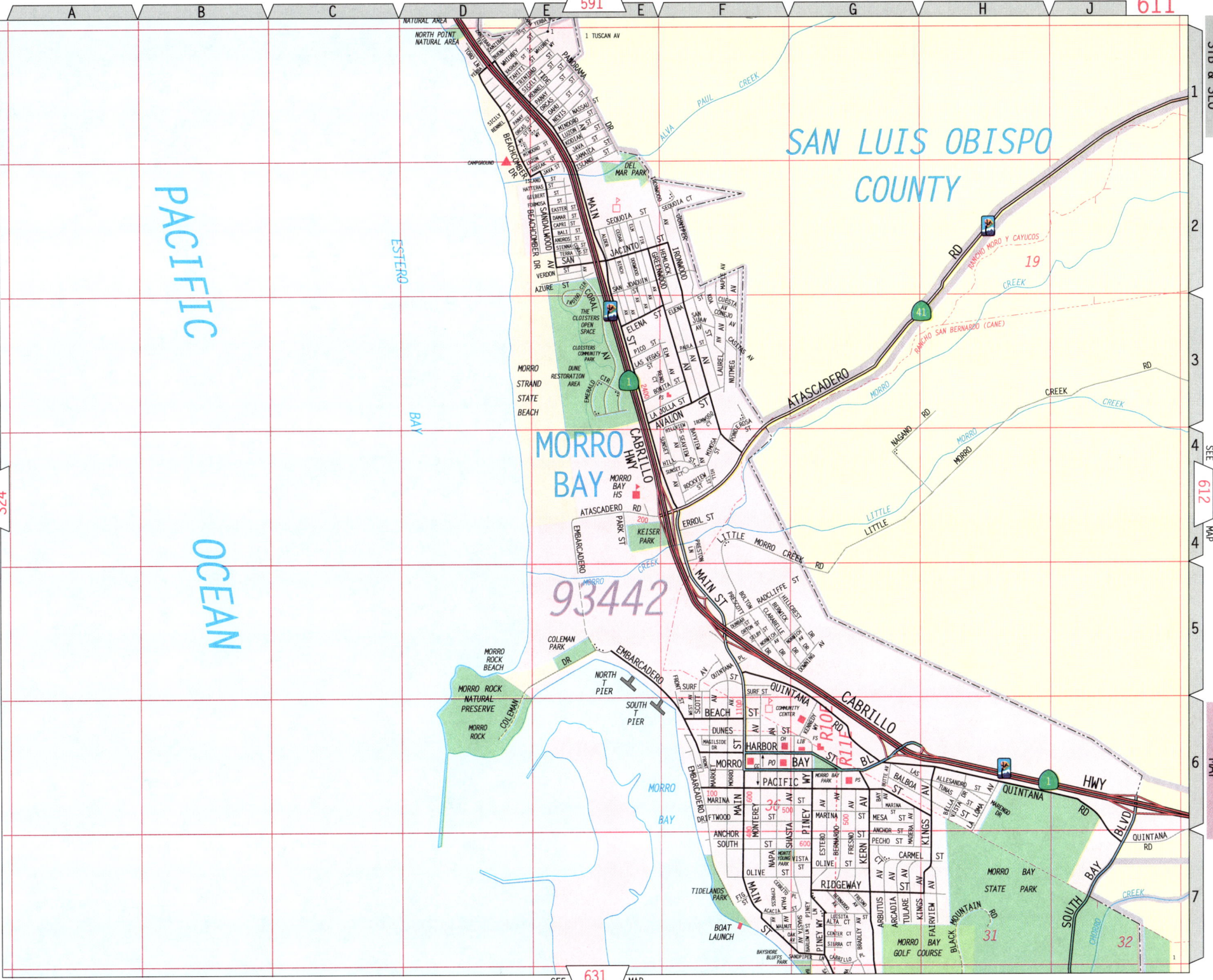

A B C D E E F G H J

Thomas Bros. Maps®
COPYRIGHT 2000

PACIFIC OCEAN

ESTERO BAY

SAN LUIS OBISPO COUNTY

MORRO BAY

93442

MORRO STRAND STATE BEACH

THE CLOISTERS OPEN SPACE

CLOISTERS COMMUNITY PARK

DUNE RESTORATION AREA

DEL MAR PARK

NORTH POINT NATURAL AREA

NATURAL AREA

MORRO BAY HS

KEISER PARK

LITTLE MORRO CREEK

COLEMAN PARK

MORRO ROCK BEACH

MORRO ROCK NATURAL PRESERVE

MORRO ROCK

NORTH T PIER

SOUTH T PIER

MORRO BAY

COMMUNITY CENTER

HARBOR

BAY

PACIFIC WY

MORRO BAY STATE PARK

MORRO BAY GOLF COURSE

BLACK MOUNTAIN RD

TIDELANDS PARK

BAYSHORE BLUFFS PARK

BOAT LAUNCH

MONTE YOUNG PARK

ATASCADERO

CABRILLO HWY

MAIN ST

QUINTANA RD

SOUTH BAY BLVD

QUINTANA RD

19
41
1
31
32

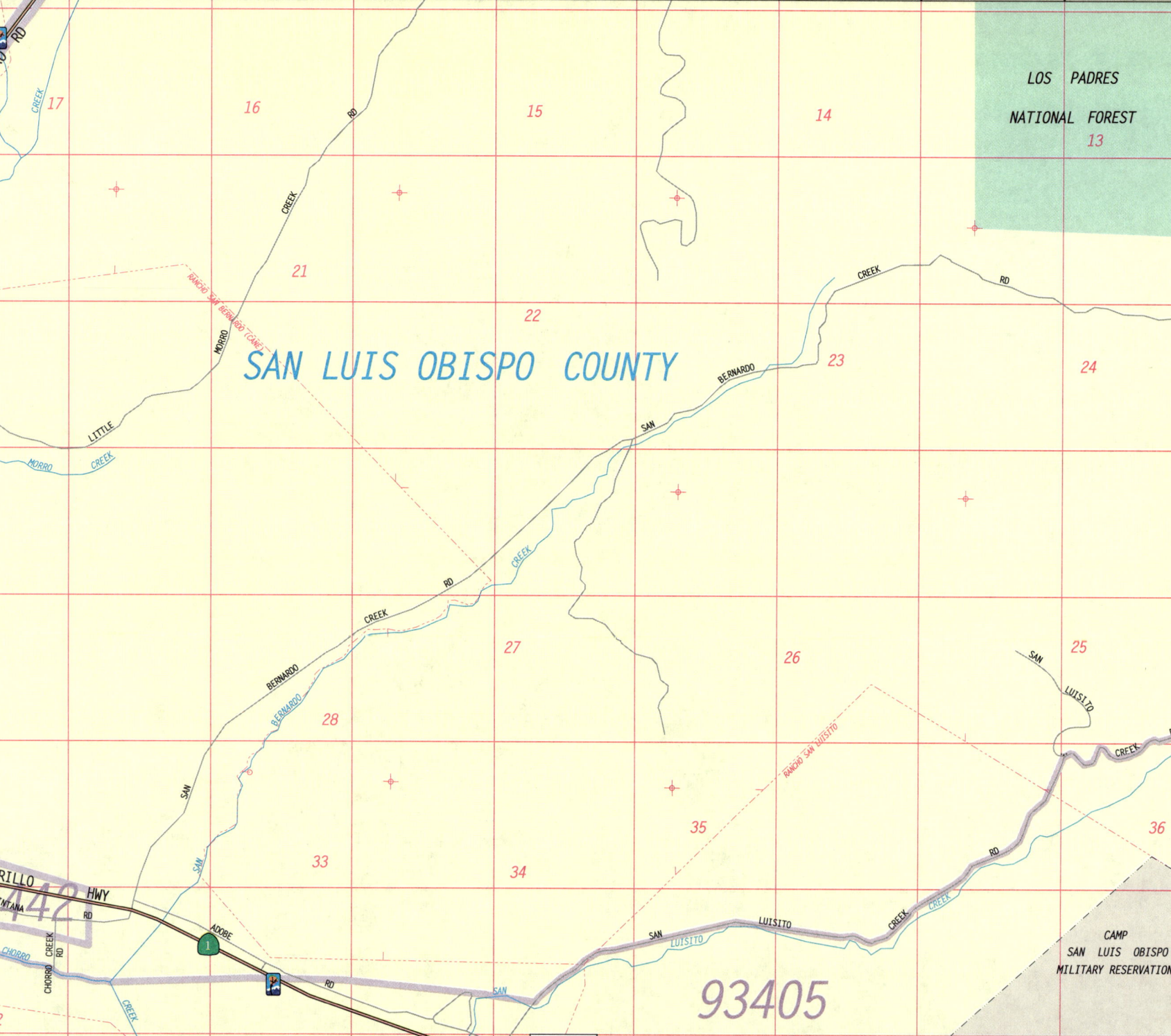

612 –613

STB & SLO

A B C D E F G H J

SEE 325 MAP

41

ATASCADERO RD

17

16

CREEK

RD

15

14

LOS PADRES

NATIONAL FOREST

13

MORRO

20

21

22

CREEK

RD

RANCHO SAN BERNARDO (CONF)

MORRO

SAN LUIS OBISPO COUNTY

LITTLE

BERNARDO

23

24

LITTLE MORRO CREEK

SAN

SEE 611 MAP

SEE 325 MAP

CREEK

RD

CREEK

27

26

SAN

LUISITO

25

BERNARDO

CREEK

BERNARDO

28

RANCHO SAN LUISITO

RD

CREEK

MAP

SAN

35

36

33

34

CABRILLO HWY

93442

QUINTANA RD

ADOBE

1

CHORRO CREEK RD

LUISITO

CREEK

CREEK

RD

CAMP
SAN LUIS OBISPO
MILITARY RESERVATION

SAN LUISITO

SAN

32

CHORRO

CREEK

RD

SAN

93405

SEE 632 MAP

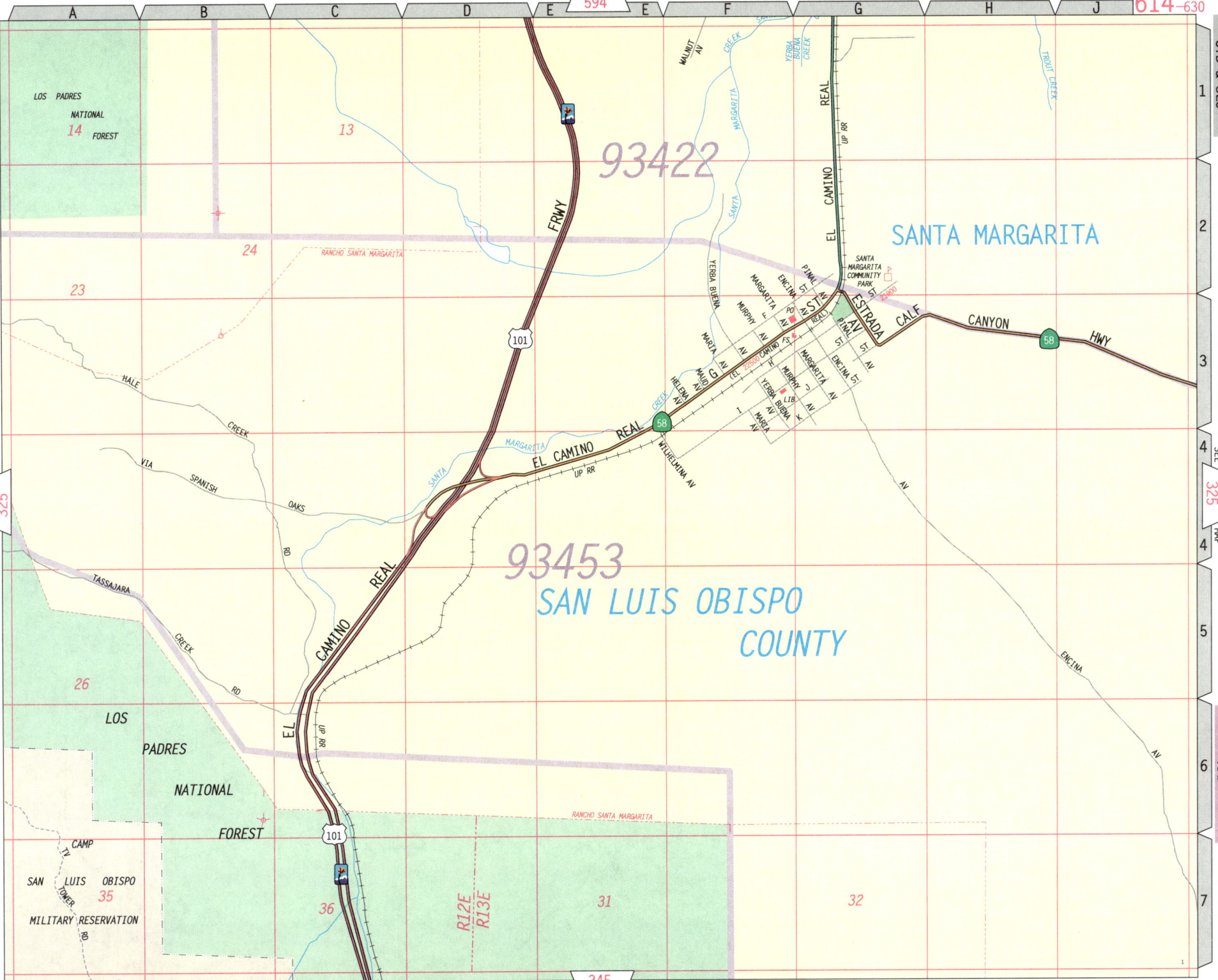

A B C D E E F G H J

1

2

3

4

4

5

6

7

Thomas Bros. Maps®

N→ COPYRIGHT 2000

LOS PADRES

NATIONAL

14 FOREST

13

93422

WALNUT AV

CREEK

YERBA BUENA CREEK

TROUT CREEK

MARGARITA

SANTA

EL CAMINO REAL

UP RR

SANTA MARGARITA

24

RANCHO SANTA MARGARITA

FRWY

101

23

HALE

CREEK

VIA SPANISH OAKS RD

TASSAJARA

CREEK

RD

26

LOS

PADRES

NATIONAL

FOREST

CAMP

TV

SAN LUIS OBISPO TOWER

35

MILITARY RESERVATION

RD

EL CAMINO REAL

UP RR

101

36

R12E

R13E

31

YERBA BUENA

MARGARITA AV

MURPHY AV

MARIA AV

MALIDO AV

HELENA AV

MARGARITA

PINAL AV

ENCINA ST

PO

EL 22500 CAMINO

G

H

I

J

K

YERBA BUENA

MARIA AV

LIB

WILHELMINA AV

EL CAMINO REAL

UP RR

CREEK

SANTA

MARGARITA

58

58

SANTA MARGARITA COMMUNITY PARK

PINAL AV

ST

ST

MARGARITA ST

ENCINA ST

MURPHY AV

ESTRADA AV

CALF

CANYON

HWY

58

93453

SAN LUIS OBISPO

COUNTY

ENCINA

AV

AV

RANCHO SANTA MARGARITA

32

SEE 325 MAP

SEE 325 MAP

A B C D E E F G H J

STB & SLO

SEE 611 MAP

COPYRIGHT 2000 Thomas Bros. Maps®

PACIFIC

OCEAN

ESTERO BAY

MORRO BAY

MONTANA DE ORO STATE PARK

MORRO BAY

MORRO BAY GOLF COURSE

Museum of Natural History

CAMPGROUND

Morro Bay State Park

MORRO BAY STATE PARK

93442

BLACK MOUNTAIN

VIEW DR

SOUTH BAY BLVD

T29S
T30S

CHORRO CREEK

LOS OSOS CREEK

TURRI RD

ELFIN FOREST ECOLOGICAL PRESERVE

SANTA LUCIA ST
SANTA PAULA AV
SANTA YSABEL AV
SANTA MARIA AV

BAYWOOD PARK

EL MORO AV

PASO ROBLES AV

SAN LUIS OBISPO COUNTY

SWEET SPRINGS NATURE RESERVE

MORRO SHORES MHP

RAMONA AV

PISMO

93402

SEA PINES GOLF COURSE

CUESTA BY-THE-SEA

MONARCH GROVE NATURAL AREA

LOS OSOS

LOS OSOS VALLEY RD

SEE 344 MAP

SEE 632 MAP

SEE 651 MAP

MAP

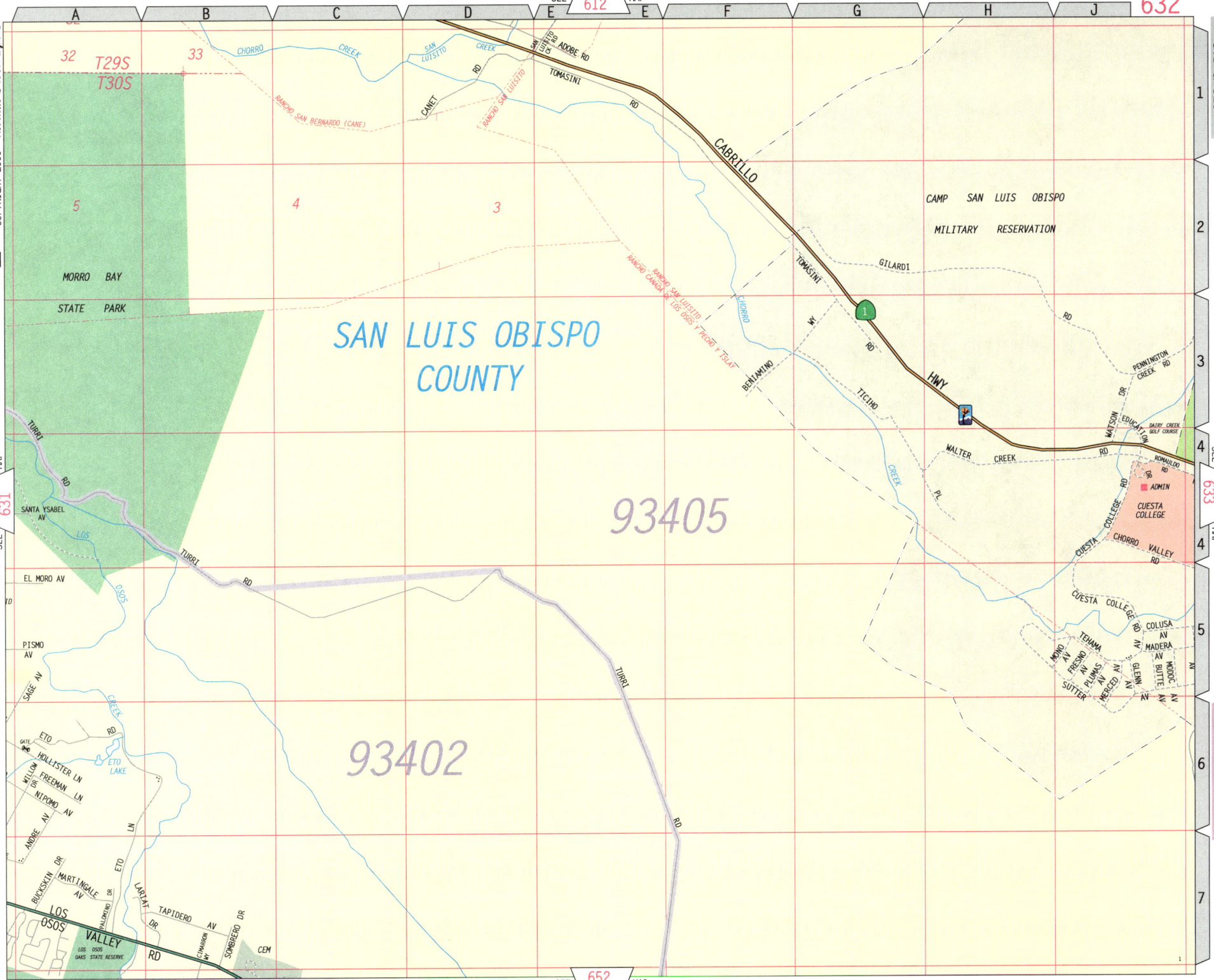

A   B   C   D   E   E   F   G   H   J

STB & SLO

Thomas Bros. Maps®
COPYRIGHT 2000
N →

32   T29S
33   T30S

CHORRO   CREEK

5   4   3

SAN LUISITO   CREEK

SAN LUISITO CK RD
ADOBE RD

RANCHO SAN BERNARDO (CANE)

CANET RD

TOMASINI RD

CABRILLO

MORRO BAY

STATE PARK

RANCHO SAN LUISITO

RANCHO CAÑADA DE LOS OSOS Y PECHO Y ISLAY

CAMP   SAN   LUIS   OBISPO
MILITARY   RESERVATION

GILARDI

SAN LUIS OBISPO
COUNTY

TOMASINI WY

RD

BENIAMINO

CHORRO

TICIHO

HWY

PENNINGTON CREEK RD

WATSON EDUCATION

DAIRY CREEK GOLF COURSE

WALTER CREEK RD

ROMAULDO RD

93405

TURRI RD

SANTA YSABEL AV

LOS

TURRI RD

CUESTA COLLEGE RD

ADMIN

CUESTA COLLEGE

CUESTA CHORRO VALLEY RD

EL MORO AV

OSOS

CUESTA COLLEGE RD
COLUSA AV
TEHAMA AV   MADERA AV
MONO AV   FRESNO AV   MODOC AV
MERCED AV   PLUMAS AV   GLENN AV   BUTTE AV
SUTTER AV   MERCED AV

PISMO AV

SAGE AV

93402

CREEK

GATE
ETO RD
HOLLISTER LN
WILLOW DR   FREEMAN LN
NIPOMO AV
ETO LAKE

ANDRE AV

ETO LN

TURRI RD

BUCKSKIN DR   MARTINGALE AV
PALOMINO DR
LARIAT DR   TAPIDERO AV
CIMARRON WY   SOMBRERO DR

LOS
OSOS   VALLEY RD

LOS OSOS OAKS STATE RESERVE

CEM

SEE 631 MAP

SEE 633 MAP

MAP

1   2   3   4   4   5   6   7

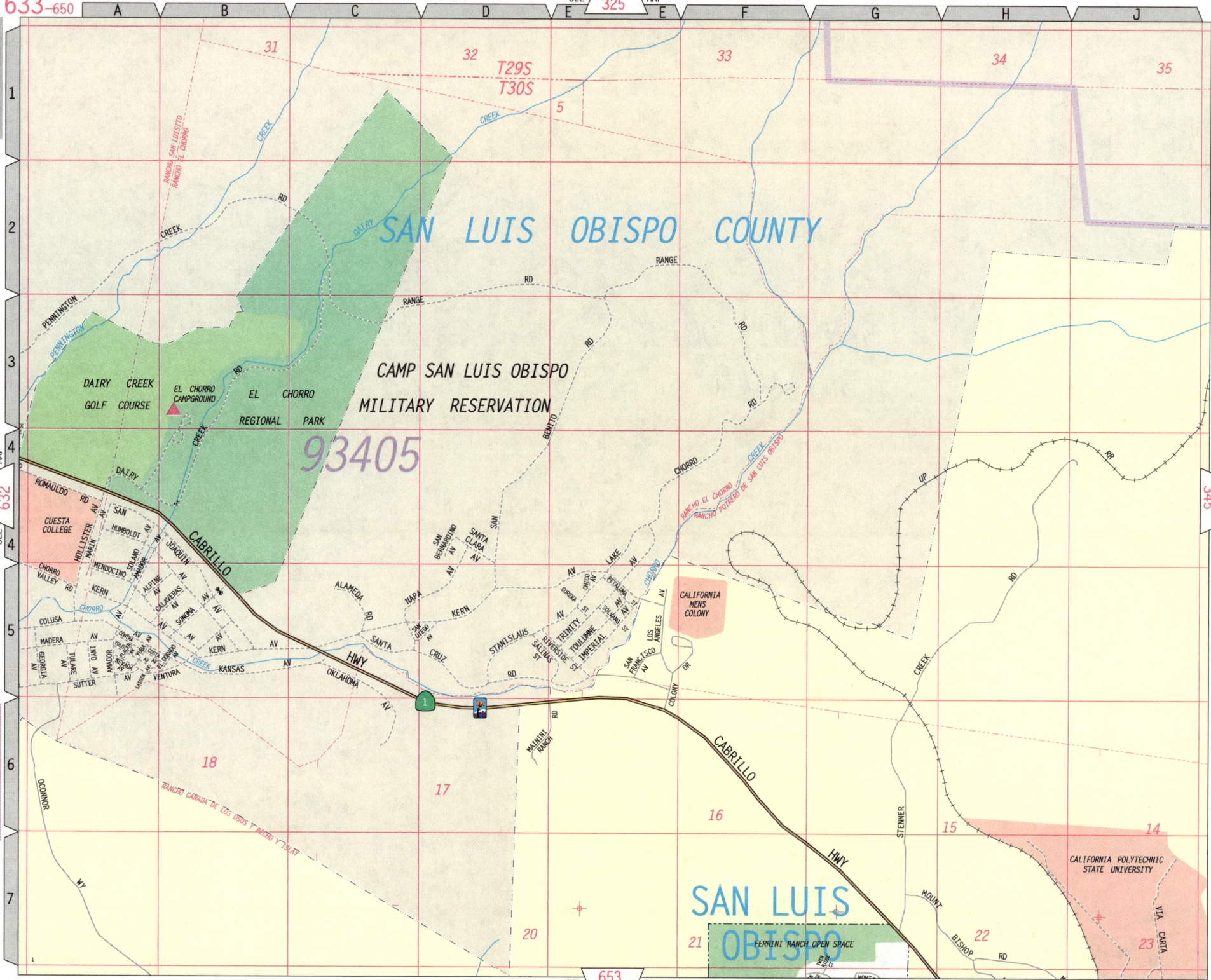

A B C D E E F G H J

STB & SLO

1

SEE 325 MAP

31 32 T29S 33 34 35
T30S

CREEK CREEK 5

—N—

SAN LUIS OBISPO COUNTY

2

RANCHO SAN LUIS/TD
RANCHO EL CHORRO

CREEK

DAIRY

RANGE

RD

PENNINGTON

3

RANGE RD

RD

CAMP SAN LUIS OBISPO

DAIRY CREEK
GOLF COURSE

EL CHORRO CAMPGROUND

EL CHORRO
REGIONAL PARK

MILITARY RESERVATION

BENITO

93405

CREEK

RD

SEE 632 MAP

4

ROMAULDO RD
CUESTA
COLLEGE

DAIRY

CABRILLO

SAN
HUMBOLDT

AV

HOLLISTER
MARIN

AV

SAN
JOAQUIN

AMADOR

CHORRO

SAN
BERNARDINO
AV

SANTA
CLARA
AV

CHORRO

RANCHO EL CHORRO
RANCHO POTRERO DE SAN LUIS OBISPO

UP

SEE 345 MAP

CHORRO
VALLEY RD

KERN

MENDOCINO

ALPINE

CALAVERAS

SOLANO

SONOMA

AV

CHORRO

ALAMEDA
RD

NAPA

SANTA

SAN

KERN

AV

EUREKA
ST

CHICO
ST

BETHANA

SOLANO
ST

CHORRO

LAKE
AV

CALIFORNIA
MENS
COLONY

RR

RD

5

COLUSA

MADERA

GEORGIA
AV

TULARE

INYO

NEVADA

CONTRA
COSTA

YOLO

YUBA

EL DORADO

KERN

AV

SANTA
CRUZ

SAN
LUIS OBISPO

STANISLAUS

RIVERSIDE

TRINITY

SALINAS
ST

TOULUMNE

IMPERIAL

SAN
FRANCISCO
AV

LOS
ANGELES
AV

COLONY
DR

CREEK

STENNER

SUTTER

AMADOR

AV

KANSAS

VENTURA

OKLAHOMA

AV

HWY

CREEK

RD

MATINNI
RANCH

CABRILLO

6

OCONNOR

18

RANCHO CAÑADA DE LOS OSOS Y PECHO Y ISLAY

17

16

HWY

MOUNT

BISHOP

15

14

CALIFORNIA POLYTECHNIC
STATE UNIVERSITY

VIA
CARTA

7

SAN LUIS
OBISPO

20

21 FERRINI RANCH OPEN SPACE

22

23

SEE 653 MAP

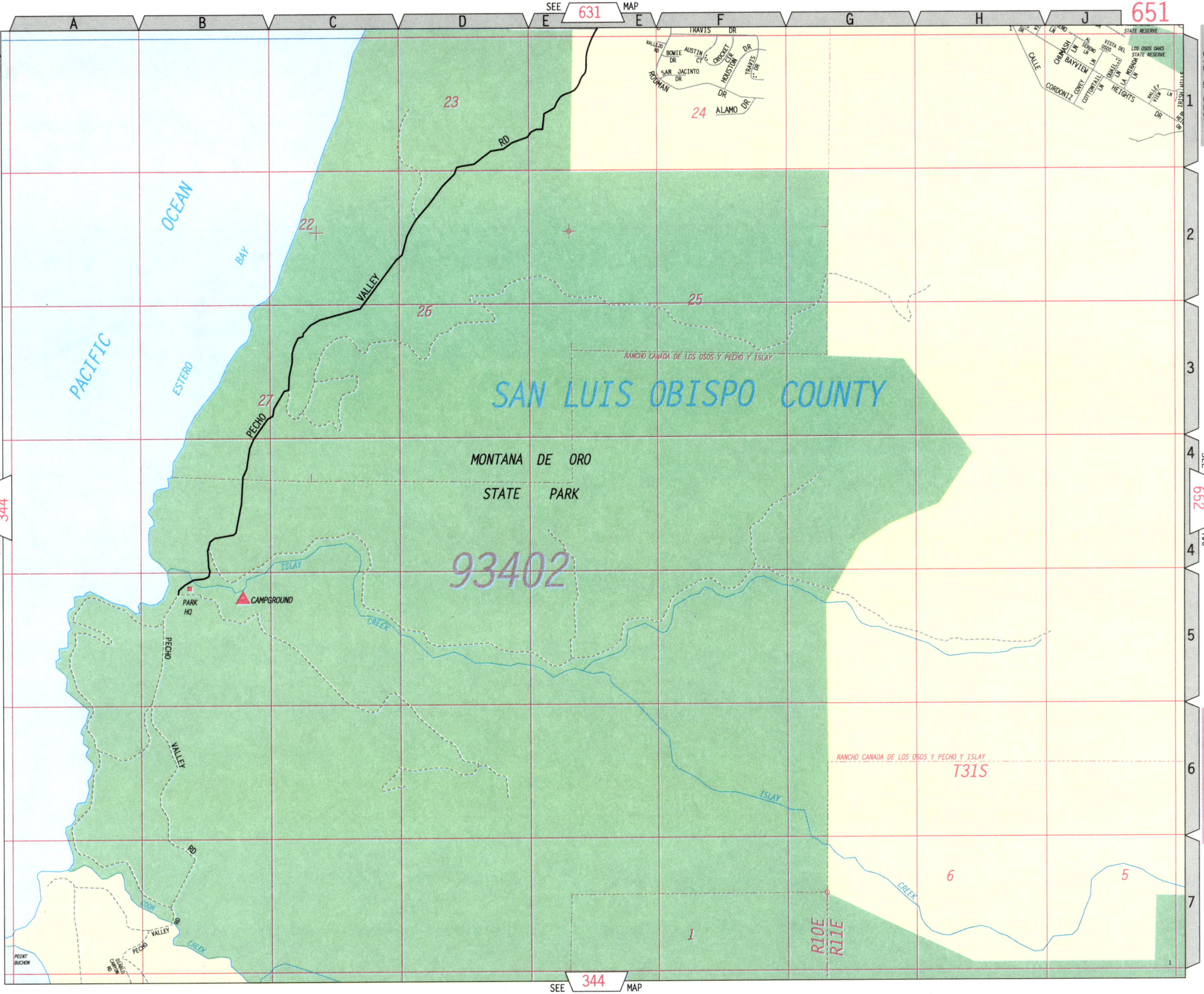

STB & SLO

SEE 344 MAP

SEE 652 MAP

MAP

A B C D E F G H J

1 2 3 4 4 5 6 7

TRAVIS DR

VALLEJO RD
BOWIE DR
AUSTIN CT
CROCKET DR
HOUSTON DR
TRAVIS DR

SAN JACINTO DR
RODMAN
ALAMO DR

24

CHUMASH LN
BAYVIEW LN
CORDONIZ
COTTONTAIL LN
QUAIL LN
HEIGHTS
LA SERENA LN
VISTA DEL
LA NEGRA LN
VALLEY DR

LOS OSOS OAKS
STATE RESERVE

STATE RESERVE

OCEAN

BAY

ESTERO

PACIFIC

23

22

26

27

25

RANCHO CANADA DE LOS OSOS Y PECHO Y ISLAY

SAN LUIS OBISPO COUNTY

MONTANA DE ORO

STATE PARK

93402

ISLAY

PECHO

VALLEY

RD

PARK HQ
CAMPGROUND

CREEK

ISLAY

PECHO

VALLEY

RD

COON RD

PECHO

VALLEY

CREEK

POINT BUCHON

DIABLO CANYON RD

1

RANCHO CANADA DE LOS OSOS Y PECHO Y ISLAY

T31S

R10E
R11E

CREEK

6

5

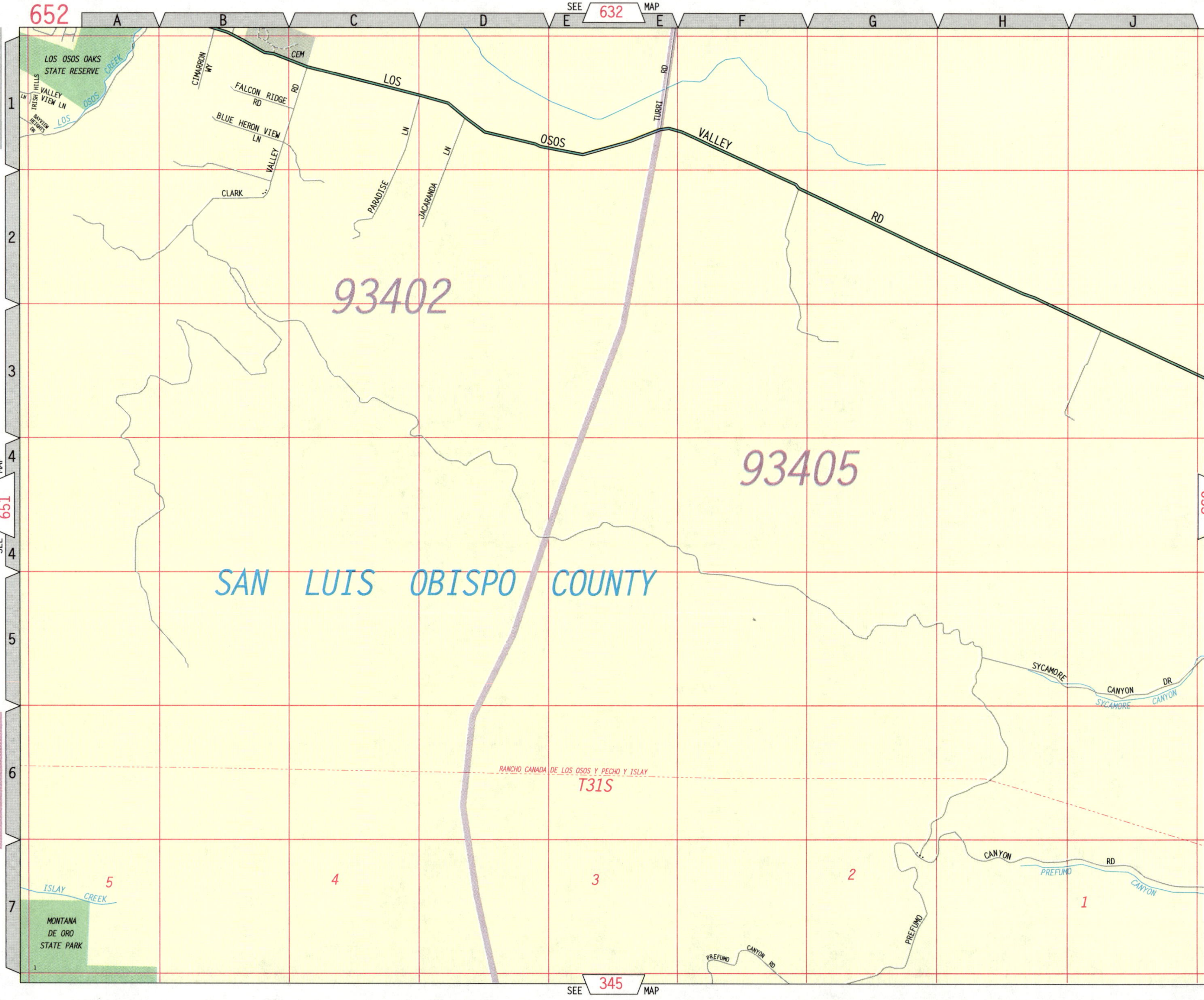

STB & SLO

A B C D E E F G H J

SEE 632 MAP

1

LOS OSOS OAKS
STATE RESERVE

CIMARRON WY

FALCON RIDGE
RD

BLUE HERON VIEW
LN

LOS

OSOS

TURRI RD

VALLEY

RD

LOS OSOS CREEK

IRISH LN

VALLEY VIEW LN

BAYWOOD HEIGHTS DR

2

VALLEY

CLARK

PARADISE LN

JACARANDA LN

93402

3

4

SEE 651 MAP

93405

SEE 653 MAP

SAN LUIS OBISPO COUNTY

5

SYCAMORE CANYON DR

SYCAMORE CANYON

MAP

6

RANCHO CANADA DE LOS OSOS Y PECHO Y ISLAY

T31S

CANYON

PREFUMO CANYON

7

ISLAY CREEK

MONTANA
DE ORO
STATE PARK

5

4

3

2

PREFUMO CANYON RD

PREFUMO CANYON RD

1

SEE 345 MAP

A B C D E E F G H J

Thomas Bros. Maps ®
© COPYRIGHT 2000
N

STB & SLO

93407

CALIFORNIA POLYTECHNIC STATE UNIVERSITY

CAMP SAN LUIS OBISPO MILITARY RESERVATION

BISHOP PEAK NATURAL AREA

FERRINI OPEN RANCH SPACE

OCONNOR

SYCAMORE CREEK

FOOTHILL BLVD

E FOOTHILL BLVD

SAN LUIS OBISPO

93405
SAN LUIS OBISPO COUNTY

SAN LUIS PEAK

LOS OSOS VALLEY RD

HAY BARN LN
PARTNER RD

LAUREATE

CHARLES A AND MAY R MAINO OPEN SPACE

EL CAMINO REAL

SYCAMORE CANYON

PREFUMO CANYON

PREFUMO CREEK

LAGUNA LAKE PARK

LAGUNA LAKE

LET IT BE NATURE PRESERVE

LAGUNA LAKE GOLF COURSE

VISTA DEL COLLADOS

MADONNA INN

MADONNA PLAZA

CENTRAL COAST MALL

EMBASSY SUITES HOTEL

93401

SOUTH HILLS OPEN SPACE

PRADO RD

DMV

101

MADONNA RD

OCEANAIRE DR

227

SEE 652 MAP

SEE 654 MAP

MAP

R11E R12E

SEE 345 MAP

A B C D E E F G H J

STB & SLO

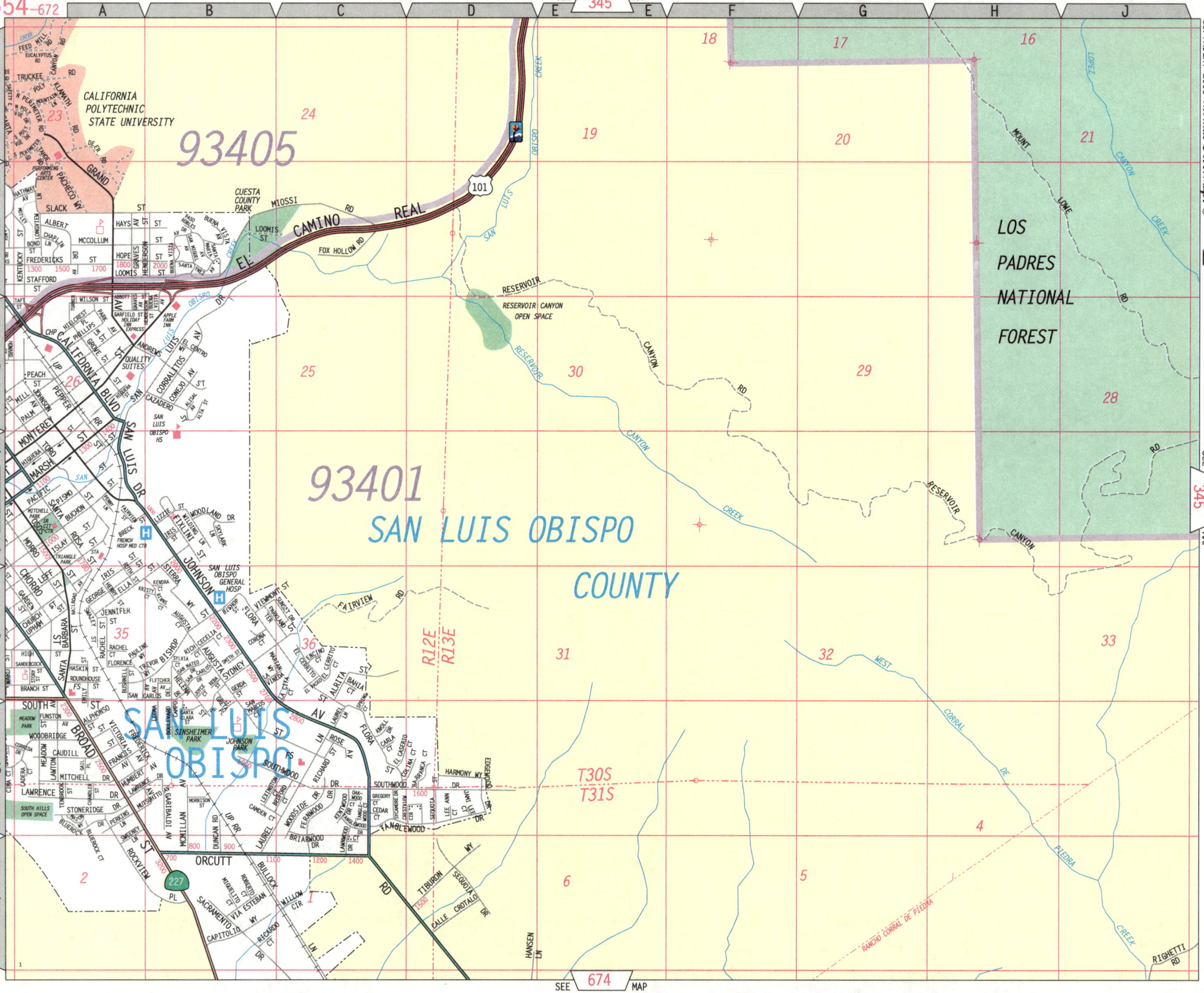

COPYRIGHT 2000 *Thomas Bros. Maps* ®

93405

CALIFORNIA POLYTECHNIC STATE UNIVERSITY

23 24 18 17 16 19 20 21

CUESTA COUNTY PARK

LOS PADRES NATIONAL FOREST

EL CAMINO REAL

101

RESERVOIR CANYON OPEN SPACE

25 26 30 29 28

93401

SAN LUIS OBISPO

SEE 653 MAP

SEE 345 MAP

COUNTY

SAN LUIS OBISPO GENERAL HOSP

FRENCH HOSP MED CTR

35 36 R12E R13E 31 32 33

SAN LUIS OBISPO

SINSHEIMER PARK

JOHNSON PARK

SOUTH HILLS OPEN SPACE

T30S T31S

227

2 6 5 4

ORCUTT RD

RANCHO CORRAL DE PIEDRA

SEE 674 MAP

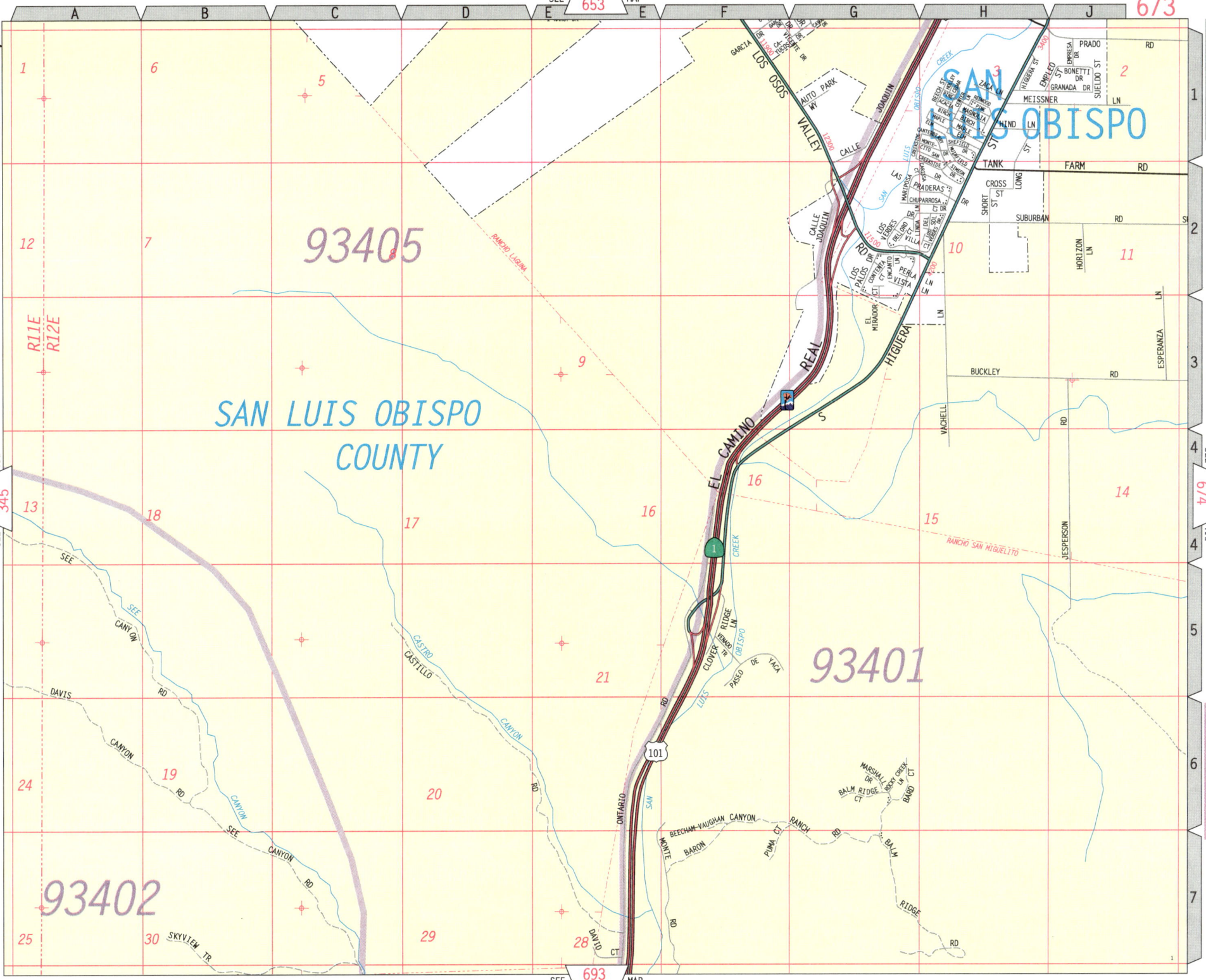

A B C D E F G H J

STB & SLO

1 6 5 3 2

1

R11E R12E

12 7 8 10 11

93405

2

SAN LUIS OBISPO

SAN LUIS OBISPO COUNTY

9

RANCHO LAGUNA

3

BUCKLEY RD

ESPERANZA LN

SEE 345 MAP

SEE 674 MAP

13 18 16 16 15 14

17

RANCHO SAN MIGUELITO

1 CREEK

4

21

93401

5

24 19 20

101

93402

25 30 SKYVIEW TR 29 28 DAVID CT

6

7

LOS OSOS VALLEY

EL CAMINO REAL

HIGUERA

ONTARIO RD

CASTRO

CASTILLO

DAVIS CANYON RD

CANYON RD

TANK FARM RD

SUBURBAN RD

CALLE JOAQUIN

AUTO PARK WY

MAP

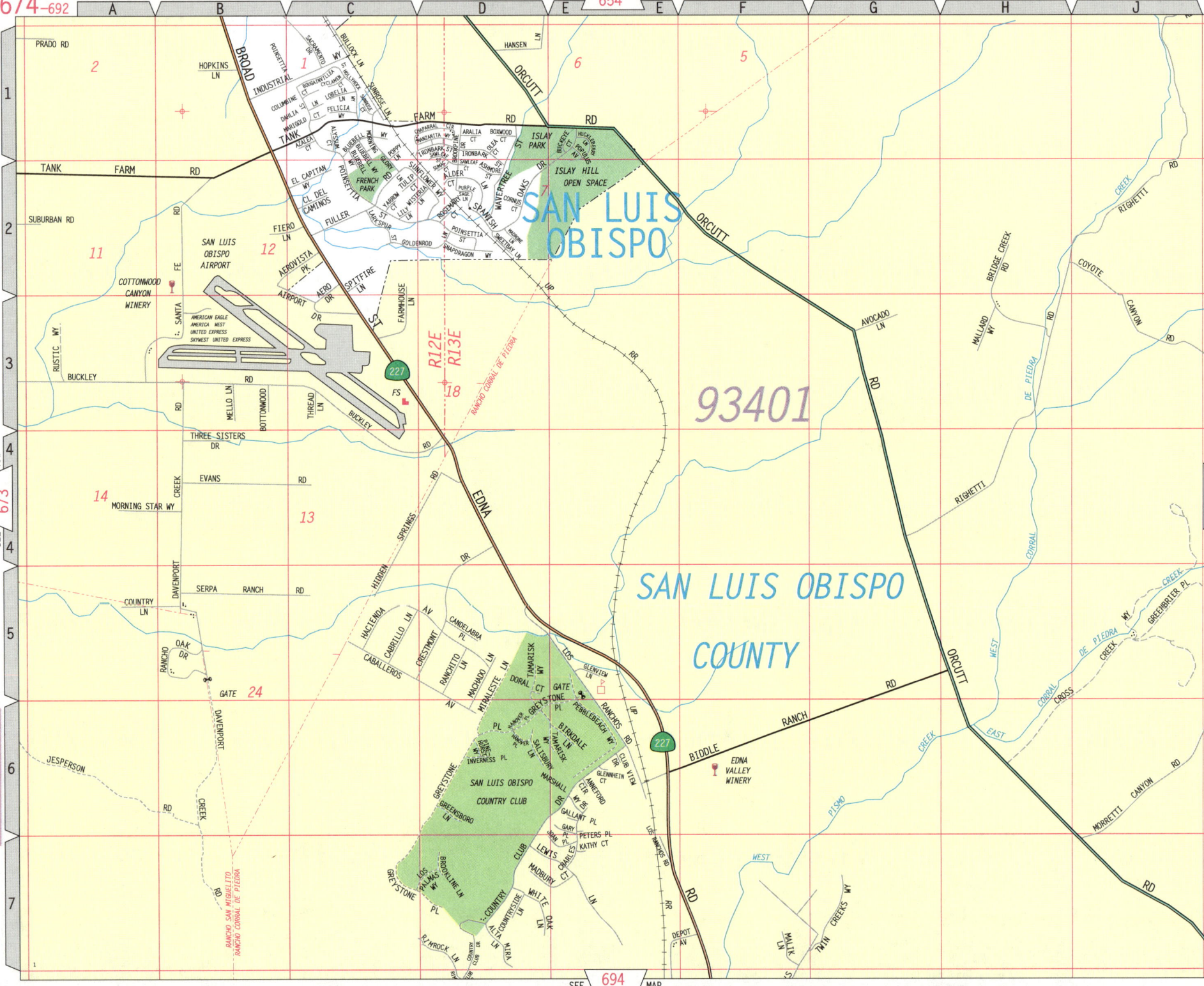

STB & SLO

SEE 673 MAP

MAP

PRADO RD

BROAD

HOPKINS LN

INDUSTRIAL

TANK FARM RD

SUBURBAN RD

TANK FARM RD

HANSEN

ORCUTT RD

ORCUTT RD

FARM

ISLAY PARK

ISLAY HILL OPEN SPACE

SAN LUIS OBISPO

FRENCH PARK

EL CAPITAN WY

CL DEL CAMINOS

POINSETTIA

FIERO LN

FULLER

GOLDENROD

SNAPDRAGON WY

SAN LUIS OBISPO AIRPORT

COTTONWOOD CANYON WINERY

AEROVISTA PK

SANTA FE

AERO DR

SPITFIRE LN

AIRPORT DR

AMERICAN EAGLE
AMERICA WEST
UNITED EXPRESS
SKYWEST UNITED EXPRESS

FARMHOUSE LN

227

R12E R13E

18

RR

93401

RUSTIC WY

BUCKLEY

MELLO LN

BOTTONWOOD

THREAD LN

BUCKLEY

RD

FS

THREE SISTERS DR

EVANS RD

MORNING STAR WY

DAVENPORT

SERPA RANCH RD

COUNTRY LN

RANCHO OAK DR

GATE

EDNA

SPRINGS

HIDDEN

DR

HACIENDA

CABRILLO LN

CABALLEROS

CRESTMONT

CANDELABRA PL

RANCHITO LN

MACHADO LN

MIRALESTE LN

AV

DORAL CT

TAMARISK WY

GREYSTONE PL

PINE PL

INVERNESS PL

GREENSBORO LN

GREYSTONE

SAN LUIS OBISPO COUNTRY CLUB

LOS PALMAS WY

BROOKLINE LN

GREYSTONE PL

RIMROCK LN

COUNTRY CLUB LN

ALTA MIRA

ALTA COUNTRYSIDE LN

WHITE OAK LN

MADBURY LN

LEWIS

PETERS PL

KATHY CT

CHARLES CT

GARY PL

GALLANT PL

JOAN PL

ANNEFORD DR

GLENNHEIM DR

CLUB VIEW DR

BIRKDALE LN

TAMARISK WY

SALISBURY WY

MARSHALL WY

HANOVER WY

PEBBLEBEACH WY

GLENVIEW LN

LOS RANCHOS RD

GATE

RANCHOS UP

227

BIDDLE

EDNA VALLEY WINERY

SAN LUIS OBISPO

COUNTY

ORCUTT RD

RANCH

RIGHETTI

AVOCADO LN

RIGHETTI RD

MALLARD WY

BRIDGE CREEK RD

COYOTE CANYON

DE PIEDRA

WEST CORRAL

EAST CORRAL

CROSS

GREENBRIER PL

GREENBRIER WY

CREEK

PISMO

CREEK

WEST

MORRETTI CANYON RD

MALIK LN

TWIN CREEKS WY

DEPOT AV

JESPERSON

DAVENPORT

RANCHO SAN MIGUELITO

RANCHO CORRAL DE PIEDRA

SEE 345 MAP

2 1 11 12 14 13 24 6 5 7 18

STB & SLO

Thomas Bros. Maps ®

COPYRIGHT 2000

N

R11E
R12E

93424

93405

93401

SKYVIEW TR

RANCHO SAN MIGUELITO

SEE A B2

1 SNOWBERRY CT
2 BRASS BUTTON CT
3 GOOSEFOOT CT LN
4 VALLEY VIEW LN
5 MEADOW VIEW
6 OAK CREST DR
7 MOON RIDGE

BASSI

CANYON RD

ONTARIO

EL CAMINO REAL

MONTE

VIA VENADO

SQUIRE

TYKES LN

SQUIRE CT

LUPINE

SEE 1900

VERDUGO

NURSERY WY

BAY

LUIS

AVILA

DR

SAN

BLUEBERRY LN

SQUIRE KNOLL DR

INDIAN

CANYON

RD

KNOB RD

GATE

LUPINE

CANYON RD

LUPINE

VALLEY

TIERRA DEL PAJARO

OAK

LN

LIVE

FERN

SAN LUIS OBISPO

COUNTY

1 SPOONBILL CT
2 SHEARWATER CT

AVILA

BOB JONES

CITY-TO-THE-SEA

BIKEWAY

OBISPO

ALLIANCE WY

PRIVATE DR

1

BLUE HERON DR

AVILA BEACH RESORT GOLF COURSE

CAVE

AVILA BEACH DR

ONTARIO

MONTE RD

HARFORD CREEK

GATE

ANA BAY RD

GATE

AVILA BEACH

2ND ST
1ST ST
SAN MIGUEL ST
SAN LUIS ST PKWY
SAN FRANCISCO ST
SAN ANTONIO ST
SAN RAFAEL ST
FRONT ST

PO
FS

AVILA BEACH

LANDING RD

GATE

PARK & RIDE

SHELL BEACH RD

93449

SEE 345 MAP

AVILA PIER

AVILA BEACH

SHELL BEACH

BONITA

BLUFFS DR

PORTAL DR

EL MIRAMAR LN

MIRAMAR

ENCANTO

INDIO

TOPAZ

LA PALOMA AV

PLAYA

BRISA

EL DORADO WY

ENCANTO CT

GATE

PALISADES PARK

FLORIN ST

FORMOSA

SEARIDGE CT

SEE 694 MAP

SAN LUIS OBISPO BAY

PALISADES

BEACHCOMBER DR

N SILVER SHOALS DR

101

BLUFF

WALKWAY

SHELL BEACH RD

EBB TIDE WY

MATTIE

RANCHO SAN MIGUELITO
RANCHO PISMO

PACIFIC

OCEAN

SPYGLASS PARK

SEACLIFF PARK

OCEAN PARK

SOLANO FS

SPYGLASS DR

RUBY CT

SEACLIFF

PADDOCK AV

BAKER AV

MONT IN 3

COBURN

PARK PL

SHORELINE DR

VIS DEL MAR

TERRACE AV

MORRO AV

MONTECITO AV

PALOMAR AV

CAPISTRANO AV

MANANA

SANTA FE AV

CASTALC AV

WINDWARD

LIB

PEARL

PALISADE AV

SEAVIEW AV

BARCELONA RD

CL CORDOVA
CL CORREA
CL GRANADA
CL VALENCIA
COSTA DEL SOL

1 CL CONSUETTA

COSTA BRAVA
COSTA DEL SOL

EMERALD

CLEO

COSTA BRAVA

CORSALLITOS CH

SEAPORT

BAYFRONT DR

FOOTHILL RD

PISMO BEACH

PRICE ST

2100

2000

A | B | C | D | E | SEE 674 MAP | E | F | G | H | J

STB & SLO

1

93401

25

EDNA

EDNA RD

TWIN CREEKS WY

GREEN GATE RD

CARPENTER CANYON RD

DEPOT AV

EMPIRE ACRE ST AV

MAXWELLTON ST

CORRAL DE PIEDRA RD

OLD PRICE CANYON RD

2

CORBETT CANYON RD

CAMINO EDNA

VIA ROBLES

PRICE CANYON

PISMO CREEK

227

WEST UP RR

3

36

CARPENTER

TOLUSA PL

93420

CANYON

PATCHETT RD

LIBRETTO LN

SAN LUIS OBISPO

COUNTY

SEE 693 MAP

4

T31S
T32S

ORMONDE

MANDARIN LN

SEE 695 MAP

1

93449

CANYON RD

PISMO CREEK

WEST UP RR

RD

RD

5

RANCHO SAN MIGUELITO
RANCHO PISMO

MAP

DELGRATIA PL

PACIFIC PINE DR

E

OBISPO PACIFIC TR

6

PRICE

CANYON

WEST PISMO

LITTLE CT

VISTA DEL ROBLES

PARK

OAK

ORMONDE

RD

NOYES RD

BURKHILL LN

1400

RANCHO CORRAL DE PIEDRA
RANCHO PISMO

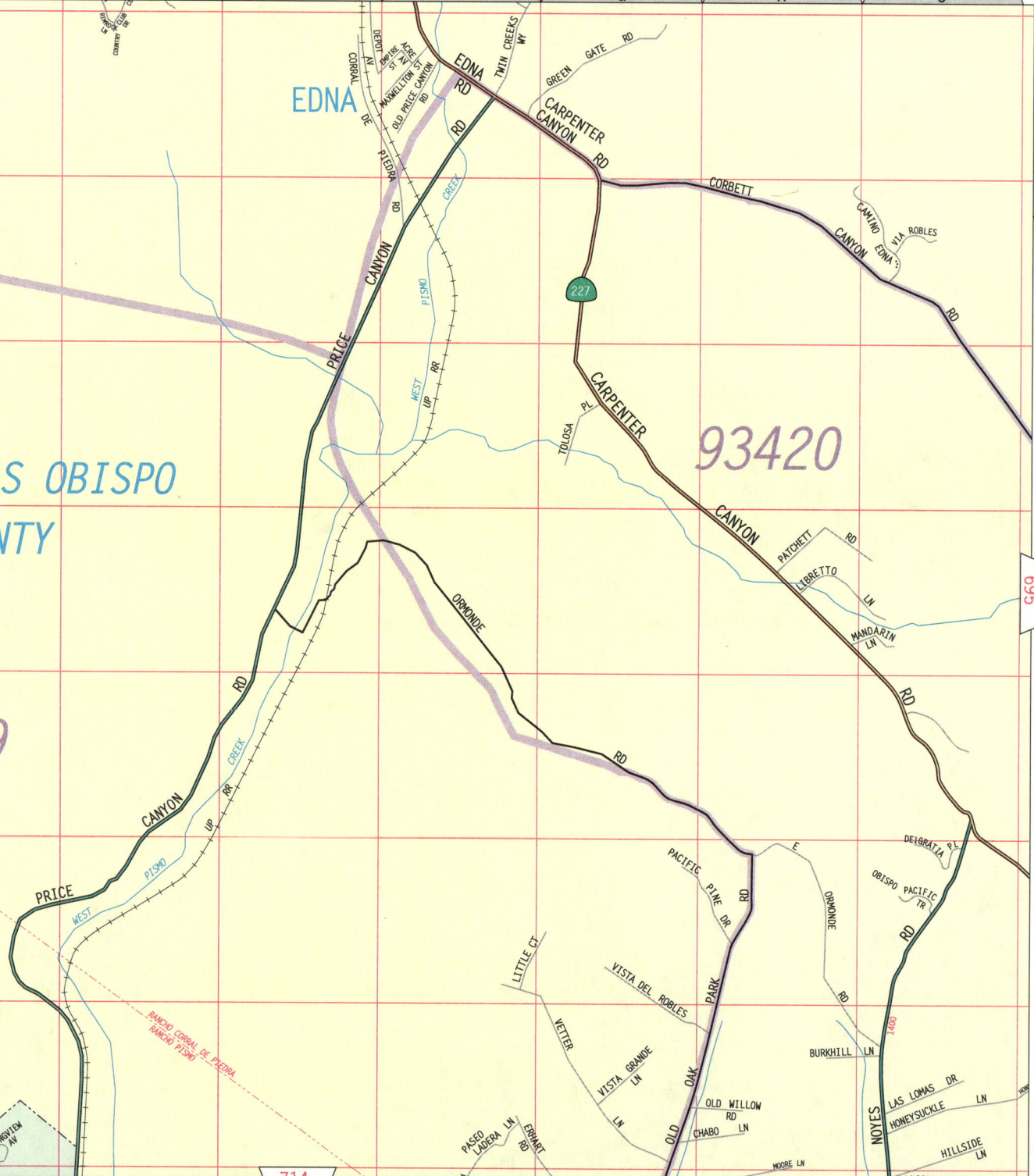

VETTER

VISTA GRANDE LN

OLD

OLD WILLOW RD

CHABO LN

LAS LOMAS DR

HONEYSUCKLE LN

7

**PISMO
BEACH**

LONGVIEW AV

PASEO LADERA LN

ERHART RD

MOORE LN

HILLSIDE LN

HILLSIDE LN

COPYRIGHT 2000 Thomas Bros. Maps ®   —N—

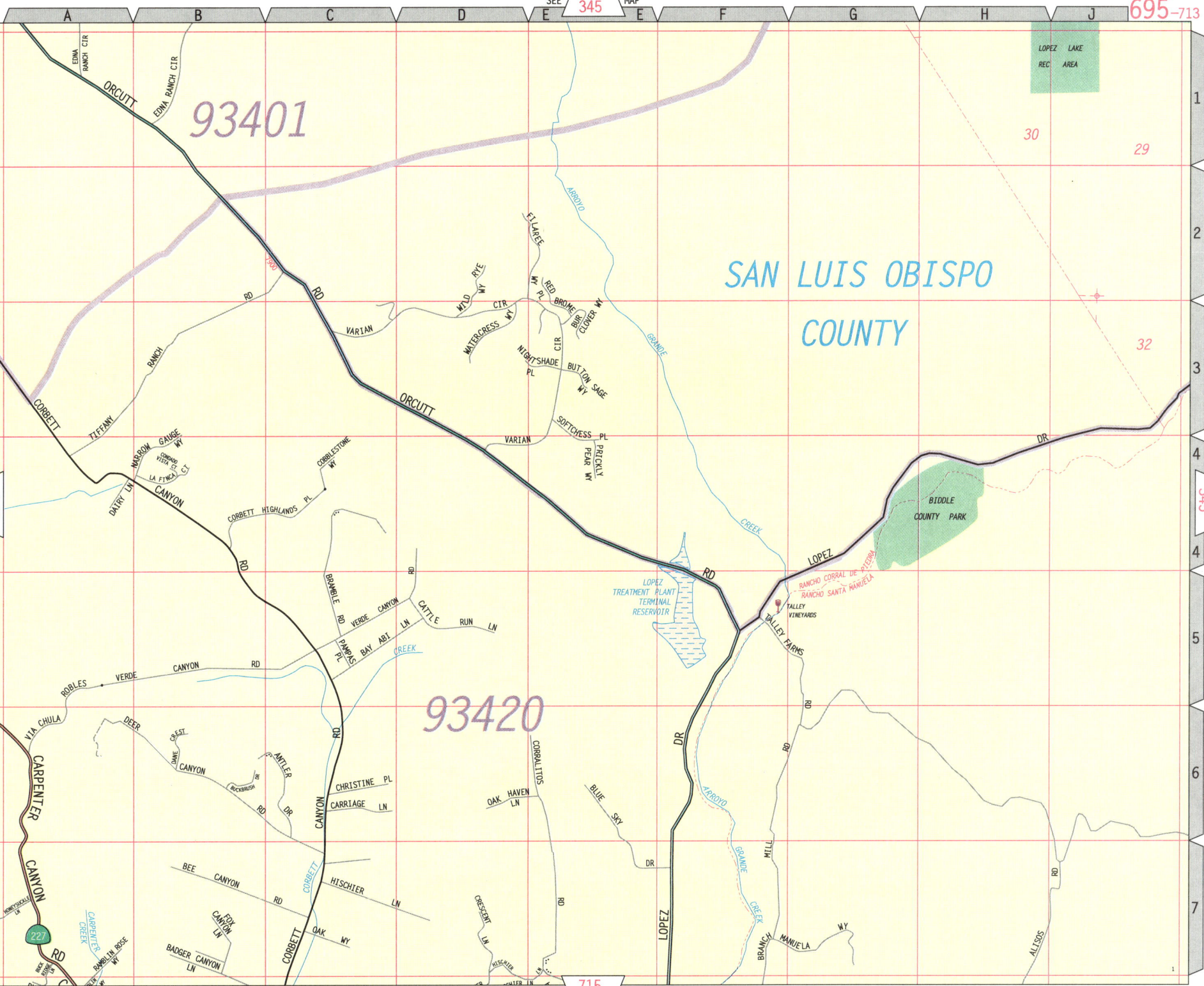

A | B | C | D | E | E | F | G | H | J

EDNA RANCH CIR

ORCUTT

93401

EDNA RANCH CIR

LOPEZ LAKE
REC AREA

1

30

29

N
COPYRIGHT 2000

RD

RD

VARIAN

FILAREE
WY

WILD RYE
WY

RED
PL

BROME
WY

BUR

CLOVER WY

ARROYO

SAN LUIS OBISPO

COUNTY

2

32

RANCH

WATERCRESS WY

CIR

NIGHTSHADE
PL

BUTTON SAGE
WY

CIR

GRANDE

TIFFANY

ORCUTT

VARIAN

SOFTCHESS PL

PRICKLY
PEAR WY

DR

3

CORBETT

NARROW GAUGE WY

DAIRY LN

CONDADO
VISTA CT

LA FINCA

CANYON

COBBLESTONE
WY

CORBETT HIGHLANDS PL

CREEK

LOPEZ

BIDDLE
COUNTY PARK

DR

4

4

RD

BRAMBLE RD

VERDE CANYON

RD

CATTLE RUN LN

LOPEZ
TREATMENT PLANT
TERMINAL
RESERVOIR

RD

RANCHO CORRAL DE PIEDRA
RANCHO SANTA MANUELA

TALLEY
VINEYARDS

TALLEY FARMS

5

ROBLES

VERDE

CANYON

BAY ABI LN

PAMPAS PL

RD

CREEK

93420

RD

VIA CHULA

DEER

DAME CREST

CANYON

ANTLER

BUCKBRUSH DR

RD

CANYON

DR

CORRALITOS

OAK HAVEN
LN

BLUE SKY

DR

ARROYO

RD

MILL

RD

6

CARPENTER

CHRISTINE PL

CARRIAGE LN

GRANDE

CREEK

CANYON

BEE CANYON

RD

CORBETT

HISCHIER LN

RD

CRESCENT LN

RD

BRANCH

MANUELA WY

ALISOS RD

7

HONEYSUCKLE LN

227

RD

CARPENTER CREEK

FOX CANYON LN

RAMBLIN ROSE WY

CORBETT

OAK WY

HISCHIER LN

LOPEZ

1

BADGER CANYON LN

A B C D E F G H J

EL CAMINO REAL

SAN LUIS OBISPO
COUNTY
93449

93420

PISMO
BEACH

PRICE CANYON RD

PACIFIC

OCEAN

93433

PISMO
STATE
BEACH

PISMO
STATE
BEACH
GOLF
COURSE

DOLLIVER ST

CABRILLO HWY

PACIFIC BLVD

GROVER BEACH

ARROYO GRANDE

EL CAMINO REAL

101

OCEANO

93444

SEE 345 MAP
SEE 715 MAP

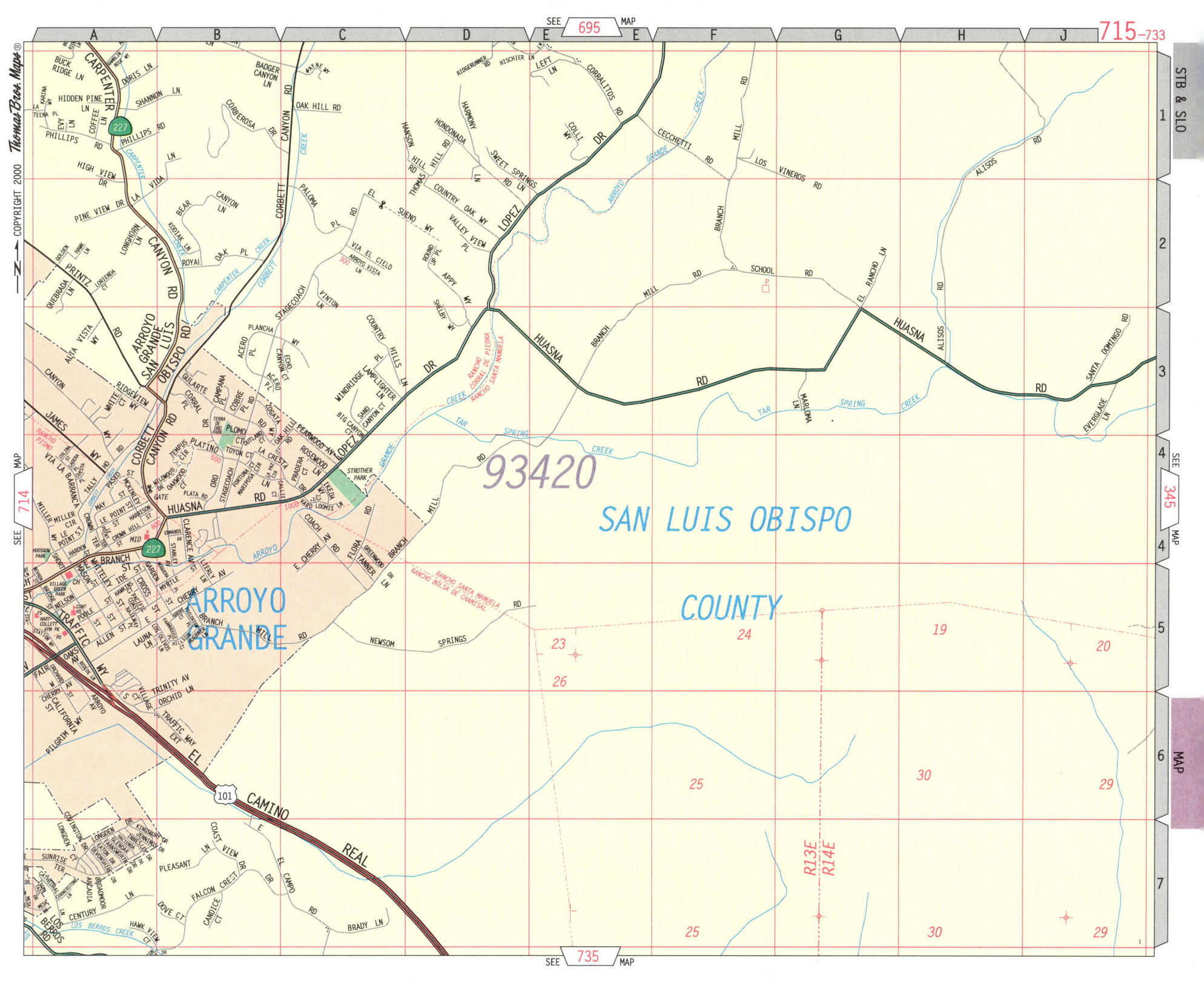

93420

SAN LUIS OBISPO

COUNTY

ARROYO GRANDE

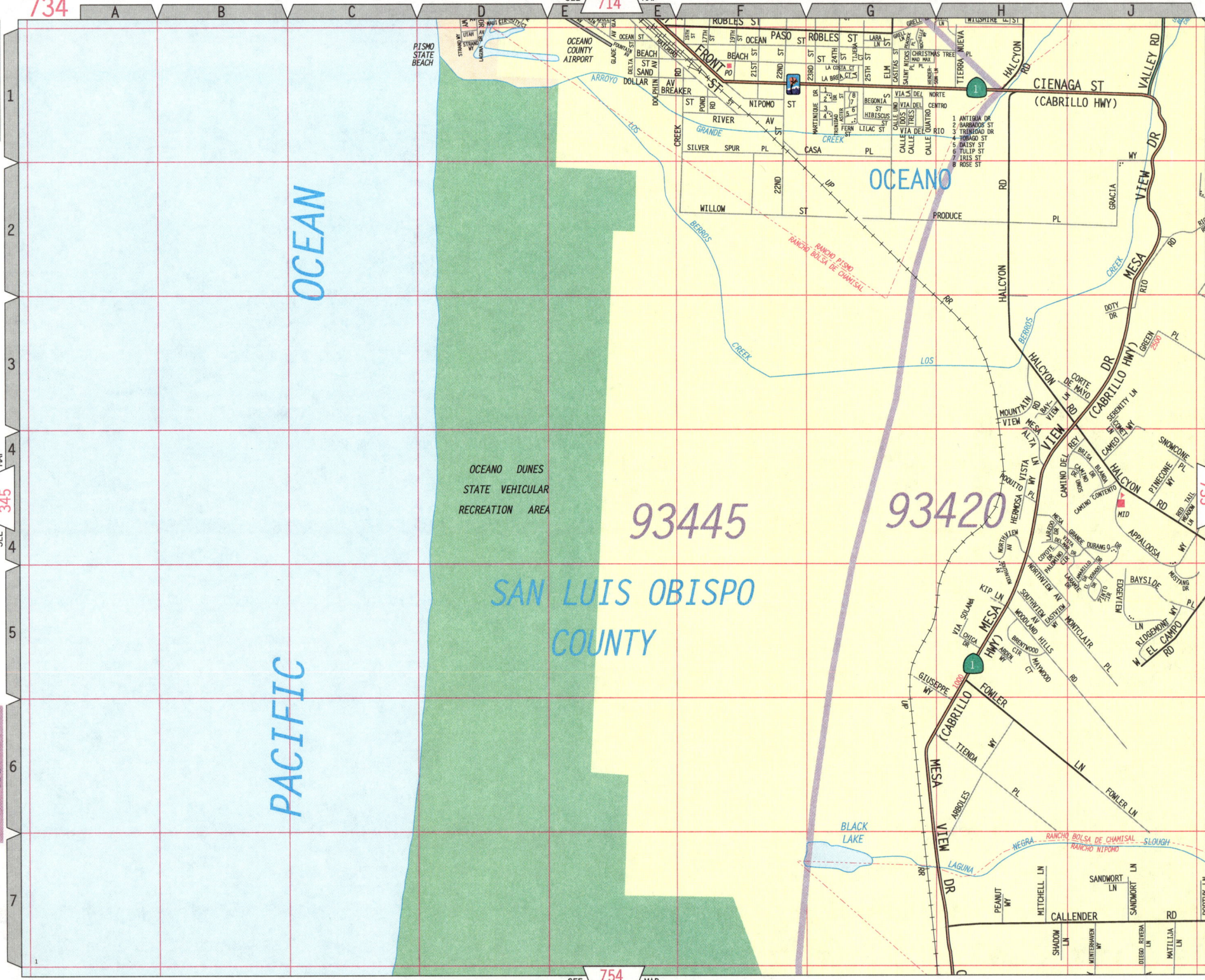

A B C D E E F G H J

1

2

4

5

6

7

COPYRIGHT 2000 Thomas Bros. Maps®

OCEAN

PACIFIC

PISMO STATE BEACH

OCEANO COUNTY AIRPORT

OCEANO DUNES STATE VEHICULAR RECREATION AREA

93445

93420

SAN LUIS OBISPO COUNTY

OCEANO

CIENAGA ST (CABRILLO HWY)

ROBLES ST
PASO ROBLES ST
OCEAN
BEACH
FRONT ST
NIPOMO AV
RIVER AV
GRANDE
SILVER SPUR PL
WILLOW ST
22ND ST
CASA
PRODUCE

VALLEY RD
HALCYON
VIEW DR
GRACIA PL
MESA RD
DOTY DR
BERROS
HALCYON
RD
MESA

1 ANTIGUA DR
2 BARBADOS ST
3 TRINIDAD DR
4 TOBAGO ST
5 DAISY ST
6 TULIP ST
7 IRIS ST
8 ROSE ST

ARROYO GRANDE CREEK
BERROS CREEK
LOS CREEK
RANCHO BOLSA DE CHAMISAL
RANCHO PISMO

HALCYON RD
(CABRILLO HWY)
MOUNTAIN VIEW
MESA ALTA
POQUITO
HERMOSA VISTA
CAMINO DEL REY
CORTE DE MAYO
SERENITY LN
CAMEO DR
PINECONE PL
SNOWCONE PL
APPALOOSA
MUSTANG DR
BAYSIDE
EDGEVIEW
RIDGEMONT
MONTCLAIR
WOODLAND HILLS
BRENTWOOD CIR
MAYWOOD
EL CAMPO RD
KIP LN
VIA SOLANA
CHICA DR
MESA VIEW DR
GIUSEPPE WY
CABRILLO HWY
FOWLER
TIENDA WY
ARROLES PL
FOWLER LN
BLACK LAKE
RANCHO BOLSA DE CHAMISAL
RANCHO NIPOMO
SLOUGH
LAGUNA
NEGRA
PEANUT WY
MITCHELL LN
SANDWORT LN
CALLENDER RD
SHADOW LN
WINTERHAVEN
DIEGO RIVERA
MATILIJA

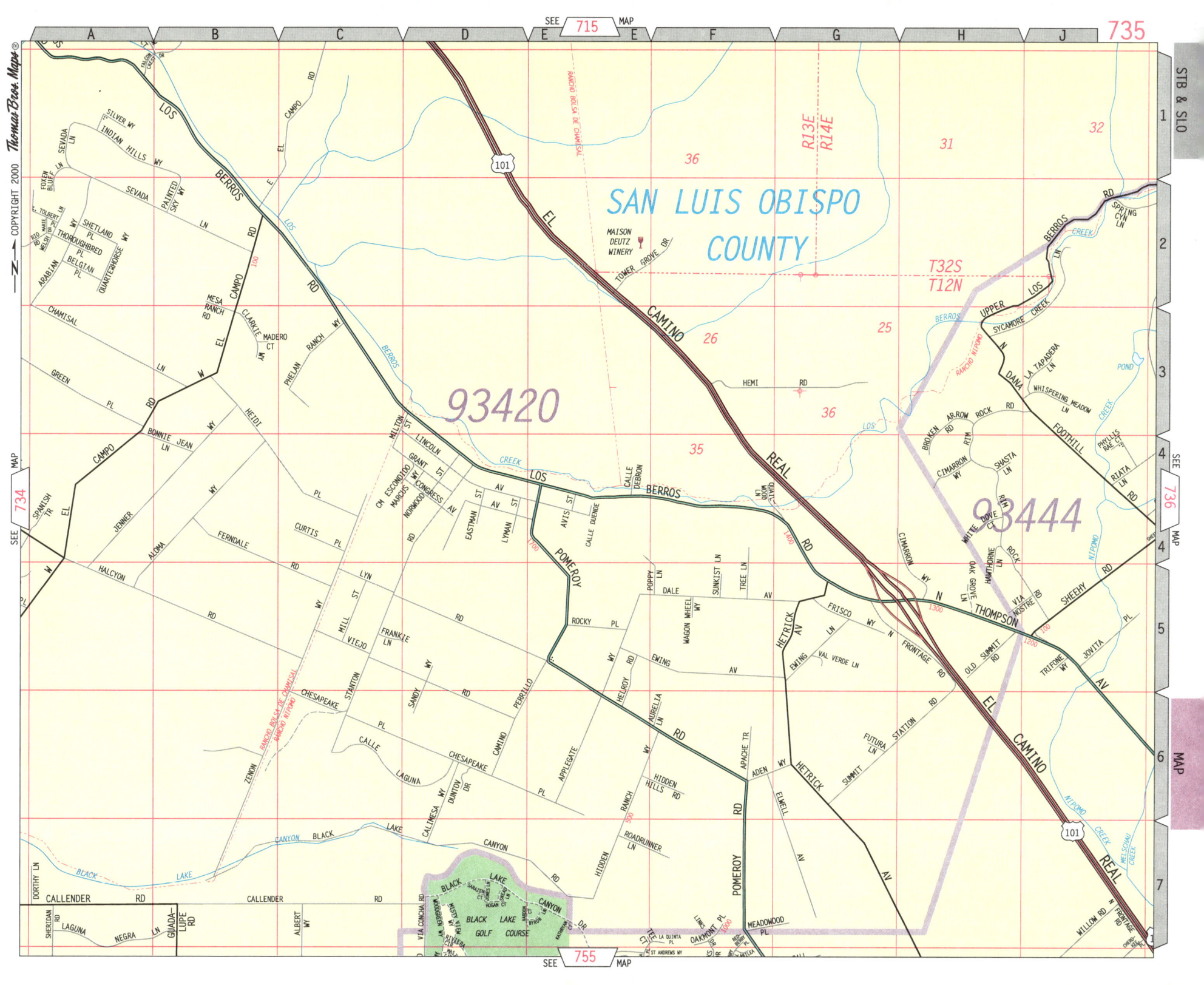

SEE 715 MAP

STB & SLO

SAN LUIS OBISPO
COUNTY

93420

93444

R13E R14E

T32S
T12N

US 101

EL CAMINO REAL

LOS BERROS RD

MAISON DEUTZ WINERY

TOWER GROVE DR

RANCHO BOLSA DE CHAMISAL

RANCHO NIPOMO

36
26
35
36
31
32
25

HEMI RD

BERROS CREEK

UPPER LOS BERROS RD

SPRING CYN LN

SYCAMORE CREEK

DANA FOOTHILL RD

LA TAPADERA LN

WHISPERING MEADOW

POND

PHYLLIS RAE CT

BROKEN ARROW RD

RTW ROCK RD

CIMARRON WY

SHASTA LN

WHITE DOVE CT

RIATA LN

RIM RD

ROCK

HAWTHORNE RD

OAK GROVE LN

VIA NOSTRE RD

SHEEHY RD

JOVITA AV

TRIFONE WY

OLD SUMMIT RD

N FRONTAGE RD

THOMPSON

FUTURA STATION RD

SUMMIT

FRISCO WY

VAL VERDE LN

EWING WY

HETRICK AV

POMEROY RD

APACHE TR

ADEN WY

ELMELL WY

MEADOWOOD PL

LOS BERROS

CALLE DEBRON

CALLE DUENDE

CALLE NOBLOOM

AVIS ST

LYMAN ST

EASTMAN

AV

LINCOLN ST

GRANT ST

CONGRESS AV

MILTON ST

MARQUS ST

NORWOOD

CM ESCONDIDO

CURTIS PL

PL

LYN ST

FRANKIE LN

VIEJO

MILL WY

STANTON

CHESAPEAKE

CALLE LAGUNA

DUNTOW DR

CALIMESA WY

CAMINO CHESAPEAKE

APPLEGATE

PEDRILLO

HELROY WY

AURELIA WY

ROCKY PL

POPPY LN

DALE WY

WAGON WHEEL WY

SUNKIST LN

TREE LN

AV

HIDDEN HILLS RD

RANCH RD

ROADRUNNER LN

HIDDEN

CANYON

BLACK LAKE CANYON

CANYON

BLACK LAKE

BLACK LAKE GOLF COURSE

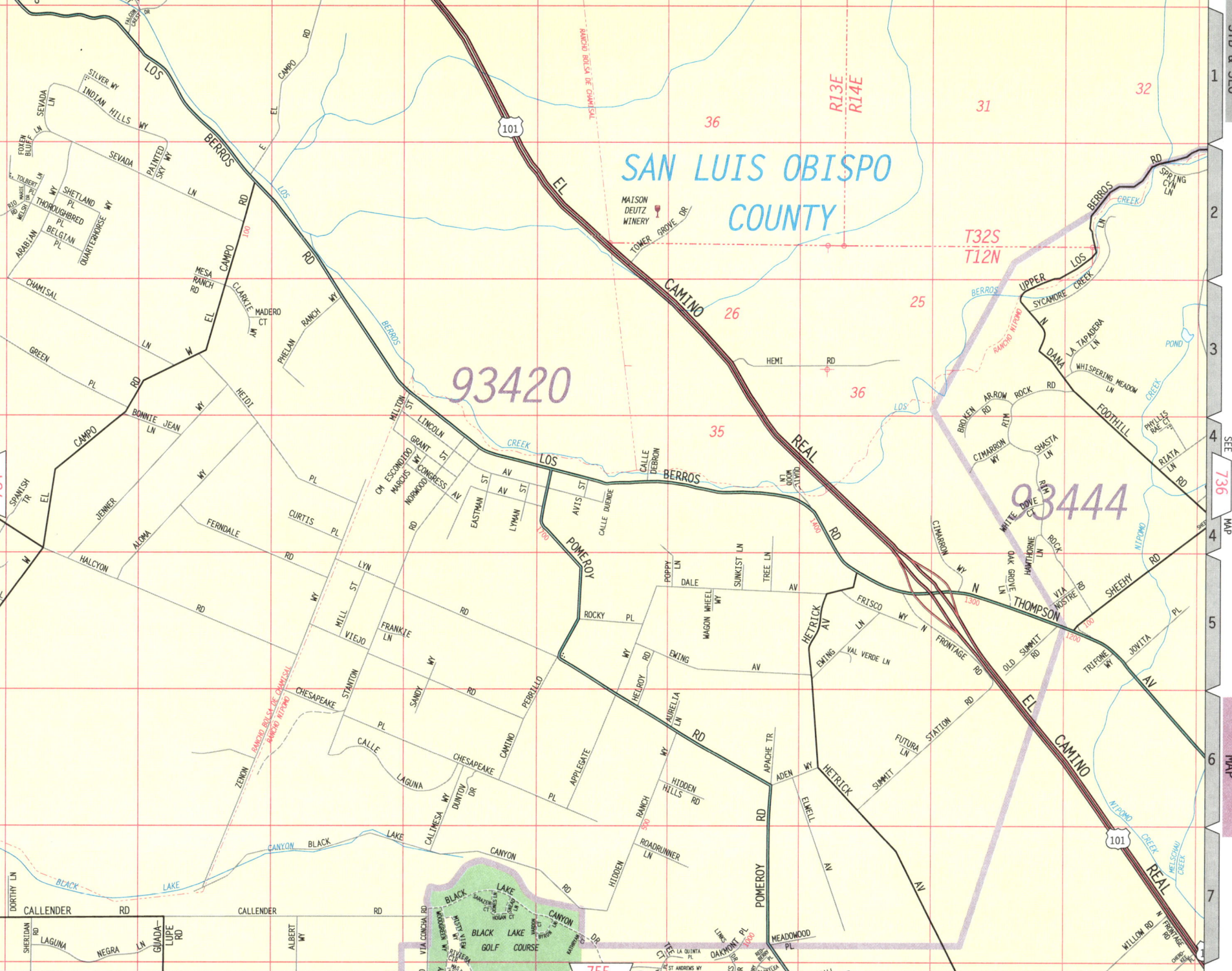

CALLENDER RD

SHERIDAN RD

LAGUNA NEGRA LN

GUADALUPE RD

ALBERT WY

VIA CONCHA RD

SARAZEN

HOGAN CT

LA QUINTA PL

ST ANDREWS WY

OAKMONT PL

DOROTHY LN

CALLENDER

SPANISH TR

EL CAMPO RD

JENNER

ALOMA

HALCYON RD

HEIDI WY

BONNIE JEAN LN

FERNDALE

GREEN PL

CHAMISAL

LOS BERROS RD

EL CAMPO RD

MESA RANCH RD

CLARKIE WY

MADERO CT

PHELAN RANCH WY

ARABIAN PL

BELGIAN PL

QUARTERHORSE

SHETLAND PL

THOROUGHBRED PL

TOLBERT PL

FOXEN BLUFF LN

SEVADA LN

SILVER WY

INDIAN HILLS WY

SEVADA

PAINTED SKY WY

RIO MESA

WILSON RD

SEE 734 MAP

SEE 736 MAP

MAP

1300

1400

1200

1100

1000

500

100

N

Thomas Bros. Maps ®

COPYRIGHT 2000

SEE 755 MAP

US 101

EL CAMINO REAL

N FRONTAGE RD

WILLOW RD

NIPOMO CREEK

MELCHIAU CREEK

A B C D E SEE 345 MAP E F G H J

STB & SLO

1

32

LOS HAVEN HILL WY

33

CREEK

BERROS

RANCHO NIPOMO

34

35

36

UPPER

SPRING

LOS CANYON LN

BERROS

RD

DAKOTA RD

OAK LN

FOX LN

JACK

ROCKY

RABBIT

RD

T32S
T12N

93420

2

LN

NIPOMO CREEK

RIDGE

LN

TEMETATTE

LN

RAMAL LN

RD

RIVITA

RIDGECREST

PL

CREEK

RD

BLUE

UPPER

28

27

26

LOS

BERROS

LOS

RD

34

35

3

SEE 735 MAP

4

CAMINO ENCANTO

SHEEHY

HILLS

RD

SHEEHY RD

DANA

SNOW LN

FOOTHILL

HIGHLAND

RD

SAN LUIS OBISPO

COUNTY

93444

BERROS

LOS

RD

UPPER

BERROS

RD

CREEK

DOS CANADAS

RD

7400

SEE 737 MAP

5

MELSCHAU

N

CREEK

N

DANA

MOUNTAIN WY

CLAMSHELL

MOUNTAIN WY

6

N

THOMPSON

PETTIT

PL

MEHLSCHAU

RD

DELESSIGUES

FOOTHILL GRADE

RD

100

S DANA

FOOTHILL RD

7

NIPOMO CREEK

101

E TEFFT ST

A   B   C   D   E   E   F   G   H   J

STB & SLO

Thomas Bros. Maps ®

COPYRIGHT 2000

—N—→

R14E R15E

36

31

35

1

RANCHO HUASNA

HUASNA

HUASNA TOWNSITE

DEER CREEK

RD

RIVER

RANCHO HUASNA RD

32

RIVER

T32S
T12N

25

30

HUASNA

HUASNA

27

2

93420

RD

CREEK

3

7200

WY

8100

CANYON WY

SAN LUIS OBISPO

COUNTY

SUEY CREEK

LOS

RIDGE

O'LEARY

BERROS

COUGAR

7900

31

SEE 736 MAP

4

SEE 345 MAP

36

EL CAZADOR
8300

8200

RD

SUEY

TEMETTATE

WY

DR

R34W R33W

CREEK

TWITCHELL

RESERVOIR

5

DOS

CANADAS

RD

RD

GOSSIP
9900

T12N
T11N

32

RANCHO HUASNA

TEMETTATE
6700

ROCK

RD

COYOTE

SPRINGS

RD

6

MAP

93444

DR

FLOWER

RD

10500

6

WILD

CREEK

RD

5

4

RANCHO NIPOMO

DANFORD
9800

CANYON

RD

SUEY
10500

CRYSTAL SPRINGS RD

7

12

STB & SLO

A   B   C   D   E   F   G   H   J

SEE 734 MAP

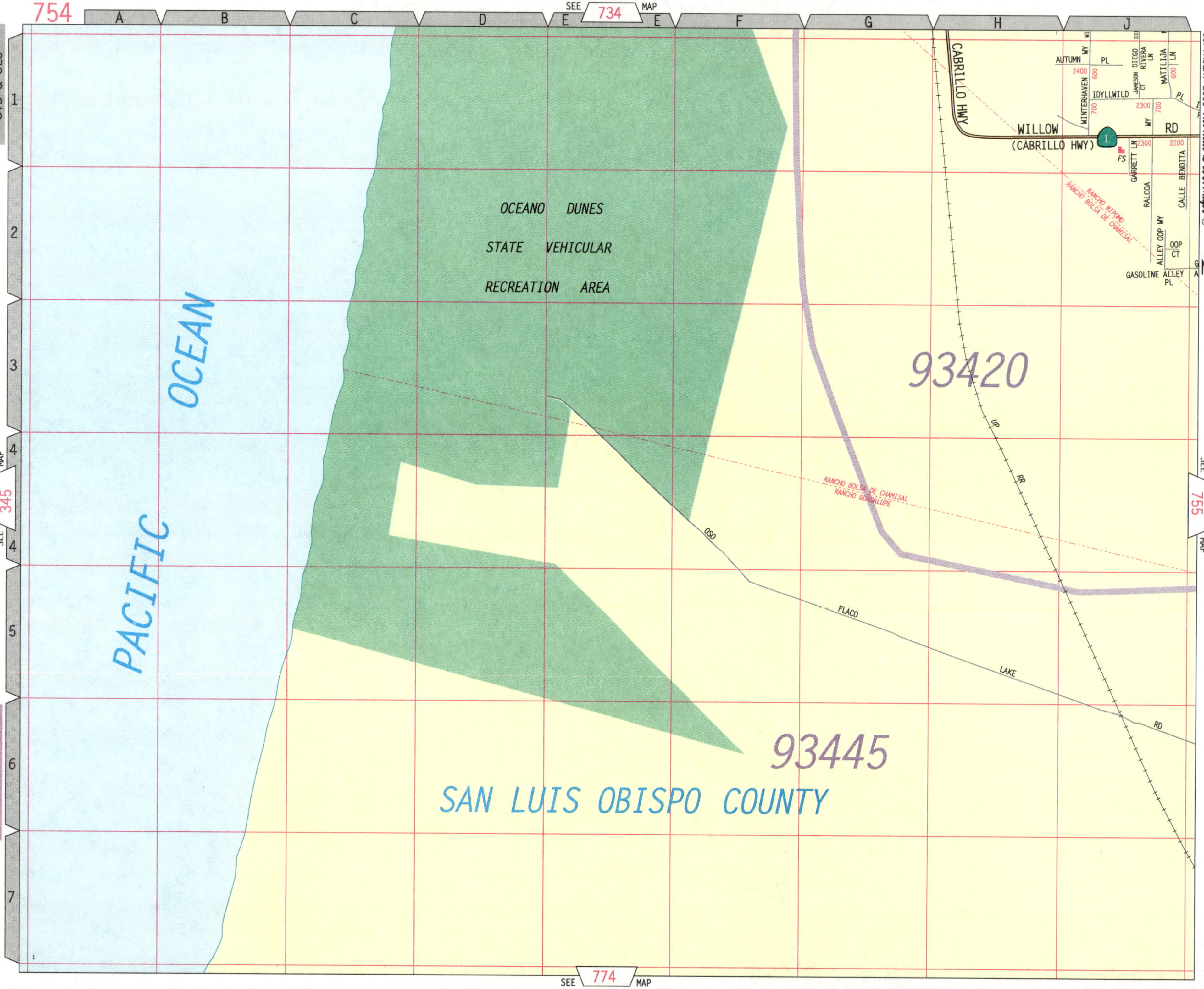

1

2

3

OCEANO   DUNES

STATE   VEHICULAR

RECREATION   AREA

PACIFIC

OCEAN

SEE 345 MAP

SEE 755 MAP

4

5

6

7

93420

93445

SAN LUIS OBISPO COUNTY

WILLOW
(CABRILLO HWY)

RD

CABRILLO HWY

AUTUMN   WY   PL
WINTERHAVEN   IDYLLWILD
DIEGO RIVERA LN
MATILIJA LN

GARRETT LN
RALCOA
CALLE BENDITA
ALLEY OOP WY
OOP CT
GASOLINE ALLEY PL

RANCHO NIPOMO
RANCHO BOLSA DE CHAMISAL

RANCHO BOLSA DE CHAMISAL
RANCHO GUADALUPE

OSO
FLACO
LAKE
RD

UP RR

COPYRIGHT 2000 Thomas Bros. Maps®

SEE 774 MAP

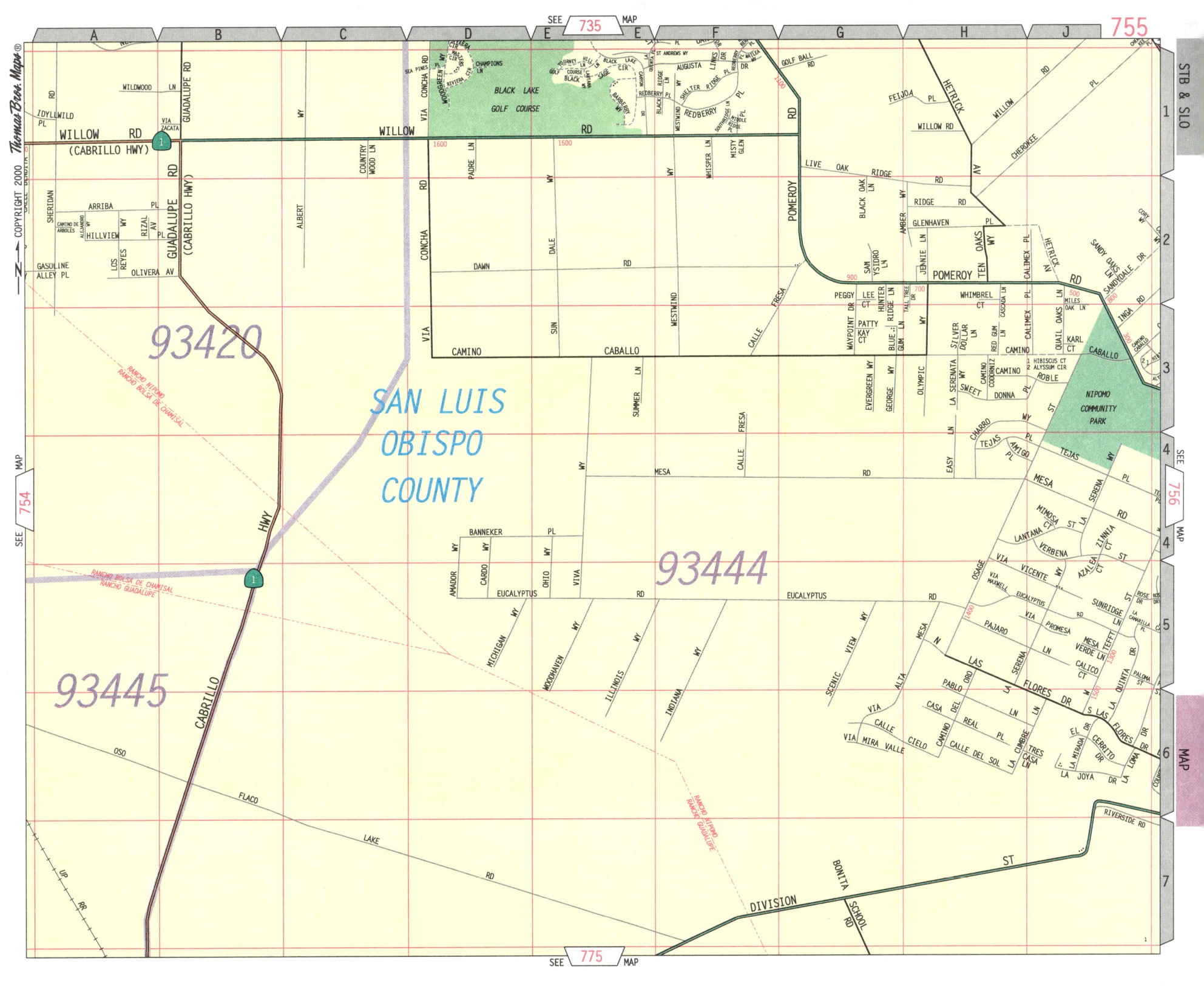

A B C D E E F G H J

STB & SLO

WILLOW RD
(CABRILLO HWY)

GUADALUPE RD

VIA ZACATA

WILDWOOD LN

IDYLLWILD PL

SHERIDAN

ARRIBA PL

CAMINO DE ARBOLES

HILLVIEW

RIZAL AV

LOS REYES

OLIVERA AV

GUADALUPE RD (CABRILLO HWY)

GASOLINE ALLEY PL

ALBERT

COUNTRY WOOD LN

CONCHA RD

WILLOW RD

PADRE LN

DALE

DAWN RD

SUN

WESTWIND

CALLE FRESA

VIA CAMINO CABALLO

SUMMER LN

CALLE FRESA

MESA

CALLE FRESA RD

BLACK LAKE GOLF COURSE

SEA PINES

CHAMPIONS LN

RIVIERA CIR

GOLF COURSE BLACK

TOURNEY

LANTANA

SAGE CIR

ST ANDREWS WY

AUGUSTA

GOLF BALL RD

REDBERRY

SHELTER RIDGE

WESTWIND LN

MISTY GLEN

WHISPER LN

WY

LIVE OAK RIDGE

POMEROY RD

BLACK OAK LN

AMBER WY

GLENHAVEN

RIDGE RD

PL

JENNIE LN

TEN OAKS WY

POMEROY RD

PEGGY

LEE CT

HUNTER

SAN YSIDRO LN

BLUE RIDGE LN

TALL TREE DR

GUM LN

WAYPOINT DR

PATTY KAY CT

WHIMBREL CT

CASCADA LN

RED GUM LN

CALIMEX PL

CAMINO

QUAIL OAKS LN

KARL CT

MILES

INGA

WY

OAK LN

CALIMEX PL

HETRICK AV

SANDY OAKS LN

SANDYDALE DR

CAMINO CABALLO

SILVER DOLLAR LN

EVERGREEN WY

GEORGE WY

OLYMPIC

LA SERENATA

SWEET

CAMINO CODORNIZ

DONNA

CAMINO ROBLE

1 HIBISCUS CT
2 ALYSSUM CIR

NIPOMO COMMUNITY PARK

EASY LN

CHARRO WY

TEJAS PL

AMIGO PL

TEJAS WY

MESA

SERENA RD

MIMOSA CT

LANTANA

VERBENA

AZALEA CT

ZINNIA ST

OSAGE

VIA VICENTE

VIA MAXWELL

EUCALYPTUS RD

VIA PROMESA

PAJARO LN

SUNRIDGE LN

MESA VERDE LN

LITEFETT

CALICO CT

ROSE DR

QUINTA ST

PALOMA ST

LAS FLORES DR

MESA N

SERENA LN

LAS FLORES DR

PABLO LN

CASA DEL

REAL PL

LA CUMBRE

TRES CASA LN

EL CERRITO DR

LA MIRADA DR

LA PALOMA DR

LA JOYA DR

VIA CALLE CIELO

VIA MIRA VALLE

CAMINO REAL

CALLE DEL SOL

SAN LUIS OBISPO COUNTY

93420

93444

93445

CABRILLO HWY

RANCHO NIPOMO
RANCHO BOLSA DE CHAMISAL

RANCHO BOLSA DE CHAMISAL
RANCHO GUADALUPE

BANNEKER PL

AMADOR WY

CARDO WY

EUCALYPTUS

OHIO WY

VIVA WY

MICHIGAN WY

WOODHAVEN WY

ILLINOIS WY

INDIANA WY

SCENIC VIEW WY

ALTA

EUCALYPTUS RD

MESA

OSO

FLACO

LAKE RD

RANCHO NIPOMO
RANCHO GUADALUPE

UP RR

BONITA

SCHOOL RD

DIVISION

RIVERSIDE RD

ST

SEE 754 MAP

756 MAP

MAP

1 2 3 4 4 5 6 7

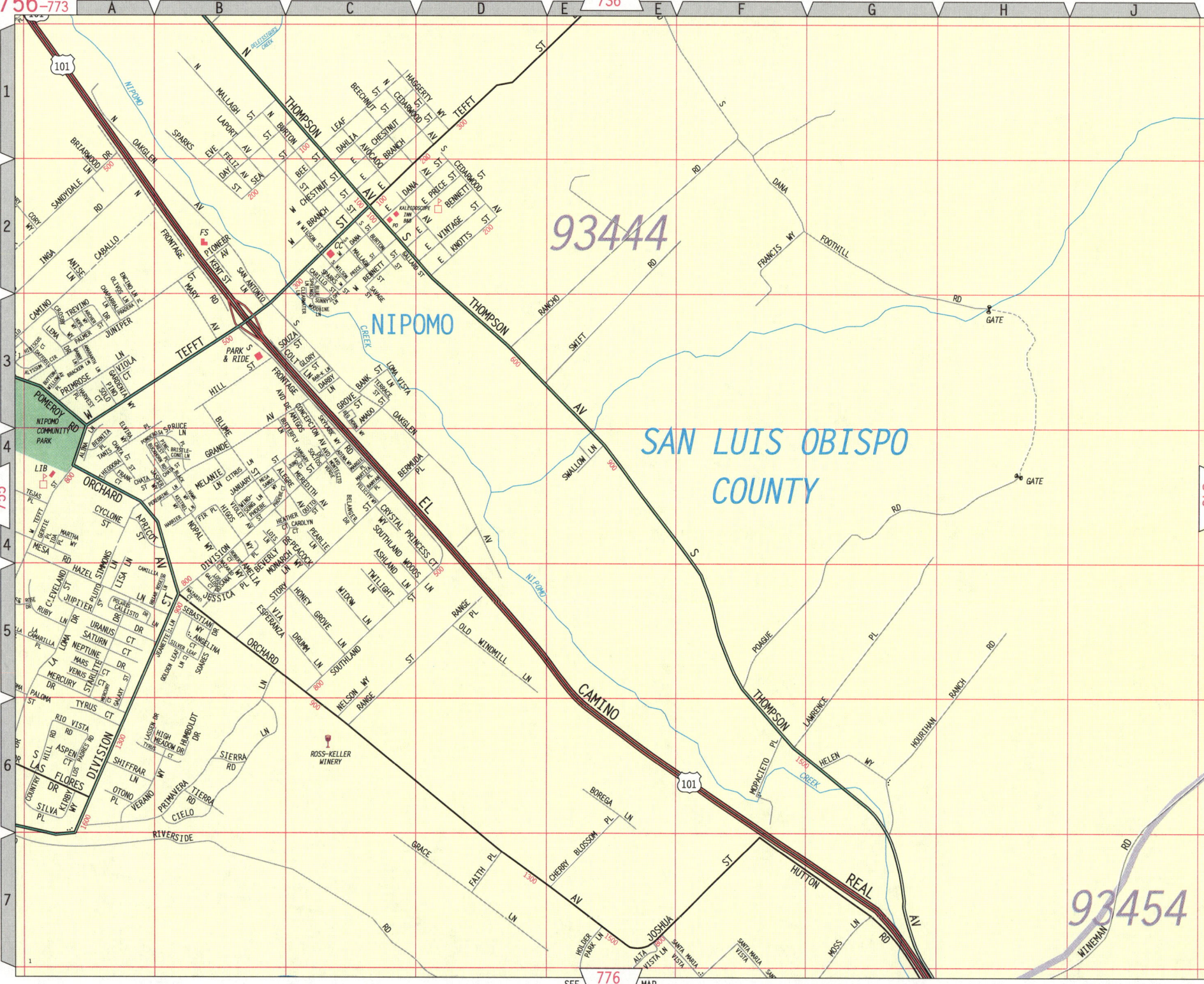

93444

93454

SAN LUIS OBISPO COUNTY

NIPOMO

STB & SLO

SEE 736 MAP

SEE 776 MAP

SEE 755 MAP

SEE 345 MAP

Grid columns: A B C D E E F G H J
Grid rows: 1 2 3 4 5 6 7

Major roads and features:
- US 101
- EL CAMINO REAL
- THOMPSON AV
- TEFFT ST
- POMEROY RD
- ORCHARD
- DIVISION ST
- FRONTAGE RD
- CAMINO
- HUTTON RD
- WINEMAN RD
- DANA RD
- FRANCIS WY
- FOOTHILL
- SWALLOW LN
- RANCHO
- MOPACITEO PL
- POAGUE
- LAWRENCE
- HOURIHAN RANCH
- HELEN WY
- NIPOMO CREEK
- MOPACITEO CREEK
- GATE

Points of interest:
- NIPOMO COMMUNITY PARK
- PARK & RIDE
- KALEIDOSCOPE INN B&B
- ROSS-KELLER WINERY
- LIB
- PO

COPYRIGHT 2000 Thomas Bros. Maps

| A | B | C | D | E | E | F | G | H | J |

1

2

3

4

5

MAP

6

7

Thomas Bros. Maps®

COPYRIGHT 2000

N →

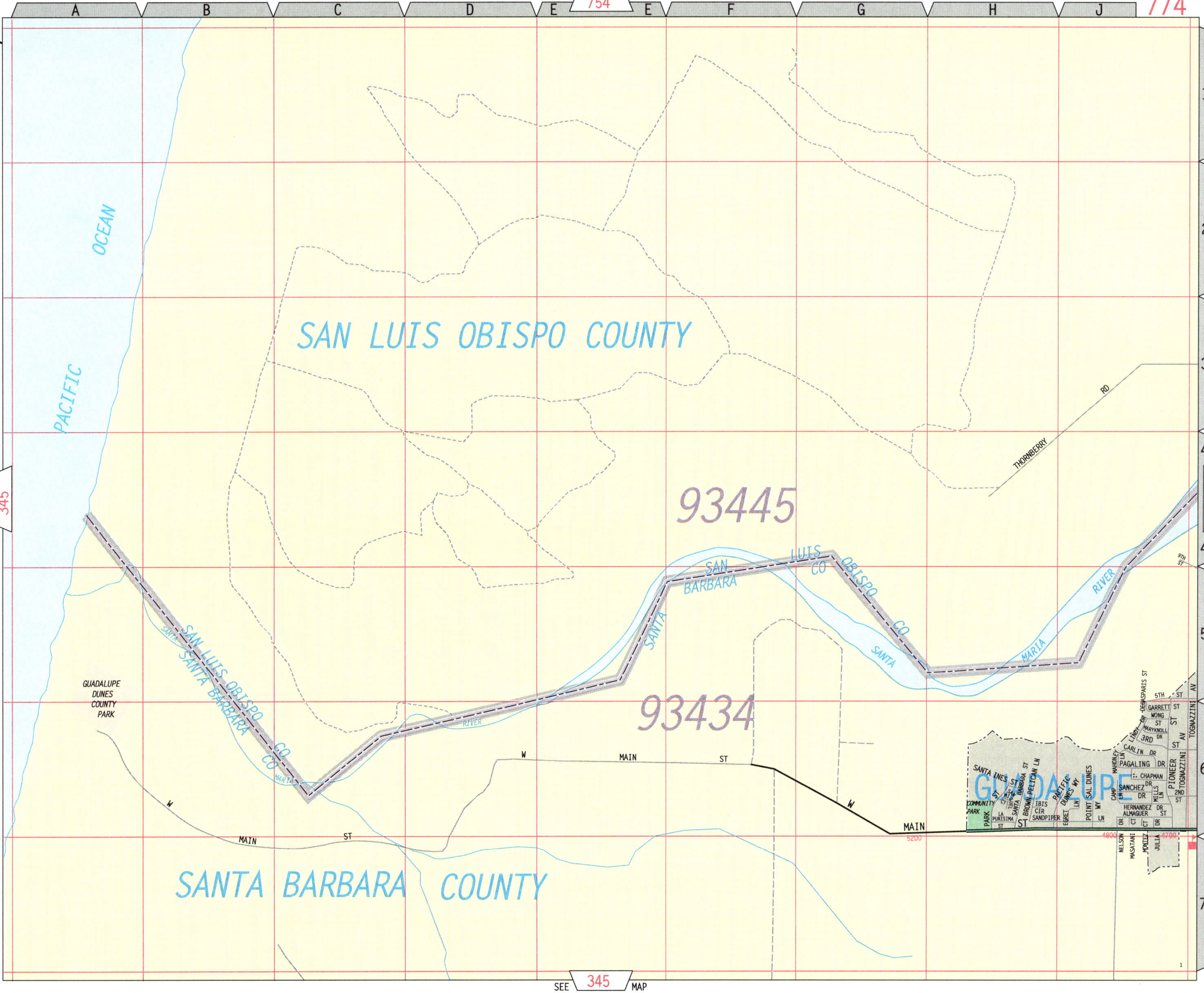

PACIFIC OCEAN

SAN LUIS OBISPO COUNTY

93445

93434

SANTA BARBARA COUNTY

SEE 345 MAP

SEE 775 MAP

GUADALUPE DUNES COUNTY PARK

SAN LUIS OBISPO CO
SANTA BARBARA CO

SANTA MARIA RIVER

SAN LUIS OBISPO CO
SANTA BARBARA CO

SANTA MARIA RIVER

THORNBERRY RD

9TH ST

W MAIN ST

W MAIN ST

MAIN ST

MAIN ST

W

W

5200

GUADALUPE

COMMUNITY PARK

5TH ST
GARRETT ST
DEE ST
SPARKS ST
WONG ST
MARYKNOLL DR
3RD ST
CARLIN DR
PAGALING DR
CHAPMAN
SANCHEZ DR
HERNANDEZ DR
ALMAGUER CT
LINDE DR
LINDE DR
MILLS
PIONEER ST
TOGNAZZINI AV
TOGNAZZINI
2ND
WHITNEY CT
CAMP
MOKLER
SANTA INES ST
SANTA BARBARA ST
BROWN ST
PELTON LN
IBIS
CIR
SANDPIPER
EGRET
POINT SAL DUNES
PACIFIC
DUNES WY
LA PURISIMA ST
ST
NELSON
MASATANI
MOKLER
JULLA
4800
4700

A B C D E E F G H J

STB & SLO

COPYRIGHT 2000 *Thomas Bros. Maps* ®   ←N→

1

93445

DIVISION

SAN LUIS OBISPO

COUNTY

2

ST

HWY

RR

CABRILLO

BONITA

SCHOOL

RD

RIVER

93444

THORNBERRY   RD

3

SAN LUIS OBISPO   CO

SANTA BARBARA   CO

MARIA

1

RANCHO NIPOMO
RANCHO GUADALUPE

RANCHO PUNTA DE LA LAGUNA
RANCHO GUADALUPE

SEE 774 MAP

4

SANTA

LEROY
PARK

RR

12TH
11TH
ST ST ST ST
PO
FS LIB
10TH
ST
9TH

93458

1600

BONITA

1600

SEE 776 MAP

5

ST
500
1100
ST CH
ST FS
ESCALANTE
PEDALTE
11TH
GILARTE LA GUARDIA
4300
LM LN
GUILARTE
4100
ST

PIONEER
OLIVERA
8TH
RUBIO
UP
PACHECO
700
800

SANTA BARBARA

COUNTY

7TH
ST

GUADALUPE

6TH
AV
5TH ST
AV
4TH   ST
AV

500

HOLLY   ST
FIR   ST
ELM   ST
3RD   ST
CEDAR   ST
BIRCH   ST
2ND   ST
AMBER   ST

FLOWER   ST

400

BONITA   LATERAL   RD

SCHOOL   RD

6

3RD   ST
TOGNAZZINI
CAMPONONICCO
GUADALUPE
OBISPO
STA
CEM
2ND   ST
W

AV
TOGNAZZINI
2ND   ST

W   MAIN

3400

W   MAIN   ST
3000

RANCHO GUADALUPE
RANCHO PUNTA DE LA LAGUNA

7

JR HS

CABRILLO   HWY
SPT CO RR

1

93434

4600
166
MAIN
4300

100
4000
ST
3800

ST
SIMAS
400

100
166
2600

RAY   RD
400

140   2400

ST

MAP

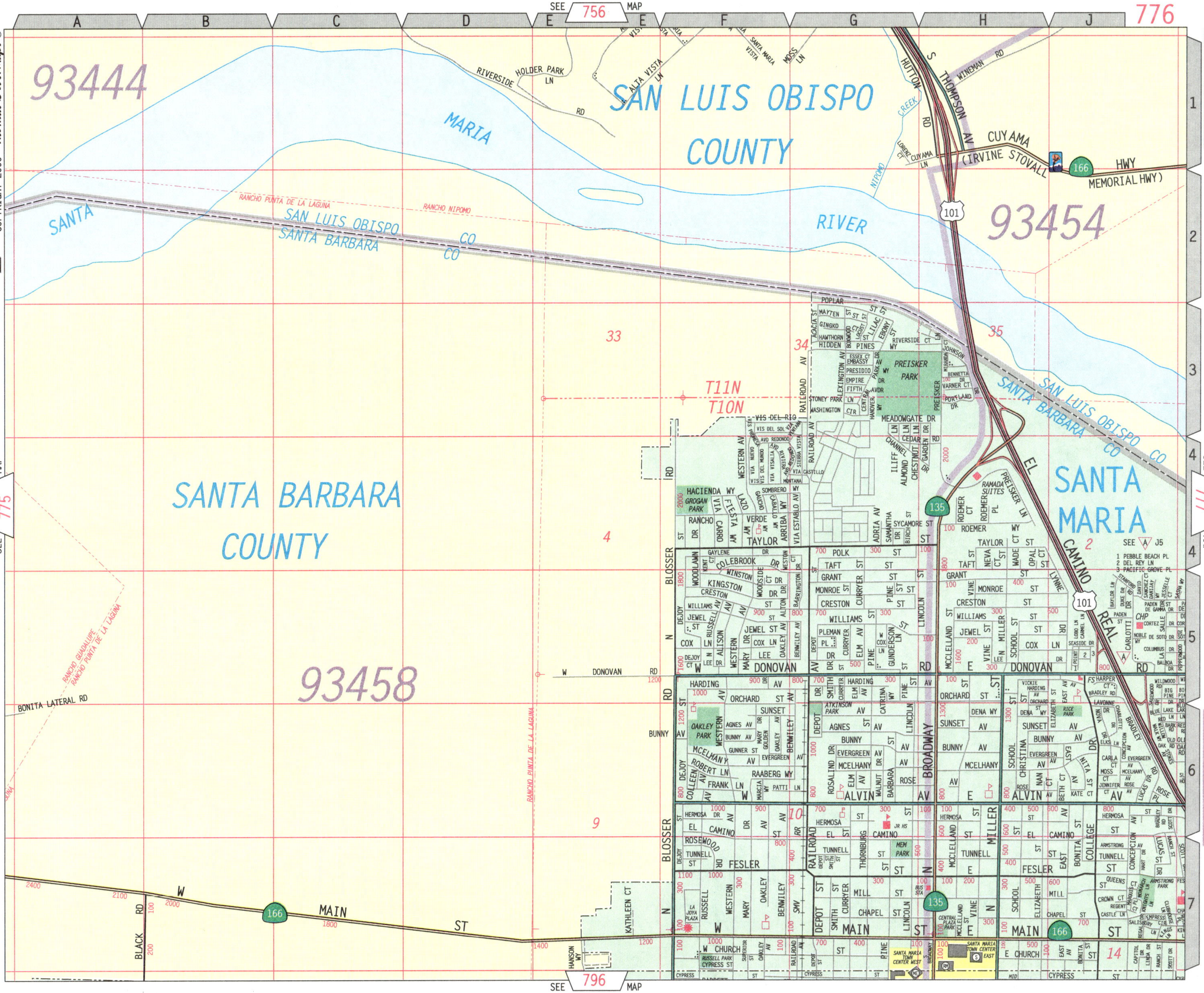

A B C D E F G H J

STB & SLO

93444

MARIA

SAN LUIS OBISPO COUNTY

RIVERSIDE HOLDER PARK LN

ALTA VISTA LN

SANTA MARIA VISTA

MOSS LN

HUTTON

S THOMPSON AV

MINEMAN RD

CUYAMA
(IRVINE STOVALL)
166 HWY
MEMORIAL HWY)

101

SANTA

SAN LUIS OBISPO CO
SANTA BARBARA CO

RANCHO PUNTA DE LA LAGUNA

RANCHO NIPOMO

RIVER

93454

COPYRIGHT 2000

N

POPLAR

33

34

35

PREISKER PARK

SANTA BARBARA CO
SAN LUIS OBISPO CO

T11N
T10N

SANTA MARIA

MEADOWGATE DR

SANTA BARBARA COUNTY

4

HACIENDA WY
GROGAN PARK

RAMADA SUITES

135

SEE A J5

1 PEBBLE BEACH PL
2 DEL REY LN
3 PACIFIC GROVE PL

TAYLOR

RANCHO
VERDE
TAYLOR

POLK
TAFT
GRANT
MONROE
CRESTON

TAFT
GRANT
MONROE
CRESTON

WILLIAMS

WILLIAMS

JEWEL ST

JEWEL

101

CHP

COX

DONOVAN

DONOVAN

W DONOVAN RD

93458

HARDING
ORCHARD
SUNSET

HARDING
ORCHARD
SUNSET

OAKLEY PARK

AGNES AV
BUNNY
MCELHANY
EVERGREEN

ATKINSON PARK

AGNES
BUNNY
MCELHANY
EVERGREEN

SUNSET
BUNNY
MCELHANY
EVERGREEN

RICE PARK

BROADWAY

ALVIN

ALVIN AV

9

10

EL CAMINO
ROSEWOOD
FESLER

HERMOSA
EL CAMINO
TUNNELL

HERMOSA
EL CAMINO
TUNNELL

MEM PARK

FESLER

FESLER

BLACK RD

166 MAIN ST

135

MAIN

BUS STA

MAIN

166 ST

SANTA MARIA TOWN CENTER WEST

SANTA MARIA TOWN CENTER EAST

W CHURCH

E CHURCH

14

CYPRESS

SEE 775 MAP
SEE 777 MAP

MAP

SEE 345 MAP

A B C D E E F G H J

COPYRIGHT 2000 Thomas Bros. Maps® —N—

1

WINEMAN RD
RANCHO NIPOMO RANCHO SUEY
166
(IRVINE STOVALL CUYAMA MEMORIAL HWY)
HWY
166
CREEK
TWITCHELL RESERVOIR

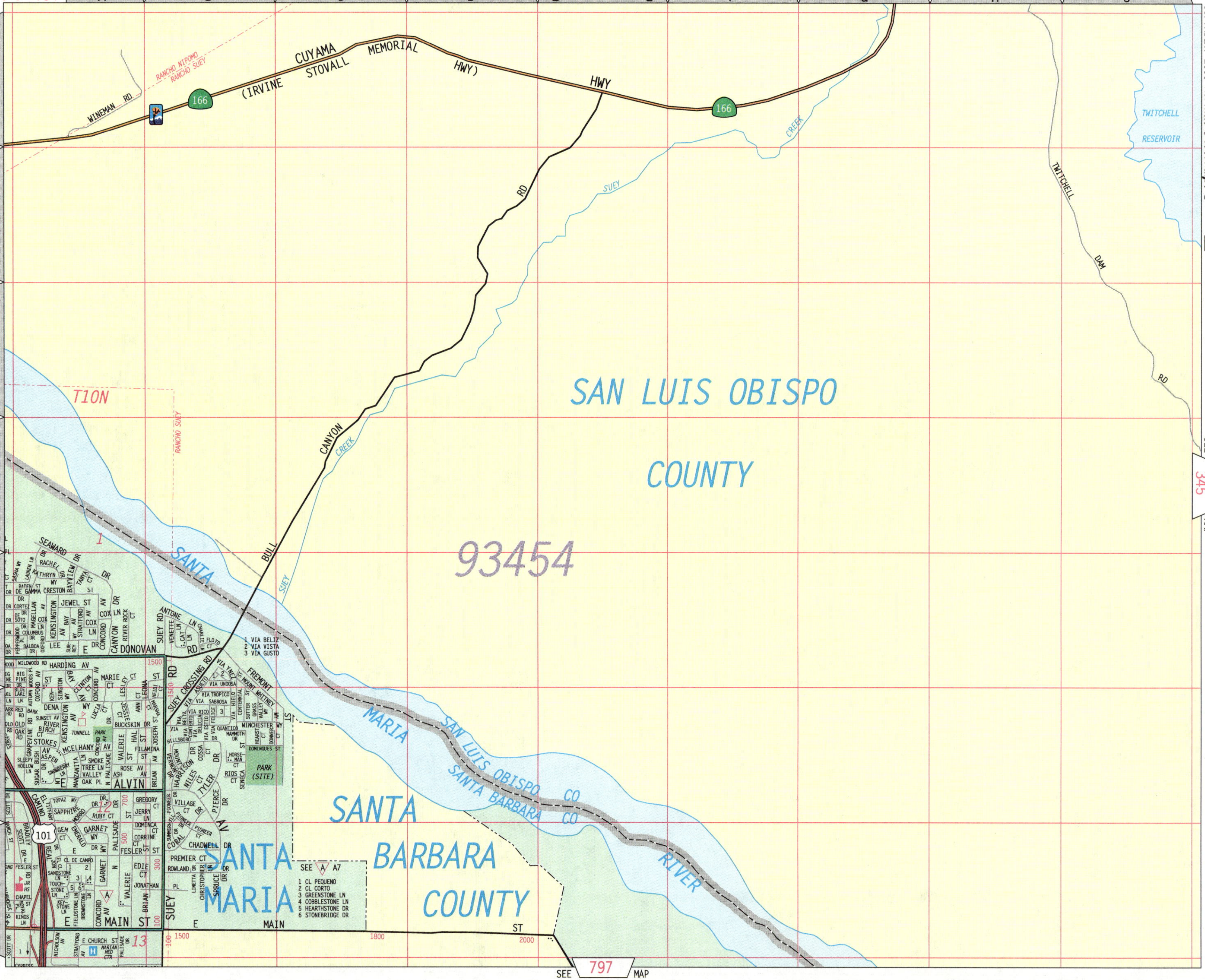

2

RD
SUEY
TWITCHELL
DAM

3

SAN LUIS OBISPO
T10N
RANCHO SUEY
RD

CANYON CREEK

4

SEE 776 MAP
SEE 345 MAP

COUNTY

SANTA
BULL
SUEY

93454

5

SEAWARD
DONOVAN
SUEY RD
ANTONE
VENETTE
CANYON RD
1 VIA BELLI
2 VIA VISTA
3 VIA GUSTO
FREMONT

6

MAP
MARIA
SAN LUIS OBISPO CO
SANTA BARBARA CO

ALVIN
PARK (SITE)
SANTA

7

101
SANTA MARIA
BARBARA
SEE A A7
1 CL PEQUENO
2 CL CORTO
3 GREENSTONE LN
4 COBBLESTONE LN
5 HEARTHSTONE DR
6 STONEBRIDGE DR
RIVER

COUNTY

MAIN ST
SUEY
MAIN
ST
13
SEE 797 MAP

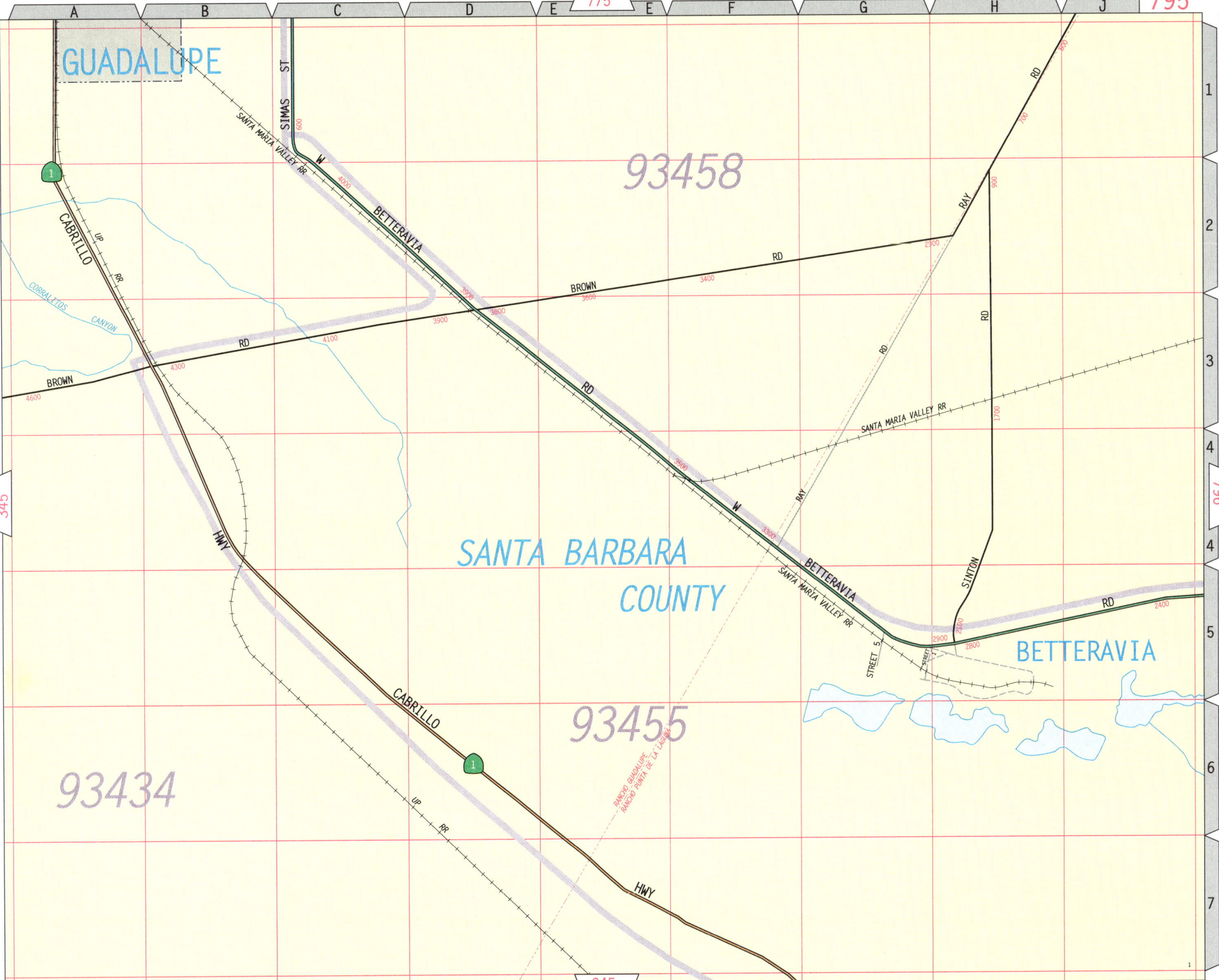

A B C D E E F G H J

Thomas Bros. Maps ®

COPYRIGHT 2000

1

GUADALUPE

93458

N

CABRILLO

UP RR

CORRALITOS CANYON

SANTA MARIA VALLEY RR

SIMS ST

600

W

BETTERAVIA

4300

3900

3900

3800

BROWN

3400

RD

2900

RAY

RD

900

700

800

2

RD

RD

BROWN

3660

3900

RD

4100

4300

3900

RD

RD

1700

SANTA MARIA VALLEY RR

3

BROWN

4600

HWY

3800

W

RAY

SANTA MARIA VALLEY RR

BETTERAVIA

SINTON

4

SANTA BARBARA

COUNTY

3900

SANTA MARIA VALLEY RR

STREET 5

STREET 1

2900 2600 2800

RD

2400

RD 2400

5

BETTERAVIA

93434

93455

CABRILLO

UP RR

1

RANCHO GUADALUPE
RANCHO PUNTA DE LA LAGUNA

6

HWY

7

1

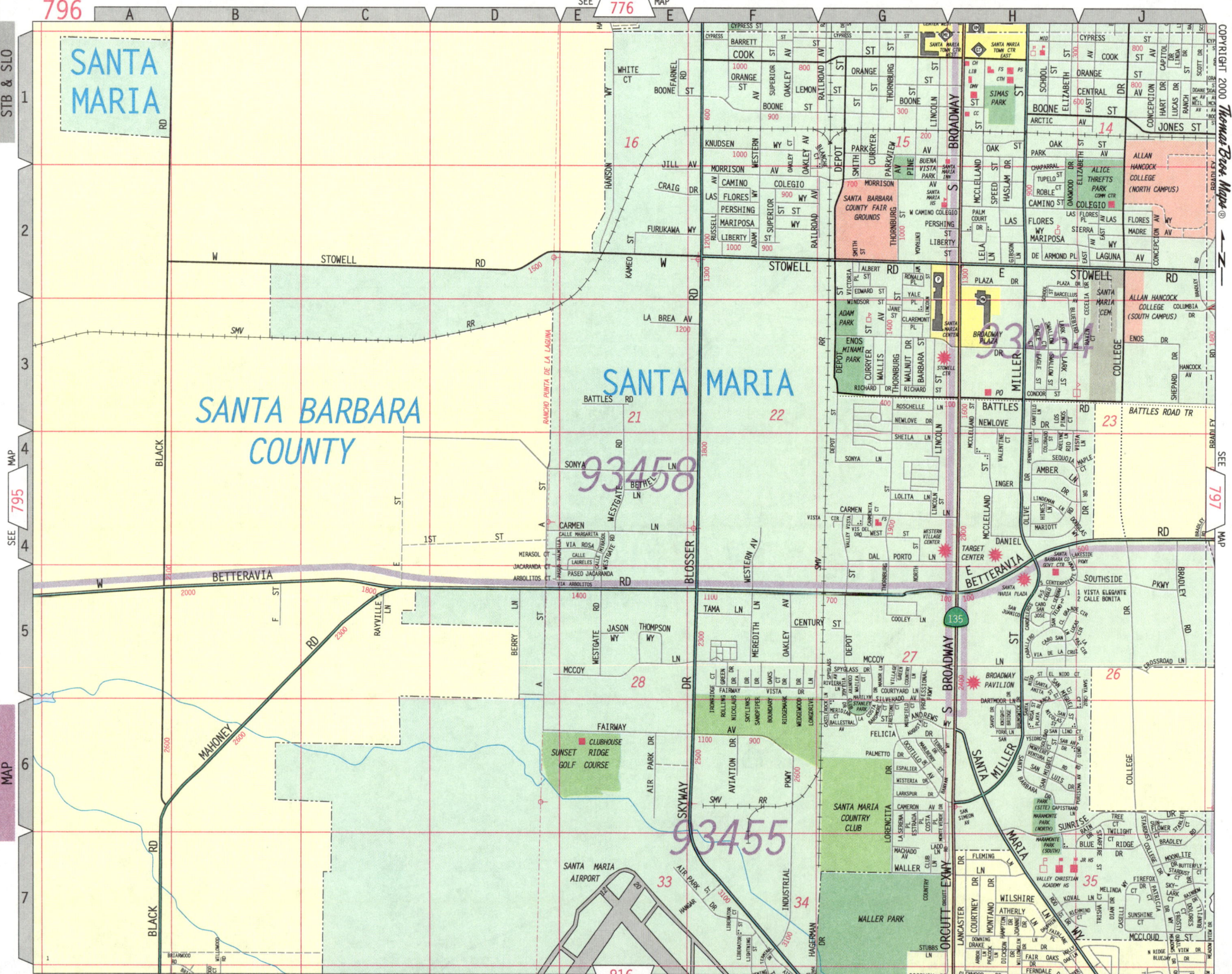

SANTA MARIA

SANTA BARBARA COUNTY

SANTA MARIA

93458
93455
93454

STB & SLO

SEE 795 MAP

SEE 797 MAP

SEE 816 MAP

COPYRIGHT 2000 Thomas Bros. Maps®

Grid columns: A B C D E F G H J
Grid rows: 1 2 3 4 5 6 7

Page numbers on map: 14 15 16 21 22 23 26 27 28 33 34 35

Major roads and places:
STOWELL RD
BETTERAVIA RD
BROADWAY
BLACK RD
MAHONEY
BLOSSER RD
SKYWAY DR
ORCUTT EXPY
COLLEGE
SANTA MARIA WY
MILLER ST
BRADLEY RD
CENTURY
LINCOLN
THORNBURG
BATTLES RD
WESTGATE

SANTA MARIA AIRPORT
SANTA MARIA COUNTRY CLUB
SUNSET RIDGE GOLF COURSE
WALLER PARK
SANTA BARBARA COUNTY FAIR GROUNDS
ALLAN HANCOCK COLLEGE (NORTH CAMPUS)
ALLAN HANCOCK COLLEGE (SOUTH CAMPUS)
BROADWAY PLAZA
BROADWAY PAVILION
TARGET CENTER
WESTERN VILLAGE CENTER
CLUBHOUSE
SIMAS PARK
SANTA MARIA TOWN CTR WEST
SANTA MARIA TOWN CTR EAST
ALICE THREFTS PARK COMM CTR
BUENA VISTA PARK

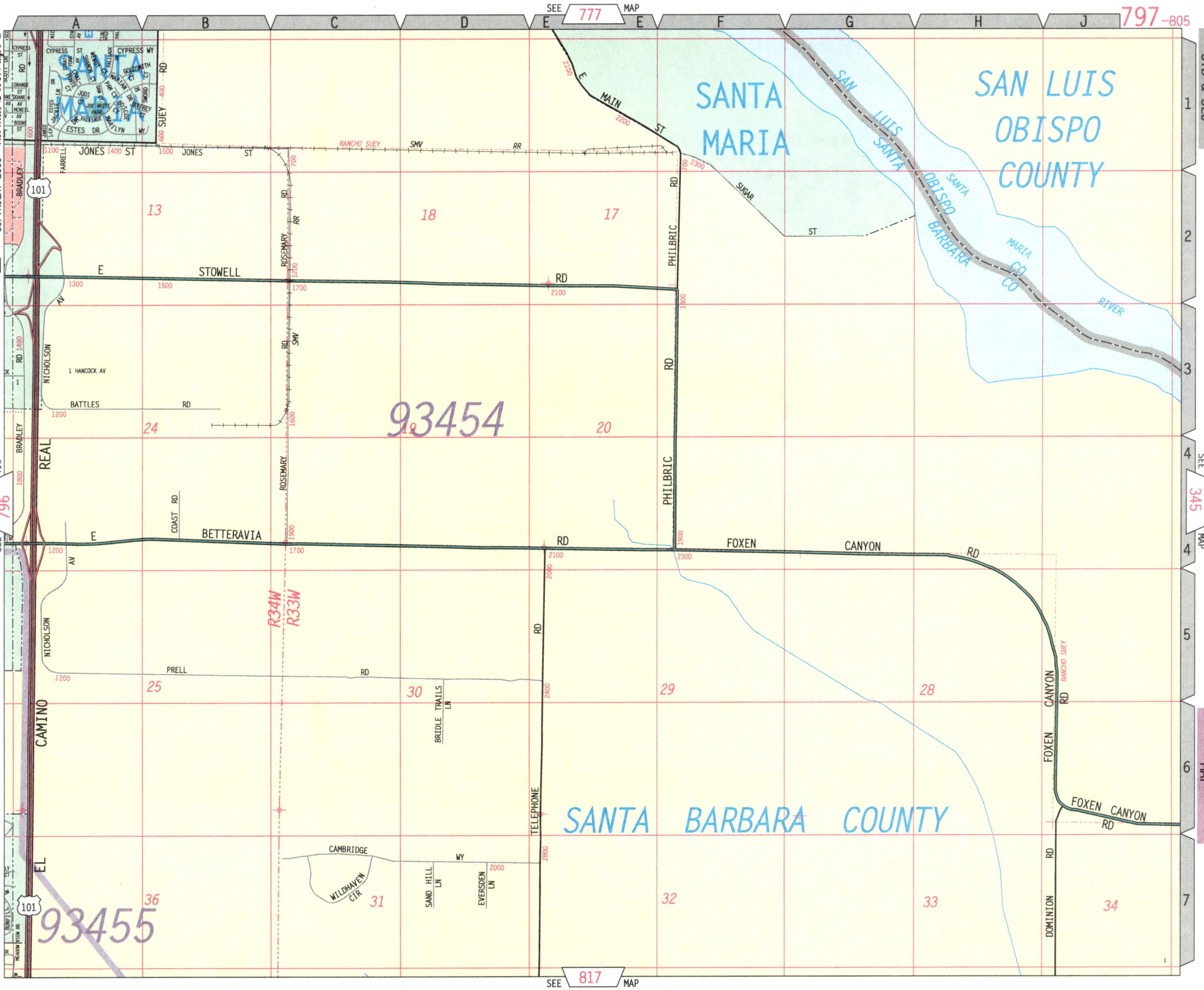

A B C D E E F G H J

STB & SLO

SANTA MARIA

SAN LUIS OBISPO COUNTY

SAN LUIS SANTA OBISPO BARBARA CO CO

SANTA MARIA RIVER

CYPRESS ST CYPRESS WY
CYPRESS ST
SANTA MARIA
ORANGE ST
SUEY RD
400 500 600
JONES ST 1400 1500 JONES ST
FARRELL
BRADLEY 1100
101
500 700

RANCHO SUEY SMV RR
MAIN ST
2100
2200
2300
SUGAR ST
700
PHILBRIC RD

13 18 17

E STOWELL RD
1300 1500 1700 1900 2100
1200 RD 2100
RD 1480
NICHOLSON

1 HANCOCK AV
BATTLES RD
1200
ROSEMARY RR RD
ROSEMARY RD SMV
1600

93454

24 19 20

REAL
BRADLEY

SEE 796 MAP

SEE 345 MAP

PHILBRIC RD
1900

COAST RD
E BETTERAVIA RD FOXEN CANYON RD
1200 1700 1900 2100 2300
R34W R33W
NICHOLSON AV

FOXEN CANYON RD RANCHO SUEY

PRELL RD
1200 2400
25 30 29 28

BRIDLE TRAILS LN

CAMINO

TELEPHONE RD

SANTA BARBARA COUNTY

FOXEN CANYON RD

EL

CAMBRIDGE WY
WILDHAVEN CIR
SAND HILL LN
EVERSDEN LN
2000
2800

101
93455
36 31 32 33 34

MEADOW VIEW DR
DOMINION RD

1 2 3 4 4 5 6 7

MAP

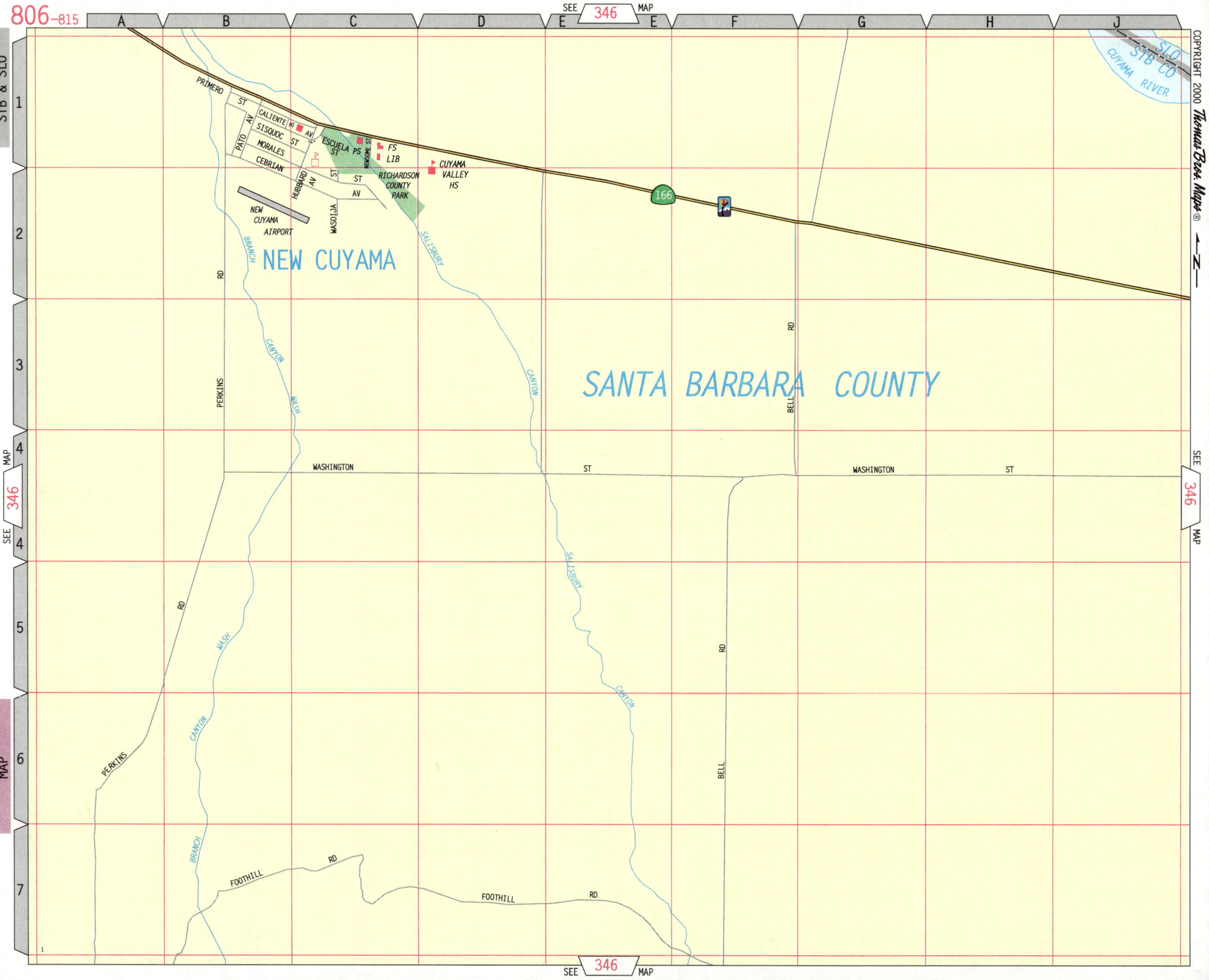

STB & SLO

SEE 346 MAP

A B C D E E F G H J

COPYRIGHT 2000 Thomas Bros. Maps ®

—N—

SLO
SLO STB CO
STB CO
CUYAMA RIVER

1

PRIMERO ST
CALIENTE RD
SISQUOC ST
PATO AV
MORALES
CEBRIAN
ESCUELA ST
PS
KEROSENE ST
FS
LIB
CUYAMA VALLEY HS

HUBBARD AV
MASOTJA
ST AV
RICHARDSON COUNTY PARK

166

2

NEW CUYAMA AIRPORT

NEW CUYAMA

BRANCH
CANYON WASH

PERKINS RD

SALISBURY

CANYON

BELL RD

SANTA BARBARA COUNTY

3

4

WASHINGTON ST
WASHINGTON ST

MAP
SEE 346 MAP

SEE 346 MAP

SALISBURY CANYON

PERKINS RD

WASH

5

CANYON

BELL RD

MAP

6

PERKINS

BRANCH

BELL

FOOTHILL RD
FOOTHILL RD

7

SEE 346 MAP

SEE 796 MAP

816

STB & SLO

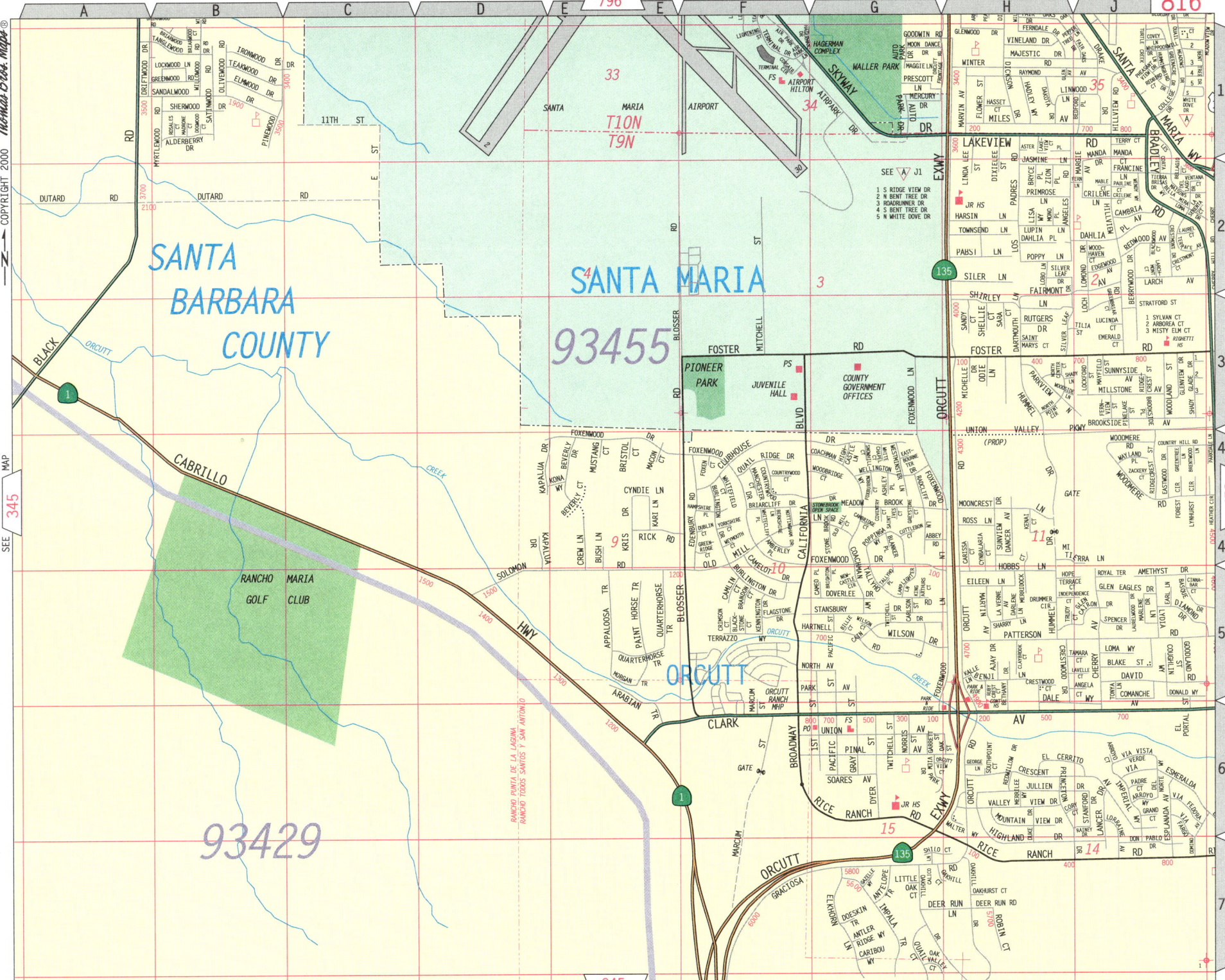

SANTA
BARBARA
COUNTY

93455

SANTA MARIA

SANTA MARIA AIRPORT

T10N
T9N

33

34

35

RANCHO MARIA
GOLF CLUB

ORCUTT

93429

PIONEER PARK

JUVENILE HALL

COUNTY GOVERNMENT OFFICES

WALLER PARK

HAGERMAN COMPLEX

AIRPORT HILTON

LAKEVIEW

FOSTER RD

UNION VALLEY PKWY

CABRILLO HWY

BLACK RD

CLARK

BROADWAY

RICE RANCH

ORCUTT

GRACIOSA

SEE 345 MAP

SEE 817 MAP

MAP

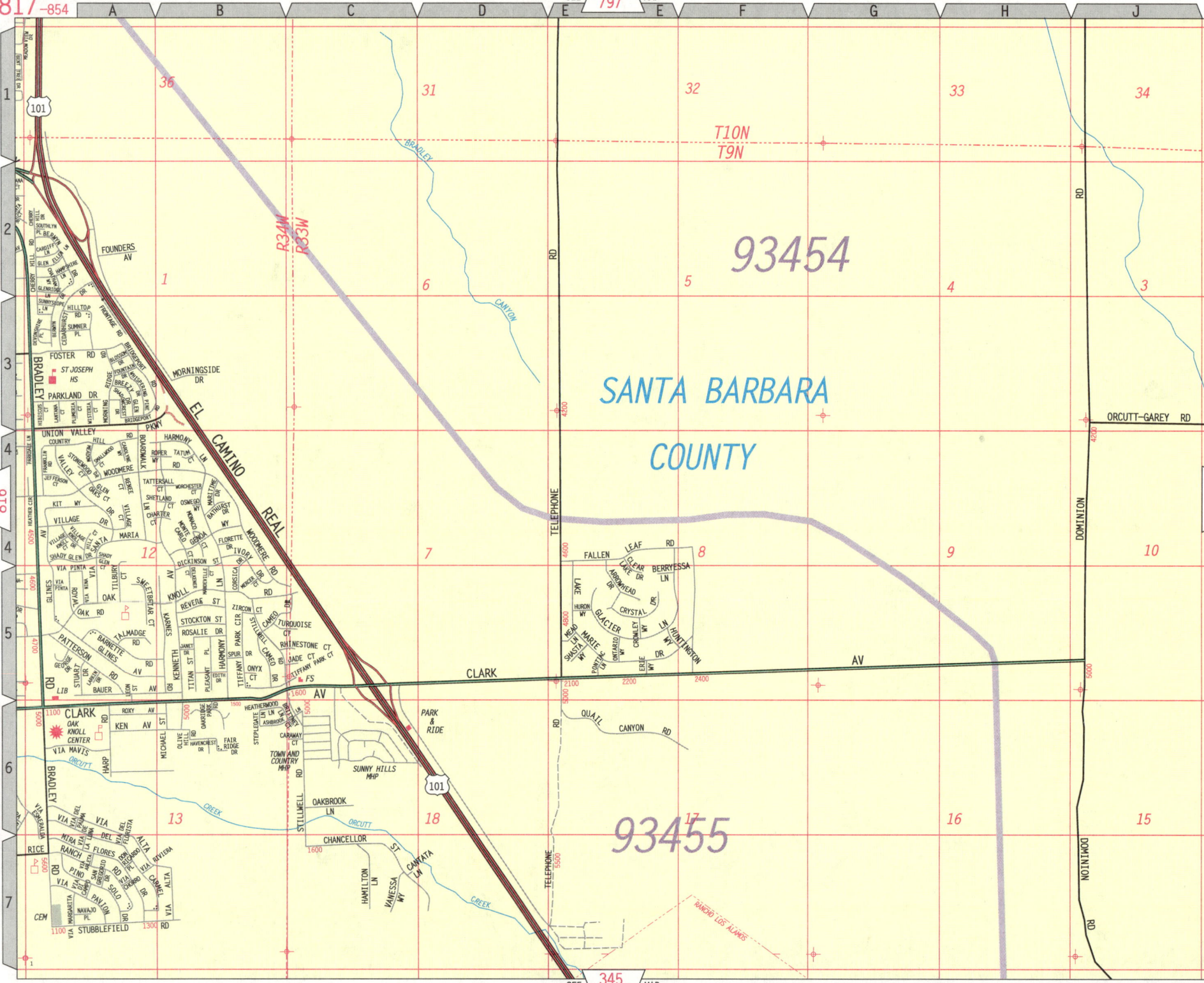

A B C D E E F G H J

SEE 797 MAP

STB & SLO

1 2 3 4 4 5 6 7

COPYRIGHT 2000 Thomas Bros. Maps ®

93454

SANTA BARBARA

COUNTY

93455

36 31 32 33 34

T10N
T9N

1 5 4 3

FOUNDERS AV

FOSTER RD
MORNINGSIDE DR
ST JOSEPH HS
PARKLAND DR
BRADLEY
UNION VALLEY PKWY

EL CAMINO REAL

R34W R33W

BRADLEY
CANYON

ORCUTT-GAREY RD

6 7 8 9 10

12 13 18 17 16 15

TELEPHONE RD

DOMINION RD

FALLEN LEAF RD
CLEAR LAKE DR
BERRYESSA LN
ARROWHEAD DR
CRYSTAL
LAKE HURON WY
MEAD LN
SHASTA WY
GLACIER WY
MARTE WY
CROMLEY LN
HUNTINGTON DR
ONTARIO WY
PONTIAC LN
ERIE WY

CLARK AV

PARK & RIDE
QUAIL CANYON RD

CLARK
OAK KNOLL CENTER
VIA MAVIS
ORCUTT

SUNNY HILLS MHP
TOWN AND COUNTRY MHP

101

BRADLEY
RICE RANCH RD
STUBBLEFIELD RD
CEM

CHANCELLOR

CREEK

RANCHO LOS ALAMOS

SEE 345 MAP
SEE 816 MAP
SEE 345 MAP

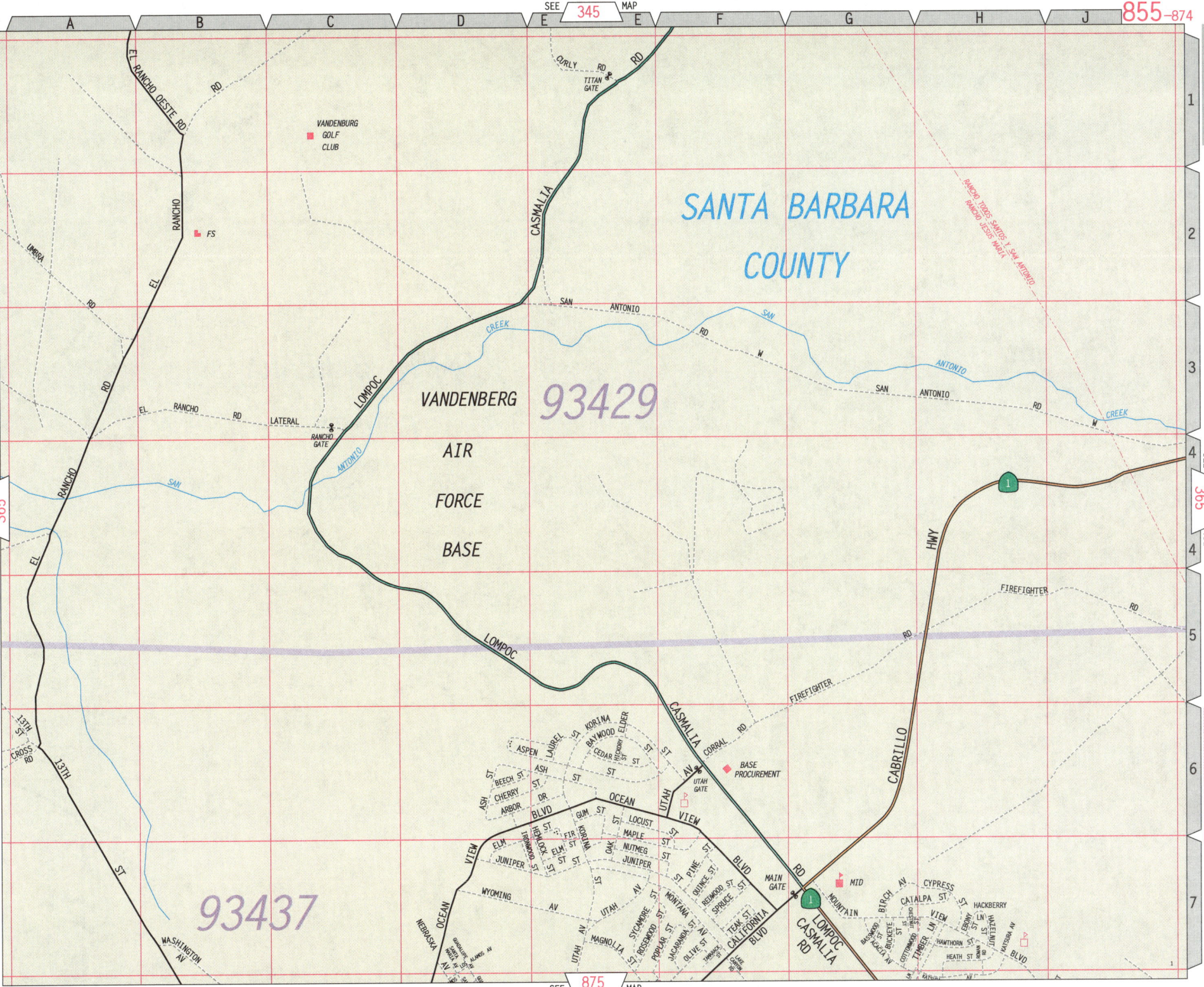

A B C D E E F G H J

1

VANDENBURG
GOLF
CLUB

OURLY RD
TITAN GATE
RD

CASMALIA

SANTA BARBARA

COUNTY

RANCHO TODOS SANTOS Y SAN ANTONIO
RANCHO JESÚS MARIA

2

EL RANCHO OESTE RD

EL RANCHO

FS

SAN ANTONIO

CREEK

SAN

RD

W

SAN ANTONIO

RD

VANDENBERG

93429

AIR

FORCE

BASE

SAN ANTONIO

CREEK

W

3

RD

RANCHO

RD

EL RANCHO RD

LATERAL

LOMPOC

RANCHO
GATE

ANTONIO

SAN

SEE 365 MAP

4

HWY

1

SEE 365 MAP

EL RANCHO

FIREFIGHTER

RD

5

LOMPOC

FIREFIGHTER

RD

CABRILLO

13TH ST
CROSS RD
13TH ST

CASMALIA

CORRAL RD

KORINA ST
BAYWOOD
ELDER ST
ASPEN
LAUREL ST
CEDAR ST
HICKORY ST
ASH ST
BEECH ST
CHERRY ST
ARBOR DR
OCEAN BLVD
GUM ST
LOCUST ST
UTAH
VIEW
MAPLE ST
BASE
PROCUREMENT
UTAH GATE

MAP

6

VIEW ST
ELM ST
JUNIPER ST
IRONWOOD ST
HEMLOCK ST
FIR ST
KORINA ST
OAK ST
NUTMEG ST
JUNIPER ST
PINE ST
QUINCE ST
REDWOOD ST
SPRUCE ST
MAIN GATE
MID
BIRCH AV
CYPRESS AV
CATALPA ST
HACKBERRY
BUCKEYE
EBONY ST
HAZELNUT
CA VIRGINIA ST

7

93437

OCEAN AV
WYOMING AV
NEBRASKA AV
SYCAMORE ST
MONTANA AV
TEAK ST
UTAH AV
MAGNOLIA ST
ROSEWOOD ST
POPLAR ST
JACARANDA ST
OLIVE ST
CALIFORNIA BLVD
BLVD
LOMPOC CASMALIA RD
MOUNTAIN RD
1
TIMBER LN
VIEW LN
HAWTHORN ST
COTTONWOOD
ACACIA ST
HEATH ST
BLVD

WASHINGTON AV

SEE 875 MAP

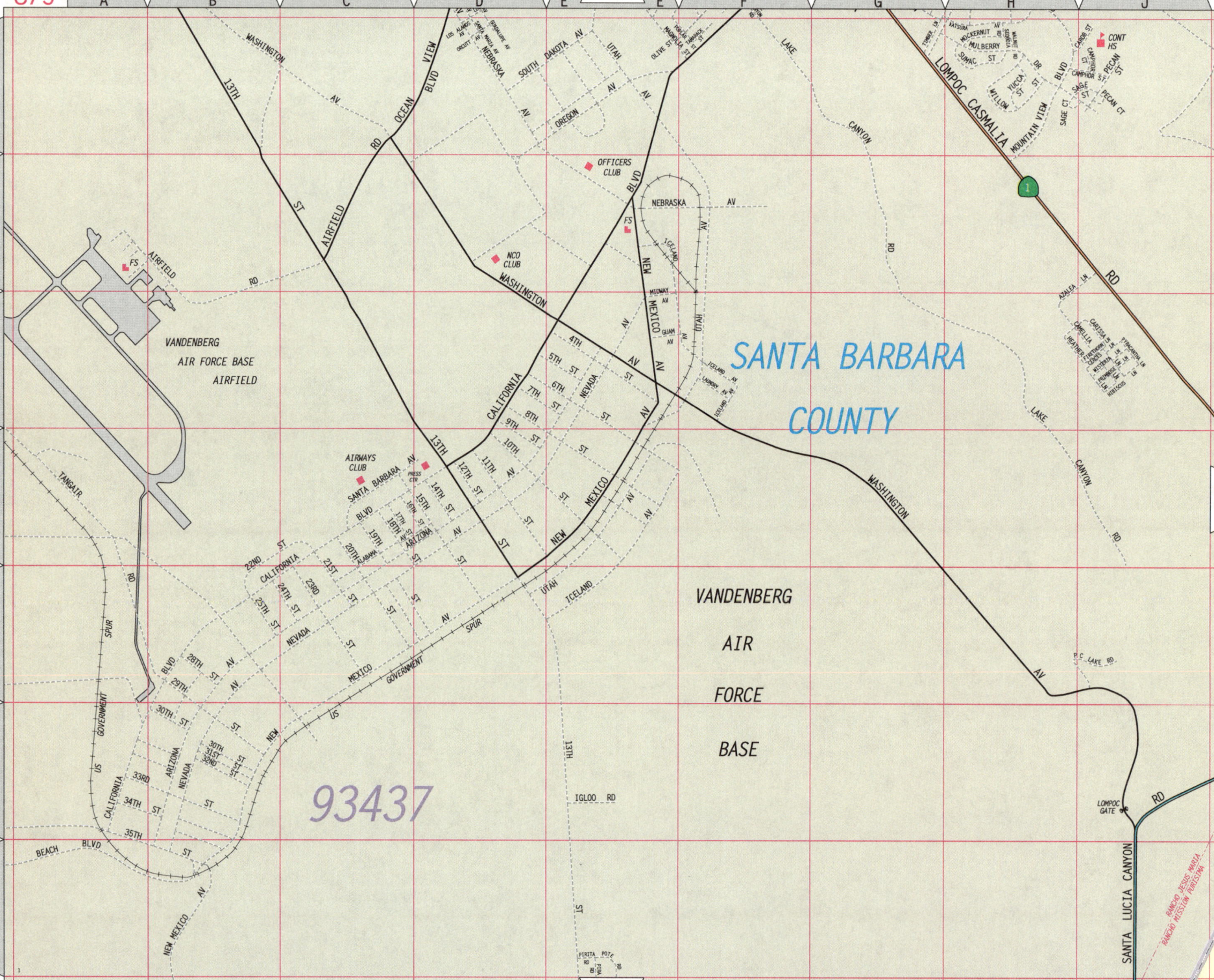

A B C D E E F G H J

COPYRIGHT 2000 Thomas Bros. Maps ®

STB & SLO

1
2
3
4
5
6
7

SEE 855 MAP

SEE 365 MAP
SEE 876 MAP
MAP
SEE 895 MAP

VANDENBERG AIR FORCE BASE AIRFIELD

SANTA BARBARA COUNTY

VANDENBERG AIR FORCE BASE

93437

LOMPOC CASMALIA RD

OFFICERS CLUB
NCO CLUB
AIRWAYS CLUB
SANTA BARBARA BLVD
PRESS CTR

WASHINGTON
OCEAN AV
AIRFIELD RD
13TH ST
OCEAN VIEW BLVD

WASHINGTON AV

NEBRASKA AV
SOUTH DAKOTA AV
OREGON AV
UTAH AV

NEW MEXICO
CALIFORNIA
NEVADA
ICELAND
MIDWAY AV
GUAM AV
LAUNDRY AV

4TH 5TH 6TH 7TH 8TH 9TH 10TH 11TH 12TH 13TH 14TH 15TH 17TH 18TH 19TH 20TH 21ST 22ND 23RD 24TH 25TH 28TH 29TH 30TH 33RD 34TH 35TH ST

ARIZONA ALABAMA
NEVADA
NEW MEXICO
GOVERNMENT
SPUR
ICELAND
IGLOO RD
13TH ST
US

CALIFORNIA BLVD
BEACH BLVD

LOMPOC GATE
P.C. LAKE RD
LAKE CANYON
CANYON RD
WASHINGTON AV

SANTA LUCIA CANYON RD

TANGAIR RD
SPUR RD

LOMPOC RD

RANCHO JESUS MARIA
RANCHO MISSION PURISIMA

PIRITA POTE RD

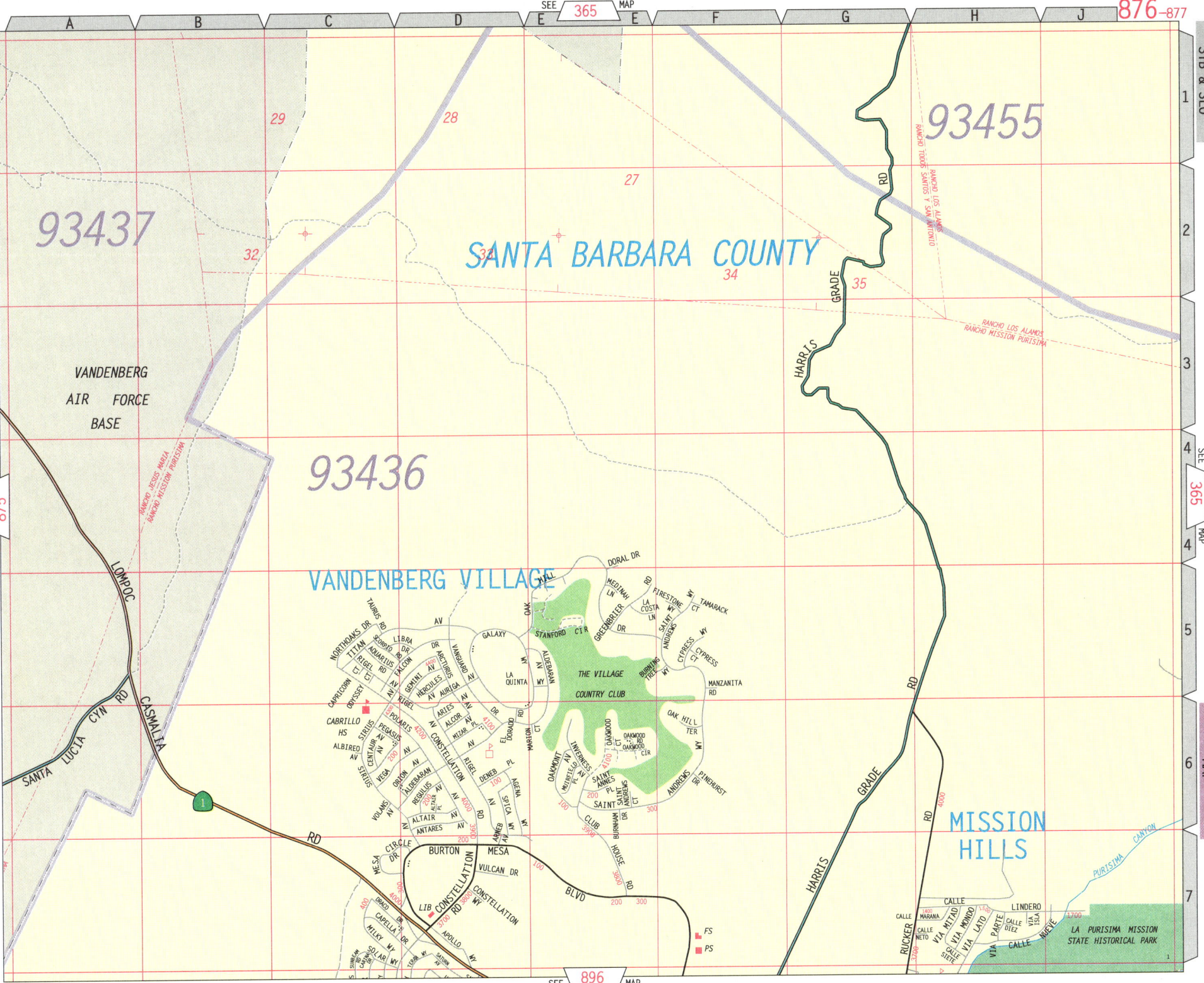

A B C D E E F G H J

1

93455

2

SANTA BARBARA COUNTY

93437

29

28

27

32

33

34

35

3

RANCHO LOS ALAMOS
SANTO Y SAN ANTONIO

RANCHO TODOS SANTOS

RANCHO LOS ALAMOS
RANCHO MISSION PURISIMA

VANDENBERG

AIR FORCE

BASE

HARRIS GRADE

RANCHO JESUS MARIA
RANCHO MISSION PURISIMA

93436

4

VANDENBERG VILLAGE

DORAL DR

MEDINAH LN

FIRESTONE WY

TAMARACK CT

GREENBRIER DR

LA COSTA LN

SAINT ANDREWS

CYPRESS WY

CYPRESS CT

5

LOMPOC CASMALIA

NORTHOAKS DR

TAURUS RD

LIBRA DR

AV

GALAXY

STANFORD CIR

OAK HILL

TITAN

AQUARIUS RD

SCORPIO RD

ARCTURUS RD

DR

VANGUARD RD

ALDEBARAN WY

THE VILLAGE
COUNTRY CLUB

BURNING TREE WY

MANZANITA RD

OAK HILL TER

SANTA LUCIA CYN RD

RIGEL CT

CAPRICORN CT

ODYSSEY CT

GEMINI AV

FALCON

HERCULES

AURIGA

LA QUINTA

AV WY

CABRILLO HS

SIRIUS PEGASUS

POLARIS

AV

ARIES

ALCOR

MIZAR PL

RIGEL

EL DORADO DR

MARRON CT

INVERNESS

OAKMONT

OAKWOOD CT

OAKWOOD RD

OAKWOOD CIR

PINEHURST

6

ALBIREO

CENTAUR AV

VEGA

ORION AV

ALDEBARAN

REGULUS

AGENA WY

MUIRFIELD PL

ANDREWS DR

MAP

SIRIUS

VOLANS AV

ALTAIR

ALTAIR PL

RIGEL

DENEB PL

SPICA WY

SAINT ANNES

SAINT ANDREWS CT

ANTARES AV

AV

AIMEB

CLUB HOUSE RD

BURNHAM DR

SAINT

MISSION

7

MESA CIRCLE DR

BURTON MESA

MESA

VULCAN DR

HILLS

CONSTELLATION WY

CONSTELLATION BLVD

LIB

CONSTELLATION RD

CAPELLA DR

DRACO

MILKY WY

APOLLO

FS

PS

CALLE MARANA

VIA MITAD

CALLE DIEZ

LINDERO

VIA VISTA

LA PURISIMA MISSION
STATE HISTORICAL PARK

RUCKER RD

SOLAR WY

SATURN

CALLE NETO

CALLE SIETE

VIA MONDO

VIA LATO

VIA PARTE

CALLE NUEVE

PURISIMA CANYON

HARRIS GRADE RD

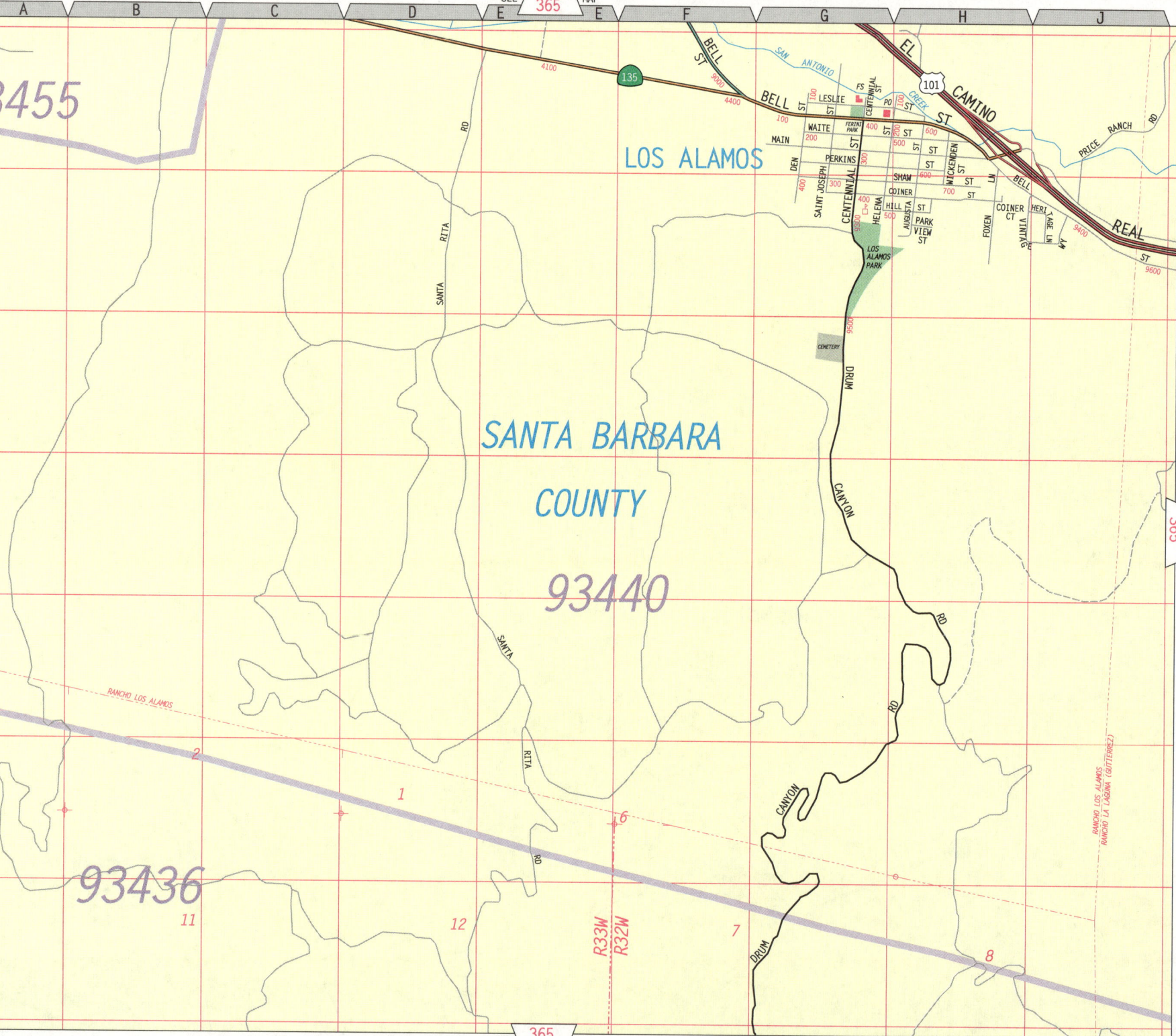

SEE 365 MAP

A B C D E E F G H J

STB & SLO

93455

1

135

4100
9000
4400

BELL ST
BELL ST

SAN ANTONIO CREEK
EL CAMINO

101

FS
LESLIE
CENTENNIAL ST
PO
100 ST

LOS ALAMOS

WAITE
MAIN
200
100
400
1200 ST
600
500
ST
PRICE RANCH RD

DEN
PERKINS
300
ST
ST
600
WICKENDEN ST
ST
700
ST
BELL

SAINT JOSEPH
CENTENNIAL ST
400
SHAW
COINER
HELENA
500
HILL
AUGUSTA
PARK VIEW ST
FOXEN
COINER CT
HERITAGE LN
VINTAGE LN
9400

2

SANTA RITA

9800

LOS ALAMOS PARK

REAL
ST 9600

CEMETERY
9950

DRUM
CANYON

3

SANTA BARBARA

COUNTY

SEE 365 MAP
SEE 365 MAP

4

93440

SANTA RITA

RD

CANYON RD

5

RANCHO LOS ALAMOS

3
2
1

RD

CANYON

6

6

RANCHO LOS ALAMOS (GUTIERREZ)
RANCHO LA LAGUNA (GUTIERREZ)

93436

10
11
12

R33W
R32W

7

DRUM

8

7

SEE 365 MAP

SEE 365 MAP

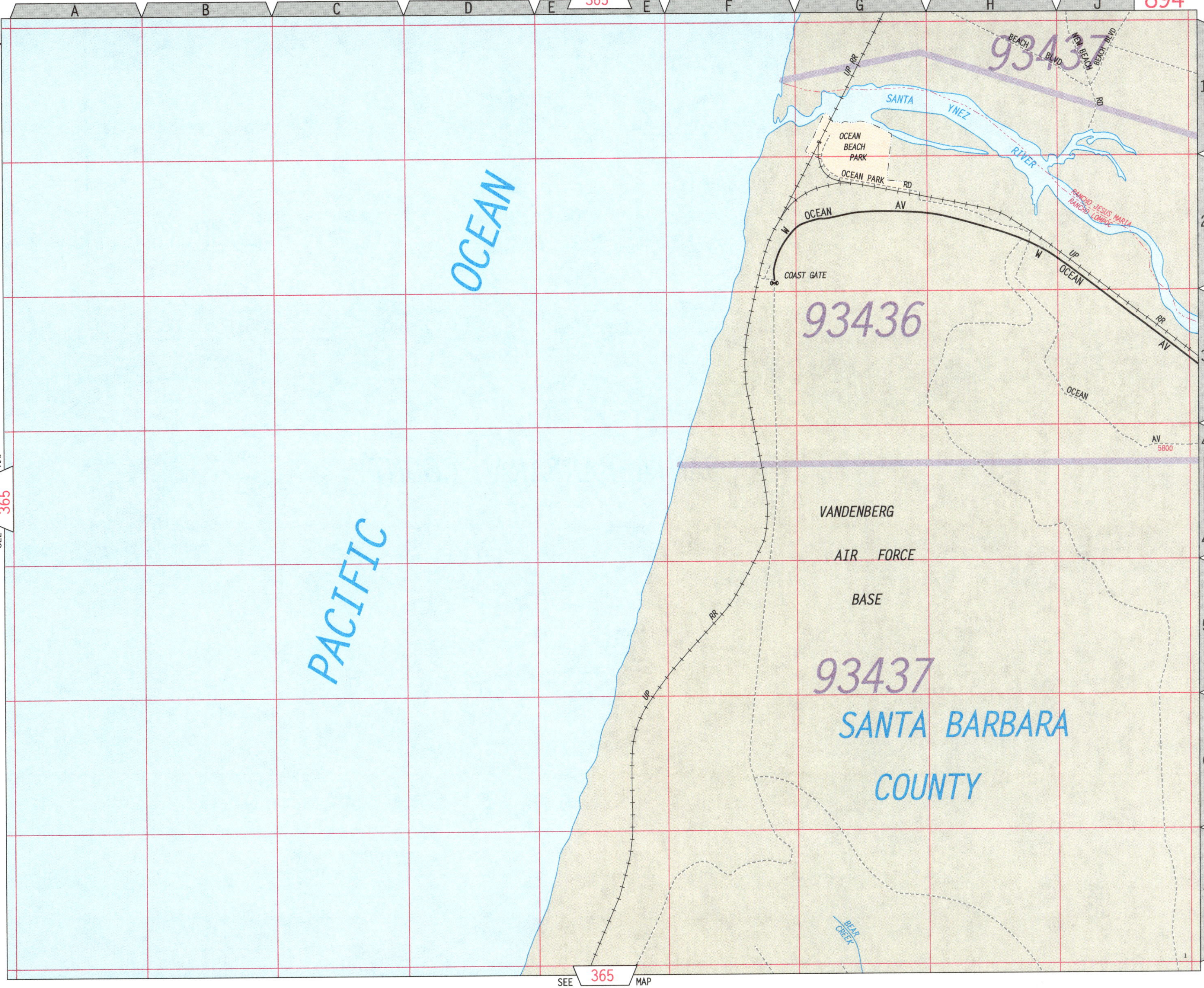

A B C D E E F G H J

STB & SLO

93437

BEACH BLVD

NEW BEACH

LOMPOC BLVD

RD

SANTA YNEZ RIVER

OCEAN BEACH PARK

OCEAN PARK RD

RAMCHO JESUS MARIA

RANCHO LOMBOC

UP RR

OCEAN

OCEAN AV

W

COAST GATE

W OCEAN

UP

RR AV

93436

OCEAN

PACIFIC

AV 5800

SEE 895 MAP

SEE 365 MAP

VANDENBERG

AIR FORCE

BASE

RR

93437

SANTA BARBARA

COUNTY

UP

MAP

OCEAN

BEAR CREEK

SEE 365 MAP

1 2 3 4 4 5 6 7

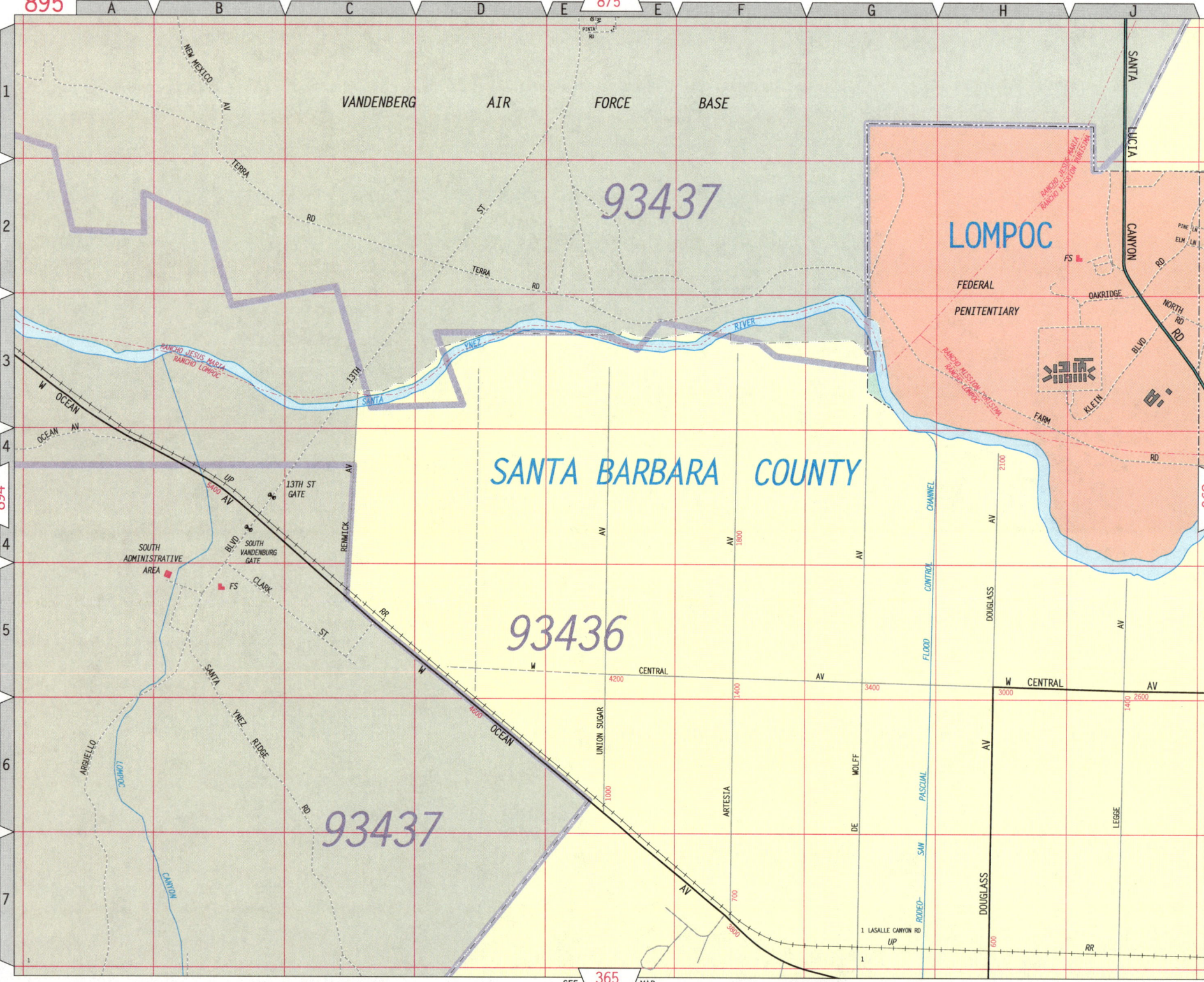

A B C D E E F G H J

STB & SLO

1

VANDENBERG AIR FORCE BASE

NEW MEXICO AV

TERRA RD

PINTA RD

SANTA LUCIA CANYON

2

93437

TERRA RD

LOMPOC

PINE LN
ELM LN

FS

FEDERAL

OAKRIDGE

PENITENTIARY

NORTH RD

RD

RANCHO JESUS MARIA
RANCHO LOMPOC

13TH ST

SANTA YNEZ

RIVER

RANCHO MISSION VIEJA
RANCHO LOMPOC

KLEIN BLVD

3

W OCEAN

OCEAN AV

SEE 894 MAP

SANTA BARBARA COUNTY

FARM RD

SEE 896 MAP

4

UP

5400

13TH ST GATE

REIMICK AV

AV

AV

AV

AV

FLOOD CONTROL CHANNEL

DOUGLASS AV

2100

AV

AV

SOUTH ADMINISTRATIVE AREA

SOUTH VANDENBURG GATE

BLVD

CLARK ST

FS

5

SANTA YNEZ RIDGE RD

ST

RR

W

4660

OCEAN

93436

4200 CENTRAL AV

1400

3400

3000

W CENTRAL AV

2600

140

MAP

ARGUELLO

LOMPOC

1000

UNION SUGAR AV

ARTESIA AV

DE WOLFF AV

SAN PASCUAL AV

FLOOD CONTROL

DOUGLASS AV

LEGGE AV

6

93437

CANYON

RODEO AV

700

3800

1 LASALLE CANYON RD

UP

DOUGLASS

600

RR

7

COPYRIGHT 2000 Thomas Bros. Maps®

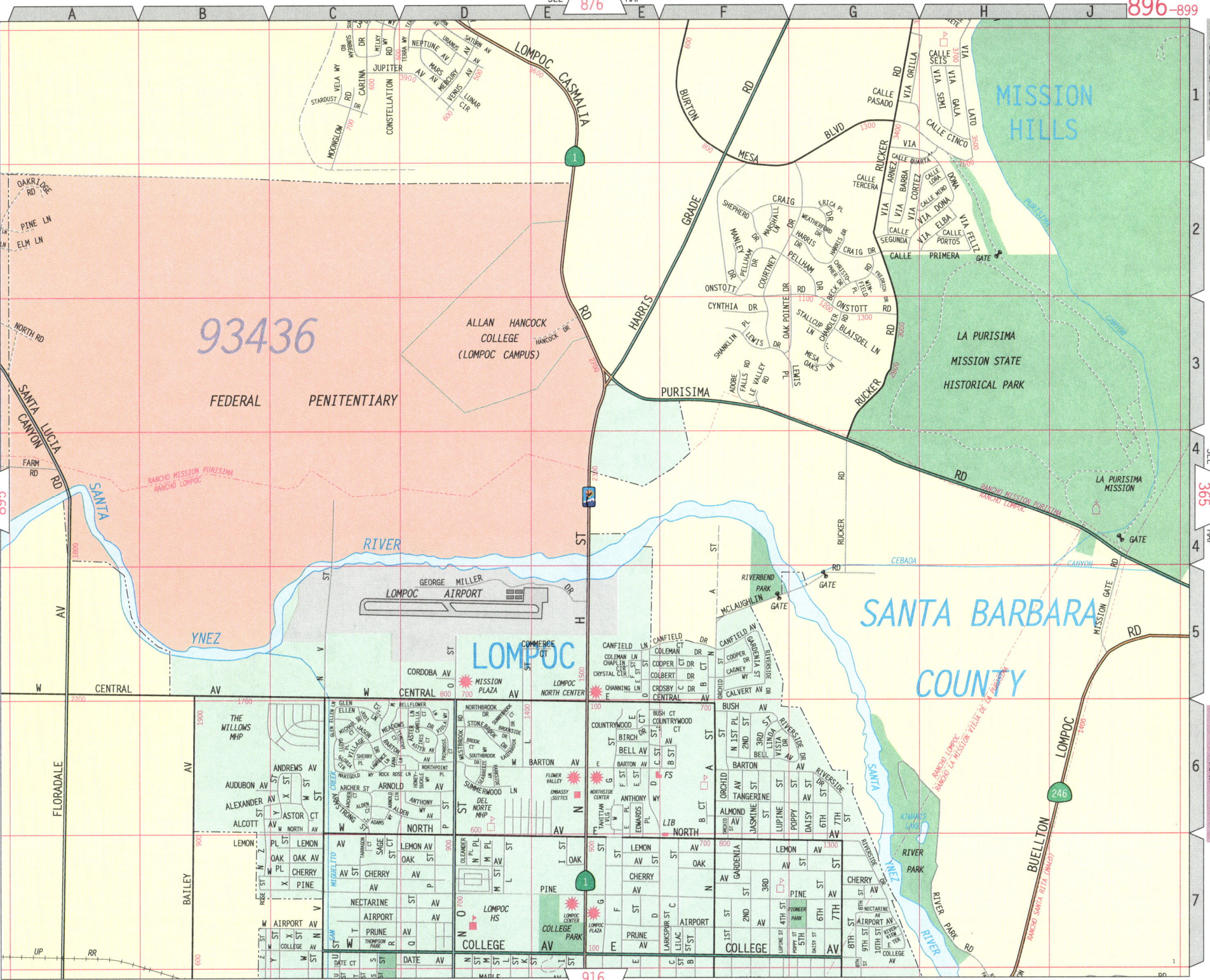

STB & SLO

MAP 365 SEE

MAP

Thomas Bros. Maps ®
COPYRIGHT 2000

MISSION HILLS

93436

FEDERAL PENITENTIARY

ALLAN HANCOCK
COLLEGE
(LOMPOC CAMPUS)

LA PURISIMA
MISSION STATE
HISTORICAL PARK

LA PURISIMA
MISSION

SANTA BARBARA

COUNTY

GEORGE MILLER
LOMPOC AIRPORT

LOMPOC

THE
WILLOWS MHP

RIVER
PARK

SEE 895

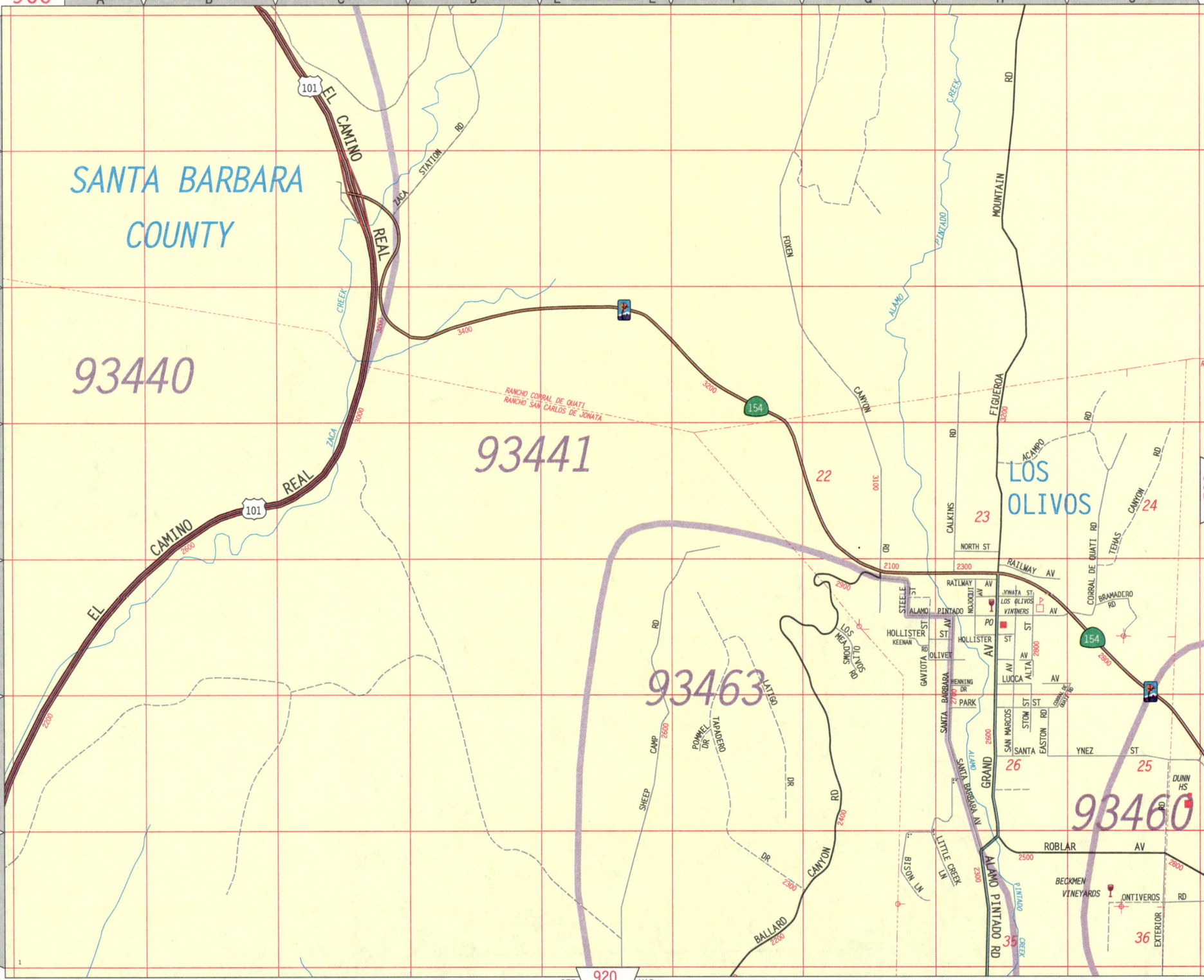

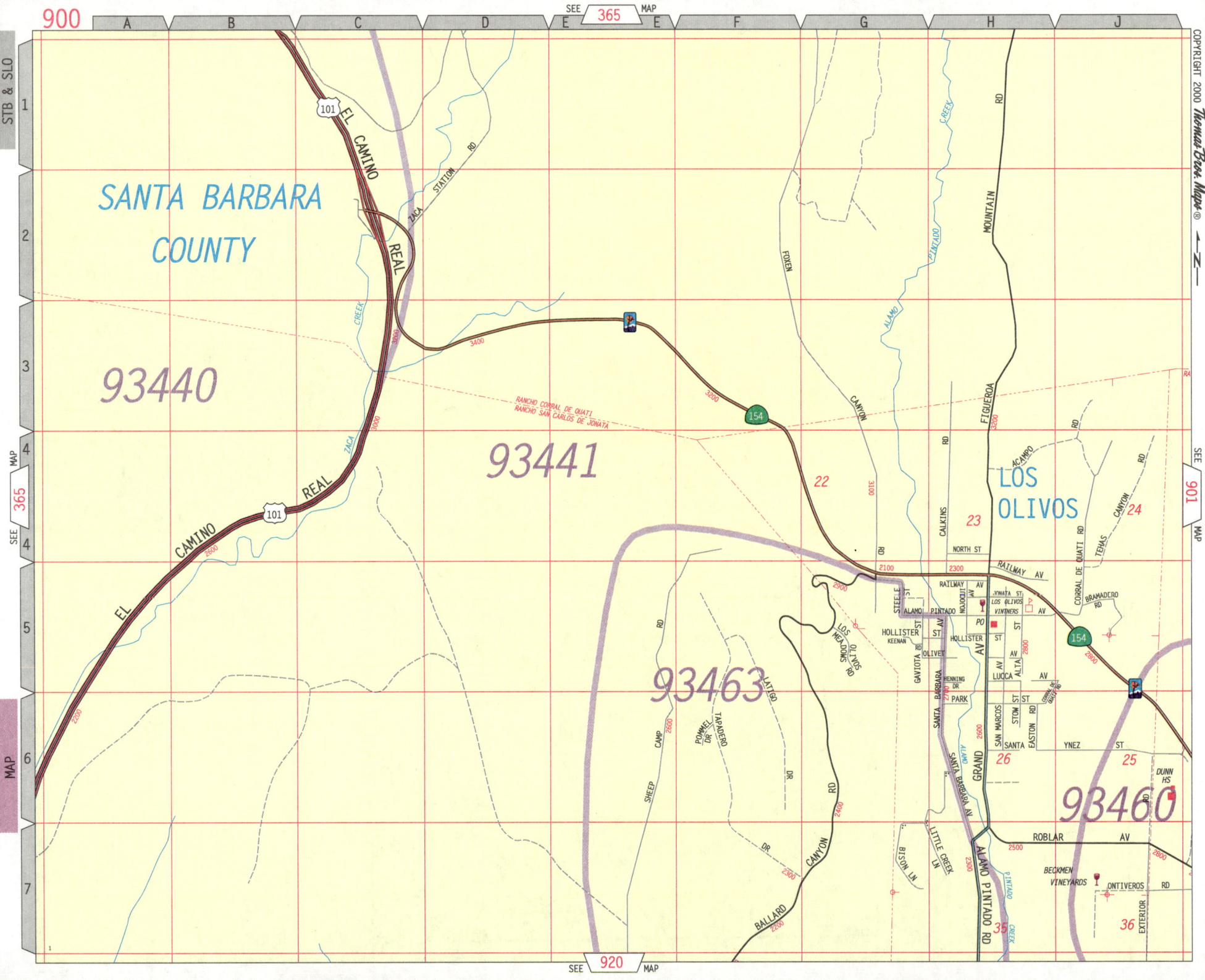

SEE 365 MAP

A B C D E E F G H J

STB & SLO

1

101

EL CAMINO

ZACA STATION RD

CREEK

SANTA BARBARA

COUNTY

2

REAL

FOXEN CANYON

ALAMO PINZADO

CREEK

FIGUEROA MOUNTAIN RD

93440

3

ZACA

CREEK

3800

3400

3200

154

RANCHO CORRAL DE QUATI
RANCHO SAN CARLOS DE JONATA

3100

3000

RA

SEE 365 MAP

4

101

EL CAMINO

REAL

2600

93441

22

3100

RD

CALKINS

FIGUEROA 3300

RD

ACAMPO

LOS
OLIVOS

23

CANYON RD

TEMAS

24

CORRAL DE QUATI RD

SEE 901 MAP

NORTH ST

RAILWAY AV

2100

2300

RAILWAY AV

5

RD

SHEEP CAMP

2600

POMMEL DR

TAPADERO DR

GAVIOTA RD

LOS OLIVOS RD

LOS MEADOWS RD

2900

STEELE ST

ALAMO PINTADO

HOLLISTER ST

KEENAN

OLIVET

HOLLISTER AV

SANTA BARBARA AV

2700

JONATA ST

LOS OLIVOS VINTNERS

PO

JONATA ST

AV

ALTA

LUCCA

HENNING DR

PARK

2800

154

2500

93463

6

CANYON RD

2400

BISON LN

GRAND AV

ALAMO PINTADO AV

2700

SAN MARCOS ST

STOW ST

SANTA

CORRAL DE QUATI RD

EASTON ST

YNEZ ST

26

25

BRAMADERO RD

DUNN HS

93460

MAP

7

DR

2300

BALLARD 2200

CANYON RD

LITTLE CREEK LN

ROBLAR AV

2500

ALAMO PINTADO RD

2500

BECKMEN VINEYARDS

PINTADO CREEK

35

ONTIVEROS RD

EXTERIOR

36

2800

SEE 920 MAP

STB & SLO

1

RANCHO CORRAL DE QUATI
RANCHO LA LAGUNA (GUTIERREZ)

SANTA BARBARA

COUNTY

TIMS

RD

WOODSTOCK

RD

LONG

VALLEY

CLOVER   LN

RD

93441

2

3

Rancho Corral de Quati
Rancho Canada de los Pinos or College Rancho

RANCHO LA LAGUNA (GUTIERREZ)
RANCHO CANADA DE LOS PINOS OR COLLEGE RANCHO

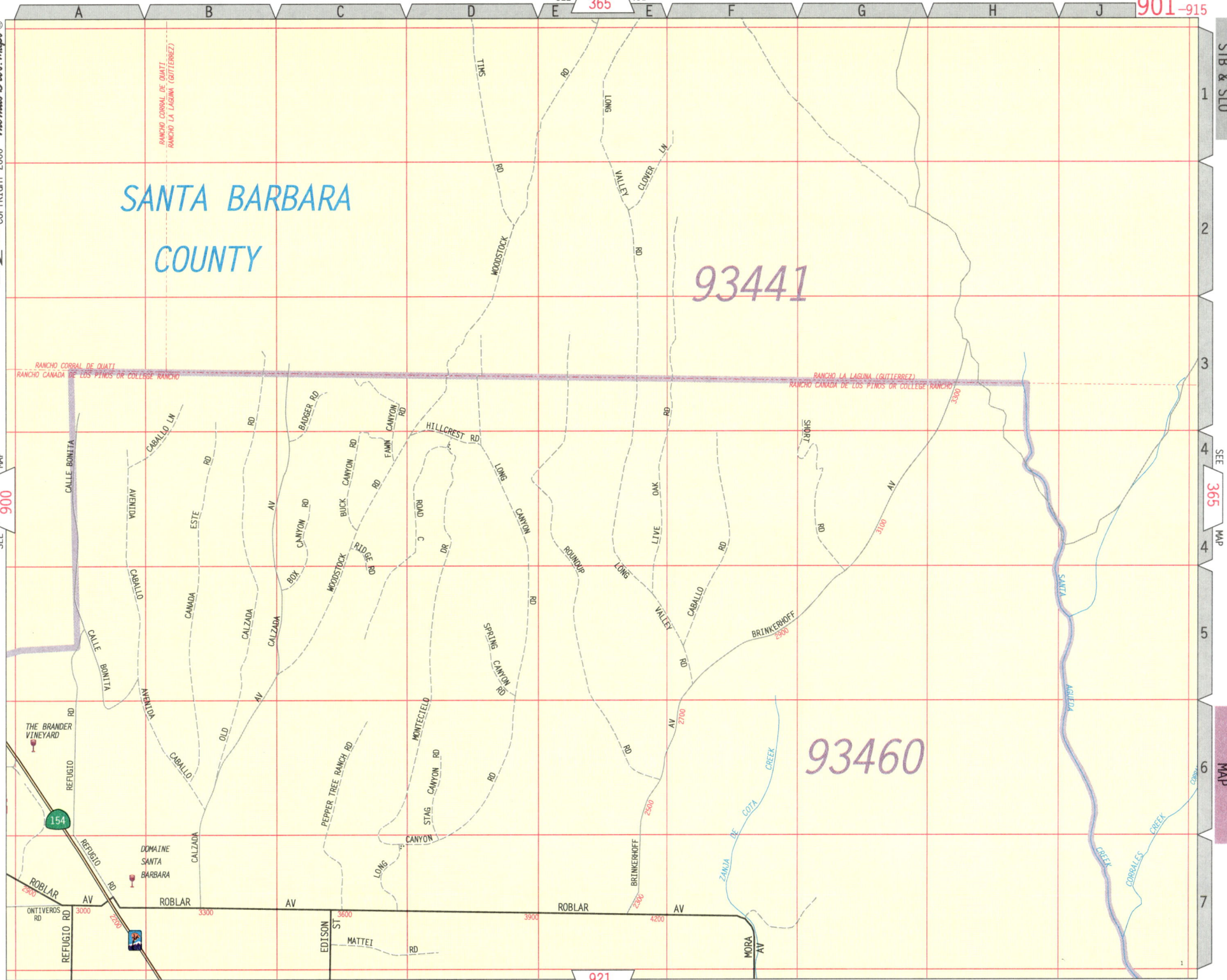

3300

CALLE BONITA

CABALLO LN

BADGER RD

FANN   CANYON   RD

HILLCREST RD

RD

RD

SHORT

AVENIDA

ESTE

RD

CANYON   AV

BUCK   CANYON   RD

ROAD   C

LONG

OAK

LIVE

RD

AV

RD

SEE 900 MAP

4

SEE 365 MAP

CABALLO

CANADA

CALZADA

CALZADA

BOX

WOODSTOCK RIDGE RD

DR

CANYON

RD

ROUNDUP

LONG

VALLEY

CABALLO

RD

BRINKERHOFF 3900

5

AVENIDA

OLD   AV

CABALLO

SPRING CANYON RD

RD

AV 2700

MAP

6

THE BRANDER
VINEYARD

REFUGIO   RD

PEPPER TREE RANCH RD

MONTECIELD

STAG   CANYON   RD

RD

RD

AV 2500

93460

COTA   CREEK

ZANJA   DE   LA

AGUEDA

SANTA

CREEK

CORRALES   CREEK

154

REFUGIO   RD

DOMAINE
SANTA
BARBARA

CALZADA

LONG

CANYON

BRINKERHOFF 2300

7

ROBLAR   AV

2500

ONTIVEROS
RD

REFUGIO RD

3000

2200

ROBLAR   3300

AV

EDISON ST

MATTEI   RD

3600

ROBLAR   AV

3900   4200

MORA   AV

1

SEE 365 MAP

SEE 921 MAP

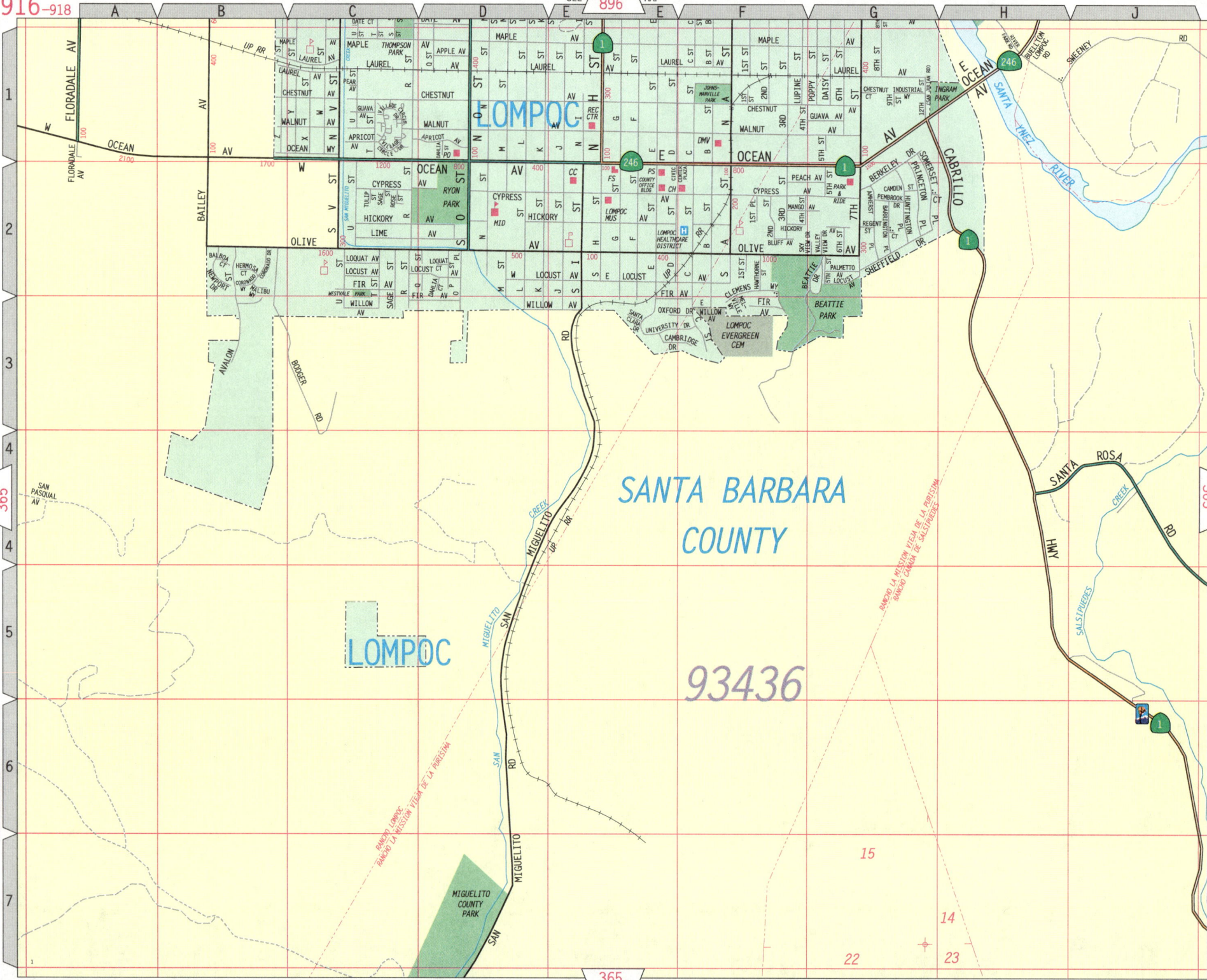

STB & SLO

SEE 896 MAP

COPYRIGHT 2000 Thomas Bros. Maps ®

A B C D E F G H J

LOMPOC

SANTA BARBARA
COUNTY

LOMPOC

93436

FLORADALE AV

OCEAN AV

MAPLE
LAUREL
CHESTNUT
WALNUT
APRICOT
OCEAN

CYPRESS
HICKORY
LIME

OLIVE

LOQUAT AV
LOCUST AV
FIR AV
WILLOW AV

THOMPSON PARK
APPLE AV

RYON PARK

MAPLE
LAUREL

CHESTNUT
WALNUT
OCEAN

CYPRESS
HICKORY

LOCUST
FIR AV
WILLOW AV

REC CTR

DMV
CC
FS
PS COUNTY OFFICE BLDG
CIVIC CENTER PLAZA
CH

LOMPOC MUS

LOMPOC HEALTHCARE DISTRICT

JOHNS-MANVILLE PARK

MAPLE
LAUREL
CHESTNUT
WALNUT
OCEAN
PEACH AV
CYPRESS
HICKORY
OLIVE

PARK & RIDE

INGRAM PARK

BERKELEY
PRINCETON
SOMERSET
CAMDEN
PEMBROOK
HUNTINGTON
BARRINGTON
AMHERST
REGENT

SHEFFIELD DR

BEATTIE PARK

E OCEAN AV

CABRILLO

BUELLTON LOMPOC RD
SWEENEY RD

SANTA YNEZ RIVER

246

SANTA ROSA

SANTA YNEZ RIVER

SALSIPUEDES CREEK

BAILEY AV

OLIVE AV

AVALON
BADGER RD

NEWPORT
BALBOA
HERMOSA
CORONADO
MALIBU

WESTVALE PARK

OXFORD DR
SANTA CLARA DR
UNIVERSITY DR
CAMBRIDGE DR

LOMPOC EVERGREEN CEM

MIGUELITO CREEK

SAN MIGUELITO RD

MIGUELITO COUNTY PARK

SANTA ROSA RD

SANTA HWY

SALSIPUEDES CREEK

RANCHO LOMPOC
RANCHO LA MISSION VIEJA DE LA PURISIMA
RANCHO CAÑADA DE SALSIPUEDES

15
14
22 23

SEE 365 MAP

SEE 365 MAP

MAP 365

MAP

A B C D E E F G H J

1 2 3 4 4 5 6 7

101

ZACA CREEK

93427

COUGAR RIDGE RD
BLUEBIRD GLEN RD
POPPY VALLEY RD
BOBCAT RD
SPRINGS
CAMINO SAN CARLOS RD

EL CAMINO REAL

SANTA BARBARA COUNTY

93436

246

SEE 365 MAP

SEE 920 MAP

1200 1000

BUELLTON

JONATA
PARK
LOS PADRES WY
EASY ST
ARTHUR EARL
COMMERCE DR
MCMURRAY
THOMAS RD
ZACA

PETERSON
VIA CHAPRA
RAY LN
PAULA PL
PITA LN
SHARON AV
Buellton Park
DAMASSA ST
Rancho Santa Barbara Marriott

RIVERVIEW
FARMLAND
CALOR DR
OAK TREE WY
2ND
LATA
LATA DR
TERI SUE LN
KIM SUE LN
NINA PL
DAMM
NINA ST

MEADOW VIEW DR
DAIRY
VALLEY DR
PARK CIR
MENLO DR
KAREN PL
DOWNEY
PALM WY
CENTRAL
AVENUE OF FLAGS
1ST
100
MCMURRAY RD
REAL
GLENRORA
FREEAR DR
GAY DR
DANITA AV
SCANDIA
WY
KENDALE
SCANDIA ST
ORENSE ST
300

PARK CIR
INDUSTRIAL WY
PO
FS
LIB
PS
ZACA ST
200
300
400
100
PEA SOUP ANDERSENS
CC

1 WESTGATE
2 EASTGATE
CHP
VICTORY
MOUNTAIN DR
FREEDOM PL
BEAR
CREEK DR
CIR
ZACA CREEK GOLF COURSE
SHADOW
SIX FLAGS
VICTORY DR
AVENUE OF FLAGS (BUELLTON PKWY)
101
246
ELISA CT
TIMBERLINE

Rancho San Carlos de Jonata
Rancho Nojoqui

YNEZ
SANTA
ROSA RD
9
RIVER
10
8600
11
8800
12
13
SANTA ROSA RD
9000
14
15

MOSBY WINERY

EL CAMINO

CREEK

SANFORD WINERY

SANTA

RANCHO SAN CARLOS DE JONATA
RANCHO SANTA ROSA (COTA)

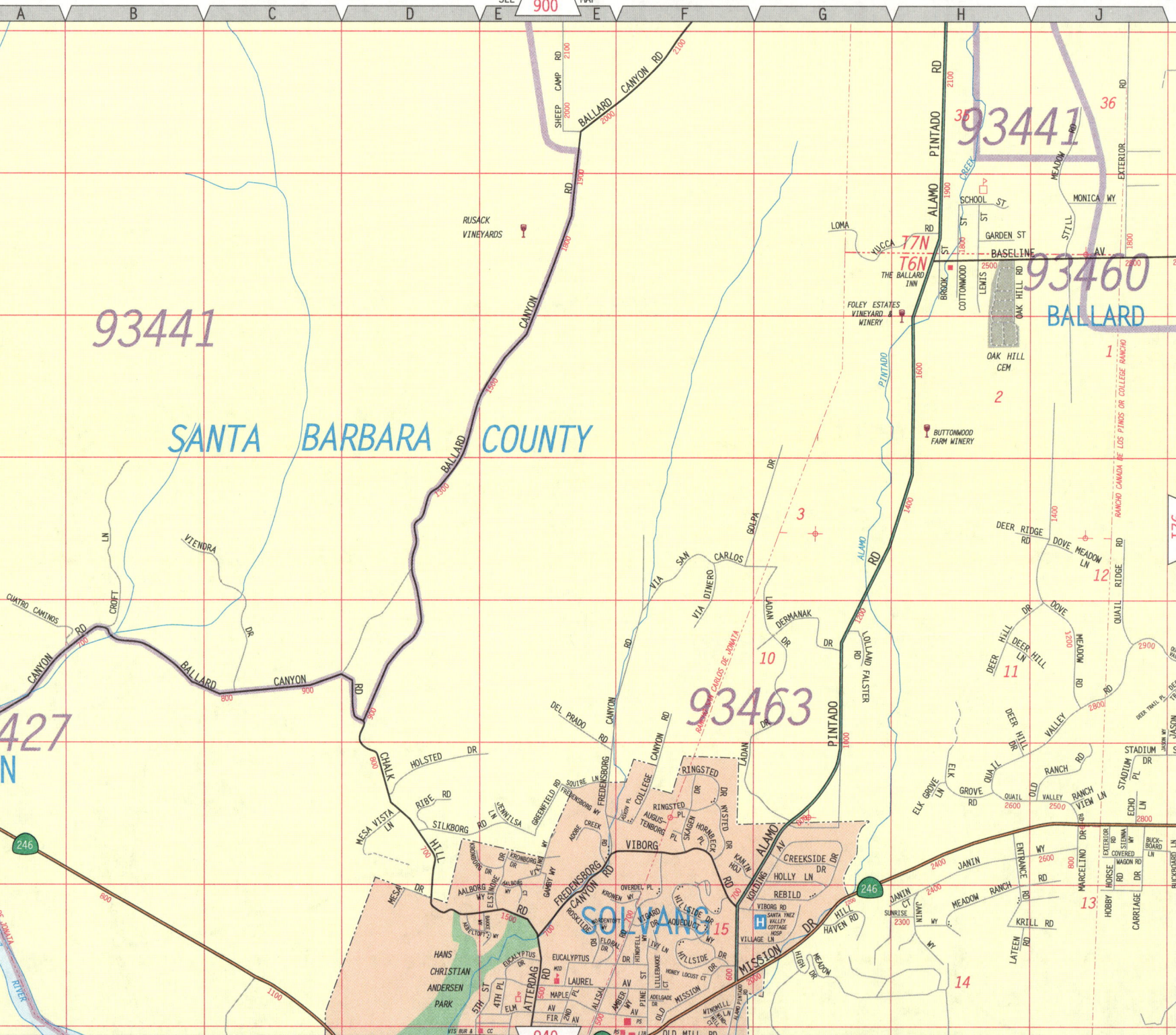

920

STB & SLO

SEE 900 MAP

A B C D E F G H J

93441

93441

SANTA BARBARA COUNTY

93441

93460
BALLARD

RUSACK VINEYARDS

FOLEY ESTATES VINEYARD & WINERY

OAK HILL CEM

BUTTONWOOD FARM WINERY

THE BALLARD INN

BASELINE

T7N
T6N

SEE 919 MAP

SEE 921 MAP

93427
BLTN

93463

SOLVANG

HANS CHRISTIAN ANDERSEN PARK

246

246

SANTA YNEZ VALLEY COTTAGE HOSP

SEE 940 MAP

COPYRIGHT 2000 Thomas Bros. Maps

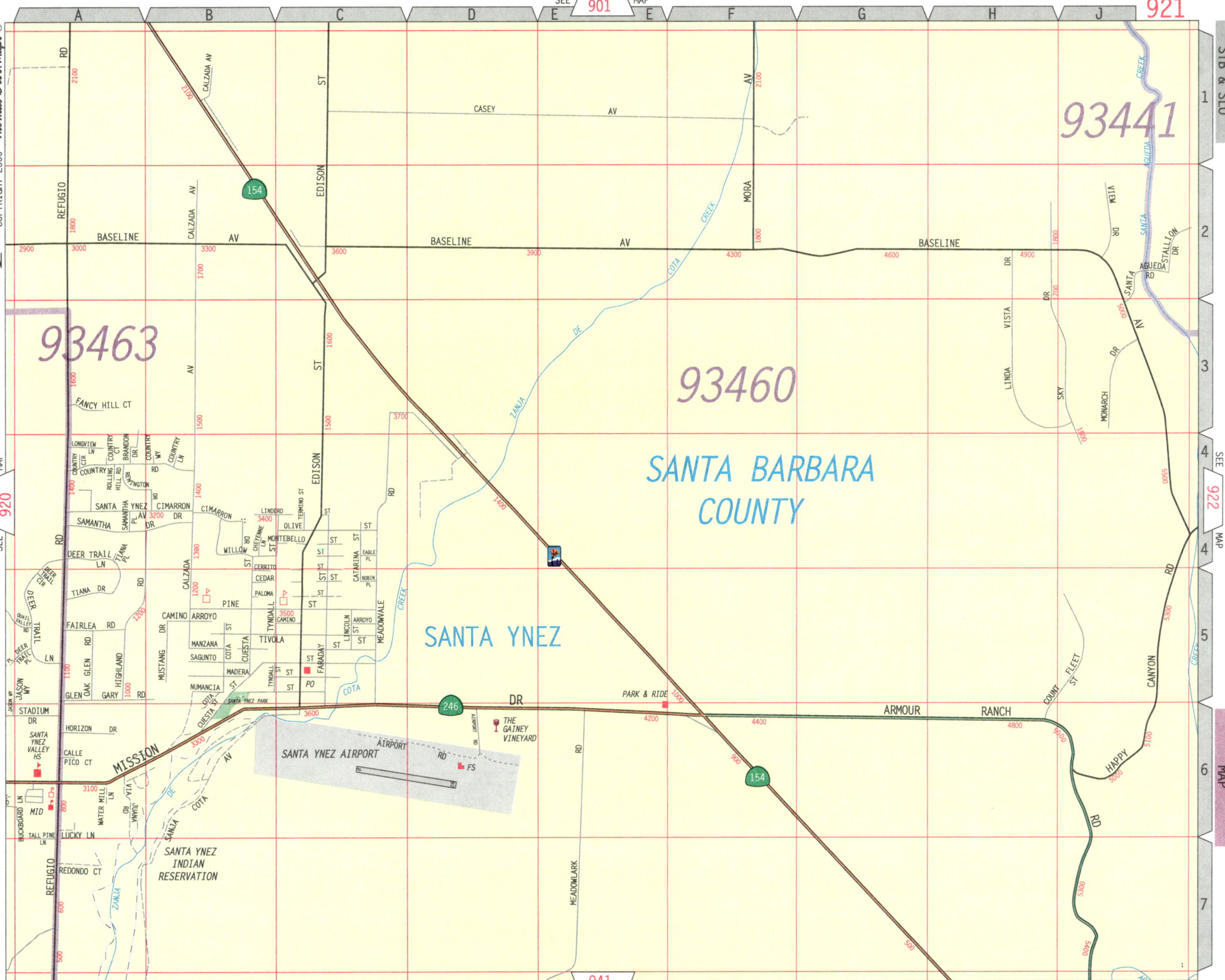

A B C D E E F G H J 921

STB & SLO

93441

1

CALZADA AV
CASEY AV
EDISON ST
MORA AV
2100

154
REFUGIO RD
2100
1800

BASELINE AV
CALZADA AV
BASELINE AV
BASELINE
2900 3000 3300 3600 3900 4300 1800 4600 4900

AV
1700
1600
ST
CALZADA
COTA
ZANJA DE CREEK
VIEW DR
SANTA AGUEDA RD
STALLION

93463

2

93460

SANTA BARBARA
COUNTY

3

FANCY HILL CT
1600
1500
EDISON ST
3700
1500
LINDA DR
VISTA DR
SKY
MONARCH DR
1600
5000
5700

SEE 920 MAP
1400
LONGVIEW LN
COUNTRY CIR
COUNTRY CT
ROLLING HILL RD
BRANDON RD
COUNTRY WY
COUNTRY LN
CIMARRON
LINDERO
TERMINO ST
OLIVE ST
EDISON ST
RD
1400

SANTA YNEZ
SAMANTHA
SAMANTHA PL
AV
CIMARRON DR
3200
3400
ST
ST
CATARINA ST
EAGLE PL
5300

DEER TRAIL LN
TIANA PL
CHEYENNE LN
MONTEBELLO
CERRITO ST
ROBIN PL
RD

4

SEE 922 MAP

DEER TRAIL CIR
TIANA DR
WILLOW
1300
ST
CEDAR ST
PALOMA ST
CREEK
1400

DEER TRAIL LN
QUAIL VALLEY RD
FAIRLEA RD
1200
PINE
1200
ARROYO
ST
ST
CAMINO
ARROYO
3500 CAMINO
SANTA YNEZ

5

JASON WY
DEER TRAIL PL
OAK GLEN RD
HIGHLAND
1000
MUSTANG DR
CAMINO ARROYO
MANZANA
SAGUNTO
COTA ST
CUESTA
TIVOLA
LINCOLN ST
MEADOWVALE
COTA

GLEN GARY RD
NUMANCIA ST
MADERA ST
TYNDALL ST
PO
ST
FARADAY
COTA
PARK & RIDE
1000
4200
4400
ARMOUR RANCH
4800
COUNT FLEET ST
CANYON
5100
5300

STADIUM DR
CUESTA ST
SANTA YNEZ PARK
246
DR
154
900
5000
5200
HAPPY

SANTA YNEZ VALLEY HS
CALLE PICO CT
MISSION
3600
3500
AV
THE GAINEY VINEYARD
AIRPORT
RD
FS

6

MAP

HORIZON DR
WATER MILL LN
VIA JUANA
ZANJA DE
COTA
SANTA YNEZ AIRPORT
RD
RD
900

3100
800
MID

BUCKBOARD LN
TALL PINE LN
LUCKY LN
REDONDO CT
SANTA YNEZ
INDIAN
RESERVATION
MEADOWLARK
5300
5500

7

REFUGIO RD
500
600
ZANJA

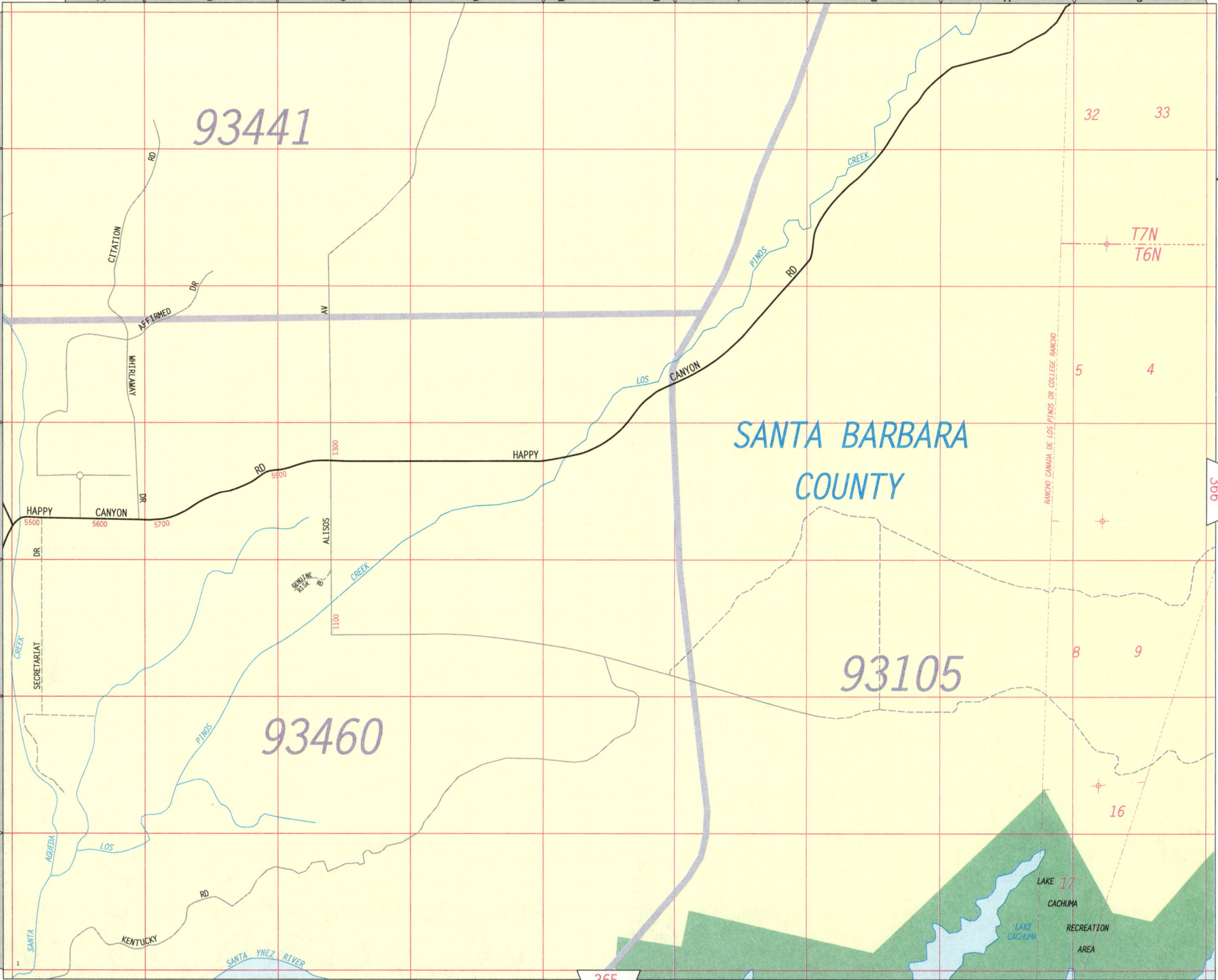

STB & SLO

SEE 365 MAP

A B C D E E F G H J

1

93441

2

CITATION RD

WHIRLAWAY

AFFIRMED DR

AV

T7N
T6N

32 33

3

LOS CANYON

PINOS RD

5 4

SANTA BARBARA

COUNTY

SEE 921 MAP

SEE 366 MAP

4

HAPPY

RD 5900

1300

RANCHO CAÑADA DE LOS PINOS OR COLLEGE RANCHO

HAPPY CANYON DR
5500 5600 5700

ALISOS

GENUINE RISK RD

CREEK

1100

5

CREEK

SECRETARIAT

93105

8 9

93460

PINOS

6

16

AGUEDA

LOS

LAKE CACHUMA
RECREATION
AREA

17

LAKE CACHUMA

7

SANTA

KENTUCKY RD

SANTA YNEZ RIVER

MAP

COPYRIGHT 2000 Thomas Bros Maps ® —N—

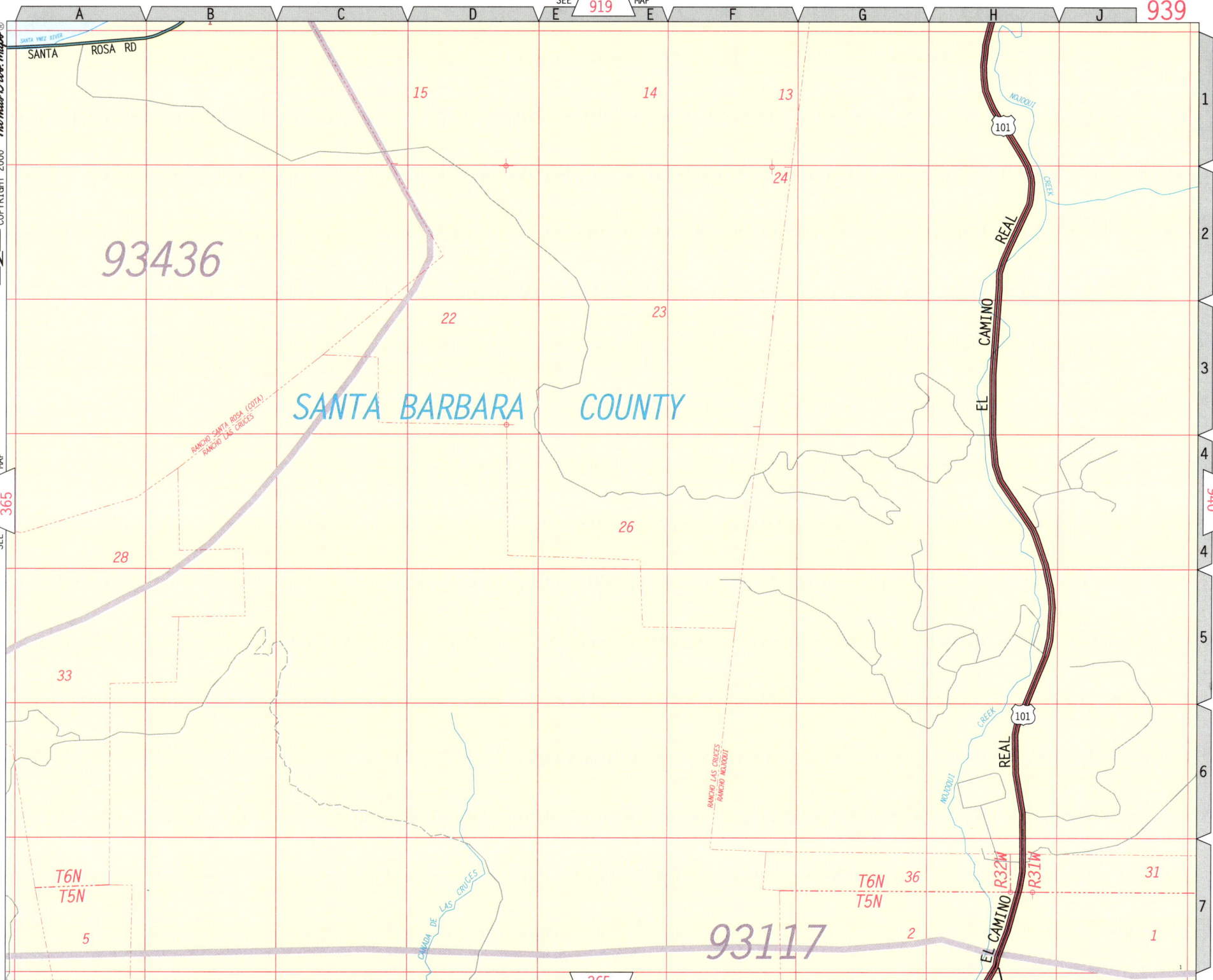

STB & SLO

A   B   C   D   E   E   F   G   H   J

1

SANTA YNEZ RIVER
SANTA   ROSA RD

15   14   13

24

101

93436

2

MOJOQUI CREEK

22   23

EL CAMINO REAL

3

SANTA BARBARA   COUNTY

RANCHO SANTA ROSA (COTA)
RANCHO LAS CRUCES

SEE 940 MAP

4

26

4

SEE 365 MAP

28

5

33

101

CREEK

6

MOJOQUI

REAL

MAP

RANCHO LAS CRUCES
RANCHO MOJOQUI

7

T6N
T5N

R32W R31W

T6N   36
T5N

31

CAÑADA DE LAS CRUCES

5

93117   2

EL CAMINO

1

A B C D E F G H J

STB & SLO

1

2

3

SEE 939 MAP

4

4

5

MAP 6

7

SANTA

SOLVANG

MISSION DR

HANS CHRISTIAN ANDERSEN PARK

SOLVANG PK

PETERSEN VLG
COPENHAGEN
OAK ST
SYCAMORE

ELVERHOY
BIRCH DR

PREMIUM OUTLET CENTER

ROYAL SCANDINAVIAN INN

SVENDBORG

SANTA INES MISSION

OLD MILL RD

246

15

14

MESA VERDE RD

22

23

RIVER COURSE AT THE ALISAL

CLUBHOUSE

YNEZ

RIVER

SANTA

ALAMO PINTADO CREEK

SUNSTONE VINEYARDS & WINERY

REFUGIO RD

RANCHO CAÑADA DE LOS PINOS OR COLLEGE RANCHO

THREE SPRINGS RD

FAIRWAY DR

FAIRWAY

FAIRWAY PL

ALISAL

RANCHO

RILEY RD

CLUBHOUSE

RINCON DR

ALISAL

ALISAL GUEST RANCH RD & GOLF COURSE

BUTTONHOOK RD

OXBOW PL

BOWL PL

DR

93463

SANTA BARBARA

COUNTY

ALISAL

RANCHO NOJOQUI

31

T6N
T5N

32

33

34

1

R32W R31W

6

5

4
RESERVOIR

3

DAM

RD

SEE 941 MAP

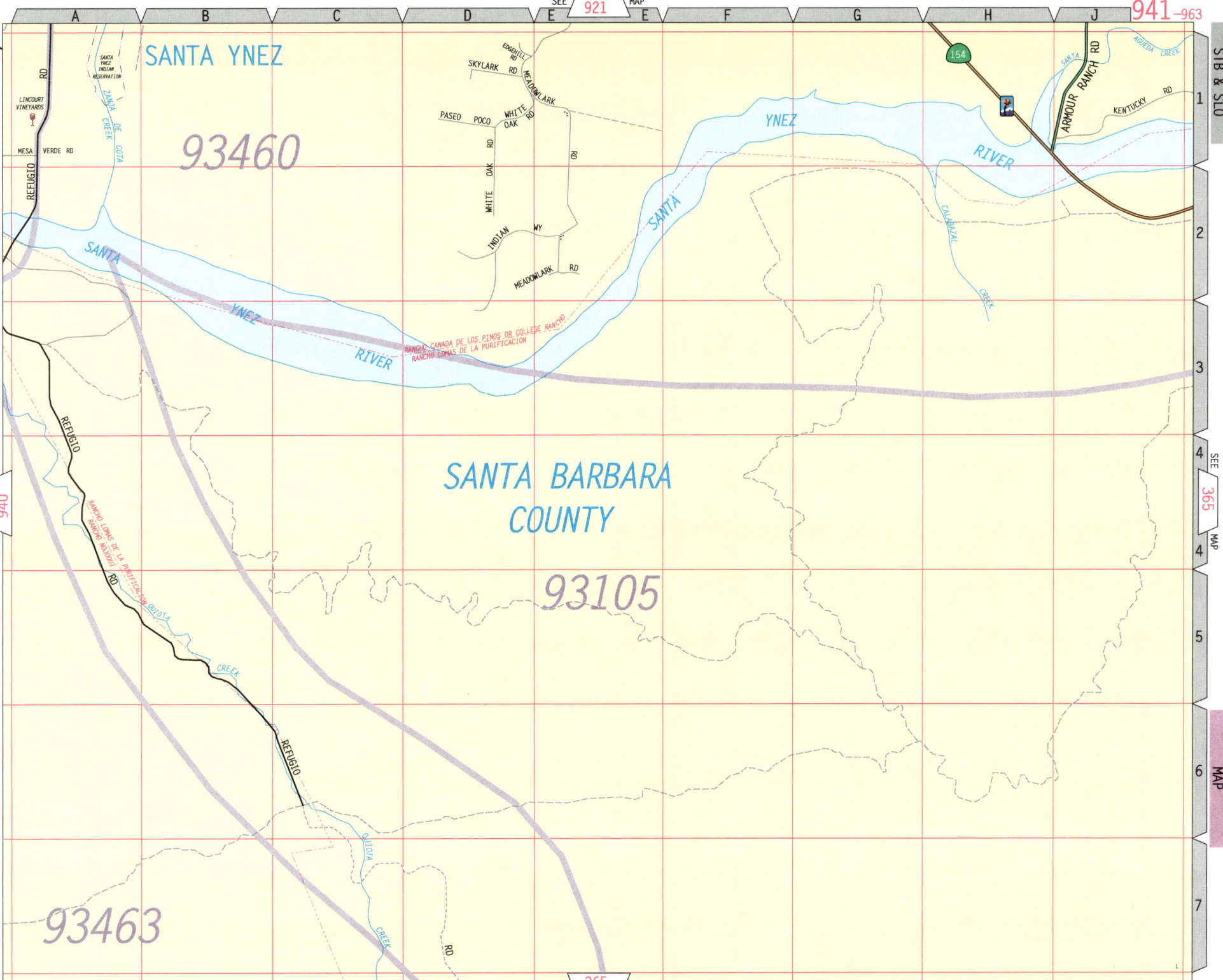

A B C D E E F G H J

STB & SLO

SANTA YNEZ

93460

SANTA YNEZ INDIAN RESERVATION

LINCOURT VINEYARDS

MESA VERDE RD

REFUGIO RD

ZANJA DE COTA CREEK

EDGEHILL RD

SKYLARK RD

MEADOWLARK RD

PASEO POCO

WHITE OAK RD

WHITE OAK RD

RD

INDIAN WY

MEADOWLARK

MEADOWLARK RD

154

SANTA YNEZ RIVER

SANTA ARMOUR RANCH RD

AGUEDA CREEK

KENTUCKY RD

CALABAZAL CREEK

1

2

SANTA YNEZ RIVER

RANCHO CANADA DE LOS PINOS OR COLLEGE RANCHO
RANCHO LOMAS DE LA PURIFICACION

3

REFUGIO RD

RANCHO LOMAS DE LA PURIFICACION
RANCHO NOJOQUI

QUIOTA CREEK

SEE 940 MAP

SANTA BARBARA COUNTY

93105

SEE 365 MAP

4

5

MAP

6

REFUGIO

QUIOTA CREEK

RD

93463

7

COPYRIGHT 2000

Thomas Bros. Maps

A B C D E E F G H J

STB & SLO

COPYRIGHT 2000

Thomas Bros. Maps ®

—N—

SANTA YNEZ RIVER

STAGECOACH

RANCHO SAN MARCOS

RD

PARADISE

PARADISE RD

CABIN LN

FREMONT PARK CAMPGROUND

MANZANITA LN

FREMONT LN

PARADISE PARK

SANTA

OAK LN

YNEZ

RIVER

PARADISE LN

FS

RANGER STATION

PARADISE RD

6

5

LA CA MES MONTE SUNSHINE VISTA LN LN

POTRERO LN

LOS PRIETOS CAMPGROUND

PARADISE PARK CAMPGROUND

SAN

RD

STAGECOACH

RANCHO LOS PRIETOS Y NAJALAYEGUA

LOS

PADRES

2

MARCOS

154

PASS

RD

LAURELES

PARADISE CANYON

NATIONAL

7

8

RD

9

10

11

3

STAGECOACH

RD

STAGECOACH

RD

CANYON

FOREST

COLD SPRINGS TAVERN

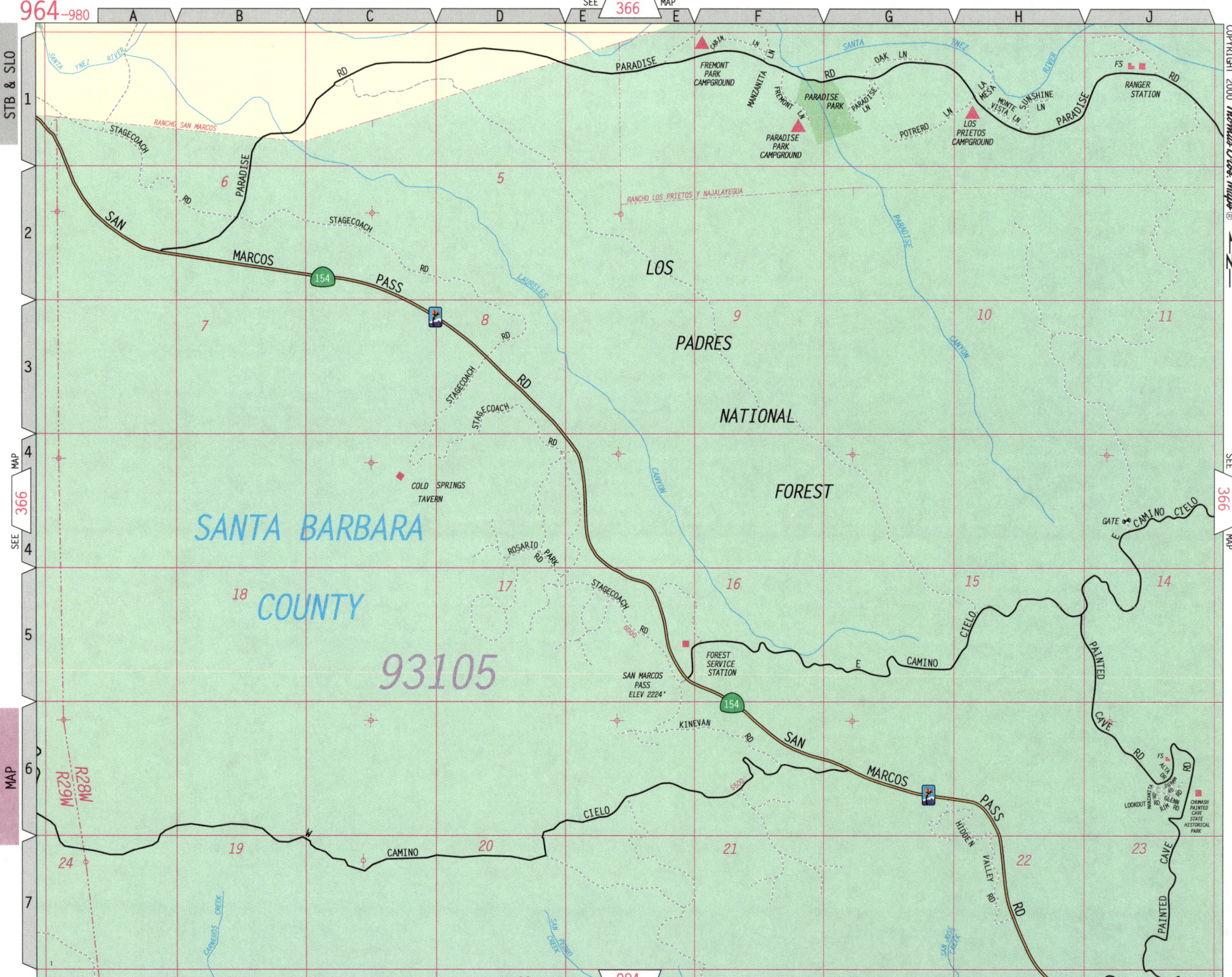

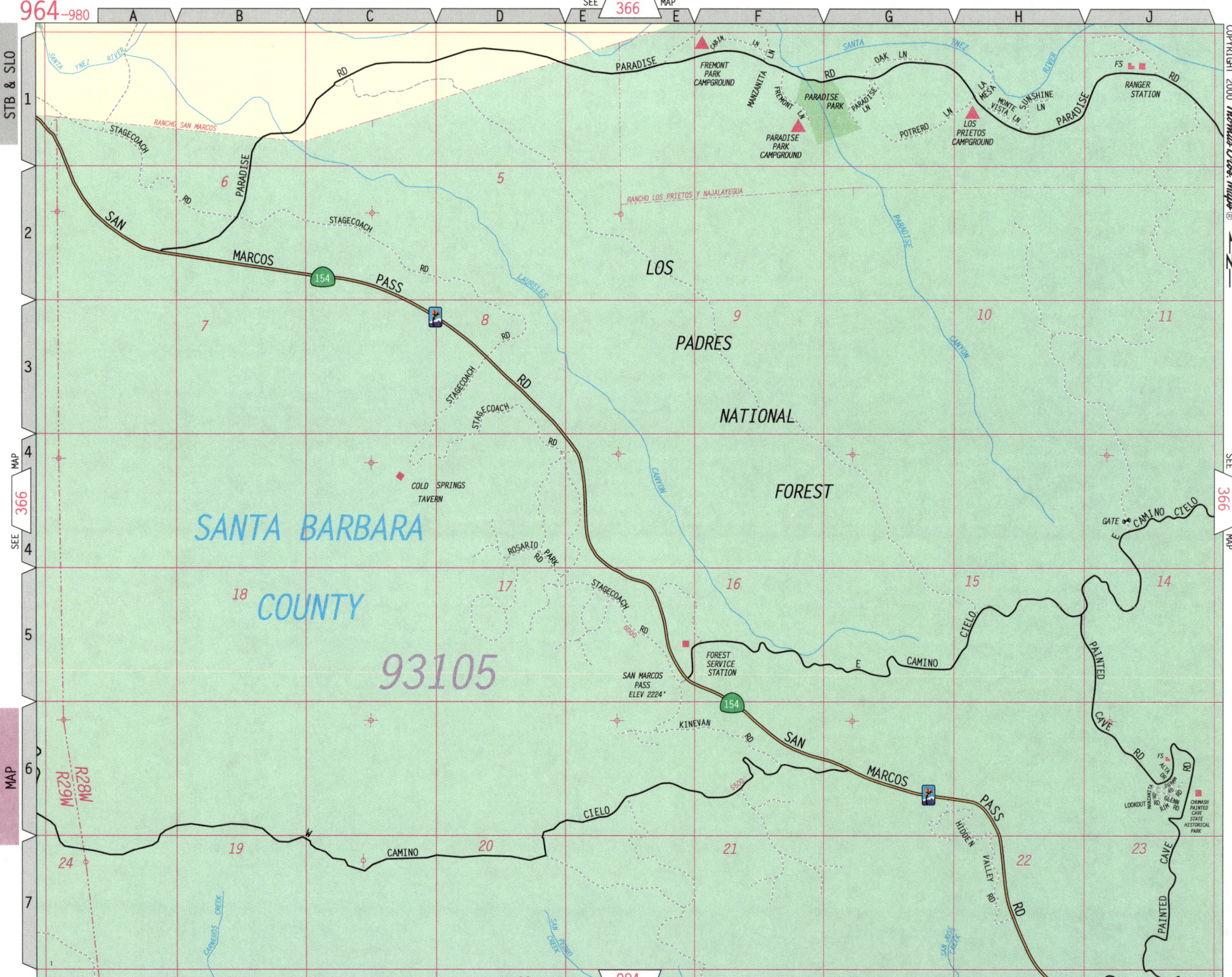

SANTA BARBARA

ROSARIO PARK RD

STAGECOACH

GATE E CAMINO CIELO

4

18

COUNTY

17

RD

16

15

14

93105

STAGECOACH 6800 RD

FOREST SERVICE STATION

E CAMINO

CIELO

PAINTED

5

SAN MARCOS PASS ELEV 2224'

154

KINEVAN

RD

SAN

MARCOS

CAVE

RD

FS ALTA DEL SOL RD

6

R28W R29W

CIELO

5500

MANZANITA RD GLENN RIM RD

LOOKOUT

CHUMASH PAINTED CAVE STATE HISTORICAL PARK

19

CAMINO

20

21

HIDDEN VALLEY RD

22

PASS

23

24

CARNEROS CREEK

SAN PEDRO CREEK

SAN JOSE CREEK

PAINTED CAVE

MAP 366

SEE 366 MAP

MAP

STB & SLO

23

LOS PADRES
NATIONAL FOREST

24

R31W
R30W

19

LOS PADRES
NATIONAL FOREST

LEON

CANYON

CREEK

AGUALITO

CANYON

TAJIGUAS

REFUGIO

RD

REFUGIO

CANADA DEL

CANADA

DEL

VENADITO

93117

SANTA BARBARA COUNTY

RESERVOIR

LAS
FLORES
CANYON

CANADA
DEL
CORRAL

RANCHO CANADA DE CORRAL
RANCHO NUESTRA SEÑORA DEL
REFUGIO

CANADA DEL CAPITAN

SEE 365 MAP

SEE 982 MAP

CALLE
REAL

REAL

CALLE   REAL

101

REFUGIO STATE
BEACH

UP

RR

EL CAPITAN
STATE
BEACH

EL CAMINO

101

UP

RR

PACIFIC   OCEAN

MAP

1

2

3

4

4

5

6

7

STB & SLO

A B C D E SEE 365 MAP E F G H J

COPYRIGHT 2000 Thomas Bros. Maps ® —N—

1

LOS PADRES NATIONAL FOREST

24 R30W R29W

93105

19

30 29

SANTA BARBARA COUNTY

2

LOS PADRES

NATIONAL

FOREST

RESERVOIR

3

CANYON RD

CANYON

CANYON

CANYON

93117

DESTILADERA

LIPPIZANA

CALLE QUEBRADA

GATO

CANYON

31 32

SEE 981 MAP

LA DE

CALLE ECUESTRE

RANCHO CANADA DEL CORRAL
RANCHO LOS DOS PUEBLOS

VARAS

SEE 983 MAP

4

AVENDA DEL CAPITAN

CALLE

LLAGAS

CANYON RD

T5N

CANADA

EL CAPITAN
STATE BEACH

EL CAPTAIN
(CALLE

RANCH

GATO

VARAS CANYON

LAS

5

REAL)

RD

101

EL CAMINO

LAS

CANYON RD

DOS PUEBLOS

PACIFIC

UP

REAL

DOS PUEBLOS

SEVILLE RD

RD

RESERVOIR

6

OCEAN

RR

DOS PUEBLOS CANYON RD

SEVILLE

7

SEE 992 MAP

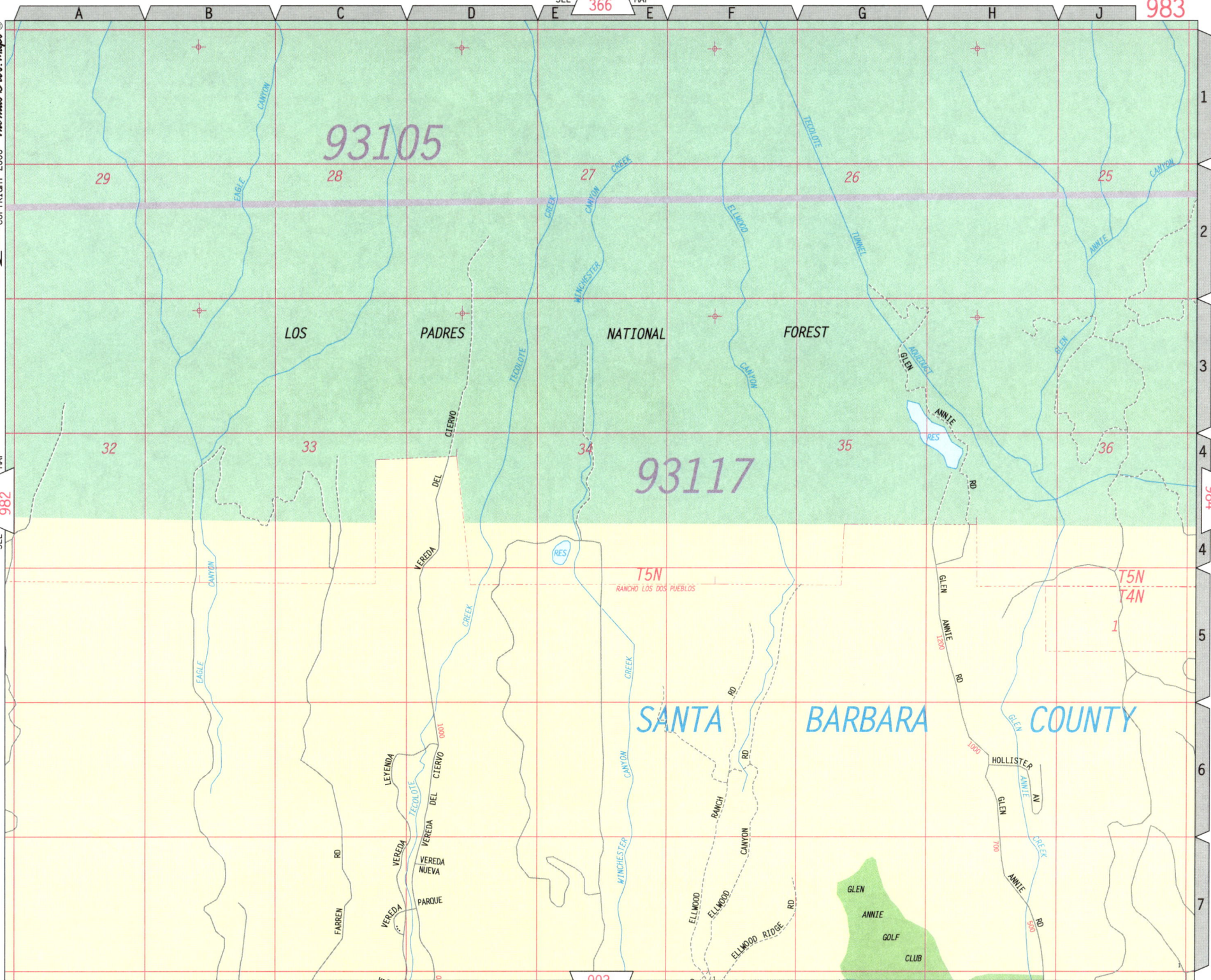

1

93105

29   28   27   26   25

2

LOS   PADRES   NATIONAL   FOREST

EAGLE CANYON

TECOLOTE CREEK

WINCHESTER

ELWOOD CANYON

TECOLOTE

TUNNEL

ARRIETA

GLEN

ANNIE

GLEN

3

ANNIE RES

SEE 982 MAP

32   33   34   35   36

SEE 984 MAP

93117

DEL

CIERVO

VEREDA

RES

RD

4

T5N
RANCHO LOS DOS PUEBLOS

T5N
T4N

1

EAGLE CANYON

TECOLOTE CREEK

WINCHESTER CANYON CREEK

GLEN ANNIE RD

5

SANTA   BARBARA   COUNTY

MAP

6

LEYENDA

DEL CIERVO

VEREDA

TECOLOTE

RD

RANCH RD

RD

ELWOOD CANYON

HOLLISTER

GLEN

ANNIE AV

GLEN ANNIE CREEK

RD

FARREN RD

VEREDA

VEREDA
NUEVA

VEREDA   PARQUE

ELWOOD

ELWOOD

ELWOOD RIDGE RD

GLEN
ANNIE
GOLF
CLUB

7

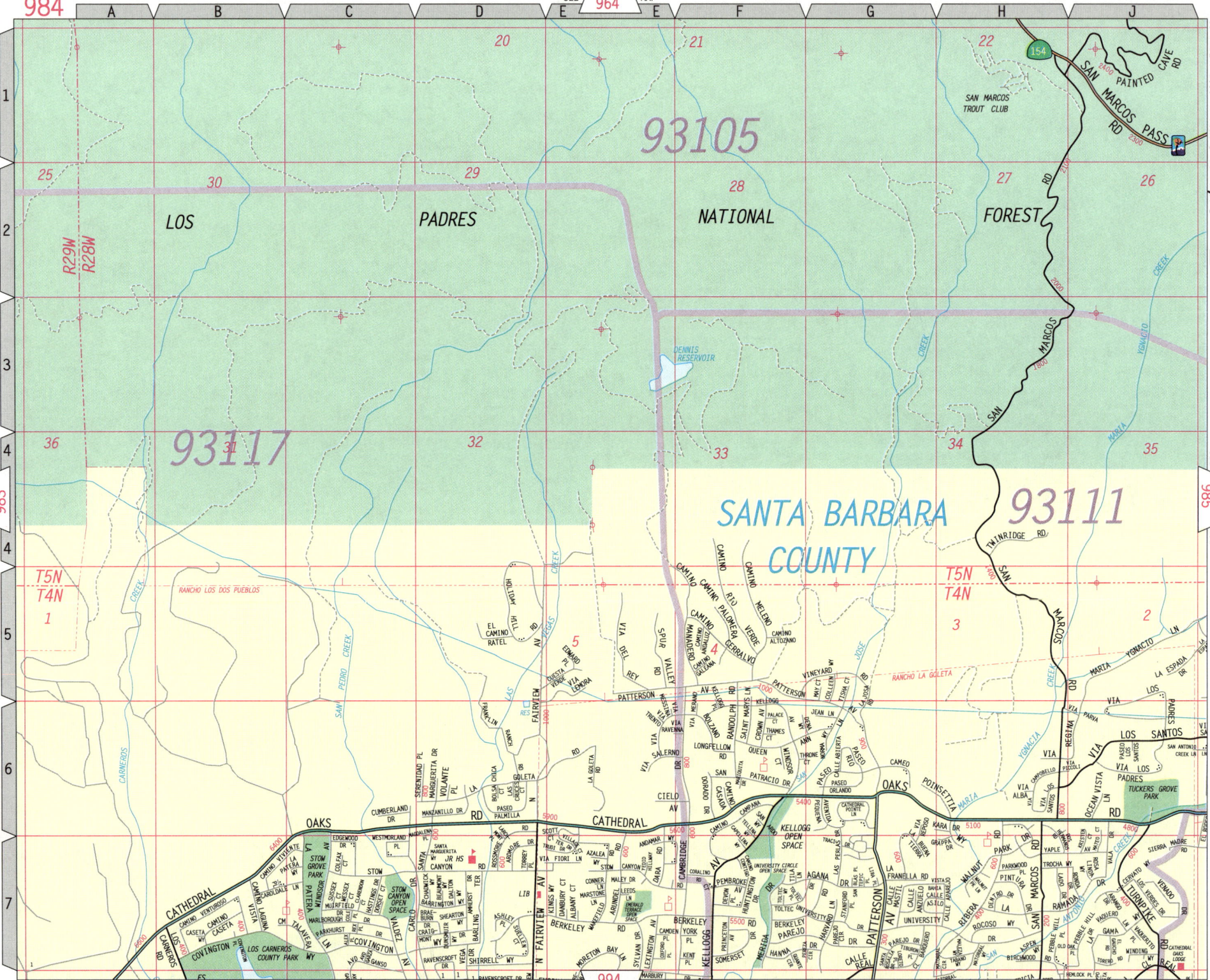

984

SEE 964 MAP

STB & SLO

93105

LOS PADRES NATIONAL FOREST

SAN MARCOS PASS RD
PAINTED CAVE RD
SAN MARCOS TROUT CLUB
154

R29W R28W

DENNIS RESERVOIR

93117

SEE 983 MAP

93111

SAN MARCOS RD

SANTA BARBARA COUNTY

T5N T4N

RANCHO LOS DOS PUEBLOS

RANCHO LA GOLETA

TWINRIDGE RD

CATHEDRAL

KELLOGG OPEN SPACE

OAKS

TUCKERS GROVE PARK

LOS CARNEROS COUNTY PARK

STOW GROVE PARK

UNIVERSITY

TURNPIKE

SEE 994 MAP

COPYRIGHT 2000 Thomas Bros. Maps

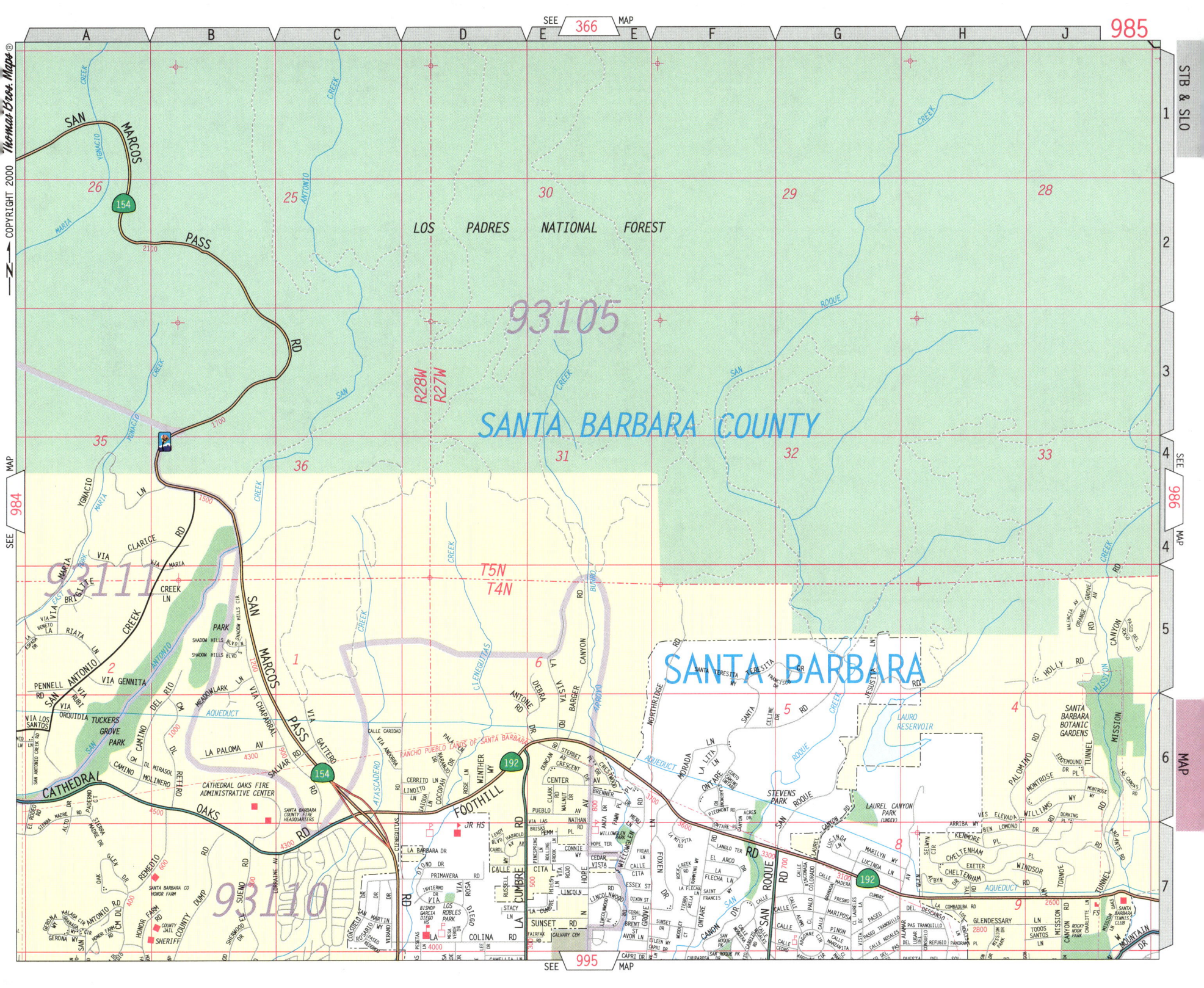

SEE 366 MAP

985

| A | B | C | D | E | E | F | G | H | J |

STB & SLO

SAN MARCOS

PASS

154

2100

26 25 30 29 28

LOS PADRES NATIONAL FOREST

93105

ROQUE

1700

1500

35 36 31 32 33

SANTA BARBARA COUNTY

SEE 984 MAP

SEE 986 MAP

93111

T5N
T4N

R28W R27W

CREEK

SANTA TERESITA BARBARA

SANTA
BARBARA
BOTANIC
GARDENS

1 6 5 4

2

Lauro Reservoir

Stevens Park

Laurel Canyon Park

MISSION
TUNNEL

AQUEDUCT

CATHEDRAL OAKS

Cathedral Oaks Fire
Administrative Center

Santa Barbara
County Fire
Headquarters

154

192

FOOTHILL

192

9

8

93110

FS

SEE 995 MAP

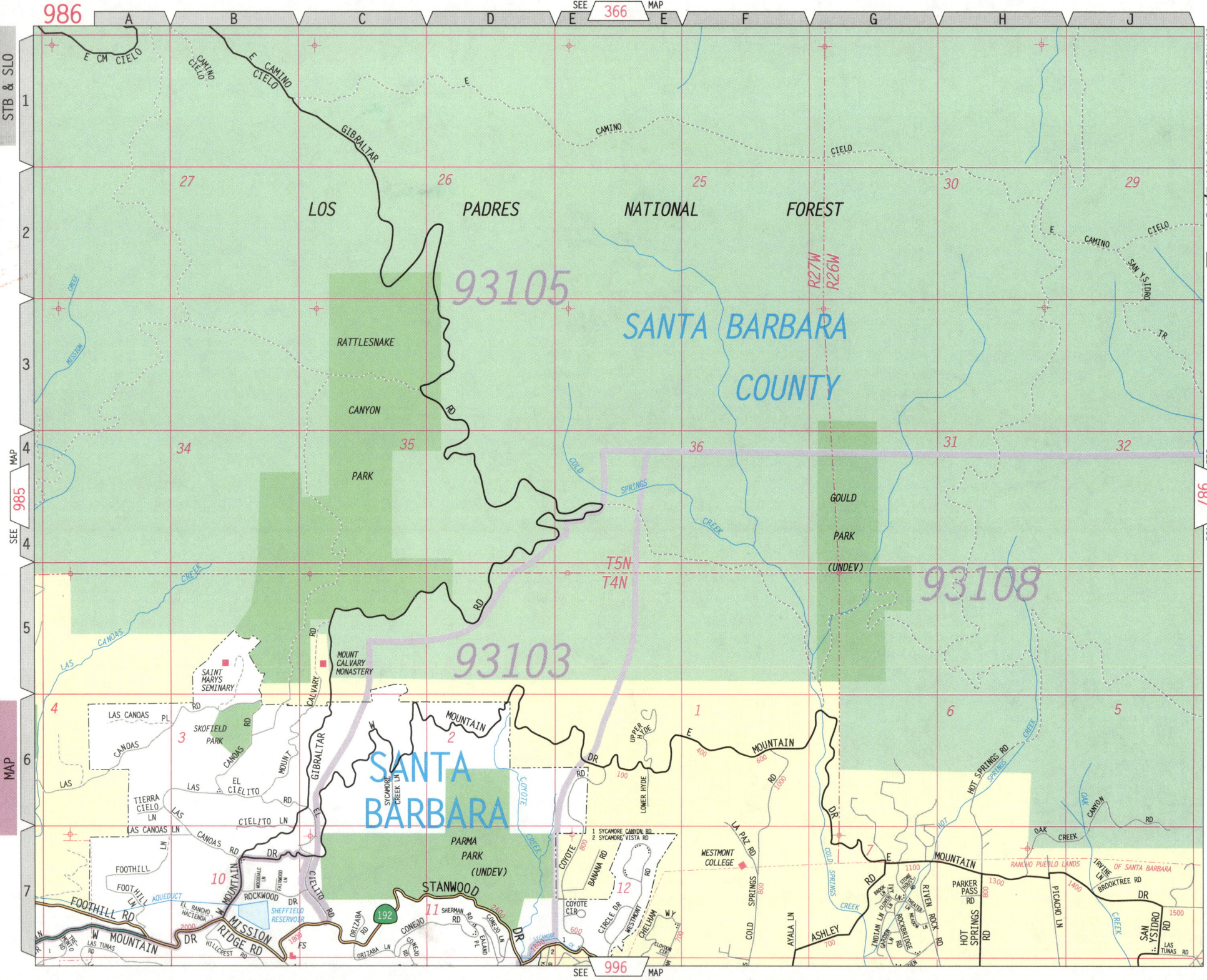

A   B   C   D   E   E   F   G   H   J

SEE 366 MAP

STB & SLO

—N→

1

27   26   25   30   29

LOS   PADRES   NATIONAL   FOREST

E   CM   CIELO

CAMINO CIELO

E CAMINO CIELO

GIBRALTAR

CAMINO

CIELO

2

E CAMINO CIELO

E CAMINO SAN YSIDRO

93105

SANTA BARBARA

R27W R26W

3

RATTLESNAKE

CANYON

COUNTY

RD

TR

PARK

MISSION CREEK

SEE 985 MAP

4

34   35   36   31   32

COLD

SPRINGS

CREEK

GOULD

PARK

(UNDEV)

SEE 987 MAP

T5N
T4N

93108

5

CANOAS CREEK

LAS CANOAS

LAS

CALVARY RD

MOUNT CALVARY MONASTERY

93103

SAINT MARYS SEMINARY

6

4   3   2   1   6   5

LAS CANOAS PL

SKOFIELD PARK

CANOAS LN

MOUNT

GIBRALTAR

MOUNTAIN

UPPER HYDE

E MOUNTAIN

100

400

600   1000

DR

LOWER HYDE

HOT SPRINGS RD

SPRINGS

OAK CANYON RD

TIERRA CIELO LN

EL CIELITO

LAS CANOAS RD

CIELITO LN

COYOTE

DR   RD

SANTA
BARBARA

SYCAMORE CREEK RD

COYOTE CREEK

PARMA PARK (UNDEV)

1 SYCAMORE CANYON RD
2 SYCAMORE VISTA RD

WESTMONT COLLEGE

LA PAZ RD

COLD SPRINGS   800

HOT SPRINGS

OAK CREEK

MOUNTAIN

RANCHO PUEBLO LANDS

OF SANTA BARBARA

IRVINE LN

BROOKTREE RD

7

FOOTHILL RD

FOOTHILL

FOOT HILL LN

AQUEDUCT

EL RANCHO HACIENDA

ROCKWOOD DR

WOODALE LN

FAIRWOOD

10

MOUNTAIN

MISSION RIDGE RD

HILLCREST

CIELITO RD

ORIZABA

ORIZABA LN

CONEJO RD

192

STANWOOD

11

SHERMAN RD

CONEJO PL

ELAND

SYCAMORE CYN RD

600

COYOTE CIR

BANANA RD

CIRCLE DR

CHELHAM WY

WESTMONT

12

1100

INDIAN LN

ROCKBRIDGE

RIVEN ROCK RD

PARKER PASS RD

1300

ROCKRIDGE

1400

PICACHO LN

1500

SAN YSIDRO

LAS TUNAS

W MOUNTAIN DR

ASHLEY

AYALA LN

COLD SPRINGS 800

HOT SPRINGS RD   700

SEE 996 MAP

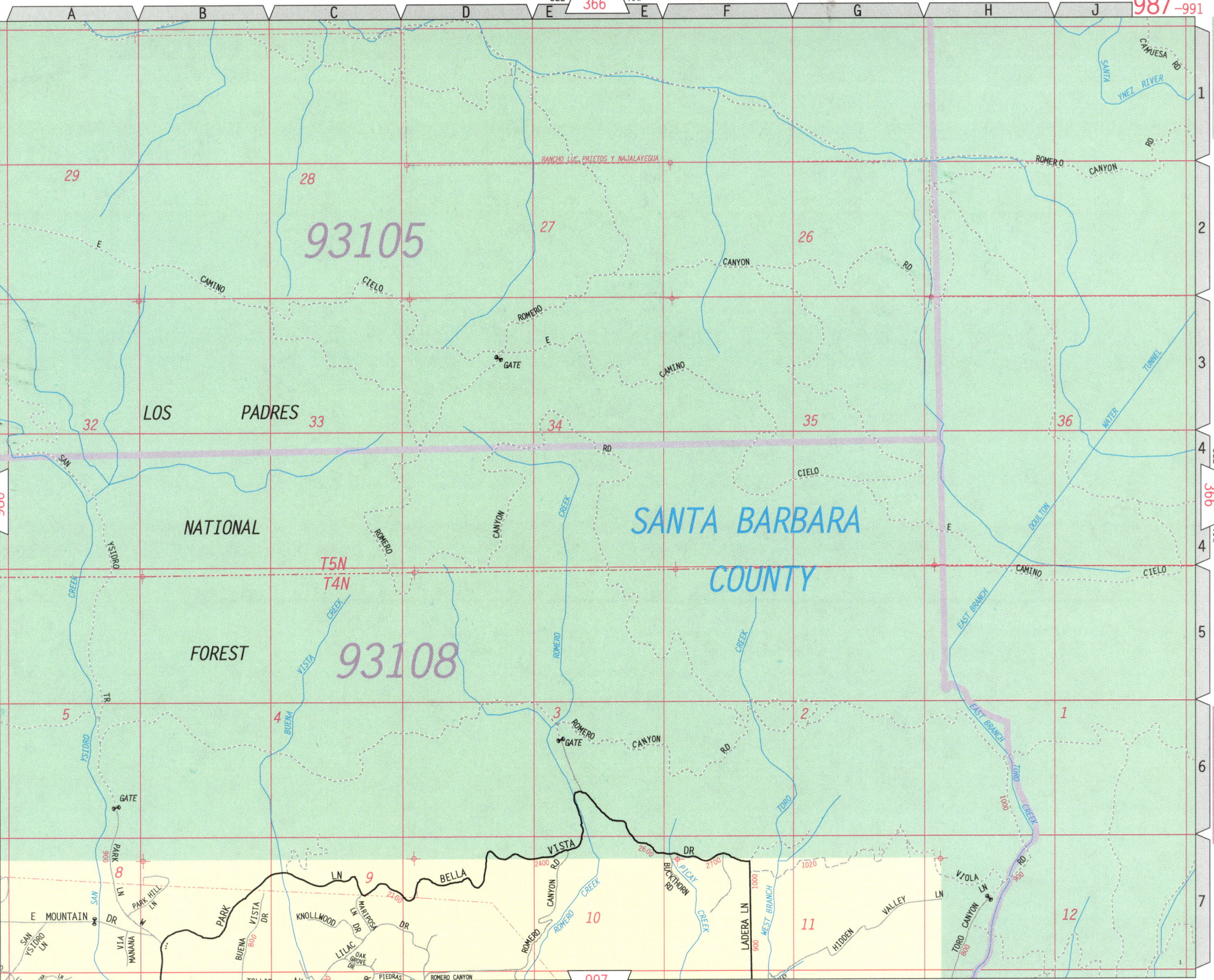

A B C D E E F G H J

STB & SLO

1

CAMUESA RD

SANTA YNEZ RIVER

RANCHO LIC. PRIETOS Y NAJALAYEGUA

29   28   27   26   ROMERO   CANYON

93105

CANYON   RD

2

E

CAMINO

CIELO

ROMERO

E

GATE

CAMINO

TUNNEL

3

32   LOS   PADRES   33   34   35   36   WATER

SEE 986 MAP

SAN

YSIDRO

NATIONAL

ROMERO

CANYON

CREEK

SANTA BARBARA

CIELO

E

BOULTON

DOULTON

SEE 366 MAP

4

CREEK

FOREST

T5N
T4N

VISTA CREEK

BUENA

93108

ROMERO

COUNTY

CAMINO   CIELO

CREEK

EAST BRANCH

5

TR

YSIDRO

5   4   3   ROMERO   CANYON   RD   2   1

GATE

EAST BRANCH

TORO   CREEK

6

MAP

GATE

PARK

SAN

VISTA

BELLA

VISTA   DR

DR

1000

VIOLA

7

E MOUNTAIN DR

VIA MANANA

SAN YSIDRO LN

BUENA VISTA DR

PARK HILL LN

KNOLLWOOD LN

MARIPOSA LN

LILAC DR

OAK GROVE DR

LN   9

2100

ROMERO CANYON RD

2400

ROMERO CANYON

2600

PICAY

BICKTHORN RD

DR

2700

10

11

LADERA LN

WEST BRANCH

1000

900

1020

TORO CANYON RD

LN

HIDDEN VALLEY LN

800

900

12

PIEDRAS

ROMERO CANYON

SEE 982 MAP

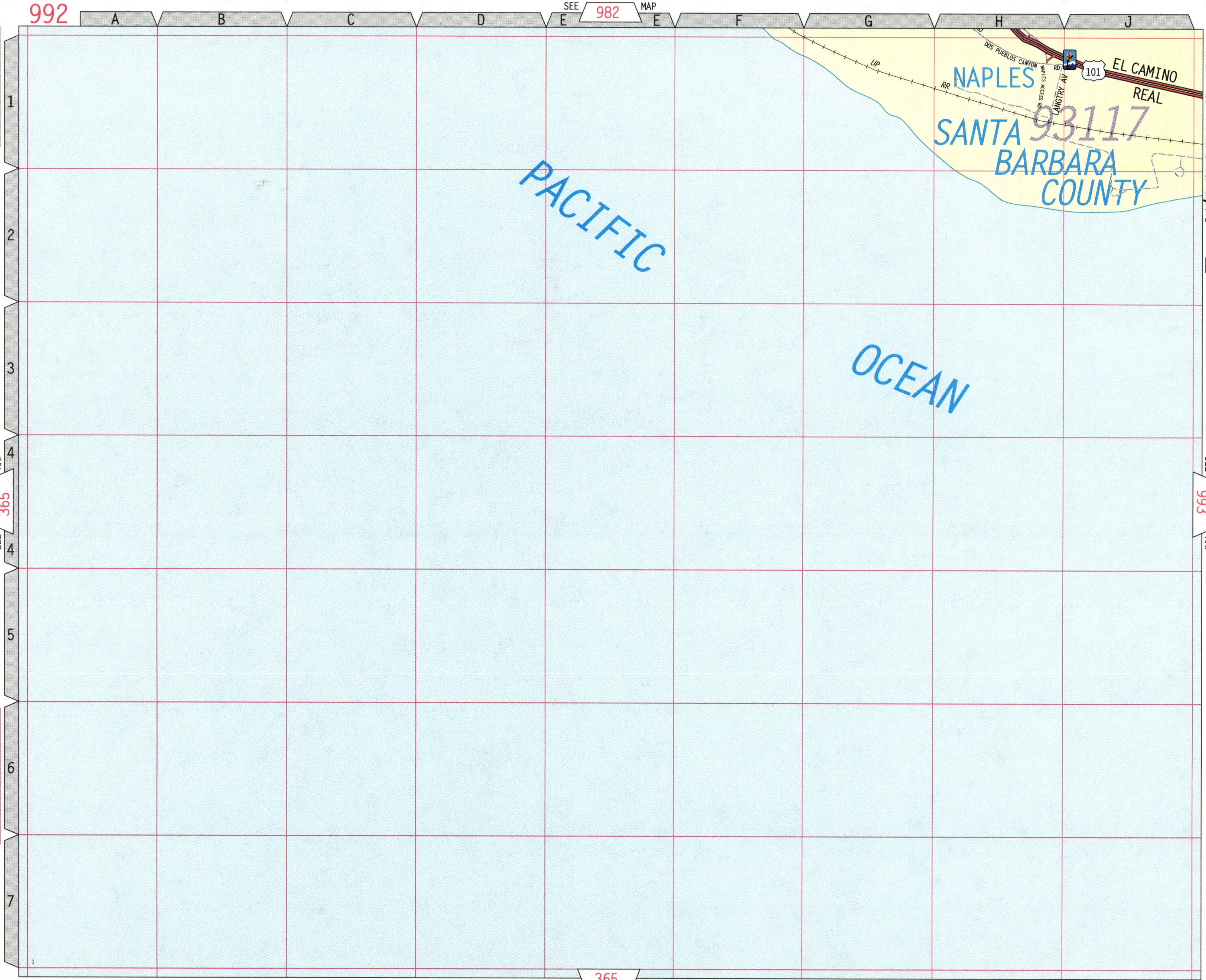

STB & SLO

1

2

3

4

4

5

6

7

MAP

SEE 365 MAP

SEE 993 MAP

MAP

PACIFIC

OCEAN

NAPLES

EL CAMINO
REAL

101

DOS PUEBLOS CANYON

UP

RR

NAPLES ACCESS RD

LANGTRY AV

RD

93117

SANTA
BARBARA
COUNTY

N

SEE 365 MAP

SANTA BARBARA COUNTY

PACIFIC

OCEAN

EL CAMINO REAL

EL CAMINO REAL

HOLLISTER AV

ELLWOOD

93117

ISLA VISTA

SANTA BARBARA SHORES COUNTY PARK (UNDEVELOPED)

SANDPIPER GOLF COURSE

OCEAN MEADOWS GOLF COURSE

DEVEREUX LAGOON

UCSB WEST CAMPUS

CAMPUS POINT

COAL OIL POINT

ISLA VISTA BEACH

HASKELLS BEACH

DOS PUEBLOS HS

GLEN ANNIE GOLF CLUB

CATHEDRAL OAKS RD

1 MEADOWLACE CT
2 SILVER FERN CT
3 EVENING SONG CT

CAMINO REAL MARKETPLACE (BIG BOX)

UNIVERSITY PLAZA

SEE 992 MAP

SEE 994 MAP

STB & SLO

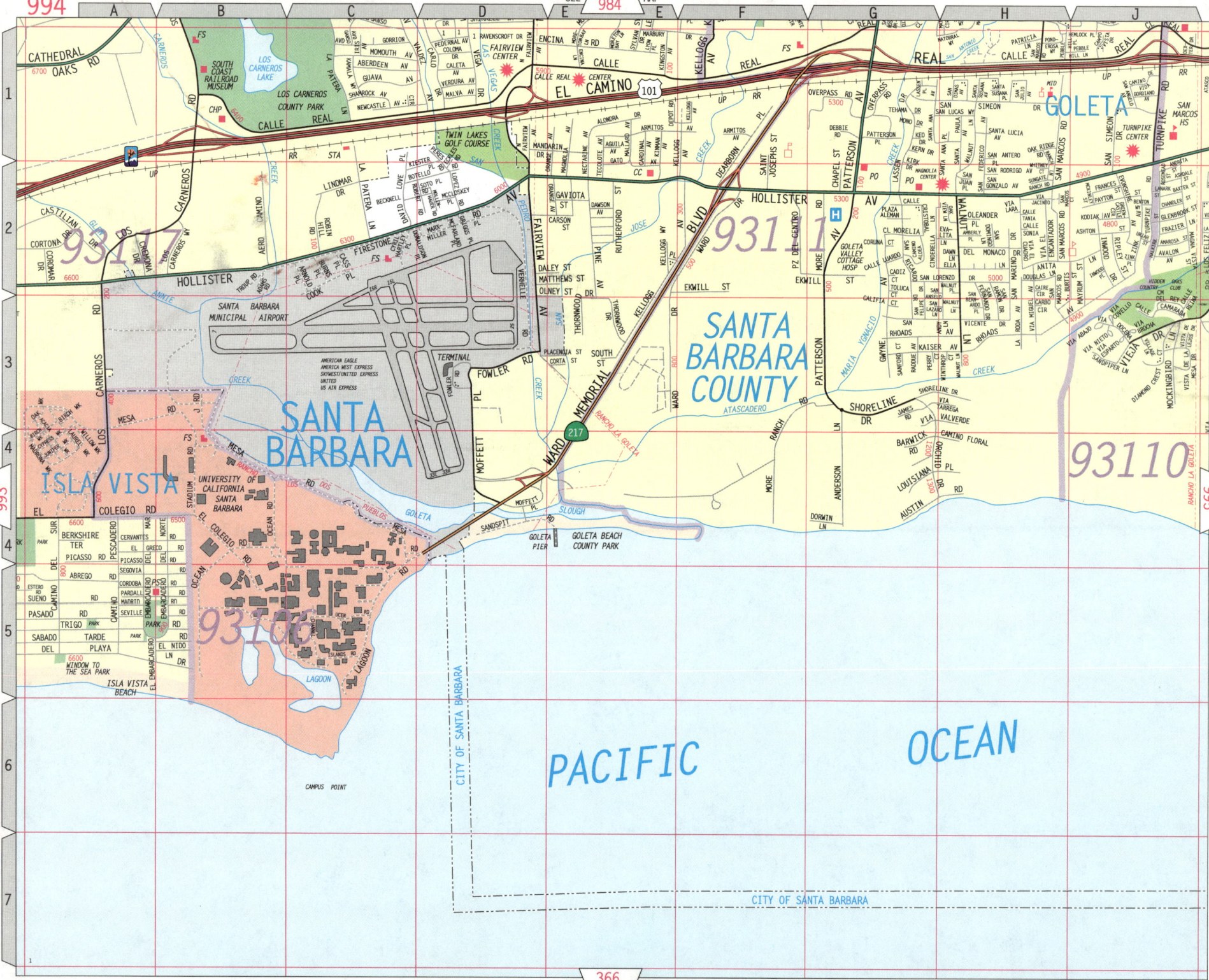

A   B   C   D   E   E   F   G   H   J

STB & SLO

COPYRIGHT 2000 Thomas Bros. Maps ®

1

CATHEDRAL OAKS RD

SOUTH COAST RAILROAD MUSEUM

LOS CARNEROS LAKE

LOS CARNEROS COUNTY PARK

CALLE REAL

EL CAMINO

101

REAL

GOLETA

GOLETA HS

TURNPIKE CENTER

TWIN LAKES GOLF COURSE

93117

2

93111

HOLLISTER

HOLLISTER AV

SANTA BARBARA MUNICIPAL AIRPORT

3

SANTA BARBARA COUNTY

TERMINAL

American Eagle
America West Express
Skywest/United Express
United
US Air Express

4

SANTA BARBARA

93110

ISLA VISTA

UNIVERSITY OF CALIFORNIA SANTA BARBARA

217

EL COLEGIO RD

SHORELINE DR

GOLETA PIER

GOLETA BEACH COUNTY PARK

5

93106

WINDOW TO THE SEA PARK

ISLA VISTA BEACH

CAMPUS POINT

CITY OF SANTA BARBARA

6

PACIFIC   OCEAN

7

CITY OF SANTA BARBARA

SANTA BARBARA COUNTY

SANTA BARBARA

MONTECITO

93103

93108

93101

93109

PACIFIC OCEAN

SANTA BARBARA CHANNEL

STB & SLO

COPYRIGHT 2000 *Thomas Bros. Maps* ®

Landmarks:
- MISSION SANTA BARBARA / Franceschi Park
- Santa Barbara County Bowl
- Brooks Institute of Photography
- Camino Viejo
- Montecito Country Club
- Andre Clark Bird Refuge
- Santa Barbara Zoological Gardens
- Santa Barbara Cemetery
- Music Academy of the West
- Four Seasons Biltmore
- East Beach
- Chase Palm Park
- Stearns Wharf / Sea Center Marine Museum / Stearns Wharf Vintners
- West Beach
- Santa Barbara City College
- Santa Barbara Yacht Club
- Point Castillo
- Leadbetter Beach
- Santa Barbara Point
- Shoreline Park
- Butterfly Beach
- Montecito Village
- Manning Park
- Fire Training Facility
- Fess Parkers Doubletree Resort
- Radisson Hotel

Highways/Roads: US 101, 192, 225, CABRILLO BLVD, EL CAMINO REAL, SHORELINE DR, CLIFF DR, OLD COAST HWY, HOT SPRINGS RD, SYCAMORE CANYON RD, ALAMEDA PADRE SERRA, STATE ST, MILPAS ST, MISSION RIDGE RD

93108

93067

SUMMERLAND

93013

SANTA BARBARA COUNTY

COLLEGE OF THE QUEEN OF PEACE SEMINARY

LOS PADRES NATIONAL FOREST

TORO CANYON PARK

LOS PADRES NATIONAL FOREST

VALLEY CLUB GOLF COURSE

VALLEY CLUB GOLF COURSE

BIRNAM WOOD GOLF COURSE

RESERVOIR

LOOKOUT PARK

LOON POINT

SANTA BARBARA POLO FIELD

PACIFIC

OCEAN

RANCHO PUEBLO LANDS OF SANTA BARBARA

FERNALD POINT

EL CAMINO REAL

VALLEY RD

FOOTHILL

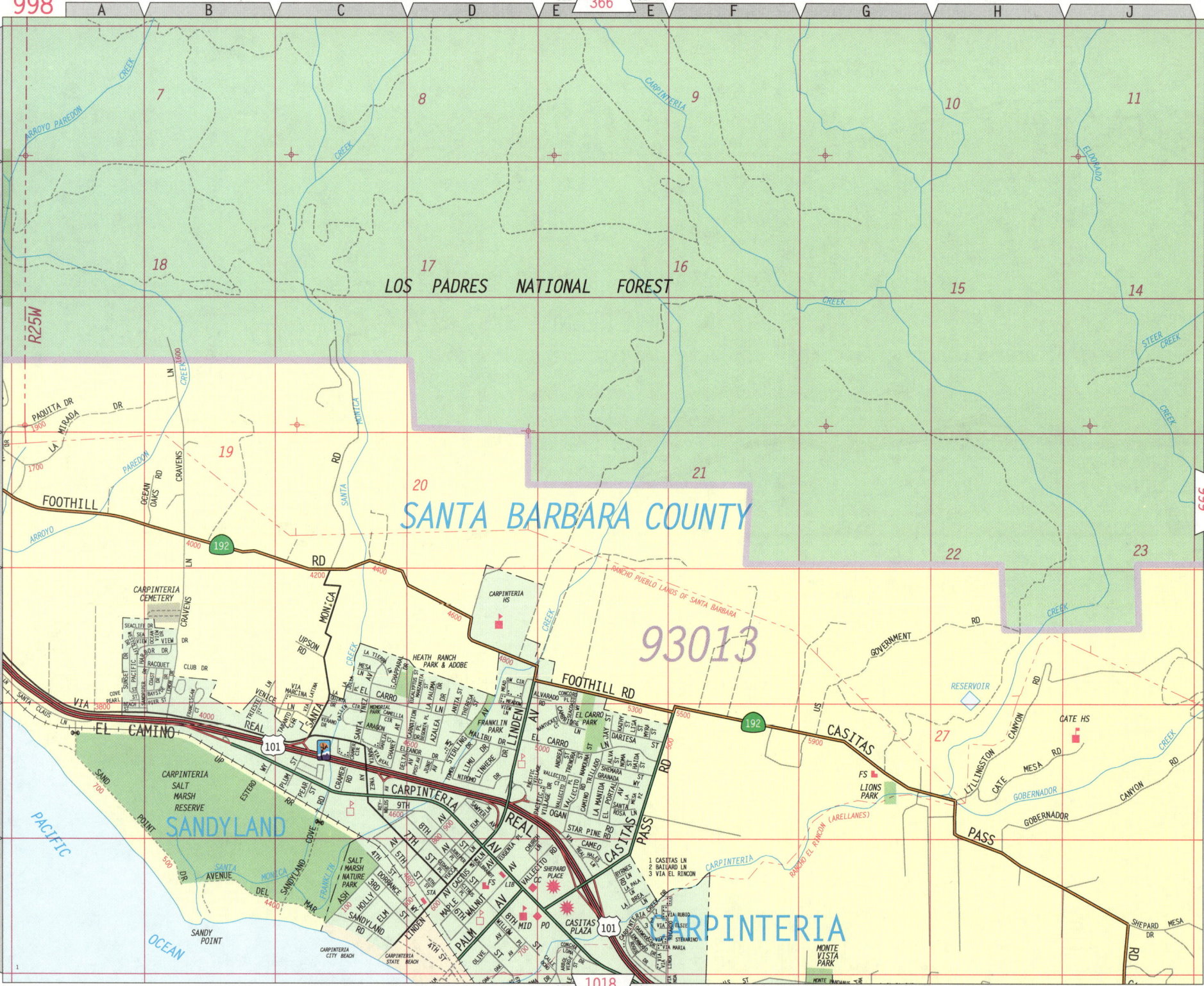

A   B   C   D   E   E   F   G   H   J

SEE 366 MAP

STB & SLO

COPYRIGHT 2000 Thomas Bros. Maps®   →N

1

7   8   9   10   11

2

18   17   16   15   14

LOS PADRES NATIONAL FOREST

R25W

3

STEER CREEK

PAQUITA DR
LA MIRADA DR
4

19   20   21

SANTA BARBARA COUNTY

FOOTHILL RD

SEE 997 MAP

SEE 999 MAP

22   23

RANCHO PUEBLO LANDS OF SANTA BARBARA

CARPINTERIA CEMETERY

CARPINTERIA HS

93013

5

HEATH RANCH PARK & ADOBE

FOOTHILL RD

RESERVOIR

GOVERNMENT

CATE HS

192

CASITAS

27

VIA EL CAMINO REAL

6

CARPINTERIA
SALT MARSH
RESERVE

CARPINTERIA

101

LIONS PARK

FS

PACIFIC

SANDYLAND

SAND POINT

CARPINTERIA SALT MARSH NATURE PARK

CASITAS PLAZA

CARPINTERIA

1 CASITAS LN
2 BAILARD LN
3 VIA EL RINCON

RANCHO EL RINCON (ARELLANES)

CARPINTERIA

MONTE VISTA PARK

SHEPARD MESA DR

7

OCEAN

SANDY POINT

CARPINTERIA CITY BEACH

CARPINTERIA STATE BEACH

101

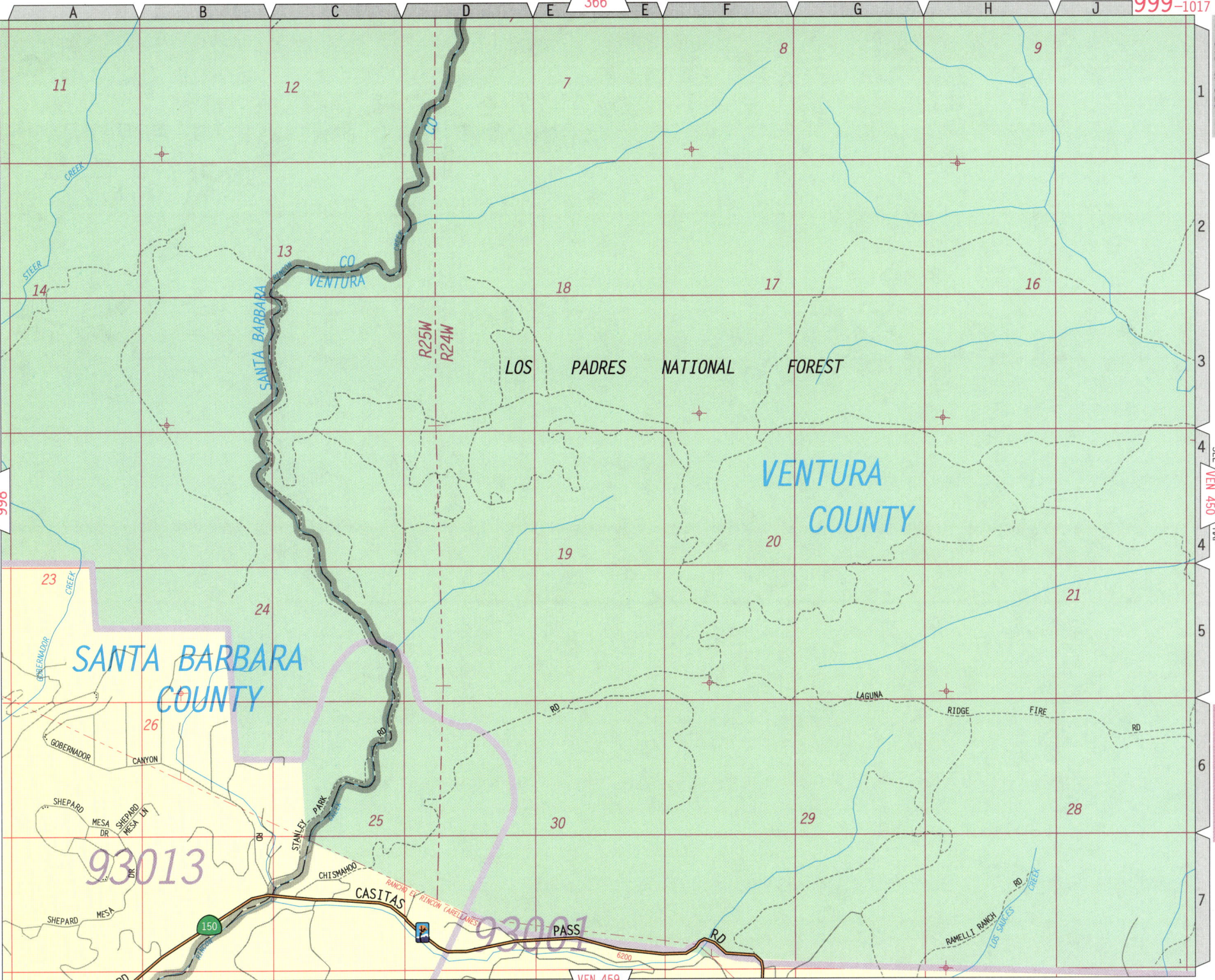

STB & SLO

SEE 366 MAP

A B C D E E F G H J

1

11   12   7   8   9

2

CREEK

STEER

14   CO VENTURA   13

SANTA BARBARA

CO

R25W R24W

18   17   16   3

LOS   PADRES   NATIONAL   FOREST

VENTURA
COUNTY

4

19   20   4

23   CREEK   24   21   5

GOBERNADOR

SANTA BARBARA
COUNTY

26

GOBERNADOR   CANYON

LAGUNA

RIDGE   FIRE   RD

MAP

SHEPARD
MESA
DR   SHEPARD
MESA LN

STANLEY PARK RD

RD

25   30   29   28   6

93013

SHEPARD   MESA

CHISMAHOO   RANCHO EL RINCON CARRETANES

CASITAS

150   PASS   RD   RAMELLI RANCH   RD   LOS SAUCES CREEK

93001   6200   7

Thomas Bros. Maps ®

COPYRIGHT 2000

1018

STB & SLO

A B C D E E F G H J

SEE 998 MAP

COPYRIGHT 2000 Thomas Bros. Maps ®

CARPINTERIA STATE BEACH

CAMPGROUND

PALM AV

CARPINTERIA BLUFFS PUBLIC OPEN SPACE

PITS PARK

TAR

CALLE 5500

CALLE PACIFIC

DUMP RD

EL CAMINO

CARPINTERIA

CARPINTERIA AV

SANTA BARBARA COUNTY

CASITAS PASS RD 192

RINCON RD

150

AROZENA LN

CAMINO CARRETA

RINCON PT

RINCON BEACH PARK

VENTURA FRWY

RINCON DEL MAR

BATES RD

BATES RANCH RD

PACIFIC

OCEAN

SEE 366 MAP

SEE VEN 459 MAP

1

2

3

4

4

5

6

7

SEE 366 MAP

93013

REAL

101

LIST OF ABBREVIATIONS

PREFIXES AND SUFFIXES

AL . . . . .ALLEY
ARC . . . . .ARCADE
AV, AVE . . . . .AVENUE
AVCT . . . . AVENUE COURT
AVD .AVENIDA
AVDR . . . . .AVENUE DRIVE
AVEX . . . . AVENUE EXTENSION
BLEX . . . . BOULEVARD EXTENSION
BL, BLVD . . . . BOULEVARD
BLCT . . . . BOULEVARD COURT
BRCH .BRANCH
BRDG .BRIDGE
BYPS .BYPASS
CIDR . . . . CIRCLE DRIVE
CIR . . . . .CIRCLE
CL . . . . .CALLE
CLJ .CALLEJON
CM . . . . CAMINO
CMTO . . . . .CAMINITO
COM .COMMON
CORR. . . . . .CORRIDOR
CRES . . . . .CRESCENT
CRLO . . . . CIRCULO
CRSG . . . . CROSSING
CSWY . . . . .CAUSEWAY
CT . . . . COURT
CTAV . . . . .COURT AVENUE
CTE . . . . .CORTE
CTO .CUTOFF
CTR .CENTER
CUR .CURVE
CV . . . . .COVE
D . . . . DE
DIAG . . . . .DIAGONAL
DR. . . . . .DRIVE
DVDR . . . . .DIVISION DRIVE
EXAV . . . . .EXTENSION AVENUE
EXBL . . . . . .EXTENSION BOULEVARD
EXRD . . . . .EXTENSION ROAD
EXST . . . . . . .EXTENSION STREET
EXT . . . . .EXTENSION
EXWY . . . . .EXPRESSWAY
FRWY . . . . .FREEWAY
GDNS . . . . .GARDENS
GN . . . . .GLEN
GRN .GREEN
HWY . . . . .HIGHWAY
JCT . . . . .JUNCTION
LN. . . . . LANE
LNDG . . . . LANDING
LP . . . . .LOOP
LS . . . . .LAS, LOS
MNR . . . . .MANOR
MTWY . . . . MOTORWAY
OH . . . . .OUTER HIGHWAY
OVL . . . . .OVAL
OVPS . . . . .OVERPASS
PAS .PASEO
PK . . . . .PARK
PKWY . . . . .PARKWAY
PL . . . . .PLACE
PLZ, PZ . . . . .PLAZA
PT . . . . .POINT
PTH .PATH
RD . . . . .ROAD
RDEX . . . . ROAD EXTENSION
RDG. . . . . .RIDGE
RW . . . . .ROW
SKWY . . . . .SKYWAY
SQ .SQUARE
ST . . . . .STREET
STAV . . . . .STREET AVENUE
STCT . . . . .STREET COURT
STDR . . . . .STREET DRIVE
STEX . . . . . . .STREET EXTENSION
STLN . . . . .STREET LANE
STLP . . . . STREET LOOP
STPL . . . . STREET PLACE
STXP . . . . . STREET EXPRESSWAY
TER . . . . TERRACE
TFWY . . . . .TRAFFICWAY
THWY . . . . .THROUGHWAY
TKTR . . . . .TRUCKTRAIL
TPKE . . . . .TURNPIKE
TR . . . . .TRAIL
TUN . . . . .TUNNEL
UNPS . . . . .UNDERPASS
VIS . . . . .VISTA
VW . . . . .VIEW
WK . . . . .WALK
WY . . . . .WAY
WYPL . . . . .WAY PLACE

DIRECTIONS

E . . . . .EAST
KPN . . . . KEY PENINSULA NORTH
KPS . . . . .KEY PENINSULA SOUTH
N . . . . .NORTH
NE . . . . NORTHEAST
NW . . . . .NORTHWEST
S . . . . .SOUTH
SE . . . . .SOUTHEAST
SW . . . . .SOUTHWEST
W . . . . .WEST

DEPARTMENT STORES

BD . . . . BLOOMINGDALES
BN . . . . THE BON MARCHE
D . . . . .DIAMONDS
DL . . . . .DILLARDS
E . . . . EMPORIUM
G . . . . .GOLDWATERS
GT . . . . .GOTTSCHALKS
H . . . . .HARRIS
IM . . . . IMAGNIN
L . . . . LAMONTS
MA . . . . MACY'S
ME . . . . MERVYN'S
MF . . . . MEIER & FRANK
MW . . . . .MONTGOMERY WARD
N . . . . .NORDSTROM
NM . . . . .NEIMAN-MARCUS
P . . . . .J C PENNEY
RM . . . . ROBINSONS MAY
S . . . . SEARS
SF . . . . .SAKS FIFTH AVENUE

BUILDINGS

CC . . . . .CHAMBER OF COMMERCE
CH . . . . .CITY HALL
CHP . . . .CALIFORNIA HIGHWAY PATROL
COMM CTR . . . .COMMUNITY CENTER
CON CTR . . . .CONVENTION CENTER
CONT HS . . . .CONTINUATION HIGH SCHOOL
CTH . . . . COURT HOUSE
DMV . . . . .DEPT OF MOTOR VEHICLES
FAA . . . FEDERAL AVIATION ADMIN
FS . . . . .FIRE STATION
HOSP . . . . .HOSPITAL
HS . . . . .HIGH SCHOOL
INT . . . . INTERMEDIATE SCHOOL
JR HS . . . . .JUNIOR HIGH SCHOOL
LIB . . . . LIBRARY
MID . . . . .MIDDLE SCHOOL
MUS . . . . MUSEUM
PO . . . . .POST OFFICE
PS . . . . POLICE STATION
SR CIT CTR . . . . . SENIOR CITIZENS CENTER
STA . . . . STATION
THTR . . . . .THEATER
VIS BUR . . . . VISITORS BUREAU

OTHER ABBREVIATIONS

BCH . . . . BEACH
BLDG . . . . .BUILDING
CEM . . . . CEMETERY
CK .CREEK
CO . . . . COUNTY
CTR . . . . .CENTER
COMM . . . . .COMMUNITY
EST . . . . .ESTATE
HIST . . . . .HISTORIC
HTS . . . . HEIGHTS
LK . . . . .LAKE
MDW . . . . .MEADOW
MED . . . . MEDICAL
MEM . . . . MEMORIAL
MHP . . . . MOBILE HOME PARK
MT . . . . MOUNT
MTN . . . . MOUNTAIN
NATL . . . . .NATIONAL
PKG . . . . .PARKING
PLGD . . . . .PLAYGROUND
RCH . . . . RANCH
RCHO . . . . RANCHO
REC . . . . .RECREATION
RES . . . . RESERVOIR
RIV . . . . RIVER
RR . . . . .RAILROAD
SPG . . . . .SPRING
STA . . . . SANTA
VLG . . . . .VILLAGE
VLY . . . . VALLEY
VW . . . . .VIEW

STREET Name City ZIP Pg-Grid

A

A AV
PBCH 93449 714-D3
A ST
MonC 93451 453-A3
SMRA 93455 796-D5
SMRA 93458 796-D4
StBC 93455 796-D5
StBC 93458 796-D4
N A ST
LMPC 93436 896-F6
LMPC 93436 916-F1
StBC 93436 896-F5
S A ST
LMPC 93436 916-F2
A-17 TANK TR
SLOC 93451 453-A6
AALBORG CT
SLVG 93463 920-E7
AALBORG WY
SLVG 93463 920-D7
AARHUS DR
SLVG 93463 940-D1
AAROE RD
SLOC 93446 514-C7
AARS AL
SLVG 93463 940-E1
ABBEY RD
StBC 93455 816-G4
ABBOTT ST
SLO 93401 654-A3
ABERDEEN AV
StBC 93117 994-C1
ABIERTO RD
SLOC 93422 594-F5
ABIGAIL LN
SBAR 93108 996-D2
ABRAMSON RD
SLOC 93465 553-D1
ABREGO RD
StBC 93117 993-J5
StBC 93117 994-A5
ACACIA
SLO 93401 673-H1
ACACIA AV
SLOC 93430 591-C5
StBC 93437 855-G7
StBC 93437 875-G1
ACACIA ST
MOBY 93442 611-F7
SMRA 93458 776-G3
ACACIA WK
StBC 93117 994-A3
ACAMPO RD
StBC 93441 900-H4
ACERO PL
SLOC 93420 715-B3
ACORN DR
ARGD 93420 714-G3
ACORN WY
SLVG 93463 940-E1
ACRE AV
SLOC 93401 694-F1
ADAIR DR
SBAR 93105 995-F1
ADAM WY
SMRA 93458 796-F2
ADAMS RD
SBAR 93117 994-B2
ADAMS ST
Cmbr 93428 548-H1
ADAMS WY
LMPC 93436 896-C6
ADDIE ST
PBCH 93449 714-C3
ADELAIDA RD
SLOC 93446 324-L6
SLOC 93446 325-A6
SLOC 93446 513-A2
ADELGADE DR
SLVG 93463 920-F7
ADELYNE LN
SMRA 93454 796-H4
ADEN WY
SLOC 93420 735-F6
ADINA WY
Npmo 93444 756-C4
ADOBE RD
PSRS 93446 494-B4
SLOC - 612-C7
SLOC 93405 612-C7
SLOC 93405 632-E1
SLOC 93446 494-B4
ADOBE CREEK RD
SLVG 93463 920-E6
ADOBE FALLS RD
StBC 93436 896-F3
ADOREE
SLOC 93430 591-C5
ADRIA AV
SMRA 93458 776-G4
AEBELTOFT WY
SLVG 93463 920-D7
AERO DR
SLO 93401 674-C2
SLOC 93401 674-C2
AERO CAMINO
SBAR 93117 994-B2
StBC 93117 994-B2
AEROPLANE AV
SLOC 93430 591-A1
AEROTECH CENTER WY
PSRS 93446 494-F7
AEROVISTA PK
SLOC 93401 674-B2
AFFIRMED DR
StBC 93441 922-B3
StBC 93460 922-B3
AFFIRMED LN
SLOC 93446 513-E3
AGANA DR
StBC 93111 984-G7
AGENA WY
StBC 93436 876-D6
AG HILL DR
SLOC 93465 553-C2
AGNES AV
SMRA 93454 776-G6
SMRA 93458 776-F6
AGUA CALIENTE RD
StBC - 366-E6
StBC 93105 366-E6
AGUACITA RD
SLOC 93422 594-F5
AGUILA AV
ATAS 93422 573-G4
StBC 93117 994-E1
AIRFIELD RD
StBC 93437 875-B2
AIR FORCE STATION RD
Cmbr 93428 324-J8
SLOC 93435 324-J8
AIR PARK DR
SLOC 93445 714-D7
SMRA 93455 796-E6
SMRA 93455 816-F1
AIRPARK DR
SMRA 93455 816-G1
AIR PARK LN
SMRA 93455 816-F1
E AIRPORT AV
LMPC 93436 896-F7
W AIRPORT AV
LMPC 93436 896-C7
StBC 93436 896-C7
AIRPORT DR
SLO 93401 674-B2
SLOC 93401 674-B2
AIRPORT RD
PSRS 93446 494-C7
PSRS 93446 514-C2
PSRS 93446 534-C1
SLOC 93446 325-C4
SLOC 93446 494-C3
SLOC 93446 514-C2
StBC 93460 921-C6
AJAY DR
StBC 93455 816-H5
ALABAMA AV
StBC 93437 875-C4
ALAMAR AV
SBAR 93105 985-H7
SBAR 93105 995-G1
ALAMEDA AV
StBC 93117 993-H1
ALAMEDA RD
SLOC 93405 633-C5
ALAMEDA PADRE SERRA
SBAR 93103 995-J1
SBAR 93103 996-A1
SBAR 93108 996-D2
ALAMO AV
ATAS 93422 573-J1
ALAMO DR
SLOC 93402 651-F1
ALAMO CREEK DR
PSRS 93446 533-J1
PSRS 93446 534-A2
ALAMO CREEK RD
SLOC 93454 345-G7
ALAMO PINTADO AV
StBC 93441 900-G5
StBC 93463 900-G5
ALAMO PINTADO RD
SLVG 93463 920-G6
SLVG 93463 940-F1
StBC 93463 900-H7
StBC 93463 920-H2
StBC 93463 940-F1
ALAN RD
SBAR 93109 995-F5
StBC 93109 995-F5
ALBAN PL
Cmbr 93428 548-G1
ALBANY CT
StBC 93117 984-E7
ALBANY WY
SLOC 93451 453-C6
ALBERT DR
SLO 93405 654-A2
ALBERT ST
SMRA 93458 796-G2
ALBERT WY
SLOC 93420 735-C7
SLOC 93420 755-C2
ALBERTA AV
SBAR 93101 995-H4
ALBIREO AV
StBC 93436 876-C6
ALCALA LN
StBC 93108 996-G2
ALCAMO PL
SBAR 93105 995-E3
ALCANTARA AV
ATAS 93422 573-J4
ALCOR AV
StBC 93436 876-D6
ALCOTT AV
LMPC 93436 896-B6
ALDEBARAN AV
StBC 93436 876-E5
ALDEN AV
LMPC 93436 896-C6
ALDEN CT
LMPC 93436 896-C6
ALDER AV
MOBY 93442 611-E2
ALDER CT
SLO 93401 674-D2
ALDER LN
SLO 93401 674-D2
ALDER ST
ARGD 93420 714-H6
ALDERBERRY DR
StBC 93455 816-B1
ALEEDA LN
SBAR 93108 996-F2
ALEGRE AV
ATAS 93422 574-A7
Npmo 93444 756-B4
ALEGRIA RD
SBAR 93105 995-G2
ALEJANDRO WY
SLOC 93420 755-A2
ALEX PL
StBC 93117 984-C7
ALEXANDER AV
LMPC 93436 896-B6
SLOC 93402 631-G7
ALHAMBRA CIR
SLOC 93430 591-C4
AL-HIL DR
SLO 93405 653-G1
ALICE PL
SLOC 93446 533-E4
ALICITA CT
SLO 93401 653-J7
ALINA LN
Npmo 93444 756-A4
ALISA LN
StBC 93110 995-C5
ALISAL AV
SLO 93401 654-B3
ALISAL RD
SBAR 93103 996-D1
SLVG - 940-D3
SLVG 93463 920-E7
SLVG 93463 940-E1
StBC - 940-E1
StBC 93117 365-J6
StBC 93463 365-J6
StBC 93463 940-E6
ALISO LN
StBC 93108 996-J3
ALISO CANYON RD
StBC - 346-C9
ALISON AV
SMRA 93458 776-F5
ALISO PARK RD
StBC - 346-B10
ALISOS AV
StBC 93441 922-C4
StBC 93460 922-C4
ALISOS DR
StBC 93108 997-C1
ALISOS RD
SLOC 93420 695-H7
SLOC 93420 715-H1
ALISOS ST
SBAR 93103 996-C2
ALISOS CANYON RD
StBC - 365-J1
StBC 93440 365-J1
ALLAIRE ST
SBAR 93103 996-D3
ALLEGRO CT
PSRS 93446 513-H4
ALLEN CT
SLOC 93465 553-B2
ALLEN RD
SLOC 93446 469-J6
SLOC 93446 470-B5
ALLEN ST
ARGD 93420 715-A5
ALLESANDRO ST
MOBY 93442 611-H6
ALLEY OOP WY
SLOC 93420 754-J2
ALLIANCE WY
SLOC 93405 693-D3
ALMA CT
GBCH 93433 714-F4
ALMAGUER ST
GDLP 93434 774-J6
ALMIRA HTS
SLOC 93446 533-F2
ALMIRA PARK WY
SLOC 93446 533-E1
ALMOND AV
LMPC 93436 896-F6
SBAR 93101 995-J4
ALMOND DR
SLOC 93465 325-C8
ALMOND LN
SMRA 93458 776-G4
ALMOND ST
PSRS 93446 513-G5
SLO 93405 653-H3
ALMOND CREST CT
PSRS 93446 513-E4
ALMOND SPRINGS DR
PSRS 93446 513-E4
ALOHA PL
SLOC 93445 714-D7
ALOMA WY
SLOC 93420 735-B4
ALONDRA DR
StBC 93117 994-E1
ALONDRA RD
ATAS 93422 594-D2
SLOC 93422 594-D2
ALPHONSE ST
SBAR 93103 996-C3
ALPHONSO ST
SLO 93401 654-A6
ALPINE AV
SLOC 93405 633-A5
ALPINE DR
StBC 93117 993-G2
N ALPINE ST
ARGD 93420 714-H5
S ALPINE ST
ARGD 93420 714-H6
ALPINE WY
SLOC 93446 325-A7
ALRITA ST
SLO 93401 654-C5
SLOC 93401 654-C5
AL SERENO LN
SLOC 93402 631-H7
SLOC 93402 651-J1
ALSTON LN
SBAR 93108 996-F2
ALSTON PL
SBAR 93108 996-E2
ALSTON RD
SBAR 93108 996-F2
StBC 93108 996-F2
ALTA CT
MOBY 93442 611-G7
ALTA DR
StBC 93105 964-J6
ALTA ST
SLO 93401 654-B3
StBC 93441 900-H5
ALTAIR AV
StBC 93436 876-D6
ALTAIR PL
StBC 93436 876-D6
ALTA MIRA LN
SLOC 93401 674-D7
ALTA VISTA
SLVG 93463 940-D1
ALTAVISTA
SLOC 93430 591-C4
ALTA VISTA AV
ATAS 93422 573-H4
ALTA VISTA LN
Npmo 93444 756-E7
Npmo 93444 776-E1
ALTA VISTA RD
SBAR 93103 996-A2
ALTA VISTA WY
SLOC 93420 715-A3
ALTO DR
StBC 93110 985-A7
ALTON DR
SMRA 93458 776-F5
ALTURAS RD
ATAS 93422 553-C7
ATAS 93422 573-C1
ALTURAS DEL SOL
SBAR 93103 996-C1
ALUFFO RD
SLOC 93446 324-K5
SLOC 93446 470-C7
ALVA ST
CARP 93013 998-E6
ALVARADO PL
SBAR 93103 996-A1
ALVARADO RD
ATAS 93422 593-F2
CARP 93013 998-D5
SLOC 93422 593-F2
E ALVIN AV
SMRA 93454 776-H6
SMRA 93454 777-A6
W ALVIN AV
SMRA 93454 776-G6
SMRA 93458 776-G6
ALYDAR PL
SLOC 93446 513-E3
ALYSSUM CIR
Npmo 93444 755-J3
Npmo 93444 756-A3
ALYSSUM CT
SLO 93401 674-C1
AMADO ST
Npmo 93444 756-C3
AMADOR AV
SLOC 93405 633-A5
StBC 93117 993-H2
AMADOR WY
Npmo 93444 755-D5
AMALFI WY
SBAR 93105 995-E2
AMAPOA AV
ATAS 93422 573-J6
AMAPOLA DR
SBAR 93105 995-F1
AMAPOLA LN
StBC 93108 997-A3
AMARANTH LN
Npmo 93444 756-A3
AMARGON RD
ATAS 93422 573-G1
AMARILLO DR
SLOC 93420 734-J5
AMAROSA ST
StBC 93110 994-J2
AMBER CT
SLOC 93446 533-E6
AMBER DR
SLOC 93446 533-E6
AMBER LN
SMRA 93454 796-H4
AMBER ST
GDLP 93434 775-A6
AMBER WY
Npmo 93444 755-H2
SLVG 93463 920-F7
AMBER GRAIN PL
PSRS 93446 534-C1
AMBERLEY PL
StBC 93455 816-F4
AMBERLY PL
StBC 93111 994-H2
AMBUSH TRAIL PL
SLOC 93446 533-E2
AMELIA WY
Npmo 93444 756-B5
AMERICAN AV
SBAR 93105 995-H2
AMETHYST DR
StBC 93455 816-J5
StBC 93455 817-A5
AMHERST DR
StBC 93117 984-D7
AMHERST PL
Cmbr 93428 548-F1
LMPC 93436 916-G2
AMIGO PL
Npmo 93444 755-H4
AMOS PL
SLOC 93422 593-C1
ANA BAY RD
SLOC 93424 345-A4
SLOC 93424 693-A3
ANACAPA CIR
SLO 93405 653-F1
ANACAPA ST
SBAR 93101 995-H1
SBAR 93101 996-A3
SBAR 93105 995-H1
ANAPAMU ST
SBAR 93101 995-J4
SBAR 93101 996-A3
SBAR 93103 996-A3
ANCHOR CIR
SLOC 93426 469-J1
ANCHOR DR
StBC 93117 993-F3
ANCHOR ST
MOBY 93442 611-F7
ANCHOR WY
SLOC 93426 469-J1
ANCONA AV
StBC 93117 993-G1
ANDAMAR WY
StBC 93117 984-E7
ANDANTE RD
StBC 93105 985-J7
ANDERSON LN
StBC 93111 994-G4
ANDERSON RD
SLOC 93446 533-A5
ANDOVER PL
Cmbr 93428 528-G7
ANDRE AV
SLOC 93402 631-J7
SLOC 93402 632-A7
ANDRE DR
ARGD 93420 714-H3
ANDREA CIR
PSRS 93446 513-J6
ANDREA ST
CARP 93013 998-E6
ANDREWS AV
LMPC 93436 896-C6
ANDREWS ST
SLO 93401 654-A3
ANDRITA RD
ATAS 93422 573-G7
ANDRITA ST
StBC 93110 994-J2
ANDROS ST
MOBY 93442 611-E2
ANDY LN
StBC 93111 994-H3
ANGELA CT
StBC 93455 816-J5
ANGELES RD
StBC 93455 816-H2
ANGELINA CT
Npmo 93444 756-B5
ANGELLO TR
GBCH 93433 714-E4
ANGUS RANCH WY
SLOC 93446 324-K5
SLOC 93446 470-E5
ANISE LN
Npmo 93444 756-A2
ANITA AV
GBCH 93433 714-F7
ANITA LN
StBC 93111 994-H2
ANITA ST
CARP 93013 998-D6
ANN CT
SMRA 93454 777-A6
ANNE AV
SLOC 93402 631-H7
ANNEFORD CIR
SLOC 93401 674-E6
ANNETTE RD
SLOC 92389 325-J6
ANTARES AV
StBC 93436 876-D6
ANTELOPE TR
StBC 93455 816-G7
ANTHONY
SLOC 93446 513-B1
E ANTHONY WY
LMPC 93436 896-E6
W ANTHONY WY
LMPC 93436 896-D6
ANTLER DR
SLOC 93420 695-C6
ANTLER RIDGE WY
StBC 93455 816-G7
ANTONE LN
SMRA 93454 777-B5
ANTONE RD
StBC 93110 985-D6
ANZA DR
SBAR 93105 985-E7
APACHE CT
PSRS 93446 513-H6
APACHE TR
SLOC 93420 735-F6
APION CT
PSRS 93446 513-J3
APOLLO WY
StBC 93436 876-D7
StBC 93436 896-D1
APPALOOSA DR
PSRS 93446 513-H6
APPALOOSA TR
StBC 93455 816-E5
APPALOOSA WY
SLOC 93420 734-J4
W APPLE AV
LMPC 93436 916-D1
APPLEGATE WY
SLOC 93420 735-E6
APPLE GROVE LN
SBAR 93105 995-E2
StBC 93105 995-E2
APPLE ORCHARD LN
SLOC 93405 693-C2
APPY WY
SLOC 93420 715-D2
W APRICOT AV
LMPC 93436 916-C1
APRICOT ST
Npmo 93444 756-A4
AQUARIUS RD
StBC 93436 876-C5
AQUEDUCT WY
SLVG 93463 920-F7
ARABIAN CIR
ARGD 93420 714-H2
ARABIAN LN
PSRS 93446 513-H7
ARABIAN TR
StBC 93455 816-E5
ARABIAN WY
SLOC 93420 735-A2
ARAGON DR
CARP 93013 998-C6
ARAGON RD
ATAS 93422 574-C3
ARALIA CT
SLO 93401 674-D1
ARANGO DR
StBC 93111 984-J7
ARBOLADO LN
PSRS 93446 533-J2
ARBOLADO RD
SBAR 93103 996-B1
SLOC 93446 533-J2
ARBOLEDA RD
StBC 93110 995-B2
N ARBOLEDA RD
StBC 93110 995-B1
ARBOLES WY
SLOC 93420 734-H6
ARBOLITOS CT
SMRA 93458 796-D5
ARBOL VERDE ST
CARP 93013 998-E7
CARP 93013 1018-E1
ARBOR DR
StBC 93437 855-D6
ARBOR LN
StBC 93455 796-H7
ARBOR RD
SLOC 93446 533-D2
ARBOREA CT
StBC 93455 816-J3
ARBUTUS AV
MOBY 93442 611-G7
ARCADE RD
ATAS 93422 574-A5
ARCADIA
ARGD 93420 715-A7
ARCADIA AV
MOBY 93442 611-G7
ARCADY RD
StBC 93108 996-F1
ARCHER CT
LMPC 93436 896-C6
ARCHER ST
LMPC 93436 896-C6
SLO 93401 653-J5
ARCHER WY
Npmo 93444 756-A3
ARCIERO CT
PSRS 93446 514-A3
ARCTIC AV
SMRA 93454 796-H1
ARCTURUS AV
StBC 93436 876-D5
ARDANA DR
SLOC 93446 513-B3
ARDATH DR
Cmbr 93428 548-G1
ARDEN RD
SBAR 93105 995-G2
ARDEN WY
SLOC 93420 734-H5
ARDILLA AV
ATAS 93422 573-G3
ARDILLA DR
SBAR 93105 995-E2
ARDILLA RD
ATAS 93422 573-E2
ARDMORE DR
StBC 93117 984-D7
ARDMORE RD
PSRS 93446 514-A4
ARENA AV
ATAS 93422 553-H7
ATAS 93422 573-H1
ARENA RD
ATAS 93422 553-G7
ARGONNE CIR
SBAR 93105 985-G7
SBAR 93105 995-G1
ARGUELLO BLVD
StBC 93437 365-D4
StBC 93437 895-A6
ARGUELLO RD
SBAR 93103 996-A1
ARIBA RD
SLOC 93446 533-E1
ARIES AV
StBC 93436 876-D6
ARIZONA AV
ATAS 93422 553-H7
ATAS 93422 573-H1
StBC 93437 875-C4
ARIZONA BLVD
MonC 93451 453-A4
SLOC 93451 453-A4
ARLEEN AV
PSRS 93446 513-F2
ARLINGTON AV
SBAR 93101 996-A3
ARLINGTON ST
Cmbr 93428 528-E6
ARLISS DR
Cmbr 93428 548-H2
ARMAS CANYON RD
StBC 93117 993-D1
ARMITOS AV
StBC 93117 994-E1
ARMOUR RANCH RD
StBC 93460 921-G6
StBC 93460 941-J1
ARMSTRONG AV
SMRA 93454 776-J7
ARMSTRONG LN
ATAS 93422 573-G4
ARMSTRONG RD
StBC 93117 993-H3
ARMSTRONG ST
LMPC 93436 896-C6
ARNEB AV
StBC 93436 876-D7
ARNOLD AV
LMPC 93436 896-C6
ARNOLD CIR
LMPC 93436 896-C6
ARNOLD PL
SBAR 93117 994-C2
AROZENA LN
StBC 93013 1018-H2
ARRELLAGA ST
SBAR 93101 995-H4
SBAR 93101 996-A2
SBAR 93103 996-A2
ARRIBA DR
StBC 93013 997-J3
ARRIBA PL
SLOC 93420 755-A2
ARRIBA WY
SBAR 93105 985-H7
SMRA 93458 776-F4
StBC 93105 985-H7
ARROQUI ST
StBC 93108 997-B3
ARROWHEAD DR
StBC 93455 817-E5
ARROYICO LN
StBC 93108 996-H2
ARROYO AV
ARGD 93420 715-A6
ATAS 93422 573-J1
SBAR 93109 995-J6
SBAR 93109 996-A6
ARROYO CT
StBC 93455 816-J6
ARROYO LN
SLOC 93405 653-C5
ARROYO RD
StBC 93110 995-A2
ARROYO WY
StBC 93455 816-J6
ARROYO GRANDE HUASNA RD
SLOC - 345-F5
SLOC 93420 345-F5
ARROYO GRANDE SAN LUIS OBISPO
ARGD 93420 715-A3
SLOC 93420 715-A3
ARROYO VISTA DR
StBC 93117 993-E2
ARROYO VISTA LN
SLOC 93420 715-C2
ARTESIA AV
StBC 93436 895-F6
ARTIGA LN
ATAS 93422 573-E2
ARUNDEL RD
StBC 93117 984-E7
ASCOT CT
Cmbr 93428 528-G7
Cmbr 93428 548-G1
ASEGRA RD
Summ 93067 997-E2
ASH AV
CARP 93013 998-C7
SLOC 93430 590-J1
SMRA 93454 777-A6
ASH LN
SLVG 93463 940-D1
ASH ST
ARGD 93420 714-F6
ATAS 93422 574-B7
GBCH 93433 714-F6
SLOC 93402 631-G6
StBC 93437 855-D6
ASHBROOK LN
StBC 93455 817-B6
ASHBY LN
Cmbr 93428 528-E5
ASHDALE ST
StBC 93110 994-J2
ASHLAND LN
Npmo 93444 756-C4
ASHLEY AV
SBAR 93103 996-D4
ASHLEY LN
SLOC 93465 553-C3
ASHLEY PL
StBC 93117 984-D7
StBC 93455 816-G4
ASHLEY RD
StBC 93108 986-G7
StBC 93108 996-F1
ASHMORE ST
SLO 93401 674-D2
ASHTON ST
StBC 93111 994-J2
ASHTON WY
SLOC 93465 553-C3
ASHWOOD PL
PSRS 93446 534-B2
ASILO
ARGD 93420 714-H2
ASKOV PL
SLVG 93463 920-F6
ASPEN CT
Npmo 93444 756-A6
ASPEN LN
SMRA 93454 777-A6
ASPEN ST
ARGD 93420 714-G6
SLOC 93402 631-F6
StBC 93437 855-D6
ASPEN WY
StBC 93111 984-H7
ASTER AV
LMPC 93436 896-D6
ASTER LN
LMPC 93436 896-D6
ASTER PL
StBC 93455 816-H1
ASTER ST
SLOC 93445 734-G1
ASTOR AV
Cmbr 93428 548-G2
ASTOR CT
LMPC 93436 896-C6
ASTORIA PL
StBC 93117 993-F3
ASUNCION RD
SLOC 93422 594-G4
ATAJO AV
ATAS 93422 573-G4
ATASCADERO AV
ATAS 93422 573-J4
ATAS 93422 574-A6
ATAS 93422 594-A1
SLOC 93422 594-A1
ATASCADERO DR
StBC 93110 995-A2
ATASCADERO MALL
ATAS 93422 573-H4
ATASCADERO RD
ATAS 93422 594-C3
MOBY 93442 611-E4
SLOC 93422 594-C3
ATASCADERO RD Rt#-41
MOBY 93442 611-G3
SLOC 92389 325-A10
SLOC 93442 325-A10
SLOC 93442 611-G3
SLOC 93442 612-A1
ATASCADERO ST
SLO 93405 653-F7
ATASCO DR
StBC 93110 995-A1
ATHERLY LN
StBC 93455 796-H7
ATLANTIC CITY AV
GBCH 93433 714-D4
ATOLL ST
SLOC 93445 714-E7
ATTERDAG RD
SLVG 93463 920-E7
SLVG 93463 940-E1
ATWELL ST
Cmbr 93428 548-F2
AUDUBON AV
LMPC 93436 896-B6
AUGUSTA CT
SLO 93401 654-B5
SMRA 93455 796-G6
AUGUSTA DR
Npmo 93444 755-F1
AUGUSTA LN
SBAR 93108 996-F2
AUGUSTA ST
SLO 93401 654-B5
StBC 93440 878-H2
AUGUSTENBORG PL
SLVG 93463 920-F6
AUHAY DR
StBC 93110 995-A1
AURELIA LN
SLOC 93420 735-F6
AURIGA AV
StBC 93436 876-D5
AURORA AV
SBAR 93109 995-H6
AURORA DR
StBC 93108 997-A3
AURORA RD
ATAS 93422 574-C4
AURORA WY
SLOC 93465 553-C1
AUSTIN CT
PSRS 93446 513-J7
SLOC 93402 651-F1
AUSTIN RD
StBC 93111 994-G4
AUTO PARK DR
SMRA 93455 816-G1
StBC 93455 816-G1
AUTO PARK WY
SLO 93405 673-G1
AUTUMN PL
SLOC 93420 754-H1
AUTUMN WOODS PL
SMRA 93454 777-A6
AVALON AV
StBC 93110 994-J2
AVALON ST
LMPC 93436 916-B3
MOBY 93442 611-F3
SLO 93405 653-F6
StBC 93436 916-B3
AVENAL AV
ATAS 93422 573-J7
AVENALES RANCH RD
SLOC - 345-G1
AVENIDA CABALLO
StBC 93460 901-A5
AVENIDA DE AMIGOS
Npmo 93444 756-C3
AVENIDA DE DIAMANTE
ARGD 93420 714-J4
AVENIDA DEL CAPITAN
StBC 93117 982-C5

STREET
Name City ZIP Pg-Grid

AVENIDA DEL SOL
PSRS 93446 513-H5
AVENIDA DE SOCIOS
Npmo 93444 756-C4
AVENIDA GANSO
StBC 93117 984-C7
StBC 93117 994-C1
AVENIDA GARZA
StBC 93117 984-C7
AVENIDA GORRION
StBC 93117 994-C1
AVENIDA MONTECITO VERDE
Npmo 93444 756-C4
AVENIDA PELICANOS
SLOC 93445 714-F7
AVENIDA PEQUENA
StBC 93111 984-G6
AVENIDA REDONDO
SMRA 93458 776-F4
AVENIDA RIVIERA
SMRA 93458 776-F4
AVENUE DEL MAR
StBC 93013 998-B7
AVENUE OF FLAGS
StBC - 919-H6
BLTN 93427 919-H5
StBC 93427 919-H6
AVERY RD
SLOC 93451 324-L3
SLOC 93451 325-A3
AVIANO AV
StBC 93117 993-G1
AVIANO PL
StBC 93117 993-H1
AVIATION DR
SMRA 93455 796-F6
AVILA WY
StBC 93108 997-A2
AVILA BEACH DR
SLOC 93405 693-C3
SLOC 93424 345-A4
SLOC 93424 693-C3
SLOC 93449 693-C3
AVILA VALLEY DR
SLOC 93405 693-C2
AVIS ST
SLOC 93420 735-E4
AVOCADO AV
Npmo 93444 756-C1
AVOCADO LN
SLOC 93401 674-G3
AVON AV
Cmbr 93428 548-G2
AVON LN
SBAR 93105 985-E7
AWAKEN PL
SLOC 93446 494-G5
AYALA LN
StBC 93108 986-F7
AZALEA CT
Npmo 93444 755-J5
SLO 93401 674-C1
AZALEA DR
CARP 93013 998-D6
AZALEA LN
StBC 93437 875-H3
AZALEA WY
StBC 93117 984-E7
AZUCENA AV
ATAS 93422 573-J6
AZURE ST
MOBY 93442 611-E2

B

B CT
LMPC 93436 896-F5
B ST
SLOC 93430 590-J1
SLOC 93451 453-B4
N B ST
LMPC 93436 896-F6
LMPC 93436 916-F1
S B ST
LMPC 93436 916-F2
BADEN AV
GBCH 93433 714-E6
BADGER RD
StBC 93460 901-C3
BADGER CANYON LN
SLOC 93420 695-B7
SLOC 93420 715-B1
BAHIA CT
SLO 93401 654-C5
BAILARD AV
CARP 93013 1018-F1
BAILARD LN
CARP 93013 998-E7
BAILEY AV
LMPC 93436 896-B7
StBC 93436 896-B7
StBC 93436 916-B2
BAJADA
SBAR 93109 995-H5
BAJADA AV
ATAS 93422 573-H2
BAJADA LN
StBC 93110 995-D5
BAJADA GRANDE
SBAR 93109 995-H5
BAKEMAN LN
ARGD 93420 714-G6
BAKER AV
PBCH 93449 693-G7
BAKERSFIELD AV
SLOC 93430 590-J1
SLOC 93430 591-A1
BAKERSFIELD ST
PBCH 93449 714-C1
BAKKE WY
SLVG 93463 920-E7
BALBOA CT
LMPC 93436 916-B2
BALBOA DR
SBAR 93109 995-G7
SMRA 93454 776-J5
SMRA 93454 777-A5
BALBOA RD
ATAS 93422 573-C1
BALBOA ST
GBCH 93433 714-F4
MOBY 93442 611-G6
SLO 93405 653-F6
BALDWIN RD
SBAR 93105 995-G2
BALI ST
MOBY 93442 611-E2
BALLARD ST
Npmo 93444 756-C2
BALLARD CANYON RD
BLTN 93427 920-A6
StBC 93427 920-B5
StBC 93441 900-F7
StBC 93441 920-D4
StBC 93463 900-F7
StBC 93463 920-E1
BALLESTRAL AV
SMRA 93455 796-G6
BALLINGER CANYON RD
StBC - 346-F10
BALM RIDGE CT
SLOC 93401 673-G6
BALM RIDGE RD
SLOC 93401 673-G7
BAMBI CT
ARGD 93420 714-J7
BANANA RD
StBC 93108 986-E7
BANBURY RD
Cmbr 93428 548-H1
BANDEROLA CT
SLO 93401 653-J6
BANE ST
ATAS 93422 574-C7
BANK ST
Npmo 93444 756-C3
BANNEKER PL
Npmo 93444 755-D4
BANNER AV
Summ 93067 997-D3
BANYAN PL
Npmo 93444 756-C4
BANYAN WY
SMRA 93455 796-G6
BARBADOS ST
SLOC 93445 734-H1
BARBARA ST
SMRA 93458 776-G6
SMRA 93458 796-G3
BARBERRY WY
Npmo 93444 755-E1
BARCA ST
GBCH 93433 714-E6
BARCELLUS AV
SMRA 93454 796-H2
BARCELONA
PBCH 93449 693-G6
BARCELONA DR
SBAR 93105 995-E3
BARD CT
SLOC 93401 673-G6
BARDMORE CT
SMRA 93455 796-G6
BARGER CANYON RD
StBC 93110 985-E6
BAR-K LN
Npmo 93444 756-C3
BARKER PASS RD
SBAR 93108 996-E2
StBC 93108 996-E2
BARLEY GRAIN RD
SLOC 93446 533-J3
SLOC 93446 534-A3
BARLING TER
StBC 93117 984-D7
BARLOW LN
MOBY 93442 611-G7
BARN RD
SLOC 93446 471-C5
BARNES RD
SLOC 93451 473-E5
SLOC 93451 493-E1
BARNETT ST
ARGD 93420 714-J5
BARNETTE RD
StBC 93455 817-A5
BARON CANYON RANCH RD
SLOC 93401 673-F7
BARRANCA AV
SBAR 93109 996-A6
BARRANCA CT
SLO 93401 654-D6
BARRANCA LN
SBAR 93109 996-A6
BARRANCO HTS
ATAS 93422 573-F7
BARRANCO RD
ATAS 93422 573-F7
BARRENDA AV
ATAS 93422 573-J2
BARRETT ST
SMRA 93458 796-F1
BARRINGTON CT
LMPC 93436 916-G2
BARRINGTON DR
SMRA 93458 776-G5
BARRINGTON PL
LMPC 93436 916-G2
BARRINGTON WY
StBC 93117 984-D7
BARRYMORE AV
SLOC 93430 591-C4
BARTON AV
LMPC 93436 896-F6
E BARTON AV
LMPC 93436 896-E6
W BARTON AV
LMPC 93436 896-C6
BARWICK RD
StBC 93111 994-G4
BASELINE AV
StBC 93460 920-H2
StBC 93460 921-A2
StBC 93460 922-A4
StBC 93463 920-H2
BASIN ST
SLOC 93445 714-G7
BASQUE DR
StBC 93455 816-J5
StBC 93455 817-A5
BASSANO DR
StBC 93117 993-G1
BASSI DR
SLOC 93401 693-D1
SLOC 93405 693-D1
BASS POINT RD
SLOC 93426 469-J2
BASSWOOD ST
StBC 93437 855-G7
BATES RD
StBC 93013 1018-J2
VeCo 93013 1018-J2
BATES RANCH RD
VeCo 93013 1018-J2
BATH ST
SBAR 93101 995-H3
SBAR 93101 996-A4
SBAR 93105 995-G2
BATHURST DR
StBC 93455 817-B4
BATTLES RD
SMRA 93454 796-H3
SMRA 93454 797-A3
SMRA 93458 796-E3
StBC 93454 796-H3
StBC 93454 797-A3
BAUER AV
StBC 93455 817-A5
BAXTER LN
PBCH 93449 714-B1
BAXTER ST
StBC 93110 994-J2
BAY AV
MOBY 93442 611-G6
SLOC 93430 591-A2
SMRA 93454 777-A5
BAY ST
PBCH 93449 714-B1
BAY ABI LN
SLOC 93420 695-C5
BAY BERRY LN
StBC 93117 993-J3
BAYCLIFF DR
PBCH 93449 693-J7
BAYFRONT DR
PBCH 93449 693-J7
BAY LAUREL PL
SLOC 93424 693-C2
BAYLOR LN
SMRA 93454 776-J5
BAY OAKS DR
SLOC 93402 631-H7
BAYSHORE DR
MOBY 93442 611-G7
MOBY 93442 631-G1
BAYSIDE DR
CARP 93013 998-B5
BAYSIDE PL
SLOC 93420 734-J5
BAYVIEW AV
MOBY 93442 611-F4
BAY VIEW CIR
SBAR 93109 995-J7
BAYVIEW DR
SMRA 93454 777-A5
BAYVIEW LN
PBCH 93449 714-D3
SLOC 93420 734-H3
BAYVIEW HEIGHTS DR
SLOC 93402 631-H7
SLOC 93402 651-J1
SLOC 93402 652-A1
BAY VISTA LN
SLOC 93402 631-H7
BAYWOOD ST
StBC 93437 855-E6
BAYWOOD WY
SLOC 93402 631-G4
BEACH
PBCH 93449 714-C3
BEACH BLVD
StBC 93437 365-C2
StBC 93437 875-A7
StBC 93437 894-H1
E BEACH CIR
SLOC 93426 470-A3
BEACH ST
CARP 93013 998-A6
MOBY 93442 611-F6
SLO 93401 653-J5
SLOC 93445 734-E1
BEACH CLUB RD
StBC 93013 997-G4
BEACHCOMBER DR
MOBY 93442 611-D1
PBCH 93449 693-E5
BEACHWOOD CT
SLOC 93446 533-E6
BEACON RD
PSRS 93446 494-F6
SLOC 93446 494-F6
BEAR CANYON LN
SLOC 93420 715-B2
BEAR CREEK DR
BLTN 93427 919-H6
BEATTIE DR
LMPC 93436 916-F2
BEAUMONT WY
StBC 93117 984-D7
BEAVER CREEK LN
SLOC 93446 533-H2
BECK RD
StBC 93436 896-G3
BECKETT PL
GBCH 93433 714-D4
BECKNELL RD
SBAR 93117 994-C2
BEDFORD CT
SLO 93401 654-C6
BEDFORD PL
StBC 93455 816-J1
BEDLOE LN
ARGD 93420 715-A5
BEE ST
Npmo 93444 756-C2
BEEBEE ST
SLO 93401 653-J6
BEE CANYON RD
SLOC 93420 695-B7
BEECH AV
SLOC 93422 594-F6
BEECH ST
ARGD 93420 714-H6
SLO 93401 673-H1
StBC 93437 855-D6
BEECHAM-VAUGHAN
SLOC 93401 673-F7
BEECHER AV
SLOC 93430 591-C4
BEECHNUT AV
Npmo 93444 756-C1
BEECHWOOD DR
PSRS 93446 534-A1
SLOC 93446 534-A2
BEE ROCK RD
SLOC 93426 324-K3
SLOC 93426 470-F1
SLOC 93451 324-L3
SLOC 93451 325-A3
SLOC 93451 473-A1
BEE TREE RD
SLOC 93451 473-D5
BEGA WY
CARP 93013 1018-G1
StBC 93013 998-G7
StBC 93013 1018-G1
BEGONIA PL
CARP 93013 998-D6
BEGONIA ST
SLOC 93445 734-G1
BEL AIR DR
SBAR 93105 995-F4
BEL AIR PL
PSRS 93446 533-J1
PSRS 93446 534-A1
BELANGER DR
Npmo 93444 756-C4
BELGIAN PL
SLOC 93420 735-A2
BELL AV
LMPC 93436 896-E6
BELL RD
StBC - 346-D10
StBC - 806-F6
StBC 93254 806-F3
BELL ST
ARGD 93420 714-H5
StBC 93440 365-G1
StBC 93440 878-F1
BELL ST Rt#-135
StBC 93440 878-G1
BELLA DR
SBAR 93105 995-F4
BELLAGIO CT
StBC 93455 816-J2
BELLA TIERRA PL
SLOC 93446 493-A5
BELLA VISTA CT
PSRS 93446 513-J3
PSRS 93446 514-A3
BELLA VISTA DR
MOBY 93442 611-H6
StBC 93108 987-D7
BELLA VISTA RD
ATAS 93422 573-G5
BELLEVUE ORCHARD LN
SLOC 93405 693-C2
BELLFLOWER LN
LMPC 93436 896-D6
BELLO ST
PBCH 93449 714-B2
BELLUNO DR
StBC 93117 993-G1
BELMONTE DR
SBAR 93101 995-H5
BELRIDGE ST
SLOC 93445 714-E7
BENCHMARK RD
PSRS 93446 514-A3
BENIAMINO WY
SLOC 93405 632-F3
BENJI LN
StBC 93455 816-H5
BEN LOMOND DR
StBC 93105 985-H7
W BENNET ST
Npmo 93444 756-C2
BENNETT AV
ARGD 93420 714-H5
E BENNETT ST
Npmo 93444 756-D2
BENNETT WY
SLOC 93465 553-C2
BENNETTA DR
SMRA 93458 776-H3
BENSON AV
Cmbr 93428 548-F2
BENTON WY
SLO 93405 653-H3
StBC 93111 994-J2
BENT TREE DR
StBC 93455 816-J1
N BENT TREE DR
StBC 93455 816-G2
S BENT TREE DR
StBC 93455 816-G2
BENWILEY AV
SMRA 93458 776-G5
BERKELEY DR
LMPC 93436 916-G2
BERKELEY RD
StBC 93111 984-F7
StBC 93117 984-E7
BERKSHIRE LN
StBC 93455 816-F4
BERKSHIRE TER
StBC 93117 994-A4
BERMUDA PL
Npmo 93444 756-C4
BERNARDO AV
MOBY 93442 611-G7
BERNITA PL
Npmo 93444 756-A4
BERRY LN
SMRA 93455 796-D5
StBC 93455 796-D5
BERRYESSA LN
StBC 93455 817-E5
BERRY PATCH LN
SLOC 93446 534-B5
SLOC 93465 534-B5
BERRYWOOD DR
StBC 93455 816-J3
BERWICK DR
Cmbr 93428 548-F2
MOBY 93442 611-F5
BERWYN DR
StBC 93455 817-A2
BETA CT
ARGD 93420 714-G5
BETH CT
SMRA 93454 776-J6
BETHANY DR
StBC 93455 816-H6
BETHEL LN
SMRA 93458 796-E4
N BETHEL RD
SLOC 93446 533-C6
SLOC 93465 533-C6
SLOC 93465 553-B1
S BETHEL RD
SLOC 93465 553-B2
E BETTERAVIA RD
SMRA 93454 796-H5
SMRA 93454 797-B4
StBC 93454 796-H5
StBC 93454 797-B4
W BETTERAVIA RD
SMRA 93454 796-B5
SMRA 93455 796-B5
StBC 93455 795-C2
StBC 93455 796-B5
BETTIGA ST
PBCH 93449 714-C2
BETTY DR
SBAR 93105 995-G2
BEVERLY AV
PSRS 93446 513-F3
BEVERLY CT
StBC 93455 816-E4
BEVERLY DR
Npmo 93444 756-B5
StBC 93455 816-E4
BIANCHI LN
SLO 93401 653-H5
BIDDLE RANCH RD
SLOC 93401 674-F6
BIG BEAR CIR
SLOC 93446 471-C7
BIG BUCK LN
SLOC 93446 471-D6
BIG CANYON CT
SLOC 93420 715-C3
BIG HORN WY
Npmo 93444 756-C3
BIG PINE DR
SMRA 93454 776-J5
SMRA 93454 777-A5
BIG SUR DR
StBC 93117 993-F3
BILLIE CT
StBC 93455 816-G5
BINNS CT
SLO 93401 654-B5
BINSCARTH RD
SLOC 93402 631-F6
BIRCH
SLO 93401 673-H1
BIRCH AV
MOBY 93442 611-E2
SLOC 93430 590-J1
StBC 93437 855-G7
E BIRCH AV
LMPC 93436 896-E6
BIRCH DR
SLVG 93463 940-E1
BIRCH LN
BLTN 93427 919-G5
BIRCH ST
ATAS 93422 574-B7
CARP 93013 1018-F1
GDLP 93434 775-A6
SMRA 93458 776-G4
BIRCH WK
StBC 93117 994-A3
BIRCHWOOD CT
SLOC 93446 533-E6
BIRCHWOOD RD
StBC 93111 984-H7
StBC 93111 994-H1
BIRDIE CT
PSRS 93446 513-J7
BIRKDALE LN
SLOC 93401 674-E6
BIRNAM WOOD DR
StBC 93108 997-B1
BISHOP ST
SLO 93401 654-B5
BISON LN
StBC 93463 900-G7
BITHYNIA RD
StBC 93110 995-D3
BITTERWATER RD
SLOC 92389 325-H5
SLOC 93461 325-H5
BITTERWATER VALLEY RD
SLOC 92389 325-K8
BIVOUAC RD
SLOC 93451 471-J1
BIXBY RD
Cmbr 93428 548-G2
BLACK RD
SMRA 93458 796-A4
StBC 93429 345-D10
StBC 93429 816-A3
StBC 93455 796-A7
StBC 93455 816-A3
StBC 93458 776-A7
StBC 93458 796-A4
BLACKBURN ST
PSRS 93446 513-E6
SLOC 93465 553-D2
BLACK HAWK WY
Npmo 93444 756-B4
BLACKHAWK WY
Npmo 93444 756-B4
BLACK HORSE LN
SLOC 93446 471-B6
BLACK LAKE CANYON DR
Npmo 93444 735-D7
Npmo 93444 755-E1
SLOC 93420 735-D7
BLACK LAKE CANYON RD
SLOC 93420 735-C7
BLACK MOUNTAIN RD
MOBY 93442 611-H7
MOBY 93442 631-G1
SLOC 93453 325-G11
SLOC 93453 345-F1
BLACK MOUNTAIN LOOKOUT RD
SLOC 93453 325-F11
BLACKOAK DR
PSRS 93446 513-G3
BLACK OAK LN
Npmo 93444 755-G2
BLACK RIDGE LN
Npmo 93444 755-F1
BLACK SAGE CIR
Npmo 93444 755-E1
BLACKSTONE CT
StBC 93455 816-F5
BLACKWOOD CT
StBC 93455 816-J2
BLAISDEL LN
StBC 93436 896-G3
BLAKE ST
StBC 93455 816-J5
BLANCA ST
MOBY 93442 591-D7
SLOC - 591-D7
BLANCHARD ST
SBAR 93103 996-C2
BLANCHE CT
SMRA 93458 796-G1
BLANKER PL
StBC 93455 816-G4
BLARNEY LN
SLOC 93405 653-D3
BLOSSER RD
SMRA 93455 796-F5
SMRA 93455 816-F3
SMRA 93458 796-F5
StBC 93455 816-F5
N BLOSSER RD
SMRA 93458 776-F5
StBC 93458 776-F5
BLOSSOM CT
PSRS 93446 513-E6
BLOSSOM DR
StBC 93455 817-A3
BLUEBELL WY
SLO 93401 674-C1
BLUEBERRY LN
SLOC 93401 693-E2
BLUEBIRD LN
SLOC 93446 471-C6
BLUEBIRD ST
SMRA 93454 796-H3
BLUEBIRD GLEN RD
StBC 93427 919-G1
BLUE FOX RD
SLOC 93420 736-E2
BLUE GUM LN
Npmo 93444 755-G3
BLUE HEAVEN LN
SLOC 93446 514-C7
BLUE HERON DR
SLOC 93424 693-A3
BLUE HERON LN
SLOC 93446 471-C6
BLUE HERON VIEW LN
SLOC 93402 652-B1
BLUE JAY
PSRS 93446 514-B7
BLUEJAY DR
StBC 93455 796-J7
StBC 93455 797-A7
BLUE LAKE LN
SMRA 93454 776-J6
SMRA 93454 777-A6
BLUE LUPINE LN
SLOC 93446 471-B5
BLUE RIDGE DR
SMRA 93455 796-J7
BLUEROCK CT
SLO 93401 654-A6
BLUEROCK DR
SLO 93401 654-A6
BLUE SAGE RD
SLOC 93446 493-C6
BLUE SKY DR
SLOC 93420 695-E6
BLUE SPRINGS LN
Npmo 93444 756-C2
BLUFF AV
LMPC 93436 916-F2
BLUFF CT
SLOC 93426 469-H2
BLUFFS DR
PBCH 93424 693-C4
SLOC 93424 693-C4
BLUME ST
Npmo 93444 756-B3
BLYTHE PL
Cmbr 93428 528-G7
Cmbr 93428 548-G1
BOARDWALK LN
StBC 93455 817-A4
BOAT HOOK RD
SLOC 93426 470-A1
BOBCAT WY
SLOC 93446 470-B5
BOBCAT SPRINGS RD
StBC 93427 919-G2
BOBWHITE
PSRS 93446 514-B7
BOCINA
ATAS 93422 594-C1
BODEGA CT
GBCH 93433 714-E7
BODEGA LN
SBAR 93110 995-D1
BODGER RD
LMPC 93436 916-C3
StBC 93436 916-C3
BOEKER ST
PBCH 93449 693-H7
BOESEKE PKWY
StBC 93108 997-A3
BOGIE LN
PSRS 93446 513-J7
BOLEN DR
PSRS 93446 513-H5
BOLERO DR
StBC 93108 996-J1
BOLINAS CT
GBCH 93433 714-D4
BOLLAY DR
StBC 93117 993-J3
BOLSA RD
ATAS 93422 573-B3
BOLSA CHICA CT
StBC 93117 984-D6
BOLTON DR
MOBY 93442 611-F5
BOLTON WK
StBC 93117 993-J4
BONANZA LN
SLOC 93446 471-B5
BOND AV
SBAR 93103 996-C3
BOND ST
SLO 93405 653-J2
SLO 93405 654-A2
BONETTI DR
SLO 93401 673-J1
BONITA AV
PSRS 93446 513-F2
SLOC 93430 591-C5
BONITA PL
SLOC 93451 473-F2
BONITA PZ
SBAR 93103 995-J1
BONITA ST
MOBY 93442 611-E3
PBCH 93449 693-E4
SMRA 93454 776-J7
SMRA 93454 796-J1
BONITA LATERAL RD
StBC 93458 775-H6
StBC 93458 776-A6
BONITA SCHOOL RD
Npmo 93444 755-G7
Npmo 93444 775-G1
StBC 93458 775-H4
BONNIE LN
StBC 93108 996-J3
BONNIE JEAN LN
SLOC 93420 735-A3
BONNYMEDE DR
StBC 93108 996-H4
BOONE ST
SMRA 93454 796-H1
SMRA 93454 797-A1
SMRA 93458 796-E1
BOREGA LN
Npmo 93444 756-E6
BORONDA ST
SLO 93405 653-F7
BORTON DR
SBAR 93109 995-F6
BOSCOE CT
SMRA 93454 797-A1
BOSTON WY
SLOC 93451 453-C6
BOTELLO RD
SBAR 93117 994-C2
BOTTONWOOD
SLOC 93401 674-B3
BOUGAINVILLEA ST
SLO 93401 674-C1
BOULEVARD DEL CAMPO
SLO 93401 654-B6
BOUNDARY DR
StBC 93108 997-C1
BOUNDARY OAKS CT
SMRA 93455 796-F6
BOWIE DR
SLOC 93402 651-F1
BOWL PL
SLVG 93463 940-E5
BOX CANYON RD
StBC 93460 901-C5
BOXWOOD CT
SLO 93401 674-D1
BOXWOOD ST
SMRA 93458 776-G3
BOY SCOUT RD
SLOC 93451 325-A4
BOYSEN AV
SLO 93405 653-H2
BRACKEN LN
Npmo 93444 756-A3
BRADBURY AV
SBAR 93101 996-A4
BRADFORD AV
Cmbr 93428 548-H2
BRADFORD CIR
Cmbr 93428 548-H2
BRADFORD DR
StBC 93117 993-E2
BRADFORD RD
Cmbr 93428 548-H2
BRADLEY AV
MOBY 93442 611-G7
MOBY 93442 631-G1
BRADLEY RD
SMRA 93454 776-J5
SMRA 93454 777-A7
SMRA 93454 796-J2
SMRA 93454 797-A2
SMRA 93455 796-J5
SMRA 93455 797-A4
StBC 93454 796-J4
StBC 93454 797-A4
StBC 93455 816-J1
StBC 93455 817-A3
BRADY LN
SLOC 93420 715-C7
BRAEBURN DR
StBC 93117 984-D7
BRAEMAR DR
SBAR 93109 995-D5
BRAMADERO RD
StBC 93441 900-J5
BRAMBLE RD
SLOC 93420 695-C5
BRAMBLES CT
SLOC 93465 533-C7
BRANCH RD
SLOC 93446 325-D6
BRANCH ST
SLO 93401 653-J5
SLO 93401 654-A5
E BRANCH ST
Npmo 93444 756-C1
E BRANCH ST Rt#-227
ARGD 93420 715-A5
W BRANCH ST
ARGD 93420 714-H4
Npmo 93444 756-C2
W BRANCH ST Rt#-227
ARGD 93420 714-J5
ARGD 93420 715-A5
BRANCH CREEK CIR
PSRS 93446 534-A1
BRANCH MILL RD
ARGD 93420 715-C4
SLOC 93420 695-F7
SLOC 93420 715-F2
BRAND PL
Cmbr 93428 548-F2
BRANDON CT
StBC 93455 816-F5
BRANDON DR
StBC 93117 993-F1
StBC 93460 921-A4
BRASS BUTTON CT
SLOC 93424 693-B1
BREAKER ST
SLOC 93445 734-E1
BREAMAR RANCH LN
SBAR 93109 995-D5
BRECK ST
SLO 93401 654-A4
BREEZY GLEN DR
StBC 93455 817-A3
BREGANTE LN
SBAR 93103 996-C3
BRENNER DR
SBAR 93105 985-E6
BRENT ST
SBAR 93105 985-E7
BRENTWOOD CIR
SLOC 93420 734-H5
BRENTWOOD LN
StBC 93455 816-J4
BRENTWOOD WY
StBC 93117 993-F1
BRESSI PL
SLO 93405 653-H3
BREWER ST
SLOC 93465 553-E2
BRIAN AV
SMRA 93454 777-B6
BRIAN ST
SMRA 93454 777-B7
BRIARCLIFF DR
StBC 93455 816-F4
BRIAR ROSE LN
Npmo 93444 756-A5
BRIARWOOD DR
SLO 93401 654-C7
BRIARWOOD LN
Npmo 93444 756-A1
BRIARWOOD PL
SLOC 93465 553-A2
BRIARWOOD RD
StBC 93455 796-A7
StBC 93455 816-B1
BRIDGE ST
ARGD 93420 715-A5
Cmbr 93428 528-F5
SLO 93401 653-H6

STREET Name City ZIP Pg-Grid

BRIDGE CANYON WY
SLOC 93451 473-C6
BRIDGE CREEK RD
SLOC 93401 674-H2
BRIDGEGATE LN
PSRS 93446 533-G1
BRIDGEPORT RD
StBC 93455 817-A3
BRIDLE TRAIL LN
SLOC 93446 471-C5
BRIDLE TRAILS LN
StBC 93454 797-D6
BRIGHTON AV
ARGD 93420 714-D4
ARGD 93433 714-D4
GBCH 93433 714-D4
BRIGHTON LN
Cmbr 93428 528-D5
BRIGHTON PL
StBC 93455 816-G5
BRINKERHOFF AV
SBAR 93101 996-B4
StBC 93441 901-F5
StBC 93460 901-F5
BRISA CT
PBCH 93449 693-E5
BRISA BLANDA DR
SLOC 93420 734-J4
BRISCO RD
ARGD 93420 714-G5
BRISTLECONE LN
Npmo 93444 756-B4
BRISTOL CT
StBC 93455 816-E4
BRISTOL PL
StBC 93117 993-E2
BRISTOL ST
Cmbr 93428 528-E6
BRITTANY CIR
SLO 93405 653-F1
BRITTNEY CT
StBC 93455 817-B6
BRITTNEY LN
StBC 93455 817-B6
BRIZZOLARA ST
SLO 93401 653-H4
BROAD ST
SLO 93401 653-J4
SLO 93401 654-A5
SLO 93405 653-H3
BROAD ST Rt#-227
SLO 93401 654-A6
SLO 93401 674-B1
SLOC 93401 654-A6
SLOC 93401 674-B1
BROADMOOR
ARGD 93420 715-A7
BROADMOOR PZ
SBAR 93105 995-F1
BROADWAY
StBC 93455 816-F6
N BROADWAY Rt#-135
SMRA 93454 776-H6
S BROADWAY Rt#-135
SMRA 93454 776-H7
SMRA 93454 796-H1
SMRA 93455 796-H5
BRODERSON AV
SLOC 93402 631-G6
BROKEN ARROW RD
Npmo 93444 735-H4
BROKEN SPUR PL
SLOC 93446 514-G7
SLOC 93446 534-G1
BROOK CT
LMPC 93436 896-D6
BROOK LN
SLOC 93446 471-D6
StBC 93108 986-G7
BROOK ST
SLO 93401 653-H6
StBC 93463 920-H2
BROOKHILL DR
PSRS 93446 514-B7
PSRS 93446 534-B1
BROOKLINE LN
SLOC 93401 674-D7
BROOKPINE DR
SLO 93401 674-D1
SLOC 93401 674-D1
BROOKSIDE AV
StBC 93455 816-J3
BROOKSIDE DR
LMPC 93436 896-D6
BROOKSIDE PL
StBC 93455 816-J3
BROOKTREE RD
StBC 93108 986-J7
BROSIAN WY
SBAR 93109 995-E5

BROSIAN WY
StBC 93109 995-E5
BROWN LN
SLOC 93430 591-D4
BROWN RD
StBC 93434 345-C9
StBC 93434 795-A3
StBC 93455 795-E2
StBC 93458 795-E2
BROWNES RD
ARGD 93420 714-G4
BROWN PELICAN LN
GDLP 93434 774-H6
BROWNSTONE LN
SMRA 93454 777-A7
BRUNSWICK DR
SMRA 93455 796-H6
BRYAN PL
Cmbr 93428 528-E7
BRYCE PL
StBC 93455 816-H2
BUCHON ST
SLO 93401 653-J5
SLO 93401 654-A4
BUCKBOARD LN
StBC 93463 920-J6
StBC 93463 921-A6
BUCKBRUSH DR
SLOC 93420 695-B6
BUCK CANYON RD
StBC 93460 901-C4
BUCKEYE CT
SLO 93401 674-E1
BUCKEYE ST
StBC 93437 855-G7
BUCKHORN RD
Npmo 93444 756-A4
BUCKINGHAM PL
Cmbr 93428 548-G1
BUCKLEY DR
Cmbr 93428 528-E4
BUCKLEY RD
SLOC 93401 673-H3
SLOC 93401 674-A3
BUCK RIDGE LN
SLOC 93420 695-A7
SLOC 93420 715-A1
BUCKSKIN DR
SLOC 93402 632-A7
SMRA 93454 777-A6
BUCKTAIL LN
SLOC 93446 471-D6
BUCKTHORN RD
StBC 93108 987-F7
BUELLTON PKWY
BLTN 93427 919-H6
StBC - 919-H6
StBC 93427 919-H6
BUELLTON LOMPOC RD Rt#-246
StBC 93436 365-F3
StBC 93436 896-H7
StBC 93436 916-H1
BUENA AV
ATAS 93422 573-J1
BUENA FORTUNA
StBC 93013 1018-J3
VeCo 93013 1018-J3
BUENAVISTA
SLOC 93430 591-C4
BUENA VISTA AV
SLO 93401 654-B3
SLO 93405 654-B2
BUENA VISTA DR
PSRS 93446 494-B6
PSRS 93446 513-J2
SLOC 93446 493-J7
SLOC 93446 494-A6
SLOC 93446 513-J2
StBC 93108 987-B7
StBC 93108 997-B1
BUGGYWHIP LN
SLOC 93446 471-E6
BULL CANYON RD
SLOC 93454 777-B5
SMRA 93454 777-B5
BULLOCK LN
SLO 93401 654-B7
SLO 93401 674-C1
SLOC 93401 654-B7
SLOC 93401 674-C1
BUMBLE BEE LN
SLOC 93465 553-B5
BUNDY CIR
BLTN 93427 919-H6
BUNFILL DR
SMRA 93455 796-J7
BUNNY AV
SMRA 93454 776-H6
SMRA 93458 776-F6

BUR CLOVER WY
SLOC - 695-E3
BURGANDY LN
SLOC 93446 514-J1
BURKET PL
PSRS 93446 513-E4
BURKHILL LN
SLOC 93420 694-H7
BURLINGTON DR
StBC 93455 816-F4
BURLWOOD LN
SLOC 93465 553-B2
BURNHAM DR
StBC 93436 876-E7
BURNING HILLS LN
SLOC 93465 553-B2
BURNING TREE WY
StBC 93436 876-E5
BURNS PL
SBAR 93117 994-C2
BURRO VERDE
PSRS 93446 513-J5
BURTIS ST
StBC 93111 994-H2
BURTON CIR
Cmbr 93428 528-G7
Cmbr 93428 548-G1
SBAR 93101 996-B5
BURTON DR
Cmbr 93428 528-G7
Cmbr 93428 548-G1
N BURTON ST
Npmo 93444 756-B1
S BURTON ST
Npmo 93444 756-C2
BURTON MESA BLVD
StBC 93436 876-D7
StBC 93436 896-F1
E BUSH AV
LMPC 93436 896-F6
BUSH CT
LMPC 93436 896-E6
BUSH DR
SLOC 93402 631-H6
BUSH LN
StBC 93455 816-E4
BUSHNELL ST
SLO 93401 654-A5
BUTTE AV
MOBY 93442 611-G6
SLOC 93405 632-J5
BUTTE DR
SLOC 93402 631-E6
StBC 93117 993-H2
BUTTERCUP LN
PSRS 93446 514-A6
BUTTERFLY CT
SMRA 93455 796-J7
SMRA 93455 797-A7
BUTTERFLY LN
Npmo 93444 756-B3
SBAR 93108 996-G3
SLOC 93402 631-E7
StBC 93108 996-G3
BUTTONHOOK RD
SLVG 93463 940-E4
BUTTON SAGE WY
SLOC - 695-E3
BUTTONWILLOW PL
Npmo 93444 756-A3
BUTTONWOOD LN
StBC 93117 993-J4
BYRNES LN
CARP 93013 998-E7
BYRON LN
Npmo 93444 735-E7

C

C CT
LMPC 93436 896-F5
C ST
SLOC 93451 453-B5
N C ST
LMPC 93436 896-F6
LMPC 93436 916-F1
S C ST
LMPC 93436 916-F2
CABALLERO LN
SMRA 93455 796-H5
CABALLEROS AV
SLO 93401 674-C5
CABALLO LN
StBC 93460 901-B4
CABALLO PL
SLOC 93446 513-E2
CABALLO RD
StBC 93460 901-F5
CABALLO WY
SMRA 93458 776-F4

CABIN LN
StBC 93105 964-F1
CABO SAN JOSE
SMRA 93455 796-H5
CABO SAN LUCAS
SMRA 93455 796-H5
CABO SAN LUCAS CIR
SMRA 93455 796-J5
CABRILLO AV
ATAS 93422 573-J2
ATAS 93422 574-A2
SLOC 93430 591-A2
E CABRILLO BLVD
SBAR 93101 996-D4
SBAR 93103 996-D4
SBAR 93108 996-D4
StBC 93108 996-D4
W CABRILLO BLVD
SBAR 93101 996-B5
CABRILLO CT
GBCH 93433 714-F4
CABRILLO HWY
SLOC 93420 734-H7
CABRILLO HWY Rt#-1
Cmbr 93428 324-J8
Cmbr 93428 528-B2
Cmbr 93428 548-J1
GBCH 93433 714-C4
GBCH 93449 714-C4
GDLP 93434 775-A3
LMPC 93436 916-H1
MOBY - 591-C6
MOBY 93430 591-C6
MOBY 93442 591-C6
MOBY 93442 611-E4
MOBY 93442 612-A6
Npmo 93444 755-B2
Npmo 93444 775-A3
PBCH 93449 714-C4
SLO 93405 633-F6
SLO 93405 653-H1
SLOC - 591-C6
SLOC - 612-A6
SLOC 93405 612-A6
SLOC 93405 632-F1
SLOC 93405 633-B4
SLOC 93405 653-H1
SLOC 93420 734-H1
SLOC 93420 754-H1
SLOC 93420 755-A1
SLOC 93430 324-J8
SLOC 93430 590-E1
SLOC 93430 591-C6
SLOC 93433 714-C4
SLOC 93435 324-J8
SLOC 93442 591-C6
SLOC 93442 611-G6
SLOC 93442 612-A6
SLOC 93445 714-C4
SLOC 93445 734-H1
SLOC 93445 755-B6
SLOC 93445 775-A3
SLOC 93452 324-F5
SLOC 93452 528-B2
StBC 93117 365-F5
StBC 93429 345-E11
StBC 93429 365-F5
StBC 93429 855-G6
StBC 93434 775-A7
StBC 93434 795-A2
StBC 93436 365-F5
StBC 93436 916-H1
StBC 93437 855-G6
StBC 93455 345-D10
StBC 93455 795-C5
StBC 93455 816-B4
CABRILLO LN
SLOC 93401 674-C5
CABRILLO PL
MOBY 93442 611-G7
CACHUMA DR
SLO 93401 653-J7
CACHUMA RD
StBC - 365-L1
StBC - 366-A1
CACIQUE ST
SBAR 93103 996-D4
CACTUS LN
CARP 93013 998-D7
CADDIE LN
PSRS 93446 513-J7
CADET PL
SLOC 93446 325-D7
SLOC 93446 534-J2
CADIZ CT
StBC 93111 994-G2
CAGNEY WY
LMPC 93436 896-F5
CAIN DR
StBC 93455 816-G5

CAIRE CIR
StBC 93111 994-H2
CALABAZA WY
SLOC 93446 494-F4
CALABRIA DR
SBAR 93105 995-E3
CALAVERAS AV
SLOC 93405 633-B5
StBC 93117 993-H2
CALETA AV
StBC 93117 994-D1
CALETA LN
ATAS 93422 574-A7
CALF CANYON HWY Rt#-58
SLOC 93422 325-D11
SLOC 93422 614-G3
SLOC 93432 325-D11
SLOC 93453 325-D11
SLOC 93453 614-G3
SLOC 93461 325-D11
SLOC 93465 325-D11
CALICO CT
Npmo 93444 755-J5
CALICO LN
StBC 93455 816-G7
CALIENTE AV
StBC 93254 806-B1
CALIFIA CT
StBC 93111 994-G3
CALIFORNIA BLVD
MonC 93451 453-A3
SLO 93401 654-A3
SLO 93405 653-J2
SLO 93405 654-A3
SLOC 93405 653-J2
SMRA 93455 816-F4
StBC 93437 855-F7
StBC 93437 875-D3
StBC 93455 816-F4
CALIFORNIA LN
SLOC 93446 514-C7
CALIFORNIA ST
ARGD 93420 714-J5
ARGD 93420 715-A6
SBAR 93103 996-A2
CALIMESA WY
SLOC 93420 735-D7
CALIMEX PL
Npmo 93444 755-J2
CALKINS RD
StBC 93441 900-H4
CALLE ABIERTA
StBC 93111 984-G6
CALLE ALAMO
SBAR 93105 985-G7
SBAR 93105 995-G1
CALLE ALLELA
SBAR 93109 995-G6
CALLE ALMONTE
SBAR 93109 995-G6
CALLE ANDALUCIA
SBAR 93109 995-G5
CALLE ANZUELO
StBC 93111 984-G7
CALLE APAREJO
StBC 93111 984-H7
CALLE ARENA
CARP 93013 1018-E1
CALLE ASILO
StBC 93111 984-G7
CALLE BARQUERO
StBC 93111 984-G7
CALLE BELLO
SBAR 93108 996-E2
CALLE BENDITA
SLOC 93420 754-J2
CALLE BOC DEL CANON
SBAR 93101 995-G4
CALLE BONITA
SMRA 93455 796-J5
StBC 93441 901-A4
StBC 93460 901-A5
CALLE BREVO
SBAR 93109 996-A7
CALLE CABALLO
SLOC 93422 594-C4
CALLE CAMARADA
StBC 93110 994-J3
CALLE CANON
SBAR 93101 995-G5
SBAR 93109 995-G5
CALLE CAPISTRANO
SBAR 93105 995-G1
CALLE CARIDAD
StBC 93110 985-C6
CALLE CARMAN
ARGD 93420 714-H4

CALLE CEDRO
SBAR 93105 985-G7
CALLE CERRITO
SBAR 93101 995-G5
CALLE CERRITO ALTO
SBAR 93101 995-H5
CALLE CERRO
SBAR 93101 995-G5
CALLE CESAR CHAVEZ
SBAR 93103 996-C4
CALLE CIELO
Npmo 93444 755-H6
CALLE CINCO
StBC 93436 896-H1
CALLE CITA
SBAR 93105 985-E7
SBAR 93110 985-E7
StBC 93110 985-E7
CALLE CONSUETTA
PBCH 93449 693-G6
CALLE CORDONIZ
SLOC 93402 631-H7
SLOC 93402 651-J1
CALLE CORDOVA
PBCH 93449 693-G6
CALLE COREA
PBCH 93449 693-G6
CALLE CORTE
SBAR 93101 995-G5
CALLE CORTITA
SBAR 93109 995-H5
CALLE CORTO
SMRA 93454 777-C7
CALLE CRESPIS
SBAR 93105 995-G1
CALLE CRISTOBAL
StBC 93111 994-G2
CALLE CROTALO
SLOC 93401 654-D7
CALLE CUERVO
ARGD 93420 714-H3
CALLE CULEBRA
Summ 93067 997-D3
CALLE CYNTHIA
ATAS 93422 594-C1
CALLE DEBRON
SLOC 93420 735-E4
CALLE DE CAMPO
SMRA 93454 777-A7
CALLE DE ESTRELLAS
CARP 93013 1018-G1
CALLE DE FRANCISCO
SLOC 93446 513-B1
CALLE DE LA LUNA
CARP 93013 1018-G1
CALLE DE LA MAR
CARP 93013 1018-G1
CALLE DE LA MONTANA
CARP 93013 1018-G1
CALLE DEL CAMINOS
SLO 93401 674-C2
SLOC 93401 674-C2
CALLE DEL ESPACIO
CARP 93013 1018-G1
CALLE DEL NORTE
CARP 93013 1018-G1
CALLE DEL ORO
SBAR 93109 995-H6
CALLE DE LOS AMIGOS
SBAR 93105 995-E3
StBC 93105 995-E3
CALLE DE LOS DESCA
SLOC 93420 714-J7
SLOC 93420 735-A7
CALLE DE LOS SUEI
SLOC 93420 714-H7
CALLE DE LOS VIENTOS
CARP 93013 1018-G1
CALLE DEL SOL
CARP 93013 1018-G1
Npmo 93444 755-H6
SBAR 93101 995-H5
CALLE DEL SUR
CARP 93013 1018-G1
CALLE DIA
CARP 93013 1018-E1
CALLE DIEZ
StBC 93436 876-H7
CALLE DOS
SLOC 93445 734-G1
CALLE DUENDE
SLOC 93420 735-E4
CALLE ECUESTRE
StBC 93117 982-C4
CALLE ELEGANTE
StBC 93108 996-E1
CALLE ESPERANZA
SBAR 93105 995-E2

CALLE FRESA
Npmo 93444 755-F3
CALLE FRESNO
SBAR 93105 985-G7
CALLE GALICIA
SBAR 93109 995-G6
CALLE GRANADA
PBCH 93449 693-G6
SBAR 93105 985-G7
SBAR 93105 995-G1
CALLE GRANDE CIR
SMRA 93455 796-H5
CALLE HERMOSA
StBC 93108 996-E1
CALLE JAZMIN
SLO 93401 653-J7
CALLE JOAQUIN
SLO 93401 673-G1
SLO 93405 673-G2
SLOC 93401 673-G1
SLOC 93405 673-G2
CALLEJON AV
CARP 93013 1018-D1
CALLE LAGUNA
SLOC 93420 735-C6
CALLE LAS CALERAS
SBAR 93109 995-D5
CALLE LAURELES
SBAR 93105 985-G7
SBAR 93105 995-G1
SMRA 93458 796-E4
CALLE LINARES
SBAR 93109 995-G6
CALLE LINDERO
StBC 93436 876-H7
CALLE LIPPIZANA
StBC 93117 982-C4
CALLE LORA
StBC 93436 896-H2
CALLE LOS CHARROS
SLOC 93446 533-J4
SLOC 93446 534-A4
CALLE LUARDO
StBC 93111 994-G2
CALLE LUPITA
StBC 93111 984-G7
CALLE MADERA
SLO 93401 653-J7
CALLE MALAGA
SBAR 93105 985-G7
CALLE MALVA
SLO 93401 653-J7
CALLE MANZANITA
SBAR 93105 985-G7
SBAR 93105 995-G1
CALLE MARANA
StBC 93436 876-H7
CALLE MARGARITA
SMRA 93458 796-E4
CALLE MARIPOSA
SBAR 93105 985-G7
CALLE MASTIL
StBC 93111 984-G7
CALLE MIRASOL
SMRA 93458 796-E4
CALLE MIRO
StBC 93436 896-H2
CALLE MONTILLA
SBAR 93109 995-G5
CALLE MORELIA
StBC 93111 994-G2
CALLENDER RD
Npmo 93444 735-B7
SLOC 93420 734-H7
SLOC 93420 735-A7
CALLE NETO
StBC 93436 876-H7
CALLE NOGUERA
SBAR 93105 985-F7
SBAR 93105 995-G1
CALLE NUEVE
StBC 93436 876-J7
CALLE OCHO
CARP 93013 998-E7
CARP 93013 1018-E1
CALLE PACIFIC
CARP 93013 1018-E1
CALLE PALO COLORADO
SBAR 93105 985-G7
SBAR 93105 995-G1
CALLE PASADO
StBC 93436 896-G1
CALLE PATTITO
SLOC 93446 534-A4
CALLE PEQUENO
SMRA 93454 777-C7
CALLE PICO CT
StBC 93460 921-A6

CALLE PINON
SBAR 93105 985-G7
CALLE PONIENTE
SBAR 93101 995-G4
CALLE PORTOS
StBC 93436 896-H2
CALLE PRIMERA
StBC 93436 896-H2
CALLE PROPANO
SLOC 93446 533-F4
CALLE PUERTA VALLARTA
SBAR 93103 996-D4
CALLE QUARTA
StBC 93436 896-G2
CALLE QUATRO
SLOC 93445 734-G1
CALLE QUEBRADA
StBC 93117 982-D4
CALLE REAL
SBAR 93105 995-G3
StBC 93105 995-F3
StBC 93110 984-J7
StBC 93110 994-J1
StBC 93110 995-C1
StBC 93111 984-G7
StBC 93111 994-F1
StBC 93117 981-G4
StBC 93117 982-C5
StBC 93117 993-C2
StBC 93117 994-C1
CALLE REAL Rt#-154
SBAR 93110 995-D1
StBC 93110 995-D1
CALLE REFUGIO
ATAS 93422 574-A6
CALLE REINA
StBC 93110 994-J3
CALLE REY MAR
CARP 93013 1018-E1
CALLE RINCONADA
SBAR 93105 985-G7
CALLE ROSALES
SBAR 93105 985-F7
SBAR 93105 995-G1
CALLE SEGUNDA
StBC 93436 896-G2
CALLE SEIS
StBC 93436 896-H1
CALLE SERENA
SMRA 93455 796-H5
CALLE SERRENTO
StBC 93117 993-E1
CALLE SIETE
StBC 93436 876-H7
CALLE SONIA
StBC 93111 994-H2
CALLE SORIA
SBAR 93109 995-G5
CALLE TANIA
StBC 93111 994-H2
CALLE TERCERA
StBC 93436 896-G2
CALLE TRES
SLOC 93445 734-G1
CALLE UNO
SLOC 93445 734-G1
CALLE VALENCIA
PBCH 93449 693-G6
CALLIE CT
ARGD 93420 715-B4
CALLISTO LN
Npmo 93444 756-A5
CALOR DR
BLTN 93427 919-G5
CALVERT AV
LMPC 93436 896-F5
CALVIN CT
GBCH 93433 714-E6
CALZADA AV
StBC 93441 901-B5
StBC 93460 901-B5
StBC 93460 921-B1
CAMATTA CREEK RD
SLOC 92389 325-G9
SLOC 93453 325-G9
SLOC 93461 325-G9
CAMBORNE PL
Cmbr 93428 548-G1
CAMBRIA
SLO 93401 653-J7
CAMBRIA AV
StBC 93455 816-J2
CAMBRIA RD
Cmbr 93428 528-F6
CAMBRIA WY
SBAR 93105 995-E3
CAMBRIA PINES RD
Cmbr 93428 528-D5

CAMBRIDGE CT
StBC 93455 816-G4
CAMBRIDGE DR
LMPC 93436 916-E3
StBC 93111 984-F7
StBC 93117 984-F7
StBC 93117 994-F1
CAMBRIDGE LN
CARP 93013 998-E6
CAMBRIDGE ST
Cmbr 93428 528-E6
CAMBRIDGE WY
StBC 93454 797-C7
CAMDEN CT
SLO 93401 654-B6
CAMDEN PL
StBC 93117 984-E7
CAMDEN ST
LMPC 93436 916-G2
CAMELLIA CIR
CARP 93013 998-C6
CAMELLIA CT
LMPC 93436 896-D6
SLO 93401 653-J7
CAMELLIA LN
SBAR 93110 995-D1
StBC 93437 875-H3
CAMELOT DR
StBC 93455 816-F4
CAMEO DR
StBC 93455 817-B5
CAMEO PL
StBC 93455 816-G5
CAMEO RD
CARP 93013 998-E7
CAMEO WY
SLOC 93420 734-J4
CAMERON AV
SMRA 93455 796-G6
CAMERON CT
ARGD 93420 714-H6
CAMETA WY
StBC 93110 995-A1
CAMILLIA DR
Npmo 93444 756-A5
CAMINO ALDEA
StBC 93111 994-G2
CAMINO AL MAR AL
SBAR 93109 995-J7
CAMINO ALTO
SBAR 93103 996-C1
CAMINO ALTOZANO
StBC 93111 984-F5
CAMINO ANDALUZ
StBC 93111 984-F5
CAMINO ARROYO
StBC 93460 921-B5
CAMINO CABALLO
Npmo 93444 755-E3
Npmo 93444 756-A2
CAMINO CALMA
SBAR 93109 995-H6
CAMINO CAMPANA
StBC 93111 984-F6
CAMINO CARRETA
StBC 93013 1018-H2
CAMINO CASADA
StBC 93111 984-F6
CAMINO CASETA
StBC 93117 984-B7
CAMINO CERRALVO
StBC 93111 984-F5
CAMINO CIELO
StBC 93105 986-B1
E CAMINO CIELO
StBC - 987-J5
StBC 93105 366-C6
StBC 93105 964-J4
StBC 93105 986-A1
StBC 93105 987-C2
StBC 93108 987-G4
W CAMINO CIELO
StBC 93105 365-L6
StBC 93105 366-A6
StBC 93105 964-E6
StBC 93460 365-L6
CAMINO CODORNIZ
Npmo 93444 755-H3
CAMINO COLEGIO
SMRA 93454 796-F2
SMRA 93458 796-F2
W CAMINO COLEGIO
SMRA 93454 796-G2
SMRA 93458 796-G2
CAMINO CONTENTO
SLOC 93420 734-J4
CAMINO CONTIGO
StBC 93111 984-F7
CAMINO CORTO
StBC 93117 993-J4

CAMINO DE ARBOLES
SLOC 93420 755-A2
CAMINO DEL MIRASOL
StBC 93110 985-B6
CAMINO DEL ORO
Npmo 93444 755-H5
CAMINO DEL REMEDIO
StBC 93110 985-A7
StBC 93110 995-A1
CAMINO DEL RETIRO
StBC 93110 985-B6
CAMINO DEL REY
SLOC 93420 734-J4
StBC 93110 994-J3
CAMINO DEL RIO
StBC 93110 985-B5
CAMINO DEL ROBLE
ATAS 93422 553-E6
StBC 93110 995-A2
CAMINO DEL ROSARIO
StBC 93108 997-D1
CAMINO DEL SUR
StBC 93117 994-A4
CAMINO DE PLAZA
ARGD 93420 714-G4
CAMINO DE UNOS
SLOC 93420 734-J4
CAMINO DE VIDA
StBC 93111 994-J1
CAMINO EDNA
SLOC 93401 694-J2
CAMINO ENCANTO
Npmo 93444 735-J4
Npmo 93444 736-A4
CAMINO ESCONDIDO
SLOC 93420 735-C4
CAMINO FLORAL
StBC 93111 994-H4
CAMINO GALEANA
StBC 93111 984-F5
CAMINO LAGUNA VISTA
StBC 93117 984-B7
CAMINO LINDO
StBC 93117 993-J5
CAMINO LOBO
PSRS 93446 514-A7
PSRS 93446 534-A1
CAMINO MAJORCA
StBC 93117 993-J5
CAMINO MANADERO
StBC 93111 984-F5
CAMINO MEDIO
StBC 93110 995-C3
CAMINO MELENO
StBC 93111 984-F5
CAMINO MERCADO
ARGD 93420 714-H4
CAMINO MOLINERO
StBC 93110 985-A6
CAMINO PALOMERA
StBC 93111 984-F5
CAMINO PERRILLO
SLOC 93420 735-D6
CAMINO PESCADERO
StBC 93117 994-A4
CAMINO RIO VERDE
StBC 93111 984-F5
CAMINO ROBLE
Npmo 93444 755-J3
CAMINO SAN CARLOS
StBC 93427 919-H2
CAMINO TALAVERA
StBC 93117 984-C7
CAMINO TRILLADO
CARP 93013 998-E6
CAMINO VENTUROSO
StBC 93117 984-B7
CAMINO VERDE
SBAR 93103 996-C1
CAMINO VIEJO
SBAR 93108 996-G2
StBC 93108 996-G2
CAMINO VIVIENTE
StBC 93117 984-B7
CAMLIN CT
StBC 93455 816-F5
CAMMATTI-SHANDON RD
SLOC 92389 325-G7
SLOC 93461 325-G7
CAMP LN
GDLP 93434 774-J6
CAMP WY
SLOC 93451 453-C6
CAMP 8 RD
SLOC 93446 325-D7
CAMPANA PL
ARGD 93420 715-B3

STREET
Name City ZIP Pg-Grid

CAMPANIL DR
SBAR 93109 995-D5
SBAR 93110 995-D4
CAMPBELL LN
ATAS 93422 573-G1
CAMPBELL RD
StBC 93436 365-G3
CAMPESINO DR
StBC 93117 993-E2
CAMPHOR CT
StBC 93437 875-J1
CAMPHOR PL
StBC 93108 996-J2
CAMPHOR ST
StBC 93437 875-H1
CAMPO RD
ATAS 93422 573-E1
CAMPONDONICO AV
GDLP 93434 775-A6
CAMPO VISTA DR
StBC 93111 994-J1
CAMPUS WY
SLOC 93405 653-J2
W CAMPUS POINT LN
StBC 93117 993-J5
CAMUESA RD
StBC - 366-E6
StBC - 987-J1
StBC 93105 366-C5
CANADA ST
SBAR 93103 996-D2
CANADA ESTE RD
StBC 93460 901-B5
CANALINO DR
CARP 93013 1018-D1
CANDELABRA PL
SLOC 93401 674-D5
CANDELEROS
SMRA 93455 796-H5
CANDICE CT
SLOC 93420 715-B7
CANDLEWOOD CT
PSRS 93446 533-J1
CANET RD
SLOC 93405 632-D1
CANFIELD AV
LMPC 93436 896-F5
CANFIELD CT
LMPC 93436 896-E5
StBC 93436 896-E5
CANFIELD DR
LMPC 93436 896-F5
StBC 93436 896-F5
CANFIELD LN
LMPC 93436 896-E5
SMRA 93454 796-H3
CANNON GREEN DR
StBC 93117 993-G3
CANON DR
SBAR 93105 985-F7
SBAR 93105 995-F1
StBC 93110 995-D3
CANON PERDIDO
SBAR 93101 995-J5
SBAR 93101 996-A4
SBAR 93103 996-B2
SBAR 93109 995-J5
CANON VIEW RD
StBC 93108 986-E7
StBC 93108 996-D1
CANTATA LN
StBC 93455 817-C7
CANTERA AV
StBC 93110 995-C4
CANTERBERRY
SLO 93401 673-H1
CANTERBURY LN
Cmbr 93428 528-E5
CANVASBACK PL
SLOC 93424 693-B2
CANYON DR
SMRA 93454 777-A5
CANYON RD
StBC - 346-C8
CANYON WY
ARGD 93420 714-J3
ARGD 93420 715-A3
CANYON ACRES DR
SBAR 93105 985-F7
CANYON CREST LN
PSRS 93446 513-G7
PSRS 93446 533-G1
CAPANNA CT
PBCH 93449 714-D2
CAPANNA ST
PBCH 93449 714-D3
CAPELLA DR
StBC 93436 876-C7
CAPELLINA WY
StBC 93111 984-F6

CAPISTRANO AV
ATAS 93422 573-J3
PBCH 93449 693-H7
CAPISTRANO AV Rt#-41
ATAS 93422 573-J3
ATAS 93422 574-A2
CAPISTRANO CT
GBCH 93433 714-F6
SLO 93405 653-D6
CAPISTRANO LN
SMRA 93455 796-H6
CAPITOL DR
SMRA 93454 776-J7
SMRA 93454 796-J1
CAPITOLA ST
GBCH 93433 714-F7
CAPITOL HILL
PSRS 93446 513-H5
CAPITOLIO WY
SLO 93401 654-B7
CAPRI DR
SBAR 93105 985-E7
SBAR 93105 995-E1
CAPRI ST
MOBY 93442 611-E2
CAPRICORN CT
StBC 93436 876-C6
CAPSTAN CIR
SLOC 93426 469-J2
CAPTAINS CIR
SLOC 93426 469-J1
CAPTAINS WK
SLOC 93426 469-J1
CARAWAY CT
StBC 93455 817-B6
CARBO CIR
StBC 93111 994-H3
CARBO RD
SLOC 93422 594-D6
CARBON CANYON TR
SLOC 93465 553-B5
CARDIFF DR
Cmbr 93428 548-G2
CARDIFF LN
StBC 93455 817-A2
CARDINAL AV
StBC 93117 994-E1
CARDINAL CT
ARGD 93420 714-G3
CARDINAL WY
PSRS 93446 534-A2
CARDO WY
Npmo 93444 755-D5
CARIBOU WY
StBC 93455 816-G7
CARILLO ST
Npmo 93444 756-C2
CARINA DR
StBC 93436 876-C7
StBC 93436 896-C1
CARINO CT
PSRS 93446 513-J3
CARISSA CT
SLO 93401 673-H2
StBC 93455 816-H4
CARISSA LN
StBC 93437 875-J3
CARLA CT
SLO 93401 654-C6
SMRA 93454 776-J6
CARLIN DR
GDLP 93434 774-J6
CARLISLE DR
StBC 93117 993-F2
CARLO DR
StBC 93117 984-C7
StBC 93117 994-D1
CARLOTTI DR
SMRA 93454 776-J5
CARLSON ST
StBC 93455 816-G5
CARLTON WY
SBAR 93109 995-G6
CARMEL CT
GBCH 93433 714-F6
MOBY 93442 611-G7
CARMEL LN
SMRA 93454 776-J5
CARMEL RD
SLOC 93422 594-E2
CARMEL ST
MOBY 93442 611-G7
SLO 93401 653-J5
CARMEL BEACH CIR
StBC 93117 993-F3
CARMELDE LN
GBCH 93433 714-D4
CARMELITA AV
ATAS 93422 573-H5

CARMELITA AV
ATAS 93422 593-F1
SBAR 93101 996-A2
CARMELLA DR
ARGD 93420 714-G6
CARMEN LN
SMRA 93454 796-G4
SMRA 93458 796-E4
CARMENITA CT
SMRA 93458 796-G4
CARNATION PL
CARP 93013 998-D6
CARNER CT
PSRS 93446 513-J7
CAROB ST
StBC 93437 875-J1
CAROL AV
StBC 93110 985-D7
CAROL PL
ARGD 93420 714-G6
CAROLDALE LN
StBC 93117 984-B7
CAROLDALE PL
StBC 93117 984-B7
CAROLYN CT
Npmo 93444 756-C4
CAROLYN DR
SLO 93405 653-E7
CAROLYNE WY
StBC 93455 817-A4
CAROSAM RD
StBC 93110 995-C3
CARPENTER ST
SLO 93405 653-J2
CARPENTER CANYON RD Rt#-227
SLOC 93401 694-G1
SLOC 93420 694-G3
SLOC 93420 695-A6
SLOC 93420 715-A1
CARPINTERIA AV
CARP 93013 998-C6
CARP 93013 1018-F1
CARPINTERIA ST
SBAR 93103 996-D4
CARPINTERIA CREEK DR
CARP 93013 998-E7
CARP 93013 1018-E1
CARRIAGE DR
StBC 93463 920-J7
CARRIAGE LN
SLOC 93420 695-C6
CARRIAGE HILL DR
StBC 93110 995-A2
CARRILLO RD
SBAR 93103 996-B2
CARRILLO ST
SBAR 93101 995-H5
SBAR 93101 996-A4
SBAR 93103 996-B2
SBAR 93109 995-H5
CARRISA HWY Rt#-58
SLOC - 345-L1
SLOC - 346-A1
SLOC 92389 325-H11
SLOC 93453 325-F9
SLOC 93453 345-L1
SLOC 93453 346-A1
SLOC 93461 325-F9
CARRIZO RD
ATAS 93422 553-E6
SBAR 93105 985-F7
SBAR 93105 995-F1
CARSON ST
StBC 93117 994-E2
CASA PL
SLOC 93445 734-G1
CASA ST
SLO 93405 653-J2
CASA DORINDA
StBC 93108 996-H3
CASALS DR
PSRS 93446 513-J7
CASANOVA AV
ATAS 93422 573-F7
CASA REAL PL
Npmo 93444 755-H6
CASCABEL RD
ATAS 93422 573-F4
CASCADA LN
Npmo 93444 755-H3
CASCADA RD
ATAS 93422 574-A6
SLOC 93422 593-F3
CASCADE LN
SLOC 93446 471-B5
CASELLI WY
SMRA 93455 796-J7

CASETA WY
StBC 93117 984-B7
CASEY AV
StBC 93460 921-D1
CASIANO DR
SBAR 93105 995-E3
CASITAS AV
ATAS 93422 573-G7
MOBY 93442 611-F3
CASITAS CT
SLO 93405 653-D6
CASITAS LN
CARP 93013 998-E7
CASITAS RD
SBAR 93103 996-C2
CASITAS ST
SLOC 93445 734-G1
CASITAS PASS RD
CARP 93013 998-E7
StBC 93013 998-E7
CASITAS PASS RD Rt#-150
StBC 93013 366-G9
StBC 93013 999-C7
VeCo - 999-C7
VeCo 93001 999-C7
VeCo 93013 999-C7
CASITAS PASS RD Rt#-192
StBC 93013 366-G9
StBC 93013 998-G6
StBC 93013 1018-J1
CASPER CT
PSRS 93446 533-J1
CASPER RD
SLOC 93465 553-C2
CASPIA LN
Summ 93067 997-E4
CASS AV
SLOC 93430 591-A2
CASS PL
SBAR 93117 994-C2
CASTAIC
SLO 93401 653-J7
CASTAIC AV
PBCH 93449 693-H7
CASTANO AV
ATAS 93422 574-B3
CASTEEL LN
SLOC 93465 553-B3
CASTENADA LN
ATAS 93422 593-G1
CASTILIAN DR
StBC 93117 993-J2
StBC 93117 994-A2
CASTILLO CT
ARGD 93420 714-H2
SLO 93405 653-D6
CASTILLO RD
SLOC 93401 673-D5
SLOC 93405 673-D5
CASTILLO ST
SBAR 93101 995-H3
SBAR 93101 996-A4
SBAR 93105 995-H3
CASTILLO ST Rt#-225
SBAR 93101 996-B5
CASTLE LN
SMRA 93454 776-J7
CASTLE ST
Cmbr 93428 548-F2
CASTLEROCK LN
SMRA 93455 796-G6
CAT LN
SMRA 93454 777-B5
CATALINA DR
SLO 93405 653-G3
CATALPA ST
ATAS 93422 574-B7
StBC 93437 855-G7
CATANIA WY
SBAR 93105 995-E3
CATARINA ST
StBC 93460 921-C5
CAT CANYON RD
StBC 93440 365-G1
StBC 93454 345-G11
CATE MESA RD
StBC 93013 998-H6
CATHEDRAL LN
SLOC 93420 715-A7
CATHEDRAL CANYON CT
PSRS 93446 533-J2
CATHEDRAL OAKS RD
StBC 93110 984-E6
StBC 93110 985-A6
StBC 93111 984-E6
StBC 93111 985-A6

CATHEDRAL OAKS RD
StBC 93117 984-E6
StBC 93117 993-G1
StBC 93117 994-A1
CATHEDRAL OAKS RD Rt#-192
StBC 93110 985-C6
CATHEDRAL POINTE LN
StBC 93111 984-G6
CATLIN CIR
CARP 93013 998-C6
CATRINA WY
SMRA 93458 776-G6
CATTAIL RD
SLOC 93465 533-E7
SLOC 93465 553-E1
CATTLEMAN WY
SLOC 93446 534-A2
CATTLE RUN LN
SLOC 93420 695-D5
CAUDILL ST
SLO 93401 654-A6
CAVALIER LN
SLO 93405 653-F7
CAVE LANDING RD
SLOC 93424 693-B3
CAYUCOS AV
ATAS 93422 573-G2
SLOC 93430 591-A2
SLOC 93465 553-D1
CAYUCOS DR
SLO 93405 653-G7
SLO 93405 673-F1
SLOC 93430 590-J1
SLOC 93430 591-A1
CAYUCOS RD
SLOC 93430 590-J1
SLOC 93430 591-A1
CAYUCOS CREEK RD
SLOC 93430 324-K9
SLOC 93430 590-J1
SLOC 93435 324-K8
CAZADERO ST
SLO 93401 654-B3
CEBADA PL
SLOC 93451 473-E4
CEBADA RD
ATAS 93422 573-D2
CEBADA CANYON RD
StBC 93436 365-F3
CEBRIAN AV
StBC 93254 806-B1
CECCHETTI RD
SLOC 93420 715-F1
CECELIA CT
SLO 93401 654-B5
CECELIA DR
SMRA 93454 796-J3
CECIL CT
PSRS 93446 513-H5
CEDAR
SLO 93401 673-H1
CEDAR AV
MOBY 93442 611-E2
CEDAR CT
SLO 93401 654-C6
CEDAR LN
SBAR 93108 996-D2
CEDAR PL
CARP 93013 998-D7
CEDAR RD
SMRA 93458 776-G4
CEDAR ST
ARGD 93420 714-G5
GDLP 93434 775-A6
StBC 93437 855-E6
StBC 93460 921-B5
CEDARHURST DR
StBC 93455 817-A3
CEDAR VISTA
SBAR 93105 985-E7
SBAR 93110 985-E7
N CEDARWOOD AV
Npmo 93444 756-C1
S CEDARWOOD AV
Npmo 93444 756-D2
CEDARWOOD DR
PSRS 93446 534-A1
CELESTIAL WY
SLOC 93465 553-C1
CELINE DR
SBAR 93105 985-F6
CEMETERY RD
ATAS 93422 574-A2
SLOC 93451 473-E3
CENCERO RD
ATAS 93422 573-A3
SLOC 93422 573-A3

CENEGAL RD
ATAS 93422 573-D5
CENTAUR AV
StBC 93436 876-C6
CENTENNIAL ST
SMRA 93454 777-B6
StBC 93440 878-G1
CENTER AV
StBC 93105 985-E6
StBC 93110 985-E6
CENTER CT
MOBY 93442 611-G7
CENTER LN
SLO 93401 673-H1
CENTER ST
Cmbr 93428 528-G7
SLOC 93405 653-J3
S CENTERPOINTE PKWY
SMRA 93454 796-H5
SMRA 93455 796-H5
CENTINELA LN
SBAR 93109 995-D4
CENTRA RD
SLOC 93451 473-D5
CENTRAL AV
BLTN 93427 919-H5
SMRA 93454 796-J1
E CENTRAL AV
LMPC 93436 896-E6
W CENTRAL AV
LMPC 93436 896-C5
StBC 93436 895-E5
StBC 93436 896-A5
CENTRAL PARK DR
SMRA 93458 776-G3
CENTRE ST Rt#-41
SLOC 93461 325-F6
CENTURY LN
SLOC 93420 715-A7
CENTURY ST
SMRA 93455 796-F5
CERCIS LN
StBC 93437 875-J3
CERRITO LN
StBC 93110 985-D6
CERRITO PL
MOBY 93442 611-F7
CERRITO ST
StBC 93460 921-B4
CERRO CT
SLO 93405 653-G2
CERRO ALTO RD
SLOC - 593-A5
SLOC 92389 325-A10
CERRO GORDO AV
SLOC 93430 591-C4
CERRO ROMAULDO AV
SLO 93405 653-G2
CERRO VISTA CIR
ARGD 93420 714-J6
CERRO VISTA DR
PBCH 93449 714-D3
CERRO VISTA LN
ARGD 93420 714-H6
CERVANTES RD
StBC 93117 994-A4
CERVATO WY
StBC 93111 984-J7
CHABO LN
SLOC 93420 694-G7
CHADWELL DR
SMRA 93454 777-B7
CHADWICK WY
StBC 93117 984-D7
CHALFONTE CT
SMRA 93454 797-A1
CHALK HILL RD
SLVG 93463 920-E7
StBC 93463 920-E7
CHAMISAL LN
SLOC 93420 735-A3
CHAMPAGNE LN
SLOC 93446 494-J7
CHAMPIONS LN
Npmo 93444 755-D1
CHANCELLOR ST
StBC 93455 817-C7
CHANDLER LN
ATAS 93422 593-H1
CHANDLER RD
StBC 93436 896-G3
CHANDLER ST
SLO 93401 654-A6
StBC 93110 994-J2
CHANEY AV
CARP 93013 998-C6
SLOC 93430 591-C5
CHANNEL DR
SBAR 93108 996-F4

CHANNEL DR
SMRA 93458 776-G4
StBC 93108 996-F4
CHANNEL ISLANDS RD
StBC 93106 994-C5
CHANNING LN
LMPC 93436 896-E5
CHANNING WY
SBAR 93109 995-G6
CHAPALA ST
SBAR 93101 995-H2
SBAR 93101 996-A3
SBAR 93105 995-H2
CHAPARRAL CIR
SLO 93401 674-D1
CHAPARRAL LN
ARGD 93420 714-J3
Npmo 93444 756-A2
SLOC 93446 471-C6
CHAPARRAL RD
SLOC 93402 631-J7
SLOC 93446 534-G3
CHAPARRAL ST
SMRA 93454 796-H2
CHAPEL ST
SMRA 93454 776-J7
SMRA 93454 777-A7
SMRA 93458 776-G7
StBC 93111 994-G2
CHAPLIN CIR
LMPC 93436 896-E5
CHAPLIN LN
SLO 93405 654-A2
CHAPMAN DR
GDLP 93434 774-J6
CHAPMAN PL
StBC 93117 993-G3
CHAPPARAL DR
CARP 93013 998-C5
CHARING LN
Cmbr 93428 528-E5
CHARLES DR
SLOC 93401 674-E7
CHARLES ST
GBCH 93433 714-E4
CHARLIE LN
SMRA 93454 777-B5
CHARLOTTE DR
SMRA 93454 776-J6
CHARLOTTE LN
StBC 93105 985-J7
CHAROLAIS RD
PSRS 93446 533-G1
PSRS 93446 534-A2
SLOC 93446 533-G1
SLOC 93446 534-A2
CHARRO WY
Npmo 93444 755-H4
CHARTER CT
StBC 93455 817-A4
CHASE DR
SBAR 93108 996-D2
CHATA ST
Npmo 93444 756-A4
CHATEAUX ELISE
SBAR 93109 995-H7
CHATHAM LN
Cmbr 93428 528-D6
CHATHAM WY
StBC 93455 817-A2
CHAUNCEY ST
SLOC 93446 533-G5
CHAUPLIN AV
ATAS 93422 573-G4
CHELHAM WY
StBC 93108 986-E7
StBC 93108 996-E1
CHELSEA CT
ARGD 93420 714-G5
CHELSEA LN
Cmbr 93428 528-D5
CHELTENHAM RD
StBC 93105 985-H7
CHENANGO CT
StBC 93117 993-J2
CHERIMOYA WY
StBC 93108 997-F2
CHERISH LN
SLOC 93465 553-E1
CHEROKEE CT
PSRS 93446 513-H6
CHEROKEE PL
Npmo 93444 735-J7
Npmo 93444 755-H1
CHERRY AV
StBC 93455 816-J5
E CHERRY AV
ARGD 93420 715-C4
LMPC 93436 896-E7

W CHERRY AV
ARGD 93420 715-A6
LMPC 93436 896-C7
CHERRY ST
PSRS 93446 513-F6
StBC 93437 855-D6
CHERRY BLOSSOM PL
Npmo 93444 756-E7
CHERRY HILL DR
StBC 93455 817-A2
CHERRY HILL RD
StBC 93455 817-A2
CHERRY WOOD
BLTN 93427 919-G5
CHESAPEAKE PL
SLOC 93420 735-C6
CHESTER LN
Cmbr 93428 548-F2
CHESTNUT AV
SLOC 93422 594-G6
E CHESTNUT AV
LMPC 93436 916-F1
W CHESTNUT AV
LMPC 93436 916-B1
E CHESTNUT CT
LMPC 93436 916-G1
CHESTNUT LN
SMRA 93458 776-G4
CHESTNUT ST
PSRS 93446 513-F4
StBC 93437 855-G7
E CHESTNUT ST
Npmo 93444 756-C1
W CHESTNUT ST
Npmo 93444 756-C2
CHEYENNE DR
PSRS 93446 513-H6
CHEYENNE LN
StBC 93460 921-B4
CHIA PL
SLOC 93465 594-F2
CHIANTI CT
SLOC 93465 553-C3
CHICA DR
SLOC 93420 734-H5
CHICAGO WY
SLOC 93451 453-C6
CHICO AV
SLOC 93405 633-E5
CHICO RD
ATAS 93422 553-G7
CHICORY LN
PSRS 93446 514-A6
CHILON WY
StBC 93110 995-A1
CHILTON ST
ARGD 93420 714-G4
CHIMNEY CANYON RD
SLOC 93454 345-H6
StBC 93454 345-H6
CHIMNEY ROCK RD
SLOC 93446 324-J5
SLOC 93446 325-A5
CHINA FLAT RD
StBC 93108 997-C2
CHINO ST
SBAR 93101 995-G3
CHIQUITA RD
SBAR 93103 996-C2
CHISMAHOO RD
VeCo - 999-C7
VeCo 93013 999-C7
CHISPA RD
SLOC 93422 594-G3
SLOC 93465 594-G3
CHISWICK WY
Cmbr 93428 528-D5
CHOLAME RD
SLOC 92389 325-F2
SLOC 93461 325-F2
CHOLARE RD
ATAS 93422 573-B6
SLOC 93422 573-B6
CHORRO ST
SLO 93401 653-J4
SLO 93401 654-A5
SLO 93405 653-H2
N CHORRO ST
SLO 93405 653-H2
CHORRO CREEK RD
SLOC - 612-A7
SLOC 93442 612-A7
CHORRO VALLEY RD
SLOC 93405 632-J4
SLOC 93405 633-A5
CHRISTINA ST
SMRA 93454 776-H6
CHRISTINA WY
PBCH 93449 714-F3
SLO 93405 653-G2

CHRISTINE PL
SLOC 93420 695-C6
CHRISTOPHER DR
StBC 93436 896-G2
CHRISTOPHER LN
SMRA 93454 777-B7
CHRSTMAS TREE PL
SLOC 93445 734-H1
CHULA VISTA DR
SLOC 93430 591-C4
CHUMASH CT
PSRS 93446 513-H6
CHUMASH DR
SLO 93401 653-J7
CHUMASH LN
SLOC 93402 651-J1
CHUPAROSA DR
SBAR 93105 995-F1
CHUPARROSA DR
SLO 93401 673-G2
CHURCH LN
CARP 93013 998-D7
CHURCH ST
SLO 93401 653-J5
SLO 93401 654-A5
E CHURCH ST
SMRA 93454 776-H7
SMRA 93454 777-A7
W CHURCH ST
SMRA 93458 776-F7
CIELITO LN
SBAR 93105 986-B6
CIELO AV
StBC 93111 984-E6
StBC 93117 984-E6
CIELO CT
PSRS 93446 513-J3
CIELO LN
Npmo 93444 756-B6
CIELO LINDO
PBCH 93449 693-H7
CIENAGA ST Rt#-1
SLOC 93420 734-H1
SLOC 93445 734-H1
CIENEGUITAS RD
SBAR 93110 985-C7
StBC 93110 985-C7
CIMA CT
SLO 93401 653-J6
CIMA LINDA LN
SBAR 93108 996-E3
CIMARRON DR
StBC 93460 921-B4
CIMARRON WY
Npmo 93444 735-H4
SLOC 93402 632-B7
SLOC 93402 652-B1
SLOC 93420 735-H4
CINCO AMIGOS
SBAR 93105 995-E2
CINDERELLA LN
StBC 93111 994-G2
CINDY LN
CARP 93013 1018-H1
CINNABAR CT
StBC 93455 816-J5
StBC 93455 817-A5
CIRCLE DR
SBAR 93108 986-E7
SLOC 93405 653-J1
SLOC 93430 591-B3
CIRCLE LN
SLOC 93430 591-B3
CIRCLE B RD
PSRS 93446 514-A1
SLOC 93446 513-J1
SLOC 93446 514-A1
CIRCLE OAK DR
ATAS 93422 574-B7
ATAS 93422 594-B1
SLOC 93426 469-H2
CIRRUS WY
PSRS 93446 494-E7
CITATION RD
StBC 93441 922-A2
StBC 93460 922-A2
CITRUS AV
SBAR 93103 996-D3
CITRUS LN
Npmo 93444 756-B4
CITRUS PL
CARP 93013 998-D7
CIVIC CENTER PZ
LMPC 93436 916-E2
CLAIRE DR
SLO 93405 653-E7
CLAMATH CT
SLOC 93446 471-D6

CLAMSHELL MOUNTAIN WY
Npmo 93444 736-D6
CLARABELLE DR
MOBY 93442 611-F5
CLAREMONT PL
SMRA 93458 796-G3
CLAREMONT RD
SBAR 93105 985-F6
CLARENCE AV
ARGD 93420 715-B4
CLARENDON CT
StBC 93117 984-C7
CLARINTA AV
SLOC 93402 631-H7
CLARK AV
StBC 93454 817-D5
StBC 93455 816-F6
StBC 93455 817-D5
CLARK RD
SLOC 93461 325-F6
StBC 93110 985-E6
CLARK ST
StBC 93437 895-B5
CLARKIE WY
SLOC 93420 735-B3
CLARK VALLEY RD
SLOC 93402 652-B2
CLASSEN RANCH LN
SLOC 93446 533-D5
CLAYBROOK CT
StBC 93455 816-H5
CLEAR LAKE DR
StBC 93455 817-E4
CLEARVIEW LN
SLO 93405 653-D6
CLEARVIEW RD
SBAR 93101 995-G4
CLEARWATER LN
Npmo 93444 756-C2
CLELLAND AV
SLOC 93402 631-F7
CLEMENS WY
LMPC 93436 916-F2
CLEVELAND AV
SBAR 93103 995-J1
SBAR 93103 996-A2
CLEVELAND ST
Npmo 93444 756-A5
CLEVENGER DR
ARGD 93420 714-G3
CLIFF AV
PBCH 93449 693-J7
CLIFF DR
SBAR 93109 995-D6
StBC 93105 995-D6
StBC 93109 995-D6
StBC 93110 995-D6
CLIFF DR Rt#-225
SBAR 93101 996-A6
SBAR 93109 995-F6
SBAR 93109 996-A6
StBC 93105 995-F6
StBC 93109 995-F6
CLIFFORD AV
SBAR 93103 996-B3
CLIFTON ST
SBAR 93103 996-D3
CLINTON CT
ARGD 93420 714-H3
SMRA 93454 777-A6
CLINTON TER
SBAR 93105 995-G2
CLOUD WY
PSRS 93446 494-D7
CLOVER DR
SLO 93405 653-G1
CLOVER LN
StBC 93108 986-G7
StBC 93441 901-E2
CLOVER RIDGE LN
SLOC 93401 673-F5
CLOYDON CIR
StBC 93108 986-E7
CLUBHOUSE CIR
ARGD 93420 714-G3
CLUBHOUSE DR
StBC 93455 816-F4
CLUBHOUSE LN
SMRA 93454 776-J7
CLUB HOUSE RD
StBC 93436 876-E6
CLUB VIEW DR
SLOC 93401 674-E6
CLYDELL WY
PBCH 93449 714-D2
CLYDESDALE CIR
PSRS 93446 513-H6
COACH RD
ARGD 93420 715-C4

STREET Name	City	ZIP	Pg-Grid
COACHMAN WY	StBC	93455	816-G4
COAST DR	CARP	93013	998-B5
COAST RD	StBC	93454	345-H9
	SLOC	93454	797-B4
COAST VIEW DR	SLOC	93420	715-B7
COAST VILLAGE CIR	SBAR	93108	996-G4
	StBC	93108	996-G4
COAST VILLAGE RD	SBAR	93108	996-G4
	StBC	93108	996-G4
COBBLE CREEK WY	SMRA	93454	533-C6
	SMRA	93454	777-A5
COBBLESTONE LN	SMRA	93454	777-C7
COBBLESTONE WY	SLOC	93420	695-C4
COBRE PL	ARGD	93420	715-B3
COBURN DR	PBCH	93449	693-G6
COCOPAH DR	StBC	93110	985-D6
CODY AV	SLOC	93430	591-C5
COFFEE LN	SLOC	93420	715-A1
COFFEEBERRY CT	SLOC	93424	693-B2
COINER CT	StBC	93440	878-H2
COINER ST	StBC	93440	878-H2
COJO BAY RD	SLOC	93436	365-D6
COLBERT DR	LMPC	93436	896-E5
COLBY ST	Summ	93067	997-E4
COLD SPRINGS RD	StBC	93108	986-F7
	StBC	93108	996-F1
COLE CT	ATAS	93422	574-A6
COLE PL	StBC	93117	984-C7
COLEBROOK DR	SMRA	93458	776-F4
COLEMAN AV	SBAR	93109	995-G6
COLEMAN DR	LMPC	93436	896-E5
	MOBY	93442	611-D6
COLEMAN LN	LMPC	93436	896-E5
COLFAX CT	StBC	93117	984-C7
COLIMA RD	ATAS	93422	553-F7
	ATAS	93422	573-G1
COLINA CT	SLO	93401	654-C6
COLINA LN	SBAR	93103	996-A2
COLINA ST	ARGD	93420	715-A4
COLLADO CTE	ARGD	93420	714-J3
COLLEEN AV	ATAS	93422	553-E7
	SMRA	93458	776-F6
COLLEEN WY	StBC	93111	984-G5
COLLEGE AV	SLOC	93405	653-J1
E COLLEGE AV	LMPC	93436	896-F7
W COLLEGE AV	LMPC	93436	896-C7
COLLEGE DR	SMRA	93454	776-J3
	SMRA	93454	796-J3
	SMRA	93454	796-J1
	StBC	93454	796-J6
	StBC	93455	816-J1
COLLEGE CANYON RD	SLVG	93463	920-F6
	SLOC	93463	920-F6
COLLI WY	SLOC	93420	715-E1
COLOMA DR	StBC	93117	994-D1
COLONY DR	SLOC	93405	633-E6
COLORADO RD	ATAS	93422	594-B1
COLORADO ST	SMRA	93454	796-H4
COLSEN CANYON RD	StBC	93454	345-H9
COLSON CANYON RD	StBC	93454	345-J9
COLT LN	Npmo	93444	756-C3
COLUMBIA DR	SMRA	93454	796-J3
	SMRA	93454	797-A3
COLUMBINE CT	StBC	93401	674-B1
COLUMBUS DR	SMRA	93454	776-J5
	SMRA	93454	777-A5
COLUSA AV	SLOC	93405	632-J5
	SLOC	93405	633-A5
COLVILLE ST	Summ	93067	997-D3
COMANCHE AV	StBC	93455	816-J5
COMBINE ST	PSRS	93446	514-B3
COMET LN	SLOC	93420	734-J3
COMMANCHE WY	SLOC	93420	471-D7
COMMERCE CT	LMPC	93436	896-D5
COMMERCE DR	BLTN	93427	919-J4
COMMERCE WY	PSRS	93446	514-B7
CONCEPCION AV	Npmo	93444	756-C3
	SMRA	93454	776-J6
	SMRA	93454	796-J1
CONCHA LOMA DR	CARP	93013	998-E7
CONCHO WY	SLOC	93446	533-H6
	SLOC	93446	533-H6
CONCORD AV	SMRA	93454	777-A5
CONCORD PL	SLOC	93013	998-E5
CONCRETE CT	SLOC	93405	533-F5
CONDADO VISTA CT	SBAR	93105	995-E2
CONDICT BLVD	StBC	93105	995-E2
CONDOR LN	SLOC	93465	553-B1
CONDOR ST	SMRA	93454	796-H3
CONEJO AV	MOBY	93442	611-F3
CONEJO CT	SLOC	93402	631-J7
CONEJO LN	SBAR	93103	986-D7
	SBAR	93103	996-D1
CONEJO WY	ATAS	93422	553-E7
	ATAS	93422	573-E1
CONGRESS AV	SLOC	93405	735-D4
CONIFER PL	SLOC	93465	533-H6
CONNER LN	StBC	93117	984-E7
CONNIE WY	StBC	93110	985-E7
CONOVER LN	SLOC	93465	533-C7
CONSTANCE AV	SBAR	93105	995-H1
CONSTANCE LN	SBAR	93105	995-H1
CONSTANCIA	SBAR	93422	574-A5
CONSTELLATION RD	StBC	93436	876-D6
	LMPC	93436	896-C1
CONSTELLATION WY	StBC	93436	876-D7
CONSUELO DR	StBC	93110	985-F2
CONTENTA CT	SLO	93401	673-G2
CONTRA COSTA AV	SLOC	93405	633-A5
COOK AV	SBAR	93101	995-H4
COOK CT	SLOC	93465	534-C7
COOK PL	SBAR	93117	994-C3
COOK ST	SMRA	93454	796-J1
COOL BROOK LN	StBC	93111	993-J4
COOLEY LN	SMRA	93455	796-G5
COOLIDGE DR	SLOC	93445	714-D6
COOL VALLEY RD	PSRS	93446	534-B2
COOPER DR	LMPC	93436	896-F5
COOPER RD	SBAR	93109	995-G7
COPENHAGEN DR	SLVG	93463	940-E1
CORAL AV	MOBY	93442	611-E2
CORAL CT	PBCH	93449	714-D3
CORAL DR	SMRA	93454	777-B7
CORAL ST	SBAR	93105	985-E7
CORALINO RD	SBAR	93105	653-F7
CORBEROSA DR	ARGD	93420	715-B1
CORBETT CANYON RD	SLOC	93401	695-A3
	SLOC	93420	694-H2
	SLOC	93420	694-H2
	SLOC	93420	715-C2
CORBETT CANYON RD Rt#-227	ARGD	93420	715-A4
CORBETT HIGHLANDS PL	SBAR	93101	995-G4
CORDERO DR	SBAR	93105	995-E2
CORDOBA AV	LMPC	93436	896-D5
CORDOBA RD	StBC	93117	994-A5
CORDOVA DR	SBAR	93109	995-H7
	SLO	93405	653-D6
CORMORANT WY	SMRA	93424	693-B3
CORNERSTONE LN	SLOC	93420	715-A7
CORNUS CT	SLOC	93401	674-D2
CORNWALL AV	ARGD	93420	714-H5
CORNWALL ST	Cmbr	93428	528-E6
COROMAR AV	ATAS	93422	574-A5
COROMAR DR	StBC	93117	994-A2
CORONA CT	PSRS	93446	513-H6
	SLOC	93401	654-B5
CORONA RD	ATAS	93422	573-B2
CORONADA CIR	SBAR	93108	996-E2
CORONA DEL MAR	SBAR	93103	996-C3
CORONA DEL TERRA	ARGD	93420	714-G5
CORONADO AV	SBAR	93105	995-H1
CORONADO CT	SLOC	93430	591-C5
CORONADO DR	LMPC	93436	916-B2
CORONADO WY	LMPC	93436	916-B2
CORONEL PL	SBAR	93101	996-A5
CORONEL ST	SBAR	93101	996-A5
	SBAR	93109	996-A5
CORRAL AV	PSRS	93446	534-A1
CORRAL PL	ARGD	93420	715-B3
CORRAL RD	StBC	93437	855-F6
CORRAL DE PIEDRA RD	SLOC	93401	694-E1
CORRAL DE QUATI RD	SLOC	93441	900-J5
CORRALITOS	PBCH	93449	693-H7
CORRALITOS AV	SLOC	93446	534-B3
CORRALITOS RD	SLOC	93420	695-D6
	SLOC	93420	715-E1
CORRIDA DR	SLOC	93401	653-J6
	SLO	93401	654-A6
CORRIENTE RD	ATAS	93422	573-C2
CORRINE CT	SMRA	93454	777-A7
CORSAIR CIR	StBC	93455	816-F1
CORSICA DR	StBC	93455	817-B5
CORTA AV	ATAS	93422	573-H4
CORTA RD	StBC	93110	995-D5
CORTA ST	StBC	93117	994-E3
CORTA BELLA WY	StBC	93455	816-J2
CORTE DE MAYO	SMRA	93454	796-G7
CORTEZ AV	ATAS	93422	574-B3
CORTEZ CT	SLO	93405	653-E6
CORTEZ DR	SMRA	93454	776-J5
	SMRA	93454	777-A5
CORTEZ WY	SBAR	93101	995-G4
CORTINA AV	ATAS	93422	574-B4
CORTO WY	PBCH	93449	714-D3
CORTO CAMINO ONTARE	SBAR	93105	985-F6
CORTONA DR	StBC	93117	993-J2
	StBC	93117	994-A2
CORUNA CT	StBC	93111	994-G2
CORY CT	StBC	93455	816-H6
CORY WY	Npmo	93420	755-J2
	Npmo	93444	756-A2
COSSA CT	SMRA	93454	777-B6
COSTA PL	SMRA	93455	796-G6
COSTA AZUL ST	SLOC	93402	631-E7
COSTA BRAVA	SLOC	93446	693-G6
COSTA DEL MAR DR	SBAR	93108	996-E4
COSTA DEL SOL	PBCH	93449	693-G6
COTA LN	SMRA	93454	796-H2
COTA ST	SBAR	93101	996-A4
	SBAR	93103	996-C3
	SBAR	93103	996-D4
	StBC	93460	921-B5
COTTAGE LN	SMRA	93454	796-G5
COTTAGE GROVE AV	SBAR	93101	996-B5
COTTONTAIL LN	SLOC	93402	651-J1
COTTONTAIL CREEK RD	SLOC	93430	324-L9
COTTONWOOD CIR	SBAR	93105	534-A1
COTTONWOOD DR	PSRS	93446	534-B1
COTTONWOOD LN	SLOC	93405	653-D4
COTTONWOOD ST	StBC	93437	855-D5
	StBC	93463	920-H2
COTTONWOOD CANYON RD	StBC	-	346-A8
COUGAR RIDGE RD	ARGD	93420	715-A6
	StBC	93427	919-G2
	StBC	93427	365-H3
COUGAR RIDGE WY	StBC	93427	984-B7
	StBC	93455	995-F4
COUGHLIN WY	StBC	93455	816-J5
COUNT FLEET ST	SLOC	93460	921-H5
COUNTRY CIR	SLOC	93460	921-A4
COUNTRY CT	StBC	93460	921-A4
COUNTRY LN	StBC	93401	674-A5
	SMRA	93455	796-G5
	SMRA	93458	776-F5
COUNTRY WY	SLOC	93460	921-B4
COUNTRY BROOK LN	SLOC	93446	533-D5
COUNTRY CLUB DR	ATAS	93422	573-J3
	PSRS	93446	513-J7
	SLOC	93401	674-J2
COUNTRY CLUB LN	SMRA	93454	796-G7
COUNTRY CLUB VILLAGE DR	SMRA	93455	796-G5
COUNTRY HILL RD	StBC	93117	984-D7
COUNTRY HILLS LN	SLOC	93436	533-D6
	ARGD	93420	715-C3
COUNTRY OAK WY	SLO	93405	653-J2
	SLO	93405	653-J2
COUNTRYSIDE LN	StBC	93401	674-D7
COUNTRYWOOD CT	LMPC	93436	896-E6
COUNTRYWOOD DR	LMPC	93436	896-E6
COUNTRY WOOD LN	StBC	93455	816-F4
COUNTY DUMP RD	StBC	93110	995-B7
COUNTY KERRY LN	SLOC	93425	593-C2
COUPER DR	SLO	93405	653-H1
COURT PL	StBC	93108	996-J2
COURT ST	SLOC	93401	653-J4
N COURT ST	SLOC	93402	631-F6
S COURT ST	SLOC	93402	631-F6
COURTLAND ST	ARGD	93420	714-F5
	ARGD	93433	714-F5
COURTNEY DR	SLVG	93463	920-G6
COURTYARD LN	SMRA	93454	796-G5
COVE CT	SLOC	93445	714-E7
COVE LN	SLOC	93426	470-A2
COVE ST	CARP	93013	998-A5
COVE MOUND DR	SLOC	93402	631-E7
COVERED WAGON RD	SLOC	93463	920-J6
COVEY LN	SLOC	93402	651-J1
	StBC	93455	816-J1
COVINA ST	StBC	93103	996-E4
COVINGTON DR	ARGD	93420	715-A6
COVINGTON PL	StBC	93427	919-G2
COVINGTON WY	StBC	93427	984-B7
COWLES RD	StBC	93108	996-E1
COW MEADOW PL	SLOC	93465	533-F6
COWPER ST	Cmbr	93428	548-G1
COX LN	SMRA	93454	776-H5
W COX LN	SMRA	93454	777-A5
COYOTE CIR	StBC	93108	986-E7
COYOTE DR	SLOC	93420	734-H4
COYOTE RD	StBC	93436	876-E7
COYOTE CANYON RD	SLOC	93401	345-D3
	StBC	93436	574-B1
COYOTE SPRINGS RD	SLOC	-	737-D6
	SLOC	93420	737-D6
CRAIG DR	SMRA	93458	796-E2
CRAIG WY	SLO	93405	653-G2
CRAIGMONT DR	StBC	93117	984-D7
CRAMER CIR	CARP	93013	998-C6
CRAMER RD	CARP	93013	998-C6
CRANDALL WY	SLO	93405	653-J2
CRANESBILL PL	SLOC	93424	693-B2
CRAVENS LN	CARP	93013	998-B5
	StBC	-	998-B4
CRAWFORD AV	SLOC	93430	591-C5
CRAZY HORSE CT	SLOC	93446	513-H6
CRAZY HORSE DR	PSRS	93446	513-H6
CRECIENTE DR	StBC	93110	995-C5
CREEK LN	StBC	93111	985-B5
CREEK RD	SLOC	93405	631-F7
	SLOC	93405	651-F1
W CREEK RD	SLOC	93405	633-H7
	SLOC	93405	653-H1
CREEKSAND LN	SLOC	93446	533-G1
CREEKSIDE	SLOC	93401	673-G1
CREEKSIDE CT	SLOC	93446	534-B1
CREEKSIDE DR	ARGD	93420	714-H6
	SLVG	93463	920-G6
CREEKSIDE RD	SLOC	93446	471-A5
CREEKSIDE RANCH RD	SLOC	93465	533-E7
CREMONA DR	StBC	93117	994-A2
CRENSHAW CT	SLOC	93402	513-J7
CRESCENT AV	SBAR	93105	995-G3
CRESCENT DR	SLO	93401	653-J7
CRESCENT ST	StBC	93455	816-H5
CRESCENT LN	SLOC	93420	695-D7
CREST AV	SLOC	93402	631-H7
CREST DR	PBCH	93449	714-F3
CREST ST	SLOC	93445	714-E7
CRESTA AV	StBC	93110	995-B4
CRESTLINE DR	PSRS	93446	513-F3
	StBC	93455	995-F4
CRESTMONT CT	StBC	93455	816-J2
CRESTMONT DR	SLOC	93465	674-D5
	SMRA	93455	816-J2
CRESTON RD	PSRS	93446	513-H5
	PSRS	93446	514-A7
	SLOC	93446	534-A2
CRESTON ST	SMRA	93454	776-H5
	SMRA	93454	777-A5
	SMRA	93454	776-F5
CRESTON EUREKA RD Rt#-41	ATAS	93422	574-B1
	StBC	93436	574-B1
CRESTON RIDGE LN	SLOC	93446	534-G6
CRESTVIEW CIR	SLOC	93401	654-D6
CRESTVIEW LN	StBC	93108	996-E1
CREST VIEW WY	SLOC	93451	473-C4
CRESTWOOD CT	StBC	93455	816-H5
CRESTWOOD DR	SLOC	93465	985-E6
	StBC	93455	816-H5
CRESTWOOD PL	SLOC	93405	985-E6
CUESTA COLLEGE RD	SLOC	93405	632-J4
CREW LN	StBC	93455	816-E4
CRILENE CT	StBC	93455	816-J2
CRILENE LN	StBC	93455	816-J2
CRIMSON CT	StBC	93455	816-F5
CRIPPLE CREEK RD	SLOC	93465	325-D8
CRISTOBAL AV	ATAS	93422	573-J5
	ATAS	93422	574-A5
CROCKER ST	StBC	93110	995-B1
CROCKER SPERRY DR	StBC	93108	997-B1
CROCKET CIR	SLOC	93422	631-F7
	SLOC	93402	651-F1
CROFT LN	SLOC	93441	920-B5
CROSBY DR	LMPC	93436	896-E5
CROSBY WY	Npmo	93444	756-A3
CROSS RD	StBC	93437	365-C1
	StBC	93437	855-A6
CROSS ST	ARGD	93420	715-A5
	SLO	93401	673-H2
CROSS CANYONS RD	SLOC	93451	325-C4
	SLOC	93451	473-H1
CROSS COUNTRY RD	SLOC	93451	325-C3
CROSS CREEK WY	SLOC	93401	674-H6
CROSSROAD LN	SMRA	93455	796-J5
CROWLEY WY	StBC	93455	817-E5
CROWN AV	StBC	93111	984-F6
CROWN CT	SLOC	93454	776-J7
CROWN TER	ARGD	93420	715-A4
CROWN WY	PSRS	93446	514-A4
CROWN HILL ST	ARGD	93420	715-A4
CROWS NEST LP	SLOC	93426	469-J2
CROYDEN LN	Cmbr	93428	528-E6
CRUISE CIR	SLOC	93446	471-B5
CRUM RD	StBC	93455	816-J2
CRYSTAL CIR	LMPC	93436	896-E5
CRYSTAL DR	StBC	93455	817-E5
CRYSTAL WY	Npmo	93444	756-C4
CRYSTAL CANYON CT	SMRA	93455	533-J2
CRYSTAL SPRINGS RD	SLOC	-	737-D7
CUATRO CAMINOS	SBAR	93454	920-A5
CUCARACHA CT	SMRA	93454	777-A5
CUERDA CORTE CIR	ARGD	93420	714-J3
CUERNO LARGO WY	SMRA	93454	797-A1
CUERVO AV	SBAR	93110	995-D4
CUESTA AV	StBC	93117	994-A4
CUESTA CT	ATAS	93422	574-B7
CUESTA DR	SLO	93405	653-G1
CUESTA PL	ARGD	93420	715-A4
CUESTA RD	SBAR	93105	995-G2
CUESTA ST	StBC	93460	921-B5
CUESTA VERDE	StBC	93117	984-E5
CUMBERLAND DR	StBC	93455	816-J2
CUMBRE CT	SLO	93401	653-J6
CUMBRE RD	PSRS	93446	533-J2
	SLOC	93446	533-J2
CUNA DR	StBC	93110	995-B1
CURBARIL AV	ATAS	93422	573-H5
	ATAS	93422	574-B3
CURBARIL AV Rt#-41	ATAS	93422	574-B3
CURLEY AV	SBAR	93101	995-J4
	SBAR	93101	996-A4
CURLY RD	SLOC	93429	345-D11
	SLOC	93429	855-E1
CURRENT LN	SLOC	93420	695-A4
CURRER ST	SMRA	93458	776-G5
CURTIS PL	SLOC	93451	735-C4
CURVADO CIR	ATAS	93422	573-H1
CUTTER RD	SLOC	93465	534-B3
CUTTLEBON CT	StBC	93455	816-G4
CUYAMA AV	PBCH	93449	693-G7
CUYAMA DR	SLO	93401	653-J7
CUYAMA HWY	Npmo	93444	776-G1
CUYAMA HWY Rt#-166	Npmo	93444	776-H1
	SLOC	93454	345-F7
	SLOC	93454	776-H1
	StBC	93455	777-C1
CYCLAMEN CT	SLOC	93401	674-C1
CYCLONE ST	SMRA	93458	796-G4
CYNBALARIA CT	StBC	93455	816-H4
CYNDIE LN	StBC	93455	816-E4
CYNTHIA DR	SLOC	93455	896-F3
CYNTHIA LN	SLOC	93465	553-C2
CYPRESS AV	MOBY	93442	611-F7
	SLOC	93430	590-J1
E CYPRESS AV	LMPC	93436	916-F2
W CYPRESS AV	LMPC	93436	916-C2
CYPRESS CT	StBC	93458	876-F5
CYPRESS LN	BLTN	93427	919-G5
CYPRESS ST	PBCH	93449	714-B2
	StBC	93455	816-H5
CYPRESS WK	StBC	93117	994-A4
CYPRESS WY	SMRA	93454	797-A1
CYPRESS GLEN CT	SLOC	93405	695-B6
CYPRESS HOLLOW RD	SLOC	-	591-G1
	SLOC	-	591-G1
CYPRESS MOUNTAIN DR	SLOC	93465	324-K6
	SLOC	93465	324-K7
CYRIL HARTLEY PL	SBAR	93117	994-C2

D

STREET Name	City	ZIP	Pg-Grid
D ST	SLOC	93430	590-J1
N D ST	LMPC	93436	896-E5
	LMPC	93436	916-E1
S D ST	LMPC	93436	916-E2
DAFFODIL AV	Npmo	93444	755-J3
	Npmo	93444	756-A3
DAHLIA CT	CARP	93013	998-C6
S DAHLIA CT	LMPC	93436	916-D2
DAHLIA LN	SLO	93401	674-B1
DAHLIA PL	StBC	93455	816-H2
DAHLIA ST	SBAR	93101	995-J4
	SBAR	93101	996-A4
N DAHLIA ST	LMPC	93436	916-D1
DAIRY LN	SLOC	93420	695-A4
DAIRY WY	BLTN	93436	919-F5
DAIRY CREEK RD	SLOC	93405	633-A4
DAIRYLAND RD	BLTN	93427	919-G5
DAISY ST	SLOC	93445	734-H1
N DAISY ST	LMPC	93436	896-G6
	LMPC	93436	916-D1
DAKOTA DR	StBC	93455	816-H1
DAKOTA LN	LMPC	93436	736-E2
DALE AV	SLOC	93430	591-C5
DALE WY	SLOC	92389	325-H5
	SLOC	93461	325-H5
DALEY ST	StBC	93117	994-D2
DALIDIO DR	SLO	93405	653-G7
DAL PORTO LN	SMRA	93454	796-G4
	SMRA	93458	796-G4
DALTON WY	StBC	93117	984-D7
DALY AV	SLOC	93405	653-G1
DALY ST	SLOC	93401	653-J4
DAMAR ST	BLTN	93427	919-J4
DAMASSA ST	StBC	93442	896-F3
DAN CT	SLOC	93465	553-C2
DANA ST	SLOC	93401	653-J4
E DANA ST	Npmo	93444	756-C2
W DANA ST	Npmo	93444	756-C2
DANA WY	MOBY	93442	611-G7
	SBAR	93403	631-G1
N DANA FOOTHILL RD	Npmo	93444	735-H3
S DANA FOOTHILL RD	Npmo	93444	736-A4
	Npmo	93444	736-E7
DANBURY CT	StBC	93484	984-E7
DANCER AV	StBC	93455	816-H4
DANDELION LN	SLOC	93465	553-C1
DANE CREST			
DANFORD CANYON RD	Npmo	93444	737-D7
DANIA AV	BLTN	93427	919-J4
DANIEL DR	SMRA	93454	796-H4
DANIELSON RD	StBC	93108	996-H4
DANIJAY WY	SLOC	93465	776-J5
DANNY LN	Npmo	93444	756-A4
DARA RD	StBC	93117	984-F7
DARBY LN	Npmo	93444	756-C2
DARIEN CT	SLOC	93445	714-G7
DARIESA ST	CARP	93013	998-E6
DARLENE LN	StBC	93455	816-H5
DARRELLONA AV	StBC	93455	473-H3
DARTMOOR AV	SBAR	93103	993-F2
DARTMOOR LN	StBC	93103	996-H6
DARTMOUTH	StBC	93455	816-H3
DARTMOUTH DR	SLOC	93405	653-H2
DARTMOUTH LN	StBC	93455	816-H3
W DATE AV	LMPC	93436	896-D7
DATE CT	LMPC	93436	896-C7
DAUPHIN ST	StBC	93455	796-H1
	StBC	93455	796-H1
DAVENPORT RD	SLOC	93405	633-A4
DAVENPORT CREEK RD	SLOC	93401	674-B5
DAVID CT	SLOC	93405	673-E7
	SLOC	93405	673-E7
DAVID RD	StBC	93455	816-J3
	StBC	93455	817-A5
DAVID LOVE PL	StBC	93117	994-C2
DAVID SANCHEZ CT	SMRA	93454	776-J5
DAVIES AV	SLOC	93430	591-C5
DAVIS RD	SLOC	92389	325-H5
	SLOC	93461	325-H5

COPYRIGHT 2000 Thomas Bros. Maps ®

STREET Name City ZIP Pg-Grid

DAVIS CANYON RD
SLOC 93402 345-A3
SLOC 93402 673-A5
DAWLISH PL
StBC 93108 996-E1
DAWN DR
BLTN 93427 919-H5
DAWN LN
StBC 93111 994-H2
DAWN RD
Npmo 93444 755-D2
DAWSON AV
StBC 93117 994-E2
DAWSON ST
MOBY 93442 591-E7
DAY
SLOC 93430 591-C5
DAY RD
StBC 93117 993-E2
DAY ST
Npmo 93444 756-B2
DAY BREAK LN
SLOC 93465 553-B6
DAYTON LN
PSRS 93446 513-H2
DAYTONA DR
StBC 93117 993-G3
DE ANZA CT
SLO 93405 653-D6
DEARBORN PL
StBC 93117 994-F2
DE ARMOND PL
SMRA 93454 796-H2
DEBBIE RD
StBC 93111 994-G1
DEBRA DR
StBC 93110 985-E5
DEER RD
SLOC 93405 654-A1
DEER CANYON RD
SLOC 93420 695-A6
DEER CREEK RD
SLOC 93420 737-F1
DEER CREEK WY
SLOC 93446 494-H7
SLOC 93446 514-H1
DEERFIELD LN
PSRS 93446 534-B1
DEERFIELD RD
StBC 93108 997-C3
DEER HILL DR
StBC 93463 920-H5
DEER HILL LN
StBC 93463 920-H5
DEERHURST DR
StBC 93117 993-F1
DEERPATH RD
SBAR 93108 996-E2
DEER RIDGE RD
StBC 93463 920-H4
DEER RUN LN
StBC 93455 816-G7
DEER RUN RD
StBC 93455 816-H7
DEER SPRINGS DR
PSRS 93446 534-B2
DEER TRAIL CIR
ARGD 93420 714-G2
StBC 93463 921-A5
DEER TRAIL CT
SLOC 93426 469-H2
DEER TRAIL LN
StBC 93460 921-A4
StBC 93463 921-A5
DEER TRAIL PL
StBC 93463 920-J5
StBC 93463 921-A5
DEER VIEW LN
SLOC 93465 534-C6
DE GAMMA DR
SMRA 93454 776-J5
SMRA 93454 777-A5
DEGASPARIS ST
GDLP 93434 774-J6
DEIGRATIA PL
SLOC 93420 694-J6
DEJOY CT
SMRA 93458 776-F5
DEJOY ST
SMRA 93458 776-F5
DEL CT
PBCH 93449 714-C2
DE LA GUERRA RD
SBAR 93103 996-C2
DE LA GUERRA ST
SBAR 93101 995-J5
SBAR 93101 996-B3
SBAR 93103 996-B3
DE LA GUERRA TER
SBAR 93103 996-C2

DELANO ST
PBCH 93449 714-C1
DE LA VINA ST
SBAR 93101 995-G1
SBAR 93101 996-A4
SBAR 93105 995-G1
DE LA VISTA AV
SBAR 93103 996-A2
DEL CANTO LN
StBC 93110 995-C1
DELKENER CT
StBC 93455 817-B5
DEL LAGO DR
StBC 93455 816-J2
DEL MAR AV
GBCH 93433 714-E7
SBAR 93109 996-A7
SLOC 93430 591-C5
DEL MAR CT
SLO 93405 653-G2
DEL MAR DR
SLOC 93402 631-H7
DEL MAR RD
SLOC 93422 572-H5
DEL MONACO DR
StBC 93111 994-H2
DEL MONTE AV
SBAR 93101 995-J5
SBAR 93101 996-A5
DEL NORTE DR
StBC 93117 993-H2
DEL NORTE ST
SLOC 93402 631-F7
DEL NORTE WY
SLO 93405 653-G2
StBC 93455 816-J6
DEL ORO
SBAR 93109 996-A7
DEL ORO CT
SLO 93401 673-G2
DEL PARQUE DR
SBAR 93103 996-E4
DEL PLAYA DR
StBC 93106 994-A5
StBC 93117 993-J5
StBC 93117 994-A5
DEL PRADO RD
StBC 93463 920-E5
DEL REY
PBCH 93449 714-C3
DEL REY LN
SMRA 93454 776-J4
DEL RIO AV
SLO 93405 653-D6
DEL RIO RD
ATAS 93422 553-C7
ATAS 93422 573-B1
DEL SOL AV
SBAR 93109 996-A6
DEL SOL CT
SLO 93401 673-H2
DEL SOL ST
ARGD 93420 714-G7
DEL SUR WY
SLO 93405 653-G2
DELTA AV
CARP 93013 998-C6
DELTA ST
SLOC 93445 714-E7
SLOC 93445 734-E1
DEN ST
StBC 93440 878-G1
DENA WY
SMRA 93454 776-H6
SMRA 93454 777-A6
StBC 93111 984-F6
DENEB PL
StBC 93436 876-D6
DENNIS LN
SLOC 93420 714-G1
SLOC 93449 714-G1
DENTRO DR
StBC 93111 984-H7
DENVER WY
SLOC 93451 453-C6
DEPOT AV
SLOC 93401 674-E7
SLOC 93401 694-E1
DEPOT DR
SMRA 93458 776-G6
DEPOT RD
StBC 93108 996-H4
StBC 93117 994-E1
DEPOT ST
SMRA 93455 796-G5
SMRA 93458 776-G5
SMRA 93458 796-G2
DERBY LN
Cmbr 93428 528-E5
PSRS 93446 513-E6

DERMANAK DR
StBC 93463 920-G5
DESCANSO ST
SLO 93405 653-E6
DESERET PL
SLO 93405 653-J2
DE SOTO DR
SMRA 93454 776-J5
SMRA 93454 777-A5
DEVAULT PL
Cmbr 93428 528-D7
DEVON CT
ATAS 93422 573-H5
DEVON PL
StBC 93111 984-F7
DEVONSHIRE DR
ARGD 93420 715-A7
DEVONSHIRE PL
StBC 93455 817-A3
DEWEY DR
SLOC 93445 714-E7
DE WOLFF AV
StBC 93436 895-G6
DEXTER DR
StBC 93110 994-J1
DEXTER RD
SLOC 93405 653-J1
SLOC 93407 653-J1
DIABLO DR
SLO 93405 653-D6
SLOC 93405 653-D6
DIABLO CANYON RD
SLOC 93402 344-L3
SLOC 93402 345-A4
SLOC 93402 651-A7
SLOC 93424 345-A4
DIAMOND CIR
ARGD 93420 714-J7
DIAMOND DR
StBC 93455 816-J5
StBC 93455 817-A5
DIAMOND CREST CT
StBC 93110 994-J3
DIAN DR
SMRA 93455 796-J7
DIANA LN
SBAR 93103 996-C2
DIANA PL
ARGD 93420 714-H6
DIANA RD
SBAR 93103 996-C2
DIBBLEE AV
SBAR 93101 996-A5
DICKINSON ST
StBC 93455 817-B4
DICKSON DR
StBC 93455 796-H7
StBC 93455 816-H1
DIEGO RIVERA LN
SLOC 93420 734-J7
SLOC 93420 754-J1
DINSMORE LN
StBC 93108 996-H2
DIVISION ST
Npmo 93444 755-F7
Npmo 93444 756-B5
Npmo 93444 775-B2
DIXIELEE ST
StBC 93455 816-H2
DIXON ST
SBAR 93105 985-E7
DIXSON ST
ARGD 93420 714-F6
DOANE AV
SMRA 93454 796-J1
SMRA 93454 797-A1
DODDS WY
SLOC 93465 574-J3
DODSON WY
ARGD 93420 714-H6
DOE LN
SLOC 93446 469-D2
DOESKIN PL
SLOC 93465 533-H6
DOESKIN TR
StBC 93455 816-G7
DOGWOOD AV
MOBY 93442 611-E2
DOGWOOD CT
StBC 93455 816-B1
DOLLIVER ST Rt#-1
GBCH 93433 714-C3
GBCH 93449 714-C3
PBCH 93449 714-C3
DOLORES AV
ATAS 93422 573-H1
DOLORES CT
SMRA 93455 796-J7
DOLORES DR
SBAR 93109 995-H6

DOLORES LN
SLOC 93465 553-C2
DOLPHIN AV
SLOC 93445 734-E1
DOMINCA CT
SMRA 93454 777-A7
DOMINGUES ST
SMRA 93454 777-B6
DOMINION RD
StBC 93454 345-F11
StBC 93454 797-J7
StBC 93454 817-J4
DOMINO AV
StBC 93455 816-J7
StBC 93455 817-A6
DON AV
SLOC 93402 631-G6
DONALD WY
StBC 93455 816-J5
DONALDSON PL
SBAR 93117 994-C2
DONEGAL DR
SLOC 93405 653-D6
DONELSON PL
SLOC 93465 553-A2
DONNA AV
SLOC 93402 631-F6
DONNA WY
SLO 93405 653-G2
DONNER CT
SMRA 93454 777-B6
E DONOVAN RD
SMRA 93454 776-H5
SMRA 93454 777-A5
W DONOVAN RD
SMRA 93454 776-F5
SMRA 93458 776-F5
StBC 93458 776-E5
DON PABLO DR
StBC 93455 816-J7
DON RICARDO PL
StBC 93455 817-A7
DONZE AV
SBAR 93101 996-A3
DORADO DR
StBC 93111 984-F6
DORAL CT
SLOC 93401 674-D5
DORAL DR
StBC 93436 876-E4
DORIS AV
SLOC 93402 631-F6
DORIS LN
SLOC 93420 715-A1
DORKING AV
Cmbr 93428 548-G1
DORKING PL
StBC 93105 985-J6
DOROTHY CT
PSRS 93446 513-J6
PSRS 93446 514-A6
DOROTHY ST
PSRS 93446 514-A6
DORRANCE WY
CARP 93013 998-C7
DORSET CT
StBC 93117 984-C7
DORSET ST
Cmbr 93428 528-E7
DORTHY LN
SLOC 93420 735-A7
DORWIN LN
StBC 93111 994-G4
DOS CANADAS RD
Npmo 93444 736-J4
Npmo 93444 737-A4
DOS CERROS
ARGD 93420 714-H4
DOS HERMANOS RD
StBC 93111 984-H7
DOS PUEBLOS CANYON RD
StBC 93117 982-H6
StBC 93117 992-H1
DOTY DR
SLOC 93420 734-J3
DOUGLAS LN
StBC 93111 994-H2
DOUGLAS WY
SMRA 93454 796-H4
DOUGLASS AV
StBC 93436 365-D4
StBC 93436 895-H5
DOVE
PSRS 93446 514-A7
DOVE CT
SLOC 93420 715-B7
DOVEDALE AV
Cmbr 93428 548-G2

DOVE MEADOW LN
StBC 93463 920-J4
DOVE MEADOW RD
StBC 93463 920-J5
DOVER CT
GBCH 93433 714-F5
DOVER LN
Cmbr 93428 528-E5
SBAR 93103 996-B1
DOVER RD
SBAR 93103 996-B1
DOVER CANYON RD
SLOC 93465 324-L7
SLOC 93465 325-A7
DOVER HILL RD
SBAR 93103 996-B1
DOVERLEE DR
StBC 93455 816-G5
DOWER AV
SLOC 93420 714-H7
DOWNEY CIR
BLTN 93427 919-H5
DOWNING AV
Cmbr 93428 548-G2
MOBY 93442 611-G5
DOWNING LN
StBC 93455 796-H7
DRACO DR
StBC 93436 876-C7
DRAKE CIR
SLO 93405 653-F6
DRAKE DR
StBC 93455 796-H7
StBC 93455 816-J1
DRAKE ST
Cmbr 93428 548-F2
DRESSER RANCH PL
SLOC 93446 325-D6
SLOC 93446 534-H2
DREXEL DR
SBAR 93103 996-D2
DREYDON AV
Cmbr 93428 548-G2
DRIFTWOOD
PBCH 93449 714-D3
DRIFTWOOD CT
PSRS 93446 534-B1
DRIFTWOOD DR
PSRS 93446 534-B1
StBC 93455 816-A1
DRIFTWOOD ST
GBCH 93433 714-F7
MOBY 93442 611-F6
DRUM CANYON RD
StBC 93436 365-G3
StBC 93436 878-G7
StBC 93440 878-G3
DRUMM LN
Npmo 93444 756-C5
DRUMMER CIR
StBC 93455 816-H5
DRY CANYON RD
SLOC 93446 325-D6
DRY CREEK RD
PSRS 93446 494-F7
PSRS 93446 514-F1
SLOC 93446 494-F7
SLOC 93446 514-F1
DRY WELL PL
PSRS 93446 534-B2
DUBLIN CT
StBC 93455 816-F4
DUGAN DR
PBCH 93449 714-F3
DUKE DR
SMRA 93454 776-J5
StBC 93455 816-H6
DULZURA AV
ATAS 93422 573-H2
DULZURA DR
StBC 93108 996-G2
DUMP RD
CARP 93013 1018-E1
DUNBAR ST
MOBY 93442 611-F5
DUNCAN RD
SLO 93401 654-B7
SLOC 93465 553-D1
StBC 93110 985-E6
DUNES
PBCH 93449 714-C3
DUNES ST
MOBY 93442 611-F6
DUNSMUIR WY
StBC 93117 984-D7
DUNTOV DR
SLOC 93420 735-D6
DURANGO DR
SLOC 93420 734-J4

DURANGO RD
SLOC 93422 594-E2
SLOC 93465 594-E2
DURHAM PL
StBC 93117 993-F2
DUSTY PL
SLOC 93446 494-G6
DUTARD RD
StBC 93455 816-A2
DUTTON AV
SBAR 93101 995-H4
DYER ST
StBC 93455 816-G6

E

N E CT
LMPC 93436 896-E6
N E PL
LMPC 93436 896-E6
E ST
SLOC 93430 590-J2
SLOC 93451 453-A4
SMRA 93455 816-C2
StBC 93455 796-C4
StBC 93455 816-C2
StBC 93458 796-C4
N E ST
LMPC 93436 896-E5
LMPC 93436 916-E1
S E ST
LMPC 93436 916-E2
EAGLE CT
PSRS 93446 513-J7
SMRA 93454 796-H3
EAGLE PL
StBC 93460 921-C4
EAGLE ST
SMRA 93454 796-H3
EAGLE CREEK CT
ATAS 93422 594-C3
EAGLE POINT LN
SLOC 93446 471-B5
EAGLE RANCH RD
SLOC - 593-H6
SLOC 93422 593-H6
EAGLE VISTA WY
SLOC 93422 594-C4
EALAND PL
SBAR 93103 986-D7
EARL LN
StBC 93455 816-J5
EAST AV
SMRA 93454 776-J5
SMRA 93454 796-J1
EAST MALL
ATAS 93422 573-J3
EAST ST
SBAR 93103 996-C2
EASTBOURNE TER
StBC 93455 816-G4
EASTBROOK DR
LMPC 93436 896-D6
EASTER ST
MOBY 93442 611-E2
EASTGATE
BLTN 93427 919-G5
EASTGATE LN
StBC 93108 997-C2
EASTMAN ST
SLOC 93420 735-D4
EASTON RD
StBC 93441 900-H6
EASTVIEW PL
PSRS 93446 534-C1
EASTVIEW WY
SLOC 93420 734-H5
EASTWOOD DR
StBC 93455 816-J4
EASY LN
Npmo 93444 755-H4
EASY ST
ARGD 93420 714-J2
BLTN 93427 919-J4
EATON DR
ARGD 93420 715-A7
EBB TIDE WY
PBCH 93449 693-F6
EBONY DR
PSRS 93446 534-A1
EBONY ST
SMRA 93458 776-G3
StBC 93437 855-H7
ECHO LN
StBC 93463 920-J6
ECHO CANYON CT
SLOC 93420 715-C3
ECKLES RD
SBAR 93117 994-D1

EDDY ST
SLOC 93465 553-D2
EDENBURY RD
StBC 93455 816-F4
EDGECLIFF LN
StBC 93108 996-J4
EDGEHILL RD
StBC 93460 941-D1
EDGEMOUND DR
StBC 93105 985-J6
EDGEVIEW LN
SLOC 93420 734-J5
EDGEWATER LN
PSRS 93446 513-G7
EDGEWATER WY
SBAR 93109 995-G7
EDGEWOOD AV
StBC 93455 816-J2
EDGEWOOD DR
SLO 93401 654-D6
SLOC 93401 654-D6
StBC 93117 984-C7
EDIE CT
SMRA 93454 777-A7
EDISON AV
SBAR 93103 996-C3
EDISON ST
StBC 93460 901-C7
StBC 93460 921-C2
EDITH DR
StBC 93455 817-B5
EDMANDS AV
ARGD 93420 715-B4
EDNA RD Rt#-227
SLOC 93401 674-D4
SLOC 93401 694-F1
SLOC 93420 694-F1
EDNA RANCH CIR
SLOC 93401 695-A1
EDUCATION DR
SLOC 93405 632-J3
EDWARD PL
StBC 93117 984-E5
EDWARD ST
SMRA 93458 796-G2
EDWARDS PL
LMPC 93436 896-E6
EFFIE WY
PBCH 93449 714-F3
EGRET LN
GDLP 93434 774-J6
SLOC 93446 471-D6
EILEEN LN
StBC 93455 816-H5
EILEEN WY
SBAR 93105 985-F7
EKWILL ST
StBC 93111 994-F2
ELAINE ST
PSRS 93446 514-A6
ELAINE WY
PBCH 93449 714-F3
EL ARCO DR
SBAR 93105 985-F7
EL BORDO AV
ATAS 93422 574-B7
EL BOSQUE RD
StBC 93108 997-A1
EL CALLE JON
SMRA 93454 777-A7
EL CAMINITO RD
SBAR 93109 995-G5
EL CAMINO ST
SMRA 93454 776-H7
SMRA 93458 776-F6
EL CAMINO DE LA LUZ
SBAR 93109 995-G7
EL CAMINO RATEL
StBC 93117 984-D5
EL CAMINO REAL
ARGD 93420 714-F3
ATAS 93422 553-E6
ATAS 93422 573-F1
ATAS 93422 574-A5
ATAS 93422 594-C1
GBCH 93420 714-F3
GBCH 93433 714-E3
GBCH 93449 714-F3
PBCH 93420 714-F3
PBCH 93433 714-E3
PBCH 93449 714-A1
SLOC 93422 553-D3
SLOC 93422 594-G7
SLOC 93422 614-G2
SLOC 93453 614-G2
EL CAMINO REAL Rt#-41
ATAS 93422 573-G2

EL CAMINO REAL Rt#-58
SLOC 93453 614-F3
EL CAMINO REAL U.S.-101
ARGD - 715-B6
ATAS - 574-A4
ATAS - 594-B1
BLTN - 919-J3
CARP - 998-A6
CARP - 1018-F1
MonC - 453-B3
Npmo - 735-H6
Npmo - 736-A7
Npmo - 756-D4
Npmo - 776-H4
PBCH - 345-B5
PBCH - 693-E3
PSRS - 513-F2
PSRS - 533-F3
SBAR - 995-D1
SBAR - 996-E3
SLO - 653-H5
SLO - 654-B2
SLO - 673-F4
SLOC - 345-C1
SLOC - 453-B3
SLOC - 473-E5
SLOC - 493-F2
SLOC - 513-F2
SLOC - 533-F3
SLOC - 553-D3
SLOC - 594-C3
SLOC - 614-C6
SLOC - 653-H5
SLOC - 654-B2
SLOC - 673-F4
SLOC - 693-E3
SLOC - 714-A1
SLOC - 715-B6
SLOC - 735-E2
SLOC - 776-H4
SMRA - 776-H4
SMRA - 777-A6
SMRA - 797-A7
StBC - 345-F11
StBC - 365-G1
StBC - 797-A7
StBC - 817-B3
StBC - 878-H1
StBC - 900-C1
StBC - 919-J3
StBC - 939-H7
StBC - 981-A5
StBC - 982-E6
StBC - 992-J1
StBC - 993-A1
StBC - 994-E1
StBC - 995-D1
StBC - 996-E3
StBC - 997-C3
StBC - 998-A6
StBC - 1018-F1
Summ - 997-C3
VeCo - 1018-F1
E EL CAMPO RD
SLOC 93420 715-B7
SLOC 93420 735-C1
W EL CAMPO RD
SLOC 93420 734-J5
SLOC 93420 735-B3
EL CAPITAN WY
SLO 93401 674-C2
SLOC 93401 674-C2
EL CAPTAIN RANCH RD
StBC 93117 982-C5
EL CARRO LN
CARP 93013 998-C5
EL CASERIO
SBAR 93101 996-B3
EL CASERIO CT
SLO 93401 654-C6
EL CAZADOR WY
Npmo 93444 737-B4
EL CENTRO RD
ATAS 93422 574-A5
EL CENTRO WY
SLO 93401 654-B3
EL CERRITO
SLO 93401 654-C5
StBC 93455 816-H6
EL CERRITO CT
SLO 93401 654-C5
EL CERRITO DR
Npmo 93444 755-J6
EL CIELITO RD
SBAR 93103 986-C6
SBAR 93105 986-B6

EL COLEGIO RD
StBC 93106 994-B4
StBC 93117 993-J4
StBC 93117 994-A4
EL CORRAL ST
SLOC 93446 533-E1
EL CORTE RD
ATAS 93422 574-B5
ELDER
StBC 93437 855-E6
EL DESCANSO AV
ATAS 93422 573-H5
EL DORADO AV
SLOC 93405 633-B5
EL DORADO CT
PSRS 93446 513-H4
EL DORADO DR
SLOC 93420 734-J5
EL DORADO LN
StBC 93108 996-J1
EL DORADO RD
ATAS 93422 574-B5
StBC 93436 876-D6
EL DORADO ST
SLOC 93402 631-E7
EL DORADO WY
PBCH 93449 693-E5
ELDRED ST
SLOC 93465 553-E1
ELEANOR DR
CARP 93013 998-C6
EL EMBARCADERO
StBC 93117 994-A5
ELENA ST
MOBY 93442 611-E3
EL ENCANTO RD
SBAR 93103 996-A1
ELEVEN OAKS LN
StBC 93108 996-H3
EL FARO
SBAR 93109 995-H6
EL GAUCHO RD
StBC 93111 984-J7
EL GRECO RD
StBC 93117 994-A4
ELISA CT
BLTN 93427 919-J6
ELISE PL
SBAR 93109 995-G7
ELISE WY
SBAR 93109 995-G6
ELIZABETH CT
SLOC 93465 553-C2
ELIZABETH ST
SBAR 93103 996-C3
SMRA 93454 776-J6
SMRA 93454 796-H1
ELK GROVE LN
StBC 93463 920-H6
ELK GROVE RD
StBC 93463 920-H6
ELKHORN LN
StBC 93455 816-G7
ELKHORN RD
SLOC - 346-B2
SLOC - 346-F7
SLOC 93453 346-B2
ELKHORN GRADE RD
SLOC - 346-G7
ELKS LN
SLO 93401 653-H6
SMRA 93454 776-J6
ELKUS WK
StBC 93117 993-J4
ELLA LN
StBC 93111 994-H2
ELLA ST
SLO 93401 654-A5
ELLEN WY
SLO 93405 653-J3
ELLIS AV
Cmbr 93428 548-H2
ELLWOOD BEACH DR
StBC 93117 993-G3
ELLWOOD CANYON RD
StBC 93117 983-F7
StBC 93117 993-F1
ELLWOOD RANCH RD
StBC 93117 983-F7
StBC 93117 993-F1
ELLWOOD RIDGE RD
StBC 93117 993-F1
ELLWOOD STATION RD
StBC 93117 993-G2
ELM
SLO 93401 673-H1
ELM AV
CARP 93013 998-C7
MOBY 93442 611-E2
SLVG 93463 920-E7

ELM AV
SMRA 93458 776-G5
ELM CT
PSRS 93446 513-H5
SLO 93405 653-H2
ELM LN
CARP 93013 998-D6
LMPC 93436 895-J2
LMPC 93436 896-A2
ELM ST
GDLP 93434 775-A6
StBC 93437 855-D7
N ELM ST
ARGD 93420 714-G5
S ELM ST
ARGD 93420 714-G6
SLOC 93420 714-G6
SLOC 93445 714-G6
SLOC 93445 734-G1
EL MERCADO
SLO 93405 653-G6
ELMHURST PL
StBC 93117 993-G3
EL MIRADOR CT
SLO 93401 673-G3
EL MONTE DR
SBAR 93109 995-H7
EL MONTE RD
ATAS 93422 572-J4
ATAS 93422 573-A2
SLOC 93422 572-J4
EL MORO AV
SLOC 93402 631-H5
SLOC 93402 632-A5
ELMWOOD DR
StBC 93455 816-B1
EL NIDO CT
SMRA 93455 796-H5
EL NIDO LN
StBC 93117 994-B5
EL NIDO ST
SMRA 93455 796-H5
EL PARQUE AV
ATAS 93422 573-H7
EL PASEO
SLO 93401 654-C5
EL PASILLO
StBC 93108 997-G2
EL PASO WY
SLOC 93451 453-D6
EL POMAR DR
SLOC 93465 325-C8
SLOC 93465 533-J7
SLOC 93465 534-A7
SLOC 93465 553-G1
S EL POMAR RD
SLOC 93465 325-C8
SLOC 93465 534-G7
EL PORTAL AV
CARP 93013 998-E6
EL PORTAL DR
PBCH 93449 693-D4
EL PORTAL ST
StBC 93455 816-J6
EL PRADO PL
SBAR 93105 995-G2
EL PRADO RD
SBAR 93105 995-G2
EL RANCHO LN
SLOC 93420 715-G2
EL RANCHO RD
SBAR 93108 996-F2
StBC 93108 996-F1
StBC 93429 345-D11
StBC 93429 855-B2
StBC 93437 855-A4
EL RANCHO HACIENDA
SBAR 93105 986-B7
EL RANCHO OESTE RD
StBC 93429 345-D11
StBC 93429 855-A1
EL RANCHO RD LATERAL
StBC 93429 855-B3
EL RETIRO AV
ATAS 93422 573-H4
EL ROBLAR
StBC 93252 346-F11
EL RODEO RD
StBC 93110 984-J7
StBC 93110 985-A7
EL SERENO AV
SLOC 93430 591-C5
ELSINORE DR
SLVG 93463 920-E7
EL SUENO RD
StBC 93110 985-B7
StBC 93110 995-B1
EL SUENO WY
SLOC 93420 715-C2

STREET Name City ZIP Pg-Grid

- EL TIGRE CT: SLO 93405 653-F7
- EL VEDADO LN: SBAR 93105 995-H1
- EL VERANO AV: ATAS 93422 573-H1
- ELVERHOY CT: SLVG 93463 940-E1
- ELVERHOY WY: SLVG 93463 940-E1
- EL VIENTO: PBCH 93449 714-E2
- ELVIRA WY: Npmo 93444 756-A3
- ELWELL AV: SLOC 93420 735-G6
- EMAN CT: ARGD 93420 714-J5
- EMBARCADERO: MOBY 93442 611-E4
- EMBARCADERO DEL MAR: StBC 93106 994-A5; StBC 93117 994-A5
- EMBARCADERO DEL NORTE E: StBC 93106 994-B5; StBC 93117 994-B5
- EMBASSY AV: SMRA 93458 776-G3
- EMERALD CIR: MOBY 93442 611-E3
- EMERALD CT: StBC 93455 816-J3
- EMERALD DR: SMRA 93454 777-A7
- EMERALD WY: PBCH 93449 693-H7; PBCH 93449 714-D3
- EMERALD BAY DR: ARGD 93420 714-J4
- EMERSON AV: SBAR 93103 995-J1
- EMERSON RD: Cmbr 93428 548-G1
- EMERSON ST: Summ 93067 997-D3
- EMILY LN: StBC 93117 993-H3
- EMILY ST: SLO 93401 654-A5
- EMMONS RD: Cmbr 93428 548-F2
- EMPIRE DR: SMRA 93458 776-G3
- EMPIRE ST: SLOC 93401 694-F1
- EMPLEO ST: SLO 93401 673-H1
- EMPRESA DR: SLO 93401 673-J1
- EMPRESS CIR: SMRA 93454 776-J7
- ENCANTO AV: PBCH 93449 693-D5
- ENCANTO CT: PSRS 93446 513-G5
- ENCANTO LN: SLO 93401 673-G2
- ENCHANTO RD: ATAS 93422 573-C2
- ENCINA AV: SLOC - 345-D1; SLOC 93453 325-D11; SLOC 93453 345-D1; SLOC 93453 614-G3
- ENCINA LN: StBC 93117 994-E1
- ENCINA RD: StBC 93117 994-D1
- ENCINAL AV: ATAS 93422 574-A4
- ENCINAL ST: SLOC 93446 513-F7; SLOC 93446 533-F1
- ENCINITAS CT: GBCH 93433 714-F6
- ENCINO AV: ATAS 93422 573-G4
- ENCINO CT: SLO 93401 654-C5
- ENCINO LN: Npmo 93444 756-A2
- ENCORE DR: StBC 93110 995-C1
- ENNISBROOK DR: StBC 93108 997-A2
- ENOS DR: SMRA 93454 796-J3; SMRA 93458 796-G3
- ENSENADA AV: ATAS 93422 573-J2; ATAS 93422 574-A2
- ENSENADA ST: SBAR 93103 996-D3
- ENTRADA W: PBCH 93449 714-D3
- ENTRADA AV: ATAS 93422 573-J3
- ENTRADA DR: PBCH 93449 714-D3
- ENTRADA WY: SMRA 93458 796-G2
- ENTRANCE RD: SLOC 93446 514-C7; StBC 93117 993-G3; StBC 93463 920-H6
- ENTRANCE WY: SLOC 93405 653-J1; SLOC 93407 653-J1
- EQUESTRIAN AV: SBAR 93101 996-A3
- EQUESTRIAN RD: SLOC 93446 471-C5
- EQUESTRIAN WY: ARGD 93420 714-G3
- ERHART RD: SLOC 93449 694-F7; SLOC 93449 714-G1
- ERIC LN: SLOC 93465 553-B2
- ERICA PL: StBC 93436 896-G2
- ERIE WY: StBC 93455 817-E5
- ERNA WY: PBCH 93449 714-F3
- ERNEST PL: Cmbr 93428 548-H1
- ERROL ST: MOBY 93442 611-F4
- ESCABROSO RD: ATAS 93422 573-A6; SLOC 93422 572-J6; SLOC 93422 573-A6
- ESCALANTE ST: GDLP 93434 775-B5
- ESCALERAS RD: SLOC 93422 572-J3
- ESCALON PL: ATAS 93422 573-J1
- ESCARPA AV: ATAS 93422 574-A3
- ESCONDIDO RD: ATAS 93422 573-E6
- ESCUELA CT: SLO 93405 653-E6
- ESCUELA ST: StBC 93254 806-C1
- ESPALIER DR: SMRA 93455 796-G6
- ESPARTO AV: PBCH 93449 693-H7
- ESPERANZA AV: ATAS 93422 574-A4
- ESPERANZA LN: SLOC 93401 673-J3
- ESPLANADA AV: StBC 93455 816-J6
- ESROM DR: SLVG 93463 940-E1
- ESSEX CT: SMRA 93458 776-G3
- ESSEX ST: SBAR 93105 985-E7
- ESTELITA CT: SLO 93401 653-J7
- ESTERO AV: MOBY 93442 611-G7
- ESTERO RD: StBC 93117 993-J5; StBC 93117 994-A5
- ESTERO WY: CARP 93013 998-B6
- ESTES DR: SMRA 93454 797-A1
- ESTRADA AV: ATAS 93422 553-H7; ATAS 93422 573-H1
- ESTRADA AV Rt#-58: SLOC 93453 614-G3
- ESTRADA PL: SMRA 93455 796-G6
- ESTRELLA CIR: SLOC 93446 494-G2
- ESTRELLA DR: StBC 93110 995-C3
- ESTRELLA RD: SLOC 93422 594-C6; SLOC 93446 325-C4; SLOC 93446 494-E1; SLOC 93451 325-C4; SLOC 93451 473-H4; SLOC 93451 494-E1
- ESTRELLA DEL MAR CT: SLOC 93424 693-B3
- ESTUARY WY: GBCH 93433 714-D4
- ETO LN: SLOC 93402 632-A7
- ETO RD: SLOC 93402 632-A6
- ETON RD: Cmbr 93428 528-H7; Cmbr 93428 548-H1
- EUCALYPTUS AV: SBAR 93101 995-G3
- EUCALYPTUS DR: SLVG 93463 920-E7
- EUCALYPTUS LN: SLOC 93465 325-D7; SLOC 93465 534-J7; StBC 93108 996-J4
- EUCALYPTUS RD: Npmo 93444 755-D5; SLOC 93405 654-A1
- EUCALYPTUS ST: CARP 93013 998-D5
- EUCALYPTUS HILL CIR: SBAR 93103 996-E3
- EUCALYPTUS HILL DR: SBAR 93108 996-F2
- EUCALYPTUS HILL RD: SBAR 93103 996-E2; SBAR 93108 996-E2; StBC 93108 996-F1
- EUCLID AV: SBAR 93101 995-J4
- EUGENIA PL: CARP 93013 998-D7
- EUREKA LN: SLOC 93465 553-H5
- EUREKA ST: SLOC 93405 633-E5
- EVALITA LN: StBC 93111 994-H2
- EVANS AV: Summ 93067 997-D3
- EVANS RD: SLOC 93401 674-B4
- EVANSTON PL: StBC 93117 993-H3
- EVE ST: Npmo 93444 756-B1
- EVELYN CT: Cmbr 93428 528-E5
- EVENING SONG CT: StBC 93117 993-J3
- EVENSONG WY: Cmbr 93428 528-H7; Cmbr 93428 548-H1
- EVERGLADE LN: SLOC 93420 715-J3
- EVERGREEN: BLTN 93427 919-G5
- EVERGREEN AV: SMRA 93454 776-H6; SMRA 93458 776-F6
- EVERGREEN DR: StBC 93117 993-F1
- EVERGREEN WY: Npmo 93444 755-G3
- EVERSDEN LN: StBC 93454 797-D7
- EVERT CT: PSRS 93446 513-J7
- EVONSHIRE AV: StBC 93111 994-J2
- EVY LN: SLOC 93420 715-A1
- EWING AV: SLOC 93420 735-F5
- EWING LN: SLOC 93420 735-G5
- EXETER LN: Cmbr 93428 528-D5
- EXETER PL: StBC 93105 985-H7
- EXLINE RD: SLOC 93446 493-D5
- EXOTIC GARDEN DR: Cmbr 93428 528-C3
- EXPERIMENTAL STATION RD: PSRS 93446 513-H3
- EXPOSITION DR: SLO 93401 653-J6
- EXTERIOR RD: StBC 93460 900-J7; StBC 93460 920-J2; StBC 93463 920-J6

F

- F ST: SLOC 93422 614-F3; SLOC 93430 590-J2; SLOC 93453 614-F3; StBC 93455 796-B5
- N F ST: LMPC 93436 896-E5; LMPC 93436 916-E1
- S F ST: LMPC 93436 916-E2
- FAEH AV: ARGD 93420 714-H5
- FAIRCHILD WY: SLOC 93402 631-J7
- FAIRFAX AV: SLOC 93430 591-A1
- FAIRFAX RD: StBC 93110 985-E7
- FAIRHILLS RD: SLOC 93446 325-A7; SLOC 93465 325-A7
- FAIRLANE PL: StBC 93455 796-H7
- FAIRLEA RD: StBC 93460 921-A5; StBC 93463 921-A5
- FAIRMONT: StBC 93455 816-J2
- FAIRMONT AV: StBC 93455 816-H2
- FAIR OAKS AV: ARGD 93420 714-J5; ARGD 93420 715-A5
- FAIR OAKS DR: StBC 93455 796-H7; StBC 93455 816-J1
- FAIR RIDGE DR: StBC 93455 817-B6
- FAIRVIEW AV: MOBY 93442 611-H7; SBAR 93117 994-D2; StBC 93117 994-D2
- N FAIRVIEW AV: SBAR 93117 994-D1; StBC 93117 984-D6; StBC 93117 994-D1
- FAIR VIEW DR: ARGD 93420 714-G5
- FAIRVIEW LN: PBCH 93449 714-D3; PSRS 93446 513-E3
- FAIRVIEW RD: SLO 93401 654-C5; SLOC 93401 654-C5
- FAIRVIEW ST: SLO 93401 654-A4
- FAIRWAY AV: SMRA 93455 796-E6
- FAIRWAY DR: PSRS 93446 513-J7; PSRS 93446 514-A7; SLO 93405 653-E7; SLVG 93463 940-E3
- FAIRWAY PL: SLVG 93463 940-D3
- FAIRWAY RD: StBC 93108 996-G4
- FAIRWAY VISTA DR: SMRA 93455 796-F5
- FAIRWOOD LN: SBAR 93103 986-B7
- FAITH PL: Npmo 93444 756-D7
- FALCON DR: PSRS 93446 534-A2; StBC 93436 876-D5
- FALCON RD: ATAS 93422 593-D2
- FALCON CREST DR: SLOC 93420 715-B7; SLOC 93420 735-A1
- FALCON RIDGE RD: SLOC 93402 652-B1
- FALDA RD: ATAS 93422 553-G7; ATAS 93422 573-G1
- FALLBROOK CT: PSRS 93446 533-J1; PSRS 93446 534-A1
- FALLBROOK ST: Cmbr 93428 548-F2
- FALLEN LEAF LN: ATAS 93422 553-E6
- FALLEN LEAF RD: StBC 93455 817-E4
- FAN CT: SLOC 93426 469-J1
- FANCY HILL CT: StBC 93460 921-A3
- FARADAY ST: StBC 93460 921-C5
- FARANHAM: SLOC 93430 591-D4
- FARM RD: LMPC 93436 895-H3; LMPC 93436 896-A4
- FARMHOUSE LN: SLOC 93401 674-C3
- FARMHOUSE PL: ARGD 93420 715-B5
- FARMLAND DR: BLTN 93427 919-F4; BLTN 93436 919-F4
- FARNEL RD: SMRA 93458 796-E1
- FARNSWORTH DR: ARGD 93420 715-A7
- FA-ROUSSE WY: SLOC 93446 494-H6; SLOC 93446 514-H1
- FARRELL DR: SMRA 93454 797-A1
- FARREN RD: StBC 93117 983-C7; StBC 93117 993-C1
- FASANO WY: SBAR 93105 995-E3
- FAWN LN: SLOC 93446 469-D2
- FAWN PL: SBAR 93105 985-E7
- FAWN CANYON RD: StBC 93460 901-C4
- FEARN AV: SLOC 93402 631-F6
- FEATHERHILL RD: StBC 93108 997-D1
- FEED MILL RD: SLOC 93405 653-J1; SLOC 93405 654-A1
- FEENSTRA RD: SLOC 93465 325-D7
- FEIJOA PL: Npmo 93444 755-G1
- FEIN AV: PSRS 93446 513-F2
- FELICIA DR: SMRA 93455 796-G6
- FELICIA WY: SLO 93401 674-C1
- FELICITY WY: Npmo 93444 756-C4
- FELIZ AV: Npmo 93444 756-B1
- FELLOWSHIP CIR: SBAR 93109 995-G5
- FELLOWSHIP LN: SBAR 93109 995-H5
- FELLOWSHIP RD: SBAR 93109 995-G6
- FEL MAR DR: SLO 93405 653-G2
- FELTON WY: SLO 93405 653-H2
- FERN DR: Cmbr 93428 548-G1
- FERN LN: StBC 93437 875-J3; StBC 93455 816-J2
- FERN ST: SLOC 93445 734-G1
- FERNALD POINT LN: StBC 93108 997-A4
- FERNANDEZ RD: SLO 93405 653-H5
- FERN CANYON LN: SLOC 93401 693-F3
- FERNDALE DR: StBC 93455 816-H1
- FERNDALE RD: SLOC 93420 735-B4
- FERNVIEW ST: StBC 93455 816-J3
- FERNWOOD DR: SLO 93401 654-C6
- FERRARA WY: SBAR 93105 995-E2
- FERRASCI RD: Cmbr 93428 528-J6
- FERRELL AV: SLOC 93402 631-G6
- FERRELO PL: SBAR 93103 996-C2
- FERRELO RD: SBAR 93103 996-B2
- FERRINI RD: SLO 93405 653-H2; SLOC 93405 653-H2
- FERRO LN: PSRS 93446 513-H5
- FERROCARIL RD: ATAS 93422 553-G6
- FESLER ST: PSRS 93446 534-A1; SMRA 93454 776-F7; SMRA 93458 776-F7
- E FESLER ST: SMRA 93454 776-H7; SMRA 93454 777-A7
- FIDDLENECK LN: SLOC 93424 693-B2
- FIELDSTONE CIR: PSRS 93446 534-B1
- FIELDSTONE LN: SMRA 93454 777-A7
- FIELDVIEW PL: ARGD 93420 715-B5
- FIERO LN: SLOC 93401 674-B2
- FIESTA DR: CARP 93013 1018-E1
- FIESTA WY: SMRA 93458 776-F4
- FIFE LN: StBC 93108 997-C2
- FIFE PL: StBC 93108 997-C2
- FIFTH AVDR: SMRA 93458 776-G3
- FIG AV: SBAR 93101 996-B4
- FIG ST: MOBY 93442 611-F7
- FIGUEROA ST: SBAR 93101 995-J5; SBAR 93101 996-A3
- FIGUEROA MOUNTAIN RD: StBC - 365-K2; StBC - 366-A3; StBC 93105 365-L3; StBC 93441 365-K2; StBC 93441 900-H3
- FILAMINA ST: SMRA 93454 777-A6
- FILAREE WY: SLOC - 695-E2
- FILBERT ST: PSRS 93446 513-E5
- FINCH ST: SLOC 93465 553-D2
- FINNEY RD: Cmbr 93428 548-J2
- E FINNEY ST: Summ 93067 997-D4
- W FINNEY ST: Summ 93067 997-D4
- FIR AV: MOBY 93442 611-E2; SLVG 93463 920-E7
- E FIR AV: LMPC 93436 916-F3
- W FIR AV: LMPC 93436 916-C2
- FIR PL: Npmo 93444 756-B4
- FIR ST: GDLP 93434 775-A6; StBC 93437 855-E6
- FIREFIGHTER RD: StBC 93429 855-H5; StBC 93437 855-G5
- FIREFOX DR: SMRA 93455 796-J7
- FIREHOUSE CANYON RD: SLOC 93424 693-B2
- FIRENZE PL: SBAR 93105 995-E3
- FIRESTONE CT: SMRA 93455 796-G6
- FIRESTONE RD: SBAR 93117 994-C2
- FIRESTONE WY: StBC 93436 876-F5
- FIRETHORN LN: PSRS 93446 514-A6; StBC 93437 875-J3
- FIR TREE PL: StBC 93117 993-F1
- FIRTREE WY: SLOC 93446 533-E6
- FISHER CT: SLOC 93465 553-E1
- FISHERMANS CT: SLOC 93446 471-A6
- FIVE CITIES DR: PBCH 93449 714-D3
- FIXLINI ST: SLO 93401 654-B4
- FJORD DR: SLVG 93463 940-D1
- FLAG WY: PSRS 93446 534-A1
- FLAGSTONE DR: StBC 93455 816-F5
- FLEMING LN: StBC 93455 796-H7
- FLETCHER AV: SLO 93401 654-B5
- FLORA RD: ARGD 93420 715-C4
- FLORA ST: SLO 93401 654-B5
- FLORADALE AV: StBC 93436 896-A6; StBC 93436 916-A1
- FLORAL DR: SLVG 93463 920-E7
- FLORA VISTA DR: SBAR 93109 995-G6
- FLORENCE AV: SLO 93401 654-A5
- FLORENCE ST: SLOC 93465 553-D2
- FLORES AV: SLOC 93430 591-B5
- FLORES RD: ATAS 93422 573-G4
- FLORETTE DR: StBC 93455 817-B4
- FLORIN ST: PBCH 93449 693-E5
- FLOWER AV: GDLP 93434 775-B6; StBC 93434 775-B6
- FLOWER ST: StBC 93455 816-H1
- FLOYD CT: SMRA 93454 777-B5
- FLYING FASTER LN: SLOC 93446 325-D7
- FONTANA: SLO 93401 653-H7
- FONTANA RD: PSRS 93446 514-B7
- E FOOTHILL BLVD: SLO 93405 653-H2
- W FOOTHILL BLVD: SLO 93405 653-E3; SLOC 93405 653-E3
- FOOTHILL LN: SBAR 93105 986-A7
- FOOTHILL RD: PBCH 93449 693-J7; StBC - 346-C9; StBC - 346-F10; StBC - 806-B7; StBC 93252 346-E10
- FOOTHILL RD Rt#-192: CARP 93013 998-E5; SBAR 93105 985-D6; SBAR 93105 986-A7; SBAR 93110 985-D6; StBC 93013 997-G3; StBC 93013 998-A4; StBC 93105 985-D6; StBC 93105 986-A7; StBC 93110 985-D6
- FORDHAM PL: StBC 93117 993-H3
- FOREMASTER LN: GBCH 93433 714-E4
- FOREST AV: SLOC 93465 553-D1
- FOREST CIR: StBC 93455 816-J4
- FOREST DR: StBC 93117 993-G1
- FOREST GLEN DR: ARGD 93420 714-H6
- FORGE RD: StBC 93108 997-C2
- FORMOSA DR: StBC 93108 996-H3
- FORMOSA ST: MOBY 93442 611-E2
- FORTINI PL: PSRS 93446 533-E4; SLOC 93446 533-E4
- FORTUNA CT: ARGD 93420 715-B4
- FORTUNA LN: StBC 93117 993-J5
- FORTUNA RD: StBC 93117 993-J5
- FORTUNATO WY: SBAR 93105 995-E3
- FOSTER RD: SMRA 93455 816-F3; StBC 93455 816-H3; StBC 93455 817-A3
- FOUNDERS AV: StBC 93455 817-A2
- FOUNTAIN AV: SLOC 93445 714-E7; SLOC 93445 734-E1
- FOUNTAIN DR: StBC 93455 817-A3
- FOUR PAWS WY: SLOC 93446 534-G6
- FOWLER LN: SLOC 93420 734-H5
- FOWLER RD: SBAR 93117 994-D3; StBC 93117 994-D3
- FOXBURROW CT: StBC 93455 816-G4
- FOX CANYON LN: SLOC 93420 695-B7
- FOXEN CT: StBC 93455 816-F4
- FOXEN DR: SBAR 93105 985-F7
- FOXEN LN: StBC 93440 878-H2
- FOXEN BLUFF LN: SLOC 93420 735-A2
- FOXEN CANYON RD: StBC - 345-H11; StBC - 365-J1; StBC 93441 365-J1; StBC 93441 900-F2; StBC 93454 345-H11; StBC 93454 797-J6; StBC 93463 900-F2
- FOXENWOOD DR: StBC 93455 816-E4
- FOXENWOOD LN: SMRA 93455 816-G3; StBC 93455 816-G4
- FOX HOLLOW RD: SLOC 93401 654-C2
- FOXTAIL LN: SLOC 93465 533-C7; SLOC 93465 553-C1
- FRADY LN: PBCH 93449 714-C2
- FRAMBUESA DR: SLO 93405 653-D6
- FRANCES ST: PSRS 93446 514-A6
- FRANCES WY: PBCH 93449 714-F3
- FRANCESCHI RD: SBAR 93103 996-B1
- FRANCIA ST: SLOC 93420 714-H7
- FRANCINE LN: StBC 93455 816-J2
- FRANCIS AV: SLO 93401 654-A6
- FRANCIS WY: Npmo 93444 756-F2
- FRANCISCAN CT: CARP 93013 998-B6
- FRANCISCO DR: SBAR 93105 985-F5
- FRANK CT: Npmo 93444 756-A4
- FRANK LN: SMRA 93458 776-F6
- FRANKIE LN: SLOC 93420 735-C5
- FRANKLIN DR: PBCH 93449 714-B1
- FRANKLIN RD: StBC 93455 817-A4
- FRANKLIN RANCH RD: SBAR 93117 984-D6
- FRAZIER LN: StBC 93110 994-J2
- FREDENSBORG WY: SLVG 93463 920-E6; StBC 93463 920-E6
- FREDENSBORG CANYON RD: SLVG 93463 920-E6; StBC 93463 920-E6
- FREDERICK AV: SLO 93401 654-A6
- FREDERICKS ST: SLO 93405 653-J2; SLO 93405 654-A2
- FREDRICH DR: StBC 93436 896-G2
- FREEAR DR: BLTN 93427 919-J5
- FREEDOM PL: BLTN 93427 919-H6
- FREEHAVEN DR: StBC 93108 997-F2
- FREEMAN LN: SLOC 93402 632-A6
- FREEMAN PL: StBC 93117 993-G3
- FREESIA DR: Summ 93067 997-E4
- FRWY U.S.-101: StBC - 365-H2
- FREMONT LN: StBC 93105 964-F1
- FREMONT PL: SBAR 93101 996-A5
- FREMONT ST: SMRA 93454 777-B5
- FRESNO AV: ATAS 93422 573-H2; MOBY 93442 611-G7; SLOC 93405 632-J5; SLOC 93430 590-J1; SLOC 93430 591-A2
- FRESNO ST: PBCH 93449 714-C1; PSRS 93446 513-E6; SLOC 93402 631-E6
- FRESNO WY: SLOC 93451 453-D6
- FREYA DR: SLVG 93463 940-E1
- FRIAR LN: SBAR 93105 985-E7
- FRISCO WY: SLOC 93420 735-G5
- FROG POND PL: SLOC 93422 593-C2
- E FRONT RD: ATAS 93422 574-B7
- W FRONT RD: ATAS 93422 574-A6
- FRONT ST: GBCH 93433 714-D4; MOBY 93442 611-F5; SLOC 93424 693-A4; SLOC 93445 734-F1
- FRONT ST Rt#-1: SLOC 93445 714-E7; SLOC 93445 734-E1
- FRONTAGE RD: StBC 93110 995-D1; StBC 93455 817-A3
- N FRONTAGE RD: Npmo 93444 735-J7; Npmo 93444 756-B2; SLOC 93420 735-H5
- S FRONTAGE RD: Npmo 93444 756-B3
- FRONTIER WY: SLOC 93465 533-C7; SLOC 93465 553-C1
- FROSTY WY: SMRA 93455 796-J7
- FUENTE PL: SLOC 93422 594-E4
- FUERA LN: StBC 93108 997-A1
- FULLER RD: SLO 93401 674-C2
- FUNSTON AV: SLO 93401 654-A6
- FURUKAWA WY: SMRA 93458 796-E2
- FUTURA LN: SLOC 93420 735-G6

G

- G ST: SLOC 93430 590-J2; SLOC 93430 591-A2
- G ST Rt#-58: SLOC 93453 614-F3
- N G ST: LMPC 93436 896-E6; LMPC 93436 916-E1
- S G ST: LMPC 93436 916-E2
- GAHAN PL: PSRS 93446 533-E4; SLOC 93446 533-E4
- GAIL PL: SLO 93401 654-A6
- GAINE ST: Cmbr 93428 548-F2
- GALAXY ST: Npmo 93444 756-A6
- GALAXY WY: StBC 93436 876-D5
- GALLANT PL: SLOC 93401 674-E6
- GALLEON WY: SLO 93405 653-F7
- GALLINA CT: ATAS 93422 573-D5
- GAMBY WY: SLVG 93463 920-E7; StBC 93427 365-H3; StBC 93427 919-H1; StBC 93436 365-G3
- GANADOR CT: SLO 93401 653-J6
- GANCHO AV: ATAS 93422 573-J2
- GARBADA RD: ATAS 93422 574-B3
- GARBO AV: SLOC 93430 591-C5
- GARCERO RD: ATAS 93422 573-A1
- GARCIA DR: SLO 93405 653-F7; SLO 93405 673-F1
- GARCIA RD: ATAS 93422 553-D6; SBAR 93103 996-B2; SLOC 93422 553-D6
- GARDEN AL: SLO 93401 653-J4
- GARDEN DR: SMRA 93458 776-H4
- GARDEN LN: StBC 93108 986-G7; StBC 93108 996-G1
- GARDEN ST: ARGD 93420 715-A5; SBAR 93101 995-J2; SBAR 93101 996-A3; SBAR 93105 995-J2; SLO 93401 653-J4; SLO 93401 654-A5; SLOC 93402 631-F5; StBC 93463 920-H2
- GARDENIA AV: LMPC 93436 896-F7
- GARDENIA CIR: PSRS 93446 513-H7
- GARDENIA CT: PSRS 93446 513-H7
- GARDENIA ST: LMPC 93436 896-F5
- GARDENIA WY: Npmo 93444 756-A3
- GARFIELD PL: ARGD 93420 714-G7
- GARFIELD ST: SLO 93401 654-A3
- GARIBALDI AV: SLO 93401 654-B6
- GARNET WY: SMRA 93454 777-A7
- GARNETTE DR: SLO 93405 653-E7
- GARRETT LN: SLOC 93420 754-J2
- GARRETT ST: GDLP 93434 774-J6; StBC 93455 816-G6
- GARY PL: SLOC 93401 674-E6
- GARY WY: SLOC 93451 453-D6
- GASOLINE ALLEY PL: SLOC 93420 754-J2; SLOC 93420 755-A2
- GATES CT: PSRS 93446 513-H6
- GATEWAY DR: SLOC 93446 471-D6
- GATHE DR: SLO 93405 653-E7
- GATO AV: StBC 93117 994-E2
- GATO CANYON RD: StBC 93105 365-L6; StBC 93105 982-E4; StBC 93117 982-E4
- GAUCHO CT: SLOC 93465 553-E1
- GAUCHO WY: SMRA 93458 776-F4

STREET Name City ZIP Pg-Grid

GAVANZA RD
ATAS 93422 593-E3
SLOC 93422 593-E3
GAVILAN RD
SLOC 93422 593-F3
GAVIOTA ST
StBC 93117 994-E2
StBC 93441 900-G5
StBC 93463 900-G5
GAY DR
BLTN 93427 919-J5
GAYLENE DR
SMRA 93458 776-F4
GAYLEY WK
StBC 93117 993-J4
GAYNFAIR TER
ARGD 93420 714-H7
GAZELLE WY
StBC 93455 816-G7
GEM CT
SMRA 93454 777-A7
GEMINI AV
StBC 93436 876-D5
GENESEO RD
SLOC 93446 325-D6
GENOA WY
StBC 93455 817-B4
GENUINE RISK RD
StBC 93460 922-C5
GEORGE DR
StBC 93455 817-A5
GEORGE LN
StBC 93455 816-H6
GEORGE ST
SLO 93401 654-A5
GEORGE WY
Npmo 93444 755-G3
GEORGE MILLER DR
LMPC 93436 896-D5
GEORGETOWN RD
StBC 93117 993-H3
GEORGIA AV
SLOC 93405 633-A5
GERAINE WY
PSRS 93446 514-B2
GERARD DR
StBC 93117 993-F1
GERDA ST
SLO 93401 654-B5
GERONA WY
StBC 93110 985-A7
GERTIE PL
Npmo 93444 756-A4
GIBRALTAR RD
SBAR 93105 986-C6
StBC 93103 986-C6
StBC 93105 366-C6
StBC 93105 986-C1
GIBSON LN
SMRA 93454 796-H2
GIBSON RD
SLOC 93465 553-E1
GILARDI RD
SLOC 93405 632-G2
GILBERT AV
SLOC 93430 591-C4
GILBERT ST
MOBY 93442 611-E2
GILEAD LN
PSRS 93446 514-A4
GILLESPIE ST
SBAR 93101 995-H4
GILLESPIE WY
SBAR 93101 995-H4
GILLIS CANYON RD
SLOC 93461 325-G6
GILROY AV
SLOC 93446 533-H4
GINGER LN
PSRS 93446 514-A7
GINGKO CT
SMRA 93458 776-G3
GIUSEPPE WY
SLOC 93420 734-G5
GLACIER LN
StBC 93455 817-E5
GLADE AV
SLOC 93445 714-E7
SLOC 93445 734-E1
GLEASON ST
Cmbr 93428 548-J2
GLEN AV
StBC 93455 816-H1
GLEN CT
PSRS 93446 513-E5
GLEN WY
SLVG 93463 940-E2
GLEN ALBYN DR
StBC 93105 985-H7
GLEN ANNIE RD
StBC 93117 983-G3
StBC 93117 993-H1
GLENBROOK ST
StBC 93110 994-J2
StBC 93111 994-J2
GLEN CAIRON DR
StBC 93455 816-J5
GLENCREST LN
PSRS 93446 513-F3
GLENDESSARY LN
SBAR 93105 985-H7
StBC 93105 985-H7
GLEN EAGLES DR
StBC 93455 816-J5
GLEN ELLEN CT
LMPC 93436 896-C6
GLEN ELLEN LN
LMPC 93436 896-C6
StBC 93455 817-A2
GLEN GARY RD
StBC 93460 921-A5
StBC 93463 921-A5
GLENHAVEN PL
Npmo 93444 755-H2
GLENN AV
SLOC 93405 632-J5
GLENN RD
StBC 93105 964-J6
GLENN ST
SLOC 93402 631-E6
GLENNHEIN CT
SLOC 93401 674-E6
GLENNORA WY
BLTN 93427 919-J5
GLENOAK DR
ARGD 93420 715-A7
GLEN OAKS CT
StBC 93455 817-A4
GLEN OAKS DR
SLO 93401 654-A2
SLO 93405 654-A2
SLOC 93405 654-A2
StBC 93441 900-H6
GLENRIDGE LN
StBC 93455 817-A2
GLENVIEW DR
StBC 93455 816-J3
GLENVIEW LN
SLOC 93401 674-E5
GLENVIEW RD
StBC 93108 996-G2
GLENWOOD DR
StBC 93455 816-H1
GLINES AV
StBC 93455 817-A5
GLORIA CIR
LMPC 93436 896-C6
GLORY ST
Npmo 93444 756-C3
GOBERNADOR CANYON RD
StBC 93013 998-H6
StBC 93013 999-A6
GODELL ST
SLOC 93465 553-B1
GOLDEN DR
SMRA 93458 776-F6
GOLDEN BRIDLE
SLOC 93465 325-C8
GOLDEN GATE AV
Summ 93067 997-D3
GOLDEN HAWK LN
SLOC 93420 715-A2
GOLDEN HILL RD
PSRS 93446 514-A3
SLOC 93446 514-A3
GOLDEN LEAF LN
Npmo 93444 756-B5
GOLDEN MEADOW DR
SLOC 93446 533-D6
GOLDENROD LN
SLO 93401 674-C2
GOLDEN WEST PL
ARGD 93420 714-G6
GOLD RUSH LN
SLOC 93446 471-B5
GOLDSMITH CT
SMRA 93454 797-A1
GOLF PL
PSRS 93446 513-J7
GOLF RD
SBAR 93108 996-G3
StBC 93108 996-G3
GOLF BALL RD
Npmo 93444 755-G1
GOLF COURSE LN
Npmo 93444 755-E1
GOLPA DR
StBC 93463 920-F4
GOODLAND ST
StBC 93455 816-J5
GOODWIN RD
StBC 93455 816-G1
GOOSEFOOT CT
SLOC 93424 693-B1
GORDIANO AV
StBC 93111 994-J1
GOSSIP ROCK RD
Npmo 93444 737-B5
GOUGH AV
SLOC 93465 553-D2
GOULD LN
StBC 93108 997-B3
GRACE DR
SLOC 93451 325-D5
GRACE LN
ARGD 93420 714-J3
Npmo 93444 756-C7
GRACIA AV
SLOC 93430 591-B5
GRACIA WY
SLOC 93420 734-J2
GRACIOSA RD
StBC 93455 345-E11
StBC 93455 365-E1
StBC 93455 816-F7
GRADE MOUNTAIN WY
Npmo 93444 736-E7
GRANA PL
SLOC 93451 473-D3
GRANADA CIR
StBC 93110 985-A7
GRANADA DR
SLO 93401 673-J1
GRANADA WY
CARP 93013 998-E6
StBC 93110 985-A7
GRAND AV
SBAR 93103 995-J1
SBAR 93103 996-A2
SLO 93401 654-A2
SLO 93405 654-A2
SLOC 93405 654-A2
StBC 93441 900-H6
E GRAND AV
ARGD 93420 714-H5
ARGD 93433 714-H5
GBCH 93433 714-H5
E GRAND AV Rt#-227
ARGD 93420 714-J5
W GRAND AV
GBCH 93433 714-D5
GRAND CT
StBC 93455 816-J6
GRANDE AV
Npmo 93444 756-B4
GRAND VIEW DR
GBCH 93433 714-E4
GRANITE RD
SLOC 93465 533-F7
GRANT AV
SLOC 93420 735-D4
GRANT ST
SMRA 93454 776-H5
SMRA 93458 776-G5
GRAPEVINE RD
SMRA 93454 777-A6
GRAPEVINE WY
SLOC 93465 553-B3
GRAPPA DR
StBC 93111 984-G7
GRASS VALLEY WY
SMRA 93454 777-B6
GRAVES AV
SLO 93401 654-A3
SLO 93405 654-A2
GRAVES CREEK RD
ATAS 93422 573-F2
GRAVILLA DR
SBAR 93109 996-A6
GRAY AV
SBAR 93101 996-C4
GRAY ST
StBC 93455 816-G6
GRAY FOX LN
SLOC 93446 471-B5
GREEN CT
PSRS 93446 534-A1
GREEN LN
SBAR 93105 995-J2
StBC 93108 997-A3
GREEN PL
SLOC 93420 734-J3
SLOC 93420 735-A3
GREEN ST
Cmbr 93428 548-H1
GREENACRE DR
StBC 93455 816-J1
GREENBRIAR CT
StBC 93455 816-J2
GREEN BRIAR LN
SLOC 93446 471-D6
GREENBRIER PL
SLOC 93401 674-J5
GREENBRIER RD
StBC 93436 876-E5
GREENBROOK LN
SLOC 93446 471-D6
GREENCASTLE CIR
StBC 93111 994-J2
GREENFIELD RD
StBC 93463 920-E6
GREEN GATE RD
SLOC 93401 694-G1
GREENLEAF CT
StBC 93117 993-J3
GREEN MEADOWS RD
StBC 93108 996-H1
GREEN OAKS DR
SLOC 93402 631-H7
GREENPINE LN
SLOC 93446 471-B6
GREENRIDGE CT
StBC 93455 816-F4
GREENRIDGE LN
SBAR 93103 996-C1
GREENSBORO LN
SLOC 93401 674-D6
GREENSBORO ST
StBC 93117 993-G3
GREENSTONE LN
SMRA 93454 777-C7
GREENTREE LN
StBC 93455 816-J4
GREEN VALLEY RD Rt#-46
Cmbr 93428 324-J8
SLOC 93435 324-J8
SLOC 93465 324-K8
GREENWELL AV
StBC 93108 997-D3
Summ 93067 997-D3
GREENWOOD AV
MOBY 93442 611-E2
GREENWOOD DR
ARGD 93420 715-C4
PSRS 93446 513-E5
GREENWOOD RD
StBC 93455 816-B1
GREENWORTH PL
StBC 93108 996-J3
GREGGORY WY
SBAR 93105 995-E1
GREGORY AV
PSRS 93446 513-G4
GREGORY CT
SLO 93401 654-C6
SMRA 93454 777-A6
GRELL LN
SLOC 93445 714-G7
SLOC 93445 734-G1
GRETA PL
SLO 93401 654-B6
GREYSTONE CT
StBC 93455 816-G4
GREYSTONE PL
SLOC 93401 674-D6
GREYSTONE WY
Cmbr 93428 528-F6
GRIEB DR
ARGD 93420 714-G3
GRIFFIN ST
GBCH 93433 714-E6
GRIGGS PL
SBAR 93117 994-D2
GROVE CT
ARGD 93420 715-B5
GROVE DR
SLOC 93446 325-D6
GROVE LN
SBAR 93105 985-E7
SBAR 93105 995-E1
GROVE ST
Cmbr 93428 528-F6
Npmo 93444 756-C3
PSRS 93446 513-E6
SLO 93401 654-A3
SLOC 93402 631-F6
GUADALUPE AV
StBC 93437 855-D7
StBC 93437 875-D1
GUADALUPE RD
SLOC 93420 735-B7
SLOC 93420 755-B1
GUADALUPE RD Rt#-1
SLOC 93420 755-B2
GUADALUPE ST Rt#-1
GDLP 93434 775-A6
GUAM AV
StBC 93437 875-E3
GUANTE CIR
StBC 93111 984-F7
GUAVA AV
StBC 93117 994-C1
E GUAVA AV
LMPC 93436 916-G1
W GUAVA AV
LMPC 93436 916-C1
GUERRA LN
SLOC 93405 653-D3
GUILDFORD DR
Cmbr 93428 528-E6
GULARTE LN
GDLP 93434 775-B5
GULARTE RD
ARGD 93420 715-B3
GULF ST
SLO 93405 653-F6
GUM ST
StBC 93437 855-E6
GUNDERSON LN
SMRA 93458 776-G5
GUNNER ST
SMRA 93458 776-F6
GUTIERREZ ST
SBAR 93101 996-C4
SBAR 93103 996-C3
GWYNE AV
StBC 93111 994-G3

H

H ST
SLOC 93422 614-F3
SLOC 93430 591-A2
SLOC 93453 614-F3
N H ST Rt#-1
LMPC 93436 896-E5
LMPC 93436 916-E1
StBC 93436 896-E5
S H ST
LMPC 93436 916-E2
HACIENDA AV
SLOC 93401 674-C5
HACIENDA DR
ARGD 93420 715-A7
SBAR 93105 995-F3
SLOC 93430 591-C4
HACIENDA WY
SBAR 93105 995-F3
SMRA 93458 776-F4
HACKBERRY LN
StBC 93437 855-H7
HACKNEY WY
SLOC 93446 471-D5
HADDON DR
Cmbr 93428 548-G1
HADLEY WY
StBC 93455 816-H1
HAGERMAN DR
SMRA 93455 796-F7
StBC 93455 796-F7
StBC 93455 816-F1
HAGGERTY WY
Npmo 93444 756-C1
HAIDA ST
CARP 93013 998-E6
HAINES AV
SLOC 93430 591-C5
HAL ST
SMRA 93454 777-A6
HALCON RD
ATAS 93422 574-D7
ATAS 93422 594-D1
ATAS 93465 574-D7
SLOC 93465 574-D7
HALCYON LN
SBAR 93101 995-G4
HALCYON RD
SLOC 93420 714-H7
SLOC 93420 734-H1
SLOC 93420 735-A5
N HALCYON RD
ARGD 93420 714-H5
S HALCYON RD
ARGD 93420 714-H6
SLOC 93420 714-H6
HALE CREEK RD
SLOC - 593-E5
SLOC 92389 325-B11
SLOC 93422 593-E5
SLOC 93453 325-B11
SLOC 93453 614-A3
HALES LN
CARP 93013 998-E7
HALEY ST
SBAR 93101 996-B4
SBAR 93103 996-B4
HALKIRK ST
StBC 93110 994-J2
HAMILTON LN
StBC 93455 817-C7
HAMMOND DR
StBC 93108 996-J4
HAMPSHIRE LN
StBC 93455 817-A2
HAMPSHIRE PL
StBC 93455 816-F4
HAMPTON CT
SLOC 93422 594-D2
HAMPTON DR
StBC 93455 796-H7
HAMPTON LN
SLOC 93446 493-A7
SLOC 93446 513-A1
HANCOCK AV
SMRA 93454 796-J3
SMRA 93454 797-A3
HANCOCK DR
LMPC 93436 896-E3
StBC 93436 896-E3
HANFORD ST
PBCH 93449 714-B1
HANGAR ST
SMRA 93455 796-E7
HANGING TREE LN
SLOC 93446 533-J5
SLOC 93446 534-A6
SLOC 93465 534-A6
HANNA DR
StBC 93111 984-F7
HANOVER PL
SLOC 93401 674-D6
HANOVER WY
SMRA 93458 776-G3
HANSEN LN
SLOC 93401 654-D7
SLOC 93401 674-D1
HANSON RD
SLOC 93446 514-D7
SLOC 93446 534-D2
HANSON WY
SMRA 93458 776-E7
SMRA 93458 796-E2
StBC 93458 776-E7
StBC 93458 796-E2
HANSON HILL RD
SLOC 93420 715-C1
HAPPY CANYON RD
StBC 93105 365-L3
StBC 93105 922-D4
StBC 93460 921-J6
StBC 93460 922-A4
HAPPY HUNTING CIR
StBC 93446 471-C7
HARBOR CIR
SLOC 93446 471-A5
HARBOR DR
CARP 93013 998-A5
HARBOR ST
MOBY 93442 611-F6
HARBOR WY
SBAR 93109 996-B6
SLOC 93420 345-E5
SLOC 93420 736-B1
HARBOR HILLS DR
SBAR 93109 995-J6
HARBOR HILLS LN
SBAR 93109 995-J6
HARBOR LIGHTS LN
SLOC 93424 693-A3
HARBOR VIEW DR
SBAR 93103 996-E3
SBAR 93108 996-E3
HARBOR VIEW ST
PBCH 93449 714-B2
HARDEN ST
ARGD 93420 715-A4
HARDING AV
SMRA 93454 776-H5
SMRA 93454 777-A5
SMRA 93458 776-F5
HARDING DR
SLOC 93445 714-D7
HARDINGE AV
Summ 93067 997-C3
HARFORD CANYON RD
SLOC 93424 693-A3
HARLEY DR
SLOC 93465 553-E1
HARLOE ST
PBCH 93449 714-B2
HARMON ST
SBAR 93103 996-E4
HARMONY LN
SLOC 93420 715-D1
StBC 93455 817-B4
HARMONY WY
SLOC 93401 654-D6
HARNESS CT
SLOC 93465 553-E1
HARP RD
StBC 93455 817-A6
HARPER CT
SMRA 93454 776-J5
HARRIER LN
Npmo 93444 756-B4
HARRIS DR
StBC 93436 896-G2
HARRIS ST
SLO 93401 653-J5
HARRIS GRADE RD
StBC 93436 876-G3
StBC 93436 896-E3
StBC 93455 365-E1
StBC 93455 876-G3
HARRISON DR
SMRA 93454 777-B6
HARRISON ST
ARGD 93420 715-A4
HARROLD AV
StBC 93110 985-D7
HARSIN LN
StBC 93455 816-H2
HART DR
SMRA 93454 776-J7
SMRA 93454 796-J1
HART LN
ARGD 93420 714-J5
ARGD 93420 715-A5
HARTFORD ST
Cmbr 93428 528-F6
HARTZELL CT
SLOC 93422 593-B2
HARVARD LN
StBC 93111 984-G7
StBC 93111 994-G1
HARVEST PL
Npmo 93444 756-A3
HARVEST MEADOW PL
PSRS 93446 534-B2
HARVEST RIDGE WY
SLOC 93446 534-G1
HARVEY ST
Cmbr 93428 548-F2
HASKIN ST
SLO 93401 654-A5
HASLAM DR
SMRA 93454 796-H2
HASSET CT
StBC 93455 816-H1
HASTINGS DR
StBC 93117 984-C7
HASTINGS ST
Cmbr 93428 528-E6
HATHWAY AV
SLO 93405 653-J2
SLO 93405 654-A2
HATTERAS ST
MOBY 93442 611-D2
HAVENCREST DR
StBC 93455 817-B6
HAVEN HILL WY
SLOC 93420 345-E5
SLOC 93420 736-B1
HAWKINS CT
ARGD 93420 715-A5
HAWK RIDGE PL
SLOC 93451 325-D4
HAWK VIEW CT
SLOC 93420 715-A7
SLOC 93420 735-B1
HAWLEY ST
SLOC 93465 553-D2
HAWTHORN ST
SMRA 93458 776-G3
StBC 93437 855-H7
HAWTHORNE LN
Npmo 93444 735-H5
HAWTHORNE ST
LMPC 93436 916-F2
HAY BARN LN
SLOC 93405 653-C3
HAYS ST
SLO 93405 654-A2
HAZEL DR
SLO 93405 653-D7
HAZEL LN
Npmo 93444 756-A5
HAZELNUT ST
StBC 93437 855-H7
HEARST CT
SMRA 93454 777-B6
HEARTHSTONE DR
SMRA 93454 777-C7
HEARTS PL
SLOC 93446 493-F2
HEATH LN
Cmbr 93428 528-E6
HEATH ST
StBC 93437 855-H7
HEATH ST
StBC 93437 875-H1
HEATHER CIR
StBC 93455 817-A4
HEATHER CT
Npmo 93444 756-B4
SLOC 93465 553-C1
HEATHER LN
StBC 93437 875-H3
HEATHERWOOD LN
StBC 93455 817-B6
HEDLEY DR
SLO 93405 653-E7
HEIDI CT
SMRA 93454 777-B6
HEIDI PL
SLOC 93420 735-B3
HELEN ST
PSRS 93446 513-J6
HELEN WY
Npmo 93444 756-G6
HELENA AV
SBAR 93101 996-B4
SLOC 93453 614-F3
HELENA ST
SLO 93401 654-B5
SLOC 93420 714-H7
StBC 93440 878-G2
HELGREN CT
SLOC 93465 553-B1
HELROY RD
SLOC 93420 735-E6
HEMI RD
SLOC 93420 735-F3
HEMINGWAY LN
SLOC 93465 553-B3
HEMLOCK AV
MOBY 93442 611-F2
HEMLOCK PL
StBC 93111 994-J1
HEMLOCK ST
StBC 93437 855-E6
HEMPSTEAD AV
StBC 93117 993-F2
HENDERSON LN
SLOC 93445 734-G1
HENDERSON ST
SLO 93401 654-B3
SLO 93405 654-B2
HENNING DR
StBC 93441 900-H5
HENRIETTA AV
StBC 93402 631-F6
HENRY ST
SLO 93401 654-A5
HERADO AV
StBC 93437 875-D2
HERBERT AV
SLOC 93430 591-C4
HERCULES AV
StBC 93436 876-D5
HERDSMAN WY
SLOC 93465 533-C5
HEREFORD LN
SLOC 93446 533-H2
HERITAGE LN
SLOC 93420 714-J1
StBC 93440 878-J2
HERITAGE RD
SLOC 93446 471-A4
HERMOSA AV
ATAS 93422 573-H5
HERMOSA CT
GBCH 93433 714-F6
LMPC 93436 916-B2
HERMOSA DR
PBCH 93449 693-E5
SMRA 93458 776-F6
HERMOSA RD
SBAR 93105 995-G1
HERMOSA ST
SMRA 93454 776-H6
SMRA 93458 776-G6
HERMOSA WY
SLO 93405 653-G3
HERMOSA VISTA WY
SLOC 93420 734-H4
HERMOSILLA AV
ATAS 93422 573-G2
HERMOSILLA DR
SBAR 93108 996-G3
StBC 93108 996-G3
HERNANDEZ DR
GDLP 93434 774-J6
HESPERIA RD
SLOC 93426 324-J3
HESPERIAN LN
Cmbr 93428 528-G7
HETRICK AV
Npmo 93444 735-G6
HETRICK AV
Npmo 93444 755-H1
SLOC 93420 735-G5
HIAWATHA LN
SLOC 93420 714-H7
HIBISCUS CT
Npmo 93444 755-J3
Npmo 93444 756-A3
StBC 93455 817-A3
HIBISCUS LN
StBC 93437 875-J3
HIBISCUS ST
SLOC 93445 734-G1
E HICKORY AV
LMPC 93436 916-F2
W HICKORY AV
LMPC 93436 916-C2
HICKORY LN
SLOC 93446 513-D7
HICKORY ST
CARP 93013 1018-F1
StBC 93437 855-E6
HICKORY WY
SLVG 93463 940-D2
HIDALGO AV
ATAS 93422 573-J1
HIDALGO ST
SLOC 93430 591-B4
HIDDEN CREEK CANYON DR
SLOC 93405 693-C2
HIDDEN HILLS RD
SLOC 93420 735-F6
HIDDEN MOUNTAIN RD
SLOC 93446 325-A6
HIDDEN OAKS RD
SBAR 93110 995-D3
HIDDEN PINE LN
SLOC 93420 715-A1
HIDDEN PINES WY
SMRA 93458 776-G3
StBC 93458 776-G3
HIDDEN RANCH WY
SLOC 93420 735-E7
HIDDEN SPRINGS RD
SLOC 93401 674-C5
HIDDEN VALLEY LN
StBC 93108 987-G7
StBC 93108 997-F1
HIDDEN VALLEY RD
StBC 93105 964-H6
HIGH RD
StBC 93108 996-G3
HIGH ST
SLO 93401 653-J5
SLO 93401 654-A5
HIGHCASTLE LN
StBC 93455 816-G4
HIGHGROVE AV
StBC 93117 993-J3
HIGHLAND DR
PBCH 93449 714-D3
SBAR 93109 995-J5
SLO 93405 653-F1
SLOC 93402 631-F7
SLOC 93405 653-H2
StBC 93455 816-H6
HIGHLAND RD
StBC 93460 921-A5
HIGHLAND WY
GBCH 93433 714-E6
HIGHLAND HILLS RD
Npmo 93444 736-A5
HIGHLAND PARK DR
PSRS 93446 513-E4
HIGH MEADOW DR
Npmo 93444 756-B6
StBC 93463 920-G7
HIGH RIDGE LN
SBAR 93103 996-C1
HIGH RIDGE RD
SLOC 93446 534-H4
HIGH SCHOOL HILL RD
ATAS 93422 573-H4
HIGH VIEW DR
SLOC 93420 715-A1
HIGHWAY Rt#-1
StBC 93455 345-E11
HIGHWAY Rt#-33
SLOC - 346-F9
StBC - 346-F10
StBC 93252 346-F11
StBC 93252 366-G1
HIGHWAY Rt#-41
SLOC 92389 325-H3
SLOC 93446 325-F6
SLOC 93461 325-G4
HIGHWAY Rt#-46
PSRS 93446 513-J3
HIGHWAY Rt#-46
PSRS 93446 514-F1
PSRS 93446 533-F3
SLOC 92389 325-E6
SLOC 93446 325-E6
SLOC 93446 514-J1
SLOC 93446 533-E3
SLOC 93451 325-E6
SLOC 93461 325-G4
SLOC 93465 324-L8
SLOC 93465 325-A7
SLOC 93465 533-C5
HIGHWAY Rt#-58
SLOC - 346-B1
HIGHWAY Rt#-135
StBC 93440 365-G1
StBC 93440 878-D1
StBC 93455 345-E11
StBC 93455 365-E1
HIGHWAY Rt#-150
CARP 93013 1018-H2
StBC 93013 1018-J1
HIGHWAY Rt#-154
StBC 93105 365-L5
StBC 93105 366-A5
StBC 93440 900-C2
StBC 93441 900-C2
StBC 93460 365-L5
StBC 93460 900-J5
StBC 93460 901-A6
StBC 93460 921-B1
StBC 93460 941-H1
HIGHWAY Rt#-166
SLOC - 345-K5
SLOC - 346-A6
SLOC - 346-F9
SLOC 93252 346-E9
SLOC 93454 345-H7
StBC - 345-K5
StBC - 346-A7
StBC - 806-H2
StBC 93252 346-E9
StBC 93254 346-C8
StBC 93254 806-A1
StBC 93454 345-J6
HIGHWAY Rt#-246
BLTN - 919-H5
BLTN - 920-A6
BLTN 93427 919-G5
BLTN 93427 920-A6
BLTN 93436 919-F4
StBC 93436 365-F3
StBC 93436 919-E4
StBC 93463 920-A6
HIGOS WY
Npmo 93444 756-B4
HIGUERA ST
SLO 93401 653-J4
SLO 93401 654-A3
SLO 93401 673-H1
HIGUERA ST Rt#-227
SLO 93401 653-H6
S HIGUERA ST
SLO 93401 653-H7
SLO 93401 673-G3
SLOC 93401 673-G3
SLOC 93405 673-G3
HILL CT
StBC 93455 817-A4
HILL RD
StBC 93108 996-G4
HILL ST
MOBY 93442 611-F4
Npmo 93444 756-B3
SLO 93405 653-H3
StBC 93440 878-G2
HILLCREST DR
ARGD 93420 714-G4
Cmbr 93428 528-F6
MOBY 93442 611-F5
PSRS 93446 513-E5
HILLCREST PL
SLO 93401 654-A3
HILLCREST RD
SBAR 93103 986-B7
SBAR 93103 996-B1
StBC 93460 901-D3
HILL HAVEN RD
StBC 93463 920-G7
HILLSBORO DR
SMRA 93454 777-B6
HILLSBORO ST
StBC 93117 993-G3
HILLSBORO WY
StBC 93117 993-H3
HILLSIDE CT
ARGD 93420 715-B5
HILLSIDE DR
SLVG 93463 920-F7

STREET Name	City	ZIP	Pg-Grid
HILLSIDE LN	SLOC	93420	694-J7
	SLOC	93420	714-J1
HILLSIDE RD	SBAR	93101	995-G6
HILLTOP DR	PSRS	93446	513-E6
	StBC	93465	553-D2
HILLTOP LN	SLOC	93451	473-C4
HILLTOP RD	StBC	93455	817-A3
HILLTOP WY	SLOC	93424	693-B2
HILLVIEW DR	StBC	93117	993-G1
HILLVIEW PL	Npmo	93444	756-A2
HILLVIEW RD	SLOC	93420	755-A2
HILLVIEW ST	SLVG	93463	920-F7
HILLVIEW ST	MOBY	93442	611-F4
HI MOUNTAIN RD	SLOC	-	345-F2
	SLOC	93420	694-J7
	SLOC	93420	695-A7
	SLOC	93420	345-E4
HIND LN	SLO	93401	673-H1
HINDFELL WY	SLVG	93463	920-F7
HINDS AV	PBCH	93449	714-B3
HINES LN	SMRA	93454	796-H4
HISCHIER LN	SLOC	93420	695-C7
	SLOC	93420	715-D1
HITCHCOCK WY	StBC	93105	995-E2
HITCHCOCK RANCH RD	StBC	93105	995-E1
HIXON DR	StBC	93108	997-A3
HOBBS LN	StBC	93455	816-H5
HOBBY HORSE RD	SLVG	93463	920-J7
HODGES LN	StBC	93108	996-J1
	StBC	93108	997-A1
HODGES RD	ARGD	93420	714-G3
HOGAN CT	Npmo	93444	735-D7
HOGAN PL	PSRS	93446	513-H7
	PSRS	93446	513-H5
HOG CANYON RD	SLOC	93446	494-H2
	SLOC	93451	325-D3
	SLOC	93451	494-H2
HOLDEN AV	SLOC	93446	714-H7
HOLDEN PL	Cmbr	93428	548-H2
HOLDER PARK LN	SLOC	93446	534-J3
HOLIDAY HILL RD	StBC	93117	984-D5
HOLLEY	SLO	93401	673-H1
HOLLISTER AV	PBCH	93449	714-B2
	SBAR	93117	994-B2
	SLOC	93405	633-A4
	StBC	93117	994-F2
	StBC	93110	995-A1
	StBC	93117	983-H6
	StBC	93117	993-F2
HOLLISTER LN	SLOC	93402	631-J6
	SLOC	93402	632-A6
HOLLISTER ST	StBC	93441	900-H5
	StBC	93446	900-G5
	Summ	93067	997-D3
HOLLY AV	CARP	93013	998-C7
HOLLY LN	SLVG	93463	920-G6
HOLLY RD	StBC	93105	985-J5
HOLLY ST	GDLP	93434	775-A6
HOLLY WY	PBCH	93449	714-B3
HOLLYHOCK LN	SLOC	93465	534-B6
HOLLYHOCK WY	SLO	93401	674-C1
HOLLY OAK LN	StBC	93455	796-H7
HOLMCREST DR	SBAR	93103	996-C2
HOLSTED DR	StBC	93463	920-D6
HOMESTEAD RD	Cmbr	93428	548-H2
HONDA CT	ATAS	93422	573-J2
HONDONADA RD	SLOC	93420	715-D1
HONEY WY	StBC	93465	553-D1
HONEY GROVE LN	Npmo	93444	756-C5
HONEY LOCUST CT	SLVG	93463	920-F7
HONEYSUCKLE LN	PSRS	93446	514-A6
	SLOC	93420	694-J7
	SLOC	93420	695-A7
HONEYSUCKLE WY	StBC	93455	896-D6
HONOLULU AV	StBC	93455	816-H3
HONOR FARM RD	StBC	93110	985-E7
	StBC	93110	995-A1
N HOPE AV	StBC	93105	985-E7
	StBC	93455	995-E1
	SBAR	93110	985-E7
	StBC	93110	995-E1
	StBC	93110	985-E1
	SBAR	93110	985-E7
	StBC	93105	985-E7
	StBC	93110	985-E1
S HOPE AV	StBC	93105	995-E1
HOPE ST	SLO	93405	654-A2
HOPE TER	StBC	93105	985-E7
HOPE TERRACE CT	StBC	93455	816-H5
HOPKINS LN	StBC	93401	674-B1
HOPKINS ST	StBC	93465	553-A2
HORIZON CT	StBC	93446	494-C6
HORIZON DR	StBC	93460	921-A6
	StBC	93463	921-A6
HORIZON LN	SLO	93401	673-J2
HORNBECK PL			
HORSEMAN CT	SMRA	93454	777-B6
HORSESHOE WY			
HORSTMAN ST	StBC	93465	553-E2
HOSMER LN	StBC	93108	996-J2
HOSPITAL DR	ATAS	93422	573-J2
HOT SPRINGS RD	SBAR	93108	996-G3
	StBC	93108	986-H6
	StBC	93108	996-H1
	Npmo	93444	756-G6
HOURIHAN RANCH RD			
HOUSTON DR	StBC	93455	651-F1
HOUSTON WY	PBCH	93449	714-F3
HOWARD AV	StBC	93465	631-E6
HOWARD ST	SLO	93401	653-J3
HUASNA DR	SLO	93405	653-F7
	SLO	93405	673-G1
HUASNA RD	ARGD	93420	715-B4
	SLOC	93420	345-E5
	SLOC	93420	715-C4
HUASNA RIVER RD	SLOC	-	345-G6
	SLOC	-	737-F2
HUASNA TOWNSITE RD	SLOC	93420	345-F5
	SLOC	93420	737-E1
HUBBARD	SLOC	93430	591-D5
HUBBARD AV	StBC	93254	806-C2
HUBER ST	GBCH	93433	714-E6
HUCKLEBERRY LN	SLO	93401	674-E1
HUDSON AV	SLOC	93405	633-A4
HUDSON DR	StBC	93109	995-G7
HUEBNER LN	ARGD	93420	715-B5
HUERHUERO RD	SLOC	93453	325-E10
HUERO RD	SLOC	93422	594-D6
HUMBERT AV	SLO	93401	654-A6
HUMBOLDT AV	PSRS	93446	514-A6
HUMBOLDT DR	Npmo	93444	756-B6
HUMBOLDT ST	SLOC	93402	631-E6
HUMMEL DR	StBC	93455	816-H3
HUMMINGBIRD	PSRS	93446	514-A7
HUMMINGBIRD LN	StBC	93455	816-J1
HUMPHREY RD	StBC	93108	996-J4
HUNT DR	Summ	93067	997-E2
HUNTER PL	SLOC	93446	493-E4
HUNTER RIDGE LN	Npmo	93444	755-G3
HUNTINGTON AV	GBCH	93433	714-F6
HUNTINGTON DR	StBC	93111	984-F7
HUNTINGTON PL	LMPC	93436	916-G2
HUNTINGTON RD	Cmbr	93428	528-E7
HUNTINGTON WY	StBC	93455	817-E5
HURON WY	StBC	93455	817-E5
HURRICANE RD	SLOC	-	346-D3
HUSTON ST	GBCH	93433	714-E6
HUTTON RD	Npmo	93444	756-F7
	Npmo	93444	776-G1
HUTTON ST	SLO	93401	653-J5

I

STREET Name	City	ZIP	Pg-Grid
I ST	LMPC	93436	896-E7
	LMPC	93436	916-E1
N I ST	LMPC	93436	896-E7
	LMPC	93436	916-E1
S I ST	LMPC	93436	916-E2
IAIQUA LN	StBC	93110	985-D6
IBIS CIR	GDLP	93434	774-H6
IBIS LN	SLOC	93446	471-D6
ICELAND AV	StBC	93437	875-E2
IDA PL	Npmo	93444	756-A4
IDE ST	ARGD	93420	715-A5
IDYLLWILD PL	SLOC	93420	754-J1
IGLOO RD	StBC	93437	875-G6
IKEDA WY	ARGD	93420	715-C4
ILENE DR	SLO	93405	653-E7
ILIFF LN	StBC	93458	776-G4
ILLINOIS WY	Npmo	93444	755-E6
IL TRENO PL	SLOC	93446	494-A6
IMPALA TR	StBC	93455	816-G7
IMPERIAL AV	SLOC	93405	633-E5
IMPERIAL WY	StBC	93455	816-J6
INDEPENDENCE CT	StBC	93455	816-H5
INDEPENDENCE RANCH PL	SLOC	93451	325-D5
INDIAN LN	StBC	93108	986-G7
INDIAN WY	StBC	93460	941-D2
INDIANA WY	Npmo	93444	755-F6
INDIAN HILLS WY	SBAR	93101	995-J3
	SBAR	93103	996-A2
INDIAN KNOB RD	SLO	93401	653-J5
	SLO	93401	654-A4
INDIAN VALLEY RD	MonC	-	453-D3
	MonC	93451	453-D3
	MonC	93451	453-D4
	SLOC	93451	473-G1
INDIGO CIR	MOBY	93442	611-E2
INDIO DR	PBCH	93449	693-E5
	PBCH	93449	693-E5
INDIO MUERTO ST	SBAR	93103	996-D4
INDUSTRIAL	SLOC	93451	453-C5
INDUSTRIAL PKWY	SMRA	93455	796-F7
INDUSTRIAL WY	BLTN	93427	919-G5
	LMPC	93436	916-G1
	SLO	93401	674-B1
	SLOC	93401	674-B1
INDUSTRIAL TAXI WY	PSRS	93446	494-C6
INGA RD	Npmo	93444	755-J3
	Npmo	93444	756-A2
INGER DR	StBC	93455	796-H4
INNESLEY DR	ARGD	93420	715-A7
INTERLAKE RD Rt#-G14	SLOC	93426	324-K3
INVERNESS AV	SMRA	93454	797-A1
INVERNESS DR	StBC	93455	876-E6
INVERNESS LN	PSRS	93446	533-J1
INVERNESS PL	StBC	93108	997-B2
INVIERNO DR	SBAR	93110	985-D7
INWOOD DR	StBC	93111	994-J2
INWOOD PL	StBC	93111	994-J2
INYO AV	SLOC	93405	633-A5
INYO ST	SLOC	93402	631-E6
IRELANE DR	BLTN	93427	919-H5
IRIS AV	StBC	93117	994-C1
IRIS CT	LMPC	93436	896-D6
IRIS ST	SLO	93401	654-B4
IRISH WY	PBCH	93449	714-E3
IRISH HILLS	SLOC	93402	652-A1
IRONBARK ST	SLO	93401	674-D1
IRONRIDGE CT	SMRA	93455	796-F6
IRONWOOD AV	MOBY	93442	611-E2
IRONWOOD CT	MOBY	93442	611-F3
IRONWOOD DR	StBC	93455	816-B1
IRONWOOD PL	SLOC	93465	553-A1
IRONWOOD ST	StBC	93437	855-D6
IRONWOOD WY	SLVG	93463	940-D2
IRVINE LN	StBC	93108	986-J7
IRVINE STOVALL MEM HWY Rt#-166	Npmo	93444	776-H1
	StBC	93454	776-H1
	StBC	93454	777-B1
ISLAND CT	SLOC	93445	714-F7
ISLAND ST	MOBY	93442	611-E2
ISLAND VIEW DR	SBAR	93109	995-H6
ISLAY ST	SBAR	93101	995-J3
	SBAR	93101	996-A2
	SBAR	93103	996-A2
ISLETA AV	StBC	93109	996-A6
IVA CT	Cmbr	93428	528-F6
IVAR ST	Cmbr	93428	548-F2
IVORY DR	StBC	93455	817-B4
IVY LN	PSRS	93446	513-J5
	SLVG	93463	920-F7

J

STREET Name	City	ZIP	Pg-Grid
J RD	StBC	93106	994-B3
J ST	LMPC	93436	916-E1
	SLOC	93430	614-G3
	SLOC	93453	614-G3
JACARANDA CT	SMRA	93458	796-D5
JACARANDA LN	SLOC	93402	652-D2
	StBC	93108	997-A3
JACARANDA ST	StBC	93437	855-F7
JACARANDA WY	CARP	93013	1018-G1
JACK CREEK RD	StBC	93465	325-A8
JACKIE LN	SMRA	93454	797-A1
JACK RABBIT RD	StBC	93436	736-E2
JACKSON DR	PSRS	93446	513-H5
JADE CT	StBC	93455	817-C5
JADE CANYON WY	StBC	93465	574-J5
JALAMA CT	GBCH	93433	714-F6
JALAMA RD	StBC	93436	365-F5
JALISCO CT	SLO	93405	653-D6
JAMAICA ST	MOBY	93442	611-E1
JAMES RD	StBC	93111	994-G3
JAMES ST	PSRS	93446	513-F6
	SLOC	93465	553-D3
JAMES WY	ARGD	93420	714-H3
	ARGD	93420	714-H3
	PBCH	93449	714-D3
JAMESON CT	SLOC	93420	754-J1
N JAMESON LN	StBC	93108	996-J3
	StBC	93108	997-A3
	Summ	93067	997-A4
S JAMESON LN	StBC	93108	996-J3
	StBC	93108	997-A4
JAMIE LP	SMRA	93454	797-A1
JAMI LEE CT	SLOC	93401	654-D6
JANE DR	SLO	93405	653-E7
JANE ST	SMRA	93458	796-G3
JANET AV	GBCH	93433	714-F7
JANET DR	PBCH	93449	714-F3
	StBC	93455	817-B5
JANICE DR	SBAR	93103	996-A2
JANICE ST	PSRS	93446	514-A6
JANIN CT	StBC	93463	920-H7
JANIN WY	SLOC	93463	920-H6
JANUARY ST	Npmo	93444	756-B4
JAQUIMA RD	ATAS	93422	573-B2
JARDINE RD	SLOC	93446	494-G4
	SLOC	93446	514-G1
JARED LN	SLO	93441	365-K2
JASMINE LN	StBC	93455	816-H2
JASMINE ST	LMPC	93436	896-C7
JASON DR	StBC	93441	900-H5
JASON WY	StBC	93463	920-J6
	StBC	93463	921-A5
JASPER WY	Npmo	93444	756-A4
JAVA ST	MOBY	93442	611-E1
JAY ST	CARP	93013	998-E6
JAYCEE DR	SLO	93405	653-G2
JEAN DR	SLO	93401	653-E7
JEAN LN	StBC	93111	984-G6
JEAN ST	Cmbr	93428	548-F2
JEANETTE LN	Npmo	93444	756-B5
JEANNE WY	PSRS	93446	514-A6
JEFFERSON CT	StBC	93455	817-A4
JEFFREY CT	SMRA	93454	797-A1
JEFFREY DR	SLO	93405	653-G2
JELINDA DR	StBC	93108	997-B2
JENNA DR	SBAR	93109	995-H5
	SLOC	93445	714-D7
JENNER WY	SLOC	93420	735-A4
JENNIE LN	SMRA	93454	755-H2
JENNIFER CT	GBCH	93433	714-F7
	SMRA	93454	776-J6
JENNIFER ST	SLO	93401	654-A5
JENNILSA LN	StBC	93463	920-E6
JENNINGS AV	SBAR	93103	996-C3
JENNINGS DR	ARGD	93420	715-A7
JENNY PL	ARGD	93420	714-H3
JENSEN RD	SLOC	93446	324-L7
	SLOC	93446	325-A6
JERRY LN	SMRA	93454	777-A5
JESMARY LN	SBAR	93105	995-H2
JESPERSON RD	SLOC	93401	673-J4
	SLOC	93401	674-A6
JESSELLE CT	SMRA	93454	776-J6
JESSICA PL	Npmo	93444	756-B5
JESSIE CT	SMRA	93454	777-A5
JESUSITA LN	SBAR	93105	985-G6
JETTY AV	SLOC	93465	714-E7
JEWEL ST	SMRA	93454	776-H5
	SMRA	93454	777-A5
	SMRA	93458	776-F5

STREET Name	City	ZIP	Pg-Grid
JILL AV	SMRA	93458	796-E2
JIMENO RD	SBAR	93103	996-A2
JOAN PL	SLOC	93401	674-D7
JOANNE DR	StBC	93455	796-H7
JODI CT	SMRA	93454	797-A1
JODI DR	LMPC	93436	896-C6
JOHE LN	SLO	93405	653-D3
JOHNSON AV	SLO	93401	654-A3
	SLO	93401	654-B4
JOHNSON DR	SMRA	93458	776-H3
JOLON RD	ATAS	93422	573-F7
JONATA ST	SLVG	93463	920-F6
JONATA PARK RD	BLTN	93427	919-H4
	StBC	93427	919-H4
JONATHAN PL	SMRA	93454	777-A7
JONES LN	StBC	93463	920-J6
	StBC	93463	921-A5
JONES ST	Npmo	93444	735-D7
JORDAN RD	StBC	93428	528-D4
JORNADA LN	BLTN	93427	919-H5
JOSEPH ST	SMRA	93454	777-B6
JOSHUA ST	Npmo	93444	756-E7
JOVITA PL	Npmo	93444	735-J5
JOYCE CT	SLO	93401	654-B5
JOYCE WY	PBCH	93449	714-F3
JUANA MARIA AV	SBAR	93103	996-C3
JUAN CRESPI LN	StBC	93108	996-J1
JUANITA AV	ATAS	93422	573-J3
	SBAR	93109	995-H5
	SLOC	93445	714-D7
JUAREZ AV	ATAS	93422	573-J2
JUDGE AV	SLOC	93420	714-H7
JULIA DR	Cmbr	93428	528-E4
JULIE LN	StBC	93465	553-D1
JULIE ST	SLO	93401	674-E7
JULLIEN DR	StBC	93455	816-H6
JUNCAL RD	StBC	93437	855-H7
	StBC	-	366-F7
JUNE AV	CARP	93013	998-D6
JUNIPER AV	SLVG	93463	940-E2
JUNIPER PL	CARP	93013	998-D7
JUNIPER ST	ARGD	93420	714-G5
	MOBY	93442	611-F2
	Npmo	93444	756-A3
	StBC	93111	994-F1
JUNIPER WK	StBC	93111	994-A4
JUNIPERO AV	ATAS	93422	574-A5
JUNIPERO PZ	SBAR	93105	995-J2
JUNIPERO ST	SBAR	93105	995-H2
JUNO CT	Npmo	93444	756-C4
JUPITER AV	StBC	93436	896-C1
JUPITER DR	Npmo	93444	756-A5
JUVENILE HALL RD			

K

STREET Name	City	ZIP	Pg-Grid
K ST	SLOC	93451	473-F2
	SLOC	93453	614-G3
N K ST	LMPC	93436	896-D7
	LMPC	93436	916-D1
S K ST	LMPC	93436	916-D2
KAISER AV	SMRA	93454	777-A5
KALLE LN	StBC	93455	816-H5
KALLEY DR	StBC	93117	993-F1
KAMALA WY	StBC	93117	994-C1
KAMEO ST	SMRA	93458	796-E2
KANIN HOJ	SLVG	93463	920-F6
KANSAS AV	SLOC	93405	633-B5
	SLOC	93460	453-A4
KAPALUA DR	StBC	93455	816-D4
KAPAREIL LN	PSRS	93446	514-A4
KARA DR	StBC	93111	984-G6
KAREN CT	SMRA	93454	796-J1
	SMRA	93454	797-A1
	SMRA	93458	796-J1
KAREN DR	SMRA	93454	797-B1
KAREN PL	PBCH	93449	714-F3
KAREN WY	PBCH	93449	714-F3
KARI LN	StBC	93455	816-E4
KARINA WY	SLOC	93420	715-A1
KARL CT	Npmo	93444	755-J3
KARNES RD	StBC	93455	817-B5
KATE CT	SMRA	93454	776-J6
KATHERINE CT	SLOC	93420	714-H7
KATHERINE DR	Npmo	93444	756-B4
KATHLEEN CT	SMRA	93454	777-A7
KATHRYAN CT	Npmo	93444	756-E7
KATHRYN DR	Cmbr	93428	528-E4
KATHRYN WY	SMRA	93454	777-A5
KATHY CT	SLOC	93401	674-E7
KATHY ST	CARP	93013	998-E6
KATSURA AV	StBC	93437	855-H7
	StBC	93437	875-H1
KAY ST	Cmbr	93428	548-H2
KEATON BLVD	SLOC	93430	591-C4
KEENAN RD	SLVG	93463	900-G5
KELLOGG AV	StBC	93111	984-F6
	StBC	93117	994-F1
KELLOGG PL	StBC	93111	984-F5
KELLOGG WY	StBC	93117	994-E2
KEN AV	StBC	93455	817-A6
KENAI CT	StBC	93455	816-H4
KENDAL LN	Cmbr	93428	528-D5
KENDALE PL	BLTN	93427	919-J5
KENDALE RD	BLTN	93427	919-H5
	StBC	93427	919-J6
KENDRA CT	SLOC	93401	654-B5
KENMORE PL	StBC	93105	985-H7

STREET Name	City	ZIP	Pg-Grid
KENNEDY LN	SLOC	93451	473-G3
KENNETH AV	StBC	93455	817-B5
KENNETH DR	Cmbr	93428	548-F2
KENNINGTON DR	StBC	93455	816-F5
KENSINGTON AV	SMRA	93454	777-A5
KENSINGTON WY	SMRA	93454	777-A6
KENT CT	StBC	93458	776-F4
KENT PL	StBC	93117	984-F7
KENT ST	Cmbr	93428	528-E6
	Npmo	93444	756-B2
KENTIA AV	SBAR	93101	995-G3
KENTUCKY AV	StBC	93430	591-A1
KENTUCKY RD	StBC	93460	365-L5
	StBC	93460	922-A7
KENTUCKY ST	StBC	93455	816-D4
KENWOOD DR	SLOC	93401	654-C6
KENWOOD RD	StBC	93109	995-G5
KEO DR	StBC	93111	994-G1
KERN CT	SMRA	93454	776-J1
KERN DR	StBC	93111	994-G1
KERRY AV	Cmbr	93428	548-H1
KERRY DR	SLO	93405	653-E7
KERWIN ST	Cmbr	93428	548-F2
KESTREL LN	SLOC	93420	693-C2
	SLOC	93424	693-C2
KESTREL WY	Npmo	93444	756-B4
KEYSTONE LN	SMRA	93454	777-A7
KEYSTONE MINE RD	SLOC	93424	324-H6
	SLOC	93452	324-H6
KIESTER PL	SBAR	93117	994-C2
KILARNEY CT	SLOC	93405	653-D6
KILER CANYON RD	SLOC	93446	325-A6
KILER CREEK PL	SLOC	93446	533-A1
KIMBALL ST	SBAR	93103	996-D4
KIMBERLY AV	SBAR	93101	996-B5
KIMBERLY DR	PSRS	93446	534-B1
KIM SUE LN	BLTN	93427	919-H5
KINEVAN RD	StBC	93105	964-E6
KING CT	SLO	93401	653-J6
KING ST	SLO	93401	653-J5
KING ARTHURS CT	StBC	93117	993-J4
KING DANIEL LN	StBC	93117	993-G1
KINGFISHER LN	StBC	93111	693-B1
KING JAMES CT	StBC	93117	993-G1
KINGS AV	MOBY	93442	611-H7
KINGS DR	PSRS	93446	534-B1
KINGS LN	SMRA	93454	776-J7
	SMRA	93454	777-A7
KINGS WY	StBC	93117	993-J4

STREET Name	City	ZIP	Pg-Grid
KINGSBURY DR	ARGD	93420	715-A7
KINGSBURY RD	SLOC	93465	574-G1
KINGSTON AV	StBC	93117	994-F3
KINGSTON DR	SMRA	93458	776-F5
KINMAN AV	StBC	93111	994-E1
KIP LN	SLOC	93420	734-H5
KIRBY WY	SLOC	93444	756-A6
KIRK DR	StBC	93111	994-G1
KIRSCHENMANN RD	Npmo	93444	756-B2
KIT WY	StBC	93455	817-A4
KLAMATH RD	SLOC	93454	654-A1
KLAU MINE RD	SLOC	93446	324-L6
	SLOC	93465	324-L6
KLECK RD	PSRS	93446	513-J4
KLEIN BLVD	LMPC	93436	895-J3
KNAPP RD	SLOC	93405	633-A5
KNIGHT CT	StBC	93108	996-F1
KNIGHTBRIDGE DR	SMRA	93455	796-H6
KNIGHTS LN	SMRA	93454	776-J7
W KNOLL CIR	SLOC	93446	469-D2
KNOLL DR	SLO	93401	654-C6
E KNOLL LN	SLOC	93446	469-D1
KNOLL CIRCLE DR	SBAR	93103	996-D2
KNOLLGLEN CT	PSRS	93446	514-A4
KNOLLWOOD DR	Cmbr	93428	528-F6
	StBC	93108	987-C2
E KNOTTS ST	Cmbr	93428	528-E6
KNUDSEN WY	SMRA	93458	796-F1
KOA AV	MOBY	93442	611-F3
KODIAK AV	StBC	93111	994-J2
KODIAK LN	SLOC	93420	715-B2
KODIAK ST	MOBY	93442	611-E1
KOLDING AV	SLVG	93463	920-G7
KONA WY	StBC	93455	816-J2
KORINA WY	StBC	93437	855-E6
KOVAL LN	SMRA	93455	796-H7
KOWALSKI AV	SBAR	93101	995-H4
KRILL RD	SLOC	93420	920-D1
KRIS DR	StBC	93455	816-E4
KRISTEN CT	StBC	93111	984-F7
KRISTY CT	SLO	93401	654-E4
KROEBER WK	StBC	93117	993-J4
KRONBORG DR	SLOC	93420	920-D6
KRONEN WY	SLVG	93463	920-E7

L

STREET Name	City	ZIP	Pg-Grid
L ST	SLOC	93451	473-F1
N L ST	LMPC	93436	896-D6
	LMPC	93436	916-D1
S L ST	LMPC	93436	916-D2
LA BARBARA DR	SBAR	93110	985-D7
	StBC	93110	985-D7

Thomas Bros. Maps® — COPYRIGHT 2000 — STB & SLO — INDEX

STREET Name	City	ZIP	Pg-Grid
LA BREA AV	SMRA	93458	796-E3
LA BREA CT	SLOC	93445	734-G1
LA BREA LN	CARP	93013	998-E7
LA BUENA TIERRA	StBC	93111	984-G6
LA CADENA ST	SBAR	93103	996-D3
LA CALERA CT	StBC	93117	993-J2
LA CAMARILLA PL	Npmo	93444	755-J5
	Npmo	93444	756-A5
LA CANADA	ARGD	93420	714-H3
LA CANADA DR	SLO	93405	653-G2
LA CANADA LN	ATAS	93422	553-C7
LA CIMA RD	SBAR	93101	995-G4
	SBAR	93105	995-G4
LA CITA CT	SLO	93401	654-C5
LA COLIMA	PBCH	93449	714-E3
LA COLINA RD	SBAR	93110	985-D7
LA COMBADURA RD	StBC	93105	985-H7
LA CORONILLA RD	SBAR	93109	995-H5
LA COSTA CT	ATAS	93422	594-C1
	SLOC	93445	734-G1
LA COSTA DR	SMRA	93455	796-G6
LA COSTA LN	StBC	93436	876-E5
LA CRESCENTA WY	SLOC	93446	594-F4
LA CRESTA CIR	SLOC	93446	995-J6
LA CRESTA DR	ARGD	93420	715-B4
LA CRUZ WY	SLOC	93446	533-F6
LA CUMBRE CIR	SBAR	93105	995-E2
LA CUMBRE LN	Npmo	93444	755-H6
LA CUMBRE RD	SBAR	93105	995-D1
	SBAR	93110	985-D1
	SBAR	93110	995-D1
	StBC	93105	995-D1
	StBC	93110	985-D7
LA CUMBRE HILLS LN	SBAR	93110	985-E7
LA CUMBRE PLAZA LN	StBC	93437	855-F7
	SBAR	93105	995-D1
LADAN DR	SLOC	93463	920-G5
LADD LN	SMRA	93455	796-G7
LADDY LN	SLOC	93446	493-F2
LADERA CT	SLO	93401	654-A6
LADERA LN	PSRS	93446	533-J2
	SLOC	93446	533-J2
	SLOC	93446	534-A2
	StBC	93108	987-F7
	StBC	93108	997-F1
LADERA ST	ARGD	93420	715-A4
LADILLO DR	SBAR	93101	996-A5
LADO DR	StBC	93111	984-H7
LADRILLOS WY	SLOC	93451	473-F1
LA DUE ST	SLOC	93446	714-H7
LA ENTRADA	SBAR	93105	995-F3
	SBAR	93105	995-F3
LA ENTRADA AV	SLO	93405	653-G2
LA ENTRADA LN	SLOC	93445	734-G1
LA ESPADA DR	StBC	93111	984-J5
	SBAR	93105	985-A5
LA FINCA CT	SLOC	93420	695-B4
LA FLECHA LN	SBAR	93105	985-F7
LA FLORICITA	PBCH	93449	714-E2
LA FRANELLA RD	StBC	93111	984-G7
LA GAMA WY	StBC	93111	984-J7
	StBC	93111	994-J1
LA GARZA	PBCH	93449	714-D2
LA GAVIOTA	PBCH	93449	714-E2
LAGO AV	ATAS	93422	573-J6
LAGO DR	SBAR	93110	995-C2
LA GOLETA RD	StBC	93117	984-D6
LAGOON RD	StBC	93106	994-C5
LA GUARDIA LN	GDLP	93434	775-B5
LAGUNA AV	GBCH	93433	714-F4
LAGUNA CT	SLOC	93445	714-D7
LAGUNA DR	SLOC	93445	714-D7
	SLOC	93445	734-D1
LAGUNA LN	SLO	93405	653-E6
LAGUNA ST	SBAR	93101	995-J1
	SBAR	93101	996-A2
	SBAR	93103	995-J1
	SLOC	93445	714-D7
LAGUNA BLANCA DR	StBC	93110	995-D2
LAGUNA DEL CAMPO	SLOC	93446	533-J4
	SLOC	93446	534-A3
LAGUNA NEGRA LN	SLOC	93420	735-A7
LAGUNA RIDGE FIRE RD	VeCo	-	999-G5
LA JOLLA LN	GBCH	93433	714-F6
LA JOLLA DR	SBAR	93109	995-G7
LA JOLLA PL	StBC	93455	796-H7
	StBC	93455	816-H1
LA JOLLA ST	MOBY	93442	611-E3
	CARP	93013	998-C5
LA JOSA RD	StBC	93111	984-G6
LA JOYA DR	Npmo	93444	755-J6
LAKE ST	SLOC	93445	714-E7
LAKE CANYON RD	StBC	93437	855-F7
	StBC	93437	875-F1
LAKE CHORRO RD	SLOC	93405	633-E4
LAKE MARIE DR	StBC	93455	817-E5
LAKESIDE AV	SLOC	93445	714-D7
LAKESIDE PKWY	SMRA	93455	796-H4
LAKEVIEW CT	StBC	93455	816-H1
LAKE VIEW DR	ATAS	93422	573-J6
LAKEVIEW DR	SLOC	93426	324-J3
	SLOC	93426	470-A1
LAKEVIEW RD	SLOC	93426	469-E1
	StBC	93455	816-H1
LAKEVIEW ST	SLO	93405	653-F7
LAKOTA WY	SLOC	93422	594-D4
LALA LN	ATAS	93422	593-B2
LA LADERA DR	StBC	93110	995-C5
LA LATA DR	SLOC	93432	325-E8
	SLOC	93461	325-E8
LA LATA PL	BLTN	93427	919-G4
LA LINIA AV	ATAS	93422	574-A6
LA LITA LN	SBAR	93105	985-F6
LA LOMA AV	MOBY	93442	611-H6
LA LOMA CT	SBAR	93101	996-A3
LA LOMA DR	Npmo	93444	755-J6
	Npmo	93444	756-A5
LA LOMA WY	SBAR	93110	995-A2
LA LUNA CT	SLOC	93405	653-D6
LA LUZ RD	ATAS	93422	553-G7
LA MANIDA	CARP	93013	998-E6
LA MARINA	SBAR	93109	995-J6
LA MESA	StBC	93105	964-H1
LA MESA PZ	CARP	93013	998-E6
LA MILPITA RD	SBAR	93105	985-F7
LA MIRADA DR	Npmo	93444	755-J6
	StBC	93013	994-J4
	StBC	93013	998-A4
LA MIRADA LN	Npmo	93444	735-F7
	Npmo	93444	755-E1
LAMPLIGHTER LN	SLOC	93420	715-C3
	StBC	93455	816-G5
LAMPTON ST	StBC	93455	816-G5
LANA LN	LMPC	93436	896-C6
LANA ST	PSRS	93446	513-J6
	PSRS	93446	514-A6
LANAI RD	SBAR	93108	996-F1
	StBC	93108	996-F1
LANARK ST	StBC	93110	994-J2
	StBC	93111	994-J2
LANCASTER DR	ARGD	93420	714-G7
	StBC	93455	796-H7
	StBC	93455	816-H1
LANCASTER PL	SLOC	93420	734-H4
	StBC	93117	993-F2
LANCASTER ST	ATAS	93422	573-H5
LANCER DR	StBC	93455	816-J6
LANDFILL RD	StBC	93437	875-E4
LANDLUBBER LN	SLOC	93426	470-A1
LANDS END RD	SLOC	93426	469-J2
LANGLO TER	SBAR	93105	985-F7
LANGLO RANCH RD	StBC	93117	983-F7
	StBC	93117	993-E1
LANGTON ST	Cmbr	93428	548-G1
LANGTRY AV	StBC	93117	992-H1
LANTANA CT	StBC	93455	817-A3
LANTANA ST	Npmo	93444	755-H4
LANTANA WY	Npmo	93444	755-H4
LA PALA LN	CARP	93013	998-E7
LA PALOMA	PBCH	93449	693-E5
LA PALOMA AV	SBAR	93105	985-B6
LA PALOMA CT	ATAS	93422	594-C1
LA PALOMA DR	CARP	93013	998-D6
LA PANZA RD	SLOC	93432	325-E8
	SLOC	93461	325-E8
LA PATERA LN	StBC	93117	994-C2
	StBC	93117	994-C1
LA PATERA WY	StBC	93117	984-C7
LA PAZ AV	SBAR	93101	995-J3
	SBAR	93101	996-A3
LA PAZ CIR	ARGD	93420	715-B4
	SMRA	93455	796-J5
LA PAZ LN	ATAS	93422	594-B2
LA PAZ RD	StBC	93108	986-J7
LA PITA PL	BLTN	93427	919-H4
LA PLATA	SBAR	93109	995-J7
	SBAR	93109	996-A7
LAPORT AV	Npmo	93444	756-B1
LA PRADERO RD	SLOC	93422	594-F5
LA PUESTA DEL SOL	StBC	93013	997-F4
	Summ	93067	997-F4
LA PURISIMA CT	SLOC	93451	473-F1
LA PURISIMA ST	GDLP	93434	774-H6
LAQUILLA LN	SBAR	93103	996-C2
LA QUINTA DR	CARP	93013	998-C5
LA QUINTA PL	Npmo	93444	755-J6
LA QUINTA WY	SLOC	93436	876-D5
LARA LN	StBC	93455	816-J2
LA RADA	SBAR	93105	995-E2
LA RAMADA DR	StBC	93111	984-H7
LARAMIE DR	SLOC	93420	734-H5
LARCH AV	StBC	93455	816-J2
	StBC	93455	817-A2
LARCHMONT CT	StBC	93455	816-J2
LARCHMONT DR	ARGD	93420	714-J5
LARCHMONT PL	StBC	93117	984-D6
LAREDO DR	SLOC	93420	734-H4
LARGA AV	ATAS	93422	573-H5
LARGA DR	SLOC	93420	694-J7
LARGURA PL	SBAR	93103	996-B2
LARIAT DR	SLOC	93402	632-A7
LARIAT LP	StBC	93110	995-A4
LA RIATA LN	StBC	93111	985-A5
LARK	PSRS	93446	514-A7
LARK CT	SMRA	93454	796-H3
LARK ST	SMRA	93454	796-H3
LARK ELLEN DR	PSRS	93446	534-B1
LARKFIELD PL	PSRS	93446	534-B1
LARKIN DR	StBC	93455	817-A5
LARKSPUR DR	SMRA	93454	796-G6
LARKSPUR LN	PSRS	93446	514-B6
LARKSPUR ST	SLO	93401	674-C2
N LARKSPUR ST	LMPC	93436	896-F7
LA RODA AV	StBC	93111	994-H3
LA SALLE DR	SMRA	93454	776-J5
LA SALLE RD	StBC	93117	993-H3
LASSEN AV	SLOC	93405	633-A5
LASSEN CT	PSRS	93446	514-B7
LASSEN DR	Npmo	93444	756-A6
	StBC	93436	365-D4
	StBC	93436	895-G7
	StBC	93436	365-D4
LASSEN PL	StBC	93111	994-G1
LAS BRISAS DR	PSRS	93446	513-G5
LAS CANOAS LN	SBAR	93105	325-A7
LAS CANOAS PL	SBAR	93105	986-A7
LAS CANOAS RD	SBAR	93105	986-A6
	SBAR	93105	986-A6
	SBAR	93103	996-A1
LAS CASITAS	ATAS	93422	594-C1
LAS CRUCES CT	StBC	93117	984-D6
LA SELVA	SBAR	93109	996-A1
LA SELVA AV	GBCH	93433	714-E6
LAS ENCINAS DR	SLOC	93402	631-J7
	SLOC	93402	651-J1
LAS ENCINAS RD	SBAR	93105	995-H1
	SBAR	93105	995-H1
LA SENDA	StBC	93105	995-F3
LAS ENTRADAS DR	StBC	93108	997-B3
LA SERENA PL	SLOC	93420	714-J1
	SLOC	93420	715-A1
LA SERENA WY	SBAR	93105	995-J4
LA SERENATA WY	Npmo	93444	755-H3
LA SERENTA CT	StBC	93455	816-J2
LAS FLORES	SLOC	93420	714-H7
N LAS FLORES DR	Npmo	93444	755-H5
S LAS FLORES DR	Npmo	93444	755-J6
	Npmo	93444	756-A6
LAS FLORES PL	SMRA	93454	796-H2
LAS FLORES WY	SMRA	93454	796-H2
	SMRA	93458	796-F2
LAS FUENTES RD	StBC	93108	997-C2
LAS GAVIOTAS	SBAR	93109	995-E6
LAS LOMAS AV	ATAS	93422	574-B6
LAS LOMAS DR	SLOC	93420	694-J7
LAS MANOS LN	SBAR	93109	995-H5
LAS OLAS AV	SBAR	93109	996-A6
LAS OLAS DR	SLO	93401	654-C6
LAS ONDAS	SBAR	93109	995-A4
	SBAR	93109	996-A6
LAS PALMAS DR	SBAR	93105	995-B4
	SBAR	93110	995-B4
LAS PERLAS DR	StBC	93111	984-G7
LAS PILITAS RD	SLOC	93453	325-E11
	SLOC	93453	345-D1
LAS POSITAS PL	PSRS	93446	995-F3
LAS POSITAS RD	SBAR	93105	995-F2
	SBAR	93105	995-F2
LAS POSITAS RD Rt#-225	SBAR	93105	995-F3
	SBAR	93105	995-F4
LAS PRADERAS DR	SLO	93401	673-G2
LAS ROSAS LN	SBAR	93105	995-H2
LAS TABLAS RD	SLOC	93465	325-A7
	SLOC	93465	553-B1
LAS TABLAS-WILLOW CREEK RD	PSRS	93446	513-G5
	SBAR	93105	325-A7
LAST CHANCE RD	SLOC	93451	325-A3
	SLOC	93451	453-A6
LAS TUNAS RD	SBAR	93103	986-A7
	SBAR	93103	986-A7
	SBAR	93103	996-J1
	SBAR	93103	996-D2
E LAS TUNAS RD	StBC	93108	987-A7
LAS TUNAS ST	MOBY	93442	611-G6
LA TAPADERA LN	SBAR	93105	996-A1
LAS VARAS CANYON RD	LMPC	93436	896-C6
LAS VEGAS ST	SBAR	93101	995-H1
	MOBY	93442	611-E3
LA TEENA PL	SLOC	93420	714-J1
	SLOC	93420	715-A1
LATHAM PL	SBAR	93105	995-J4
LA TIERRA LN	CARP	93013	998-C5
LATIGO DR	StBC	93463	900-F5
LA TIJERA CT	SLOC	93445	734-G1
LAUNA LN	ARGD	93420	715-A5
LAUNDRY AV	StBC	93437	875-F3
LAURA CT	SLOC	93465	553-B2
LAURA WY	PSRS	93446	513-J6
LAUREATE LN	SLOC	93405	653-D3
LAUREL AV	MOBY	93442	611-F3
	SLVG	93463	920-E7
E LAUREL AV	LMPC	93436	916-E1
W LAUREL AV	LMPC	93436	916-B1
LAUREL CT	StBC	93455	816-J2
LAUREL LN	SLO	93401	654-C6
LAUREL PL	Cmbr	93428	548-F2
LAUREL RD	StBC	93436	365-D4
	ATAS	93422	573-E7
LAUREL ST	SLOC	93424	693-A4
	StBC	93437	855-E6
LAUREL WK	StBC	93117	994-A4
LAUREL CANYON RD	SBAR	93105	985-G7
	SBAR	93105	985-G7
LAURELWOOD DR	PSRS	93446	534-B1
	StBC	93455	816-J5
LAUREN LN	SMRA	93454	777-A5
LA UVA LN	ATAS	93422	573-F1
LAVELLE CT	StBC	93455	816-J5
LA VENTA DR	StBC	93110	995-A1
LA VEREDA LN	StBC	93108	996-J3
LA VEREDA RD	StBC	93108	996-J3
LA VERNE AV	StBC	93455	816-H5
LA VERNE ST	SLOC	93445	714-F7
LA VIDA LN	SLOC	93420	715-A2
LA VINEDA	SLO	93401	654-B5
LA VIRADA WY	SLOC	93465	553-A1
LA VISTA CT	ARGD	93420	714-G7
LA VISTA RD	StBC	93105	985-E5
	StBC	93110	985-E5
LA VISTA DEL OCEANO	SBAR	93109	995-H6
LA VISTA GRANDE	SBAR	93103	996-D2
	SBAR	93108	996-D2
LA VUELTA RD	StBC	93108	997-A3
LAWNWOOD CT	SLOC	93401	654-C7
LAWNWOOD DR	SLO	93401	654-C7
LAWRENCE DR	SLO	93401	654-A6
LAWRENCE LN	LMPC	93436	896-C6
LAWRENCE PL	Npmo	93444	756-G6
LAWRENCE ST	SBAR	93103	996-C4
LAWSON PL	Cmbr	93428	548-H2
LAWTON AV	SLO	93401	654-A6
LAWTON LN	SLOC	93465	553-B3
LAZO WY	SBAR	93458	776-F4
LAZY LN	SLOC	93445	714-F7
LEAF ST	SLOC	93446	756-C1
LEANNA DR	ARGD	93420	714-J7
LEDO PL	ARGD	93420	714-G5
LEE	StBC	93430	591-C5
LEE DR	SBAR	93110	985-D7
	SBAR	93110	995-D1
LEE ANN CT	SLO	93401	654-D6
LEEDS LN	StBC	93117	984-E7
LEEWARD AV	PBCH	93449	693-H7
LEFF ST	SLO	93401	653-J5
LEFT LN	SLOC	93420	715-E1
LEGADO	ATAS	93422	573-G3
LEGGE AV	ARGD	93420	715-B5
LEIGHTON ST	Cmbr	93428	528-E7
LEISURE DR	ARGD	93420	714-G3
LELA LN	SMRA	93454	796-H2
LELAND ST	PSRS	93446	513-E6
LEMA DR	Npmo	93444	756-A3
E LEMON AV	LMPC	93436	896-E7
W LEMON AV	LMPC	93436	896-C7
LEMON DR	CARP	93013	998-B5
W LEMON PL	LMPC	93436	896-B7
LEMON ST	SLO	93405	653-J5
	SMRA	93458	796-F1
LEMON GROVE LN	StBC	93108	996-D2
LEMON RANCH RD	StBC	93108	997-C1
LEMONWOOD DR	SLOC	93445	714-G1
LEMOORE ST	PBCH	93449	714-C1
LENOSA LN	ATAS	93422	553-A7
LEON ST	StBC	93455	817-A1
LEONA AV	SLO	93401	654-B6
LEONA DR	Cmbr	93428	548-G1
LEONA ST	SMRA	93454	777-B6
LEONARD PL	Cmbr	93428	548-H3
LEONI DR	GBCH	93433	714-D6
LE POINT ST	ARGD	93420	715-A4
LE POINT TER	ARGD	93420	715-A4
LEROY BLVD	StBC	93110	985-D7
LE SAGE DR	GBCH	93433	714-C5
LESLEY CT	SMRA	93454	777-A6
LESLIE DR	SBAR	93105	995-G3
LESLIE ST	SLOC	93440	878-G1
LES MAISONS DR	StBC	93455	816-J1
	StBC	93455	817-A2
LE VALLEY RD	StBC	93436	896-F3
LEWIS AV	ATAS	93422	573-J3
LEWIS DR	StBC	93436	896-F3
LEWIS PL	StBC	93436	896-G3
LEXINGTON AV	SMRA	93454	776-G3
	StBC	93117	984-E7
LEXINGTON CT	StBC	93117	994-E1
LIBERATOR CT	SBAR	93110	985-D6
	SBAR	93110	995-D1
LIBERATOR ST	SMRA	93454	776-F7
LIBERTY ST	SBAR	93113	996-E3
	SMRA	93454	777-B7
LIBRA DR	StBC	93436	876-C5
LIBRARY AV	SBAR	93101	996-A3
LIBRETTO LN	SLOC	93420	694-H4
LICHEN PL	SLOC	93465	534-A7
LIDO WY	SBAR	93105	995-E3
LIERLY LN	ARGD	93420	715-B5
LIGA RD	ATAS	93422	553-G7
LIGHTHOUSE PL	SBAR	93109	995-H7
LIGHTHOUSE RD	SBAR	93109	995-H7
LIGHTNING ST	SMRA	93454	796-F7
LILA PL	StBC	93111	984-G7
LILAC DR	SLOC	93402	631-F7
	StBC	93108	987-C7
	StBC	93108	997-C1
LILAC ST	LMPC	93436	896-F7
LILLEBAKKE CT	LMPC	93436	896-B7
LILLIE AV	Summ	93067	997-D3
LILLINGSTON CANYON RD	StBC	93013	998-H6
LILY LN	SLO	93401	674-C2
LIMA DR	SLO	93401	653-J7
LIMERICK LN	PBCH	93449	714-E2
LIMU DR	SLOC	92389	325-A10
LINCOLN AV	SLOC	93455	816-G7
LINCOLN AV	SLOC	93465	553-C2
LINCOLN RD	SBAR	93110	985-E7
LINCOLN ST	SLO	93405	653-H3
	SMRA	93458	776-H5
	SMRA	93458	796-G1
LINCOLNWOOD DR	SBAR	93110	985-E7
LINCOLNWOOD PL	SBAR	93110	985-E7
LINDA CIR	PSRS	93446	513-J6
	PSRS	93446	514-A6
LINDA DR	ARGD	93420	714-G5
	SMRA	93454	776-J7
	SMRA	93458	796-J1
LINDA LN	SLO	93401	673-H2
LINDA RD	SBAR	93109	995-F6
LINDA LEE ST	StBC	93455	816-H2
LINDA VISTA AV	ATAS	93422	573-H5
LINDA VISTA DR	LMPC	93436	896-F6
LINDEMAN DR	SMRA	93454	796-H4
LINDEN AV	CARP	93013	998-D6
	SLOC	93442	594-G7
LINDEN CT	Cmbr	93428	548-J2
LINDERO ST	StBC	93117	994-E1
LINDITO LN	SLOC	93430	985-D6
LINDMAR DR	StBC	93117	994-C2
LINDY DR	GDLP	93434	774-H7
LINETTA DR	SMRA	93454	777-B7
LINFIELD ST	StBC	93117	993-J3
LINGATE LN	StBC	93108	996-J3
LINHERE DR	CARP	93013	998-D6
LINKS DR	Npmo	93444	735-F7
LINNE RD	PSRS	93446	514-B7
	SLOC	93446	325-D7
	SLOC	93446	514-D7
	SLOC	93446	534-F1
LINWOOD LN	StBC	93455	816-H1
LIPPIZAN ST	PSRS	93446	513-H7
LIRA PL	StBC	93111	984-G7
LIRIO CT	SLO	93401	653-J7
LISA LN	Npmo	93444	756-A5
LISA ST	CARP	93013	998-E6
LISA WY	StBC	93455	816-H2
LISTOWEL LN	SLOC	93013	1018-H1
	SLOC	93013	1018-H1
LITCHFIELD LN	SBAR	93103	995-G5
LITCHFIELD PL	SBAR	93109	995-G5
LITTLE CT	SLOC	93446	654-G1
LITTLE CREEK LN	SLOC	93463	471-B5
	SLOC	93463	900-F7
LITTLE FAWN PL	SLOC	93446	325-D7
	SLOC	93446	534-J2
LITTLE MORRO CREEK RD	LMPC	93436	876-D1
	SLOC	-	876-G1
LITTLE OAK CT	StBC	93455	816-G7
LITTLE QUAIL PL	PSRS	93446	534-C2
LIVE OAK DR	BLTN	93427	919-G5
LIVE OAK LN	StBC	93105	995-F4
	SBAR	93105	693-F3
LIVE OAK RD	SLOC	93446	325-B3
	SLOC	93446	533-B3
	StBC	93460	901-E4
	StBC	93460	901-E4
LIVE OAK RIDGE RD	SLOC	93446	755-G1
LIVE OAKS RD	StBC	93108	997-A1
LIZZIE ST	SLO	93401	654-B4
LLANO AV	SBAR	93110	995-B4
LLANO RD	ATAS	93422	573-B3
LLOYD AV	SBAR	93101	996-A3
LLOYD PL	LMPC	93436	896-C6
LOBELIA LN	SLO	93401	674-C1
LOBO LN	StBC	93455	816-H2
LOBOS AV	ATAS	93422	573-G2
LOBOS CT	ATAS	93422	573-H2
LOBOS LN	ATAS	93422	573-H2
LOCH LOMOND DR	StBC	93455	816-J3
LOCKFORD ST	StBC	93455	816-J3
LOCKWOOD LN	StBC	93455	816-B1
E LOCUST AV	LMPC	93436	916-F2
W LOCUST AV	LMPC	93436	916-C2
LOCUST ST	PSRS	93446	513-E4
	SMRA	93458	776-G3
LOIS LN	Npmo	93444	756-B4
LOLITA LN	SMRA	93458	796-G4
LOLITA ST	ATAS	93422	573-J1
LOLLAND FALSTER RD	SLVG	93463	920-D2
LOMA ST	SBAR	93103	996-A2
	SLOC	93446	631-G6
LOMA WY	StBC	93455	816-J5
LOMA ALTA DR	SBAR	93109	995-J5
	SBAR	93109	996-A5
LOMA BONITA	SLO	93401	653-J6
LOMA MEDIA RD	SBAR	93103	996-A3
LOMA VISTA AV	ATAS	93422	573-H5
LOMA VISTA LN	Npmo	93444	756-C3
LOMA YUCCA RD	SLOC	93463	920-G2
LOMITA LN	CARP	93013	1018-H1
	CARP	93013	1018-H1
LOMITA RD	SBAR	93109	995-G5
LOMITAS RD	ATAS	93422	573-B3
LOMPOC	SLO	93401	653-J6
LOMPOC CASMALIA RD	StBC	93429	325-D11
	StBC	93429	855-C3
	StBC	93437	855-D5
LOMPOC CASMALIA RD Rt#-1	LMPC	93436	896-D1
	LMPC	93436	876-D1
	SLOC	93437	855-G1
	StBC	93437	876-G1
LONDON LN	Cmbr	93428	548-J2

Column format: STREET Name — City ZIP Pg-Grid

LONDONDERRY LN
- Cmbr 93428 548-H1

LONE OAK WY
- SLOC 93465 553-C1

LONE PALM DR
- Cmbr 93428 528-B1
- SLOC 93452 528-B1

LONG ST
- SLOC 93401 673-H2

LONGBRANCH AV
- GBCH 93433 714-E5

LONG CANYON RD
- StBC 93117 994-A2
- StBC 93454 345-G10
- StBC 93460 901-D4

LONGDEN CT
- ARGD 93420 715-A7

LONGDEN DR
- ARGD 93420 715-A7

LONGDRIVE LN
- SMRA 93455 796-F6

LONGFELLOW RD
- SLOC 93111 984-F6

LONG HILL PL
- SLOC 93446 325-D7
- SLOC 93446 534-J1

LONGHORN LN
- SLOC 93405 715-A2
- SLOC 93446 471-D6

LONG VALLEY RD
- StBC 93441 365-K2
- StBC 93441 901-E1
- StBC 93460 901-E5

LONGVIEW AV
- PBCH 93449 694-C7
- PBCH 93449 714-C1

LONGVIEW LN
- SLO 93405 654-A2
- SLOC 93405 654-A2
- SLOC 93446 471-B5

LONGVIEW RD
- StBC 93460 921-A4
- StBC 93463 921-A4

LOOKOUT LP
- SLOC 93426 469-J2

LOOKOUT RD
- StBC 93105 964-J6

LOOKOUT PARK RD
- Summ 93067 997-D4

LOOMIS ST
- SLO 93401 654-B2
- SLO 93405 654-A2
- SLO 93405 654-B2

LOPEZ DR
- ARGD 93420 715-C4
- SLOC - 345-E4
- SLOC 93420 695-G4
- SLOC 93420 345-E4
- SLOC 93420 695-F7
- SLOC 93420 715-D2

LOPEZ RD
- SBAR 93117 994-D2

LOPEZ CANYON RD
- SLOC - 345-E3

W LOQUAT AV
- LMPC 93436 916-C2

W LOQUAT CT
- LMPC 93436 916-D2

LORENA ST
- ATAS 93422 573-J1

LORENCITA DR
- SMRA 93455 796-G7

LORENZ CT
- Npmo 93444 776-G1

LORETO PL
- SLOC 93111 984-G7

LORIENDA CT
- SLOC 93420 715-A2

LORINDA PL
- SLOC 93101 995-H3

LORINDA WY
- SBAR 93101 995-G3

LORRAINE AV
- SLOC 93110 985-C7
- SLOC 93116 816-J6

LOS AGUAJES AV
- SBAR 93101 996-B5

LOS ALAMOS
- SLO 93401 653-J7

LOS ALAMOS AV
- SBAR 93109 995-J7
- StBC 93455 855-D7
- StBC 93437 875-D1

LOS ALAMOS LN
- SBAR 93109 995-J7

LOS ALTOS RD
- ATAS 93422 573-D7
- ATAS 93422 593-C1

LOS ANGELES AV
- SLOC 93405 633-E5

LOS ARBOLES
- SLOC 93402 631-F7

LOS ARBOLES AV
- ATAS 93422 573-J4

LOS BERROS RD
- SLOC 93420 714-J7
- SLOC 93420 715-A7
- SLOC 93420 735-B1

LOS CARNEROS RD
- StBC 93106 994-A2
- StBC 93106 994-A2
- StBC 93117 984-B7
- StBC 93117 994-A2

LOS CARNEROS WY
- StBC 93117 994-B2

LOS CERRITOS AV
- ATAS 93422 573-H4

LOS CERROS DR
- SLOC 93405 653-F2

LOS CIERVOS
- ARGD 93420 714-H2

LOS FELIZ
- SLO 93401 653-J7

LOS FELIZ DR
- SLOC 93110 995-A2

LOS GALLOS CT
- SMRA 93454 776-J6

LOS GATOS RD
- ATAS 93422 573-G5

LOS OLIVOS
- SLOC 93402 631-H6

LOS OLIVOS LN
- ARGD 93420 715-A5

LOS OLIVOS ST
- SBAR 93103 995-J2
- SBAR 93105 995-J2

LOS OLIVOS MEADOWS RD
- SLOC 93463 900-G5

LOS OSOS RD
- ATAS 93422 593-G1
- ATAS 93422 593-G1

LOS OSOS VALLEY RD
- SLO 93401 673-F1
- SLO 93405 653-D6
- SLO 93405 673-F1
- SLO 93402 631-F6
- SLO 93402 632-A7
- SLO 93405 652-C1
- SLO 93405 652-C1
- SLOC 93405 653-A3
- SLOC 93405 673-F1

LOS PADRES CT
- SLOC 93402 631-F7

LOS PADRES RD
- Npmo 93444 756-A6
- StBC 93455 816-H2

LOS PADRES WY
- BLTN 93427 919-J3

LOS PALMAS WY
- SLO 93401 674-D7

LOS PALOS ST
- SLO 93405 673-G2

LOS PALOS CT
- ATAS 93465 594-E1
- SLOC 93465 594-E1
- SLOC 93465 594-E1
- SLOC 93465 594-E1

LOS PATOS WY
- SBAR 93103 996-F3
- SBAR 93108 996-F3

LOS PINOS CT
- SMRA 93454 796-H3

LOS PINOS DR
- SBAR 93105 995-F1

LOS PUEBLOS
- ATAS 93422 594-C1

LOS PUEBLOS RD
- SBAR 93103 996-C2

LOS RANCHOS RD
- SLOC 93401 674-E5

LOS REYES WY
- SLOC 93420 755-A2

LOS ROBLES
- SLOC 93405 653-G1

LOS ROBLES LN
- SBAR 93105 995-H7

LOS ROBLES RD
- SLOC 93465 533-A7
- SLOC 93465 553-A1

LOST OAK DR
- SLOC 93402 631-J6

LOST SPRINGS LN
- GBCH 93433 714-F7

LOS VERDES DR
- SLO 93401 673-G2
- SLO 93111 984-J7

LOS VINEROS RD
- StBC 93110 995-C1

LOTHAR LN
- SLOC 93446 534-A5

LOU DILLON CT
- SBAR 93103 996-E3

LOU DILLON LN
- SBAR 93103 996-E3

LOUISA AV
- SLOC 93109 995-H6

LOUISIANA PL
- SLOC 93111 994-G4

LOUREYRO ST
- SLOC 93108 997-B3

LOWELL WY
- SLOC 93117 993-G3

LOWENA DR
- SBAR 93103 996-B2

LOWER HYDE
- SLOC 93108 986-E6

LOWES CANYON RD
- SMRA 93455 796-G7

LOYOLA DR
- SBAR 93109 995-H7

L P RANCH RD
- SLOC 93465 534-C7

LUCAS DR
- SMRA 93454 776-J6
- SMRA 93455 796-J1

LUCCA AV
- SLOC 93441 900-H5

LUCERNE RD
- SLOC 93430 590-H2

LUCIA CT
- SMRA 93454 777-A6

LUCILLE AV
- Cmbr 93428 548-H1

LUCINDA CT
- StBC 93455 816-J3

LUCINDA LN
- ATAS 93422 573-F7
- SBAR 93105 985-G7

LUCKY LN
- SLOC 93460 735-B3

LUCY BROWN RD
- SLOC 92389 325-G5
- SLOC 93461 325-G5

LUDLOW AV
- Cmbr 93428 548-G1

LUGAR DEL CONSUELO
- SBAR 93105 985-H1
- SBAR 93105 995-H1

LUISITA ST
- MOBY 93442 611-G7

LUNAR CIR
- StBC 93436 896-D1

LUNETA DR
- SLOC 93405 653-G3

LUNETA PZ
- SBAR 93109 996-A6

LUPIN LN
- StBC 93455 816-H2

LUPINE LN
- SLOC 93465 325-C8
- SLOC 93465 534-B7
- SLOC 93465 553-J4

LUPINE ST
- SLOC 93402 631-F5

N LUPINE ST
- SLOC 93405 653-B2
- LMPC 93436 916-F6

LUPINE CANYON RD
- SLOC 93405 693-B2
- SLOC 93424 693-B1

LUZON ST
- MOBY 93442 611-E1

LYDIA LN
- SLOC 93451 473-J3

LYLE AV
- Cmbr 93428 548-H2

LYLE DR
- PSRS 93446 513-J4

LYMAN ST
- SLOC 93420 735-D4

LYN RD
- SLOC 93420 735-C5

LYNCH CANYON RD
- SLOC 93426 324-J3
- SLOC 93405 469-F1

LYNHURST CIR
- StBC 93455 816-J4

LYNN DR
- SLO 93405 653-E7

LYNN ST
- GBCH 93433 714-F7

LYNNE DR
- SMRA 93454 776-J5

LYON PL
- SLO 93117 994-E1

LYRIC LN
- StBC 93110 995-C1

LYSANDRA CT
- SLOC 93465 553-C2

M

M PL
- LMPC 93436 896-D7

N M ST
- LMPC 93436 896-D7

S M ST
- LMPC 93436 916-D2

MABLE CT
- StBC 93455 816-J2

MACADAMIA ST
- StBC 93108 997-F2

MACETA LN
- StBC 93108 996-H4

MACHADO AV
- SMRA 93455 796-G7

MACHADO LN
- SMRA 93454 797-C1

MACHADO ST
- SLOC 93401 674-D5

MACLEOD WY
- Cmbr 93428 548-H1

MACON CT
- StBC 93455 816-E4

MADBURY CT
- SLOC 93401 674-D7

MADERA AV
- MOBY 93442 611-G7

MADERA DR
- StBC 93117 993-H2

MADERA PL
- ATAS 93422 553-F7

MADERA ST
- SLOC 93402 631-E7
- SLOC 93460 921-B5

MADERO CT
- SLOC 93420 735-B3

MADISON ST
- Cmbr 93428 548-F2

MAD MAX PL
- StBC 93445 734-G1

MADONNA RD
- SLO 93405 653-F7
- SLO 93405 653-F7

MADONNA RD Rt#-227
- SLO 93405 653-G6
- SLO 93405 653-G6

MADRID CT
- SLO 93401 653-J6

MADRID RD
- SLO 93401 653-J7

MADRONA DR
- SBAR 93105 995-F1

MADRONA WK
- StBC 93117 994-A4

MADRONE CT
- StBC 93455 816-B1

MADRONE LN
- SLO 93401 674-D2

MADRONE RD
- ATAS 93422 573-B5

MADRONE ST
- StBC 93446 533-F1

MADURO
- ATAS 93422 594-C1

MAGDALENA AV
- StBC 93454 574-A2

MAGDALENA DR
- SLOC 93451 473-J3

MAGDALENA PL
- StBC 93117 984-C7

MAGELLAN DR
- SMRA 93454 777-A5

MAGGIE LN
- StBC 93423 573-G1

MAGILSIDE DR
- MOBY 93442 611-F6

MAGNA VISTA ST
- StBC 93110 994-J2

MAGNOLIA
- ATAS 93422 548-H1

MAGNOLIA AV
- ATAS 93422 573-J4
- ATAS 93422 574-A2

MAGNOLIA DR
- ARGD 93420 714-H7

MAGNOLIA ST
- StBC 93437 855-E7
- StBC 93437 875-E1

MANDA CT
- StBC 93455 816-J1

MANDA DR
- StBC 93455 816-J1

MAHONEY LN
- SLOC 93446 493-A2

MAHONEY RD
- SLOC 93446 493-A2

MAHONEY RD
- SLOC 93451 325-A4
- SLOC 93451 493-A2
- StBC 93451 796-B6

MAHONEY CANYON RD
- SLOC 93451 325-C3
- SLOC 93451 453-J7
- SLOC 93451 473-H1

MAIL RD
- StBC 93436 365-G4

MAIN AV
- PBCH 93449 714-B2

MAIN ST
- Cmbr 93428 528-F6
- Cmbr 93428 528-F6
- MOBY 93442 611-E2
- MOBY 93440 878-G1

E MAIN ST
- SMRA 93454 777-B7
- SMRA 93454 797-C1
- SMRA 93454 777-B7
- SMRA 93454 797-A1

E MAIN ST Rt#-166
- SMRA 93454 776-H7
- SMRA 93454 777-A7

N MAIN ST
- SLOC 93446 533-E7
- SLOC 93465 533-E7
- SLOC 93465 553-E1

S MAIN ST
- SLOC 93422 553-D3
- SLOC 93465 553-D2

W MAIN ST
- GDLP 93434 774-G6
- GDLP 93434 775-B6
- GDLP 93434 774-E6
- SMRA 93454 775-B6

W MAIN ST Rt#-166
- GDLP 93434 775-G6
- SLOC 93434 964-F1

MANZANITA RD
- SMRA 93458 775-G6
- SMRA 93436 876-F5

MANZANITA ST
- CARP 93013 998-D5

MANZANITA WY
- SLO 93401 674-D1

MAININI RANCH RD
- SLOC 93436 633-D6

MAJESTIC DR
- StBC 93455 816-H1

MALAGA CIR
- StBC 93110 985-A7

MALAGA DR
- StBC 93108 996-J2

MALEY DR
- StBC 93117 984-E7

MALEZA AV
- ATAS 93422 574-B3

MALEZA WY
- StBC 93111 984-H7

MALIBU CT
- GBCH 93433 714-F5

MALIBU DR
- CARP 93013 998-D6
- SLO 93401 653-J7

MALIBU WY
- LMPC 93436 916-B2

MALIK LN
- SLOC 93401 674-F7

S MALL EXT
- ATAS 93422 573-J3

N MALLAGH ST
- Npmo 93444 756-B1

S MALLAGH ST
- Npmo 93444 756-C2

MALLARD
- PSRS 93446 514-B6

MALLARD AV
- StBC 93117 994-E1

MALLARD CT
- SLOC 93446 471-C6

MALLARD WY
- SLOC 93401 674-H1

MALVA AV
- MOBY 93442 611-F6

MALVERN ST
- StBC 93117 994-D1

MAMMOTH DR
- MOBY 93442 611-H6

MAMMOTH LN
- SLO 93401 653-J7
- SLOC 93446 471-B5

MANANITA AV
- ATAS 93422 573-H1

MANCHESTER CT
- StBC 93455 816-F4

MANCHESTER PL
- StBC 93117 993-F2

MANDA CT
- StBC 93455 816-J1

MANDA DR
- StBC 93455 816-J1

MANDARIN DR
- StBC 93117 994-D1

MANDARIN WY
- Summ 93067 997-E4

MANDERINA CT
- StBC 93105 995-E2

MANDEVILLE CT
- StBC 93455 817-B5

E MANGO AV
- LMPC 93436 916-F2

MANHATTAN AV
- GBCH 93433 714-E5

MANITOU CIR
- StBC 93455 995-E3

MANITOU LN
- SLOC 93101 995-G4

MANITOU RD
- SLOC 93101 995-F4
- SBAR 93105 995-F4

MANLEY DR
- StBC 93436 896-F2

MANNIX AV
- SLOC 93430 591-C5

MANOR LN
- StBC 93455 816-H5

MANOR WY
- Cmbr 93428 528-F6

MANUELA WY
- SLOC 93420 735-A2

MANZANA ST
- StBC 93460 921-B5

MANZANILLO DR
- StBC 93117 984-D6

MANZANITA DR
- SLOC 93402 631-F7

MANZANITA LN
- StBC 93455 797-A1

MANZANITA RD
- SLOC 93405 633-A4

MANZANITA WY
- MOBY 93442 611-F6

MARBELLA LN
- SLOC 93465 553-B1

MARBURY DR
- StBC 93111 994-E1

MARCELINO DR
- StBC 93463 920-J7

MARCHANT AV
- ATAS 93422 573-J4
- ATAS 93422 574-A5

MARCIA WY
- SMRA 93458 776-F6

MARCO LN
- SMRA 93455 796-G6

MARCUM ST
- StBC 93111 984-C7

MARCUS WY
- Cmbr 93428 548-F2

MARENGO DR
- MOBY 93442 611-H6

MARGARITA AV
- GBCH 93433 714-E4
- SLO 93401 653-J7

MARGATE AV
- Cmbr 93428 528-G7

MARGETTS AV
- SLOC 93465 553-B2

MARGIE AV
- StBC 93455 816-J2

MARGIE PL
- SLOC 93445 533-F5

MARGO ST
- SBAR 93109 995-H5

MARGO WY
- PBCH 93449 714-F3

MARGUERITE WY
- Summ 93067 997-E4

MARIA AV
- SLOC 93453 614-F3

MARIAH LN
- PSRS 93446 513-H4

MARIAN DR
- SMRA 93454 797-A1

MARIAN WY
- PBCH 93449 714-F3

MARIANA WY
- SLOC 93405 653-E7

MARIANELA ST
- SLOC 93402 631-E7

MARICOPA DR
- StBC 93117 984-E7

MARICOPA RD
- ATAS 93422 573-F2

MARIE CT
- StBC 93455 816-H5

MARIE DR
- SLOC 93465 553-D1

MARIGOLD CT
- SLOC 93401 674-C1

MARIGOLD LN
- SLOC 93465 534-B1

MARIGOLD WY
- SLOC 93402 632-A7

MARILLA AV
- SBAR 93101 995-J5

MARILYN WY
- SBAR 93105 985-G7

MARIN AV
- StBC 93455 816-H1

MARINA DR
- SBAR 93110 995-B5

MARINA ST
- MOBY 93442 611-F6

MARINERS CV
- SLOC 93405 653-F6

MARION AV
- PSRS 93446 513-F2

MARION CT
- StBC 93436 876-E6

MARIOTT RD
- SMRA 93454 796-H4

MARIPOSA CIR
- ARGD 93420 715-B4

MARIPOSA DR
- GDLP 93434 774-J7

MARIPOSA LN
- StBC 93108 987-C7

MARIPOSA WY
- SMRA 93454 796-H2

MARIQUITA AV
- ATAS 93422 573-H3

MARIQUITA DR
- StBC 93437 984-F6

MARITIME DR
- StBC 93117 993-G3

MARJORIE PL
- Cmbr 93428 548-H1

MARK AV
- CARP 93013 1018-H1

MARKET AV
- MOBY 93442 611-F6

MARLBERRY ST
- SMRA 93454 796-G6

MARLBOROUGH DR
- StBC 93117 984-C7

MARLBOROUGH LN
- Cmbr 93428 548-F2

MARLEE LN
- PSRS 93446 513-C6

MARLENE DR
- SLOC 93405 653-G1

MARLOMA LN
- SLOC 93446 614-G3

MARQUARD TER
- SLOC 93453 614-F3

MARQUIS PL
- SLOC 93445 714-D7

MARQUITA AV
- SLOC 93446 533-F5

MARS AV
- StBC 93111 984-G5

MARS CT
- StBC 93436 896-D1

MARSALA DR
- GBCH 93433 714-E6

MARSH RD
- SLOC - 572-A5
- SLOC 93430 572-A5

MARSH ST
- SLO 93401 654-A4
- SLO 93405 653-J5

MARSHA CT
- Cmbr 93428 548-H1

MARSHA DR
- Cmbr 93428 548-H1

MARSHALL DR
- StBC 93436 896-F2

MARSHALL LN
- SLOC 93401 674-D6

MARSHALL WY
- SLOC 93401 674-D6

MARSTONE LN
- StBC 93117 984-E7

MARTHA WY
- Npmo 93444 756-A4

MARTIN AV
- StBC 93455 816-H5

MARTIN RD
- SLOC 93465 553-D1

MARTINDALE RD
- Cmbr 93428 528-G7

MARTINEZ
- SLOC 93451 473-G3

MARTINGALE AV
- SMRA 93454 796-H6
- SMRA 93458 776-F6

MARTINIQUE DR
- SLOC 93402 632-A7

MARTITA PL
- Npmo 93444 756-C4

MARVIN AV
- StBC 93455 816-H1

MAR VISTA DR
- SLOC 93402 631-F7

MAR VISTA PL
- LMPC 93436 896-F5

MARXMILLER PL
- LMPC 93436 896-C6

MARYMOUNT WY
- StBC 93117 993-H3

MARY AV
- Npmo 93444 756-B2

MARY DR
- SMRA 93458 776-F5

MARY AUSTIN WY
- PSRS 93446 513-F2

MARYKNOLL DR
- GDLP 93434 774-J6

MASATANI CT
- GDLP 93434 774-J7

MASON ST
- ARGD 93420 715-A5
- SBAR 93101 996-B5

MASON WY
- SLOC 93401 654-A6

MASTERS CIR
- Npmo 93444 755-D1

MATEO CT
- StBC 93111 984-J7

MATHILDA DR
- StBC 93117 993-G3

MATILIJA LN
- SLOC 93420 734-J7

MATORRAL CIR
- StBC 93455 984-H7

MATORRAL WY
- StBC 93455 816-G4

MATTEI RD
- StBC 93460 901-C7

MATTHEW WY
- ARGD 93420 714-H3

MATTHEWS ST
- StBC 93117 994-D2

MATTIE RD
- PBCH 93449 693-F6

MAUD AV
- SLOC 93453 614-F3

MAUI CIR
- SLOC 93445 714-D7

MAXWELLTON ST
- StBC 93460 941-D1

MAY CT
- StBC 93111 984-G5

MAY ST
- ARGD 93420 694-F1

MAYA LN
- ATAS 93422 573-G1

MAYER AV
- SLOC 93430 591-C5

MAYFIELD ST
- StBC 93455 816-J3

MAYRUM ST
- StBC 93111 994-J3

MAYTEN ST
- SMRA 93458 776-G3

MAYWOOD CT
- SLOC 93420 734-H5

MCCABE DR
- Cmbr 93428 548-H1

MCCARTHY AV
- SLOC 93445 714-D7

MCCAW AV
- SBAR 93105 995-F1

MCCLELLAND ST
- SMRA 93454 776-H5
- SMRA 93454 796-H2

MCCLOSKEY PL
- StBC 93117 994-D2

MCCLOUD ST
- StBC 93455 796-J7

MCCOLLUM ST
- SLOC 93405 654-A2

MCCOY LN
- SMRA 93454 796-G5
- SMRA 93455 796-E5

MCELHANY AV
- SMRA 93454 796-H6
- SMRA 93458 776-F6

MCFARLAND PL
- SLOC 93420 734-G1

MCGINNIS CREEK RD
- SLOC 93453 325-G11

MCKINLEY ST
- ARGD 93420 715-A4
- StBC 93111 994-J2

MCLAUGHLIN RD
- LMPC 93436 896-F5

MCLEAN LN
- StBC 93108 997-C2

MCMILLAN AV
- SLOC 93401 654-B7

MCMILLAN CANYON RD
- SLOC 93461 325-F5

MCMURRAY RD
- BLTN 93427 919-H6
- BLTN 93427 919-J4

MCNEIL AV
- SMRA 93454 796-J1

MEAD LN
- ARGD 93420 715-A5

MEADOW CIR
- CARP 93013 998-D5

MEADOW DR
- StBC 93455 817-A4

MEADOW LN
- StBC 93108 986-G7

MEADOW RD
- BLTN 93436 919-F5

MEADOW ST
- SLO 93401 654-A6

MEADOW VW
- SLOC 93424 693-B1

MEADOW WY
- ARGD 93420 714-G3

MEADOW VIEW DR
- BLTN 93436 919-F5

MEADOW VIEW LN
- StBC 93455 796-J7
- StBC 93455 797-A7

MEADOW VIEW RD
- StBC 93455 816-J1
- StBC 93455 817-A1

MEADOW WOOD LN
- StBC 93108 996-G2

MEADOWWOOD PL
- SLOC 93108 996-G2

MEDCLIFF ST
- SLOC 93109 995-F7

MEDINAH LN
- StBC 93436 876-E5

MEDIO RD
- SBAR 93103 996-B2

MEGAN CT
- SLOC 93465 553-C2

MEHLSCHAU RD
- Npmo 93444 736-B7

MEIGS RD
- SLOC 93109 995-H7

MEINECKE AV
- SLOC 93405 654-A2

MEISSNER LN
- SLO 93401 673-H1

MELANIE LN
- Npmo 93444 756-B4

MELINDA CT
- SMRA 93455 796-J2

MELLIFONT AV
- SBAR 93103 996-D2

MELLO LN
- SLOC 93401 674-B3

MELODY DR
- PSRS 93446 514-A6

MELROSE AV
- Cmbr 93428 548-G2

MELVILLE WY
- StBC 93117 916-F3

MENDEL DR
- StBC 93445 714-D7

MENDOCINO AV
- SLOC 93405 654-B7

MENDOCINO DR
- StBC 93455 654-B7

MENLO DR
- BLTN 93427 919-J5

MENTONE AV
- GBCH 93433 714-D6

MERCED AV
- SLOC 93405 632-G6

MERCED ST
- PBCH 93449 714-C1

MERCEDES AV
- StBC 93427 574-A2
- ATAS 93422 574-A2

MERCEDES AV Rt#-41
- ATAS 93422 573-J3
- ATAS 93422 574-A2

MERCEDES LN
- ARGD 93420 714-A4

MERCER CT
- StBC 93455 817-B5

MERCURY AV
- StBC 93436 896-D1

MERCURY CT
- Npmo 93444 756-A6

MEREDITH AV
- Npmo 93444 756-A5

MEREDITH LN
- StBC 93455 816-G1

MERIDA DR
- StBC 93117 984-F7

MERIDIAN CT
- StBC 93117 993-J3

MERLOT ST
- SLOC 93494 494-J7

MERLYN AV
- StBC 93455 548-H2

MERRIDOCK CT
- StBC 93455 816-H5

MERRILEE WY
- StBC 93455 816-H6

MERRY HILL RD
- PSRS 93446 513-J6
- PSRS 93446 513-C6

MERU LN
- SBAR 93105 985-E6

MESA DR
- ARGD 93420 714-J7
- ARGD 93420 715-A7
- SLVG 93463 920-D7

MESA LN
- CARP 93013 998-C5

STREET Name City ZIP Pg-Grid

Street	City ZIP	Pg-Grid
MESA LN	SBAR 93109	995-G7
MESA RD	Npmo 93444	755-F4
	Npmo 93444	756-A4
	PSRS 93446	513-J3
	SBAR 93106	994-B4
	SBAR 93117	994-B4
	SLOC 93422	594-E4
	StBC 93106	994-B4
	StBC 93108	996-H3
	StBC 93117	994-B4
MESA ST	MOBY 93442	611-G6
MESA ALTA LN	SLOC 93420	734-H3
MESA CIRCLE DR	StBC 93436	876-C7
MESA GRANDE DR	SLOC 93420	734-H4
MESA OAKS LN	StBC 93436	896-G3
MESA RANCH RD	SLOC 93420	735-B2
MESA SANDS WY	Npmo 93444	756-B4
MESA SCHOOL LN	SBAR 93109	995-F6
MESA VERDE DR	StBC 93110	985-D7
	StBC 93110	995-D1
MESA VERDE LN	Npmo 93444	755-J5
MESA VERDE RD	StBC 93463	940-H1
	StBC 93441	941-A1
MESA VIEW DR Rt#-1	SLOC 93420	734-J2
MESA VISTA CT	PSRS 513-J3	
MESA VISTA LN	StBC 93463	920-D6
MESETA PL	SLO 93110	714-J7
MESQUITE LN	ARGD 93420	714-J2
	ARGD 93420	715-A3
MESSINA CT	SLOC 93401	674-D6
MICHAEL DR	GBCH 93433	714-E6
MICHAEL ST	LMPC 93436	896-C6
MICHELLE DR	StBC 93455	817-B6
MICHELTORENA ST	StBC 93108	816-H3
	SBAR 93105	995-H5
	SBAR 93101	996-A2
	SBAR 93101	996-A2
MICHIGAN AV	SLOC 93451	453-A5
MICHIGAN WY	Npmo 93444	755-D5
MIDDLE RD	SBAR 93108	996-H3
	StBC 93108	996-H3
MIDDLE RIDGE PL	Npmo 93444	755-F1
MIDDLETREE LN	StBC 93422	594-C2
	SLOC 93422	594-C2
MIDTEN HOF	SLVG 93463	940-D1
MIDWAY AV	StBC 93437	875-E3
MIDWICK PL	StBC 93108	997-A2
MIGUELITO CT	SLOC 93401	654-B7
MILES AV	StBC 93455	816-H1
MILES OAK LN	Npmo 93444	755-J2
MILKY WY	StBC 93436	876-C7
	StBC 93436	896-C1
MILL RD	SLOC 93446	514-E3
MILL ST	SLO 93401	653-J4
	SLO 93401	653-J4
	SLOC 93420	735-C5
	SMRA 93454	776-J7
	SMRA 93458	776-G7
MILLER CIR	ARGD 93420	715-A4
MILLER ST	SMRA 93454	776-H6
	SMRA 93454	796-H3

Street	City ZIP	Pg-Grid
MILLER ST	SMRA 93455	796-H6
N MILLER ST	SMRA 93454	776-H5
MILLER WY	ARGD 93420	714-J4
	ARGD 93420	715-A4
MILLS LN	GDLP 93434	774-J6
MILLS ST	Cmbr 93428	548-H1
MILLS WY	StBC 93117	993-H4
MILLSTONE AV	StBC 93455	816-J3
MILPAS ST	SBAR 93103	996-C3
MILTON ST	SLOC 93420	735-C4
MIMOSA CT	Npmo 93444	755-J4
MIMOSA LN	StBC 93108	996-J3
MIMOSA ST	MOBY 93442	611-F4
MINDORO ST	MOBY 93442	611-D1
MINDORO WY	MOBY 93442	611-D1
MINT LN	StBC 93110	995-A2
MIOSSI RD	SLOC 93405	654-C2
	SLOC 93405	654-C2
MIRACANON LN	SLOC 93405	653-E6
MIRADA DR	ATAS 93422	574-A6
MIRADA LN	ATAS 93422	574-A6
MIRADERO DR	StBC 93105	995-H1
MIRA FLORES AV	ATAS 93422	573-H4
MIRA FLORES DR	StBC 93110	994-J3
MIRALESTE LN	SLOC 93401	674-D6
MIRA LOMA DR	StBC 93455	816-J2
	StBC 93455	817-A2
MIRA LOMA WY	StBC 93455	513-E2
MIRAMAR AV	PBCH 93449	693-D5
	StBC 93108	996-J3
MIRA MAR CT	GBCH 93433	714-F4
MIRAMAR LN	PBCH 93449	693-D5
	StBC 93108	997-A3
MIRA MESA DR	StBC 93109	995-H6
MIRAMON AV	SBAR 93101	573-J1
MIRA MONTE AV	SBAR 93108	996-J2
MIRAMONTE DR	SBAR 93101	995-J5
MIRANDA CT	GBCH 93433	714-F6
	SMRA 93458	776-H3
MIRANO DR	StBC 93117	993-G1
MONA LEI CT	SLOC 93420	714-G7
MIRASOL CT	SMRA 93458	796-D4
MIRA SOL DR	SLOC 93405	653-G1
MIRA VISTA AV	SBAR 93103	996-A1
MIRA VISTA WY	SMRA 93454	776-J7
MISSION DR	StBC 93108	997-A2
	SLOC 93451	473-H3
MISSION DR Rt#-246	StBC 93460	920-J2
	StBC 93463	920-J2
MISSION LN	SLVG 93463	920-F7
	SLVG 93463	940-D1
	StBC 93460	921-A6
	StBC 93463	920-F7
	StBC 93463	921-A6
MISSION ST	SBAR 93101	995-H4
	SBAR 93105	995-H3
	SLOC 93451	653-H3

Street	City ZIP	Pg-Grid
MISSION CANYON RD	SBAR 93105	995-J1
	StBC 93105	985-J6
	SMRA 93458	776-G5
	SBAR 93105	986-A5
	SBAR 93105	995-J1
MISSION GATE RD	StBC 93436	896-J5
MISSION OAKS LN	StBC 93105	985-J7
MISSION PARK DR	StBC 93105	985-H7
	StBC 93105	995-H1
MISSION RIDGE RD	SBAR 93105	995-J1
	SBAR 93105	996-A1
MISSION RIDGE RD Rt#-192	SBAR 93103	986-B7
	SBAR 93103	996-B1
MISTY CANYON WY	SLOC 93405	574-F2
MISTY ELM CT	StBC 93455	816-J3
MISTY GLEN PL	Npmo 93444	755-F1
MISTY VIEW WY	SLOC 93446	735-D7
MITCHELL DR	SLO 93401	654-A6
MITCHELL DR	SLOC 93402	631-F5
MITCHELL LN	SLOC 93420	734-H7
MITCHELL ST	SMRA 93455	816-F3
MI TIERRA LN	StBC 93455	816-H4
MIZAR PL	StBC 93436	876-D6
MIZPAH PL	SLO 93401	673-H1
MOCCASIN LN	SLOC 93446	471-B5
MOCKERNUT	StBC 93437	875-H1
MOCKINGBIRD LN	SLOC 93405	553-B1
MODENA WY	StBC 93455	995-E3
MODOC AV	SLOC 93405	632-J5
MODOC RD	SBAR 93101	995-F3
	SBAR 93105	995-F3
	SBAR 93105	995-F3
MOFFETT PL	SBAR 93117	994-D4
MONTEREY CT	StBC 93117	994-D4
MOHAWK CT	PSRS 93446	513-H7
MOHAWK RD	StBC 93109	995-G7
MOJAVE LN	SLOC 93446	533-H2
MOLLE WY	SLVG 93463	940-E1
MOLLENHAUER RD	SBAR 93117	994-D2
MOMOUTH AV	StBC 93117	994-C1
MONA WY	PSRS 93446	513-J6
MONACO CT	GBCH 93433	714-F4
MONARCH DR	StBC 93460	921-J3
MONARCH LN	Npmo 93444	756-B5
MONETA AV	SLOC 93430	591-C4
MONICA WY	StBC 93460	920-J2
	StBC 93463	920-J2
MONITA RD	ATAS 93422	573-G7
MONO AV	SLOC 93405	632-J5
MONO CT	GBCH 93433	714-F4
MONO DR	StBC 93111	994-G1
MONO PL	SLOC 93405	653-H3
MONROE DR	SLOC 93445	714-D7

Street	City ZIP	Pg-Grid
MONROE ST	SMRA 93454	776-H5
	StBC 93458	776-G5
MONTALBAN ST	SLO 93405	653-J3
MONTALVO WY	StBC 93436	896-J5
MONTANA AV	StBC 93437	855-F7
MONTANA BLVD	MonC 93437	453-A3
	SLOC 93451	453-A3
MONTANA WY	StBC 93402	631-F7
MONTANO DR	StBC 93455	796-H7
MONTCLAIR PL	SLOC 93420	734-J5
MONTE DR	SBAR 93110	995-D3
MONTE RD	SLOC 93401	673-E7
	SLOC 93401	693-E1
	SLOC 93449	693-E4
MONTE ST	PSRS 93110	995-A2
MONTEBELLO ST	StBC 93460	921-B4
MONTE CARLO CT	StBC 93455	817-B4
MONTECIELO DR	StBC 93460	901-B4
MONTECITO AV	ATAS 93422	574-B7
	PBCH 93449	693-H7
MONTECITO DR	SLO 93401	673-H1
MONTECITO PL	SBAR 93103	996-D2
MONTECITO RD	SLOC 93430	324-L9
MONTECITO ST	SLOC 93430	591-D3
	SBAR 93101	996-C4
	SBAR 93103	996-C4
MONTECITO ST Rt#-225	SBAR 93101	996-A5
MONTE CRISTO LN	StBC 93108	996-G4
MONTEGO ST	ARGD 93420	714-G4
MONTEREY AV	MOBY 93442	611-F7
MONTEREY CT	ATAS 93422	573-G2
MONTEREY RD	ATAS 93422	553-E7
	ATAS 93422	573-E1
	SLOC 93446	473-F3
	SLOC 93451	473-F3
	SMRA 93455	796-H6
MONTEREY ST	SBAR 93101	995-G3
	SLO 93401	653-J4
	SLOC 93401	654-A4
MONTEREY PINES	StBC 93105	995-E1
MONTE VERDE DR	SMRA 93455	796-G7
MONTE VISTA	SLOC 93405	653-J4
MONTE VISTA LN	StBC 93105	964-H1
MONTE VISTA RD	StBC 93108	996-J3
MONTEZ CT	GDLP 93434	774-J7
MONTGOMERY ST	SLOC 93420	995-J2
MONTROSE DR	SLOC 93420	653-G1
MONTROSE PL	StBC 93105	985-J6
MONTROSE WY	StBC 93105	985-J6
MONTURA LN	SLOC 93446	553-H2
MOODY CT	PSRS 93446	513-J7
MOON RDG	SLOC 93424	693-B1
MOONCREST LN	StBC 93455	816-H4
MOON DANCE DR	StBC 93455	816-G1

Street	City ZIP	Pg-Grid
MOONGLOW RD	StBC 93436	896-C1
MOONLITE DR	SMRA 93455	796-J7
MOONSTONE BEACH DR	Cmbr 93428	528-C4
MOORE LN	SLOC 93420	694-H7
	StBC 93420	714-G1
MOORE RD	StBC 93108	997-A1
MOPACIETO PL	Npmo 93444	756-F6
MORA AV	StBC 93460	901-F7
	SBAR 93460	921-F2
MORADA LN	SBAR 93105	985-F6
MOUNTAIN LN	SLOC 93405	654-A1
MOUNTAIN LOOKOUT RD	SLOC	345-F2
MOUNTAIN RANCH RD	SLOC 93446	470-A6
MOUNTAIN SPRINGS RD	SLOC 93446	513-E3
	SLOC 93446	513-B3
MOUNTAIN VIEW AV	SLOC 93430	591-A1
MOUNTAIN VIEW BLVD	StBC 93437	855-G7
	StBC 93437	855-H1
MOUNTAIN VIEW DR	ATAS 93422	573-J6
	ATAS 93422	574-A7
	SLOC 93402	631-J6
	SLVG 93463	940-D1
	StBC 93455	816-H6
MOUNTAIN VIEW RD	PSRS 93446	513-H7
	SBAR 93109	995-H5
	SLOC 93420	734-H3
MOUNTAIN VIEW ST	SLOC 93426	324-L3
	SLOC 93426	324-L3
	SLOC 93426	324-A5
	SLOC 93426	325-A5
	SLOC 93446	471-C1
	SLOC 93446	493-A5
	SLOC 93405	653-J1
MOUNT CALVARY RD	SLOC 93405	986-C6
	SLOC 93405	986-C6
MOUNT LOWE RD	SLOC	345-C1
	SLOC	654-H2
	SLOC	654-H2
MOUNT VERNON DR	SMRA 93454	777-B6
MOUNT WHITNEY WY	SMRA 93454	777-B6
MOURNING DOVE LN	SLOC 93424	693-B1
MUGU LN	SLO 93401	653-J7
MUIRFIELD	SLO 93401	673-H1
MUIRFIELD CT	StBC 93455	796-G6
MUIRFIELD DR	ARGD 93420	714-J7
MUIRFIELD PL	CARP 93013	998-E6
MULBERRY AV	SBAR 93101	995-H4
MULBERRY DR	StBC 93437	875-H1
MULBERRY LN	ARGD 93420	714-H7
MURL DR	SLOC 93405	653-E7
MURPHY AV	SLOC 93453	614-F3
MURRAY PL	Cmbr 93428	528-E7
MURRAY ST	SLO 93405	653-J3
MURRELL RD	SLOC 93109	995-F6
MUSSELMAN DR	ATAS 93422	574-B7
MUSTANG CIR	ARGD 93420	714-H3
MUSTANG CT	StBC 93455	816-E4
MUSTANG DR	SLO 93405	653-J2
	SLOC 93420	734-J5
	StBC 93460	921-B5
MUSTANG SPRINGS RD	StBC 93108	986-F6

Street	City ZIP	Pg-Grid
E MOUNTAIN DR	StBC 93108	987-A7
W MOUNTAIN DR	SBAR 93103	985-J7
	SBAR 93103	986-B6
	SBAR 93103	986-A6
	SBAR 93103	995-J1
	SBAR 93103	985-J7
	SBAR 93103	995-J1
	StBC 93103	986-B7
	SBAR 93108	986-D6
	StBC 93108	986-D6
W MOUNTAIN DR Rt#-192	SBAR 93105	986-A7
	SBAR 93105	986-A7
MOUNTAIN LN	SLOC 93405	654-A1
MOUNTAIN LOOKOUT RD	SLOC	345-F2
MOUNTAIN RANCH RD	SLOC 93446	470-A6
MOUNTAIN SPRINGS RD	SLOC 93451	473-F2
MOUNTAIN VIEW AV	SLOC 93430	591-A1
MOUNTAIN VIEW DR	ATAS 93422	574-A7
MOUNTAIN VIEW RD	SLOC 93451	325-A3
MOUNTAIN VIEW ST	SLOC 93426	324-L3
MOUNT BISHOP RD	SLOC 93405	653-J1
MOUNT CALVARY RD	SLOC 93405	986-C6
MORGAN	SLOC 93430	591-D5
MORGAN DR	SLOC 93402	631-J6
MORGAN LN	PBCH 93449	714-E2
MORGAN LN	PSRS 93446	513-H7
	StBC 93013	997-G4
MORGAN TR	StBC 93455	816-E5
MORNING GLORY LN	SLO 93401	674-C1
MORNING RIDGE RD	StBC 93455	817-A3
MORNING RISE LN	ARGD 93420	714-G6
MORNINGSIDE DR	SLOC 93422	594-C4
MORNING STAR WY	ARGD 93420	674-A4
MORRETTI CANYON RD	SLOC	345-D2
	SLOC 93401	674-J6
MORRISON AV	SMRA 93454	796-F2
	SMRA 93458	796-F2
MORRISON ST	SLO 93401	654-B6
MORRO AV	MOBY 93442	611-F6
	PBCH 93449	693-H7
MORRO DR	SMRA 93454	777-A6
MORRO RD Rt#-41	SLOC 93422	573-H7
	ATAS 93422	593-D1
	SLOC	572-J7
	SLOC 93422	573-A7
	SLOC 93422	573-J7
	ATAS 93422	593-D1
MORRO ST	SLO 93401	653-J3
	SLO 93401	654-A4
	SLO 93401	654-A3
MORRO BAY BLVD	MOBY 93442	611-F6
MOSS AV	PSRS 93446	513-H5
MOSS CT	SMRA 93454	776-J6
MOSS LN	Npmo 93444	776-G1
	Npmo 93444	776-G1
MOSS BEACH CT	GBCH 93433	714-F4
MOTLEY	SLO 93401	654-A2
MOTOR WY	SBAR 93101	996-B4
MOUNTAIN AV	SLOC 93405	654-A4
E MOUNTAIN DR	StBC 93108	986-F6

Street	City ZIP	Pg-Grid
MUSTARD CREEK RD	SLOC 93446	493-B5
MUTSUHITO AV	SLO 93454	654-A6
MYRA ST	CARP 93013	998-E6
MYRTLE AV	StBC 93101	995-J4
MYRTLE DR	SLO 93405	653-E7
MYRTLE ST	ARGD 93420	715-B5
MYRTLEWOOD DR	PSRS 93446	534-A1
MYRTLEWOOD RD	StBC 93455	816-B1

N

Street	City ZIP	Pg-Grid
N PL	LMPC 93436	896-D7
N ST	MonC 93451	453-A1
N N ST	SLOC	591-H4
N N ST	BLTN 93427	919-H5
S N ST	ARGD 93420	715-A5
NACIMIENTO AV	ATAS 93422	573-H4
NACIMIENTO RD	SLOC 93451	325-A3
NACIMIENTO LAKE DR	PSRS 93446	513-C2
NACIMIENTO LAKE DR Rt#-G14	SLOC 93446	513-E3
	SLOC 93426	324-L3
	SLOC 93426	324-L3
	SLOC 93426	324-L3
	SLOC 93426	325-A5
	SLOC 93426	325-A5
	SLOC 93420	715-A5
NACIMIENTO LAKE DR Rt#-G19	SLOC 93426	324-L2
NACIMIENTO SHORES RD	SLOC 93426	324-K3
	SLOC 93426	470-C2
NAGANO RD	StBC 93117	994-C1
NAMOUNA ST	CARP 93013	998-E6
NAN CT	SMRA 93454	776-H6
NANCY AV	SLOC 93402	631-F6
NANCY DR	StBC 93455	653-E7
NANETTE LN	PSRS 93446	513-J6
	PSRS 93446	514-A6
NANTUCKET CT	CARP 93013	998-E6
NAOMI AV	PBCH 93449	693-G7
NAPA AV	MOBY 93442	611-F7
	SLOC 93405	633-C5
NAPA LN	StBC 93117	993-H2
NAPLES AV	GBCH 93433	714-F6
NAPLES ACCESS RD	StBC 93117	982-H7
NARANJO DR	SLOC 93420	715-C5
NARLENE WY	SLOC 93445	714-D6
NARROW CT	Cmbr 93428	548-G1
NARROW GAUGE WY	SLOC 93420	695-B4
NASSAU ST	MOBY 93442	611-E1
NATHAN RD	StBC 93110	985-E6
NATOMA AV	SBAR 93101	996-B5
NAULT RD	Cmbr 93428	548-G2
NAVAHO AV	PSRS 93446	513-H6

Street	City ZIP	Pg-Grid
NAVAJO PL	StBC 93455	817-A7
NAVAJOA AV	ATAS 93422	573-J5
NAVARETTE AV	ATAS 93422	573-G4
NAVIDAD DR	ATAS 93422	573-H1
NAZARIO CT	Npmo 93444	756-B5
NEAL SPRINGS RD	SLOC 93465	534-C5
	SLOC 93465	533-J7
	SLOC 93465	534-A6
NEBRASKA AV	StBC 93437	855-D7
NECTARINE AV	PSRS 93446	534-A1
E NECTARINE AV	LMPC 93436	896-G7
W NECTARINE AV	LMPC 93436	896-C7
NEGRANTI RD	SLOC	591-H4
NELSON DR	GDLP 93434	774-J7
NELSON ST	ARGD 93420	715-A5
NELSON WY	Npmo 93444	756-C6
NEPTUNE AV	StBC 93436	896-D1
NEPTUNE DR	Npmo 93444	756-A5
NEVA CT	SMRA 93454	776-H4
NEVADA AV	MonC 93451	453-A3
	SLOC 93405	633-A5
NEVADA CT	SLOC 93402	631-E6
NEVADA ST	SMRA 93454	776-J5
NEVIS ST	MOBY 93442	611-E1
	SLOC	611-E1
NEW BEACH RD	StBC 93436	894-J1
	StBC 93437	365-C2
	StBC 93437	894-J1
NEWCASTLE AV	StBC 93117	994-C1
NEWCASTLE CIR	StBC 93117	994-C1
	StBC 93455	816-G5
NEWHALL AV	Cmbr 93428	548-G2
NEWLOVE DR	SMRA 93454	796-H3
	SMRA 93454	796-G3
NEWMAN DR	Npmo 93444	756-B4
NEW MEXICO AV	StBC 93437	875-E2
	StBC 93437	895-B1
NEWPORT AV	ARGD 93420	714-F4
	Cmbr 93428	528-D6
NEWPORT DR	LMPC 93436	916-B2
NEWPORT ST	GBCH 93433	714-F6
W NEWPORT ST	SMRA 93454	553-E6
NEWSOME ST	StBC 93254	806-C1
NEWSOM SPRINGS RD	SLOC 93420	715-C5
NEWTON DR	Cmbr 93428	528-F7
NEWTON RD	Cmbr 93428	548-G1
NORTH AV	StBC 93436	816-F5
E NORTH AV	LMPC 93436	896-F7
W NORTH AV	LMPC 93436	896-C6
NORTH RD	LMPC 93436	895-J3
NORTH ST	SMRA 93458	796-G5
	StBC 93441	900-H4
NORTHAMPTON ST	SBAR 93108	528-F6

Street	City ZIP	Pg-Grid
NORTHBROOK DR	SMRA 93454	797-A3
	LMPC 93436	896-D6
NORTH CENTER	StBC 93455	816-H3
NORTH CENTER CT	StBC 93455	816-H3
NORTHERLY BRANCH GREEN VALLEY	Cmbr 93428	324-J8
NORTHFORK PL	SLOC 93446	471-D6
NIDERER RD	SLOC 93446	325-A6
NORTHGATE DR	StBC 93117	993-E2
NIDEVER RD	StBC 93013	997-H4
NORTHOAKS DR	StBC 93436	876-C5
NIEL PARK ST	SBAR 93103	996-D3
NORTH POINT CIR	StBC 93455	816-H3
NIGHTHAWK DR	StBC 93117	994-E2
NORTHPOINT PL	LMPC 93436	896-D6
NIGHTINGALE	PSRS 93446	514-A6
NORTHRIDGE RD	SBAR 93105	985-F6
NIGHTSHADE PL	SLOC	695-D3
NORTH STAR LN	StBC 93105	985-F6
NILES CT	SMRA 93454	777-B6
NORTH STAR LN	SLOC 93446	493-F3
NINA PL	BLTN 93427	919-H5
NINOS DR	StBC 93455	996-E4
NORTHVIEW AV	StBC 93455	734-H4
NIPOMO AV	SLOC 93402	632-A6
NORTHVIEW PL	PSRS 93446	534-C1
NIPOMO DR	CARP 93013	998-D6
NORTHVIEW RD	SBAR 93105	995-E2
	SLOC 93422	595-E2
NIPOMO ST	SLOC 93401	653-J4
	SLOC 93402	632-A6
NORTON LN	SLOC 93405	693-C2
NIRVANA RD	SBAR 93101	995-G4
NORWICH AV	Cmbr 93428	548-G2
	MOBY 93442	611-F5
NITA ST	SMRA 93454	776-J6
NORWOOD ST	SLOC 93420	735-D4
NOBLE LN	StBC 93455	816-F4
NOTTINGHAM DR	StBC 93455	528-D7
NOBLE WY	SLOC 93465	325-A7
NOEL ST	SMRA 93454	776-J5
NOVA DR	SMRA 93454	776-J6
NOGAL DR	StBC 93110	995-B1
NOVARRO AV	SLOC 93430	591-C5
NOGALES AV	ATAS 93422	573-H1
NOYES RD	ARGD 93420	714-G2
	ARGD 93449	714-G2
NOGUERA PL	ARGD 93420	715-B5
NUECES DR	StBC 93110	995-A2
NOJOQUI	SLO 93401	653-J7
NUMANCIA ST	StBC 93460	921-B5
NOJOQUI AV	SLOC 93441	900-H5
NURSERY WY	SLOC 93405	693-C2
NOMA ST	CARP 93013	998-E6
NUTMEG AV	MOBY 93442	611-F3
NOPAL ST	SBAR 93103	996-B2
NUTMEG ST	StBC 93437	855-E7
NOPAL WY	Npmo 93444	756-B4
NUTWOOD CIR	SLOC 93451	533-E5
NOPALITOS WY	StBC 93436	896-D4
NYGREN RD	SLOC 93451	473-B4
NORDENTOFT WY	SLVG 93463	920-E7
NYKOBING	SLVG 93463	940-D1
NORFOLK ST	Cmbr 93428	528-D6
NYSTED DR	SLVG 93463	920-F6
NORMA DR	PBCH 93449	714-F3
NORMA LN	GBCH 93433	714-E4

O

Street	City ZIP	Pg-Grid
S O PL	LMPC 93436	916-D2
O ST	MonC 93451	453-A1
N O ST	LMPC 93436	896-D5
S O ST	LMPC 93436	916-D1
OAHU ST	MOBY 93442	611-E1
OAK AV	CARP 93013	998-D6
	CARP 93013	1018-D1
	MOBY 93442	611-F6
E OAK AV	SBAR 93101	995-H3
	SLOC 93422	594-F6
W OAK AV	LMPC 93436	896-C6
OAK DR	SLOC 93451	473-G3
OAK LN	SLOC 93446	533-G1
	SMRA 93455	964-C5
W OAK PL	LMPC 93436	896-C6

STREET Name	City	ZIP	Pg-Grid
OAK RD	StBC	93108	996-H3
OAK ST	ARGD	93420	714-J5
	PSRS	93446	513-F2
	SBAR	93103	996-D3
	SLO	93405	653-J3
	SLVG	93463	940-E1
	SMRA	93454	796-H1
	StBC	93437	855-E7
	StBC	93455	816-H6
OAK WK	StBC	93117	994-A3
OAK WY	SLOC	93420	695-C7
OAKBROOK LN	StBC	93455	817-C6
OAK CREEK CANYON RD	StBC	93108	986-H7
OAK CREST DR	SLOC	93424	693-B1
OAKCREST DR	SBAR	93105	995-G2
OAKDALE RD	SLOC	93446	325-A7
	SLOC	93465	325-A7
OAK FLAT RD	SLOC	93446	493-A6
N OAKGLEN AV	Npmo	93444	756-A1
S OAKGLEN AV	Npmo	93444	756-C3
OAK GLEN DR	StBC	93110	985-A7
OAK GLEN RD	StBC	93460	921-A5
OAK GROVE DR	StBC	93108	987-C7
	StBC	93108	997-C1
OAK GROVE LN	SLOC	93420	735-H5
OAK HAVEN LN	SLOC	93420	695-D6
OAKHILL CT	StBC	93455	816-G7
OAK HILL DR	StBC	93436	876-E5
OAKHILL DR	StBC	93455	816-G7
OAK HILL RD	ARGD	93420	715-B4
	SLOC	93420	715-C1
	SLOC	93463	920-H2
OAK HILL TER	StBC	93436	876-F6
OAKHURST CT	StBC	93455	816-H7
OAKHURST DR	Cmbr	93428	528-F6
OAK KNOLL DR	SLOC	93446	533-E6
OAK KNOLL RD	StBC	93455	817-B5
OAK LEAF CIR	ARGD	93420	714-G3
OAKLEY AV	SMRA	93455	796-F5
	SMRA	93458	776-F5
	SMRA	93458	796-F1
OAKLEY CT	SMRA	93458	796-F2
OAK MEADOW LN	PSRS	93446	514-A6
OAKMONT AV	StBC	93436	876-E6
OAKMONT PL	Npmo	93444	735-F7
	SLOC	93420	735-F7
OAK PARK BLVD	ARGD	93420	714-G3
	ARGD	93433	714-F5
	ARGD	93449	714-G3
	GBCH	93420	714-F5
	GBCH	93433	714-F5
	PBCH	93420	714-G3
	PBCH	93449	714-G3
	SLOC	93420	714-G3
	SLOC	93449	714-G3
OAK PARK LN	SBAR	93105	995-G3
OAK POINTE DR	StBC	93436	896-G3
OAKRIDGE DR	SLO	93405	653-F1
	SLOC	93402	631-J7
OAK RIDGE RD	StBC	93111	994-H1
OAKRIDGE RD	LMPC	93436	895-J3
	LMPC	93436	896-A2
OAKRIDGE PARK RD	StBC	93455	817-B6
OAK SHORES DR	SLOC	93426	324-J3
	SLOC	93426	469-H2
OAKSPRINGS LN	StBC	93108	996-G1
OAK TREE PL	StBC	93108	997-C3
OAK TREE WY	BLTN	93427	919-G4
OAK TREE VALLEY PL	SLOC	93446	494-G5
OAK VALLEY CT	StBC	93455	816-G7
OAK VIEW CT	SLOC	93424	693-B2
OAK VIEW LN	StBC	93111	994-H2
OAKWOOD CIR	StBC	93436	876-E6
OAKWOOD CT	ARGD	93420	715-B4
	SLO	93401	654-C6
	StBC	93436	876-E6
OAK WOOD DR	PBCH	93449	714-E2
OAKWOOD DR	CARP	93013	998-E7
	SMRA	93454	796-H2
OAKWOOD RD	StBC	93436	876-E6
OAKWOOD ST	PSRS	93446	514-A3
OBISPO AV	SLOC	93430	591-B4
OBISPO RD	ATAS	93422	553-F7
OBISPO ST	GDLP	93434	775-A6
OBISPO PACIFIC TR	SLOC	93420	694-J6
OCEAN	PBCH	93449	714-C3
OCEAN AV	StBC	93436	365-D4
E OCEAN AV Rt#-1	LMPC	93436	916-F1
E OCEAN AV Rt#-246	LMPC	93436	916-H1
	StBC	93436	916-H1
N OCEAN AV	SLOC	93430	590-H1
S OCEAN AV	SLOC	93430	590-J2
	SLOC	93430	591-A2
W OCEAN AV	LMPC	93436	916-C2
	StBC	93436	365-D4
	StBC	93436	894-G2
	StBC	93436	895-A3
	StBC	93436	916-A1
	StBC	93437	895-D6
OCEAN BLVD	PBCH	93449	693-G7
	SLOC	93430	591-B4
OCEAN RD	StBC	93106	994-B4
OCEAN ST	SLOC	93445	734-E1
OCEAN VW	SLOC	93430	591-A1
OCEAN WY	PBCH	93449	714-B1
W OCEAN WY	LMPC	93436	916-C1
OCEANAIRE CT	SLO	93405	653-G7
OCEANAIRE DR	SLO	93405	653-F6
OCEAN FRONT LN	SLOC	93430	590-J2
OCEAN MEADOWS PL	StBC	93108	996-J4
OCEANO AV	SBAR	93109	996-A6
OCEAN OAKS RD	StBC	93013	998-B4
OCEAN PARK RD	StBC	93436	894-G2
OCEAN VIEW AV	GBCH	93433	714-D4
	PBCH	93449	714-C2
	SBAR	93103	996-E3
OCEANVIEW AV	StBC	93013	997-G4
OCEAN VIEW BLVD	StBC	93437	855-E6
	StBC	93437	875-C1
OCEAN VIEW CT	SLOC	93430	591-B5
OCEAN VIEW DR	CARP	93013	998-B5
OCEAN VIEW PL	SLOC	93402	631-H7
OCEAN VISTA LN	StBC	93117	993-E1
OCONNOR WY	SLOC	93405	633-A6
	SLOC	93405	653-B1
OCOTILLO AV	SMRA	93455	796-G6
ODBY AL	SLVG	93463	940-E1
ODENSE ST	BLTN	93427	919-J6
	BLTN	93427	920-A5
ODIE LN	StBC	93455	816-H3
ODIN WY	SLVG	93463	940-E2
ODONOVAN RD	SLOC	93432	325-D9
ODYSSEY CT	StBC	93436	876-C6
OGAN RD	CARP	93013	998-E6
OGDEN DR	Cmbr	93428	548-F2
OGRAM RD	StBC	93105	964-J6
OHARA	SLOC	93430	591-D4
OHIO WY	Npmo	93444	755-E5
OJAI	PBCH	93449	714-C3
OJAI DR	SLO	93401	653-J7
OKLAHOMA AV	SLOC	93405	633-C5
OLD LP	SLOC	93451	473-G2
OLD ADOBE WY	SLOC	93465	574-G4
OLD CALZADA RD	StBC	93441	901-B6
	StBC	93460	901-B6
OLD COAST HWY	SBAR	93103	996-E3
	SBAR	93108	996-E3
	StBC	93117	365-H6
	StBC	93117	939-H7
OLD COUNTY RD	SLOC	93422	553-D3
	SLOC	93465	553-D2
OLD CREEK RD	SLOC	93430	324-L9
	SLOC	93430	591-C3
	SLOC	93465	324-L9
OLD DAIRY RD	BLTN	93436	919-G5
OLD FORD RD	SLOC	93446	325-D7
	SLOC	93465	325-D7
OLD GLEN ANNIE PL	StBC	93117	993-J2
OLD MILL CT	StBC	93455	816-G4
OLD MILL LN	StBC	93455	816-F5
OLD MILL RD	SLVG	93463	940-F1
	StBC	93110	985-C7
	StBC	93110	995-C1
OLD MISSION DR	SLVG	93463	920-F7
OLD MORRO RD	ATAS	93422	573-B7
	ATAS	93422	593-D1
	SLOC	93422	573-B7
	SLOC	93422	593-D1
OLD MORRO RD E	ATAS	93422	573-H7
	ATAS	93422	593-G1
OLD MORRO RD W	SLOC	93422	572-J7
	SLOC	93422	573-A7
OLD OAK PL	StBC	93111	984-H7
OLD OAK RD	SMRA	93454	776-J6
	SMRA	93454	777-A6
OLD OAK PARK RD	ARGD	93420	714-G2
	ARGD	93449	714-G2
	SLOC	93420	694-G7
	SLOC	93420	714-G2
	SLOC	93449	694-G7
	SLOC	93449	714-G2
OLD PRICE CANYON RD	SLOC	93401	694-F1
OLD RANCH DR	StBC	93117	993-E1
OLD RANCH RD	ARGD	93420	714-J5
	StBC	93463	920-J6
OLD SANTA BARBARA RD	ATAS	93422	594-C3
OLD SANTA ROSA RD	ATAS	93422	574-B7
OLD SETTLER RD	SLOC	93446	513-C6
OLD SUMMIT RD	SLOC	93420	735-H5
OLD WILLOW RD	SLOC	93420	694-H7
OLD WINDMILL LN	Npmo	93444	756-D5
OLD WRANGLER LN	SLOC	93446	471-B6
OLEA CT	SLO	93401	674-D1
OLEANDER LN	PSRS	93446	514-A6
OLEANDER PL	LMPC	93436	896-D7
	StBC	93111	994-H2
OLEARY CANYON WY	SLOC	93420	737-C4
OLIVE AV	CARP	93013	998-D7
	LMPC	93436	916-F2
	SBAR	93101	995-J2
	SBAR	93101	996-A2
	SBAR	93103	995-J2
	SBAR	93103	996-A2
	StBC	93436	916-C2
OLIVE DR	PSRS	93446	513-F6
	SMRA	93454	796-H4
OLIVE RD	StBC	93108	997-C1
OLIVE ST	ARGD	93420	714-H6
	MOBY	93442	611-F7
	PSRS	93446	513-F4
	SBAR	93101	996-A2
	SBAR	93103	996-A2
	SLO	93405	653-J3
	StBC	93446	513-F7
	StBC	93437	855-F7
	StBC	93437	875-E1
	StBC	93460	921-C4
	Summ	93067	997-D4
S OLIVE ST	SBAR	93103	996-C4
OLIVE HILL RD	StBC	93455	817-B6
OLIVE MILL LN	StBC	93108	996-H3
OLIVE MILL RD	SBAR	93108	996-H3
	StBC	93108	996-H3
OLIVER RD	SBAR	93109	995-G7
OLIVERA AV	SLOC	93420	755-A2
OLIVERA ST	GDLP	93434	775-A5
OLIVET AV	StBC	93441	900-G5
	StBC	93463	900-G5
OLIVEWOOD RD	StBC	93455	816-B1
OLIVIA CT	PSRS	93446	513-J6
OLIVOS LN	Npmo	93444	756-A2
OLMEDA AV	ATAS	93422	573-H2
OLNEY ST	SBAR	93117	994-D2
	StBC	93117	994-D2
OLYMPIC WY	Npmo	93444	755-H3
ONSTOTT RD	StBC	93436	896-F2
ONTARE PL	SBAR	93105	985-F7
ONTARE RD	SBAR	93105	985-F6
	SBAR	93105	995-F1
ONTARIO RD	SLOC	93401	673-E6
	SLOC	93401	693-E1
	SLOC	93405	673-E6
	SLOC	93405	693-D3
ONTARIO WY	StBC	93455	817-E5
ONTIVEROS RD	StBC	93460	900-J7
	StBC	93460	901-A7
ONYX CT	StBC	93455	817-B5
OOP CT	SLOC	93420	754-J2
OPAL CIR	ARGD	93420	714-J7
OPAL CT	SMRA	93454	776-H4
ORAMAS RD	SBAR	93103	996-A1
ORANGE AV	SBAR	93101	996-A5
	StBC	93117	994-E2
ORANGE DR	SLO	93405	653-J2
ORANGE ST	SMRA	93454	796-J1
	SMRA	93454	797-A1
	SMRA	93458	796-F1
ORANGE BLOSSOM LN	StBC	93117	993-J3
ORANGE GROVE AV	StBC	93105	985-J5
ORCAS ST	MOBY	93442	611-D1
ORCAS WY	MOBY	93442	611-E1
ORCHARD AV	Npmo	93444	756-A4
	StBC	93108	997-C1
ORCHARD DR	PSRS	93446	513-J5
ORCHARD RD	SLOC	93465	553-A4
ORCHARD ST	ARGD	93420	715-A5
	SMRA	93454	776-H5
	SMRA	93458	776-F5
ORCHID DR	StBC	93111	994-G4
ORCHID LN	ARGD	93420	715-B6
ORCHID ST	LMPC	93436	896-F5
ORCUTT AV	StBC	93437	875-D1
ORCUTT EXWY Rt#-1	StBC	93455	345-E11
ORCUTT EXWY Rt#-135	SMRA	93455	796-H7
	SMRA	93455	816-F7
	StBC	93455	345-E11
	StBC	93455	796-H7
	StBC	93455	816-F7
ORCUTT RD	SLO	93401	654-B7
	SLO	93401	674-D1
	SLOC	-	695-D3
	SLOC	93401	345-D3
	SLOC	93401	654-B7
	SLOC	93401	674-D1
	SLOC	93401	695-A1
	SLOC	93420	695-A1
	SMRA	93455	796-H7
	StBC	93455	796-H7
	StBC	93455	816-H5
ORCUTT RD Rt#-1	StBC	93455	345-E11
ORCUTT FRONTAGE RD	SMRA	93455	816-G1
	StBC	93455	796-H7
	StBC	93455	816-G1
ORCUTT-GAREY RD	StBC	93454	345-G10
	StBC	93454	817-J3
ORCUTT VIEW CT	StBC	93455	816-G6
OREGON AV	MonC	93451	453-A3
	SLOC	93451	453-A3
	StBC	93437	875-E1
ORELLA ST	SBAR	93105	995-G2
ORENA ST	SBAR	93103	995-J1
ORILLA DEL MAR DR	SBAR	93103	996-D4
ORIN	Cmbr	93428	548-H1
ORIOLE RD	StBC	93108	996-G3
ORIOLE WY	PSRS	93446	534-B2
ORION AV	StBC	93436	876-C6
ORIZABA LN	SBAR	93103	986-C7
	SBAR	93103	996-C1
ORIZABA RD	SBAR	93103	986-C7
ORLANDO DR	Cmbr	93428	548-F2
ORLEN LN	SLOC	93465	553-A1
ORME PL	Cmbr	93428	528-G7
	Cmbr	93428	548-G1
ORMONDE RD	SLOC	93420	694-F4
	SLOC	93449	694-F4
E ORMONDE RD	SLOC	93420	694-H6
ORO DR	ARGD	93420	715-B4
ORTEGA RD	ATAS	93422	594-A3
	SLOC	93422	593-J3
	SLOC	93422	594-A3
ORTEGA ST	SBAR	93101	996-A4
	SBAR	93101	996-B4
ORTEGA HILL RD	Summ	93067	997-B3
ORTEGA RANCH LN	StBC	93108	997-C3
ORTEGA RANCH RD	StBC	93108	997-D3
ORTEGA RIDGE RD	StBC	93108	997-C3
	Summ	93067	997-C3
ORTON ST	MOBY	93442	611-F5
ORVILLE AV	Cmbr	93428	548-H2
	SLOC	93430	591-B4
ORVILLE PL	Cmbr	93428	548-H2
OSAGE ST	Npmo	93444	755-H5
OSITO CT	SBAR	93105	995-E2
OSO FLACO LAKE RD	Npmo	93444	755-A6
	SLOC	93445	754-F4
	SLOC	93445	755-A6
OSOS CT	SLOC	93402	631-J7
OSOS ST	SLO	93401	653-J3
	SLO	93401	654-A4
OSOS WY	PSRS	93446	513-J5
	PSRS	93446	514-A5
OSPREY CT	SLOC	93465	553-B1
OSTER STED	SLVG	93463	940-D1
OSWEGO WY	StBC	93455	817-B4
OTERO LN	SLOC	93446	533-H2
OTERO RD	ATAS	93422	573-C2
OTONO DR	SBAR	93110	985-D7
OTONO PL	Npmo	93444	756-A6
OUR PL	SLOC	93446	494-F6
OUR HILL LN	SLOC	93446	513-A3
OUTLAND CT	ARGD	93420	715-B4
OVERDEL PL	SLVG	93463	920-F7
OVERLOOK LN	SBAR	93103	996-E2
	SBAR	93108	996-D2
OVERPASS RD	StBC	93111	994-G1
OWEN CT	GBCH	93433	714-F4
OWEN RD	SBAR	93108	996-F3
OXBOW PL	SLVG	93463	940-E4
OXFORD AV	Cmbr	93428	548-F2
	SMRA	93454	777-A5
OXFORD DR	LMPC	93436	916-E3
OXFORD PL	StBC	93117	984-E7
OXFORD ST	SMRA	93454	777-A5
P			
P ST	MonC	93451	453-A1
N P ST	LMPC	93436	896-D6
S P ST	LMPC	93436	916-D2
PABLO LN	Npmo	93444	755-H5
PABST LN	StBC	93455	816-H2
PACHECO ST	GDLP	93434	775-A5
PACHECO WY	SLOC	93405	654-A2
PACIFIC AV	PSRS	93446	513-E6
	SBAR	93109	995-J7
	SLOC	93430	590-J2
	SLOC	93430	591-A2
PACIFIC BLVD Rt#-1	GBCH	93433	714-D5
	SLOC	93433	714-D5
	SLOC	93445	714-D5
PACIFIC CT	SLOC	93430	591-A1
PACIFIC DR	PBCH	93449	714-D3
PACIFIC ST	MOBY	93442	611-F6
	SLO	93401	653-J5
	SLO	93401	654-A4
	StBC	93455	816-G5
PACIFIC VW	SBAR	93109	995-J6
PACIFICA DR	GBCH	93433	714-E4
PACIFIC COAST RAILWAY PL	ARGD	93420	715-A5
PACIFIC DUNES WY	GDLP	93434	774-J6
PACIFIC GROVE PL	SMRA	93454	776-J5
PACIFIC OAKS RD	StBC	93117	993-H3
PACIFIC PINE DR	SLOC	93449	694-G6
PACIFIC POINTE WY	ARGD	93420	714-G6
PACIFIC VIEW DR	CARP	93013	998-A5
PACIFIC VILLAGE CT	CARP	93013	998-D6
PACIFIC VILLAGE DR	CARP	93013	998-E6
PACKING HOUSE RD	StBC	93108	997-B2
PADARO LN	StBC	93013	997-H4
N PADARO LN	StBC	93013	997-F4
	Summ	93067	997-F4
S PADARO LN	StBC	93013	997-J5
PADDOCK AV	PBCH	93449	693-G7
PADEN ST	SMRA	93454	776-J5
	SMRA	93454	777-A5
PADERNO CT	StBC	93110	985-A6
PADOVA DR	StBC	93117	993-F1
PADRE CT	StBC	93455	816-J6
PADRE LN	Npmo	93444	755-D1
PADRE ST	StBC	93117	993-F3
PAGALING DR	GDLP	93434	774-J6
PAGE	SLOC	93430	591-D4
PAINTED CAVE RD	StBC	93105	964-J5
	StBC	93105	984-J1
PAINTED SKY WY	SLOC	93420	735-B2
PAINT HORSE PL	SLOC	93446	533-D3
PAINT HORSE TR	StBC	93455	816-E5
PAJARO LN	ATAS	93422	574-A6
	Npmo	93444	755-H5
PALA LN	StBC	93110	985-D6
PALACE AV	SLOC	93445	714-E7
PALACE CT	StBC	93111	984-F6
PALA MISSION WY	SLOC	93451	473-F1
PALERMO DR	SBAR	93105	995-E3
PALISADE AV	PBCH	93449	693-H7
PALISADE DR	SMRA	93454	777-A7
	SMRA	93454	797-A1
N PALISADE DR	SMRA	93454	777-A6
PALISADES AV	SLOC	93402	631-G6
PALISADES DR	SBAR	93109	995-G7
PALM AV	CARP	93013	998-D7
	CARP	93013	1018-D1
	MOBY	93442	611-F7
	SBAR	93101	996-B4
PALM CT	ARGD	93420	714-G6
	PSRS	93446	513-H5
PALM ST	SLO	93401	653-J4
	SLO	93401	654-A3
PALM WY	BLTN	93427	919-H5
PALMA AV	ATAS	93422	573-H2
PALM COURT DR	SMRA	93454	796-H2
PALM DESERT CT	PSRS	93446	533-J1
PALMER RD	StBC	93454	345-G11
	StBC	93454	365-F1
PALMER ST	Npmo	93444	756-A3
PALMETTO AV	LMPC	93436	916-G2
PALMETTO DR	SMRA	93455	796-G6
PALMETTO WY	CARP	93013	1018-G1
PALM TREE LN	StBC	93108	996-G3
PALO ALTO DR	StBC	93117	993-F3
PALOMA DR	StBC	93110	995-C4
PALOMA PL	SLOC	93420	715-C2
PALOMA ST	Npmo	93444	755-J5
	Npmo	93444	756-A5
	StBC	93460	921-B5
PALOMAR AV	ATAS	93422	574-B4
	PBCH	93449	693-H7
	SLO	93405	653-H2
PALOMINO	PBCH	93449	714-D3
PALOMINO CIR	PSRS	93446	513-H7
	SLOC	93420	734-H5
PALOMINO DR	SLOC	93402	632-A7
PALOMINO LN	PSRS	93446	513-H7
PALOMINO RD	StBC	93105	985-H6
PALOS SECOS	ARGD	93420	714-H3
PALOS VERDES CT	SBAR	93105	995-F3
PALO VERDE RD	ATAS	93422	593-D1
	SLOC	93422	593-D1
PAM CT	SMRA	93454	797-A1
PAMELA CT	SLOC	93465	553-B1
PAMELA DR	PBCH	93449	714-F3
PAMPAS AV	SBAR	93101	995-H4
PAMPAS PL	SLOC	93420	695-C5
PANAY ST	MOBY	93442	611-D1
PANCHITA PL	SBAR	93103	996-A2
PANDANUS ST	CARP	93013	1018-G1
	StBC	93013	1018-F1
PANORAMA DR	MOBY	93442	591-D7
	MOBY	93442	611-E1
	PBCH	93449	714-F3
	PSRS	93446	513-F3
	SLOC	-	591-D7
	SLOC	-	611-E1
	SLOC	93442	591-D7
	SLOC	93442	611-E1
PANORAMA PL	SBAR	93105	985-H7
PAQUITA DR	StBC	93013	997-J4
	StBC	93013	998-A3
PAR AV	PSRS	93446	513-J7
PARADISE LN	SLOC	93402	652-C2
	StBC	93105	964-G1
PARADISE RD	StBC	93105	366-C5
	StBC	93105	964-E1
PARAISO	ARGD	93420	714-H2
PARDALL RD	StBC	93117	994-A5
PAREJO CIR	StBC	93111	984-G7
PAREJO DR	StBC	93111	984-F7
PARK AV	PBCH	93449	714-C3
	SLO	93401	654-A3
	SLOC	93430	591-A2
	SMRA	93454	796-H1
	SMRA	93458	796-G1
	StBC	93455	816-F5
PARK CIR	BLTN	93427	919-G5
	StBC	93117	993-G1
PARK LN	GBCH	93433	714-D4
	StBC	93108	987-B7
	StBC	93108	997-B1
PARK LN W	StBC	93108	987-A7
PARK PL	PBCH	93449	693-G7
	SBAR	93103	996-E3
PARK ST	BLTN	93427	919-H5
	GDLP	93434	774-H6
	MOBY	93442	611-E4
	PSRS	93446	513-F2
	StBC	93441	900-H6
PARK WY	ARGD	93420	714-H5
	SLVG	93463	940-E1
PARKDALE LN	StBC	93455	817-A4
PARKER ST	SLO	93401	653-H5
PARKER WY	SBAR	93101	996-B5
PARKER PASS RD	StBC	93108	986-H7
PARK HILL LN	StBC	93108	987-A7
PARKHILL RD	SLOC	93453	325-D11
	SLOC	93453	345-F1
PARKHURST DR	StBC	93117	984-C7
PARKLAND DR	StBC	93455	817-A3
PARKLAND TER	SLO	93401	654-B5
PARKS RD	SBAR	93105	995-F3
PARKSIDE WY	LMPC	93436	896-D6
PARKVIEW N	StBC	93455	816-H3
PARK VIEW AV	GBCH	93433	714-D4
PARKVIEW AV	SMRA	93458	796-G2
PARK VIEW DR	MOBY	93442	631-G1
PARKVIEW LN	PSRS	93446	534-C1
PARKVIEW RD	BLTN	93436	919-F5
PARK VIEW ST	StBC	93440	878-H2
PARKWAY DR	SBAR	93105	995-H3
PARKWAY CIRCLE DR	SLOC	93446	471-E4
PARKWOOD PL	StBC	93111	984-H7
PARRA GRANDE LN	StBC	93108	996-H1
PARTNER RD	SLOC	93405	653-C3
PARTRIDGE	PSRS	93446	514-A6
PARTRIDGE DR	SLO	93405	653-E7
PARTRIDGE LN	SLOC	93446	471-B5
PASADENA DR	SLOC	93402	631-G4
PASADENA RD	SLOC	93422	594-D5
PASADO RD	StBC	93117	993-J5
	StBC	93117	994-A5
PASATIEMPO DR	SLO	93405	653-G1
PASEO	PBCH	93449	714-C3
PASEO ST	ARGD	93420	715-A4
PASEO ALICANTE	SBAR	93103	995-J1
PASEO ALMERIA	SBAR	93103	996-A1
PASEO CAMEO	StBC	93111	984-G6
PASEO CIELO	SMRA	93455	796-H5
PASEO DEL DESCANSO	SBAR	93105	985-H7
	SBAR	93105	995-H1
PASEO DEL OCASO	StBC	93105	985-J5
PASEO DEL PINON	StBC	93117	993-F1
PASEO DEL REFUGIO	SBAR	93105	985-G7
	SBAR	93105	995-G1
PASEO DEL RIO	SLVG	93463	940-D1
PASEO DE YACA	SLOC	93401	673-F5
PASEO FERRELO	SBAR	93103	996-C2
PASEO JACARANDA	SMRA	93458	796-E5
PASEO LADERA	PBCH	93449	714-E3
PASEO LADERA LN	SLOC	93449	694-F7
	SLOC	93449	714-F1
PASEO LOS SANTOS	StBC	93111	984-J6
PASEO ORLANDO	StBC	93111	984-G6
PASEO PACIFICO	ATAS	93422	553-C6
PASEO PALMILLA	SMRA	93458	796-E4
PASEO POCO	StBC	93460	941-D1
PASEO REDONDO	SBAR	93110	985-C7
PASEO RIO	StBC	93111	984-G6
PASEO TRANQUILLO	SBAR	93105	985-G7
PASO ROBLES AV	SLOC	93402	631-H5
PASO ROBLES BLVD	PSRS	93446	514-B3
PASO ROBLES DR	SLO	93405	654-B2
	StBC	93108	996-E1
PASO ROBLES HWY Rt#-46	SLOC	92389	325-H4
	SLOC	93461	325-H4
PASO ROBLES ST	PSRS	93446	513-G5
	SLOC	93445	714-F7
	SLOC	93445	734-F1
PATCHETT RD	SLOC	93420	694-H4
PATERNA RD	SBAR	93103	996-A1

COPYRIGHT 2000 Thomas Bros Maps®

STREET Name City ZIP Pg-Grid

PATO AV
StBC 93254 806-B1
PATRIA CIR
ATAS 93422 594-C1
PATRICIA CT
SLO 93405 653-G1
SMRA 93455 796-J7
PATRICIA DR
SLO 93405 653-G1
PATRICIA LN
PSRS 93446 513-J7
PSRS 93446 514-A7
StBC 93111 994-H1
PATTERSON AV
StBC 93111 984-F5
StBC 93111 994-G2
StBC 93117 984-E5
PATTERSON PL
Cmbr 93428 528-G7
Cmbr 93428 548-H1
StBC 93111 994-G1
PATTERSON RD
StBC 93455 816-H5
StBC 93455 817-A5
PATTI LN
SMRA 93458 776-F6
PATTY KAY CT
Npmo 93444 755-G3
PAUL PL
ARGD 93420 714-G7
PAULA ST
MOBY 93442 611-F3
PAULA RAY LN
BLTN 93427 919-H4
PAULINE CT
StBC 93455 816-J2
PAULINE WY
SLO 93401 654-A5
PAWNEE CT
PSRS 93446 513-H6
PAXTON CT
StBC 93117 993-E1
PAYERAS ST
SBAR 93109 995-H6
PAYTON ST
StBC 93111 994-J2
P C LAKE RD
StBC 93437 875-H5
PEACH AV
LMPC 93436 916-F2
PEACH ST
SLO 93401 653-J4
SLO 93401 654-A3
PEACH GROVE LN
SBAR 93105 995-E2
PEACHTREE CT
PSRS 93446 513-E6
PEACHTREE LN
PSRS 93446 513-F6
PEACHY CT
PSRS 93446 513-F6
PEACHY CANYON RD
PSRS 93446 513-E6
SLOC 93446 325-A7
SLOC 93446 513-A6
PEACOCK CT
SLOC 93465 553-B1
PEACOCK LN
StBC 93455 796-H7
PEACOCK PL
SLOC 93445 734-G1
PEACOCK WY
Npmo 93444 756-C4
PEANUT WY
SLOC 93420 734-H7
W PEAR AV
LMPC 93436 916-C1
PEAR ST
CARP 93013 998-C6
PEARL DR
ARGD 93420 714-J7
PEARL ST
CARP 93013 998-A5
PBCH 93449 693-H7
PEARLIE LN
Npmo 93444 756-C4
PEAR VALLEY RD
SLOC 93451 473-D2
PEAR VALLEY WY
SLOC 93451 473-C1
PEARWOOD AV
ARGD 93420 715-C3
SLOC 93420 715-C3
PEBBLE ST
GBCH 93433 714-F6
PEBBLE BEACH CT
PSRS 93446 533-J1
PEBBLE BEACH DR
StBC 93117 993-F3

PEBBLE BEACH PL
SMRA 93454 776-J4
PEBBLEBEACH WY
SLOC 93401 674-E6
PEBBLE HILL DR
StBC 93111 984-J7
PEBBLE HILL LN
StBC 93111 994-J1
PEBBLE HILL PL
StBC 93111 984-H7
StBC 93111 994-H1
PECAN CT
StBC 93437 875-J1
PECAN PL
ARGD 93420 714-H6
PECAN ST
ARGD 93420 714-H6
StBC 93437 875-J1
PECHO RD
SLOC 93402 631-F6
PECHO ST
MOBY 93442 611-G7
PECHO VALLEY RD
SLOC 93402 344-L3
SLOC 93402 631-E7
SLOC 93402 651-B3
PEDERNAL AV
StBC 93117 994-D1
PEDREGOSA ST
SBAR 93101 995-H4
SBAR 93103 995-H4
SBAR 93103 996-A1
PEGASUS AV
StBC 93436 876-C6
PEGGY LEE CT
Npmo 93444 755-G2
PELLHAM DR
StBC 93436 896-F2
PEMBROKE AV
StBC 93111 984-F7
PEMBROKE CT
StBC 93111 984-F7
PEMBROOK DR
Cmbr 93428 528-D6
LMPC 93436 916-G2
PEMM PL
SBAR 93110 985-E7
StBC 93110 985-E7
PENDLETON LN
SLOC 93465 553-B1
PENMAN WY
SLO 93405 653-H3
PENMAN SPRINGS RD
SLOC 93446 514-F7
SLOC 93446 534-F1
PENNELL RD
StBC 93111 985-A5
PENNINGTON CREEK RD
SLOC 93405 632-J3
SLOC 93405 633-A3
PENNSYLVANIA ST
SMRA 93454 796-H4
PENNY LN
SLO 93401 654-A4
StBC 93108 997-B3
PEPPER LN
StBC 93108 996-H2
E PEPPER LN
StBC 93108 996-H2
PEPPER ST
SLO 93401 654-A3
PEPPERDINE CT
StBC 93117 993-H3
PEPPER TREE LN
StBC 93455 816-H1
PEPPER TREE RANCH RD
StBC 93460 901-C6
PEPPERWOOD PL
SMRA 93454 777-A5
PEPPERWOOD WY
SLVG 93463 940-D2
PEQUENIA AV
ATAS 93422 573-H5
PERALTA ST
GDLP 93434 775-B5
PEREGRINA RD
SBAR 93105 995-G2
PEREGRINE LN
Npmo 93444 756-A4
PEREIRA DR
SLO 93405 653-F7
PERES RD
SBAR 93117 994-D1
PEREZA CIR
StBC 93111 984-F7
PERIMETER RD
SLOC 93451 325-A3
SLOC 93451 471-H1

E PERIMETER RD
SLOC 93451 325-A4
SLOC 93451 453-A7
SLOC 93451 473-B1
N PERIMETER RD
SLOC 93405 653-J1
SLOC 93405 654-A1
SLOC 93407 653-J1
S PERIMETER RD
SLOC 93405 653-J2
SLOC 93405 654-A1
PERIWINKLE LN
StBC 93108 996-J1
PERKINS LN
SLO 93401 654-A6
PERKINS RD
StBC - 346-D10
StBC - 806-A6
StBC 93254 806-B3
PERKINS ST
StBC 93440 878-G1
PERLA LN
SLO 93401 673-G2
PERRY CT
StBC 93111 994-G3
PERSHING DR
SLOC 93445 714-D7
PERSHING ST
SMRA 93454 796-G2
SMRA 93458 796-F2
PERUVIAN WY
SLOC 93446 471-C5
PESCADERO DR
SBAR 93105 995-E3
PESCADO CT
ATAS 93422 573-H4
PESETAS LN
SBAR 93110 985-D7
SBAR 93110 995-D1
PETALUMA ST
SLOC 93405 633-E5
PETERS PL
SLOC 93401 674-E7
PETERSEN RANCH RD
SLOC 93465 553-C1
PETTIT PL
Npmo 93444 736-B7
PHEASANT
PSRS 93446 514-B7
PHEASANT LN
SLOC 93446 471-B5
PHEASANT VIEW DR
StBC 93455 816-J1
PHELAN RANCH WY
SLOC 93420 735-C3
PHELPS RD
StBC 93117 993-H3
PHILBRIC RD
SMRA 93454 797-F2
StBC 93454 797-F2
PHILINDA AV
SBAR 93103 996-B2
PHILLIPS LN
SLO 93401 653-J3
SLO 93401 654-A3
PHILLIPS RD
SLOC 93420 715-A1
PHOEBE CT
Npmo 93444 756-B4
PHOEBE ST
Npmo 93444 756-B4
PHULLAHARI RD
SLOC - 572-A5
SLOC 93430 572-A5
PHYLLIS RAE CT
Npmo 93444 735-J4
PICACHIO RD
SLOC 93430 324-K9
PICACHO LN
StBC 93108 986-H7
StBC 93108 996-H1
PICASSO RD
StBC 93117 994-A4
PICAY LN
StBC 93108 997-F1
PICKWICK LN
Cmbr 93428 548-H2
PICO AV
SBAR 93103 996-B3
PICO CT
SLO 93405 653-F7
PICO ST
MOBY 93442 611-E3
PIEDMONT PL
PSRS 93446 513-E5
PIEDMONT RD
SBAR 93105 985-F6
PIEDRAS DR
StBC 93108 997-C1

PIEDRAS ALTOS
ATAS 93422 573-H5
PIER AV
PBCH 93449 693-H7
SLOC 93445 714-D7
PIER ST
CARP 93013 998-B6
PIERCE AV
Cmbr 93428 548-H1
PIERCE DR
SMRA 93454 777-B6
PIERPONT ST
Summ 93067 997-C3
PIKE LN
SLOC 93445 714-E7
PILGRIM WY
ARGD 93420 715-A6
PILGRIM TERRACE DR
SBAR 93101 995-G3
PIMIENTO LN
StBC 93108 996-J2
PINAL AV
ATAS 93422 574-A3
SLOC 93453 614-G3
StBC 93455 816-G6
PINA SELVA PL
SLOC 93465 533-H6
PINE
SLO 93401 673-H1
PINE AV
SLOC 93402 631-G6
SLOC 93422 594-G6
StBC 93117 994-E2
E PINE AV
LMPC 93436 896-E7
W PINE AV
LMPC 93436 896-C7
PINE CT
Cmbr 93428 528-G7
PINE DR
SBAR 93105 995-G3
PINE LN
LMPC 93436 895-J2
LMPC 93436 896-A2
PINE ST
ARGD 93420 714-G5
PSRS 93446 513-F2
PSRS 93446 513-G2
SLVG 93463 920-F7
SLVG 93463 940-F1
SMRA 93458 776-G5
SMRA 93458 796-G2
StBC 93437 855-F7
StBC 93460 921-B5
PINE BRANCH RD
SLOC 93426 470-A2
PINE CANYON RD
StBC - 345-H7
StBC 93454 345-H7
PINECONE WY
SLOC 93420 734-J4
PINECOVE DR
SLO 93405 653-G7
PINECREST PL
Npmo 93444 756-B4
PINEDORADO RD
ATAS 93422 573-J7
ATAS 93422 574-A6
PINEHURST DR
StBC 93436 876-F6
PINEHURST WY
SLOC 93401 674-D6
PINEKNOLLS DR
Cmbr 93428 528-F6
PINELAKE ST
StBC 93455 816-J3
PINERIDGE DR
Cmbr 93428 548-H1
PINE RIDGE RD
SLOC 93426 470-A2
PINESPRING LN
SBAR 93110 985-E7
PINETREE LN
SLOC 93449 714-G1
PINE TREE PL
StBC 93117 993-F1
PINE VIEW DR
SLOC 93420 715-A2
PINEWOOD CT
ATAS 93422 574-B7
PINEWOOD DR
Cmbr 93428 528-F6
StBC 93455 816-B1
PINEY LN
MOBY 93442 611-G7
PINEY WY
Cmbr 93428 528-G7
MOBY 93442 611-G6
PINNACLE CT
PSRS 93446 514-A4

PINO WY
PSRS 93446 513-J5
PINO SOLO AV
ATAS 93422 574-B6
PINO SOLO CT
Npmo 93444 756-A3
PINO SOLO DR
StBC 93455 817-A7
PINTA RD
StBC 93437 895-E1
PINTAIL AV
SLOC 93446 471-D6
PINTO
PBCH 93449 714-D3
PINTO CIR
SLOC 93420 734-J5
PINTO LN
SLOC 93446 471-C6
PINTURA DR
StBC 93111 984-H7
PIONEER AV
Npmo 93444 756-B2
PIONEER CT
SMRA 93454 777-B7
PIONEER DR
SMRA 93454 777-B6
PIONEER ST
GDLP 93434 774-J6
GDLP 93434 775-A5
StBC 93434 775-A5
PIONEER TRAIL RD
PSRS 93446 534-C1
PIRA RD
StBC 93437 875-E7
StBC 93437 895-E1
PIRITA RD
StBC 93437 875-E7
PISMO AV
ATAS 93422 573-H6
PBCH 93449 714-B2
SLOC 93402 631-J5
SLOC 93402 632-A5
PISMO ST
SLO 93401 653-J5
SLO 93401 654-A4
PISMO BEACH CIR
StBC 93117 993-F3
PITOS ST
SBAR 93103 996-E4
PITT PL
Cmbr 93428 548-G2
PITZER CT
StBC 93117 993-H3
PLACENCIA ST
SBAR 93117 994-E3
StBC 93117 994-E3
PLACENTIA AV
PBCH 93449 693-H7
PLACER AV
SLOC 93405 633-A5
PLACER DR
StBC 93117 993-G2
PLACIDA AV
SBAR 93101 996-A4
PLANCHA WY
SLOC 93420 715-B3
PLATA LN
ATAS 93422 574-A6
PLATA RD
ARGD 93420 715-B4
PLATINO LN
ARGD 93420 715-B4
PLAYA PL
PBCH 93449 693-E5
PLAYA BLANCA CT
SMRA 93455 796-H5
PLAYA BLANCA ST
SMRA 93455 796-H6
PLAYA DEL SOL
PBCH 93449 693-H7
PLAYA VISTA PL
SLOC 93424 693-A3
PLAYER LN
PSRS 93446 513-J7
PSRS 93446 533-J1
PLAZA
PBCH 93449 714-C3
PLAZA DR
SMRA 93454 796-H2
PLAZA LN
SBAR 93105 995-E1
PLAZA ALEMAN
StBC 93111 994-G2
PLAZA DEL CENTRO
StBC 93111 994-F2
PLAZA DEL MAR
SBAR 93101 996-B5
PLAZA DEL MONTE
SBAR 93101 995-H5

PLAZA DE SONODORES
StBC 93108 996-H4
PLAZA PACIFICA
StBC 93108 996-H4
PLAZA RUBIO
SBAR 93103 995-J1
PLEASANT LN
SLOC 93420 715-B7
PLEASANT PL
StBC 93455 817-B5
PLEASANT RD
SLOC 93451 325-C4
PLEMAN PL
SMRA 93458 776-G5
PLOMO CT
ARGD 93420 715-B3
PLUM ST
CARP 93013 998-C6
PLUMAS AV
SLOC 93405 632-J5
StBC 93117 993-H2
PLUMAS CT
PSRS 93446 514-B7
PSRS 93446 534-B1
PLUMERIA CT
StBC 93455 817-A3
PLUM ORCHARD LN
SLOC 93465 553-B4
PLUTO ST
Npmo 93444 756-A5
PLYMOUTH ST
Cmbr 93428 528-E6
PLYMOUTH HILL ST
SLOC 93446 513-F2
POAGUE RD
Npmo 93444 756-F5
POCAHONTAS CT
PSRS 93446 513-H6
POCO RD
SLOC 93465 574-G1
POINSETTIA ST
SLO 93401 674-C2
POINSETTIA WY
StBC 93111 984-G6
POINT LOBO LN
SMRA 93454 776-J5
POINT SAL RD
StBC 93429 345-D11
StBC 93434 345-D11
POINT SAL DUNES WY
GDLP 93434 774-J6
POLARIS AV
StBC 93436 876-C6
POLARIS DR
Npmo 93444 756-A5
POLK ST
SMRA 93458 776-G4
POLY CANYON RD
SLOC 93405 345-C1
SLOC 93405 654-A1
N POLY VUE DR
SLOC 93405 653-J1
SLOC 93405 654-A1
S POLY VUE DR
SLOC 93405 653-J1
SLOC 93405 654-A1
POMAR LN
StBC 93108 997-A3
POMAR RD
SLOC 93422 593-F3
POMEROY AV
PBCH 93449 714-B2
POMEROY RD
Npmo 93444 735-F7
Npmo 93444 755-G2
Npmo 93444 756-A3
SLOC 93420 735-E4
POMMEL DR
StBC 93463 900-F6
POMONA CT
StBC 93117 993-H3
POND RD
SLOC 93445 734-F1
PONDEROSA LN
PSRS 93446 534-B1
PONDEROSA PL
Npmo 93444 756-A4
PONDEROSA ST
MOBY 93442 611-F4
PONDEROSA WY
StBC 93111 994-H1
PONTIAC LN
StBC 93455 817-E5
POOLE ST
ARGD 93420 715-A5
POOPOUT HILL RD
SLOC 93451 473-A1
POPLAR AV
SLOC 93422 594-F7

POPLAR ST
ARGD 93420 714-G5
CARP 93013 1018-F1
SMRA 93458 776-G2
StBC 93013 1018-F1
StBC 93437 855-E7
StBC 93437 875-E1
POPPINGA WY
StBC 93455 816-G4
POPPY LN
PSRS 93446 514-C7
PSRS 93446 534-C1
SLO 93401 674-C1
SLOC 93420 735-F5
StBC 93455 816-H2
N POPPY ST
LMPC 93436 896-G6
LMPC 93436 916-G1
POPPY VALLEY RD
StBC 93427 919-G1
POPULUS AV
SLO 93401 674-E1
POQUITA LN
SLOC 93451 473-F2
POQUITO PL
SLOC 93420 734-H4
POR LA MAR CIR
SBAR 93103 996-E4
POR LA MAR DR
SBAR 93103 996-E4
PORTAL RD
ATAS 93422 573-E5
PORTER ST
PBCH 93449 714-B2
PORTERVILLE ST
PBCH 93449 714-C2
PORTESUELLO AV
SBAR 93101 995-F4
SBAR 93105 995-F4
PORTLAND DR
SMRA 93458 776-H3
PORTOFINO WY
SBAR 93105 995-E3
PORTOLA LN
SBAR 93105 995-G3
PORTOLA RD
ATAS 93422 573-G3
ATAS 93422 574-A6
PORTOLA ST
SLO 93405 653-D6
PORTOLA WY
ATAS 93422 573-G3
POSADA LN
SLOC 93465 553-C1
POSILIPO LN
StBC 93108 997-A4
POST AV
CARP 93013 998-D6
POTE RD
StBC 93437 875-E7
StBC 93437 895-E1
POTRERO LN
StBC 93105 964-G1
POTRERO RD
ATAS 93422 553-F7
POWER RD
SLOC 93451 473-G2
POWERLINE RD
SLOC 93422 594-D5
POWERS AV
SBAR 93103 996-D4
POZO RD
SLOC - 345-G1
SLOC 93453 345-G1
E POZO RD
SLOC - 345-F1
SLOC 93453 325-H11
SLOC 93453 345-H1
W POZO RD
SLOC - 345-E2
SLOC 93453 325-D11
SLOC 93453 345-E2
PRADERA CT
ARGD 93420 715-C4
PRADERA PL
Npmo 93444 756-A3
PRADO LN
ATAS 93422 593-H1
PRADO PL
SLOC 93451 473-F2
PRADO RD
SLO 93401 653-H7
SLO 93401 673-J1
SLOC 93401 673-J1
SLOC 93401 674-A1
PRAIRIE RD
SLOC 93446 494-G7
SLOC 93446 514-G1
PREFUMO CANYON RD
SLO 93405 653-D6

PREFUMO CANYON RD
SLOC 93402 345-A3
SLOC 93405 345-A3
SLOC 93405 652-F7
SLOC 93405 653-A6
PREISKER LN
SMRA 93454 776-H4
SMRA 93458 776-H3
PRELL RD
StBC 93454 797-B5
PREMIER CT
SMRA 93454 777-B7
PRESCOTT DR
MOBY 93442 611-F5
PRESCOTT LN
StBC 93455 816-G1
PRESIDIO AV
SBAR 93101 996-B3
PRESIDIO WY
SMRA 93458 776-G3
PRESTON LN
MOBY 93442 611-F4
PRESTON ST
Cmbr 93428 548-H2
PRETTY DOE LN
SLOC 93446 471-D6
PRICE ST
PBCH 93449 693-J7
PBCH 93449 714-A1
SLO 93401 653-J5
E PRICE ST
Npmo 93444 756-D2
W PRICE ST
Npmo 93444 756-C2
PRICE CANYON RD
PBCH 93449 714-C2
SLOC 93420 694-E3
SLOC 93449 694-E3
SLOC 93449 714-C2
PRICE RANCH RD
StBC 93440 878-J1
PRICKLY PEAR WY
SLOC - 695-E4
PRIMAVERA LN
Npmo 93444 756-B6
PRIMAVERA RD
SBAR 93110 985-D7
PRIMERO ST
StBC 93254 806-B1
PRIMROSE CT
LMPC 93436 896-D6
PRIMROSE LN
Npmo 93444 756-A3
PSRS 93446 514-A6
StBC 93437 875-J3
StBC 93455 816-H2
PRINCESS CT
Npmo 93444 756-C4
PRINCETON AV
StBC 93111 984-F7
PRINCETON DR
StBC 93455 816-H6
PRINCETON PL
LMPC 93436 916-G2
SLO 93405 653-G1
PRINCIPAL AV
ATAS 93422 574-B6
PRINTZ RD
ARGD 93420 714-J1
ARGD 93420 715-A2
SLOC 93420 714-J1
SLOC 93420 715-A2
PRISCILLA LN
ARGD 93420 714-G5
PRIVATE DR
SLOC 93401 693-E3
PRODUCE PL
SLOC 93420 734-H2
SLOC 93445 734-H2
PROFESSIONAL PKWY
SMRA 93455 796-G6
PROMONTORY PL
PSRS 93446 514-A4
PRONGHORN CT
SLOC 93426 469-H2
PROPELLER DR
PSRS 93446 494-C6
PROSPECT AV
PSRS 93446 514-A3
SBAR 93103 995-J2
SBAR 93103 996-A2
SLOC 93446 533-H4
E PRUNE AV
LMPC 93436 896-E7
W PRUNE AV
LMPC 93436 896-C7
PUEBLO AV
ATAS 93422 574-A4
StBC 93110 985-E6

PUEBLO ST
SBAR 93105 995-H3
PUEBLO VISTA RD
SBAR 93103 996-C2
PUENTE DR
StBC 93110 994-J3
StBC 93110 995-A2
PUENTE PZ
StBC 93110 995-A2
PUERTO DR
StBC 93117 993-H2
PUESTA DEL SOL
ARGD 93420 714-H2
StBC 93013 1018-J3
VeCo 93013 1018-J3
PUESTA DEL SOL RD
SBAR 93105 995-H1
StBC 93105 995-J1
PUFFIN WY
SLOC 93465 553-B2
PUMA CT
SLOC 93401 673-F7
PUMP HANDLE LN
SLOC 93446 533-G2
PUNTA GORDA ST
SBAR 93103 996-E4
PURISIMA AV
SMRA 93455 796-J6
PURISIMA RD
LMPC 93436 896-F3
StBC 93436 365-F3
StBC 93436 896-F3
PURPLE SAGE LN
SLO 93401 674-D2
PUTTER AV
PSRS 93446 513-J7
PSRS 93446 514-A7
PYRACANTHA LN
StBC 93437 875-J3

Q

N Q ST
LMPC 93436 896-D7
LMPC 93436 916-D1
S Q ST
LMPC 93436 916-D2
QUAIL CIR
SLO 93405 653-E7
QUAIL CT
ARGD 93420 714-G3
StBC 93455 816-G7
QUAIL DR
SLO 93405 653-E7
QUAIL LN
SLOC 93402 651-J1
QUAIL RUN
PSRS 93446 514-B7
QUAIL WY
SLOC 93424 693-C2
QUAIL CANYON RD
StBC 93455 817-E6
QUAILCROSSING
SLOC 93446 470-B5
QUAILHILL LN
SLOC 93420 714-H1
QUAIL MEADOWS CT
StBC 93455 816-J1
QUAIL MEADOWS DR
StBC 93455 796-J7
StBC 93455 816-J1
QUAIL OAKS LN
Npmo 93444 755-J3
QUAIL RIDGE DR
StBC 93455 816-F4
QUAIL RIDGE RD
StBC 93463 920-J5
QUAIL SUMMIT
PSRS 93446 514-A6
QUAIL VALLEY RD
StBC 93463 920-H6
StBC 93463 921-A5
QUAILWOOD LN
SLOC 93420 735-F4
QUAN AV
SLOC 93420 714-H7
QUARANTINA ST
SBAR 93103 996-B3
QUARTERHORSE LN
PSRS 93446 513-H7
QUARTERHORSE TR
StBC 93455 816-E5
QUARTERHORSE WY
SLOC 93420 735-A2
SLOC 93446 471-C4
QUATAL CANYON RD
StBC 93252 346-G11
QUEBRADA LN
SLOC 93420 715-A2

QUEEN ANN LN
StBC 93111 984-F6
QUEENANNE RD
PSRS 93446 534-B1
QUEENS CT
SMRA 93454 776-J7
QUICKSILVER WY
SLOC 93465 553-B3
QUINCE ST
StBC 93437 855-F7
QUINIENTOS ST
SBAR 93103 996-D3
QUINTANA PL
MOBY 93442 611-F5
QUINTANA RD
MOBY 93442 611-F5
MOBY 93442 612-A7
SLOC - 612-A7
SLOC 93442 611-J7
SLOC 93442 612-A7
QUINTO ST
SBAR 93105 995-G2
QUITO ST
Npmo 93444 756-C4

R

R ST
MonC 93451 453-A1
N R ST
LMPC 93436 896-C7
LMPC 93436 916-C1
S R ST
LMPC 93436 916-C2
RAABERG WY
SMRA 93458 776-F6
RACHEL CT
SLO 93401 654-A5
RACHEL DR
SMRA 93454 777-A5
RACHEL LN
PSRS 93446 513-J6
RACHEL ST
SLO 93401 654-A5
RACQUET CLUB DR
CARP 93013 998-B5
RADCLIFF AV
Cmbr 93428 548-G2
RADCLIFF LN
StBC 93455 816-G4
RADCLIFFE ST
MOBY 93442 611-F5
RADDUE AV
StBC 93111 994-G3
RAFAEL WY
SLO 93405 653-G3
RAFTER WY
SLOC 93446 513-J2
RAGIN WY
SLOC 93465 325-C8
RAILROAD AV
SLO 93401 654-A5
SMRA 93458 776-G4
SMRA 93458 796-G1
StBC 93458 776-G3
RAILROAD ST
PSRS 93446 513-G5
SLOC 93445 714-E7
SLOC 93445 734-E1
SLOC 93465 553-E1
RAILWAY AV
StBC 93441 900-H5
RAINBOW CT
PSRS 93446 513-H6
SLOC 93465 553-C1
RAINBOW DR
SMRA 93455 796-J7
RAINBOWS END WY
SLOC 93422 593-C1
RAINEY DR
StBC 93455 816-J6
RAIN TREE CT
SMRA 93455 796-J6
RAIN TREE DR
SMRA 93455 796-J6
RALCOA WY
SLOC 93420 754-J2
RAMADA DR
PSRS 93446 533-F3
SLOC 93446 533-F4
SLOC 93465 533-E6
RAMAGE DR
ATAS 93422 573-G3
RAMAL LN
Npmo 93444 736-A3
RAMBLIN ROSE WY
SLOC 93420 695-A7
SLOC 93420 715-A1
RAMBOUILLET RD
PSRS 93446 513-J7

STREET Name City ZIP Pg-Grid

RAMBOUILLET RD
PSRS 93446 533-J1
RAMELLI RANCH RD
VeCo - 999-H7
VeCo 93001 999-H7
RAMETTO LN
SBAR 93108 996-F2
RAMETTO RD
SBAR 93108 996-F3
RAMITAS RD
StBC 93110 995-C3
RAMMING WY
SBAR 93105 985-F7
RAMONA AV
GBCH 93433 714-D5
SLOC 93402 631-G5
SLOC 93430 591-C4
RAMONA DR
SLO 93405 653-G2
RAMONA LN
StBC 93108 996-J3
StBC 93108 997-A3
RAMONA RD
ATAS 93422 553-E7
ATAS 93422 573-F1
RAMSEY ST
Cmbr 93428 528-F7
Cmbr 93428 548-F1
RANCH LN
StBC 93111 994-H1
RANCH RD
BLTN 93436 919-G5
RANCH ST
SMRA 93454 776-J7
SMRA 93454 796-J1
RANCH CLUB DR
BLTN 93427 919-G5
RANCHERIA ST
SBAR 93101 996-A5
RANCHITA CANYON RD
PSRS 93446 494-B7
SLOC 93446 494-B7
SLOC 93451 325-C4
SLOC 93451 494-F1
RANCHITA OAKS PL
SLOC 93451 325-C3
RANCHITA VISTA WY
SLOC 93451 325-C3
RANCHITO LN
SLOC 93401 674-D5
RANCHITO VISTA RD
SBAR 93108 996-D1
StBC 93108 996-D1
RANCHO DR
SLO 93405 653-G1
RANCHO PKWY
ARGD 93420 714-H4
RANCHO RD
Npmo 93444 756-D3
RANCHO ALISAL DR
SLVG - 940-D3
SLVG 93463 940-D3
StBC 93463 940-D3
RANCHO ASOLEADO DR
StBC 93110 995-B1
RANCHO CARO RD
SLOC 93446 534-A4
RANCHO LA LOMA LINDA DR
SLOC 93446 325-D8
RANCHO LOMA LINDA DR
SLOC 93446 325-D8
RANCHO OAK DR
SLOC 93401 674-B5
RANCHO VERDE
SMRA 93458 776-F4
RANCH VIEW LN
StBC 93463 920-J6
RANDALL DR
Cmbr 93428 548-G2
StBC 93108 997-A1
RANDOLPH RD
StBC 93111 984-F6
RANDOM OAKS DR
SLOC 93422 594-E4
RANGE PL
Npmo 93444 756-D5
RANGE RD
SLOC 93405 633-E2
RANGE ST
Npmo 93444 756-C6
RAPF AV
SLOC 93430 591-C5
RAVEN CT
SMRA 93454 796-J3
RAVENNA AV
SLOC 93402 631-G7
RAVENSCROFT DR
StBC 93117 984-D7
RAVENSCROFT DR
StBC 93117 994-D1
RAWHIDE PL
SLOC 93446 325-D7
SLOC 93446 534-J4
RAY RD
StBC 93455 795-G4
StBC 93458 775-J7
StBC 93458 795-H2
RAYAR RD
ATAS 93422 573-C3
RAYMOND AV
StBC 93455 816-H1
RAYVILLE LN
StBC 93455 796-C5
READY RD
SLOC 93426 470-A1
REALITO AV
ATAS 93422 573-E7
REBA ST
SLO 93401 654-B5
REBECCA LN
StBC 93105 995-F4
REBECCA ST
GBCH 93433 714-F7
REBILD DR
SLVG 93463 920-G7
RED BARK RD
SMRA 93454 776-J6
SMRA 93454 777-A6
REDBERRY PL
Npmo 93444 735-F7
Npmo 93444 755-E1
REDBIRD CT
StBC 93455 816-J1
RED BROME PL
SLOC - 695-E2
RED CLOUD RD
PSRS 93446 513-H6
REDDICK ST
SBAR 93103 996-C3
RED GUM LN
Npmo 93444 755-H3
REDONDO CT
GBCH 93433 714-F6
StBC 93460 921-A7
REDONDO LN
SLOC 93465 553-H1
REDONDO RD
SLOC 93422 593-G4
RED ROBIN LN
SLOC 93446 514-C7
RED ROCK RD
SLOC 93420 714-J1
RED ROSE LN
SBAR 93109 995-H6
RED ROSE WY
SBAR 93109 995-G6
RED TAIL HAWK LN
SLOC 93446 493-F3
RED TAIL MEADOW LN
SLOC 93420 734-J4
REDWILLOW DR
StBC 93455 816-H6
REDWOOD
BLTN 93427 919-G5
SLO 93401 673-H1
REDWOOD AV
StBC 93455 816-J2
REDWOOD CT
PSRS 93446 534-B1
SLOC 93402 631-J7
REDWOOD DR
PSRS 93446 534-B1
REDWOOD ST
StBC 93437 855-F7
REDWOOD WY
StBC 93117 993-F1
REED CT
StBC 93117 993-H3
REEF CT
PBCH 93449 714-D2
SBAR 93109 995-H7
REFLECTION PL
SLOC 93465 533-E7
REFUGIO AV
StBC 93460 901-A7
REFUGIO PL
ARGD 93420 714-H3
REFUGIO RD
StBC 93105 365-K6
StBC 93117 365-K6
StBC 93117 981-D3
StBC 93460 365-K6
StBC 93460 901-A6
StBC 93460 921-A2
StBC 93460 940-J3
StBC 93460 941-A3
StBC 93463 921-A7
StBC 93463 940-J3
REFUGIO RD
StBC 93463 941-A2
REFUGIO ST
GBCH 93433 714-F6
REGAL DR
SMRA 93454 776-J7
REGENT CT
SMRA 93454 776-J7
REGENT ST
LMPC 93436 916-G2
REGIS
Cmbr 93428 548-G1
REGULUS AV
StBC 93436 876-D6
REMINGTON CT
SLOC 93446 514-A2
REMINGTON DR
StBC 93460 921-A4
N RENA ST
ARGD 93420 714-H5
S RENA ST
ARGD 93420 714-H6
RENATE WY
PSRS 93446 513-J4
RENEE CT
StBC 93455 817-A4
RENNEL ST
MOBY 93442 611-D1
RENO CT
MOBY 93442 611-E3
RENWICK AV
StBC 93436 895-C4
StBC 93437 895-C4
RESERVOIR RD
ARGD 93420 714-J5
SLOC 93446 471-E4
SLOC 93451 471-E4
RESERVOIR CANYON RD
SLOC - 345-D2
SLOC - 654-H4
SLOC 93401 654-D2
RETORNO DR
CARP 93013 1018-E1
REVERE ST
StBC 93455 817-B5
REX PL
StBC 93117 984-C7
REY RD
SBAR 93101 996-B4
REYNOLDS AV
CARP 93013 998-C6
RHINESTONE CT
StBC 93455 817-B5
RHOADS AV
StBC 93111 994-G3
RIALTO LN
SBAR 93105 995-F4
RIATA LN
Npmo 93444 735-J4
Npmo 93444 736-A3
RIBE RD
StBC 93463 920-D6
RIBERA RD
StBC 93111 984-H7
StBC 93111 994-G1
RICARDO AV
SBAR 93109 995-H6
RICARDO CT
SLO 93401 654-B7
RICE CT
ARGD 93420 714-G6
RICE ST
SLOC 93445 714-E7
RICE RANCH RD
StBC 93455 816-G6
StBC 93455 817-A7
RICH CT
SLO 93401 654-B5
RICHARD AV
Cmbr 93428 548-H2
SLOC 93430 591-B4
RICHARD DR
SMRA 93458 796-G3
RICHARD ST
SLO 93401 654-C6
SMRA 93458 796-G3
RICHARDSON AV
SBAR 93103 996-B4
RICHELLE LN
SBAR 93105 995-E4
StBC 93105 995-E4
RICHLAND DR
SBAR 93105 995-F1
RICHMIND CT
SMRA 93455 796-H7
RICK RD
StBC 93455 816-E4
RIDGE LN
SBAR 93103 995-J1
RIDGE RD
Npmo 93444 755-H2
PBCH 93449 714-F3
SLOC 93465 553-B4
StBC 93460 901-C4
RIDGECREST DR
StBC 93108 997-D2
RIDGECREST PL
Npmo 93444 736-B3
RIDGECREST ST
StBC 93455 816-J3
RIDGEMARK DR
SMRA 93455 796-F6
RIDGEMONT WY
SLOC 93420 734-J5
RIDGE RIDER RD
SLOC 93426 469-J1
RIDGERUNNER RD
SLOC 93420 695-D7
SLOC 93420 715-D1
RIDGEVIEW CT
PSRS 93446 513-E5
RIDGEVIEW DR
PSRS 93446 513-E5
N RIDGE VIEW DR
StBC 93455 796-J7
S RIDGE VIEW DR
StBC 93455 816-G2
RIDGEVIEW RD
StBC 93108 996-E1
RIDGEVIEW WY
ARGD 93420 715-A3
SLOC 93420 715-A3
RIDGEWAY CT
ATAS 93422 573-H3
RIDGEWAY ST
MOBY 93442 611-G7
RIGEL AV
StBC 93436 876-C5
RIGHETTI RD
SLOC 93401 345-D2
SLOC 93401 654-J7
SLOC 93401 674-J2
RILEY RD
SLVG 93463 940-E3
RIM RD
StBC 93105 964-J6
RIMROCK LN
SLOC 93401 674-D7
SLOC 93401 694-D1
RIM ROCK RD
Npmo 93444 735-H4
RINCON CT
GBCH 93433 714-F6
RINCON DR
SLVG 93463 940-D4
RINCON RD
SLOC 93422 593-J3
RINCON RD Rt#-150
StBC 93013 366-G9
StBC 93013 1018-J1
RINCONADA RD
SBAR 93101 996-B3
SBAR 93103 996-B3
RINCON HILL RD
StBC 93013 1018-J2
RINCON POINT LN
StBC 93013 1018-J3
RINCON POINT RD
StBC 93013 1018-J3
RINCON VISTA RD
SBAR 93103 996-C1
RINGSTED DR
SLVG 93463 920-F6
RINGSTED PL
SLVG 93463 920-F6
RIO RD
SLOC 93420 734-J2
SLOC 93420 735-A2
RIO RITA
ATAS 93422 553-F7
RIOS CT
SMRA 93454 777-B6
RIO VISTA
SLVG 93463 940-D1
RIO VISTA DR
StBC 93117 993-E1
RIO VISTA LN
SLOC 93465 574-B2
SMRA 93454 796-H4
RIO VISTA PL
SLOC 93451 473-F2
RIO VISTA RD
Npmo 93444 756-A6
RIPARIAN WY
SLOC 93446 471-A5
RIPLEY ST
StBC 93111 994-J2
RITCHIE CT
GBCH 93433 714-E4
RITCHIE RD
GBCH 93433 714-E4
RIVEN ROCK RD
StBC 93108 986-G7
StBC 93108 996-H1
RIVER AV
SLOC 93445 734-F1
RIVER RD
SLOC 93446 471-D1
SLOC 93451 324-L3
SLOC 93451 471-H1
SLOC 93453 345-F1
N RIVER RD
MonC 93451 453-A2
PSRS 93446 513-G2
SLOC 93446 473-G6
SLOC 93446 493-H2
SLOC 93446 513-F1
SLOC 93451 473-G2
S RIVER RD
PSRS 93446 513-H6
PSRS 93446 533-G1
SLOC 93446 533-H3
SLOC 93446 534-A5
RIVER VW
SLOC 93424 693-C2
RIVERA
ATAS 93422 594-C1
RIVERBANK LN
PSRS 93446 533-G1
RIVER BIRCH CT
SMRA 93454 777-A6
RIVERGLEN DR
PSRS 93446 513-H4
RIVER PARK RD
StBC 93436 896-H7
StBC 93436 916-H1
RIVER ROCK CT
SMRA 93454 777-A5
RIVERSIDE AV
PSRS 93446 513-F1
RIVERSIDE CT
SMRA 93458 776-G3
RIVERSIDE DR
LMPC 93436 896-F5
RIVERSIDE RD
Npmo 93444 755-J6
Npmo 93444 756-B7
Npmo 93444 776-D1
RIVERSIDE ST
SLOC 93405 633-D5
RIVERVIEW DR
BLTN 93436 919-F4
RIVER VIEW LN
SLOC 93465 574-C1
RIVERVIEW TER
LMPC 93436 896-G7
RIVIERA CIR
Npmo 93444 735-D7
Npmo 93444 755-D1
RIVIERA LN
SMRA 93455 796-G5
RIZAL AV
SLOC 93420 755-A2
ROAD C
StBC 93460 901-D4
ROAD CLOSED
StBC 93437 875-B6
ROADRUNNER DR
StBC 93455 816-G2
ROAD RUNNER LN
SLOC 93465 574-D1
ROADRUNNER LN
SLOC 93420 735-E7
ROBBIE CIR
StBC 93117 993-E1
ROBBINS ST
SBAR 93101 995-H4
ROBERT CT
Npmo 93444 756-B4
ROBERT LN
SMRA 93458 776-F6
ROBERT RD
SBAR 93117 994-C2
ROBERTA DR
SLOC 93420 714-H7
ROBERT EMMET WY
SLOC 93422 593-C1
ROBERTO AV
SBAR 93109 995-H6
ROBERTO CT
SLO 93401 654-B7
ROBIN
PSRS 93446 514-A7
ROBIN CIR
ARGD 93420 714-G3
ARGD 93449 714-G3
ROBIN CT
StBC 93455 816-H7
ROBIN PL
StBC 93460 921-C5
ROBIN HILL RD
StBC 93117 994-C2
ROBLAR AV
StBC 93441 900-H7
StBC 93460 900-H7
StBC 93460 901-A7
ROBLE DR
StBC 93110 995-B4
ROBLE LN
SBAR 93103 996-C1
ROBLE ST
SMRA 93454 796-H2
ROBLES AV
ATAS 93422 574-A4
ROBLES RD
ARGD 93420 714-G4
ROBLES ST
SLOC 93446 533-F1
ROBLES PERDIDO DR
SLOC 93402 631-J6
ROCHELLE WY
SLOC 93445 734-G1
ROCHESTER PL
StBC 93117 993-F2
ROCKAWAY AV
GBCH 93433 714-D5
ROCKBRIDGE RD
StBC 93108 986-G7
ROCKCREEK RD
SBAR 93105 985-F7
ROCK ROSE LN
LMPC 93436 896-C6
ROCKVIEW PL
SLO 93401 654-A7
SLOC 93401 654-A7
ROCKVIEW ST
MOBY 93442 611-F4
ROCKWOOD DR
SBAR 93103 986-B7
SBAR 93105 986-B7
ROCKY PL
SLOC 93420 735-E5
ROCKY BUTTE TKTR
SLOC 93446 324-H4
ROCKY CANYON RD
SLOC 93422 574-C3
SLOC 93465 325-D9
SLOC 93465 574-C3
ROCKY CREEK LN
SLOC 93401 673-G6
ROCKY OAK LN
SLOC 93420 736-F2
ROCKY POINT LN
SLOC 93422 593-C1
ROCOSO WY
StBC 93111 984-H7
ROD DR
SMRA 93455 796-H7
RODEO
SLOC 93405 653-J1
RODEO DR
ARGD 93420 714-J3
RODEO WY
SLOC 93446 534-J4
RODEO GROUNDS RD
Cmbr 93428 528-G7
RODMAN AV
Cmbr 93428 548-G1
RODMAN DR
SLOC 93402 631-F7
SLOC 93402 651-E1
ROEMER CT
SMRA 93454 776-H4
ROEMER PL
SMRA 93454 776-H4
ROEMER WY
SMRA 93454 776-H4
ROGERS CT
ARGD 93420 714-G7
ROGERS DR
Cmbr 93428 528-G7
ROGUE DR
CARP 93013 998-E7
ROLFE LN
SLOC 93465 553-B2
ROLLIE GATES DR
PSRS 93446 494-C6
ROLLING BROOK LN
SBAR 93110 985-E7
ROLLING GREEN DR
SMRA 93455 796-F6
ROLLING HILL RD
PSRS 93446 513-J6
PSRS 93446 514-A5
StBC 93460 921-A4
ROMAINE DR
SBAR 93105 995-G2
ROMAULDO RD
SLOC 93405 632-J4
SLOC 93405 633-A4
ROMERO CANYON RD
StBC - 366-F7
StBC - 987-H2
StBC 93105 987-D3
StBC 93108 987-C4
StBC 93108 997-D1
ROMNEY DR
Cmbr 93428 548-G1
RONALD PL
SMRA 93458 796-G2
RONAN AV
PSRS 93446 513-H2
RONDA DR
StBC 93111 984-J7
ROPA CT
ATAS 93422 553-D6
ROPER WY
StBC 93455 817-A4
ROSALES CT
StBC 93455 816-B1
ROSALIE DR
StBC 93455 817-B5
ROSALIND DR
SMRA 93458 776-G6
ROSA LINDA WY
StBC 93111 984-J7
ROSANA PL
Npmo 93444 756-B5
ROSARIO AV
ATAS 93422 573-H3
ROSARIO DR
SBAR 93110 985-C7
ROSARIO PARK RD
StBC 93105 964-D4
ROSARITA LN
StBC 93105 995-H1
ROSCHELLE LN
SMRA 93458 796-G3
ROSCOE PL
Cmbr 93428 548-H2
ROSE AL
SLO 93401 653-J4
ROSE AV
SBAR 93101 996-B4
SLO 93401 654-C6
SMRA 93454 776-H6
SMRA 93454 777-A6
SMRA 93458 776-G6
ROSE CT
GBCH 93433 714-F6
ROSE DR
Npmo 93444 755-J5
Npmo 93444 756-A5
ROSE LN
CARP 93013 1018-H1
PSRS 93446 513-H6
StBC 93110 985-D6
ROSE PL
SMRA 93454 776-J6
ROSE ST
SLOC 93445 734-H2
N ROSE ST
LMPC 93436 896-B7
S ROSE ST
LMPC 93436 916-C2
ROSEMARY CT
ARGD 93420 714-H2
SLO 93401 674-D2
ROSEMARY DR
PSRS 93446 514-A7
ROSEMARY LN
ARGD 93420 714-J3
SBAR 93108 996-E2
ROSEMARY RD
StBC 93454 797-C2
ROSEMEAD ST
StBC 93110 994-J2
ROSEWOOD DR
SMRA 93458 776-F7
ROSEWOOD LN
ARGD 93420 715-C4
ROSEWOOD ST
StBC 93437 855-E7
ROSINA DR
SLOC 93402 631-F6
ROSITA AV
ATAS 93422 573-G1
ROSITA ST
SLO 93405 653-G2
ROSKILDE RD
SLVG 93463 920-E7
ROSS DR
SLOC 93451 325-D6
ROSS LN
SLOC 93420 714-H7
StBC 93455 816-H4
ROSS RD
Cmbr 93428 548-H2
ROSSI RD
SLOC 93465 553-C3
ROSSIER LN
SBAR 93101 995-J2
ROSSMORE RD
StBC 93117 984-D7
ROTHBURY PL
StBC 93117 993-F2
ROUGEOT PL
SLO 93405 653-H2
ROUGH RD
SLOC 93426 470-A1
ROUNDHOUSE ST
SLO 93401 654-A5
ROUND UP PL
SLOC 93420 715-D2
ROUNDUP RD
StBC 93441 901-E4
StBC 93460 901-E4
ROWAN RD
StBC 93437 855-H7
StBC 93437 875-H1
ROWLAND DR
SMRA 93454 777-B7
ROXY AV
StBC 93455 817-A6
ROYAL CT
PSRS 93446 513-F3
SLO 93405 653-E7
ROYAL PL
SMRA 93454 776-J7
SMRA 93454 777-A7
ROYAL TER
StBC 93455 816-J5
ROYAL WY
SLO 93405 653-E7
ROYAL LINDA DR
StBC 93117 993-G1
ROYAL LINDA RD
StBC 93117 993-G1
ROYAL OAK PL
SLOC 93420 715-B2
ROYAL OAK RD
StBC 93455 817-A5
RUBIO
GDLP 93434 775-A5
RUBIO LN
SLO 93405 653-E7
RUBIO RD
SBAR 93103 996-C2
RUBY CT
PBCH 93449 693-G6
SMRA 93454 777-A6
RUBY LN
Npmo 93444 756-A5
RUBY CREST CT
StBC 93455 816-H5
RUCKER RD
StBC 93436 876-G7
StBC 93436 896-G2
RUNNING BEAR CT
SLOC 93446 471-D7
RUNNING RABBIT CIR
SLOC 93446 471-C7
RUNNING STAG WY
PSRS 93446 534-B2
RUSS CT
ARGD 93420 714-G7
RUSSELL AV
SMRA 93458 776-F7
SMRA 93458 796-F2
N RUSSELL AV
SMRA 93458 776-F5
RUSSELL WY
StBC 93110 985-D7
RUSTIC WY
SLOC 93401 674-A3
RUSTLER WY
SLOC 93446 325-D7
RUTGERS DR
StBC 93455 816-H3
RUTH AV
SBAR 93101 996-A5
RUTH ST
SLO 93401 654-A5
RUTH ANN WY
ARGD 93420 714-G5
RUTHERFORD ST
StBC 93117 994-E2
RYAN RD
SLOC 93432 325-E8

S

N S ST
LMPC 93436 896-C7
LMPC 93436 916-C1
SABADO TARDE RD
StBC 93106 994-A5
StBC 93117 993-J5
StBC 93117 994-A5
SABLON RD
ATAS 93422 553-G6
SACAGAWEA CT
PSRS 93446 513-H6
SACRAMENTO DR
SLO 93401 654-B7
SLO 93401 674-C1
SADDLE WY
SLOC 93426 469-H2
SADDLE BACK LN
SLOC 93446 471-C6
SAFETY E
SLOC 93405 653-J1
SAFETY W
SLOC 93405 653-J1
SAGE AV
SLOC 93402 631-J6
SLOC 93402 632-A5
SAGE CT
LMPC 93436 896-C7
StBC 93437 875-H1
SAGE LN
SLOC 93446 471-B5
SAGE ST
ARGD 93420 714-G5
LMPC 93436 916-C2
StBC 93437 875-H1
SAGE HILL DR
SBAR 93109 995-G5
SAGEWOOD DR
SMRA 93454 776-J5
SAGUNTO ST
StBC 93460 921-B5
SAINT ALBANS PL
StBC 93117 993-F2
SAINT ANDREWS CIR
PSRS 93446 533-J1
SAINT ANDREWS CT
StBC 93436 876-E6
SAINT ANDREWS WY
Npmo 93444 755-F1
SMRA 93455 796-H6
StBC 93436 876-F5
SAINT ANN DR
PSRS 93446 533-J1
SBAR 93109 995-G5
SAINT ANNES PL
StBC 93436 876-E6
SAINT CHARLES PL
StBC 93117 993-F2
SAINT FRANCIS WY
SBAR 93105 985-F7
SLOC 93451 473-F1
SAINT GEORGE PL
StBC 93117 993-F2
SAINT IVES CT
StBC 93455 816-G4
SAINT IVES PL
StBC 93117 993-F2
SAINT JAMES DR
SBAR 93105 995-F4
SAINT JAMES RD
Cmbr 93428 548-G2
SAINT JOHN CIR
GBCH 93433 714-F6
SAINT JOSEPH ST
StBC 93440 878-G2
SAINT JOSEPHS ST
StBC 93111 994-F2
SAINT MARY AV
SLOC 93430 590-J2
SLOC 93430 591-A2
SAINT MARYS CT
StBC 93455 816-H3
SAINT MARYS LN
StBC 93111 984-F6
SAINT NICKS PL
SLOC 93445 734-G1
SAINT THOMAS AV
Cmbr 93428 548-F2
SAINT VINCENT AV
SBAR 93101 996-A4
SALIDA DEL SOL
ARGD 93420 714-J3
SBAR 93109 995-H7
SALINAS AV
SLOC 93446 533-G4
SLOC 93465 553-D2
SALINAS PL
SBAR 93103 996-D3
SALINAS RD
SLOC 93422 594-F3
SLOC 93465 594-F2
SALINAS ST
SBAR 93103 996-D3
SLOC 93405 633-D5
SALISBURY AV
StBC 93117 993-F2
SALISBURY LN
SLOC 93401 674-D6
SMRA 93454 776-J7
SALSIPUEDES ST
SBAR 93103 996-A2
SALVAR RD
StBC 93105 985-B6
SAMANTHA DR
PSRS 93446 513-J7
SMRA 93458 776-G4
StBC 93460 921-A4
StBC 93463 921-A4
SAMANTHA PL
StBC 93460 921-A4
SAMARKAND DR
SBAR 93105 995-G1
SAN ADRIANO CT
SLO 93405 653-E6
SAN ADRIANO ST
SLO 93405 653-E6
SAN ANDREAS ST
SBAR 93101 995-H4
SAN ANDRES AV
ATAS 93422 573-H4
ATAS 93422 574-A4
SAN ANGELO AV
StBC 93111 994-J1
SAN ANSELMO RD
ATAS 93422 553-H7
ATAS 93422 573-G2
SAN ANSELO
StBC 93111 994-G2
SAN ANTERO PL
StBC 93111 994-H1
SAN ANTONIO DR
SMRA 93455 796-H6
SAN ANTONIO LN
Npmo 93444 756-B2
SAN ANTONIO RD
ATAS 93422 594-C3
SLOC 93422 594-D4
StBC 93110 985-A7
StBC 93110 995-A1
StBC 93429 365-E1
StBC 93455 365-E1
SAN ANTONIO RD W
StBC 93429 855-E3
SAN ANTONIO ST
SLOC 93424 693-A4
SAN ANTONIO CREEK LN
StBC 93111 984-J6
StBC 93111 985-A6
SAN ANTONIO CREEK RD
StBC 93111 985-A6
SAN ANZIO WY
StBC 93117 993-G2
SAN ARDO AV
ATAS 93422 573-H1
SAN ARDO WY
StBC 93111 984-F6
SAN AUGUSTIN DR
PSRS 93446 514-A7
PSRS 93446 534-A1
SAN BARI WY
StBC 93117 993-F2
SAN BENITO RD
ATAS 93422 553-F7
ATAS 93422 573-F1
SLOC 93405 633-D4
SAN BENITO WY
StBC 93108 996-H3
SAN BERGAMO WY
StBC 93117 993-G2
SAN BERNARDINO AV
SLOC 93405 633-D4
SAN BERNARDO PL
StBC 93111 994-H2
SAN BERNARDO CREEK RD
SLOC - 612-F3
SLOC 92389 325-B11
SAN BLANCO DR
StBC 93117 993-G2
SAN BLAS PL
StBC 93111 984-G7
SAN BUENAVENTURA WY
SLOC 93451 473-F1
SAN CARLOS DR
PSRS 93446 514-A7
PSRS 93446 534-A1
SLO 93401 654-A5
SAN CARLOS RD
ATAS 93422 593-J1
SBAR 93103 996-A1
SLOC 93422 593-J1

STREET Name City ZIP Pg-Grid

SAN CARPINO DR
StBC 93117 993-G2
SAN CASSINO WY
StBC 93117 993-G2
SAN CAYETANO RD
ATAS 93422 573-B4
SLOC 93422 572-J4
SLOC 93422 573-A4
SANCHEZ DR
GDLP 93434 774-J6
SAN CLEMENTE
SBAR 93109 995-J6
SBAR 93109 996-A7
SAN CLEMENTE AV
ATAS 93422 573-H5
SAN COMO WY
StBC 93117 993-F2
SANDALWOOD AV
ARGD 93420 714-H6
MOBY 93442 611-E2
SANDALWOOD DR
StBC 93455 816-B1
SANDALWOOD LN
SLOC 93465 553-A2
SANDALWOOD WY
SLVG 93463 940-D2
SANDBAR CT
PSRS 93446 533-G1
SAND CANYON CT
SLOC 93420 715-C3
SAND CASTLE CT
GBCH 93433 714-E4
SANDCOVE LN
PSRS 93446 533-G1
SAND DOLLAR AV
SLOC 93445 734-E1
SANDERCOCK ST
SLO 93401 653-H5
SLO 93401 654-A5
SAND HILL LN
StBC 93454 797-D7
SAN DIEGO AV
SLOC 93405 633-C5
SAN DIEGO LP
GBCH 93433 714-F4
SAN DIEGO RD
ATAS 93422 593-G2
ATAS 93422 594-B2
SBAR 93103 996-B2
SLOC 93422 593-H2
SLOC 93422 594-A2
SAN DIEGO WY
ATAS 93422 594-C1
SAN DIEGO CREEK RD
SLOC - 346-B3
SLOC 93453 346-B3
SAN DIMAS AV
StBC 93111 994-H1
SAN DIMAS CT
ATAS 93422 593-H1
SAN DIMAS RD
ATAS 93422 593-G2
SLOC 93422 593-G2
SAN DOMINGO LN
StBC 93111 994-H2
SAN DOMINICO AV
SLOC 93402 631-F7
SANDOVAL RD
SLOC 93422 594-F3
SLOC 93465 594-F3
SANDOWN PL
Cmbr 93428 548-G1
SANDPIPER CIR
MOBY 93442 631-G1
SANDPIPER DR
CARP 93013 998-B5
SMRA 93455 796-F6
SANDPIPER LN
GDLP 93434 774-H6
MOBY 93442 611-G7
MOBY 93442 631-G1
SLOC 93445 714-D7
SLOC 93446 471-C6
StBC 93110 994-J3
SAND POINT DR
StBC 93013 998-A6
SANDSPIT RD
StBC 93117 994-D4
SANDSTONE LN
SMRA 93454 777-A7
SANDWORT LN
SLOC 93420 734-J7
SANDY CT
StBC 93455 816-H3
SANDY PL
StBC 93108 997-B2
SANDY WY
SLOC 93420 735-D6
SLOC 93446 325-D7

SANDY CREEK WY
SLOC 93446 325-D7
SLOC 93446 534-J4
SANDYDALE DR
Npmo 93444 755-J2
Npmo 93444 756-A2
SANDYLAND RD
CARP 93013 998-C7
SANDYLAND COVE RD
CARP 93013 998-C7
StBC 93013 998-C7
SANDY OAKS LN
Npmo 93444 755-J2
SAN FEDERICO AV
StBC 93111 994-H2
SAN FELIPE DR
StBC 93111 994-G3
SAN FELIPE RD
ATAS 93422 573-B5
SLOC 93422 572-J5
SLOC 93422 573-A6
SAN FERMO
StBC 93117 993-G2
SAN FERNANDO DR
PSRS 93446 514-A7
PSRS 93446 534-A1
SAN FERNANDO RD
ATAS 93422 553-D7
ATAS 93422 573-D1
SANFORD CT
StBC 93111 994-G3
SAN FRANCISCO AV
ATAS 93422 573-J6
SLOC 93405 633-E5
SAN FRANCISCO ST
SLOC 93424 693-A4
SAN GABRIEL LN
SBAR 93105 995-F1
SAN GABRIEL RD
ATAS 93422 573-E4
ATAS 93422 574-A7
ATAS 93422 593-J1
ATAS 93422 594-A1
SAN GERONIMO RD
SLOC 93430 324-K9
SLOC 93430 590-F1
SAN GONZALO AV
StBC 93111 994-H2
SAN GREGORIO DR
StBC 93455 817-A7
SAN GREGORIO RD
ATAS 93422 553-D6
ATAS 93422 573-B1
SAN GUILLERMO LN
ATAS 93422 594-A1
SANITARY FILL RD
SLOC 93451 453-B6
SAN JACINTO AV
ATAS 93422 573-H2
SAN JACINTO DR
SLOC 93402 651-F1
SAN JACINTO ST
MOBY 93442 611-E2
SANJA COTA AV
StBC 93460 921-B7
SAN JANO DR
StBC 93117 993-G2
SAN JOAQUIN AV
SLOC 93405 633-A4
SLOC 93430 591-A1
SAN JOAQUIN ST
MOBY 93442 611-E2
SAN JOSE CT
SLO 93405 653-G3
SAN JOSE LN
SBAR 93105 995-F2
SAN JUAN AV
MOBY 93442 611-F3
SAN JUAN PL
StBC 93111 994-H2
SAN JUAN RD
SLOC 93422 594-A3
SLOC 93461 325-F6
SAN JUAN ST
SLOC 93424 693-A4
SAN JUAN BAUTISTA ST
SLOC 93451 473-F1
SAN JUANICO
SMRA 93455 796-H5
SAN JULIAN AV
SBAR 93109 995-J6
SAN JULIAN PL
SBAR 93109 995-J7
SAN JULIAN RD
LMPC 93436 916-G1
SAN JULIO AV
StBC 93111 994-H1

SAN LAZARO LN
StBC 93111 994-G3
SAN LEANDRO CT
SLOC 93402 631-F7
SAN LEANDRO LN
StBC 93108 996-J3
StBC 93108 997-A3
SAN LEANDRO PIKE
StBC 93108 996-J3
SAN LEANDRO PL
StBC 93108 997-B3
SAN LINO CT
SMRA 93455 796-H6
SAN LORENZO DR
StBC 93111 994-G2
SAN LUCAS
ATAS 93422 573-A3
SAN LUCAS WY
StBC 93111 994-G1
SAN LUIS AV
ATAS 93422 574-A5
SLOC 93402 631-H6
SAN LUIS DR
SLO 93401 654-A3
SMRA 93455 796-H6
SAN LUIS ST
PBCH 93449 714-B2
StBC 93111 994-H2
SAN LUIS BAY DR
SLOC 93401 693-C2
SLOC 93405 693-C2
SLOC 93424 693-C2
SAN LUISITO CREEK RD
SLOC - 612-H5
SLOC 92389 325-B11
SLOC 93405 325-B11
SLOC 93405 612-H5
SLOC 93405 632-E1
SAN LUIS OBISPO RD
SLOC 93451 473-F3
SAN LUIS ST PKWY
SLOC 93424 693-A4
SAN MARCOS AV
ATAS 93422 573-H5
StBC 93441 900-H6
SAN MARCOS CT
SLO 93401 654-B6
StBC 93111 994-H2
SAN MARCOS RD
ATAS 93422 573-B6
ATAS 93422 593-D1
SLOC 93422 572-J5
SLOC 93422 573-A5
SLOC 93446 325-A5
SLOC 93446 473-E7
SLOC 93446 493-D2
SLOC 93451 325-A5
SLOC 93451 473-E7
SLOC 93451 493-D2
StBC 93105 984-H3
StBC 93111 984-H3
StBC 93111 994-H1
SAN MARCOS PASS RD
StBC 93110 995-C1
SAN MARCOS PASS RD Rt#-154
SBAR 93110 985-B5
StBC 93105 365-L5
StBC 93105 366-A5
StBC 93105 964-A2
StBC 93105 984-J1
StBC 93105 985-A1
StBC 93110 985-B5
StBC 93110 995-C1
StBC 93111 985-B5
SAN MARINO DR
StBC 93111 994-H2
SAN MARTIN WY
SBAR 93110 985-C7
SAN MATEO AV
StBC 93117 993-H2
SAN MATEO DR
SLO 93401 654-B5
SAN MIGUEL AV
SBAR 93109 995-J7
SLO 93405 654-B2
SLOC 93451 453-B5
SAN MIGUEL CT
GDLP 93434 774-H6
SAN MIGUEL RD
SLOC 93422 573-B7
SLOC 93422 593-A1
SAN MIGUEL ST
SLOC 93424 693-A4
SMRA 93455 796-H5
SAN MIGUELITO RD
LMPC 93436 365-D4
LMPC 93436 916-D5
StBC 93436 365-D4

SAN MIGUELITO RD
StBC 93436 916-D5
StBC 93437 365-D4
SAN MILANO DR
StBC 93117 993-G2
SAN NAPOLI DR
StBC 93117 993-F1
SAN NICOLAS AV
SBAR 93109 995-J6
SAN NICOLAS ST
SMRA 93455 796-H6
SAN ONOFRE RD
SBAR 93105 995-F2
SAN PABLO DR
SLOC 93451 473-H3
SAN PABLO LN
SBAR 93105 995-E1
SAN PALO RD
ATAS 93422 573-G2
SAN PAREDES RD
SLOC 93422 572-J5
SAN PASCUAL ST
SBAR 93101 995-H3
SBAR 93101 996-A5
SAN PASQUAL AV
StBC 93436 365-D4
StBC 93436 916-A4
SAN PATRACIO DR
StBC 93111 984-F6
SAN PEDRO AV
ATAS 93422 573-J1
SAN PEDRO LN
SBAR 93105 995-F1
SAN PESARO WY
StBC 93117 993-G2
SAN PICA WY
StBC 93117 993-G2
SAN RAFAEL AV
SBAR 93109 995-J7
SAN RAFAEL CT
ATAS 93422 574-B7
SAN RAFAEL DR
PSRS 93446 514-A7
SAN RAFAEL RD
ATAS 93422 573-H7
ATAS 93422 574-B7
ATAS 93422 593-H1
ATAS 93422 594-A1
SLOC 93422 593-H1
SAN RAFAEL ST
SLOC 93424 693-A4
SAN RAMON DR
StBC 93111 994-H2
SAN RAMON RD
ATAS 93422 553-E6
SAN REMO DR
SBAR 93105 995-E1
SAN RICARDO DR
StBC 93111 994-G2
SAN RICARDO LN
SLOC 93402 631-E7
SAN RODRIGO AV
StBC 93111 994-H2
SAN ROQUE RD
SBAR 93105 985-F7
SBAR 93105 995-F1
StBC 93105 985-G7
SAN ROSSANO DR
StBC 93117 993-G1
SAN SEBASTIAN CT
GBCH 93433 714-F6
SAN SEBASTIAN LN
SLOC 93402 631-F7
SAN SIMEON AV
SMRA 93455 796-H6
SAN SIMEON DR
SLO 93401 673-H1
StBC 93111 994-H1
SAN SIMEON RD
SLOC 93452 324-G6
SAN SIMEON CREEK RD
Cmbr 93428 324-H6
Cmbr 93428 528-G1
SLOC 93446 324-H6
SLOC 93452 324-H6
SLOC 93452 528-G2
SAN SORRENTO CT
GBCH 93433 714-F7
SANTA AGUEDA RD
StBC 93441 921-J2
StBC 93460 921-J2
SANTA ANA AV
StBC 93111 994-G1
SANTA ANA PL
StBC 93111 994-H2
SANTA ANA RD
ATAS 93422 573-A1
SANTA ANGELA LN
StBC 93108 996-J1

SANTA ANITA RD
SBAR 93105 995-G2
SANTA ANITA ST
SMRA 93455 796-H5
SANTA BARBARA AV
SLOC 93430 591-B4
StBC 93437 875-C4
StBC 93441 900-H6
StBC 93463 900-H6
SANTA BARBARA DR
SMRA 93455 796-H6
SANTA BARBARA RD
ATAS 93422 594-C2
SLOC 93422 593-J4
SLOC 93422 594-A4
SANTA BARBARA ST
GDLP 93434 774-H6
SBAR 93101 995-H1
SBAR 93101 996-A3
SBAR 93105 995-H1
SLO 93401 654-A5
SANTA BARBARA CANYON RD
StBC - 346-F10
SANTA BARBARA SHORES DR
StBC 93117 993-F3
SANTA BELLA AV
PSRS 93446 514-A7
SANTA CATALINA
SBAR 93109 995-J6
SBAR 93109 996-A6
SANTA CLARA AV
SLOC 93405 633-D4
SANTA CLARA DR
LMPC 93436 916-E3
SANTA CLARA RD
SLOC 93422 594-D3
SLOC 93465 594-F3
SANTA CLARA ST
SLO 93401 654-B6
SANTA CLARA WY
StBC 93108 996-H3
SANTA CLAUS LN
StBC 93013 997-J5
StBC 93013 998-A5
SANTA CRUZ AV
PSRS 93446 514-A7
SANTA CRUZ BLVD
SBAR 93109 995-J7
SANTA CRUZ CT
SMRA 93455 796-J5
SANTA CRUZ RD
ATAS 93422 553-E5
ATAS 93422 573-A1
SLOC 93405 633-C5
SANTA DOMINGO RD
SLOC 93420 715-J3
SANTA ELENA LN
StBC 93108 996-H3
SANTA FE
SBAR 93109 995-J6
SANTA FE AV
PBCH 93449 693-H7
PSRS 93446 514-A7
SANTA FE RD
ATAS 93422 574-B5
SLOC 93401 674-B3
SLOC 93422 593-J4
SLOC 93422 594-A5
SANTA FELICIA DR
StBC 93117 993-H2
SANTA INES ST
GDLP 93434 774-H6
SANTA ISABEL
SLOC 93430 591-A2
SANTA ISABEL LN
StBC 93108 996-H3
SANTA LUCIA AV
SLOC 93402 631-G4
StBC 93111 994-H1
SANTA LUCIA DR
SLO 93405 653-G2
SANTA LUCIA RD
ATAS 93422 573-A2
SLOC 93422 573-B4
SANTA LUCIA CANYON RD
LMPC 93436 895-J1
LMPC 93436 896-A3
StBC 93436 895-J1
StBC 93436 896-A3
StBC 93437 875-J7
StBC 93437 876-A6
StBC 93437 895-J1
SANTA MARGARITA RD
SLOC 93422 594-C5
N SANTA MARGARITA RD
SLOC 93422 594-D4

SANTA MARGARITA LAKE RD
SLOC 93453 345-D1
SANTA MARGUERITA DR
StBC 93117 984-D7
SANTA MARGUERITA WY
StBC 93117 984-D7
SANTA MARIA AV
SLO 93405 654-B2
SLOC 93402 631-G4
StBC 93437 855-D7
StBC 93437 875-D1
SANTA MARIA LN
SBAR 93105 995-F1
SANTA MARIA WY
SMRA 93455 796-H6
StBC 93455 796-H6
StBC 93455 816-J1
SANTA MARIA MESA RD
StBC 93454 345-G10
SANTA MARIA VISTA
Npmo 93444 756-E7
Npmo 93444 776-F1
SANTA MONICA RD
CARP 93013 998-C6
StBC - 998-C6
StBC 93013 998-C6
SANTA MONICA WY
SBAR 93109 995-G7
SANTA PAULA AV
SLOC 93402 631-H4
StBC 93111 994-H1
SANTA RITA CIR
SBAR 93109 995-J7
SANTA RITA RD
SLOC - 572-A5
SLOC 93422 325-A8
SLOC 93422 572-C1
SLOC 93430 324-L9
SLOC 93430 572-A5
SLOC 93465 325-A8
SLOC 93465 553-B3
SLOC 93465 572-C1
StBC 93436 365-G3
StBC 93436 878-E5
StBC 93440 878-D2
SANTA ROSA AV
ATAS 93422 573-J7
ATAS 93422 574-A7
SBAR 93109 995-H7
SANTA ROSA LN
CARP 93013 998-E6
StBC 93108 996-J2
StBC 93108 997-A2
SANTA ROSA PL
SBAR 93109 995-J7
SBAR 93109 996-A7
SANTA ROSA RD
ATAS 93422 574-A7
StBC - 919-F6
StBC 93427 919-F6
StBC 93436 365-F4
StBC 93436 916-H4
StBC 93436 919-B7
StBC 93436 939-A1
SANTA ROSA ST
SLO 93401 653-J3
SLO 93401 654-A4
SMRA 93455 796-H6
SANTA ROSA ST Rt#-1
SLO 93401 653-H2
SLO 93405 653-H2
SLOC 93405 653-H2
SANTA ROSA CREEK RD
Cmbr 93428 324-J7
Cmbr 93428 528-H6
SLOC 93465 324-J7
SANTA ROSALIA WY
StBC 93111 984-G7
SANTA SUSANA AV
StBC 93111 994-H1
SANTA SUSANA PL
StBC 93111 994-H1
SANTA TERESITA DR
SBAR 93105 985-F6
SANTA TERESITA WY
SBAR 93105 985-F5
SANTA YNEZ AV
ATAS 93422 573-J5
CARP 93013 998-C6
PSRS 93446 534-A1
SLO 93405 654-B2
SLOC 93402 631-H6
StBC 93460 921-A4
StBC 93463 921-A4

SANTA YNEZ CT
SBAR 93103 996-E3
SANTA YNEZ ST
SBAR 93103 996-D3
StBC 93441 900-H6
StBC 93460 900-H6
StBC 93460 901-A6
SANTA YNEZ RIDGE RD
StBC 93437 895-B5
SANTA YSABEL AV
ATAS 93422 573-J4
ATAS 93422 574-A4
PSRS 93446 514-A7
SLOC 93402 631-G4
SLOC 93402 632-A4
SLOC 93446 533-G2
SANTA YSABEL AV Rt#-41
ATAS 93422 573-J4
SANTA YSABEL DR
SLOC 93430 591-A2
SANTECITO DR
SBAR 93108 996-G2
SAN TELMO
SMRA 93455 796-H5
SANTIAGO RD
SBAR 93103 996-A1
SANTO THOMAS CT
GBCH 93433 714-E4
SANTO TOMAS LN
StBC 93108 996-H3
SAN VICENTE AV
ATAS 93422 573-H1
SAN VICENTE DR
StBC 93111 994-G3
SAN YSIDRO LN
Npmo 93444 755-G2
StBC 93108 987-A7
StBC 93108 996-J1
StBC 93108 997-A1
SAN YSIDRO RD
StBC 93108 986-J7
StBC 93108 996-J1
SAN YSIDRO ST
SMRA 93455 796-H6
SAN YSIDRO TR
StBC 93105 986-J2
StBC 93105 987-A4
StBC 93108 987-A4
SAPPHIRE DR
SMRA 93454 777-A6
SARA CT
StBC 93455 816-H3
SARATOGA AV
GBCH 93433 714-D4
SARATOGA CT
StBC 93117 993-G3
SARAZEN CT
Npmo 93444 735-D7
SASHA WY
SMRA 93454 777-A5
SATINWOOD RD
StBC 93455 816-B1
SATURN AV
StBC 93436 876-D7
StBC 93436 896-D1
SATURN CT
Npmo 93444 756-A5
SAVAGE ST
Npmo 93444 756-C2
SAVONA AV
StBC 93117 993-G1
SAVOY DR
SMRA 93455 796-H6
SAWLEAF CT
SLO 93401 674-D2
SAWLEAF ST
SLO 93401 674-D1
SAWYER AV
CARP 93013 998-D6
SCANDIA DR
BLTN 93427 919-J5
SCANDIA WY
BLTN 93427 919-J5
SCENIC CIR
ARGD 93420 714-H3
SCENIC DR
SBAR 93103 996-E3
SCENIC WY
SLOC 93402 631-J4
SCENIC VIEW WY
Npmo 93444 755-G6
SCHAEFFER RD
StBC - 346-E9
StBC 93252 346-E9
SCHOOL RD
SLOC 93420 715-F2
SCHOOL ST
SMRA 93454 776-H5

SCHOOL ST
SMRA 93454 796-H1
StBC 93463 920-H2
SCHOOLHOUSE LN
Cmbr 93428 528-H7
SCHOOL HOUSE RD
StBC 93108 996-H2
SCHOOL HOUSE CANYON RD
StBC - 346-A8
SCORPIO RD
StBC 93436 876-C5
SCOTT AV
MOBY 93442 611-F6
SCOTT CT
StBC 93117 984-D6
SCOTT DR
SMRA 93454 776-J6
SMRA 93454 777-A7
SMRA 93454 796-J1
SCOTT ST
PSRS 93446 534-A1
SCOTT LEE DR
SLOC 93420 714-G7
SLOC 93445 714-G7
SCRIPPS CRES
StBC 93117 993-H4
SEA ST
Npmo 93444 756-B2
SEA VW
CARP 93013 998-A5
SEA BREEZE
PBCH 93449 714-D3
SEABREEZE WY
LMPC 93436 896-D6
SEABRIGHT AV
GBCH 93433 714-D5
SEACLIFF DR
CARP 93013 998-A5
PBCH 93449 693-F6
SEACLIFF RD
SBAR 93109 995-E6
SEACOAST WY
CARP 93013 998-E6
SEA GULL DR
StBC 93117 993-F3
SEA HORSE LN
SLOC 93402 631-F7
SEA LEDGE LN
SBAR 93109 995-D6
SEA PINES PL
Npmo 93444 755-D1
SEAPORT DR
PBCH 93449 693-J7
SEA RANCH DR
SBAR 93109 995-D5
SBAR 93110 995-D5
SEARIDGE CT
PBCH 93449 693-E5
SEARS ST
Summ 93067 997-C3
SEASCAPE PL
SLOC 93402 631-E7
SEASIDE DR
SMRA 93454 776-J5
SEA VIEW AV
PBCH 93449 693-H7
SEAVIEW AV
MOBY 93442 611-F4
SEAVIEW CIR
PBCH 93449 714-C3
SEAVIEW DR
StBC 93108 996-H4
SEAVIEW LN
PBCH 93449 714-D3
SEAVIEW RD
StBC 93108 996-J2
SEAWARD DR
SMRA 93454 777-A4
SEAWARD ST
SLO 93405 653-G7
SEA WIND WY
SLOC 93402 631-E7
SEBASTIAN WY
Npmo 93444 756-B5
SECOND WIND WY
PSRS 93446 494-E7
SECRETARIAT DR
StBC 93460 922-A5
SECURITY CT
SLOC 93445 714-D7
SEE CANYON RD
SLOC 93402 345-A3
SLOC 93402 673-A4
SLOC 93402 693-C2
SLOC 93405 345-A3
SLOC 93405 693-C2
SLOC 93424 693-C2
SEGOVIA RD
StBC 93117 994-A5

SELBY ST
MOBY 93442 611-F5
SELMA ST
PBCH 93449 714-C2
SELROSE LN
SBAR 93109 995-F6
SELWYN CIR
StBC 93105 985-H7
SENDA VERDE
GBCH 93433 714-F7
SBAR 93105 995-D3
SENDERO ST
SLO 93401 653-J6
SENECA ST
SMRA 93454 777-B6
SENTAR RD
StBC 93013 997-G4
SENTIMENTAL LN
SLOC 93446 514-C7
SEPERADO AV
ATAS 93422 553-H7
ATAS 93422 573-J1
SEQUOIA CT
MOBY 93442 611-F2
PSRS 93446 514-B7
SEQUOIA DR
SLOC 93401 654-D7
SMRA 93454 796-H4
SEQUOIA RD
StBC 93437 875-H1
SEQUOIA ST
MOBY 93442 611-E2
SLO 93401 654-D6
SERAFIN WY
StBC 93013 997-G4
SERENA AV
SLOC 93430 591-A2
StBC 93013 997-G4
SERENA CT
ATAS 93422 573-J3
ATAS 93422 574-A3
SERENA RD
SBAR 93105 995-G1
SERENIDAD PL
StBC 93117 984-D6
SERENITY LN
SLOC 93420 734-J3
SERPA RANCH RD
SLOC 93401 674-B5
SERPOLLA DR
StBC 93013 997-G4
SERRA AV
ATAS 93422 573-J4
SERRANO DR
SLO 93405 653-H3
SERRANO HTS
SLO 93405 653-H3
SESPE LN
StBC 93117 993-H2
SEVADA LN
SLOC 93420 735-A1
SEVEN MILE RD
SLOC - 346-A2
SLOC 93453 346-A2
SEVILLE RD
StBC 93117 982-H6
StBC 93117 994-A5
SHADOW LN
SLOC 93420 734-H7
SHADOWBROOK DR
StBC 93117 993-J3
SHADOW CANYON RD
SLOC 93465 324-L7
SLOC 93465 325-A8
SHADOW CREEK LN
PSRS 93446 533-G1
SHADOWCREST DR
StBC 93455 817-A3
SHADOW HILLS BLVD N
StBC 93105 985-B5
SHADOW HILLS CIR
StBC 93105 985-B5
SHADOW MOUNTAIN DR
BLTN 93427 919-G6
SHADY LN
StBC 93455 816-H3
SHADY CREEK DR
SLOC 93446 471-A5
SHADY GLADE DR
StBC 93455 816-J3
SHADY GLEN CT
StBC 93455 817-A4
SHADY GLEN DR
StBC 93455 817-A4
SHAFFER LN
PBCH 93449 714-B1
SHAMROCK AV
StBC 93117 994-C1
SHAMROCK LN
PBCH 93449 714-E3

SHANDON-SAN JUAN RD
SLOC 93461 325-F7
SHANE LN
SLOC 93465 553-C3
SHANKLIN PL
StBC 93436 896-F3
SHANNA PL
GBCH 93433 714-F7
SHANNON LN
SLOC 93420 715-A1
SHANNON HILL DR
PSRS 93446 513-H5
SHANON CT
SMRA 93454 797-A1
SHARON LN
GBCH 93433 714-E4
SHARON PL
BLTN 93427 919-H4
SHARRY LN
StBC 93455 816-H5
SHASTA AV
MOBY 93442 611-G7
SHASTA LN
Npmo 93444 735-H4
SBAR 93101 996-A2
SLOC 93446 471-B5
SHASTA WY
StBC 93455 817-E5
SHAW ST
StBC 93440 878-H2
SHEARER AV
SLOC 93430 591-C5
SHEARTON WY
StBC 93117 984-D7
SHEARWATER CT
SLOC 93424 693-B3
SHEEHY RD
Npmo 93444 735-J5
Npmo 93444 736-A4
SHEEP CAMP RD
StBC 93463 900-E6
StBC 93463 920-E1
SHEFFIELD DR
LMPC 93436 916-G2
StBC 93108 997-C2
Summ 93067 997-C2
SHEFFIELD ST
Cmbr 93428 528-F6
SHEFIELD DR
SLO 93401 673-H1
SHEILA LN
SMRA 93458 796-G4
SHELBY ST
Summ 93067 997-D3
SHELBY WY
SLOC 93420 715-D2
SHELL BEACH RD
PBCH 93449 693-F6
SLOC 93449 693-E4
SHELL CREEK RD
SLOC 93453 325-G9
SLOC 93461 325-G9
SHELLIE CT
StBC 93455 816-H3
SHELTER RIDGE PL
Npmo 93444 755-F1
SHEMARA ST
CARP 93013 998-E6
SHEPARD DR
SMRA 93454 796-J3
SHEPARD MESA DR
StBC 93013 998-J7
StBC 93013 999-A6
SHEPARD MESA LN
StBC 93013 999-A6
SHEPHERD DR
PSRS 93446 534-B1
StBC 93436 896-F2
SHERIDAN AV
SBAR 93101 995-H3
SHERIDAN RD
SLOC 93420 735-A7
SLOC 93420 755-A2
SHERMAN RD
SBAR 93103 986-D7
SHERRY PL
LMPC 93436 896-C6
SHERWOOD DR
Cmbr 93428 548-F2
StBC 93110 985-B7
StBC 93110 995-B1
StBC 93455 816-B1
SHERWOOD RD
PSRS 93446 514-A7
SHETLAND CT
StBC 93455 817-A4
SHETLAND PL
SLOC 93420 735-A2

STB & SLO

STREET Name City ZIP Pg-Grid

SHETLAND WY
SLOC 93446 471-C4
SHIFFRAR LN
Npmo 93444 756-A6
SHILO CT
StBC 93455 816-G7
SHILOH PL
SLOC 93465 553-B1
SHIRLEY LN
StBC 93455 816-H3
SHIRRELL WY
StBC 93117 984-D7
S SHORE DR
SLOC 93446 469-E2
SHORELINE DR
PBCH 93449 693-G7
SBAR 93101 996-A6
SBAR 93109 995-H7
SBAR 93109 996-A6
StBC 93111 994-G3
SHORT LN
SLOC 93446 469-D2
SHORT RD
StBC 93460 901-G3
SHORT ST
ARGD 93420 715-A4
SLO 93401 673-H2
SHOSHONE DR
PSRS 93446 513-H6
SICILY ST
MOBY 93442 611-D1
SIENNA ST
MOBY 93442 611-E2
SIENNA WY
StBC 93463 920-J6
SIERRA CT
MOBY 93442 611-G7
SIERRA DR
ARGD 93420 714-G4
SIERRA LN
PSRS 93446 514-C7
PSRS 93446 534-C1
SIERRA RD
Npmo 93444 756-B6
SIERRA ST
SBAR 93103 995-J1
SIERRA WY
SLO 93401 654-B5
SIERRA MADRE AV
SMRA 93454 796-H2
SMRA 93454 797-A2
SIERRA MADRE DR
StBC 93110 985-A6
SIERRA MADRE RD
StBC 93110 984-J7
StBC 93110 985-A7
StBC 93111 984-J7
SIERRA VISTA
SLVG 93463 940-D1
SMRA 93458 776-G4
SIERRA VISTA RD
ATAS 93422 573-G6
StBC 93108 996-E1
SILER LN
StBC 93455 816-H2
SILKBORG RD
StBC 93463 920-D6
SILLA RD
ATAS 93422 573-F1
SILVA PL
Npmo 93444 756-A6
SILVER WY
SLOC 93420 735-A1
SILVERADO AV
SMRA 93455 796-G6
SILVER DOLLAR LN
Npmo 93444 755-H3
SILVER FERN CT
StBC 93117 993-J3
SILVER LEAF CT
Npmo 93444 756-B5
SILVER LEAF DR
StBC 93455 816-H2
SILVER SADDLE LN
SLOC 93446 471-B6
N SILVER SHOALS DR
PBCH 93449 693-F5
SILVER SPUR PL
SLOC 93445 734-F1
SILVERY MOON LN
SLOC 93446 514-C7
SILVESTRE RD
StBC 93110 995-D4
SIMAS ST
StBC 93434 775-C7
StBC 93455 795-C1
StBC 93458 775-C7
StBC 93458 795-C1
SIMMONS LN
Npmo 93444 756-A5

SIMMS AV
PSRS 93446 513-F2
SINALOA AV
ATAS 93422 574-A4
SINALOA DR
StBC 93108 996-J3
StBC 93108 997-A3
SINTON RD
StBC 93455 795-H5
StBC 93458 795-H5
SIRIUS AV
StBC 93436 876-C6
SISQUOC
SLO 93401 653-J7
SISQUOC ST
StBC 93254 806-B1
SIX FLAGS CIR
BLTN 93427 919-H5
SKAGEN DR
SLVG 93463 920-F6
SKIPJACK LN
SLOC 93446 471-B5
SKY DR
StBC 93460 921-J3
SKYE ST
Cmbr 93428 528-F7
SKYLARK CT
SMRA 93455 796-J7
SMRA 93455 797-A7
SKYLARK LN
SLO 93401 654-B4
SKYLARK RD
StBC 93460 941-D1
SKYLARK WY
Npmo 93444 756-C3
SKYLINE CIR
SBAR 93109 995-G5
SKYLINE DR
PBCH 93449 714-F3
SLO 93405 653-G1
SLOC 93402 631-F6
SKYLINE WY
SBAR 93109 995-G5
SKYLINK LN
SLOC 93446 471-B5
SKYLINKS DR
SMRA 93455 796-F6
SKY VIEW DR
LMPC 93436 916-F2
SKYVIEW DR
PSRS 93446 513-H4
SBAR 93108 996-F2
StBC 93108 996-F2
SKYVIEW TR
SLOC 93402 673-B7
SLOC 93402 693-B1
SKYWAY DR
SMRA 93455 796-E6
SMRA 93455 816-G1
StBC 93455 816-G1
SLACK ST
SLO 93405 654-A2
SLOC 93405 654-A2
SLEEPY HOLLOW LN
SMRA 93454 777-A6
SLEEPY HOLLOW RD
PSRS 93446 533-J2
SMALLWOOD CT
StBC 93455 817-A4
SMILEY PL
SLOC 93422 593-C2
SMITH AV
SLOC 93445 714-D7
SMITH CT
Cmbr 93428 548-H1
SMITH DR
SMRA 93458 776-G5
SMITH ST
SLO 93401 654-B5
SMRA 93458 776-G7
SMRA 93458 796-G2
SMITH POINT RD
SLOC 93426 469-J3
SLOC 93426 470-A3
SMOKE TREE LN
SMRA 93454 777-A6
SMUGGLERS POINT LN
SLOC 93446 471-B6
SNAPDRAGON WY
SLO 93401 674-D2
SNEAD LN
Npmo 93444 735-D7
SNEAD ST
PSRS 93446 533-H1
SNOW LN
Npmo 93444 736-A4
SNOWBERRY CT
SLOC 93424 693-B1
SNOWBERRY LN
SMRA 93454 777-A6

SNOWCONE PL
SLOC 93420 734-J4
SNOWHILL CT
StBC 93455 816-G4
SOARES AV
StBC 93455 816-G6
SOARES DR
Npmo 93444 756-B5
SODA LAKE RD
SLOC - 345-L1
SLOC - 346-B4
SLOC 92389 325-L10
SLOC 93252 346-B4
SLOC 93453 345-L1
SLOC 93453 346-B4
SODA LAKE SAN DIEGO CREEK RD
SLOC - 345-L4
SLOC - 346-A2
SOFTCHESS PL
SLOC - 695-E3
SOLA CT
SLO 93405 653-F7
SOLA ST
SBAR 93101 995-J3
SBAR 93101 996-A3
SBAR 93103 996-A3
SOLANA CT
GBCH 93433 714-F6
SBAR 93109 995-F5
SOLANO AV
SLOC 93405 633-A5
SOLANO RD
ATAS 93422 574-A6
PBCH 93449 693-F6
SLOC 93422 593-F3
SOLANO ST
SLOC 93402 631-F6
SOLAR WY
PBCH 93449 714-C2
StBC 93436 876-C7
SOLEDAD AV
SBAR 93103 996-C2
SOLEDAD CT
SMRA 93455 796-H6
SOLEDAD RD
ATAS 93422 573-A4
SLOC 93422 573-A4
SOLEDAD ST
SBAR 93103 996-C2
SOLOMON RD
StBC 93455 816-D5
SOLVANG ST
SLOC 93405 633-E5
SOMBRERO DR
SLOC 93402 632-B7
SOMBRERO WY
SMRA 93458 776-F4
SOMBRILLA AV
ATAS 93422 574-A4
SOMBRILLO
ARGD 93420 714-J3
SOMERS LN
PSRS 93446 513-H2
SOMERSET CT
LMPC 93436 916-G2
SOMERSET DR
StBC 93111 984-F7
SOMERSET PL
LMPC 93436 916-G1
SOMERSET WY
Cmbr 93428 528-D5
SOMMER LN
StBC 93117 993-E2
SONGBIRD ST
SLOC 93424 693-B1
SONOMA AV
SLOC 93405 633-B5
StBC 93117 993-H2
SONORA AV
ATAS 93422 574-A3
SONORA DR
SBAR 93105 995-F3
SONRIENTE RD
StBC 93110 995-D4
SONRISA CT
SLO 93405 653-E6
SONYA LN
SMRA 93458 796-E4
SORO AL
SLVG 93463 940-E1
SORREL LN
SLOC 93446 471-B6
SOTO PL
SBAR 93117 994-D2
SOUTH ST
MOBY 93442 611-F7
SLO 93401 653-H5
SLO 93401 654-A6
StBC 93117 994-E3

SOUTH ST Rt#-227
SLO 93401 653-J5
SLO 93401 654-A5
SOUTH BAY BLVD
MOBY 93402 631-J1
MOBY 93405 631-J1
MOBY 93442 611-J7
MOBY 93442 631-J1
SLOC - 611-J7
SLOC 93402 631-J6
SLOC 93405 631-J1
SLOC 93442 611-J7
SLOC 93442 631-J1
SOUTHBROOK DR
LMPC 93436 896-D6
SOUTH DAKOTA AV
SLOC 93451 453-A5
StBC 93437 875-D1
SOUTHFORK PL
SLOC 93446 471-D7
SOUTHLAND ST
Npmo 93444 756-C5
SOUTHLAND WOODS LN
Npmo 93444 756-C4
SOUTHLYN PL
StBC 93455 817-A2
SOUTHPOINT CT
StBC 93455 816-H6
SOUTHRIDGE LN
Npmo 93444 755-F1
SOUTHSIDE PKWY
SMRA 93455 796-J5
SOUTHVIEW AV
SLOC 93420 734-H5
SOUTHVIEW CIR
PSRS 93446 534-C1
SOUTHWOOD DR
SLO 93401 654-B6
SLOC 93401 654-C6
SOUZA ST
Npmo 93444 756-B3
SPANISH TR
SLOC 93420 734-J4
SLOC 93420 735-A4
SPANISH CAMP RD
SLOC 93446 533-H2
SPANISH MOSS LN
ARGD 93420 714-J3
SPANISH OAKS DR
SLO 93401 674-D2
SPARKS ST
Npmo 93444 756-B1
SPARKS TRAIL WY
SLOC - 345-F5
SLOC 93420 345-F5
SPARROW ST
SLOC 93405 693-C2
SPARROW HAWK LN
SLOC 93446 471-C6
SPEED ST
SMRA 93454 796-H2
SPENCE
SLOC 93430 591-D4
SPENCER DR
StBC 93455 816-J5
SPENCER ST
Cmbr 93428 548-H2
SPICA WY
StBC 93436 876-D6
SPIKE CT
SLOC 93426 469-H2
SPITFIRE LN
SLO 93401 674-C2
SLOC 93401 674-C2
SPOONBILL CT
SLOC 93424 693-B3
SPRING CT
SLO 93401 654-C6
SPRING RD
StBC 93108 996-H4
SPRING ST
PSRS 93446 513-F3
SBAR 93103 996-C2
SLOC 93446 513-F3
SPRING CANYON LN
Npmo 93444 735-J2
Npmo 93444 736-A2
SPRING CANYON RD
StBC 93460 901-D5
SPRING MEADOW LN
SLOC 93422 593-C1
SPRUCE DR
SMRA 93454 777-B7
StBC 93117 993-G1
SPRUCE LN
Npmo 93444 756-B4
SPRUCE ST
ARGD 93420 714-G6
StBC 93437 855-F7

SPRUCEWOOD CT
SLOC 93446 533-E6
SPUR DR
StBC 93455 817-B5
SPUR VALLEY RD
StBC 93117 984-E5
SPYGLASS AV
SMRA 93455 796-G5
SPYGLASS CT
PSRS 93446 533-J1
SPYGLASS DR
PBCH 93449 693-F6
SMRA 93455 796-G5
SPYGLASS LN
SLOC 93446 471-B5
SQUASH CT
SLOC 93465 553-A2
SQUIRE CT
SLOC 93401 693-G1
SQUIRE LN
SLVG 93463 920-E6
StBC 93463 920-E6
SQUIRE CANYON RD
SLOC 93401 693-F2
SQUIRE KNOLL DR
SLOC 93401 693-F1
STACY LN
SBAR 93110 985-D7
STADIUM
StBC 93463 920-J6
STADIUM DR
StBC 93463 920-J6
StBC 93463 921-A6
STADIUM PL
StBC 93463 920-J6
STADIUM RD
StBC 93106 994-B4
STAFFORD ST
Cmbr 93428 528-D6
SLO 93405 653-J2
SLO 93405 654-A2
STAG CANYON RD
StBC 93460 901-D6
STAGE COACH RD
SLOC 93446 534-J7
SLOC 93465 325-C8
SLOC 93465 534-J7
STAGECOACH RD
ARGD 93420 715-B4
SLOC 93420 715-C3
StBC 93105 366-A5
StBC 93105 964-A1
STAGE SPRINGS RD
SLOC 93432 325-E9
STAGS LEAP WY
SLOC 93446 513-A2
STALLCUP LN
StBC 93436 896-G3
STALLION DR
StBC 93441 921-J2
StBC 93441 922-A2
STALLION WY
SLOC 93446 534-J4
STANFORD CIR
StBC 93436 876-E5
STANFORD DR
SLO 93405 653-G1
StBC 93455 816-J6
STANFORD PL
StBC 93111 984-G7
STANFORD RD
SMRA 93454 776-J5
STANISLAUS AV
SLOC 93405 633-D5
STANLEY AV
ARGD 93420 715-D4
STANLEY DR
SBAR 93105 995-G2
STANLEY PARK RD
StBC - 999-C7
StBC 93013 999-C7
VeCo - 999-C7
VeCo 93013 999-C7
STANSBURY DR
StBC 93455 816-G5
STANTON RD
SLOC 93420 735-C6
STANWOOD DR Rt#-192
SBAR 93103 986-D7
SBAR 93103 996-D1
SBAR 93105 986-D7
SBAR 93108 996-D1
STARDUST CT
SMRA 93455 796-J7
STARDUST DR
SMRA 93455 796-J6
StBC 93436 896-C1
STARDUST LN
SLOC 93446 514-C7

STARFIRE ST
SMRA 93455 796-J7
STARKEY RD
SLOC 93461 325-F6
STARLIGHT LN
ARGD 93420 714-H6
STARLING CT
PSRS 93446 534-A1
STARLING DR
PSRS 93446 534-A2
STARLITE CT
SMRA 93455 796-J6
STARLITE DR
Npmo 93444 756-A5
STAR PINE RD
CARP 93013 998-E6
STATE ST
SBAR 93101 995-J3
SBAR 93101 996-A3
SBAR 93105 995-F1
SBAR 93110 995-D1
StBC 93105 995-D1
StBC 93110 995-C1
STATE PARK RD
MOBY 93442 611-G7
MOBY 93442 631-G1
STATION WY
ARGD 93420 714-J5
ARGD 93420 715-A5
STEELE ST
StBC 93441 900-G5
StBC 93463 900-G5
STELLA CT
PSRS 93446 514-A3
STENNER ST
SLO 93405 653-J2
STENNER CREEK RD
SLOC 93405 633-G6
STEPHANIE DR
SLO 93405 653-E6
STEPLEGATE LN
StBC 93455 817-B6
STERLING AV
CARP 93013 998-D6
STERLING LN
SLO 93405 653-D7
STERLING WY
CARP 93013 998-D6
STERN DECK RD
SLOC 93426 469-J1
STERRET AV
StBC 93110 985-E6
STEVENS RD
SBAR 93105 995-E2
StBC 93105 995-E2
STEVENSON DR
ARGD 93420 714-H3
STILL MEADOW RD
StBC 93441 920-J2
StBC 93463 920-J2
STILLWATER CT
PSRS 93446 533-G1
STILLWELL RD
StBC 93455 817-B5
STIMSON AV
PBCH 93449 714-C2
STINSON CT
GBCH 93433 714-F5
STOCKDALE RD
SLOC 93446 493-F4
STOCKTON ST
StBC 93455 817-B5
STODDARD LN
StBC 93108 996-F1
STOKES AV
SMRA 93454 776-J6
SMRA 93454 777-A6
STONEBRIDGE DR
SMRA 93454 777-C7
STONEBRIDGE LN
PSRS 93446 533-G1
STONEBROOK DR
LMPC 93436 896-D6
STONE BROOK RD
StBC 93455 816-G4
STONECREEK RD
StBC 93105 995-F4
STONEHOUSE LN
StBC 93108 997-D1
STONE HOUSE RD
StBC 93108 986-G7
STONE MEADOW LN
StBC 93108 996-H1
STONERIDGE DR
SLO 93401 654-A6
STONEWOOD CT
StBC 93455 817-A4
STONEY PL
SLOC 93446 325-D6
SLOC 93446 514-J7

STONEY PL
SLOC 93446 534-J1
STONEY CREEK DR
PSRS 93446 533-J1
PSRS 93446 534-A1
STONEY PARK LN
SMRA 93458 776-G3
STORKE RD
StBC 93117 993-J4
STORMY WY
PSRS 93446 513-H4
STORY ST
Npmo 93444 756-C4
SLO 93401 654-A5
STOW ST
StBC 93441 900-H6
STOW CANYON RD
StBC 93117 984-C7
E STOWELL RD
SMRA 93454 796-H2
SMRA 93454 797-B2
StBC 93454 797-B2
W STOWELL RD
SMRA 93454 796-F2
SMRA 93458 796-F2
StBC 93458 796-C2
STRAND WY
SLOC 93445 714-D7
SLOC 93445 734-D1
STRATFORD AV
SMRA 93454 777-A5
SMRA 93454 797-A1
STRATFORD PL
StBC 93108 997-C1
STRATFORD ST
PBCH 93449 714-C1
StBC 93455 816-J3
STREHLE LN
StBC 93117 993-G3
STUART AV
SLOC 93430 591-C4
STUART DR
StBC 93455 817-A5
STUART ST
Cmbr 93428 548-H2
STUBBLEFIELD RD
StBC 93455 817-A7
STUBBS LN
StBC 93455 796-G7
STUB END CIR
SLOC 93426 469-J2
STUDIO DR
SLOC 93430 591-B4
STUPID RULE LN
SLOC 93446 493-H7
SUBURBAN RD
SLO 93401 673-H2
SLOC 93401 673-H2
SLOC 93401 674-A2
SUELDO ST
SLO 93401 673-J1
SUELLEN CT
StBC 93117 984-D7
SUENO RD
StBC 93117 993-J5
StBC 93117 994-A5
SUEY RD
SMRA 93454 777-B5
SMRA 93454 797-B1
StBC 93454 777-B7
StBC 93454 797-B1
SUEY CREEK RD
Npmo 93444 345-F7
Npmo 93444 737-D7
SLOC - 345-F7
SLOC - 737-D7
SLOC 93420 737-A4
SLOC 93454 345-F7
SUEY CROSSING RD
SMRA 93454 777-B6
SUFFOLK ST
Cmbr 93428 528-F6
SUGAR ST
SMRA 93454 797-F2
StBC 93454 797-F2
SUGAR BUSH DR
SMRA 93454 777-A6
SULPHUR SPRINGS DR
PSRS 93446 513-G2
SUMAC CT
SLO 93401 674-D2
SUMAC ST
StBC 93437 875-H1
SUMMER LN
Npmo 93444 755-E3
SUMMER CREEK LN
PSRS 93446 513-G7
PSRS 93446 533-G1
SUMMER FALLOW PL
PSRS 93446 534-C1

SUMMERHILL DR
SMRA 93454 777-B7
SUMMERLAND HEIGHTS LN
StBC 93108 997-C3
Summ 93067 997-C3
SUMMER RANCH RD
SLOC 93446 325-D7
SUMMERWOOD LN
LMPC 93436 896-D6
SUMMIT DR
PBCH 93449 714-F3
PSRS 93446 514-A4
SUMMIT LN
SBAR 93108 996-F2
SUMMIT RD
SBAR 93108 996-F2
StBC 93108 996-G3
SUMMIT STATION RD
SLOC 93420 735-G6
SUMNER PL
StBC 93455 817-A3
SUNBEAM RD
StBC 93436 876-C7
StBC 93436 896-C1
SUNBURY AV
Cmbr 93428 528-E6
SUNCREST DR
SLOC 93465 553-B1
SUN DALE WY
Npmo 93444 755-E3
SUNDANCE LN
PSRS 93446 513-H4
SUNFLOWER CT
SMRA 93455 796-J6
SUNFLOWER WY
SLO 93401 674-C2
SUNGATE RANCH RD
StBC 93111 994-H2
SUNKIST LN
SLOC 93420 735-F5
SUNNYBROOK CT
LMPC 93436 896-D6
SUNNY HILL AV
SLOC 93402 631-F6
SUNNY RIDGE PL
SLOC 93446 534-H1
SUNNYSIDE AV
StBC 93455 816-J3
SUNNYSIDE WY
SLOC 93465 553-C1
SUNNYSLOPE LN
Npmo 93444 756-C3
StBC 93455 817-A3
SUNRIDGE LN
Npmo 93444 755-J5
SUNRISE CT
PSRS 93446 533-J1
PSRS 93446 534-A1
SUNRISE DR
SMRA 93455 796-H6
SMRA 93455 797-A6
SUNRISE TER
ARGD 93420 714-J7
ARGD 93420 715-A7
SUNRISE TR
SLOC 93424 693-C2
SUNRISE WY
StBC 93463 920-G7
SUNRISE HILL LN
StBC 93108 996-E1
SUNRISE VISTA WY
SBAR 93109 995-G6
SUNROSE CT
SLO 93401 674-C1
SUNROSE LN
SLO 93401 674-C1
SUNSET AV
MOBY 93442 611-F4
SBAR 93101 995-H3
SMRA 93454 776-H6
SMRA 93454 777-A6
SMRA 93458 776-F6
SUNSET CT
MOBY 93442 611-F4
SUNSET DR
ARGD 93420 714-G5
CARP 93013 998-A5
PSRS 93446 513-F3
SBAR 93105 985-F7
SLO 93401 654-C5
SLOC 93402 631-H7
SUNSET LN
SLOC 93445 714-D7
SUNSET RD
SBAR 93110 985-E7
StBC 93110 985-E7
SUNSHINE CT
SMRA 93455 796-J7

SUNSHINE LN
StBC 93105 964-H1
SUNVIEW DR
StBC 93455 816-H4
SUPERIOR ST
SMRA 93458 776-F7
SMRA 93458 796-F1
SURF
PBCH 93449 714-C3
SURF AV
SLOC 93445 714-D7
SURF ST
MOBY 93442 611-F5
PBCH 93449 714-D2
SURF VIEW DR
SBAR 93109 995-H6
SURREY WY
SMRA 93454 777-A5
SURRY PL
StBC 93117 993-F2
SUSSEX CT
StBC 93117 984-C7
SUTLIFF RD
SLOC 93451 473-B5
SUTTER AV
SLOC 93405 632-J5
SLOC 93405 633-A5
SUTTER ST
SMRA 93454 777-B6
SUTTON AV
SBAR 93101 996-A5
SVENDBORG RD
SLVG 93463 940-E1
SWALLOW CT
SMRA 93454 796-H3
SWALLOW LN
Npmo 93444 756-E4
SWALLOW ST
SMRA 93454 796-H3
SWAN LN
SLOC 93446 471-D5
SWAZEY ST
SLO 93401 654-A5
SWEENEY LN
SLO 93401 654-A7
SWEENEY RD
StBC 93436 365-F4
StBC 93436 916-J1
SWEETBAY LN
SLO 93401 674-D2
SWEETBRIAR CT
StBC 93455 817-A5
SWEET DONNA PL
Npmo 93444 755-H3
SWEETHEART LN
SLOC 93446 514-C7
SWEETIE LN
SLOC 93451 325-D4
SWEET SPRINGS LN
SLOC 93420 715-D1
SWEETWATER WY
StBC 93117 993-J4
SWIFT RD
Npmo 93444 756-E3
SWORD CT
SMRA 93454 797-B1
SYCAMORE CT
ARGD 93420 714-H7
SYCAMORE DR
ARGD 93420 714-H7
SLO 93401 654-C6
SYCAMORE LN
SBAR 93103 996-D3
SYCAMORE RD
ATAS 93422 573-J1
ATAS 93422 574-A2
SYCAMORE RD Rt#-41
ATAS 93422 574-A2
SYCAMORE ST
SMRA 93458 776-G4
StBC 93437 855-E7
SYCAMORE WY
SLVG 93463 940-E1
SYCAMORE CANYON DR
PSRS 93446 534-B1
SLOC 93405 652-H5
SLOC 93405 653-A5
SYCAMORE CANYON RD
PSRS 93446 534-B1
SBAR 93108 996-D2
StBC 93108 996-H2
SYCAMORE CANYON RD Rt#-192
SBAR 93108 986-D7
SBAR 93108 996-F1
StBC 93108 986-D7
StBC 93108 996-F1
SYCAMORE CREEK LN
Npmo 93444 735-H3
SBAR 93103 986-C6

SYCAMORE VISTA RD
StBC 93108 986-E7
StBC 93108 996-D1
SYDNEY ST
SLO 93401 654-B5
SYLVAN CT
StBC 93455 816-J3
SYLVAN DR
StBC 93117 984-E7
StBC 93117 994-E1
SYLVESTER WY
SLOC 93446 494-A6
SYLVIA CIR
PSRS 93446 513-J6
SYLVIA CT
SLO 93401 654-B5
SYRAH CT
SLOC 93465 553-A3

T

N T ST
LMPC 93436 896-C7
LMPC 93436 916-C1
S T ST
LMPC 93436 916-C2
TABANO WY
StBC 93111 984-H7
TABOR LN
StBC 93108 997-C1
TADPOLE CT
SLOC 93465 553-F1
TAFT AV
SLOC 93430 590-J1
SLOC 93430 591-A1
TAFT PL
Cmbr 93428 548-H1
TAFT ST
PBCH 93449 714-C1
SLO 93405 653-J3
SLO 93405 654-A3
SMRA 93454 776-H4
SMRA 93458 776-G4
TAHITI ST
MOBY 93442 611-D1
TAHITIAN VILLAGE W
LMPC 93436 896-E6
TAHOE RD
SLOC 93405 654-A1
TAJO DR
StBC 93110 995-A1
TALLANT RD
SBAR 93105 995-G2
TALLEY FARMS RD
SLOC 93420 695-F5
TALL PINE LN
StBC 93463 921-A6
TALL TREE DR
Npmo 93444 755-H3
TALLYHO PL
StBC 93455 816-G5
TALLY HO RD
ARGD 93420 715-A4
TALLYHO RD
StBC 93455 816-G5
TALMADGE RD
StBC 93455 817-A5
TAMA LN
SMRA 93455 796-F5
TAMARA CT
StBC 93455 816-H5
TAMARA LN
SLOC 93465 574-F1
TAMARACK CT
StBC 93436 876-F5
TAMARACK ST
StBC 93437 855-F7
StBC 93437 875-F1
TAMARACK WY
SLOC 93465 553-E1
TAMARISK WY
SLOC 93401 674-D5
TAMERA DR
SLOC 93445 714-G7
TAMPICO RD
ATAS 93422 574-B4
TAMSEN ST
Cmbr 93428 528-F7
TANAGER CT
SLOC 93465 553-B1
TANGAIR RD
StBC 93437 365-C2
StBC 93437 875-A4
E TANGERINE AV
LMPC 93436 896-F6
TANGLEWOOD CT
PSRS 93446 534-B1
SLO 93401 654-C6
TANGLEWOOD DR
PSRS 93446 534-A1

INDEX

COPYRIGHT 2000 Thomas Bros. Maps ®

STREET Name City ZIP Pg-Grid

TANGLEWOOD DR
SLO 93401 654-C6
StBC 93455 816-B1
TANIS PL
Npmo 93444 756-A4
TANK FARM RD
SLO 93401 673-H2
SLO 93401 674-C1
SLOC 93401 673-H2
SLOC 93401 674-A2
TANNER DR
PSRS 93446 513-H5
TANNER LN
ARGD 93420 715-C4
TANYA CT
SMRA 93454 777-A5
TANYA DR
PSRS 93446 513-J7
TAPADERO DR
StBC 93463 900-F6
TAPIDERO AV
SLOC 93402 632-B7
TARANTO CIR
StBC 93013 998-C6
TARRAGON CT
LMPC 93436 896-C7
TARSUS CIR
PSRS 93446 494-F7
N TASSAJARA DR
SLO 93405 653-G2
S TASSAJARA DR
SLO 93405 653-G2
TASSAJARA CREEK RD
SLOC - 614-A5
SLOC 92389 325-B11
SLOC 93453 614-A5
TATTERSALL CT
StBC 93455 817-A4
TATUM CT
StBC 93455 817-B4
TAURUS RD
StBC 93436 876-C5
TAYLOR PL
ARGD 93420 714-J5
TAYLOR ST
SMRA 93454 776-H4
SMRA 93458 776-F4
TEAK DR
PSRS 93446 534-A1
TEAK ST
StBC 93437 855-F7
TEAKWOOD DR
StBC 93455 816-B1
TEAL
PSRS 93446 514-A7
TECOLOTE AV
StBC 93117 994-E2
TECOLOTE RD
ATAS 93422 573-E5
TECORIDA AV
ATAS 93422 573-J5
TEDDY BEAR LN
GBCH 93433 714-E4
TEE CT
Npmo 93444 735-E7
PSRS 93446 513-J7
E TEFFT ST
Npmo 93444 736-E7
Npmo 93444 756-D1
W TEFFT ST
Npmo 93444 755-J5
Npmo 93444 756-B3
TEHAMA AV
SLOC 93405 632-J5
TEHAMA DR
StBC 93111 994-G1
TEHAS CANYON RD
StBC 93441 900-J4
TEJAS PL
Npmo 93444 755-H4
Npmo 93444 756-A4
TELEPHONE RD
StBC 93454 797-E6
StBC 93454 817-E4
StBC 93455 817-E4
TELFORD RD
SLOC 93446 469-J4
SLOC 93446 470-A4
TELLINA WY
StBC 93111 984-F6
TEMETATTE RIDGE LN
Npmo 93444 736-B3
TEMETTATE DR
Npmo 93444 737-B4
TEMPLE ST
SLOC 93420 714-H7
Summ 93067 997-D4
TEMPLETON RD
SLOC 93422 553-D3
SLOC 93465 325-C8
TEMPLETON RD
SLOC 93465 553-D3
SLOC 93465 574-A1
TEMPLETON RD Rt#-41
SLOC 93422 574-B2
SLOC 93465 574-B2
TEMPLETON CEMETERY RD
SLOC 93446 533-E6
TEMPLETON HILLS RD
SLOC 93465 553-B2
TEMPLETON PARK RD
SLOC 93465 553-C2
TEMPUS CIR
ARGD 93420 715-B4
TEN ACRE RD
StBC 93108 997-C2
TENBROOK ST
SLO 93401 654-A6
TENNESSEE WALKER WY
SLOC 93446 471-C5
TEN OAKS WY
Npmo 93444 755-H2
TEPIC PL
StBC 93111 984-G7
TEPUSQUET RD
StBC 93454 345-H10
TEREBINTH LN
SLOC 93465 553-C1
TERESA ST
ATAS 93422 573-J1
TERI SUE LN
BLTN 93427 919-H4
TERMINAL DR
SMRA 93455 796-F7
SMRA 93455 816-F1
TERMINO ST
StBC 93460 921-C4
TERNI LN
SBAR 93105 995-E3
TERRA RD
StBC 93437 895-B2
TERRA ST
MOBY 93442 611-E2
TERRA WY
StBC 93436 876-D7
StBC 93436 896-D1
TERRACE AV
PBCH 93449 693-G7
StBC 93455 816-J2
TERRACE CT
BLTN 93427 919-G4
TERRACE DR
SMRA 93455 796-G6
TERRACE RD
SBAR 93103 996-C1
SBAR 93109 995-J6
TERRACE ST
Npmo 93444 756-C3
TERRACE HILL DR
PSRS 93446 513-E5
TERRACE VISTA LN
SBAR 93103 996-D3
TERRAZZO WY
StBC 93455 816-F5
TERRY CT
PBCH 93449 714-F3
StBC 93455 816-J1
TERRY DR
PBCH 93449 714-F3
TEXAS RD
SLOC 93451 473-A7
SLOC 93451 493-A1
THALBERG AV
SLOC 93430 591-C5
THAMES CT
StBC 93111 984-F6
THE PIKE
ARGD 93420 714-G7
GBCH 93433 714-E7
SLOC 93420 714-G7
SLOC 93445 714-E7
THEATER DR
PSRS 93446 533-F5
SLOC 93446 533-E6
SLOC 93465 533-E7
THEATER LN
StBC 93108 986-G7
THELMA DR
SLO 93405 653-E7
THEODORA ST
Npmo 93444 756-A4
THERESA ST
CARP 93013 998-D6
THOMAS AV
SBAR 93101 995-H3
THOMAS CT
SLOC 93465 553-E1
THOMAS RD
BLTN 93427 919-J4
THOMAS HILL RD
SLOC 93420 715-D2
N THOMPSON AV
Npmo 93444 735-H5
Npmo 93444 736-A7
Npmo 93444 756-C1
SLOC 93420 735-H5
S THOMPSON AV
Npmo 93444 756-D3
Npmo 93444 776-H1
THOMPSON ST
SBAR 93101 996-B4
THOMPSON WY
SMRA 93455 796-E5
THORNBERRY RD
SLOC 93445 774-H4
SLOC 93445 775-A3
THORNBURG ST
SMRA 93455 796-G5
SMRA 93458 776-G7
SMRA 93458 796-G1
THORNTON CT
SLOC 93422 593-B1
THORNWOOD DR
StBC 93117 994-E3
THOROUGHBRED PL
SLOC 93420 735-A2
THREAD LN
SLOC 93401 674-C3
THREE SISTERS DR
SLOC 93401 674-B4
THREE SPRINGS RD
SLVG 93463 940-E2
StBC 93463 940-E2
THRONE CT
StBC 93111 984-F6
THUMBELINA DR
BLTN 93427 919-J6
BLTN 93427 920-A5
THUNDER CANYON RD
SLOC 93430 324-K9
SLOC 93465 324-K9
TIANA DR
StBC 93460 921-A5
StBC 93463 921-A5
TIANA PL
StBC 93460 921-A4
TIBURON CIR
ATAS 93422 574-B7
TIBURON PL
StBC 93111 984-G7
TIBURON WY
SLOC 93401 654-D7
TICIHO PL
SLOC 93405 632-G3
TIDE AV
MOBY 93442 611-E1
TIENDA PL
SLOC 93420 734-H6
TIERRA DR
SLOC 93402 631-J7
TIERRA RD
Npmo 93444 756-B6
SLOC 93422 594-E5
TIERRA ST
ARGD 93420 714-G7
TIERRA BELLA
SBAR 93105 985-F7
TIERRA BRISAS DR
StBC 93455 816-J2
TIERRA CIELO LN
SBAR 93105 986-A6
TIERRA DEL PAJARO
SLOC 93405 693-D2
TIERRA NUEVA
SLOC 93420 714-H7
SLOC 93420 734-H1
SLOC 93445 734-H1
TIERRA NUEVA LN
SLOC 93420 714-G7
SLOC 93420 734-G1
SLOC 93445 734-G1
TIERRA REDONDA RD
SLOC 93426 470-B1
TIERRA VISTA RD
SLOC 93446 513-E2
TIFFANY DR
SMRA 93454 777-A6
TIFFANY PARK CIR
StBC 93455 817-B5
TIFFANY PARK CT
StBC 93455 817-C5
TIFFANY RANCH RD
SLOC - 695-A4
SLOC 93420 695-A4
TIGER TAIL DR
ARGD 93420 714-J7
ARGD 93420 715-A7
TILA LN
StBC 93111 984-F7
TILBURY CT
StBC 93455 817-A5
TILIA ST
StBC 93455 816-J3
TIMBER LN
StBC 93437 855-H7
StBC 93437 875-G1
TIMOTHY CT
LMPC 93436 896-C6
TIMS RD
StBC 93441 365-K2
StBC 93441 901-D1
TINKER WY
SBAR 93101 995-H3
TIPTON ST
Cmbr 93428 548-F1
TISHA CT
StBC 93111 984-G5
TISHLINI LN
SLOC 93465 553-B3
TITAN AV
StBC 93436 876-C5
TITAN ST
StBC 93455 817-B5
TIVOLA ST
StBC 93460 921-B5
TOBAGO ST
SLOC 93445 734-H1
TODD LN
ARGD 93420 714-H6
TODOS SANTOS LN
StBC 93105 985-J7
TOGNAZZINI AV
GDLP 93434 774-J6
GDLP 93434 775-A6
TOLBERT PL
SLOC 93420 735-A2
TOLLIS AV
StBC 93108 997-B1
TOLOSA PL
SLOC 93420 694-G3
TOLOSA WY
SLO 93405 653-G2
TOLOSO RD
ATAS 93422 593-G1
TOLTEC DR
StBC 93111 984-F7
TOLTEC PL
StBC 93111 984-F7
TOLTEC WY
StBC 93111 984-F7
TOLUCA CT
StBC 93111 994-G2
TOMASINI RD
SLOC 93405 632-E1
TOMOL DR
CARP 93013 998-D6
TONYA LN
StBC 93455 816-J5
TOPAZ
PBCH 93449 714-D3
TOPAZ ST
PBCH 93449 693-E5
TOPAZ WY
SMRA 93454 777-A6
TORERO RD
StBC 93111 984-J7
TORINO DR
SBAR 93105 995-E3
SBAR 93110 995-D4
TORITO RD
StBC 93108 997-G2
TORNOE RD
StBC 93105 985-J7
TORO LN
MOBY 93442 611-D1
TORO ST
SLO 93401 653-J3
SLO 93401 654-A4
TORO CANYON RD
StBC - 987-H7
StBC 93013 997-G4
StBC 93108 987-H7
StBC 93108 997-G2
TORO CANYON RD Rt#-192
StBC 93013 997-G3
StBC 93108 997-G3
TORO CANYON PARK RD
StBC - 997-G2
StBC 93108 997-G2
TORO CREEK RD
MOBY 93430 591-D6
SLOC - 572-F7
SLOC - 591-G4
SLOC 92389 325-A10
SLOC 93430 591-D6
TORREON RD
SLOC 93422 594-E2
SLOC 93465 594-E2
TORREY PL
StBC 93117 984-D7
TORREY PINE PL
SLOC 93420 714-H1
TORREY PINES DR
PSRS 93446 533-J1
TOUCHSTONE LN
SMRA 93454 777-A7
TOULUMNE AV
SLOC 93405 633-E5
TOURAN LN
StBC 93117 993-E2
TOURNEY HILL LN
Npmo 93444 755-E1
TOWER RD
PSRS 93446 494-D4
SLOC 93446 494-D4
SLOC 93451 324-L3
SLOC 93451 325-A4
SLOC 93451 471-J1
TOWER GROVE DR
SLOC 93420 735-E2
TOWN CREEK LN
SLOC 93446 470-A5
TOWN CREEK TKTR
SLOC 93446 324-J5
TOWNHOUSE TER
PSRS 93446 513-F5
TOWNSEND LN
StBC 93455 816-H2
TOWNSHIP RD
SLOC 93446 325-A7
TOYON CT
ARGD 93420 715-B4
TOYON DR
SBAR 93105 995-F1
TOYON PL
SLOC 93424 693-B2
TRACI DR
StBC 93111 984-G7
TRACK WY
SLOC 93451 453-D6
TRACTOR ST
PSRS 93446 514-A2
TRAFFIC WY
ARGD 93420 714-J5
ARGD 93420 715-A5
ATAS 93422 553-F6
ATAS 93422 573-J3
S TRAFFIC WAY EXT
ARGD 93420 715-B6
TRANQUILLA AV
ATAS 93422 573-G1
TRANSFER AV
SBAR 93101 996-A4
TRAVIS DR
SLOC 93402 631-F7
SLOC 93402 651-F1
TREASURE DR
SBAR 93105 995-G2
TREE LN
SLOC 93420 735-F5
TREE TRAP RD
SLOC 93426 469-J2
TREMONTO RD
SBAR 93103 986-A7
SBAR 93103 995-J1
SBAR 93103 996-A1
TRENORA ST
CARP 93013 998-E6
TRENTON AV
Cmbr 93428 548-G1
TRES CASA LN
Npmo 93444 755-J6
TREVINO CT
PSRS 93446 513-J7
PSRS 93446 533-J1
TREVINO DR
Npmo 93444 756-A3
TREVOR WY
SLO 93401 654-A5
TRIESTE LN
CARP 93013 998-B6
StBC 93013 998-B6
TRIFONE WY
Npmo 93444 735-J5
TRIGO LN
PSRS 93446 513-H5
N TRIGO LN
PSRS 93446 513-J5
TRIGO RD
StBC 93117 993-J5
StBC 93117 994-A5
TRINIDAD DR
SLOC 93445 734-G1
TRINIDAD ST
MOBY 93442 611-D1
TRINITY AV
ARGD 93420 715-B6
SLOC 93405 633-E5
TRINITY CT
PSRS 93446 514-B7
PSRS 93446 534-B1
TRISHA CT
SMRA 93455 796-J7
TROCHA WY
StBC 93111 984-H7
TROUP RD
SBAR 93117 994-B2
TROUVILLE AV
GBCH 93433 714-D5
TRUCKEE RD
SLOC 93405 653-J1
SLOC 93405 654-A1
TRUDI CT
StBC 93117 984-E7
TRUDI DR
StBC 93117 984-D7
TRUDY CT
StBC 93455 816-H5
TRUESDALE RD
SLOC 93461 325-F6
TRUMAN DR
SLOC 93445 714-D7
TUCKER AV
PSRS 93446 513-H5
TUCKER CANYON RD
SLOC 93461 325-G6
TULARE AV
MOBY 93442 611-G7
SLOC 93405 633-A5
TULARE ST
PBCH 93449 714-C1
TULIP CT
SLO 93401 674-C2
TULIP ST
SLOC 93445 734-H1
S TULIP ST
LMPC 93436 916-C2
TULIPWOOD DR
PSRS 93446 514-A7
PSRS 93446 534-A1
TULLY PL
Cmbr 93428 548-G2
TUMBLEWEED WY
SLOC 93446 471-D6
TUNITAS AV
ATAS 93422 573-J2
TUNNEL RD
StBC 93105 985-J6
TUNNELL ST
SMRA 93454 776-H7
SMRA 93458 776-F7
TUOLUMNE DR
StBC 93117 993-G2
TUPELO CT
SMRA 93454 796-H2
TURKEY COVE LN
StBC 93426 469-J2
TURKEY RANCH RD
SLOC 93465 553-C2
TURNER AV
SLO 93401 654-A3
SLO 93405 654-A3
TURNPIKE RD
StBC 93111 984-J7
StBC 93111 994-J2
TURQUOISE CT
StBC 93455 817-B5
TURQUOISE DR
ARGD 93420 714-J7
TURRI RD
SLOC 93402 631-J3
SLOC 93402 632-A3
SLOC 93402 652-E1
SLOC 93405 631-J3
SLOC 93405 632-A3
SLOC 93405 652-E1
TURTLE CREEK DR
StBC 93455 816-J1
TURTLE CREEK RD
PSRS 93446 514-B7
PSRS 93446 534-B1
TUSCAN AV
MOBY - 591-E7
MOBY 93442 591-E7
MOBY 93442 611-E1
SLOC - 591-E7
TV TOWER RD
SLOC - 345-C1
SLOC - 593-A7
SLOC - 614-A7
SLOC 92389 325-A10
TWEED AV
Cmbr 93428 548-G2
TWELVE OAKS DR
SLOC 93446 533-D4
TWILIGHT CT
SMRA 93455 796-J7
TWILIGHT LN
Npmo 93444 756-C5
TWINBERRY CIR
SLOC 93424 693-B2
TWIN CREEKS WY
SLOC 93401 674-G7
SLOC 93401 694-F1
TWIN OAK DR
BLTN 93427 919-G5
TWIN RIDGE CT
SLO 93405 633-G7
SLO 93405 653-G1
TWIN RIDGE DR
SLO 93405 653-G1
TWINRIDGE RD
StBC 93111 984-H4
TWITCHELL ST
StBC 93455 816-G5
TWITCHELL DAM RD
SLOC 93454 345-F7
SLOC 93454 777-H2
TYE RD
StBC 93105 985-H7
TYKES LN
SLOC 93401 693-F1
TYLER DR
SMRA 93454 777-B6
TYNDALL ST
StBC 93460 921-B5
TYRUS CT
Npmo 93444 756-A6

U

N U ST
LMPC 93436 896-C7
LMPC 93436 916-C1
S U ST
LMPC 93436 916-C2
UCEN RD
StBC 93106 994-C5
UHLAN CT
SBAR 93103 996-E3
UKIAH ST
StBC 93111 994-J2
UMBRA RD
StBC 93429 345-C11
StBC 93429 365-C1
StBC 93429 855-A2
UNION AV
StBC 93455 816-G6
UNION RD
PSRS 93446 513-G5
PSRS 93446 514-B3
SLOC 93446 325-D6
SLOC 93446 514-G5
UNION ST
SBAR 93103 996-C4
UNION SUGAR AV
StBC 93436 895-E6
UNION VALLEY PKWY
StBC 93455 816-H4
StBC 93455 817-A4
UNIVERSITY DR
LMPC 93436 916-E3
SLOC 93405 653-J1
StBC 93111 984-G7
UPHAM ST
SLO 93401 653-J5
SLO 93401 654-A5
UPPER HYDE
StBC 93108 986-E6
UPPER LOPEZ CANYON RD
SLOC - 345-D1
SLOC 93401 345-D1
UPPER LOS BERROS RD
Npmo 93444 735-H3
Npmo 93444 736-A2
SLOC 93420 735-H3
SLOC 93420 736-A2
UPSON RD
StBC 93013 998-C5
URANUS AV
StBC 93436 896-D1
URANUS CT
Npmo 93444 756-A5
US GOVERNMENT RD
StBC - 998-G6
StBC 93013 998-G6
UTAH AV
SLOC 93445 734-D1
StBC 93437 855-F6
StBC 93437 875-E1

V

N V ST
LMPC 93436 896-C5
LMPC 93436 916-C1
StBC 93436 896-C7
S V ST
LMPC 93436 916-C2
StBC 93436 916-C2
VACHELL LN
SLO 93401 673-H4
SLOC 93401 673-H4
VALA DR
StBC 93111 984-J7
VALDEZ AV
ATAS 93422 573-G2
StBC 93117 984-C7
StBC 93117 994-C1
VALDIVIA DR
StBC 93110 995-A1
VALENCIA AV
StBC 93105 985-J5
VALENCIA DR
SBAR 93105 995-H1
VALENCIA RD
Summ 93067 997-D3
VALENTINA AV
ATAS 93422 573-J1
VALENTINE CT
SMRA 93454 796-H4
VALERIE ST
SMRA 93454 777-A6
VALERIO PL
SBAR 93103 996-A2
VALERIO ST
SBAR 93101 995-H4
SBAR 93101 996-A2
SBAR 93103 996-A2
VALES ST
SBAR 93109 995-H6
VALHALLA DR
SLVG 93463 940-E1
VALLE AV
ATAS 93422 574-A3
VALLECITO CT
CARP 93013 998-E6
SLO 93405 653-E6
VALLECITO PL
CARP 93013 998-E6
VALLECITO RD
CARP 93013 998-E6
VALLEJO RD
SLOC 93402 651-E1
VALLE VISTA PL
SLOC 93405 653-C6
VALLEY DR
StBC 93455 817-A4
VALLEY LN
SLOC 93446 471-C5
E VALLEY LN
StBC 93108 997-A2
VALLEY RD
ARGD 93420 714-J7
SLOC 93420 714-J7
SLOC 93420 734-J1
E VALLEY RD Rt#-192
StBC 93108 996-H2
StBC 93108 997-B1
VALLEY CLUB RD
StBC 93108 997-B2
VALLEY DAIRY RD
BLTN 93436 919-G5
VALLEY OAK PL
SMRA 93454 777-A6
VALLEY QUAIL PL
SLOC 93446 493-C6
VALLEY VIEW DR
LMPC 93436 916-G2
PBCH 93449 714-D2
StBC 93455 816-H6
VALLEY VIEW LN
SLOC 93402 651-J1
SLOC 93402 652-A1
SLOC 93424 693-B1
VALLEY VIEW PL
SLOC 93420 715-D2
VALLEY VISTA
SMRA 93458 796-G4
VAL VERDE
SLVG 93463 940-D1
VAL VERDE LN
SLOC 93420 735-G5
VANDERLIP CT
PSRS 93446 514-A3
VAN DOLLEN RD
SLOC 93451 325-C4
VANESSA WY
StBC 93455 817-C7
VAN GORDON CREEK RD
SLOC 93452 324-H6
SLOC 93452 528-C1
VANGUARD DR
StBC 93436 876-D5
VAQUERITO PL
StBC 93111 984-J7
VAQUERO DR
SLOC 93465 533-G7
SLOC 93465 553-G1
VAQUERO LN
StBC 93111 984-J7
VARD LOOMIS CT
ARGD 93420 715-C4
VARD LOOMIS LN
ARGD 93420 715-C4
VARDON CT
Npmo 93444 735-D7
VARIAN CIR
SLOC - 695-C3
VARLEY ST
Summ 93067 997-D3
VARNER CT
SMRA 93458 776-H3
VASHON ST
MOBY 93442 611-D1
VEGA AV
ATAS 93422 573-H3
StBC 93436 876-C6
VEGA DR
StBC 93117 984-D7
StBC 93117 994-D1
VEGA WY
SLO 93405 653-E6
VELA WY
StBC 93436 896-C1
VELOZ DR
StBC 93108 997-C1
VENABLE ST
SLO 93405 653-J3
VENADO AV
ATAS 93422 573-G3
VENADO DR
StBC 93111 984-J7
VENADO TR
SLOC 93401 673-F5
VENDELS CIR
PSRS 93446 533-F3
VENETTE LN
SMRA 93454 777-B5
VENICE LN
CARP 93013 998-B5
StBC 93013 998-B5
VENITIA LN
SBAR 93105 995-E2
VENTANA CT
StBC 93455 816-J2
VENTANA DR
PBCH 93449 714-E3
VENTANA DEL ROBLES LN
SLOC 93465 553-C2
VENTURA AV
SLOC 93405 633-A5
VENTURA DR
SBAR 93105 995-H1
VENTURA FRWY U.S.-101
StBC - 1018-J3
VeCo - 1018-J3
VENTURA RD
SLOC 93422 572-J5
SMRA 93455 796-H6
VENUS AV
StBC 93436 896-D1
VENUS CT
Npmo 93444 756-A5
VERANO DR
CARP 93013 998-C6
SBAR 93110 985-C7
VERANO WY
Npmo 93444 756-A6
VERBENA ST
Npmo 93444 755-J4
VERDE DR
SLO 93405 653-H2
VERDE PL
ARGD 93420 714-G7
SLOC 93451 473-F2
VERDE CANYON RD
SLOC 93420 695-A5
VERDE MAR DR
SBAR 93103 996-E4
VERDE VISTA DR
SBAR 93105 995-G1
VERDON ST
MOBY 93442 611-E2
VERDUGO PL
StBC 93110 995-A2
VERDUGO RANCH WY
SLOC 93405 693-C1
VERDURA AV
StBC 93117 994-D1
VEREDA CORDILLER
StBC 93117 993-D2
VEREDA DEL CIERVO
StBC 93117 983-D5
StBC 93117 993-D1
VEREDA DEL PADRE
StBC 93117 993-C1
VEREDA ESCOLAR
StBC 93117 993-C1
VEREDA GALERIA
StBC 93117 993-C1
VEREDA LEYENDA
StBC 93117 983-C7
StBC 93117 993-C1
VEREDA NUEVA
StBC 93117 983-D7
VEREDA PARQUE
StBC 93117 983-C7
VEREDA PRADERA
StBC 93117 993-D1
VERHELLE RD
SBAR 93117 994-D2
VERNAL AV
SBAR 93105 995-H1
VERNALIS RD
ATAS 93422 574-B3
VERNON RD
SBAR 93105 995-G2
VERNON ST
ARGD 93420 714-J5
VERONA AV
StBC 93117 993-H1
VERONICA DR
PSRS 93446 513-J7
VERONICA PL
SBAR 93105 995-F4
VERONICA SPRINGS RD
SBAR 93105 995-E3
StBC 93105 995-E3
StBC 93109 995-E5
VESTER HOF
SLVG 93463 940-D1
VESTER STED
SLVG 93463 940-D1
VETTER LN
SLOC 93449 694-G7
VIA AV
ATAS 93422 573-J2
VIA ABAJO
StBC 93110 994-J3
VIA ABRIGADA
StBC 93110 995-B3
VIA AIROSA
StBC 93110 995-B2
VIA ALBA
StBC 93111 984-H6
VIA ALEGRE
StBC 93110 995-B2
VIA ALICIA
SBAR 93108 996-E2
VIA ALTA
StBC 93455 817-A7
VIA ALTA MESA
Npmo 93444 755-G5
VIA ANDORRA
StBC 93110 985-C6
VIA ARBOLITOS
SMRA 93458 796-E5
VIA ARLETA
StBC 93455 817-A7
VIA ARNEZ
StBC 93436 896-G2
VIA ARROYO
PSRS 93446 513-H4
VIA ASUETO
SMRA 93454 777-B6
VIA BANDOLERO
ARGD 93420 714-H4
VIA BARBA
StBC 93436 896-G2
VIA BELIZ
SMRA 93454 777-B5
VIA BENDITA
StBC 93110 995-A4
VIA BERROS
ARGD 93420 714-J7
VIA BOLZANO
StBC 93111 984-F6
StBC 93117 984-F6
VIA BRIGITTE
StBC 93111 985-A5
VIA BROCHA
StBC 93110 994-J3
VIA CAMELIA
PSRS 93446 513-H4

STREET	City	ZIP	Pg-Grid
VIA CAMPOBELLO	StBC	93111	984-H6
VIA CARISMA	SBAR	93109	995-H7
VIA CARRETAS	SBAR	93110	995-A3
VIA CARRO	SMRA	93458	776-F4
VIA CARTA	SLO	93405	653-J1
	SLO	93405	654-A2
	SLOC	93405	633-J7
	SLOC	93405	653-J1
VIA CASTILLO	StBC	93458	776-G4
VIA CAYENTE	SBAR	93109	995-B3
VIA CHAPARRAL RD	StBC	93105	985-B6
	StBC	93110	985-B6
VIA CHORRO	StBC	93455	817-A7
VIA CHULA ROBLES	SLOC	93446	695-A6
VIA CLARICE	StBC	93111	985-A4
VIA CONCHA RD	Npmo	93444	735-D7
	Npmo	93444	755-D1
VIA CONTENTO	SMRA	93454	777-B6
VIA CORONA	StBC	93110	995-C2
VIA CORONA DR	BLTN	93427	919-G4
VIA CORTEZ	StBC	93436	896-G2
VIA COVELLO	StBC	93110	994-J3
	StBC	93110	995-A3
VIA DE LA CRUZ	SMRA	93454	796-H5
VIA DE LA LUNA	StBC	93455	817-A6
VIA DEL CARMEL	StBC	93117	993-F2
VIA DEL CENTRO	SLOC	93445	734-G1
VIA DEL CIELO	SBAR	93109	995-J5
	SBAR	93109	996-A5
VIA DEL FLORISTA	StBC	93455	817-A7
VIA DELICIA	SMRA	93454	777-B6
VIA DEL MAR	StBC	93108	996-J4
VIA DEL NORTE	SLOC	93445	734-G1
VIA DEL PALMA	CtBC	00155	017-AG
VIA DEL REY	StBC	93111	984-E5
VIA DEL RIO	SLOC	93445	734-G1
VIA DEL SOL	SLVG	93463	940-D1
VIA DI CAMPO	StBC	93455	817-A7
VIA DICHOSA	StBC	93110	995-C2
VIA DIEGO	SBAR	93109	985-D7
VIA DINERO	SLVG	93463	920-F4
VIA DOCENA	StBC	93110	994-J3
VIA DONA	StBC	93436	896-H2
VIA ELBA	StBC	93436	896-H2
VIA EL CIELO	SLOC	93420	715-C2
VIA EL CUADRO	StBC	93111	994-H2
VIA EL ENCANTADOR	StBC	93111	994-H2
VIA EL RINCON	CARP	93013	998-E7
VIA ELSIE	CARP	93013	998-F7
	Npmo	93444	755-H5
VIA ENSENADA	SLO	93401	653-J7
VIA ESMERALDA	StBC	93455	816-J6
	StBC	93455	817-A6
VIA ESPARTO	StBC	93110	994-J3
VIA ESPERANZA	Npmo	93444	756-B5
	StBC	93110	995-C2
VIA ESTABLO	SMRA	93458	776-G4
VIA ESTEBAN	SLO	93401	654-B7
VIA ESTIO	SMRA	93454	777-B6
VIA FARGO	StBC	93455	816-J6
VIA FEDORA	StBC	93455	816-J6
VIA FELICE	SMRA	93454	777-B6
VIA FELIZ	StBC	93436	896-H2
VIA FIORI LN	StBC	93117	984-E7
VIA FRUTERIA	StBC	93436	876-H7
VIA GAITERO	StBC	93105	985-C6
VIA GALA	StBC	93436	896-H1
VIA GENNITA	StBC	93111	985-A5
VIA GLORIETA	SBAR	93109	995-B3
VIA GRANADA	SBAR	93103	995-J1
	SBAR	93103	996-A1
VIA GUSTO	SMRA	93454	777-B5
VIA HIELO	SMRA	93454	777-B6
VIA HIERBA	StBC	93110	995-C2
VIA HUERTO	StBC	93110	994-J3
	StBC	93110	995-A3
VIA ISLA	StBC	93436	876-H7
VIA JACINTO	StBC	93111	994-H2
VIAJERO DR	StBC	93117	993-F2
VIA JUANA RD	StBC	93460	921-A6
VIA LA BARRANCA	ARGD	93420	715-A4
VIA LAGUNA DR	StBC	93110	995-D2
VIA LAGUNA VISTA	SLOC	93401	653-C6
VIA LA PAZ	SLO	93401	653-J7
VIA LARA	StBC	93111	994-H2
VIA LAS AGUILAS	ARGD	93420	714-H4
VIA LAS BRISAS	SMRA	93454	777-B6
VIA LATINA	StBC	93013	998-C5
VIA LATO	StBC	93436	876-H7
	StBC	93436	896-H1
VIA LEMORA	StBC	93117	984-E5
VIA LINDA	CARP	93013	998-F7
	StBC	93013	1018-F1
VIA LOS PADRES	StBC	93111	984-J5
VIA LOS SANTOS	SBAR	93110	985-D7
	SMRA	93458	796-E4
VIA LUCERO	StBC	93110	995-C3
VIA MANANA	StBC	93108	987-A7
VIA MARCINA	StBC	93013	998-C5
VIA MARGARITA	StBC	93455	817-A7
VIA MARIA	CARP	93013	998-E7
	StBC	93111	985-B5
VIA MAVIS	StBC	93455	817-A6
VIA MAXWELL	SLO	93401	653-J7
	Npmo	93444	755-H5
VIA MERANO	StBC	93111	984-F6
VIA MESSINA	StBC	93117	984-E5
VIA MIGUEL AV	StBC	93111	994-H3
VIA MIRA VALLE	Npmo	93444	755-G6
VIA MITAD	StBC	93436	876-H7
VIA MONDO	StBC	93436	876-H7
VIA NIETO	StBC	93110	994-J3
VIA NINA	StBC	93455	817-A5
VIA NOSTRE	Npmo	93444	735-H5
VIA NUEVO	SMRA	93458	776-F4
VIA ORILLA	StBC	93436	896-G1
VIA ORQUIDIA	StBC	93111	985-A6
VIA PARTE	StBC	93436	876-H7
VIA PARVA	StBC	93111	984-J6
VIA PAVION	StBC	93455	817-A7
VIA PICCOLI	StBC	93111	984-H6
VIA PINTA	StBC	93455	817-A5
VIA POCA	ARGD	93420	714-H4
VIA PRESADA	SLOC	93401	693-F1
VIA PROMESA	StBC	93110	995-C2
VIA PROMESA DR	PSRS	93446	513-G5
VIA QUANTICO	SMRA	93454	777-B6
VIA RAMONA	PSRS	93446	514-A7
	PSRS	93446	534-A1
VIA RAVENNA	StBC	93111	984-E6
	StBC	93117	984-E6
VIA REAL	CARP	93013	998-B6
	StBC	93013	997-H4
	StBC	93013	998-B6
	Summ	93067	997-E4
N VIA REAL	CARP	93013	1018-G1
	StBC	93013	1018-G1
VIA REGINA	StBC	93111	984-J6
VIA REPOSA	SLVG	93463	940-D1
VIA REPOSO	StBC	93111	984-G6
VIA RICARDO	CARP	93013	998-F7
VIA RICO	SMRA	93454	777-B8
VIA RIVIERA	StBC	93013	817-B7
VIA ROBLADA	StBC	93110	995-A3
VIA ROBLES	SLOC	93401	694-J2
VIA ROJO	StBC	93117	985-E7
VIA ROMA	SBAR	93101	996-A3
	SBAR	93103	996-A3
VIA ROSA	PSRS	93446	513-H4
VIA ROSITA	StBC	93110	995-C3
VIA RUBI	StBC	93111	985-A6
VIA RUBIO	CARP	93013	998-F7
VIA RUEDA	StBC	93110	995-A2
VIA SABROSA	SMRA	93454	777-B6
VIA SALERNO	StBC	93111	984-E6
VIA SAN BLAS	StBC	93111	984-E6
VIA SAN CARLOS	SLVG	93463	920-F4
VIA SANTA MARIA	StBC	93455	817-A4
VIA SEMI	StBC	93436	896-H1
VIA SENDA	StBC	93110	995-D2
VIA SEVILLA	SBAR	93109	995-G7
VIA SINUOSA	StBC	93110	995-C2
VIA SOLANA	SLOC	93420	734-H5
VIA SPANISH OAKS	SLOC	93453	614-B4
VIA STEVARINO	CARP	93013	998-F7
VIA TARREGA	StBC	93111	994-H3
VIA TORTUGA	ATAS	93422	574-A6
VIA TRANQUILA	StBC	93110	995-C3
VIA TRENTO	StBC	93117	984-E6
VIA TREPADORA	StBC	93110	995-B2
VIA TROPICO	SMRA	93454	777-B6
VIA UNDOSA	SMRA	93454	777-B5
VIA VALVERDE	StBC	93111	994-H3
VIA VAQUERO	ARGD	93420	714-H4
VIA VENADO	SLOC	93401	693-F1
VIA VENETO	StBC	93111	985-A5
VIA VENTANA	SMRA	93458	776-G3
VIA VICENTE	Npmo	93444	755-H5
VIA VISALIA	SMRA	93458	776-F4
VIA VISTA	PSRS	93446	514-A7
	PSRS	93446	534-A1
VIA VISTA WY	SLOC	93465	574-E1
VIA VISTA VERDE	StBC	93455	816-J6
VIA VISTOSA	SLOC	93402	631-J7
	SLOC	93402	631-J7
	StBC	93110	995-B2
VIA YNEZ	SMRA	93454	777-B5
VIA ZACATA	SLOC	93420	755-B1
VIA ZORRO	StBC	93110	995-D1
VIBORG RD	SLOC	93446	493-E3
VICENTE DR	SLO	93405	653-F7
VICENTI PL	StBC	93108	996-J4
VICKIE AV	SMRA	93454	776-H5
VICTORIA AV	SLOC	93401	654-A3
VICTORIA PL	SMRA	93458	796-G2
VICTORIA ST	SBAR	93101	995-J4
	SBAR	93101	996-A3
VICTORIA WY	ARGD	93420	714-H7
	Cmbr	93428	548-F1
VICTORIAN CT	ARGD	93420	714-H6
VICTORY DR	BLTN	93427	919-H5
VIDA AV	ATAS	93422	573-H2
VIEJA DR	StBC	93110	994-J3
VIEJO RD	SLOC	93420	735-C5
VIEJO CAMINO	ATAS	93422	594-C1
	ATAS	93422	594-D2
VIENDRA DR	StBC	93441	920-B4
VIEW DR	BLTN	93427	919-H5
VIEWMONT ST	SLO	93401	654-B5
VIEW PARK DR	StBC	93436	816-G6
VIGARD DR	SLVG	93463	920-F7
VILLA AV	StBC	93101	995-H4
VILLA CT	PBCH	93449	714-D2
VILLA DR	PSRS	93446	513-F4
VILLA CREEK RD	SLOC	93430	324-K9
	SLOC	93435	324-K9
VILLAGE CT	ARGD	93420	715-A6
VILLAGE DR	StBC	93110	817-A4
VILLAGE GRN	SMRA	93455	796-G5
VILLAGE LN	Cmbr	93428	528-H7
	SLVG	93463	920-F7
VILLAGE RD	SLOC	93446	471-A5
VILLAGE CIRCLE DR	LMPC	93436	916-C1
VILLAGE CREST	StBC	93110	995-C1
VILLAGE KNOLL CT	StBC	93110	995-A4
VILLAGE KNOLL DR	SBAR	93105	995-G1
VILLAGE MEADOWS DR	LMPC	93436	896-C6
VILLAGE TERRACE DR	StBC	93110	994-J3
VILLA LOTS RD	PSRS	93446	513-F1
VINA WY	SLOC	93451	473-D3
VINCENTE WY	SLOC	93465	574-E1
VINE AV	SLOC	93401	996-B3
VINE ST	PSRS	93446	513-F2
	SLOC	93402	631-G5
	SLOC	93420	755-B1
S VINE ST	PSRS	93446	513-F7
VINELAND DR	SLO	93405	653-F7
VINEYARD DR	StBC	93455	816-H1
VINEYARD RD	StBC	93111	984-G5
VINEYARD CANYON RD	MonC	-	453-H3
VINEYARD RANCH WY	ARGD	93420	714-H7
VINEYARD RANCH LN	StdC	93110	995-A2
VINTON LN	SLOC	93420	715-C2
VIOLA CT	Npmo	93444	756-A3
VIOLA LN	StBC	93108	987-H7
VIOLA WY	LMPC	93436	896-D6
VIOLET AV	Npmo	93444	756-B4
VIOLETA AV	ATAS	93422	573-H4
VIRGINIA DR	ARGD	93420	714-H7
VIRGINIA LN	StBC	93108	997-G1
VIRGINIA RD	StBC	93108	996-H4
VISALIA ST	PBCH	93449	714-C1
VISCAINO RD	SBAR	93103	996-B1
VISCANO AV	ATAS	93422	573-J1
VISTA CIR	ARGD	93420	714-H2
	SMRA	93458	796-F4
VISTA CT	PSRS	93446	513-F3
	SLOC	93402	631-F7
VISTA DR	ARGD	93420	714-H2
	SLOC	93430	591-A2
VISTA LN	SLO	93401	673-G2
VISTA RD	ATAS	93422	573-E7
	ATAS	93422	593-F1
VISTA ST	StBC	93110	984-D6
VISTA ARROYO	SBAR	93109	995-E6
VISTA BAHIA	StBC	93111	984-G7
VISTA BONITA	ATAS	93422	574-C6
VISTA BUENA PL	StBC	93110	995-A1
VISTA CLARA RD	StBC	93110	995-C1
VISTA DE AVILA	SLOC	93424	693-B3
VISTA DE LA CUMBRE	SBAR	93105	985-G7
VISTA DE LA MESA DR	PBCH	93449	714-B1
VISTA DE LA MONTANA	SLO	93405	653-E6
VISTA DE LA PLAYA LN	SBAR	93109	995-E6
VISTA DEL ARROYO	SLO	93405	653-E6
VISTA DEL ASTA	SLOC	93420	714-J2
VISTA DE LA VINA	SLOC	93446	534-A4
VISTA DEL BRISA	SLO	93405	653-E6
VISTA DEL CAMPO	SBAR	93101	995-G3
VISTA DEL COLLADOS	SLO	93405	653-E6
VISTA DE LEJOS DR	SLO	93401	994-J3
VISTA DEL LAGO	SLO	93405	653-F6
VISTA DEL MAR	PBCH	93449	693-G7
VISTA DEL MAR DR	SBAR	93109	995-F5
	SLOC	93420	734-H4
VISTA DEL MUNDO	SMRA	93458	776-F4
VISTA DEL ORO	Summ	93067	997-D4
VISTA DEL OSOS	SLOC	93401	651-J7
VISTA DEL PUEBLO	SBAR	93101	995-J5
VISTA DEL RIO	SMRA	93458	776-F3
VISTA DEL ROBLES	SLOC	93420	694-G6
VISTA DEL SOL	SMRA	93458	776-F3
VISTA DE ROBLES PL	SLOC	93446	325-D6
VISTA ELEGANTE	SMRA	93458	796-J5
VISTA ELEVADA	SBAR	93105	985-H6
VISTA GRANDE LN	SLOC	93420	694-G7
VISTA GRANDE ST	PSRS	93446	513-J4
	PSRS	93446	514-A5
VISTA LINDA LN	StBC	93108	997-G1
VISTA MADERA	SBAR	93101	994-H1
VISTA MONTANA	SMRA	93458	776-F4
VISTA OCEANO LN	Summ	93067	997-F4
VISTA PACIFICA	MOBY	93442	611-F7
VISTA PACIFICA CIR	PBCH	93449	714-E3
VISTA PROMESA	SMRA	93458	776-F3
VISTA SERRANO WY	SLOC	93446	493-A5
VISTA VALLEJO	SBAR	93105	995-F2
VIVA WY	Npmo	93444	755-E5
VOLANS AV	PSRS	93446	534-A2
VOLANTE PL	StBC	93436	876-C6
VOLPI YSABEL RD	SLOC	93445	533-F5
VOLUNTARIO ST	SBAR	93103	996-C2
VULCAN DR	StBC	93436	876-D7

W

STREET	City	ZIP	Pg-Grid
N W ST	LMPC	93436	896-C6
	LMPC	93436	916-C1
WADE CT	PSRS	93446	513-J7
WADE DR	PSRS	93446	513-H7
WADSWORTH AV	PBCH	93449	714-B1
WAGON WHEEL DR	StBC	93437	855-B7
	StBC	93437	875-B1
WAGON WHEEL PL	SLOC	93446	325-A3
WAGON WHEEL WY	SLOC	93446	325-D7
WAH KON TAH LN	ATAS	93422	594-C2
WAILEA CT	SMRA	93455	796-G5
WAILEA WY	Npmo	93444	755-F1
WAITE ST	StBC	93440	878-G1
WAKEFIELD RD	PBCH	93449	693-H7
WALDRON AV	SBAR	93103	996-C2
WALES RD	Cmbr	93428	548-G2
WALKER ST	SLO	93401	653-H5
WALL ST	Cmbr	93428	528-G6
WALLACE AV	SLOC	93446	548-H1
WALLACE DR	SLOC	93446	632-J4
WALLACE PL	PSRS	93446	514-A3
WALLBRIDGE DR	Cmbr	93428	528-E7
WALLER LN	StBC	93455	796-G7
WALLIS AV	SMRA	93458	796-G3
WALNUT AV	CARP	93013	998-D7
E WALNUT AV	SBAR	93101	995-J4
W WALNUT AV	SBAR	93101	995-J4
WALNUT DR	PSRS	93446	513-J4
WALNUT PL	SMRA	93458	776-F4
WALNUT RD	StBC	93437	875-H1
WALNUT ST	SLO	93401	653-J3
WALNUT PARK DR	StBC	93111	984-H7
WALNUT PARK LN	StBC	93111	984-H7
WALTER WY	StBC	93455	816-H6
WALTER CREEK RD	SLOC	93446	632-H4
WARBLER CT	PSRS	93446	534-A2
WARD CT	StBC	93465	553-D2
WARD DR	StBC	93111	994-F2
WARD ST	SLO	93401	653-J5
WARD MEMORIAL BLVD Rt#-217	SBAR	93117	994-E4
	StBC	93106	994-E4
	StBC	93111	994-E4
	StBC	93117	994-E4
WARNER ST	SLOC	93445	714-F7
WARREN RD	Cmbr	93428	548-F1
WARREN WY	SLO	93405	653-G2
WARWICK PL	SBAR	93117	993-F2
WARWICK ST	Cmbr	93428	528-D5
WASHINGTON AV	SBAR	93101	995-H4
	SMRA	93458	796-F5
WASHINGTON BLVD	SLOC	93445	325-A3
	SLOC	93451	453-A4
WASHINGTON CIR	SMRA	93458	776-F4
WASHINGTON ST	BLTN	93427	919-G5
WASHINGTON RD	StBC	-	346-E9
	StBC	-	806-G4
	StDC	93254	806-C4
WASIOJA RD	StBC	93455	816-G4
WASOIJA ST	StBC	93254	806-C4
WATER ST	PBCH	93449	693-H7
WATERCRESS WY	SLOC	-	695-D3
WATERFALL LN	PSRS	93446	533-G1
WATERFALL RD	SLOC	93446	533-E7
WATER MILL LN	SLOC	93446	921-A6
WATER VIEW DR	SLOC	93446	471-B5
WATSON DR	SLOC	93465	632-J4
WAVE AV	MOBY	93442	611-D1
WAVERTREE ST	SLO	93401	674-D2
WAWONA AV	PBCH	93449	693-H7
WAYLAND PL	StBC	93455	816-J4
WAYNE WY	SLOC	93420	715-C1
WAYPOINT DR	SLOC	93460	922-A3
WEATHERFORD DR	Npmo	93444	755-F1
WEBSTER RD Rt#-229	SLOC	93432	325-D8
WEDGEWOOD DR	SMRA	93458	796-F6
WEDGEWOOD ST	Cmbr	93428	548-F2
WEEPING WILLOW WY	StBC	93455	816-J4
WELDON PL	SBAR	93109	996-A5
WELDON RD	SBAR	93109	996-A6
WELL RD	StBC	93465	553-B2
WELLINGTON AV	SLOC	93446	494-G7
WELLINGTON DR	StBC	93455	816-G4
WELLINGTON LN	Cmbr	93428	528-D6
WELLSONA RD	SLOC	93446	493-D2
	SLOC	93446	494-A3
	SLOC	93451	493-D2
WELSH LN	SLOC	93420	735-A2
WELSH WY	SLOC	93446	471-C4
WENDY CT	SMRA	93454	797-A1
WENDY WY	StBC	93455	816-J2
WENTWORTH ST	SBAR	93101	996-A5
WESLEY ST	ARGD	93420	714-J4
WESSELS WY	StBC	93465	553-D1
WESSEX CT	SBAR	93117	984-C7
WEST AV	StBC	93111	994-E4
WEST MALL Rt#-41	ATAS	93422	573-J3
WEST ST	Cmbr	93428	528-G7
	SLO	93405	653-H3
WESTBROOK RD	LMPC	93436	896-D6
WESTCLIFF DR	CARP	93013	998-A5
WESTERN AV	SBAR	93101	995-H4
	SMRA	93458	776-F4
WESTFIELD RD	PSRS	93446	534-B1
WESTGATE	BLTN	93427	919-G5
WESTGATE RD	SMRA	93455	796-E5
WESTMINSTER LN	PSRS	93446	494-G7
WESTMONT AV	SLOC	93465	553-G1
WESTMONT RD	Npmo	93444	737-D2
WESTMORLAND PL	SBAR	93117	984-C7
WESTON CT	SMRA	93458	776-F4
WESTWIND WY	Npmo	93444	755-F1
WESTWOOD DR	SMRA	93455	796-G6
WEYMOUTH CT	StBC	93455	816-F4
WEYMOUTH ST	Cmbr	93428	528-D5
WHIDBEY ST	SLO	93401	654-B4
WHIDBEY WY	PSRS	93446	514-E1
WHIMBREL CT	PSRS	93446	534-H2
WHIPPOORWILL DR	StBC	93455	816-J1
WHIPPOORWILL LN	StBC	93455	553-B1
WHIRLAWAY DR	SLOC	93460	922-A3
WHISPER LN	Npmo	93444	755-G3
WHISPERING MEADOW LN	Npmo	93444	735-J3
WHISPERING OAK WY	StBC	93455	817-A3
WHISPERING PINE LN	StBC	93455	817-A3
WHITBY ST	SLOC	93446	494-G7
WHITE AV	SBAR	93109	995-G6
WHITE CT	ARGD	93420	715-A3
	SBAR	93109	995-G5
WHITE CHAPEL CT	StBC	93455	816-G4
WHITECLIFF PL	StBC	93455	816-F4
WHITE CLOVER LN	PSRS	93446	514-A6
WHITE DOVE LN	Npmo	93444	735-H4
N WHITE DOVE DR	StBC	93455	816-G2
S WHITE DOVE DR	StBC	93455	816-J1
WHITEFIELD CT	StBC	93455	816-F4
WHITEHALL AV	Cmbr	93428	528-E7
WHITELEY ST	ARGD	93420	715-A4
WHITE OAK AV	PBCH	93449	714-B1
WHITE OAK LN	SLO	93401	674-D7
WHITE OAK RD	SLOC	93465	553-A5
WHITEWATER RD	ATAS	93422	573-J3
WHITLEY GARDENS DR	SLOC	93451	325-D5
	SLOC	93451	325-D5
WHITMAN ST	StBC	93117	993-J3
WHITNEY AV	SLOC	93465	553-B4
WHITNEY CT	Summ	93067	997-D3
WHITTIER DR	StBC	93117	993-J3
WICKENDEN ST	StBC	93458	878-H2
WIDOW LN	Npmo	93444	756-C5
WILCOMBE DR	Cmbr	93428	548-G1
WILD ASS TIMES TR	SLOC	92389	325-B11
WILD DEER CT	PSRS	93446	513-F4
WILDERNESS LN	PSRS	93446	494-C7
WILD FLOWER RD	SLOC	93446	494-B1
WILDHAVEN CIR	SLOC	93446	797-C2
WILD HORSE LN	SLOC	93446	493-E7
WILD HORSE PL	SLOC	93446	513-E1
WILD HORSE WY	SLOC	93446	325-D7
WILD HORSE WINERY CT	SLOC	93446	325-D7
WILDING LN	SLO	93401	654-B4
WILD MUSTARD LN	PSRS	93446	514-E1
WILD OATS WY	PSRS	93446	514-E1
WILD RICE LN	SLOC	93446	533-C6
WILD RYE WY	SLOC	-	695-D3
WILDWOOD DR	ARGD	93420	715-B4
	SLOC	93465	553-A2
WILDWOOD LN	SLOC	93446	755-A4
WILDWOOD RD	SMRA	93458	776-J5
	SMRA	93458	777-A5
WILHELMINA DR	SLOC	93446	614-E4
WILHOIT LN	SLOC	93465	553-D2
WILLIAM ST	SMRA	93454	776-F5
WILLIAMS ST	SMRA	93454	776-F5
	SMRA	93458	776-F5
WILLIAMS WY	SBAR	93109	995-G6
WILLINA LN	SLOC	93105	985-H6
E WILLOW AV	LMPC	93436	916-F3
W WILLOW AV	LMPC	93436	916-F3

STREET Name City ZIP Pg-Grid

W WILLOW AV
StBC 93436 916-D3
WILLOW CIR
SLO 93401 654-C7
WILLOW CT
ATAS 93422 574-B7
WILLOW DR
SLOC 93402 631-J7
SLOC 93402 632-A6
SLVG 93463 940-E1
WILLOW LN
ARGD 93420 714-H7
WILLOW PL
CARP 93013 998-D7
WILLOW RD
Npmo 93444 735-J7
Npmo 93444 755-H1
SLOC 93420 755-C1
WILLOW RD Rt#-1
SLOC 93420 754-H1
SLOC 93420 755-A1
WILLOW ST
SLOC 93445 734-F2
StBC 93437 875-H1
StBC 93460 921-B4
WILLOW WK
StBC 93117 994-A4
WILLOWBANK LN
PSRS 93446 533-G1
WILLOW BROOK LN
SLOC 93446 471-D6
WILLOW CREEK RD
SLOC 93446 325-A7
WILLOWGLEN DR
StBC 93455 796-H7
StBC 93455 816-H1
WILLOWGLEN PL
SBAR 93105 985-E6
WILLOWGLEN RD
SBAR 93105 985-E7
WILLOWGROVE DR
StBC 93117 993-J4
WILLOWOOD RD
StBC 93455 796-B7
StBC 93455 816-B1
WILLOW WALK WY
SMRA 93454 776-J6
WILMAR AV
PBCH 93449 714-B2
SLOC 93445 714-F7
WILSHIRE LN
StBC 93455 796-H7
WILSHIRE ST
SLOC 93420 714-H7
WILSON
SLOC 93430 591-D4
WILSON AV
SBAR 93103 996-D3
WILSON CT
ARGD 93420 714-G6
StBC 93455 816-G5
WILSON DR
StBC 93455 816-G5
WILSON ST
SBAR 93101 996-B5
SLO 93401 654-A3
N WILSON ST
Npmo 93444 756-C2
S WILSON ST
Npmo 93444 756-C2
WILTON DR
Cmbr 93428 528-F7
Cmbr 93428 548-G1
WILTON PL
ARGD 93420 714-J5
WINCHESTER CIR
StBC 93117 993-E2
WINCHESTER DR
StBC 93117 993-E1
WINCHESTER PL
StBC 93117 993-E2
WINCHESTER WY
SMRA 93454 777-B6
WINCHESTER CANYON RD
StBC 93117 993-E1
WINDERMERE LN
SLOC 93420 714-J2
WINDING WY
StBC 93111 984-J7
WINDING BROOK RD
PSRS 93446 534-C2
WINDING CREEK LN
StBC 93108 987-D7
StBC 93108 997-D1
WINDMILL CT
SLVG 93463 920-F7
WINDMILL LN
SLVG 93463 920-F7

WINDMILL PL
SLOC 93446 325-D7
SLOC 93446 534-J4
WINDMILL RD
SLOC 93446 471-E5
WINDRIDGE PL
SLOC 93420 715-C3
WINDSONG LN
SLOC 93420 734-H5
WINDSONG WY
PSRS 93446 513-H4
WINDSOR AV
StBC 93117 984-C7
WINDSOR BLVD
Cmbr 93428 528-D6
Cmbr 93428 548-F2
WINDSOR CT
StBC 93111 984-F6
WINDSOR ST
SMRA 93458 796-G3
WINDSOR WY
StBC 93105 985-H7
WINDWARD AV
PBCH 93449 693-H7
WINDWARD WY
SLOC 93446 471-B5
WINDWOOD RD
SLOC 93446 534-J2
WINE COUNTRY PL
SLOC 93465 553-B2
WINEGRAPE CT
SLOC 93465 533-C7
WINEMAN RD
Npmo 93444 345-F7
Npmo 93444 756-J7
Npmo 93444 776-H1
SLOC 93454 345-F7
SLOC 93454 756-J7
SLOC 93454 776-H1
WINFIELD PL
StBC 93436 896-G2
WING
SLOC 93430 591-D4
WING WY
PSRS 93446 494-C7
WINNELL AV
SLOC 93402 631-H7
WINSTON DR
SMRA 93458 776-F5
WINTER RD
StBC 93455 816-H1
WINTERHAVEN WY
SLOC 93420 734-J7
SLOC 93420 754-J1
WINTER WHEAT PL
PSRS 93446 534-C1
WINTHER WY
StBC 93110 985-D6
WINTHROP CT
StBC 93111 994-H3
WISTERIA CT
StBC 93455 817-A3
WISTERIA DR
SMRA 93458 796-G6
WISTERIA LN
SLO 93401 674-C2
SLOC 93446 514-A2
StBC 93437 875-J3
WONG ST
GDLP 93434 774-J6
WOOD DR
Cmbr 93428 528-H7
Cmbr 93428 548-H1
WOOD PL
ARGD 93420 714-H6
WOODBINE LN
Npmo 93444 756-C3
WOODBRIDGE CT
StBC 93455 816-G4
WOODBRIDGE ST
SLO 93401 653-J6
SLO 93401 654-A6
WOODDALE LN
SBAR 93103 986-B7
WOOD DUCK LN
SLOC 93446 471-C6
WOODGREEN WY
Npmo 93444 735-D7
Npmo 93444 755-D1
WOODHAVEN CT
PSRS 93446 533-J1
StBC 93455 816-J2
WOODHAVEN WY
Npmo 93444 755-E5
WOODLAND CT
ARGD 93420 714-H7
WOODLAND DR
ARGD 93420 714-H6
SBAR 93108 996-E2
SLO 93401 654-B4

WOODLAND DR
SLOC 93402 631-F6
WOODLAND RD
SLOC 93446 493-E4
WOODLAND ST
StBC 93455 816-J3
WOODLAND HILLS RD
SLOC 93420 734-H5
WOODLAWN DR
SMRA 93458 776-F5
WOODLEY CT
SBAR 93105 985-F7
WOODLEY RD
StBC 93108 996-G2
WOODMANSEE WY
SLOC 93451 473-D2
WOODMERE RD
StBC 93455 816-J4
StBC 93455 817-A4
WOODPECKER LN
SLOC 93424 693-B1
WOODSIDE CT
SMRA 93458 776-F5
WOODSIDE DR
SLO 93401 654-C6
WOODSIDE LN
StBC 93455 816-H3
WOODSTOCK RD
StBC 93441 365-K2
StBC 93441 901-D2
StBC 93460 901-C5
WOODVIEW AV
Cmbr 93428 548-G1
WOODY POINT LN
SLOC 93426 469-J2
WORCESTER DR
Cmbr 93428 528-E7
WORCHESTER CT
StBC 93455 817-B4
WRANGLER PL
SLOC 93446 534-J4
WRANGLER WY
SLOC 93465 533-D7
WULLBRANDT WY
CARP 93013 998-D7
WYANT RD
StBC 93108 996-J3
WYE RD
SBAR 93110 995-D1
WYOLA RD
SBAR 93105 995-G2
WYOMING AV
SLOC 93451 453-A4
StBC 93437 855-D7

X

N X ST
LMPC 93436 896-C6
LMPC 93436 916-C1

Y

N Y ST
LMPC 93436 896-C6
LMPC 93436 916-C1
YALE PL
SMRA 93458 796-G2
YAMA LN
SLOC 93402 631-J5
YANKEE FARM RD
SBAR 93109 995-E5
YANONALI ST
SBAR 93101 996-C4
SBAR 93103 996-D3
YAPLE AV
StBC 93111 984-H7
YARROW CT
SLO 93401 674-C2
YEDID HILLWAY
StBC 93117 984-E7
YELLOW FEATHER CIR
SLOC 93446 471-D6
YELLOW GOLD CIR
SLOC 93446 471-D7
YERBA AV
ATAS 93422 573-H1
YERBA BUENA AV
SLOC 93422 614-F2
SLOC 93453 614-F2
YERBA BUENA ST
MOBY 93442 591-E7
MOBY 93442 611-D1
YESAL AV
ATAS 93422 574-B4
YOLO AV
SLOC 93405 633-A5
YOLO LN
StBC 93117 993-G2

YORK
Cmbr 93428 528-D6
YORK AV
SLOC 93445 714-D7
YORK LN
SMRA 93455 796-H6
YORK PL
StBC 93117 984-F7
YORK MOUNTAIN RD
SLOC 93465 324-L8
SLOC 93465 325-A8
YORKSHIRE CT
StBC 93455 816-F4
YORKSHIRE ST
Cmbr 93428 528-G7
Cmbr 93428 548-G1
YOUNG AV
SLOC 93430 591-C5
YOUNGER AV
SLOC 93430 591-C4
YSABEL AV
PSRS 93446 513-G3
YUBA AV
SLOC 93405 633-A5
YUBA LN
StBC 93117 993-G2
YUCCA LN
CARP 93013 998-D7
YUCCA ST
StBC 93437 875-H1

Z

N Z ST
LMPC 93436 896-B7
LMPC 93436 916-B1
ZACA LN
SLO 93401 673-H1
ZACA ST
BLTN 93427 919-H5
ZACA STATION RD
StBC - 365-J2
StBC 93440 900-C2
StBC 93441 365-J2
StBC 93441 900-C2
ZACKERY CT
StBC 93455 816-J4
ZANZIBAR ST
MOBY 93442 591-E7
MOBY 93442 611-D1
SLOC - 591-E7
SLOC - 611-D1
SLOC 93442 591-E7
ZANZIBAR TER
MOBY 93442 611-D1
ZENON WY
SLOC 93420 735-B6
ZIA LUCIA LN
Cmbr 93428 528-F7
ZINFANDEL CT
SLOC 93465 553-A3
ZINK AV
StBC 93111 994-J2
ZINK PL
StBC 93111 994-J2
ZINNIA CT
Npmo 93444 755-J4
ZION PL
StBC 93455 816-H2
ZIRCON CT
StBC 93455 817-B5
ZOGATA WY
ARGD 93420 715-B3

#

AVENUE 1
SLOC 93451 453-B5
STREET 1
StBC 93455 795-H5
1ST CT
SLVG 93463 940-E2
N 1ST PL
LMPC 93436 896-F6
LMPC 93436 916-F2
1ST ST
BLTN 93427 919-H5
LMPC 93436 896-F7
LMPC 93436 916-F1
PSRS 93446 513-F7
SLOC 93402 631-G4
SLOC 93424 693-A4
SLOC 93430 590-J2
SLOC 93430 591-A2
SLOC 93465 553-E1
SLVG 93463 940-E1
StBC 93455 816-G6
StBC 93458 796-C4

N 1ST ST
GBCH 93433 714-D4
AVENUE 2
SLOC 93451 453-B5
2ND PL
SLVG 93463 920-E7
2ND ST
BLTN 93427 919-G4
GDLP 93434 774-J6
GDLP 93434 775-A6
LMPC 93436 896-F6
LMPC 93436 916-F1
PSRS 93446 513-F7
SLOC 93402 631-G4
SLOC 93424 693-A4
SLOC 93430 591-A2
SLOC 93465 553-E2
SLVG 93463 940-E1
N 2ND ST
GBCH 93433 714-D4
AVENUE 3
SLOC 93451 453-B4
3RD ST
CARP 93013 998-C7
GDLP 93434 774-J6
GDLP 93434 775-A6
LMPC 93436 896-F6
LMPC 93436 916-F1
PSRS 93446 513-F7
SLOC 93402 631-G5
SLOC 93465 553-E2
SLVG 93463 940-D1
N 3RD ST
GBCH 93433 714-D4
SLOC 93430 591-A2
S 3RD ST
GBCH 93433 714-D5
SLOC 93430 591-A2
4TH PL
SLVG 93463 920-E7
SLVG 93463 940-E1
4TH ST
CARP 93013 998-C7
GDLP 93434 775-A6
LMPC 93436 896-F7
LMPC 93436 916-F1
PSRS 93446 513-F6
SLOC 93402 631-G5
SLOC 93430 591-A2
SLOC 93446 513-E6
SLOC 93465 553-E2
StBC 93437 875-E3
N 4TH ST
GBCH 93433 714-D4
PBCH 93449 714-E4
S 4TH ST
GBCH 93433 714-D5
GBCH 93445 714-E7
SLOC 93433 714-D5
SLOC 93445 714-E7
W 4TH ST
SLOC 93446 513-E6
STREET 5
StBC 93455 795-G5
5TH ST
CARP 93013 998-C7
GDLP 93434 774-J5
GDLP 93434 775-A5
LMPC 93436 896-G7
LMPC 93436 916-G1
PSRS 93446 513-F6
SLOC 93402 631-G5
SLOC 93430 591-A2
SLOC 93465 553-D2
SLVG 93463 920-D7
SLVG 93463 940-D1
StBC 93434 774-J5
StBC 93437 875-E3
N 5TH ST
GBCH 93433 714-D4
S 5TH ST
GBCH 93433 714-D5
AVENUE 6
SLOC 93451 453-A4
6TH ST
CARP 93013 998-D7
CARP 93013 1018-D1
GDLP 93434 775-A5
LMPC 93436 896-G6
LMPC 93436 916-G1
PSRS 93446 513-F6
SLOC 93402 631-H5
SLOC 93430 591-A2
SLOC 93465 553-D2
StBC 93437 875-E3
N 6TH ST
GBCH 93433 714-E4
S 6TH ST
GBCH 93433 714-E5

AVENUE 7
SLOC 93451 453-A4
7TH ST
CARP 93013 998-D7
GDLP 93434 775-A5
LMPC 93436 896-G6
LMPC 93436 916-G2
PSRS 93446 513-F6
SLOC 93402 631-H5
SLOC 93430 591-A2
SLOC 93465 553-D2
StBC 93437 875-D3
N 7TH ST
GBCH 93433 714-E4
S 7TH ST
GBCH 93433 714-E5
AVENUE 8
MonC 93451 453-B4
SLOC 93451 453-A4
8TH ST
CARP 93013 998-D6
GDLP 93434 775-A5
LMPC 93436 896-G7
LMPC 93436 916-G1
PSRS 93446 513-F6
SLOC 93402 631-H5
SLOC 93430 591-A2
SLOC 93465 553-D2
StBC 93437 875-D3
N 8TH ST
GBCH 93433 714-E5
S 8TH ST
GBCH 93433 714-E5
AVENUE 9
MonC 93451 453-A3
SLOC 93451 453-A4
9TH ST
CARP 93013 998-C6
GDLP 93434 775-A5
LMPC 93436 896-G7
LMPC 93436 916-G1
PSRS 93446 513-F6
SLOC 93402 631-H6
SLOC 93430 591-A2
SLOC 93445 734-F1
SLOC 93451 473-F3
StBC 93434 774-J4
StBC 93434 775-A5
StBC 93437 875-D3
N 9TH ST
GBCH 93433 714-E4
S 9TH ST
GBCH 93433 714-E5
AVENUE 10
MonC 93451 453-A3
SLOC 93451 453-A4
10TH ST
GDLP 93434 775-A5
LMPC 93436 896-G7
PSRS 93446 513-F6
SLOC 93402 631-H5
SLOC 93430 591-A2
SLOC 93451 473-D2
StBC 93437 875-D4
N 10TH ST
GBCH 93433 714-E4
S 10TH ST
GBCH 93433 714-E5
AVENUE 11
MonC 93451 453-A3
SLOC 93451 453-A4
11TH ST
GDLP 93434 775-A4
PSRS 93446 513-F5
SLOC 93402 631-H6
SLOC 93430 591-A3
SLOC 93451 473-F2
SMRA 93455 816-C1
StBC 93434 775-B5
StBC 93437 875-D4
StBC 93455 816-C1
N 11TH ST
GBCH 93433 714-E4
S 11TH ST
GBCH 93433 714-E6
AVENUE 12
MonC 93451 453-A3
SLOC 93451 453-A4
12TH ST
GDLP 93434 775-A4
LMPC 93436 916-G1
PSRS 93446 513-E5
SLOC 93402 631-H5
SLOC 93430 591-A3
SLOC 93451 473-F2
StBC 93437 875-D4
N 12TH ST
GBCH 93433 714-F4
S 12TH ST
GBCH 93433 714-E5

12TH STEX
PSRS 93446 513-D5
SLOC 93446 513-D5
AVENUE 13
MonC 93451 453-A3
13TH ST
PSRS 93446 513-F5
SLOC 93402 631-H5
SLOC 93430 591-B2
SLOC 93445 714-E7
SLOC 93451 473-F2
StBC 93429 365-C1
StBC 93436 895-C3
StBC 93437 365-C1
StBC 93437 855-A6
StBC 93437 875-B1
StBC 93437 895-C3
N 13TH ST
GBCH 93433 714-F4
S 13TH ST
GBCH 93433 714-E6
AVENUE 14
MonC 93451 453-A3
14TH ST
PSRS 93446 513-F5
SLOC 93402 631-J5
SLOC 93430 591-A3
SLOC 93445 714-E7
SLOC 93451 473-F2
StBC 93437 875-D4
N 14TH ST
GBCH 93433 714-F5
S 14TH ST
GBCH 93433 714-F6
AVENUE 15
MonC 93451 453-A3
15TH ST
PSRS 93446 513-E5
SLOC 93402 631-J5
SLOC 93430 591-A3
SLOC 93445 714-F7
SLOC 93445 734-F1
SLOC 93451 473-F2
StBC 93437 875-D4
16TH ST
PSRS 93446 513-F5
SLOC 93402 631-J5
SLOC 93430 591-A3
SLOC 93445 714-F7
SLOC 93451 473-F1
StBC 93437 875-C4
N 16TH ST
GBCH 93433 714-F5
S 16TH ST
GBCH 93433 714-F5
17TH ST
PSRS 93446 513-E5
SLOC 93402 631-J5
SLOC 93430 591-B3
SLOC 93445 714-F7
SLOC 93445 734-F1
SLOC 93446 513-E5
SLOC 93451 473-F1
StBC 93437 875-C4
18TH ST
PSRS 93446 513-F4
SLOC 93402 631-J5
SLOC 93430 591-B3
SLOC 93445 714-F7
SLOC 93451 473-F1
StBC 93437 875-C4
19TH ST
PSRS 93446 513-F4
SLOC 93430 591-B3
SLOC 93445 714-F7
SLOC 93445 734-F1
SLOC 93451 473-F1
StBC 93437 875-C4
20TH CT
SLOC 93445 714-F7
20TH ST
PSRS 93446 513-F4
SLOC 93430 591-B3
SLOC 93445 714-F7
SLOC 93451 473-F1
StBC 93437 875-C4
21ST CT
SLOC 93445 714-F7
21ST ST
PSRS 93446 513-E4
SLOC 93430 591-B3
SLOC 93445 714-F7
SLOC 93445 734-F1
SLOC 93446 513-E4
SLOC 93451 473-F1
StBC 93437 875-C4
22ND ST
PSRS 93446 513-F4
SLOC 93430 591-B3
SLOC 93445 714-F7
SLOC 93445 734-F1

22ND ST
StBC 93437 875-B5
23RD ST
PSRS 93446 513-F4
SLOC 93430 591-B3
SLOC 93445 714-G7
SLOC 93445 734-G1
StBC 93437 875-C5
24TH ST
PSRS 93446 513-F4
SLOC 93420 714-G7
SLOC 93430 591-B3
SLOC 93445 714-G7
SLOC 93445 734-G1
StBC 93437 875-B5
25TH ST
SLOC 93445 714-G7
SLOC 93445 734-G1
StBC 93437 875-B5
26TH ST
PSRS 93446 513-F3
28TH ST
PSRS 93446 513-F3
StBC 93437 875-B5
29TH ST
StBC 93437 875-B5
30TH ST
PSRS 93446 513-F3
StBC 93437 875-B6
31ST ST
StBC 93437 875-B6
32ND ST
PSRS 93446 513-F2
StBC 93437 875-B6
33RD ST
StBC 93437 875-A6
34TH ST
PSRS 93446 513-F2
StBC 93437 875-A6
35TH ST
StBC 93437 365-C2
StBC 93437 875-A6
36TH ST
PSRS 93446 513-F2
38TH ST
PSRS 93446 513-F2
AVENUE 50
MonC 93451 453-A1
AVENUE 51
MonC 93451 453-A1
AVENUE 52
MonC 93451 453-A1
Rt#-G14 INTERLAKE RD
SLOC 93426 324-K3
Rt#-G14 NACIMIENTO LAKE DR
PSRS 93446 513-E3
SLOC 93426 324-L3
SLOC 93446 324-L3
SLOC 93446 471-C1
SLOC 93446 493-A5
SLOC 93446 513-B1
SLOC 93451 325-A5
Rt#-G19 NACIMIENTO LAKE DR
SLOC 93426 324-L2
Rt#-1 CABRILLO HWY
Cmbr 93428 324-J8
Cmbr 93428 528-B2
Cmbr 93428 548-J1
GBCH 93433 714-C4
GBCH 93449 714-C4
GDLP 93434 775-A3
LMPC 93436 916-H1
MOBY - 591-C6
MOBY 93430 591-C6
MOBY 93442 591-C6
MOBY 93442 611-E4
MOBY 93442 612-A6
Npmo 93444 755-B2
Npmo 93444 775-A3
PBCH 93449 714-C4
SLO 93405 633-F6
SLO 93405 653-H1
SLOC - 591-C6
SLOC - 612-A6
SLOC 93405 612-A6
SLOC 93405 632-F1
SLOC 93405 633-B4
SLOC 93405 653-H1
SLOC 93420 734-H1
SLOC 93420 754-H1
SLOC 93420 755-A1
SLOC 93430 324-J8
SLOC 93430 590-E1
SLOC 93430 591-C6
SLOC 93433 714-C4
SLOC 93435 324-J8

Rt#-1 CABRILLO HWY
SLOC 93442 591-C6
SLOC 93442 611-G6
SLOC 93442 612-A6
SLOC 93445 714-C4
SLOC 93445 734-H1
SLOC 93445 755-B6
SLOC 93445 775-A3
SLOC 93452 324-F5
SLOC 93452 528-B2
StBC 93117 365-F5
StBC 93429 345-E11
StBC 93429 365-F5
StBC 93429 855-G6
StBC 93434 775-A7
StBC 93434 795-A2
StBC 93436 365-F5
StBC 93436 916-H1
StBC 93437 855-G6
StBC 93455 345-D10
StBC 93455 795-C5
StBC 93455 816-B4
Rt#-1 CIENAGA ST
SLOC 93420 734-H1
SLOC 93445 734-H1
Rt#-1 DOLLIVER ST
GBCH 93433 714-C3
PBCH 93449 714-C3
PBCH 93449 714-C3
Rt#-1 FRONT ST
SLOC 93445 714-E7
SLOC 93445 734-E1
Rt#-1 GUADALUPE RD
SLOC 93420 755-B2
Rt#-1 GUADALUPE ST
GDLP 93434 775-A6
Rt#-1 HIGHWAY
StBC 93455 345-E11
Rt#-1 N H ST
LMPC 93436 896-E5
LMPC 93436 916-E1
StBC 93436 896-E5
Rt#-1 LOMPOC CASMALIA RD
LMPC 93436 896-D1
StBC 93436 876-A4
StBC 93436 896-D1
StBC 93437 855-G7
StBC 93437 875-G1
StBC 93437 876-A4
Rt#-1 MESA VIEW DR
SLOC 93420 734-J2
Rt#-1 E OCEAN AV
LMPC 93436 916-F1
Rt#-1 ORCUTT EXWY
StBC 93455 345-E11
Rt#-1 ORCUTT RD
StBC 93455 345-E11
Rt#-1 PACIFIC BLVD
GBCH 93433 714-D5
SLOC 93433 714-D5
SLOC 93445 714-D5
Rt#-1 SANTA ROSA ST
SLO 93401 653-H2
SLO 93405 653-H2
SLOC 93405 653-H2
Rt#-1 WILLOW RD
SLOC 93420 754-H1
SLOC 93420 755-A1
Rt#-33 HIGHWAY
SLOC - 346-F9
StBC - 346-F10
StBC 93252 346-F11
StBC 93252 366-G1
Rt#-41 ATASCADERO RD
MOBY 93442 611-G3
SLOC 92389 325-A10
SLOC 93442 325-A10
SLOC 93442 611-G3
SLOC 93442 612-A1
Rt#-41 CAPISTRANO AV
ATAS 93422 573-J3
ATAS 93422 574-A2
Rt#-41 CENTRE ST
SLOC 93461 325-F6
Rt#-41 CRESTON EUREKA RD
ATAS 93422 574-B1
SLOC 93422 574-B1
SLOC 93432 325-C8
SLOC 93446 325-C8
SLOC 93465 325-C8
SLOC 93465 574-B1
Rt#-41 CURBARIL AV
ATAS 93422 574-B3
SLOC 93422 574-B3
SLOC 93465 574-B3

Rt#-41 EL CAMINO REAL
ATAS 93422 573-G2
Rt#-41 HIGHWAY
SLOC 92389 325-H3
SLOC 93446 325-F6
SLOC 93461 325-G4
Rt#-41 MERCEDES AV
ATAS 93422 573-J3
ATAS 93422 574-A2
Rt#-41 MORRO RD
ATAS 93422 573-H7
ATAS 93422 593-D1
SLOC - 572-J7
SLOC 92389 325-A10
SLOC 93422 572-J7
SLOC 93422 573-A7
SLOC 93422 593-D1
Rt#-41 SANTA YSABEL AV
ATAS 93422 573-J4
Rt#-41 SYCAMORE RD
ATAS 93422 574-A2
Rt#-41 TEMPLETON RD
SLOC 93422 574-B2
SLOC 93465 574-B2
Rt#-41 WEST MALL
ATAS 93422 573-J3
Rt#-46 GREEN VALLEY RD
Cmbr 93428 324-J8
SLOC 93435 324-J8
SLOC 93465 324-K8
Rt#-46 HIGHWAY
PSRS 93446 513-J3
PSRS 93446 514-F1
PSRS 93446 533-F3
SLOC 92389 325-E6
SLOC 93446 325-E6
SLOC 93446 514-J1
SLOC 93446 533-E3
SLOC 93451 325-E6
SLOC 93461 325-G4
SLOC 93465 324-L8
SLOC 93465 325-A7
SLOC 93465 533-C5
Rt#-46 PASO ROBLES HWY
SLOC 92389 325-H4
SLOC 93461 325-H4
Rt#-58 CALF CANYON HWY
SLOC 93422 325-D11
SLOC 93422 614-G3
SLOC 93432 325-D11
SLOC 93453 325-D11
SLOC 93453 614-G3
SLOC 93461 325-D11
SLOC 93465 325-D11
Rt#-58 CARRISA HWY
SLOC - 345-L1
SLOC - 346-A1
SLOC 92389 325-H11
SLOC 93453 325-F9
SLOC 93453 345-L1
SLOC 93453 346-A1
SLOC 93461 325-F9
Rt#-58 EL CAMINO REAL
SLOC 93453 614-F3
Rt#-58 ESTRADA AV
SLOC 93453 614-G3
Rt#-58 G ST
SLOC 93453 614-F3
Rt#-58 HIGHWAY
SLOC - 346-B1
Rt#-135 BELL ST
StBC 93440 878-G1
Rt#-135 N BROADWAY
SMRA 93454 776-H6
Rt#-135 S BROADWAY
SMRA 93454 776-H7
SMRA 93454 796-H1
SMRA 93455 796-H5
Rt#-135 HIGHWAY
StBC 93440 365-G1
StBC 93440 878-D1
StBC 93455 345-E11
StBC 93455 365-E1
Rt#-135 ORCUTT EXWY
SMRA 93455 796-H7
SMRA 93455 816-F7
StBC 93455 345-E11
StBC 93455 796-H7
StBC 93455 816-F7
Rt#-150 CASITAS PASS RD
StBC 93013 366-G9

STB & SLO

INDEX

STREET — Name City ZIP Pg-Grid

Rt#-150 CASITAS PASS RD
StBC 93013 999-C7
VeCo - 999-C7
VeCo 93001 999-C7
VeCo 93013 999-C7

Rt#-150 HIGHWAY
CARP 93013 1018-H2
StBC 93013 1018-J1

Rt#-150 RINCON RD
StBC 93013 366-G9
StBC 93013 1018-J1

Rt#-154 CALLE REAL
SBAR 93110 995-D1
SBAR 93110 995-D1

Rt#-154 HIGHWAY
StBC 93105 365-L5
StBC 93105 366-A5
StBC 93440 900-C2
StBC 93441 900-C2
StBC 93460 365-L5
StBC 93460 900-J5
StBC 93460 901-A6
StBC 93460 921-B1
StBC 93460 941-H1

Rt#-154 SAN MARCOS PASS RD
SBAR 93110 985-B5
StBC 93105 365-L5
StBC 93105 366-A5
StBC 93105 964-A2
StBC 93105 984-J1
StBC 93105 985-A1
StBC 93110 985-B5
StBC 93110 995-C1
StBC 93111 985-B5

Rt#-166 CUYAMA HWY
Npmo 93444 776-H1
SLOC 93454 345-F7
SLOC 93454 776-H1
SLOC 93454 777-C1

Rt#-166 HIGHWAY
SLOC - 345-K5
SLOC - 346-A6
SLOC - 346-F9
SLOC 93252 346-E9
SLOC 93454 345-H7
StBC - 345-K5
StBC - 346-A7
StBC - 806-H2
StBC 93252 346-E9
StBC 93254 346-C8
StBC 93254 806-A1
StBC 93454 345-J6

Rt#-166 IRVINE STOVALL MEM HW
Npmo 93444 776-H1
SLOC 93454 776-H1
SLOC 93454 777-B1

Rt# 166 E MAIN ST
SMRA 93454 776-H7
SMRA 93454 777-A7

Rt#-166 W MAIN ST
GDLP 93434 775-G6
SMRA 93454 776-G7
SMRA 93458 776-G7
StBC 93434 775-G6
StBC 93458 776-C7

Rt#-192 CASITAS PASS RD
StBC 93013 366-G9
StBC 93013 998-G6
StBC 93013 1018-J1

Rt#-192 CATHEDRAL OAKS RD
StBC 93110 985-C6

Rt#-192 FOOTHILL RD
CARP 93013 998-E5
SBAR 93105 985-D6
SBAR 93105 986-A7
SBAR 93110 985-D6
StBC 93013 997-G3
StBC 93013 998-A4
StBC 93105 985-D6
StBC 93105 986-A7
StBC 93110 985-D6

Rt#-192 MISSION RIDGE RD
SBAR 93103 986-B7
SBAR 93103 996-B1

Rt#-192 W MOUNTAIN DR
SBAR 93103 986-A7
SBAR 93105 986-A7

Rt#-192 STANWOOD DR
SBAR 93103 986-D7
SBAR 93103 996-D1

Rt#-192 STANWOOD DR
SBAR 93108 996-D1

Rt#-192 SYCAMORE CANYON RD
SBAR 93108 986-D7
StBC 93108 986-D7
StBC 93108 996-F1

Rt#-192 TORO CANYON RD
StBC 93013 997-G3
StBC 93108 997-G3

Rt#-192 E VALLEY RD
StBC 93108 996-H2
StBC 93108 997-B1

Rt#-217 WARD MEMORIAL BLVD
SBAR 93117 994-E4
StBC 93106 994-E4
StBC 93111 994-E4
StBC 93117 994-E4

Rt#-225 CASTILLO ST
SBAR 93101 996-B5

Rt#-225 CLIFF DR
SBAR 93101 996-A6
SBAR 93109 995-F6
SBAR 93109 996-A6
SBAR 93105 995-F6
StBC 93109 995-F6

Rt#-225 LAS POSITAS RD
StBC 93105 995-F4
StBC 93105 995-F4

Rt#-225 MONTECITO ST
SBAR 93101 996-A5

Rt#-227 ARROYO GRANDE SAN LUI
ARGD 93420 715-A3
SLOC 93420 715-A3

Rt#-227 E BRANCH ST
ARGD 93420 715-A5

Rt#-227 W BRANCH ST
ARGD 93420 714-J5
ARGD 93420 715-A5

Rt#-227 BROAD ST
SLO 93401 654-A6
SLO 93401 674-B1
SLOC 93401 654-A6
SLOC 93401 674-B1

Rt#-227 CARPENTER CANYON RD
SLOC 93401 694-G1
SLOC 93420 694-G3
SLOC 03420 605-A6
SLOC 93420 715-A1

Rt#-227 CORBETT CANYON RD
ARGD 93420 715-A4

Rt#-227 EDNA RD
SLOC 93401 674-D4
SLOC 93401 694-F1
SLOC 93420 694-F1

Rt#-227 E GRAND AV
ARGD 93420 714-J5

Rt#-227 HIGUERA ST
SLO 93401 653-H6

Rt#-227 MADONNA RD
SLO 93401 653-G6
SLO 93405 653-G6

Rt#-227 SOUTH ST
SLO 93401 653-J5
SLO 93401 654-A5

Rt#-229 WEBSTER RD
SLOC 93432 325-D8
SLOC 93465 325-D10

Rt#-246 BUELLTON LOMPOC RD
StBC 93436 365-F3
StBC 93436 896-H7
StBC 93436 916-H1

Rt#-246 HIGHWAY
BLTN - 919-H5
BLTN - 920-A6
BLTN 93427 919-G5
BLTN 93427 920-A6
BLTN 93436 919-F4
StBC 93436 365-F3
StBC 93436 919-E4
StBC 93463 920-A6

Rt#-246 MISSION DR
SLVG 93463 920-F7
SLVG 93463 940-D1
StBC 93460 921-A6
StBC 93463 920-F7

Rt#-246 MISSION DR
StBC 93463 921-A6

Rt#-246 E OCEAN AV
LMPC 93436 916-H1
StBC 93436 916-H1

U.S.-101 EL CAMINO REAL
ARGD - 715-B6
ATAS - 574-A4
ATAS - 594-B1
BLTN - 919-J3
CARP - 998-A6
CARP - 1018-F1
MonC - 453-B3
Npmo - 735-H6
Npmo - 736-A7
Npmo - 756-D4
Npmo - 776-H4
PBCH - 345-B5
PBCH - 693-E3
PSRS - 513-F2
PSRS - 533-F3
SBAR - 995-D1
SBAR - 996-E3
SLO - 653-H5
SLO - 654-B2
SLO - 673-F4
SLOC - 345-C1
SLOC - 453-B3
SLOC - 473-E5
SLOC - 493-F2
SLOC - 513-F2
SLOC - 533-F3
SLOC - 553-D3
SLOC - 594-C3
SLOC - 614-C6
SLOC - 653-H5
SLOC - 654-B2
SLOC - 673-F4
SLOC - 693-E3
SLOC - 714-A1
SLOC - 715-B6
SLOC - 735-E2
SLOC - 776-H4
SMRA - 777-A6
SMRA - 797-A7
StBC - 345-F11
StBC - 365-G1
StBC - 797-A7
StBC - 817-B3
StBC - 878-H1
StBC - 900-C1
StBC - 919-J3
StBC - 939-H7
StBC - 981-A5
StBC - 982-E6
StBC - 992-J1
StBC - 993-A1
StBC - 004-E1
StBC - 995-D1
StBC - 996-E3
StBC - 997-C3
StBC - 998-A6
StBC - 1018-F1
Summ - 997-C3
VeCo - 1018-F1

U.S.-101 FRWY
StBC - 365-H2

U.S.-101 VENTURA FRWY
StBC - 1018-J3
VeCo - 1018-J3

COPYRIGHT 2000 Thomas Bros. Maps ®

AIRPORTS

FEATURE NAME	Address City, ZIP Code	PAGE-GRID
LOMPOC	1801 N H ST, LMPC, 93436	896 - C5
NEW CUYAMA	PERKINS RD & CEBRIAN AV, StBC, 93254	806 - B2
OCEANO COUNTY	AIR PARK DR, SLOC, 93445	714 - D7
PASO ROBLES MUNICIPAL	AIRPORT RD, PSRS, 93446	494 - D6
SAN LUIS OBISPO	HIGHWAY 227, SLOC, 93401	674 - B2
SANTA BARBARA MUNICIPAL	500 FOWLER RD, SBAR, 93117	994 - B3
SANTA MARIA	3233 SKYWAY DR, SMRA, 93455	816 - D1
SANTA YNEZ	AIRPORT RD, StBC, 93460	921 - C6

BEACHES & HARBORS

FEATURE NAME	Address City, ZIP Code	PAGE-GRID
ARROYO BURRO BEACH CO PK	2981 CLIFF DR, SBAR, 93109	995 - E6
AVILA BEACH	FRONT ST, SLOC, 93424	693 - A4
BUTTERFLY BEACH	CHANNEL DR & BUTTERFLY LN, StBC, 93108	996 - G4
CARPINTERIA CITY BEACH	LINDEN AV, CARP, 93013	998 - C7
CARPINTERIA ST BCH	PALM AV, CARP, 93013	998 - C7
CAYUCOS ST BCH	OCEAN FRONT LN, SLOC, 93430	590 - J2
EAST BEACH	E CABRILLO BLVD, SBAR, 93103	996 - E4
EL CAPITAN ST BCH	EL CAMINO REAL, StBC, 93117	981 - H5
GAVIOTA STATE PK	EL CAMINO REAL & CABRILLO HWY, StBC, 93117	365 - J7
GOLETA BEACH COUNTY PK	5990 SANDSPIT RD, StBC, 93117	994 - E4
GUADALUPE DUNES COUNTY PK	W MAIN ST, StBC, 93434	774 - A5
HASKELLS BEACH	EL CAMINO REAL, StBC, 93117	993 - C2
ISLA VISTA BEACH	DEL PLAYA DR, StBC, 93117	993 - J5
JALAMA BEACH COUNTY PK	JALAMA RD & COJO BAY RD, StBC, 93436	365 - D6
LEADBETTER BEACH	SHORELINE DR & LOMA ALTA DR, SBAR, 93109	996 - A6
LEFFINGWELL LANDING ST BCH	MOONSTONE BEACH DR, Cmbr, 93428	528 - C5
LOOKOUT PK	LOOKOUT PARK RD, Summ, 93067	997 - D4
MOONSTONE BEACH	MOONSTONE BEACH DR, Cmbr, 93428	528 - D5
MORRO ROCK BEACH	COLEMAN DR, MOBY, 93442	611 - D5
MORRO STRAND ST BCH	SANDALWOOD AV, MOBY, 93442	611 - D3
MORRO STRAND ST BCH	STUDIO DR, SLOC, 93430	591 - B4
OCEAN BEACH PK	OCEAN PARK RD, StBC, 93436	894 - G1
PISMO ST BCH	OFF HIGHWAY 1, SLOC, 93433	714 - D6
REFUGIO ST BCH	EL CAMINO REAL & REFUGIO RD, StBC, 93117	981 - D5
SAN SIMEON ST BCH	CABRILLO HWY, Cmbr, 93428	528 - B2
SAN SIMEON ST BCH	MOONSTONE BEACH DR, Cmbr, 93428	528 - C4
SANTA BARBARA SHORES CO PK	HOLLISTER AV & LAS ARMAS RD, StBC, 93117	993 - F3
WEST BEACH	W CABRILLO BLVD, SBAR, 93101	996 - B5

BED & BREAKFAST

FEATURE NAME	Address City, ZIP Code	PAGE-GRID
ARBOR INN B&B	2130 ARBOR RD, SLOC, 93446	533 - C4
ARROYO VILLAGE INN B&B	407 EL CAMINO REAL, ARGD, 93420	714 - J5
BATH STREET INN B&B	1720 BATH ST, SBAR, 93101	995 - J3
BEACH HOUSE B&B	6360 MOONSTONE BEACH DR, Cmbr, 93428	528 - D5
BLUE WHALE INN B&B	6736 MOONSTONE BEACH DR, Cmbr, 93428	528 - D5
CAMBRIA LANDING INN B&B	6530 MOONSTONE BEACH DR, Cmbr, 93428	528 - D5
CAPTAINS COVE LODGE	6454 MOONSTONE BEACH DR, Cmbr, 93428	528 - D5
CHESHIRE CAT INN B&B	36 W VALERIO ST, SBAR, 93101	995 - J3
EAGLE INN B&B	232 NATOMA AV, SBAR, 93101	996 - B5
GARDEN STREET INN B&B	1212 GARDEN ST, SLO, 93401	653 - J4
GLENBOROUGH INN B&B	1327 BATH ST, SBAR, 93101	995 - J4
HERITAGE INN	978 OLIVE ST, SLO, 93405	653 - J3
HITCHCOCK HOUSE B&B	427 CORONA DEL MAR, SBAR, 93103	996 - D4
INN ON SUMMER HILL B&B	2520 LILLIE AV, Summ, 93067	997 - E4
KALEIDOSCOPE INN B&B	130 E DANA ST, Npmo, 93444	756 - C2
MARY MAY INN B&B	111 W VALERIO ST, SBAR, 93101	995 - J3
OLD YACHT CLUB INN B&B	431 CORONA DEL MAR, SBAR, 93103	996 - E4
OLIVE HOUSE B&B	1604 OLIVE ST, SBAR, 93103	996 - A2
OLLALIEBERRY INN B&B	2476 MAIN ST, Cmbr, 93428	528 - H6
PARSONAGE B&B	1600 OLIVE ST, SBAR, 93103	996 - A2
SECRET GARDEN B&B	1908 BATH ST, SBAR, 93101	995 - H3
SIMPSON HOUSE INN B&B	121 E ARRELLAGA ST, SBAR, 93103	996 - A2
STORYBOOK INN B&B	409 1ST ST, SLVG, 93463	940 - E1
SUMMERLAND INN B&B	2161 ORTEGA HILL RD, Summ, 93067	997 - C3
SYLVIAS RIGDON HALL INN B&B	4936 BURTON DR, Cmbr, 93428	528 - H7
THE BALLARD INN B&B	2436 BASELINE AV, StBC, 93463	920 - G2
THE INN AT MORRO BAY B&B	60 STATE PARK RD, MOBY, 93442	631 - G1
THE IVANHOE INN B&B	1406 CASTILLO ST, SBAR, 93101	995 - J4
THE J PATRICK HOUSE B&B	2990 BURTON DR, Cmbr, 93428	528 - H7
TIFFANY INN B&B	1323 DE LA VINA ST, SBAR, 93101	995 - J3
VILLA ROSA B&B	15 CHAPALA ST, SBAR, 93101	996 - B5

BUILDINGS - GOVERNMENTAL

FEATURE NAME	Address City, ZIP Code	PAGE-GRID
FOR DOWNTOWN BUILDINGS SEE PAGE viii		-
CALIFORNIA MENS COLONY	COLONY DR, SLOC, 93405	633 - F5
CATHEDRAL OAKS FIRE ADMIN	4410 CATHEDRAL OAKS RD, StBC, 93110	985 - B6
COURTHOUSE	312 E COOK ST, SMRA, 93454	796 - H1
EL PASO DE ROBLES STATE YOUTH AUTH	4545 AIRPORT RD, PSRS, 93446	494 - B7
FEDERAL PENITENTIARY	3901 KLEIN BLVD, LMPC, 93436	895 - H2
FIRE TRAINING FACILITY	S OLIVE ST, SBAR, 93103	996 - C4
JUVENILE HALL	812 W FOSTER RD, SMRA, 93455	816 - F3
JUVENILE HALL	JUVENILE HALL RD, StBC, 93110	995 - B1
SAN LUIS OBISPO CO COURT HOUSE	1050 MONTEREY ST, SLO, 93401	653 - J4
STB CO ADMIN & BOARD OF-SUPERVISORS	ANAPAMU ST, SBAR, 93101	996 - A3
SANTA BARBARA CO BLDG	401 CYPRESS AV, LMPC, 93436	916 - E2
SANTA BARBARA CO COURT HOUSE	1110 ANACAPA ST, SBAR, 93101	996 - A3
SANTA BARBARA CO FIRE HQ	CATHEDRAL OAKS RD, StBC, 93110	985 - C6
SANTA BARBARA COUNTY-GOVERNMENT CTR	2100 S CENTERPOINTE PKWY, SMRA, 93455	796 - H4
SANTA BARBARA CO HONOR FARM	4436 CL REAL, StBC, 93110	985 - B7
SANTA BARBARA COUNTY JAIL	4436 CL REAL, StBC, 93110	985 - B7
SOUTH ADMINISTRATIVE AREA	ARGUELLO BLVD, StBC, 93437	895 - A4

CEMETERIES

FEATURE NAME	Address City, ZIP Code	PAGE-GRID
CALVARY CEM	199 N HOPE AV, SBAR, 93110	995 - E1
CAMBRIA CEM	BRIDGE ST, Cmbr, 93428	528 - F5
CARPINTERIA CEM	1500 CRAVENS LN, StBC, 93013	998 - A5
CAYUCOS MORRO BAY CEM	CABRILLO AV, SLOC, 93430	591 - B3
GOLETA CEM	44 S SAN ANTONIO RD, StBC, 93110	995 - A1
LOMPOC EVERGREEN CEM	C ST, StBC, 93436	916 - F3
OAK HILL CEM	2560 BASELINE AV, StBC, 93463	920 - H3
SANTA BARBARA CEM	E CABRILLO BLVD, StBC, 93108	996 - F4
SANTA MARIA CEM	730 STOWELL RD, SMRA, 93454	796 - J2

CHAMBERS OF COMMERCE

FEATURE NAME	Address City, ZIP Code	PAGE-GRID
ARROYO GRANDE	800 W BRANCH ST, ARGD, 93420	714 - H4
ATASCADERO	6550 EL CAMINO REAL, ATAS, 93422	573 - J3
BUELLTON	376 AV OF FLAGS, BLTN, 93427	919 - H5
CAMBRIA	767 MAIN ST, Cmbr, 93428	528 - E6
CARPINTERIA	5320 CARPINTERIA AV, CARP, 93013	998 - D7
CAYUCOS	80 S OCEAN AV, SLOC, 93430	590 - J2
GOLETA VALLEY	5730 HOLLISTER AV, StBC, 93117	994 - E2
GROVER BEACH	177 S 8TH ST, GBCH, 93433	714 - E5
LOMPOC VALLEY	111 I ST, LMPC, 93436	916 - E2
LOS OSOS-BAYWOOD PK	781 LOS OSOS VALLEY RD, SLOC, 93402	631 - H7
MORRO BAY	850 MAIN ST, MOBY, 93442	611 - F6
NIPOMO	257 W TEFFT ST, Npmo, 93444	756 - C2
PASO ROBLES	1225 PARK ST, PSRS, 93446	513 - F5
PISMO BEACH	581 DOLLIVER ST, PBCH, 93449	714 - C2
SAN LUIS OBISPO	1039 CHORRO ST, SLO, 93401	653 - J4
SANTA BARBARA	12 E CARRILLO ST, SBAR, 93101	996 - A4
SANTA MARIA	614 S BROADWAY, SMRA, 93454	796 - H1
SOLVANG VISITORS BUREAU	1511 MISSION DR, SLVG, 93463	940 - E1
VISITOR BUREAU	1639 COPENHAGEN DR, SLVG, 93463	940 - E1
VISITORS CTR	1 SANTA BARBARA ST, SBAR, 93101	996 - C5

CITY HALLS

FEATURE NAME	Address City, ZIP Code	PAGE-GRID
ARROYO GRANDE	214 E BRANCH ST, ARGD, 93420	715 - A5
ATASCADERO	6500 PALMA AV, ATAS, 93422	573 - J3
BUELLTON	107 W HWY 246, BLTN, 93427	919 - H5
CARPINTERIA	5775 CARPINTERIA AV, CARP, 93013	1018 - E1
GROVER BEACH	154 S 8TH ST, GBCH, 93433	714 - E5
GUADALUPE	918 OBISPO ST, GDLP, 93434	775 - A5
LOMPOC	100 CIVIC CENTER PZ, LMPC, 93436	916 - F2
MORRO BAY	595 HARBOR ST, MOBY, 93442	611 - F6
PASO ROBLES	1000 SPRING ST, PSRS, 93446	513 - F6
PISMO BEACH	760 MATTIE RD, PBCH, 93449	693 - J7
SAN LUIS OBISPO	990 PALM ST, SLO, 93401	653 - J4
SANTA BARBARA	735 ANACAPA ST, SBAR, 93101	996 - B4
SANTA MARIA	110 E COOK ST, SMRA, 93454	796 - H1
SOLVANG	1644 OAK ST, SLVG, 93463	940 - E1

COLLEGES & UNIVERSITIES

FEATURE NAME	Address City, ZIP Code	PAGE-GRID
ANTIOCH UNIV	801 GARDEN ST, SBAR, 93101	996 - B3
BROOKS INSTITUTE OF PHOTO-GRAPHY	801 ALSTON RD, SBAR, 93108	996 - F2
CAL POLY STATE UNIV	1 GRAND AV, SLOC, 93407	653 - J1
COLL OF THE QUEEN OF PEACE SEMINARY	E VALLEY RD, StBC, 93108	997 - F1
CUESTA COLLEGE	EDUCATION DR, SLOC, 93405	632 - J4
HANCOCK COLLEGE (LOMPOC CAMPUS)	HANCOCK DR, LMPC, 93436	896 - D3
HANCOCK COLLEGE (NORTH CAMPUS)	800 COLLEGE DR, SMRA, 93454	796 - J2
HANCOCK COLLEGE (SOUTH CAMPUS)	1300 COLLEGE DR, SMRA, 93454	796 - J3
MUSIC ACADEMY OF THE WEST	1070 FAIRWAY RD, StBC, 93108	996 - G4
SAINT MARYS SEMINARY	1964 LAS CANOAS RD, SBAR, 93105	986 - B5
SANTA BARBARA CITY COLLEGE	721 CLIFF DR, SBAR, 93109	996 - A6
UC SANTA BARBARA WEST CAMPUS	EL COLEGIO RD & STORKE RD, StBC, 93117	993 - H5
UNIV OF CALIF SANTA BARBARA	END OF WARD MEMORIAL BLVD, StBC, 93106	994 - C5
WESTMONT COLLEGE	955 LA PAZ RD, StBC, 93108	986 - F7

DEPARTMENT OF MOTOR VEHICLES

FEATURE NAME	Address City, ZIP Code	PAGE-GRID
GOLETA DMV	7127 HOLLISTER AV, StBC, 93117	993 - H3
LOMPOC DMV	138 B ST, LMPC, 93436	916 - F1
PASO ROBLES DMV	841 PARK ST, PSRS, 93446	513 - F6
SAN LUIS OBISPO DMV	3190 S HIGUERA ST, SLO, 93401	653 - H7
SANTA BARBARA DMV	535 CASTILLO ST, SBAR, 93101	996 - A5
SANTA MARIA DMV	523 MCCLELLAND ST, SMRA, 93454	796 - H1

ENTERTAINMENT & SPORTS

FEATURE NAME	Address City, ZIP Code	PAGE-GRID
COUNTY FAIRGROUNDS	24TH ST & RIVERSIDE AV, PSRS, 93446	513 - G4
EARL WARREN SHOWGROUNDS	LAS POSITAS RD & EL CAMINO REA, StBC, 93105	995 - F2
PEABODY STADIUM	ANAPAMU ST, SBAR, 93103	996 - B2
SANTA BARBARA CITY COLLEGE-STADIUM	721 CLIFF DR, SBAR, 93109	996 - B6
SANTA BARBARA COUNTY FAIR-GROUNDS	STOWELL RD & DEPOT ST, SMRA, 93458	796 - G2

GOLF COURSES

FEATURE NAME	Address City, ZIP Code	PAGE-GRID
ALISAL GUEST RANCH & GC	1054 ALISAL RD, SLVG, 93463	940 - D4
AVILA BEACH RESORT GC	6680 BAY LAUREL PL, SLOC, 93424	693 - B3
BIRNAM WOOD GC	2031 PACKING HOUSE RD, StBC, 93108	997 - C2
BLACK LAKE GC	1490 GOLF COURSE LN, Npmo, 93444	735 - D7
CHALK MTN GC	10000 EL BORDO AV, ATAS, 93422	574 - B6
DAIRY CREEK GC	CABRILLO HWY & DAIRY CREEK RD, SLOC, 93405	633 - A3
GLEN ANNIE GC	405 N GLEN ANNIE RD, StBC, 93117	983 - G7
HIDDEN OAKS CC	4760 CL CAMARADA, StBC, 93110	994 - J2
HUNTER RANCH GC	4041 HWY 46, SLOC, 93446	514 - E2
LA CUMBRE GOLF & CC	4015 VIA LAGUNA DR, StBC, 93110	995 - D2
LAGUNA LAKE GC	11175 LOS OSOS VALLEY RD, SLO, 93405	653 - E7
LINKS COURSE AT PASO ROBLES	5151 JARDINE RD, PSRS, 93446	494 - F5
MONTECITO CC	920 SUMMIT RD, SBAR, 93108	996 - F3
MORRO BAY GC	101 STATE PARK RD, MOBY, 93442	631 - G1
OCEAN MEADOWS GC	6925 WHITTIER DR, StBC, 93117	993 - H4
PASO ROBLES GC	1600 COUNTRY CLUB DR, PSRS, 93446	514 - A7
PISMO ST BCH GC	25 GRAND AV, GBCH, 93433	714 - C4
RANCHO MARIA GC	1950 CABRILLO HWY, StBC, 93429	816 - B5
RIVER COURSE AT THE ALISAL	150 ALISAL RD, StBC, 93463	940 - F2
SANDPIPER GC	7925 HOLLISTER AV, StBC, 93117	993 - E3
SAN LUIS OBISPO CC	255 COUNTRY CLUB DR, SLOC, 93401	674 - D6
SANTA BARBARA GC	3500 MCCAW AV, SBAR, 93105	995 - F2
SANTA MARIA CC	505 WALLER LN, SMRA, 93455	796 - G6
SEA PINES GC	250 HOWARD AV, SLOC, 93402	631 - E6
SUNSET RIDGE GC	1425 FAIRWAY AV, SMRA, 93455	796 - D6
THE VILLAGE CC	4300 CLUBHOUSE RD, StBC, 93436	876 - E5
TWIN LAKES GC	6034 HOLLISTER AV, SBAR, 93117	994 - D1
VALLEY CLUB GC	1901 E VALLEY RD, StBC, 93108	997 - D2
ZACA CREEK GC	223 SHADOW MOUNTAIN DR, BLTN, 93427	919 - G6

HOSPITALS

FEATURE NAME	Address City, ZIP Code	PAGE-GRID
ARROYO GRANDE COMM HOSP	345 S HALCYON RD, ARGD, 93420	714 - H6
ATASCADERO STATE HOSP	10333 EL CAMINO REAL, ATAS, 93422	574 - C6
FRENCH HOSP MED CTR	1911 JOHNSON AV, SLO, 93401	654 - A4
GOLETA VILLAGE COTTAGE HOSP	351 S PATTERSON AV, StBC, 93111	994 - G2
LOMPOC HEALTHCARE DIST	508 HICKORY AV, LMPC, 93436	916 - E2
MARIAN MED CTR	1400 E CHURCH ST, SMRA, 93454	777 - A7
SAINT FRANCIS MED CTR	601 MICHELTORENA ST, SBAR, 93103	996 - A2
SAN LUIS OBISBO GENERAL HOSP	2180 JOHNSON AV, SLO, 93401	654 - B5
SANTA BARBARA COTTAGE HOSP	PUEBLO ST & BATH ST, SBAR, 93105	995 - H2
SANTA YNEZ VLY COTTAGE HOSP	700 ALAMO PINTADO RD, SLVG, 93463	920 - G7
SIERRA VISTA REGL MED CTR	1010 MURRAY ST, SLO, 93405	653 - J2
TWIN CITIES COMM HOSP	1100 LAS TABLAS RD, SLOC, 93465	553 - C1

HOTELS & MOTELS

FEATURE NAME	Address City, ZIP Code	PAGE-GRID
APPLE FARM INN	2015 MONTEREY ST, SLO, 93401	654 - B3
BEST WESTERN BIG AMERICA	1725 N BROADWAY, SMRA, 93454	776 - H5
BEST WESTERN BLACK OAK MOTOR LODGE	1135 24TH ST, PSRS, 93446	513 - G3
BEST WESTERN CARPINTERIA INN	4558 CARPINTERIA AV, CARP, 93013	998 - C6
BEST WESTERN CASA GRANDE INN	850 OAK PARK BLVD, ARGD, 93420	714 - G3
BEST WESTERN COLONY INN	3600 EL CAMINO REAL, ATAS, 93422	573 - G2
BEST WESTERN EL RANCHO MOTEL	2460 MAIN ST, MOBY, 93442	611 - E3
BEST WESTERN ENCINA LODGE	2220 BATH ST, SBAR, 93105	995 - H2
BEST WESTERN FIRESIDE INN	6700 MOONSTONE BEACH DR, Cmbr, 93428	528 - D5
BEST WESTERN KING FREDERIK-MOTEL	1617 COPENHAGEN DR, SLVG, 93463	940 - E1
BEST WESTERN KRONBERG INN	1440 MISSION DR, SLVG, 93463	940 - D1
BEST WESTERN MARINERS INN	6180 MOONSTONE BEACH DR, Cmbr, 93428	528 - D4
BEST WESTERN OLIVE TREE INN	1000 OLIVE ST, SLO, 93405	653 - J3
BEST WESTERN PEA SOUP-ANDERSENS INN	51 E HWY 246, BLTN, 93427	919 - H5
BEST WESTERN PEPPER TREE INN	3850 STATE ST, SBAR, 93110	995 - E1
BEST WESTERN ROYAL OAK	214 MADONNA RD, SLO, 93405	653 - H6
BEST WESTERN SAN MARCOS	250 PACIFIC AV, MOBY, 93442	611 - F6

FEATURE NAME	Address City, ZIP Code	PAGE-GRID
BEST WESTERN SEA PINES GOLF-RESORT	1945 SOLANO ST, SLOC, 93402	631 - F6
BEST WESTERN SHELTER COVE LODGE	2651 PRICE ST, PBCH, 93449	693 - J7
BEST WESTERN SHORE CLIFF LODGE	2555 PRICE ST, PBCH, 93449	714 - A1
BEST WESTERN SOMERSET MANOR	1895 MONTEREY ST, SLO, 93401	654 - B3
BEST WESTERN SOUTH COAST INN	5620 CL REAL, StBC, 93117	994 - E1
BEST WESTERN TRADEWINDS	225 BEACH ST, MOBY, 93442	611 - F6
BREAKERS MOTEL	MORRO BAY BL & MARKET, MOBY, 93442	611 - F6
CAMBRIA PINES LODGE	2905 BURTON DR, Cmbr, 93428	528 - H7
CATHEDRAL OAKS LODGE	4770 CALLE REAL, StBC, 93110	984 - J7
DANISH COUNTRY INN	1455 MISSION DR, SLVG, 93463	940 - D1
EDGEWATER MOTEL	280 WADSWORTH AV, PBCH, 93449	714 - B2
EMBASSY SUITES HOTEL	1117 N H ST, LMPC, 93436	896 - E6
EMBASSY SUITES HOTEL	333 MADONNA RD, SLO, 93405	653 - H7
FESS PARKERS DOUBLETREE RESORT STB	633 E CABRILLO BLVD, SBAR, 93103	996 - D4
FOUR SEASONS BILTMORE HOTEL	1260 CHANNEL DR, StBC, 93108	996 - H4
HILTON HOTEL	3455 SKYWAY DR, SMRA, 93455	816 - F1
HOLIDAY INN EXPRESS	1800 MONTEREY ST, SLO, 93401	654 - A3
HOLIDAY INN SANTA-BARBARA/GOLETA	5650 CL REAL, StBC, 93117	994 - E1
HOWARD JOHNSON	1585 CL JOAQUIN, SLO, 93405	673 - G3
INN AT MORRO BAY	60 STATE PARK RD, MOBY, 93442	631 - G1
INN OF LOMPOC	1122 N H ST, LMPC, 93436	896 - E6
KON TIKI INN	1621 PRICE ST, PBCH, 93449	714 - B2
MADONNA INN	100 MADONNA RD, SLO, 93405	653 - H6
MONTECITO INN	1295 COAST VILLAGE RD, SBAR, 93108	996 - H4
MOONSTONE INN MOTEL	5860 MOONSTONE BEACH DR, Cmbr, 93428	528 - D6
PACIFICA SUITES	5490 HOLLISTER AV, StBC, 93111	994 - F2
PETERSEN VILLAGE INN	1576 MISSION DR, SLVG, 93463	940 - E1
PORTO FINALE INN	940 OCEAN AV, LMPC, 93436	916 - F2
QUALITY INN & EXECUTIVE SUITES	1621 N H ST, LMPC, 93436	896 - E5
QUALITY INN OF SOLVANG	1450 MISSION DR, SLVG, 93463	940 - D1
QUALITY SUITES	1631 MONTEREY ST, SLO, 93401	654 - A3
QUALITY SUITES	651 FIVE CITIES DR, PBCH, 93449	714 - E3
RADISSON HOTEL SANTA BARBARA	1111 E CABRILLO BLVD, SBAR, 93103	996 - E4
RAMADA INN AT THE WINDMILL	114 E HWY 246, BLTN, 93427	919 - H5
RAMADA SUITES	2050 PREISKER LN, SMRA, 93454	776 - H4
RANCHO SANTA BARBARA MARRIOTT	555 MCMURRAY RD, BLTN, 93427	919 - J5
ROSE GARDEN INN	1007 E MAIN ST, SMRA, 93454	776 - J7
SANDMAN INN	3714 STATE ST, SBAR, 93105	995 - E1
SANTA MARIA INN	801 S BROADWAY, SMRA, 93458	796 - G2
SEA CREST RESORT	2241 PRICE ST, PBCH, 93449	714 - A1
SEA GYPSY MOTEL	1020 CYPRESS ST, PBCH, 93449	714 - B2
SOLVANG ROYAL SCANDANAVIAN INN	400 ALISAL RD, SLVG, 93463	940 - E1
SPYGLASS INN	2705 SPYGLASS DR, PBCH, 93449	693 - F6
SYCAMORE MINERAL SPRINGS RESORT	1215 AVILA BEACH DR, SLOC, 93424	693 - D3
THE CLIFFS AT SHELL BEACH	2757 SHELL BEACH RD, PBCH, 93449	693 - F6
UPHAM HOTEL	1404 DE LA VINA ST, SBAR, 93101	995 - J3

LIBRARIES

FEATURE NAME	Address City, ZIP Code	PAGE-GRID
ATASCADERO	6850 MORRO RD, ATAS, 93422	573 - J4
BUELLTON	140 W HWY 246, BLTN, 93427	919 - H5
CAMBRIA	900 MAIN ST, Cmbr, 93428	528 - F6
CARPINTERIA	5141 CARPINTERIA AV, CARP, 93013	998 - D7
CAYUCOS	201 OCEAN FRONT LN, SLOC, 93430	590 - J1
CUYAMA	HWY 166 & NEWSOME ST, StBC, 93254	806 - C1
EASTSIDE	1102 MONTECITO ST, SBAR, 93103	996 - D3
GOLETA	500 N FAIRVIEW AV, StBC, 93117	984 - D7
GUADALUPE	1005 GUADALUPE ST, GDLP, 93434	775 - A5
LOMPOC	501 E NORTH AV, LMPC, 93436	896 - F6
LURIA	721 CLIFF DR, SBAR, 93109	996 - A6
MONTECITO	1469 E VALLEY RD, StBC, 93108	996 - J1
MORRO BAY	625 HARBOR ST, MOBY, 93442	611 - G6
NIPOMO	918 W TEFFT ST, Npmo, 93444	756 - A4
ORCUTT	1157 E CLARK AV, StBC, 93455	817 - A5
PASO ROBLES	1000 SPRING ST, PSRS, 93446	513 - F5
SAN LUIS OBISPO	995 PALM ST, SLO, 93401	653 - J4
SAN MIGUEL	254 13TH ST, SLOC, 93451	473 - F2
SANTA BARBARA CENTRAL	40 ANAPAMU ST, SBAR, 93101	996 - A3
SANTA MARGARITA	22501 I ST, SLOC, 93453	614 - F3
SANTA MARIA	420 S BROADWAY, SMRA, 93454	796 - H1
SHELL BEACH	230 LEEWARD AV, PBCH, 93449	693 - H7
SOLVANG	1745 MISSION DR, SLVG, 93463	940 - F1
SOUTH BAY	2075 PALISADES AV, SLOC, 93402	631 - G6
SOUTH COUNTY	800 W BRANCH ST, ARGD, 93420	714 - H5
VANDENBERG VILLAGE	3755 CONSTELLATION RD, StBC, 93436	876 - D7

MILITARY INSTALLATIONS

FEATURE NAME	Address City, ZIP Code	PAGE-GRID
CAMP ROBERTS MILITARY RES	SLOC, 93451	471 - H2
CAMP SAN LUIS OBISPO MIL RES	CABRILLO HWY, SLOC, 93405	633 - C3
VANDENBERG AIR FORCE BASE	HWY 1, StBC, 93429	855 - D3

MUSEUMS

FEATURE NAME	Address City, ZIP Code	PAGE-GRID
CONTEMPORARY ARTS FORUM	653 PASEO NUEVO, SBAR, 93101	996 - A4
HANS CHRISTIAN ANDERSEN MUS	1680 MISSION DR, SLVG, 93463	940 - E1
KARPELES MANUSCRIPT	21 W ANAMAPU ST, SBAR, 93101	995 - J4
LOMPOC MUS	200 H ST, LMPC, 93436	916 - E2
MUS OF NATURAL HIST	STATE PARK RD, MOBY, 93442	631 - G2
SAN LUIS OBISPO ART CTR	1010 BROAD ST, SLO, 93401	653 - J4
SAN LUIS OBISPO CHILDRENS MUS	1010 NIPOMO ST, SLO, 93401	653 - J4
SANTA BARBARA HIST SOC MUS	136 E DE LA GUERRA ST, SBAR, 93101	996 - B3
SANTA BARBARA MUS OF ART	1130 STATE ST, SBAR, 93101	996 - A3
SANTA BARBARA MUS OF NAT HIST	2559 PUESTA DEL SOL RD, SBAR, 93105	995 - J1
SEA CTR MARINE MUS	211 STEARNS WHARF, SBAR, 93101	996 - C5
SAN LUIS OBISPO CO HIST MUS	696 MONTEREY ST, SLO, 93401	653 - J4
SOUTH COAST RAILROAD MUS	300 LOS CARNEROS RD, StBC, 93117	994 - B1

OPEN SPACE PRESERVES

FEATURE NAME	Address City, ZIP Code	PAGE-GRID
ANDRE CLARK BIRD REFUGE	1400 E CABRILLO BLVD, SBAR, 93103	996 - F4
BELLA VISTA OPEN SPACE	ALPINE DR & PADOVA DR, StBC, 93117	993 - G1
BISHOP PEAK NATURAL AREA	FOOTHILL BLVD & OCONNOR WY, SLOC, 93405	653 - E1
CARPINTERIA BLUFFS PUB OPEN SPACE	CARPINTERIA AV & BAILARD AV, CARP, 93013	1018 - F1
CARPINTERIA SALT MARSH RES	SANDYLAND COVE RD & AV DEL MAR, StBC, 93013	998 - B6
DOUGLAS FAMILY PRESERVE	2981 CLIFF DR, SBAR, 93109	995 - E6
DUNE RESTORATION AREA	CABRILLO PK, MOBY, 93442	611 - E3
ELFIN FOREST ECOLOGICAL PRESERVE	SOUTH BAY BLVD, SLOC, 93402	631 - H3
EMERALD TERRACE OPEN SPACE	BERKELEY RD & ARUNDEL RD, StBC, 93117	984 - E7
EVERGREEN OPEN SPACE	CATHEDRAL OAKS RD & BRANDON DR, StBC, 93117	993 - F1
FERRINI RANCH OPEN SPACE	CABRILLO HWY & STENNER CK RD, SLO, 93405	633 - F7
ISLAY HILL OPEN SPACE	ORCUTT RD, SLO, 93401	674 - E2
KELLOGG OPEN SPACE	KELLOGG AV & CATHEDRAL OAKS RD, StBC, 93111	984 - F6
LET IT BE NATURE PRESERVE	LOS OSOS VALLEY RD & DIABLO DR, SLO, 93405	653 - E5
LOS OSOS OAKS STATE RESERVE	LOS OSOS VALLEY RD, SLOC, 93402	652 - A1
MAINO, CHARLES A & MAY R OPEN SPACE	EL CAMINO REAL & MARSH ST, SLO, 93405	653 - H4
MONARCH GROVE NATURAL AREA	SEA WIND WY & PECHO VALLEY RD, SLOC, 93402	631 - E7
MORRO ROCK NATURAL PRESERVE	COLEMAN DR, MOBY, 93442	611 - D5
NORTH POINT NATURAL AREA	CABRILLO HWY, MOBY, 93442	591 - D7
RESERVOIR CYN OPEN SPACE	RESERVOIR CANYON RD, SLOC, 93401	654 - D3
SAN MIGUEL OPEN SPACE	WINCHESTER CANYON RD, StBC, 93117	993 - E1
SOUTH HILLS OPEN SPACE	EXPOSITION DR & WOODBRIDGE ST, SLO, 93401	653 - J6
STONEBROOK OPEN SPACE	CALIFORNIA BLVD & OLD MILL LN, StBC, 93455	816 - G4
STOW CANYON OPEN SPACE	STOW CANYON RD & CARLO DR, StBC, 93117	984 - C7
SWEET SPRINGS NATURE RES	RAMONA AV & BRODERSON AV, SLOC, 93402	631 - G5
THE CLOISTERS OPEN SPACE	CABRILLO PK, MOBY, 93442	611 - E3
UNIV CIRCLE OPEN SPACE	MERIDA DR, StBC, 93111	984 - F7
WINCHESTER OPEN SPACE	WINCHESTER CANYON RD & CALLE R, StBC, 93117	993 - F2

PARK & RIDE

FEATURE NAME	Address City, ZIP Code	PAGE-GRID
ARROYO GRANDE 101	HWY 101 & N HALCYON RD, ARGD, 93420	714 - H5
ATASCADERO 101	CURBARIL AV & SAN LUIS AV, ATAS, 93422	574 - A5
ATASCADERO 101	SANTA BARBARA & SAN ANTONIO RD, ATAS, 93422	594 - C3
ATASCADERO 101	SANTA YSABEL AV & CAPISTRANO A, ATAS, 93422	573 - J4
AVILA 101	AVILA BEACH & SHELL BEACH, SLOC, 93424	693 - E4
LOS OSOS	LOS OSOS VALLEY RD, SLOC, 93402	631 - H7
NIPOMO 101	HILL ST & S FRONTAGE RD, Npmo, 93444	756 - B3
ORCUTT 101	CLARK AV & HWY 101, StBC, 93455	817 - C6
ORCUTT 135	CLARK AV & ORCUTT EXWY, StBC, 93455	816 - H6
ORCUTT 135	CLARK AV & ORCUTT RD, StBC, 93455	816 - H5
PARK & RIDE	7TH ST & OCEAN AV, LMPC, 93436	916 - G2
PARK & RIDE	NIBLICK RD & S RIVER RD, PSRS, 93446	513 - G7
PARK & RIDE	SANTA YSABEL AV & S BAY BLVD, SLOC, 93402	631 - J4
PASO ROBLES	10TH ST AND PINE ST, PSRS, 93446	513 - G6
PISMO BEACH	FIVE CITIES DR, PBCH, 93449	714 - D3
SANTA YNEZ 154	HWY 246 & HWY 154, StBC, 93460	921 - E6

PARKS & RECREATION

FEATURE NAME	PAGE-GRID
16TH STREET PK, GBCH	714 - F6
ADAM PK, SMRA	796 - G3
ADAMS, SPENCER PK, SBAR	996 - A3
ALAMEDA PK, SBAR	996 - A3
ALISAL COMMONS PK, SLVG	940 - E1
AMBASSADOR PK, SBAR	996 - B5
ARMSTRONG PK, SMRA	776 - J7
ATASCADERO LAKE PK, ATAS	573 - J6
ATKINSON PK, SMRA	776 - G6
BAYSHORE BLUFFS PK, MOBY	631 - F1
BEATTIE PK, LMPC	916 - G3
BETHEL ROAD PK, SLOC	553 - B1
BIDDLE COUNTY PK, SLOC	695 - H4
BOHNETT PK, SBAR	995 - J4
BOOSINGER PK, PBCH	714 - C1
BUELLTON PK, BLTN	919 - H4
BUENA VISTA PK, SMRA	796 - G1
CABRILLO BALL PK, SBAR	996 - D4
CENTENNIAL PK, PSRS	513 - J6
CENTRAL PLAZA PK, SMRA	776 - H7
CHANNEL IS NATL PK, StBC	385 - E4
CHANNEL IS NATL PK, StBC	386 - B6
CHASE PALM PK, SBAR	996 - C5
CITY PK, PSRS	513 - F5
CLOISTERS COMM PK, MOBY	611 - E3
COLEMAN PK, MOBY	611 - E5
COLLEGE PK REC AREA, LMPC	896 - E7
COMMUNITY PK, GDLP	774 - H6
COSTA BELLA PK, GBCH	714 - F6
CUESTA COUNTY PK, SLOC	654 - B2
DEL MAR PK, MOBY	611 - E2
EAST SIDE NEIGHBRHD PK, SBAR	996 - D3
EL CAMINO REAL PK, ARGD	714 - H4
EL CARRO PK, CARP	998 - E6
EL CHORRO REGL PK, SLOC	633 - B3
ELM STREET PK, ARGD	714 - G6
EMERSON PK, SLO	653 - J5
ESCONDIDO PK, SBAR	995 - G5
FERINI PK, StBC	878 - G1
FRANCESCHI PK, SBAR	996 - B1
FRANKLIN PK, CARP	998 - D6
FRENCH PK, SLO	674 - C2
GAVIOTA STATE PK, StBC	365 - G6
GOULD PK (UNDEV), StBC	986 - G4
GROGAN PK, SMRA	776 - F4
GROVER HEIGHTS PK, GBCH	714 - E4
HAGERMAN COMPLEX, StBC	816 - G1
HALE PK (UNDEVELOPED), SBAR	996 - F2
H CHRISTIAN ANDRSN PK, SLVG	940 - D1
HARDIE PK, SLOC	590 - J1
HARRINGTON, MARY PK, PBCH	714 - C3
HART-COLLETT VFM PK, ARGD	715 - A5
HEATH RNCH PK & ADOBE, CARP	998 - D5
HEILMANN REGL PK, ATAS	574 - B5
HIDDEN VALLEY PK, SBAR	995 - E3
HILDA RAY PK, SBAR	995 - H5
HONDA VLY PK (UNDEV), SBAR	995 - H5
HOOSGOW PK, ARGD	715 - A4
INGRAM PK, StBC	916 - G1
ISLAY PK, SLO	674 - D1
JOE WHITE PK, SMRA	797 - A1
JOHNS-MANVILLE PK, LMPC	916 - F1
JOHNSON PK, SLO	654 - B6
KECK PK MEM GARDEN, SBAR	996 - A2
KEISER PK, MOBY	611 - E4
LA CORONILLA PK (UNDV), SBAR	995 - H6
LAGUNA HILLS PK, SLO	653 - E6
LAGUNA LAKE PK, SLO	653 - F5
LAKE CACHUMA REC AREA, StBC	922 - H7
LA MESA PK, SBAR	995 - H7
LA MESA VILLAGE PK, ARGD	714 - J7
LAMPTON CLIFFS CO PK, Cmbr	548 - F3
LAS POSITAS PK, StBC	995 - F5
LAUREL CYN PK (UNDEV), SBAR	995 - G6
LAWRENCE MOORE PK, PSRS	533 - G1
LEASE, IRA PK, PBCH	714 - C3
LENCO PK, PSRS	513 - H7
LEROY PK, GDLP	775 - A4
LIONS PK, StBC	998 - G6
LOPEZ LAKE REC AREA, SLOC	695 - H1
LOS ALAMOS PK, StBC	878 - G2
LOS CARNEROS CO PK, StBC	984 - B7
LOS OSOS COMM PK, SLOC	631 - H6
LOS PADRES NATL FOR, SLOC	572 - C6
LOS ROBLES PK, SBAR	985 - D7
MACKENZIE PK, SBAR	995 - F1
MANNING PK, StBC	996 - J2
MARAMONTE PK (NORTH), SMRA	796 - H6
MARAMONTE PK (SOUTH), SMRA	796 - H7
MEADOW PK, SLO	654 - A6
MELODY PK, PSRS	513 - J7
MEMORIAL PK, SMRA	776 - G7
MEMORIAL PK, CARP	998 - C6
MENTONE BASIN PK, GBCH	714 - F6
MIGUELITO COUNTY PK, StBC	916 - D7
MINAMI PK, SMRA	796 - G3
MISSION PK, SBAR	995 - J1
MITCHELL PK, SLO	654 - A4
MONTANA DE ORO ST PK, SLOC	631 - D4
MONTE VISTA PK, StBC	998 - G7
MONTE YOUNG PK, MOBY	611 - F7
MORRO BAY PK, MOBY	611 - G6
MORRO BAY STATE PK, MOBY	611 - H7
MURPHY, DWIGHT FIELD, SBAR	996 - E4
NIPOMO COMM PK, Npmo	755 - J3
NOJOQUI FALLS CO PK, StBC	365 - J6
OAK CREEK PK, PSRS	534 - A1
OAKLEY PK, SMRA	776 - F6
OAK PK, SBAR	995 - G2
OCEANO COUNTY PK, SLOC	714 - D7
OCEANO DUNES ST VEH REC AREA, SLOC	754 - E2
OCEANO MEM PK, SLOC	714 - D7
OCEAN PK, PBCH	693 - G7
ORPET PK, SBAR	996 - A1
ORTEGA PK, SBAR	996 - B3
PALISADES BLF WKWY, PBCH	693 - E5
PALISADES PK, PBCH	693 - E5
PALOMA CREEK PK, ATAS	594 - D1
PARADISE PK, StBC	964 - F1
PARMA PK (UNDEV), SBAR	986 - D7
PAUL ANDREW PK, SLOC	591 - A2
PERSHING PK, SBAR	996 - B5
PILGRIM TERRACE PK, SBAR	995 - G3
PIONEER PK, LMPC	896 - G7
PIONEER PK, SMRA	816 - F3
PIONEER PK, PSRS	513 - G4
PLAZA DEL MAR PK, SBAR	996 - B5
PLAZA VERA CRUZ, SBAR	996 - B4
PREISKER PK, SMRA	776 - G3
PRIOLO MARTIN PK, SLO	653 - E6
RAMONA GARDEN PK, GBCH	714 - E5
RATTLESNAKE CANYON PK, StBC	986 - C3
RICE PK, SMRA	776 - J6
RICHARDSON COUNTY PK, StBC	806 - C2
RINCON BEACH PK, StBC	1018 - H2
RIVERBEND PK, StBC	896 - F5
RIVER PK, StBC	896 - G7
ROBINS FIELD, PSRS	513 - F6
ROCKY NOOK PK, StBC	985 - J7
ROYAL OAK MEADOWS PK, PSRS	534 - C1
RUSSELL PK, SMRA	776 - F7
RYON PK, LMPC	916 - D2
SALT MARSH NATURE PK, CARP	998 - C7
SAN MIGUEL PK, SLOC	473 - F2
SAN ROQUE PK, SBAR	985 - F7
SAN SIMEON ST BCH, Cmbr	528 - C2
SANTA BARBARA BOT GRDNS, StBC	985 - J6
SANTA MARGARITA COM PK, SLOC	614 - G2
SANTA ROSA PK, SLO	653 - J3
SANTA YNEZ PK, StBC	921 - B5
SEACLIFF PK, PBCH	693 - F7
SHAMEL PK, Cmbr	528 - D6
SHERWOOD PK, PSRS	534 - A1
SHORELINE PK, SBAR	996 - A7
SIMAS PK, SMRA	796 - H1
SINSHEIMER PK, SLO	654 - B6
SKOFIELD PK, SBAR	986 - B6
SMITH PK, SLO	653 - F7
SOLVANG PK, SLVG	940 - E1
SOTO SPORTS COMPLEX, ARGD	714 - G6
SPYGLASS PK, PBCH	693 - F7
STANLEY, MARILYN PK, SMRA	796 - G6
STEVENS PK, SBAR	985 - F6
STOW GROVE PK, StBC	984 - C7
STROTHER PK, ARGD	715 - C4
SUNFLOWER PK, SBAR	996 - D3
TAR PITS PK, CARP	1018 - E1
TEMPLETON PK, SLOC	553 - D2
TERRA DE ORO PK, ARGD	715 - B3
THOMPSON PK, LMPC	896 - C7
THORNBURY PK (UNDEV), SBAR	995 - J5
THREFTS, ALICE PK, SMRA	796 - J2
THROOP PK, SLO	653 - H2
TIDELANDS PK, MOBY	611 - F7
TORO CANYON PK, StBC	997 - J2
TRAFFIC WAY PK, ATAS	573 - J2
TRIANGLE PK, SLO	654 - A4
TUCKERS GROVE PK, StBC	984 - J6
TUNNELL PK, SMRA	777 - A6
TURTLE CREEK PK, PSRS	514 - B7

COPYRIGHT 2000 Thomas Bros. Maps ®

FEATURE NAME Address City, ZIP Code	PAGE-GRID
VILLAGE GREEN PK, ARGD	715 - A5
WALLER PK, StBC	796 - G7
WENTWORTH PK, SBAR	996 - A5
WESTVALE PK, LMPC	916 - C2
WILLOWGLEN PK, SBAR	985 - E7
WINDOW TO THE SEA PK, StBC	994 - A5

PERFORMING ARTS

FEATURE NAME Address City, ZIP Code	PAGE-GRID
ARLINGTON THEATRE 1317 STATE ST, SBAR, 93101	996 - A3
GRANADA THEATER 1216 STATE ST, SBAR, 93101	996 - A3
LOBERO THEATER 33 CANON PERDIDO ST, SBAR, 93101	996 - A4
PERFORMING ARTS CTR TAHOE RD & GRAND AV, SLOC, 93405	654 - A2
SANTA BARBARA COUNTY BOWL 1122 MILPAS ST, SBAR, 93103	996 - B2

POINTS OF INTEREST

FEATURE NAME Address City, ZIP Code	PAGE-GRID
BOY SCOUT COUNTY HQ 4000 MODOC RD, StBC, 93110	995 - D2
BRAILLE INSTITUTE 2031 DE LA VINA ST, SBAR, 93105	995 - H2
CHARLES PADDOCK ZOO LAGO AV & MORRO RD, ATAS, 93422	573 - H6
MORETON BAY FIG TREE CHAPALA ST & MONTECITO ST, SBAR, 93101	996 - B5
MOUNT CALVARY MONASTERY GIBRALTAR RD, StBC, 93105	986 - C5
SANTA BARBARA POLO FIELD 3375 FOOTHILL RD, StBC, 93013	997 - H4
SANTA BARBARA ZOOLOGICAL-GARDENS 500 NINOS DR, SBAR, 93103	996 - E4

POINTS OF INTEREST - HISTORIC

FEATURE NAME Address City, ZIP Code	PAGE-GRID
CASA DE LA GUERRA 15 E DE LA GUERRA ST, SBAR, 93101	996 - A4
CHUMASH PAINTED CAVE STATE HIST PK PAINTED CAVE RD, StBC, 93105	964 - J6
COLD SPRINGS TAVERN 5995 STAGECOACH RD, StBC, 93105	964 - C4
DE LA GUERRA PLAZA DE LA GUERRA ST, SBAR, 93101	996 - B4
EL PRESIDIO DE STB ST HIST PK 123 CANON PERDIDO ST, SBAR, 93101	996 - A3
FERNALD HSE & TRUSSELL-WINCHSTER ADOBE 414 MONTECITO ST, SBAR, 93101	996 - A5
LA PURISIMA MISSION LOMPOC-CASMALIA RD, StBC, 93436	896 - J4
LA PURISIMA MISN ST HIST PK PURISIMA RD & RUCKER RD, StBC, 93436	896 - H3
MISSION SAN LUIS OBISPO DE-TOLOSA CHORRO ST & MONTEREY ST, SLO, 93401	653 - J4
MISSION SAN MIGUEL ARCANGEL 700 MISSION ST, SLOC, 93451	473 - F3
MISSION SANTA BARBARA LAGUNA ST, SBAR, 93105	995 - H1
RIOS CALEDONIA ADOBE MONTEREY RD, SLOC, 93451	473 - F4
SANTA INES MISSION 1760 MISSION DR, SLVG, 93463	940 - F1

REGIONAL SHOPPING

FEATURE NAME Address City, ZIP Code	PAGE-GRID
BROADWAY PLAZA 1450 S BROADWAY, SMRA, 93454	796 - H3
CENTRAL COAST MALL 321 MADONNA RD, SLO, 93405	653 - G7
LA CUMBRE PLAZA 140 S HOPE AV, SBAR, 93105	995 - E1
MADONNA PLAZA 221 MADONNA RD, SLO, 93405	653 - H6
PASEO NUEVO 651 PASEO NUEVO, SBAR, 93101	996 - A4
SANTA MARIA CTR 1425 S BROADWAY, SMRA, 93458	796 - G3
SANTA MARIA TOWN CTR EAST S BROADWAY & COOK ST, SMRA, 93454	776 - H7
SANTA MARIA TOWN CTR WEST S BROADWAY & COOK ST, SMRA, 93458	776 - G7

SCHOOLS - PRIVATE ELEMENTARY

FEATURE NAME Address City, ZIP Code	PAGE-GRID
ADVANCED CHRISTIAN TRAINING-SCHOOL 1030 VINE ST, PSRS, 93446	513 - F6
CHRISTIAN LIFE 709 CURRYER ST, SMRA, 93458	776 - G6
COASTAL CHRISTIAN 1220 FARROLL AV, ARGD, 93420	714 - G6
CRANE 1795 SAN LEANDRO LN, StBC, 93108	997 - A3
DEVEREUX CALIFORNIA STORKE RD & EL COLEGIO RD, StBC, 93117	993 - H5
LAGUNA BLANCA 4125 PALOMA DR, StBC, 93110	995 - C4
LA PURISIMA 219 OLIVE AV, LMPC, 93436	916 - E2
LAUREATE SCHOOL 880 LAUREATE LN, SLOC, 93405	653 - D3
MARYMOUNT 2130 MISSION RIDGE RD, SBAR, 93103	995 - J1
MONTESSORI CTR 3970 LA COLINA RD, SBAR, 93110	985 - D7
NORTH COUNTY CHRISTIAN 6225 ATASCADERO MALL, ATAS, 93422	573 - J4
NOTRE DAME SCHOOL 33 E MICHELTORENA ST, SBAR, 93101	995 - J3
OLD MISSION 761 BROAD ST, SLO, 93401	653 - J4
OUR LADY OF MT CARMEL 530 HOT SPRINGS RD, StBC, 93108	996 - H1
PACIFIC CHRISTIAN 3435 SANTA MARIA WY, StBC, 93455	816 - J1
SAINT LOUIS DE MONTFORT 5095 HARP RD, StBC, 93455	817 - A6
SAINT MARY OF THE ASSUMPTION 424 E CYPRESS ST, SMRA, 93454	796 - H1
SAINT PATRICK 900 W BRANCH ST, ARGD, 93420	714 - H4
SAINT RAPHAEL 160 SAINT JOSEPHS ST, StBC, 93111	994 - F1
SAINT ROSE SCHOOL 900 TUCKER AV, PSRS, 93446	513 - H6
SAN ROQUE 3214 CL CEDRO, SBAR, 93105	985 - G7
SANTA BARBARA CHRISTIAN SCH 4200 CL REAL, StBC, 93110	995 - C1
SANTA YNEZ VALLEY CHRISTIAN-ACADEMY 891 REFUGIO RD, StBC, 93463	921 - A6
TRINITY LUTHERAN 940 CRESTON RD, PSRS, 93446	513 - J6
VALLEY CHRISTIAN ACADEMY 2970 SANTA MARIA WY, SMRA, 93455	796 - H7
VALLEY VIEW ACADEMY 230 VERNON ST, ARGD, 93420	714 - J5
WALDORF SCHOOL OF SANTA - BARBARA 2300-B GARDEN ST, SBAR, 93105	995 - J1

SCHOOLS - PRIVATE HIGH

FEATURE NAME Address City, ZIP Code	PAGE-GRID
ADVANCED CHRISTIAN TRAINING 1030 VINE ST, PSRS, 93446	513 - F5
BISHOP GARCIA DIEGO 4000 LA COLINA RD, SBAR, 93110	985 - D7
CATE 1960 CATE MESA RD, StBC, 93013	998 - J6
COASTAL CHRISTIAN 1220 FARROLL AV, ARGD, 93420	714 - G6
DUNN COLLEGE PREP 2555 HWY 154, StBC, 93460	900 - J6
LAGUNA BLANCA 4125 PALOMA DR, StBC, 93110	995 - C4
MISSION COLLEGE PREP 682 PALM ST, SLO, 93401	653 - J4
NORTH COUNTY CHRISTIAN 6225 ATASCADERO MALL, ATAS, 93422	573 - J4
SAINT JOSEPH 4120 BRADLEY RD, StBC, 93455	817 - A3
VALLEY CHRISTIAN ACADEMY 2970 SANTA MARIA WY, SMRA, 93455	796 - H7

SCHOOLS - PRIVATE JUNIOR HIGH

FEATURE NAME Address City, ZIP Code	PAGE-GRID
MARYMOUNT 2130 MISSION RIDGE RD, SBAR, 93103	995 - J1
VALLEY CHRISTIAN ACADEMY 2970 SANTA MARIA WY, SMRA, 93455	796 - H7

SCHOOLS - PRIVATE MIDDLE

FEATURE NAME Address City, ZIP Code	PAGE-GRID
CRANE SCHOOL 1795 SAN LEANDRO LN, StBC, 93108	997 - A3
NOTRE DAME SCHOOL 33 E MICHELTORENA ST, SBAR, 93101	995 - J3
OLD MISSION SCHOOL 761 BROAD ST, SLO, 93401	653 - J4
SAINT MARY OF THE ASSUMPTION 424 E CYPRESS ST, SMRA, 93454	796 - H1
SANTA BARBARA 2300-A GARDEN ST, SBAR, 93105	995 - J1
SANTA BARBARA CHRISTIAN SCH 5020 SAN SIMEON DR, StBC, 93111	994 - H1
SANTA YNEZ VALLEY CHRISTIAN-ACADEMY 891 REFUGIO RD, StBC, 93463	921 - A6
WALDORF SCHOOL OF SANTA - BARBARA 2300-B GARDEN ST, SBAR, 93105	995 - J1

SCHOOLS - PUBLIC ELEMENTARY

FEATURE NAME Address City, ZIP Code	PAGE-GRID
ADAM 500 WINDSOR ST, SMRA, 93458	796 - G3
ADAMS 2701 LAS POSITAS RD, SBAR, 93105	995 - F2
ALISO 4545 CARPINTERIA AV, CARP, 93013	998 - C6
ALVIN 301 ALVIN AV, SMRA, 93454	776 - H6
ARELLANES 1890 SANDALWOOD DR, StBC, 93455	816 - B1
BALLARD 2425 SCHOOL ST, StBC, 93463	920 - H2
BATTLES, GEORGE W 605 BATTLES RD, SMRA, 93454	796 - H3
BAUER-SPECK 401 17TH ST, PSRS, 93446	513 - F4
BAYWOOD 1330 9TH ST, SLOC, 93402	631 - H4
BELLEVUE-SANTA FE 1401 SAN LUIS BAY DR, SLOC, 93405	693 - C2
BISHOPS PEAK 451 JAYCEE DR, SLO, 93405	653 - G2
BONITA 2715 W MAIN ST, StBC, 93458	775 - H6
BRANCH 970 SCHOOL RD, SLOC, 93420	715 - F2
BRANDON SCHOOL 195 BRANDON DR, StBC, 93117	993 - F2
BROWN, GEORGIA 525 36TH ST, PSRS, 93446	513 - F2
BRUCE 601 W ALVIN AV, SMRA, 93458	776 - G6
BUENA VISTA 100 ALDEBARAN AV, StBC, 93436	876 - D6
BUREN, MARY 1050 PERALTA ST, GDLP, 93434	775 - A5
BUTLER, PAT 700 NICKLAUS ST, PSRS, 93446	513 - H7
CAMBRIA 1350 MAIN ST, Cmbr, 93428	528 - F7
CANALINO 1480 N LINDEN AV, CARP, 93013	998 - D6
CAYUCOS 301 CAYUCOS DR, SLOC, 93430	590 - J1
CLEVELAND 123 ALAMEDA PADRE SERRA, SBAR, 93103	996 - D2
COLD SPRING 2243 SYCAMORE CANYON RD, StBC, 93108	996 - F1
COLLEGE 3525 PINE ST, StBC, 93460	921 - C5
CRESTVIEW UTAH AV, StBC, 93437	855 - F6
CUYAMA MORALES ST & HUBBARD AV, StBC, 93254	806 - C1
DANA 920 W TEFFT ST, Npmo, 93444	756 - A4
DEL MAR 501 SEQUOIA ST, MOBY, 93442	611 - E2
DUNLAP, RALPH 1220 OAK KNOLL RD, StBC, 93455	817 - A5
EL CAMINO 5020 SAN SIMEON DR, StBC, 93111	994 - H1
ELLWOOD 7686 HOLLISTER AV, StBC, 93117	993 - F2
EL RANCHO 7421 MIRANO DR, StBC, 93117	993 - G1
FAIRLAWN 120 MARY DR, SMRA, 93458	776 - F7
FILLMORE, LEONORA 1211 E PINE AV, LMPC, 93436	896 - F7
FOOTHILL 711 RIBERA RD, StBC, 93111	984 - H7
FRANKLIN 1111 MASON ST, SBAR, 93103	996 - D3
GRISHAM, MAY 610 PINAL AV, StBC, 93455	816 - G6
GROVER BEACH 356 S 10TH ST, GBCH, 93433	714 - E5
GROVER HEIGHTS 770 N 8TH ST, GBCH, 93433	714 - E4
HAPGOOD, ARTHUR 324 A ST, LMPC, 93436	916 - F2
HARDING 1625 ROBBINS ST, SBAR, 93101	995 - H4
HARLOE 901 FAIR OAKS AV, ARGD, 93420	714 - H6
HAWTHORNE 2125 STORY ST, SLO, 93401	654 - A5
HOLLISTER 4950 ANITA LN, StBC, 93111	994 - J2
ISLA VISTA 6875 EL COLEGIO RD, StBC, 93117	993 - J4
JONATA 301 2ND ST, BLTN, 93427	919 - G4
KELLOGG 475 CAMBRIDGE DR, StBC, 93117	984 - E7
LA CANADA 620 W NORTH AV, LMPC, 93436	896 - D6
LA HONDA 1213 N A ST, LMPC, 93436	896 - F6
LA PATERA 555 LA PATERA LN, StBC, 93117	984 - B7
LARSEN, LILLIAN 1601 L ST, SLOC, 93451	473 - F1
LOS BERROS 3745 VIA LATO, StBC, 93436	896 - H1
LOS OLIVOS 2540 ALAMO PINTADO AV, StBC, 93441	900 - H5
LOS PADRES MOUNTAIN VIEW BLVD, StBC, 93437	855 - H7
LOS RANCHOS 5785 LOS RANCHOS DR, SLOC, 93401	674 - E5
MAIN 5241 8TH ST, CARP, 93013	998 - D7
MCKINLEY 350 LOMA ALTA DR, SBAR, 93101	996 - A5
MIGUELITO 1600 OLIVE AV, LMPC, 93436	916 - C2
MILLER 410 CM COLEGIO, SMRA, 93454	796 - H2
MONARCH GROVE 348 LOS OSOS VALLEY RD, SLOC, 93402	631 - F6
MONROE 431 FLORA VISTA DR, SBAR, 93109	995 - G6
MONTECITO 385 SAN YSIDRO RD, StBC, 93108	996 - J2
MONTEREY ROAD 3355 MONTEREY RD, ATAS, 93422	573 - F2
MONTESSORI SCH MONTEREY RD & GRAVES CREEK RD, ATAS, 93422	573 - F2
MONTE VISTA 730 N HOPE AV, SBAR, 93105	985 - E7
MORRO 1130 NAPA AV, MOBY, 93442	611 - F6
MTN VIEW 5465 QUEEN ANN LN, StBC, 93111	984 - F6
NIGHTINGALE, JOE 255 WINTER RD, StBC, 93455	816 - H1
NIPOMO 190 E PRICE ST, Npmo, 93444	756 - D2
NORTH OCEANO 2101 THE PIKE, GBCH, 93433	714 - G7
OAKLEY 1120 HARDING AV, SMRA, 93458	776 - F6
OCEANO 520 17TH ST, SLOC, 93445	714 - F7
OCEAN VIEW 1208 LINDA DR, ARGD, 93420	714 - G5
ONTIVEROS 930 RANCHO VERDE, SMRA, 93458	776 - F4
OPEN ALTERNATIVE SCHOOL 4025 FOOTHILL RD, SBAR, 93110	985 - D7
PACHECO 165 GRAND AV, SLO, 93405	654 - A2
PATTERSON RD 400 PATTERSON RD, StBC, 93455	816 - H5
PEABODY 3018 CL NOGUERA, SBAR, 93105	995 - G1
PETERSON, VIRGINIA 2501 BEECHWOOD DR, PSRS, 93446	534 - A2
PIFER, WINIFRED 1350 CRESTON RD, PSRS, 93446	514 - A6
PINE GROVE 1050 RICE RANCH RD, StBC, 93455	817 - A7
PLEASANT VALLEY 7000 RANCHITA CANYON RD, SLOC, 93451	494 - F1
REED, OLGA 480 CENTENNIAL ST, StBC, 93440	878 - G2
RICE 700 VICKIE AV, SMRA, 93454	776 - J5
ROOSEVELT 1990 LAGUNA ST, SBAR, 93103	995 - J1
RUTH, CLARENCE 501 W ST, LMPC, 93436	916 - C1
SAN BENITO 4300 SAN BENITO RD, ATAS, 93422	553 - G7
SAN GABRIEL 8500 SAN GABRIEL RD, ATAS, 93422	593 - J1
SANTA MARGARITA 21900 H ST, SLOC, 93422	614 - G2
SANTA ROSA 8655 SANTA ROSA RD, ATAS, 93422	574 - A7
SANTA YNEZ 3325 PINE ST, StBC, 93460	921 - B5
SHAW, ALICE 759 DAHLIA PL, StBC, 93455	816 - J2
SHELL BEACH 2100 SHELL BEACH RD, PBCH, 93449	693 - G7
SINSHEIMER 2755 AUGUSTA ST, SLO, 93401	654 - B6
SMITH, C L 1375 BALBOA ST, SLO, 93405	653 - F6
SOLVANG 565 ATTERDAG RD, SLVG, 93463	920 - E7
SUMMERLAND SCHOOL 135 VALENCIA RD, Summ, 93067	997 - D4
SUNNYSIDE 880 MANZANITA DR, SLOC, 93402	631 - H7
TEACH, CHARLES 375 FERRINI RD, SLO, 93405	653 - H2
TEMPLETON 215 8TH ST, SLOC, 93465	553 - D2
TUNNELL 1248 E DENA WY, SMRA, 93454	777 - A6
VIEJA VALLEY 434 NOGAL DR, StBC, 93110	995 - B2
VINEYARD 2121 VINEYARD DR, SLOC, 93465	553 - C3
WASHINGTON 290 LIGHTHOUSE RD, SBAR, 93109	995 - H7

SCHOOLS - PUBLIC HIGH

FEATURE NAME Address City, ZIP Code	PAGE-GRID
ARROYO GRANDE 495 VALLEY RD, ARGD, 93420	714 - J6
ATASCADERO 1 HIGH SCHOOL HILL RD, ATAS, 93422	573 - H4
CABRILLO 4350 CONSTELLATION RD, StBC, 93436	876 - C6
CARPINTERIA 4810 FOOTHILL RD, CARP, 93013	998 - D5
COAST UNION 2950 SANTA ROSA CREEK RD, Cmbr, 93428	528 - J6
CUYAMA VALLEY HWY 166, StBC, 93254	806 - D1
DELTA 251 CLARK AV, StBC, 93455	816 - H6
DOS PUEBLOS 7266 ALAMEDA AV, StBC, 93117	993 - H1
LA CUESTA 905 NOPAL ST, SBAR, 93103	996 - B2
LOMPOC 515 W COLLEGE AV, LMPC, 93436	896 - D7
LOPEZ 227 BRIDGE ST, ARGD, 93420	715 - A5
MAPLE CAROB ST, StBC, 93437	875 - J1
MORRO BAY 235 ATASCADERO RD, MOBY, 93442	611 - E4
OAK HILLS CONTINUATION SCH 4507 DEL RIO RD, ATAS, 93422	553 - G7
PASO ROBLES 801 NIBLICK RD, PSRS, 93446	513 - J6
RIGHETTI, ERNEST 941 FOSTER RD, StBC, 93455	816 - J3
SAN LUIS OBISPO 1350 CALIFORNIA BLVD, SLO, 93401	654 - B3
SAN MARCOS 4750 HOLLISTER AV, StBC, 93110	994 - J1
SANTA BARBARA 700 ANAPAMU ST, SBAR, 93103	996 - B2
SANTA MARIA 901 S BROADWAY, SMRA, 93458	796 - G2
SANTA YNEZ VALLEY 2975 E HWY 246, StBC, 93463	921 - A6
TEMPLETON 1200 MAIN ST, SLOC, 93422	553 - D3
WEST MALL ALTERNATIVE 6495 LEWIS AV, ATAS, 93422	573 - J3

SCHOOLS - PUBLIC JUNIOR HIGH

FEATURE NAME Address City, ZIP Code	PAGE-GRID
ATASCADERO 6501 LEWIS AV, ATAS, 93422	573 - J3
EL CAMINO 219 EL CAMINO ST, SMRA, 93458	776 - G6
FESLER, ISAAC 1100 E FESLER ST, SMRA, 93454	777 - A7
GOLETA VALLEY 6100 STOW CANYON RD, StBC, 93117	984 - D7
LA COLINA 4025 FOOTHILL RD, SBAR, 93110	985 - D7
LAKEVIEW 3700 ORCUTT RD, StBC, 93455	816 - H2
MCKENZIE, KERMIT 4710 W MAIN ST, StBC, 93434	775 - A7
ORCUTT RICE RANCH RD & DYER ST, StBC, 93455	816 - G6
SANTA BARBARA 721 COTA ST, SBAR, 93103	996 - C3

FEATURE NAME / Address City, ZIP Code	PAGE-GRID

SCHOOLS - PUBLIC MIDDLE

FEATURE NAME / Address City, ZIP Code	PAGE-GRID
CARPINTERIA 5351 CARPINTERIA AV, CARP, 93013	998 - D7
FLAMSON, GEORGE 655 24TH ST, PSRS, 93446	513 - F4
JUDKINS 680 WADSWORTH AV, PBCH, 93449	714 - C2
LA CUMBRE 2255 MODOC RD, SBAR, 93101	995 - G3
LAGUNA 11050 LOS OSOS VALLEY RD, SLO, 93405	653 - E6
LEWIS, DANIEL 900 CRESTON RD, PSRS, 93446	513 - J6
LOMPOC VALLEY 234 S N ST, LMPC, 93436	916 - D2
LOS OSOS 1555 EL MORO AV, SLOC, 93402	631 - J5
MESA 2555 HALCYON RD, SLOC, 93420	734 - J4
PAULDING 600 CROWN HILL ST, ARGD, 93420	715 - A4
SANTA LUCIA 2850 SCHOOLHOUSE LN, Cmbr, 93428	528 - H7
SOLVANG 565 ATTERDAG RD, SLVG, 93463	920 - E7
TEMPLETON 925 OLD COUNTY RD, SLOC, 93465	553 - D2
VANDENBERG MOUNTAIN VIEW BLVD, StBC, 93437	855 - G7

SHOPPING CENTERS - COMMUNITY

FEATURE NAME / Address City, ZIP Code	PAGE-GRID
ADOBE PLAZA 7305 EL CAMINO REAL, ATAS, 93422	573 - J4
ARROYO TOWN & COUNTRY SQ 1440 GRAND AV, ARGD, 93420	714 - G5
ATASCADERO FACTORY OUTLETS 2290 EL CAMINO REAL, ATAS, 93422	553 - F7
BROADWAY PAVILION S BROADWAY & MCCOY LN, SMRA, 93455	796 - H5
CALLE REAL CTR CALLE REAL & FAIRVIEW AV, StBC, 93117	994 - D1
CAMINO REAL MARKETPLACE SANTA FELICIA DR, StBC, 93117	993 - H3
CASITAS PLAZA CARPINTERIA AV, CARP, 93013	998 - E7
FAIRVIEW CTR FAIRVIEW AV & CALLE REAL, StBC, 93117	994 - D1
FIVE POINTS LA CUMBRE RD & STATE ST, SBAR, 93105	995 - D1
FLOWER VALLEY H ST & BARTON AV, LMPC, 93436	896 - E6
LA JOYA PLAZA W MAIN ST & BLOSSER RD, SMRA, 93458	776 - F7
LOMPOC CTR H ST & PINE AV, LMPC, 93436	896 - E7
LOMPOC NORTH CTR H ST & CENTRAL AV, LMPC, 93436	896 - E5
LOMPOC PLAZA H ST & PINE AV, LMPC, 93436	896 - E7
LORETO PLAZA STATE ST & LAS POSITAS RD, SBAR, 93105	995 - F1
LOS OSOS CTR 1130 LOS OSOS VALLEY RD, SLOC, 93402	631 - H6
LUCKY CTR EL CAMINO REAL & SOLANO RD, ATAS, 93422	574 - B6
MAGNOLIA CTR HOLLISTER AV & WALNUT LN, StBC, 93111	994 - G2
MESA CTR CLIFF DR & MEIGS RD, SBAR, 93109	995 - H6
MISSION PLAZA CENTRAL AV & O ST, LMPC, 93436	896 - D5
MONTECITO VILLAGE SAN YSIDRO RD & E VALLEY RD, StBC, 93108	996 - J1
NORTHSIDE CTR H ST & BARTON AV, LMPC, 93436	896 - E6
OAK KNOLL CTR CLARK AV & BRADLEY RD, StBC, 93455	817 - A6
OAK PK PLAZA 1590 W BRANCH ST, ARGD, 93420	714 - G4
PACIFIC COAST PLAZA JAMES WY & OAK PARK BLVD, PBCH, 93449	714 - F3
PISMO COAST PLAZA 555 FIVE CITIES DR, PBCH, 93449	714 - E3
PREMIUM OUTLET CTR 320 N ALISAL RD, SLVG, 93463	940 - E1
PRIME OUTLETS AT PISMO BEACH 333 FIVE CITIES DR, PBCH, 93449	714 - D3
SANTA MARIA PLAZA BETTERAVIA RD & MILLER ST, SMRA, 93455	796 - H5
SHEPARD PLACE SHOPPING CTR CASITAS PASS RD & CARPINTERIA, CARP, 93013	998 - E7
STOWELL CTR S BROADWAY & ENOS DR, SMRA, 93458	796 - G3

FEATURE NAME / Address City, ZIP Code	PAGE-GRID
TARGET CTR BETTERAVIA RD & S BROADWAY, SMRA, 93454	796 - H4
TURNPIKE CTR HOLLISTER AV & TURNPIKE RD, StBC, 93111	994 - J1
UNIVERSTIY PLAZA HOLLISTER AV & GLEN ANNIE RD, StBC, 93117	993 - J3
WESTERN VILLAGE CTR S BROADWAY & DAL PORTO LN, SMRA, 93458	796 - G4
WILLIAMS PLAZA 1191 CRESTON RD, PSRS, 93446	514 - A6
WOODLAND PLAZA S RIVER RD & NIBLICK RD, PSRS, 93446	513 - G7
WOODLAND PLAZA II S RIVER RD & NIBLICK RD, PSRS, 93446	513 - G7

TRANSPORTATION

FEATURE NAME / Address City, ZIP Code	PAGE-GRID
AMTRAK CARPINTERIA STA 475 LINDEN AV, CARP, 93013	998 - D7
AMTRAK GOLETA STA 25 LA PATERA LN, StBC, 93117	994 - C1
AMTRAK GROVER BEACH STA 180 GRAND AV, GBCH, 93433	714 - D5
AMTRAK RAIL STA 330 GUADALUPE ST, GDLP, 93434	775 - A6
AMTRAK SANTA BARBARA STA 209 STATE ST, SBAR, 93101	996 - B5
GREYHOUND TERMINAL 150 SOUTH ST, SLO, 93401	653 - H5
GREYHOUND TERMINAL 313A N BROADWAY, SMRA, 93454	776 - H7
GREYHOUND TERMINAL 34 CABRILLO ST, SBAR, 93101	996 - A4
GREYHOUND TERMINAL 5945 ENTRADA AV, ATAS, 93422	573 - J3
GREYHOUND TERMINAL 945 9TH RR, PSRS, 93446	513 - G6
SAN LUIS OBISPO AMTRAK STA 1011 RAILROAD AV, SLO, 93401	654 - A4

WINERIES

FEATURE NAME / Address City, ZIP Code	PAGE-GRID
ARCIERO HIGHWAY 46, SLOC, 93446	514 - H1
ARTHUR EARL 90 EASY ST, BLTN, 93427	919 - J4
BECKMEN VINEYARDS 2670 ONTIVEROS RD, StBC, 93460	900 - H7
BUTTONWOOD FARM 1500 ALAMO PINTADO RD, StBC, 93463	920 - H3
CASTORO CELLARS HWY 46 & BETHEL RD, SLOC, 93465	533 - C5
COTTONWOOD CANYON 4330 SANTA FE RD, SLOC, 93401	674 - A2
CRESTON VINEYARDS VINEYARD DR & HWY 101, SLOC, 93465	553 - C3
DOMAINE SANTA BARBARA HWY 154 & ROBLAR AV, StBC, 93460	901 - A7
DOVER CANYON HWY 46 & BETHEL RD, SLOC, 93446	533 - C5
EBERLE HIGHWAY 46, PSRS, 93446	514 - D2
EDNA VALLEY 2585 BIDDLE RANCH RD, SLOC, 93401	674 - F6
FOLEY ESTATES VINEYARD 1711 ALAMO PINTADO RD, StBC, 93463	920 - G2
LAURAS VINEYARD 5620 HIGHWAY 46, SLOC, 93446	514 - H1
LINCOURT VINEYARDS 343 N REFUGIO RD, StBC, 93463	941 - A1
LIVE OAK VINEYARDS 1480 N BETHEL RD, SLOC, 93446	533 - C5
LOS OLIVOS VINTNERS 2923 GRAND AV, StBC, 93441	900 - H5
MAISON DEUTZ 453 DEUTZ DR, SLOC, 93420	735 - E2
MARTIN BROTHERS 2610 BUENA VISTA DR, SLOC, 93446	513 - J1
MISSION VIEW ESTATE VINEYDS WELLSONA RD & HWY 101, SLOC, 93446	493 - F2
MOSBY 9496 SANTA ROSA RD, StBC	919 - H7
PESENTI 2900 VINEYARD DR, SLOC, 93465	553 - A3
ROSS-KELLER 985 ORCHARD RD, Npmo, 93444	756 - C6
RUSACK VINEYARDS 1825 BALLARD CANYON RD, StBC, 93441	920 - D2
SANFORD 7250 SANTA ROSA RD, StBC, 93436	919 - B7
SANTA BARBARA 202 ANACAPA ST, SBAR, 93101	996 - B4
STEARNS WHARF VINTNERS 217 STEARNS WHARF, SBAR, 93101	996 - C5
SUNSTONE VINEYARDS 125 REFUGIO RD, StBC, 93463	940 - J2

FEATURE NAME / Address City, ZIP Code	PAGE-GRID
SYLVESTER 5115 BUENA VISTA DR, SLOC, 93446	493 - J6
TALLEY VINEYARDS 3031 LOPEZ DR, SLOC, 93420	695 - G5
THE BRANDER VINEYARD 2401 REFUGIO RD, StBC, 93460	901 - A6
THE GAINEY VINEYARD 3950 E HWY 246, StBC, 93460	921 - D6
TREANA 2175 ARBOR RD, SLOC, 93446	533 - C4
TWIN HILLS 2025 NACIMIENTO LAKE DR, SLOC, 93446	513 - B1
WILD HORSE 1437 WILD HORSE WINERY CT, SLOC, 93465	553 - J4

STB & SLO

INDEX

Express Wall Maps™

Features

- Quality and detail of the Thomas Guide
- Customized coverages made from Thomas Bros. Maps digital data
- Tag up to 10 locations
- ZIP code coverage available for detail maps
- Thomas Guide page and grid available

Map Description

- Standard sizes ranging from 17"x 22" to 66"x 86"
- Full color or black & white maps
- Full street detail or arterial view
- Ask about our mounting and laminating options

Who will find Express Wall Maps Useful?

- Sales Executives - Charting Territory
- Real Estate Agents - map out your farm areas
- Delivery Services - fast food, courier, etc.
- Government Agencies and Municipalities - police, fire, emergency
- Court Room Illustrations

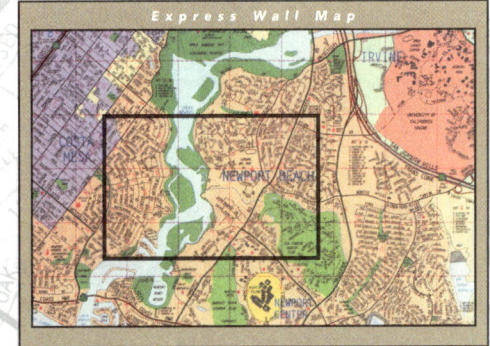

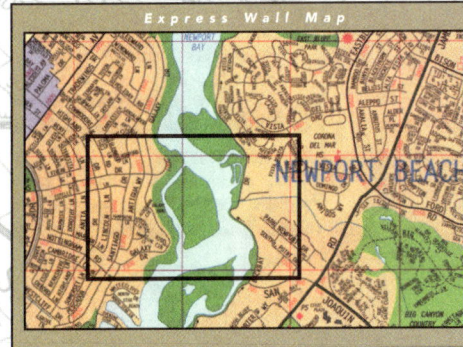

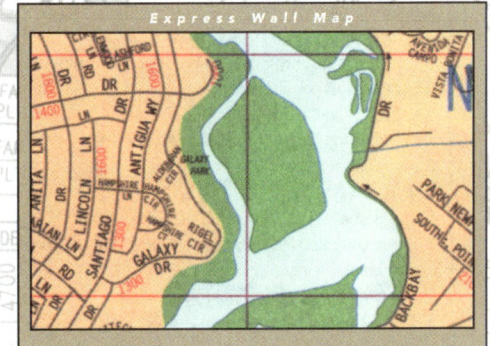

Thomas Bros. Maps®
A RAND M^cNALLY COMPANY

1-800-899-6277
www.thomas.com

PRODUCT INFORMATION LIST

THOMAS GUIDES®
NOW INCLUDING ZIP CODES AND BOUNDARIES FOR 2001 EDITIONS

CALIFORNIA

Alameda County
Alameda / Contra Costa Counties
Alameda / Santa Clara Counties
Central Valley Cities
   (Coverage includes all urban areas from Stockton to Bakersfield)
Contra Costa County
Fresno / Madera Counties *(NEW - available 12/2000)*
Golden Gate
   (Marin, San Francisco, San Mateo, and Santa Clara Counties)
Kern County *(NEW - available 10/2000)*
Los Angeles County
* Los Angeles / Orange Counties
* Los Angeles / Ventura Counties
Marin County
Metropolitan Monterey Bay
Napa / Sonoma Counties
Orange County
Orange / Los Angeles Counties
Riverside County
Riverside / Orange Counties
Riverside / San Diego Counties
Sacramento County
   (Coverage includes portions of Placer & El Dorado Counties)
* Sacramento / Solano Counties
San Bernardino County
San Bernardino / Riverside Counties
* San Diego County including portions of Imperial County
San Diego / Orange Counties
San Francisco County
San Francisco / Alameda / Contra Costa Counties
San Francisco / San Mateo Counties
San Mateo County
Santa Barbara and San Luis Obispo Counties
* Santa Barbara and San Luis Obispo / Ventura Counties
Santa Clara County
Santa Clara / San Mateo Counties
Solano County including portions of Napa & Yolo Counties
Ventura County

*Thomas Guide & Thomas Guide *DigitalEdition*™ Combo Packs

ARIZONA - NEVADA - OREGON - WASHINGTON

* Clark County, NV
Metropolitan Phoenix Area, AZ *(NEW - available 7/2000)*
Metropolitan Tucson Area, AZ *(NEW - available 9/2000)*
* Portland Metro Area, OR
   (Coverage includes Clackamas, Columbia, Multnomah, Washington
   & Yamhill Counties and Greater Vancouver Area)
King County, WA
King / Pierce Counties, WA
King / Snohomish Counties, WA
Pierce County, WA
Snohomish County, WA

WASHINGTON, D.C. & VICINITY

Anne Arundel County, MD
Frederick County, MD
Howard County, MD
Loudoun County, VA
Montgomery County, MD
Northern Virginia & the Beltway
Prince George's County, VA
Prince William County, VA

ROAD ATLAS & DRIVER'S GUIDES

California Road Atlas & Driver's Guide
Pacific Northwest Road Atlas & Driver's Guide

METROPOLITAN THOMAS GUIDES®

CALIFORNIA

* Metropolitan Bay Area
   (Coverage includes Metro areas of Alameda, Contra Costa, Marin,
   San Francisco, San Mateo, and Santa Clara Counties)
* Metropolitan Inland Empire
   (Coverage includes Metro areas of San Bernardino, Riverside,
   Eastern Los Angeles, and Northeastern Orange Counties)

WASHINGTON

* Metropolitan Puget Sound
   (Coverage includes Metro areas of King, Pierce, and Snohomish
   Counties)

METROPOLITAN BALTIMORE & METROPOLITAN WASHINGTON, D. C.

* Metropolitan Baltimore, MD
* Metropolitan Washington DC includes Montgomery & Prince George's
   Counties, MD, and Northern Virginia

THOMAS GUIDE *DIGITALEDITION*™ (CD-ROM)

Tool Box *(NEW)* - Tool Box is a companion to any Thomas Guide *DigitalEdition*™ CD-ROM. It allows you to customize your maps and e-mail them to others with a full set of drawing tools, address locator, GPS interface, and query tools.

CALIFORNIA

State of California *(NEW)*

SOUTHERN CALIFORNIA

Los Angeles / Orange Counties
Los Angeles / Ventura Counties
Metropolitan Inland Empire
   (Coverage includes all of San Bernardino and Riverside,
   Eastern Los Angeles and Northeastern Orange Counties)
Santa Barbara / Ventura Counties

NORTHERN CALIFORNIA

Bay Area
   (Coverage includes Alameda, Contra Costa, Marin,
   San Francisco, San Mateo, and Santa Clara Counties)
Sacramento / Solano Counties

ARIZONA

Phoenix / Tucson, AZ *(NEW - available 9/2000)*

OREGON - WASHINGTON

Portland Metro Area, OR
Metropolitan Puget Sound, WA
   (Coverage includes all of King, Pierce, and Snohomish Counties)

NEVADA

Clark County

THOMAS GUIDE & *DIGITALEDITION*™ COMBO PACKS

Our Thomas Guide and Thomas Guide *DigitalEdition*™ sold together in one convenient package. Call for more information.

EXPRESS MAPS & EXPRESS WALL MAPS™

Affordable, high quality custom maps designed to your specifications. You select the coverage, choose black & white or full-color, optional ZIP & Census overlays. Lamination & mounting additional. Call for more information.

For more information, or to order, please contact Customer Service at 1-800-899-6277 or e-mail us at cust-serv@thomas.com or visit our web site at www.thomas.com
Our Secure On-line Store is Now Open!

Information subject to change without notice

The Thomas Guide®

VENTURA COUNTY

OUR MAPS ARE PUBLISHED TO PROVIDE ACCURATE STREET INFORMATION AND TO ASSIST IN RELATING DEMOGRAPHICS AND CULTURAL FEATURES TO STREET GEOGRAPHY. HOWEVER, THIS PRODUCT IS BEING SOLD ON AN "AS-IS" BASIS AND WE ASSUME NO LIABILITY FOR DAMAGES ARISING FROM ERRORS OR OMISSIONS.

Thomas Bros. Maps®

A RAND MCNALLY COMPANY

Call Toll Free:
1-800-899-MAPS
1-800-899-6277

Corporate Office & Showroom
17731 Cowan, Irvine, CA 92614 (949) 863-1984 or 1-888-826-6277

Thomas Bros. Maps & Books
550 Jackson St., San Francisco, CA 94133 (415) 981-7520 or 1-800-969-3072
521 W. 6th St., Los Angeles, CA 90014 (213) 627-4018 or 1-888-277-6277
Customer Service: 1-800-899-6277
World Wide Web: www.thomas.com
e-mail: comments@thomas.com
For more information regarding licensing and copyright permission, please contact us at:
licensing@thomas.com

Introduction — INTRO

- How to Use — ii
- Legend — iii
- Area Maps — iv-v
- Key Map — vi
- Cities & Communities Index — vii
- Downtown Map — viii

Map Pages — MAP

- Arterial Maps — 366-387
- Detail Maps — 441-625

Indexes — INDEX

- List of Abbreviations — 626
- Street Index — 627-649
- Points of Interest Index — 650-654

How To Use This Thomas Guide
Modo De Empleo Del Thomas Guide

To Find a City or Community:
Manera de Localizar una Ciudad o Comunidad:

Start with the Key Map to Detail Pages, then turn to the Detail Page indicated.

Empiece con el mapa clave de páginas detalladas, luego pase a la página detallada que se indica.

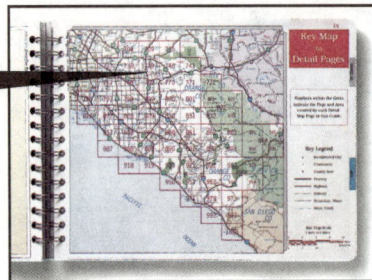

or
o

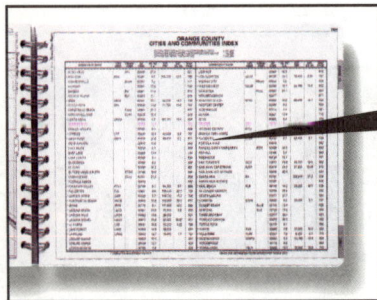

Look up the name in the Cities and Communities Index, then turn to the Detail Page indicated.

Busque el nombre en el Indice de Ciudades y Comunidades, luego pase a la página detallada que se indica.

To Find an Address:
Manera de Localizar una Dirección:

1 Look up the street name in the Street Index. If there are multiple listings, choose the proper city and/or address range. (All city abbreviations are listed in the Cities and Communities Index.)

Localice el nombre de la calle en el Indice de Calles. Si aparecen varias listas, seleccione el área apropiada de la ciudad y/o el domicilio. (Todas las abreviaturas de las ciudades figuran en la lista del Indice de Ciudades y Comunidades).

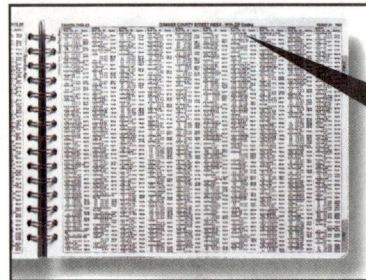

2 The street name will include a Thomas Bros. Maps Page and Grid™ where the address is located.

El nombre de la calle incluye un cuadro de Thomas Bros. Maps Page and Grid™ con el número de página y de coordenadas que indican la ubicación del domicilio.

3 Turn to the Page indicated.

Pase a la página que se indica.

4 Locate the address by following the indicated Letter column and Number row until the two intersect. The street name is within this Grid area.

Localice el domicilio siguiendo la columna con letras y la hilera con números indicadas hasta que intersecten. El nombre de la calle se encuentra dentro de dicho cuadro.

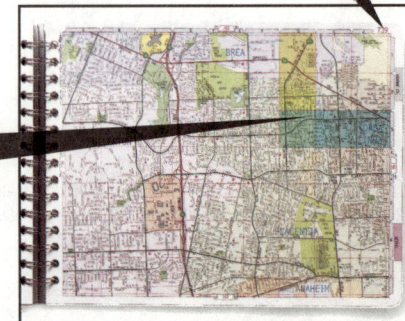

Thomas Bros. Maps®
A RAND MCNALLY COMPANY

www.thomas.com

1-800-899-MAPS
1-800-899-6277

LEGEND OF MAP SYMBOLS

NORTH

Roads

Freeway	
Interchange/Ramp	
Highway	
Primary Road	
Secondary Road	
Minor Road	
Restricted Road	
Alley	
Unpaved Road	
Tunnel	
Toll Road	
High Occupancy Veh. Lane	
Stacked Multiple Roadways	
Proposed Road	
Proposed Freeway	
Freeway Under Construction	
One-Way Road	
Two-Way Road	
Trail, Walkway	
Stairs	
Railroad	
Rapid Transit	
Rapid Transit, Underground	
City Boundary	
County Boundary	
State Boundary	
International Boundary	
Military Base, Indian Resv.	
Township, Range, Rancho	
River, Creek, Shoreline	
Ferry	
ZIP Code Boundary	

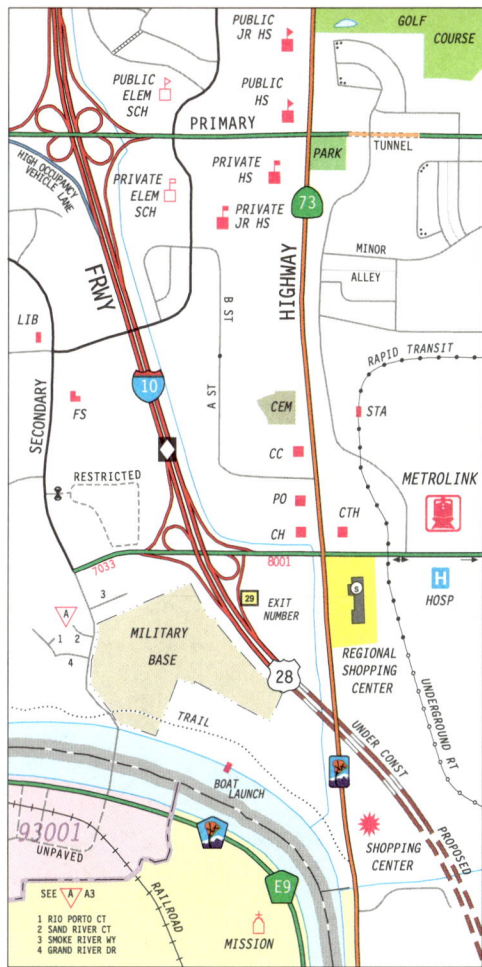

93001

COPYRIGHT 2000

Symbols

- Interstate
- Interstate (Business)
- U.S. Highway
- State Highway
- County Highway
- State Scenic Highway
- County Scenic Highway
- Carpool Lane
- Street List Marker
- Street Name Continuation
- Street Name Change
- Airport
- Station (Train, Bus)
- Building (see List of Abbr. page)
- Building Footprint
- Public Elementary School
- Public High School
- Private Elementary School
- Private High School
- Shopping Center
- Fire Station
- Library
- Mission
- Winery
- Campground
- Hospital
- Mountain
- Boat Launch
- Gates, Locks, Barricades
- Lighthouse

Areas

- County Seat
- County
- Incorporated City
- Incorporated City
- Incorporated City
- Incorporated City
- Incorporated City
- Incorporated City
- City, County, State Park
- National Forest, Park
- Water
- Intermittent Lake, Marsh
- Dry Lake, Beach
- Dam
- Point of Interest
- Golf Course, Country Club
- Cemetery
- Military Base
- Airport
- Parking Lot
- Structure Footprint
- Regional Shopping Center
- Major Dept. Store (List of Abbr. page)

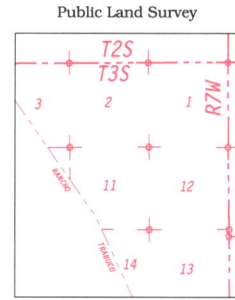

Public Land Survey

T2S / T3S / R7W

Detail Map Scale
1 Inch to 2400 Feet
Miles / Kilometers

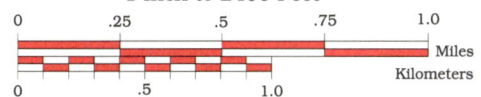

Detail Grid Equivalents
1 Grid Equals:
.5 x .5 Miles
2640 x 2640 Feet
1.1 x 1.1 Inches

Arterial Map Scale
1 Inch to 5 Miles
Miles / Kilometers

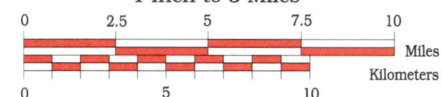

Arterial Grid Equivalents
1 Grid Equals:
1 Detail Page
4.5 x 3.5 Miles
.9 x .7 Inches

iv

VENTURA CO.

INTRO

AREA MAP

PACIFIC OCEAN

324 325 326

344 345 346

365 366

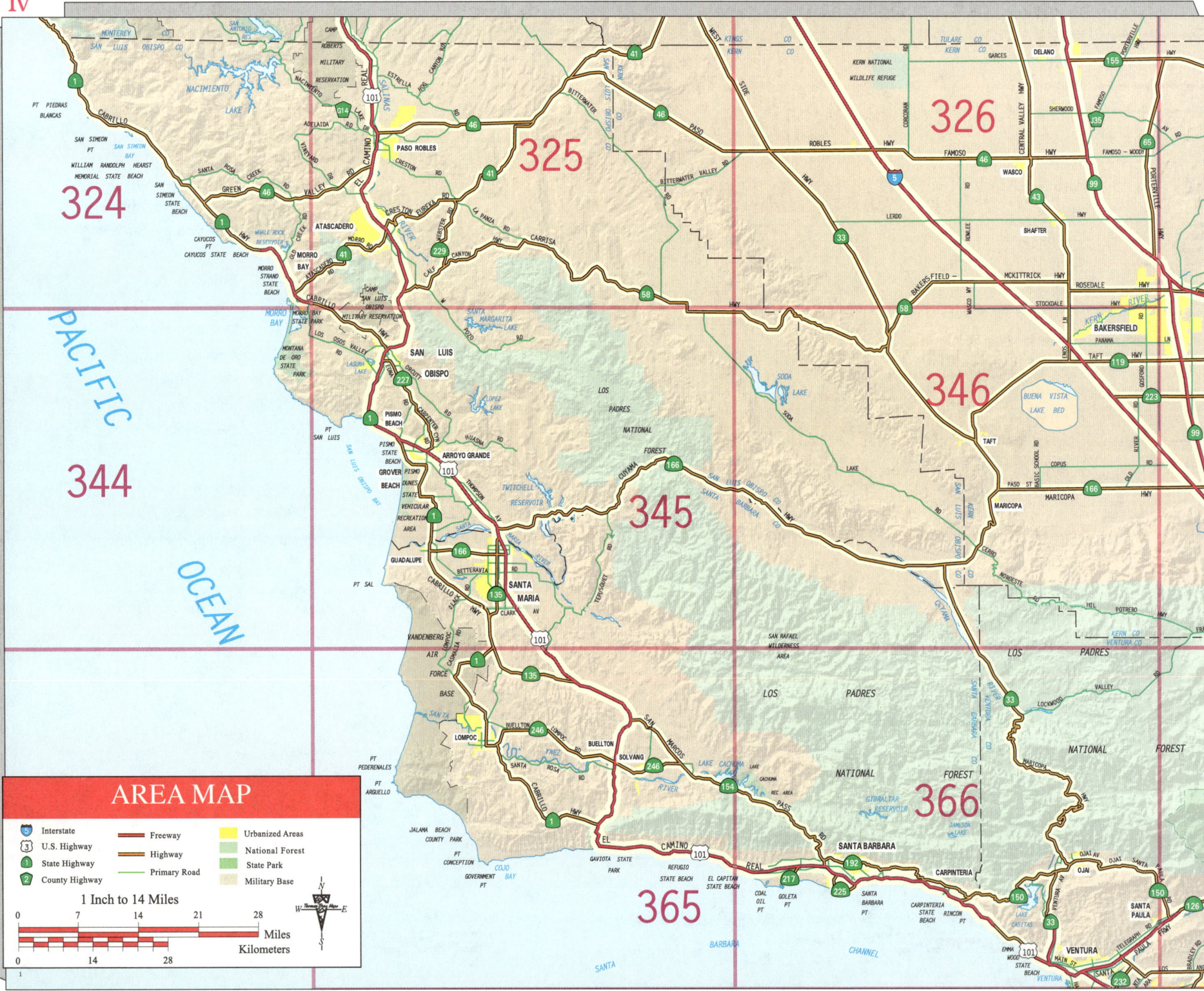

Legend
- Interstate
- U.S. Highway
- State Highway
- County Highway
- Freeway
- Highway
- Primary Road
- Urbanized Areas
- National Forest
- State Park
- Military Base

1 Inch to 14 Miles

Miles
Kilometers

COPYRIGHT 2000 Thomas Bros. Maps ®

Cities and places: PASO ROBLES, ATASCADERO, MORRO BAY, SAN LUIS OBISPO, PISMO BEACH, ARROYO GRANDE, GROVER BEACH, GUADALUPE, SANTA MARIA, BETTERAVIA, LOMPOC, BUELLTON, SOLVANG, SANTA BARBARA, CARPINTERIA, GOLETA, VENTURA, SANTA PAULA, OJAI, BAKERSFIELD, WASCO, SHAFTER, DELANO, TAFT, MARICOPA, MCKITTRICK, FAMOSO, PORTERVILLE

LOS PADRES NATIONAL FOREST

SAN RAFAEL WILDERNESS AREA

KERN NATIONAL WILDLIFE REFUGE

VANDENBERG AIR FORCE BASE

WILLIAM RANDOLPH HEARST MEMORIAL STATE BEACH

MONTEREY BAY, SAN SIMEON BAY, MORRO BAY, ESTERO BAY, SAN LUIS OBISPO BAY, COJO BAY, SANTA BARBARA CHANNEL

PT PIEDRAS BLANCAS, SAN SIMEON PT, PT SAN LUIS, PT SAL, PT PEDERNALES, PT ARGUELLO, PT CONCEPTION, GOVERNMENT PT, PT SAL

NACIMIENTO LAKE, SAN ANTONIO RES, WHALE ROCK RESERVOIR, SANTA MARGARITA LAKE, LOPEZ LAKE, TWITCHELL RESERVOIR, LAKE CACHUMA, GIBRALTAR RESERVOIR, JAMESON LAKE, LAKE CASITAS, SODA LAKE, BUENA VISTA LAKE BED

Highways: 1, 41, 46, 33, 58, 5, 99, 43, 65, 155, 135, 119, 223, 166, 154, 227, 229, 101, 225, 192, 217, 150, 126, 232, 246, G14

VENTURA CO.

INTRO

346
348
345
366
367
368
365
386
385
387
388

LOS PADRES NATIONAL FOREST

CUYAMA

166

TAFT

BUENA VISTA LAKE BED

SODA LAKE

99

223

GOSFORD RD

RIDGE RD

RIVER RD

COPUS RD

166 HWY

MARICOPA

PASO ST

BASIC SCHOOL RD

MARICOPA

DESERT TORTOISE NATURAL AREA

CALIFORNIA CITY

14

OAK CREEK RD

MIDLAND TR

5

GOLDEN STATE FRWY

ROSAMOND BLVD

90TH ST

ROSAMOND LAKE

BUCKHORN LAKE

ROGERS LAKE

KERN CO
VENTURA CO

SAN RAFAEL WILDERNESS AREA

SAN LUIS OBISPO CO HWY

SANTA BARBARA CO

NORDESTE

MIL POTRERO HWY

FRAZIER MTN PARK RD

LOS PADRES
VENTURA CO

LANCASTER

KERN CO
LOS ANGELES CO

EDWARDS AIR FORCE BASE

138 AVENUE

14

138 LANCASTER

N5

CALIFORNIA

LOS PADRES NATIONAL FOREST

33

LOCKWOOD

VALLEY

HUNGRY VALLEY STATE VEHICULAR REC AREA

ANGELES NATIONAL FOREST

N2

PYRAMID LAKE

CASTAIC LAKE STATE REC AREA

CASTAIC LAKE

PALMDALE

138 PEARBLOSSOM

BUELLTON

SOLVANG

246

SAN MARCOS

154

LAKE CACHUMA

CACHUMA LAKE REC AREA

GIBRALTAR RESERVOIR

JAMESON LAKE

NATIONAL FOREST

366

SESPE CONDOR PRESERVE

LAKE PIRU

HENRY MAYO

SANTA CLARITA

14

ANTELOPE VALLEY

N3

CREST HWY

ANGELES NATIONAL FOREST

EL CAMINO REAL

101

SANTA BARBARA

192

CARPINTERIA

OJAI AV

OJAI

OJAI SANTA PAULA

150

FILLMORE

TELEGRAPH

126

5

SAN GABRIEL CANYON RD

GAVIOTA STATE PARK

REFUGIO STATE BEACH

EL CAPITAN STATE BEACH

COAL OIL PT

GOLETA PT

217

225

SANTA BARBARA PT

CARPINTERIA STATE BEACH

RINCON PT

150

LAKE CASITAS

33

SANTA PAULA

126

SANTA CLARA RIVER

23

CLARA

MOORPARK

118

SAN FERNANDO

210

FOOTHILL FRWY

2

ANGELES

365

BARBARA CHANNEL

EMMA WOOD STATE BEACH

101

VENTURA

TELEGRAPH RD

SANTA PAULA FRWY

BRADLEY RD

LOS ANGELES AV

MOORPARK

118

RONALD REAGAN FRWY

SIMI VALLEY

405

SAN FERNANDO

BURBANK

170

GLENDALE

210

MONROVIA

PASADENA

AZUSA

210

SANTA

HARBOR

232

5TH ST

OXNARD

34

CAMARILLO

SANTA ROSA RD

101

THOUSAND OAKS

23

AGOURA HILLS

HIDDEN HILLS

CALABASAS

27

134

GLENDALE VENTURA FRWY

101

19

ALHAMBRA

10

605

COVINA

210

BERNARDINO FRWY

PACIFIC OCEAN

CHANNEL ISLANDS NATIONAL PARK

SANTA CRUZ ISLAND

SANTA BARBARA CO

ANACAPA ISLAND

VENTURA CO

ANACAPA PASSAGE

SANTA CRUZ CHANNEL

SANTA ROSA ISLAND

PORT HUENEME HARBOR

HUENEME

PORT HUENEME

1

SAN BUENAVENTURA STATE BEACH

POINT MUGU STATE PARK

PT MUGU

LEWIS RD

POTRERO RD

WESTLAKE VILLAGE

N1

WESTLAKE

SANTA MONICA MTNS NAT REC AREA

23

THOUSAND OAKS BLVD

AGOURA RD

MULHOLLAND HWY

TOPANGA STATE PARK

TOPANGA CANYON BLVD

BEVERLY HILLS

SANTA MONICA

10

110

LOS ANGELES

5

60

POMONA

MONTEBELLO

WHITTIER

72

57

386

387

PACIFIC OCEAN

PT DUME

MALIBU

1

SANTA MONICA

PACIFIC COAST HWY

MARINA DEL REY

INGLEWOOD

L A INT AIRPORT

EL SEGUNDO

MANHATTAN BEACH

HERMOSA BEACH

REDONDO BEACH

105

DOWNEY

405

COMPTON

BELLFLOWER

ARTESIA FRWY

LAKEWOOD

19

605

LOS ALAMITOS

39

ANAHEIM

FULLERTON

PLACENTIA

RIVERSIDE FRWY

385

TORRANCE

110

CARSON

710

RANCHO PALOS VERDES

LONG BEACH

GARDEN GROVE

22

WESTMINSTER

SANTA ANA

55

HUNTINGTON BEACH

LOS ANGELES HARBOR

HUNTINGTON HARBOUR

LOS ANGELES CO
ORANGE CO

COSTA MESA

388

vi

Key Map to Detail Pages

The Thomas Guide® contains two types of map pages: Arterial and Detail

367 Arterial Page–Small scale area map, shown with a wide border

478 Detail Page–Full scale map page, shown with a solid thin border

Key Legend

- ○ Community
- Freeway
- Highway
- Primary
- Secondary, Minor
- River, Creek

Key Map Scale
1 Inch to 8 Miles

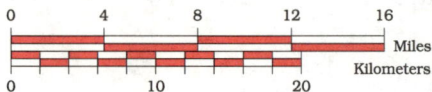

Miles: 0 4 8 12 16
Kilometers: 0 10 20

VENTURA COUNTY
Cities And Communities

Community Name	City Abbr.	ZIP Code	Miles To Ventura	Est. Sq. Mi.	Map Page	Community Name	City Abbr.	ZIP Code	Miles To Ventura	Est. Sq. Mi.	Map Page
BARDSDALE		93015	25.0		465	OAK PARK		91377	30.0		558
BELL CANYON		91307	82.0		529	OAK VIEW		93022	10.1		451
BUCKHORN		93015	31.6		457	❖ OJAI	OJAI	93023	14.2	4.48	441
❖ CAMARILLO	CMRL	93010	16.6	19.12	524	ORTONVILLE		93001	3.2		471
CASITAS SPRINGS		93001	7.4		460	❖ OXNARD	OXN	93030	10.2	24.49	522
CHRISMAN		93001	1.1		471	PIERPONT BAY		93003	2.2		491
COLONIA		93030	10.1		522	PIRU		93040	33.2		457
EL RIO		93030	8.2		522	POINT MUGU		93041	22.3		387
FARIA BEACH		93001	5.5		470	❖ PORT HUENEME	PHME	93041	12.3	4.31	552
❖ FILLMORE	FILM	93015	25.6	2.63	456	❖ SAN BUENAVENTURA					
FOSTER PARK		93001	6.2		461	(SEE VENTURA)					
HOLLYWOOD BEACH		93035	11.0		552	❖ SANTA PAULA	SPLA	93060	15.8	4.61	464
HOLLYWOOD-BY-THE-SEA		93035	11.2		552	SANTA SUSANA		93063	36.4		499
LA CONCHITA		93001	10.1		459	SATICOY		93004	7.2		473
LAKE SHERWOOD		91361	29.1		556	SEACLIFF		93001	8.0		459
LEISURE VILLAGE		93010	17.2		525	SILVER STRAND		93030	11.7		552
LIVE OAK ACRES		93022	11.2		451	❖ SIMI VALLEY	SIMI	93065	32.4	34.18	478
LOCKWOOD VALLEY			32.0		367	SOLIMAR BEACH		93001	4.8		470
MEINERS OAKS		93023	13.2		441	SOMIS		93066	19.2		495
MIRA MONTE		93023	12.2		451	SOUTH COAST		90265	29.1		625
MONTALVO		93003	5.9		492	SPRINGVILLE		93010	11.9		523
❖ MOORPARK	MRPK	93021	27.6	12.39	476	SULPHUR SPRINGS		93060	19.5		453
MOORPARK HOME ACRES		93021	24.6		496	SUMMIT		93023	22.3		453
NEWBURY PARK		91320	22.5		525	❖ THOUSAND OAKS	THO	91360	25.2	55.98	526
NORTH FILLMORE		93015	26.0		455	❖ VENTURA	VEN	93001		20.96	491
NORWEGIAN GRADE		91360	29.2		526	-- VENTURA COUNTY	VeCo				
NYELAND ACRES		93030	11.3		523	WHEELER SPRINGS		93023	17.5		366
OAKBROOK VILLAGE		91360	27.0		527						

❖ INDICATES INCORPORATED CITY

MILES ARE ESTIMATED FROM DOWNTOWN CIVIC CENTER

COPYRIGHT 2000 Thomas Bros. Maps®

VENTURA CO.

INTRO

Downtown Ventura

Points of Interest

1	A J Comstock Fire Museum	C2
2	Albinger Archaeological Museum	C2
3	Amtrak Station	C2
4	California Street Plaza	D2
5	Chamber of Commerce	G4
6	Channel Islands National Park HQ & Visitors Center	G7
7	City Hall	D1
8	Doubletree Hotel	F4
9	E P Foster Library	D2
10	Father Serra Cross	C1
11	Greyhound Bus Station	C2
12	Holiday Inn Beach Resort	C2
13	Main Post Office	D2
14	Ortega Adobe	B1
15	San Buenaventura Mission	C2
16	Ventura Concert Theater	D2
17	Ventura County Fairgrounds	B3
18	Ventura County Historical Courthouse	D1
19	Ventura County Museum of History and Art	C2
20	Ventura Historical Pier	D3
21	Visitors Bureau	C2

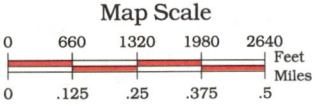

VENTURA CO.

INTRO

Map Scale

```
0    660   1320   1980   2640
                              Feet
                              Miles
0     .125    .25   .375    .5
```

GRID REFERENCES THIS PAGE ONLY

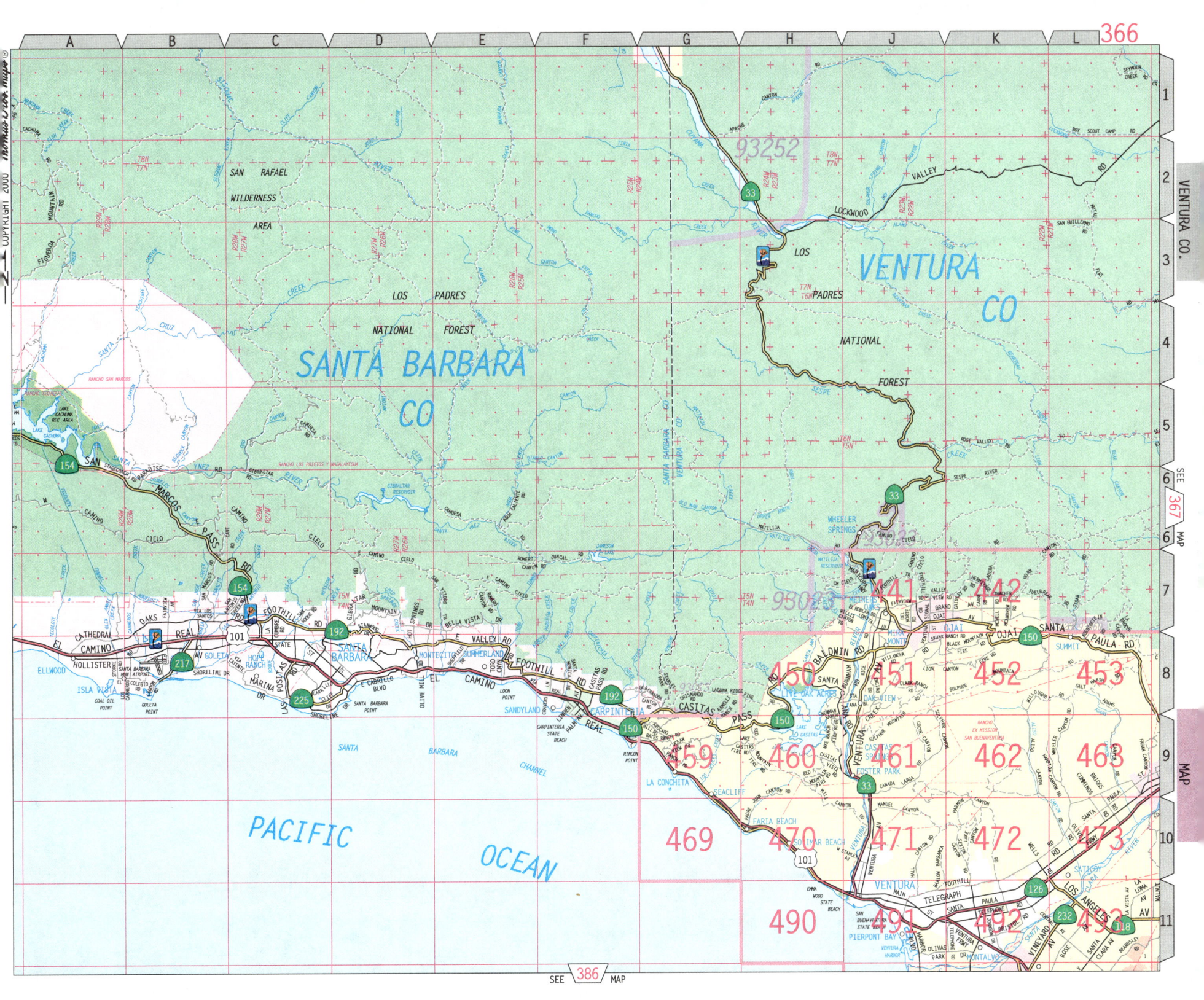

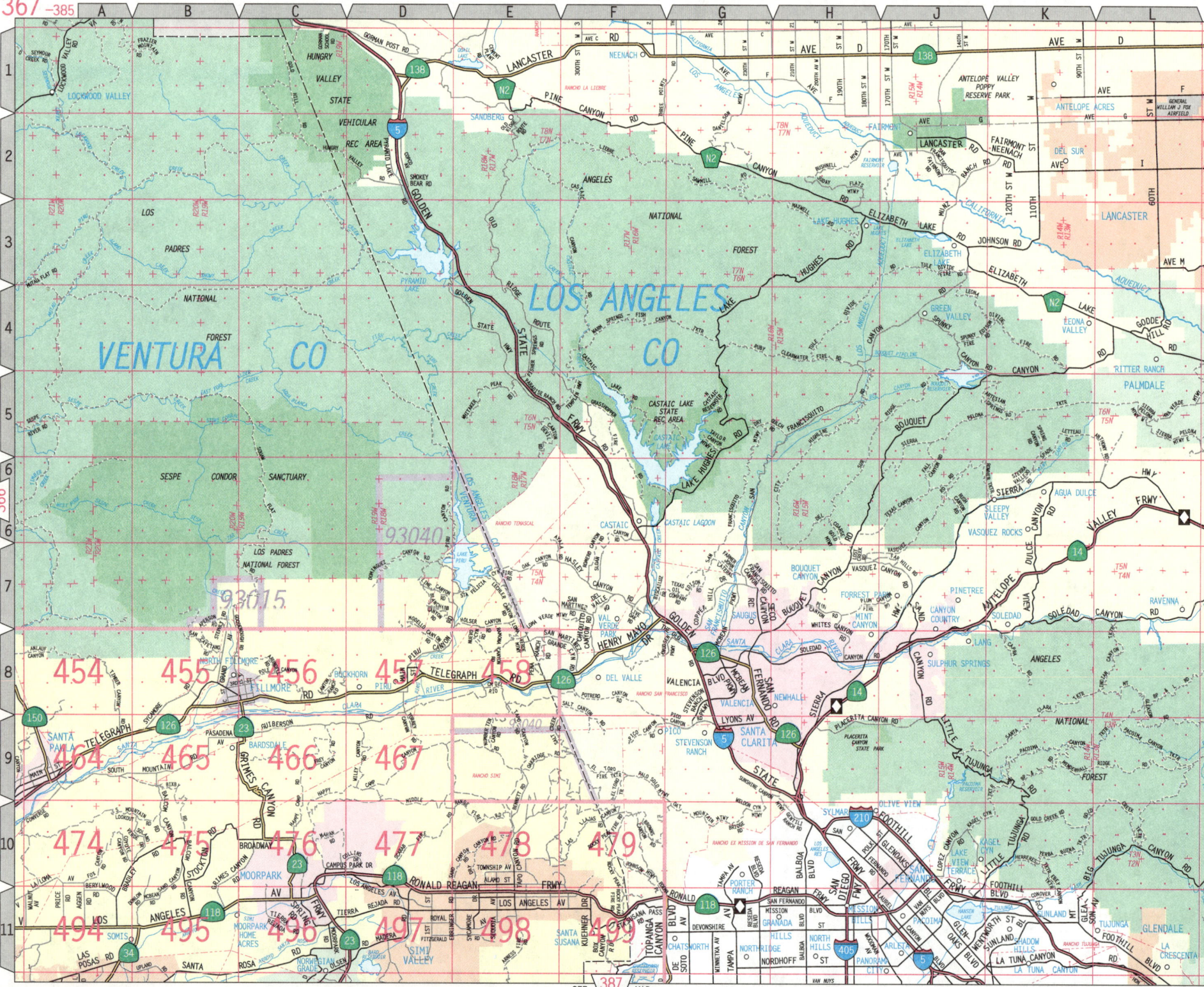

A B C D E F G H J K L

VENTURA CO.

LOS ANGELES CO.

VENTURA CO

LOS PADRES NATIONAL FOREST

SESPE CONDOR SANCTUARY

HUNGRY VALLEY STATE VEHICULAR REC AREA

ANGELES NATIONAL FOREST

ANTELOPE VALLEY POPPY RESERVE PARK

LANCASTER

PALMDALE

CASTAIC LAKE STATE REC AREA

SANTA CLARITA

VALENCIA

NEWHALL

SAN FERNANDO

FILLMORE

MOORPARK

SIMI VALLEY

SANTA PAULA

GLENDALE

454 455 456 457 458
464 465 466 467
474 475 476 477 478 479
494 495 496 497 498 499

SEE 366 MAP

SEE 387 MAP

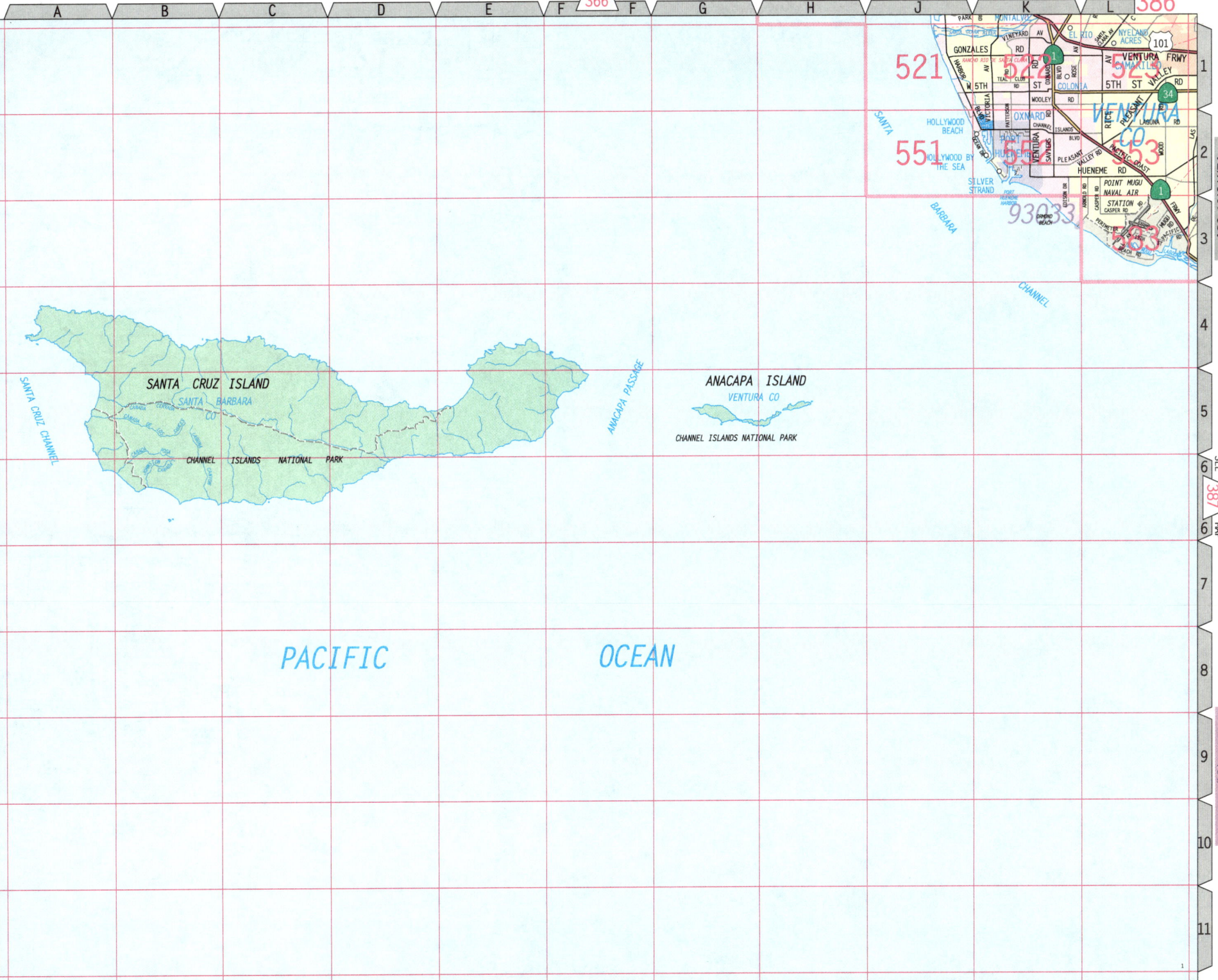

A B C D E F F G H J K L

521   522   523

551   552   553

93033

563

SANTA CRUZ ISLAND

SANTA BARBARA CO.

CHANNEL ISLANDS NATIONAL PARK

ANACAPA ISLAND
VENTURA CO

CHANNEL ISLANDS NATIONAL PARK

ANACAPA PASSAGE

SANTA CRUZ CHANNEL

PACIFIC   OCEAN

SEE 387 MAP

SEE 367 MAP

A B C D E F F G H J K L

VENTURA CO.

LOS ANGELES CO

VENTURA CO

PACIFIC OCEAN

PACIFIC

Grid map numbers:
524, 525, 526, 527, 528, 529
554, 555, 556, 557, 558
584, 585, 586, 625

Cities and places:
CAMARILLO, LEISURE VILLAGE, NEWBURY PARK, THOUSAND OAKS, OAKBROOK, OAK PARK, BELL CANYON, HIDDEN HILLS, WOODLAND HILLS, TARZANA, ENCINO, CANOGA PARK, RESEDA, VAN NUYS AIRPORT, ROSCOE BLVD, SUN VALLEY, BURBANK, VERDUGO CITY, LA TUNA CANYON, GLENDALE

WESTLAKE VILLAGE, LAKE SHERWOOD, AGOURA, AGOURA HILLS, CALABASAS, CALABASAS PARK, CALABASAS HIGHLANDS, GLENVIEW, OLD CANYON, SYLVIA PARK, TOPANGA, NORTH HOLLYWOOD, STUDIO CITY, VALLEY VILLAGE, SHERMAN OAKS, UNIVERSAL CITY, TOLUCA LAKE, HOLLYWOOD, ATWATER VILLAGE, SILVER LAKE

POINT MUGU STATE PARK, SANTA MONICA MOUNTAINS NATIONAL RECREATION AREA, MALIBU CREEK STATE PARK, MALIBU LAKE, MONTE NIDO, FERNWOOD, BIG ROCK, TOPANGA STATE PARK, PACIFIC PALISADES, BRENTWOOD, BEL AIR ESTATES, WEST HOLLYWOOD, BEVERLY HILLS, WESTWOOD

LEO CARRILLO STATE BEACH, ROBERT H MEYER MEMORIAL STATE BEACH, MALIBU PARK, MALIBU BOWL, EL NIDO, MALIBU, MALIBU LAGOON STATE BEACH, CASTELLAMMARE, SANTA MONICA, OCEAN PARK, VENICE, MAR VISTA, CULVER CITY, PALMS, CRENSHAW, BALDWIN HILLS, VIEW PARK, WINDSOR HILLS, LEIMERT PARK, VERNON

POINT MUGU, PT DUME COUNTY BEACH, POINT DUME, 90265

MARINA DEL REY, PLAYA DEL REY, LOS ANGELES INTERNATIONAL AIRPORT, WESTCHESTER, INGLEWOOD, MORNINGSIDE PARK, HYDE PARK, FLORENCE, WALNUT PARK, LADERA HEIGHTS, CENTURY CITY, LENNOX, IMPERIAL, WATTS

EL SEGUNDO, EL PORTO, MANHATTAN BEACH, HAWTHORNE, LAWNDALE, GARDENA, EL CAMINO VILLAGE, ROSECRANS, WILLOWBROOK, ATHENS, ROSEWOOD

HERMOSA BEACH, REDONDO BEACH, TORRANCE, HARBOR GATEWAY, CARSON, DEL AMO, EL NIDO

HOLLYWOOD RIVIERA, PALOS VERDES ESTATES, LOMITA, HARBOR CITY, WILMINGTON, ROLLING HILLS, ROLLING HILLS ESTATES

RANCHO PALOS VERDES, MIRALESTE, PORTUGUESE BEND, SAN PEDRO, TERMINAL ISLAND, LOS ANGELES HARBOR

SEE 386 MAP

A B C D E F G H J

1

2

3

4

5

6

7

MATILIJA RESERVOIR

SCHMIDT ROCK QUARRY

MARICOPA

DAM MATILIJA

29

MATILIJA HOT SPRINGS

GATE

CAMINO CIELO

28

LOS PADRES NATIONAL FOREST

CM CIELO

CIELO

26

25

27

CAMINO

RICE RD

RIVER RD

DELL CANYON

FOOTHILL

TR

CANYON

32

CIELO

33

CAMINO

KENNEDY

CANYON

HWY

COZY TR

34

FOOTHILL

35

36

FOOTHILL 1500

PIRIE RD

STEWART

VALLEY VIEW RD

93023

RES

RES

T5N
T4N

FARNHAM

CAMP RAMAH

RANCHO OJAI

1

LAYTON ST

2

FAIRVIEW CT

E FAIRVIEW

DALY RD

RED HILL

PLEASANT

PATRICIA

TOPAZ CT

MEINERS OAKS

4

33

3

RICE RD

MEYER RD

OSO RD

FAIRVIEW RD

DOMINION DR

FAIRVIEW

MCDONALD

CAMP RAMAH

DEL NORTE

PALOMAR RD

FOOTHILL LN

EL CAMINO

VISTA DEL ORO DR

HERMOSA DR

MONTGOMERY

DALY

OJAI

MOUNTAIN VIEW

DOUGLAS

ANDREW DR

SUNSET

GRANDVIEW

FRANCE CIR

TICO AV

MCKEE ST

BUENA VISTA AV

LA LUNA AV

MARICOPA

EL CONEJO

RANCHO CT

RANCHO DR

RANCHO DR

DEVEREUX DR

FERNANDO AV

CARPAZIO ST

N POLI

N ALVARADO

N ENCINAL

N PADRE JUAN AV

MULBERRY LN

JUNIPER

SYCAMORE LN

ASH LN

MEINERS RD

MONTANA CIR

FOOTHILL RD

PALOMAR

N TICO

DEL ORO DR

EL TORO

RANCHO

RAYMOND ST

PAULINE ST

SUMMER

BLANCHE ST

EUCALYPTUS

OAK ST

QUAIL OAKS

VENTURA ST

SIGNAL ST

GRAND

FRANKLIN DR

COMM CTR

SARZOTTI PARK

EL ROBLAR

MESA

N ARNAZ

N POLI

N ALVARADO

N ENCINAL

N JUAN AV

FELIX

CRES DR

CARTER

CHRISTOPHER

SAINT THOMAS

LIB

OJAI VALLEY ESTATE

RANCHO SANTA ANA

RANCHO OJAI

EL TORO RD

SIERRA RD

CANADA

ALISO

RINCON

MALLORY

MATILIJA ST

CONT HS

PARK & RIDE

MATILIJA ST

ALISO ST

LION

MONTGOMERY

FULTON

PARK

ALISO ST

LA LUNA AV

LOMITA AV

WALLBRIDGE WY

EL RIO

EL PLANO

EL CAMINO DR

PUEBLO DR

STOCKBRIDGE

CUYAMA

VERANO DR

BONITA DR

NORDHOFF CEM

JR HS

CUYAMA

PASEO

OJAI VLY HS

LIBBEY PARK

PO

E TOPA

W TOPA TOPA

S BLANCHE

E TOPA

SANTA ANA

CH

OAK CREEK LN

WILLOW ST

FOX ST

PEARL ST

BALD ST

FULTON ST

BRYANT PL

LOMITA AV

EL CAMINO CORTO

EL SOL

PALA RD

TICO RD

NORDHOFF HS

33

HWY

CHURCH

OAKMORE ST

CARRILLO RD

OJAI VALLEY COMMUNITY HOSP

CREEKSIDE WY

DESCANSO AV

DEL NORTE RD

W OJAI

OJAI

150

OJAI VALLEY INN AND SPA

COUNTRY CLUB DR

SAN ANTONIO RD

CREEKSIDE

OAK CREEK LN

CRESTVIEW

MONTGOMERY ST

E OJAI

E OJAI AV

POPE LN

BRYANT CIR

BRYANT PL

BUCKBOARD LN

SADDLE LN

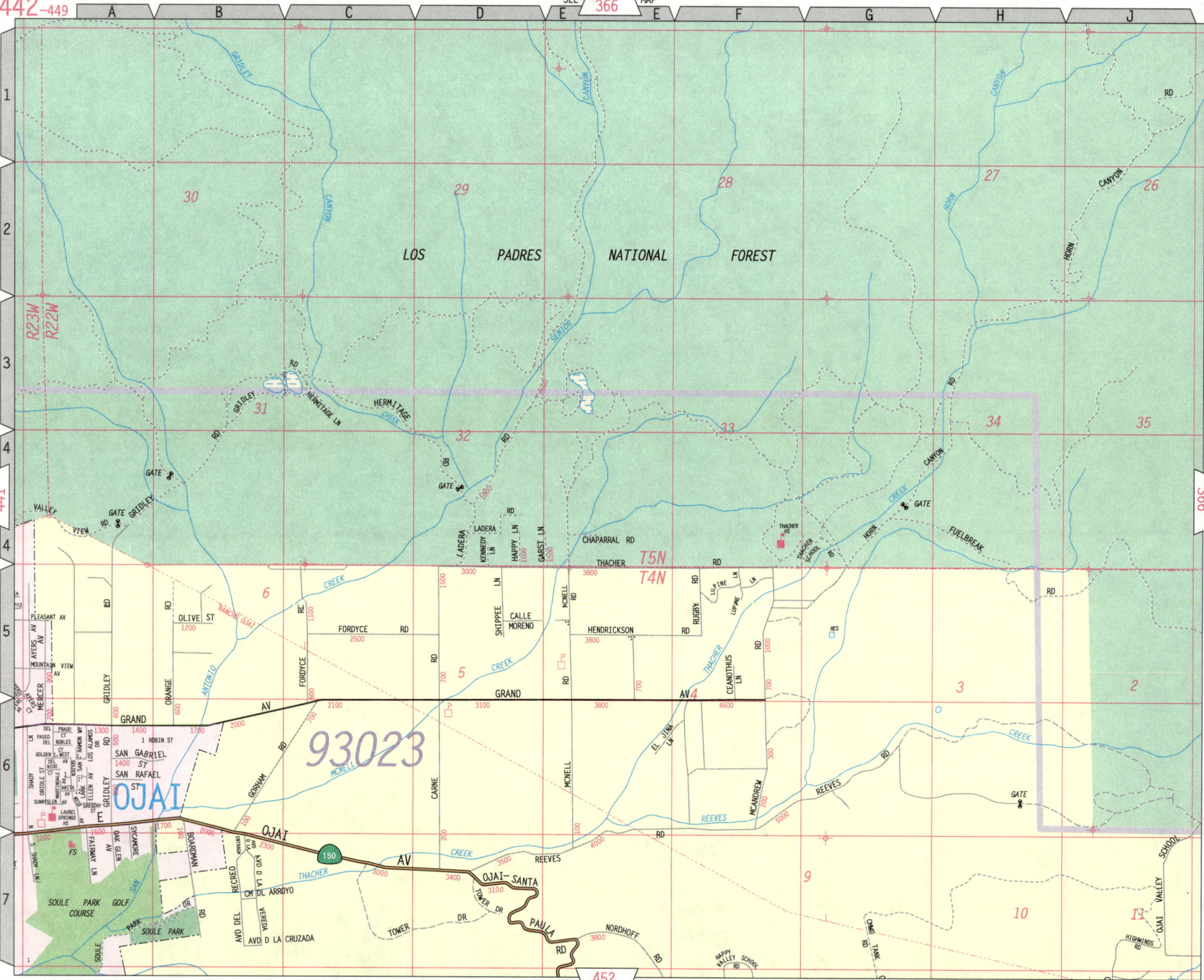

SEE 366 MAP

A B C D E E F G H J

1

VENTURA CO.

30 29 28 27 26

2

LOS PADRES NATIONAL FOREST

R23W / R22W

SENIOR

CANYON

HORN

3

GRIDLEY CANYON

HORN CANYON

RD

HERMITAGE LN

HERMITAGE CREEK

GRIDLEY RD

31 32 33 34 35

4

SEE 441 MAP

SEE 366

GATE

GATE

VALLEY VIEW

GRIDLEY RD GATE

LADERA

KENNEDY LN

HAPPY LN

GARST LN

CHAPARRAL RD

THACHER RD

T5N / T4N

THACHER HS

THACHER SCHOOL RD

HORN CANYON CREEK GATE

FUELBREAK

RD

5

PLEASANT AV

AYERS AV

MOUNTAIN VIEW AV

MERCER

GRIDLEY

ORANGE

OLIVE ST 1200

RANCHO OJAI

ANTONIO

CREEK

FORDYCE RD 2500

FORDYCE

RD

CREEK

SHIPPEE LN

CALLE MORENO

MCNELL RD

HENDRICKSON RD 3800

RUGBY

LUPINE LN

LUPINE LN

THACHER RD

RES

5 3 2

6

GRAND

PRADO CT

PASEO DEL ROBLES

GOLDEN ST

WEST ST

SHADY LN

ORIOLE ST

ANITA

SUNNYGLEN AV

SAN GABRIEL ST

SAN RAFAEL

LARK

ELLEN AV

GREGORY ST

1 ROBIN ST

DEL NIDO AV

LOS ALAMOS DR

RAMON DR

93023

GRAND

GORHAM RD

MCNELL

CARNE

MCNELL RD

CEANOTHUS LN

EL JINK LN

AV

GRAND AV

MCANDREW

REEVES RD

REEVES

CREEK

GATE

OJAI

LAUREL SPRINGS HS

FS

FAIRWAY AV

OAK GLEN AV

SYCAMORE

BOARDMAN

OJAI

150

AV

THACHER

CREEK

REEVES

REEVES RD

9

7

SOULE PARK GOLF COURSE

SOULE

SOULE PARK

RECREO

AVD DEL

AVD D LA VEREDA

AVD D LA CRUZADA

CM DL ARROYO

TOWER DR

OJAI-SANTA PAULA RD

NORDHOFF RD

HAPPY VALLEY SCHOOL RD

CMNO TANK RD

OJAI VALLEY SCHOOL

HIGHWINDS RD

10 11

SEE 452 MAP

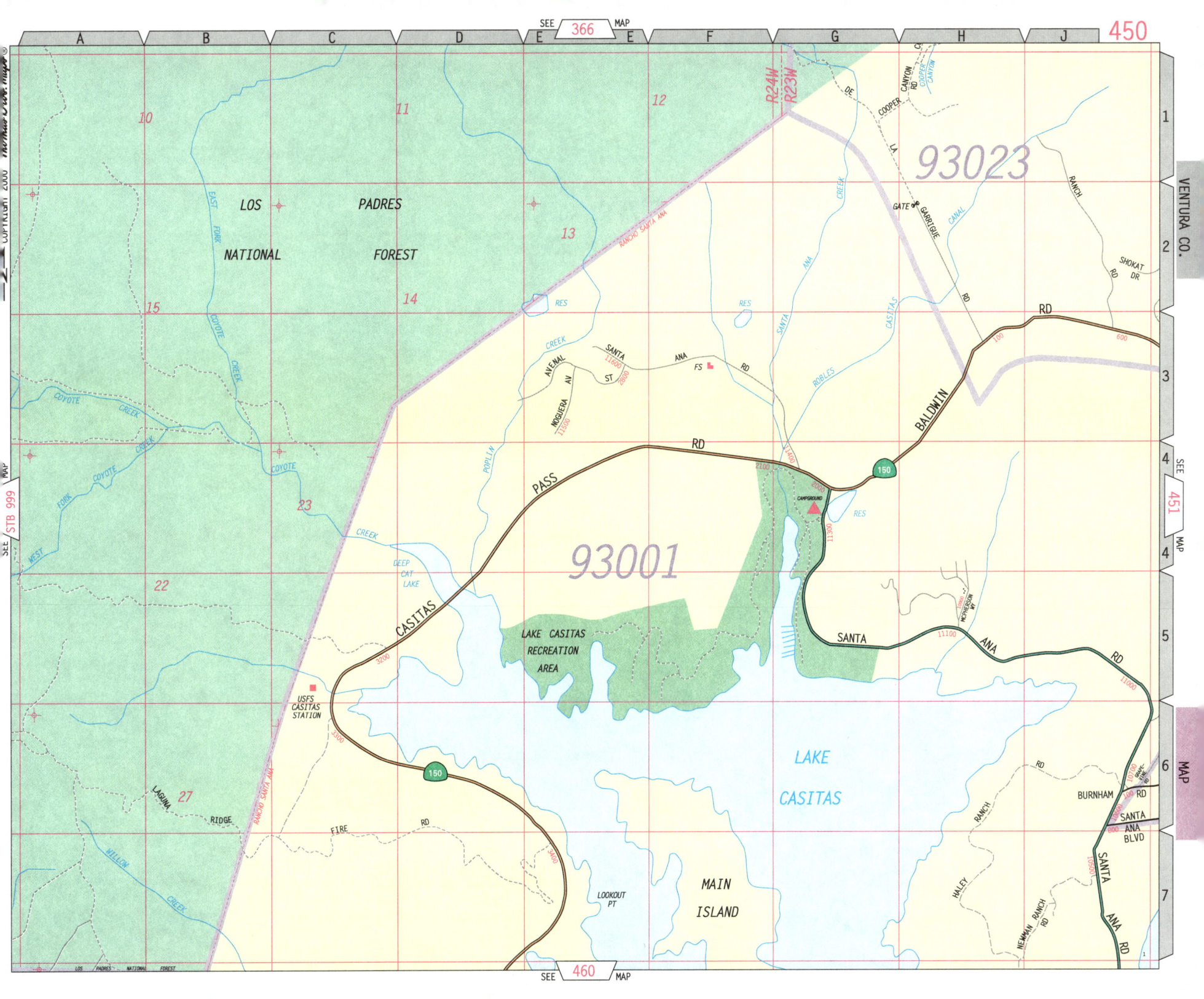

A B C D E E F G H J **450**

1

2

3

4

4

5

6

7

93023

93001

LOS PADRES

NATIONAL FOREST

10 11 12

13

14

15

23

22

27 LAGUNA

RIDGE

WILLOW CREEK

COYOTE CREEK

EAST FORK COYOTE CREEK

WEST FORK

COYOTE CREEK

CREEK

DEEP CAT LAKE

USFS CASITAS STATION

CASITAS PASS RD

FIRE RD

3200

3000

3400

LAKE CASITAS RECREATION AREA

LAKE CASITAS

MAIN ISLAND

LOOKOUT PT

150

150

RANCHO SANTA ANA

RANCHO SANTA ANA

R24W R23W

AVENAL AV

NOGUERA AV

SANTA 11600 2800 ST

ANA FS RD

POPL LW

CREEK

RES

RES

SANTA ANA CREEK

CASITAS ROBLES

2100

2000

11400

11300

CAMPGROUND

RES

BALDWIN

150

DE

COOPER CANYON RD

COOPER CANYON

LA

GATE GARRIGUE

CANAL

RD

RANCH

SHOKAT DR

RD

RD

100

600

SANTA 11100 ANA RD

11000

MCPHERSON WY

SANTA ANA BLVD

HALEY RANCH RD

NEWMAN RANCH RD

SANTA ANA RD

BURNHAM RD

RD

10100

10500

10000 100 600

MAP

LOS PADRES NATIONAL FOREST

11500

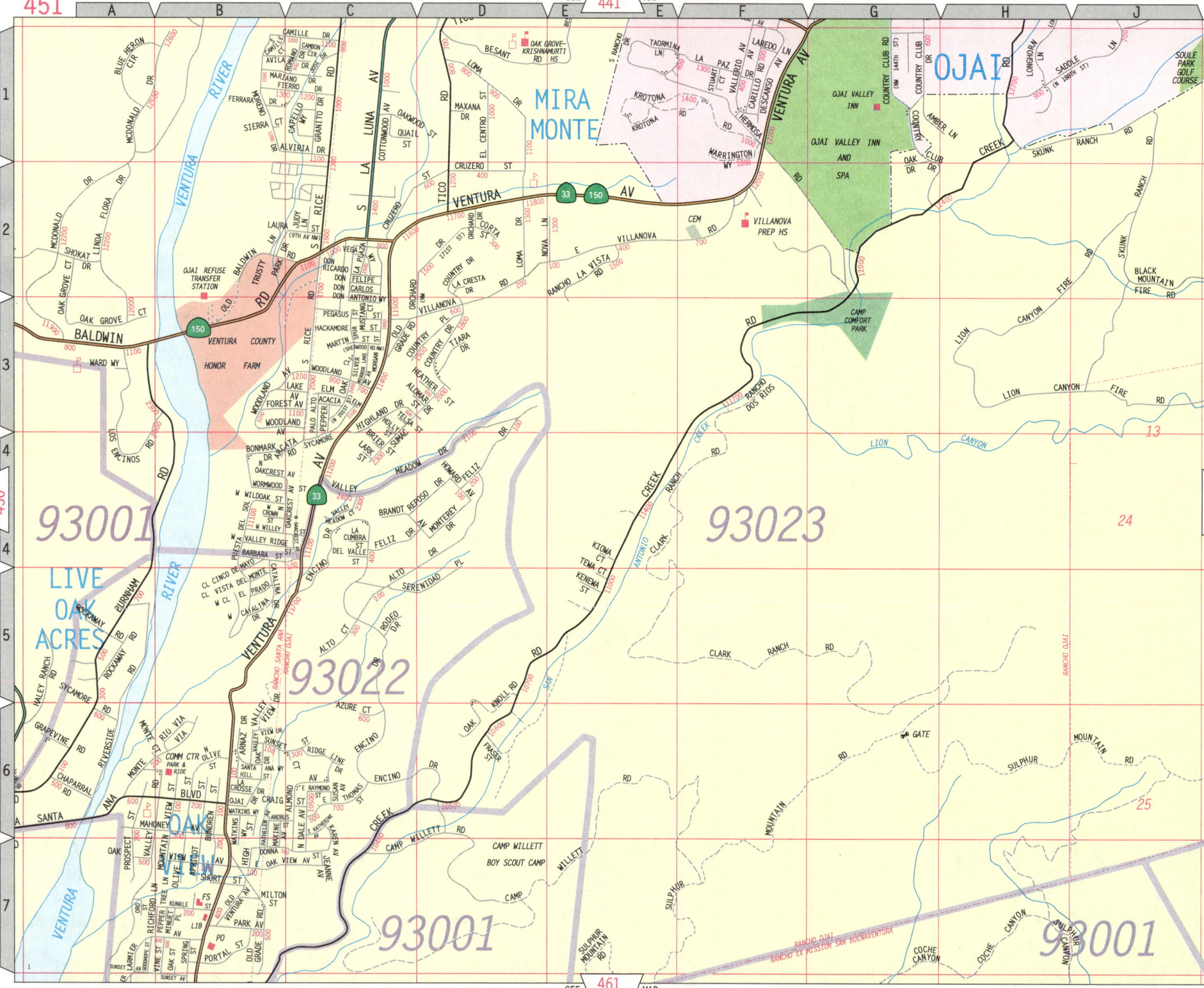

A B C D E F G H J

VENTURA CO.

OJAI

MIRA MONTE

SOULE PARK GOLF COURSE

OAK GROVE-KRISHNAMURTI RD HS

BESANT

KROTONA

OJAI VALLEY INN

OJAI VALLEY INN AND SPA

VILLANOVA PREP HS

COUNTRY CLUB RD

COUNTRY CLUB

VENTURA AV

33 150 AV

BLACK MOUNTAIN FIRE RD

SKUNK RANCH

CAMP COMFORT PARK

LION CANYON FIRE RD

LION CANYON FIRE RD

LION CANYON

BALDWIN

150

OJAI REFUSE TRANSFER STATION

VENTURA COUNTY HONOR FARM

WARD WY

13

93001

LIVE OAK ACRES

93022

93023

24

RANCHO DOS RIOS

CLARK RANCH

KNOLL RD

CLARK RANCH RD

RANCHO OJAI

GATE

MOUNTAIN RD

SULPHUR MOUNTAIN RD

93001

OAK VIEW

CAMP WILLETT BOY SCOUT CAMP

CAMP WILLETT

SULPHUR MOUNTAIN RD

RANCHO OJAI

RANCHO EX MISSION SAN BUENAVENTURA

COCHE CANYON

COCHE CANYON

SULPHUR CANYON

93001

VENTURA RIVER

SEE 450 MAP

SEE 452 MAP

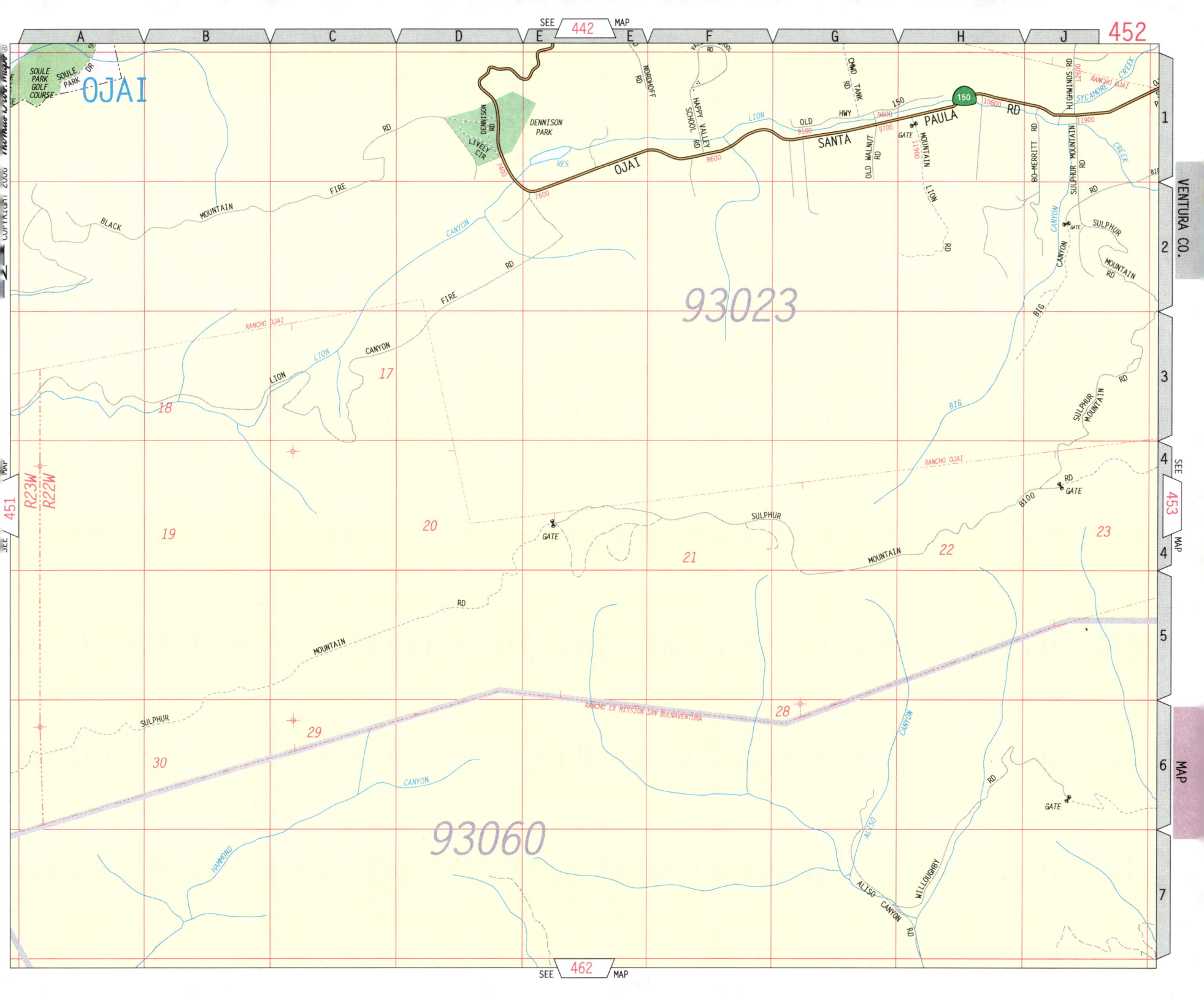

OJAI

SOULE PARK GOLF COURSE

SOULE PARK DR

DENNISON RD

LIVELY CIR

DENNISON PARK

NORDHOFF RD

HAPPY VALLEY SCHOOL RD

VALLEY SCHOOL RD

CMD TANK RD

NORDHOFF RD

150

150

HIGHWINDS RD

12600

RANCHO OJAI

SYCAMORE CREEK

11900

BLACK

MOUNTAIN

FIRE

RD

RES

7400

7600

OJAI

8600

LION

RD

OLD 9100

HWY

9700

9800

OLD WALNUT RD

SANTA

PAULA

GATE

MOUNTAIN 11900

LION

RD

10800

RD

BO-MERRITT RD

SULPHUR MOUNTAIN RD

CANYON

GATE

SULPHUR

MOUNTAIN RD

BIG

93023

CANYON

FIRE

RD

RANCHO OJAI

LION

LION

CANYON

17

LION

18

19

20

GATE

SULPHUR

21

MOUNTAIN

22

RANCHO OJAI

8100

GATE RD

23

SEE 451 MAP

R23W R22W

MOUNTAIN

RD

SULPHUR

29

30

MOUNTAIN

CANYON

RANCHO EX MISSION SAN BUENAVENTURA

28

ALISO CANYON

RD

GATE

HAMMOND

CANYON

93060

ALISO CANYON RD

WILLOUGHBY RD

SEE 453 MAP

VENTURA CO.

MAP

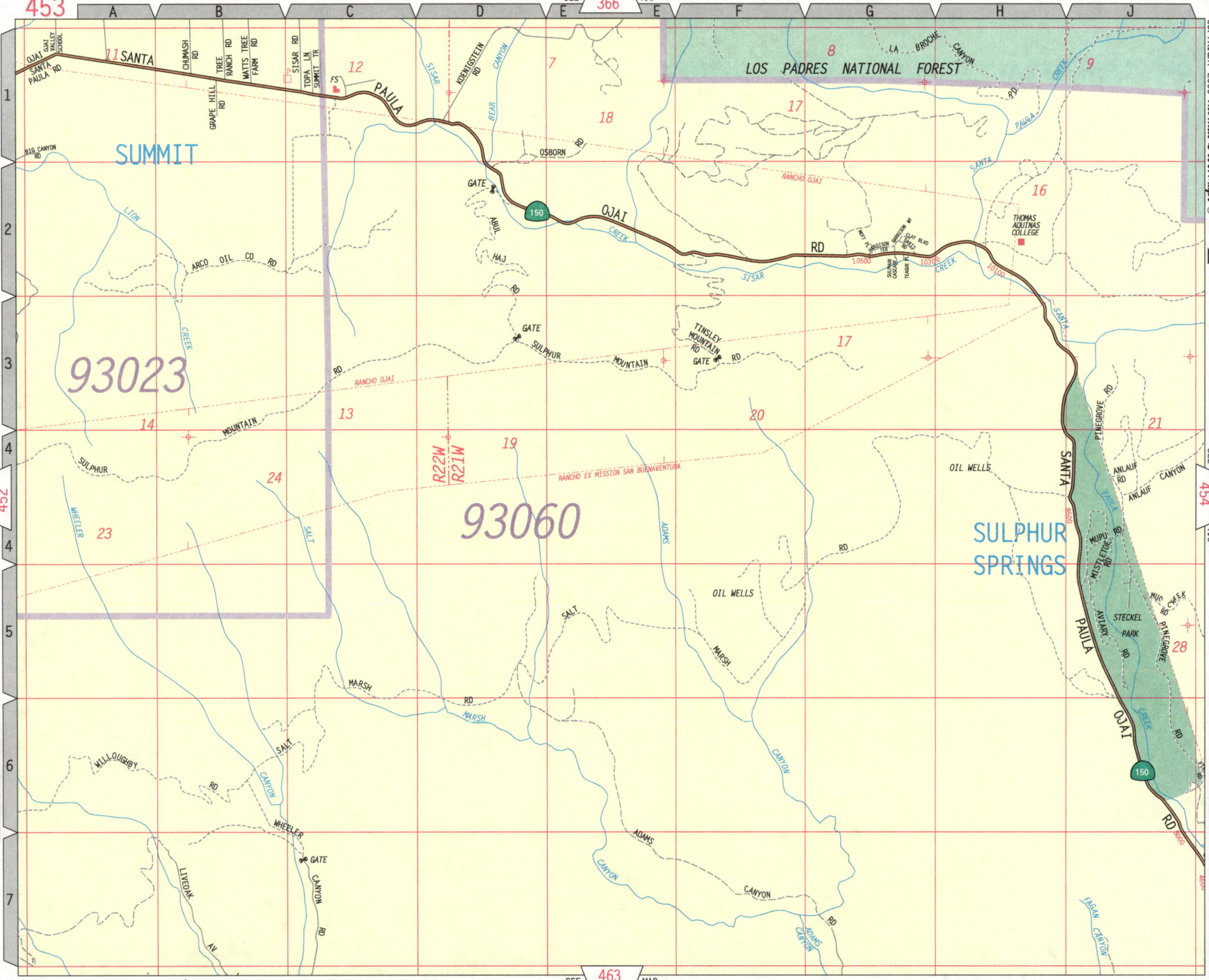

453

A B C D E SEE 366 MAP E F G H J

VENTURA CO.

11 SANTA
OJAI SANTA PAULA RD
OJAI VALLEY SCHOOL
CHUMASH RD
GRAPE HILL RD
TREE RANCH RD
WATTS TREE FARM RD
SISAR RD
TOPA LN
SUMMIT TR
FS
12
PAULA
SISAR
KOENIGSTEIN RD
CANYON
7
8 LA BROCHE CANYON
LOS PADRES NATIONAL FOREST
9
CREEK

1

BEAR
18
17
SANTA PAULA RD

SUMMIT
BIG CANYON RD
OSBORN RD
RANCHO OJAI
SANTA

GATE
150
OJAI
CREEK
RD
NOTT PL
HARDISON TER
SANDSTONE WY
RESALES
BARCLAY BLVD
SULPHUR CASCADE
TEAGUE PL
10500
10300
10100
16
THOMAS AQUINAS COLLEGE

2
LION
ABUL
HAJ
ARCO OIL CO. RD
CREEK
SISAR CREEK
SANTA

93023
CREEK
RD
GATE
SULPHUR
MOUNTAIN
TINSLEY MOUNTAIN RD
GATE RD
17
PINEGROVE RD
21

3
RD
RANCHO OJAI
13
MOUNTAIN
20
SANTA
ANLAUF RD
ANLAUF CANYON

14
R22W R21W
19
RANCHO EX MISSION SAN BUENAVENTURA
OIL WELLS
PAULA
MUPU RD

4
SULPHUR
24
SALT
93060
ADAMS
RD
SULPHUR SPRINGS
MISTLETOE RD
AVIARY RD
STECKEL PARK
PINEGROVE RD
MUD CREEK
RD
28

SEE 452 MAP
SEE 454 MAP

5
WHEELER
23
SALT
MARSH
OIL WELLS
SALT
MARSH
OJAI

6
WILLOUGHBY
SALT
CANYON
MARSH
RD
CANYON
CANYON
150
CREEK
RD

MAP

7
LIVEOAK
WHEELER
GATE
CANYON RD
AV
ADAMS
CANYON
ADAMS CANYON
RD
FAGAN CANYON

SEE 463 MAP

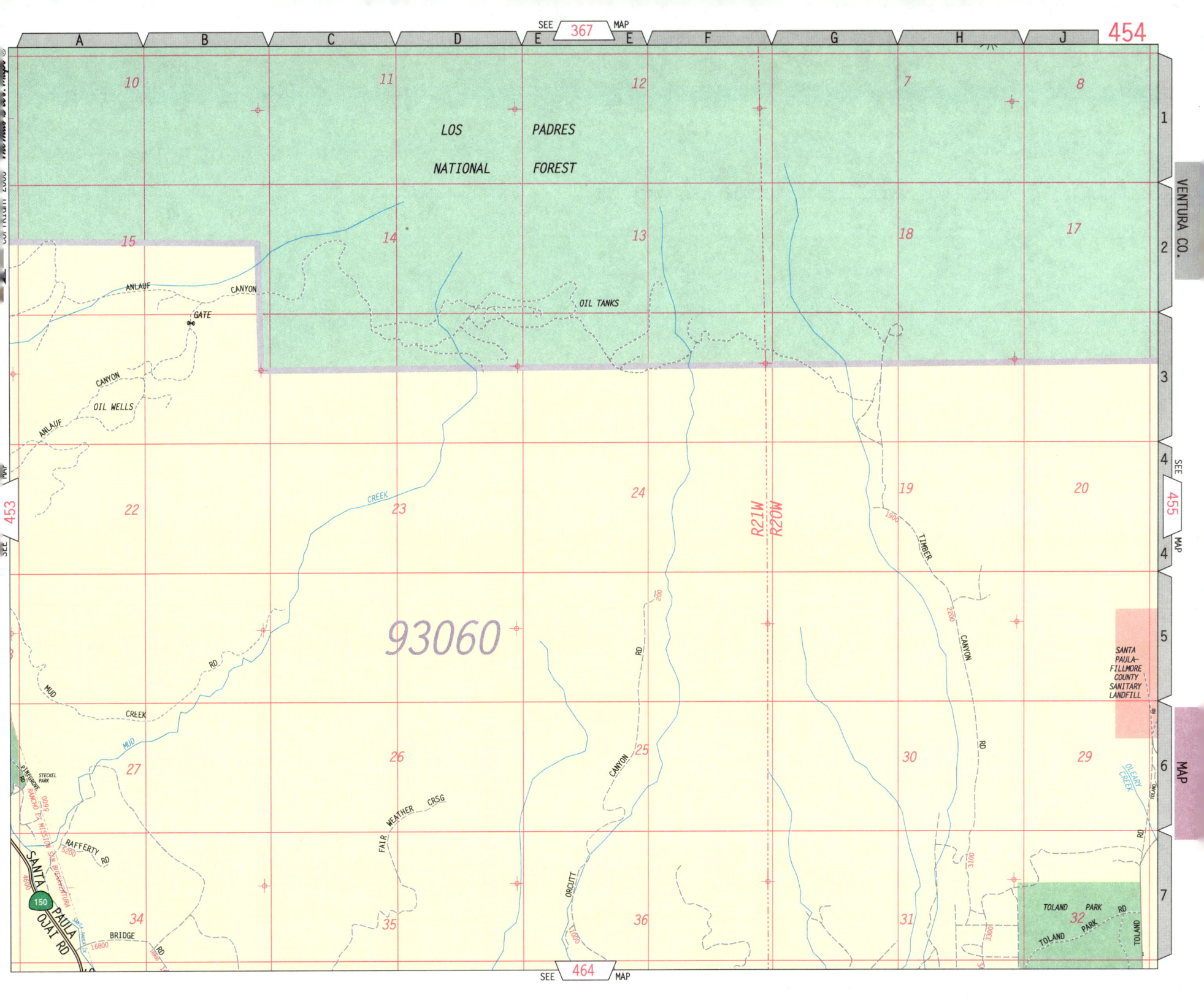

A	B	C	D	E	E	F	G	H	J

1

10

11

12

7

8

LOS   PADRES

NATIONAL   FOREST

2

15

14

13

18

17

ANLAUF   CANYON

GATE

OIL TANKS

3

CANYON

OIL WELLS

ANLAUF

4

22

CREEK

23

24

R21W R20W

19

20

TIMBER

1900

2200

5

93060

RD

CANYON

RD

SANTA PAULA– FILLMORE COUNTY SANITARY LANDFILL

6

MUD

CREEK

MUD

26

25

CANYON

RD

30

29

O'LEARY CREEK

27

STECKEL PARK

RANCHO EX–MISSION SAN BUENAVENTURA

0095

FAIR WEATHER CRSG

FAIR

7

RAFFERTY RD

5200

150

SANTA PAULA OJAI RD

34

BRIDGE

RD

16800

35

36

ORCUTT

1000

31

TOLAND PARK RD

32 PARK

TOLAND PARK

TOLAND RD

3000

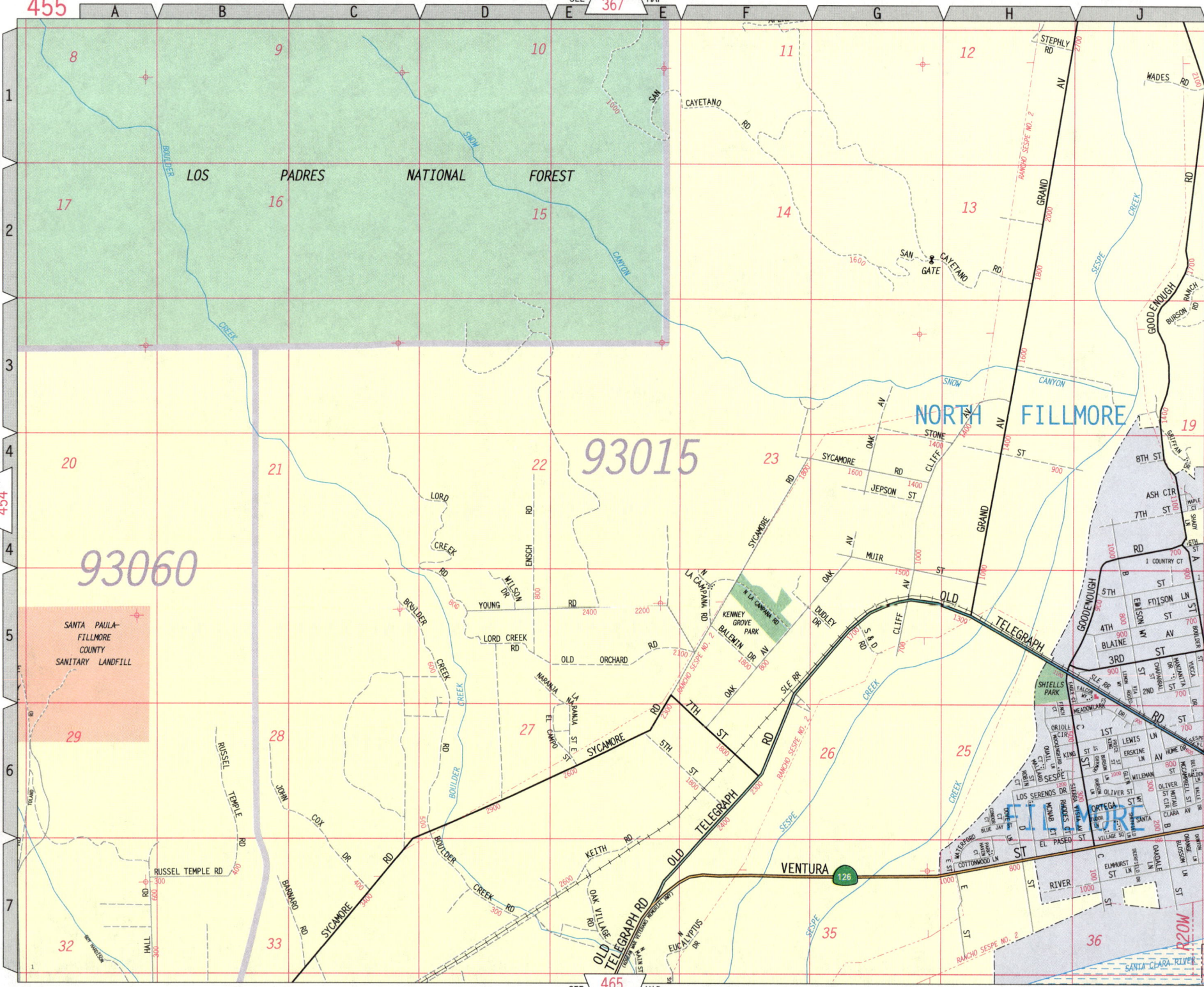

A B C D E F G H J

SEE 367 MAP

VENTURA CO.

8   9   10   11   12

STEPHLY RD
WADES RD

1

CAYETANO RD

SAN

LOS   PADRES   NATIONAL   FOREST

17   16   15   14   13

2

SAN CAYETANO GATE
RD

BOULDER

CREEK

SNOW CANYON

BURSON RD
GOODENOUGH RD

3

NORTH FILLMORE

93015

19

20   21   22   23

STONE ST
OAK AV
CLIFF AV
SYCAMORE RD
GRAND AV
8TH ST
ASH CIR
7TH ST

4

SEE 454 MAP

JEPSON ST

93060

LORD
CREEK
RD

WILSON DR
YOUNG RD

LA CAMPANA RD
N LA CAMPANA RD
KENNEY GROVE PARK
OAK AV
MUIR ST
DUDLEY DR

OLD
TELEGRAPH

5TH ST
EDISON LN
BLAINE ST
3RD ST

5

SANTA PAULA-
FILLMORE
COUNTY
SANITARY LANDFILL

LORD CREEK RD
OLD   ORCHARD

BALEWIN DR
CLIFF AV
S & D RD
SLE RR
SHIELLS PARK

1ST ST
LEWIS LN
ERSKINE AV

28   27   26   25

NARANJA ST
EL CAMPO ST

SYCAMORE RD
7TH ST
5TH ST

OAK ST

SESPE

FILLMORE

6

29

RUSSEL
TEMPLE
RD

JOHN RD
COX DR
BOULDER RD
KEITH ST

OLD
TELEGRAPH
RD

VENTURA 126

RIVER ST

7

RUSSEL TEMPLE RD

HALL RD

BARNARD RD
SYCAMORE

CREEK RD

OAK VILLAGE RD
EUCALYPTUS DR

OLD TELEGRAPH RD

SESPE

SANTA CLARA RIVER

32   33   35   36

R20W

SEE 465 MAP

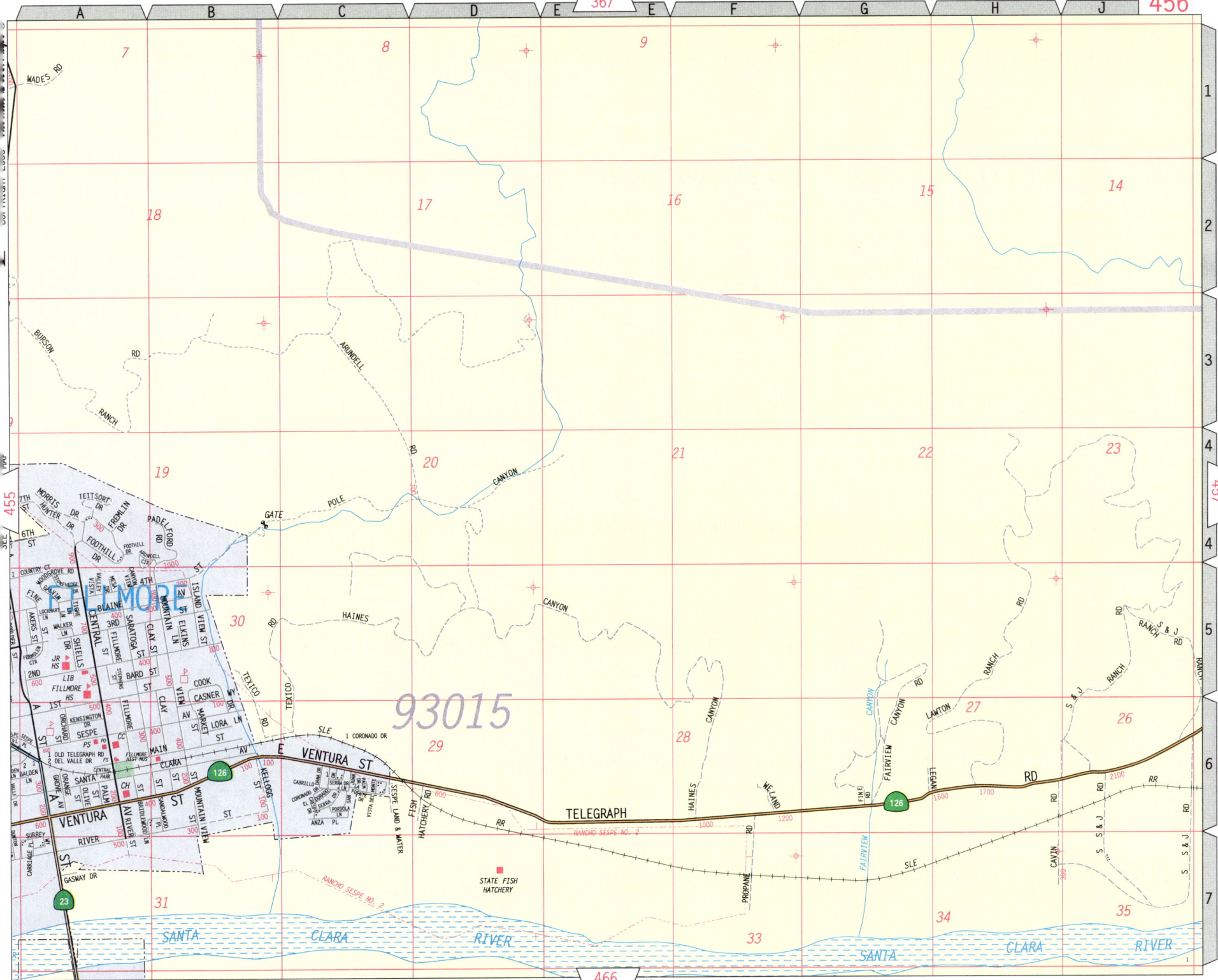

SEE 367 MAP

456

A B C D E E F G H J

VENTURA CO.

7 8 9

1

WADES RD

18 17 16 15 14

2

BURSON RANCH RD

ARUNDELL

3

19 20 21 22 23

SEE 455

SEE 457 MAP

GATE POLE CANYON

FILLMORE

30 CANYON

HAINES RD

93015

28 27 26

S & J RANCH RD

SESPE

E VENTURA ST 126

29 CANYON FAIRVIEW CANYON LAWTON DR RANCH

TELEGRAPH RD 126

VENTURA 23 RR

STATE FISH HATCHERY PROPANE RD

31 33 34 35

SANTA CLARA RIVER SANTA CLARA RIVER

SEE 466 MAP

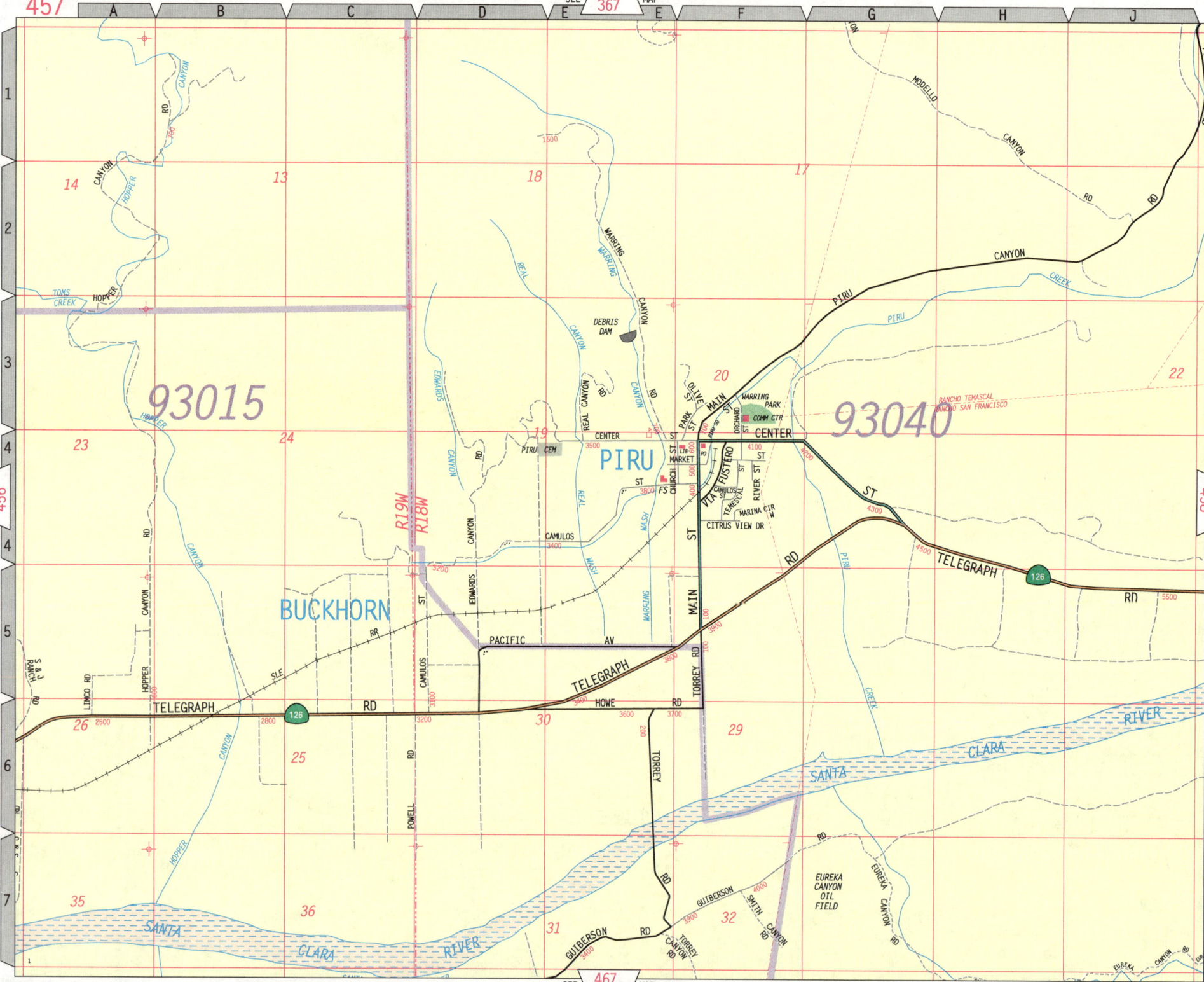

A B C D E SEE 367 MAP E F G H J

VENTURA CO.

1

14 13 18 17

2

TOMS CREEK
HOPPER
HOPPER CANYON RD

93015

3

1500

WARRING CANYON
WARRING
REAL
REAL CANYON
DEBRIS DAM
CANYON
20
RANCHO TEMASCAL
RANCHO SAN FRANCISCO
PIRU
22

93040

SEE 456 MAP
SEE 458 MAP

4

23 24 19
CENTER
3500
PIRU CEM
MARKET
PIRU
OLIVE ST
PARK ST
MAIN ST
WARRING PARK
COMM CTR
ORCHARD ST
CENTER

R19W R18W
CAMULOS
REAL
WASH
CHURCH ST
3800 FS
Lib 600
PO
500
4000
VIA FUSTERO
CAMULOS ST
TEMESCAL
RIVER ST
4100
ST
4300
ST
TELEGRAPH
4500
126

4

CAMULOS 3400
MARINA CIR W
CITRUS VIEW DR

5

CANYON
CANYON RD
EDWARDS
EDWARDS
3200
CANYON RD
BUCKHORN
ST
RR
PACIFIC AV
WARRING
MAIN ST
TORREY RD
100
3900
CREEK
PIRU
RD
4300
126

6

S & J RANCH RD
LIMCO RD
HOPPER
CANYON
SLE
2800
126
RD
CAMULOS 3700
POWELL RD
3200
TELEGRAPH
3600 HOWE RD
3600 3700
200
TELEGRAPH
3800
TORREY RD
TORREY
29
SANTA
CLARA RIVER
RD
EUREKA CANYON OIL FIELD

TELEGRAPH 2500 26 25 30

7

35 36 31
GUIBERSON RD
3400
3900
GUIBERSON RD
TORREY CANYON RD
32
SMITH CANYON RD
4000
EUREKA CANYON RD
EUREKA CANYON RD
SANTA CLARA RIVER

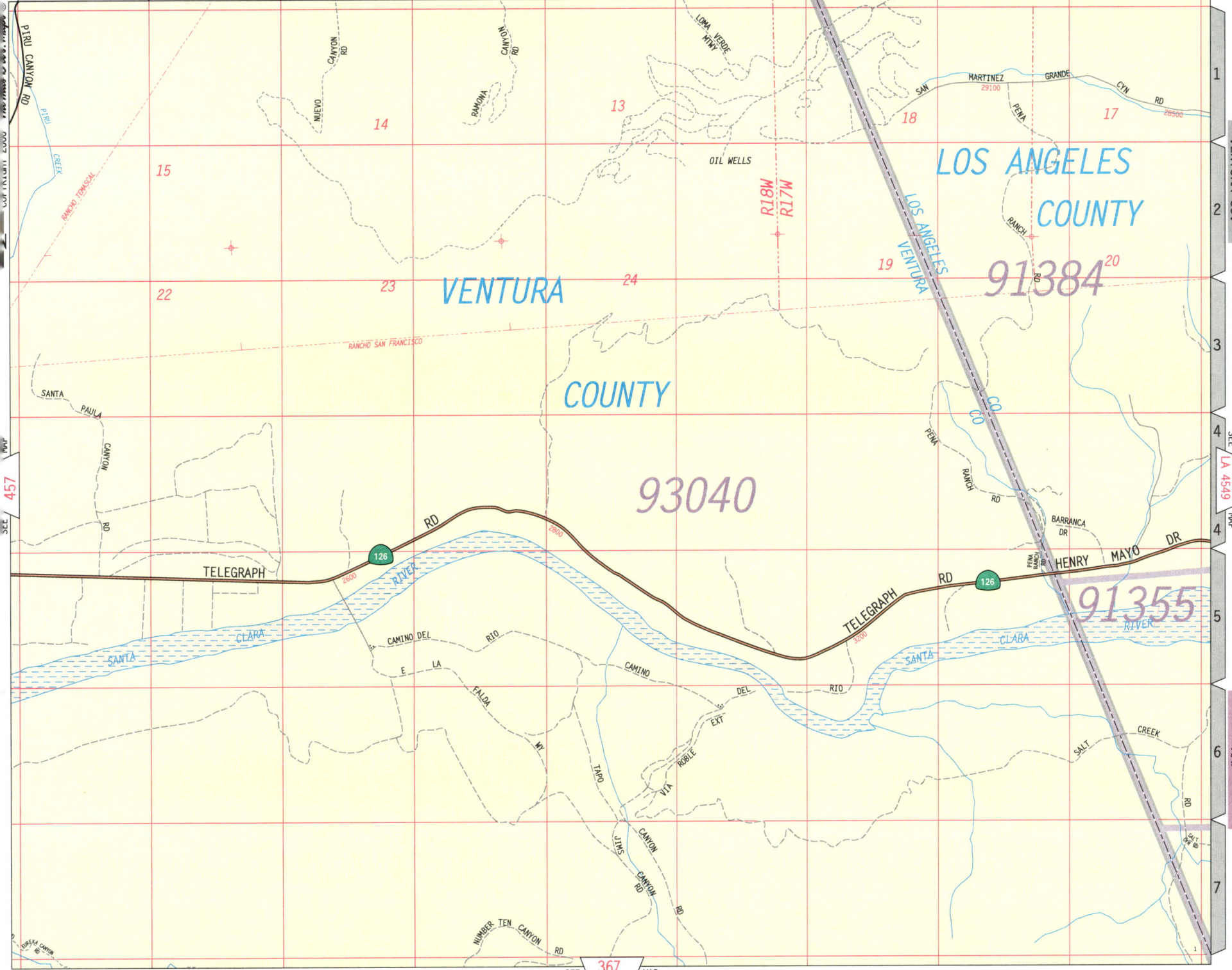

458

VENTURA CO.

PIRU CANYON RD

PIRU CREEK

RANCHO TEMASCAL

CANYON RD

NUEVO

RAMONA

CANYON RD

LOMA VERDE MTWY

13

14

15

22

23

24

OIL WELLS

R18W R17W

VENTURA

COUNTY

RANCHO SAN FRANCISCO

SANTA PAULA CANYON RD

CANYON RD

SAN

MARTINEZ GRANDE
29100

PENA

CYN RD
28500

LOS ANGELES

COUNTY

18

19

17

20

91384

VENTURA

LOS ANGELES

CO

PENA

RANCH RD

RANCH RD

93040

RD

2800

126

TELEGRAPH

2600

RIVER

SANTA CLARA

CAMINO DEL

RIO

E LA FALDA

WY

TAPO

VIA ROBLE

CANYON RD

JIMS CANYON RD

RD

NUMBER TEN CANYON RD

CAMINO

RIO

DEL EXT

DEL

RIO

SANTA

CLARA

TELEGRAPH RD
3200

126

PENA RANCH RD

BARRANCA DR

HENRY MAYO DR

91355

RIVER

SALT CREEK

SALT CYN RD

SALT CW RD

SEE 457 MAP

SEE LA 4549 MAP

MAP

1

2

3

4

4

5

6

7

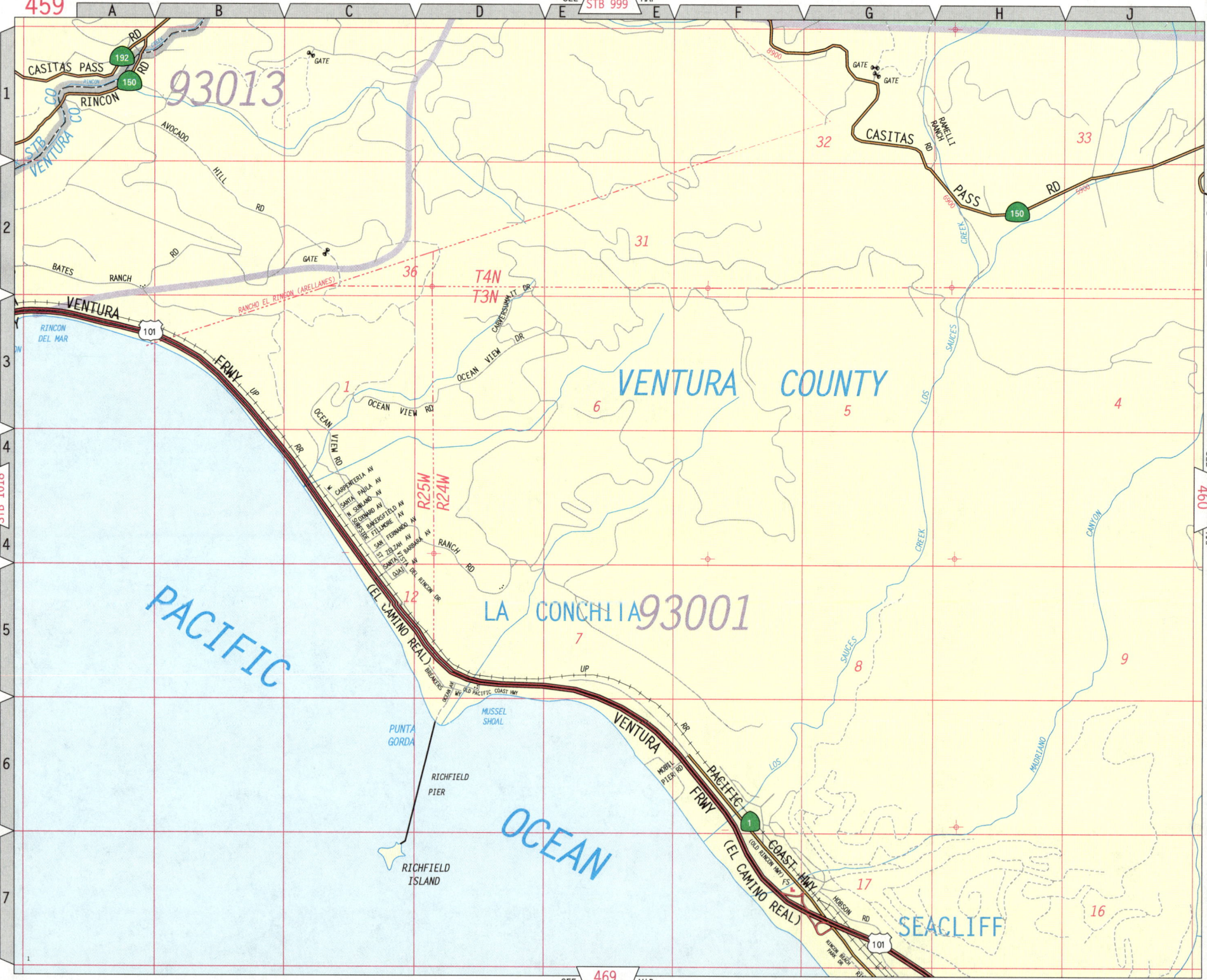

A   B   C   D   E   F   G   H   J

SEE STB 999 MAP

VENTURA CO.

CASITAS PASS
192
150
RINCON

93013

AVOCADO

HILL

RD

BATES   RANCH

GATE

GATE

GATE

CASITAS

RAMELLI RANCH RD

32

33

PASS   RD

150

31

36

T4N
T3N

RANCHO EL RINCON (ARELLANES)

CARVERSHAM IT   DR

VENTURA

101

FRWY

RINCON DEL MAR

OCEAN VIEW   DR

VENTURA   COUNTY

1

OCEAN VIEW   RD

6

5

4

SEE STB 1018 MAP

CARPENTERIA AV
SANTA PAULA AV
N SUNLAND
SO OXNARD AV
BAKERSFIELD AV
FILLMORE AV
SAN FERNANDO AV
LT ZIB ZAH AV
SANTA CLARA AV
QUAIL AV
SANTA DEL RINCON DR

R25W
R24W

RANCH   RD

LOS

SAUCES

CANYON

CREEK

PACIFIC

12

LA   CONCHITA 93001

7

SEE 460 MAP

8

9

BREAKERS

OCEAN WY

OLD PACIFIC COAST HWY

UP

VENTURA

FRWY

MUSSEL SHOAL

PACIFIC

LOS

SAUCES

MADRIANO

PUNTA GORDA

RICHFIELD PIER

MOBIL PIER RD

1

OCEAN

RICHFIELD ISLAND

COAST HWY

(OLD RINCON HWY) FS

(EL CAMINO REAL)

17

HORSON   RD

16

RINCON BEACH PARK DR

SEACLIFF

101

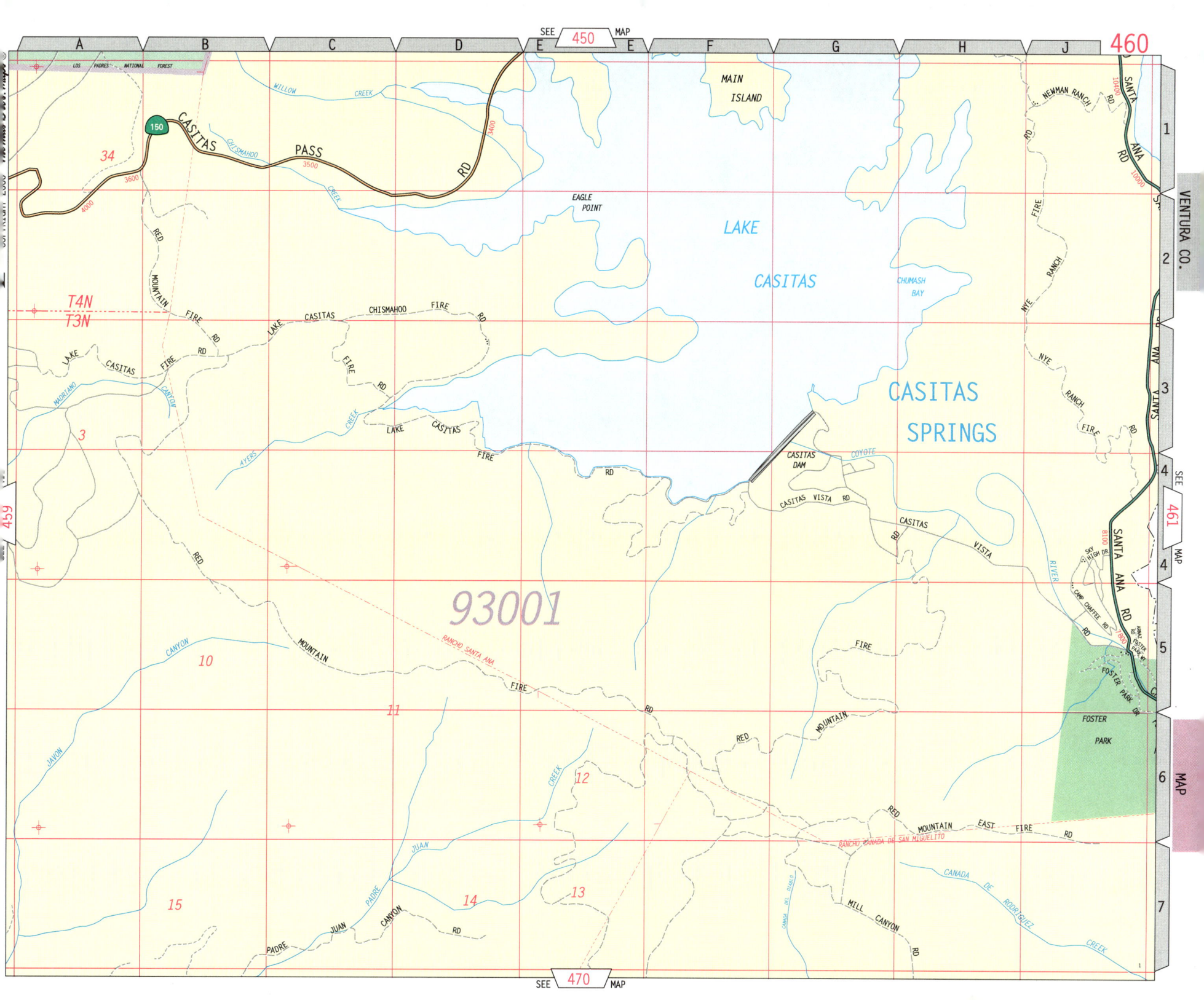

SEE 450 MAP

A B C D E E F G H J **460**

1

LOS PADRES NATIONAL FOREST

MAIN ISLAND

CASITAS
150
PASS
34
WILLOW CREEK
CHISMAHOO
3500
3600
4000

NEWMAN RANCH RD

SANTA ANA RD

2

RED MOUNTAIN FIRE RD

EAGLE POINT

LAKE

CASITAS

CHUMASH BAY

FIRE RANCH

NYE RANCH

T4N
T3N

LAKE CASITAS FIRE RD

CHISMAHOO FIRE RD

3

LAKE CASITAS FIRE RD

MADRIANO CANYON

FIRE RD

CREEK

CASITAS SPRINGS

NYE RANCH

NYE RANCH FIRE RD

3

AYERS CREEK

LAKE CASITAS FIRE RD

COYOTE

SANTA ANA

SEE 461 MAP

RD

CASITAS DAM

CASITAS VISTA RD

RIVER

SANTA ANA RD

4

SKY HIGH DR

CAMP CHAFFEE RD

ANIMAL FOSTER PARK RD

93001

RANCHO SANTA ANA

CANYON

MOUNTAIN

FIRE

RD

CASITAS VISTA

8100

7800

10

11

FIRE

MOUNTAIN FIRE

FOSTER PARK DR

5

JAVON

CREEK

12

RED

RED MOUNTAIN

FOSTER PARK

6

JUAN

RED MOUNTAIN EAST FIRE RD

RANCHO CANADA DE SAN MIGUELITO

CANADA DE RODRIGUEZ CREEK

15

PADRE JUAN CANYON RD

14

13

CANADA DEL GADO

MILL CANYON RD

7

PADRE

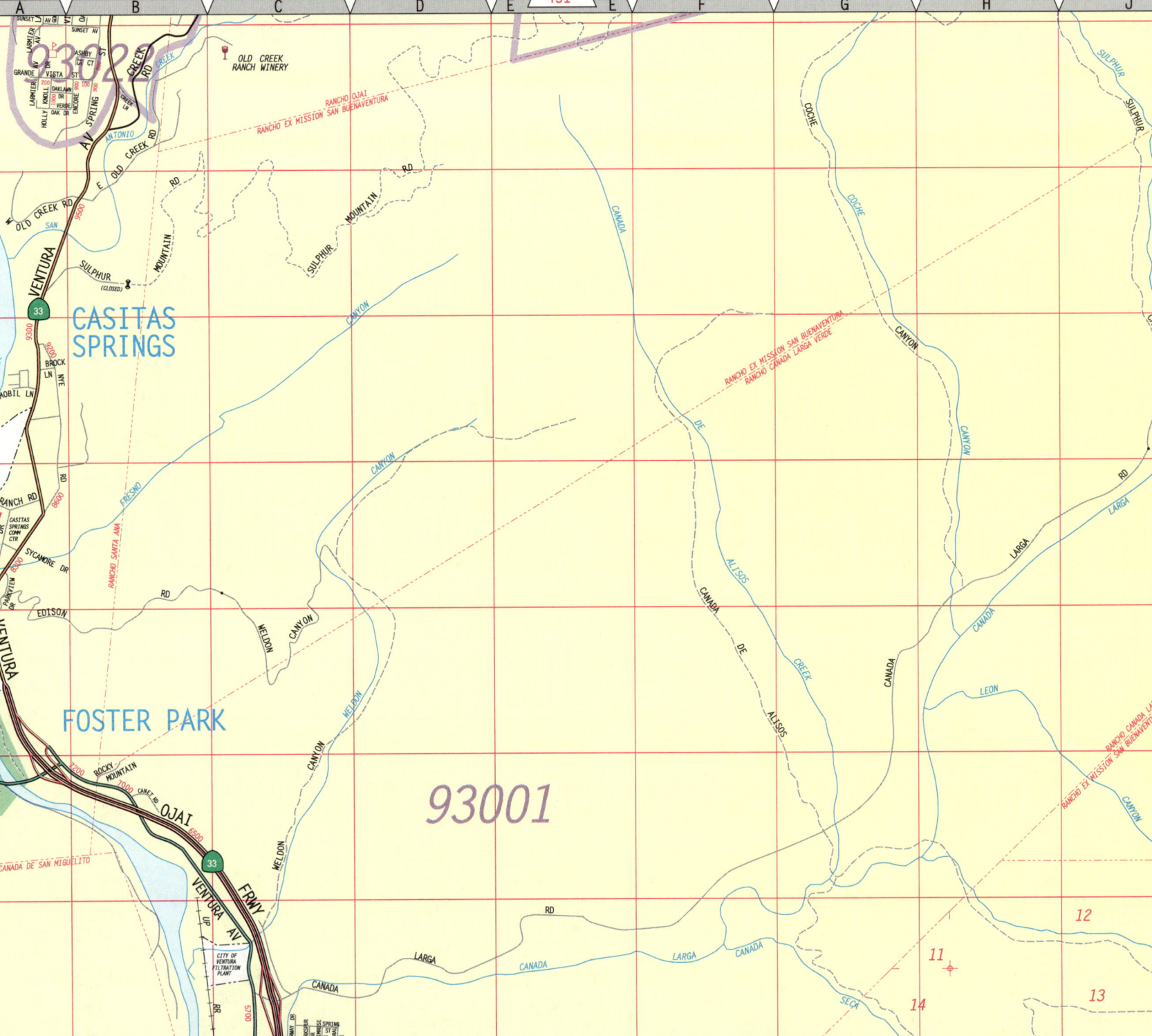

A B C D E SEE 451 MAP E F G H J

VENTURA CO.

1

SUNSET AV
LARIMER AV GR
SUNSET AV
ASHBY CT
93022
GRANDE VISTA
LARIMER
OAKLAWN DR
KNOLL
HOLLY
OAK DR
OAK
200
1000
960 190
OLD CREEK RANCH WINERY

ANTONIO
E OLD CREEK RD
OLD CREEK RD
RD
RANCHO OJAI
RANCHO EX MISSION SAN BUENAVENTURA

SANTA ANA RD
SAN
9500
MOUNTAIN
SULPHUR MOUNTAIN
RD
COCHE
SULPHUR
SULPHUR

2

VENTURA
SULPHUR (CLOSED)
CANADA
COCHE
CANYON
CANYON

33
CASITAS SPRINGS

SANTA ANA RD
RIVER
9300
9200
BROCK LN
NYE
MOBIL LN
CANYON
RANCHO EX MISSION SAN BUENAVENTURA
RANCHO CANADA LARGA VERDE
DE
CANYON
CANYON

3

SANTA
9000
RD
8600
RANCH RD
CASITAS SPRINGS COMM CTR
SYCAMORE DR
EDISON DR
8800
RD
FRESNO
CANYON
RANCHO SANTA ANA
DE
ALLSOS
CANADA
LARGA
RD

VEN
4

8100
PARKVIEW DR
EDISON
RD
CANYON
WELDON
CANADA
DE
CREEK
CANADA
LARGA
LEON

SEE 460 MAP
4

VENTURA AV
CANYON
WELDON
ALLSOS

5
FOSTER PARK
VENTURA

CASITAS VISTA RD
FOSTER PARK DR
FOSTER PARK
9200
ROCKY MOUNTAIN
7000
CANET RD
OJAI
6500
WELDON
CANYON
ALLSOS
RANCHO CANADA LARGA VERDE
RANCHO EX MISSION SAN BUENAVENTURA
CANYON

MAP 6

RANCHO CANADA DE SAN MIGUELITO
33
VENTURA AV FRWY
UP
93001
WELDON
RD

7

CITY OF VENTURA FILTRATION PLANT
6700
RR
CANADA
LARGA
CANADA
LARGA
CANADA
SECA
11
12
14
13
NORWAY DR
LARKSHIRE DR
PRIMROSE ST
SPRING ST
FLORAL DR

1

SEE 471 MAP

VENTURA CO.
MAP
462

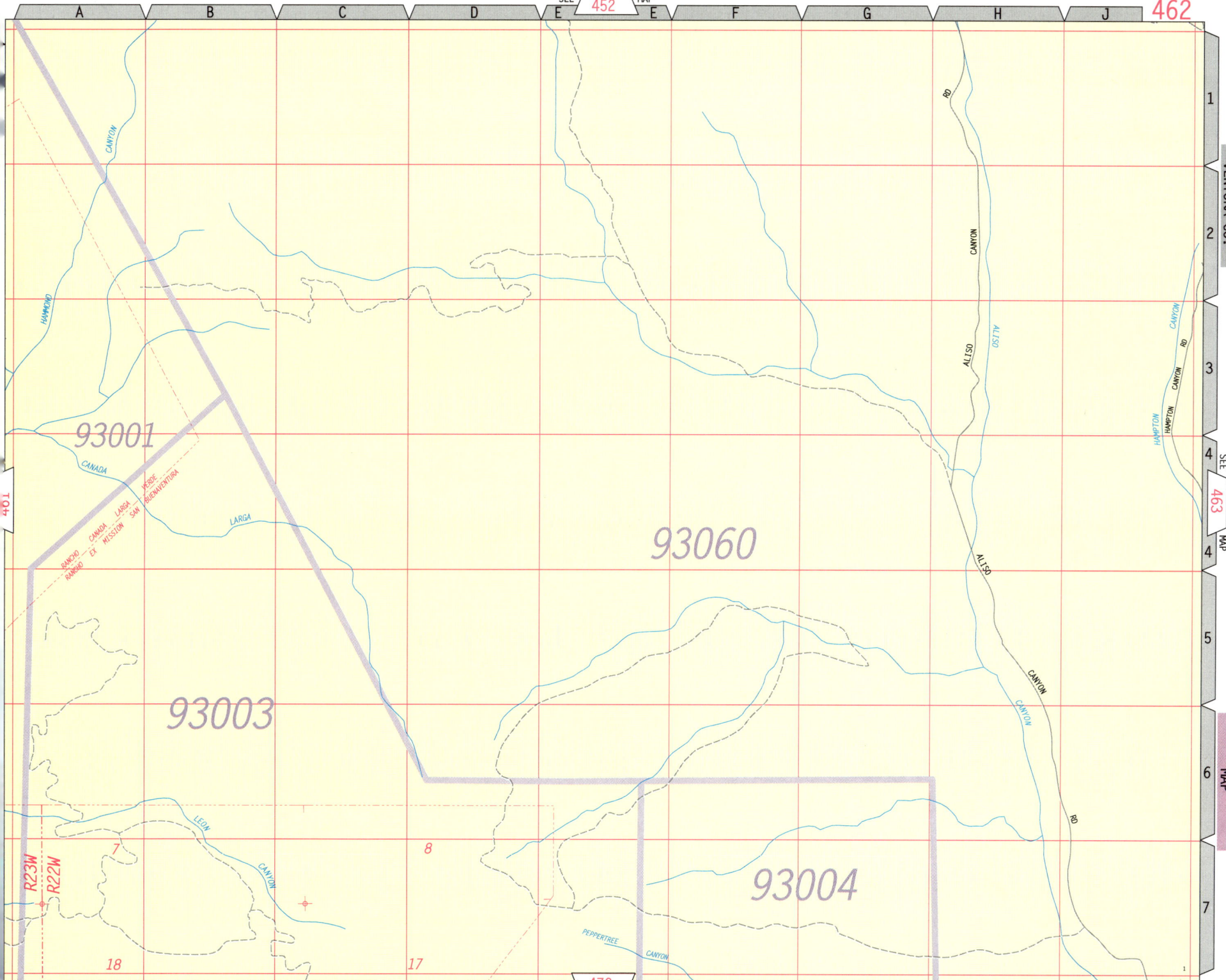

VENTURA CO.

93001

93060

93003

93004

R23W R22W

7

8

18

17

CANYON

CANADA

LARGA

LEON

CANYON

PEPPERTREE CANYON

ALISO

CANYON

HAMPTON CANYON RD

RD

RANCHO CANADA LARGA VERDE
RANCHO EX MISSION SAN BUENAVENTURA

401

1 2 3 4 4 5 6 7

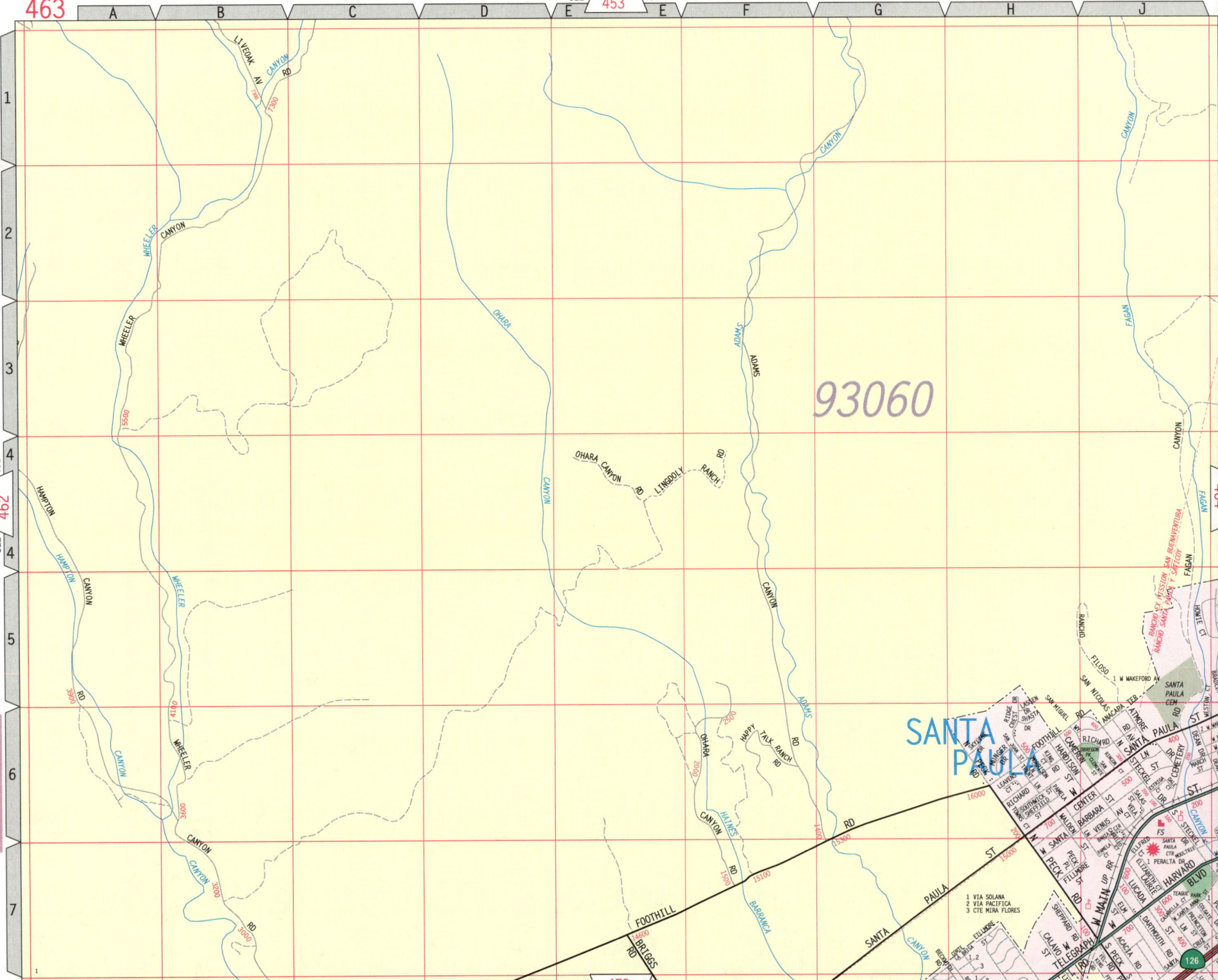

SEE 453 MAP

A	B	C	D	E	E	F	G	H	J

VENTURA CO.

93060

LIVEOAK AV

WHEELER CANYON RD

WHEELER CANYON

7300

5500

HAMPTON

HAMPTON CANYON

WHEELER

WHEELER

3900

4100

3900

CANYON

CANYON 3200

CANYON 3000

OHARA

OHARA CANYON

CANYON

OHARA CANYON RD   LINGDOLY   RANCH RD

ADAMS

ADAMS

ADAMS CANYON

CANYON

HAPPY TALK RANCH RD

OHARA

CANYON

HAINES RD

CANYON RD

2500

2000

16000

1400

1500

15100

15300

14600

BARRANCA

FAGAN

FAGAN CANYON

FAGAN

CANYON

SEE 462 MAP
MAP

SEE 464 MAP

SANTA PAULA

SANTA PAULA CEM

RANCHO FILOSO

W WAKEFORD AV

RANCHO SANTA PAULA Y SATICOY
RANCHO SANTA PAULA Y SATICOY
S.M. MISSION SAN BUENAVENTURA

HOWIE CT

BRADLEY DR

RANCHO

SAN NICOLAS

SAN MIGUEL

AMACARA TER

HARDISON

CAMERON

OBREGON

RICHARD

N SANTA PAULA

STECKEL ST

DEAN DR

SANTA PAULA ST

MARCH ST

CENTER

BARBARA

N STECKEL DR

VENUS AV

WALNUT ST

SOUTHWICK ST

SHEFFIELD ST

RICHARD

LEAVENS

LN

500

400

500

700

200

FOOTHILL

W PECK ST

N SANTA PAULA ST

PECK

FILLMORE

ELFRED

CURIE

ELIZABETH

LUCADA

PERALTA DR

SANTA PAULA CTR

MISTLETREE

SANTA PAULA

ELM

HARVARD BLVD

W MAIN

S PECK RD

SHEPARD RD

CALAVO DR

W MALN UP RR

TELEGRAPH RD

DARTMOUTH ST

ACACIA ST

1 VIA SOLANA
2 VIA PACIFICA
3 CTE MIRA FLORES

1 PERALTA DR

FS

126

FOOTHILL RD

BRIGGS RD

SANTA PAULA

SANTA

CANYON

BEGG

FILLMORE

SEE 473 MAP

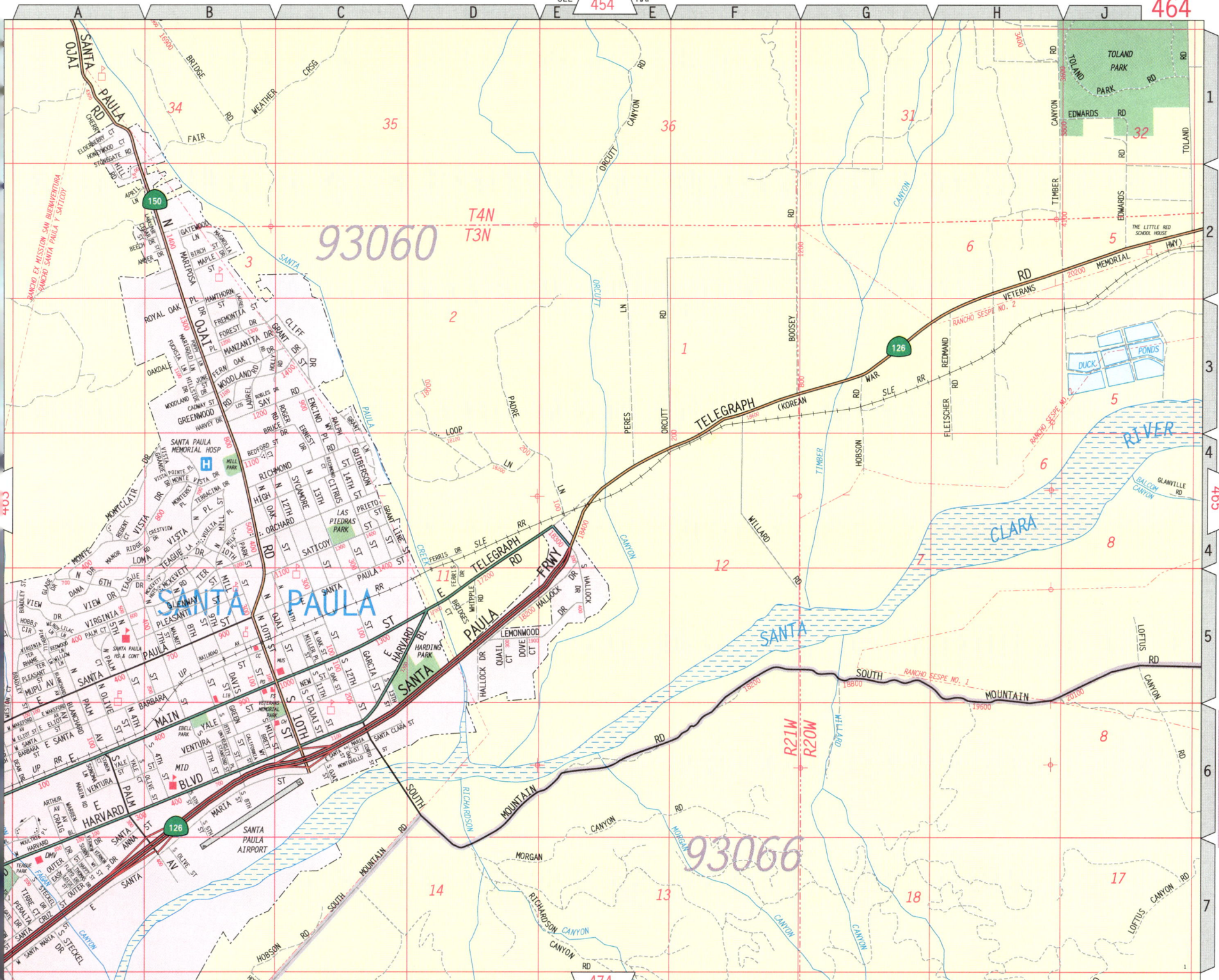

464

SEE 454 MAP

SEE 454 MAP

A B C D E E F G H J

VENTURA CO.

93060

T4N
T3N

SANTA PAULA

SANTA CLARA RIVER

93066

TOLAND PARK

THE LITTLE RED SCHOOL HOUSE

SANTA PAULA MEMORIAL HOSP

SANTA PAULA AIRPORT

RANCHO SESPE NO. 2
RANCHO SESPE NO. 1

DUCK PONDS

TELEGRAPH RD (KOREAN WAR SLE RR)

VETERANS MEMORIAL HWY

SOUTH MOUNTAIN RD

R21W R20W

1 2 3 4 5 6 7

SEE 465 MAP

MAP

SEE 474 MAP

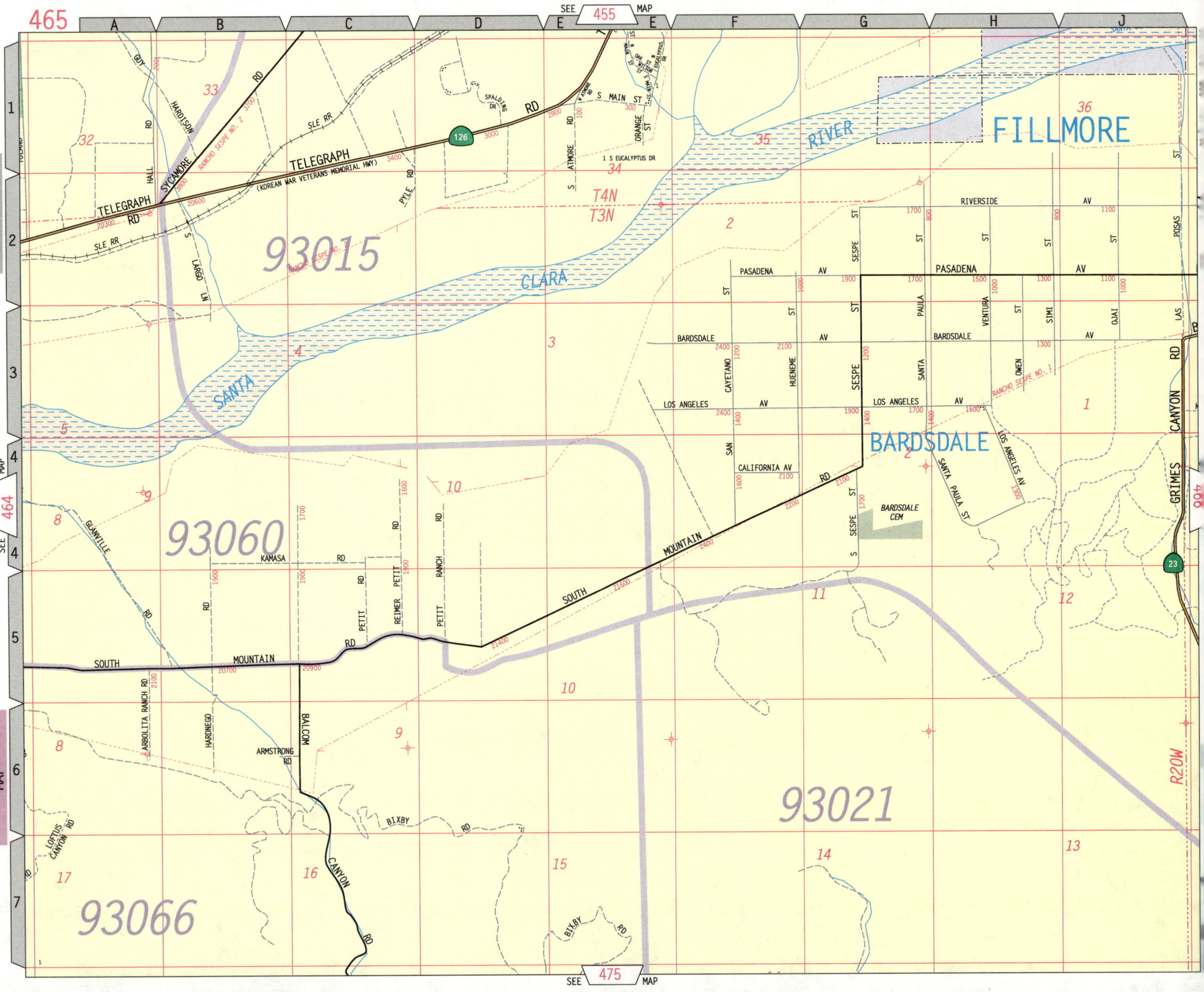

SEE 455 MAP

A B C D E E F G H J

1

2

3

4

4

5

6

7

VENTURA CO.

MAP 464 SEE

MAP

33

32

HARDISON RD

HALL RD

TOLAND RD

SYCAMORE RD

S SYCAMORE

SLE RR

TELEGRAPH
(KOREAN WAR VETERANS MEMORIAL HWY)

TELEGRAPH RD

SLE RR

20300

20600

3400

3900

RANCHO SESPE NO. 2

126

3000

3100

PYLE RD

SPALDING DR

S ATMORE RD

ORANGE ST

S MAIN ST

OLD TELEGRAPH RD

A ST

B ST

EUCALYPTUS DR

100

300

200

1 S EUCALYPTUS DR

34

35

RIVER

FILLMORE

36

SANTA ST

POSAS RD

93015

CLARA

SANTA

2

T4N
T3N

RIVERSIDE AV

1700 800 1100

SESPE ST

PASADENA AV

1900 1700 1500 1300 1100

PASADENA AV

1000 1000

4

3

PAULA ST

VENTURA ST

SIMI ST

OJAI ST

LAS POSAS RD

BARDSDALE AV

2400 1200 2100

1900

SANTA PAULA ST

BARDSDALE AV

1300

5

CAYETANO ST

HUENEME ST

SESPE ST

RANCHO SESPE NO. 1

LOS ANGELES AV

2400 1400

LOS ANGELES AV

1900 1400 1700

1500

OWEN RD

1

BARDSDALE

2

93060

9

8

GLANVILLE RD

KAMASA RD

10

1700

1600

SAN RD

CALIFORNIA AV

1600 2100

MOUNTAIN RD

2100

2200

S SESPE ST

1700

BARDSDALE CEM

LOS ANGELES AV

1500

RD 1900

PETIT RD

REIMER RD

PETIT RD

PETIT RANCH RD

RD

1900

1900

21600

MOUNTAIN

2400

11

12

23

SOUTH

RD

21400

20900

20700

SOUTH MOUNTAIN

ARBOLITA RANCH RD 2100

HARDNEGO RD

BALCOM

ARMSTRONG RD

9

8

10

93021

R20W

LOFTUS CANYON RD

RD

17

16

CANYON RD

BIXBY RD

15

BIXBY RD

14

13

93066

SEE 475 MAP

R20W

GRIMES CANYON RD

R20W

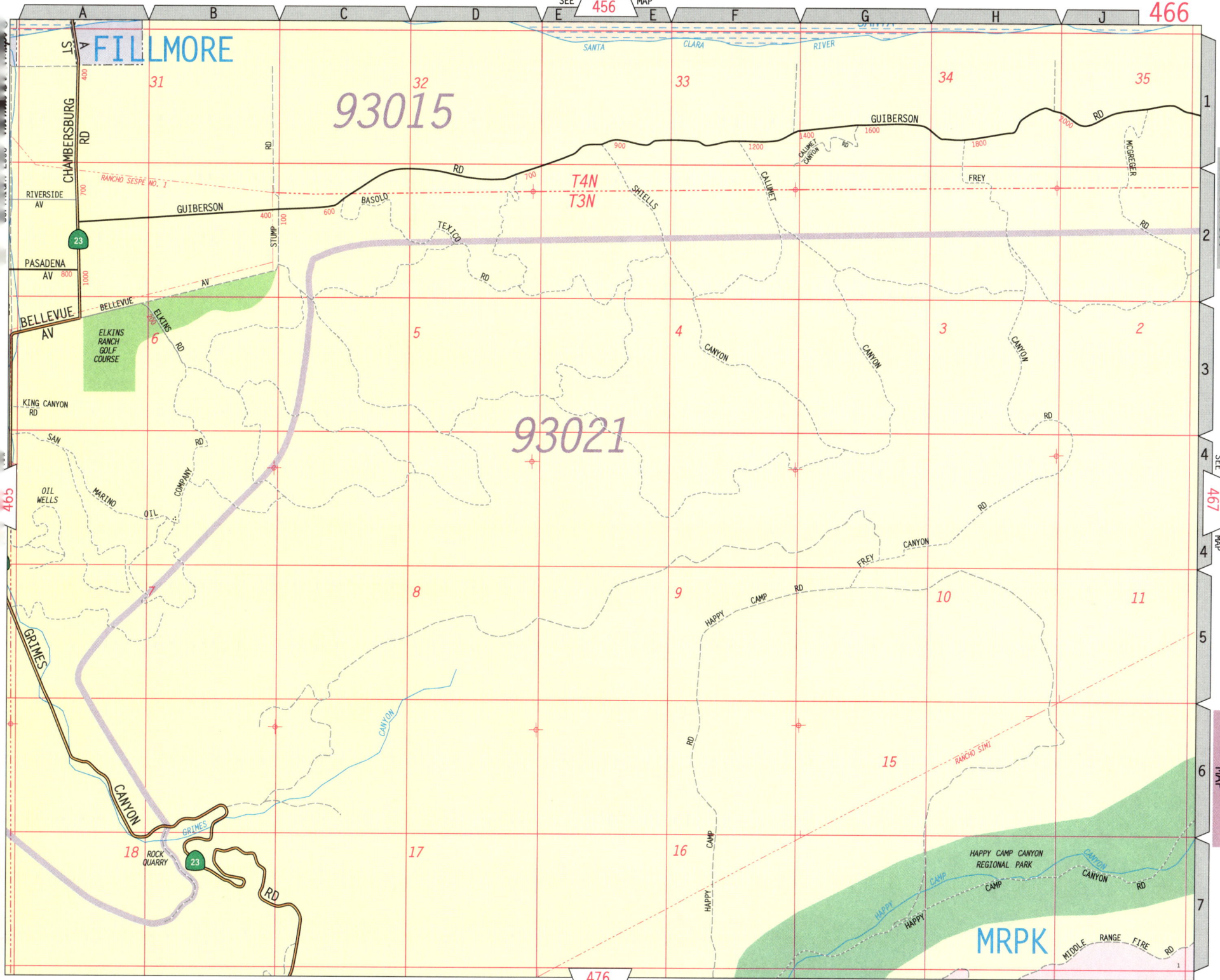

| A | B | C | D | E | E | F | G | H | J |

FILLMORE

ST
A

93015

31   32   33   34   35

CHAMBERSBURG RD

400

SANTA   CLARA   RIVER

GUIBERSON   RD

RD   900   1200   1400   1600   1800   2000

CALUMET CANYON   RD

MCGREGER

700   RANCHO SESPE NO. 1

RIVERSIDE AV   700   GUIBERSON   RD   BASOLO   T4N   T3N   SHELLS   CALUMET   FREY   RD

400   100   600   STUMP

23

PASADENA AV   800   TEXICO

1000   RD

BELLEVUE   AV   RD

BELLEVUE AV   ELKINS RD   200   6   5   4   CANYON   CANYON   3   CANYON   2

ELKINS RANCH GOLF COURSE   AV

KING CANYON RD

SAN   RD

OIL WELLS   MARINO   COMPANY   OIL   93021   RD   RD

SEE 467 MAP

FREY   CANYON   4

7   8   9   CAMP   RD   10   11

HAPPY CAMP RD   5

GRIMES

CANYON   CANYON

RD   15   RANCHO SIMI   6

GRIMES   CAMP

18   ROCK QUARRY   23   17   16   HAPPY CAMP CANYON REGIONAL PARK   CANYON   RD

RD   HAPPY   CAMP   MRPK   7

HAPPY   CAMP

MIDDLE   RANGE   FIRE   RD

VENTURA CO.

46b

MAP

1

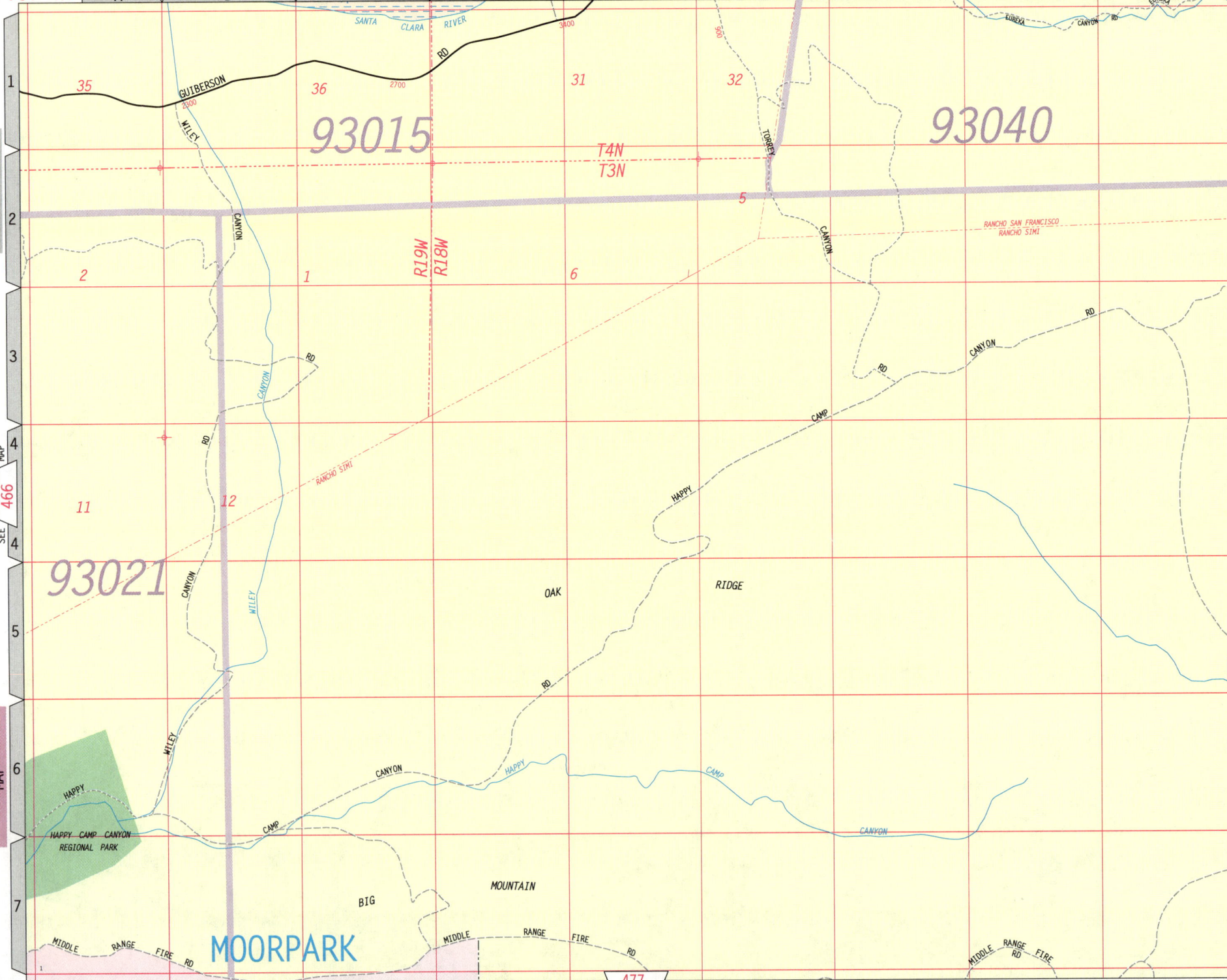

A B C D E SEE 457 MAP E F G H J

VENTURA CO.

SANTA CLARA RIVER

GUIBERSON

1

35 36 2700 3400 31 900 32

WILEY

93015

TORREY

93040

T4N
T3N

5

2

CANYON

R19W
R18W

2 1 6

RANCHO SAN FRANCISCO
RANCHO SIMI

CANYON

3

CANYON

RD

RD

CANYON

RD

RD CANYON

SEE 466 MAP

SEE 367 MAP

4

RANCHO SIMI

CAMP

11 12

93021

CANYON

HAPPY

RIDGE

OAK

5

WILEY

RD

6

WILEY

HAPPY

CANYON

HAPPY

CAMP

CANYON

HAPPY CAMP CANYON
REGIONAL PARK

CAMP

MAP

7

BIG

MOUNTAIN

MOORPARK

MIDDLE RANGE FIRE RD

MIDDLE RANGE FIRE RD

MIDDLE RANGE FIRE
RD

SEE 477 MAP

SEE 470 MAP

PACIFIC

OCEAN

VENTURA CO.

MAP

93001

(EL CAMINO REAL)

VENTURA

PACIFIC COAST HWY

FRWY

FARIA COUNTY PARK

HOBSON COUNTY PARK

RINCON BEACH

RINCON BEACH PARK

(OLD RINCON HWY)

HOBSON

RD

101

JAVON

CANYON

VENTURA CO.

A | B | C | D | E | E | F | G | H | J

1

15

14

13

RANCHO CAÑADA DE SAN MIGUELITO

OIL WELLS

MILL CANYON

RD

2

22

23

CANYON

JUAN

JUAN

PADRE

CAÑADA

DEL

FARIA BEACH

PADRE

VENTURA

3

HOBSON RD

PACIFIC

101

FRWY

UP COAST

A LEASE

CANYON

RD

DIABLO

FARIA COUNTY PARK

FARIA RD

MANDOS COVE

RD

RD

GRUB

OIL WELLS

SEE 469 MAP

PITAS POINT

4

RR

HWY

HIGH

RD

AMPHITHEATER

RD

SOLIMAR BEACH

TAYLOR RANCH RD

4/1

SOLIMAR

BEACH

EAST

LEASE

RD

4

RD

(EL CAMINO REAL)

PACIFIC

PACIFIC

5

101

93001

OCEAN

UP

VENTURA

MAP 6

COAST

RR

FRWY

(OLD RINCON HWY)

1

HWY

7

EMMA WOOD STATE BEACH

1

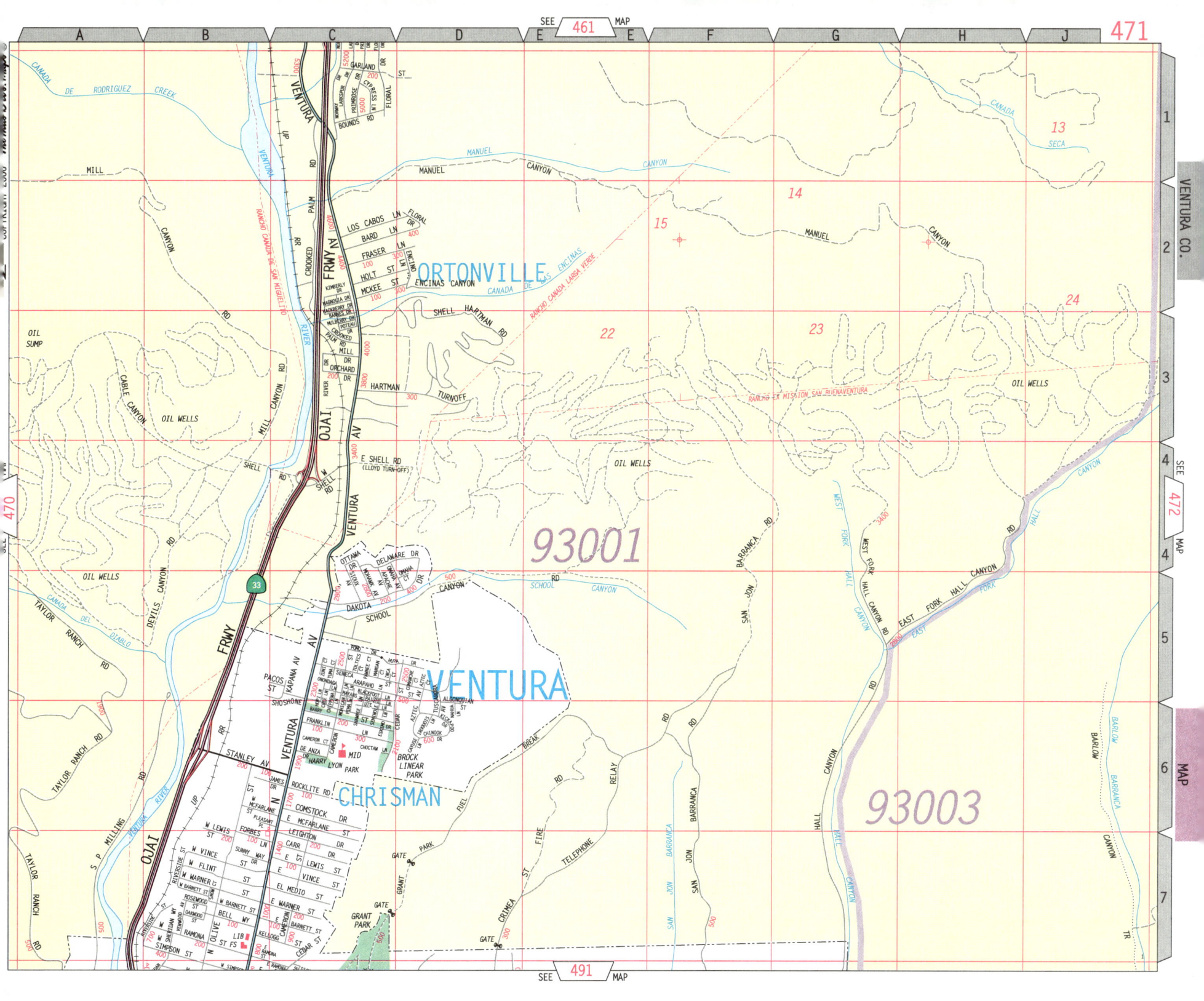

471

SEE 461 MAP

A B C D E E F G H J

VENTURA CO.

470

SEE 472 MAP

MAP

1
2
3
4
4
5
6
7

CANADA DE RODRIGUEZ CREEK

MILL

VENTURA

UP

RR

PALM

CROOKED

FRWY

GARLAND DR
LARKSPUR
PRIMROSE LN
CYPRESS
BOUNDS RD
FLORAL ST

5200
200
5000

LOS CABOS LN
FLORAL DR
BARD LN
FRASER LN
HOLT ST
MCKEE ST

ENCINO

400
300
100

KIMBERLY DR
MAGNOLIA DR
HACKBERRY DR
BARNES DR
MULBERRY DR
CROTEAU DR
CROOKED RD

10500

ORTONVILLE

ENCINAS CANYON

MANUEL CANYON CANYON

CANADA DE LAS ENCINAS
CANADA DE LAS LARGA VERDE

RANCHO CANADA LARGA VERDE

13
SECA

14

15

24

23

22

MANUEL CANYON

OIL WELLS

OIL SUMP

CABLE CANYON

OIL WELLS

MILL CANYON RD

CANYON RD

OJAI AV

VENTURA AV

SHELL

MILL DR
ORCHARD DR
RIVER

HARTMAN

4000
3800
200
300

SHELL HARTMAN RD

TURNOFF

E SHELL RD
(LLOYD TURNOFF)

3400

RAMIING EX MISSION SAN BUENAVENTURA

OIL WELLS

OIL WELLS

93001

WEST FORK HALL CANYON

HALL CANYON RD

WEST FORK HALL CANYON

EAST FORK HALL CANYON

3450
3800

HALL CANYON

SHELL RD

33

TAYLOR RANCH RD

CANADA DEL DIABLO

DEVILS CANYON

OIL WELLS

OTTAWA DR
DELAMARE DR
OMAHA

DAKOTA

SCHOOL

CANYON DR

SCHOOL RD

CANYON

SAN JON BARRANCA RD

EAST FORK

BARLOW

BARLOW BARRANCA

FRWY

OJAI

UP

RR

VENTURA AV

KAPANA AV

PACOS ST

SHOSHONE

FRANKLIN LN

CAMERON CT

DE ANZA DR

HARRY LYON PARK

MID

STANLEY AV

JAMES ST

ROCKLITE RD

COMSTOCK DR

E MCFARLANE

LEIGHTON DR

W MCFARLANE

W LEWIS ST
FORBES LN
SUNNY WAY

W VINCE
W FLINT
W WARNER ST
W BARNETT ST

RIVERSIDE ST

ROSEWOOD
OAKWOOD
REDWOOD

N OLIVE ST

W SHERIDAN WY

RAMONA ST

RIVERSIDE

W SIMPSON ST

CARR

E LEWIS ST

VINCE ST

EL MEDIO ST

E WARNER ST

BELL WY

E BARNETT ST

CEDAR ST

KELLOGG

LIB FS

N SIMPSON ST

E RAMONA

GRANT PARK

GATE

GATE

GATE

GRANT PARK RD

CRIMEA ST

FIRE ST

TELEPHONE RD

RELAY RD

FUEL RD

BREAK RD

SAN JON BARRANCA

SAN JON

HALL CANYON

93003

CHRISMAN

VENTURA

BROCK LINEAR PARK

VENTURA AV

VINCE ST

VENTURA ST

200
100
1400
100
1700
200
100
100
1000
700
200
400
900
800

2800
2600
200
400
500

2500
2300
2200
200
100
300
2500
500
2600
2100

SEE 491 MAP

A B C D E | SEE 462 MAP | E F G H J

VENTURA CO.

R23W R22W

SEE 462 MAP

1

13

18

HALL

FORK

CANYON

HARMON CANYON

HARMON

CANYON

17

17

RANCHO EX MISSION SAN BUENAVENTURA

ALISO CANYON

ALISO CANYON RD

WASON

BARRANCA

2

EAST

24

20

19

CANYON

HARMON

CANYON RD

PEPPERTREE

3

OIL WELLS

SEXTON CANYON

SEXTON CANYON

CANYON RD

CANYON

CANYON

CANYON RD

93060

CANYON RD

700

SEE 471 MAP
SEE 473 MAP

4

SEXTON

SEXTON

LAKE

LAKE

93003

HARMON CANYON

93004

LONG CANYON RD

LONG CANYON

LONG

GATE

GATE

WILLIAMS CANYON

FRANKLIN BARRANCA

RANCHO VISTA LN

FOOTHILL RD

5

BARLOW BARRANCA

GATE

1300

FRANKLIN CANYON

PINKERTON RANCH RD

N WELLS RD

WELLS RD

6

GATE

SOUTHVIEW VIA ARROYO CIR
HARBORVIEW CT
VIEW POINT CIR
CHANNEL HEIGHTS CT
HILLMAY CIR
GRAND RIDGE CT
COLINA VISTA
CROWNHILL
GLENCREST
LONGRIDGE
VIA PAZ
ARROYO MORADA
GREENVIEW CIR
HILLHAVEN CT
WESTRIDGE DR
LA CUESTA
SONORA
ETNA CIR
HORIZON
MEADOW-VIEW DR
LOS PADRES
SAN ORICIO
PARKHILL CIR
SUNNYCREST
VIA CIELITO
BRIDGEVIEW DR
PLAINVIEW
VICTORIA
MAYVIEW
SUNNYHILL
COLINA VIA
SCENIC
SONATO
RIDGECREST
ELIZABETH RD
HARMON CANYON
HARMON CANYON RD

7

GATE
GATE
GATE
GATE

ARROYO VERDE PARK

VENTURA

SKYLINE RD
TOPA TOPA DR
CRESTONE CT
KAILAS ST
RUSHMORE ST
CANON CT
VIEWCREST CT
SENTINE
VIEWCREST
SUNSET VIEW CT
VIA CIELITO
MONTCLAIR DR
SKYVIEW TER
NOB HILL LN
CORTE DE CHARD
ONDULANDO
MONTE VISTA AV
GREENPOINT
HIGH POINT AV
EL MALABAR
RASTO
VISTA
900
600
6500
CORONA CIR
1 MESA CIR
2 BRIARCLIFF CIR
3 LA CUMBRE CIR

CONTRA COSTA ST
SAN FRANCISCO
SAN MATEO
COLUSA
IMPERIAL
CALAVERAS ST
PETIT AV
SISKIYOU ST
FOOTHILL RD
RANCHO EX MISSION SAN BUENAVENTURA RD
RANCHO SANTA PAULA Y SATICOY 9600
N SATICOY AV
GALVIN ST
SALLY PL
ROSEDALE
LONGS
DEL NORTE
NEVADA ST
SACRAMENTO DR
ALPINE
MERCED DR
ALPINE CIR
LASSEN
LINDER
ORANGE CIR
MENDOCINO
N WELLS RD
WOODSIDE LINEAR PARK
S WELLS RD
CARLOS ST
LA JOLLA ST
S LINDEN DR
CITRUS DR
S SATICOY AV
TELEGRAPH RD

SEE 492 MAP

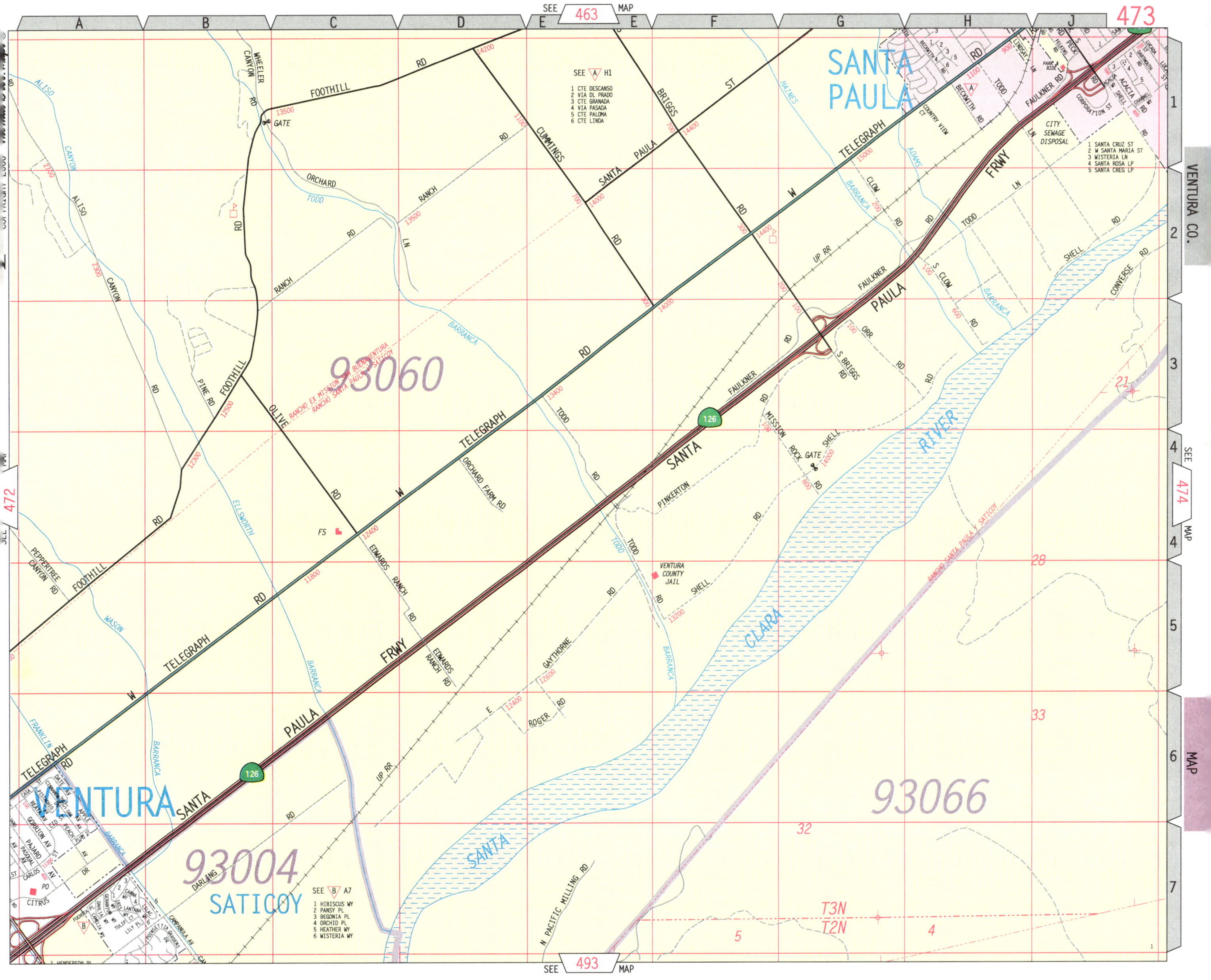

473

SANTA PAULA

VENTURA CO.

SEE 474 MAP

MAP

472

SEE 472

SANTA PAULA FRWY

TELEGRAPH RD

93060

93066

93004

SATICOY

VENTURA

CITY SEWAGE DISPOSAL

VENTURA COUNTY JAIL

SANTA CLARA RIVER

SEE A H1
1 CTE DESCANSO
2 VIA DL PRADO
3 CTE GRANADA
4 VIA PASADA
5 CTE PALOMA
6 CTE LINDA

1 SANTA CRUZ ST
2 W SANTA MARIA ST
3 WISTERIA LN
4 SANTA ROSA LP
5 SANTA CREG LP

SEE B A7
1 HIBISCUS WY
2 PANSY PL
3 BEGONIA PL
4 ORCHID PL
5 HEATHER WY
6 WISTERIA WY

FOOTHILL RD
WHEELER CANYON RD
ORCHARD RD
RANCH RD
PINE RD
OLIVE RD
EDWARDS RANCH RD
TELEGRAPH RD
ELLSWORTH
PEPPERTREE CANYON RD
FRANKLIN
MASON
BARRANCA
ALISO CANYON
BRIGGS ST
CUMMINGS
SANTA PAULA RD
HAINES
ADAMS
TELEGRAPH
FAULKNER
CLOM
BARRANCA
TODD RD
SHELL RD
CONVERSE RD
PINKERTON
MISSION ROCK RD
GATE
PAULA
S CLOM
OBR
S BRIGGS RD
GAYTHORNE
ROGER PL
UP RR
N PACIFIC MILLING RD
BEGINTH RD
LINDSAY
FAULKNER RD
TODD
PARK RIDE
ACACIA
SHELL
CORPORATION ST
COUNTRY VIEW CT
PECK
LUCY

RANCHO EX MISSION SAN BUENAVENTURA
RANCHO SANTA PAULA Y SATICOY

126

FS

GATE

ORCHARD FARM RD

T3N
T2N

21
28
33
32
4
5

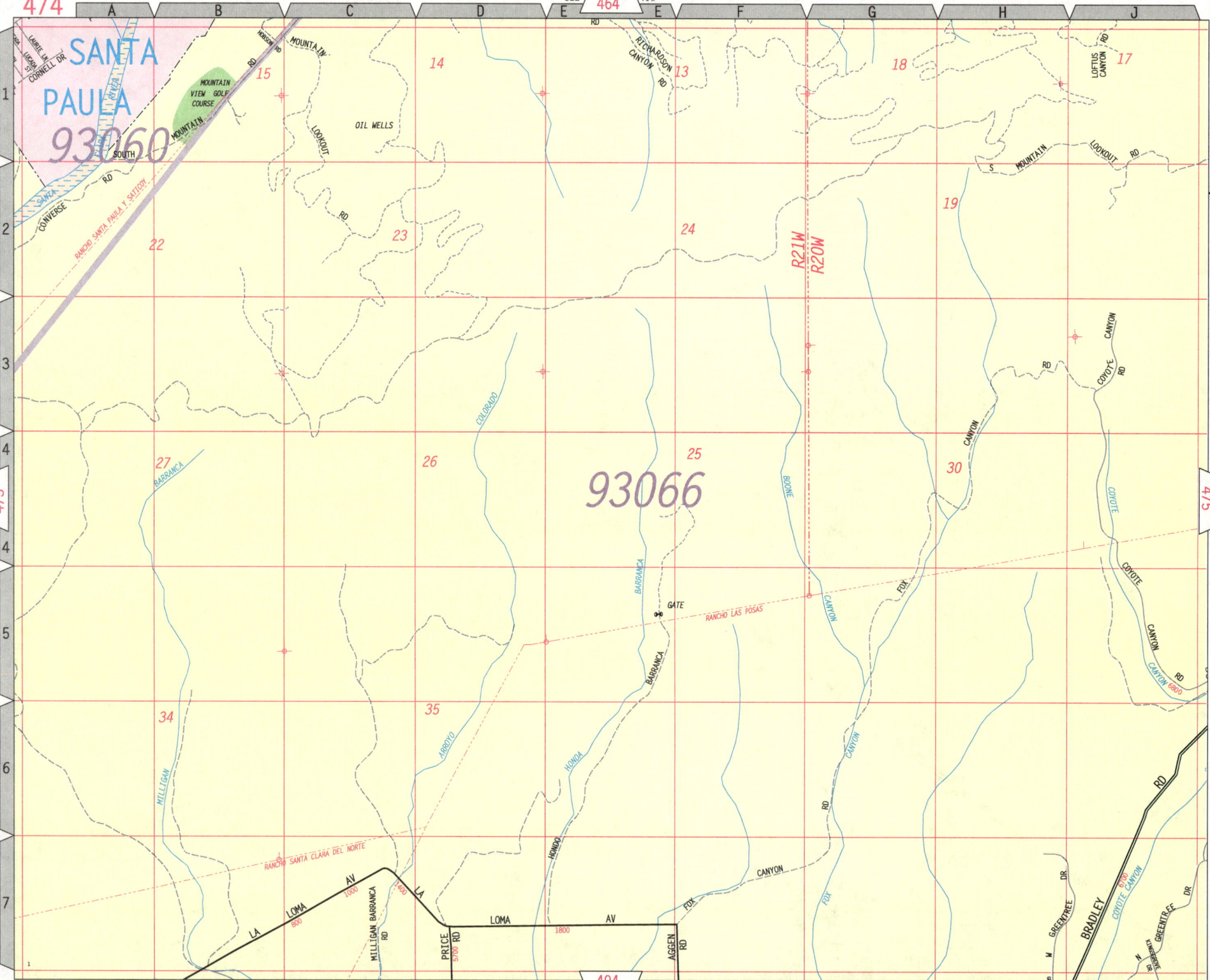

SANTA PAULA
93060

93066

SEE 464 MAP

A B C D E F G H J

VENTURA CO.

1
2
3
4
SEE 473 MAP
5
MAP
6
7

SEE 494 MAP

MOUNTAIN VIEW GOLF COURSE

OIL WELLS

LAURIE LN
LUCHA ST
CORNELL DR
RIVERA

RANCHO SANTA PAULA Y SATICOY

CONVERSE RD

SANTA

MOSSON RD

MOUNTAIN

LOOKOUT RD

SOUTH

MOUNTAIN

RD

RICHARDSON CANYON RD

S MOUNTAIN

LOOKOUT RD

LOFTUS CANYON RD

R21W R20W

COLORADO

BOONE

BARRANCA

BARRANCA

BARRANCA

GATE

RANCHO LAS POSAS

CANYON

FOX

CANYON

COYOTE

COYOTE CANYON

COYOTE CANYON RD

CANYON 6800

CANYON

RD

COYOTE RD

MILLIGAN

ARROYO

HONDA

HONDA

FOX

FOX

CANYON

RANCHO SANTA CLARA DEL NORTE

LA LOMA AV 800

AV 1000

MILLIGAN BARRANCA RD

PRICE RD 5700

LA

LOMA AV 1800

FOX RD

AGGEN RD

CANYON

GREENTREE DR

W GREENTREE

N GREENTREE

BRADLEY RD

15 14 13 18 17
22 23 24 19
27 26 25 30
34 35

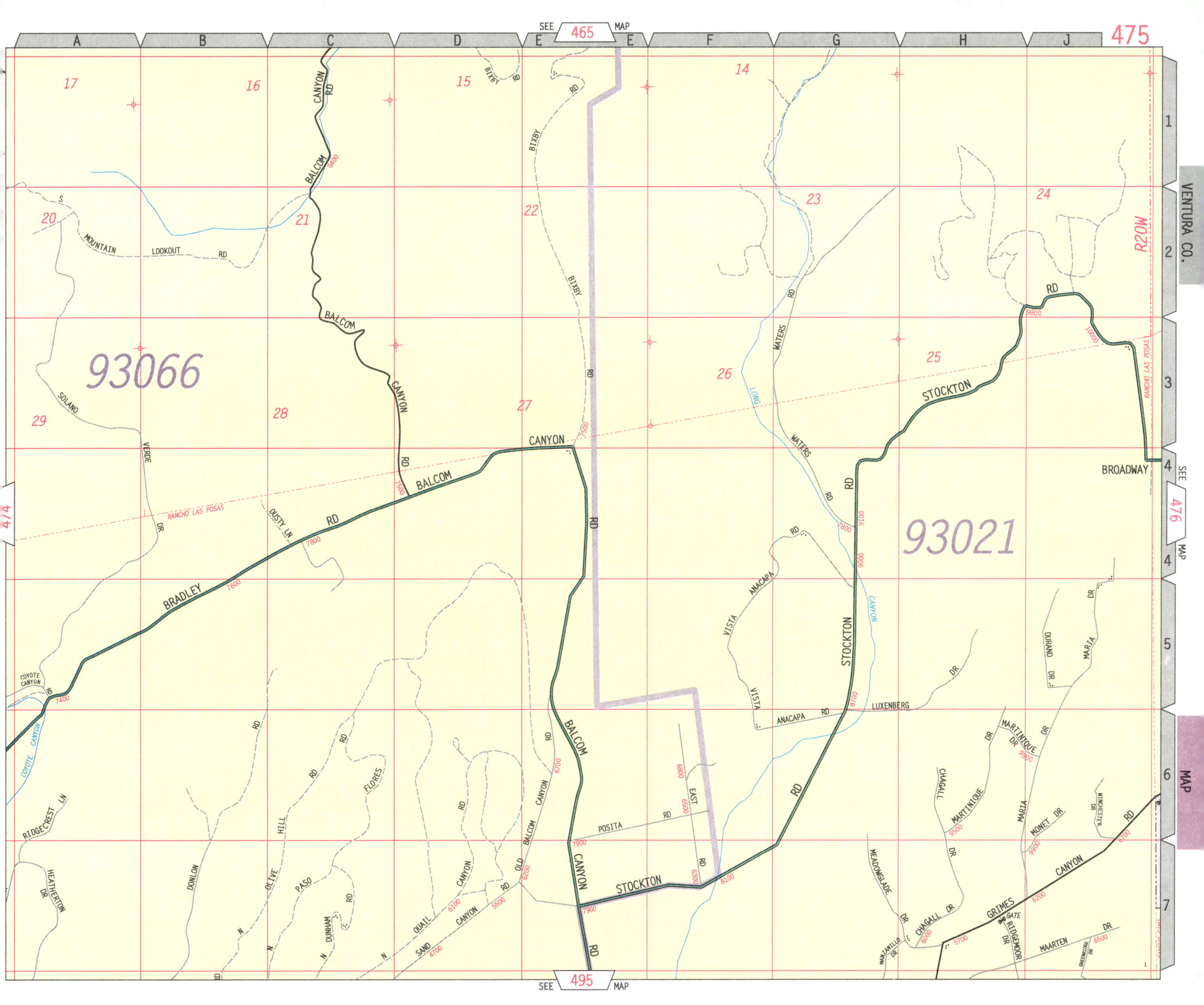

475

A B C D E E F G H J

VENTURA CO.

17 16 15 14

R20W

1

20 S 22 23 24

MOUNTAIN LOOKOUT RD

2

BIXBY RD

BIXBY RD

BALCOM CANYON RD

9800

BIXBY RD

BALCOM

93066

21

SOLANO

WATERS RD

RD

9800

10800

3

27

28

29

VERDE

CANYON

RD

BIXBY RD

7500

26

25

STOCKTON

RANCHO LAS POSAS

LONG

WATERS RD

RANCHO LAS POSAS

CANYON

BALCOM

RD

CANYON

7500

DUSTY LN 7900

RANCHO LAS POSAS

93021

BROADWAY

4/4

DR

7800

8006

SEE 476 MAP

4

BRADLEY 7600

ANACAPA RD

STOCKTON CANYON

8008

VISTA

LUXENBERG

DURAND DR

MARIA

5

COYOTE CANYON RD 7400

RD

FLORES RD

RD

BALCOM CANYON

6700

VISTA

ANACAPA RD

STOCKTON RD

DR

MARTINIQUE DR 9800

CHAGALL DR

MARIA

MONET DR

WINCHESTER DR

MAP

6

RIDGECREST LN

HILL

PASO

RD

OLD BALCOM CANYON RD 6500

EAST RD 6500

POSITA RD

7900

RD 6000

8100

MARTINIQUE DR

MEADOWGLADE DR

CHAGALL DR

9800

MARIA 9800

CANYON RD 6700

7

HEATHERTON DR

OLIVE

DUNHAM

RD

N

QUAIL CANYON RD 6100

SAND CANYON 5500

N

4700

BALCOM CANYON RD 7900

STOCKTON

MANZANILLO DR

CHAGALL DR 6600

5700

GRIMES GATE RIDGEMOOR DR

MAARTEN DR

GREENRIDGE DR 6500

6200

1

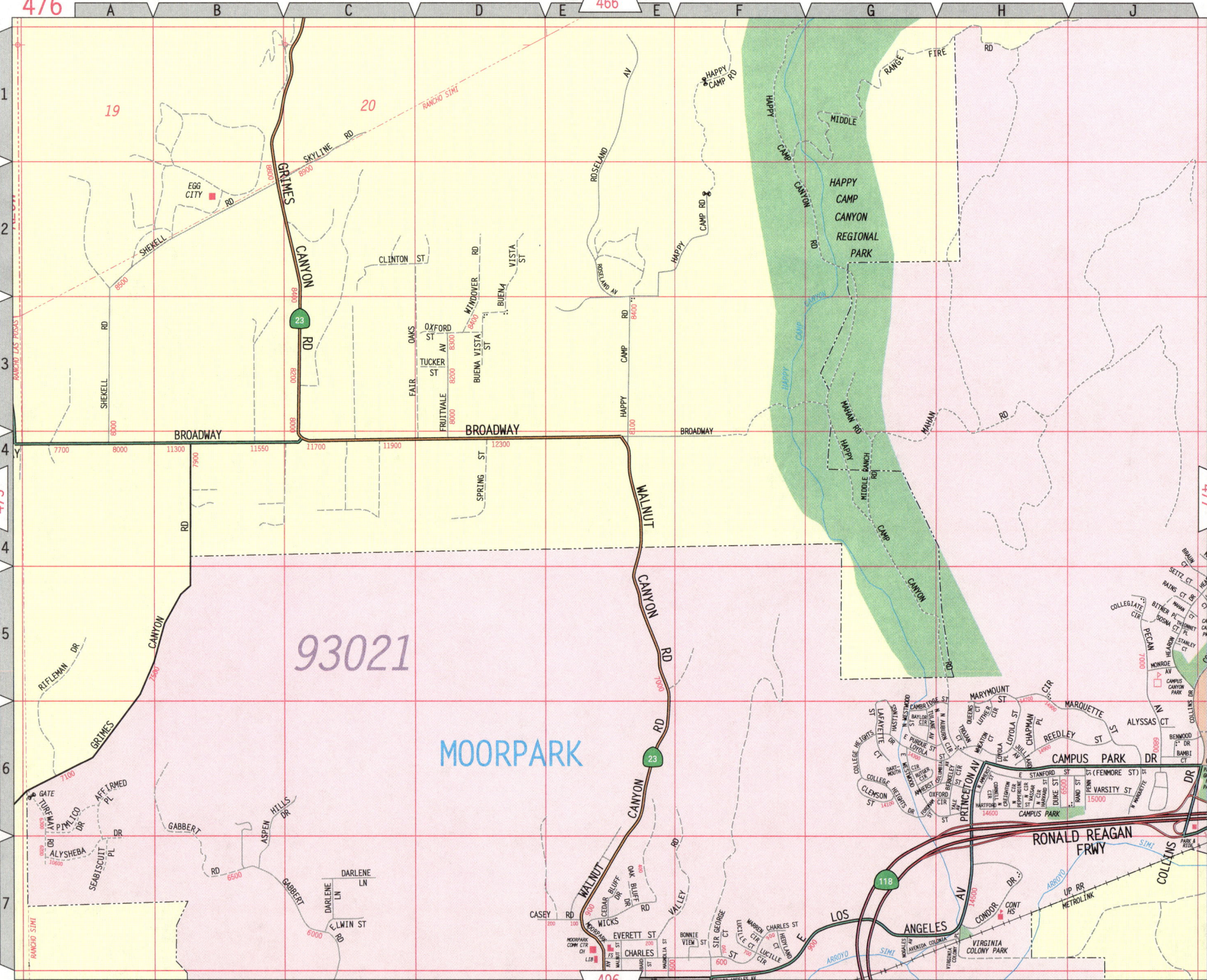

A B C D E **SEE 466 MAP** E F G H J

Ventura Co.

1
19   20
RANCHO SIMI

SKYLINE RD
GRIMES CANYON RD

8800 8900

2
EGG CITY
SHEKELL RD
8500
CLINTON ST
WINDOVER RD
BUENA VISTA ST
ROSELAND AV

HAPPY CAMP RD

8400

HAPPY CAMP CANYON RD

HAPPY CAMP CANYON REGIONAL PARK

MIDDLE

RANGE   FIRE   RD

3
SHEKELL RD
8800
8600
8400
23
8200
8000

OXFORD ST
OAKS AV
FAIR OAKS
TUCKER ST
BUENA VISTA ST
FRUITVALE
8000

8300
8200

HAPPY CAMP RD
8100

ROSELAND AV

MAHAN RD
MAHAN RD

4
BROADWAY
7700 8000 11300
7900
11550
11700
11900
BROADWAY
12300
BROADWAY

SPRING ST

WALNUT CANYON RD

MIDDLE RANCH RD
HAPPY CAMP CANYON RD

SEE 475 MAP

4A
CANYON RD
7600

5
RIFLEMAN DR
GRIMES CANYON RD
7600

93021

7000
700

MAP

6
7100
GATE
TURFWAY
PIMLICO DR
AFFIRMED PL
GABBERT

ASPEN HILLS DR

23

MOORPARK

14900

MARYMOUNT ST
CAMBRIDGE ST
COLLEGE HEIGHTS CT
LAFAYETTE DR
WESTMONT
BAYLOR ST
QUEENS ST
TULANE ST
N AUBURN CIR
LOYOLA PL
LOYOLA ST
CHAPMAN PL
REEDLEY ST
MARQUETTE ST
ALYSSAS CT
BENWOOD
BAMBI
CAMPUS PARK DR
MONROE AV
COLLEGIATE CIR
SEITZ CT
RATES CT DR
BITNER PL
THONNET
SOSNA CT
PL
PECAN
7000
STANLEY
HEXRON
CAMPUS CANYON PARK

7
ALYSHEBA
SEABISCUIT
10600
GABBERT RD
6500
DARLENE LN
DARLENE LN
ELWIN ST
6000

CASEY RD
200 100
WICKS
MOORPARK AV
WALNUT
OAK BLUFF DR
CEDAR BLUFF DR
VALLEY RD
EVERETT ST
BONNIE VIEW
CHARLES ST
SIR GEORGE CT
WARREN ST
LUCILLE CT
LUCILLE CT
CHARLES ST
LOS ANGELES AV
VIRGINIA COLONY PARK

CLEMSON ST
COLLEGE HEIGHTS DR
E STANFORD ST
E PURDUE ST
WESTWOOD
N BERKELEY CIR
HARVARD ST
PEPPERDINE
E PEPPERDINE
DUKE ST
HARTFORD ST
14600
OXFORD CIR
PRINCETON AV
PENN ST
RAND ST
VARSITY ST
15000
CAMPUS PARK
6500

RONALD REAGAN FRWY

118

CONDOR DR
CONT HS
PARK & RIDE
COLLINS DR

ARROYO SIMI
UP RR
METROLINK

SEE 496 MAP

477

MIDDLE   RANGE   FIRE   RD   MIDDLE   RANGE
FIRE
RD

1

2

RD

FIRE

RD

FIRE

3

SCARAB

CANYON

NO. 2

FIRE

SEE 478 MAP

MOORPARK

4

4

ALAMOS   CANYON

FIRE   RD

93065

5

SCARAB   FIRE   RD

BORGES   15300
HARTE   LN   GRIFFITH   GRADUATE   CIR
ALUMNI   LN   SWIFT   PL
MALLORY   CT   SOPHOMORE   UNIVERSITY   DR
HEARON   CT   BRAUN   FRESMAN   CT
SEITZ   CT   IMBACH   PL   MILNE   CT
CT   DR. BORGES   CT
CAMPUS   CANYON   PK   DORIS   TRUELOVE   CT
COLLINS   SHAKESPEARE   CT   7000   CAMPUS   RD
DR   6900

MOORPARK COLLEGE

93021

CAMPUS   RD

6

CAMPUS PARK   DR
PAUL   GRIFF   BELFER   ST
FIN   PARK   COLLEGE   AV   KERNVALE   AV
OVERN   AV   DRACENA   AV
LITTLE   AV   GRANDVIEW   AV
MEDEA   ST
BERGAN   ST
RONALD   REAGAN   SIMI VALLEY
SANITARY LANDFILL

15400

118   FRWY

OAK   PARK   LIONS   CIR   16400

VILLA DEL ARROYO
MOBILE HOME
ESTATES

ARROYO   LOS   UP   SIMI   VALLEY
SIMI   ANGELES   QUI/MESA   DR   RR   METROLINK
800   500   AV

ALAMOS   CANYON   RD

VIEW   LINE   DR
WESTHILLS CT   BREA   GATE
COCHRAN   ST   MADERA   CANYON   RD

AMERICAN   ST
AMERITE   WY
COUNTRY   WIDE   WY

COUNTRY WIDE WY

FLOWER
GLEN ST

FLOWER GLEN ST

7

SEE 497 MAP

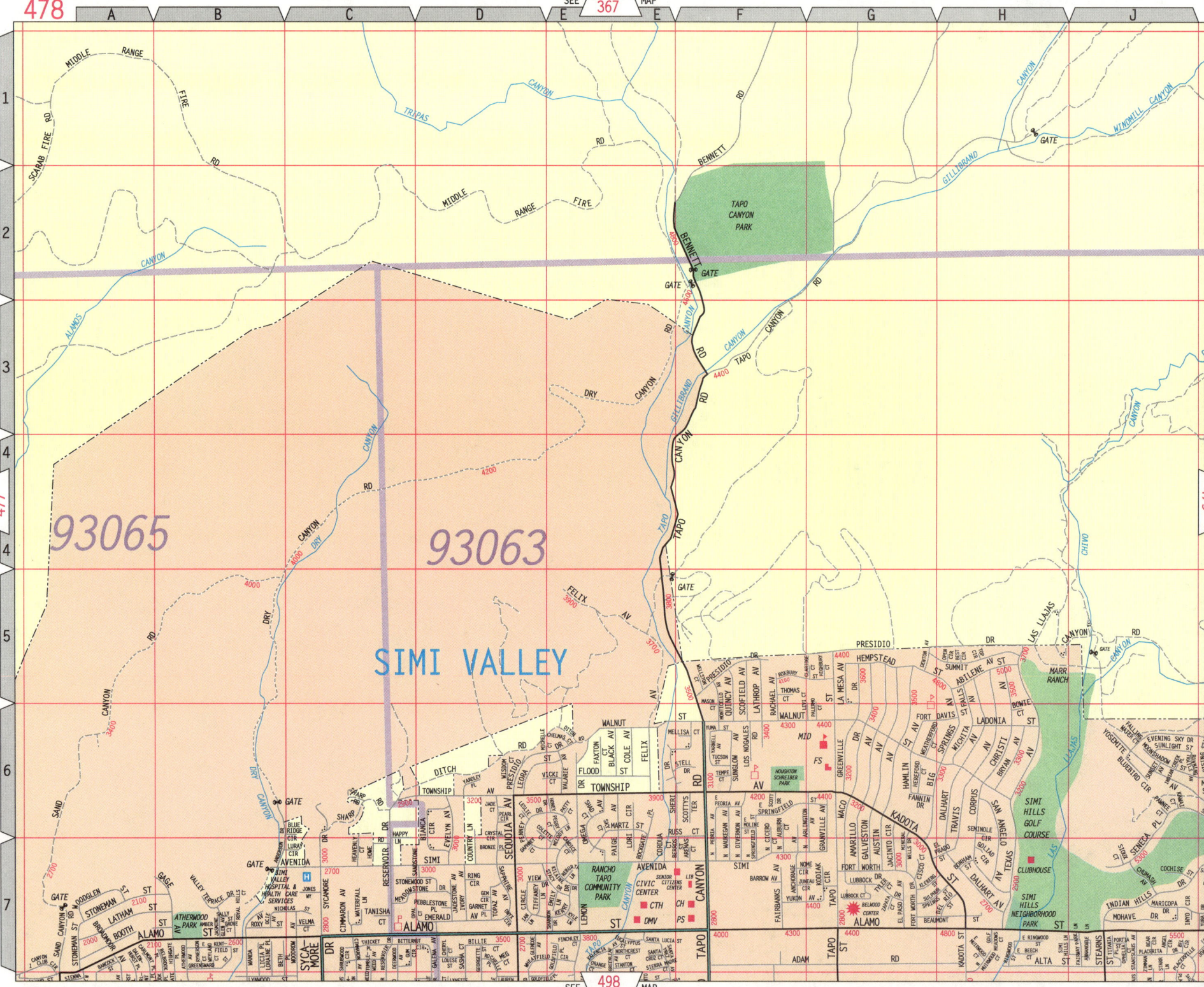

SEE 367 MAP

A B C D E E F G H J

VENTURA CO.

SEE 477 MAP

MAP

TAPO CANYON PARK

93065

93063

SIMI VALLEY

MIDDLE RANGE FIRE RD
SCARAB FIRE RD
TRIPAS CANYON
BENNETT RD
MIDDLE RANGE FIRE RD
ALAMOS CANYON
GILLIBRAND RD
WINDMILL CANYON
GATE
GILLIBRAND
DRY CANYON RD
TAPO CANYON RD
CHIVO CANYON
DRY CANYON RD
FELIX AV
PRESIDIO DR
MARR RANCH
HEMPSTEAD AV
SUMMIT AV
ABILENE AV
BOWIE ST
SIMI HILLS GOLF COURSE
SIMI HILLS NEIGHBORHOOD PARK
CANYON RD
LAS LLAJAS
WALNUT AV
WALNUT ST
MID AV
HOUGHTON SCHREIBER PARK
SIMI VALLEY HOSPITAL & HEALTH SERVICES
ATHERWOOD PARK
RANCHO TAPO COMMUNITY PARK
CIVIC CENTER
SENIOR CITIZENS CENTER
DMV
CLUBHOUSE
ALAMO ST
ALAMO
SYCAMORE DR
TAPO ST
TAPO CANYON
KADOTA ST
STEARNS ST
INDIAN HILLS DR
SEE 498 MAP

A   B   C   D   E   E   F   G   H   J

VENTURA CO.

91382

91381

23   24

91311

26   25

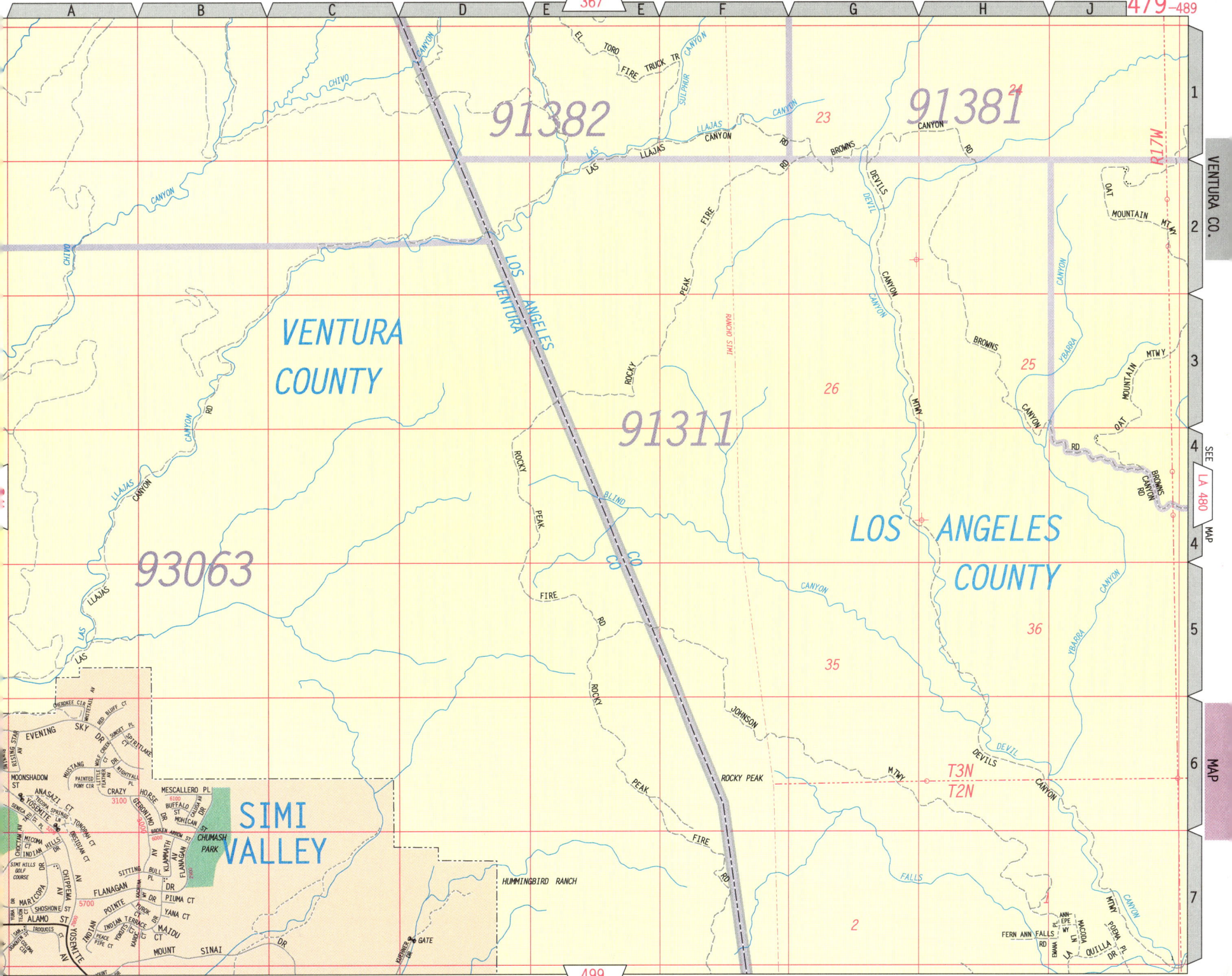

VENTURA COUNTY

LOS ANGELES COUNTY

93063

35   36

SEE LA 480 MAP

MAP

SIMI VALLEY

CHUMASH PARK

HUMMINGBIRD RANCH

KUEHNER GATE

T3N
T2N

FERN ANN FALLS

CHIVO CANYON
EL TORO FIRE TRUCK TR
SULPHUR CANYON
LLAJAS CANYON
BROWNS
DEVILS CANYON
OAT MOUNTAIN MTWY
R1W
LAS LLAJAS CANYON
FIRE PEAK
DEVIL CANYON
YBARRA CANYON
BROWNS
OAT MOUNTAIN MTWY
LOS ANGELES VENTURA
RANCHO SIMI
ROCKY PEAK
BROWNS CANYON RD
ROCKY PEAK
BLIND
FIRE RD
CANYON
YBARRA CANYON
LLAJAS CANYON RD
LAS LLAJAS CANYON
FIRE RD
ROCKY PEAK
JOHNSON MTWY
DEVILS CANYON
DEVIL
ROCKY PEAK MTWY
FIRE RD
FALLS
MACODA LN
PUBNA PL
QUILLA DR
2

SEE 470 MAP

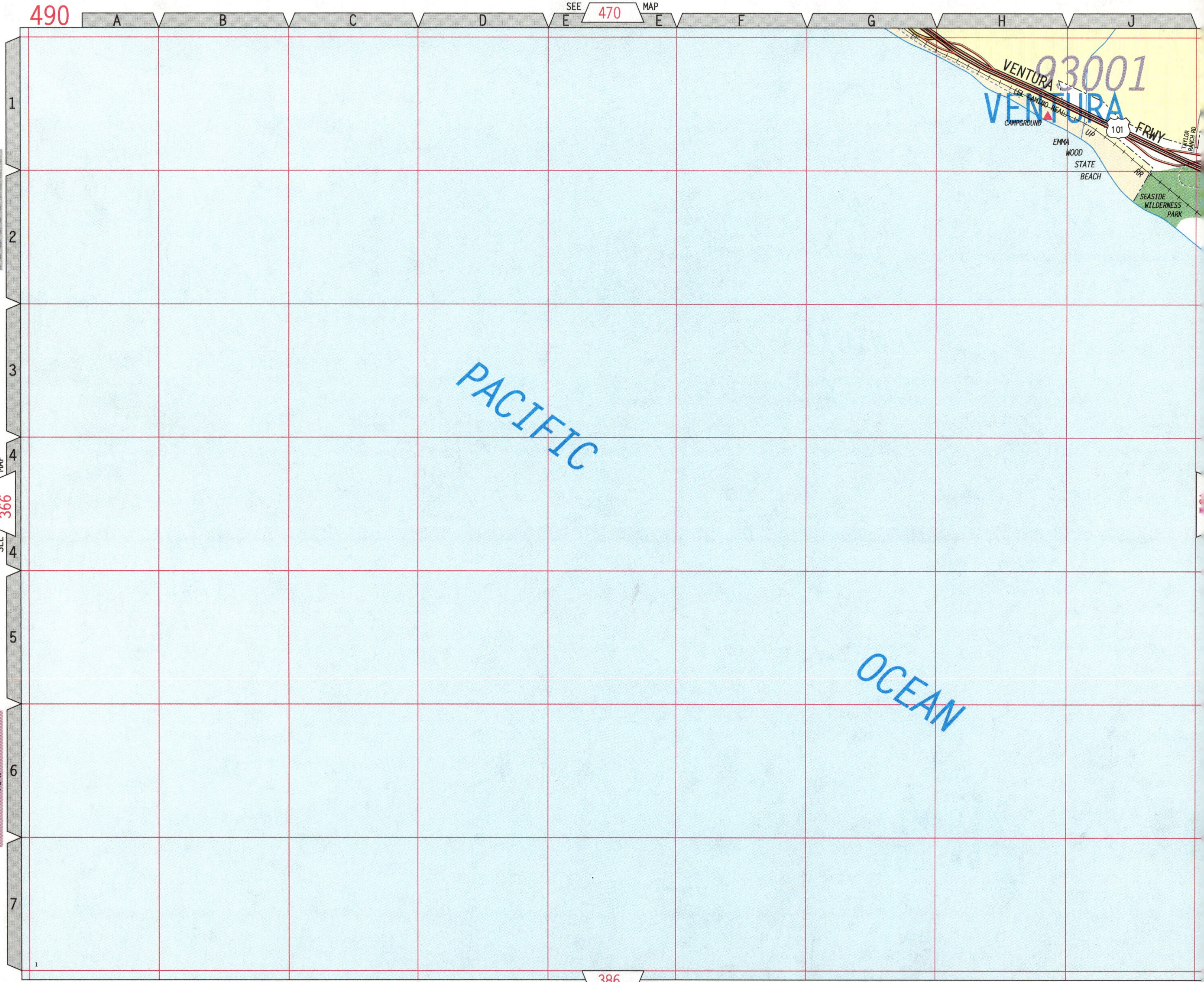

A　B　C　D　E　E　F　G　H　J

1

VENTURA CO.

2

3

PACIFIC

SEE 366 MAP

4

4

OCEAN

5

MAP

6

7

93001

VENTURA

VENTURA FRWY

EL CAMINO REAL

CAMPGROUND

EMMA WOOD STATE BEACH

SEASIDE WILDERNESS PARK

TAYLOR RANCH RD

UP RR

101

SEE 386 MAP

A B C D E E F G H J

93001

VENTURA

OJAI FRWY

VENTURA FRWY
(EL CAMINO REAL)
101

Seaside Wilderness Park

MCBRIDE BRIDGE

W MAIN ST
POLI ST
MAIN ST
THOMPSON

GRANT PARK

FATHER SERRA CROSS

SEASIDE PARK & VENTURA COUNTY FAIRGROUNDS

SHORELINE
PROMENADE
FIGUEROA

SURFERS POINT AT SEASIDE PARK

VENTURA PIER

HARBOR BLVD

SAN BUENAVENTURA STATE BEACH

ALESSANDRO

PIERPONT

SEAWARD AV

OCEAN

VANCOUVER AV

VENTURA COLLEGE

PACIFIC VIEW MALL

MAIN ST

TELEGRAPH RD

POLI

CAMINO REAL PARK

E MAIN ST

SEE 492 MAP

VENTURA FRWY
(EL CAMINO REAL)
101

PACIFIC

OCEAN

PIERPONT BAY

93003

SEAVIEW AV

SEAHORSE AV

SAILOR AV

SEAHORSE AV

BAYSHORE BLVD

GREENOCK

MARINA PARK

BREAKWATER

VENTURA HARBOR

ANCHORS WY

VENTURA MARINA MHP

CHANNEL ISLANDS NATIONAL PARK HDQTRS & VISITORS CENTER

SCHOONER DR

NAVIGATOR

COLONY HARBORTOWN MARINA RESORT DR

VENTURA COVE BEACH

VENTURA MARINA

VENTURA YACHT CLUB

PIERPONT BAY YACHT CLUB

SPINNAKER DR

ANGLER CT

HELIPORT DR

VENTURA HARBOR VILLAGE

OLIVAS PARK DR

OLIVAS ADOBE

HARBOR BLVD

OLIVAS PARK GOLF COURSE

Grid reference columns: A B C D E E F G H J
Grid reference rows: 1 2 3 4 5 6 7

Major labels: VENTURA CO. • FOOTHILL • VENTURA COLLEGE • CENTRAL CAMPUS • VENTURA • MONTALVO • OXNARD • BUENAVENTURA GOLF COURSE • IVY LAWN CEMETERY • TELEPHONE ROAD PLAZA • DONLON ST PLAZA • CAMINO REAL PARK • ARROYO VERDE PARK • SANTA PAULA FRWY • VENTURA FRWY • NORTHBANK LINEAR PARK • RIVERVIEW LINEAR PARK • LEEWARD WINERY • GATEWAY VILLAGE CENTER • BRISTOL BAY LINEAR PARK

ZIP codes: 93009 • 93001 • 93003 • 93030

SEE B D3 (index box)

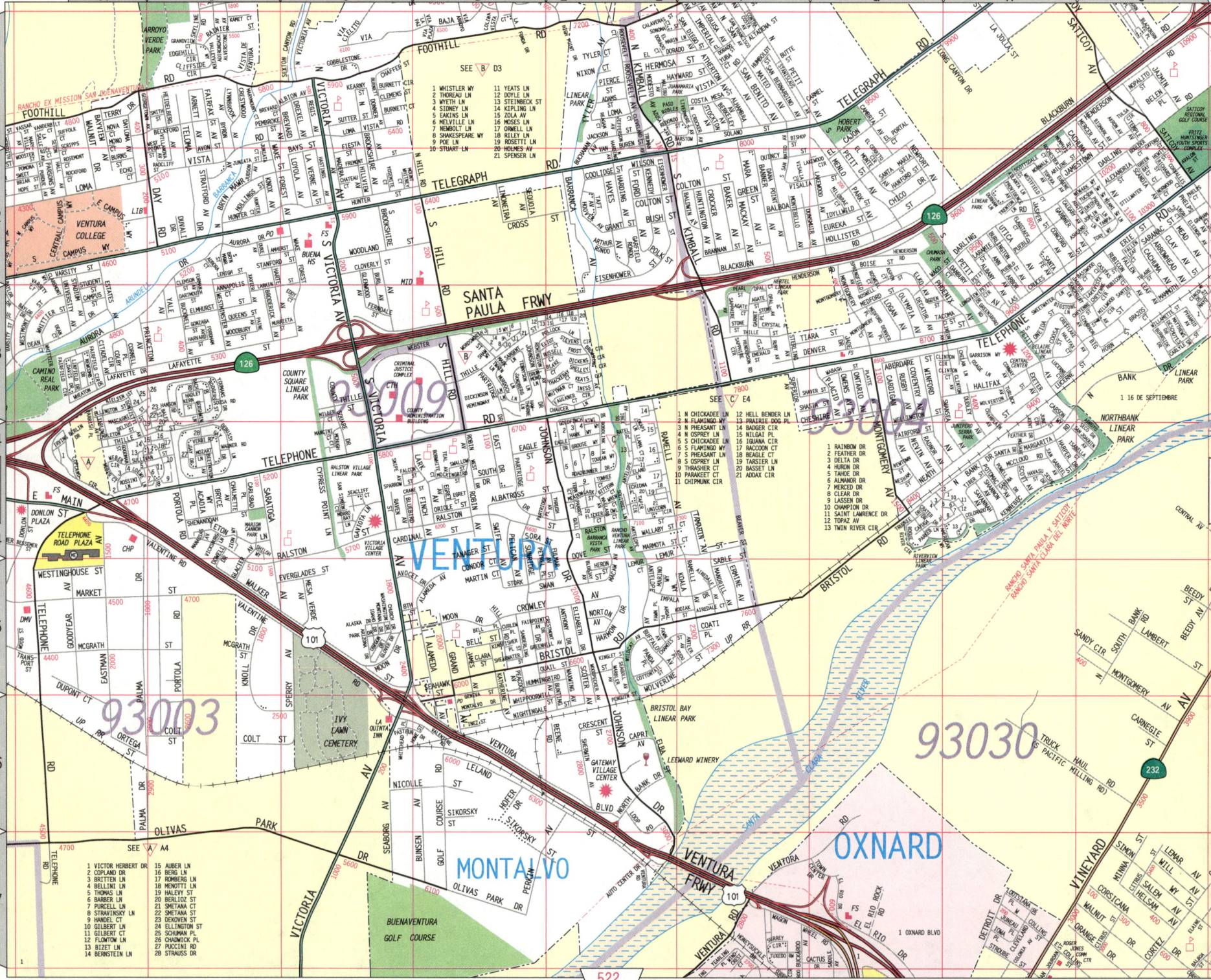

1 WHISTLER WY	11 YEATS LN
2 THOREAU LN	12 DOYLE LN
3 WYETH LN	13 STEINBECK ST
4 SIDNEY LN	14 KIPLING LN
5 EAKINS LN	15 ZOLA AV
6 MELVILLE LN	16 MOSES LN
7 NEWBOLT LN	17 ORWELL LN
8 SHAKESPEARE LN	18 RILEY LN
9 POE LN	19 ROSETTI LN
10 STUART LN	20 HOLMES LN
	21 SPENSER LN

SEE C E4 (index box)

1 N CHICKADEE LN	12 HELL BENDER LN
2 N FLAMINGO WY	13 PRAIRIE DOG PL
3 N PHEASANT LN	14 BADGER CIR
4 N OSPREY LN	15 NILGAI PL
5 S CHICKADEE LN	16 IGUANA CIR
6 S FLAMINGO WY	17 RACCOON CT
7 S PHEASANT LN	18 BEAGLE CT
8 S OSPREY LN	19 TARSIER LN
9 THRASHER CT	20 BASSET LN
10 PARAKEET CT	21 ADDAX CIR
11 CHIPMUNK CIR	

(index box, 93001)

1 RAINBOW DR
2 FEATHER DR
3 DELTA DR
4 TAHOE DR
5 HURON DR
6 ALMANOR DR
7 MERCED DR
8 CLEAR DR
9 LASSEN DR
10 CHAMPION DR
11 SAINT LAWRENCE DR
12 TOPAZ AV
13 TWIN RIVER CIR

SEE A A4 (index box)

1 VICTOR HERBERT DR	15 AUBER LN
2 COPLAND DR	16 BERG LN
3 BRITTEN LN	17 ROMBERG LN
4 BELLINI LN	18 MENOTTI PL
5 THOMAS LN	19 HALEVY ST
6 BARBER LN	20 BERLIOZ ST
7 PURCELL LN	21 SMETANA CT
8 STRAVINSKY LN	22 SMETANA ST
9 HANDEL CT	23 DEKOVEN ST
10 GILBERT LN	24 ELLINGTON ST
11 GILBERT CT	25 SCHUMAN PL
12 FLOWTON LN	26 CHADWICK PL
13 BIZET LN	27 PUCCINI RD
14 BERNSTEIN LN	28 STRAUSS DR

Highway shields: 101 • 126 • 232

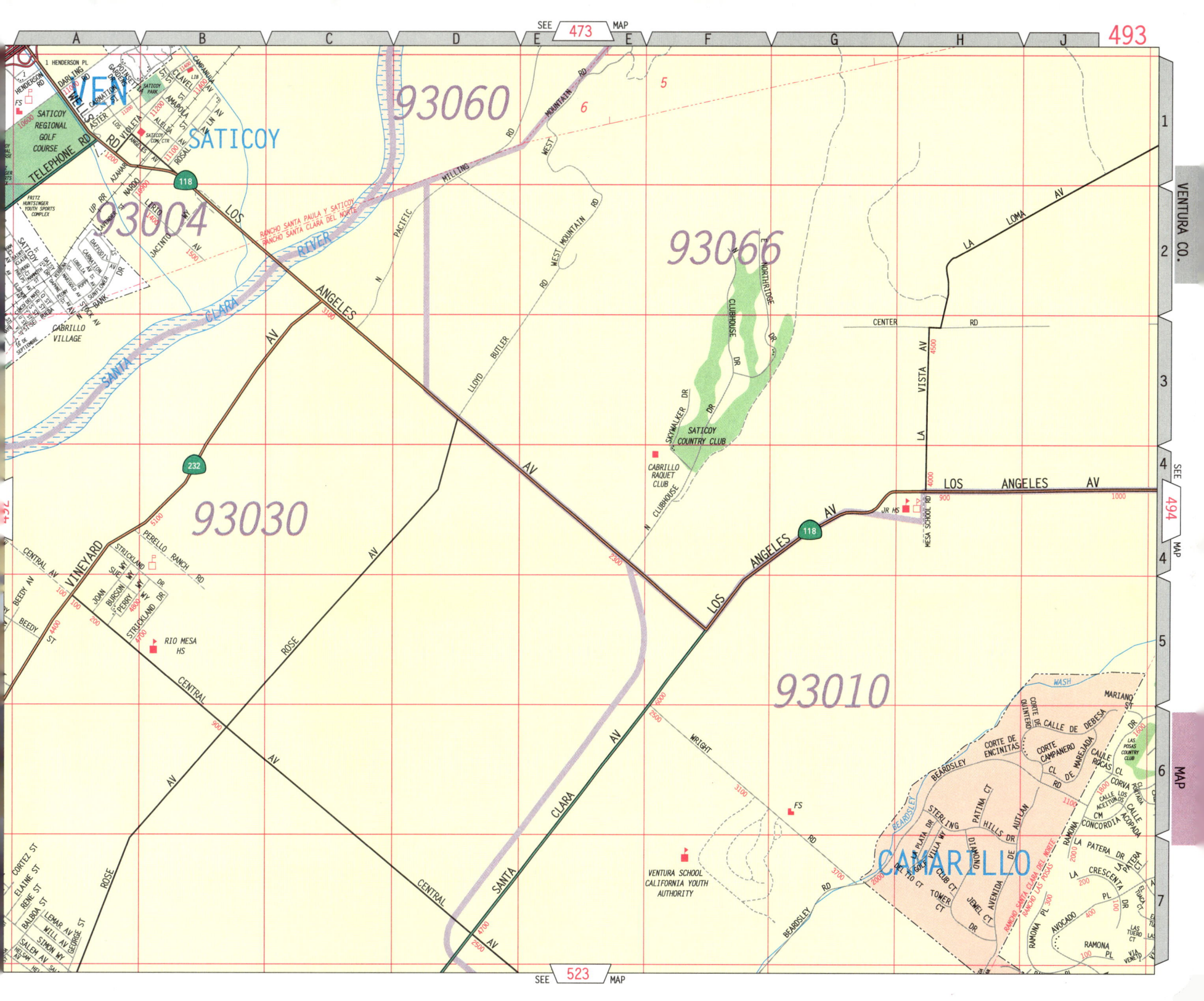

A B C D E E F G H J

1 HENDERSON PL
DARLING
HENDERSON RD
FS
VEN
WELLS
TELEPHONE RD

SATICOY REGIONAL GOLF COURSE

Fritz Huntsinger Youth Sports Complex

SATICOY PARK
GASSNETT
POINSETT ST
CAMPANILLA
CLAVEL
AMAPOLA AV
LOS ANGELES
SATICOY
SATICOY COM. CTR

93060

5

6

WEST MOUNTAIN RD

MILLING

PACIFIC

93066

LA LOMA AV

VENTURA CO.

1

93004
AZAHAR
LIRIO AV
JACINTO
NAPOD

RANCHO SANTA PAULA Y SATICOY
RANCHO SANTA CLARA DEL NORTE

SANTA CLARA RIVER

N

WEST MOUNTAIN RD

CLUBHOUSE DR

NORTHRIDGE DR

CENTER RD

2

CABRILLO VILLAGE

ANGELES

LLOYD

BUTLER

SKYWALKER DR

SATICOY COUNTRY CLUB

LA VISTA AV

3

232

93030

VINEYARD
STRICKLAND
PERELLO RANCH RD
CENTRAL AV
BEEDY AV
SUE WY
JOAN WY
BURSON WY
PIERRI WY
STRICKLAND DR

AV

AV

CABRILLO RAQUET CLUB

CLUBHOUSE

N

LOS ANGELES AV

JR HS
MESA SCHOOL RD

LOS ANGELES AV

118

SEE 494 MAP

4

BEEDY ST

RIO MESA HS

ROSE

CENTRAL

AV

AV

93010

WASH

MARIANO ST

LAS POSAS COUNTRY CLUB

5

CORTEZ ST
ELAINE ST
RENE ST
BALBOA ST
LEMAR AV
WILL AV
GEORGE ST
SALEM AV
SIMON WY

ROSE

CENTRAL

SANTA CLARA AV

WRIGHT

FS

VENTURA SCHOOL CALIFORNIA YOUTH AUTHORITY

BEARDSLEY RD

RANCHO SANTA CLARA DEL NORTE
RANCHO LAS POSAS

BEARDSLEY
STERLING
PATINA
HILLS DR
AUTLAN
TOWER CT
DIAMOND AVENIDA DE
JEWEL CT
RAMONA DR
RAMONA PL
AVOCADO
LA PATERA DR
LA CRESCENTA DR
LAS TUERO CT
RAMONA PL
VIA VENETO

CORTE DE CALLE DE DEBESA
CORTE DE ENCINITAS
CORTE CAMPANERO
CL DE ROCAS CL
CAULE ROCAS CL
CORVA PORTADA
CALLE ACOPADA
CM CONCORDIA DR
LA PATERA

CAMARILLO

6

7

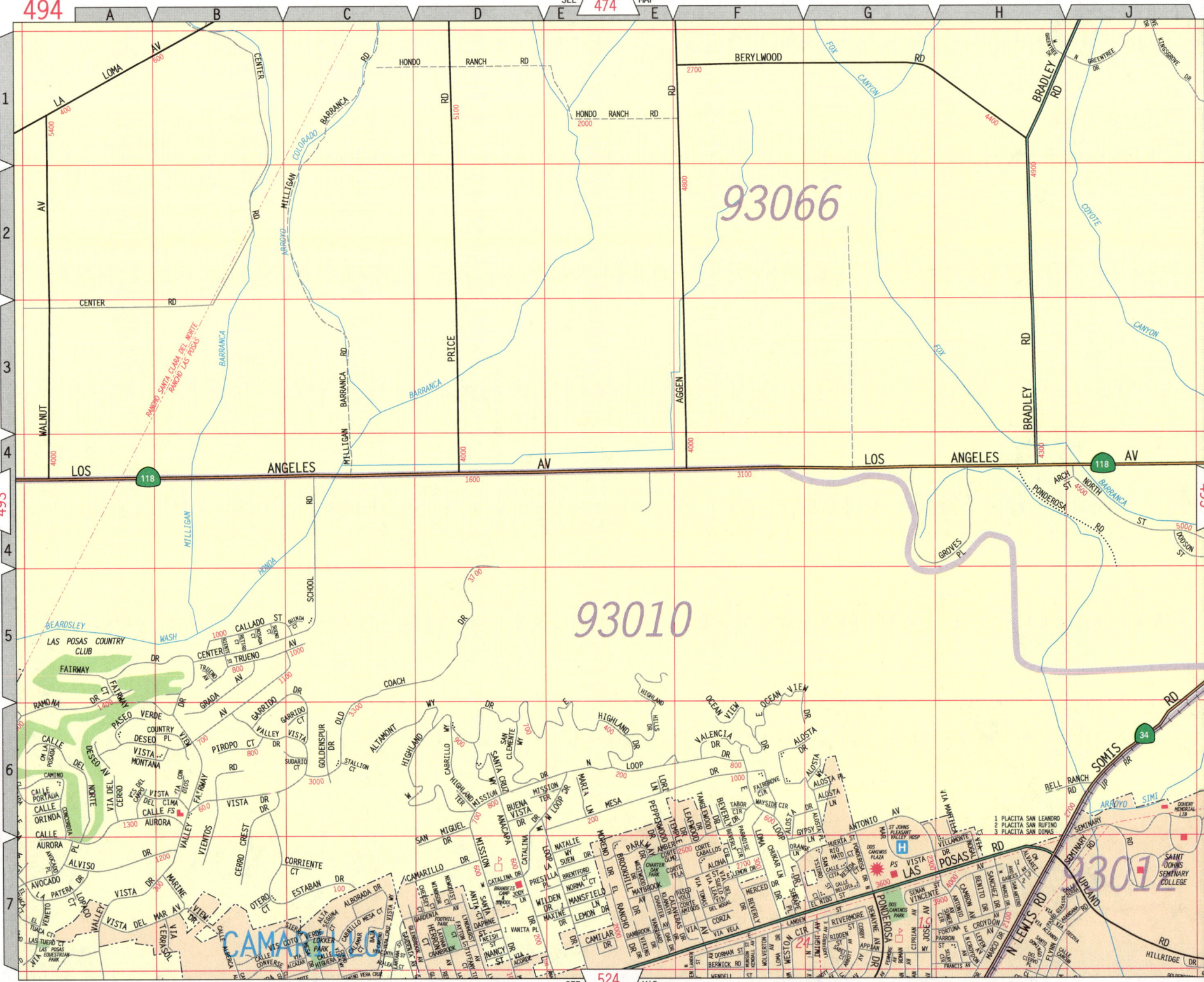

SEE 474 MAP

A B C D E E F G H J

VENTURA CO.

1
2
3
4
4
5
MAP
6
MAP
7

93066

93010

93012

LA LOMA AV
LA LOMA AV
CENTER RD
BARRANCA RD
COLORADO RD
HONDO RANCH RD
RANCH RD
HONDO RANCH RD
BERYLWOOD RD
FOX CANYON
BRADLEY RD
GREENTREE DR
KINGSGROVE DR

CENTER RD
WALNUT
MILLIGAN RD
BARRANCA
BARRANCA
PRICE
AGGEN
BRADLEY RD
COYOTE CANYON

RANCHO SANTA CLARA DEL NORTE
RANCHO LAS POSAS
BARRANCA

LOS ANGELES AV
118
LOS ANGELES AV
118
MILLIGAN
SCHOOL RD
HONDA
ARCH ST
NORTH BARRANCA
PONDEROSA RD
GODSON ST
GROVES PL

SEE 493 MAP

BEARDSLEY WASH
LAS POSAS COUNTRY CLUB
FAIRWAY
CALLADO ST
CENTER
TRUENO AV
GRADA AV
COACH
ALTAMONT
HIGHLAND
OCEAN VIEW
OCEAN VIEW DR
SOMIS RD
34

FAIRWAY DR
RAMONA
PASEO VERDE
COUNTRY PL
DESEO
VISTA MONTANA
PIROPO CT
GARRIDO AV
GARRIDO CT
VALLEY
VISTA
GOLDENSPUR DR
STALLION CT
HIGHLAND WY
CABRILLO
SANTA CRUZ
SANTA CLEMENTE
MISSION TER
MARIA LN
MESA
VALENCIA DR
ALOSTA
FAIRGROVE CIR
MAYSIDE CIR
BELL RANCH RD
ARROYO SIMI
DOHENY MEMORIAL LIB

CALLE PORTADA
CALLE ORINDA
AURORA
VIA DEL CERRO
DEL CIMA
VISTA DR
CERRO CREST
SAN MIGUEL DR
BUENA VISTA
ANACAPA
N LOOP DR
S LOOP
ANTONIO AV
VISTA
LAS POSAS RD
VIA MARTELL
PLEASANT VALLEY HOSP
ST JOHNS
RIO NIDO
VIA VELA

CAMARILLO
ALVISO
AVOCADO DR
PATERA
VETETO
TIACA CT
TIERO CT
LAS POSAS EQUESTRIAN PARK
VIA TERRASOL
VISTA DEL MAR AV
MARINE AV
VIENTOS DR
VALLEY DR
CERRO CREST
CORRIENTE CT
ESTABAN DR
ALBORADA DR
OTERO CT
CAMARILLO DR
CATALINA DR
BRANDEIS CAMP JODY
NATALIE WY
SUEN DR
BRENTFORD
NORMA CT
WILDEN PL
MANSFIELD LN
MAXINE LN
LEMON AV
CAMILAR DR
PARK AV
BROOKHILL DR
WESTWOOD DR
MAYBROOK DR
EL RANCHO DR
DANBROOK DR
CORTE
ALOHA
CHARTER
LEMON DR
BEVERLY
CORZA
VIA
MERCED DR
VIA SERENE
LANDEN
RIVERMORE
RIDDEN
CONBY
PONDEROSA DR
DEMINE AV
N LEWIS RD
SAINT JOHNS SEMINARY COLLEGE
SEMINARY RD
HILLRIDGE RD

DOS CAMINOS PLAZA
H
PS VISTA
LAS POSAS RD
1 PLACITA SAN LEANDRO
2 PLACITA SAN RUFINO
3 PLACITA SAN DIMAS

SEE 524 MAP

A B C D E E F G H J

1 2 3 4 5 6 7

VENTURA CO.

SEE 496 MAP

MAP

93021

93066

93012

SOMIS

MOORPARK
HOME ACRES

CAMARILLO

BALCOM CANYON RD

LOS ANGELES AV

HEATHERTON DR
KINGSGROVE
FAIRCREST LN
CRESTON LN
DONLON RD
OLIVE HILL RD
N PASO FLORES RD
DUNHAM
SAND CANYON RD
CANYON RD
MANZANILLO DR
MAARTEN DR
RIDGEMOOR DR
LEMONWOOD DR
GREENRIDGE DR
PHLEGER RD
HACKNEY RD
QUAIL
SAND RD
MCBEAN RD
BUSHELL RD
GRIMES CANYON RD
PALOMINO
PALOMINO DR
CIR
LA CUMBRE
PEPPER LN
BLACKBERRY LN
ASPEN LN
RES
CHARI LN
HITCH DR
LOS ANGELES AV
SIMI
ARROYO
VALLEY CREST DR
VENTAVO
TERNEZ DR
CITRUS DR
VENTAVO
CHAUCER
CHAUCER
LOS ANGELES AV
COYOTE
DONLON RD
CANYON RD
FOX
NORTH
RICE ST
EAST ST
BELL ST
MID
LIB
WEST ST
SOMIS
BARRANCA
ARROYO
UP
WORTH WY
PRESILLA
RANCHO SIMI RD
CHESTNUT LN
GATE
RANCHO LAS POSAS
RANCHO CALLEGUAS
RD
BUGGY LN
OATFIELD WY
VOLTAIRE WY
SUMMER VIEW CIR
ROSITA RD
CHURCHMAN LN
ROSITA
GATE
BARBARA DR
BLANCHARD PL
LA SIERRA
TERRA BELLA
GABRIELA CT
RIANE CT
CIELO CT
VISTA CT
ARMITOS
LOS COYOTES
CAMINITO LOS RAMBLAS
EL BOSQUE PL
HILLTOP
GATE
NORTH WY
JEFFREY RD
STACY LN
TERRA BELLA CT
VIA LOMA
PASEO
AVIANO DR
NOCHE DR
CALLE DIA
CORTE PINTA
SOLANO DR
ALCEDO DR
QUITO PARK
QUITO DR
GATE
PRINCIPE PL
YUCCA WY
CHIPPENHAM RD
BARBARA
PALOMAR
CERVATO
RAMADA DR
SAN ONOFRE DR
SAN ARDO CT
LA SENDA CT
VIA MONTECITO
CL TANIA
VIS
CAMROSA WATER DISTRICT HEADQUARTERS
SANTA ROSA RD
GERRY RD
GATE
UPLAND

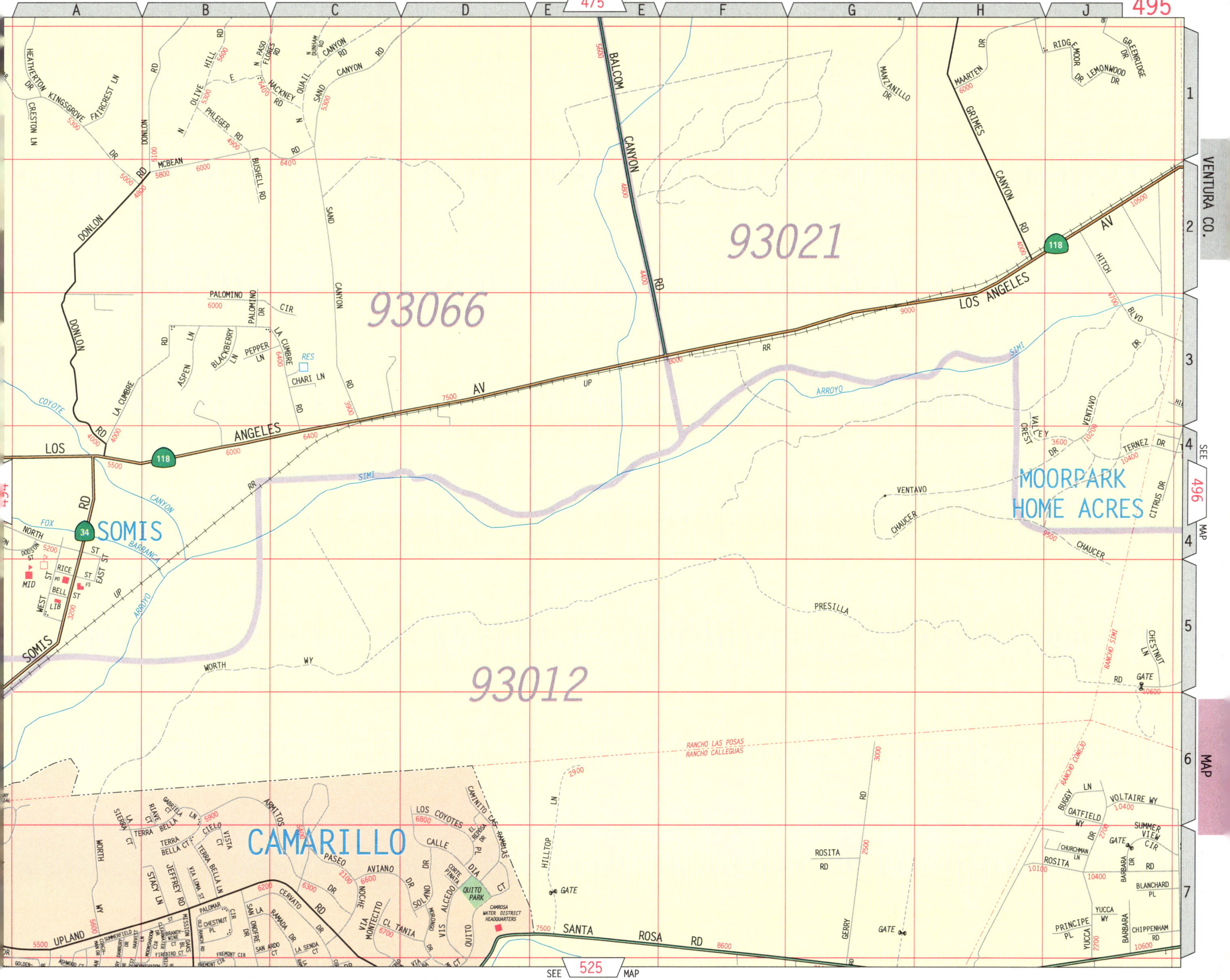

MOORPARK

93021

93012

MOORPARK HOME ACRES

THOUSAND OAKS

91360

NORWEGIAN GRADE

VENTURA CO.

SEE 476 MAP
SEE 526 MAP
SEE 495 MAP
SEE 496

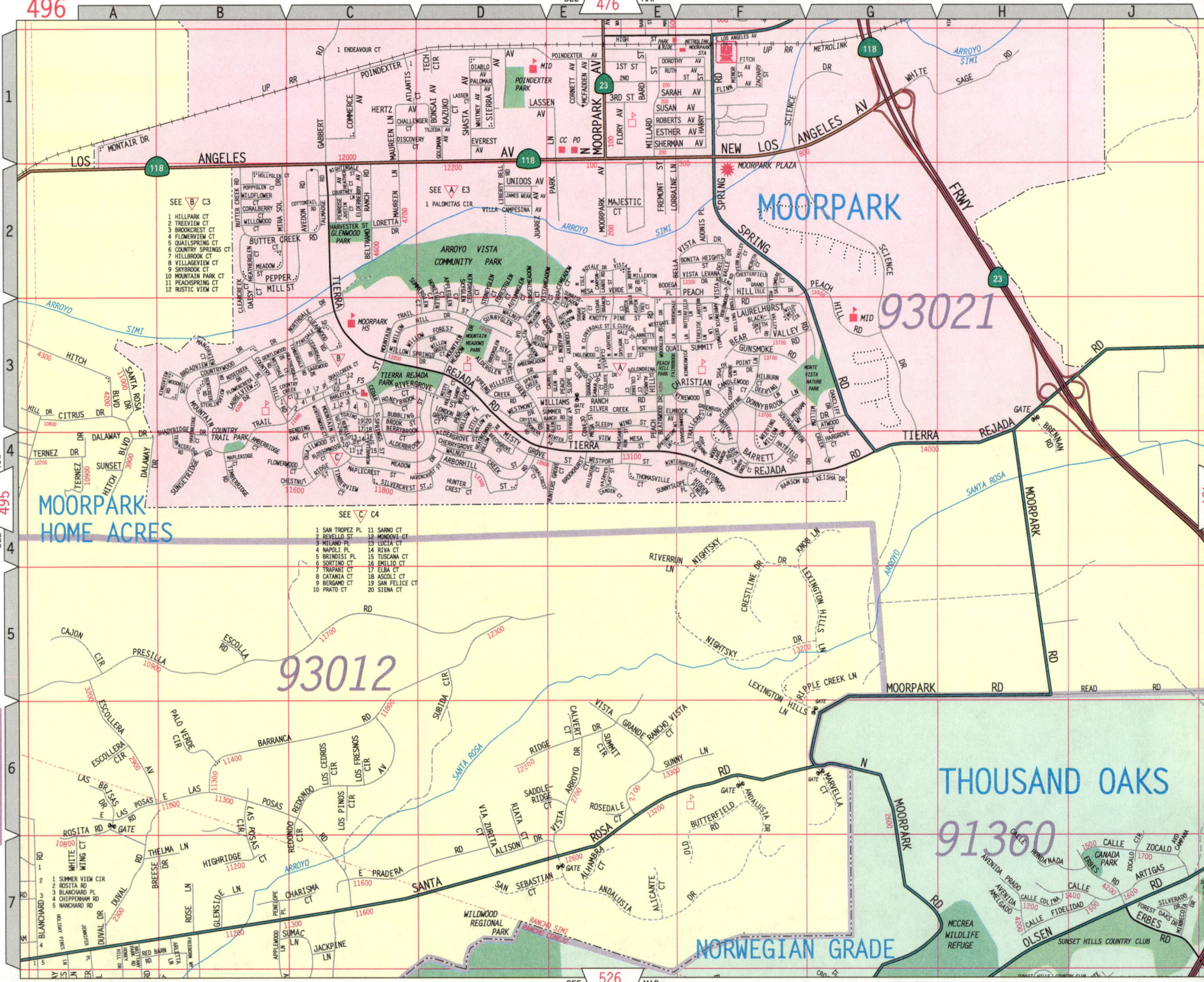

SEE B C3
1 HILLPARK CT
2 TREEVIEW CT
3 BROOKCREST CT
4 FLOWERVIEW CT
5 QUAILSPRING CT
6 COUNTRY SPRINGS CT
7 HILLBROOK CT
8 VILLAGEVIEW CT
9 SKYBROOK CT
10 MOUNTAIN PARK CT
11 PEACHSPRING CT
12 RUSTIC VIEW CT

SEE C C4
1 SAN TROPEZ PL
2 REVELLO ST
3 MILANO PL
4 NAPOLI PL
5 BRINDISI PL
6 SORTINO CT
7 TRAPANI CT
8 CATANIA CT
9 BERGAMO CT
10 PRATO CT
11 SARNO CT
12 MONDOVI CT
13 LUCIA CT
14 RIVA CT
15 TUSCANA CT
16 EMILIO CT
17 ELBA CT
18 ASCOLI CT
19 SAN FELICE CT
20 SIENA CT

ARROYO VISTA COMMUNITY PARK

TIERRA REJADA PARK

POINDEXTER PARK

WILDWOOD REGIONAL PARK

MCCREA WILDLIFE REFUGE

SUNSET HILLS COUNTRY CLUB

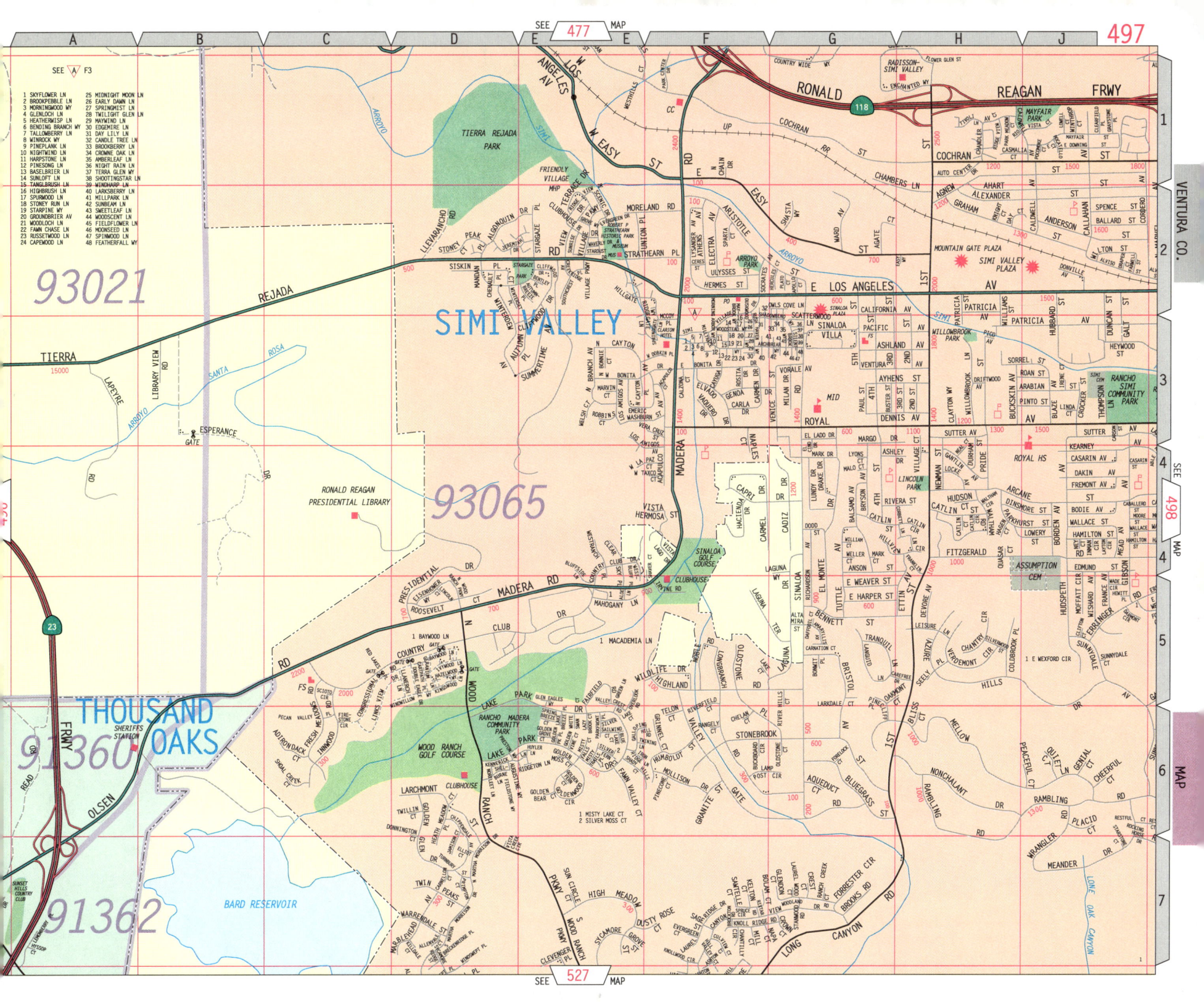

SEE 477 MAP

497

| A | B | C | D | E | F | G | H | J |

SEE F3

1 SKYFLOWER LN
2 BROOKPEBBLE LN
3 MORNINGWOOD WY
4 GLENLOCH LN
5 HEATHERWISP LN
6 BENDING BRANCH WY
7 TALLOWBERRY LN
8 WINROCK WY
9 PINEPLANK LN
10 NIGHTWIND LN
11 HARPSTONE LN
12 PINESONG LN
13 BASELBRIER LN
14 SUNLOFT LN
15 TANGLBRUSH LN
16 HIGHBRUSH LN
17 SPURWOOD LN
18 STONEY RUN LN
19 STARPINE WY
20 GROUNDBRIER AV
21 WOODLOCH LN
22 FAWN CHASE LN
23 RUSSETWOOD LN
24 CAPEWOOD LN
25 MIDNIGHT MOON LN
26 EARLY DAWN LN
27 SPRINGMIST LN
28 TWILIGHT GLEN LN
29 MAYWIND LN
30 EDGEMIRE LN
31 DAY LILY LN
32 CANDLE TREE LN
33 BROOKBERRY LN
34 CROWNE OAK LN
35 AMBERLEAF LN
36 NIGHT RAIN LN
37 TERRA GLEN WY
38 SHOOTINGSTAR LN
39 WINDHARP LN
40 LARKSBERRY LN
41 MILLPARK LN
42 SUNBEAM LN
43 SWEETLEAF LN
44 WOODSCENT LN
45 FIELDFLOWER LN
46 MOONSEED LN
47 SPINWOOD LN
48 FEATHERFALL LN

93021

93065

SIMI VALLEY

THOUSAND OAKS

91360

91362

BARD RESERVOIR

RONALD REAGAN FRWY

RONALD REAGAN PRESIDENTIAL LIBRARY

TIERRA REJADA PARK

VENTURA CO.

SEE 498 MAP

SEE 527 MAP

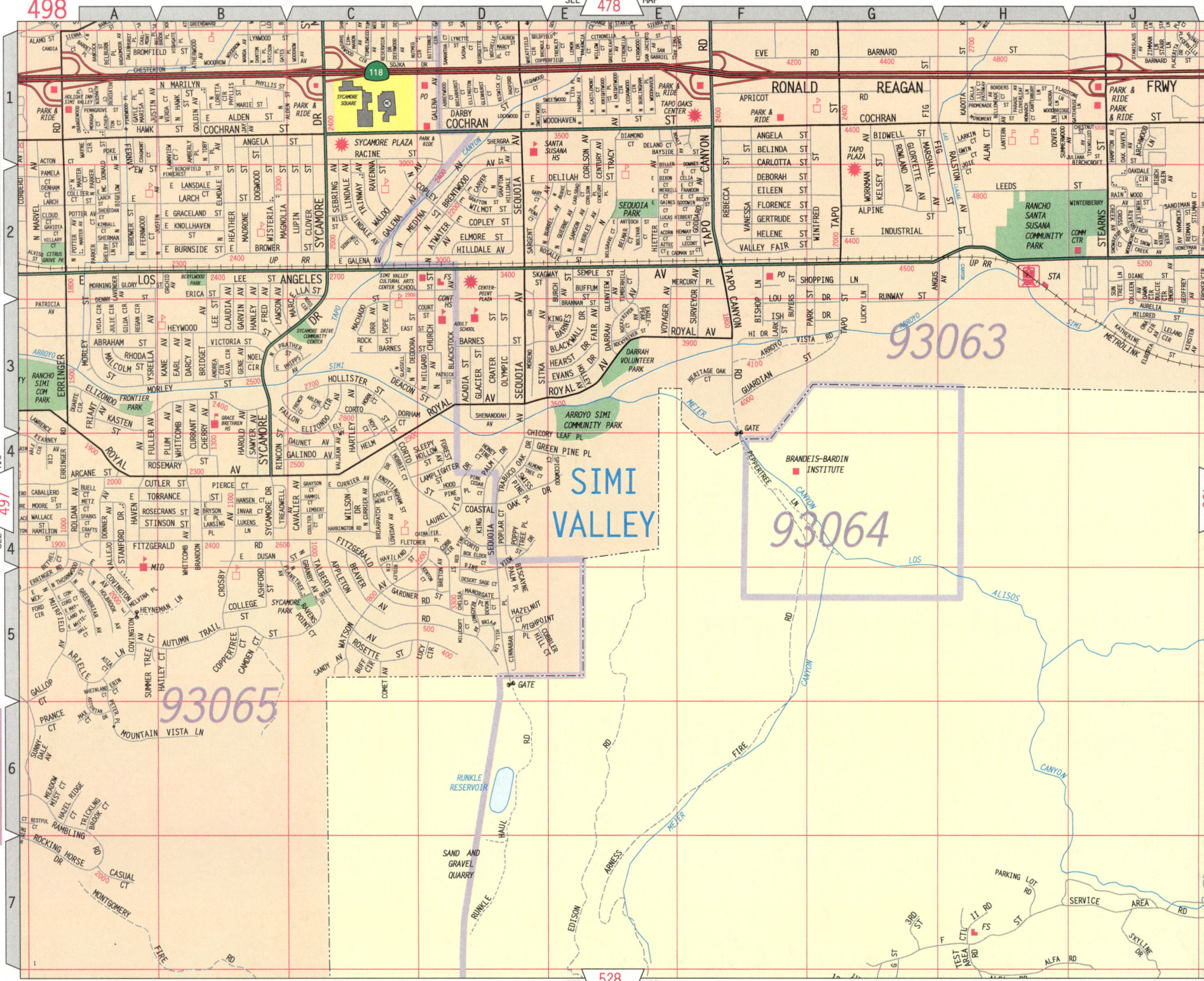

A B C D E F G H J

SEE 478 MAP

VENTURA CO.

RONALD REAGAN FRWY

118

SYCAMORE SQUARE

DARBY COCHRAN

SYCAMORE PLAZA RACINE

SANTA SUSANA HS

TAPO OAKS CENTER

PARK & RIDE

TAPO PLAZA

SEQUOIA PARK

RANCHO SANTA SUSANA COMMUNITY PARK

COMM CTR

STEARNS

LOS ANGELES AV

SIMI VALLEY CULTURAL ARTS CENTER SCHOOL

CENTER-POINT PLAZA

CONT HS

SYCAMORE DRIVE COMMUNITY CENTER

ADULT SCHOOL

DARRAH VOLUNTEER PARK

93063

STA

METROLINK

RANCHO SIMI COM PARK

ELIZONDO FRONTIER PARK

GRACE BRETHREN HS

ARROYO SIMI COMMUNITY PARK

CHICORY LEAF PL

GATE

BRANDEIS-BARDIN INSTITUTE

SIMI VALLEY

93064

SLEEPY HOLLOW

FITZGERALD

SYCAMORE RAVENS PARK POINT

COLLEGE

93065

GATE

MOUNTAIN VISTA LN

RUNKLE RESERVOIR

SAND AND GRAVEL QUARRY

PARKING LOT RD

SERVICE AREA

TEST AREA II RD

SKYLINE DR

SEE 528 MAP

MAP 497

LOS ANGELES COUNTY

93063

SIMI VALLEY

LOS ANGELES
91311

CHATSWORTH

SANTA SUSANA

VENTURA COUNTY

91304

CORRIGANVILLE REGIONAL PARK

FOOTHILL PARK

VERDE PARK

SANTA SUSANA PARK

KNOLLS PARK

CHATSWORTH PARK NORTH

CHATSWORTH PARK SOUTH

OAKWOOD MEMORIAL PARK

CHATSWORTH OAKS PARK

CHATSWORTH NATURE PRESERVE/RESERVOIR

CHATSWORTH RESERVOIR

DETENTION BASIN NO. 1

VENTURA CO.

LA 500 MAP

MAP

RONALD REAGAN FRWY

118

SANTA SUSANA PASS

SANTA SUSANA PASS RD

DEVONSHIRE ST

LASSEN ST

PLUMMER ST

NORDHOFF ST

RANCHO EX MISSION DE SAN FERNANDO

RANCHO SIMI

VENTURA CO LOS ANGELES CO

LAKE MANOR

VALLEY CIRCLE BLVD

WOOLSEY CANYON RD

ROCKETDYNE

SERVICE AREA

1 HAPPY VALLEY RD

AREA I

MOUNT SINAI DR

KUEHNER DR

COCHRAN ST

LOS ANGELES AV

YOSEMITE AV

KATHERINE RD

SMITH RD

SANTA SUSANA

BOX CANYON RD

STUDIO RD

FIRE RD

MESA

AMERICAN CANYON RD

NORTH

BRYANT DR

SHIRLEY DR

MESA RD

SECKER DR

A B C D E E F G H J

SEE 491 MAP

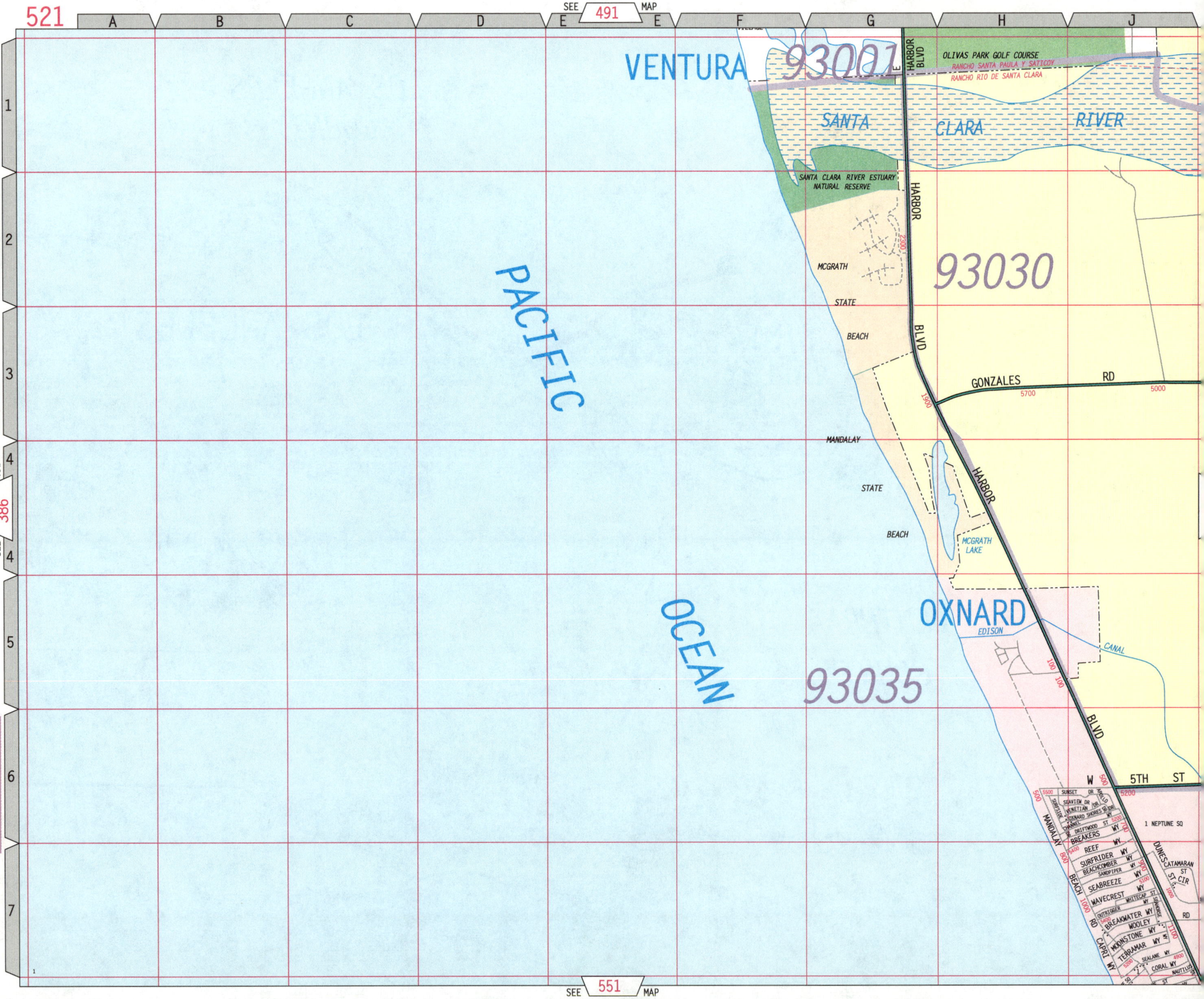

1

VENTURA CO.

VENTURA

93001

OLIVAS PARK GOLF COURSE

RANCHO SANTA PAULA Y SATICOY

RANCHO RIO DE SANTA CLARA

SANTA   CLARA   RIVER

HARBOR BLVD

2

SANTA CLARA RIVER ESTUARY
NATURAL RESERVE

MCGRATH

93030

2200

STATE

3

BEACH

HARBOR

BLVD

GONZALES   RD

1500   5700   5000

MANDALAY

4

SEE 386 MAP

STATE

HARBOR

BEACH

MCGRATH
LAKE

PACIFIC

OXNARD

EDISON

5

OCEAN

93035

CANAL

100 100

BLVD

6

MAP

W   500   5TH   ST

5200

1 NEPTUNE SQ

5500

SUNSET DR

SEAVIEW DR

VENETIAN

SURFSIDE DR

OXNARD SHORES

ONNARD SHORES

ST

DRIFTWOOD WY

BREAKERS WY

REEF WY

MANDALAY

SURFRIDER WY

BEACHCOMBER WY

SANDPIPER

SEABREEZE WY

BEACH

WAVECREST WY

WHITECAP ST

WOOLEY

7

CATAMARAN

DUNES

ST

CIR

RD

BREAKWATER WY

BREAKWATER WY

MOONSTONE WY

CAPRI WY

TERRAMAR WY

SEALANE WY

CORAL WY

NAUTILUS

SEE 551 MAP

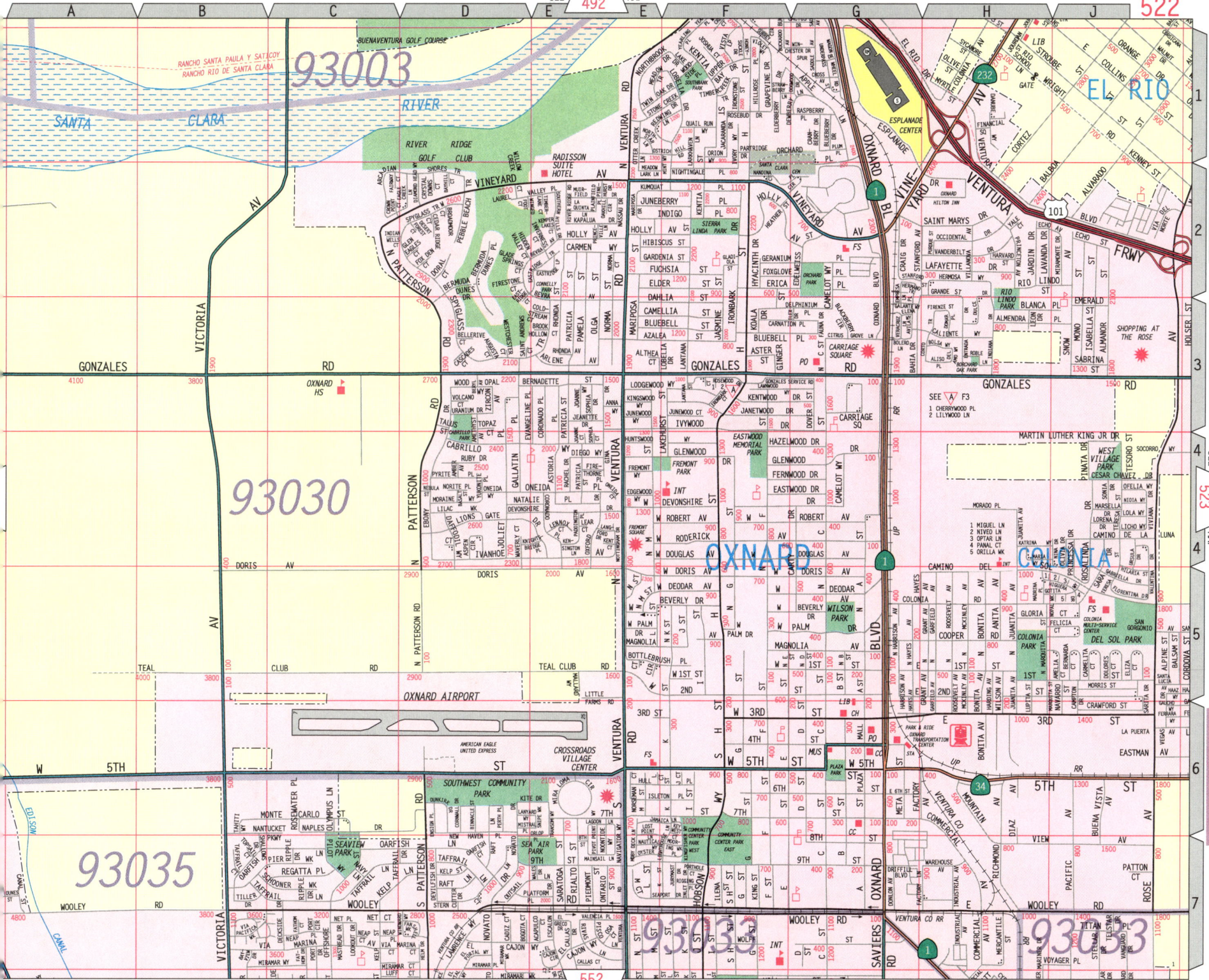

93003

SANTA CLARA RIVER

Rancho Santa Paula y Saticoy
Rancho Rio de Santa Clara

Buenaventura Golf Course

River Ridge Golf Club

RADISSON SUITE HOTEL

EL RIO

VENTURA CO.

93030

OXNARD HS

VICTORIA AV

N PATTERSON

PATTERSON AV

GONZALES RD

OXNARD

COLONIA

GONZALES RD

MARTIN LUTHER KING JR DR

WEST VILLAGE PARK
CESAR CHAVEZ DR

RIO LINDO PARK

SHOPPING AT THE ROSE

CARRIAGE SQUARE

DEL SOL PARK

COLONIA PARK

WILSON PARK

DORIS AV

TEAL CLUB RD

OXNARD AIRPORT

AMERICAN EAGLE UNITED EXPRESS

CROSSROADS VILLAGE CENTER

VENTURA RD

OXNARD BLVD

W 5TH ST

SOUTHWEST COMMUNITY PARK

SEAVIEW PARK

SEA AIR PARK

COMMUNITY CENTER PARK EAST

OXNARD TRANSPORTATION CENTER

93035

WOOLEY RD

93036

93033

VENTURA CO RR

SAVIERS RD

EDISON CANAL

SEE 492 MAP

SEE 552 MAP

SEE 523 MAP

523

A B C D E E F G H J

VENTURA CO.

1

CENTRAL

93010

SPANISH HILLS GOLF AND COUNTRY CLUB

CRESTVIEW

SPRINGVILLE PARK

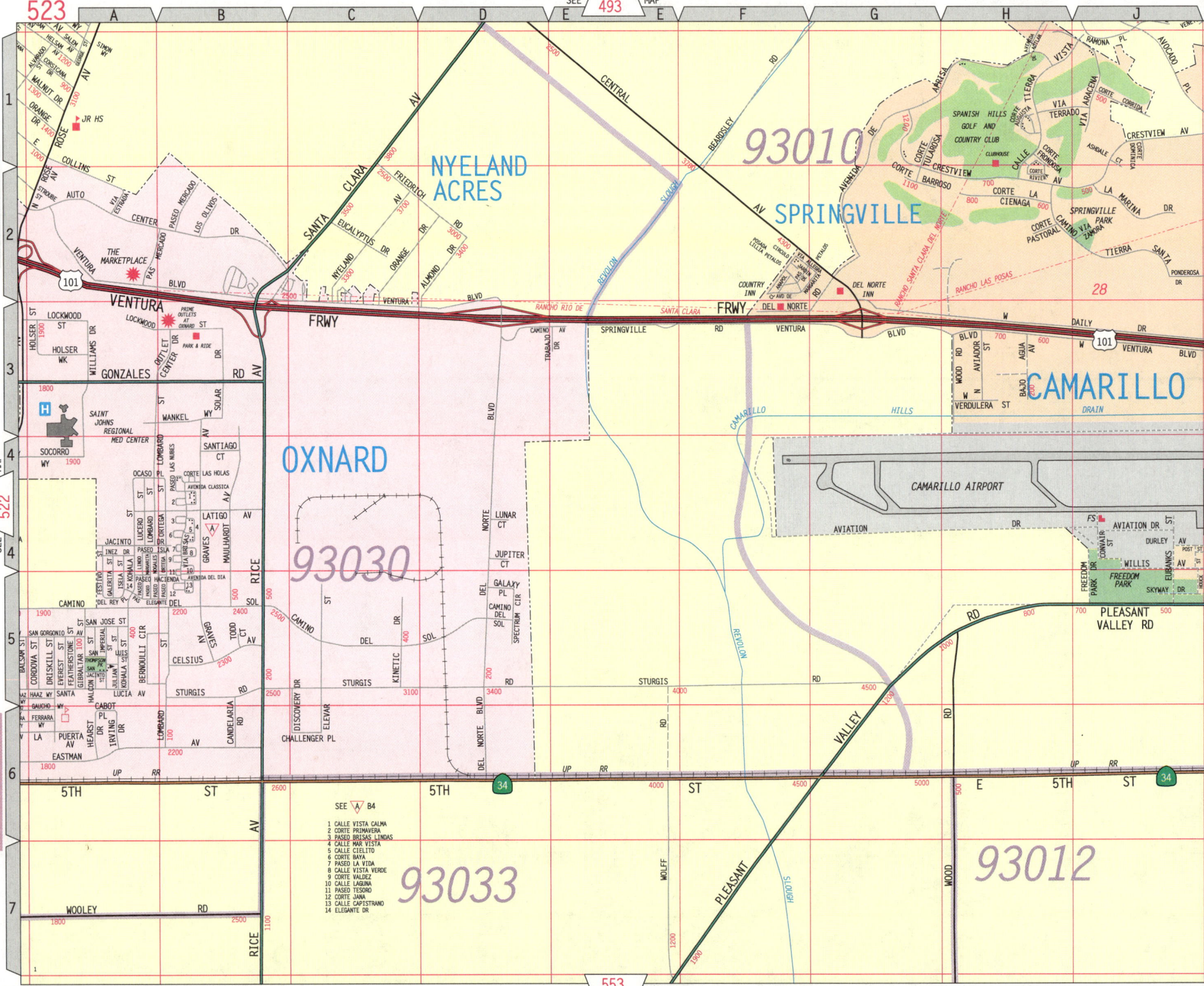

NYELAND ACRES

2

SANTA CLARA AV

SPRINGVILLE

28

THE MARKETPLACE

PRIME OUTLETS AT OXNARD

VENTURA BLVD

COUNTRY INN

DEL NORTE INN

CAMARILLO

101

VENTURA FRWY

RANCHO RIO DE SANTA CLARA FRWY

DEL NORTE

SPRINGVILLE RD

VENTURA BLVD

101 VENTURA BLVD

3

GONZALES RD

SAINT JOHNS REGIONAL MED CENTER

H SOCORRO WY

CAMARILLO HILLS DRAIN

4

OXNARD

93030

CAMARILLO AIRPORT

AVIATION DR

FREEDOM PARK

WILLIS

5

LUNAR CT

JUPITER CT

GALAXY PL

CAMINO DEL SOL

REVOLON

STURGIS RD

STURGIS RD

PLEASANT VALLEY RD

6

5TH ST

5TH ST

34

5TH ST

34

SEE B4

1 CALLE VISTA CALMA
2 CORTE PRIMAVERA
3 PASEO BRISAS LINDAS
4 CALLE MAR VISTA
5 CALLE CIELITO
6 CORTE BAYA
7 PASEO LA VIDA
8 CALLE VISTA VERDE
9 CORTE VALDEZ
10 CALLE LAGUNA
11 PASEO TESORO
12 CORTE JANA
13 CALLE CAPISTRANO
14 ELEGANTE DR

7

WOOLEY RD

93033

PLEASANT VALLEY RD

93012

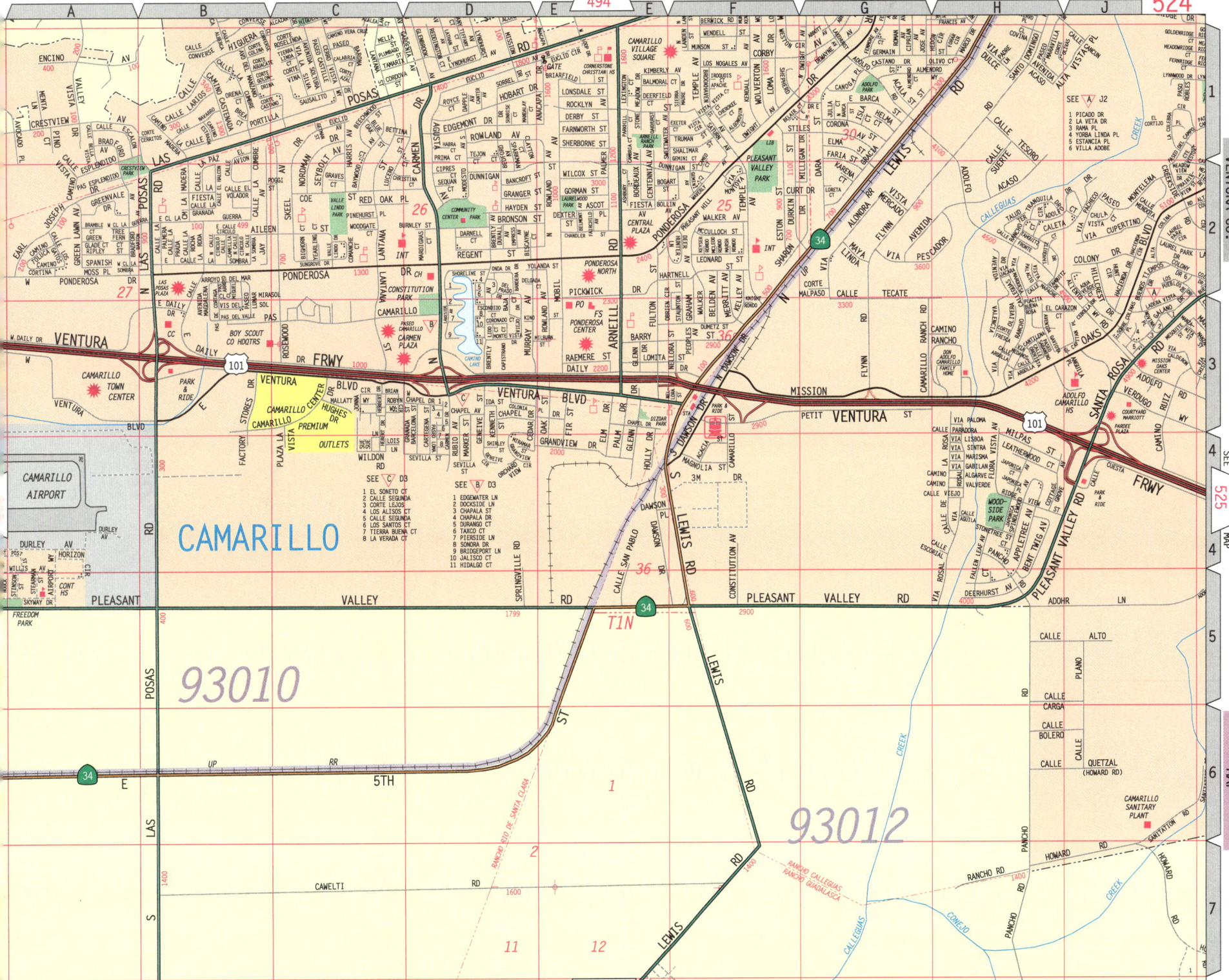

CAMARILLO

CAMARILLO AIRPORT

93010

93012

VENTURA FRWY 101

PLEASANT VALLEY RD

VENTURA BLVD

CAMARILLO PREMIUM OUTLETS

CAMARILLO TOWN CENTER

VENTURA CO.

SEE 494 MAP

SEE 554 MAP

SEE 524

SEE 525 MAP

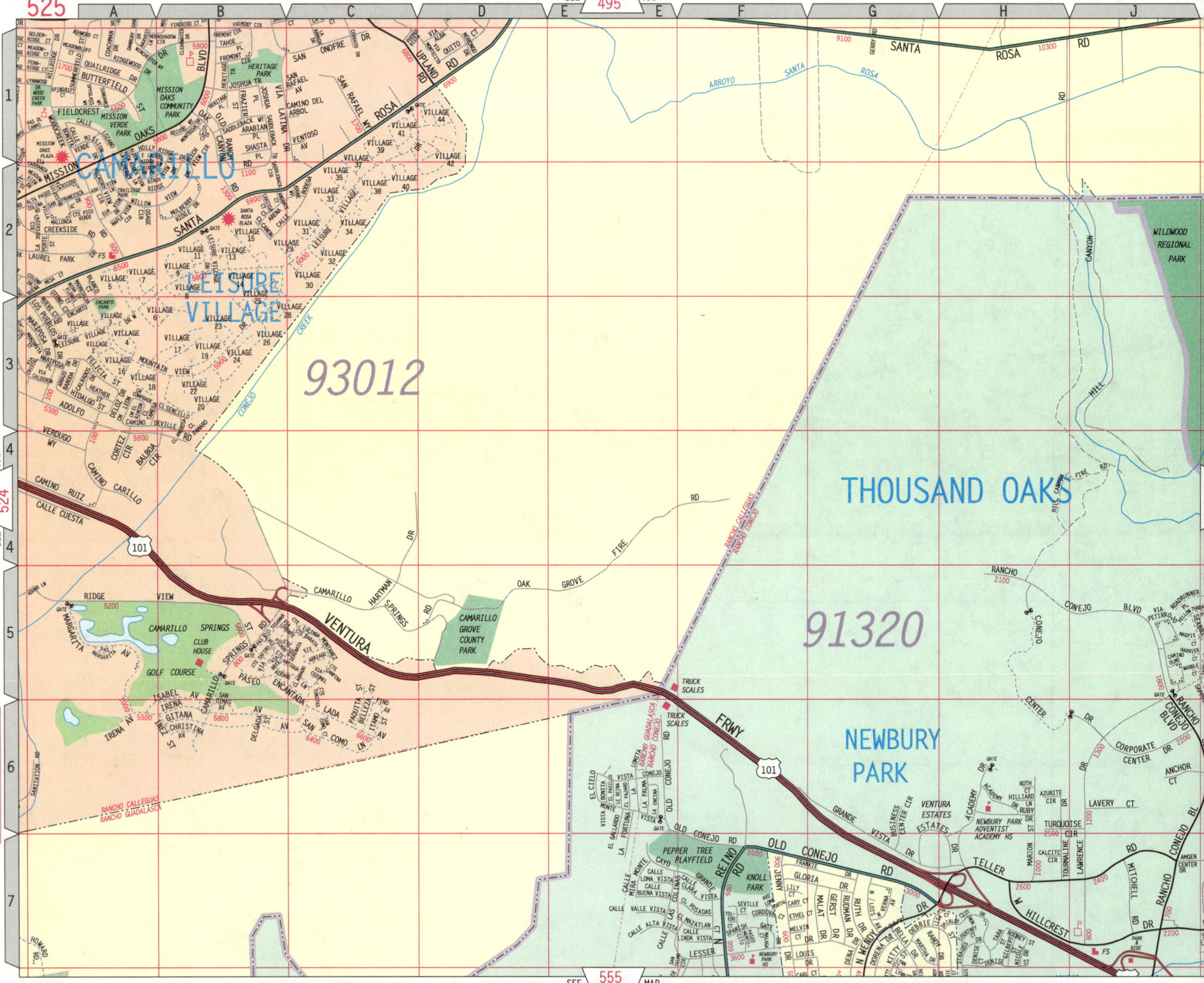

525

SEE 495 MAP

A B C D E E F G H J

VENTURA CO.

SANTA ROSA RD

CAMARILLO

LEISURE VILLAGE

WILDWOOD REGIONAL PARK

93012

MAP 524 SEE

THOUSAND OAKS

91320

CAMARILLO SPRINGS CLUB HOUSE

GOLF COURSE

VENTURA

CAMARILLO GROVE COUNTY PARK

101

MAP

NEWBURY PARK

FRWY

101

VENTURA ESTATES

CORPORATE CENTER

PEPPER TREE PLAYFIELD

KNOLL PARK

NEWBURY PARK HS

W HILLCREST DR

RANCHO CONEJO BLVD

SEE 555 MAP

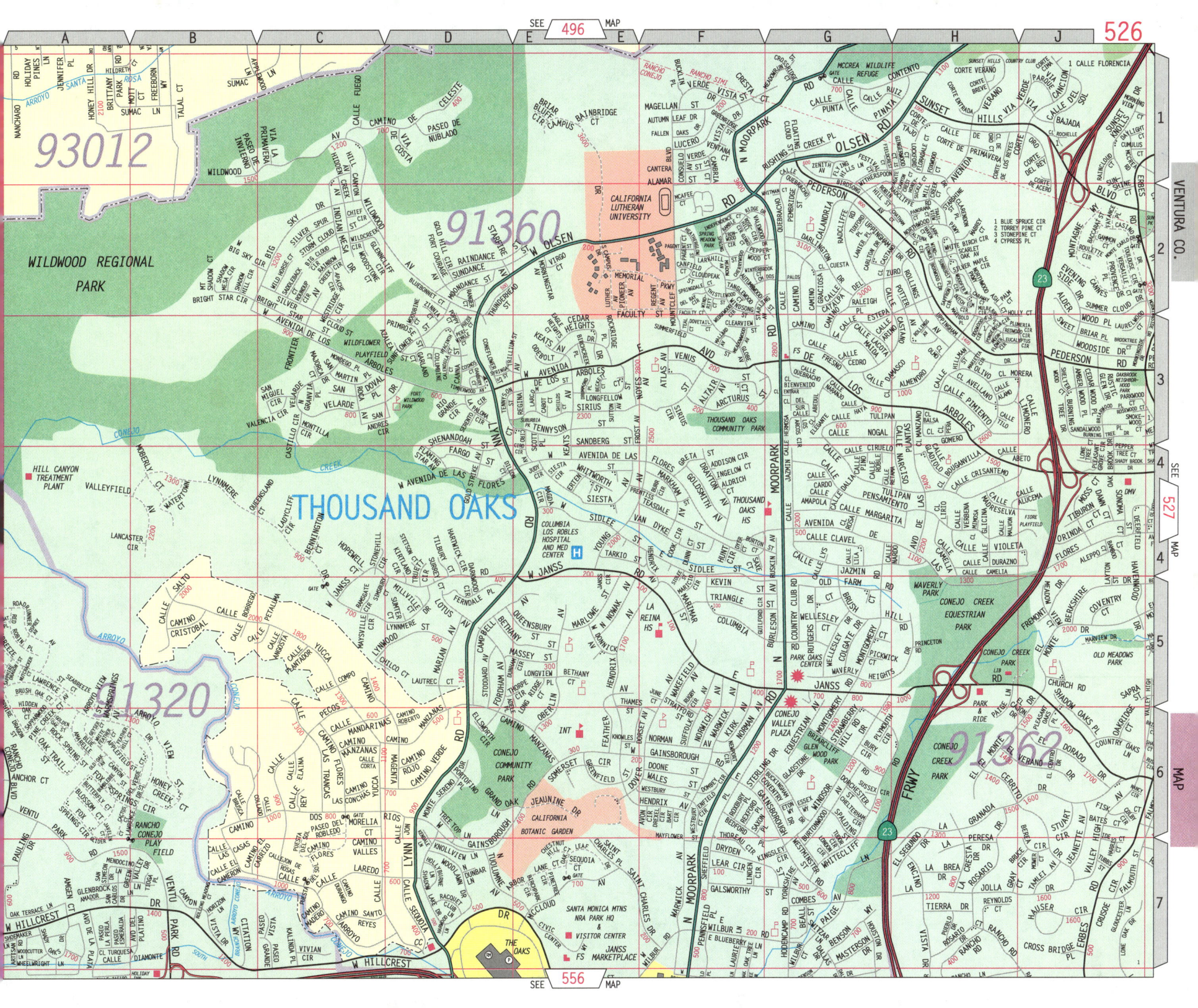

THOUSAND OAKS

93012
91360
91320
91362

WILDWOOD REGIONAL PARK

CALIFORNIA LUTHERAN UNIVERSITY

SEE 496 MAP
SEE 526 MAP
SEE 527 MAP
SEE 556 MAP

VENTURA CO.

MAP

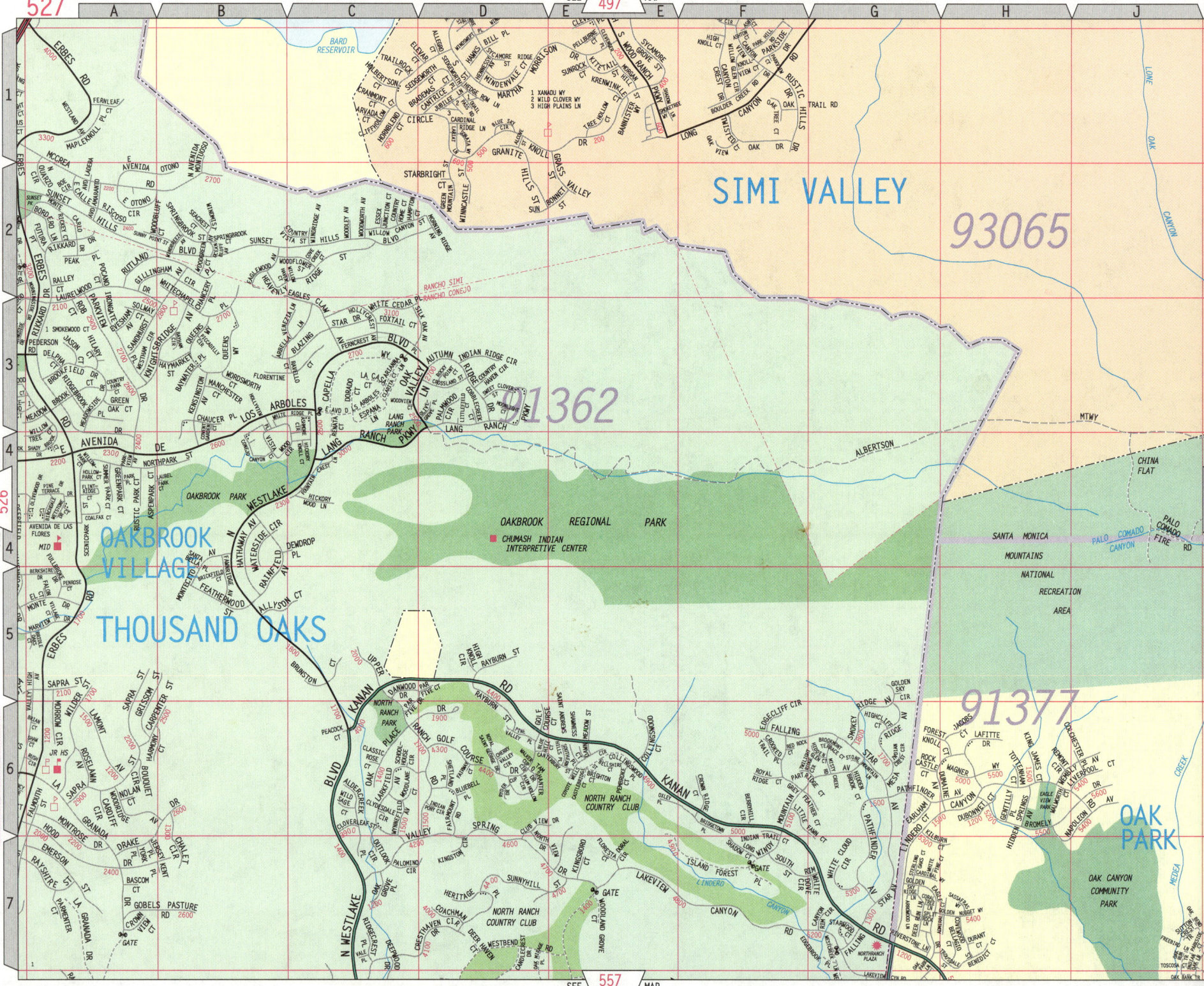

A B C D E E F G H J

SEE 497 MAP

SIMI VALLEY

93065

91362

91377

BARD RESERVOIR

VENTURA CO.

SEE 526 MAP

OAKBROOK VILLAGE

THOUSAND OAKS

OAKBROOK REGIONAL PARK

CHUMASH INDIAN INTERPRETIVE CENTER

SANTA MONICA MOUNTAINS NATIONAL RECREATION AREA

CHINA FLAT

PALO COMADO CANYON

PALO COMADO FIRE RD

NORTH RANCH COUNTRY CLUB

OAK PARK

OAK CANYON COMMUNITY PARK

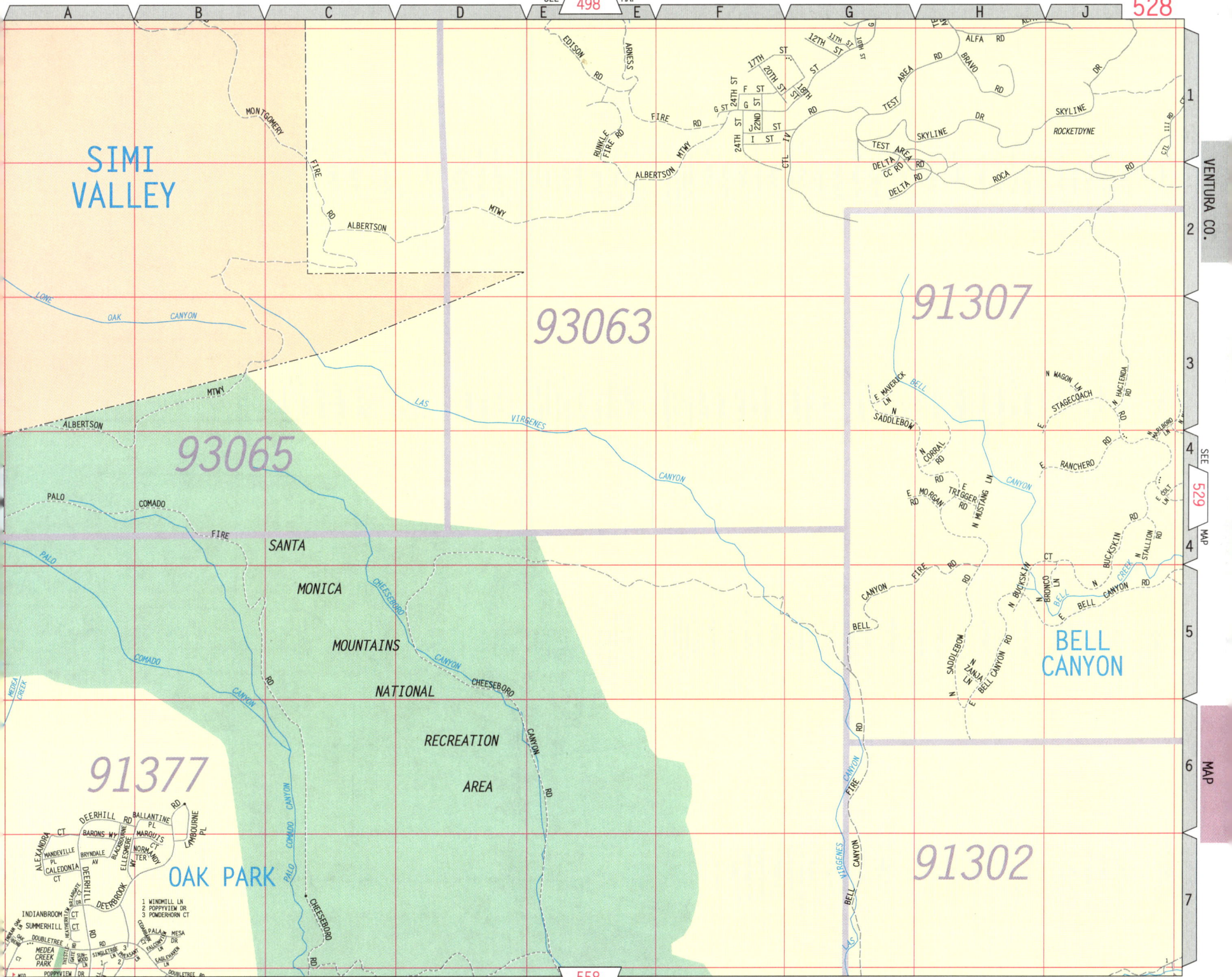

A   B   C   D   E   E   F   G   H   J

VENTURA CO.

SIMI VALLEY

MONTGOMERY

EDISON RD
ARNESS
FIRE RD
RUNKLE FIRE RD
ALBERTSON MTWY
FIRE RD
24TH ST   17TH ST   12TH ST   11TH ST   10TH ST
20TH ST   18TH ST
22ND ST
24TH ST   I ST   J ST   G ST   F ST
CTL IV   CTL III RD
ALFA RD
BRAVO RD
SKYLINE
ROCKETDYNE
TEST AREA
SKYLINE DR
DELTA CC RD
DELTA RD
ROCA

FIRE RD
ALBERTSON MTWY

91307

93063

MTWY
ALBERTSON
LONE OAK CANYON
LAS VIRGENES
CANYON

N MAVERICK LN   BELL
N SADDLEBOW
N WAGON LN
STAGECOACH
HACIENDA RD
N CORRAL RD
E RANCHERO
RD
E MORGAN RD   E TRIGGER RD   N MUSTANG LN
BELL CANYON
E COLT LN
N WILBURD

93065

PALO
COMADO
FIRE
SANTA
MONICA
MOUNTAINS
NATIONAL
RECREATION
AREA

COMADO
PALO
MEDEA CREEK
CANYON
CHEESEBORO
CANYON
CHEESEBORO
CANYON RD

CANYON FIRE RD
RD
BRONCO LN
N BUCKSKIN   BUCKSKIN RD
STALLION RD
BELL CANYON RD
BELL
BELL CANYON CREEK
CT

BELL CANYON

N SADDLEBOW   N ZANJA LN   E BELL CANYON RD

91377

DEERHILL RD
BALLANTINE PL
BARONS WY   MARQUIS PL
LAMBOURNE PL
MANDEVILLE PL
BRYNDALE AV   NORMANDY TER
ALEXANDRA CT   CALEDONIA CT   ELLESMERE WY   BLACKBOURNE CT
DEERHILL CT
DEERBROOK
INDIANBROOM CT
SUMMERHILL CT
DOUBLETREE
MEDEA CREEK PARK
THISTLE   HEATHERVIEW   SINGLETREE LN   PHEASANT LN
GATEWOOD
ESPALA   MESA DR
FALCON   EAGLEVIEW
DOUBLETREE RD
POPPYVIEW DR

1 WINDMILL LN
2 POPPYVIEW DR
3 POWDERHORN CT

OAK PARK

PALO COMADO CANYON
CHEESEBORO RD

BELL CANYON FIRE RD
LAS VIRGENES
BELL CANYON

91302

SEE 529 MAP

MAP

1 2 3 4 4 5 6 7

SEE 499 MAP

A B C D E E F G H J

93063

91304

VENTURA CO.

MAP 528 SEE MAP

VENTURA CO

LOS ANGELES CO

BELL CANYON

LA CO

91302

CHATSWORTH NATURE PRESERVE/RESERVOIR

CHATSWORTH RESERVOIR

DAM

HIDDEN LAKE

ROSCOE BLVD

JUSTICE

STRATHERN

INGOMAR

SATICOY

WEST HILLS

LOS ANGELES

MEDICAL CENTER DR

SHERMAN

CANOGA PARK

91303

91307

VANOWEN

FALLBROOK MALL

VICTORY BLVD

WOODLAND HILLS

91367

SEE LA 559 MAP

SEE A E1
1 OAKRIDGE RD
2 LAKELAND TER
3 TODD VIEW CT
4 HOMEZELL TR
5 YUKON TR

SEE 521 MAP
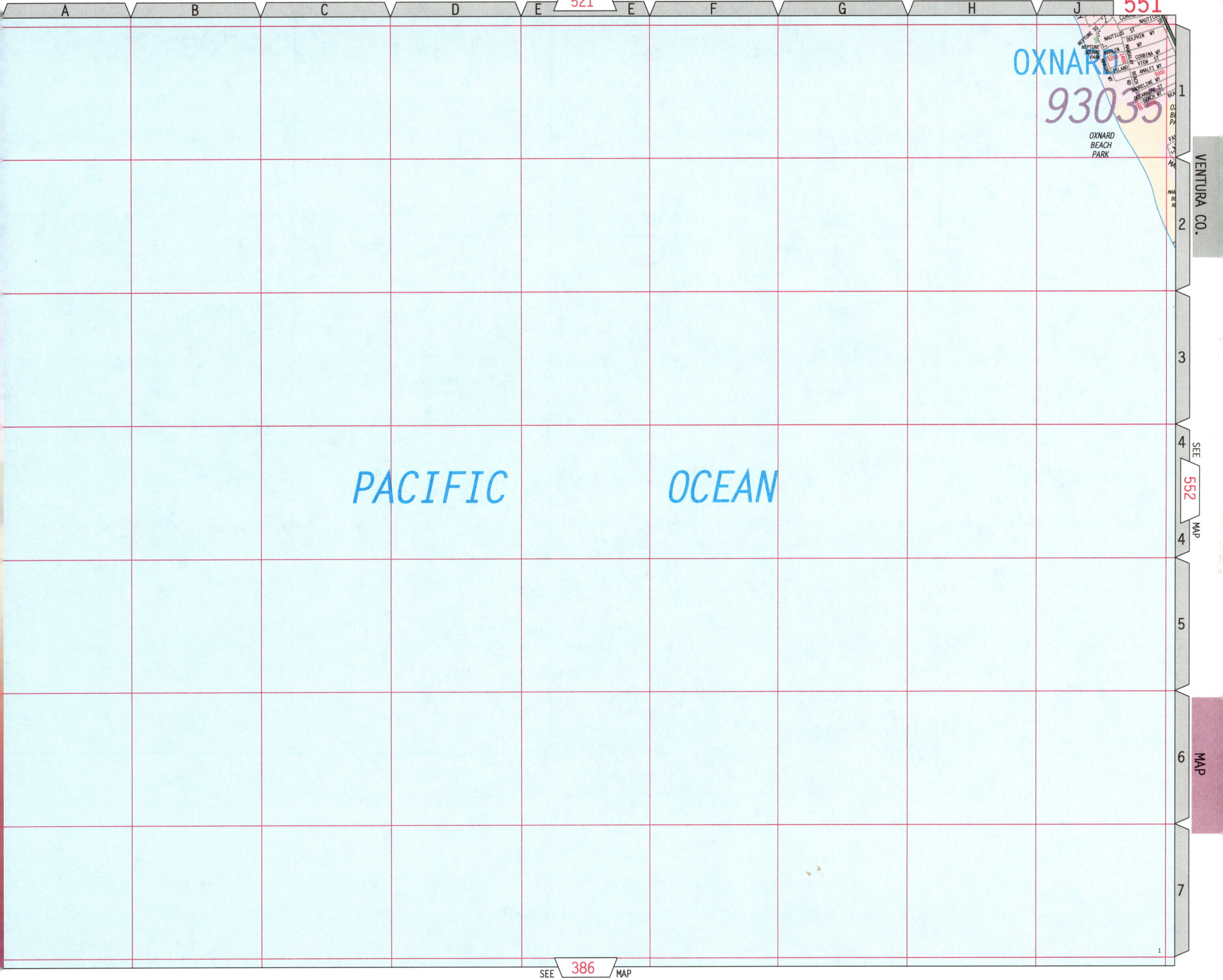
A
B
C
D
E
F
G
H
J
1
2
3
4
5
6
7
OXNARD
93035
OXNARD BEACH PARK
PACIFIC OCEAN
VENTURA CO.
MAP
SEE 552 MAP
SEE 386 MAP

93030

HOLLYWOOD BEACH

HOLLYWOOD BY-THE-SEA

SILVER STRAND

93043

OXNARD

93033

PORT HUENEME

PACIFIC OCEAN

CHANNEL ISLANDS HARBOR

PORT HUENEME HARBOR

CBC PORT HUENEME GOLF CLUB

US NAVAL CONSTRUCTION BATTALION CENTER

VENTURA CO.

W CHANNEL ISLANDS BLVD

CHANNEL ISLANDS BLVD

W HUENEME RD

OXNARD COLLEGE

POINT HUENEME LIGHTHOUSE

PORT HUENEME FISHING PIER

PORT HUENEME BEACH PARK

SEE 551 MAP

SEE 523 MAP

A B C D E E F G H J

VENTURA CO.

OXNARD

93033

93012

930

COLLEGE PARK

OXNARD COLLEGE

LEMONWOOD PARK

EMERSON AV

CHANNEL ISLANDS BL

PLEASANT VALLEY RD

RICE AV

LAGUNA RD

ETTING RD

ETTING RD

PACIFIC COAST

SIESTA WY

DUFAU RD

RAYTHEON RD

E HUENEME RD

E HUENEME RD

HUENEME RD

HAILES RD

DODGE

NAUMAN RD

WOOD RD

WOOD RD

REVOLON

SLOUGH

SLOUGH

REVOLON

BROOME

RANCH

GATE RD

OLDS RD

CASPER RD

ARNOLD RD

NAVAL AIR

CALIFORNIA AIR NATIONAL GUARD

POINT MUGU NAVAL AIR WEAPONS STATION

PERIMETER RD

FRWY

GATE

NAVAL AIR

MULCAHEY

POL DR

RANCHO RIO DE SANTA CLARA
RANCHO GUADALASCA

SEE 554 MAP

MAP

1 YELLOWSTONE DR
2 WHITNEY CIR
3 ARROWHEAD CIR

1 PACKARD ST
2 MURPHY LN
3 NASH LN

SEE A3

1 TAHOE LN   10 PERSIMMON LN
2 TORREY PINES CT 11 PEACH LN
3 SHASTA DR   12 AVOCADO AV
4 YOSEMITE DR   13 CHERRY AV
5 SEQUOIA DR   14 LIME AV
6 ARROWHEAD LN   15 CARDINAL AV
7 KINGS CANYON CT 16 BLUEBIRD LN
8 PONDEROSA LP   17 RAVEN LN
9 APRICOT LN   18 BLUEJAY AV

JR HS

F & AM CEM
JAPANESE CEM

SEE 583 MAP

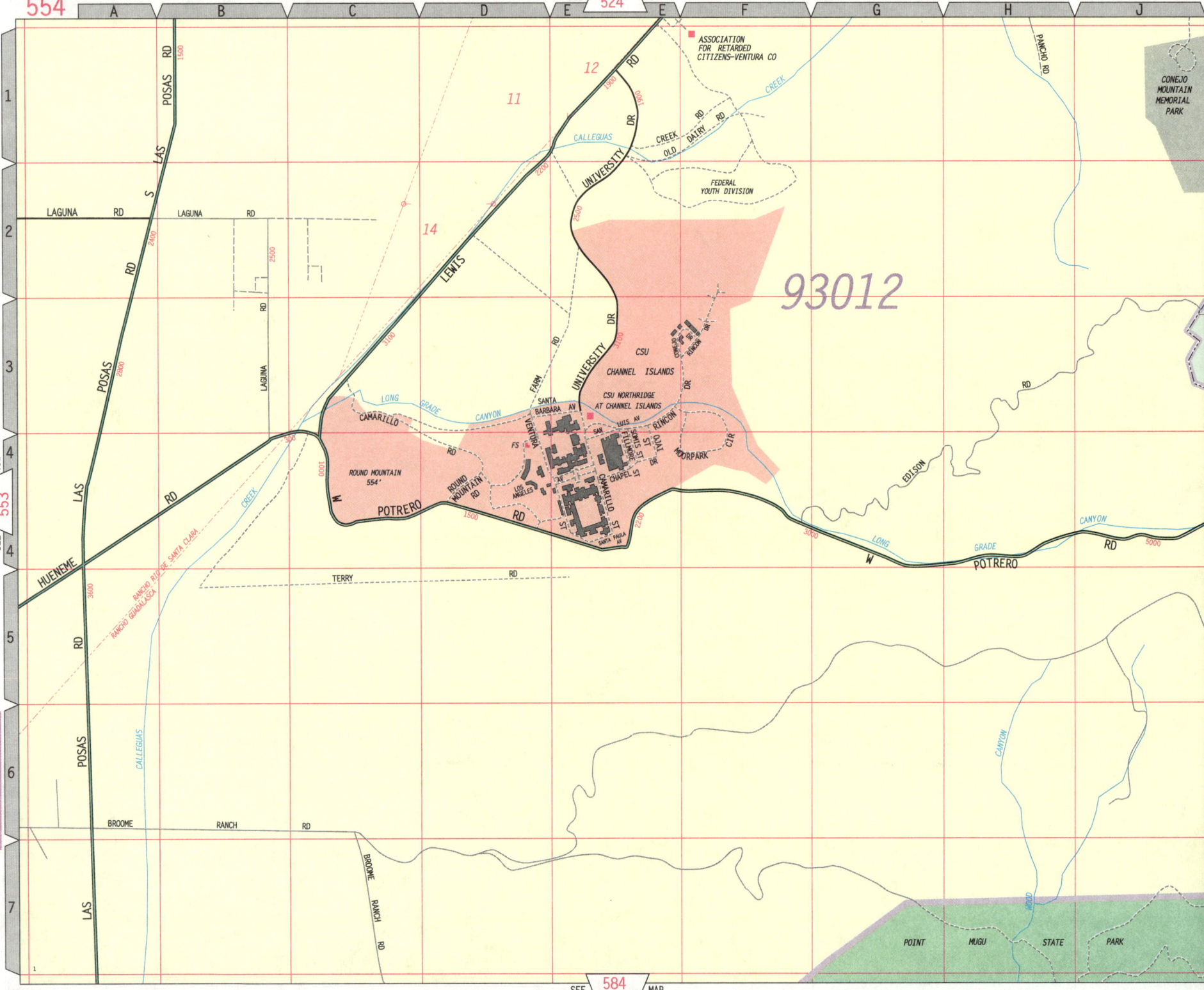

93012

VENTURA CO.

SEE MAP 553

MAP

1

2

3

4

4

5

6

7

POSAS RD S LAS

1500

1900
1900

2200

12

11

14

CALLEGUAS CREEK

UNIVERSITY DR

CREEK OLD DAIRY RD RD

ASSOCIATION FOR RETARDED CITIZENS-VENTURA CO

FEDERAL YOUTH DIVISION

CONEJO MOUNTAIN MEMORIAL PARK

PANCHO RD

LAGUNA RD

LAGUNA RD

LAGUNA RD

POSAS RD

2400

2800

2500

LEWIS

3100

2500

2500

LONG GRADE CANYON

500

1000

CAMARILLO

FARM RD

SANTA BARBARA AV

VENTURA ST

FS

RINCON DR

UNIVERSITY DR

CSU CHANNEL ISLANDS

CSU NORTHRIDGE AT CHANNEL ISLANDS

CONEJO RINCON DR

LUIS AV SAN

LEWIS ST FILLMORE ST

QUAL DR

MOORPARK

RD

EDISON RD

RD

RD

RINCON DR CIR

CANYON

5000

ROUND MOUNTAIN 554'

W

ROUND MOUNTAIN RD

POTRERO RD

1500

LOS ANGELES ST

CHAPEL ST

CAMARILLO ST

SANTA PAULA AV

2200

3000

LONG GRADE

W POTRERO RD

HUENEME

LAS

RD

3600

RANCHO RIO DE SANTA CLARA

RANCHO GUADALASCA

CREEK

TERRY RD

POSAS

CALLEGUAS

BROOME RANCH RD

BROOME RANCH RD

CANYON

WOOD CANYON

POINT MUGU STATE PARK

SEE 525 MAP

555

A B C D E F G H J

VENTURA CO.

93012

91320

THOUSAND OAKS

NEWBURY PARK

91361

93012

SANTA MONICA MOUNTAINS
NATIONAL RECREATION AREA

POINT MUGU STATE PARK

SANTA MONICA MOUNTAINS
NATIONAL RECREATION AREA

SEE 556 MAP

MAP

SEE 585 MAP

CONEJO MOUNTAIN MEM PARK

NEWBURY PARK

BORCHARD PARK

CYPRESS PARK

POTRERO OPEN SPACE

VENTU PARK

SEE A F1
1 MARIPOSA DR
2 PADUA LN
3 PADUA CIR
4 DAMIANA DR
5 OAK GLEN DR

SEE C G4
1 FAWNGLEN PL
2 DEER SPRING PL
3 SADDLEHORN PL
4 LODESTONE CT
5 BEARCLAW CT
6 DEERFOOT PL
7 RAWHIDE PL
8 SAGEBRUSH PL
9 LARAMIE CT
10 MIRAGE CT
11 PRAIRIE CT
12 CONESTOGA CIR
13 ELMWOOD ST
14 HOLLOWAY CT

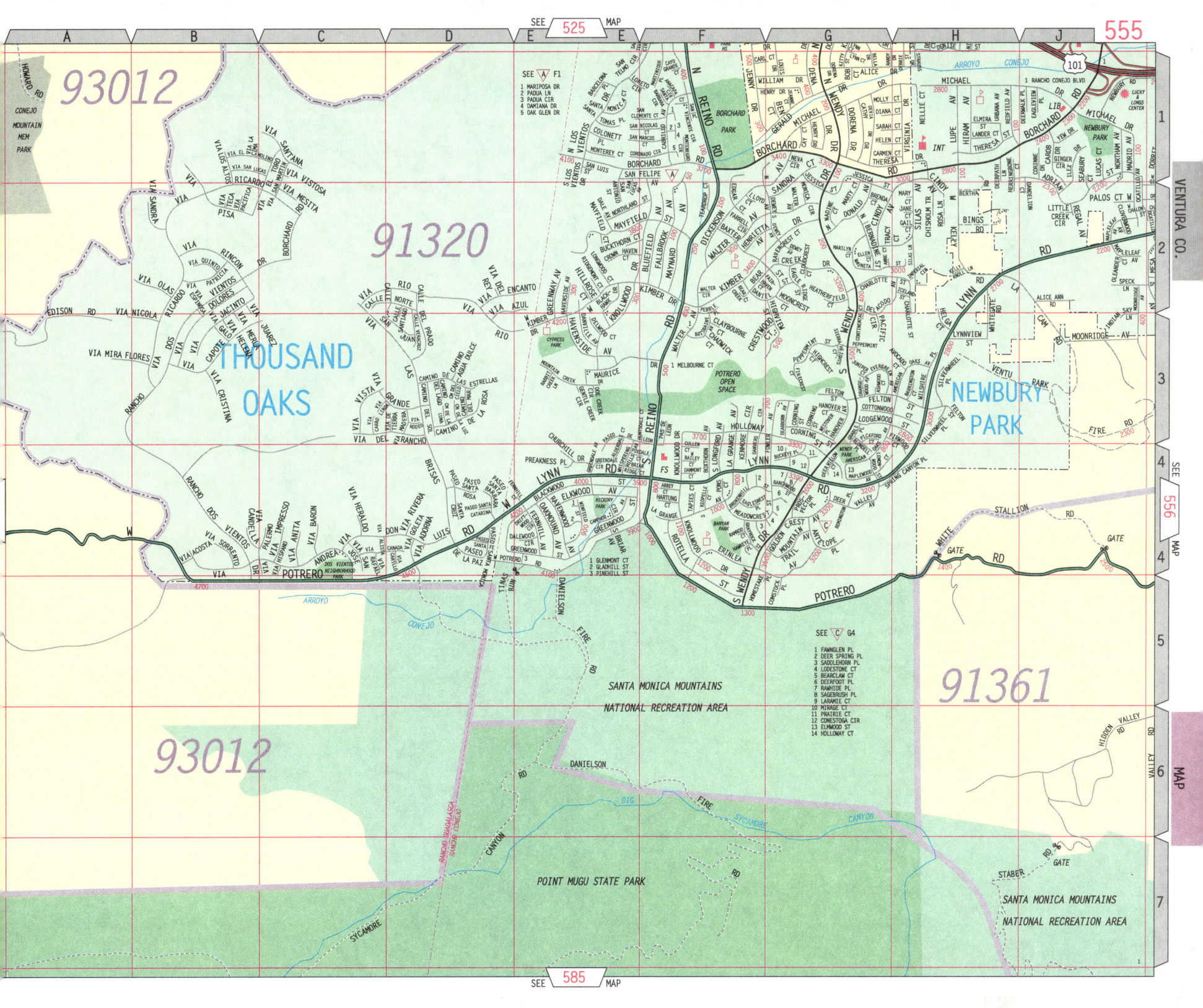

1 GLENMONT CT
2 GLADHILL ST
3 PINEHILL ST

ARROYO CONEJO

A B C D E SEE 526 MAP E F G H J

VENTURA CO.

SEE 555 MAP
SEE 555 MAP
MAP

1
2
3
4
4
5
6
7

91320

91361

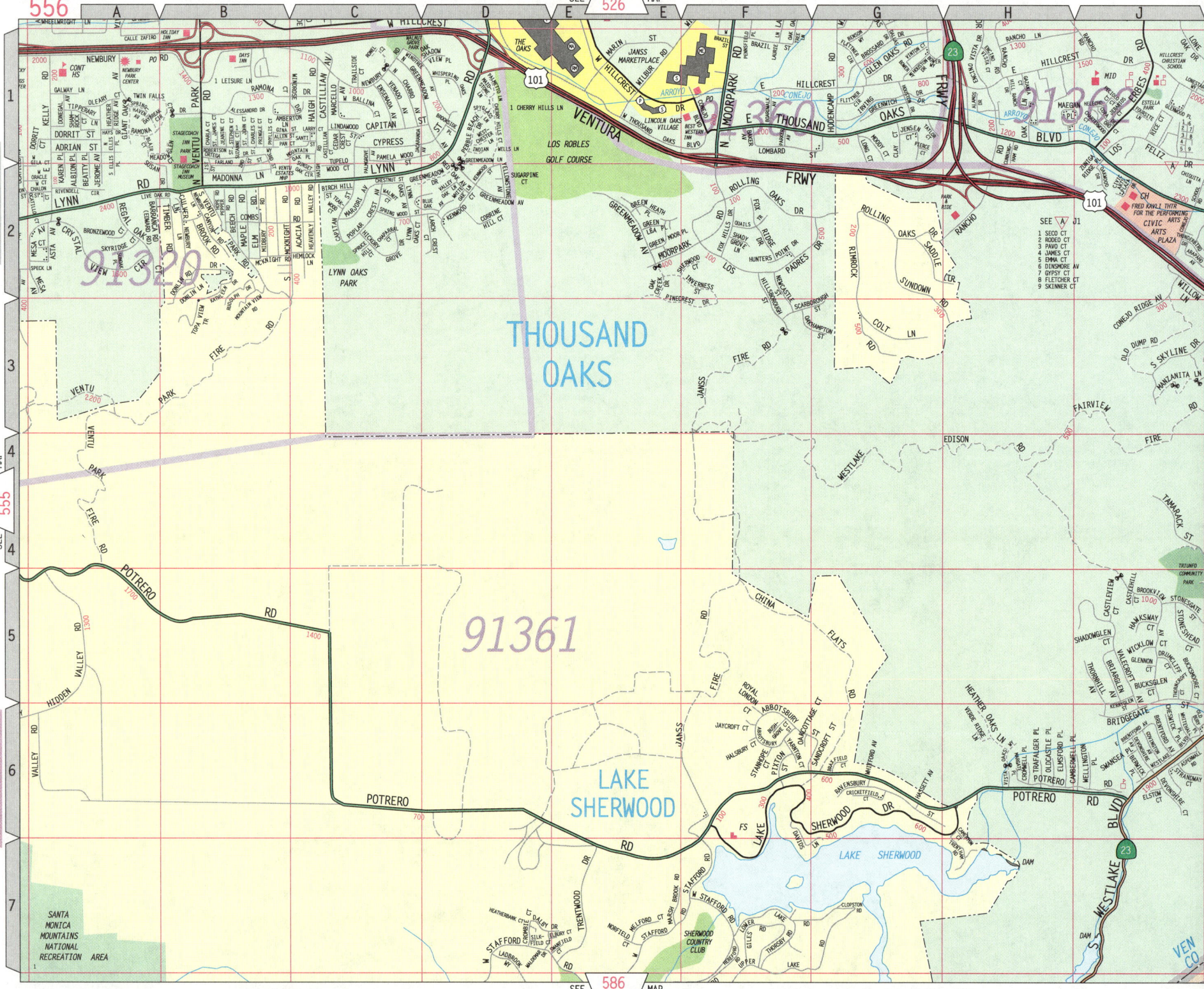

THOUSAND OAKS

LAKE SHERWOOD

SANTA MONICA MOUNTAINS NATIONAL RECREATION AREA

NEWBURY PARK

LOS ROBLES GOLF COURSE

VENTURA FRWY

LYNN OAKS PARK

LYNN RD

POTRERO RD

HIDDEN VALLEY RD

CHINA FLATS

ROLLING OAKS

CONEJO

HILLCREST

THOUSAND OAKS BLVD

FRED KAVLI THTR FOR THE PERFORMING ARTS CIVIC ARTS PLAZA

SEE A 01
1 SECO CT
2 RODEO CT
3 PAVO CT
4 JAMES CT
5 EMMA CT
6 DINSMORE AV
7 GYPSY CT
8 FLETCHER CT
9 SKINNER CT

POTRERO RD

LAKE SHERWOOD

SHERWOOD COUNTRY CLUB

WESTLAKE BLVD

VEN CO

101

23

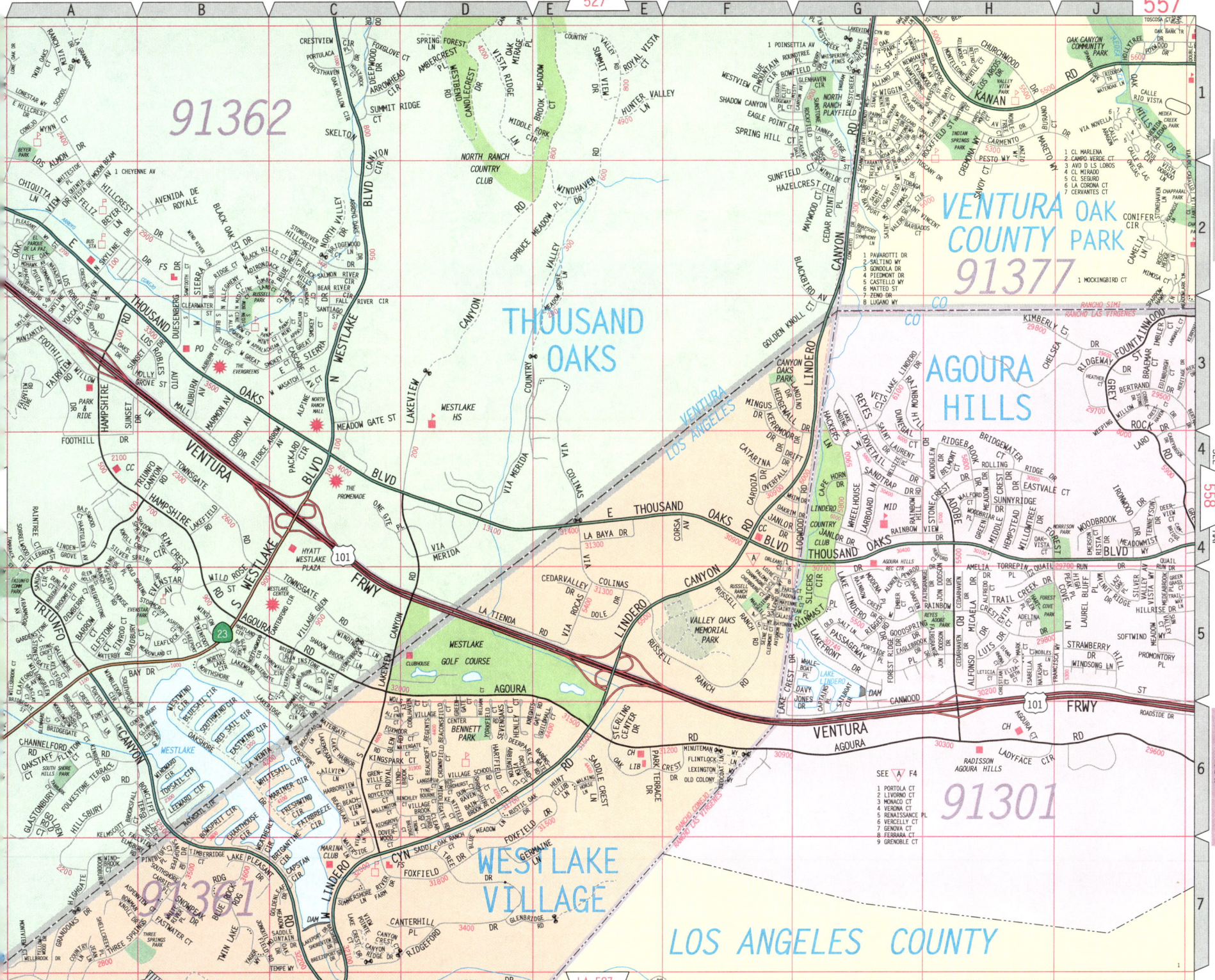

A B C D E E F G H J

91362

THOUSAND OAKS

VENTURA COUNTY

OAK PARK

91377

AGOURA HILLS

91301

WESTLAKE VILLAGE

91361

LOS ANGELES COUNTY

VENTURA CO.

NORTH RANCH COUNTRY CLUB

OAK CANYON COMMUNITY PARK

KANAN RD

VENTURA BLVD

THOUSAND OAKS BLVD

E THOUSAND OAKS BLVD

VENTURA FRWY

101 FRWY

VENTURA LOS ANGELES CO

WESTLAKE GOLF COURSE

WESTLAKE

RUSSELL RANCH

VALLEY OAKS MEMORIAL PARK

LINDERO CANYON RD

AGOURA RD

LAKEVIEW CANYON RD

SEE 558 MAP

SEE A F4

MAP

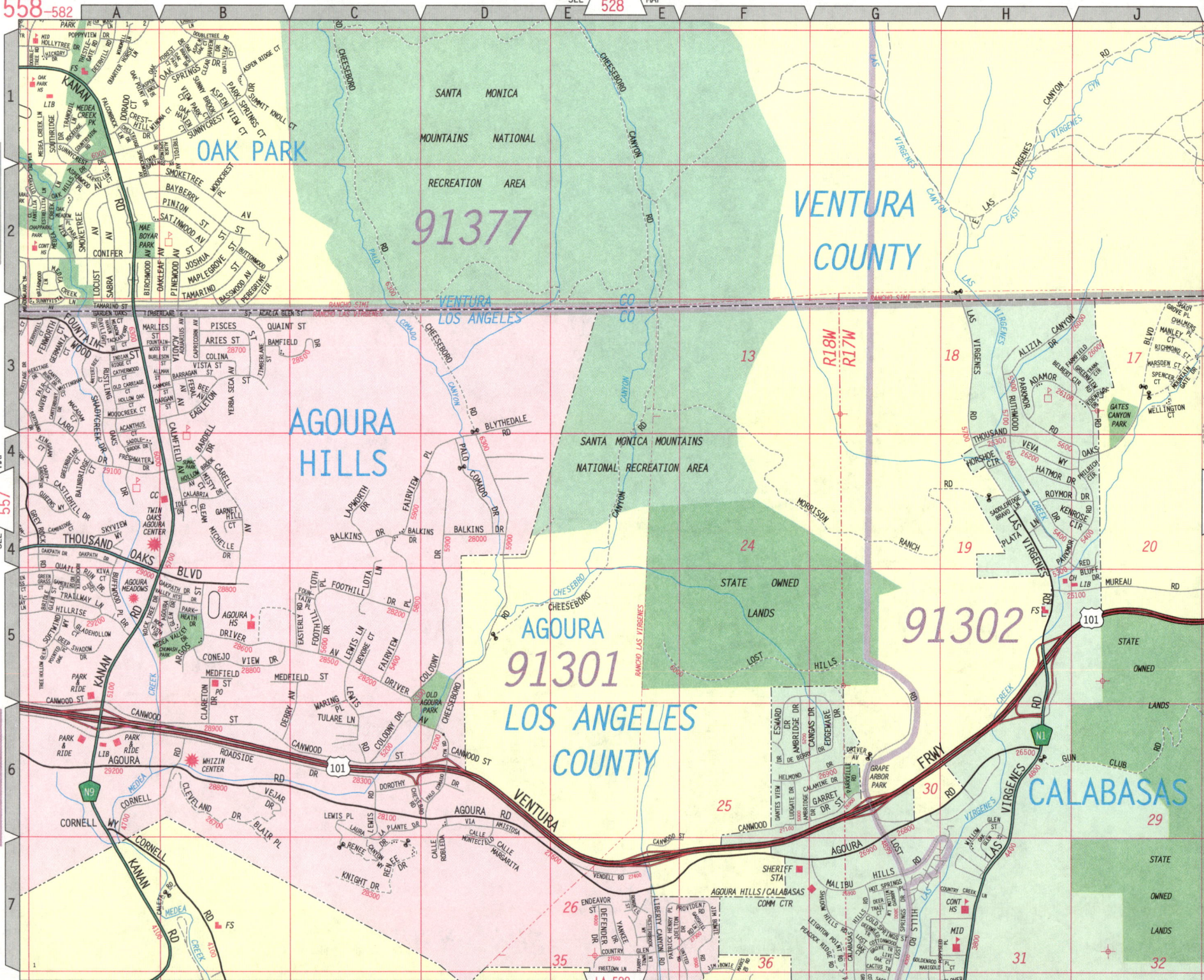

A B C D E E F G H J

OAK PARK

SANTA MONICA

MOUNTAINS NATIONAL

RECREATION AREA

91377

VENTURA COUNTY

VENTURA CO.

RANCHO SIMI
VENTURA
LOS ANGELES

CO
CO

13

R18W R17W

18

17

AGOURA
HILLS

SANTA MONICA MOUNTAINS
NATIONAL RECREATION AREA

24

19

20

THOUSAND
OAKS

STATE OWNED

LANDS

91302

STATE
OWNED

AGOURA

91301

LOS ANGELES
COUNTY

LOST HILLS

LANDS

CALABASAS

101

MAP 557   SEE

MAP

N9

CORNELL

N1

29

VENTURA

25

30

FRWY

AGOURA

MALIBU HILLS

STATE

OWNED

LANDS

31

32

26

35

36

SEE LA 588 MAP

A B C D E E F G H J

OXNARD

93033

POINT MUGU GAME RESERVE

SEE 584 MAP

VENTURA CO.

93012

POINT MUGU
GOLF CLUB

93041

VENTURA COUNTY GAME RESERVE

NAVAL AIR
WARFARE CENTER
WEAPONS DIVISION

BASE
DISPENSARY

93042

POINT MUGU
NAVAL AIR
WEAPONS
STATION

MUGU
LAGOON

PACIFIC

OCEAN

CALIFORNIA EXIT GATE 8

VENTURA CO FAIR GRND

SEE 386 MAP

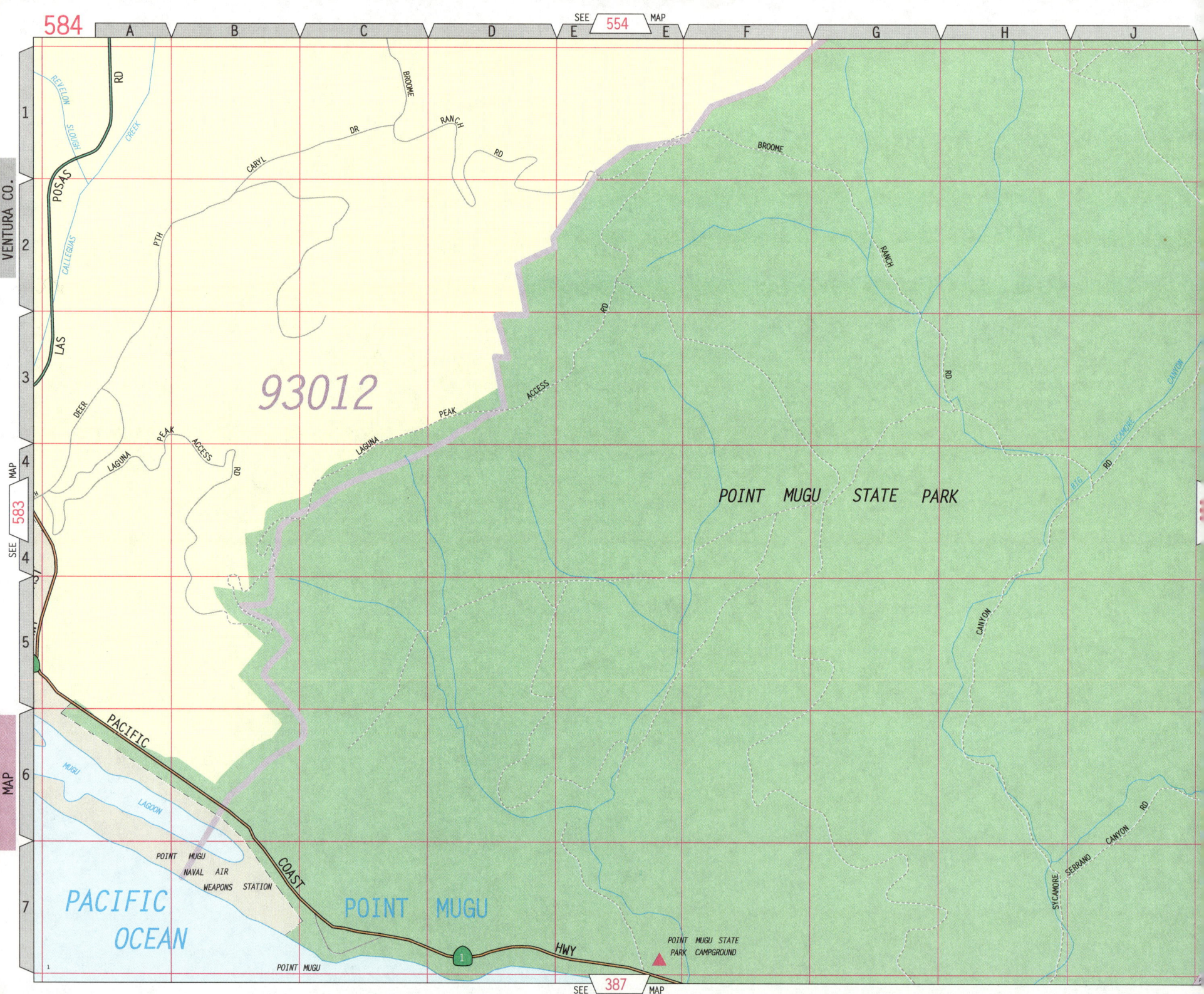

SEE 554 MAP

A B C D E E F G H J

1

2

3

4

4

5

6

7

VENTURA CO.

SEE 583 MAP

MAP

REVELON SLOUGH

CALLEGUAS CREEK

POSAS RD

LAS

PTH

DEER

LAGUNA PEAK ACCESS RD

CARYL

DR

BROOME

RANCH RD

RD

93012

ACCESS

LAGUNA PEAK ACCESS

BROOME

RANCH

RD

RD

SYCAMORE CANYON

BIG RD

POINT MUGU STATE PARK

CANYON

PACIFIC

MUGU LAGOON

POINT MUGU NAVAL AIR WEAPONS STATION

COAST

PACIFIC OCEAN

POINT MUGU

POINT MUGU

1

HWY

POINT MUGU STATE PARK CAMPGROUND

SYCAMORE CANYON RD

SERRANO

SEE 387 MAP

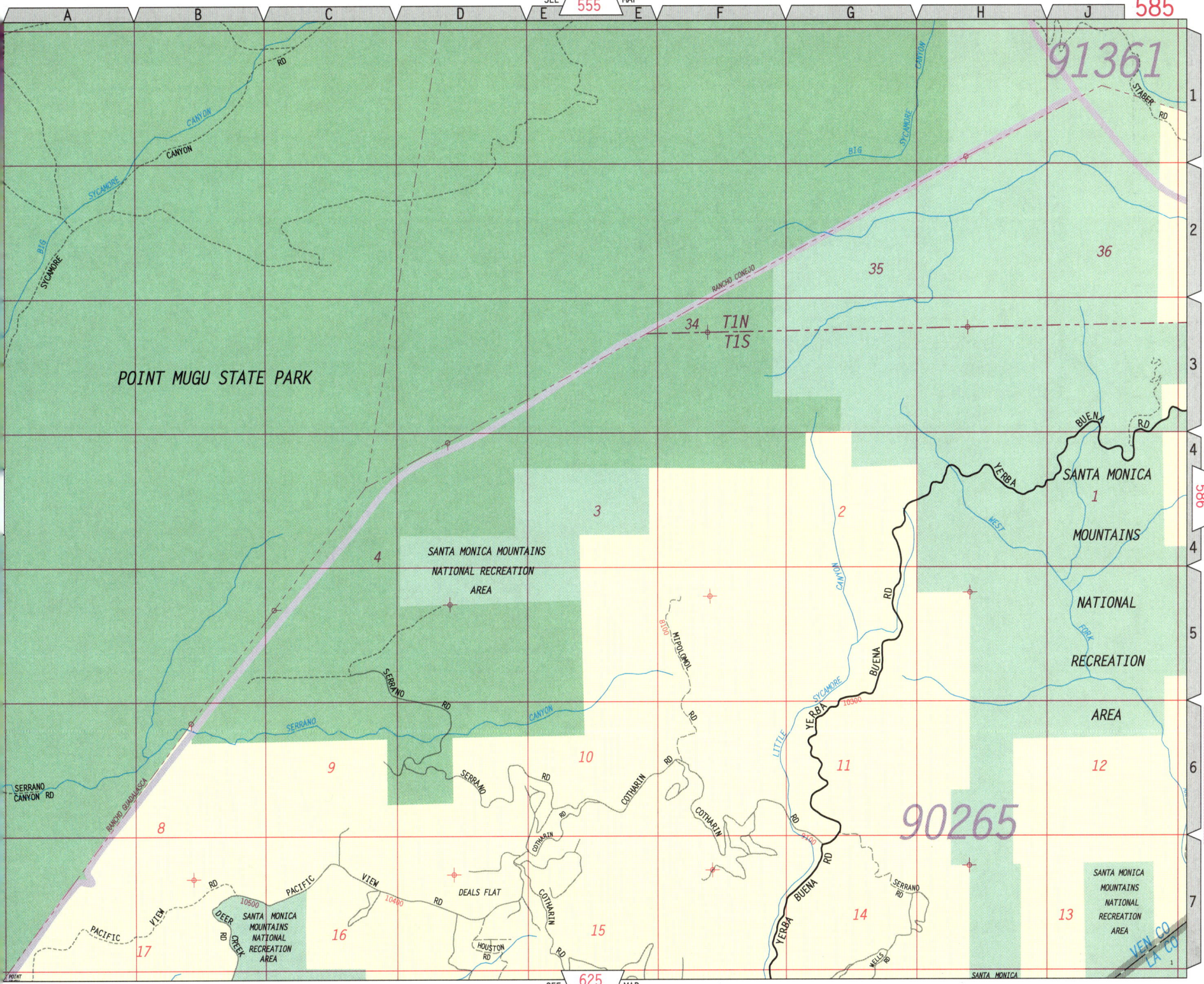

91361

SEE 555 MAP

A B C D E E F G H J

VENTURA CO.

1

2

35 36

34 T1N
T1S

3

POINT MUGU STATE PARK

SEE 586 MAP

4

SANTA MONICA
3
2
1
MOUNTAINS

SANTA MONICA MOUNTAINS
NATIONAL RECREATION
AREA

NATIONAL

4

5

RECREATION

SERRANO RD

AREA

MAP

SERRANO CANYON

CANYON

MIPOLOMOL RD

YERBA BUENA RD

LITTLE SYCAMORE CANYON

YERBA WEST FORK

10500

9 10 11 12

SERRANO
CANYON RD

8

90265

RANCHO GUADALASCA

COTHARIN RD

COTHARIN RD

SERRANO RD

SANTA MONICA
MOUNTAINS
NATIONAL
RECREATION
AREA

PACIFIC VIEW RD

VIEW

DEALS FLAT

10490

COTHARIN RD

YERBA BUENA RD

WELLS RD

13

7

DEER CREEK RD

SANTA MONICA
MOUNTAINS
NATIONAL
RECREATION
AREA

10500

16 15 14

17

PACIFIC

HOUSTON RD

POINT

SANTA MONICA

VEN CO
LA CO

SEE 625 MAP

SYCAMORE CANYON

BIG SYCAMORE CANYON

RANCHO CONEJO

STABER RD

BIG SYCAMORE CANYON

BUENA RD

YERBA

10560

SEE 556 MAP

A B C D E E F G H J

VENTURA CO.

SEE 585 MAP

MAP

1

2

3

4

5

6

7

SANTA MONICA MOUNTAINS NATIONAL RECREATION AREA

91361

STABER RD

SANTA MONICA MOUNTAINS NATIONAL RECREATION AREA

31

36

2500 DUCHY WY
MORVALE DR FARTING FORD RD

VENTURA COUNTY

CARLISLE

32 RD

CARLISLE

T1N
T1S

CARLISLE RD

600

CARLISLE

300

33

RANCHO CONEJO

SANTA MONICA MOUNTAINS NATIONAL RECREATION AREA

YERBA

VEDDER

1

5

36

R20W R19W

6

BUENA

RD

LITTLE
100

SANTA
MONICA

MTWY

4

(TRIUNFO
ETZ

LOS ANGELES

COUNTY

90265

3

2

BODLE PEAK MTWY

MULHOLLAND HWY
32400

SANTA MONICA MOUNTAINS

NATIONAL RECREATION

AREA

7

12

SYCAMORE

8

RIDGE

Mountains

MELOY FIRE

NATIONAL

9
RECREATION

AREA

MTWY

HWY
38100

10

33000
32800

ZUMA

CANYON

11

CANYON

500

RD

900

MULHOLLAND

34100

IBOLD RD

TRANCAS
LAKES

MALIBU COUNTRY CLUB

TRANCAS LAKES DR

MULHOLLAND

CLARKE RANCH RD

13

WEST

SEQUIT

FORK

ARROYO

18

34300

EAST

FORK

BARDMAN AV

34200

17

MASON RD

SANTA MONICA MOUNTAINS NATIONAL RECREATION AREA

HASSTED DR

900

SEQUIT

1300

33600

HWY

33400

DAVIS RD

16

DECKER RD
1500

23

MULHOLLAND
33200

33300

SANTA MONICA MOUNTAINS
NATIONAL RECREATION AREA

ENCINAL
1300

STATE OWNED LANDS

CLUB HOUSE

CANYON

TRANCAS CANYON RD

15

1700

STATE OWNED LANDS

14 700

EDISON

QUINO AV

MULHOLLAND
34500

SANTA MONICA MOUNTAINS NATIONAL RECREATION AREA

BATTLESNAKE RD COUNTY FIRE DEPT CAMP 13

SANTA MONICA MOUNTAINS NATIONAL RECREATION AREA

SEE LA 626 MAP

MNTNS WY
STAFFORD RD
2400
GREENBANK RD

LADBROOK WY

LADBROOK WY

W STAFFORD

W STAFFORD

ELDEROAK LN
ELDEROAK DR

2600

CLUBHOUSE

W STAFFORD RD

SHERWOOD COUNTRY CLUB

QUEENS RD
HEREFORD RD
UPPER LAKE RD

QUEENS GARDEN DR
QUEENS GARDEN CT

STAFFORD

2500 RD

LAKE SHERWOOD

LAKE

100

800

RD

THOUSAND OAKS

COUNTRY RANCH RD
1600

1300

RANCHGROVE DR
2500

LEE DR

DENVER SPRINGS DR

1600

KIRSTEN

WESTLAKE VILLAGE

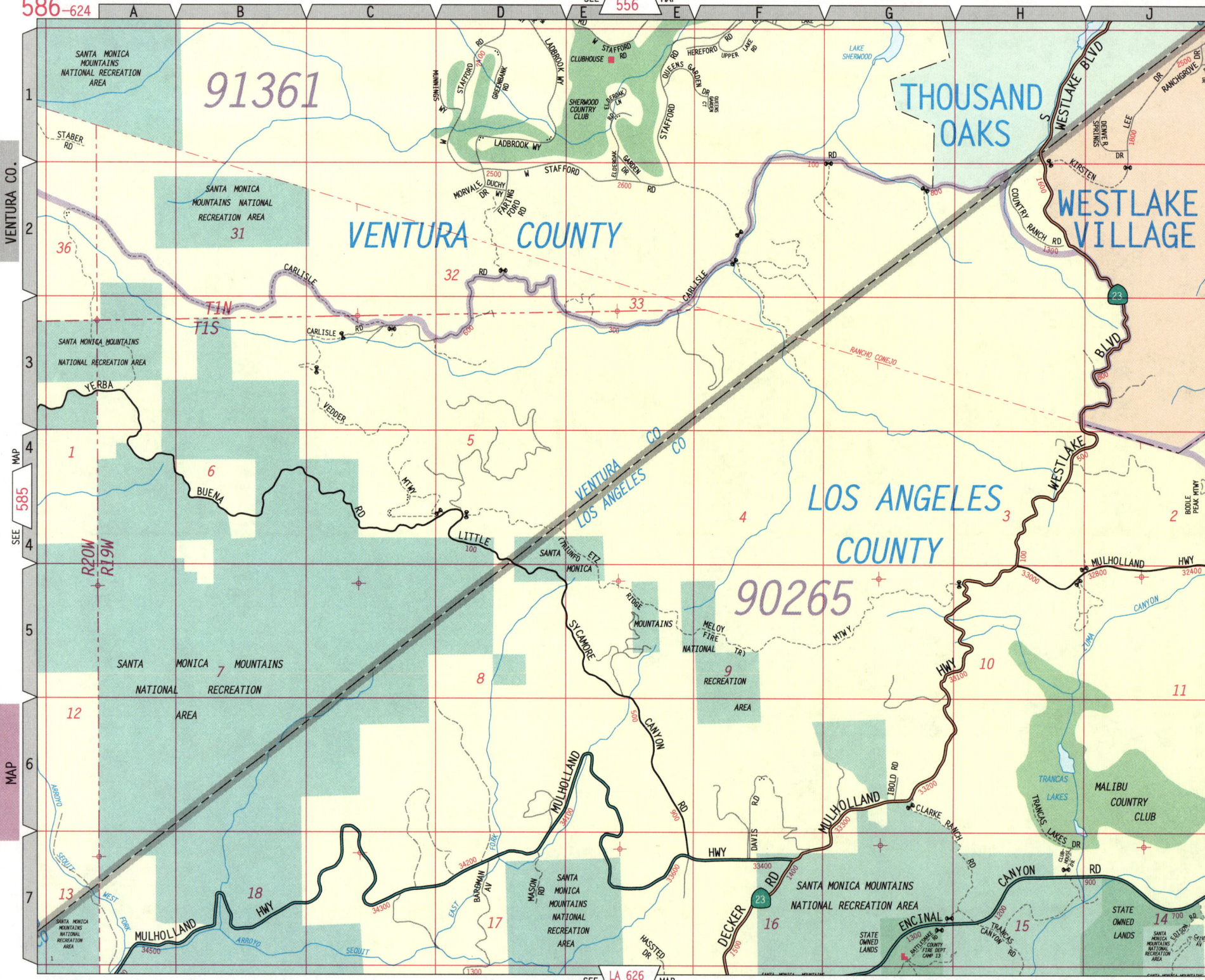

23

BLVD

WESTLAKE

WESTLAKE BLVD

500

100

33000

SEE 585 MAP

POINT
MUGU
STATE
PARK

PACIFIC

SANTA MONICA
MOUNTAINS
NATIONAL
RECREATION
AREA

PACIFIC VIEW RD

SANTA MONICA
MOUNTAINS
NATIONAL
RECREATION
AREA

SANTA MONICA
MOUNTAINS NATIONAL
RECREATION AREA

SANTA MONICA
MOUNTAINS NATIONAL
RECREATION AREA

CAMP
BLOOMFIELD

SANTA MONICA
MTNS NATL
REC AREA

17

16

15

14

13

90265

VENTURA
COUNTY

VENTURA CO.

VENTURA CO.
LOS ANGELES CO.

20

21

22

23

24

LEO

LOS ANGELES
COUNTY

DEER

CREEK

RD

HOUSTON

COTHARIN RD

RD

SYCAMORE CANYON

YERBA

BUENA

RD

HASLER RD

CHUMASH TR

DRY GULCH TR

HASLER RD

DRY GULCH RANCH

WELLS RD

11500

MOTOR HWY

YELLOW HILL

SANTA
MONICA

MOUNTAINS

NATIONAL

RECREATION

AREA

RD

YELLOW

RANCHO TOPANGA MALIBU SEQUIT

MULHOLLAND HWY

SEQUIT

CARRILLO

STATE

DEER

CREEK

RD

12200

PACIFIC

COAST

HWY

28

YERBA

BUENA

RD

13200

CAMP
HESS
KRAMER

CAMP
JOAN
MIER

27

FS

ELLICE

COUNTY
LINE
BEACH

12000

14200

SOUTH COAST

26

1 STARFISH LN
2 CORAL REEF LN
3 EBBTIDE LN
4 OCEANAIRE LN
5 WHALERS LN
6 WHITEWATER LN

TONGA REVA

TONGA ST

REEF WY

S BEACH CLUB WY

LEO

CARRILLO

STATE

BEACH

PACIFIC

COAST

HWY

36500

36000

35800

35600

35500

35900

HILL

MULHOLLAND

RD

CAMPGROUND

BEACH

YELLOW CREEK

NICHOLAS
CANYON
COUNTY
BEACH

PACIFIC

OCEAN

SEQUIT
POINT

1

SEE 387 MAP

SEE LA 626 MAP

LIST OF ABBREVIATIONS

PREFIXES AND SUFFIXES

AL . . . . .ALLEY
ARC .ARCADE
AV, AVE . . . . .AVENUE
AVCT . . . . AVENUE COURT
AVD . . . . .AVENIDA
AVDR . . . . .AVENUE DRIVE
AVEX . . . . AVENUE EXTENSION
BLEX . . . . BOULEVARD EXTENSION
BL, BLVD . . . . BOULEVARD
BLCT . . . . BOULEVARD COURT
BRCH . . . . .BRANCH
BRDG . . . . .BRIDGE
BYPS . . . . .BYPASS
CIDR . . . . CIRCLE DRIVE
CIR . . . . .CIRCLE
CL . . . . .CALLE
CLJ . . . . .CALLEJON
CM . . . . CAMINO
CMTO . . . . CAMINITO
COM . . . . .COMMON
CORR. . . . . CORRIDOR
CRES . . . . .CRESCENT
CRLO . . . . CIRCULO
CRSG . . . . CROSSING
CSWY . . . . .CAUSEWAY
CT . . . . COURT
CTAV . . . . .COURT AVENUE
CTE . . . . CORTE
CTO . . . . .CUTOFF
CTR . . . . .CENTER
CUR . . . . CURVE
CV .COVE
D . . . . DE
DIAG . . . . .DIAGONAL
DR. . . . . .DRIVE
DVDR . . . . .DIVISION DRIVE
EXAV . . . . .EXTENSION AVENUE
EXBL . . . . . .EXTENSION BOULEVARD
EXRD . . . . .EXTENSION ROAD
EXST . . . . .EXTENSION STREET
EXT . . . . .EXTENSION
EXWY . . . . .EXPRESSWAY
FRWY . . . . .FREEWAY
GDNS . . . . .GARDENS
GN . . . . .GLEN

GRN .GREEN
HWY . . . . .HIGHWAY
JCT . . . . .JUNCTION
LN. LANE
LNDG . . . . .LANDING
LP .LOOP
LS . . . . .LAS, LOS
MNR . . . . .MANOR
MTWY . . . . MOTORWAY
OH . . . . .OUTER HIGHWAY
OVL . . . . .OVAL
OVPS . . . . .OVERPASS
PAS . . . . .PASEO
PK . . . . .PARK
PKWY . . . . .PARKWAY
PL . . . . .PLACE
PLZ, PZ . . . . .PLAZA
PT . . . . .POINT
PTH . . . . .PATH
RD . . . . .ROAD
RDEX . . . . ROAD EXTENSION
RDG. . . . . .RIDGE
RW . . . . .ROW
SKWY . . . . SKYWAY
SQ . . . . .SQUARE
ST . . . . .STREET
STAV . . . . .STREET AVENUE
STCT . . . . .STREET COURT
STDR . . . . .STREET DRIVE
STEX . . . . .STREET EXTENSION
STLN . . . . .STREET LANE
STLP . . . . STREET LOOP
STPL . . . . STREET PLACE
STXP . . . . . STREET EXPRESSWAY
TER . . . . TERRACE
TFWY . . . . .TRAFFICWAY
THWY . . . . .THROUGHWAY
TKTR . . . . .TRUCKTRAIL
TPKE . . . . .TURNPIKE
TR . . . . .TRAIL
TUN . . . . .TUNNEL
UNPS . . . . .UNDERPASS
VIS . . . . .VISTA
VW . . . . .VIEW
WK . . . . .WALK
WY . . . . .WAY
WYPL . . . . .WAY PLACE

DIRECTIONS

E . . . . .EAST
KPN . . . . .KEY PENINSULA NORTH
KPS . . . . .KEY PENINSULA SOUTH
N .NORTH
NE . . . . NORTHEAST
NW . . . . .NORTHWEST
S .SOUTH
SE . . . . .SOUTHEAST
SW . . . . .SOUTHWEST
W .WEST

DEPARTMENT STORES

BD . . . . BLOOMINGDALES
BN . . . . THE BON MARCHE
D . . . . .DIAMONDS
DL . . . . .DILLARDS
E . . . . EMPORIUM
G . . . . .GOLDWATERS
GT . . . . .GOTTSCHALKS
H .HARRIS
IM . . . . .IMAGNIN
L . . . . LAMONTS
MA . . . . MACY'S
ME . . . . MERVYN'S
MF . . . . MEIER & FRANK
MW . . . . .MONTGOMERY WARD
N . . . . .NORDSTROM
NM . . . . .NEIMAN-MARCUS
P . . . . .J C PENNEY
RM . . . . ROBINSONS MAY
S . . . . SEARS
SF . . . . .SAKS FIFTH AVENUE

BUILDINGS

CC . . . . .CHAMBER OF COMMERCE
CH . . . . .CITY HALL
CHP . . . .CALIFORNIA HIGHWAY PATROL
COMM CTR . . . .COMMUNITY CENTER
CON CTR . . . . . .CONVENTION CENTER
CONT HS . . . .CONTINUATION HIGH SCHOOL
CTH . . . . COURT HOUSE
DMV . . . . . . .DEPT OF MOTOR VEHICLES
FAA . . . FEDERAL AVIATION ADMIN

FS . . . . .FIRE STATION
HOSP . . . . .HOSPITAL
HS . . . . .HIGH SCHOOL
INT . . . . INTERMEDIATE SCHOOL
JR HS . . . . .JUNIOR HIGH SCHOOL
LIB . . . . .LIBRARY
MID . . . . .MIDDLE SCHOOL
MUS . . . . MUSEUM
PO . . . . .POST OFFICE
PS . . . . POLICE STATION
SR CIT CTR . . . . . SENIOR CITIZENS CENTER
STA . . . . STATION
THTR . . . . .THEATER
VIS BUR . . . . VISITORS BUREAU

OTHER ABBREVIATIONS

BCH . . . . .BEACH
BLDG . . . . .BUILDING
CEM . . . . CEMETERY
CK . . . . .CREEK
CO . . . . .COUNTY
CTR . . . . .CENTER
COMM . . . . .COMMUNITY
EST . . . . .ESTATE
HIST . . . . .HISTORIC
HTS . . . . .HEIGHTS
LK .LAKE
MDW . . . . .MEADOW
MED . . . . .MEDICAL
MEM . . . . .MEMORIAL
MHP . . . . .MOBILE HOME PARK
MT . . . . MOUNT
MTN . . . . .MOUNTAIN
NATL . . . . .NATIONAL
PKG . . . . .PARKING
PLGD . . . . .PLAYGROUND
RCH . . . . .RANCH
RCHO . . . . .RANCHO
REC . . . . .RECREATION
RES . . . . .RESERVOIR
RIV . . . . .RIVER
RR . . . . .RAILROAD
SPG . . . . .SPRING
STA . . . . SANTA
VLG . . . . .VILLAGE
VLY . . . . .VALLEY
VW . . . . .VIEW

STREET
Block City ZIP Pg-Grid

A

A AV
- VeCo 93042 583-H3
A CT
3600 OXN 93033 552-G3
A ST
100 OXN 93030 522-G5
400 FILM 93015 456-A6
800 FILM 93015 455-J4
2900 OXN 93033 552-G3
A ST Rt#-23
- FILM 93015 456-A6
- FILM 93015 466-A1
E A ST
100 PHME 93041 552-E5
N A ST
100 OXN 93030 522-G5
W A ST
100 PHME 93041 552-E5
ABALONE CV
2600 PHME 93041 552-C2
ABALONE DR
2600 OXN 93035 552-A2
ABBEY CT
3600 THO 91320 555-F4
ABBEYWOOD CT
2400 SIMI 93063 498-D1
ABBEYWOOD DR
23900 CanP 91307 529-D5
ABBINGTON CT
4200 WLKV 91361 557-D6
ABBOTSBURY ST
23600 VeCo 91361 556-F6
ABBOTT AV
1700 CMRL 93010 524-G1
1700 CMRL 93010 494-G7
ABBOTT ST
2000 OXN 93033 553-A5
ABERDARE ST
8500 VEN 93004 492-G3
ABILENE ST
4700 SIMI 93063 478-H5
10100 VEN 93004 492-H2
ABLE CIR
1200 SIMI 93065 498-A4
ABRAHAM ST
2000 SIMI 93065 498-A3
ABRAZO DR
100 CMRL 93012 525-A3
ABUL HAJ RD
- VeCo 93060 453-D2
ACACIA
1000 VeCo 93023 451-C3
ACACIA RD
100 VeCo 91320 556-C2
300 SPLA 93060 463-J7
400 SPLA 93060 473-J1
ACACIA ST
2500 OXN 93033 552-H2
2700 CMRL 93012 524-F4
ACACIA WY
23600 SPLA 93060 473-J1
ACACIA GLEN ST
28600 AGRH 91301 558-B3
ACADEMY DR
- THO 91320 525-H6
ACADIA AV
6100 AGRH 91301 558-B3
ACADIA PL
1100 VEN 93003 492-B4
ACADIA ST
1300 SIMI 93063 498-D3
ACALA ST
3500 CMRL 93010 524-G1
ACANTHUS CT
29000 AGRH 91301 558-A3
ACAPULCO AV
1200 SIMI 93065 497-F4
ACAPULCO CT
- SIMI 93065 497-F3
1100 OXN 93035 522-E7
ACORN CT
3800 SIMI 93063 498-E2
ACORN RD
- PHME 93043 552-C5
ACORN ST
22100 Chat 91311 499-J6
ACTON CT
1800 SIMI 93065 498-A1
ADAK ST
1100 PHME 93041 552-E4
ADAM RD
4000 SIMI 93063 478-F7
ADAMOR RD
26000 CALB 91302 558-H3
ADAMS ST
7300 VEN 93003 492-E1
ADAMS CANYON RD
1400 VeCo 93060 463-F3
1800 VeCo 93060 453-E7
ADDAX CIR
1600 VEN 93003 492-F4
ADDISON CIR
300 THO 91360 526-F4
ADDOR ST
- PHME 93041 552-E5
900 PHME 93043 552-E3
ADELAIDE CT
1700 OXN 93035 552-C1
ADELE PL
1400 THO 91360 526-D5
ADELINA CT
5500 AGRH 91301 557-H5
ADIRONDACK AV
600 VEN 93003 472-B7
600 VEN 93003 492-B1
ADIRONDACK CT
2100 SIMI 93065 497-C6
E ADIRONDACK CT
3300 THO 91362 557-C2
W ADIRONDACK CT
3000 THO 91362 557-B2
ADLENA PL
13500 MRPK 93021 496-F2
ADMIRAL CT
1300 VeCo 91377 527-H7
ADOBE WY
800 CMRL 93012 525-C2
ADOHR LN
4500 CMRL 93012 524-H5
5100 CMRL 93012 525-A5
ADOLFO RD
3400 CMRL 93010 524-G1
3900 CMRL 93012 524-H2
5200 CMRL 93012 525-A3
ADONIS PL
4600 MRPK 93021 496-F2
ADRIAN ST
1700 THO 91320 556-A1
1900 THO 91320 555-J1
AFFIRMED PL
6300 MRPK 93021 476-A6
AGATE CT
2100 SIMI 93065 497-G2
7900 VEN 93004 492-F3
AGATE ST
3500 THO 91360 526-H1
8000 VEN 93004 492-F3
AGGEN RD
4000 VeCo 93066 494-F3
5100 VeCo 93066 474-E7
AGNEW ST
1100 SIMI 93065 497-H2
AGNUS DR
200 VEN 93003 491-H2
AGOURA CT
29900 AGRH 91301 557-H6
AGOURA RD
2600 THO 91361 557-B5
2900 WLKV 91361 557-D5
26400 CALB 91302 558-G7
26600 LACo 91302 558-G7
26800 CALB 91301 558-G7
27000 Ago 91301 558-D6
27400 AGRH 91301 558-A6
29200 AGRH 91301 557-G6
AGOURA GLEN DR
5500 AGRH 91301 558-B5
AGUSTA AV
1000 CMRL 93010 524-D1
AHART ST
1200 SIMI 93065 497-H2
AILEEN ST
500 CMRL 93010 524-B2
AIREDALE AV
2000 VEN 93003 492-F5
AIREDALE CT
7300 VEN 93003 492-F5
AIRPORT WY
100 CMRL 93010 524-A5
AKERS ST
700 FILM 93015 456-A5
AKRON AV
700 VEN 93004 492-J1
AL WY
6000 SIMI 93063 499-B2
ALAMAR ST
- THO 91360 526-F2
ALAMEDA AV
1800 VEN 93003 492-D5
2000 VeCo 93003 492-D5
ALAMO ST
1700 SIMI 93065 497-J1
1700 SIMI 93065 498-A1
1900 SIMI 93065 478-A7
3300 SIMI 93063 478-C7
5400 SIMI 93063 479-A7
ALAMOS DR
1100 THO 91362 556-H1
ALAMOS CANYON RD
23600 SIMI 93065 477-D7
23600 VeCo 93065 477-D7
ALAN CT
23600 SIMI 93063 498-H1
ALANDIA CT
4200 MRPK 93021 496-E3
ALASKA DR
5700 VEN 93003 492-C5
ALBACORE WY
200 OXN 93035 552-B4
ALBANY AV
700 VEN 93004 492-H2
ALBANY DR
2800 OXN 93033 552-H2
ALBATROSS ST
6400 VEN 93003 492-D4
ALBERTSON MTWY
- VeCo 93065 527-G4
23600 SIMI 93065 527-G4
23600 SIMI 93065 528-C2
23600 THO 91362 527-G4
23600 VeCo 93063 528-E2
23600 VeCo 93065 528-C2
ALBION AV
5700 VEN 93003 492-C1
ALBION PL
- THO 91320 556-A2
ALBORADA DR
23600 CMRL 93010 494-C7
ALCOVE ST
500 SIMI 93065 527-D1
E ALDEN ST
2300 SIMI 93065 498-B1
N ALDEN ST
2400 SIMI 93065 498-C1
ALDERBROOK ST
11700 MRPK 93021 496-C4
ALDERCREEK PL
1300 THO 91362 527-C6
ALDERDALE CT
23600 THO 91320 555-E4
ALDERGLEN ST
12300 MRPK 93021 496-D3
ALDERGROVE ST
12100 MRPK 93021 496-D4
ALDER SPRINGS DR
300 VeCo 91377 558-B1
ALDER VIEW LN
23600 CMRL 93012 525-A1
ALDER WOOD PL
1500 THO 91362 526-J2
ALDREN CT
5500 AGRH 91301 557-G5
ALDRICH CT
300 THO 91360 526-F4
A LEASE CANYON RD
23600 VeCo 93001 470-D3
ALELIA AV
1200 VeCo 93004 493-B1
ALEPPO CT
1700 THO 91362 526-J4
ALESSANDRO DR
1200 THO 91320 556-B1
1500 VEN 93001 491-D3
ALEXANDER DR
4700 OXN 93033 553-A5
ALEXANDER ST
1100 SIMI 93065 497-H2
1700 OXN 93033 553-A2
ALEXANDRA CT
23600 VeCo 91377 528-A7
ALEXANDRIA ST
10200 VEN 93004 492-J2
ALFA RD
23600 VeCo 93063 498-H7
23600 VeCo 93063 528-H1
ALFONSO DR
5300 AGRH 91301 557-H5
ALFREDO CT
5500 AGRH 91301 557-H5
ALGONQUIAN ST
700 VEN 93001 471-D5
ALGONQUIN CT
2900 CMRL 93010 524-F1
ALGONQUIN DR
2100 SIMI 93065 497-D2
ALHAMBRA AV
- VEN 93004 492-F1
ALHAMBRA CT
- VeCo 93012 496-E7
ALIANO DR
4800 VeCo 91377 557-G1
ALICANTE CT
- VeCo 93012 496-E7
ALICE DR
3000 THO 91320 555-G1
3000 VeCo 91320 555-G1
ALICE ANN RD
2400 THO 91320 555-J2
2400 VeCo 91320 555-J2
ALIENTO WY
600 CMRL 93012 524-J2
ALISO LN
100 VEN 93001 491-E2
ALISO PL
300 OXN 93030 522-H3
1300 VEN 93001 491-D1
ALISO ST
100 OJAI 93023 441-H6
200 VEN 93001 491-D1
400 VEN 93001 471-D7
N ALISO ST
100 VEN 93001 491-E1
W ALISO ST
100 OJAI 93023 441-H6
ALISO CANYON RD
2900 VeCo 93060 462-H3
6200 VeCo 93060 472-J1
6700 VeCo 93060 473-A2
23600 VeCo 93060 452-G7
ALISON DR
12400 VeCo 93012 496-D7
ALIZIA CANYON DR
26000 CALB 91302 558-H3
26000 VeCo 91302 558-H3
N ALLEGHENY CT
200 THO 91362 557-B3
S ALLEGHENY CT
100 THO 91362 557-B3
ALLEGRO CT
200 SIMI 93065 527-D1
ALLEN ST
1100 THO 91320 556-B1
ALLENBY CT
32000 WLKV 91361 557-C6
ALLENVALE CT
500 SIMI 93065 497-D7
ALLMAN ST
28900 AGRH 91301 558-A3
ALLYSON CT
23600 THO 91362 527-B5
ALMADEN CT
2500 SIMI 93065 498-A1
ALMANOR DR
8600 VEN 93004 492-G4
ALMANOR ST
1800 OXN 93030 522-J3
ALMAR ST
6300 SIMI 93063 499-C2
ALMENDRA PL
800 OXN 93030 522-H3
ALMENDRO CT
1500 CMRL 93010 524-G1
ALMENDRO WY
3500 CMRL 93010 524-G1
ALMON DR
200 THO 91362 557-A2
ALMOND AV
10400 VeCo 93022 451-C6
ALMOND DR
3400 VeCo 93030 523-D2
ALMOND TREE CT
23600 SIMI 93063 498-D4
ALOE LN
23600 SIMI 93065 497-E5
ALOHA LN
1800 OXN 93033 552-J1
1800 OXN 93033 553-A1
ALOHA ST
2600 CMRL 93010 494-F7
2600 VeCo 93010 494-F7
ALOMAR ST
600 VeCo 93023 451-C3
ALOSTA DR
100 VeCo 93010 494-F6
ALOSTA LN
1300 CMRL 93010 494-G6
1300 VeCo 93010 494-G6
ALOSTA PL
300 VeCo 93010 494-G6
600 CMRL 93010 494-G6
ALOSTA WY
600 VeCo 93010 494-G6
ALPINE AV
100 VEN 93004 472-H6
ALPINE CT
400 VEN 93004 472-H6
2800 THO 91362 557-C3
ALPINE ST
100 OXN 93030 522-J5
4400 SIMI 93063 498-G2
ALSCOT AV
1800 SIMI 93063 499-B1
ALTA ST
4800 SIMI 93063 478-H7
ALTA WY
23200 Chat 91311 499-F6
ALTA COLINA RD
4900 CMRL 93012 524-J2
5100 CMRL 93012 525-A2
ALTADENA ST
8300 VEN 93004 492-F1
E ALTA GREEN ST
100 PHME 93041 552-E2
W ALTA GREEN ST
100 PHME 93041 552-D2
ALTAIR AV
2700 THO 91360 526-F3
ALTA MIRA ST
400 VeCo 93065 497-G5
14100 SIMI 93065 497-G5
ALTAMONT WY
- VeCo 93010 494-C6
ALTA SEGUNDA CT
23600 CMRL 93010 494-C7
ALTA VISTA PL
23600 CMRL 93012 524-H1
ALTA VISTA RD
600 VeCo 93063 499-B4
ALTA VISTA RIDGE RD
6300 VeCo 93063 499-C4
ALTHEA CT
1300 OXN 93030 522-E3
ALTO CT
300 VeCo 93022 451-C5
ALTO DR
- VeCo 93022 451-C5
ALTUNA CT
3300 THO 91360 526-H2
ALTURAS ST
1300 OXN 93035 552-D1
ALTUS WY
2700 OXN 93035 552-D1
ALUMNI WY
7300 MRPK 93021 477-A4
ALVA CIR
1500 SIMI 93065 498-B3
N ALVARADO AV
100 VeCo 93023 441-D6
S ALVARADO AV
100 VeCo 93023 441-D7
ALVARADO ST
2400 OXN 93030 522-J2
2400 VeCo 93030 522-J2
3000 VeCo 93030 523-A1
ALVERSTONE AV
600 VEN 93003 492-B1
600 VEN 93003 472-B7
ALVIRIA DR
1100 VeCo 93023 451-B1
ALVISO DR
1200 VeCo 93010 494-A7
ALVISO ST
1500 SIMI 93065 497-J2
1700 SIMI 93065 498-A2
ALYSHEBA DR
10600 MRPK 93021 476-A7
ALYSSAS CT
23600 MRPK 93021 476-J6
AMADOR AV
300 VEN 93004 472-H6
400 VeCo 93004 472-H6
AMADOR LN
1500 THO 91320 526-A7
AMAGRO WY
100 OXN 93033 552-G5
AMALFI DR
1300 SIMI 93063 499-C3
AMALFI WY
5000 OXN 93035 551-J1
5000 OXN 93035 552-A1
AMAPOLA AV
1200 VeCo 93004 493-B1
AMARELLE ST
1000 THO 91320 526-A6
AMARILLO AV
3000 SIMI 93063 478-G7
AMARYLLIS AV
23600 SIMI 93065 497-G5
AMBER AV
1100 OXN 93030 522-D4
AMBER DR
1000 SPLA 93060 464-A2
2600 CMRL 93010 494-E7
2700 VeCo 93010 494-E7
AMBER LN
800 OJAI 93023 451-G1
800 VeCo 93023 451-G1
AMBERCREST PL
4000 THO 91362 557-D1
AMBER GROVE CT
2300 SIMI 93065 478-B7
AMBERLEAF LN
23600 SIMI 93065 497-A1
AMBERLY PL
2300 SIMI 93065 498-B1
AMBERMEADOW ST
12500 MRPK 93021 496-D3
AMBERRIDGE CT
11500 MRPK 93021 496-B4
AMBERTON LN
1100 THO 91320 556-B1
AMBERWICK LN
4300 MRPK 93021 496-F3
AMBER WOOD PL
2600 THO 91362 526-J3
AMBRIDGE DR
5000 CALB 91301 558-F6
AMBROSE AV
1400 OXN 93035 552-D1
AMELIA CT
100 OXN 93030 522-J5
AMELIA DR
30100 AGRH 91301 557-H5
AMERICAN ST
400 SIMI 93065 477-G7
AMERICAN WY
1800 VEN 93004 492-G4
AMERICAN OAKS AV
100 THO 91320 555-H3
AMERITE WY
2800 SIMI 93065 477-G7
AMETHYST AV
1400 OXN 93030 522-D4
AMGEN CT
600 THO 91320 526-A7
AMGEN CENTER DR
2000 THO 91320 525-J7
2000 THO 91320 526-A7
AMHERST ST
5500 VEN 93003 492-B2
14300 MRPK 93021 476-G6
N AMHERST ST
6400 MRPK 93021 476-H6
AMIGO RD
100 Chat 91311 499-F6
AMOND LN
8300 LA 91304 529-F2
AMONDO CIR
5900 SIMI 93063 499-A1
AMPHITHEATER RD
23600 VeCo 93001 470-E4
AMY PL
2600 PHME 93041 552-D2
ANACAPA AV
100 VeCo 93035 552-B5
ANACAPA CIR
400 THO 91320 555-F1
ANACAPA DR
100 CMRL 93010 524-E1
100 VeCo 93010 494-D6
100 VeCo 93010 524-E1
100 CMRL 93010 494-D6
ANACAPA ST
- VEN 93001 491-E3
ANACAPA TER
400 SPLA 93060 463-J6
400 VeCo 93060 463-J6
ANASAZI CT
23600 SIMI 93063 479-A6
ANASTASIA AV
6200 SIMI 93063 499-B2
ANCHOR AV
2500 PHME 93041 552-B2
2700 PHME 93035 552-B2
ANCHOR CT
2200 THO 91320 525-J6
2200 THO 91320 526-A6
ANCHORAGE AV
2900 SIMI 93063 478-F7
ANCHORAGE ST
3700 OXN 93033 552-J4
ANCHORS WY
1200 VEN 93001 491-F6
ANDALUSIA DR
- VeCo 93012 496-F6
ANDANTE CT
800 CMRL 93012 525-B2
ANDERSON DR
3100 VeCo 93065 478-B7
3100 SIMI 93065 478-B7
ANDERSON ST
1400 SIMI 93065 497-J2
ANDORA AV
9600 Chat 91311 499-J4
ANDORA PL
9800 Chat 91311 499-H5
ANDREA CIR
1500 SIMI 93065 498-B3
ANDREA CT
700 OXN 93033 552-H5
ANDREA DR
400 OXN 93033 552-H5
ANDREW DR
400 OJAI 93023 441-J5
ANDRUS ST
- VeCo 93022 451-B6
ANGEL CIR
2700 SIMI 93063 478-J7
ANGELA AV
7200 CanP 91307 529-F5
ANGELA ST
2400 SIMI 93065 498-B1
4000 SIMI 93063 498-F1
ANGLER CT
23600 VEN 93001 491-G7
ANGUILA PL
100 CMRL 93012 524-J3
ANGUS AV
1800 SIMI 93063 498-G2
ANITA AV
200 OXN 93030 522-H5
1100 OJAI 93023 441-G6
ANLAUF RD
- VeCo 93060 453-J4
ANLAUF CANYON
- VeCo - 454-A2
- VeCo 93060 453-J4
- VeCo 93060 454-A2
ANN AV
100 PHME 93041 552-F6
N ANN ST
- VEN 93001 491-D2
S ANN ST
- VEN 93001 491-D2
ANNA WY
1400 OXN 93030 522-E3
ANNANDALE LN
2600 SIMI 93063 478-J7
ANNAPOLIS CT
5300 VEN 93003 492-B3
ANN ARBOR AV
700 VEN 93004 492-H2
ANNE CT
200 THO 91320 555-G2
ANNEPE WY
22400 Chat 91311 479-J7
E ANNETTE ST
13000 MRPK 93021 496-E3
ANSON ST
600 SIMI 93065 497-G4
ANTELOPE AV
1100 VEN 93003 492-E4
ANTELOPE PL
1100 THO 91320 555-G4
ANTHONY DR
2000 VEN 93003 492-E5
ANTIGUA PL
6400 CanP 91307 529-C7
ANTIGUA WY
2300 OXN 93035 552-A2
E ANTIOCH ST
3400 SIMI 93063 498-E2
ANTLER AV
2300 VEN 93003 492-F5
ANTONIO AV
2100 CMRL 93010 494-G6
2400 VeCo 93010 494-G6
ANZA CT
1300 OXN 93035 552-E1
ANZA PL
200 FILM 93015 456-C6
ANZIO WY
600 VeCo 91377 557-H1
APACHE AV
- THO 91362 557-A2
2800 VEN 93001 471-C5
APACHE CIR
3000 THO 91360 526-C2
APACHE CT
1400 CMRL 93010 524-F1
APACHE CANYON RD
- VeCo - 366-G1
- VeCo 93252 366-G1
APERSON RD
- VeCo 93015 367-B7
- VeCo 93015 455-F1
APOLLO CT
2000 SIMI 93065 497-G2
APOLLO DR
500 OXN 93035 521-J6
E APPALACHIAN CT
2800 THO 91362 557-C3
W APPALACHIAN CT
2700 THO 91362 557-B3
N APPALOOSA LN
- VeCo 91307 529-B3
APPIAN WY
300 VEN 93003 491-J2
3400 CMRL 93010 494-G7
APPLE AV
200 VEN 93004 473-A6
APPLE LN
2300 OXN 93030 522-G1
APPLEFIELD ST
1500 THO 91320 526-A6
APPLEGATE TER
9200 Chat 91311 499-F7
APPLEGLEN CT
4400 MRPK 93021 496-D2
APPLETON RD
400 SIMI 93065 498-C4
APPLETREE AV
200 CMRL 93012 524-H4
APPLETREE CT
400 CMRL 93012 524-H5
APPLEWOOD LN
2000 VeCo 93012 496-B7
2000 VeCo 93012 526-B1
APRICOT LN
1400 OXN 93033 553-B5
23600 VeCo 93063 499-B4
APRICOT RD
4000 SIMI 93063 498-F1
APRICOT ST
- VeCo 93022 451-B7
APRIL LN
1000 SPLA 93060 464-A2
1000 VeCo 93060 464-A2
AQUARIUS AV
6300 AGRH 91301 558-B3
AQUA VERDE CT
4700 CMRL 93012 524-J2
AQUEDUCT CT
600 SIMI 93065 497-G6
ARABIAN PL
6000 CMRL 93012 525-B1
ARABIAN ST
1400 SIMI 93065 497-J3
ARANMOOR AV
900 THO 91361 557-A5
ARAPAHO AV
2300 THO 91362 556-J2
2300 THO 91362 557-A2
ARAPAHO ST
200 VEN 93001 471-C5
ARBELLA LN
- THO 91362 527-B3
ARBOL LN
6400 VeCo 93063 499-C4
ARBOLITA RANCH RD
2100 VeCo 93066 465-A6
ARBOR AV
600 VEN 93003 491-H4
ARBORHILL ST
12100 MRPK 93021 496-D4
ARBOR LANE CT
200 THO 91360 526-D7
ARCADE DR
- VEN 93003 491-F3
ARCADIA ST
1700 OXN 93033 552-H1
ARCADIAN SHORES TR
2400 OXN 93030 522-C2
ARCANE ST
1100 SIMI 93065 497-H4
1700 SIMI 93065 498-A4
ARCATA RD
1100 VeCo 93023 451-B4
ARCH ST
4500 VeCo 93066 494-H4
ARCHBRIAR WY
300 SIMI 93065 497-F3
ARCHWOOD LN
2300 SIMI 93063 498-J1
ARCHWOOD ST
22100 CanP 91303 529-J6
22600 CanP 91307 529-D6
ARCO OIL CO RD
- VeCo 93023 453-B2
- VeCo 93060 453-B2
ARCTURUS AV
5500 OXN 93033 552-H6
ARCTURUS ST
100 THO 91360 526-F3
ARDENWOOD AV
1800 SIMI 93063 499-D2
E ARDENWOOD AV
6500 SIMI 93063 499-C2
N ARDENWOOD CIR
6600 SIMI 93063 499-D2
AREA I RD
23600 VeCo 93063 499-A7
23600 VeCo 93063 529-A1
ARENAS CT
3000 SIMI 93063 478-F7
ARGAL PL
2200 VEN 93003 492-E5
ARGOS ST
5300 AGRH 91301 558-B5
ARIANNA LN
2600 THO 91362 527-C3
ARIELLE LN
23600 SIMI 93065 498-A5
ARIES ST
28700 AGRH 91301 558-B3
ARISTOTLE ST
100 SIMI 93065 497-F2
ARIZONA DR
1900 VEN 93003 492-C5
ARLENE AV
1700 OXN 93030 522-E3
ARLENE CT
2600 SIMI 93065 498-C3
ARLETTA LN
2200 VeCo 93012 496-B7
N ARLINGTON AV
3000 SIMI 93063 478-G6
ARMADA DR
3100 VEN 93003 491-G4
ARMINTA ST
22900 LA 91304 529-E3
ARMITOS DR
5900 CMRL 93012 495-B6
ARMSTRONG AV
- VEN 93003 491-J3
ARMSTRONG RD
3700 VeCo 93066 465-B6
N ARNAZ AV
100 VeCo 93023 441-D6
S ARNAZ AV
100 VeCo 93023 441-D6
ARNAZ DR
- VeCo 93022 451-B6
ARNAZ RD
- VeCo 93001 460-J5
ARNEILL RD
- CMRL 93010 524-E3
1500 CMRL 93010 494-E7
ARNESS FIRE RD
23600 VeCo 93063 498-E7
23600 VeCo 93063 528-E1
23600 VeCo 93064 498-E7
ARNETT AV
300 VEN 93003 492-B1
ARNOLD RD
6000 OXN 93033 583-A2
6000 OXN 93033 553-A7
6000 VeCo 93033 583-A2
6000 VeCo 93033 553-A7
6600 OXN 93033 386-K3
6600 OXN 93042 386-K3
ARROWHEAD AV
1200 VEN 93004 492-J2
ARROWHEAD CIR
100 OXN 93030 553-C3
3900 THO 91362 557-C1
ARROWHEAD LN
2200 OXN 93033 553-B5
ARROWOOD LN
5300 VeCo 91377 527-G7
ARROYO DEL MAR
200 CMRL 93010 524-B2
ARROYO OAKS DR
500 THO 91362 557-C2
ARROYO SECO DR
1700 VEN 93004 492-J4
ARROYO VIEW ST
1000 THO 91320 526-A6
ARROYO VISTA RD
4000 SIMI 93063 498-F3
ARROYO WILLOW LN
4100 CALB 91301 558-G7
ARTEMISIA AV
200 VEN 93001 491-E1
ARTHUR AV
100 SPLA 93060 464-A6
ARTHUR RONDO
7200 VEN 93003 492-E2
ARTISAN RD
400 THO 91320 526-A7
ARUNDELL AV
500 VEN 93003 491-H5
ARUNDELL CIR
300 FILM 93015 456-A4
3400 VEN 93003 491-H5
ARUNDELL RD
700 VeCo 93015 456-C3
ARVADA CT
800 SIMI 93065 527-C1
ASCOLI CT
23600 MRPK 93021 496-C5
ASCOT PL
2100 CMRL 93010 524-E2
ASH CIR
500 FILM 93015 455-J4
ASH CT
3000 THO 91360 526-H2
ASH LN
- VeCo 93023 441-E6
ASH ST
- VeCo 93063 499-B4
100 OXN 93033 552-G1
N ASH ST
- VEN 93001 491-C2
S ASH ST
- VEN 93001 491-C2
ASHBOURNE LN
3900 MRPK 93021 496-F4
ASHBROOK LN
13500 MRPK 93021 496-F4
ASHBURY CT
1000 CMRL 93010 524-E2
ASHBY CT
100 VeCo 93022 461-B1
ASHDALE CT
400 CMRL 93010 523-J1
ASHFORD CT
900 THO 91361 557-B5
ASHFORD ST
800 SIMI 93065 498-B5
ASHLAND AV
700 SIMI 93065 497-G3
ASHLAND ST
10000 VEN 93004 492-H2
ASHLEY DR
800 SIMI 93065 497-G4
ASHMORE CIR
2800 THO 91362 527-C3
ASHTON CT
7500 LA 91304 529-E4
23600 SIMI 93065 497-F7
23600 SIMI 93065 527-F1
ASHTON ST
200 OXN 93033 552-G5
N ASHTREE ST
4300 MRPK 93021 496-E3
ASH VIEW LN
5600 CMRL 93012 525-A2
N ASHWOOD AV
- VEN 93003 491-J2
S ASHWOOD AV
- VEN 93003 491-J3
ASHWOOD CT
500 THO 91320 555-G3
4000 VEN 93003 491-J2
5300 CMRL 93012 495-A7
5300 CMRL 93012 525-A1
ASIA CT
23600 SIMI 93065 498-A5
ASMAN AV
7100 CanP 91307 529-H5
ASPEN CIR
800 OXN 93030 522-D4
ASPEN CT
700 VEN 93004 492-G2
ASPEN GN
5100 OXN 93033 552-G6
ASPEN LN
4200 VeCo 93066 495-B3
ASPEN HILLS DR
6000 MRPK 93021 476-B7
ASPEN KNOLL DR
6100 VeCo 91377 558-A1
ASPEN OAK CT
700 VeCo 91377 558-B1
ASPENPARK CT
2100 THO 91362 527-A4
ASPEN RIDGE CT
500 VeCo 91377 558-B1
ASPEN TREE CT
4400 MRPK 93021 496-E3
ASPEN VIEW CT
500 VeCo 91377 558-B1
ASPENVIEW CT
32500 WLKV 91361 557-A7
ASPENWALL RD
1500 THO 91361 556-J6
ASPENWOOD PL
5900 VeCo 91377 558-A2
ASTA AV
200 THO 91320 556-A2
ASTA CT
2000 THO 91320 556-A2
ASTER ST
600 OXN 93030 522-F3
1200 VeCo 93063 499-B4
11000 VeCo 93004 493-A1
ASTORIA PL
1000 OXN 93030 522-E4
ASTORIAN DR
23600 SIMI 93065 498-A5
ATHELING WY
7100 CanP 91307 529-G5
ATHENS AV
2000 SIMI 93065 497-F2
ATHERTON AV
200 VEN 93004 492-F1
ATHERTON CT
2400 SIMI 93065 498-A1
ATHERTON LN
7400 LA 91304 529-D4
ATHERWOOD AV
2600 SIMI 93065 498-B1
2600 SIMI 93065 478-B7
ATLANTA LN
600 VEN 93004 492-H2
ATLANTIS CT
5400 MRPK 93021 496-C1
ATLAS AV
2700 THO 91360 526-F3
ATMORE DR
200 SPLA 93060 463-J6
N ATMORE RD
100 VeCo 93015 465-E1
S ATMORE RD
100 VeCo 93015 465-E1
ATRON AV
7600 LA 91304 529-F3
N ATWATER AV
2000 SIMI 93063 498-D2
ATWOOD CT
14000 MRPK 93021 496-G3
AUBER LN
800 VEN 93003 492-B7
AUBURN AV
- THO 91362 557-B3
N AUBURN CIR
6600 MRPK 93021 476-H6
AUBURN CT
- THO 91362 557-B3
N AUBURN CT
3000 SIMI 93063 478-F6
AUGUSTA CT
1900 OXN 93030 522-D3
AUGUSTINE WY
300 SIMI 93065 497-D6
AURELIA ST
5300 SIMI 93063 498-J3
5400 SIMI 93063 499-A3
AURORA CT
100 VEN 93003 492-B2
AURORA DR
4400 VEN 93003 492-B2
AURORA LN
- SIMI 93063 498-H1
AUSTIN AV
3000 SIMI 93063 478-G7
AUSTIN LN
800 VEN 93004 492-H2
AUTO CENTER DR
1100 SIMI 93065 497-H1
1500 OXN 93030 523-A2
23600 VeCo 93003 492-E7
AUTO MALL DR
3000 THO 91362 557-B3
AUTUMN PL
23600 SIMI 93065 497-D3
AUTUMNBREEZE PL
1800 SIMI 93065 497-E2
AUTUMNGLEN CT
4400 MRPK 93021 496-D3
AUTUMN LEAF DR
- THO 91360 526-F1
AUTUMN MEADOW CIR
4300 MRPK 93021 496-E3
AUTUMN RIDGE DR
2500 THO 91362 527-D3
AUTUMN TRAIL ST
23600 SIMI 93065 498-B5
AUTUMNWOOD ST
200 THO 91360 526-F2
AVALON PL
200 OXN 93033 552-H4
AVALON ST
10400 VEN 93004 492-J2
AVALON WY
700 OXN 93033 552-H4
AVEDON RD
4700 MRPK 93021 496-C2
AVENAL ST
2800 VeCo 93001 450-E3
AVENIDA ACASO
600 CMRL 93012 524-H1
AVENIDA AMARANTO
3100 THO 91362 527-A2
AVENIDA AMELGADO
4300 THO 91360 496-H7
AVENIDA CAMPANA
4400 THO 91360 496-J7
AVENIDA CLASSICA
23600 OXN 93030 523-B4
AVENIDA COLONIA
14300 MRPK 93021 476-G7
AVENIDA DE APRISA
1900 CMRL 93010 523-G1
AVENIDA DE AUTLAN
- CMRL 93010 493-H6
- CMRL 93010 523-H1
- VeCo 93010 523-H1

STREET / Block City ZIP Pg-Grid

AVENIDA DE LA CRUZADA
2000 VeCo 93023 442-B7
AVENIDA DE LA ENTRADA
100 VeCo 93023 442-B7
AVENIDA DE LA PLATA
400 THO 91320 526-A7
400 THO 91320 556-A1
AVENIDA DE LAS FLORES
- THO 91360 526-F4
1600 THO 91362 526-J4
2000 THO 91362 527-A4
W AVENIDA DE LAS FLORES
- THO 91360 526-D4
AVENIDA DE LAS PLANTAS
2200 THO 91360 526-H4
AVENIDA DE LA VEREDA
100 VeCo 93023 442-B7
AVENIDA DEL DIA
23600 OXN 93030 523-B5
AVENIDA DEL MANZANO
1300 CMRL 93010 524-B1
E AVENIDA DE LOS ARBOLES
- THO 91360 526-E3
1700 THO 91362 526-H3
1800 THO 91362 527-B3
W AVENIDA DE LOS ARBOLES
- THO 91360 526-C3
AVENIDA DE LOS LOBOS
700 VeCo 91377 557-J2
AVENIDA DEL PLATINO
400 THO 91320 526-B7
400 THO 91320 556-B1
AVENIDA DEL RECREO
100 VeCo 93023 442-B7
AVENIDA DE MARGARITA
1300 CMRL 93010 523-F2
AVENIDA DE ROYALE
200 THO 91362 557-B2
AVENIDA ENCANTO
4900 CMRL 93012 525-A3
AVENIDA GAVIOTA
200 CMRL 93012 524-H3
AVENIDA LADERA
3200 THO 91362 527-A2
AVENIDA LOMA PORTAL
700 THO 91320 525-F7
AVENIDA MAGDALENA
600 CMRL 93010 524-B3
N AVENIDA MONTUOSO
3300 THO 91362 527-B2
E AVENIDA OTONO
2200 THO 91362 527-B2
AVENIDA PLACIDA
2000 SIMI 93063 499-B2
AVENIDA PRADO
4200 THO 91360 496-H7
N AVENIDA REFUGIO
2000 SIMI 93063 499-B2
AVENIDA SAN ANTERO
2200 CMRL 93010 494-H7
AVENIDA SIMI
2400 VeCo 93065 478-D7
2400 SIMI 93065 478-D7
2900 SIMI 93063 478-D7
2900 VeCo 93063 478-D7
AVENIDA SOLEDAD
700 VeCo 91377 557-J1
AVENIDA SOLTURA
1400 CMRL 93010 524-C1
1600 CMRL 93010 494-C7
AVENIDA VALENCIA
23600 CMRL 93012 524-H3
AVENIDA VERANO
3600 THO 91360 526-H1
N AVENIDA VISTA DEL MONTE
2000 SIMI 93063 499-B2
N AVIADOR ST
2000 CMRL 93010 523-H3
AVIANO DR
6600 CMRL 93012 495-C7
AVIARY RD
- VeCo 93060 453-J5
AVIATION DR
300 CMRL 93010 523-G4
600 VeCo 93010 523-G4
AVIGNON CT
5400 WLKV 91362 557-F5
AVILA DR
1100 VeCo 93023 451-B1
AVILA PL
2000 OXN 93030 522-G3
AVOCADO AV
3600 OXN 93033 553-B5
AVOCADO CT
3000 THO 91320 555-G3
AVOCADO PL
- CMRL 93010 524-A1
100 CMRL 93010 523-J1
100 VeCo 93010 493-J7
AVOCADO PL
100 VeCo 93010 523-J1
100 VeCo 93010 524-A1
400 VeCo 93010 494-A7
AVOCADO HILL RD
23600 VeCo 93013 366-G9
23600 VeCo 93013 459-B1
AVOCET DR
5900 VEN 93003 492-C5
AVON CIR
1000 THO 91360 526-F6
AVON ST
5300 VEN 93003 492-B2
AWENITA CT
11400 Chat 91311 499-H1
AYALA ST
2000 VEN 93001 491-E3
AYERS AV
800 OJAI 93023 441-J6
900 OJAI 93023 442-A5
AYERS CT
700 OJAI 93023 441-J5
700 OJAI 93023 442-A5
AYHENS ST
700 SIMI 93065 497-G3
AZAHAR ST
11000 VeCo 93004 493-A1
AZALEA CT
300 VeCo 93010 494-C7
300 VeCo 93010 524-C1
AZALEA ST
400 THO 91360 526-C3
800 OXN 93030 522-E3
AZTEC AV
2200 VEN 93001 471-D6
AZTEC CT
2500 VEN 93001 471-D5
3800 SIMI 93063 498-E2
AZUL CIR
8800 LA 91304 529-E1
AZUL DR
8700 WHil 91304 529-D1
8700 LA 91304 529-D1
AZURE CT
600 VeCo 93022 451-C6
AZURE HILLS DR
500 SIMI 93065 497-H5
AZURITE CIR
2500 THO 91320 525-H6
AZUSA AV
100 VEN 93004 492-E1

B

B AV
- VeCo 93042 583-H3
B ST
- FILM 93015 455-J5
100 OXN 93030 522-G5
1500 OXN 93033 552-G1
E B ST
100 PHME 93041 552-E5
N B ST
100 OXN 93030 522-G5
W B ST
100 PHME 93041 552-E5
BACCARAT ST
3200 THO 91362 526-J2
BACH RD
500 VEN 93003 492-B3
BADEN AV
9500 Chat 91311 499-H5
BADGER CIR
7200 VEN 93003 492-F4
BAHAMA ST
22000 LA 91304 529-J1
BAHIA CIR
- SPLA 93060 463-J7
BAHIA DR
2000 OXN 93030 522-G3
W BAILEY CT
3600 THO 91320 555-F4
BAINBRIDGE CT
- THO 91360 526-E1
5900 AGRH 91301 558-A4
BAINBROOK CT
31700 WLKV 91361 557-D6
BAJA CT
400 CMRL 93010 524-D3
BAJA VISTA WY
1700 CMRL 93010 494-C7
BAJO AGUA AV
100 CMRL 93010 523-H3
BAKER AV
- THO 91360 556-F1
200 VEN 93004 492-F2
BAKERSFIELD AV
6900 VeCo 93001 459-C4
BALBOA CIR
- CMRL 93012 525-A4
BALBOA ST
2400 OXN 93030 522-H2
2400 VeCo 93030 522-H2
2600 PHME 93041 552-E2
3200 VeCo 93004 492-J7
3300 VeCo 93030 493-A7
8000 VEN 93004 492-F2
BALCOM CANYON RD
1700 VeCo 93060 465-C6
4000 VeCo 93021 495-E1
BALCOM CANYON RD
4000 VeCo 93066 495-E1
5500 VeCo 93021 475-E6
5500 VeCo 93066 475-C1
8400 VeCo 93066 465-C6
BALD ST
100 OJAI 93023 441-J7
BALDEN LN
700 FILM 93015 455-J6
700 FILM 93015 456-A6
BALDWIN AV
200 VEN 93004 492-F2
BALDWIN RD Rt#-150
- VeCo 93001 450-H3
- VeCo 93023 450-H3
600 VeCo 93023 451-A3
BALEWIN DR
1800 VeCo 93015 455-F5
BALFE ST
700 VEN 93003 492-B3
BALI LN
1800 OXN 93033 552-J1
1800 OXN 93033 553-A1
BALKINS DR
28000 AGRH 91301 558-C4
BALLANTINE PL
7000 VeCo 91377 528-B6
BALLARD ST
1600 SIMI 93065 497-J2
W BALLINA CT
900 THO 91320 556-C1
BALLINGER ST
22000 Chat 91311 499-H6
BALMORAL CT
2400 CMRL 93010 524-E1
BALMORAL LN
23300 CanP 91307 529-F5
BALSAM ST
100 OXN 93030 522-J5
BALSAMO AV
1000 SIMI 93065 497-G4
BALTAR ST
22100 LA 91304 529-E3
BAMBI CT
15300 MRPK 93021 476-J6
BAMBOO CT
2100 THO 91362 526-J4
BAMFIELD DR
28500 AGRH 91301 558-B3
BANCOCK ST
2600 SIMI 93065 498-A1
2600 SIMI 93065 478-A7
BANCROFT ST
1800 CMRL 93010 524-D2
BANDERA DR
500 CMRL 93010 524-D2
BANG RD
- WHil 91304 499-C7
- WHil 91304 529-C1
BANGOR LN
1000 VEN 93001 491-E4
N BANK DR
8400 VEN 93004 492-H4
9500 VeCo 93004 492-J3
10300 VeCo 93004 493-A2
10300 VEN 93004 493-A2
BANNER AV
- VEN 93004 492-F2
BANNISTER WY
400 SIMI 93065 527-E1
BANTA CT
1300 OXN 93035 522-E7
1300 OXN 93035 552-E1
BARBADOS CT
4900 VeCo 91377 557-G2
BARBARA DR
1800 VeCo 93012 495-J7
BARBARA ST
- VeCo 93022 451-B4
BARBER LN
800 VEN 93003 492-A7
E BARCA ST
3400 CMRL 93010 524-G1
N BARCA ST
1400 CMRL 93010 524-G1
BARCELONA PL
3900 THO 91320 555-E1
BARCELONA ST
100 CMRL 93010 524-D4
BARCLAY CT
1900 THO 91361 557-A5
BARD LN
- PHME 93041 552-E4
- VeCo 93001 471-C2
BARD RD
400 PHME 93041 552-E4
700 OXN 93033 553-A4
1800 OXN 93033 552-E4
E BARD RD
- OXN 93033 552-G4
W BARD RD
- OXN 93033 552-G4
800 PHME 93033 552-G4
800 PHME 93041 552-G4
BARD ST
300 FILM 93015 456-A5
300 MRPK 93021 496-E1
600 MRPK 93021 476-E7
BARDELL DR
28900 AGRH 91301 558-B4
BARDET PL
1900 SIMI 93065 498-A1
BARDMAN AV
1300 LACo 90265 586-D7
BARDSDALE AV
100 VeCo 93035 552-B5
800 VeCo 93015 465-F3
BARLETTA PL
23600 MRPK 93021 496-C3
BARLOW CANYON RD
600 VEN 93003 491-H1
BARNACLE CV
2600 PHME 93041 552-C1
BARNARD ST
4400 SIMI 93063 498-G1
5400 SIMI 93063 499-A1
BARNARD WY
1600 VEN 93001 491-E2
BARNARO RD
300 VeCo 93015 455-B7
BARNES DR
- VeCo 93001 471-C3
BARNES ST
1500 SIMI 93063 498-E3
E BARNES ST
2700 SIMI 93065 498-C3
3200 SIMI 93063 498-D3
BARNETT ST
2000 OXN 93033 553-A4
E BARNETT ST
- VEN 93001 471-C7
W BARNETT ST
- VEN 93001 471-B7
BARODA DR
- CMRL 93012 525-A3
BARONS WY
23600 VeCo 91377 528-A7
BARONSGATE RD
4200 WLKV 91361 557-E6
BARR DR
500 VEN 93003 491-J4
BARRACUDA WY
200 OXN 93035 552-A3
BARRAGAN ST
28800 AGRH 91301 558-B3
BARRANCA AV
- VEN 93003 492-E2
200 VeCo 93003 492-E2
BARRANCA DR
- Cstc 91384 458-H4
BARRANCA RD
200 THO 91320 556-A2
200 VeCo 91320 556-A2
11200 VeCo 93012 496-B6
BARRETT DR
32700 WLKV 91361 586-J1
BARRINGTON CT
500 THO 91320 555-H3
BARROW AV
4200 SIMI 93063 478-F7
BARROW CT
1000 THO 91361 557-A5
BARRY DR
- VEN 93001 471-C6
BARRY ST
2300 CMRL 93010 524-E3
BARRYMORE DR
5200 OXN 93033 552-G5
BARSTOW AV
7700 VEN 93004 492-F1
BART CIR
1000 THO 91360 526-F6
BARTON AV
800 CMRL 93010 524-B2
BASALT ST
300 OXN 93030 522-D4
BASCOM CT
2300 THO 91362 527-A7
BASELBRIER LN
23600 SIMI 93065 497-A1
BASOLO TEXICO RD
- VeCo 93015 466-C2
- VeCo 93021 466-C2
BASS CT
2600 OXN 93035 552-A2
BASSET LN
1600 VEN 93003 492-F4
BASSETT ST
2700 CanP 91307 529-F6
22000 CanP 91307 529-H6
BASSWOOD AV
- VeCo 91377 558-B3
BASSWOOD CT
1100 VEN 93004 492-J2
2100 THO 91361 557-A4
BATES CT
1700 THO 91362 526-J6
BATES RANCH RD
23600 VeCo 93013 366-G9
23600 VeCo 93013 459-A2
BATH CT
5000 VeCo 91377 557-H1
BATH LN
1000 VEN 93001 491-E4
BATTEN LN
500 OXN 93033 552-G5
BAXTER ST
3300 THO 91320 555-F2
E BAY BLVD
100 PHME 93041 552-E2
E BAY BLVD
300 OXN 93033 552-E2
300 PHME 93033 552-E2
BAY DR
2200 THO 91361 557-A5
BAYBERRY ST
6300 VeCo 91377 558-B2
BAYBRIDGE CT
2500 PHME 93041 552-C2
BAYHAM CIR
2800 THO 91362 527-B3
BAYHILL CT
2300 OXN 93030 522-D2
BAYLOR CIR
14400 MRPK 93021 476-G6
BAYLOR DR
- VEN 93003 491-J2
- VEN 93003 492-A3
E BAYMARE RD
- VeCo 91307 529-A4
BAYONNE CT
30800 WLKV 91362 557-F5
BAYPORT WY
300 VeCo 91377 557-G2
BAYS ST
5700 VEN 93003 492-C2
BAYSHORE AV
2400 VEN 93001 491-F5
BAYSHORE DR
32000 WLKV 91361 557-C7
BAYSIDE CT
2300 THO 91361 557-B6
BAYSIDE ST
3800 SIMI 93063 498-E1
BAYVIEW AV
300 VEN 93003 492-A1
BAYVIEW DR
1300 OXN 93035 522-B7
1400 OXN 93035 552-B1
BAYWATER PL
2600 THO 91362 527-B3
BAYWOOD AV
1100 CMRL 93010 524-C2
BAYWOOD CT
1100 CMRL 93010 524-C1
BAYWOOD LN
400 SIMI 93065 497-D5
BEACH RD
- VeCo 93042 583-B4
BEACH WY
5000 OXN 93035 551-J1
5000 OXN 93035 552-A1
S BEACH CLUB WY
11800 VeCo 90265 625-F5
BEACHCOMBER WY
5000 OXN 93035 521-J7
BEACHFRONT LN
32100 WLKV 91361 557-C6
BEACH HAVEN WY
600 PHME 93041 552-F6
BEACHLAKE LN
32100 WLKV 91361 557-C6
BEACHMEADOW LN
4100 WLKV 91361 557-C6
BEACHMONT ST
1200 VeCo 93001 491-F5
1200 VEN 93001 491-F5
BEACHNUT AV
700 SIMI 93065 498-D5
BEACHPORT DR
500 PHME 93041 552-F6
BEACHVIEW LN
32100 WLKV 91361 557-C6
BEACON AV
2600 VEN 93003 491-G4
BEACON PL
1100 OXN 93033 552-J1
BEACONSFIELD CT
4400 WLKV 91361 557-D6
BEAGLE CT
7200 VEN 93003 492-F4
BEALL ST
500 THO 91360 526-G7
BEAR CIR
2600 SIMI 93063 478-J7
BEARCLAW CT
900 THO 91320 555-G5
BEAR CREEK CT
3400 THO 91320 555-F2
BEAR CREEK DR
3200 THO 91320 555-F2
BEARDEN CT
1800 OXN 93035 552-C1
BEARDSLEY RD
5600 VeCo 93010 493-G7
5600 VeCo 93010 523-F1
6100 CMRL 93010 493-H6
BEAR RIVER CIR
3400 THO 91362 557-C2
BEAR VALLEY RD
13500 MRPK 93021 496-F3
BEATTY PL
- THO 91320 556-A2
BEAUCROFT CT
4200 WLKV 91361 557-D6
BEAUFORT DR
1800 OXN 93033 553-A2
BEAUMONT AV
4300 OXN 93033 553-A5
5000 VeCo 93033 553-A5
BEAUMONT ST
4600 SIMI 93063 478-G7
BEAVER AV
2700 SIMI 93065 498-C5
BEAVER ST
1800 VEN 93003 492-F4
BECKETT CT
2700 THO 91360 526-E3
BECKFORD ST
4900 VEN 93003 492-B1
BECKWITH RD
100 SPLA 93060 473-H1
400 SPLA 93060 463-G7
BECKY ST
3900 SIMI 93063 498-F2
BEDFORD CT
700 SPLA 93060 464-B4
1700 CMRL 93010 524-D1
BEDFORD DR
1000 CMRL 93010 524-D2
BEDFORD PL
100 THO 91360 526-F6
BEDFORD ST
1100 SPLA 93060 464-B4
BEDFORDHURST CT
31700 WLKV 91361 557-D6
BEE AV
6200 AGRH 91301 558-B3
BEE CANYON
10800 Chat 91311 499-J2
E BEECH CT
4900 SIMI 93063 478-H7
BEECH DR
1000 SPLA 93060 464-A2
BEECH RD
- THO 91320 556-B2
BEECHGROVE CT
12400 MRPK 93021 496-D4
BEECH VIEW CIR
1100 CMRL 93012 525-B2
BEECHWOOD ST
1000 CMRL 93010 524-C1
BEEDY AV
23600 VeCo 93030 492-J5
23600 VeCo 93030 493-A5
BEEDY ST
100 VeCo 93030 492-J5
100 VeCo 93030 493-A5
BEENE RD
2600 VEN 93003 492-E6
BEETHOVEN AV
900 VEN 93003 492-B4
BEGONIA PL
- VEN 93004 473-C7
BEL CIR
2700 SIMI 93063 478-J7
BELAIR CT E
1300 CMRL 93010 524-F1
BELAIR CT S
3100 CMRL 93010 524-F1
BELBERT CIR
5800 CALB 91302 558-H3
BELBROOK PL
2700 SIMI 93065 478-B7
2700 SIMI 93065 498-B1
BELBURN PL
2600 SIMI 93065 498-A1
BELCARO WY
500 VeCo 91377 557-G1
BELDEN AV
400 CMRL 93010 524-F3
BELEN PL
10500 VEN 93004 492-J1
BELFAST LN
1000 VEN 93001 491-E4
BELFORD CT
24000 LA 91304 529-D4
N BELGRAVE CT
2000 SIMI 93063 498-E2
BELHAM CT
4500 WLKV 91361 557-D6
N BELHAVEN AV
1800 SIMI 93063 499-C2
BELINDA ST
4000 SIMI 93063 498-F1
BELL PL
6200 VeCo 93003 492-D5
6200 VEN 93003 492-D5
BELL ST
5300 VeCo 93066 495-A5
6200 VeCo 93003 492-D5
6200 VEN 93003 492-D5
BELL WY
- VEN 93001 471-B7
BELLA DR
400 VeCo 91320 525-G7
400 VeCo 91320 555-G1
600 THO 91320 525-G7
BELLAGIO CT
1100 VeCo 91377 527-H7
BELLA VISTA DR
4400 MRPK 93021 496-F2
BELL CANYON RD
- CanP 91307 529-C4
- VeCo 91307 529-C4
E BELL CANYON RD
- VeCo 91307 528-H5
- VeCo 91307 529-A4
BELL CANYON FIRE RD
23600 VeCo 91302 528-G7
BELL CANYON FIRE RD
23600 VeCo 91307 528-G5
BELLEMEADE CT
- SIMI 93063 498-H1
BELLERIVE CT
2600 OXN 93030 522-D3
BELLEVUE AV
100 VeCo 93015 466-A3
BELLEVUE AV Rt#-23
700 VeCo 93015 465-J3
700 VeCo 93015 466-A3
BELLEZA ST
1000 CMRL 93012 525-C6
BELLINI LN
900 VEN 93003 492-A7
BELL RANCH RD
4500 VeCo 93010 494-H6
BELLSHIRE CT
4800 THO 91362 527-E6
N BELMAR CT
2000 SIMI 93063 498-E2
BELMONT AV
900 CMRL 93010 524-E2
BELMONT CT
27300 AGRH 91301 557-H4
BELSIZE PL
5800 AGRH 91301 557-G4
BELTRAMO RANCH RD
4600 MRPK 93021 496-C2
BELVEDERE CT
2500 SIMI 93065 498-A1
BEN CT
400 VeCo 91320 555-G1
BENCHLEY CT
30900 WLKV 91361 557-C6
BENDING BRANCH WY
23600 SIMI 93065 497-A1
BENDING OAK CT
11600 MRPK 93021 496-C4
BENECIA WY
100 OXN 93033 553-C3
BENEDICT CT
5300 VeCo 91377 527-H7
BENITO DR
2100 CMRL 93010 494-H7
BENNETT RD
4400 SIMI 93063 478-F2
4400 VeCo 93063 478-F2
4600 VeCo - 478-F1
23600 VeCo - 367-E9
BENNETT ST
500 SIMI 93065 497-G5
BENNINGTON CT
2000 THO 91360 526-C4
BENSON WY
600 THO 91360 526-G7
600 THO 91360 556-G1
BENTCREEK RD
4100 MRPK 93021 496-B3
BENTLEY PL
300 SIMI 93065 497-E2
BENTON WY
1300 OXN 93033 552-G1
BENT TWIG AV
300 CMRL 93012 524-H4
BENWOOD DR
15300 MRPK 93021 476-J6
15300 MRPK 93021 477-A6
BERAGAN ST
23600 MRPK 93021 477-A6
BEREA CIR
1400 THO 91362 526-J6
BERG LN
4600 VEN 93003 492-B7
BERGAMO CT
23600 MRPK 93021 496-C5
BERING ST
100 OXN 93033 552-G6
BERKELEY AV
- VEN 93004 492-F1
BERKELEY CIR
6400 MRPK 93021 476-H6
BERKSHIRE CT
4300 OXN 93033 553-A4
BERKSHIRE DR
1600 THO 91362 526-J5
1800 THO 91362 527-A5
BERKSHIRE PL
600 VEN 93003 492-H5
BERKSHIRE ST
1000 OXN 93033 552-J5
1700 OXN 93033 553-A4
BERLIOZ ST
4900 VEN 93003 492-B7
BERMUDA CT
4000 VEN 93003 491-J3
BERMUDA DUNES DR
2300 OXN 93030 522-D2
BERMUDA DUNES PL
2000 OXN 93030 522-D2
BERNADETTE ST
1600 OXN 93030 522-D3
BERNADINE AV
7200 CanP 91307 529-F5
7400 LA 91304 529-F5
N BERNADINE ST
3000 THO 91320 555-G2
BERNAL ST
6500 SIMI 93063 499-C2
BERNARDA CT
100 OXN 93030 522-J5
BERNICE DR
23600 WHil 91304 499-E6
BERNINI CT
600 VeCo 91377 557-G1
BERNOULLI CIR
100 OXN 93030 523-A5
BERNSTEIN LN
800 VEN 93003 492-A7
BERQUIST AV
6200 WdHl 91367 529-F7
6400 CanP 91307 529-F7
BERROS ST
3000 SIMI 93063 478-F7
BERRYBROOK CT
11900 MRPK 93021 496-C3
BERRYHILL CIR
1400 THO 91360 527-F6
BERTHA RD
2700 THO 91320 555-H2
BERTRAND DR
29400 AGRH 91301 557-J3
29400 AGRH 91301 558-A3
BERWICK PL
1500 THO 91361 556-J6
BERWICK RD
2700 CMRL 93010 494-F7
BERYL AV
1800 OXN 93030 522-D3
BERYLWOOD RD
2700 VeCo 93066 494-F1
BESANT RD
100 VeCo 93023 441-E7
100 VeCo 93023 451-D1
BESSEMER ST
4000 VEN 93003 491-J4
4000 VEN 93003 492-A4
BEST CIR
4700 SIMI 93063 478-H5
BETH PL
2700 SIMI 93065 478-B7
2700 SIMI 93065 498-B1
BETHANY CT
200 THO 91360 526-E5
BETHANY ST
300 THO 91360 526-D5
BETHEL AV
200 VEN 93003 491-J2
BETHEL CT
900 SIMI 93065 498-A5
4200 VEN 93003 491-J2
BETTINA CT
1300 CMRL 93010 524-C1
BEVERLY CIR
300 VeCo 93010 494-F6
BEVERLY DR
- CMRL 93010 494-F7
100 VeCo 93010 494-F6
W BEVERLY DR
400 OXN 93030 522-F5
BEVRA AV
1500 OXN 93030 522-E2
BEYER LN
200 THO 91362 557-A2
BIANCA CIR
3000 SIMI 93063 478-D6
BIDWELL ST
4400 SIMI 93063 498-G1
BIENVILLE WK
5200 OXN 93033 552-G5
BIG BEAR WY
100 OXN 93033 553-C3
BIG CANYON RD
23600 VeCo 93023 452-J3
23600 VeCo 93023 453-A1
BIG CLOUD CIR
3300 THO 91360 526-C2
N BIGELOW AV
2000 SIMI 93065 498-A2
BIGHORN CT
800 CMRL 93010 524-C2
BIG HORN ST
9800 VEN 93004 492-J3
BIG ROCK TR
8500 LA 91304 529-E1
8500 WHil 91304 529-E1
W BIG SKY CIR
900 THO 91360 526-B2
BIG SKY DR
2900 THO 91360 526-C2
BIG SPRINGS AV
3000 SIMI 93063 478-G6
BIGSTONE LN
9800 VEN 93004 492-H3
BILLIE CT
3200 SIMI 93063 478-D7
BILLINGS ST
1400 OXN 93033 552-J4
BINGS RD
2600 THO 91320 555-H2
2600 VeCo 91320 555-H2
BINNACLE ST
600 OXN 93035 522-D6
BIRCH ST
1200 SPLA 93060 464-B2
1500 OXN 93035 552-D1
3700 VEN 93003 491-J3
6000 VeCo 93063 499-B4
E BIRCH ST
100 OXN 93033 552-G1
W BIRCH ST
100 OXN 93033 552-F1
BIRCHCREEK PL
2900 THO 91360 526-E3
BIRCHCROFT ST
5200 SIMI 93063 498-J2
BIRCHDALE CT
2000 THO 91362 527-A4
BIRCHDALE DR
1800 THO 91362 527-A4
BIRCHFIELD ST
2200 SIMI 93065 498-B2
BIRCH GLEN AV
2200 SIMI 93063 498-J2
BIRCH HILL ST
800 THO 91320 556-C2
BIRCHPARK CIR
500 THO 91360 526-E7
BIRCHTON AV
6600 CanP 91307 529-F6
BIRCH VIEW LN
5600 CMRL 93012 525-A2
BIRCHWOOD AV
- VeCo 91377 558-A2
BIRDSONG AV
3300 THO 91360 526-G2
BISCAYNE CT
800 CMRL 93010 524-D2
BISCAYNE PALM PL
23600 SIMI 93065 498-D5
BISHOP LN
1600 SIMI 93063 498-F3
BISHOP ST
8200 VEN 93004 492-F1
BISMARK AV
600 VEN 93004 492-J1
BISMARK WY
800 OXN 93033 552-H3
BITNER PL
15300 MRPK 93021 476-J5
BITTERN CT
6900 VEN 93003 492-E4
BITTERNUT CIR
2600 SIMI 93065 498-D1
2700 SIMI 93065 478-C7
BIXBY RD
8400 VeCo 93066 465-C6
8400 VeCo 93066 475-D1
BIZET LN
4600 VEN 93003 492-A7
BLACK AV
3200 VeCo 93063 478-E6
BLACKBERRY CIR
2000 OXN 93030 522-G3
BLACKBERRY LN
4200 VeCo 93066 495-B3
BLACKBIRD AV
100 THO 91362 557-G2
BLACKBOURNE
23600 VeCo 91377 528-A7
BLACKBURN PL
- VEN 93004 472-J7
- VEN 93004 492-J1
BLACKBURN RD
7700 VEN 93004 492-F2
9200 VeCo 93004 492-H1
10600 VEN 93004 472-J7
BLACK CANYON RD
- VeCo 93063 499-B4
BLACKFOOT LN
200 VEN 93001 471-C5
BLACKHAWK DR
300 THO 91320 555-E2
BLACKHAWK ST
- Chat 91311 499-J4
E BLACK HILLS CT
3300 THO 91362 557-C2
W BLACK HILLS CT
3000 THO 91362 557-B2
BLACK MOUNTAIN FIRE RD
23600 VeCo 93023 451-J2
23600 VeCo 93023 452-A2
BLACK OAK ST
2800 THO 91362 557-B2
BLACKPOOL AV
800 VeCo 91377 557-H1
BLACKSMITH CT
13600 MRPK 93021 496-F3
BLACKSTOCK AV
1400 SIMI 93065 498-D3
BLACKWALL DR
1500 SIMI 93063 498-E3
BLACKWOOD ST
3700 THO 91320 555-E4
BLAINE AV
200 FILM 93015 456-A5
700 FILM 93015 455-J5
BLAIR CT
- THO 91320 556-A1
BLAIR PL
4800 AGRH 91301 558-B6
BLAIRWOOD DR
3900 MRPK 93021 496-E3
BLAKE CT
6800 VEN 93003 492-E3
BLANCA PL
800 OXN 93030 522-H3
BLANCHARD AV
200 SPLA 93060 464-A5
BLANCHARD PL
10600 VeCo 93012 495-J7
10600 VeCo 93012 496-A7
BLANCHARD RD
2200 VeCo 93012 496-A7
BLANCHARD CANYON RD
23600 VeCo 93040 367-D7
BLANCHE ST
100 OJAI 93023 441-H6
S BLANCHE ST
100 OJAI 93023 441-H7
BLANCO CT
300 CMRL 93012 525-A2
BLAZE AV
1400 SIMI 93065 497-J3
BLAZING STAR DR
3000 THO 91362 527-C3
BLISS CT
400 SIMI 93065 497-H6
BLONDELL PL
3000 THO 91320 555-G3
BLOOMFIELD ST
5600 SIMI 93063 499-A2
BLOSSOM CT
1600 THO 91320 526-A6
BLOSSOMWOOD CT
11700 MRPK 93021 496-C4
BLUEBELL PL
300 OXN 93030 522-F3
4300 THO 91362 527-D6
BLUEBELL ST
900 OXN 93030 522-E3
BLUEBERRY DR
2400 OXN 93030 522-G1
E BLUEBERRY LN
200 THO 91360 526-F7
BLUEBIRD AV
1300 VEN 93003 492-C4
BLUEBIRD CIR
23600 SIMI 93063 478-J6
BLUEBIRD LN
3900 OXN 93033 553-B5
BLUEBONNET CT
600 THO 91360 526-D2
BLUE CANYON ST
1500 THO 91320 526-A6
BLUE DOLPHIN DR
400 PHME 93041 552-F7
BLUEFIELD AV
1600 THO 91320 555-F2
BLUEFIN CIR
200 OXN 93035 552-B4
BLUEGRASS ST
600 SIMI 93065 497-G6
BLUE HERON CIR
12500 VeCo 93023 451-A1
BLUE HILL CT
1700 THO 91362 527-D6
BLUEJAY AV
1900 VEN 93003 492-E5
2100 OXN 93033 553-B5
BLUE JAY ST
1400 FILM 93015 455-H6
BLUE LAKE CT
400 SIMI 93065 497-E6
BLUE MEADOW LN
31600 WLKV 91361 557-D7
BLUE MESA ST
2900 THO 91362 557-C2
BLUE MOUNTAIN CIR
700 THO 91362 557-F1
BLUE OAK AV
600 THO 91320 556-D2
BLUE OAK ST
1100 CMRL 93010 524-C1
BLUE RIDGE CIR
2500 VeCo 93065 478-C6
N BLUE RIDGE CT
2000 THO 91362 557-B2
S BLUE RIDGE CT
100 THO 91362 557-B3
BLUE ROCK RDG
32300 WLKV 91361 557-B7
BLUESAIL CIR
1300 THO 91361 557-B6
BLUE SKY CIR
400 SIMI 93065 527-D1
BLUE SKY CT
24400 CanP 91307 529-D5
BLUESPRING DR
800 THO 91361 557-A5
BLUE SPRUCE CIR
2900 THO 91360 526-H2
BLUEWATER WY
600 PHME 93041 552-F7
BLUFFSIDE LN
23600 SIMI 93065 497-E4
BLYTHE ST
22100 LA 91304 529-E3
BLYTHEDALE RD
27800 AGRH 91301 558-D3
BOALT AV
2300 SIMI 93063 498-E1
BOARDMAN RD
100 OJAI 93023 442-B7
100 VeCo 93023 442-B7
BOARDWALK AV
100 THO 91360 556-F1

STREET
Block City ZIP Pg-Grid

BOB CT
400 VeCo 91320 555-G1
BOBBYBOYAR AV
6400 CanP 91307 529-G4
7500 LA 91304 529-G3
BOBOLINK LN
1100 VEN 93003 492-E4
BOBWHITE CT
1200 VEN 93003 492-D4
BODEGA PL
13200 MRPK 93021 496-E2
BODIE AV
1500 SIMI 93065 497-J4
BODLE PEAK MTWY
600 LACo 90265 586-J4
BOE CIR
2100 THO 91362 527-A2
BOGART ST
2500 CMRL 93010 524-E2
BOGOTA CT
1100 OXN 93035 522-D7
BOISE ST
8300 VEN 93004 492-G2
BOLAM CT
23600 SIMI 93065 497-F7
BOLERO LN
200 OXN 93030 522-G3
N BOLIVAR CT
2000 SIMI 93063 498-E2
BOLKER DR
2500 PHME 93041 552-D1
2700 PHME 93035 552-D1
BOLKER WY
2600 PHME 93041 552-D2
BOLLIN AV
1000 CMRL 93010 524-E2
BOLSA WY
300 OXN 93030 522-H3
BO-MERRITT RD
23600 VeCo 93023 452-J1
BONANZA ST
1700 SIMI 93063 499-C3
BONHAM ST
4700 SIMI 93063 478-H7
BONITA AV
100 OXN 93030 522-H6
N BONITA AV
100 OXN 93030 522-H5
BONITA CT
1100 VEN 93001 491-G5
BONITA DR
300 VeCo 93023 441-F7
E BONITA DR
100 SIMI 93065 497-F3
W BONITA DR
- SIMI 93065 497-E3
BONITA HEIGHTS ST
13300 MRPK 93021 496-F2
BONMARK DR
1100 VeCo 93023 451-B4
N BONNIE CT
1600 SIMI 93065 497-E3
BONNIE VIEW ST
300 MRPK 93021 476-F7
BONSAI AV
200 MRPK 93021 496-D1
BONWIT PL
600 SIMI 93065 497-G5
BOOSEY RD
800 VeCo 93060 464-F3
BOOTH ST
2000 SIMI 93065 478-A7
S BORCHARD DR
- VEN 93003 491-G3
BORCHARD RD
2200 THO 91320 555-E1
2900 VeCo 91320 555-F1
BORDEAUX AV
1000 CMRL 93010 524-E2
BORDEN AV
1000 SIMI 93065 497-J4
BORDERO LN
3100 THO 91362 527-A2
BORDERS ST
- SIMI 93063 498-H1
BORGES CT
15700 MRPK 93021 477-A5
BORGES DR
15300 MRPK 93021 477-A4
BORREGO AV
3900 OXN 93033 552-G4
BORREGO CT
200 OXN 93033 552-H4
BORREGO WY
700 OXN 93033 552-H4
BOSTON DR
3500 OXN 93033 552-J4
BOSTON WY
4400 OXN 93033 552-J5
BOTTLEBRUSH CIR
100 OXN 93030 522-E5
BOTTLEBRUSH CT
100 OXN 93030 522-E5
BOTTLEBRUSH PL
1000 OXN 93030 522-E5
BOULDER CT
10400 VEN 93004 492-J2
BOULDER ST
600 FILM 93015 455-J5

BOULDER CREEK RD
300 VeCo 93015 455-C5
23600 SIMI 93065 527-F1
BOULDER RIDGE TER
10500 Chat 91311 499-H3
BOUNDS RD
- VeCo 93001 471-C1
BOUQUET CIR
1200 THO 91362 527-A6
BOUQUET DR
7200 CanP 91307 529-F5
BOWCLIFF TER
1600 THO 91361 557-B6
BOWER WY
200 THO 91360 556-G1
BOWFIELD ST
4800 THO 91362 557-F1
4900 VeCo 91362 557-F1
5000 VeCo 91377 557-F1
BOWIE CT
4900 SIMI 93063 478-H6
BOWL RD
23600 VeCo 93063 529-A1
BOWLINE PL
5100 OXN 93033 552-G5
E BOWLING GREEN ST
100 PHME 93041 552-E2
W BOWLING GREEN ST
100 PHME 93041 552-D2
BOWMAN KNOLL DR
32500 WLKV 91361 557-A7
BOWSPRIT CIR
3800 WLKV 91361 557-B6
BOX CANYON RD
1000 VeCo 93063 499-E5
1000 WHil 91304 499-E5
23600 Chat 91311 499-E6
23600 LA 91304 499-E6
23700 WHil 91304 499-E6
BOX ELDER CT
23600 SIMI 93065 498-D4
BOXTHORN AV
600 THO 91320 555-F4
BOXWOOD CIR
3100 THO 91360 526-H2
BOY SCOUT CAMP RD
- VeCo - 366-L1
BRADBURY CT
1000 THO 91361 557-A5
BRADEMAS CT
600 SIMI 93065 527-C1
BRADFIELD DR
3700 OXN 93033 552-G4
BRADFIELD PL
4700 OXN 93033 552-H5
BRADFORD AV
- CMRL 93010 524-A1
BRADLEY RD
3900 VeCo 93066 494-H1
5300 VeCo 93066 474-J7
5300 VeCo 93066 475-B5
BRADLEY ST
200 SPLA 93060 464-A5
BRAEMAR CT
6100 AGRH 91301 557-J3
BRAKEY RD
100 VEN 93001 491-C1
BRAMBLE CT
- CMRL 93010 524-A2
BRAMWELL PL
1200 THO 91361 557-C6
N BRANCH AV
1400 SIMI 93065 497-E3
BRANDON AV
900 SIMI 93065 498-B4
BRANDT AV
- VeCo 93022 451-C4
BRANDYWINE CT
5700 CMRL 93012 495-B7
BRANNAN ST
3500 SIMI 93063 498-E3
7700 VEN 93004 492-F2
BRAUN CT
15300 MRPK 93021 476-J4
15300 MRPK 93021 477-A5
BRAVO LN
26300 CALB 91302 558-H4
BRAVO RD
23600 VeCo 93063 528-H1
BRAXFIELD CT
23600 VeCo 91361 556-G6
E BRAZIL ST
- THO 91360 556-F1
W BRAZIL ST
- THO 91360 556-F1
BRAZOS CT
10000 VEN 93004 492-J3
BREA CT
400 CMRL 93010 524-B1
BREA CANYON RD
2600 SIMI 93065 477-F7
2600 VeCo 93065 477-F7
BREAKER CT
3100 VEN 93003 491-G1
BREAKER DR
300 VEN 93003 491-G1
BREAKERS WY
5100 OXN 93035 521-J7
23600 VeCo 93001 459-D5

BREAKWATER WY
5100 OXN 93035 521-J7
BRECKENRIDGE PL
500 SIMI 93065 497-D7
500 SIMI 93065 527-D1
BRECKFORD CT
1300 THO 91361 557-A5
BREESE DR
2500 VeCo 93012 496-A7
BREEZEPORT DR
3300 WLKV 91361 557-C7
BREEZEWATER CT
2500 PHME 93041 552-C2
BRENDA CT
3000 THO 91320 555-G2
BRENNAN
- PHME 93041 552-E4
BRENNAN AV
6600 CanP 91307 529-F6
BRENNAN RD
3900 VeCo 93021 496-H3
N BRENT ST
100 VEN 93003 491-G2
S BRENT ST
100 VEN 93003 491-G4
BRENTFORD AV
1500 THO 91361 556-J6
E BRENTFORD AV
1600 THO 91361 556-J6
BRENTFORD CT
100 VeCo 93010 494-E7
BRENTLY AV
100 CMRL 93010 524-D2
BRENTWOOD AV
- VEN 93003 491-J3
N BRENTWOOD AV
2000 SIMI 93063 498-D2
BRETON AV
800 SIMI 93065 498-D5
BRETT WY
200 SPLA 93060 464-B6
BREVARD AV
300 VEN 93003 492-C1
BREVARD CT
5600 VEN 93003 492-B1
BRIAN CIR
- CMRL 93010 524-C3
BRIAN CT
1900 THO 91362 527-A6
S BRIAR AV
800 THO 91320 555-E4
BRIAR BLUFF CIR
3800 THO 91360 526-E1
BRIARCLIFF CIR
7200 VEN 93003 472-D7
BRIARCLIFF RD
600 THO 91360 526-G6
BRIARFIELD ST
2100 CMRL 93010 524-E1
BRIARGATE CT
1200 VeCo 91377 528-A7
BRIARGLEN AV
1400 THO 91361 556-J5
BRIAR HILL CIR
700 SIMI 93065 498-D5
BRIARHURST CT
2400 SIMI 93063 498-D1
BRIARPATCH DR
2600 SIMI 93065 498-C4
BRIAR RIDGE CT
23600 THO 91320 555-E4
BRIARSTONE LN
7100 CanP 91307 529-D5
BRIARWOOD LN
5400 VeCo 91377 558-A2
BRIARWOOD PL
2600 THO 91362 526-J3
BRIARWOOD TER
300 VEN 93001 491-G1
BRICKFIELD CT
23600 THO 91362 527-B5
BRIDGE RD
16800 VeCo 93060 454-A7
16900 VeCo 93060 464-B1
BRIDGEGATE CT
2000 THO 91361 557-A6
BRIDGEGATE ST
1700 THO 91361 556-J6
1800 THO 91361 557-A5
BRIDGEPORT LN
1500 CMRL 93010 524-D4
BRIDGES CT
23600 VeCo 93060 464-D5
BRIDGET AV
1500 SIMI 93065 498-B3
BRIDGETOWN PL
4900 THO 91362 527-F6
BRIDGEVIEW DR
5800 VEN 93003 472-C6
BRIDGEWATER CT
5900 AGRH 91301 557-H4
BRIDGEWOOD LN
3400 THO 91362 557-C2
N BRIDLE LN
- VeCo 91307 529-A5
BRIDLE GLEN ST
5500 AGRH 91301 558-A5
BRIDLE OAKS CT
1600 THO 91362 527-A5

BRIDLEWOOD LN
100 FILM 93015 456-A6
BRIER ST
600 VeCo 93023 451-C4
BRIGANTINE CIR
3700 WLKV 91361 557-C7
BRIGGS RD
100 VeCo 93060 473-F1
700 VeCo 93060 463-E7
S BRIGGS RD
100 VeCo 93060 473-G3
BRIGHAM ST
2000 OXN 93033 553-A4
BRIGHT GLEN CIR
2800 THO 91361 557-C5
BRIGHTON CT
4700 THO 91362 527-E6
BRIGHT STAR CIR
800 THO 91360 526-B2
BRIGHT STAR ST
700 THO 91360 526-C2
BRIGHTSTONE CT
900 THO 91361 557-A5
BRINDISI PL
23600 MRPK 93021 496-C4
BRINDLE CT
2600 SIMI 93063 498-D1
BRISBAINE AV
300 THO 91320 555-F3
BRISTOL AV
400 SIMI 93065 497-G5
BRISTOL RD
- OJAI 93023 441-G7
6000 VeCo 93003 492-D5
6300 VEN 93003 492-D5
7600 VEN 93004 492-G5
7600 VeCo 93004 492-G5
BRITTANY PARK RD
1800 VeCo 93012 526-A1
2000 VeCo 93012 496-A7
BRITTEN LN
900 VEN 93003 492-A7
BROADMOOR AV
2600 SIMI 93065 498-A1
2700 SIMI 93065 478-A7
BROADMOOR CT
2300 OXN 93030 522-D2
BROADVIEW DR
11100 MRPK 93021 496-B3
BROADWAY
13000 VeCo 93021 476-B4
23100 VeCo 93021 475-J4
BROADWAY Rt#-23
14900 VeCo 93021 476-D4
BROCK LN
- VeCo 93001 461-A3
BROCKTON LN
800 VEN 93001 491-E4
BROCKTON RD
23600 SIMI 93065 497-F7
BRODERICK AV
200 VEN 93003 492-B3
BRODERICK WY
400 PHME 93041 552-C2
BRODIEA AV
1300 VEN 93001 491-E1
BRODIEA PL
300 VEN 93001 491-E1
BROKEN ARROW ST
6000 SIMI 93063 479-B7
BROKENHILL ST
3400 THO 91320 555-F4
BROMELY DR
5400 VeCo 91377 527-H6
BROMFIELD ST
2100 SIMI 93065 498-A1
N BRONCO LN
- VeCo 91307 528-J5
BRONSON ST
1700 CMRL 93010 524-D2
BRONZE PL
3300 SIMI 93063 478-D7
BRONZEWOOD CT
1700 THO 91320 556-A2
BROOK RD
200 VeCo 91320 556-B2
BROOKBERRY LN
23600 SIMI 93065 497-A1
BROOKCREST CT
4100 MRPK 93021 496-B2
BROOKDALE LN
4300 MRPK 93021 496-E3
BROOKE AV
10100 Chat 91311 499-J4
BROOKFIELD DR
2000 THO 91362 527-A3
BROOKGLEN ST
4300 MRPK 93021 496-D3
BROOKHAVEN AV
1200 CMRL 93010 524-F1
BROOKHILL DR
2600 CMRL 93010 494-E7
BROOK HOLLOW CT
2000 OXN 93030 522-E3
BROOKHURST CT
3900 MRPK 93021 496-E4
BROOK MEADOW CT
800 THO 91362 557-E1
BROOKMONT PL
7600 LA 91304 529-E4

BROOKMONT TERRACE CT
5100 THO 91362 527-G6
BROOKPEBBLE LN
23600 SIMI 93065 497-A1
BROOKS AV
200 VEN 93001 491-B2
BROOKS RD
23400 Chat 91311 499-F7
23600 SIMI 93065 497-G7
BROOKSFALL CT
1700 THO 91361 557-A6
N BROOKSHIRE AV
- VEN 93003 492-C1
S BROOKSHIRE AV
- VEN 93003 492-C2
BROOKSIDE AV
1400 OXN 93035 552-D1
BROOKSIDE PL
100 THO 91320 556-D1
BROOKTREE CT
1800 THO 91362 526-J3
BROOKTREE DR
1300 SIMI 93063 499-C3
BROOKVIEW AV
900 THO 91361 556-J5
BROOME RANCH RD
- VeCo - 584-F1
- VeCo 93012 554-A6
200 VeCo 93012 553-H6
23600 VeCo 93012 584-C1
BROOMFIRTH CT
2000 THO 91361 557-A5
BROSSARD DR
500 THO 91360 556-G1
E BROWER ST
2100 SIMI 93065 498-B2
N BROWER ST
2000 SIMI 93065 498-A2
BROWNING AV
600 VEN 93003 492-E3
BROWNING DR
4200 OXN 93033 552-J4
4400 OXN 93033 553-A4
BROWNS CANYON RD
- StvR 91381 479-G1
2500 Nor 91326 479-J4
2500 Chat 91311 479-H3
BROWNSTONE CREEK AV
2100 SIMI 93063 499-A2
BRUCE CIR
900 THO 91362 526-H7
BRUCE DR
1200 SPLA 93060 464-B3
BRUCKER RD
200 OXN 93033 552-F4
BRUNSTON CT
2900 THO 91362 527-C5
BRUNSWICK LN
800 VEN 93001 491-E5
BRUSH HILL RD
700 THO 91360 526-G5
BRUSH OAK CT
1800 THO 91320 526-A5
BRYAN AV
3200 SIMI 93063 478-H6
BRYANT CIR
400 OJAI 93023 441-J7
BRYANT DR
500 WHil 91304 499-D5
BRYANT PL
800 OJAI 93023 441-J7
BRYANT ST
100 OJAI 93023 441-J7
22100 LA 91304 529-J1
BRYCE WY
1100 VEN 93003 492-B4
BRYCE CANYON AV
100 OXN 93033 552-F3
700 PHME 93033 552-F3
700 PHME 93041 552-F3
BRYNDALE AV
23600 VeCo 91377 528-A7
N BRYN MAWR ST
5300 VEN 93003 492-B2
S BRYN MAWR ST
- VEN 93003 492-B2
BRYSON AV
1100 SIMI 93065 497-G4
E BRYSON PL
2300 SIMI 93065 498-B4
BUBBLING BROOK ST
11900 MRPK 93021 496-C3
BUCHANAN AV
- VEN 93003 492-E2
BUCKAROO AV
2600 OXN 93030 492-F7
2600 OXN 93030 522-F1
BUCKBOARD CIR
300 SIMI 93065 497-F6
BUCKBOARD LN
200 OJAI 93023 441-H7
500 OJAI 93023 451-J1
BUCKEYE PL
3300 THO 91320 555-G4
BUCKINGHAM DR
1000 THO 91360 526-G6
BUCKLIN PL
3900 THO 91360 526-F1

BUCKNELL AV
100 VEN 93003 492-B3
BUCKSGLEN CT
1600 THO 91361 556-J5
BUCKSKIN AV
1400 SIMI 93065 497-H3
N BUCKSKIN RD
- VeCo 91307 528-J4
BUCKSMOORE CT
1300 THO 91361 556-J5
BUCKTHORN CT
3800 THO 91320 555-E2
BUELL CT
1900 SIMI 93065 498-A4
BUENA MESA CT
5200 CMRL 93012 525-A2
BUENA VISTA
100 VEN 93001 491-D1
BUENA VISTA AV
500 OXN 93030 522-J6
BUENA VISTA DR
- VeCo 93010 494-D6
400 OJAI 93023 441-J6
BUENA VISTA ST
600 VEN 93001 491-C1
8200 VeCo 93021 476-D3
BUENOS TIEMPOS DR
500 CMRL 93012 524-J3
BUFF CIR
2800 SIMI 93065 498-C5
BUFFALO AV
2200 VEN 93003 492-E5
BUFFALO ST
6100 SIMI 93063 479-B6
BUFFUM ST
3500 SIMI 93063 498-E2
BUFFWOOD PL
5500 AGRH 91301 558-A5
BUGGY LN
10300 VeCo 93012 495-J6
BULL PUP CIR
- VeCo 93041 583-G1
BUMBLEBEE AV
1000 THO 91320 526-A6
BUNDREN ST
- VeCo 93022 451-B6
BUNSEN AV
2800 VEN 93003 492-D7
BUNTING AV
2500 VEN 93003 492-E5
BURANO CT
700 VeCo 91377 557-H1
BURBANK AV
100 VeCo 93035 552-C6
BURCH AV
1800 SIMI 93063 498-E2
N BURKE CT
2200 SIMI 93063 498-E2
BURL AV
200 VEN 93003 492-C2
BURLESON AV
1800 THO 91360 526-G5
BURLESON ST
28900 AGRH 91301 558-A3
N BURLINGHAM PL
2400 SIMI 93063 498-E1
BURLINGTON AV
700 VEN 93004 492-H2
BURNETT AV
200 VEN 93003 492-C1
BURNETT CIR
6300 VEN 93003 492-C1
BURNETT CT
6300 VEN 93003 492-C1
BURNHAM RD
- VeCo 93001 450-J6
- VeCo 93022 450-J6
100 VeCo 93022 451-A5
700 VeCo 93022 451-A5
700 VeCo 93023 451-A5
BURNING TREE DR
1700 THO 91362 526-J3
BURNLEY ST
1400 CMRL 93010 524-C2
BURNS ST
4900 VEN 93003 492-A2
BURNSIDE DR
1500 VEN 93004 492-J3
E BURNSIDE ST
2200 SIMI 93065 498-B2
BURR CIR
2300 THO 91360 526-F4
N BURREL AV
2000 SIMI 93063 498-E2
BURSON LN
200 FILM 93015 455-J6
BURSON WY
4700 VeCo 93030 493-A5
BURSON RANCH RD
- VeCo 93015 455-J3
- VeCo 93015 456-A3
BURTON CT
300 THO 91360 526-F4
BURTON ST
300 THO 91360 526-G4
22100 LA 91304 529-E2
BURTONWOOD AV
1000 THO 91360 526-G7
BURY CIR
800 THO 91360 526-G6

BUSH ST
23600 VEN 93003 492-E2
BUSHELL RD
4700 VeCo 93066 495-B2
BUSHGROVE CT
23600 VeCo 91361 556-F6
BUSINESS CENTER CIR
1000 THO 91320 525-G6
BUSTER ST
1400 SIMI 93065 497-G3
BUTLER RD
2200 OXN 93033 553-A3
BUTTE ST
8400 VEN 93004 492-F1
BUTTER CREEK RD
4900 MRPK 93021 496-B2
BUTTERFIELD LN
4300 MRPK 93021 496-F3
BUTTERFIELD ST
5300 CMRL 93012 525-A1
BUTTERFLY CT
1600 THO 91320 526-A6
BUTTONWOOD AV
6600 VeCo 91377 558-B2
BUYERS ST
1600 SIMI 93063 498-F3
BYRD DR
2100 OXN 93033 552-J2
BYRON AV
200 VEN 93003 492-B1

C

C ST
- VeCo 93042 583-H3
- FILM 93015 455-J6
100 OXN 93033 522-G7
1000 OXN 93033 522-G7
1200 OXN 93033 552-G2
E C ST
100 PHME 93041 552-E5
N C ST
100 OXN 93030 522-G3
W C ST
- PHME 93041 552-E5
CABALLERO ST
1700 SIMI 93065 497-J4
1700 SIMI 93065 498-A4
CABEZONE WY
200 OXN 93035 552-A3
CABIN CV
2500 PHME 93041 552-C3
CABLE CANYON
- VeCo 93001 471-A3
CABLE RACK RD
- VeCo 93042 583-D4
CABOT CT
2700 THO 91360 526-E3
CABOT PL
2000 OXN 93030 523-A6
CABRILLO AV
- THO 91320 555-F1
CABRILLO CT
100 SPLA 93060 463-J6
CABRILLO DR
2700 VEN 93003 491-G3
CABRILLO LN
300 FILM 93015 456-C6
CABRILLO WY
1000 VeCo 93010 494-D6
1600 OXN 93030 522-D4
CABRILLO MESA CT
23600 CMRL 93010 494-C7
CACHUMA AV
500 VEN 93004 492-H1
CACTUS AV
9600 Chat 91311 499-H5
CACTUS CT
800 THO 91320 526-A6
CACTUS DR
300 OXN 93030 492-G7
CACTUS TR
26800 CALB 91301 558-G7
CADIZ CT
1100 OXN 93035 522-D7
CADIZ DR
1000 VeCo 93065 497-G4
E CADMAN ST
3800 SIMI 93063 498-E2
CADWAY ST
1000 SPLA 93060 464-B3
CAHUENGA DR
200 VeCo 93035 552-B5
CAIRD AV
1700 LACo 90265 586-J7
CAJON CIR
10600 VeCo 93012 496-A5
CALABASAS HILLS RD
- CALB 91301 558-G7
CALABRIA
28800 AGRH 91301 558-B4
CALABRIA CT
800 CMRL 93010 524-C1
CALAISE CT
30800 WLKV 91362 557-F5
CALAMAR CT
23600 CMRL 93010 494-C7
CALAMINE DR
26900 CALB 91301 558-F6

CALAVERAS DR
2300 CMRL 93010 494-E7
CALAVERAS ST
8000 VEN 93004 472-F7
8000 VEN 93004 492-E1
S CALAVO ST
100 SPLA 93060 463-H7
CALCITE CIR
2500 THO 91320 525-H7
CALDWELL AV
2100 SIMI 93065 497-H1
CALEDONIA CT
23600 VeCo 91377 528-A7
CALENDULA CT
2800 THO 91360 526-D3
CALETA CT
- CMRL 93012 524-J2
CALETA DR
- CMRL 93012 524-H2
CALETA RD
4300 Ago 91301 558-B7
CALGARY AV
800 VEN 93004 492-H2
CALIENTE LN
800 VEN 93001 491-C1
CALIENTE WY
600 OXN 93030 522-H3
CALIFORNIA AV
700 SIMI 93065 497-G2
2100 VeCo 93015 465-F4
CALIFORNIA ST
200 SPLA 93060 464-B6
1300 OXN 93033 552-H1
N CALIFORNIA ST
- VEN 93001 491-C2
S CALIFORNIA ST
- VEN 93001 491-C2
S CALIFORNIA STREET MALL
300 VEN 93001 491-C2
CALLADO ST
700 VeCo 93010 494-B5
CALLAHAN AV
2100 SIMI 93065 497-J2
CALLA LILY CT
- SIMI 93063 498-H1
CALLAS CT
1700 OXN 93035 522-E7
CALLAS DR
1100 OXN 93035 522-E7
1200 OXN 93035 552-E1
CALLE ABEDUL
2500 THO 91360 526-G3
CALLE ABETO
2600 THO 91360 526-H4
CALLE ACOPADA
600 VeCo 93010 493-J6
CALLE AGRADO
600 CMRL 93012 525-C5
CALLE AGUILA
3900 CMRL 93012 524-H4
CALLE ALAMO
1500 THO 91360 526-H3
CALLE ALBERCA
1700 CMRL 93010 494-B7
1700 CMRL 93010 524-B1
CALLE ALMENDRO
800 THO 91360 526-H3
CALLE ALTA VISTA
3700 THO 91320 525-E7
CALLE ALTO
4500 CMRL 93012 524-J5
CALLE ALUCEMA
2300 THO 91360 526-J4
CALLE AMAPOLA
500 THO 91360 526-G4
CALLE AMOROSA
- CMRL 93012 525-B4
CALLE ANAPOL
23600 CMRL 93010 523-F2
CALLE ANGOSTA
1800 VeCo 91360 526-C5
CALLE ARAGON
600 VeCo 91377 557-J1
CALLE ARENA
5900 CMRL 93012 525-B2
CALLE ARGOLLA
4200 CMRL 93012 524-H3
CALLE ARINO
2900 THO 91360 526-G3
CALLE ARROYO
600 VeCo 91360 526-C7
CALLE ARTIGAS
1300 THO 91360 496-J7
CALLE AURORA
1200 VeCo 93010 494-A6
CALLE AVELLANO
1300 THO 91360 526-H3
CALLE BALSA
1200 THO 91360 526-H3
CALLE BELLA VISTA
1400 CMRL 93010 524-A1
CALLE BELLOTA
3500 CMRL 93010 494-G7
CALLE BIENVENIDO
2600 THO 91360 526-G3
CALLE BODEGA
5900 CMRL 93012 525-C2
CALLE BOLERO
4500 CMRL 93012 524-H6

CALLE BONITA
1200 CMRL 93012 525-A1
CALLE BORREGO
1900 VeCo 91360 526-B5
CALLE BOUGANVILLA
2400 THO 91360 526-H4
CALLE BRUSCA
900 VeCo 91360 526-B6
CALLE BUENA VISTA
3800 THO 91320 525-E7
CALLE CAMELIA
1100 THO 91360 526-H4
CALLE CAMELLIA
800 CMRL 93010 524-B2
CALLE CANCUN
23600 CMRL 93012 494-H7
23600 CMRL 93012 524-J1
CALLE CANON
600 CMRL 93012 525-B2
CALLE CAPISTRANO
23600 OXN 93030 523-C7
CALLE CARDO
500 THO 91360 526-G4
CALLE CARGA
4500 CMRL 93012 524-H6
CALLE CASTANO
2700 THO 91360 526-G2
CALLE CATALPA
600 THO 91360 526-G2
CALLE CEDRO
2800 THO 91360 526-G3
CALLE CIELITO
23600 OXN 93030 523-C7
CALLE CINCO DE MAYO
- VeCo 93022 451-B5
E CALLE CIRCULO
300 CMRL 93010 524-B2
N CALLE CIRCULO
800 CMRL 93010 524-B2
CALLE CIRUELO
600 THO 91360 526-G4
CALLE CITA
3500 CMRL 93010 494-G7
CALLE CLARA VISTA
3700 THO 91320 525-F7
CALLE CLAVEL
600 THO 91360 526-G4
CALLE COLINA
1200 THO 91360 496-H7
CALLE COLLADO
900 VeCo 91360 526-B6
CALLE COMPO
1400 VeCo 91360 526-C5
CALLE CONTENTO
700 THO 91360 526-H1
CALLE CONVERSE
100 CMRL 93010 524-B1
400 CMRL 93010 494-B7
CALLE CORTA
600 VeCo 91360 526-C6
CALLE CORVA
1700 VeCo 93010 493-J6
CALLE COVINA
- CMRL 93012 524-H1
CALLE CRISANTEMO
1300 THO 91360 526-H4
CALLE CUESTA
600 THO 91360 526-G2
4900 CMRL 93012 524-J4
4900 CMRL 93012 525-A4
CALLE DALIA
2300 THO 91360 526-G4
CALLE DAMASCO
2700 THO 91360 526-G3
CALLE DE DEBESA
3000 CMRL 93010 493-J6
CALLE DE LA ROSA
- CMRL 93012 524-H4
CALLE DE LAS OVEJAS
500 VeCo 91377 557-J2
CALLE DEL NORTE
800 VeCo 93010 494-A6
CALLE DEL PRADO
23600 THO 91320 555-D3
CALLE DEL SOL
3700 THO 91360 526-J1
CALLE DEL SUR
500 THO 91360 526-G3
CALLE DE MAREJADA
3000 CMRL 93010 493-J6
CALLE DE ORO
1200 THO 91360 526-J1
CALLE DE ORO CT
3300 THO 91360 526-H1
CALLE DIA
2000 CMRL 93012 495-D7
CALLE DIAMONTE
1500 THO 91320 526-B7
CALLE DURAZNO
1300 THO 91360 526-H4
CALLE ELAINA
1000 VeCo 91360 526-C6
CALLE EL AVION
300 CMRL 93010 524-B1
CALLE EL CAMERON
1200 VeCo 91360 526-B7
CALLE ELEGANTE
2500 THO 91360 526-G3
CALLE EL HALCON
1000 CMRL 93010 524-B2

W CALLE EL PRADO
- VeCo 93022 451-B5
CALLE EL VOLADOR
300 CMRL 93010 524-B2
CALLE ENTRAR
500 THO 91360 526-G3
CALLE ESCALON
1400 CMRL 93010 524-A1
CALLE ESCORIAL
3900 CMRL 93012 524-G4
CALLE ESTEPA
2900 THO 91360 526-G3
CALLE FANILLIA
200 VeCo 91377 558-A2
CALLE FIDELIDAD
1200 THO 91360 496-H7
CALLE FLORENCIA
1600 THO 91360 526-J1
CALLE FRESNO
500 THO 91360 526-G3
CALLE FRONTE
- CMRL 93012 524-H2
CALLE FUEGO
3500 THO 91360 526-C1
CALLE GALVEZ
5900 CMRL 93012 525-B5
CALLE GLADIOLO
2400 THO 91360 526-H4
CALLE GLICINA
2100 THO 91360 526-H4
CALLE GOMERO
1200 THO 91360 526-H3
CALLE HAYA
2600 THO 91360 526-G3
CALLE HERMOSA
2500 THO 91360 526-G3
CALLE HIGUERA
200 CMRL 93010 524-B1
800 CMRL 93010 494-C7
CALLE HONDANADA
1400 THO 91360 496-H7
CALLE JAZMIN
700 THO 91360 526-G4
CALLE JON
800 VeCo 91360 526-D6
CALLEJON DE ROSAS
900 VeCo 91360 526-C7
CALLE LACOTA
800 THO 91360 526-G3
CALLE LA CUMBRE
900 CMRL 93010 524-B1
CALLE LA FIESTA
- CMRL 93010 524-B2
CALLE LA GRANADA
- CMRL 93010 524-B2
E CALLE LA GUERRA
- CMRL 93010 524-B2
W CALLE LA GUERRA
- CMRL 93010 524-A2
CALLE LAGUNA
23600 OXN 93030 523-C7
CALLE LA PALMERA
800 CMRL 93010 524-B2
CALLE LA PAZ
1100 CMRL 93010 524-B1
CALLE LA PRADA
800 CMRL 93010 524-B2
CALLE LAREDO
500 THO 91360 526-C7
500 VeCo 91360 526-C7
CALLE LARIOS
- CMRL 93010 524-B1
CALLE LA ROCHA
800 CMRL 93010 524-B2
CALLE LA RODA
600 CMRL 93010 524-B2
CALLE LAS CASAS
1300 VeCo 91360 526-B7
CALLE LAS COLINAS
800 THO 91320 525-E7
CALLE LA SOMBRA
2000 SIMI 93063 499-B2
E CALLE LA SOMBRA
- CMRL 93010 524-B2
N CALLE LA SOMBRA
800 CMRL 93010 524-B2
W CALLE LA SOMBRA
- CMRL 93010 524-A2
CALLE LAS TRANCAS
900 VeCo 91360 526-C6
CALLE LILA
2100 THO 91360 526-G4
CALLE LIMONERO
2600 THO 91360 526-J3
CALLE LINDA VISTA
3700 THO 91320 525-E7
CALLE LIRIO
2300 THO 91360 526-H4
CALLE LOMA VISTA
3800 THO 91320 525-E7
CALLE LOS ACEITUNOS
600 VeCo 93010 493-J6
CALLE LOS GATOS
800 CMRL 93010 524-A2
CALLE LOZANO
1100 CMRL 93012 525-A1
CALLE LYS
2100 THO 91360 526-G4
CALLE MADRESELVA
1300 THO 91360 526-H4

STREET
Block City ZIP Pg-Grid

CALLE MALVON
2300 THO 91360 526-H4
CALLE MANDARINAS
600 VeCo 91360 526-C6
CALLE MANZANO
2500 THO 91360 526-H3
CALLE MAPACHE
4600 CMRL 93012 524-H2
CALLE MARGARITA
500 THO 91360 526-G4
27800 AGRH 91301 558-D7
CALLE MARLENA
600 VeCo 91377 557-J1
CALLE MAR VISTA
23600 OXN 93030 523-C7
CALLE MAZATLAN
3700 THO 91320 525-F7
CALLE MENDOTA
23600 CMRL 93012 524-J2
CALLE MIGUEL
23600 CMRL 93010 524-B2
CALLE MILAGROS
22000 Chat 91311 499-J3
CALLE MIMOSA
2300 THO 91360 526-H4
CALLE MIRADO
600 VeCo 91377 557-J2
CALLE MIRA MONTE
900 THO 91320 525-E7
CALLE MIRASOL
23600 CMRL 93010 524-B2
CALLE MONTECILLO
4900 AGRH 91301 558-D7
CALLE MORENO
3400 VeCo 93023 442-D5
CALLE MORERA
1500 THO 91360 526-H3
CALLE NARANJO
600 THO 91360 526-G3
CALLE NARCISO
2400 THO 91360 526-H4
CALLE NARDO
2100 THO 91360 526-H4
CALLE NAVARRO
- CMRL 93010 524-B1
CALLE NOGAL
500 THO 91360 526-G3
CALLE NORTE
23600 THO 91320 555-D2
CALLENS RD
500 VEN 93003 491-J5
CALLE OLIVO
2600 THO 91360 526-H3
CALLE OLMO
1200 THO 91360 526-H3
CALLE ORINDA
1400 VeCo 93010 494-A6
CALLE OROVISTA
100 CMRL 93012 524-H3
CALLE PAMARO
5800 CMRL 93012 525-B4
CALLE PARADORA
3900 CMRL 93012 524-H3
CALLE PECOS
700 VeCo 91360 526-C6
CALLE PENSAMIENTO
500 THO 91360 526-G4
CALLE PERA
2500 THO 91360 526-H3
CALLE PETALUMA
1800 VeCo 91360 526-C5
CALLE PIMIENTO
1200 THO 91360 526-H3
CALLE PINATA
800 THO 91360 526-G1
CALLE PINO
2400 THO 91360 526-G4
CALLE PLANO
700 CMRL 93012 524-J5
CALLE PLANTADOR
1800 VeCo 91360 526-C5
CALLE PORTADA
1400 VeCo 93010 493-J6
1400 VeCo 93010 494-A6
CALLE PORTILLA
100 CMRL 93010 524-B1
CALLE POSADAS
3700 THO 91320 525-F7
CALLE PUNTA
600 THO 91360 526-G1
CALLE QUEBRACHO
2700 THO 91360 526-G1
CALLE QUETZAL
4500 CMRL 93012 524-J6
CALLE RETAMA
2400 THO 91360 526-H4
CALLE REY
900 VeCo 91360 526-C6
CALLE RIO VISTA
5600 VeCo 91377 557-J1
E CALLE RISCOSO
2000 THO 91362 527-A2
CALLE ROBLE
2400 THO 91360 526-G4
CALLE ROBLEDA
4900 AGRH 91301 558-D7
CALLE ROCAS
1700 VeCo 93010 493-J6
CALLE ROCHELLE
3600 THO 91360 526-J1

CALLE ROSA
2200 THO 91360 526-G4
CALLE RUIZ
800 THO 91360 526-G1
CALLE SALTO
1700 VeCo 91360 526-B5
CALLE SAN JUAN
23600 THO 91320 555-C3
CALLE SAN PABLO
500 CMRL 93012 524-E5
CALLE SANTIAGO
23600 THO 91320 555-D3
CALLE SEGUNDA
23600 CMRL 93010 524-C4
CALLE SEGURO
600 VeCo 91377 557-J2
CALLE SENCILLO
5700 CMRL 93012 525-B3
CALLE SEQUOIA
400 THO 91360 526-D7
400 VeCo 91360 526-D7
CALLE SERRA
23600 CMRL 93012 494-J7
CALLE SUERTE
900 CMRL 93012 524-H2
CALLE TAMEGA
- CMRL 93012 525-A3
CALLE TANIA
6700 CMRL 93012 495-C7
CALLE TECATE
3600 CMRL 93012 524-G2
CALLE TESORO
4100 CMRL 93012 524-H1
CALLE TIERRA VISTA
1300 CMRL 93010 523-H1
1700 VeCo 93010 523-H1
CALLE TILO
1500 THO 91360 526-H3
CALLE TULIPAN
1000 THO 91360 526-G3
CALLE TURQUESA
1500 THO 91320 526-A7
CALLE VALLE VISTA
3800 THO 91320 525-E7
CALLE VERACRUZ
23600 THO 91320 555-D3
CALLE VERBENA
2300 THO 91360 526-H4
CALLE VIEJO
3900 CMRL 93012 524-H4
CALLE VIOLETA
1300 THO 91360 526-H4
CALLE VISTA
1200 CMRL 93010 524-A2
CALLE VISTA CALMA
23600 OXN 93030 523-C6
CALLE VISTA DEL MONTE
- VeCo 93022 451-B5
CALLE VISTA VERDE
23600 OXN 93030 523-C7
CALLE YUCCA
400 THO 91360 526-C6
400 VeCo 91360 526-C5
CALLE ZAFIRO
1700 THO 91320 556-A1
CALLE ZOCALO
1500 THO 91360 496-J7
CALLICOTT AV
6200 WdHl 91367 529-F7
6600 CanP 91307 529-F6
CALMFIELD AV
5800 AGRH 91301 558-B3
CALUMET CANYON
- VeCo 93015 466-F2
- VeCo 93021 466-F2
CALUMET CANYON RD
23600 VeCo 93015 466-G1
CALUSA AV
3000 SIMI 93063 479-B6
CALVADOS DR
- CMRL 93012 525-A3
CALVERT CT
3000 VeCo 93012 496-E6
CALVERT ST
23800 WdHl 91367 529-C7
CALZONA CT
1500 SIMI 93065 497-F3
CAMARILLO AV
100 VeCo 93035 552-C6
CAMARILLO DR
- CMRL 93010 494-C7
- VeCo 93010 494-C7
CAMARILLO RD
- VeCo 93012 554-C3
CAMARILLO ST
- VeCo 93012 554-E4
- VeCo 93012 524-F4
CAMARILLO CENTER DR
300 CMRL 93010 524-B3
CAMARILLO RANCH RD
23600 CMRL 93012 524-G3
CAMARILLO SPRINGS RD
600 CMRL 93012 525-B6
600 VeCo 93012 525-C5
CAMBERWELL PL
1500 THO 91361 556-J6
CAMBON AV
2100 CMRL 93010 494-H7

CAMBON CIR
1100 VeCo 93023 451-C1
CAMBRIA AV
- VEN 93004 492-G1
CAMBRIA CT
1100 CMRL 93010 524-E1
3600 THO 91360 526-F1
CAMBRIDGE CT
29300 AGRH 91301 558-A4
29400 AGRH 91301 557-J4
CAMBRIDGE ST
14300 MRPK 93021 476-G6
CAMDEN CT
12900 MRPK 93021 496-E4
23600 SIMI 93065 498-B5
CAMDEN LN
1300 VEN 93001 491-F5
CAMELIA DR
800 PHME 93041 552-F5
CAMELIA LN
200 VeCo 91377 557-J2
CAMELIA WY
100 VEN 93004 473-A7
CAMELLIA ST
900 OXN 93030 522-E3
CAMELOT WY
1000 OXN 93030 522-G3
CAMEO CT
1100 CMRL 93010 524-F2
CAMERON CT
- VEN 93001 471-C6
CAMERON ST
100 SPLA 93060 463-H6
800 VEN 93001 471-C6
CAMERTON CT
2000 VeCo 91361 556-H6
CAMILAR DR
2200 CMRL 93010 494-E7
S CAMILLE CT
800 VeCo 93023 451-B1
CAMILLE DR
1100 VeCo 93023 451-C1
CAMINITO LAS RAMBLAS
23600 CMRL 93012 495-D6
CAMINO AV
3400 OXN 93030 523-D3
CAMINO AGUA DULCE
500 THO 91320 555-D3
CAMINO ALGARVE
3900 CMRL 93012 524-H4
CAMINO ALVAREZ
2200 CMRL 93010 494-H7
2200 VeCo 93010 494-H7
CAMINO CALANDRIA
2800 THO 91360 526-G2
CAMINO CARILLO
- CMRL 93012 525-A4
CAMINO CASTENADA
1300 CMRL 93010 524-B1
CAMINO CIELO
- VeCo - 366-J6
- VeCo - 441-G1
- VeCo 93023 366-J6
15400 VeCo 93023 441-D1
CAMINO COMPRADE
5600 CMRL 93012 525-A3
CAMINO CONCORDIA
500 VeCo 93010 493-J6
600 VeCo 93010 494-A6
CAMINO CORTINA
200 CMRL 93010 524-A2
CAMINO CRISTOBAL
1300 VeCo 91360 526-B5
CAMINO DE CELESTE
400 THO 91360 526-D1
CAMINO DE LA LUNA
600 THO 91320 555-D3
23600 OXN 93030 522-J4
CAMINO DE LA LUZ
600 THO 91320 555-D3
CAMINO DEL ARBOL
6200 CMRL 93012 525-C1
CAMINO DE LA ROSA
4300 THO 91320 555-D3
CAMINO DEL ARROYO
2000 VeCo 93023 442-B7
CAMINO DE LAS ESTRELLAS
4300 THO 91320 555-D3
CAMINO DEL CIELO
500 THO 91320 555-D3
CAMINO DEL LAGO
500 THO 91320 555-D3
CAMINO DEL MAR
600 THO 91320 555-D3
CAMINO DEL RIO
23600 VeCo 93040 458-D5
CAMINO DEL SOL
300 OXN 93030 522-H5
600 THO 91320 555-D3
1800 OXN 93030 523-B5
1800 VeCo 93030 522-H5
1800 VeCo 93030 523-B5
CAMINO DEL ZURO
2900 THO 91360 526-G2
CAMINO DEVILLE
5600 CMRL 93012 525-B3
CAMINO DOS PALOS
300 THO 91360 526-G2

CAMINO DOS RIOS
600 VeCo 91360 526-C6
CAMINO DURANGO
600 VeCo 91360 526-C7
CAMINO EL CARRIZO
700 VeCo 91360 526-C7
CAMINO EL RINCON
- CMRL 93012 525-A3
CAMINO ESPLENDIDO
- CMRL 93012 524-A2
CAMINO ESTRADA
1300 CMRL 93010 524-B1
CAMINO FLORES
700 VeCo 91360 526-C6
CAMINO GRACIOSA
2900 THO 91360 526-G2
CAMINO LA MADERA
900 CMRL 93010 524-B1
CAMINO LA MAIDA
500 THO 91360 526-G3
CAMINO LA POSADA
500 VeCo 93010 494-A6
CAMINO LAS CONCHAS
700 VeCo 91360 526-C6
CAMINO LAS RAMBLAS
700 CMRL 93012 495-D7
CAMINO LEON
- CMRL 93012 525-A3
CAMINO MADERO
800 VeCo 91360 526-C7
CAMINO MAGENTA
1000 VeCo 91360 526-D6
CAMINO MANZANAS
200 THO 91360 526-E6
400 VeCo 91360 526-C6
CAMINO OLMO
23600 THO 91320 525-J5
CAMINO RANCHO
23600 CMRL 93012 524-G3
CAMINO ROBERTO
500 VeCo 91360 526-D6
CAMINO ROJO
500 VeCo 91360 526-D6
CAMINO RUIZ
100 CMRL 93012 524-J3
1300 CMRL 93012 525-A4
CAMINO SANTO REYES
600 VeCo 91360 526-C7
CAMINO TIERRA SANTA
300 CMRL 93010 523-J2
CAMINO TOLUCA
200 CMRL 93010 524-A2
CAMINO VALLES
600 VeCo 91360 526-C7
CAMINO VALVERDE
3900 CMRL 93012 524-H4
CAMINO VERA CRUZ
1700 CMRL 93010 494-C7
1700 CMRL 93010 524-C1
CAMINO VERDE
500 VeCo 91360 526-D6
CAMPANULA AV
1000 VeCo 93004 473-B7
1000 VeCo 93004 493-B1
CAMPBELL AV
1400 THO 91360 526-D5
CAMPBELL WY
200 OXN 93033 552-G5
CAMP CHAFFEE RD
7900 VeCo 93001 460-J5
CAMPHOR AV
3800 THO 91320 555-E4
CAMPHOR CIR
900 THO 91320 555-E4
CAMPO VERDE CT
600 VeCo 91377 557-J2
CAMP RAMAH RD
1100 VeCo 93023 441-F5
CAMPTON DR
100 OXN 93030 522-J6
CAMPUS DR
3400 THO 91360 526-E1
N CAMPUS DR
1800 OXN 93033 552-J3
1800 OXN 93033 553-A3
S CAMPUS DR
1800 OXN 93033 552-J4
1800 OXN 93033 553-A4
3200 THO 91360 526-E2
CAMPUS RD
7000 MRPK 93021 477-B5
CAMPUS ST
4600 VEN 93003 492-A3
E CAMPUS WY
4800 VEN 93003 492-A2
S CAMPUS WY
4300 VEN 93003 492-A2
W CAMPUS WY
4300 VEN 93003 491-J2
4300 VEN 93003 492-A2
CAMPUS PARK DR
14300 MRPK 93021 476-H6
15400 MRPK 93021 477-A6
CAMP WILLETT RD
23600 VeCo 93001 451-C7
23600 VeCo 93023 451-D7
CAMULOS ST
3100 VeCo 93015 457-D5
3100 VeCo 93040 457-E4

CANADA ST
100 OJAI 93023 441-H6
CANADA DE ALISOS
23600 VeCo 93001 461-F4
CANADA LARGA RD
- VeCo 93001 461-G5
CANAL ST
1000 OXN 93035 522-A7
CANARIO CT
4200 MRPK 93021 496-E3
CANARY LN
4000 OXN 93033 553-A4
CANDELARIA RD
100 OXN 93030 523-B6
CANDIA CT
1000 SIMI 93065 498-A1
CANDICE CT
3000 SIMI 93063 478-E7
CANDLECREST DR
600 THO 91362 557-D1
800 THO 91362 527-D7
CANDLE TREE LN
23600 SIMI 93065 497-A1
CANDLEWOOD CT
13500 MRPK 93021 496-F3
CANDLEWOOD WY
23400 CanP 91307 529-E5
CANET RD
23600 VeCo 93001 461-B6
CANFIELD CT
- THO 91360 526-F2
CANGAS DR
5200 CALB 91301 558-G6
CANMORE ST
28900 AGRH 91301 558-A3
CANNA ST
2700 THO 91360 526-D3
CANNA WY
200 VEN 93004 473-A7
CANNES DR
1700 THO 91362 526-J2
CANNES SQ
4600 OXN 93035 552-A2
CANOGA PL
3300 CMRL 93010 524-G1
CANON CT
5700 VEN 93003 472-C7
CANON ST
5600 VEN 93003 472-B7
CANTARA ST
22100 LA 91304 529-J2
CANTER AV
1500 CMRL 93010 524-D1
CANTERA ST
- THO 91360 526-F1
CANTERBURY CT
100 VeCo 93023 441-E7
CANTERBURY DR
6000 AGRH 91301 558-A3
CANTERBURY LN
- SIMI 93063 498-H1
CANTERBURY ST
4600 THO 91362 527-D6
CANTERBURY WY
200 OXN 93033 552-G5
CANTERFORD CIR
1100 THO 91361 557-C5
CANTERHILL PL
32000 WLKV 91361 557-C7
CANTLAY ST
22000 CanP 91303 529-J5
22400 CanP 91307 529-G5
CANTRICE ST
500 SIMI 93065 527-D1
CANWOOD ST
26800 Ago 91301 558-F6
26800 CALB 91301 558-F6
28000 AGRH 91301 558-A6
29300 AGRH 91301 557-G6
CANYON RD
200 VeCo 91320 556-B2
23600 VeCo 93063 529-A1
CANYON WY
4800 AGRH 91301 558-C7
CANYON CLUB CIR
1800 SIMI 93065 497-J1
1800 SIMI 93065 478-A7
1800 SIMI 93065 498-A1
CANYON CREST CT
3500 THO 91360 526-H2
32100 WLKV 91361 557-C7
CANYON CREST DR
23600 SIMI 93065 497-F7
23600 SIMI 93065 527-F1
N CANYONLANDS RD
4500 MRPK 93021 496-E2
CANYON OAKS DR
6500 SIMI 93063 499-C1
CANYON RIDGE DR
32100 WLKV 91361 557-C7
CANYON RIM CIR
1300 THO 91362 527-G7
CANYON VIEW
800 FILM 93015 456-A5
CANYON VIEW DR
23600 SIMI 93065 497-F7
23600 SIMI 93065 527-F1
CANYON VISTA DR
1100 THO 91320 526-B7

CANYONWOOD CT
13400 MRPK 93021 496-F4
CANYONWOOD DR
24600 CanP 91307 529-C5
CAPE HORN DR
5800 AGRH 91301 557-G4
CAPELLA WY
2600 THO 91362 527-C3
CAPELLO WY
1100 VeCo 93023 451-C1
CAPEWOOD LN
23600 SIMI 93065 497-A2
CAPISTRANO AV
6100 WdHl 91367 529-J7
6500 CanP 91307 529-H5
7600 LA 91304 529-F2
9500 Chat 91311 499-H6
CAPISTRANO CT
300 CMRL 93010 524-D3
CAPITAN ST
100 THO 91320 556-C1
CAPRI AV
2700 VEN 93003 492-E6
CAPRI DR
100 VeCo 93065 497-F4
400 SIMI 93065 497-F4
CAPRI WY
1000 OXN 93035 521-J7
1200 OXN 93035 551-J1
CAPRICORN AV
6300 AGRH 91301 558-B3
CAPSTAN CIR
3700 WLKV 91361 557-C7
CAPSTAN DR
1700 OXN 93035 552-C1
CAPTAINS AV
2500 PHME 93041 552-D2
CAPTAINS PL
5300 AGRH 91301 557-G6
CARAWAY CT
3000 THO 91360 526-H2
CARDIFF CIR
1100 THO 91362 527-A6
CARDIGAN AV
1100 VEN 93004 492-G3
CARDINAL AV
2100 OXN 93033 553-B5
CARDINAL ST
5900 VEN 93003 492-C4
CARDINAL WY
5300 VeCo 91377 527-G7
CARDINAL RIDGE LN
23600 SIMI 93065 527-D1
CARDOZA DR
5800 WLKV 91361 557-F4
CAREFREE DR
900 SIMI 93065 497-G5
CARELL AV
5700 AGRH 91301 558-B4
CAREYBROOK DR
5900 AGRH 91301 558-A4
5900 AGRH 91301 557-J4
CARGO RD
- PHME 93043 552-C5
CARILLO RD
200 OJAI 93023 441-F7
200 OJAI 93023 451-F1
CARISSA CT
800 CMRL 93012 525-B2
CARL CT
3400 VeCo 91320 555-F1
CARLA DR
200 SIMI 93065 497-F3
CARLA LN
8400 LA 91304 529-G2
CARLISLE CT
100 OXN 93033 552-G6
CARLISLE RD
100 VeCo 90265 586-C3
100 VeCo 91361 586-B2
600 THO 90265 586-E3
600 THO 91361 586-E3
CARLMONT PL
2700 SIMI 93065 478-A7
2700 SIMI 93065 498-A1
CARLOS ST
11000 VEN 93004 472-J7
11000 VEN 93004 473-A7
CARLOTTA ST
4000 SIMI 93063 498-F2
CARLSBAD CT
1900 SIMI 93063 498-E2
CARLSBAD PL
1100 VEN 93003 492-B4
CARLSON CIR
22200 CanP 91303 529-J5
22200 CanP 91307 529-J5
CARLTON DR
3200 THO 91360 526-G2
CARLYLE ST
10000 VEN 93004 492-J3
CARMEL CT
200 OXN 93033 553-C4
CARMEL DR
1000 VeCo 93065 497-F4
CARMEL ST
8400 VEN 93004 492-G1
E CARMEL GREEN ST
100 PHME 93041 552-E2

W CARMEL GREEN ST
100 PHME 93041 552-D2
CARMELITA CT
100 OXN 93030 522-J5
CARMEN CT
2900 VeCo 91320 555-G1
CARMEN DR
1400 SIMI 93065 497-F3
23600 CMRL 93010 524-D4
N CARMEN DR
100 CMRL 93010 524-D2
CARMEN WY
1500 OXN 93030 522-E2
CARMENITA LN
7500 LA 91304 529-D4
CARMENTO DR
5300 VeCo 91377 557-H1
CARNATION AV
1500 VEN 93004 493-A2
CARNATION CT
23600 SIMI 93065 497-G5
CARNATION PL
300 OXN 93030 522-F3
CARNATION ST
- VEN 93004 493-A1
CARNE RD
500 VeCo 93023 442-D6
CARNEGIE CT
1800 OXN 93033 553-A2
CARNEGIE ST
100 VeCo 93030 492-J6
CARNELLON CT
200 SIMI 93065 497-D7
CAROB DR
- THO 91320 555-J1
CAROB ST
1900 OXN 93035 552-D1
CAROL DR
200 VEN 93003 491-H2
CAROLINE AV
6200 SIMI 93063 499-B3
CARPENTER ST
1400 THO 91362 527-A6
CARPENTERIA AV
7100 VeCo 93001 459-C4
CARR DR
- VEN 93001 471-C7
CARRIAGE PL
100 FILM 93015 456-A7
CARRIAGE SQ
- OXN 93030 522-G3
CARRIE PL
32500 WLKV 91361 557-B7
CARRIZO ST
200 VeCo 93023 441-D6
CARSON ST
1400 SIMI 93065 497-J3
CARSON WY
1500 VEN 93004 492-H3
CARTEGENA ST
100 CMRL 93010 524-D4
CARTPATH PL
- SIMI 93065 497-D5
CARTY DR
400 OXN 93030 522-G5
CARVER CT
2200 SIMI 93063 498-D2
CARVERSUMMIT DR
23600 VeCo 93001 459-D3
CARY CT
3400 VeCo 91320 525-F7
CARYL DR
23600 VeCo 93012 584-B1
CASA ST
11100 VEN 93004 472-J6
11200 VEN 93004 473-A6
CASABELLA CT
500 SPLA 93060 463-J7
CASA GRANDE RD
1000 VeCo 93063 499-C4
CASARIN AV
1500 SIMI 93065 497-J4
CASARIN ST
1700 SIMI 93065 497-J4
CASA SAN CARLOS
1300 OXN 93033 552-E2
CASCADE AV
100 THO 91362 557-C3
200 OXN 93033 552-G4
CASCADES CT
1900 OXN 93030 522-D3
CASE ST
4200 VEN 93003 491-J1
CASEY RD
100 MRPK 93021 476-D7
CASINO DR
2900 THO 91362 526-J2
2900 THO 91362 527-A2
CASITAS CT
1100 VEN 93004 492-J2
CASITAS PASS RD
Rt#-150
2000 VeCo 93001 450-D5
3500 VeCo 93001 460-B1
4000 VeCo 93001 366-G8
4000 VeCo 93001 459-G1
5800 VeCo - 366-G8
6100 VeCo 93013 366-G8
7100 StBC 93013 459-G1

CASITAS PASS RD
Rt#-192
6800 StBC 93013 459-A1
CASITAS VISTA RD
500 VeCo 93001 460-G4
7200 VeCo 93001 461-A5
CASMALIA CT
1300 SIMI 93065 497-H1
CASMALIA LN
800 VEN 93001 491-C1
CASNER WY
100 FILM 93015 456-B5
CASPER CT
4300 OXN 93033 553-A4
CASPER RD
900 MRPK 93021 476-E7
2900 VeCo 93033 583-B2
2900 VeCo 93042 583-C2
4700 VeCo 93033 553-B7
CASTANO DR
3500 CMRL 93010 524-G1
CASTANO ST
1600 CMRL 93010 524-G1
CASTELLO WY
4800 VeCo 91377 557-G2
CASTILLIAN AV
100 THO 91320 556-C1
CASTILLIAN CT
- THO 91320 556-C1
CASTILLO CIR
2600 THO 91360 526-C4
CASTLE CT
2200 SIMI 93063 499-B1
CASTLEBRIDGE CT
1600 THO 91362 527-E6
CASTLEHILL CT
1600 THO 91361 556-J5
CASTLEHILL DR
29300 AGRH 91301 558-A4
29300 AGRH 91301 557-J4
CASTLEMERE CT
1100 SIMI 93065 498-C4
N CASTLEMONT CT
2400 SIMI 93063 498-E1
CASTLE PEAK DR
6900 CanP 91307 529-C5
CASTLEVIEW CT
1500 THO 91361 556-J5
CASUAL CT
1900 SIMI 93065 498-A7
CATALINA DR
- VeCo 93010 494-D7
10500 VeCo 93022 451-B4
W CATALINA DR
- VeCo 93010 494-D7
10500 VeCo 93022 451-B5
N CATALINA ST
- VEN 93001 491-F2
S CATALINA ST
- VEN 93001 491-F2
CATAMARAN ST
900 OXN 93035 521-J7
CATANIA CT
23600 MRPK 93021 496-C5
CATARINA DR
30800 WLKV 91362 557-F4
CATHERWOOD CT
29000 AGRH 91301 558-A3
CATHY DR
100 VeCo 91320 555-G1
CATLIN CIR
800 SIMI 93065 497-H4
CATLIN CT
1100 SIMI 93065 497-H4
CATLIN ST
700 SIMI 93065 497-G4
CAVALIER AV
1000 SIMI 93065 498-C4
CAVENWAY LN
3000 THO 91361 557-C5
CAVIN RD
300 VeCo 93015 456-H7
CAWELTI RD
- VeCo 93012 524-C7
CAY CT
200 VeCo 91320 555-G1
CAYO GRANDE CT
500 THO 91320 525-E7
500 THO 91320 555-F1
N CAYTON AV
1600 SIMI 93065 497-E3
N CAYTON PL
1500 SIMI 93065 497-E3
CAYUGA DR
1500 SIMI 93065 497-F3
8300 VEN 93004 492-G4
CAYUSE LN
2200 VEN 93001 471-D6
CEANOTHUS LN
700 VeCo 93023 442-F5
CEANOTHUS PL
3900 CALB 91302 558-G7
CEBOLLA DR
23600 CMRL 93012 524-J3
CEDAR
5100 OXN 93033 552-G6
CEDAR CT
800 OXN 93033 552-F1
CEDAR DR
- CMRL 93010 524-D4

CEDAR PL
200 VEN 93001 491-C1
CEDAR ST
- VEN 93001 491-B1
800 VEN 93001 471-D6
1400 SPLA 93060 464-A2
6000 VeCo 93063 499-B4
E CEDAR ST
100 OXN 93033 552-G1
W CEDAR ST
200 OXN 93033 552-E1
CEDARBARK CT
6600 VeCo 91377 528-B7
CEDAR BLUFF DR
900 MRPK 93021 476-E7
CEDAR BRANCH CT
4400 MRPK 93021 496-E3
CEDARCLIFF CT
600 THO 91362 557-F1
CEDAR CREST CT
- THO 91320 556-C1
CEDARDALE RD
4300 MRPK 93021 496-C3
CEDARGLEN CT
4400 MRPK 93021 496-D3
CEDAR GROVE LN
4200 MRPK 93021 496-F3
CEDARHAVEN DR
5300 AGRH 91301 557-H5
CEDAR HEIGHTS DR
100 THO 91360 526-E3
CEDAR MEADOW CT
4300 MRPK 93021 496-D3
CEDARPINE LN
3900 MRPK 93021 496-F3
CEDAR POINT PL
300 THO 91362 557-G2
CEDAR RIDGE CT
2200 OXN 93030 522-D2
CEDAR SPRINGS ST
3900 MRPK 93021 496-C3
CEDARVALLEY DR
31200 WLKV 91362 557-E5
N CEDARWOOD CIR
2400 SIMI 93063 498-E1
CEDAR WOOD PL
2600 THO 91362 526-J3
E CELIA CT
3900 SIMI 93063 498-F2
CELSIUS AV
2200 OXN 93030 523-B5
CEMETERY RD
100 SPLA 93060 463-J6
CENTENNIAL AV
1000 CMRL 93010 524-E2
CENTER LN
400 SPLA 93060 463-H6
CENTER RD
- VeCo 93066 493-G3
900 VeCo 93066 494-B1
1000 VeCo 93066 474-B7
CENTER ST
3400 VeCo 93040 457-E4
E CENTER ST
- VEN 93001 491-B1
W CENTER ST
- VEN 93001 491-B1
CENTER COURT DR
2300 THO 91361 557-A6
CENTER SCHOOL RD
3100 VeCo 93010 494-B5
CENTINELLA ST
6100 SIMI 93063 499-B2
CENTRAL AV
100 FILM 93015 456-A5
100 VeCo 93030 492-J4
100 VeCo 93030 493-A4
1000 VeCo 93010 493-D7
2500 VeCo 93010 523-E1
3000 VEN 93003 491-G3
3600 CMRL 93010 523-E1
CENTRAL CAMPUS WY
100 VEN 93003 492-A2
CENTURY AV
2200 SIMI 93063 498-E2
CENTURY PL
2100 SIMI 93063 498-E2
CERES ST
100 SIMI 93065 497-F2
CERRO CREST DR
- VeCo 93010 494-B7
CERRO VISTA WY
1300 CMRL 93010 524-C1
1700 CMRL 93010 494-C7
CERVANTES CT
600 VeCo 91377 557-J2
CERVATO DR
1700 CMRL 93012 525-C1
1800 CMRL 93012 495-C7
CESAR CHAVEZ DR
3400 OXN 93030 522-J4
CHADWICK CT
3500 THO 91320 555-F3
CHADWICK PL
23600 VEN 93003 492-B7
CHAFFEE ST
6300 VEN 93003 492-C1
CHAGALL DR
6000 VeCo 93021 475-H6

N CHAIN DR
2400 SIMI 93065 497-F1
CHALET CIR
1000 THO 91362 527-B7
CHALLENGER CT
11900 MRPK 93021 496-C1
CHALLENGER PL
23600 OXN 93030 523-B6
CHALMERS PL
25800 LACo 91302 558-J3
CHALMETTE AV
1100 VEN 93003 492-B4
W CHALON CT
- THO 91320 556-A2
W CHALON ST
1900 THO 91320 556-A2
1900 THO 91320 555-J2
CHAMBERS LN
500 SIMI 93065 497-G1
CHAMBERSBURG RD
Rt#-23
300 FILM 93015 466-A2
300 VeCo 93015 466-A2
CHAMINADE AV
7400 LA 91304 529-F4
CHAMOIS ST
7100 VEN 93003 492-E5
CHAMPAGNE CT
30800 WLKV 91362 557-F5
CHAMPION DR
8500 VEN 93004 492-G4
CHAMPLAIN AV
1400 VEN 93004 492-H3
CHANCERY PL
2800 THO 91362 527-B3
CHANDLER AV
2400 SIMI 93065 497-H1
CHANDLER ST
2100 CMRL 93010 524-E2
CHANNEL DR
1800 VEN 93001 491-E3
2300 VEN 93003 491-F3
CHANNEL WY
900 SPLA 93060 473-J1
5200 OXN 93035 521-H6
CHANNELFORD RD
1900 THO 91361 557-A6
CHANNEL HEIGHTS CT
6200 VEN 93003 472-C6
CHANNEL ISLANDS BLVD
1800 OXN 93033 553-A2
2200 VeCo 93033 553-A2
E CHANNEL ISLANDS BLVD
100 OXN 93033 552-H2
100 PHME 93041 552-H2
300 PHME 93033 552-H2
300 PHME 93043 552-H2
W CHANNEL ISLANDS BLVD
100 OXN 93033 552-F2
100 PHME 93041 552-C2
300 PHME 93043 552-E2
500 PHME 93035 552-C2
3800 OXN 93035 552-A2
4500 VeCo 93035 552-A2
CHANTILLY CIR
23600 SIMI 93065 497-F7
CHANTRY CIR
700 SIMI 93065 497-H5
CHAPALA DR
1300 CMRL 93010 524-D4
CHAPALA ST
400 CMRL 93010 524-D4
CHAPARRAL CT
700 THO 91320 556-C2
CHAPARRAL RD
500 VeCo 93022 451-A6
3800 VeCo 93023 442-E4
9200 Chat 91311 499-E7
9200 LA 91304 499-E7
9200 WHil 91304 499-E7
CHAPARRAL ST
600 FILM 93015 455-J5
CHAPEL AV
1600 CMRL 93010 524-D3
CHAPEL DR
- VeCo 93012 554-E4
300 VEN 93003 491-J3
1300 CMRL 93010 524-D3
CHAPMAN PL
6700 MRPK 93021 476-H6
CHAPS CT
1700 SIMI 93063 499-C3
CHARI LN
6600 VeCo 93066 495-C3
CHARING CT
1800 SIMI 93063 499-D2
CHARING ST
6500 SIMI 93063 499-C2
CHARISMA CT
11200 VeCo 93012 496-C7
CHARLA CT
- THO 91320 556-B1
CHARLES ST
100 MRPK 93021 476-E7
5100 OXN 93033 552-G5
CHARLOTTE ST
3000 THO 91320 555-G2

STREET	Block	City	ZIP	Pg-Grid
N CHARRO AV	100	THO	91320	556-C1
CHARTER OAK DR	2000	CMRL	93010	494-E7
CHARTERWOOD CT	1300	THO	91362	556-J1
CHARTHOUSE CIR	3800	WLKV	91361	557-B6
CHASE PL	22700	LA	91304	529-H2
CHASE ST	8400	LA	91304	529-F2
CHATEAU CT	5900	VEN	93003	492-C2
CHATHAM CT	1000	THO	91360	526-H2
CHATLAKE DR	8700	LA	91304	529-E1
CHATSWORTH ST	22000	Chat	91311	499-J3
CHAUCER	9000	VeCo	93012	495-G4
	9000	VeCo	93021	495-G4
CHAUCER LN	6800	VEN	93003	492-E3
CHAUCER PL	2500	THO	91362	527-B3
CHAUTAUGUA DR	1300	SIMI	93063	499-C3
N CHEAM AV	2000	SIMI	93063	499-C2
CHEERFUL CT	200	SIMI	93065	497-J6
CHEESEBORO RD	5200	AGRH	91301	558-D3
	5300	Ago	91301	558-D3
	6300	VeCo	91377	528-C7
	6300	VeCo	91377	558-D3
CHEESEBORO CANYON RD	-	VeCo	91377	528-D5
	-	VeCo	91377	558-E1
	5800	Ago	91301	558-E5
CHEESEBRO RD	5000	AGRH	91301	558-C6
CHELAN CT	300	SIMI	93065	497-F6
CHELAN LN	1100	VEN	93004	492-H3
CHELMAS CT	23600	SIMI	93063	478-E6
CHELSEA CT	800	SIMI	93065	498-D5
	6300	AGRH	91301	557-H3
CHELSEY CT	2200	CMRL	93010	494-D7
CHELTERHAM CIR	800	THO	91360	526-G6
CHENAULT PL	2000	SIMI	93065	497-D2
CHERBOURG CT	30800	WLKV	91362	557-F5
CHEROKEE CIR	23600	SIMI	93063	479-A6
CHEROKEE CT	1300	CMRL	93010	524-F1
CHERRY AV	1200	SIMI	93065	498-B4
	1500	OXN	93033	553-B5
CHERRY ST	3700	VEN	93003	491-J3
CHERRY CREEK CIR	800	THO	91362	557-G1
CHERRYGROVE ST	12100	MRPK	93021	496-D4
CHERRY HILL RD	1600	SPLA	93060	464-A1
CHERRY HILLS CT	-	THO	91320	556-D1
CHERRY HILLS LN	400	THO	91320	556-D1
CHERRY RIDGE DR	5500	CMRL	93012	525-A2
CHERRY VALLEY CIR	4500	THO	91362	527-D6
CHERRYWOOD DR	3000	THO	91360	526-F2
CHERRYWOOD PL	900	OXN	93030	522-H3
CHERYL CT	2700	SIMI	93063	478-D7
CHESHIRE ST	8100	VEN	93004	492-F4
CHESSHIRE CT	100	VeCo	93023	441-E7
CHESTER WY	200	OXN	93033	552-G5
CHESTERFIELD DR	13600	MRPK	93021	496-F2
CHESTERTON ST	2000	SIMI	93065	498-A1
CHESTNUT LN	3300	VeCo	93012	495-J5
CHESTNUT PL	5800	CMRL	93012	495-B7
CHESTNUT ST	-	SIMI	93063	498-J1
	700	THO	91320	556-C2
N CHESTNUT ST	-	VEN	93001	491-C2
S CHESTNUT ST	-	VEN	93001	491-C2
CHESTNUT HILL CT	300	THO	91360	526-E7
CHESTNUT RIDGE ST	11600	MRPK	93021	496-B4
CHESWICK PL	1500	THO	91361	556-J6
CHEYENNE AV	-	THO	91362	557-A2
	11200	Chat	91311	499-J1
CHEYENNE CIR	9900	VEN	93004	492-J3
CHEYENNE ST	9800	VEN	93004	492-H3
CHEYENNE WY	900	OXN	93033	552-J3
N CHICKADEE LN	1100	VEN	93003	492-F3
S CHICKADEE LN	1300	VEN	93003	492-F4
CHICO CT	2300	VeCo	93035	552-B5
CHICO DR	9200	VEN	93004	492-G2
CHICO RD	100	OJAI	93023	441-G7
CHICORY LEAF PL	23600	SIMI	93063	498-D4
CHIEF CIR	3400	THO	91360	526-C2
CHILCO CT	1600	THO	91360	526-C5
CHINA FIR PL	23600	SIMI	93065	498-D4
CHINA FLATS RD	1000	VeCo	91361	556-F5
CHINOOK DR	600	VEN	93001	471-D6
CHIPMUNK CIR	7000	VEN	93003	492-F4
CHIPPENDALE AV	-	SIMI	93065	497-D6
CHIPPENHAM RD	10600	VeCo	93012	495-J7
	10600	VeCo	93012	496-A7
CHIPPEWA AV	2800	SIMI	93063	479-A7
CHIPPEWA LN	2300	VEN	93001	471-C6
CHIQUITA LN	2200	THO	91362	556-J2
	2200	THO	91362	557-A2
CHISHOLM TR	-	THO	91320	555-H2
CHISMAHOO RD	-	VeCo	-	366-G8
	23600	VeCo	93013	366-G8
CHISMAHOO FIRE RD	23600	VeCo	93001	460-C2
CHOCTAW AV	2900	SIMI	93063	479-A7
CHOCTAW LN	400	VEN	93001	471-C6
CHRISMAN AV	-	VEN	93001	491-E2
CHRISTIAN CT	5300	AGRH	91301	557-H5
CHRISTIAN BARRETT DR	13300	MRPK	93021	496-F3
CHRISTINA AV	5600	CMRL	93012	525-B6
CHRISTINA CT	1200	CMRL	93010	524-C2
CHRISTINE AV	1400	SIMI	93063	499-B2
CHRISTOPHER LN	100	VeCo	93023	441-E7
CHUKAR LN	200	VeCo	93010	494-F7
CHULA VISTA CT	4700	CMRL	93012	524-J2
CHUMASH AV	2900	SIMI	93063	478-J7
CHUMASH RD	12000	VeCo	93023	453-B1
CHUMASH TR	23600	VeCo	90265	625-G1
CHURCH DR	2000	VEN	93003	492-C5
CHURCH RD	400	OJAI	93023	441-F7
	1500	THO	91362	526-J5
CHURCH ST	500	VeCo	93040	457-F4
	700	VEN	93001	491-C1
N CHURCH ST	1400	SIMI	93065	498-D3
CHURCHILL DR	2100	OXN	93033	553-A2
	4000	THO	91320	555-E3
CHURCHMAN LN	10200	VeCo	93012	495-J7
CHURCHWOOD DR	5100	VeCo	91377	557-H1
N CICERO CT	3000	SIMI	93063	478-F7
CID ST	11300	VEN	93004	473-A7
CIELO VISTA CT	5800	CMRL	93012	495-B7
CIMA DE LAGO ST	9200	Chat	91311	499-E7
CIMARRON AV	1200	VEN	93004	492-J3
CIMMARON AV	2600	SIMI	93065	478-C7
	2600	SIMI	93065	498-C1
N CINCH RD	-	VeCo	91307	529-A4
CINCO DE MAYO	10200	VEN	93004	492-J3
	10200	VEN	93004	493-A2
CINDY AV	-	THO	91320	555-H1
CINDY PL	2600	PHME	93041	552-D2
CINNABAR PL	700	SIMI	93065	498-D5
CINNAMON OAK AV	-	VEN	93004	473-A6
CIPRES CT	1400	CMRL	93010	524-D2
CIPRIAN AV	1700	CMRL	93010	494-G7
	1700	CMRL	93010	524-G1
CIRCLE DR	2900	OXN	93033	552-H3
CIRCLE KNOLL DR	-	SIMI	93065	527-C1
CIRCLE VIEW DR	2700	SIMI	93063	478-D7
CIRCULO JARDIN	23600	CMRL	93010	523-F2
CIRO AV	2400	THO	91360	526-E3
CIRO CIR	300	THO	91360	526-E4
CIRRUS WY	7200	CanP	91307	529-F5
CISCO CT	2900	SIMI	93063	478-G7
CITADEL AV	300	VEN	93003	492-A3
CITATION WY	400	THO	91320	526-B7
CITRONELLA CT	2600	SIMI	93063	498-E1
CITRONELLA ST	3600	SIMI	93063	498-E1
CITRUS DR	4000	VeCo	93021	496-A3
	10700	VeCo	93021	495-J4
	11000	VEN	93004	472-J7
	11000	VEN	93004	473-A7
	11100	VeCo	93004	473-A7
CITRUS ST	300	SPLA	93060	464-C4
	3000	VeCo	93030	492-J7
CITRUS GROVE LN	-	OXN	93030	522-G3
CITRUS VIEW DR	4000	VeCo	93040	457-F4
CIVIC ARTS PLAZA DR	1600	THO	91362	556-J2
CIVIC CENTER WY	23600	THO	91360	526-E7
CLARA ST	6200	VeCo	93003	492-D5
E CLARA ST	100	OXN	93033	552-G5
	100	PHME	93041	552-E5
	800	PHME	93033	552-E5
W CLARA ST	100	OXN	93033	552-F5
	100	PHME	93041	552-E5
CLAREMONT DR	1500	OXN	93035	552-D1
CLAREMONT WY	-	VEN	93003	492-A2
CLARENDON PL	3300	THO	91360	526-H2
CLARETON DR	5100	AGRH	91301	558-B6
CLARIDGE CT	3500	SIMI	93063	478-G5
CLARINGTON DR	23900	LA	91304	529-D4
CLARITA CT	2500	THO	91362	527-C3
CLARK CT	200	OXN	93033	552-G6
CLARKE RANCH RD	-	LACo	90265	586-G6
CLARK RANCH RD	23600	VeCo	93023	451-E4
CLASSIC ROSE CT	1700	THO	91362	527-C6
CLAUDIA AV	1600	SIMI	93065	498-B3
CLAVEL AV	1200	VeCo	93004	493-B1
	1200	VEN	93004	493-B1
CLAVELE AV	4300	MRPK	93021	496-E3
CLAVELE CT	4300	MRPK	93021	496-E3
CLAY AV	1100	VEN	93004	492-J2
CLAY BLVD	23600	VeCo	93060	453-G2
CLAY CT	-	THO	91360	556-G1
CLAY ST	200	FILM	93015	456-A5
CLAYBOURNE CT	3500	THO	91320	555-F3
CLAYFORD AV	1100	THO	91361	557-A5
CLAYTON CT	1200	CMRL	93010	524-D1
CLAYTON WY	1400	SIMI	93065	497-H3
CLEAR DR	8600	VEN	93004	492-G4
CLEARCREEK CT	4400	MRPK	93021	496-B3
CLEARFIELD PL	2500	SIMI	93065	497-J1
CLEARFORD CT	3900	WLKV	91361	557-D6
CLEAR HAVEN DR	700	VeCo	91377	558-B1
CLEAR SKY PL	23600	SIMI	93065	497-E4
CLEAR SPRINGS RD	6400	VeCo	93063	499-C4
CLEARVIEW AV	2500	VEN	93001	491-F4
CLEARVIEW ST	100	THO	91360	526-F3
CLEARWATER DR	1700	CMRL	93012	495-B7
	1700	CMRL	93012	525-B1
CLEARWATER ST	2500	THO	91362	557-B3
CLEARWOOD RD	4300	MRPK	93021	496-C3
CLEE CT	5500	AGRH	91301	558-A5
CLEMENS AV	8000	LA	91304	529-F3
CLEMENS ST	6300	VEN	93003	492-C1
CLEMSON ST	5200	VEN	93003	492-B2
	14100	MRPK	93021	476-G6
CLEOMOORE AV	6500	CanP	91307	529-E6
CLERMONT CT	5400	WLKV	91362	557-F5
CLEVELAND CT	100	VEN	93003	492-E1
CLEVELAND DR	2800	OXN	93030	492-H7
	28600	AGRH	91301	558-B6
CLEVENGER PL	100	SIMI	93065	497-E7
	100	SIMI	93065	527-E1
CLIFF AV	700	VeCo	93015	455-G4
CLIFF DR	900	SPLA	93060	464-C3
CLIFFHOLLOW CT	500	SIMI	93065	527-C1
CLIFFROSE AV	4000	MRPK	93021	496-E4
CLIFFSIDE CIR	5300	VEN	93003	492-B1
CLIFFSIDE CT	-	LA	91304	529-E4
CLIFFWOOD DR	200	SIMI	93065	497-E2
CLIFTON CT	700	SIMI	93065	497-J5
CLINTON AV	1000	VEN	93004	492-H3
CLINTON CIR	3100	OXN	93033	552-H3
	8800	VEN	93004	492-G3
CLINTON CT	8800	VEN	93004	492-G3
CLINTON ST	3000	OXN	93033	552-H3
	11800	VeCo	93021	476-C2
CLIPPER DR	500	OXN	93033	552-G5
CLIPPERS CIR	2300	THO	91361	557-B6
CLOUD CT	1800	SIMI	93065	498-A2
CLOUDCREST CT	200	THO	91320	555-G2
CLOUDPEAK ST	-	THO	91360	526-F2
CLOVER DR	4300	OXN	93033	552-H5
CLOVER ST	2000	SIMI	93065	498-C2
E CLOVERDALE ST	4300	MRPK	93021	496-E3
N CLOVERDALE ST	12800	MRPK	93021	496-E3
CLOVERLEAF LN	-	SIMI	93063	498-H1
CLOVERLEAF ST	3900	THO	91362	527-C6
CLOVERLY ST	5900	VEN	93003	492-C2
CLOVERWOOD AV	100	THO	91320	555-J2
CLOW RD	200	VeCo	93060	473-G2
S CLOW RD	100	VeCo	93060	473-H2
CLOYNE ST	2900	OXN	93033	552-H3
CLUB CT	-	CMRL	93010	493-H7
CLUBHOUSE DR	-	LACo	90265	586-H7
	200	SIMI	93065	497-E2
N CLUBHOUSE DR	3900	VeCo	93066	493-F2
CLUB VIEW DR	4500	THO	91362	527-D6
CLYDESDALE CIR	4100	THO	91362	527-C6
CMWD TANK RD	-	VeCo	93023	442-G7
	-	VeCo	93023	452-G1
COACHMAN CIR	4200	THO	91362	527-D7
COACHMAN DR	1700	CMRL	93012	495-A7
	1700	CMRL	93012	525-A1
COALFAX CT	2200	THO	91362	527-A4
COASTAL OAK DR	23600	SIMI	93063	498-D4
	23600	SIMI	93065	498-D4
COATI PL	7300	VEN	93003	492-F5
COATS ST	-	PHME	93041	552-E4
	-	PHME	93043	552-E4
COBB CIR	3000	SIMI	93065	498-D4
COBBLECREEK CT	2500	THO	91362	527-D3
COBBLER HILL CT	700	SIMI	93065	498-D5
COBBLESTONE DR	6000	AGRH	91301	557-J3
	6000	VEN	93003	492-C1
COCHE CANYON	23600	VeCo	93001	451-G7
	23600	VeCo	93001	461-G1
COCHISE ST	5400	SIMI	93063	478-J7
COCHRAN ST	-	SIMI	93065	497-G1
	200	SIMI	93065	477-E7
	1700	SIMI	93065	498-B1
	3100	SIMI	93063	498-D1
	5400	SIMI	93063	499-A1
COCOS CT	4000	VEN	93003	491-J3
CODY AV	1600	SIMI	93063	499-C3
COE ST	700	CMRL	93010	524-C2
COHASSET ST	22000	CanP	91303	529-J4
	22600	CanP	91307	529-G4
	23200	LA	91304	529-F4
COLBY CIR	300	VEN	93003	492-A3
	1000	THO	91362	526-J6
COLCHESTER PL	1500	VeCo	91377	527-H6
COLDBROOK PL	600	SIMI	93065	497-H5
COLD SPRINGS ST	26800	CALB	91301	558-G7
COLD STREAM CT	2000	OXN	93030	522-E3
COLE AV	3200	VeCo	93063	478-E6
COLEMAN CT	2000	SIMI	93063	499-A2
COLETTE CT	3100	SIMI	93063	478-D6
COLGATE DR	1700	THO	91360	526-G5
COLGATE ST	300	SPLA	93060	463-J7
	300	SPLA	93060	464-A7
COLIBRI CT	4200	MRPK	93021	496-E3
COLINA RD	23600	VeCo	93063	499-F3
COLINA VISTA	400	VEN	93003	472-C6
	400	VEN	93003	492-D1
COLINA VISTA ST	28700	AGRH	91301	558-B3
COLISEUM ST	4100	VEN	93003	491-J2
COLLEEN AV	1700	SIMI	93063	498-J3
COLLEGE DR	-	VEN	93003	491-J3
COLLEGE ST	2400	SIMI	93065	498-B5
COLLEGE HEIGHTS DR	6400	MRPK	93021	476-G6
COLLEGE VIEW AV	6400	MRPK	93021	477-A6
COLLEGIATE CIR	15200	MRPK	93021	476-J5
COLLIER CT	2200	SIMI	93065	498-A2
COLLINGSWOOD CT	1700	THO	91362	527-E6
COLLINGSWOOD PL	4800	THO	91362	527-E6
COLLINS DR	6400	MRPK	93021	476-J6
	6500	MRPK	93021	477-A5
E COLLINS ST	200	VeCo	93030	492-H7
	200	VeCo	93030	522-J1
	700	VeCo	93030	523-A1
	1000	OXN	93030	523-A1
W COLLINS ST	100	OXN	93030	492-H7
COLODNY DR	5200	AGRH	91301	558-D5
COLOMA CIR	5500	SIMI	93063	479-A7
COLONETT PL	3900	THO	91320	555-E1
COLONIA AV	2400	OXN	93030	522-H1
	2500	VeCo	93030	522-H1
	2700	VeCo	93030	492-H7
COLONIA PL	1700	CMRL	93010	524-D3
COLONIA RD	1300	OXN	93030	522-G5
COLONY DR	4600	CMRL	93012	524-J2
	5100	CMRL	93012	525-A2
COLORADO DR	8500	VEN	93004	492-H4
COLT LN	100	VeCo	91361	556-G3
E COLT LN	-	VeCo	91307	528-J4
	-	VeCo	91307	529-A4
COLT ST	4800	VEN	93003	492-B6
COLTON ST	7700	VEN	93004	492-F2
	23600	VEN	93003	492-E2
COLUMBIA AV	6500	MRPK	93021	476-H6
COLUMBIA CT	800	OXN	93033	552-H4
COLUMBIA DR	700	OXN	93033	552-H4
COLUMBIA PL	100	OXN	93033	552-H4
COLUMBIA RD	-	THO	91360	526-F5
COLUMBINE CT	2800	THO	91360	526-D3
COLUMBUS PL	5100	OXN	93033	552-G5
COLUSA AV	300	VEN	93004	472-F7
	300	VEN	93004	492-F1
COMANCHE AV	2700	THO	91362	557-A2
COMANCHE CT	900	CMRL	93010	524-C2
	2500	VEN	93001	471-D5
COMBES AV	500	THO	91360	526-G7
COMBS RD	1100	VeCo	91320	556-B2
	1200	THO	91320	556-B2
COMET AV	600	SIMI	93065	498-C5
COMMERCE AV	23600	MRPK	93021	496-C1
COMMERCIAL AV	100	OXN	93030	522-H6
	1200	OXN	93030	552-H1
COMMUNITY ST	23200	LA	91304	529-E2
COMSTOCK DR	-	VEN	93001	471-C6
COMSTOCK PL	1200	THO	91320	555-G5
CONCERTO DR	200	VeCo	91377	557-G2
N CONCHO LN	-	VeCo	91307	529-B3
CONCORD AV	700	VEN	93004	492-H2
CONCORD CT	3700	OXN	93033	552-J3
E CONCORD CT	1900	SIMI	93065	498-A5
CONCORD DR	2900	OXN	93033	552-J3
CONCORD WY	4400	OXN	93033	552-J4
CONDOR CT	300	FILM	93015	455-H6
	6300	VEN	93003	492-D5
CONDOR DR	5700	MRPK	93021	476-H7
CONEFLOWER ST	2800	THO	91360	526-D3
CONEJO BLVD	-	THO	91360	556-F1
CONEJO DR	-	VeCo	93012	554-E3
CONEJO CANYON CT	2600	THO	91362	527-B4
CONEJO CENTER DR	23600	THO	91320	525-H5
CONEJO MESA ST	4000	MRPK	93021	496-E4
CONEJO RIDGE AV	200	THO	91361	556-J3
CONEJO SCHOOL RD	100	THO	91361	556-J2
	100	THO	91362	556-J2
	200	THO	91362	557-A1
CONEJO VIEW DR	28500	AGRH	91301	558-B5
CONESTOGA CIR	800	THO	91320	555-G6
CONGRESSIONAL RD	600	SIMI	93065	497-C6
CONIFER CIR	5600	VeCo	91377	557-J2
CONIFER ST	5700	VeCo	91377	557-J2
	5700	VeCo	91377	558-A2
N CONNELL AV	2100	SIMI	93063	499-A2
CONSTITUTION AV	400	CMRL	93012	524-F5
CONSUELO AV	3600	THO	91360	526-F1
CONTAINER WY	-	PHME	93043	552-C6
CONTINENTAL CT	300	THO	91320	555-G3
CONTRA COSTA AV	200	VEN	93004	492-F1
	200	VEN	93004	472-F7
CONVAIR ST	400	CMRL	93010	523-J4
CONVERSE RD	23600	VeCo	93060	473-J2
	23600	VeCo	93060	474-A2
CONWAY AV	1200	VEN	93004	492-H3
COOK CIR	2100	THO	91360	526-F4
COOK DR	100	FILM	93015	456-B5
COOLHAVEN CT	4500	WLKV	91361	557-D6
COOLIDGE ST	7200	VEN	93003	492-E2
N COOLWATER RD	-	VeCo	91307	529-A3
	-	WHil	91304	529-A3
COOPER RD	100	OXN	93030	522-H5
COOPER CANYON RD	-	VeCo	93023	366-H7
	-	VeCo	93023	450-G1
COOSA ST	9600	VEN	93004	492-H3
COPA DE ORO CT	1600	THO	91362	556-J1
COPLAND CIR	-	VEN	93003	492-A4
	-	VeCo	93003	492-A4
COPLAND DR	4500	VEN	93003	492-A7
E COPLEY ST	3100	SIMI	93063	498-D2
N COPLEY ST	2100	SIMI	93063	498-D2
	2100	SIMI	93065	498-D2
COPPERFIELD ST	3500	SIMI	93063	498-D1
COPPERTREE CT	23600	SIMI	93065	498-B5
CORAL LN	1800	OXN	93033	552-J2
	1800	OXN	93033	553-A2
CORAL ST	1100	VEN	93001	491-F5
CORAL WY	4900	OXN	93035	521-J7
	4900	OXN	93035	551-J1
CORALBELL LN	22200	WdHl	91367	529-J7
CORALBERRY CT	11500	MRPK	93021	496-B2
CORALCREST CT	12600	MRPK	93021	496-D4
CORAL PINK CIR	6100	WdHl	91367	529-J7
CORAL REEF LN	11800	VeCo	90265	625-F5
CORAL TREE LN	5300	VeCo	91377	527-G7
CORBETT LN	1100	SIMI	93065	497-H4
CORBINA WY	5000	OXN	93035	551-J1
	5000	OXN	93035	552-A1
CORBY AV	3000	CMRL	93010	524-F1
	3400	CMRL	93010	494-G7
CORD AV	-	THO	91362	557-B4
CORDERO AV	2100	SIMI	93065	497-J2
	2100	SIMI	93065	498-A2
CORDOVA CT	3500	THO	91320	525-F7
	3500	VeCo	91320	525-F7
CORDOVA ST	100	OXN	93030	523-A5
	500	VeCo	93010	524-C1
CORDUA CT	3000	SIMI	93063	478-E7
CORIE LN	6700	LACo	91307	529-D6
CORINNE DR	-	THO	91320	555-J1
CORINTH WEIGH	1900	OXN	93035	552-B1
CORLSON AV	2200	SIMI	93063	498-E2
CORLSON PL	2200	SIMI	93063	498-E2
CORNELL CIR	6400	MRPK	93021	476-H6
CORNELL DR	500	SPLA	93060	473-J1
	500	SPLA	93060	474-A1
CORNELL PL	300	VEN	93003	492-A3
CORNELL RD	3900	Ago	91301	558-A7
	4400	AGRH	91301	558-A6
CORNELL WY	4600	AGRH	91301	558-A6
CORNETT AV	300	MRPK	93021	496-E1
CORNING ST	3300	THO	91320	555-G3
CORNWALL DR	600	OXN	93035	522-D6
CORNWALL LN	1100	VEN	93001	491-E4
N CORONA CIR	500	VEN	93003	472-E7
CORONA ST	3300	CMRL	93010	524-G1
CORONADO CIR	3700	THO	91320	555-E1
CORONADO CT	1600	CMRL	93010	524-D3
CORONADO DR	100	FILM	93015	456-C6
CORONADO PL	500	OXN	93030	522-E4
CORONADO ST	-	VEN	93001	491-F3
CORPORATE CENTER DR	2000	THO	91320	525-J6
CORPORATION ST	600	SPLA	93060	473-J1
CORPUS CHRISTI AV	2800	SIMI	93063	478-H6
N CORRAL RD	-	VeCo	91307	528-H4
CORRIENTE CT	1100	VeCo	93010	494-C7
CORRINE HILL CT	200	THO	91320	556-D2
CORSA AV	5700	WLKV	91362	557-F4
CORSICANA DR	-	VeCo	93030	492-J7
	600	VeCo	93030	522-J1
	700	VeCo	93030	523-A1
CORTA ST	300	VeCo	93023	451-D2
CORTE AGUACATE	600	CMRL	93010	524-B1
CORTE AMIGOS	2600	CMRL	93010	494-F7
CORTE ANTIGUA	6000	CMRL	93012	525-B5
CORTE AUGUSTA	800	CMRL	93010	523-H1
CORTE AZAL	800	CMRL	93010	524-C1
CORTE BARATA	6100	CMRL	93012	525-C5
CORTE BARROSO	900	CMRL	93010	523-G2
CORTE BAYA VISTA	23600	OXN	93030	523-C7
CORTE BREVE	1400	THO	91360	526-H1
CORTE CABALLOS	2700	CMRL	93010	494-F7
CORTE CAMPANERO	1200	CMRL	93010	493-J6
CORTE CAMPINA	6300	CMRL	93012	525-C5
CORTE CANCION	3600	THO	91360	526-J1
CORTE CASTANO	600	CMRL	93010	524-B1
CORTE CERRITOS	-	CMRL	93010	524-B1
CORTE CIMA	1600	THO	91360	526-J1
CORTE COLINA	600	CMRL	93010	524-B1
CORTE CORRIDA	300	CMRL	93010	523-J1
	300	VeCo	93010	523-J1
CORTE DE ACERO	3600	THO	91360	526-J2
CORTE DE CHARCO	6500	VEN	93003	472-D7
CORTE DE ENCINITAS	1500	CMRL	93010	493-H6
CORTE DE LOS REYES	3600	THO	91360	526-H1
CORTE DEL REY	3600	THO	91360	526-J1
CORTE DE PRIMAVERA	1200	THO	91360	526-H1
CORTE DE QUINTERO	600	CMRL	93010	493-J5
CORTE DESCANSO	1000	SPLA	93060	473-E1
CORTE DE TAJO	1000	THO	91360	526-H1
CORTE DOMINICA	1400	CMRL	93010	523-J1
CORTE ENTRADA	1300	THO	91360	526-H1
CORTE FRESCA	23600	CMRL	93012	524-H3
CORTE FRONDOSA	600	CMRL	93010	523-H1
CORTE GOLONDRINA	600	CMRL	93010	524-B1
CORTE GRANADA	1000	SPLA	93060	473-E1
CORTE JANA	23600	OXN	93030	523-C7
CORTE LA BRISA	15500	SPLA	93060	463-H7
CORTE LA CIENAGA	600	CMRL	93010	523-H2
CORTE LAS HOLAS	23600	OXN	93030	523-B4
CORTE LEJOS	23600	CMRL	93010	524-C4
CORTE LINDA	200	SPLA	93060	473-E1
CORTE LUCINDA	6100	CMRL	93012	525-C5
CORTE MALPASO	3200	CMRL	93012	524-G2
CORTE MIRA FLORES	1000	SPLA	93060	463-H7
	1000	SPLA	93060	473-H1
CORTE OLIVAS	23600	CMRL	93012	524-J1
CORTE OLMO	2600	CMRL	93010	494-E7
CORTE PALOMA	1000	SPLA	93060	473-E1
CORTE PASTORAL	600	CMRL	93010	523-H2
CORTE PICADO	6000	CMRL	93012	525-B5
CORTE PICO VERDE	5300	CMRL	93012	525-A2
CORTE PINATA	6900	CMRL	93012	495-D7
CORTE PRIMAVERA	23600	OXN	93030	523-C6
CORTE RIVIERA	23600	CMRL	93010	523-H2
CORTE ROSELINDA	700	CMRL	93010	524-C1
CORTE SAFIRO	800	CMRL	93012	525-B5
CORTE TELA	2600	CMRL	93010	494-E7
CORTE TULAROSA	1000	CMRL	93010	523-G1
CORTE TUNITAS	700	CMRL	93012	525-C5
CORTE VALDEZ	23600	OXN	93030	523-C7
CORTE VERANO	1400	THO	91360	526-H1
CORTE VINA	700	CMRL	93010	524-C1
CORTE VISTORA	23600	CMRL	93012	524-J2
CORTEZ CIR	-	CMRL	93012	525-A4
CORTEZ ST	2400	VeCo	93030	522-H1
	3000	VeCo	93030	492-J7
	3500	VeCo	93030	493-A7
CORTO DR	6000	VeCo	93063	499-B3
CORTO ST	300	SPLA	93060	464-C6
	2700	SIMI	93065	498-C3
	14600	SIMI	93063	498-D4
CORTO TR	1900	OXN	93030	522-H3
CORVALLIS CT	1100	VEN	93004	492-J2
CORVETTE ST	400	PHME	93041	552-C1
CORVUS DR	-	VeCo	93041	583-G2
CORY ST	6200	SIMI	93063	499-B2
COSMOS CT	400	THO	91360	526-D3
COSTA DE ORO	4400	OXN	93035	552-A1
COSTA MESA ST	7800	VEN	93004	492-F1
COTA CIR	3000	OXN	93033	552-J3
COTHARIN RD	9100	VeCo	90265	585-E6
	11700	VeCo	90265	625-E1
COTTAGE CT	1100	VEN	93001	491-D2
COTTAGE GROVE AV	100	CMRL	93012	524-H4
COTTONTAIL AV	-	SIMI	93063	498-J1
COTTONTAIL RD	23600	MRPK	93021	496-C2
COTTONTAIL ST	7000	VEN	93003	492-E5
COTTONWOOD AV	900	VeCo	93023	451-C1
COTTONWOOD CT	2800	THO	91320	555-G3
COTTONWOOD LN	1400	FILM	93015	455-H7
COTTONWOOD GROVE TR	3800	CALB	91301	558-G7
COULTER CT	1000	SIMI	93065	498-C4
COUNTRY CT	600	FILM	93015	455-J4
	600	FILM	93015	456-A5
COUNTRY DR	500	VeCo	93023	451-D2
COUNTRY LN	2600	WLKV	91361	557-A7
	3000	SIMI	93063	478-D7
	3000	VeCo	93063	478-D7
COUNTRY PL	1800	VeCo	93023	451-C3
COUNTRY CLUB DR	400	OJAI	93023	441-G7
	400	SIMI	93065	497-D5
	500	OJAI	93023	451-G1
	900	VeCo	93023	451-G1
	16800	VeCo	93065	497-E5
COUNTRY CLUB RD	400	OJAI	93023	451-G1
	1800	THO	91360	526-G5
COUNTRY CREEK CT	11500	MRPK	93021	496-B3
COUNTRY CREEK LN	-	CALB	91302	558-H7
COUNTRY GLEN RD	27200	AGRH	91301	558-E7
COUNTRY HAVEN CIR	3400	THO	91362	527-D3
COUNTRY HILL RD	4100	MRPK	93021	496-B3
COUNTRY HOME CT	-	THO	91362	527-C2
COUNTRY MEADOW ST	4200	MRPK	93021	496-E3
COUNTRY OAKS LN	1700	THO	91362	526-J6
COUNTRY PARK CT	2300	THO	91362	527-A3
COUNTRY RANCH RD	1300	LACo	91361	586-H2
	1300	THO	91361	586-H2
COUNTRYSIDE RD	300	VeCo	91377	558-A1
COUNTRY SPRINGS CT	11600	MRPK	93021	496-B2
COUNTRY VALLEY RD	100	THO	91362	557-E1
COUNTRY VIEW CT	100	SPLA	93060	473-H1
COUNTRY VIEW PL	500	VeCo	93010	494-A6
COUNTRY VISTA ST	-	THO	91362	527-B2
COUNTRY WIDE WY	400	SIMI	93065	477-G7
	400	SIMI	93065	497-G1
	400	VeCo	93065	477-G7
COUNTRYWOOD DR	11300	MRPK	93021	496-B3
COUNTY LINE RD	23200	Chat	91311	499-F6
COUNTY OAK RD	6000	WdHl	91367	529-C7
	6200	CanP	91307	529-C7
COUNTY SQUARE DR	500	VEN	93003	492-C3
COURT AV	200	VEN	93003	491-J2
COURT ST	3000	SIMI	93065	498-D3
COURTLAND ST	5100	OXN	93033	552-G6
COURTNEY CT	600	THO	91320	525-H7
COURTNEY LN	11700	MRPK	93021	496-C2
COURTYARD DR	100	PHME	93041	552-F6
	100	PHME	93033	552-F6

VENTURA COUNTY STREET INDEX - With ZIP Codes

STREET / Block	City	ZIP	Pg-Grid
COURTYARD WY			
800	PHME	93041	552-F6
COVE DR			
400	PHME	93041	552-C1
COVE ST			
900	VEN	93001	491-F4
COVE CREEK CT			
-	THO	91362	527-C2
COVELLO ST			
22000	CanP	91303	529-J4
22400	CanP	91307	529-G4
23200	LA	91304	529-F4
COVENT GARDEN CT			
2400	THO	91362	527-B4
COVENTRY AV			
1100	VEN	93004	492-G3
COVENTRY CT			
1900	THO	91362	526-J5
COVENTRY DR			
400	THO	91360	526-F6
COVEWOOD ST			
1100	VeCo	91377	527-H7
COVINGTON AV			
1500	THO	91361	556-J6
23600	SIMI	93065	498-A5
E COVINGTON AV			
1900	SIMI	93065	498-A5
COWBOY CT			
1500	SIMI	93063	499-D3
COWBOY ST			
6700	SIMI	93063	499-D3
COWGIRL CT			
6700	SIMI	93063	499-D3
COWPER AV			
7800	LA	91304	529-E3
COYOTE CANYON RD			
6800	VeCo	93066	474-J3
6800	VeCo	93066	475-A5
COYOTE WELLS CIR			
-	THO	91362	527-E6
CRABAPPLE CT			
24500	CanP	91307	529-D5
CRAFTS CT			
1900	SIMI	93065	498-A4
CRAGGY VIEW ST			
22200	Chat	91311	499-J4
CRAGGYVIEW ST			
22000	Chat	91311	499-J4
CRAGMONT CT			
2300	SIMI	93065	498-A1
CRAIG DR			
100	SPLA	93060	464-A6
2000	OXN	93030	522-G2
CRAIG ST			
400	VeCo	93022	451-B6
CRANBERRY DR			
2400	OXN	93030	522-G1
CRANBROOK ST			
1400	CMRL	93010	494-D7
CRANE ST			
6000	VEN	93003	492-C4
CRANMONT CT			
800	SIMI	93065	527-C1
CRAPE MYRTLE CT			
6100	WdHI	91367	529-J7
CRATER DR			
1800	VEN	93004	492-G4
CRATER ST			
1400	SIMI	93063	498-D3
CRAWFORD ST			
1300	OXN	93030	522-J6
CRAZY HORSE DR			
3000	SIMI	93063	479-A6
CREE LN			
2400	VEN	93001	471-C6
CREEK LN			
9700	VeCo	93001	461-B1
9700	VeCo	93022	461-B1
CREEK RD			
-	VeCo	93012	554-E1
9600	VeCo	93001	461-B1
10200	VeCo	93001	451-C6
10200	VeCo	93022	451-C6
10200	VeCo	93022	461-B1
10400	VeCo	93023	451-H1
12000	OJAI	93023	451-H1
CREEKMONT CT			
500	VEN	93003	472-D7
CREEKRIDGE AV			
-	SIMI	93065	497-E2
CREEKSIDE CIR			
800	CMRL	93012	525-A2
CREEKSIDE RD			
5000	CMRL	93012	524-J2
5000	CMRL	93012	525-A2
CREEKSIDE WY			
100	OJAI	93023	441-F7
CREEKWOOD ST			
2100	THO	91361	557-A6
N CREIGHTON CIR			
6400	MRPK	93021	476-H6
CREMONA WY			
600	VeCo	91377	557-H2
CRESCENT ST			
6600	VEN	93003	492-E6
CRESCENT WY			
2800	THO	91362	557-A2
CRESCENT MEADOW CT			
4300	MRPK	93021	496-D3
CRESPI DR			
100	FILM	93015	456-C6
1600	OXN	93033	552-J3
CRESPI LN			
2100	THO	91361	557-A5
CREST CT			
1400	OXN	93035	552-B1
23600	SIMI	93065	497-G7
CRESTA CT			
3800	THO	91360	526-F1
CRESTHAVEN CT			
29400	AGRH	91301	557-J3
CRESTHAVEN DR			
3600	THO	91362	527-D7
3600	THO	91362	557-C1
CRESTHILL DR			
400	VeCo	91377	558-A1
CRESTLAKE AV			
1200	VEN	93004	492-H3
CRESTLINE DR			
13500	VeCo	93012	496-F5
CRESTMONT DR			
2100	VEN	93003	492-D5
CRESTON LN			
5100	VeCo	93066	495-A1
CRESTONE CT			
5500	VEN	93003	472-B7
CRESTRIDGE DR			
400	VeCo	91377	558-A1
CRESTVIEW AV			
-	CMRL	93010	524-A1
-	VeCo	93010	524-A1
200	CMRL	93010	523-G2
200	VeCo	93010	523-J1
CRESTVIEW CIR			
3900	THO	91362	557-C1
CRESTVIEW DR			
300	OJAI	93023	441-H7
700	SPLA	93060	464-B4
CRESTWOOD AV			
300	VEN	93003	492-B1
CRESTWOOD CT			
400	THO	91320	555-F3
CRICKETFIELD CT			
400	VeCo	91361	556-G6
N CRIMEA ST			
100	VEN	93001	491-D1
S CRIMEA ST			
-	VEN	93001	491-D2
CRIMEA ST FIRE RD			
300	VeCo	93001	471-D7
300	VEN	93001	471-D7
300	VEN	93001	491-D1
CRINKLAW LN			
5600	SIMI	93063	499-A3
5600	VeCo	93063	499-A3
CRISWELL ST			
22200	CanP	91303	529-J6
22400	CanP	91307	529-H6
N CROCKER AV			
-	VEN	93004	492-F1
S CROCKER AV			
-	VEN	93004	492-F2
CROCKER ST			
1300	SIMI	93065	497-J3
CROMBIE CT			
-	VeCo	91361	556-D7
CROMWELL PL			
1500	THO	91361	556-H6
CROOKED PALM RD			
4200	VeCo	93001	471-C2
CROOKED TRAIL PL			
1700	THO	91362	527-F6
CROSBY AV			
700	SIMI	93065	498-B5
CROSS AV			
100	OXN	93030	522-G1
CROSS ST			
6900	VeCo	93003	492-D2
7000	VEN	93003	492-D2
CROSS BRIDGE PL			
1600	THO	91362	526-J7
CROSS CREEK AV			
2000	SIMI	93063	498-J2
CROSSJACK ST			
400	PHME	93041	552-B2
CROSSLAND ST			
3200	THO	91362	527-D3
CROSSRIDGE CT			
3800	THO	91360	526-G1
CROTHERS CT			
8000	LA	91304	529-E3
CROWLEY AV			
6300	VEN	93003	492-D5
CROWN CT			
23600	SIMI	93065	497-G7
W CROWN ST			
-	VeCo	93023	451-B4
CROWNE OAK LN			
23600	SIMI	93065	497-A1
CROWNFIELD CT			
4200	WLKV	91361	557-D6
CROWN HAVEN CT			
3700	THO	91320	555-E2
CROWNHILL CT			
6200	VEN	93003	472-C6
CROWN HILL DR			
800	VeCo	93063	499-B4
CROWN POINT CT			
2300	OXN	93030	522-C2
CROWN RIDGE CT			
1500	THO	91362	527-F6
CROWN VIEW CT			
2300	THO	91362	527-A7
E CROYDON AV			
4100	CMRL	93010	494-H7
N CROYDON AV			
1800	CMRL	93010	494-H7
CRUSOE CIR			
800	THO	91362	526-J7
CRUZERO ST			
200	VeCo	93023	451-C2
CRYSTAL CIR			
3300	SIMI	93063	478-D6
CRYSTAL PL			
8000	VEN	93004	492-F3
CRYSTAL DOWNS CT			
2300	OXN	93030	522-D2
CRYSTAL RANCH RD			
12400	MRPK	93021	496-D3
CRYSTAL VIEW CIR			
1600	THO	91320	556-A2
CTL II RD			
23600	VeCo	93063	498-H7
CTL III RD			
23600	VeCo	93063	528-J1
23600	VeCo	93063	529-A1
CTL IV RD			
23600	VeCo	91307	528-G2
23600	VeCo	93063	528-G2
CUESTA DEL MAR DR			
200	OXN	93033	552-F6
CULLEN CT			
3600	THO	91320	555-F4
CULVER LN			
100	THO	91320	556-B2
100	VeCo	91320	556-B2
CULVIEW CT			
23600	SIMI	93065	497-F7
E CUMBERLAND CT			
3300	THO	91362	557-C2
W CUMBERLAND CT			
3000	THO	91362	557-B2
CUMMINGS RD			
300	VeCo	93060	473-E1
CUMULUS CT			
1900	THO	91362	526-J1
CUNNINGHAM RD			
-	THO	91362	556-H1
CURLEW PL			
6300	VEN	93003	492-D5
CURLEW WY			
3800	OXN	93035	552-B3
CURRAN ST			
2000	OXN	93033	553-A4
CURRANT AV			
1200	SIMI	93065	498-B4
E CURRIER AV			
2700	SIMI	93065	498-C4
N CURRIER AV			
1000	SIMI	93065	498-C4
CURT DR			
3100	CMRL	93010	524-F2
CUSHMAN CT			
2000	SIMI	93063	499-A2
CUTLER ST			
2000	SIMI	93065	498-A4
CUTTER DR			
900	OXN	93035	522-D7
CUTTING RD			
400	PHME	93041	552-C3
400	PHME	93043	552-C3
CUYAMA RD			
400	OJAI	93023	441-F7
400	VeCo	93023	441-F7
CYNTHIA ST			
6200	SIMI	93063	499-B2
CYPRESS LN			
5000	VeCo	93001	471-C1
CYPRESS PL			
1300	THO	91360	526-H2
6000	VeCo	93063	499-B4
CYPRESS RD			
5100	OXN	93033	552-H6
CYPRESS ST			
600	THO	91320	556-C1
1500	OXN	93030	552-H1
CYPRESS POINT LN			
1100	VEN	93003	492-C4

D

STREET / Block	City	ZIP	Pg-Grid
D ST			
-	FILM	93015	455-H6
-	VeCo	93015	455-H6
100	OXN	93030	522-G6
1200	OXN	93033	522-G7
1500	OXN	93033	552-G1
N D ST			
100	OXN	93030	522-G5
DAFFODIL AV			
1500	VEN	93004	493-A2
DAFFODIL CT			
2700	OXN	93030	522-D4
23600	SIMI	93065	497-G5
DAFFODIL WY			
500	OXN	93030	522-D4
DAHL AV			
400	PHME	93041	552-F5
DAHLIA ST			
900	OXN	93030	522-E3
DAHLIA WY			
100	VEN	93004	473-A7
DAILY DR			
100	CMRL	93010	524-B3
E DAILY DR			
-	CMRL	93010	524-B3
W DAILY DR			
-	CMRL	93010	524-A3
300	CMRL	93010	523-J3
DAISY CT			
4400	MRPK	93021	496-B3
DAISY DR			
10500	VEN	93004	493-A2
DAISY ST			
-	SIMI	93063	499-A2
DAKIN AV			
1400	SIMI	93065	497-J4
DAKOTA DR			
-	VEN	93001	471-C5
DALAWAY DR			
3800	MRPK	93021	496-A4
3800	VeCo	93021	496-A4
DALBY DR			
-	VeCo	91361	556-D7
DALE AV			
100	THO	91320	555-E2
N DALE AV			
10400	VeCo	93022	451-C7
DALE CT			
100	SPLA	93060	463-J6
22700	Chat	91311	499-H5
DALECREST AV			
6100	WdHI	91367	529-F7
DALENHURST PL			
2700	SIMI	93065	478-A7
2700	SIMI	93065	498-A1
DALEWOOD CIR			
4200	THO	91320	555-D4
DALHART AV			
2700	SIMI	93063	478-H6
DALLAS DR			
500	THO	91360	526-G7
500	THO	91360	556-G1
1000	OXN	93033	552-J2
DALLAS ST			
2600	OXN	93033	552-J3
DALTON ST			
-	VEN	93003	491-G2
DALY RD			
700	OJAI	93023	441-J5
DAMIANA DR			
100	THO	91320	555-E1
DAMON ST			
5700	SIMI	93063	499-A3
DANA AV			
6200	SIMI	93063	499-C3
DANA DR			
300	FILM	93015	456-C6
300	SPLA	93060	464-A5
DANA POINT AV			
-	VEN	93004	492-F2
DANBROOK AV			
2300	CMRL	93010	494-E7
DANBURY CT			
800	VEN	93004	492-H2
DANBURY DR			
1700	CMRL	93012	495-A7
1700	CMRL	93012	525-A1
DANDELION CT			
-	THO	91320	555-J2
DANETTE ST			
6400	SIMI	93063	499-C2
DANIEL ST			
3300	THO	91320	555-F2
DANIELSON FIRE RD			
-	VeCo	-	555-E6
-	VeCo	91320	555-E5
DANMONT CT			
3600	THO	91320	555-F4
DANNYBOYAR AV			
6300	CanP	91307	529-G6
DANTE WY			
500	VeCo	91377	557-G1
DANTES VIEW DR			
5000	CALB	91301	558-F6
N DANTON PL			
2600	SIMI	93065	498-B1
DANUBE WY			
-	OXN	93030	522-H1
DANVERS CIR			
700	THO	91320	555-F4
DANVILLE AV			
300	THO	91320	555-E3
DANWOOD DR			
4100	THO	91362	527-C5
DAPHNE AV			
1500	VEN	93004	493-A2
DAPHNE ST			
1600	CMRL	93010	494-D7
DAPHNEY CT			
3000	SIMI	93063	478-D7
DAPPER CT			
4300	OXN	93033	553-A4
DAPPLE AV			
1500	CMRL	93010	524-D1
N DAPPLEGRAY RD			
-	VeCo	91307	529-B4
DARA ST			
800	CMRL	93010	524-G2
DARBY ST			
3100	SIMI	93063	498-D1
3100	SIMI	93065	498-D1
DARCY AV			
1500	SIMI	93065	498-B3
DARGAN ST			
28900	AGRH	91301	558-A3
DARKWOOD CIR			
1900	THO	91360	526-D4
DARLENE LN			
6000	MRPK	93021	476-C7
8400	LA	91304	529-G2
DARLING RD			
9400	VEN	93004	492-H2
10600	VeCo	93004	493-A1
10600	VEN	93004	493-A1
10900	VEN	93004	473-B7
10900	VeCo	93004	473-B7
DARLINGTON DR			
2900	THO	91360	526-G2
DARMONT CIR			
700	SIMI	93065	497-J5
DARNELL CT			
1600	CMRL	93010	524-D2
DARNOCH WY			
6900	CanP	91307	529-E4
DARRAH AV			
1500	SIMI	93063	498-E3
DART CT			
5500	AGRH	91301	557-G5
DARTMOUTH CIR			
14300	MRPK	93021	476-G6
DARTMOUTH RD			
100	SPLA	93060	463-J7
400	SPLA	93060	473-J1
400	SPLA	93060	474-A1
DARTMOUTH ST			
5200	VEN	93003	492-B3
DARYN DR			
6600	LACo	91307	529-D6
DATE AV			
-	VEN	93004	473-A6
DATE ST			
100	OXN	93033	552-G1
600	OXN	93030	552-H1
W DATE ST			
100	OXN	93033	552-E1
DAUNET AV			
2500	SIMI	93065	498-C4
DAVIDS LN			
200	VeCo	91361	556-F6
DAVIDSON LN			
1600	SIMI	93063	499-B2
DAVIS CT			
4300	OXN	93033	552-H4
DAVIS DR			
300	VEN	93003	492-A3
DAVIS RD			
-	LACo	90265	586-F7
23600	VeCo	93060	453-G2
DAVIS ST			
100	SPLA	93060	464-B5
DAVIS WY			
23300	Chat	91311	499-F7
DAVY JONES DR			
30700	AGRH	91301	557-G5
DAWN CIR			
1700	SIMI	93063	498-J2
DAWN CT			
2100	THO	91362	526-J4
DAWN MEADOW ST			
1700	THO	91362	527-E6
DAWSON AV			
2600	VEN	93003	491-G3
N DAWSON DR			
-	CMRL	93012	524-F3
S DAWSON DR			
-	CMRL	93012	524-E4
DAWSON PL			
2500	CMRL	93012	524-E4
DAY CT			
2200	SIMI	93065	497-H2
DAY RD			
-	VEN	93003	492-B2
DAYBREAK CIR			
-	THO	91320	556-A1
DAYLIGHT CT			
1900	THO	91362	526-J1
DAYLIGHT DR			
6300	AGRH	91301	558-A3
DAY LILY LN			
23600	SIMI	93065	497-A1
DAYLOMA AV			
200	VEN	93003	492-A1
DAYTON CANYON DR			
24100	LA	91304	529-C2
24100	WHil	91304	529-C2
DEACON ST			
2900	SIMI	93065	498-C3
DEAN CT			
100	VEN	93003	492-A3
DEAN DR			
100	SPLA	93060	463-J6
100	SPLA	93060	464-A6
3500	VEN	93003	491-H3
4300	VEN	93003	492-A3
DEANNA AV			
1600	SIMI	93063	499-A3
DE ANZA DR			
-	VEN	93001	471-C6
DE ANZA WY			
200	OXN	93033	552-H3
DEARBORN AV			
700	THO	91320	555-G3
DEBBIE ST			
500	VeCo	91320	525-G7
500	VeCo	91320	555-H1
DE BERRY DR			
26000	CALB	91301	558-F6
DEBORAH ST			
4000	SIMI	93063	498-F2
DEBS AV			
6100	WdHI	91367	529-E7
6500	CanP	91307	529-E7
DEBUSSY LN			
-	VEN	93003	492-B4
DECATUR AV			
700	VEN	93004	492-G3
DECKER RD Rt#-23			
1400	LACo	90265	586-F7
DECKSIDE CT			
1400	OXN	93035	552-C1
DECKSIDE DR			
900	OXN	93035	522-C7
DEEP SHADOW DR			
29200	AGRH	91301	558-A5
DEEPWELL LN			
4300	MRPK	93021	496-F3
DEEPWOOD DR			
800	THO	91362	557-C1
1000	THO	91362	527-C7
DEER PTH			
-	VeCo	93012	583-J4
-	VeCo	93012	584-A3
DEERBROOK RD			
6700	VeCo	91377	528-A7
DEER CREEK AV			
2000	SIMI	93063	498-J2
DEER CREEK RD			
14700	VeCo	90265	585-B7
14700	VeCo	90265	625-B1
DEERFIELD CT			
2400	CMRL	93010	524-E1
DEERFIELD DR			
100	FILM	93015	455-J7
DEERFIELD ST			
2100	THO	91362	526-J4
2100	THO	91362	527-A4
DEERFOOT PL			
800	THO	91320	555-G5
DEER HAVEN CT			
-	THO	91362	527-D7
DEERHILL RD			
800	VeCo	91377	528-A6
800	VeCo	91377	558-A1
DEER HUNTER LN			
600	CMRL	93010	524-F2
DEERHURST AV			
400	CMRL	93012	524-H5
DEERING LN			
13600	MRPK	93021	496-F3
DEER LICK DR			
23900	LA	91304	529-E2
DEER MEADOW ST			
12600	MRPK	93021	496-D3
DEERPARK CT			
4300	WLKV	91361	557-D6
DEERPATH LN			
-	THO	91320	555-H2
DEER RUN LN			
1200	VeCo	91377	527-G7
DEER SPRING PL			
900	THO	91320	555-G5
DEER TRAIL CT			
26900	CALB	91301	558-G7
DEER VALLEY AV			
3100	THO	91320	555-G4
DEERVIEW CT			
29400	AGRH	91301	557-J4
DEERWALK PL			
300	THO	91320	555-J1
DEERWEED TR			
20900	CALB	91301	558-G7
DEER WILLOW CT			
700	THO	91320	555-G4
DEERWOOD AV			
2600	SIMI	93065	478-C7
2600	SIMI	93065	498-C1
DEFENDER DR			
4000	AGRH	91301	558-E7
DEKOVEN ST			
4900	VEN	93003	492-B7
DELACODO AV			
3000	THO	91320	555-G2
DE LA GARRIGUE RD			
-	VeCo	-	366-H7
-	VeCo	93023	366-H7
23600	VeCo	93023	450-G1
DEL AMO WY			
2000	OXN	93030	522-H3
DELANO CT			
3800	SIMI	93063	498-E1
DELAWARE DR			
200	VEN	93001	471-C4
DEL CERRO CIR			
23600	LA	91304	529-E4
DEL CIERVO PL			
-	CMRL	93012	494-H7
DELFEN ST			
6500	MRPK	93021	477-A6
DELGADA CT			
1900	CMRL	93010	524-D2
DELGADA ST			
1000	CMRL	93012	525-B6
E DELILAH ST			
3500	SIMI	93063	498-E2
DELIUS ST			
4900	VEN	93003	492-A4
DEL MAR PL			
4000	OXN	93033	552-G4
DEL MAR TR			
6800	VeCo	93063	499-D4
DELMONICO AV			
8600	LA	91304	529-J1
DEL NIDO CT			
1100	OJAI	93023	442-A6
DEL NORTE BLVD			
100	OXN	93030	523-D5
DEL NORTE RD			
100	OJAI	93023	441-G7
300	VeCo	93023	441-F6
1300	CMRL	93010	523-F3
DEL NORTE ST			
10800	VEN	93004	472-J6
DEL ORO DR			
800	OJAI	93023	441-G5
DEL ORO PL			
4800	OXN	93033	552-G5
DELOZ DR			
-	CMRL	93012	525-A3
DELPHA CT			
2100	THO	91362	527-A3
DELPHINIUM PL			
200	OXN	93030	522-F3
DEL PRADO CT			
1100	OJAI	93023	442-A6
DEL PRADO DR			
1700	CMRL	93010	524-D2
DEL RAY CIR			
-	THO	91360	526-F2
DEL REY PL			
-	OXN	93030	523-A5
DEL RIO ST			
4600	SIMI	93063	478-H7
DEL ROBLES DR			
6300	VeCo	93063	499-C4
DEL ROBLES PL			
1000	VeCo	93063	499-C4
DEL SUR WY			
300	OXN	93033	552-H3
DELTA DR			
8600	VEN	93004	492-G4
DELTA RD			
23600	VeCo	93063	528-G2
DELTA CC RD			
23600	VeCo	93063	528-G2
W DELTA GREEN ST			
100	PHME	93041	552-D2
DEL TIO CT			
-	CMRL	93010	493-G7
DEL VALLE DR			
200	FILM	93015	455-J6
500	FILM	93015	456-A6
DEL VALLE ST			
-	VeCo	93022	451-C4
DEL VERDE CT			
1000	THO	91320	526-B6
DELWOOD CT			
400	THO	91320	555-E3
DENA DR			
100	VeCo	91320	555-G1
500	VeCo	91320	525-G7
DENBY CT			
6500	SIMI	93063	499-C2
DENHAM CT			
1800	SIMI	93065	498-A2
DENISE CT			
500	THO	91320	525-H7
DENISE LN			
8300	LA	91304	529-G2
DENISE ST			
2600	THO	91320	525-H7
DENNIS AV			
700	SIMI	93065	497-G3
DENNIS LN			
7200	CanP	91307	529-F5
DENNIS WY			
9300	Chat	91311	499-F6
DENNISON RD			
-	VeCo	93023	452-D1
DENNY ST			
2000	SIMI	93065	498-A3
DENTON AV			
3500	SIMI	93063	478-G5
3500	VeCo	93063	478-G5
DENVER PL			
900	OXN	93033	552-J3
900	VEN	93004	492-G3
DENVER ST			
8000	VEN	93004	492-F3
DENVER SPRINGS DR			
32900	WLKV	91361	586-J1
W DEODAR AV			
100	OXN	93030	522-F5
N DEODORA ST			
1400	SIMI	93065	498-C3
DE PAUL ST			
4200	VEN	93003	491-J3
DE QUINCY CT			
24100	LA	91304	529-D3
DERBY ST			
2100	CMRL	93010	524-E1
DERRY AV			
5300	AGRH	91301	558-B6
DESCANSO AV			
100	OJAI	93023	441-F7
200	OJAI	93023	451-F1
DESCANSO CT			
1300	OXN	93035	552-E1
DESCHUTES DR			
1500	VEN	93004	492-J3
DESEO AV			
400	VeCo	93010	494-A6
DESERT CREEK AV			
2100	SIMI	93063	499-B2
DESERT FOREST CT			
2200	OXN	93030	522-D2
DESERT SAGE CT			
23600	SIMI	93065	498-D5
DETROIT DR			
2800	OXN	93030	492-H7
DEVEREUX DR			
900	VeCo	93023	441-D6
DEVERON RIDGE RD			
6900	CanP	91307	529-E5
DEVIA DR			
-	VeCo	91320	555-G1
DEVILFISH DR			
800	OXN	93035	522-D7
DEVILS CANYON MTWY			
-	Chat	91311	479-G2
-	Chat	91311	499-J1
DEVILS CANYON RD			
-	VeCo	93001	471-B5
DEVON CT			
800	SIMI	93065	498-D5
DEVON LN			
1200	VEN	93001	491-F5
DEVONSHIRE AV			
1500	THO	91361	556-J6
DEVONSHIRE CT			
1600	THO	91361	556-J6
DEVONSHIRE DR			
800	OXN	93030	522-D4
W DEVONSHIRE DR			
300	OXN	93030	522-F4
DEVONSHIRE ST			
10300	Chat	91311	499-J4
DEVORE AV			
700	SIMI	93065	497-H5
DEVORE CT			
5500	AGRH	91301	558-C5
DEWAYNE AV			
1600	CMRL	93010	524-G1
1700	CMRL	93010	494-G7
DEWBERRY CT			
2000	THO	91361	557-A5
DEWBERRY LN			
400	OXN	93030	522-G1
DEWDROP PL			
23600	THO	91362	527-C4
DEWEY AV			
200	THO	91320	555-G2
N DEWEY AV			
-	THO	91320	555-G2
S DEWEY AV			
100	THO	91320	555-G2
DEXTER ST			
2100	CMRL	93010	524-E2
DIABLO AV			
600	MRPK	93021	496-D1
DIABLO WY			
100	OXN	93033	553-C3
DIAMOND AL			
200	VEN	93001	491-C1
DIAMOND CT			
3700	SIMI	93063	498-E1
DIAMOND DR			
-	CMRL	93010	493-H7
DIAMOND HEAD WY			
2300	OXN	93030	522-D2
DIANA CT			
2900	VeCo	91320	555-G1
30100	AGRH	91301	557-H5
DIANE ST			
5300	SIMI	93063	498-J2
DIAZ AV			
500	OXN	93030	522-H6
DICKENS CIR			
6900	VEN	93003	492-E3
DICKENS DR			
5300	OXN	93033	552-G5
DICKENSON AV			
-	THO	91320	555-F2
DICKINSON LN			
6600	VEN	93003	492-D3
DICKINSON PL			
2100	OXN	93033	553-A1
DIEGO WY			
1600	OXN	93030	522-E4
DILLER CT			
3800	SIMI	93063	498-E2
DILLON CT			
2300	THO	91360	526-D4
DINSMORE AV			
100	THO	91362	556-H2
DINSMORE ST			
1300	SIMI	93065	497-H4
DISCOVERY CT			
11900	MRPK	93021	496-C1
DISCOVERY CV			
2600	PHME	93041	552-C2
DISCOVERY DR			
23600	OXN	93030	523-C6
DISPENSARY RD			
-	VeCo	93041	583-G3
-	VeCo	93042	583-G3
DITCH RD			
-	VeCo	93042	583-C4
2800	VeCo	93063	478-D6
2800	VeCo	93065	478-D6
2800	SIMI	93063	478-D6
N DIVERNON AV			
3000	SIMI	93063	478-F7
DIVIDE TER			
8300	LA	91304	529-E2
E DIXON CT			
3800	SIMI	93063	498-E2
DOANE ST			
4000	VEN	93003	491-J2
W DOBKIN PL			
-	SIMI	93065	497-F3
DOCK RD			
-	PHME	93043	552-D5
DOCKSIDE LN			
1500	CMRL	93010	524-D4
DOCKSON PL			
2500	PHME	93041	552-D2
DODD ST			
500	SIMI	93065	497-G4
DODGE RD			
23600	OXN	93033	553-C4
23600	VeCo	93033	553-C4
DODSON ST			
-	PHME	93041	552-E4
-	PHME	93043	552-E3
5000	VeCo	93066	494-J4
5000	VeCo	93066	495-A4
DOE CREEK CIR			
500	THO	91320	555-E3
DOGWOOD CIR			
2900	THO	91360	526-H3
DOGWOOD DR			
2500	OXN	93030	522-G1
DOGWOOD ST			
2200	SIMI	93065	498-B2
DOLE DR			
-	WLKV	91362	557-E5
DOLLIE ST			
100	OXN	93033	552-G5
W DOLLIE ST			
-	OXN	93033	552-G5
DOLORES CT			
100	OXN	93030	522-J5
DOLPHIN CT			
1000	VEN	93001	491-G5
DOLPHIN WY			
5000	OXN	93035	551-J1
DOMAR PL			
2100	OXN	93030	522-H3
DOMBEY CIR			
-	THO	91360	526-F6
DOMINGUEZ CANYON RD			
-	VeCo	-	367-D7
-	VeCo	93040	367-D7
DOMINION DR			
1000	VeCo	93023	441-D6
N DONALD AV			
-	THO	91320	555-G2
DON ANTONIO WY			
800	VeCo	93023	451-C3
DON CARLOS			
800	VeCo	93023	451-C2
DON CARLOS ST			
300	VEN	93001	491-D2
DONEGAL AV			
100	THO	91320	556-A1
DONEVA RD			
4000	MRPK	93021	496-D3
DON FELIPE			
800	VeCo	93023	451-C2
DONIZETTI AV			
600	VEN	93003	492-A3
DONLIN LN			
200	VeCo	91320	556-B3
DONLIN RD			
300	VeCo	91320	556-B2
DONLON AV			
800	OXN	93030	522-G7
DONLON RD			
2900	VeCo	93066	495-B1
5300	VeCo	93066	475-B7
DONLON ST			
100	VEN	93003	492-A4
600	VEN	93003	491-J5
DONNA ST			
100	VeCo	93022	451-B7
DONNER AV			
100	VEN	93003	492-C1
1100	SIMI	93065	498-A4
DONNER ST			
600	OXN	93033	552-H4
W DONNICK AV			
100	THO	91360	526-E5
DONNINGTON CT			
700	SIMI	93065	497-C6
DONNYBROOK LN			
13600	MRPK	93021	496-F3
DON RICARDO			
800	VeCo	93023	451-C2
DONVILLE AV			
2000	SIMI	93065	497-J2
DOONE ST			
-	THO	91360	526-F6
DORA CT			
2200	SIMI	93063	499-B1
DORADO CT			
500	VeCo	91377	558-A1
2400	THO	91362	527-C3
DORAL CIR			
1400	THO	91362	527-E7
DORAL CT			
2600	OXN	93030	522-D2
DORCHESTER ST			
800	THO	91360	526-G6
DOREEN WY			
3100	VEN	93003	491-H3
DORENA DR			
100	VeCo	91320	555-G1
400	VeCo	91320	525-G7
DORHAM CT			
2900	SIMI	93065	498-C3
DORIE DR			
7400	LA	91304	529-E4
DORIS AV			
1400	OXN	93030	522-D5
1400	VeCo	93030	522-B5
W DORIS AV			
200	OXN	93030	522-F5
DORIS CT			
15400	MRPK	93021	477-A5
DORMAN ST			
2700	CMRL	93010	494-F7
DOROTHY AV			
200	MRPK	93021	496-E1
200	VEN	93003	491-J2
400	VeCo	93003	491-J2
1400	SIMI	93063	499-C3
DOROTHY DR			
28000	AGRH	91301	558-C6
DORRIT CT			
-	THO	91320	556-A1
DORRIT ST			
1800	THO	91320	556-A1
DORSET AV			
1400	THO	91360	526-F6
DORY LN			
5100	OXN	93033	552-G5
N DOS CAMINOS AV			
-	VEN	93003	491-G2
S DOS CAMINOS AV			
-	VEN	93003	491-G3
DOUBLE EAGLE DR			
600	SIMI	93065	497-D5
DOUBLETREE RD			
800	VeCo	91377	558-A1
900	VeCo	91377	528-A7
W DOUGLAS AV			
200	OXN	93030	522-F4
DOUGLAS ST			
300	OJAI	93023	441-H5
DOVE CT			
300	FILM	93015	455-H6
300	SPLA	93060	464-D5
DOVE ST			
6800	VEN	93003	492-E4
DOVER AV			
1100	THO	91360	526-E6
DOVER LN			
-	SIMI	93063	498-H1
1000	VEN	93001	491-E4
DOVER ST			
1500	OXN	93030	522-G3
DOVERWOOD CT			
31900	WLKV	91361	557-C6
DOVETAIL CT			
-	THO	91360	526-F3
DOVETAIL DR			
5800	AGRH	91301	557-G4
DOWEL DR			
6400	SIMI	93063	499-C2
DOWELL DR			
1400	VEN	93003	492-B5
DOWNEY CT			
3900	SIMI	93063	498-F2
E DOWNING ST			
1400	SIMI	93065	497-J1
DOWNWIND WY			
500	OXN	93033	552-G5
DOYLE LN			
500	VEN	93003	492-D1
DRACENA AV			
15400	MRPK	93021	477-A6
DRACO WY			
23600	CanP	91307	529-F5
DRAKE DR			
1200	SIMI	93065	497-G4
2300	THO	91362	527-B6
4200	OXN	93033	553-A4
DRAPER CT			
2000	SIMI	93065	497-J2
DRAYTON AV			
2200	THO	91360	526-F4
DREXEL AV			
200	VEN	93003	492-C1
DREXEL CIR			
1000	THO	91360	526-F6

Right margin: VENTURA CO.   INDEX

STREET — Block / City / ZIP / Pg-Grid

Street	Block	City	ZIP	Pg-Grid
DRIFFILL BLVD	-	OXN	93030	522-G7
DRIFT DR	5900	WLKV	91362	557-F4
DRIFTWOOD CT	1200	SIMI	93065	497-H3
DRIFTWOOD CIR	900	THO	91320	555-E4
DRIFTWOOD LN	1000	VEN	91E4	491-E4
DRIFTWOOD ST	5100	OXN	93035	521-J6
DRISKILL ST	3900	VeCo	93063	523-A5
DRIVER AV	5200	Ago	91301	558-G6
	5200	CALB	91301	558-G6
	28100	AGRH	91301	558-B5
DROWN AV	100	OJAI	93023	441-J6
DRUMCLIFF CT	1700	SIMI	93065	556-J5
DRUMMOND LN	6700	VeCo	93063	492-D3
DRUMMOND PL	2700	THO	91360	556-E3
DRY CANYON RD	3400	SIMI	93065	478-B5
	4000	SIMI	93063	478-E3
	4000	VeCo	93063	478-E3
DRYDEN ST	2300	VeCo	93012	496-A7
DRY GULCH TR	23600	VeCo	90265	625-G1
DUARTE CIR	1400	SIMI	93065	498-A3
DUBBERS ST	100	SIMI	91361	491-B1
DUBONNET CT	1400	OXN	91377	527-H6
DUCHY WY	2500	SIMI	91361	586-D2
DUCOR AV	7600	LA	91304	529-G2
DUDLEY AV	1200	VEN	93004	492-H3
DUDLEY DR	1600	VEN	93015	455-H7
DUESENBERG DR	2700	SIMI	91362	557-B3
DUFAU RD	3600	VeCo	93030	553-E5
DUKE AV	100	VEN	93003	492-B2
DUKE ST	6400	MRPK	93021	476-H6
DULCE DR	600	OXN	93030	522-H3
DULCIE CIR	1700	SIMI	93063	498-J2
DUMAINE AV	1400	SIMI	91377	527-G6
DUMETZ ST	2500	CMRL	93010	524-F3
DUMP RD	-	VeCo	93042	583-G4
N DUNBAR LN	400	THO	91360	526-D7
DUNCAN ST	1700	SIMI	93065	497-J3
DUNEGAL CT	5900	AGRH	91301	557-G3
DUNES CIR	900	OXN	93035	521-J7
DUNES ST	800	OXN	93035	521-J7
	4800	OXN	93035	522-A7
DUNHAM CIR	1600	THO	91360	526-D5
N DUNHAM RD	5600	VeCo	93066	475-C7
	5600	VeCo	93066	495-C1
DUNKIRK DR	600	OXN	93035	522-D6
	600	VeCo	93035	522-D6
DUNLIN LN	800	THO	91361	557-A5
DUNLO PL	6400	CanP	91307	529-D7
DUNN CT	2100	THO	91360	526-F4
DUNNIGAN ST	1600	CMRL	93010	524-D2
N DUNNING ST	-	VEN	93003	491-H2
S DUNNING ST	-	VEN	93003	491-H3
DUNRAVEN ST	31700	WLKV	91362	557-D6
DUNSMUIR AV	-	VEN	93004	492-F2
DUNSMUIR DR	2500	SIMI		552-D1
DUNSMUIR ST	5900	OXN	93035	522-D1
DUNTON ST	100	FILM	93015	455-J6
DUPONT	4400	VEN	93003	492-A5
DUPONT ST	1800	OXN	93033	553-A1
DURAND DR	6900	VeCo	93021	475-J5
DURANGO CT	1600	CMRL	93010	524-D4
DURANT CT	5400	OXN	91377	527-H7
DURHAM LN	9800	VeCo	93004	492-H2
DURHAM ST	1200	SIMI	93065	497-H4
DURKIN ST	700	CMRL	93010	524-F2
DURLEY AV	100	CMRL	93010	524-A4
E DUSAN ST	2300	SIMI	93065	498-B4
DUSKWOOD WY	1600	SIMI	93065	497-F2
DUSTY LN	7800	VeCo	93066	475-C4
DUSTY ROSE CT	200	SIMI	93065	497-E7
DUTCH ELM CIR	1200	THO	91320	526-H2
DUVAL DR	2200	VeCo	93012	496-A7
DUVAL RD	2300	VeCo	93012	496-A7
DUVALI DR	100	VEN	93003	492-B2
DUVALL AV	700	CMRL	93010	524-D2
N DWIGHT AV	1500	OXN	93033	524-G1
DWIGHT AV S	3000	CMRL	93010	524-F1
DYER CT	200	THO	91360	526-F4

E

Street	Block	City	ZIP	Pg-Grid
E ST	-	VeCo	93015	455-H7
	100	OXN	93033	522-F7
	200	FILM	93015	455-H7
	1300	OXN	93033	552-G3
	23600	OXN	93033	552-F7
N E ST	100	OXN	93030	522-F5
EAGLE CIR	-	VeCo	93041	583-J3
EAGLE CT	600	FILM	93015	455-H5
EAGLE DR	6800	VEN	93003	492-E4
EAGLE ST	1300	OXN	93033	522-J2
N ECROYD AV	2100	SIMI	93063	499-A2
EAGLEBROOK DR	30300	AGRH	91301	557-G5
EAGLE CREEK LN	23600	SIMI	93065	522-D2
EAGLE HEIGHTS CT	2800	THO	91360	526-D1
EAGLEHAVEN LN	6800	VeCo	91377	528-B7
EAGLE MOUNTAIN RD	24000	LA	91304	529-D2
EAGLE MOUNTAIN ST	24000	LA	91304	529-D1
EAGLEPEAK AV	-	THO	91360	555-F2
EAGLE POINT CIR	4800	THO	91362	527-F1
EAGLE RIDGE ST	1600	THO	91320	555-G2
EAGLE ROCK AV	100	OXN	93035	552-C6
EAGLES CLAW AV	2800	THO	91362	527-B2
EAGLESNEST PL	3400	THO	91362	555-F4
EAGLETON ST	28600	AGRH	91301	558-B3
EAGLEVIEW PL	300	THO	91360	555-J1
EAGLEWOOD AV	-	THO	91362	527-B2
EAKINS LN	500	VEN	93003	492-D1
EARHART CT	1800	VEN	93033	553-A1
EARL AV	1500	SIMI	93065	498-B3
EARLHAM CT	1400	OXN	91377	527-G6
EARL JOSEPH DR	6100	AGRH	91301	557-J3
EARLY DAWN LN	23600	VEN	93003	497-A1
EAST DR	-	VeCo	93021	475-F6
	6300	VeCo	93021	475-F6
EAST RD	6300	VeCo	93021	475-F6
	6300	VeCo	93066	475-F6
EAST ST	3000	SIMI	93065	498-C3
	3400	SIMI	93065	495-A5
EASTBOURNE BAY	4400	OXN	93035	552-A1
EASTERLY RD	5500	AGRH	91301	558-C5
EAST FORK HALL CANYON RD	2800	SIMI	93001	471-H5
EASTMAN AV	1500	VEN	93003	492-A5
	1800	OXN	93030	523-A6
	1800	OXN	93030	523-A6
EASTRIDGE CT	2200	SIMI	93065	522-D3
EASTRIDGE LP	2100	SIMI	93065	522-E2
EASTRIDGE TR	2000	SIMI	93065	522-E2
EASTVALE CT	29900	AGRH	91301	557-H4
EASTWARD ST	23600	Chat	91311	499-F6
EASTWIND CIR	200	SIMI	93065	557-B6
EASTWOOD DR	400	OXN	93030	522-F2
EASY ST	100	SIMI	93065	497-D5
E EASY ST	100	SIMI	93065	497-F1
W EASY ST	-	SIMI	93065	497-E1
EASY WY	2000	SIMI	93065	497-H2
EATOUGH AV	8500	LA	91304	529-J1
EATOUGH PL	8500	LA	91304	529-J2
EBB CT	1400	OXN	93035	552-C1
EBB TIDE CIR	600	PHME	93041	552-F7
EBBTIDE LN	11800	VeCo	90265	625-F5
EBONY DR	6100	WdHI	91367	529-E7
ECCLES ST	22100	LA	91304	529-H2
ECHIDNA PL	7000	VEN	93003	492-E4
ECHO AV	700	OXN	93030	522-H2
ECHO CT	4900	VEN	93003	492-A2
ECHO ST	1300	OXN	93033	522-J2
EDDINGHAM WY	-	LA	91304	529-E4
EDDY CT	5500	VEN	93003	492-C3
EDELWEISS ST	2000	OXN	93033	522-G2
EDEN ST	3000	OXN	93033	553-A3
EDENPARK DR	24000	LA	91304	529-D2
EDGAR CT	26000	CALB	91302	558-J3
EDGEBROOK PL	5100	VeCo	93013	386-E8
EDGECLIFF CIR	1800	THO	91362	527-F6
EDGEHILL CIR	5300	VEN	93003	492-B1
EDGEMIRE LN	23600	VEN	93015	455-D6
EDGEMONT DR	1400	CMRL	93010	524-D1
EDGERTON PL	2500	PHME	93041	552-E5
EDGEWARE DR	5200	CALB	91301	558-G6
EDGEWATER LN	1500	OXN	93035	552-D4
EDGEWOOD DR	1700	SIMI	93063	499-D3
EDGEWOOD WY	1300	VEN	93004	492-G1
EDINBURGH CT	6100	AGRH	91301	557-J3
EDISON DR	5500	OXN	93033	552-H7
	6100	VeCo	93033	386-K3
	6100	VeCo	93033	386-K3
	6100	VeCo	93066	386-K3
EDISON LN	700	FILM	93015	455-J5
EDISON RD	5600	VeCo	93012	554-G4
	23600	VeCo	93063	498-E7
	23600	VeCo	93063	528-E1
EDISON WY	800	FILM	93015	455-J5
EDMUND ST	1500	SIMI	93065	497-J4
EDWARD RD	200	THO	91320	556-A2
	200	THO	91320	556-A2
EDWARDS RD	23600	VeCo	93060	464-J1
EDWARDS CANYON RD	23600	VeCo	93015	457-D5
	23600	VeCo	93015	457-D5
EDWARDS RANCH RD	100	VeCo	93060	473-C4
EGRET AV	1300	VEN	93003	492-D4
EGRET CT	6300	VEN	93003	492-D4
EHLERS DR	9300	Chat	91311	499-F6
	23400	Chat	91311	499-F6
EILEEN ST	23600	VEN	93003	498-F2
EISENHOWER CIR	600	OXN	93030	552-H6
EISENHOWER ST	7200	VEN	93003	492-E2
EISENHOWER WY	-	SIMI	93065	497-D5
ELAINE ST	3400	VeCo	93030	492-F3
	3400	VeCo	93030	493-A7
ELAND LN	7000	VEN	93003	492-E4
EL AZUL CIR	500	OXN	91377	557-J1
ELBA CT	23600	MRPK	93021	496-C5
ELBA PL	6100	VEN	93003	498-J3
ELBA ST	2800	VEN	93003	492-E6
ELBERTA AV	1600	VEN	93063	498-J3
ELBURY CT	1100	OXN	91361	556-F7
EL CAJON CIR	1900	OXN	93035	522-E7
EL CAJON CT	1200	OXN	93035	552-E1
	1200	OXN	93035	552-E1
EL CAJON DR	1400	THO	91362	526-J5
EL CAJON ST	9200	VEN	93004	492-G2
EL CAJON WY	1600	OXN	93035	522-D7
EL CAMINO	2100	OJAI	93023	441-G6
EL CAMINO DR	100	OJAI	93023	441-E7
EL CAMINO CORTO	800	OJAI	93023	441-C7
EL CAMINO REAL	1000	VEN	93063	499-B4
EL CAMINO REAL U.S.-101	-	VeCo	93001	366-E8
	-	VeCo	93001	459-C5
	-	VeCo	93001	469-H1
	-	THO	91320	470-E5
	26000	CALB	91302	558-J3
	-	THO	91320	470-E4
EL CAMPO ST	600	VEN	93015	455-D6
EL CANON AV	6100	WdHI	91367	529-D7
EL CAPITAN PL	4200	CMRL	93012	524-J3
EL CARAZON CT	4900	CMRL	93012	524-H3
EL CENTRO DR	1500	CMRL	93010	524-D4
EL CENTRO ST	1700	SIMI	93063	499-D3
EL CERRITO CIR	1300	VEN	93004	492-G1
EL CERRITO DR	100	VEN	93004	492-G1
EL CIELO	6100	AGRH	91301	557-J3
EL CINO DR	5500	OXN	93033	552-H7
EL CONEJO DR	1200	THO	91320	526-H6
EL CORTIJO PL	5100	CMRL	93012	524-J1
ELDER ST	900	OXN	93030	522-E2
ELDERBERRY AV	4700	MRPK	93021	496-C2
ELDERBERRY CT	1000	SPLA	93060	499-B3
ELDERBERRY DR	2400	OXN	93030	522-F1
ELDEROAK LN	2600	VEN	91361	586-E1
ELDEROAK RD	2700	VEN	91361	586-E2
ELDER VINE LN	1100	CMRL	93012	525-A2
EL DORADO AV	2300	VEN	93033	553-B2
EL DORADO CT	300	VEN	93004	492-E1
EL DORADO DR	100	FILM	93015	456-C6
	1400	THO	91362	526-J6
EL DORADO ST	7600	VEN	93004	492-F3
ELECTRA AV	2000	SIMI	93063	478-G7
ELEGANTE DR	3300	OXN	93030	523-C7
ELENA WY	2700	OXN	93030	522-G3
EL ESCORPION RD	6000	WdHI	91367	529-E3
ELEVAR CT	700	SIMI	93065	527-C1
ELEVAR ST	-	OXN	93030	523-C6
ELFIN GRN	100	PHME	93041	552-D2
W ELFIN GRN	100	PHME	93041	552-E2
ELFSTONE CT	1000	VEN	91361	557-A5
EL GALLARDO	13200	MRPK	93021	496-E3
EL GRECO DR	1000	OXN	93035	522-E7
ELINOR CT	2900	SIMI	93063	525-H1
ELIOT CT	6800	VEN	93003	492-D3
ELIOT DR	4200	VEN	93033	553-A4
E ELIOT ST	100	SPLA	93060	464-A6
W ELIOT ST	100	SPLA	93060	463-J6
	100	SPLA	93060	464-A6
ELIZA CT	2200	SIMI	93065	525-E6
ELIZABETH CT	100	SPLA	93060	463-J7
	30100	AGRH	91301	557-H5
ELIZABETH DR	2000	VEN	93003	492-E1
ELIZABETH RD	500	VEN	93004	472-G6
ELIZONDO AV	2500	SIMI	93065	498-C3
ELIZONDO ST	1900	SIMI	93065	498-A3
EL JARDIN AV	100	VEN	93001	491-G1
EL JINA LN	400	OXN	93023	442-E6
ELKINS LN	1100	FILM	93015	456-B5
ELKINS RD	100	FILM	93015	466-B3
ELKO AV	700	VEN	93004	492-G2
ELKWOOD AV	3700	THO	91362	555-E4
ELKWOOD ST	1400	LA	91304	529-E3
EL LADO DR	500	SIMI	93065	497-G3
EL LAZO CT	1300	CMRL	93012	525-B1
ELLEN CT	3000	VEN	93004	492-G2
ELLENVIEW AV	5900	WdHI	91367	529-D7
ELLESMERE WY	1300	VEN	93004	492-A2
ELLFRED CT	600	SPLA	93060	464-A6
ELLICE ST	11700	VeCo	90265	625-F5
ELLINGTON CT	2400	SIMI	93065	498-D1
ELLINGTON ST	23600	VEN	93003	492-B7
ELLIOT CT	1200	THO	91320	526-D6
N ELLIS PL	-	SIMI	93065	556-A1
S ELLIS PL	-	THO	91320	556-A1
ELLSWORTH CIR	400	THO	91360	526-D6
ELM	-	OXN	93030	522-E2
ELM CT	800	OXN	93033	552-F1
ELM DR	-	CMRL	93010	524-E4
ELM RD	100	THO	91320	556-B2
ELM ST	100	THO	91320	556-B2
	200	SPLA	93060	463-J7
	23600	VEN	93033	552-G1
W ELM ST	2700	SIMI	93065	498-C3
ELMA ST	5500	AGRH	91301	557-G5
N ELMDALE AV	3000	SIMI	93063	478-D7
ELMHURST LN	1600	VEN	93004	492-F3
ELMHURST ST	1600	SIMI	93065	552-A1
ELMIRA ST	100	THO	91320	556-H1
EL MONTE AV	700	SIMI	93065	497-G5
EL MONTE DR	900	SIMI	93065	497-G5
	1100	THO	91362	526-J5
	2000	THO	91362	527-A5
ELMORE ST	3200	SIMI	93063	498-D2
ELMROCK AV	13200	MRPK	93021	496-E3
ELMSBURY LN	7000	CanP	91307	529-D5
ELMSBURY PL	1900	SIMI	91361	557-A7
ELMSFORD ST	1500	THO	91360	556-H6
ELM VIEW DR	5400	CMRL	93012	525-A2
ELMWOOD ST	23600	THO	91320	555-G6
EL NIDO CT	2200	CMRL	93010	494-G7
EL NIDO ST	3200	CMRL	93010	494-G7
ELOISE CIR	1600	VEN	93063	499-A3
EL PAJARO	2100	OXN	93030	522-G3
EL PASEO RD	300	OJAI	93023	441-G7
EL PASEO ST	1000	FILM	93015	455-H7
EL PASILLO	100	THO	91320	526-E6
EL PASO AV	2500	SIMI	93065	498-C3
EL PLANO DR	1900	SIMI	93065	498-A3
EL PORTAL CT	9500	VEN	93004	492-G1
EL PORTAL WY	1300	OXN	93035	522-D1
EL PRADO ST	4600	SIMI	93063	478-H7
EL RANCHO DR	1900	OXN	93030	494-E7
EL REPOSA DR	2200	CMRL	93012	495-D7
EL RETIRO CT	900	VeCo	91377	557-H1
EL RIO DR	100	VeCo	93030	441-D7
EL RIO ROCK RD	300	VEN	93030	522-G1
EL ROBLAR DR	100	VeCo	93023	441-C6
EL SEGUNDO DR	6200	CanP	91307	529-D7
ELSINOR AV	1200	VEN	93004	492-A2
	1200	VEN	93004	441-A2
ELSINOR CT	1100	VEN	93004	492-J2
ELSINORE AV	1300	VEN	93004	552-D1
ELSINORE CIR	2600	VEN	93004	552-D1
ELSINORE CT	1900	VEN	93004	552-D1
EL SOL AV	500	SIMI	93023	441-D7
ELSTOW CT	100	PHME	93041	552-E4
EL TORO DR	700	OJAI	93023	441-G6
	900	VEN	93023	441-F6
EL TORO FIRE TRUCK TR	-	NwhI	91382	479-E1
EL TUACA CT	300	VEN	93010	493-J7
	300	VEN	93010	494-A7
ELVADO DR	1400	SIMI	93065	497-F3
EL VERANO DR	1100	THO	91360	526-G6
ERBES RD	11800	MRPK	93021	476-C7
ELWIN ST	500	THO	91361	526-J1
ELY WY	2700	SIMI	93065	498-C3
EMBER CT	5500	AGRH	91301	557-G5
EMERALD AV	3000	SIMI	93063	478-D7
EMERALD CT	400	VEN	93001	491-F1
EMERALD ISLE WY	1600	OXN	93035	552-A1
EMERIC AV	1400	SIMI	93065	497-E3
EMERSON AV	1100	VEN	93003	552-J1
	1100	VEN	93003	553-A1
EMERSON CT	900	SIMI	93065	497-G5
	1100	THO	91362	526-J5
	2000	THO	91362	527-A5
EMERSON ST	700	AGRH	91301	557-J4
EMILIO CT	23600	MRPK	93021	496-C4
EMILY LN	2800	SIMI	93063	478-E7
EMILY ST	600	OJAI	93023	441-H6
EMMA AV	-	VEN	93003	491-G3
EMMA CT	2000	THO	91362	556-H2
N EMMETT AV	2100	SIMI	93063	499-A2
EMORY AV	1700	SIMI	93063	498-J2
EMPIRE AV	600	VEN		491-H4
EMPRESA LN	2100	OXN	93030	522-G3
EMPRESS AV	2100	OXN	93030	522-G3
EMPTY SADDLE AV	1700	OXN	93035	499-D3
ENADIA WY	22500	CanP	91307	529-G5
ENCANTO DR	2600	VEN	93003	491-G2
N ENCINAL AV	100	VeCo	93023	441-D6
S ENCINAL AV	100	VeCo	93023	441-D7
ENCINAL PL	-	VEN	93001	491-E2
ENCINAL WY	1300	OXN	93035	522-D1
ENCINAS CANYON RD	300	VeCo	93015	471-D2
ENCINO AV	300	CMRL	93010	524-A1
	900	CMRL	93010	524-A1
ENCINO DR	900	VeCo	93023	451-C5
	10500	VeCo	93023	451-C6
ENCINO PL	300	OXN	93030	522-G1
ENCINO VISTA CT	4200	VEN	93001	471-D2
ENCINO VISTA DR	2800	VEN	93001	471-D2
ENCORE ST	800	VEN	93022	461-B1
END ST	6000	VeCo	93063	499-B3
ENDEAVOR ST	27500	AGRH	91301	558-E7
ENDEAVOUR CT	700	MRPK	93021	496-C1
ENDICOTT ST	-	PHME	93041	552-E4
ENFIELD CIR	100	THO	91360	526-F6
ENGLISH OAKS CT	2400	THO	91362	527-C3
ENID WY	10100	VEN	93004	492-J2
ENSCH RD	700	THO	91320	526-H3
ENSENADA AV	100	THO	91320	556-C6
ENSIGN PL	600	VeCo	93035	522-D6
ENTRADA DR	2000	OXN	93030	522-H3
	3100	OXN	93030	491-G4
EQUESTRIAN AV	100	THO	91320	478-E7
ERBURU AV	-	VEN	93003	491-G2
ERICA CIR	7000	CanP	91307	529-F5
ERICA PL	300	OXN	93030	522-F2
ERICA ST	2400	SIMI	93065	498-B2
N ERICSON PL	2600	SIMI	93065	498-B1
ERIE ST	10100	VEN	93004	492-J2
ERIN CT	23600	VEN	93003	498-A5
ERINLEA AV	1500	OXN	93030	522-D4
ERMINE AV	2300	VEN	93001	471-C6
ERNEST DR	3500	SIMI	93063	498-E3
ERRINGER RD	900	OXN	93033	552-J3
ERSKINE LN	800	SIMI	93065	498-A3
ERTEN ST	100	THO	91360	526-E4
ERWIN ST	22100	WdHI	91367	529-F7
ESCALON DR	1300	OXN	93035	552-E1
ESCOLLA RD	23600	VeCo	93012	496-B5
ESCOLLERA AV	2800	VeCo	93012	496-A6
ESCOLLERA CIR	10900	VeCo	93012	496-A6
ESCONDIDO CT	1600	CMRL	93010	524-D3
ESKIMO LN	2300	VEN	93001	471-C6
ESPANA LN	3000	THO	91362	527-C3
ESPERANCE DR	23600	SIMI	93065	497-B3
ESPLANADE DR	-	VEN	93001	491-F2
ESSEX WY	2300	VEN	93001	471-C6
ESSEX JUNCTION CT	1100	THO	91362	527-C2
ESTABAN DR	-	VEN	93001	491-E2
ESTANCIA PL	200	CMRL	93012	495-D7
ESTATES AV	-	VEN	93003	492-A2
ESTATES DR	500	THO	91320	525-D6
ESTER AV	300	MRPK	93021	496-C1
ESTON ST	1600	CMRL	93010	524-F2
ESTRELLA ST	2300	VEN	93001	491-G2
ESTRELLITA LN	200	VEN	91377	558-A2
ESTRIGA CT	400	SPLA	93060	463-J6
ESWARD DR	27000	CALB	91301	558-B7
ETHEL CT	3400	VeCo	93020	525-C2
ETNA CT	7000	VEN	93003	472-D6
ETON WY	100	THO	91360	526-H3
ETTIN AV	800	SIMI	93065	497-H5
ETTING RD	1100	OXN	93033	553-B4
	23600	VeCo	93012	553-E4
	17600	VeCo	93012	553-E4
ETZ MELOY MTWY	-	VeCo	90265	586-E4
EUBANKS ST	400	SIMI	93023	441-D7
EUCALYPTUS AV	10100	VEN	93004	492-J2
EUCALYPTUS CIR	1500	THO	91360	526-H3
N EUCALYPTUS DR	-	CMRL	93010	524-B4
	-	VeCo	93015	455-E7
S EUCALYPTUS DR	100	VeCo	93015	465-E1
EUCALYPTUS ST	100	OJAI	93023	441-H6
	3700	SIMI	93065	478-E7
W EUCALYPTUS ST	400	OJAI	93023	441-G6
EUCLID AV	900	CMRL	93010	524-C1
EUCLID CIR	1900	CMRL	93010	524-E1
EUGENE AV	700	VEN	93003	492-H2
EUGENIA ST	-	VEN	93003	491-G2
EUNICE AV	7000	CanP	91307	529-F5
EUREKA ST	400	PHME	93041	552-E5
	8300	VEN	93004	492-G2
EUREKA CANYON RD	23600	VeCo	93040	457-G7
EVA ST	100	VEN	93003	491-G4
EVANGELINE PL	1500	OXN	93030	522-D4
EVANS AV	1700	VEN	93001	491-E2
EVANS DR	3500	SIMI	93063	498-E3
EVANSTON PL	900	OXN	93033	552-J3
EVANWOOD AV	800	SIMI	93065	498-A3
EVE RD	4200	SIMI	93063	478-D7
EVELYN AV	100	THO	91360	526-E4
EVENING SIDE DR	22100	WdHI	91367	529-F7
EVENING SKY DR	2900	THO	91362	526-J2
EVENSTAR AV	800	THO	91361	557-B5
EVEREST AV	2800	VeCo	93012	496-A6
EVEREST ST	23600	VEN	93003	523-A5
EVERETT ST	-	MRPK	93021	476-C7
	2300	VEN	93001	471-C6
EVERGLADES ST	5300	VEN	93003	492-C5
EVERGREEN AV	-	OJAI	93023	441-G5
	500	THO	91320	555-G3
EVERGREEN CT	23600	SIMI	93063	497-F7
EVERGREEN DR	2100	SIMI	93065	497-E2
N EVERGREEN DR	-	VEN	93001	491-E2
S EVERGREEN DR	-	VEN	93001	491-F3
EVERGREEN LN	400	PHME	93041	552-E5
	1100	OXN	93033	552-F5
	1100	PHME	93033	552-F5
EVERGREEN SQ	400	PHME	93041	552-F5
EVESHAM AV	2800	THO	91362	527-A3
EVITA CT	5500	AGRH	91301	557-H5
EWANA PL	-	Chat	91311	479-A7
EXETER AV	1300	VEN	93003	492-H3
EXETER CT	2500	CMRL	93010	524-F1
EXPLORER CV	2500	PHME	93041	552-C3

F

Street	Block	City	ZIP	Pg-Grid
F AV	-	VeCo	93042	583-F6
F ST	-	VeCo	93041	583-G2
	-	VeCo	93041	583-G2
	100	OXN	93030	522-F6
	1300	OXN	93033	552-F1
	23600	VEN	93003	498-H7
	1100	VEN	93003	553-B4
	23600	VeCo	93012	553-E4
N F ST	100	OXN	93030	522-F5
FABLE AV	2600	LA	91304	529-H3
FACILITY RD	23600	VeCo	93012	499-B7
FACTORY AV	500	THO	91320	526-G6
FACTORY LN	300	OXN	93030	522-H7
FACTORY STORES DR	-	CMRL	93010	524-B4
FACULTY CT	-	THO	91360	526-F2
FACULTY ST	100	THO	91360	526-E3
FAGAN CANYON	23600	SPLA	93060	463-J5
	23600	SPLA	93060	463-J5
FAIR AV	1500	SIMI	93065	498-E3
FAIRBANKS AV	2800	SIMI	93063	478-E3
FAIRBOURNE PL	300	OXN	93033	552-G5
FAIRBREEZE CIR	3900	WLKV	91362	557-C6
FAIRBROOK LN	4300	MRPK	93021	496-C1
FAIRCHILD AV	900	CMRL	93010	524-E2
FAIRCREST LN	5100	VeCo	93063	495-A1
FAIRFAX AV	200	VEN	93003	492-B1
FAIRFIELD CIR	1600	VeCo	93040	457-H1
FAIRFIELD RD	10100	VEN	93004	492-J2
FAIRFORD ST	8500	VEN	93004	492-G4
FAIRGRANGE DR	5400	AGRH	91301	557-H5
FAIRGROVE CIR	1000	VEN	93063	494-F6
FAIRHAVEN CT	300	THO	91320	555-G2
	6100	AGRH	91301	558-A3
FAIRMONT DR	3300	VEN	93033	491-H2
FAIRMOUNT RD	1400	THO	91362	527-D6
FAIR OAKS	8000	VeCo	93063	476-D3
FAIRPOINT AV	6500	VEN	93003	492-D5
FAIRVIEW CT	1200	OJAI	93023	441-G5
	23600	SIMI	93063	479-A6
FAIRVIEW DR	800	VEN	93001	491-F2
	5400	AGRH	91301	558-C4
FAIRVIEW RD	100	THO	91361	557-A3
	100	VeCo	93023	441-E5
	100	VeCo	93023	441-D5
E FAIRVIEW RD	100	OJAI	93023	441-G5
	500	THO	91361	557-A3
FAIRVIEW CANYON RD	23600	SIMI	93063	456-G6
FAIRVIEW FIRE RD	400	THO	91361	556-J3
	400	THO	91361	557-A3
FAIRWAY CT	1300	VeCo	93010	494-A5
	1600	THO	91362	527-D6
	2300	OXN	93030	522-C2
FAIRWAY DR	500	VeCo	93010	494-A5
FAIRWAY LN	100	OJAI	93023	442-A7
FAIRWAY PARK LN	2600	SIMI	93063	478-J7
FAIR WEATHER CRSG	23600	SPLA	93060	464-B7
	23600	SPLA	93060	464-C7
	23600	VeCo	93060	464-B7
FAITH CT	6400	SIMI	93063	499-C3
FALCON CT	-	VEN	93003	492-C4
FALCON WY	1000	FILM	93015	455-J5
FALCONROCK LN	400	VeCo	91377	558-A1
FALCONVIEW LN	400	VeCo	91377	528-B7
FALKIRK AV	1500	SIMI	93065	552-A1
FALKIRK BAY	4400	OXN	93035	552-A1
FALKNER PL	1900	OXN	93033	553-A1
FALLBROOK AV	6100	WdHI	91367	529-H7
	6400	CanP	91307	529-H3
	7400	LA	91304	529-H3
FALLEN LEAF AV	300	VEN	93012	524-H5
FALLEN LEAF CT	2400	VEN	93004	492-J2
FALLEN OAKS DR	23600	THO	91360	526-F1
FALLING STAR AV	1200	THO	91362	527-B4
FALLING WATER CT	23600	SIMI	93063	478-J6

VENTURA CO. INDEX

Street	Block	City	ZIP	Pg-Grid
FALLON CIR	2500	SIMI	93065	498-B3
FALL RIVER CIR	3400	THO	91362	557-C3
FALLVIEW RD	1800	SIMI	93061	557-A6
	1800	WLKV	91361	557-A6
FALMOUTH ST	800	THO	91362	526-J7
	900	THO	91362	527-A6
FALON CT	1900	THO	91362	527-A5
FANNIN DR	4600	SIMI	93063	478-G6
FANSHELL WK	1100	OXN	93035	522-D7
FARGO ST	400	THO	91360	526-D4
FARIA RD	4000	VeCo	93001	470-A3
FARIA ST	3300	CMRL	93010	524-G1
FARING FORD RD	2900	SIMI	93061	586-D2
FARLAND ST	100	THO	91320	556-B2
FARLEY ST		PHME	93043	552-E4
FARM RD	1900	SIMI	93064	554-D3
FARMFIELD RD	26000	CALB	91342	558-H3
FARNHAM RD	100	VeCo	93023	441-F4
FARNWORTH ST	2100	CMRL	93010	524-E1
FARRAGUT CT	1900	OXN	93033	553-A1
FARRAGUT DR	2600	OXN	93033	553-A2
FARRALONE AV	6400	CanP	91303	529-J6
	7600	LA	91304	529-J1
	8900	LA	91304	499-J7
	9000	Chat	91311	499-J3
FARRELL CT	3500	THO	91320	555-F2
FARWELL ST	2000	SIMI	93065	497-J2
FASHION PARK PL		OXN	93033	552-G4
E FASLEY AV	5800	SIMI	93063	499-A1
FASTWATER CT	32400	WLKV	91362	557-B7
FATHOM CT	1000	OXN	93035	522-C7
FATHOM DR	1300	OXN	93035	522-C7
	1300	OXN	93035	522-C1
FAULKNER CT	6800	VEN	93003	492-E3
FAULKNER RD	14900	VeCo	93060	473-G2
	23600	SPLA	93060	473-H1
FAUNA DR	2000	SIMI	93065	523-A6
FAUST AV	6700	CanP	91307	529-H4
	7600	LA	91304	529-H2
FAWN AV	2300	VEN	93003	492-E5
FAWN PL	2100	VEN	93003	492-E5
FAWN CHASE LN	2300	SIMI	93065	497-A2
FAWNGLEN CT	900	THO	91361	555-G5
FAWNRIDGE AV	23600	THO	91362	527-B4
FAWN VALLEY CT	200	SIMI	93065	497-E6
FAXTON CT	3200	SIMI	93063	478-E6
FAYANCE PL	3300	THO	91362	526-J2
FAYTON CT	2000	CMRL	93010	494-D7
E FEARING ST	5600	SIMI	93063	499-A2
FEATHER AV	1300	THO	91360	526-E6
FEATHER DR	1800	VEN	93004	492-G4
FEATHER ST	9000	VEN	93004	492-H4
FEATHERFALL WY	23600	SIMI	93065	497-A2
FEATHER HILL CT	1300	THO	91362	526-A6
FEATHERSTONE ST	23600	SIMI	93065	523-A5
FEATHERWOOD ST	23600	THO	91362	527-B5
FELICIA LN	1200	OXN	93030	522-J5
FELICIA ST	5200	CMRL	93012	525-A3
FELIX AV	3200	VeCo	93063	478-E6
FELIX AV	3400	SIMI	93063	478-E5
	2000	SIMI	93063	499-C2
FELIX DR	100	VeCo	93023	441-E7
FELIZ DR		VeCo	93022	451-C4
FELKINS RD	200	SPLA	93060	463-J7
	200	SPLA	93060	463-J7
	200	SPLA	93060	473-J1
FELTON ST	2700	THO	91320	555-G3
FENMORE AV	1700	CMRL	93010	524-G1
	1700	CMRL	93010	494-G7
FENMORE CT	1700	CMRL	93010	524-G1
FENMORE ST	14600	MRPK	93021	476-J6
FENWOOD AV	6100	WdHl	91367	529-G7
FENWORTH CT	6300	AGRH	91301	558-A3
FERAL AV	6200	AGRH	91301	558-B3
FERNANDO DR	100	VeCo	93023	441-D6
FERN ANN FALLS RD		Chat	91311	479-H7
FERNBROOK RD	8600	LA	91304	529-E1
FERNCREST PL	3000	THO	91362	527-C3
FERNDALE PL	300	THO	91360	526-D5
FERNDALE ST	6000	VEN	93003	492-C3
FERNGLEN CIR	600	FILM	93015	456-A5
FERNHILL AV	800	THO	91320	555-E4
FERNHILL CT	800	THO	91320	555-D4
FERNLEAF CT	2100	THO	91362	527-A1
FERN OAK DR	1100	SPLA	93060	464-B3
FERNRIDGE CT	5200	CMRL	93012	524-J1
	5200	CMRL	93012	525-A1
FERN VALLEY CT	4500	MRPK	93021	496-F2
FERNVIEW ST	2100	SIMI	93065	498-A1
N FERNWOOD ST	2000	SIMI	93065	498-A2
FERNWOOD DR	400	OXN	93030	522-F4
	2400	VEN	93001	491-J4
FERRARA CT	30800	WLKV	91362	557-G7
FERRARA DR	1100	VeCo	93023	451-B1
FERRARA WY	1800	OXN	93030	523-A6
	1800	OXN	93030	523-A6
FERRIS DR		VeCo	93060	464-D4
FERRO DR	200	VEN	93001	491-B1
FESTIVAL CT	3600	THO	91360	526-G1
FESTIVO ST	3600	OXN	93030	523-A5
FIELDCREST CT	5300	CMRL	93012	525-A1
FIELDCREST DR	5300	CMRL	93012	525-A1
FIELDFLOWER LN	23600	SIMI	93065	497-A2
FIELDMONT PL	24400	CanP	91307	529-D5
FIELDSTONE WY	300	SIMI	93065	497-D6
FIERRO DR	1100	VeCo	93023	451-B1
FIESTA AV	2300	CMRL	93010	524-E2
E FIESTA GRN	100	PHME	93041	552-D2
W FIESTA GRN	100	PHME	93041	552-D1
FIESTA CT	5900	VEN	93003	492-C2
FIG ST	1400	SIMI	93063	498-G1
FIGUEROA ST	1800	SIMI	93063	491-B2
FILLMORE AV	100	SIMI	93035	552-B5
	100	SIMI	93043	552-B5
FILLMORE ST	6900	VeCo	93012	554-E4
	100	FILM	93015	456-A5
	700	SPLA	93060	463-H7
FINANCIAL SQ	2400	SIMI	93063	522-H1
FINCH AV	1300	VEN	93003	492-D4
FINCH CT	500	FILM	93015	455-H5
	2000	SIMI	93063	499-C2
FINCHLEY CT	3500	SIMI	93063	478-E7
FINE RD	700	VeCo	93015	456-G6
FINE ST	700	FILM	93015	456-A5
FINO AV	6500	CMRL	93012	525-C6
FINROD CT	1000	THO	91361	557-A5
E FIR AV	1700	OXN	93033	552-G1
W FIR AV	100	OXN	93033	552-G1
FIR CT	1600	OXN	93033	552-H1
FIR ST		CMRL	93010	524-E3
N FIR ST		VEN	93001	491-C1
S FIR ST		VEN	93001	491-C2
FIREBIRD CT	5700	CMRL	93012	495-B7
FIRECREST CT	500	THO	91320	555-G3
FIRENZE ST	300	OXN	93030	522-H3
FIRESIDE LN	4300	MRPK	93021	496-F3
FIRESTONE CIR	900	SIMI	93065	497-C6
FIRESTONE CT	2100	OXN	93030	522-D2
FIRETHORNE PL	1600	OXN	93033	522-E4
FIRWOOD CT	2900	THO	91320	555-G3
FISHER CT	3600	SIMI	93035	552-C1
FISHER DR	1700	OXN	93035	552-C1
FISH HATCHERY RD	100	VeCo	93015	456-D6
FISK CT	1700	THO	91362	526-J6
FISKE PL	1200	OXN	93033	552-J1
FITCH AV	600	MRPK	93021	496-F1
FITZGERALD RD	1000	SIMI	93065	497-H4
	1700	SIMI	93065	498-A4
FITZGERALD ST	23600	LA	91304	529-E3
FIVE OAK CT	5600	SIMI	93063	499-A1
FIX WY		VEN	93001	491-B1
FLAGSTAFF CT	700	VEN	93004	492-H2
FLAGSTONE LN	1800	SIMI	93063	498-H1
N FLAMINGO WY	1100	VEN	93004	492-F4
S FLAMINGO WY	1300	VEN	93004	492-F4
FLAMING STAR AV	600	THO	91360	526-D4
FLANAGAN DR	5700	SIMI	93063	479-A7
FLEET AV	700	VEN	93001	491-J4
FLEET ST		VeCo	93042	583-D4
	400	PHME	93041	552-D2
FLEISCHER REDMAN RD	23600	VeCo	93030	464-H3
FLETCHER CT	2100	THO	91360	556-H7
FLETCHER ST	2700	SIMI	93065	498-C4
FLEURY LN	6100	WdHl	91367	529-J7
FLICKER CT	6900	VEN	93003	492-E4
FLINN AV	500	MRPK	93021	496-F1
W FLINT ST		VEN	93001	471-B7
FLINTLOCK LN	4200	WLKV	91361	557-F6
	4200	AGRH	91301	557-F6
N FLINTLOCK LN		VeCo	91307	529-A5
FLINTON CT	1400	THO	91360	557-A6
FLINTRIDGE CT	2200	THO	91360	527-B4
FLITTNER CIR	3600	SIMI	93063	556-G1
FLOATING CLOUD ST	3600	THO	91360	526-G1
FLOOD ST	2400	SIMI	93063	522-H1
FLORADALE CT	3600	THO	91360	526-H1
FLORAL DR	4000	VeCo	93001	471-C1
	4700	VeCo	93001	461-C7
FLORA VISTA AV	100	THO	91360	526-D2
		CMRL	93012	524-H1
FLORENCE AV	200	PHME	93041	552-F5
FLORENCE ST	4000	SIMI	93063	498-F2
FLORENTINA DR	23600	VeCo	93030	522-J5
FLORENTINE CT	1700	THO	91362	527-B3
FLORESTA CT	4800	THO	91362	527-E7
FLORY AV		MRPK	93021	496-E1
FLOWER ST	3900	VEN	93003	491-J3
FLOWERCREEK DR	11500	MRPK	93021	496-B3
FLOWERDALE ST	1600	SIMI	93065	499-C3
FLOWER GLEN ST	900	SIMI	93065	477-G7
	900	SIMI	93065	497-H1
FLOWERVIEW CT	4200	MRPK	93021	496-B2
FLOWERWOOD CT	11600	MRPK	93021	496-B4
FLOWTOW LN	900	THO	91362	556-J1
FLOYD DR	300	SPLA	93060	464-A7
FLYING HILLS LN	2600	THO	91362	526-G1
FLYNN RD		CMRL	93012	524-G2
	18300	CMRL	93012	494-H7
FOGHORN CV	2600	PHME	93041	552-D1
FOLKESTONE TERRACE RD		THO	91361	557-A6
FONT LN		THO	91361	557-A6
FONTANA DR	100	OXN	93030	553-C4
FOOTHILL DR	400	FILM	93015	456-A4
	1200	VeCo	93063	499-B3
	1900	THO	91361	557-A7
	5500	AGRH	91301	558-C5
FOOTHILL LN	100	OJAI	93023	441-G6
FOOTHILL RD	100	OJAI	93023	441-F6
	500	SPLA	93060	463-H6
	700	VeCo	93060	463-E7
	1100	VeCo	93060	441-G4
	2800	VeCo	93003	491-H1
	2800	VeCo	93003	491-H1
	3800	VeCo	93003	492-A1
	3800	VeCo	93003	492-A1
	7500	VEN	93004	492-D1
	7500	VEN	93004	492-D1
	7600	VEN	93004	472-F7
	8000	VEN	93004	472-J6
	10600	VeCo	93060	472-J6
	11000	VeCo	93060	472-J6
	11400	VeCo	93060	473-C1
FOOTHILL TR		VeCo		441-F3
FORAR CIR	1700	CMRL	93010	524-H1
FORBES LN		VEN	93001	471-B6
FORD AV	23600	VeCo	93030	492-A2
FORDHAM AV	300	VEN	93003	492-A3
	1200	THO	91360	526-D5
FORDHAM ST	14300	MRPK	93021	476-G6
FORDYCE RD	700	VeCo	93023	442-C5
FORELOCK CT	700	SIMI	93065	497-G6
FOREST AV	1100	OJAI	93023	451-B3
	1200	SIMI	93065	497-H4
FOREST DR	1200	SPLA	93060	464-B3
FOREST COVE LN	5300	WLKV	91361	557-H4
FORESTGLEN CT	4400	MRPK	93021	496-D3
FOREST HILLS RD	7100	CanP	91307	529-F5
FOREST KNOLL CT	5300	WLKV	91377	557-G6
FOREST LOOP DR	600	PHME	93041	552-F5
FOREST OAKS DR	4100	OXN	93036	496-J7
FOREST RIDGE DR	5400	AGRH	91301	557-G5
FORNEY LN	6400	VeCo	93063	499-C4
FORRESTER CIR	2800	SIMI	93065	497-G7
FORT COURAGE AV	100	THO	91360	526-D2
FORT DAVIS ST	4600	SIMI	93063	478-G6
FORTUNA AV	2100	SIMI	93063	496-B7
FORTUNA CT	3900	CMRL	93010	494-H7
FORTUNA LN	4100	OXN	93033	553-C4
FORT WORTH DR	4000	SIMI	93063	478-G7
FOSTER AV	1800	VEN	93001	491-E2
FOSTER PARK DR		VeCo	93001	460-J5
FOSTER PARK WY		VeCo	93001	460-J5
FOUNTAIN PL	28500	AGRH	91301	558-C5
FOUNTAIN CREST LN	2300	THO	91362	527-C4
FOUNTAINWOOD ST	28900	AGRH	91301	558-A3
FOUR OAK CT	5600	SIMI	93063	499-A1
FOURSITE LN	300	THO	91362	556-J1
FOURNIER ST	2900	OXN	93033	552-H3
FOX ST	100	OJAI	93023	441-J7
FOXBORO LN	7600	LA	91304	529-E4
FOX CANYON RD	2600	VeCo	93066	474-G5
FOXDALE CT	2200	THO	91360	556-H1
FOX DEN CT	300	OXN	93030	522-D2
FOXFIELD DR	3900	WLKV	91361	557-D7
FOXGLOVE CT	3900	THO	91362	557-C1
FOXGLOVE PL	300	THO	91362	522-F2
FOX HILL LN	9400	Chat	91311	499-H6
FOX HILLS DR	200	THO	91362	556-F7
FOXMOOR CT	200	THO	91360	556-F7
FOX RIDGE DR	1100	THO	91361	556-F7
FOX SPRINGS CIR	300	VeCo	93060	523-C2
FOXTAIL CT	3100	THO	91362	527-C3
FOXWOOD CT	3600	THO	91360	526-H1
FOXWOOD DR	5600	VeCo	93377	557-J1
FRAGRANS WY	6100	WdHl	91367	529-J7
FRANCE AV	200	OJAI	93023	441-H6
FRANCE CIR	200	OJAI	93023	441-H6
FRANCES ST	100	VEN	93001	491-G3
FRANCIS AV	3900	CMRL	93010	494-H7
FRANCISCA WY	5300	AGRH	91301	557-J5
FRANCISCO PL	300	VEN	93003	492-G4
E FRANDON CT	3900	SIMI	93063	498-F2
FRANK AV	200	THO	91360	526-D5
FRANKFORT CT	700	SIMI	93065	552-J3
FRANKIE DR	3200	THO	91320	525-F7
FRANKLIN CT	1200	SIMI	93065	497-H4
FRANKLIN DR	1200	SPLA	93060	464-B3
FRANKLIN LN		VEN	93004	471-C6
FRANKLIN ST	9200	Chat	91311	499-F7
FRANRIVERS AV	6400	CanP	91307	529-D7
FRANTZ DR	23600	WHll	91304	499-E6
FRASER AV		VEN	93001	471-C2
FRASER ST	23600	VeCo	93033	451-D6
FRAZIER ST	1400	CMRL	93012	525-B1
FRAZIER MOUNTAIN RD		VeCo		367-B1
FRED AV	1700	SIMI	93065	498-B3
FREEBIRD LN		VeCo	91377	527-J7
FREEBORN WY	2100	SIMI	93012	496-B7
FREEDOM PARK DR	500	CMRL	93010	523-J5
FREEPORT CT	1000	THO	91361	557-B5
FREETOWN LN	27400	AGRH	91301	558-E7
FRWY Rt#-23		MRPK		496-G1
		THO		496-J7
		THO		497-A5
		THO		526-J1
		THO		556-H1
		VeCo		496-H3
		THO		497-A4
FREMLIN DR	1800	SIMI	93015	456-A4
FREMONT AV	1500	SIMI	93063	497-J4
FREMONT CIR	5900	CMRL	93012	525-B1
	5900	CMRL	93012	525-B7
FREMONT DR	1800	THO	91362	526-J5
FREMONT ST		MRPK	93021	496-E2
	3400	SIMI	93063	523-D5
FREMONT WY	1900	VeCo	93012	496-C3
FREMONTIA ST	2300	SIMI	93065	523-A5
FRENCH CT	2500	SIMI	93065	498-D1
FRESHMAN CT	15700	MRPK	93021	477-A5
FRESH MEADOWS RD	2800	SIMI	93063	498-C2
FRESHWATER DR	29000	AGRH	91301	558-A3
FRESHWIND CIR	3900	WLKV	91361	557-C6
FRESNO CT	10700	VEN	93004	472-H7
FREY CANYON RD		VeCo	93060	466-H2
FRIANT AV	1300	SIMI	93065	498-A3
FRIAR ST	22400	WdHl	91362	529-D7
FRIEDRICH LN	1300	OXN	93033	552-E2
FRIEDRICH RD	500	OXN	93033	523-C2
E FRONT ST	1700	SIMI	93065	498-A1
W FRONT ST	3000	SIMI	93063	478-G7
FRONTAGE RD	400	VEN	93004	472-H6
FRONTIER AV	2900	THO	91360	526-C3
FRONTIER PL	11300	Chat	91311	499-J2
FROST AV	2500	THO	91360	526-F3
FROST CIR	6900	VEN	93003	492-E3
FROST DR	4200	OXN	93033	552-H4
FRUITVALE AV	8000	SIMI	93021	476-D3
FUCHSIA AV	1100	SPLA	93060	464-B3
FUCHSIA PL		VeCo	93063	473-A7
FUCHSIA ST	900	OXN	93030	522-E2
FUELBREAK RD	5300	VeCo	93023	366-L7
	5300	VeCo	93023	366-L7
	5300	VeCo	93023	442-H4
FULBROKE DR	1900	VeCo	91320	558-A4
FULLER AV	1900	SIMI	93065	498-A4
FULMAR AV	6900	VEN	93003	492-E4
FULTON DR		THO	91320	555-B1
FULTON ST		CMRL	93010	524-E3
S FULTON ST		CMRL	93010	524-E3
FURMAN AV	1200	THO	91362	526-J3
FUTURA PT	3100	THO	91362	527-A2

G

Street	Block	City	ZIP	Pg-Grid
G ST		VeCo	93042	583-F6
	100	VeCo	93042	522-F6
	1200	OXN	93033	552-F7
N G ST	300	OXN	93030	522-F5
GABBERT RD	5000	MRPK	93021	496-C1
	5200	MRPK	93021	476-B6
GABRIELA CT	2400	CMRL	93012	495-B6
GABRIELLA DR	23600	OXN	93030	522-J5
GADSHILL LN	6300	AGRH	91301	558-F7
GAGE AV	4100	AGRH	91301	557-J6
GAIL CT	2900	THO	91320	555-H2
E GAINES CT	3800	SIMI	93063	498-E2
E GAINSBOROUGH RD	1800	THO	91360	526-F6
W GAINSBOROUGH RD	500	THO	91360	526-F6
GALANO DR	4900	CMRL	93012	524-J3
GALANTE WY	200	OXN	93030	522-G3
GALAXY PL	3400	OXN	93030	523-D5
GALE WY	3300	VEN	93003	491-H2
GALENA AV	2100	SIMI	93063	498-D1
	2100	SIMI	93065	498-D1
	2700	SIMI	93063	478-D7
E GALENA AV	2700	SIMI	93065	498-C2
GALERITA ST	2800	OXN	93030	523-A5
GALESMORE CT	1000	THO	91361	557-A5
GALINDO AV	2500	SIMI	93065	498-C4
GALLATIN PL	1100	OXN	93030	522-D4
GALLEON AV	2600	PHME	93041	552-D1
GALLOP CT	1800	SIMI	93065	497-J6
GALLOPING HILL RD	400	SIMI	93065	497-E6
GALSWORTHY ST	100	THO	91360	526-F7
GALT ST	1700	SIMI	93065	497-J3
GALVESTON AV	3000	SIMI	93063	478-G7
GALVIN CIR	400	VEN	93004	472-H6
GALVIN LN	700	FILM	93015	456-A4
GALVIN ST	10500	VEN	93004	472-H6
GALWAY LN	1800	THO	91320	556-A1
GAMEBIRD CT	29300	AGRH	91301	558-A3
GAMMON CT	1800	THO	91362	526-J2
GANTLIN AV	1100	SIMI	93065	497-H4
GARCES AV	4400	CMRL	93010	494-H7
GARCIA ST	100	SPLA	93060	464-C5
GARDEN DR	200	THO	91361	586-E1
E GARDEN GRN	100	PHME	93041	552-E1
W GARDEN GRN	100	PHME	93041	552-D1
N GARDEN ST		VEN	93001	491-B1
S GARDEN ST		VEN	93001	491-B2
GARDENIA AV	1400	CMRL	93010	494-D7
	1600	VeCo	93041	552-B5
	1600	VeCo	93041	524-C1
GARDENIA ST	100	THO	91320	555-B7
GARDEN OAKS CT	29000	AGRH	91301	558-A3
GARDENSTONE CT	1800	SIMI	93065	498-J3
GARDENSTONE LN	1800	SIMI	93065	499-A2
GARDNER AV	700	VEN	93004	492-E2
GARDNER ST	2800	SIMI	93065	498-C5
GARFIELD AV	100	OXN	93030	522-H6
N GARFIELD AV	100	OXN	93030	522-H5
	1200	OXN	93033	552-F1
	1200	OXN	93033	552-F1
	23600	VeCo	93063	528-F1
GARFIELD RONDO	300	CMRL	93010	492-E2
GERALD DR	3100	VeCo	91320	555-G1
GARLAND CT	2800	THO	91360	526-D3
GARLAND ST	300	VeCo	93001	471-C1
GARNET PL	200	OXN	93030	522-F2
GARNET HILL CT	28800	AGRH	91301	558-A3
GARRET DR	26900	CALB	91302	495-B6
GARRIDO CT	1000	VeCo	93060	494-B6
GARRIDO DR	6300	AGRH	91301	558-A3
GARRISON WY	8900	VEN	93004	492-H3
GARST LN	1500	VeCo	93023	442-E4
GARVIN AV	1700	SIMI	93065	498-B3
GARY CT	3400	SIMI	93063	499-B4
GARY DR	4900	CMRL	93012	524-J3
GASTON RD	1000	OXN	93033	553-A3
GASWAY DR		FILM	93015	456-A7
GATEHOUSE LN	1400	CMRL	93010	524-C1
GATES PL	2600	SIMI	93065	498-B1
GATESHEAD BAY	4400	OXN	93035	522-A1
GATESHEAD WY	7100	CanP	91307	529-F5
GATEWAY DR	6400	SIMI	93063	499-C3
GATEWOOD LN	1200	SPLA	93060	464-B2
GAUCHO WY	1800	OXN	93030	522-J6
GAULT ST	22200	CanP	91303	529-J5
	22700	CanP	91307	529-J5
GAVIOTA CT	400	SIMI	93065	498-A2
GAVIOTA LN	1300	VEN	93003	492-C4
GAVIOTA PL	100	OXN	93033	552-G4
GAVIOTA WY	700	OXN	93033	552-H4
GAY DR		VEN	93003	492-B4
GAYLE PL	2400	SIMI	93065	498-A1
E GAYTHORNE RD	12600	VeCo	93060	473-E5
GAZANIA CT	200	THO	91362	556-H1
GEM CIR	3600	SIMI	93063	478-D7
GEMINI AV	1000	OXN	93030	524-F2
GEMINI CT	2600	CMRL	93010	524-F1
GENE AV	1500	SIMI	93065	498-B3
GENEIVE CIR	6000	VeCo	93003	492-D6
GENEIVE CT		CMRL	93010	524-D4
GENEVA ST	100	PHME	93041	552-E1
GENEVA WY	2000	OXN	93036	552-D1
GENIAL CT	2500	SIMI	93065	497-A3
GENOA DR	900	OXN	93033	497-F3
GENOVA CT	30800	WLKV	91362	557-G6
GENTILLY PL	1400	VeCo	91377	527-J6
GENTLE CREEK CIR	500	THO	91320	555-F2
GENTLEWOOD DR	11500	MRPK	93021	496-B3
GEOFFREY AV	1800	SIMI	93065	498-J3
GEORGE ST	1800	SIMI	93065	499-A2
GEORGETOWN AV	700	VEN	93004	492-A1
GEORGETTE ST	2600	SIMI	93065	498-D1
	2700	SIMI	93065	478-D7
GEORGIA ST	3900	VEN	93003	491-J3
GEORGIA WY	9200	Chat	91311	499-E7
GERANIUM LN	600	SIMI	93065	497-D5
GERANIUM PL	200	OXN	93030	522-F2
GERANIUM WY	23600	SIMI	93060	473-A7
GERMAIN ST	3400	CMRL	93010	524-G1
	22100	Chat	91311	499-J3
GERMANIA ST	6300	AGRH	91301	558-A3
GERONIMO AV	2900	SIMI	93063	479-A6
GERONIMO DR	23600	VeCo	93060	453-G2
GERRAD WY	23600	CanP	91307	529-E4
GERRY RD	1800	VeCo	93012	495-G7
GERSHWIN LN	1800	OXN	93033	552-G1
GERSHWIN PL	2100	OXN	93033	553-A1
GERST DR	1300	THO	91320	525-F2
GERTRUDE ST	4000	SIMI	93063	498-F2
GETMAN ST	1400	CMRL	93010	524-C1
GETTYSBURG ST	4000	VEN	93003	491-J2
GEYSER CT	1300	THO	91320	526-A6
GIANT OAK AV	2600	THO	91362	556-A1
GIBRALTAR ST	100	VEN	93003	497-E5
GIBSON AV	800	SIMI	93065	497-J5
GIERSON AV	9400	Chat	91311	499-J5
GIFFORD ST	7200	CanP	91307	529-E5
W GILA CT	1900	THO	91320	555-J2
N GILA CT	2400	THO	91320	556-J1
GILBERT CT	4700	VEN	93003	492-A7
GILBERT LN	200	SIMI	93063	492-A1
GILBERT ST	500	VEN	93003	525-H7
GILDA CIR	1700	SIMI	93065	498-A3
GILES RD	100	THO	91361	556-F7
GILL AV	400	PHME	93041	552-F4
GILLIARD ST	200	VEN	93001	491-D1
GILLINGHAM CIR	200	THO	91362	527-A2
GILMORE ST	22000	CanP	91307	529-J7
	22300	CanP	91307	529-C7
GINA DR	1200	OXN	93030	522-E4
GINA ST	1200	THO	91320	556-B1
GINGER CIR	2300	THO	91320	555-J1
GINGER DR	3200	OXN	93033	552-F4
GINGER ST	2200	THO	91320	522-F3
GINGERWOOD CT	3600	THO	91360	526-H1
GINKO CT	3200	THO	91360	526-F2
GISLER AV	5600	CMRL	93012	525-B6
GITANA AV	5600	OXN	93033	522-H5
GLACIER CT	1400	OXN	93030	552-H2
GLACIER DR	30800	WLKV	91362	557-G6
GLACIER ST	1400	SIMI	93063	498-D3
GLADE AV	6400	CanP	91303	529-J2
	7600	LA	91304	529-J2
	9200	Chat	91311	499-J4
GLADE DR	500	SPLA	93060	464-A5
GLADEHOLLOW CT	5500	AGRH	91301	558-H5
GLADE SPRINGS CT	2100	OXN	93030	522-D2
GLADHILL ST	4000	THO	91320	555-E4
GLADIOLA ST	800	THO	91320	522-F2
GLADSTONE ST	500	THO	91360	526-E6
GLAMOUR TER		LA	91304	529-D2
GLANVILLE RD	23600	SIMI	93060	464-J4
N GLASSELL AV	1500	SIMI	93063	465-A4
GLASTONBURY RD	1900	THO	91363	557-A6
GLEAM CT	5900	AGRH	91301	558-B4
GLEDHILL ST	22000	Chat	91311	499-J6
GLEN ST	2300	VEN	93003	491-G3
GLEN WY	200	FILM	93015	455-J6
GLENBRIDGE CIR	1100	THO	91361	557-B5
GLENBRIDGE RD	31400	WLKV	91361	557-D7
GLENBROCK LN	1500	THO	91320	526-A7
GLENBROOK AV		CMRL	93010	524-D1
	700	CMRL	93010	524-D1
GLENCOE AV	2600	SIMI	93063	478-D7
GLENCREST CIR	6300	VEN	93003	472-C6
GLENDALE AV	100	VeCo	93035	552-H5
GLENDON CT	23600	VEN	93003	497-A7
GLEN EAGLES AV	2600	OXN	93030	522-D2
GLEN EAGLES CT	500	SIMI	93065	498-A1
GLEN ELLEN DR	2300	VEN	93003	491-H2
GLENHAVEN CIR	4800	THO	91362	557-G1
GLENHAVEN CT	7200	CanP	91307	529-E5
GLEN HOLLOW ST	1900	THO	91320	555-J2
GLENHURST CT	2400	SIMI	93063	498-D1
GLENLOCH LN	23600	SIMI	93063	497-A1
GLENMARE CT	1300	THO	91361	557-A6
GLENMONT CT	4000	THO	91320	555-E4
GLENN DR		CMRL	93010	524-E3
S GLENN DR		CMRL	93010	524-E4
GLENNCLIFF CIR	3100	THO	91360	526-C2
GLENNON CT	1600	THO	91361	556-J5
GLEN OAKS RD	600	THO	91360	556-G1
GLENSIDE LN	2300	VEN	93003	491-H2
GLENVIEW AV	1700	SIMI	93065	498-E3
GLENWAY ST	700	SIMI	93065	464-B5
GLENWOOD AV	200	VEN	93003	492-C2
GLENWOOD DR	200	OXN	93030	522-F4
GLENWOOD PL	2300	THO	91320	556-J1
GLIDE AV	6100	WdHl	91367	529-F7
GLIDER CT	1900	THO	91320	526-A6
GLOBE AV	2800	THO	91320	555-F1
GLORIA CT	5600	CMRL	93012	525-B6
GLORIA DR	3200	VeCo	91320	525-F7
GLORIA LN	23600	SIMI	93063	498-B3
GLORYETTE AV	2100	SIMI	93063	498-G1
GLOUCESTER LN	2100	THO	91320	526-J7
GLOVER DR	2100	VEN	93003	492-C5
GOBELS PASTURE RD	2300	THO	91320	527-A7
GODDARD ST	3400	SIMI	93063	498-E2
GOLD CV	2500	PHME	93041	552-D7

STREET
Block City ZIP Pg-Grid

GOLD DUST CT
1600 SIMI 93063 499-C3
GOLDEN BEAR CT
800 SIMI 93065 497-E6
GOLDEN CANYON CIR
11200 Chat 91311 499-H2
GOLDEN CREST AV
3200 THO 91320 555-G4
GOLDEN EAGLE DR
1200 VeCo 91377 527-G7
GOLDEN FERN CT
200 SIMI 93065 497-E6
GOLDEN GLEN DR
- SIMI 93065 497-D6
GOLDEN GROVE CT
800 SIMI 93065 497-E6
GOLDEN KNOLL CT
4900 THO 91362 557-F3
GOLDENLEAF DR
3600 WLKV 91361 557-C7
GOLDEN MOSS CT
700 SIMI 93065 497-E6
GOLDEN NUGGET WY
5300 VeCo 91377 527-H7
GOLDEN OAK ST
- THO 91320 526-A6
GOLDEN PARK PL
400 SIMI 93065 497-E6
GOLDENRIDGE CT
5200 CMRL 93012 524-J1
5200 CMRL 93012 525-A1
GOLDEN ROD CT
1900 THO 91361 557-A6
GOLDENROD PL
26600 CALB 91302 558-G7
GOLDEN SKY CIR
1900 THO 91362 527-G5
GOLDENSPUR DR
3000 VeCo 93010 494-C6
GOLDEN VINE CT
400 SIMI 93065 497-E6
GOLDEN WEST AV
200 OJAI 93023 442-A6
200 VeCo 93023 442-A6
GOLDENWOOD CIR
500 SIMI 93065 497-E6
GOLDFIELD PL
2700 SIMI 93063 478-E7
2700 SIMI 93063 498-D1
GOLDFINCH DR
6800 VEN 93003 492-E4
GOLD HILL CIR
3100 THO 91360 526-D2
GOLD HILL RD
- VeCo - 367-C1
GOLDIN AV
2400 SIMI 93065 498-B1
GOLDMAN AV
- MRPK 93021 496-D1
GOLDSMITH AV
2200 THO 91360 526-F4
GOLD SPRING PL
800 THO 91361 557-A5
GOLD STRIKE AV
2300 THO 91360 526-D4
GOLF COURSE CT
1800 THO 91362 527-D6
GOLF COURSE DR
4300 THO 91362 527-D6
GOLF COURSE RD
2800 VEN 93003 492-D7
GOLF MEADOWS CT
2600 SIMI 93063 478-H7
GOLF VILLA WY
- CMRL 93010 493-H7
GOLIAD CIR
4800 SIMI 93063 478-H7
GOLONDRINA ST
13100 MRPK 93021 496-E3
GONDOLA DR
4800 VeCo 91377 557-G2
GONZAGA ST
5200 VEN 93003 492-B3
GONZALES RD
- OXN 93030 522-F3
1100 VeCo 93063 499-A4
1300 VeCo 93030 522-A3
1800 OXN 93030 523-A3
3900 VeCo 93030 521-H3
5000 VeCo 93035 521-H3
GONZALES SERVICE RD
500 OXN 93030 522-F3
GOODENOUGH RD
700 FILM 93015 455-J5
1000 VeCo 93015 455-J3
2100 VeCo 93015 367-B7
GOODHOPE ST
500 VeCo 93022 451-A7
GOODMAN ST
800 VEN 93003 492-A4
GOODSPEED ST
1000 PHME 93041 552-E5
GOODSPRING DR
30300 AGRH 91301 557-G5
E GOODWIN CT
3900 SIMI 93063 498-F2
GOODYEAR AV
1700 VEN 93003 492-A5
GORGON DR
- VeCo 93041 583-G2
GORHAM RD
100 VeCo 93023 442-B6
GORMAN ST
2100 CMRL 93010 524-E2
GORRION AV
- VEN 93004 472-J6
- VEN 93004 473-A6
GOSHEN ST
6100 SIMI 93063 499-B2
GOTITA WY
1200 OXN 93030 522-H5
E GOULD ST
2600 SIMI 93065 498-C5
GRABLE PL
700 THO 91320 555-G3
E GRACELAND ST
2200 SIMI 93065 498-B2
GRACIA ST
800 CMRL 93010 524-G2
GRADA AV
600 VeCo 93010 494-B6
GRADUATE CIR
15800 MRPK 93021 477-A4
E GRAFTON ST
3100 SIMI 93063 498-D2
N GRAFTON ST
2200 SIMI 93063 498-D2
GRAHAM AV
400 CMRL 93010 524-F3
GRAHAM CT
10100 VEN 93004 492-J2
GRAHAM ST
1100 SIMI 93065 497-H2
GRANADA ST
- CMRL 93010 524-D4
GRANADILLA DR
4200 MRPK 93021 496-E3
N GRANBY AV
800 SIMI 93065 498-C4
GRAND AV
200 OJAI 93023 441-H6
900 VeCo 93015 455-H2
900 OJAI 93023 442-A6
1100 VeCo 93023 442-D5
1900 VEN 93003 492-D5
2000 VeCo 93003 492-D5
2700 VeCo 93015 367-B7
GRANDE ST
200 OXN 93030 522-H2
GRANDE VISTA DR
3000 THO 91320 525-G6
GRANDE VISTA ST
100 VeCo 93022 461-A1
GRAND ISLE DR
13600 MRPK 93021 496-F2
GRAND OAK LN
300 THO 91360 526-D6
GRANDOAKS DR
2600 WLKV 91361 557-A7
GRAND RIDGE CT
6200 VEN 93003 472-C6
GRANDSEN CT
6400 MRPK 93021 477-A6
GRANDVIEW AV
700 OJAI 93023 441-J6
GRANDVIEW CIR
100 CMRL 93010 524-D4
GRANDVIEW CT
5300 VEN 93003 492-B1
GRANDVIEW DR
2000 CMRL 93010 524-E4
GRANDVIEW TER
23200 Chat 91311 499-G6
GRANGER ST
1800 CMRL 93010 524-D2
GRANITE ST
100 SIMI 93065 497-F6
GRANITE HILLS ST
500 SIMI 93065 527-D1
GRANITO DR
1000 VeCo 93023 451-C1
GRANT AV
100 OXN 93030 522-H6
N GRANT AV
100 OXN 93030 522-H5
GRANT LN
500 SPLA 93060 464-C3
GRANT ST
900 SPLA 93060 464-B3
7300 VEN 93003 492-E2
GRANT WY
600 OXN 93033 552-F4
GRANT LINE ST
300 SPLA 93060 464-C4
GRANT PARK FUEL BREAK
500 VeCo 93001 471-D7
500 VEN 93001 471-D7
500 VEN 93001 491-C1
N GRANVIA PL
2600 THO 91360 526-C3
GRANVILLE AV
3000 SIMI 93063 478-G7
GRAPE HILL RD
300 VeCo 93023 453-B1
GRAPEVINE DR
2400 OXN 93030 522-F1
GRAPEVINE RD
- VeCo 93001 450-J6
- VeCo 93001 451-A6
GRAPEVINE RD
- VeCo 93022 450-J6
- VeCo 93022 451-A6
GRASS VALLEY ST
500 SIMI 93065 527-E1
GRAVES AV
300 OXN 93030 523-B4
GRAVES CT
1000 CMRL 93010 524-C2
GRAY CT
800 THO 91362 526-H7
GRAYROCK ST
900 THO 91320 555-F4
GRAYSON CT
2600 SIMI 93065 498-C4
GRAYSTONE DR
7600 LA 91304 529-D4
GRAYSTONE PL
2500 SIMI 93065 497-J1
E GREAT SMOKEY CT
2800 THO 91362 557-C3
W GREAT SMOKEY CT
2700 THO 91362 557-B3
GREELY CT
2000 OXN 93033 553-A1
GREEN LN
600 SIMI 93065 497-E5
GREEN ST
100 SPLA 93060 464-B6
8000 VEN 93004 492-F2
GREENBANK RD
2400 VeCo 91361 586-D1
GREEN BAY CT
10400 VEN 93004 492-J2
N GREENBRIAR AV
700 SIMI 93065 498-A5
GREENBRIAR CT
5900 AGRH 91301 558-A4
GREENBROOK DR
2100 OXN 93033 552-J2
2600 OXN 93033 553-A2
GREENBUSH LN
4100 MRPK 93021 496-F3
GREENCASTLE CT
2500 OXN 93035 552-B2
GREENCASTLE LN
2200 OXN 93035 552-B2
GREENCASTLE WY
2000 OXN 93035 552-B1
GREENDALE AV
800 THO 91320 555-E4
GREENDALE CIR
700 THO 91320 555-E4
GREENFIELD ST
100 THO 91360 526-E6
GREENGATE CT
4500 WLKV 91361 557-D6
GREEN GLADE CT
- CMRL 93010 524-A2
GREEN GRASS CT
29400 AGRH 91301 557-J5
29400 AGRH 91301 558-A5
GREEN HEATH PL
200 THO 91361 556-E2
GREENHILL AV
6500 VEN 93003 492-D5
GREEN LAWN AV
800 CMRL 93010 524-A2
GREEN LEA PL
200 THO 91361 556-E2
GREENLEAF AV
2600 SIMI 93063 498-E1
2700 SIMI 93063 478-E7
GREENMEADOW AV
- THO 91320 556-D2
100 THO 91361 556-E2
N GREENMEADOW AV
- THO 91320 556-C1
GREEN MEADOW DR
5700 AGRH 91301 557-H4
GREENMEADOW DR
- THO 91320 556-C2
GREENMEADOW LN
600 THO 91320 556-D1
GREEN MOOR PL
200 THO 91361 556-E2
GREEN MOUNTAIN ST
500 SIMI 93065 527-D2
GREEN OAK CT
2300 THO 91362 527-A3
GREENOCK LN
1300 VEN 93001 491-F5
GREENPARK CT
2100 THO 91362 527-A4
GREEN PINE PL
23600 SIMI 93063 498-D4
GREENRIDGE DR
5200 VeCo 93021 475-J7
5200 VeCo 93021 495-J1
GREENRIDGE ST
100 THO 91360 526-F1
GREENSBORO RD
800 VEN 93004 492-H3
GREENSWARD ST
2200 SIMI 93065 478-B7
N GREENTREE DR
5400 VeCo 93066 474-J7
5400 VeCo 93066 494-J1
5700 VeCo 93066 475-A7
W GREENTREE DR
5400 VeCo 93066 474-H7
5400 VeCo 93066 494-H1
GREENVALE DR
- CMRL 93010 524-A2
GREEN VALLEY DR
800 THO 91320 526-A7
GREENVIEW CIR
6300 VEN 93003 472-C6
GREENVIEW RD
5800 CALB 91302 558-J3
GREENVILLE DR
3200 SIMI 93063 478-G6
GREEN VISTA CIR
7000 CanP 91307 529-F5
GREENWAY AV
200 THO 91320 555-E2
GREENWICH DR
500 THO 91360 556-G1
GREENWOOD RD
900 SPLA 93060 464-B3
GREENWOOD ST
3700 THO 91320 555-D4
GREGORY ST
1200 OJAI 93023 442-A6
GRENOBLE CT
30800 WLKV 91362 557-G7
GRENVILLE CT
32000 WLKV 91361 557-C6
GRESHAM ST
22000 LA 91304 529-J1
GRETA ST
100 THO 91360 526-F4
GREY FEATHER CT
1500 THO 91362 527-F6
GREY ROCK RD
5600 AGRH 91301 558-A4
5700 AGRH 91301 557-J3
GRIDLEY RD
100 OJAI 93023 442-A6
400 VeCo 93023 442-B3
2300 VeCo - 442-B3
GRIFFAN DR
23600 VeCo 93015 455-J3
GRIFFITH LN
7300 MRPK 93021 477-A4
GRIMES CANYON RD
8600 VeCo 93021 476-A6
9600 MRPK 93021 476-A6
15000 VeCo 93021 475-H7
19300 VeCo 93021 495-H1
GRIMES CANYON RD Rt#-23
1300 VeCo 93015 465-J4
4800 VeCo 93015 466-A5
4800 VeCo 93021 466-A5
8000 VeCo 93021 476-B2
GRINNEL CT
400 SIMI 93065 497-F6
GRISSOM ST
1400 THO 91362 527-A6
GROSS AV
6400 CanP 91307 529-F7
GROUNDBRIER AV
23600 SIMI 93065 497-A2
GROUSE WY
6800 VEN 93003 492-E4
GROVE LN
200 VEN 93001 491-G1
200 VEN 93003 491-G1
GROVE ST
2800 VEN 93003 491-G2
GROVE WY
200 SIMI 93065 497-E2
GROVEDALE LN
13500 MRPK 93021 496-F3
GROVER CIR
1700 SIMI 93063 499-A2
GROVES PL
3700 VeCo 93066 494-H4
GRUB LEASE RD
- VeCo 93001 470-G4
GRUNDY LN
9100 Chat 91311 499-E7
GUADALCANAL ST
- PHME 93041 552-E5
N GUAM DR
1000 PHME 93041 552-E5
S GUAM DR
1000 PHME 93041 552-E5
GUARDIAN ST
4000 SIMI 93063 498-F3
GUAVA CT
1800 OXN 93033 552-F1
E GUAVA ST
100 OXN 93033 552-G1
W GUAVA ST
100 OXN 93033 552-F1
N GUERNE AV
2000 SIMI 93063 498-E2
GUIBERSON RD
- VeCo 93040 457-F7
- VeCo 93015 466-G1
2400 VeCo 93015 467-B1
3700 VeCo 93015 457-E7
GUIBERSON ST
300 SPLA 93060 464-C4
GUILDHALL CT
4400 WLKV 91361 557-E6
GUILFORD CIR
1800 THO 91360 526-F5
GUINDA CT
1100 VeCo 93010 494-C5
GULL CT
1600 VEN 93003 492-E4
GUM CIR
2600 SIMI 93065 478-C7
GUN CLUB RD
25300 CALB 91302 558-H6
GUNNER LN
1500 SIMI 93063 499-B3
GUNSMOKE RD
13500 MRPK 93021 496-F3
GUSTAV LN
8300 LA 91304 529-F2
GUY HARDISON
100 VeCo 93015 465-A1
100 VeCo 93060 465-A1
300 VeCo 93060 455-A7
GWIN CT
4700 SIMI 93063 498-H1
GYPSY CT
2100 THO 91362 556-H2
GYPSY LN
- VeCo 93010 494-F6

H

H
- PHME 93035 552-B3
- PHME 93043 552-B3
H AV
- VeCo 93042 583-F4
H ST
100 OXN 93030 522-F1
S H ST
100 OXN 93030 522-F6
1100 OXN 93033 522-F7
1200 OXN 93033 552-F1
HAAZ WY
1800 OXN 93030 522-J5
1800 OXN 93030 523-A5
HABRA CT
1400 CMRL 93010 524-D1
HACIENDA CIR
800 CMRL 93012 524-J2
HACIENDA DR
500 CMRL 93012 524-J2
900 VeCo 93065 497-F4
N HACIENDA RD
- VeCo 91307 528-J3
N HACKAMORE LN
- VeCo 91307 529-A4
HACKAMORE ST
800 VeCo 93023 451-C3
HACKBERRY DR
- VeCo 93001 471-C3
HACKERS LN
6000 AGRH 91301 557-G3
E HACKNEY RD
6000 VeCo 93066 495-C1
HACKNEY ST
22000 LA 91304 529-J2
HADJIAN LN
22100 CanP 91303 529-J5
HADLEY DR
300 VEN 93003 492-B3
HAGEN CT
1000 SIMI 93065 497-H4
HAIGH RD
100 THO 91320 556-C1
HAILES RD
3100 VeCo 93033 553-D3
HAILEY CT
23600 SIMI 93065 498-B5
HAINES CANYON
23600 VeCo 93015 456-C5
HALCON ST
100 OXN 93030 523-A5
HALEVY ST
600 VEN 93003 492-B7
HALEY RANCH RD
100 VeCo 93001 450-H7
100 VeCo 93001 451-A5
HALIFAX CT
1200 VEN 93004 492-H3
HALIFAX ST
8800 VEN 93004 492-H3
HALL RD
100 VeCo 93060 465-A2
300 VeCo 93060 455-A7
HALL CANYON RD
100 VEN 93001 491-G2
500 VeCo 93001 471-G6
500 VEN 93001 471-G6
HALLOCK DR
200 SPLA 93060 464-D5
S HALLOCK DR
200 SPLA 93060 464-E5
HALSBURY CT
23600 VeCo 91361 556-F6
HALSEY WY
4800 OXN 93033 552-H5
HALSTED ST
22100 Chat 91311 499-J6
HALYARD ST
600 PHME 93041 552-B1
HAMILTON AV
300 VEN 93003 491-J2
HAMILTON AV
4200 OXN 93033 552-J5
HAMILTON ST
1500 SIMI 93065 497-J4
1700 SIMI 93065 498-A4
HAMLIN AV
3200 SIMI 93063 478-G6
HAMLIN ST
22200 CanP 91303 529-J6
22600 CanP 91307 529-F6
HAMMIL CT
2600 SIMI 93065 498-C4
HAMPSHIRE RD
- THO 91362 557-A3
100 THO 91361 557-A3
HAMPTON AV
2300 SIMI 93063 498-J1
HAMPTON CT
- THO 91362 527-C2
HAMPTON CANYON RD
3600 VeCo 93060 463-A4
3900 VeCo 93060 462-J3
HANCOCK PL
2100 OXN 93033 553-A2
HANDEL CT
4700 VEN 93003 492-A7
HANFORD ST
9300 VEN 93004 492-G2
HANLEY AV
1700 SIMI 93065 498-B3
HANNA AV
8500 LA 91304 529-J1
9300 Chat 91311 499-J4
HANNAH CIR
1700 SIMI 93063 499-A3
HANOVER AV
500 THO 91320 555-G3
HANOVER CT
3200 THO 91320 555-G3
HANOVER LN
1200 VEN 93001 491-F5
HANSEN CT
2400 SIMI 93065 498-B4
HANSON RD
4900 VEN 93003 492-B3
HAPPY LN
1500 VeCo 93023 442-D4
2900 VeCo 93063 478-C6
HAPPY ST
300 SPLA 93060 464-A7
HAPPY CAMP RD
7900 VeCo 93021 476-F1
9400 VeCo 93021 466-F5
HAPPY CAMP CANYON RD
- MRPK 93021 476-G4
- VeCo 93021 466-G7
- VeCo 93021 476-F1
23600 VeCo - 367-E9
23600 VeCo - 467-E4
23600 VeCo 93021 467-A6
HAPPY TALK RANCH RD
14800 VeCo 93060 463-F6
HAPPY VALLEY RD
23600 VeCo 93063 499-A7
23600 VeCo 93063 529-B1
HAPPY VALLEY SCHOOL RD
23600 VeCo 93023 442-F7
23600 VeCo 93023 452-F1
HARBOR BLVD
100 OXN 93035 521-G2
100 VeCo 93030 521-G2
100 VeCo 93035 521-H4
1200 OXN 93035 552-A1
1900 OXN 93030 521-G2
2500 VEN 93030 521-G2
2500 VEN 93035 521-G2
3000 VeCo 93035 552-B4
E HARBOR BLVD
- VEN 93001 491-B2
2500 VeCo 93001 491-D3
3300 VEN 93001 521-G1
3300 VEN 93030 521-G1
3300 VEN 93035 521-G1
HARBOR RD
4600 PHME 93043 552-D6
HARBOR LIGHTS LN
400 PHME 93041 552-C2
HARBORVIEW CT
6100 VEN 93003 472-C5
HARBORVIEW LN
32100 WLKV 91361 557-C6
HARBOUR ISLAND LN
4200 OXN 93035 552-A1
HARDING AV
- VEN 93003 492-E2
100 OXN 93030 522-H6
N HARDING AV
- VEN 93003 492-E1
HARDISON ST
300 SPLA 93060 463-H6
HARDISON TER
23600 VeCo 93060 453-G2
HARDNEGO RD
1800 VeCo 93060 465-B6
2100 VeCo 93066 465-B6
HARGROVE CT
14000 MRPK 93021 496-G4
HARMON DR
6800 VEN 93003 492-E5
HARMON CANYON RD
23600 VeCo 93003 472-D1
23600 VeCo 93003 492-E1
23600 VEN 93003 492-E1
HARMONY CT
1400 THO 91362 527-A6
HAROLD AV
1200 SIMI 93065 498-B4
HARPER DR
1700 VEN 93004 492-H4
E HARPER ST
600 SIMI 93065 497-G5
HARPSTONE LN
23600 SIMI 93065 497-A1
HARRIER CT
- THO 91320 525-J5
- THO 91320 526-A5
HARRIET ST
300 VEN 93001 491-A1
HARRINGTON RD
2700 SIMI 93065 498-C4
HARRIS AV
1000 CMRL 93010 524-C1
HARRIS CT
900 THO 91362 526-J7
HARRIS ST
- PHME 93043 552-E4
HARRISON AV
100 OXN 93030 522-G6
E HARRISON AV
- VEN 93001 491-B1
N HARRISON AV
100 OXN 93030 522-G5
W HARRISON AV
- VEN 93001 491-B1
HARRY ST
- MRPK 93021 496-F1
HART ST
22000 CanP 91303 529-J5
HARTE AV
200 VEN 93003 492-B2
HARTE LN
15500 MRPK 93021 477-A4
HARTFIELD CT
4200 WLKV 91361 557-D6
HARTFORD ST
14600 MRPK 93021 476-H6
HARTGLEN AV
800 THO 91361 557-A4
HARTGLEN PL
5500 AGRH 91301 557-H5
HARTLAND CIR
2600 THO 91361 557-B5
HARTLAND ST
22200 CanP 91303 529-H6
22400 CanP 91307 529-E6
HARTLEY AV
1200 SIMI 93065 498-C4
HARTMAN DR
- VeCo 93012 525-C5
- VEN 93003 491-G3
HARTMAN WY
9300 WHil 91304 499-E7
HARTMAN TURNOFF
- VeCo 93001 471-C3
HARTNELL ST
2500 CMRL 93010 524-E2
HARTUNG CT
3600 THO 91320 555-F4
HARTWICK CIR
2000 THO 91360 526-D4
E HARVARD BLVD
100 SPLA 93060 464-C5
1300 VeCo 93060 464-C5
W HARVARD BLVD
100 SPLA 93060 464-A7
200 SPLA 93060 463-J7
HARVARD ST
300 OXN 93030 522-H2
5200 VEN 93003 492-B3
N HARVARD ST
6400 MRPK 93021 476-H6
HARVEST LN
1700 CMRL 93012 525-A1
1800 CMRL 93012 495-A7
HARVESTER ST
11800 MRPK 93021 496-C2
HARVEY DR
1000 SPLA 93060 464-B3
HARWICH PL
23700 CanP 91307 529-E5
HARWOOD LN
500 THO 91360 526-D7
HASLER RD
11500 VeCo 90265 625-G1
HASSETT AV
23600 VeCo 91361 556-G6
HASSTED DR
33100 LACo 90265 586-E7
HASTINGS
6700 MRPK 93021 476-G6
HASTINGS AV
- VEN 93003 492-C2
HASTINGS CT
5000 VeCo 91377 557-H1
HATFIELD CT
13700 MRPK 93021 496-F4
HATHAWAY AV
23600 THO 91362 527-B5
HATMOR DR
26100 CALB 91302 558-H4
HAUSER CIR
1500 THO 91362 526-J7
HAVASU ST
9000 VEN 93004 492-H4
HAVEN AV
1000 SIMI 93065 498-A4
HAVENCREST ST
12000 MRPK 93021 496-C4
HAVENRIDGE CT
4000 MRPK 93021 496-B4
HAVENSIDE AV
300 THO 91320 555-E2
HAVENWOOD DR
1800 THO 91362 526-J4
HAVILAND ST
800 SIMI 93065 498-C4
HAWK CIR
- VeCo 93041 583-H3
HAWK DR
- VeCo 93041 583-J3
HAWK ST
2100 SIMI 93065 498-A1
N HAWK ST
2400 SIMI 93065 498-B1
HAWK WY
6800 VEN 93003 492-E4
HAWKEYE PL
3600 THO 91320 555-F4
HAWKS BILL PL
500 SIMI 93065 527-D1
HAWKSWAY CT
1600 THO 91361 556-J5
HAWTHORN ST
1200 SPLA 93060 464-B3
HAWTHORNE DR
5000 VeCo 91377 557-G1
HAWTHORNE LN
900 VEN 93003 492-D3
HAYDEN ST
1700 CMRL 93010 524-D2
HAYES AV
- VEN 93003 492-E2
100 OXN 93030 522-G5
N HAYES AV
100 OXN 93030 522-G5
HAYMARKET ST
2400 THO 91362 527-B3
HAYNES ST
22200 CanP 91303 529-J6
22400 CanP 91307 529-E6
HAYS DR
1700 THO 91320 556-A1
HAYWARD ST
7600 VEN 93004 492-E1
HAZEL CIR
6400 SIMI 93063 499-C2
HAZEL ST
9200 Chat 91311 499-G7
HAZELCREST CIR
4800 THO 91362 557-F2
HAZELNUT CT
3400 SIMI 93065 498-D5
HAZEL RIDGE CT
200 SIMI 93065 498-A6
HAZELWOOD DR
400 OXN 93030 522-F4
HAZELWOOD WY
400 SIMI 93065 497-D5
HEALY TER
9300 Chat 91311 499-E6
HEALY TR
9300 Chat 91311 499-F7
HEARON DR
6900 MRPK 93021 476-J5
7200 MRPK 93021 477-A5
HEARST DR
300 OXN 93030 523-A6
3500 SIMI 93063 498-E3
HEATHER CT
4800 MRPK 93021 496-C2
29600 AGRH 91301 557-J3
HEATHER ST
100 OXN 93030 522-F2
600 VeCo 93023 451-C3
2000 SIMI 93065 498-B2
5300 CMRL 93012 525-A3
HEATHER WY
- VEN 93004 473-C7
HEATHERBANK CT
- VeCo 91361 556-D7
HEATHERDALE CT
4200 MRPK 93021 496-B3
HEATHERFIELD CT
3200 THO 91320 555-G2
HEATHERGLEN CT
4500 MRPK 93021 496-B2
HEATHERGLOW ST
3200 THO 91360 526-F2
HEATHER OAKS LN
1400 THO 91361 556-H5
HEATHER RIDGE AV
100 THO 91320 556-A1
HEATHERTON DR
5200 VeCo 93066 475-A7
5200 VeCo 93066 495-A1
HEATHERVIEW DR
1100 VeCo 91377 528-A7
HEATHERWISP LN
23600 SIMI 93065 497-A1
HEATHERWOOD HOLLOW AV
3900 MRPK 93021 496-D4
HEATH MEADOW CT
100 SIMI 93065 497-D6
HEATH MEADOW PL
100 SIMI 93065 497-D7
HEAVENLY CT
3000 SIMI 93065 478-C7
24500 CanP 91307 529-D4
HEAVENLY RIDGE ST
- THO 91362 527-B2
HEAVENLY VALLEY RD
100 VeCo 91320 556-C2
HEBERT DR
100 CMRL 93010 524-C4
HEBRIDES CIR
7000 CanP 91307 529-F5
HEDGE ROW LN
600 SIMI 93065 527-D1
HEDGEWALL DR
6000 WLKV 91362 557-F3
HEDON CIR
1700 CMRL 93010 524-H1
HEDYLAND CT
600 MRPK 93021 476-F7
HEIDELBERG AV
300 VEN 93003 492-B1
HEIDEMARIE ST
22100 Chat 91311 499-J6
HELECHO CT
- THO 91362 556-J1
HELEN CT
2900 VeCo 91320 555-G1
HELEN ST
600 PHME 93041 552-F4
HELENA CT
700 OXN 93033 552-H5
3900 VEN 93003 491-J3
HELENA WY
400 OXN 93033 552-H5
HELENE ST
4000 SIMI 93063 498-F2
HELGA CT
400 THO 91320 555-H2
HELL BENDER LN
7000 VEN 93003 492-F3
HELM DR
1200 OXN 93035 522-D7
1400 OXN 93035 552-D1
HELM ST
2800 SIMI 93065 498-C4
HELMA CT
3500 CMRL 93010 524-G1
HELMOND DR
26900 CALB 91301 558-F6
HELMSDALE CIR
7100 CanP 91307 529-F5
HELMSDALE RD
7000 CanP 91307 529-E5
HELSAM AV
200 VeCo 93030 492-J7
700 VeCo 93030 493-A7
700 VeCo 93030 523-A1
HEMINGWAY LN
6600 VEN 93003 492-D3
HEMLOCK LN
1100 VeCo 91320 556-C2
1200 VEN 93001 491-D2
E HEMLOCK ST
200 OXN 93033 552-H1
N HEMLOCK ST
- VEN 93001 491-D2
S HEMLOCK ST
- VEN 93001 491-D2
W HEMLOCK ST
400 OXN 93033 552-F1
1500 OXN 93035 552-B1
2300 PHME 93035 552-B1
22400 PHME 93041 552-D1
HEMMINGWAY ST
22100 LA 91304 529-J3
HEMPSTEAD DR
5700 AGRH 91301 557-H4
HEMPSTEAD ST
4400 SIMI 93063 478-G5
HEMWAY CT
3900 SIMI 93063 498-F2
HENDERSON PL
10900 VEN 93004 493-A1
HENDERSON RD
7500 VEN 93004 492-J1
10800 VEN 93004 493-A1
HENDRICKSON RD
700 VeCo 93023 442-E5
HENDRIX AV
900 THO 91360 526-F4
HENLEY CT
4400 WLKV 91361 557-D6
HENNESSY AV
300 SIMI 93065 527-D1
HENRIETTA AV
200 THO 91320 555-F2
HENRY DR
200 VeCo 91320 555-F1
HENRY MAYO DR Rt#-126
31100 Cstc 91384 458-H5
31800 VeCo 93040 458-H5
HERBERT DR
- CMRL 93010 524-C3
HERCULES CT
2000 SIMI 93065 497-G2
HEREFORD CT
3200 SIMI 93063 478-G6
HEREFORD RD
- VeCo 91361 586-E1
2400 VeCo 91361 556-F7
HERITAGE DR
6100 AGRH 91301 557-J3
6100 AGRH 91301 558-A3
HERITAGE PL
1200 THO 91362 527-D7
5900 CMRL 93012 525-B1
HERITAGE TR
1500 CMRL 93012 525-B1
HERITAGE OAK CT
3800 SIMI 93063 498-F3
HERITAGE PASS PL
22300 Chat 91311 499-H2
HERMANO TR
200 OXN 93030 522-G2
HERMES ST
100 SIMI 93065 497-F2
HERMITAGE LN
- VeCo - 442-C3
- VeCo 93023 442-C3
HERMITAGE RD
2600 VeCo - 442-C3
2600 VeCo 93023 442-C3
HERMOSA RD
23600 OJAI 93023 451-F1
23600 VeCo 93023 451-F1
HERMOSA ST
7600 VEN 93004 492-E1
HERMOSA WY
200 OXN 93030 522-H2
HERON ST
6900 VEN 93003 492-E5
HERRINGBONE CT
- THO 91320 555-H2
HERRON CT
2000 CMRL 93010 494-D7
HERTZ ST
12000 MRPK 93021 496-C1
HEWITT PL
1700 SIMI 93065 497-J5
HEWITT ST
10400 VEN 93004 492-J2
HEYNEMAN LN
2100 SIMI 93065 498-A5
HEYWOOD ST
1600 SIMI 93065 497-J3
1700 SIMI 93065 498-B3
HI DR
4000 SIMI 93063 498-F3
HIAWATHA ST
22000 Chat 91311 499-J4
HIBBERT CT
3900 SIMI 93063 498-F2
HIBISCUS ST
1100 OXN 93030 522-E2
HIBISCUS WY
- VEN 93004 473-C7
HICKORY DR
5800 VeCo 91377 558-A1
HICKORY GROVE DR
200 THO 91320 556-C2
HICKORY KNOLL CT
2800 THO 91362 527-C4
HICKORY VIEW CIR
900 CMRL 93012 525-A2
HICKORY WOOD LN
2800 THO 91362 527-C4
HIDALGO CT
300 CMRL 93010 524-D4
HIDALGO ST
5200 CMRL 93012 525-A3
HIDDEN BROOK CT
1600 THO 91362 527-G6
HIDDEN CREEK AV
3100 THO 91360 526-C1
HIDDEN GLEN CT
5100 THO 91362 527-G6
HIDDEN OAK CT
1800 THO 91320 526-A5
HIDDEN PINES CT
3800 MRPK 93021 496-F4
HIDDEN SPRINGS AV
1400 VeCo 91377 527-H7
HIDDEN VALLEY CT
2100 OXN 93030 522-D2
HIDDEN VALLEY RD
1100 VeCo 91361 556-A6
1400 VeCo 91361 555-J6
HIETTER AV
2000 SIMI 93063 498-E2
HIGH RD
- VeCo 93001 470-D4
HIGH ST
100 MRPK 93021 496-E1
100 VeCo 93022 451-B7
1100 SPLA 93060 464-B4
HIGHBRUSH LN
23600 SIMI 93065 497-A2

STREET
Block City ZIP Pg-Grid

HIGHBURY CT
3500 SIMI 93063 478-G5
HIGHCLIFF CT
5800 THO 91362 527-G6
HIGHCREST CT
400 THO 91320 555-G3
HIGHGATE PL
2700 SIMI 93065 478-B7
2700 SIMI 93065 498-B1
HIGHGATE RD
2100 THO 91361 557-A7
2100 WLKV 91361 557-A7
HIGH KNOLL CIR
1900 THO 91362 527-D5
HIGH KNOLL CT
23600 SIMI 93065 527-F1
HIGHLAND AV
4200 OXN 93033 552-J5
HIGHLAND DR
100 VeCo 93035 552-B5
500 VeCo 93023 451-C3
E HIGHLAND DR
- VeCo 93010 494-E6
W HIGHLAND DR
600 VeCo 93010 494-C6
HIGHLAND RD
100 SIMI 93065 497-F5
HIGHLAND TER
- VeCo 93010 494-D6
HIGHLANDER RD
23700 CanP 91307 529-D5
HIGHLAND HILLS DR
200 VeCo 93010 494-E5
HIGH MEADOW ST
100 SIMI 93065 497-E7
HIGH PEAK PL
5600 AGRH 91301 557-J5
HIGH PLAINS LN
600 SIMI 93065 527-D1
HIGH POINT DR
500 VEN 93003 472-D7
500 VEN 93003 492-E1
HIGHPOINT PL
3300 SIMI 93065 498-D5
HIGHRIDGE CT
11200 VeCo 93012 496-B7
HIGH TREE RD
1300 SIMI 93063 499-C3
HIGHVIEW ST
300 THO 91320 555-G2
HIGHWAY Rt#-33
- VeCo - 366-H3
- VeCo 93023 366-J6
- VeCo 93252 366-G1
HIGHWINDS RD
12600 VeCo 93023 442-J7
12600 VeCo 93023 452-J1
HIGHWOOD CT
3500 SIMI 93063 498-D1
HIGUERA DR
1100 OXN 93030 522-J5
HILA LN
4900 OXN 93033 552-J5
HILARIA ST
23600 OXN 93030 522-J5
HILARY CT
2700 THO 91362 527-A3
HILBURN CT
13600 MRPK 93021 496-F3
HILDRETH CT
11000 VeCo 93012 526-A1
N HILGARD AV
1400 SIMI 93065 498-D3
HILL DR
10600 VeCo 93021 495-J3
10600 VeCo 93021 496-A3
HILL RD
2000 VEN 93003 492-D5
N HILL RD
100 VEN 93003 492-D2
100 VeCo 93003 492-D2
S HILL RD
- VeCo 93003 492-D2
- VEN 93003 492-D2
500 VEN 93009 492-D3
HILL ST
- VeCo 93022 451-B6
100 OXN 93033 552-F1
1400 OXN 93035 552-D1
HILLARY CT
1800 SIMI 93065 498-A2
HILLARY DR
7800 LA 91304 529-F2
HILLBROOK CT
4200 MRPK 93021 496-B2
HILL CANYON AV
3300 THO 91360 526-C1
HILL CANYON RD
1800 VeCo 93012 525-J3
8300 THO 91320 525-J3
8300 THO 93012 525-J3
HILL CANYON FIRE RD
23600 THO 91320 525-H4
HILLCREST DR
500 CMRL 93012 524-J2
1700 VEN 93001 491-E1
2400 THO 91362 557-A2
E HILLCREST DR
- THO 91360 556-F1
1000 THO 91362 556-H1
2000 THO 91362 557-A1
W HILLCREST DR
- THO 91360 556-E1
300 THO 91360 526-C7
600 THO 91320 526-A7
600 VeCo 91360 526-C7
1000 THO 91320 556-E1
2000 THO 91320 525-H7
HILLCREST LN
400 VEN 93001 491-F1
HILLCROFT DR
8200 LA 91304 529-D1
HILLDALE AV
2000 SIMI 93063 498-D2
HILLGATE WY
1900 SIMI 93065 497-E2
HILLHAVEN CT
6300 VEN 93003 472-C6
HILLHURST DR
- CanP 91307 529-D5
- LA 91304 529-D5
HILLIARD AV
1700 SIMI 93063 499-A3
HILLIARD LN
2600 THO 91320 525-H6
HILLMAN ST
2800 THO 91360 526-H3
HILLMONT AV
200 VEN 93003 491-G2
HILLPARK CT
4100 MRPK 93021 496-B2
HILL RANCH DR
200 THO 91362 556-H1
HILLRIDGE DR
1600 CMRL 93012 525-A1
2300 CMRL 93012 494-J7
2300 CMRL 93012 495-A7
HILLRISE DR
29100 AGRH 91301 558-A5
29400 AGRH 91301 557-J5
HILLROSE CT
300 THO 91320 555-E2
HILLROSE PL
2400 OXN 93030 522-F1
HILLSBOROUGH ST
400 THO 91361 556-F2
HILLSBURY RD
2200 THO 91361 557-A6
HILLSHIRE CT
3800 MRPK 93021 496-E4
HILLSIDE DR
1000 SPLA 93060 464-B3
12400 MRPK 93021 496-D3
HILLSVIEW CT
7300 LA 91304 529-E4
HILLTOP DR
3000 VEN 93003 491-G1
HILLTOP LN
1900 VeCo 93012 495-E7
HILLTOP RD
1100 VeCo 93063 499-B3
HILL VALLEY CT
23600 SIMI 93065 497-F7
23600 SIMI 93065 527-F1
HILLVIEW AV
- VEN 93003 492-C2
HILLVIEW CIR
800 SIMI 93065 497-G4
HILLVIEW LN
1100 SIMI 93065 497-H4
HILLWAY CIR
6100 VEN 93003 472-C6
HINGHAM LN
1000 VEN 93001 491-E4
HIRAM AV
100 THO 91320 555-H1
HITCH BLVD
3800 VeCo 93021 496-A3
4000 VeCo 93021 495-J2
HITCHING POST LN
- VeCo 91307 529-A5
HOBART DR
1400 CMRL 93010 524-D1
HOBBIT CT
1200 SIMI 93065 498-C4
HOBBS CIR
- SPLA 93060 464-A5
HOBSON RD
5200 VeCo 93001 469-H2
5200 VeCo 93001 470-A3
5200 VeCo 93001 459-G7
23600 VeCo 93060 464-G4
23600 VeCo 93060 474-B1
HOBSON WY
500 OXN 93030 522-F7
HODENCAMP RD
- THO 91360 556-G1
500 THO 91360 526-G7
HOFER DR
3100 VEN 93003 492-D6
HOLBERTSON CT
700 SIMI 93065 527-C1
N HOLBROOK AV
700 SIMI 93065 498-A5
HOLIDAY PINES LN
2100 VeCo 93012 496-A7
2100 VeCo 93012 526-A1
HOLLEY AV
1400 SIMI 93063 498-E3
HOLLINGS ST
- VEN 93003 492-B2
HOLLISTER ST
2500 SIMI 93065 498-C3
8100 VEN 93004 492-G2
HOLLOWAY CT
3100 THO 91320 555-G6
HOLLOWAY ST
3300 THO 91320 555-F3
HOLLOW BROOK AV
28900 AGRH 91301 558-B4
HOLLOW OAK CT
29000 AGRH 91301 558-A3
HOLLOWPARK CT
2200 THO 91362 527-A4
HOLLY AV
400 OXN 93030 522-E2
HOLLY CT
1500 THO 91360 526-H3
HOLLY DR
100 CMRL 93010 524-E4
HOLLY RD
900 SPLA 93060 464-B3
HOLLY ST
600 VeCo 93023 451-C3
HOLLYBURNE LN
500 THO 91360 526-D7
HOLLYCREST AV
2800 THO 91362 527-C3
HOLLYGLEN CT
4900 MRPK 93021 496-B2
HOLLY GROVE ST
3300 THO 91362 557-B3
HOLLYHOCK CT
900 THO 91362 557-C1
HOLLY KNOLL DR
900 VeCo 93022 461-A1
HOLLY RIDGE DR
5500 CMRL 93012 525-A1
HOLLYTREE DR
5600 VeCo 91377 557-J1
5600 VeCo 91377 558-A1
HOLLYVIEW PL
2400 THO 91362 527-B3
HOLLYWOOD AV
100 VeCo 93035 552-C6
HOLLYWOOD BLVD
200 VeCo 93035 552-B4
400 PHME 93035 552-B4
400 PHME 93043 552-B4
HOLMES AV
500 VEN 93003 492-D2
HOLSER ST
1900 OXN 93030 523-A3
HOLSER WK
1800 OXN 93030 523-A3
HOLSER CANYON RD
23600 VeCo 93040 367-E7
N HOLSTER LN
- VeCo 91307 529-B4
HOLT ST
- VeCo 93001 471-C2
HOMER AV
200 VEN 93003 491-G2
HOMER ST
100 OXN 93033 552-G3
HOMESTAKE PL
1200 THO 91320 555-F5
HOMEWOOD AV
2200 SIMI 93063 499-C1
HOMEWOOD CT
6400 SIMI 93063 499-C1
HOMEZELL DR
23900 LA 91304 529-E1
HOMEZELL TR
24000 LA 91304 529-C1
HOMOJA CIR
- PHME 93041 552-E4
HOMOJA DR
1100 PHME 93041 552-D4
HONDO BARRANCA
23600 VeCo 93066 474-E7
HONDO RANCH RD
1400 VeCo 93066 494-C1
HONEY DR
3100 SIMI 93063 478-E6
E HONEYBEE ST
13100 MRPK 93021 496-E3
HONEYBROOK CT
11900 MRPK 93021 496-C3
HONEY CREEK CT
1300 THO 91320 526-B6
HONEYGLEN CT
4400 MRPK 93021 496-D2
HONEY HILL DR
2100 VeCo 93012 496-A7
2100 VeCo 93012 526-A1
HONEYMAN ST
5400 SIMI 93063 498-J2
5400 SIMI 93063 499-A2
HONEY PINE CT
23600 SIMI 93063 498-D4
HONEYSUCKLE CT
3500 THO 91360 526-H2
HONEYSUCKLE DR
2600 OXN 93030 492-F7
2600 OXN 93030 522-F1
HONEYWOOD CT
1000 SPLA 93060 464-A1
HOOD DR
2000 THO 91362 526-J6
2000 THO 91362 527-A6
HOOD PINE PL
23600 SIMI 93065 498-D4
HOOVER AV
- VEN 93003 492-E2
HOPE RD
100 THO 91320 556-B2
HOPE ST
4300 VEN 93003 491-J2
4300 VEN 93003 492-A2
6100 SIMI 93063 499-B3
HOPEWELL CT
2000 THO 91360 526-C4
HOPI LN
2300 VEN 93001 471-C6
HOPPER CANYON RD
500 VeCo 93015 457-A5
1600 VeCo - 457-A3
HORIZON CIR
100 CMRL 93010 524-A4
HORIZON DR
1000 VEN 93003 472-D6
HORIZON LN
600 THO 91320 526-B7
HORIZON PL
22200 Chat 91311 499-J2
HORN CT
2800 SIMI 93065 498-C3
HORNBLEND CT
400 SIMI 93065 527-C1
HORN CANYON RD
- VeCo - 366-L6
- VeCo - 442-J2
5100 VeCo 93023 442-G4
E HORSESHOE RD
- VeCo 91307 529-A4
HORSHOE CIR
- CALB 91302 558-H4
HOSPITAL RD
23600 VEN 93003 491-G2
HOT SPRINGS PL
26800 CALB 91301 558-G7
HOUCK ST
500 CMRL 93010 523-J5
HOUSTON DR
- THO 91360 556-G1
400 THO 91360 526-G7
HOUSTON PL
1500 OXN 93033 552-J3
HOUSTON RD
9500 VeCo 90265 585-D7
9500 VeCo 90265 625-D1
HOWARD AV
- VeCo 93022 451-D4
HOWARD RD
- CMRL 93012 524-J6
600 VeCo 93012 524-J7
1400 VeCo 93012 525-A7
1400 VeCo 93012 555-A1
HOWARD ST
- VEN 93003 491-F3
1000 FILM 93015 455-J6
HOWE RD
2700 VeCo 93065 478-C7
3400 VeCo 93015 457-E6
3700 VeCo 93040 457-E6
HOWE ST
23600 VEN 93003 492-D6
HOWELL RD
300 OXN 93033 552-H5
HOWIE CT
400 SPLA 93060 463-J5
400 SPLA 93060 464-A5
HOYT CT
1300 SIMI 93065 498-C3
HUBBARD ST
1800 SIMI 93065 497-J3
HUDSON CT
1100 SIMI 93065 497-H4
HUDSON LN
400 PHME 93041 552-D2
HUDSPETH AV
500 SIMI 93065 497-J5
HUENEME AV
100 PHME 93035 552-B5
100 VeCo 93035 552-B5
HUENEME RD
- PHME 93041 552-D6
- PHME 93043 552-D6
500 VeCo 93012 553-H6
500 VeCo 93012 554-A5
E HUENEME RD
100 OXN 93033 552-H6
900 VeCo 93033 552-H6
900 VeCo 93033 553-B6
W HUENEME RD
- OXN 93033 552-G6
HUENEME ST
1000 VeCo 93015 465-F3
HUERTA ST
3500 CMRL 93010 494-G7
HUGHES DR
100 OXN 93033 552-G3
1000 CMRL 93010 524-C3
HUGO CT
10100 VEN 93004 493-A2
HULA DR
23600 OXN 93033 553-A2
HULL CT
2100 SIMI 93063 499-B2
HULL PL
1000 OXN 93030 522-E6
HUMBOLDT ST
100 SIMI 93065 497-F6
8300 VEN 93004 492-F1
HUME DR
400 FILM 93015 455-J6
HUMMINGBIRD ST
6300 VEN 93003 492-D5
HUNGRY VALLEY RD
- VeCo - 367-D2
HUNT CIR
100 THO 91360 526-F4
600 CMRL 93012 524-J2
HUNT CLUB LN
4200 WLKV 91361 557-E6
9500 Chat 91311 499-H6
HUNTER CT
- VEN 93003 492-B2
HUNTER DR
500 FILM 93015 456-A4
HUNTER ST
5400 VEN 93003 492-B2
HUNTER CREST CT
3800 MRPK 93021 496-D4
HUNTERS GROVE CT
3800 MRPK 93021 496-E4
HUNTERS POINT DR
200 THO 91361 556-F2
HUNTER VALLEY LN
4900 THO 91362 557-E1
HUNTINGTON AV
200 VEN 93004 492-F2
HUNTLEY ST
5200 SIMI 93063 498-J2
HUNTSDALE CT
23600 THO 91320 555-F3
HUNTSWOOD WY
900 OXN 93030 522-E4
HUPA DR
300 VEN 93001 471-C5
HURFORD CT
5600 AGRH 91301 557-H4
N HURLES AV
1900 SIMI 93063 498-E2
HURON DR
1800 VEN 93004 492-G4
HURRICANE CV
2600 PHME 93041 552-C3
HURST AV
- VEN 93001 491-E3
HUSTON RD
9100 Chat 91311 499-E7
9300 Chat 91311 499-E7
HUYLER LN
900 SIMI 93065 497-E6
HYACINTH CT
2900 THO 91360 526-D3
HYACINTH DR
2000 OXN 93030 522-F2
HYACINTH ST
800 CMRL 93010 494-C7
800 VeCo 93010 494-C7
HYANNIS DR
7200 CanP 91307 529-F4
HYLAND AV
2100 VEN 93001 491-F1
HYSSOP CT
2200 THO 91362 497-A7

I

I AV
- VeCo 93042 583-F6
I ST
100 OXN 93030 522-F5
1100 OXN 93033 522-F6
23600 VeCo 93063 528-F1
S I ST
1200 OXN 93033 522-F7
1200 OXN 93033 552-F1
IAN LN
2700 SIMI 93063 478-D7
IBEX SQ
1100 VEN 93003 492-E3
IBOLD RD
600 LACo 90265 586-G6
IBSEN PL
100 OXN 93033 552-G4
ICELAND ST
2900 THO 91320 555-H2
IDA PL
23200 Chat 91311 499-F7
IDA ST
1700 CMRL 93010 524-D3
IDA WY
23600 WHil 91304 499-E6
IDAHO DR
1900 VEN 93003 492-C5
IDE CT
1700 THO 91362 526-J7
IDLE DR
28900 AGRH 91301 558-B4
IDYLLWILD ST
8300 VEN 93004 492-G2
IGUANA CIR
1300 VEN 93003 492-F4
ILENA ST
900 OXN 93030 522-F7
ILEX DR
- THO 91320 555-J1
2000 OXN 93030 522-G3
IMBACH PL
7100 MRPK 93021 477-A5
IMBLER CT
6300 AGRH 91301 557-J3
IMPALA DR
7100 VEN 93003 492-E5
IMPERIAL AV
- VEN 93004 492-F1
300 VEN 93004 472-E7
400 VeCo 93004 472-E7
IMPERIAL CIR
3000 THO 91320 555-H2
IMPERIAL ST
200 OXN 93030 523-A5
INCA CT
2500 VEN 93001 471-C5
INDEPENDENCE CT
3200 THO 91360 526-F2
INDIAN DR
22000 Chat 91311 499-J1
INDIANA DR
2000 OXN 93030 522-H3
2000 VeCo 93030 522-H3
INDIANBROOM CT
6600 VeCo 91377 528-A7
INDIAN CREEK PL
23600 SIMI 93063 478-J6
INDIAN CREST CIR
1700 THO 91362 527-G6
INDIAN HILL LN
24400 CanP 91307 529-D4
INDIAN HILLS DR
5100 SIMI 93063 478-J7
5400 SIMI 93063 479-A7
INDIAN MESA DR
3100 THO 91360 526-C2
INDIAN OAK LN
- VeCo 91377 527-J7
- VeCo 91377 528-A7
- VeCo 91377 557-J1
- VeCo 91377 558-A1
INDIAN POINTE DR
23600 SIMI 93063 479-A7
INDIAN PONY CIR
4200 THO 91362 527-D6
INDIAN RIDGE CIR
3200 THO 91362 527-D3
INDIAN RIDGE CT
29000 AGRH 91301 558-A3
INDIAN SKY LN
2100 THO 91320 555-J3
INDIAN TERRACE DR
23600 SIMI 93063 479-A7
INDIAN TRAIL CT
5000 THO 91362 527-F7
INDIAN WELLS CT
2700 OXN 93030 522-C2
INDIAN WELLS LN
600 THO 91320 556-D1
INDIGO PL
800 OXN 93030 522-F2
INDUSTRIAL AV
600 PHME 93041 552-F7
900 OXN 93030 522-H7
E INDUSTRIAL ST
4400 SIMI 93063 498-G2
INESS CIR
6900 VEN 93003 492-E3
INEZ DR
- OXN 93030 523-A4
INEZ ST
1000 CMRL 93012 525-A6
6000 VeCo 93003 492-D6
6000 VEN 93003 492-D6
INGELOW CT
300 THO 91360 526-F4
INGLEWOOD ST
12800 MRPK 93021 496-E3
INGOMAR ST
22100 LA 91304 529-D3
INGRAM PL
4900 THO 91362 557-G1
INLET DR
900 OXN 93030 522-F7
INMAN CIR
1000 SIMI 93065 497-J4
INNWOOD RD
100 SIMI 93065 497-C6
INSPIRATION WY
100 VEN 93001 491-D1
INSTONE CT
2900 THO 91361 557-C5
INVAR CT
2400 SIMI 93065 498-B4
INVERNESS CT
2100 OXN 93030 522-E2
INVERNESS ST
- THO 91361 556-F2
INYO CIR
2800 SIMI 93063 478-J7
INYO ST
10600 VEN 93004 472-H6
IOWA PL
200 OXN 93030 492-H7
IRENA AV
5400 CMRL 93012 525-A6
IRENE CT
1500 SIMI 93065 497-J3
IRIS ST
- SIMI 93063 499-A2
1200 VeCo 93063 499-B4
E IRIS ST
100 OXN 93033 552-G2
W IRIS ST
100 OXN 93033 552-E1
IRIS WY
200 VEN 93004 473-A7
IRONBARK CT
1700 OXN 93030 522-F3
IRONBARK DR
2000 OXN 93030 522-F3
IRONGATE PL
2600 THO 91362 527-A2
IRON RIDGE LN
300 SIMI 93065 497-E6
IRONSIDE CV
2600 PHME 93041 552-C3
IRONSTONE ST
2500 OXN 93030 522-F1
IRONWOOD CIR
200 THO 91360 526-F2
IRONWOOD DR
5700 AGRH 91301 557-J4
IROQUOIS CT
1500 CMRL 93010 524-F1
5500 SIMI 93063 479-A7
IROQUOIS LN
2300 VEN 93001 471-D6
IRVINE RD
700 SIMI 93065 497-F5
IRVING DR
300 OXN 93030 523-A6
500 THO 91360 556-G1
IRVING BERLIN DR
- VEN 93003 492-A4
ISABEL AV
5600 CMRL 93012 525-B6
ISABELLA CT
1700 VEN 93004 492-H4
5300 AGRH 91301 557-H5
ISABELLA ST
1900 OXN 93030 522-J3
ISCHIA DR
4000 OXN 93035 552-B2
ISELA ST
- OXN 93030 523-A5
ISH DR
4100 SIMI 93063 498-F3
ISLA CT
1300 CMRL 93010 524-G1
ISLAND AV
- VeCo 93042 583-E4
ISLAND FOREST PL
4900 THO 91362 527-F7
ISLAND VIEW AV
100 PHME 93043 552-B5
100 VeCo 93035 552-B5
900 VeCo 93043 552-B5
1700 PHME 93035 552-B5
ISLAND VIEW CIR
400 PHME 93041 552-E6
ISLAND VIEW DR
3000 VEN 93003 491-G1
3200 VeCo 93003 491-G1
ISLAND VIEW ST
600 FILM 93015 456-B5
1300 OXN 93035 552-A1
1600 OXN 93035 551-J1
ISLE WY
2900 OXN 93035 552-C1
N ISLE ROYALE DR
4500 MRPK 93021 496-E2
ISLETON PL
1000 OXN 93030 522-E6
ITAMO ST
1100 CMRL 93012 525-C6
ITASCA ST
22100 Chat 91311 499-H6
IVAN DR
4800 OXN 93033 552-H5
IVANHOE AV
1500 OXN 93030 522-D4
IVERSON LN
11100 Chat 91311 499-J2
IVERSON RD
11300 Chat 91311 499-H2
11400 Chat 91311 499-H2
IVES AV
1100 OXN 93033 552-J1
1800 OXN 93033 553-A2
IVES CT
2000 OXN 93033 553-A1
IVES PL
1900 OXN 93033 553-A2
IVORY AV
2800 SIMI 93063 478-D7
IVORY WY
2300 OXN 93030 522-F1
IVY ST
4000 VEN 93003 491-J3
IVYWOOD DR
400 OXN 93030 522-F3
IVYWOOD LN
400 SIMI 93065 497-D5

J

J CT
500 OXN 93030 522-F6
J ST
- VeCo 93042 583-E5
100 OXN 93030 522-F5
1100 OXN 93033 522-F7
1100 OXN 93033 552-F1
4300 PHME 93033 552-F5
23600 VeCo 93063 528-F1
JACARANDA AV
- THO 91320 556-C1
JACARANDA DR
2400 OXN 93030 522-F1
JACINTO CIR
3000 SIMI 93063 478-G7
JACINTO DR
- OXN 93030 523-A4
JACINTO WY
10000 VeCo 93004 493-B2
JACKIE AV
6200 WdHl 91367 529-F7
JACKLIGHT CV
2600 PHME 93041 552-C3
JACKPINE LN
11400 VeCo 93012 496-C7
JACKSON ST
2200 OXN 93033 552-F2
3400 PHME 93033 552-F3
3400 PHME 93041 552-F3
7300 VEN 93003 492-E1
7400 VEN 93004 492-E1
JACKTAR AV
2900 OXN 93035 552-C1
JACOBS CT
5300 VeCo 91377 527-H6
JADE CT
3300 SIMI 93063 478-D6
JADE DR
900 VEN 93004 492-G3
JADESTONE AV
2800 SIMI 93063 478-D7
JALISCO CT
1600 CMRL 93010 524-D4
JAMAICA LN
1100 OXN 93030 522-E6
JAMES AV
100 OXN 93033 552-G3
2100 VeCo 93003 492-D5
JAMES CT
2000 THO 91362 556-H2
JAMES DR
- VEN 93001 471-C6
JAMES WY
5900 SIMI 93063 499-B3
JAMES ALAN CIR
22100 Chat 91311 499-J4
JAMESTOWN CT
2400 OXN 93035 552-A2
JAMESTOWN LN
2200 OXN 93035 552-A2
JAMESTOWN ST
9800 VEN 93004 492-H2
JAMESTOWN WY
2000 OXN 93035 552-A1
JAMES WEAK AV
12400 MRPK 93021 496-D2
JAMISON CT
100 SIMI 93065 497-D7
JANE CT
700 OXN 93033 552-F6
2900 THO 91320 555-H2
JANE DR
700 OXN 93033 552-F6
700 PHME 93033 552-F6
700 PHME 93041 552-F6
JANET LN
1500 SIMI 93063 499-B3
JANET WY
5900 SIMI 93063 499-B3
JANETWOOD DR
500 OXN 93030 522-F3
JANIS LN
1500 SIMI 93063 499-B3
JANIS WY
6000 SIMI 93063 499-B3
JANLOR DR
30600 AGRH 91301 557-G4
30800 WLKV 91362 557-F4
JANSS CIR
1800 THO 91360 526-E5
E JANSS RD
- THO 91360 526-G5
1000 THO 91362 526-G5
1800 THO 91362 527-A6
W JANSS RD
- THO 91360 526-E4
JANSS FIRE RD
500 THO 91361 556-F3
700 VeCo 91361 556-F6
JAPONICA AV
100 CMRL 93012 524-H4
JAPONICA CT
4300 CMRL 93012 524-H4
JAPONICA PL
4300 CMRL 93012 524-H4
JARDIN DR
2200 OXN 93030 522-H2
JARED CT
6100 WdHl 91367 529-D7
JASMINE ST
2000 OXN 93030 522-F3
JASMINE GLEN AV
2700 SIMI 93065 478-B7
JASON AV
7400 CanP 91307 529-F4
7700 LA 91304 529-F2
JASON CT
2700 THO 91362 527-A3
JASON LN
23200 CanP 91307 529-F4
JASON PL
1000 OXN 93033 552-J3
JASPER AV
500 VEN 93004 492-H2
JAVELIN CT
1600 THO 91320 526-A6
JAY AV
800 CMRL 93010 524-B2
2400 SIMI 93065 498-B1
JAYCROFT CT
23600 VeCo 91361 556-F6
JAZMIN AV
600 VEN 93004 492-J1
JEAN LN
2800 WLKV 91361 557-A7
JEANETTE AV
800 THO 91362 526-J7
JEANETTE DR
1500 OXN 93030 522-E3
JEANINE CT
- THO 91320 556-B1
JEANNE AV
10300 VeCo 93022 451-C7
JEANNE CT
400 VeCo 91320 555-G1
JEAUNINE DR
100 THO 91360 526-E6
JEFFERSON AV
100 VEN 93003 492-E1
JEFFERSON SQ
5100 OXN 93033 552-H5
JEFFREY RD
2300 CMRL 93012 495-B7
JEFFREY MARK CT
22400 Chat 91311 499-H4
JEFFREYS PL
1900 OXN 93033 553-A4
JELLEY DR
- PHME 93041 552-D4
JENNIFER CT
6200 SIMI 93063 499-B2
JENNIFER PL
2000 VeCo 93012 496-A7
2000 VeCo 93012 526-A1
JENNY DR
300 VeCo 91320 555-F1
500 VeCo 91320 525-F7
JENSEN CT
100 THO 91360 556-G1
JENSEN DR
23900 LA 91304 529-E2
JEPSON ST
1500 VeCo 93015 455-G4
JERANIOS CT
100 THO 91362 556-J1
JEREMIAH DR
400 SIMI 93065 497-D2
JEROME AV
- THO 91320 556-A2
JERRY DR
400 PHME 93041 552-F5
JERSEY PL
1100 THO 91362 527-A7
JESSICA ST
3000 THO 91320 555-G1
JETTY ST
1800 OXN 93035 552-C1
2000 PHME 93035 552-C1
2000 PHME 93041 552-C1
JEWEL CT
- CMRL 93010 493-H7
JILL CT
2000 SIMI 93063 499-C2
JILL PL
2700 PHME 93041 552-D1
JIM BOWIE RD
3900 Ago 91301 558-F7
3900 AGRH 91301 558-F7
JIMILYN ST
6400 SIMI 93063 499-C2
JIMS CANYON RD
23600 VeCo 93040 367-E9
23600 VeCo 93040 458-E7
JOAN DR
800 PHME 93041 552-F5
JOAN LN
8300 LA 91304 529-F2
JOAN WY
4700 VeCo 93030 493-A5
N JOANNE AV
- VEN 93003 491-G3
S JOANNE AV
100 VEN 93003 491-G4
JOANNE CT
1500 OXN 93030 522-E4
JOANNE WY
1600 OXN 93030 522-E3
JODY LN
- VeCo 93010 494-D7
100 VEN 93001 491-C1
JOELTON DR
4000 AGRH 91301 558-E7
JOHN WY
6000 SIMI 93063 499-B3
JOHN COX DR
400 VeCo 93015 455-B6
JOHNELL RD
9200 Chat 91311 499-F7
JOHNSON DR
500 VEN 93003 492-D3
3000 VeCo 93003 492-E6
JOHNSON MTWY
23600 Chat 91311 479-F6
23600 VeCo 93063 479-F6
JOHNSON PL
9300 Chat 91311 499-F6
JOHNSON RD
100 OXN 93033 552-G4
JOIE CT
4700 SIMI 93063 498-H2
JOLIET PL
700 OXN 93030 522-D4
JONATHAN ST
23100 LA 91304 529-F3
JON DODSON DR
5300 AGRH 91301 557-H5
JONES ST
300 VEN 93003 491-F3
JONES WY
2100 OXN 93033 552-J2
23600 SIMI 93065 478-C7
JONESBORO AV
2200 SIMI 93063 499-C1
JONNA CIR
- CMRL 93010 524-C3
JONQUIL FIELD RD
3300 WLKV 91361 557-B7
JOPLIN WY
10100 VEN 93004 492-J2
JORDAN AV
- VEN 93001 491-F3
JOSE AV
1600 CMRL 93010 524-G1
1700 CMRL 93010 494-G7
JOSE DR
800 VeCo 93023 451-C1
JOSHUA CT
2500 OXN 93030 522-F1
JOSHUA PL
1500 CMRL 93012 525-B1
JOSHUA ST
6400 VeCo 91377 558-B2
JOSHUA TR
5900 CMRL 93012 525-B1
JOSHUA TREE CT
23600 SIMI 93063 499-C3
JOURDAN ST
2800 VeCo 93030 492-H7
2800 VeCo 93030 522-H1
JOYCE DR
500 PHME 93041 552-F5
JOYCE PL
2100 OXN 93033 553-A2
JUANITA AV
100 OXN 93030 522-H4
N JUANITA AV
100 OXN 93030 522-H5
JUAREZ AV
4800 MRPK 93021 496-D2
JUBILEE LN
500 SIMI 93065 527-D1
JUDSON AV
200 VEN 93003 492-B2
JUDY CIR
300 THO 91360 526-E4
JUDY LN
1300 VeCo 93023 451-C2
JULIA CT
1400 CMRL 93010 524-G1
JULIAN ST
- VEN 93001 491-A2
100 OXN 93030 523-A5
JULIANA ST
- SIMI 93063 498-H1
JULIE CIR
1700 SIMI 93065 498-A3
JULIE LN
6600 LACo 91307 529-D6
JULLIARD AV
6600 MRPK 93021 476-H6
JUNE CIR
1500 VEN 93004 492-H3
JUNE CT
- THO 91360 526-F5
JUNE ST
1000 SPLA 93060 464-B3
JUNEAU CIR
4300 SIMI 93063 478-F7
JUNEAU PL
200 OXN 93030 492-H7
JUNEBERRY PL
800 OXN 93030 522-E2
JUNEWOOD CT
900 OXN 93030 522-F3
JUNEWOOD WY
1300 OXN 93030 522-E3

INDEX

STREET
Block City ZIP Pg-Grid

JUNIATA CT
5600 VEN 93003 492-B1
JUNIATA ST
5600 VEN 93003 492-B2
JUNIPER CT
500 THO 91320 555-G3
JUNIPER LN
- VeCo 93023 441-E6
JUNIPER ST
300 OXN 93033 552-H2
W JUNIPER ST
200 OXN 93033 552-E2
JUNIPERO ST
100 VEN 93001 491-B2
3500 VeCo 93063 499-B4
JUPITER CT
3400 OXN 93030 523-D4
JURYMAST DR
900 OXN 93030 522-F7
JUSTICE ST
23200 LA 91304 529-F3
N JUSTIN AV
2000 SIMI 93065 498-B2
JUSTIN CT
4700 MRPK 93021 496-C2
7700 LA 91304 529-G4
JUSTIN WY
4100 OXN 93033 552-H4

K

K ST
- OXN 93030 522-F6
1100 OXN 93033 522-F7
1100 OXN 93033 552-F1
N K ST
- OXN 93030 522-F5
KACHINA WY
23600 SIMI 93063 479-B7
KADOTA ST
2500 SIMI 93063 498-H1
2600 SIMI 93063 478-G6
KAILAS ST
5500 VEN 93003 472-B7
KAITIS ST
- PHME 93043 552-D3
KALINDA PL
400 THO 91320 526-C7
KALORAMA
800 VEN 93001 491-D1
KALORAMA DR
200 VEN 93001 491-D1
N KALORAMA ST
- VEN 93001 491-D2
S KALORAMA ST
- VEN 93001 491-D2
KAMALA ST
300 OXN 93033 552-H2
W KAMALA ST
400 OXN 93033 552-F2
KAMASA RD
3500 VeCo 93060 465-B4
KAMET CT
5500 VEN 93003 492-B1
KANAINA CT
- Chat 91311 499-J1
KANAN RD
1800 VeCo 91377 527-E6
1800 VeCo 91377 557-H1
1900 THO 91362 527-C6
3100 VeCo 91362 527-E6
5200 AGRH 91301 558-A5
5500 VeCo 91377 558-A1
KANAN RD Rt#-N9
4100 Ago 91301 558-A7
4100 AGRH 91301 558-A7
KANE AV
1500 SIMI 93065 498-B3
KAPALUA DR
1600 OXN 93030 522-E2
KAPANA AV
- VEN 93001 471-C5
KAREN AV
10400 VeCo 93022 451-C6
KAREN PL
- THO 91320 556-A1
KARENA CT
3500 CMRL 93010 524-G2
KAROC CT
3500 SIMI 93063 479-A7
KASTEN ST
2000 SIMI 93065 498-A3
KATHERINE AV
2100 VeCo 93003 492-D5
2500 VEN 93003 492-D5
E KATHERINE AV
500 VeCo 93022 451-C6
N KATHERINE DR
- VEN 93003 491-G2
S KATHERINE DR
- VEN 93003 491-G3
KATHERINE LN
1500 SIMI 93063 499-B3
KATHERINE RD
600 VeCo 93063 499-B4
6500 SIMI 93063 499-B3
KATHERINE ST
5300 SIMI 93063 498-J3
5500 SIMI 93063 499-A3
KATHERINE WY
5900 SIMI 93063 499-B3
KATHLEEN DR
500 VeCo 91320 556-B3
500 THO 91320 556-B3
KATRINA WY
23600 OXN 93030 522-H4
KATY LN
1100 VeCo 93063 499-B4
KAWAI CT
3100 SIMI 93063 478-J6
KAY AV
1600 SIMI 93063 499-C3
KAYAK CV
2600 PHME 93041 552-C3
KAZUKO CT
200 MRPK 93021 496-D1
KEARNEY AV
1400 SIMI 93065 497-J4
1700 SIMI 93065 498-A4
KEARNY ST
6200 VEN 93003 492-C1
KEATS AV
2400 THO 91360 526-E3
KEATS CIR
100 VEN 93003 492-E3
KEATS PL
1800 OXN 93033 552-J4
1800 OXN 93033 553-A4
KEEL AV
3400 OXN 93035 552-B1
KEEL WY
2900 OXN 93035 552-C1
KEISHA DR
13900 MRPK 93021 496-G4
KEITH RD
2400 VeCo 93015 455-E7
KELLEY AV
400 CMRL 93010 524-F3
KELLOGG ST
- VEN 93001 471-B7
100 FILM 93015 456-B6
KELLWOOD CT
900 VeCo 91377 557-H1
E KELLY RD
- THO 91320 556-A1
W KELLY RD
- THO 91320 555-H2
- VeCo 91320 555-H2
KELLY KNOLL LN
2700 VeCo 91320 555-H2
KELMSCOTT CT
2200 THO 91361 557-A6
KELP LN
2800 OXN 93035 522-C7
KELP ST
1100 OXN 93035 522-C7
1300 OXN 93035 552-C1
KELSEY ST
2200 SIMI 93063 498-G2
KELSFORD CT
1100 THO 91361 557-A5
KELTON CT
23600 SIMI 93065 497-F7
KEMPER LAKES CT
1900 OXN 93030 522-E2
KENDALE LN
600 THO 91360 526-D6
KENDALL AV
1300 CMRL 93010 524-F1
1700 CMRL 93010 494-F7
KENEWA ST
1600 VeCo 93023 451-E5
KENMORE CIR
700 THO 91320 555-F4
KENNEBEC ST
8800 VEN 93004 492-H4
KENNEDY AV
23600 VEN 93003 492-E2
KENNEDY LN
1500 VeCo 93023 442-D4
KENNEDY PL
1800 OXN 93033 552-J2
1800 OXN 93033 553-A2
KENNERICK LN
900 SIMI 93065 497-D6
KENNETH ST
- CMRL 93010 524-D3
KENNEY ST
900 VeCo 93030 522-J1
KENROSE CIR
26100 CALB 91302 558-H4
KENSINGTON AV
2400 THO 91362 527-B3
KENSINGTON CT
7400 CanP 91307 529-E4
KENSINGTON DR
500 FILM 93015 456-A6
KENSINGTON LN
1700 OXN 93030 522-E4
KENT CT
1500 OXN 93030 522-E4
KENT DR
1500 VEN 93004 492-H3
KENT PL
1000 THO 91362 527-B7
KENTFIELD CT
31700 WLKV 91361 557-D6
E KENTFIELD ST
2200 SIMI 93065 478-B7
KENTIA ST
2200 OXN 93030 522-F1
KENTLAND AV
6100 WdHl 91367 529-H7
6500 CanP 91307 529-H5
7600 LA 91304 529-H2
9600 Chat 91311 499-H6
KENTON CT
3000 SIMI 93065 498-D5
KENTWOOD DR
500 OXN 93030 522-F3
KENWATER AV
6100 WdHl 91367 529-E7
6400 CanP 91307 529-E7
KENWATER PL
6400 CanP 91307 529-E7
KENWOOD CT
600 THO 91320 556-D2
KENWOOD ST
500 THO 91320 556-D2
KEPLER DR
1800 OXN 93033 553-A2
KERN ST
300 VEN 93003 492-B3
1700 OXN 93033 552-F3
1700 PHME 93033 552-F3
1700 PHME 93041 552-F3
KERNVALE AV
15500 MRPK 93021 477-A6
KERRMOOR DR
6000 WLKV 91362 557-F3
KERRY DR
2700 SIMI 93063 478-E7
KERRYGLEN ST
1500 THO 91361 556-J6
KERRYHILL CT
6300 AGRH 91301 558-A3
KESWICK CT
2400 SIMI 93063 498-D1
KESWICK ST
22200 LA 91304 529-F4
KETCH AV
3300 OXN 93035 552-B1
KETCH PL
2900 OXN 93035 552-C1
KEVIN ST
100 THO 91360 526-F5
KEY LARGO CT
4800 VeCo 91377 557-G2
KEYSER RONDO
700 CMRL 93010 524-F2
KEYSTONE ST
2200 SIMI 93063 499-C1
KEY WEST CT
1100 OXN 93030 522-F6
KHYBER DR
700 VEN 93001 491-C1
KICKAPOO DR
600 VEN 93001 471-D6
KILAINE DR
2900 SIMI 93063 478-E7
KILBURN CT
5300 VeCo 91377 527-G6
KILLDALE CT
600 SIMI 93065 497-D7
KILTY AV
7100 CanP 91307 529-F5
KILTY PL
23400 CanP 91307 529-F5
KIMBALL CT
2000 SIMI 93065 498-A2
N KIMBALL RD
- VEN 93004 492-E1
S KIMBALL RD
- VEN 93004 492-F2
KIMBER DR
3300 THO 91320 555-F2
W KIMBER DR
3700 THO 91320 555-F2
KIMBERLY AV
2400 CMRL 93010 524-E1
KIMBERLY DR
- VeCo 93001 471-C2
29600 AGRH 91301 557-H3
KIMBERWICK LN
4300 MRPK 93021 496-F3
KINETIC DR
200 OXN 93030 523-C5
KING CT
400 SPLA 93060 463-H6
KING PL
3500 SIMI 93063 498-E3
KING ST
400 FILM 93015 455-H6
900 OXN 93030 522-F7
KING CANYON RD
700 VeCo 93015 465-J3
700 VeCo 93015 466-A3
KINGFISHER PL
6300 VEN 93003 492-D5
KINGFISHER WY
700 OXN 93030 522-F7
KINGHAM CT
5900 AGRH 91301 558-A4
KING JAMES CT
1500 VeCo 91377 527-H6
KINGLET ST
6800 VEN 93003 492-E5
KINGMAN AV
2000 SIMI 93063 498-J2
KING PALM DR
23600 SIMI 93063 498-D4
23600 SIMI 93065 498-D4
KINGS RD
10800 VEN 93004 472-H6
KINGSBORO CT
1400 THO 91362 527-E7
KINGSBRIDGE LN
2200 OXN 93035 552-A2
KINGSBRIDGE WY
2000 OXN 93035 552-A1
KINGS CANYON CT
2200 OXN 93033 553-B5
KINGSGROVE DR
5000 VeCo 93066 495-A1
5200 VeCo 93066 474-J7
5200 VeCo 93066 494-J1
KINGSLEY CIR
400 THO 91360 526-F7
KINGSPARK CT
31900 WLKV 91361 557-C6
KINGSTON CIR
1300 THO 91362 527-D7
KINGSTON LN
1100 VEN 93001 491-E4
KINGSVIEW RD
4100 MRPK 93021 496-B3
KINGSWOOD LN
400 SIMI 93065 497-D5
KINGSWOOD WY
1300 OXN 93030 522-E3
KINO ST
1900 CMRL 93010 524-D3
KINROSS CT
2200 THO 91361 557-A6
KINZIE ST
22000 Chat 91311 499-J5
KIOWA CT
1600 VeCo 93023 451-E4
KIPLING CT
1500 OXN 93033 552-J4
KIPLING LN
500 VEN 93003 492-D1
KIPLING PL
1000 OXN 93033 552-J4
KIRK AV
600 VEN 93003 491-H4
1400 THO 91360 526-F6
KIRKCALDY CIR
24000 CanP 91307 529-E5
KIRKFORD WY
1200 THO 91361 557-C5
KIRKWOOD CT
2600 SIMI 93063 498-E1
KIRSTEN AV
1600 SIMI 93063 498-J3
KIRSTEN LEE DR
1700 WLKV 91361 586-H2
KIRTLAND CIR
2000 THO 91360 526-D4
KITE DR
2000 OXN 93035 522-D6
KITETAIL ST
100 SIMI 93065 527-E1
KITSY LN
1500 SIMI 93063 499-B3
KITTRIDGE ST
22000 CanP 91303 529-H6
22300 CanP 91307 529-D6
24500 LACo 91307 529-C6
KITTY ST
500 VeCo 91320 525-G7
500 VeCo 91320 555-G1
KIVA CT
29100 AGRH 91301 558-A5
KIWI WY
6900 VEN 93003 492-E4
KLAMATH DR
1900 CMRL 93010 494-E7
KLAMMATH AV
2800 SIMI 93063 479-B7
KLEBERG ST
4600 SIMI 93063 478-G7
KNAPP RD
7600 Chat 91311 499-F6
KNAPP WY
9300 Chat 91311 499-F7
KNAPP RANCH RD
- WHil 91304 499-C7
- WHil 91304 529-C1
KNIGHT CT
2200 SIMI 93065 497-H2
KNIGHT DR
28200 AGRH 91301 558-C7
KNIGHT RONDO
2900 CMRL 93010 524-F3
KNIGHTSBRIDGE AV
2600 THO 91362 527-A3
KNIGHTSBRIDGE PL
2100 OXN 93030 522-D4
KNIGHTSGATE RD
4500 WLKV 91361 557-D6
N KNIGHTWOOD CIR
2500 SIMI 93063 498-E1
N KNIGHTWOOD PL
2400 SIMI 93063 498-E1
KNOB LN
13500 VeCo 93012 496-F4
KNOLL DR
1800 VEN 93003 492-B5
KNOLL CREST PL
2200 THO 91361 557-A4
E KNOLLHAVEN ST
2200 SIMI 93065 498-B2
KNOLL RIDGE RD
23600 SIMI 93065 497-F7
KNOLLVIEW CT
23600 SIMI 93065 527-F1
KNOLLVIEW LN
400 THO 91360 526-D7
KNOLLWOOD CIR
23600 SIMI 93065 497-F7
KNOLLWOOD CT
- CanP 91307 529-E5
KNOLLWOOD DR
- THO 91320 555-E3
KNOTTINGHAM ST
1100 SIMI 93065 498-C4
KNOTTY PINE ST
12900 MRPK 93021 496-E3
KNOWLES ST
100 THO 91360 526-E6
KNOX AV
- VEN 93003 492-B2
KOALA DR
2000 OXN 93030 522-F3
KOALA WY
2000 VEN 93003 492-F5
KODIAK CIR
2700 SIMI 93063 478-G7
KODIAK ST
7100 VEN 93003 492-F5
KOENIGSTEIN RD
12400 VeCo 93060 366-L7
12400 VeCo 93060 453-D1
12900 VeCo - 366-L7
KOHALA ST
100 OXN 93030 523-A5
KONA DR
23600 OXN 93033 552-J1
KONA LN
4800 OXN 93033 552-J5
KOREAN WAR VET MEM HWY RT#-126
2300 VeCo 93015 455-F6
2600 VeCo 93015 455-E7
2700 VeCo 93015 465-B2
17900 VeCo 93060 464-F3
18400 SPLA 93060 464-F3
20100 VeCo 93060 465-B2
KRENWINKLE CT
100 SIMI 93065 527-E1
KROTONA RD
- OJAI 93023 451-E1
KUDU PL
2300 VEN 93003 492-F5
KUEHNER DR
1300 SIMI 93063 499-C1
2500 SIMI 93063 479-D7
KUMQUAT PL
800 OXN 93030 522-E2
KUNKLE ST
- VeCo 93022 451-B7
KYLE CT
7400 CanP 91307 529-G4
KYLE LN
2800 SIMI 93063 478-E7

L

L AV
- VeCo 93042 583-D5
L CT
500 OXN 93030 522-E6
L ST
100 OXN 93030 522-E5
1100 OXN 93033 522-F7
1100 OXN 93033 552-F1
LA BAYA DR
5600 WLKV 91362 557-E4
LA BREA DR
1200 THO 91362 526-H7
LA BREA ST
100 VeCo 93035 552-A3
4500 OXN 93035 552-A3
LA BROCHE CANYON RD
- VeCo - 453-G1
- VeCo 93060 366-L7
- VeCo 93060 453-G1
23600 VeCo - 366-L7
LA CAM RD
2200 THO 91320 555-H2
2200 VeCo 91320 555-H2
N LA CAMPANA RD
800 VeCo 93015 455-F5
LA CANADA AV
100 OXN 93033 552-G3
LA CASA CT
3100 THO 91362 527-C3
LA CORONA CT
600 VeCo 91377 557-J2
LA COSTA PL
3500 OXN 93033 552-G3
LA CRESCENTA DR
- VeCo 93010 493-J7
LA CRESCENTA ST
- VeCo 93035 552-A3
LA CRESTA DR
800 THO 91362 526-H7
23600 VeCo 93023 451-D2
LA CROSSE DR
- VeCo 93022 451-B6
LA CUESTA CT
6500 VEN 93003 472-D6
LA CULEBRA CIR
1200 CMRL 93012 524-J1
LA CUMBRA ST
- VeCo 93022 451-C4
LA CUMBRE CIR
7200 VEN 93003 472-D7
LA CUMBRE RD
5800 VeCo 93066 495-A3
LADA AV
6300 CMRL 93012 525-C6
LADBROOK WY
2500 VeCo 91361 556-D7
2500 VeCo 91361 586-D1
LADERA RD
1500 VeCo 93023 442-D4
2600 VeCo - 442-D4
3800 VeCo - 366-K6
LADERA VISTA DR
4900 CMRL 93012 524-J3
LADONIA ST
4800 SIMI 93063 478-H6
LADYCLIFF CIR
2000 THO 91360 526-C4
LADYFACE CIR
29800 AGRH 91301 557-H6
LA ENCINA
- THO 91320 525-E6
E LA FALDA WY
23600 VeCo 93040 458-D5
LAFAYETTE CT
6500 MRPK 93021 476-G6
LAFAYETTE DR
200 OXN 93033 522-H2
4700 VEN 93003 492-A3
LAFAYETTE ST
4900 VEN 93003 492-B3
6700 MRPK 93021 476-G6
LAFITTE DR
1500 VeCo 91377 527-H6
LA FONDA CT
7000 VEN 93003 492-D1
LA FONDA DR
400 VEN 93003 492-D1
LA FONDA DR E
400 VEN 93003 472-D7
400 VEN 93003 492-D1
LA FORTUNA
100 THO 91320 525-E7
LAGOON LN
- OXN 93035 522-E6
LA GRANADA DR
700 THO 91362 527-A6
1100 THO 91362 526-H6
1400 THO 91362 557-A1
LA GRANADA ST
100 VeCo 93035 552-A4
LA GRANGE AV
500 THO 91320 555-F4
LAGROSS WY
9400 Chat 91311 499-F6
LAGUNA DR
600 SIMI 93065 497-G5
600 VeCo 93065 497-G5
LAGUNA RD
- VeCo 93042 583-G4
- VeCo 93012 553-F2
- VeCo 93012 554-A2
1600 VeCo 93033 553-F2
LAGUNA TER
300 VeCo 93065 497-F5
LAGUNA WY
300 VeCo 93065 497-G4
LAGUNA PEAK ACCESS RD
- VeCo - 584-C4
23600 VeCo 93012 583-J4
23600 VeCo 93012 584-A4
LAGUNA RIDGE FIRE RD
- VeCo - 366-G8
- VeCo - 450-B6
- VeCo 93001 450-B6
LA JOLLA DR
1100 THO 91362 526-H7
LA JOLLA ST
100 VEN 93004 472-H7
100 VEN 93004 492-H1
LAKE AV
1100 VeCo 93023 451-C3
LAKE CT
300 SIMI 93065 497-F5
LAKE DR
2500 OXN 93030 522-F1
LAKE BREEZE PL
500 SIMI 93065 497-E6
LAKE CANYON
- VeCo 93003 472-C4
LAKE CASITAS FIRE RD
23600 VeCo 93001 460-A3
LAKE CREST CT
3300 WLKV 91361 557-C7
LAKE CREST DR
5300 AGRH 91301 557-F6
LAKEFIELD RD
100 THO 91361 557-B4
LAKEFRONT DR
30600 AGRH 91301 557-G5
LAKE HARBOR LN
3800 WLKV 91361 557-C6
LAKEHURST AV E
1700 CMRL 93010 524-G1
1700 CMRL 93010 494-G7
LAKEHURST ST
1400 OXN 93030 522-F4
LAKELAND TER
24000 LA 91304 529-C1
LAKE LINDERO DR
5300 AGRH 91301 557-G3
LAKE MANOR DR
23200 Chat 91311 499-F7
23400 Chat 91311 499-F7
LAKEMEADOW LN
32100 WLKV 91361 557-C6
LAKE NADINE PL
6000 AGRH 91301 557-G3
LAKE PARK DR
500 SIMI 93065 497-D6
LAKE PLEASANT DR
32300 WLKV 91361 557-B7
LAKEPORT DR
3300 WLKV 91361 557-C7
LAKERIDGE LN
1300 THO 91361 557-B5
LAKE SHERWOOD DR
- VeCo 91361 556-F7
900 THO 91361 556-F7
LAKE SHORE DR
200 VeCo 93035 552-B4
200 VeCo 93043 552-B4
200 PHME 93035 552-B4
200 PHME 93043 552-B4
LAKESIDE AV
300 CMRL 93010 524-D3
LAKEVIEW TER
9200 Chat 91311 499-F7
LAKEVIEW CANYON RD
- THO 91362 557-G1
100 THO 91361 557-C5
300 WLKV 91361 557-C5
1100 THO 91362 527-E7
5200 VeCo 91362 557-G1
LAKEVISTA ST
9900 VEN 93004 492-J3
LAKEWOOD AV
100 VEN 93004 492-G2
LAKEWOOD CIR
8300 VEN 93004 492-F2
LAKEWOOD CT
1300 THO 91361 557-C5
LAKEWOOD PL
2700 THO 91361 557-B5
LA LOMA AV
- VeCo 93066 493-H2
500 VeCo 93066 494-A1
600 VeCo 93066 474-B7
LA LOMITA
- THO 91320 525-E6
N LA LUNA AV
100 VeCo 93023 441-D6
S LA LUNA AV
100 VeCo 93023 441-D7
600 VeCo 93023 451-C2
LA MARINA DR
300 CMRL 93010 523-J2
LAMBERT ST
100 VeCo 93030 492-J5
LAMBOURNE PL
7000 VeCo 91377 528-B7
LA MESA AV
3400 SIMI 93063 478-G5
LAMONT AV
1200 THO 91362 527-A6
LAMPLIGHTER ST
2900 SIMI 93065 498-D4
LAMP POST CIR
400 SIMI 93065 497-F6
LANA CT
2200 SIMI 93063 499-C1
LA NARANJA ST E
600 VeCo 93015 455-E5
LANARK ST
22100 LA 91304 529-G3
LANCASTER CIR
1400 THO 91360 526-A4
LANCE PL
24000 CanP 91307 529-E5
E LANDEN ST
2600 CMRL 93010 494-F7
N LANDEN ST
1700 CMRL 93010 494-F7
1700 CMRL 93010 524-F1
LANDER CT
2600 THO 91320 555-H1
LANDINO DR
6100 WLKV 91362 557-F3
LANDSBURN CIR
1100 THO 91361 557-C5
LANG ST
100 VEN 93003 491-H3
LANGDON WY
1700 VEN 93001 491-E2
LANGFORD DR
1500 OXN 93030 522-E4
LANGHALL CT
6300 AGRH 91301 557-J3
LANGLEY ST
2000 OXN 93033 553-A4
LANG RANCH PKWY
3000 THO 91362 527-C4
LANGSPUR CT
31800 WLKV 91361 557-D6
LANGUID LN
600 SIMI 93065 497-G5
LANIER PL
3200 THO 91360 526-G2
E LANSDALE CT
2200 SIMI 93065 498-B2
E LANSING PL
2300 SIMI 93065 498-B4
LANTANA ST
100 CMRL 93010 524-C2
1400 VeCo 93010 524-C1
1600 VeCo 93010 494-C7
1800 OXN 93030 522-F3
LANTANA WY
100 VEN 93004 473-A7
LANTERN AV
- SIMI 93063 498-H1
LANTERN LN
4300 MRPK 93021 496-F3
LANYARD WY
2000 OXN 93035 522-D6
LA PALMA
100 THO 91320 525-E6
LA PALOMA CIR
2500 THO 91360 526-D3
LA PATERA CT
- VeCo 93010 493-J7
- VeCo 93010 494-A7
LA PATERA DR
- VeCo 93010 494-A7
- VeCo 93010 493-J7
W LA PAZ CT
- SIMI 93065 497-E4
LA PAZ DR
1100 OJAI 93023 451-F1
LA PERESA DR
1200 THO 91362 526-H7
LAPEYRE RD
23600 VeCo 93021 497-A3
LA PLATA DR
- CMRL 93010 493-H7
LA PLAZA
1400 VeCo 93023 451-C2
LA PORTE ST
600 CMRL 93012 525-A2
LA PUENTE DR
23600 FILM 93015 456-C6
LA PUERTA AV
1800 OXN 93030 522-J6
1800 OXN 93030 523-A6
LAPWORTH DR
5800 AGRH 91301 558-C4
LA QUILLA DR
22300 Chat 91311 479-J7
22400 Chat 91311 499-H1
LA QUINTA LN
1600 OXN 93030 522-E2
LA RAMADA DR
1800 CMRL 93012 495-B7
1800 CMRL 93012 525-C1
LARAMIE CT
700 THO 91320 555-G5
LARAMIE ST
9500 VEN 93004 492-H2
LARBOARD LN
5800 AGRH 91301 557-G4
LARCH ST
1800 SIMI 93065 498-A2
E LARCH ST
2000 SIMI 93065 498-A2
LARCH CREST CT
200 THO 91320 556-D2
LARCHMONT ST
1200 SIMI 93065 497-D6
LARCHWOOD CIR
6900 CanP 91307 529-F6
LARCOM ST
2700 THO 91360 526-E3
LAREDO LN
200 OJAI 93023 451-F1
S LARGO LN
800 VeCo 93015 465-B2
LARIAT LN
23600 SIMI 93065 527-D1
LARK AV
1100 VEN 93003 492-D4
LARK DR
- VeCo 93041 583-G2
LARK ST
100 OXN 93033 552-G3
600 VeCo 93023 451-C4
1600 SIMI 93063 498-F3
LARKDALE CT
600 SIMI 93065 497-G6
LARK ELLEN AV
200 OJAI 93023 442-A6
LARKELLEN CT
6000 VeCo 91377 558-A2
LARKFIELD AV
1300 THO 91362 527-C6
LARKHAVEN CT
3300 THO 91360 526-H2
LARKHAVEN LN
2400 OXN 93030 522-F2
LARKHILL ST
100 THO 91360 526-F2
LARKIN CT
4700 SIMI 93063 498-H1
LARKIN ST
5400 VEN 93003 492-B3
LARKSBERRY LN
23600 SIMI 93065 497-A2
LARKSPUR AV
- SIMI 93063 499-A2
LARKSPUR DR
5000 VeCo 93001 471-C1
5200 VeCo 93001 461-C7
LARKSPUR ST
1200 VeCo 93063 499-B4
1400 SPLA 93060 464-B2
LARMIER AV
100 VeCo 93022 451-A7
600 VeCo 93022 461-A1
LARO DR
28900 AGRH 91301 558-A3
29300 AGRH 91301 557-J4
LA ROSA DR
4800 VeCo 91377 557-G1
LARRY CT
23600 THO 91320 556-C1
LARSON WY
9300 Chat 91311 499-F6
9300 Chat 91311 499-F6
LARWIN AV
10000 Chat 91311 499-H4
LA SALLE AV
300 VEN 93003 492-A1
LAS BRISAS DR
2700 VeCo 93012 496-A6
LAS CRUCES ST
9500 VEN 93004 492-H3
LA SENDA CT
6400 CMRL 93012 495-C7
LA SIERRA CT
2300 CMRL 93012 495-A6
LAS LLAJAS CANYON RD
- Nwhl 91382 479-E2
- StvR 91381 479-E2
4900 SIMI 93063 478-H5
4900 VeCo 93063 478-H5
5100 VeCo 93063 479-A5
5500 Chat 91311 479-E2
5500 VeCo - 479-E2
LAS PALMAS ST
100 VeCo 93035 552-A4
LAS PALOMAS DR
400 PHME 93041 552-C2
LAS POSAS CIR
2500 VeCo 93012 496-B6
LAS POSAS RD
- CMRL 93010 524-B2
900 VeCo 93010 524-B2
2100 CMRL 93010 494-G7
2400 VeCo 93012 554-A4
3200 VeCo 93010 494-G7
5400 VeCo 93012 583-J3
5400 VeCo 93012 584-A3
E LAS POSAS RD
10800 VeCo 93012 496-A6
N LAS POSAS RD
300 CMRL 93010 524-B2
S LAS POSAS RD
100 CMRL 93010 524-B6
700 VeCo 93010 524-B6
1400 VeCo 93012 524-B6
1500 VeCo 93012 554-B1
LAS POSAS ST
300 VeCo 93015 465-J3
LASSEN AV
300 MRPK 93021 496-D1
LASSEN CT
10700 VEN 93004 472-H7
23600 MRPK 93021 496-D1
LASSEN DR
600 SPLA 93060 463-H6
1800 VEN 93004 492-G4
LASSEN ST
2200 OXN 93033 552-F2
22000 Chat 91311 499-H5
LAS TUERO CT
300 VeCo 93010 493-J7
300 VeCo 93010 494-A7
LAS TUNAS PL
3500 OXN 93033 552-H3
LA SUEN DR
100 CMRL 93010 494-E7
100 VeCo 93010 494-E7
LAS VIRGENES RD
4900 CALB 91302 558-H3
4900 LACo 91302 558-H3
5700 VeCo 91302 558-H3
LAS VIRGENES RD Rt#-N1
3700 CALB 91302 558-H7
4800 LACo 91302 558-H7
E LAS VIRGENES CANYON RD
23600 VeCo 91302 528-J7
23600 VeCo 91302 529-A7
23600 VeCo 91302 558-H2
LATHAM ST
2000 SIMI 93065 478-A7
LATHAN AV
1700 CMRL 93010 494-D7
1700 CMRL 93010 524-D1
LATHROP AV
3300 SIMI 93063 478-F6
LA TIENDA RD
31600 THO 91362 557-D5
31600 WLKV 91362 557-D5
LATIGO AV
2200 OXN 93030 523-B4
LATIMER RD
6300 SIMI 93063 499-C3
LAURA ST
1100 VeCo 93023 451-B2
LAURA LA PLANTE DR
28100 AGRH 91301 558-C6
LAUREL CT
200 VeCo 93035 552-B4
LAUREL RD
900 SPLA 93060 464-B2
LAUREL ST
100 OXN 93033 552-H2
N LAUREL ST
- VEN 93001 491-D2
S LAUREL ST
- VEN 93001 491-D2
W LAUREL ST
100 OXN 93033 552-F2
LAUREL BLUFF PL
5600 AGRH 91301 557-J5
LAUREL FIG DR
23600 SIMI 93063 498-D4
23600 SIMI 93065 498-D4
LAUREL GLEN DR
4200 MRPK 93021 496-E3
LAURELHURST RD
13200 MRPK 93021 496-F3
LAUREL PARK CIR
800 CMRL 93012 524-J2
LAUREL PARK CT
2100 THO 91362 527-B4
LAUREL PARK DR
5000 CMRL 93012 524-J2
5000 CMRL 93012 525-A2
LAUREL RIDGE DR
23600 SIMI 93065 497-F7
E LAUREL RIDGE LN
5600 CMRL 93012 525-A1
LAUREL VALLEY PL
1900 OXN 93030 522-D2
LAURELVIEW DR
4100 MRPK 93021 496-B3
LAURELWOOD AV
- SIMI 93063 499-A2
LAUREL WOOD CT
23600 SIMI 93065 497-G7
LAURELWOOD CT
1800 THO 91362 526-J3
1800 THO 91362 527-A3
LAURELWOOD DR
1900 THO 91362 527-A3
LAUREN ST
3300 SIMI 93063 498-D1
LAURIE LN
100 SPLA 93060 463-J7
300 THO 91360 526-F7
300 THO 91360 556-F1
400 SPLA 93060 473-J1
400 SPLA 93060 474-A1
LAUTREC CT
400 THO 91360 526-D5
LAVA PL
8700 LA 91304 529-E1
LAVANDA DR
2200 OXN 93030 522-H2
LA VELLA DR
4800 VeCo 91377 557-G1
LAVENDER AV
1900 SIMI 93065 498-A2
LAVENDER ST
10700 VEN 93004 493-A2
LAVENDER BELL LN
22300 WdHl 91367 529-J7
LA VENTA DR
1200 THO 91361 557-B6
LA VERADA CT
23600 CMRL 93010 524-C4
LA VERNE AV
- VEN 93003 492-C2
LAVERY CT
2600 THO 91320 525-J6
LA VETA DR
5000 CMRL 93012 524-J1
LA VISTA AV
4000 VeCo 93066 493-H3
LA VUELTA PL
900 SPLA 93060 464-B4
LAWNVIEW CT
2300 SIMI 93065 498-B2
LAWNWOOD WY
500 OXN 93030 522-F3
LAWRENCE CIR
1200 SIMI 93065 498-A3
LAWRENCE DR
800 THO 91320 525-J7
800 THO 91320 526-A5
LAWRENCE WY
1100 OXN 93035 522-D7
1200 OXN 93035 552-D1

STREET
Block City ZIP Pg-Grid

LAWSON AV
1700 SIMI 93065 498-B3
LAWTON RANCH RD
23600 VeCo 93015 456-G6
LAYTON CIR
1000 SIMI 93065 497-J4
LAYTON ST
100 VeCo 93023 441-G5
2000 THO 91362 526-J5
LAZIO WY
4900 VeCo 91377 557-G2
LAZY BROOK CT
500 SIMI 93065 497-E6
LAZY OAK PL
29600 AGRH 91301 557-J5
LEADWELL ST
22000 CanP 91303 529-J4
22500 CanP 91307 529-H4
LEAFLOCK AV
2400 THO 91361 557-B5
LEAFWOOD DR
2500 CMRL 93010 494-F6
LEAR CIR
100 THO 91360 526-F7
LEAR CT
1600 OXN 93030 522-E4
LEATHERWOOD CT
4300 CMRL 93012 524-H4
LEAVENS CT
400 SPLA 93060 463-H6
LECHLER CANYON RD
23600 VeCo 93040 367-E7
E LECONT CT
3500 SIMI 93063 498-F2
LEDERER AV
6100 WdHl 91367 529-F7
6400 CanP 91307 529-F7
LEE PL
2800 OXN 93035 552-C1
LEE ST
1600 SIMI 93065 498-B2
LEEDS ST
4800 SIMI 93063 498-H2
LEEWARD CIR
2300 THO 91361 557-B6
LEEWARD WY
2900 OXN 93035 552-B1
LEGAN
23600 VeCo 93015 456-G6
LEHIGH ST
5300 VEN 93003 492-B2
LEHMAN RD
- PHME 93043 552-C4
LEI DR
1000 OXN 93033 552-J5
LEI LN
1800 OXN 93033 552-J1
1800 OXN 93033 553-A1
LEIGHTON DR
- VEN 93001 471-C7
LEIGHTON POINT RD
3800 CALB 91301 558-G7
LEISURE LN
900 SIMI 93065 497-H5
1300 THO 91320 556-B1
LEISURE VILLAGE DR
5600 CMRL 93012 525-B2
LEISURE VILLAGE DR W
5100 CMRL 93012 525-A3
LELAND CIR
5300 SIMI 93063 498-J3
LELAND ST
6000 VEN 93003 492-D6
LE MAR AV
- VeCo 93042 583-F5
LEMAR AV
300 VeCo 93030 492-J7
700 VeCo 93030 493-A7
LEMARSH ST
22000 Chat 91311 499-J4
LEMAY ST
24000 CanP 91307 529-D6
LEMBERT ST
2600 SIMI 93065 498-C4
LEMON AV
3600 OXN 93033 553-B3
LEMON DR
2600 SIMI 93063 498-E1
2700 SIMI 93063 478-E7
2800 VeCo 93010 494-E6
3200 VeCo 93063 478-E7
E LEMON DR
800 VeCo 93010 494-F7
2200 CMRL 93010 494-F7
LEMON WY
600 FILM 93015 455-J5
LEMONBERRY PL
3900 THO 91362 497-A7
3900 THO 91362 527-A1
LEMON GROVE AV
500 VEN 93003 491-H4
LEMONWOOD DR
1700 SPLA 93060 464-D5
10400 VeCo 93021 495-J1
LEMONWOOD ST
700 THO 91320 555-G4
LEMUR CT
6900 VEN 93003 492-E5
LEMUR ST
7000 VEN 93003 492-E4
LENA AV
6200 WdHl 91367 529-G7
6800 CanP 91307 529-G4
7600 LA 91304 529-G3
LENNOX CT
1800 OXN 93030 522-E4
LEON DR
1900 OXN 93030 522-H3
LEONARD ST
500 CMRL 93010 524-F2
LEORA ST
3400 SIMI 93063 478-D6
LEOTA LN
7100 WHil 91304 499-E6
22700 WHil 91304 499-E6
LE REINA
100 THO 91320 525-E6
LE SAGE AV
6100 WdHl 91367 529-F7
LESLIE CT
3100 SIMI 93063 478-D6
LESSER DR
3200 VeCo 91320 525-F7
3500 THO 91320 525-F7
LESTER LN
8300 LA 91304 529-F2
LETICIA CT
30100 AGRH 91301 557-H5
LEVEN AV
2000 CMRL 93010 494-H7
LEVI CT
3400 SIMI 93063 478-F6
LEVI WY
1600 OXN 93033 552-J3
LEWIS LN
900 FILM 93015 455-J6
5500 AGRH 91301 558-C5
LEWIS PL
28400 AGRH 91301 558-C6
LEWIS RD
600 VeCo 93012 524-F5
1800 VeCo 93012 554-D2
4900 AGRH 91301 558-C5
N LEWIS RD Rt#-34
- CMRL 93010 524-G2
1700 CMRL 93010 494-H7
S LEWIS RD Rt#-34
- CMRL 93010 524-F4
200 CMRL 93012 524-F4
E LEWIS ST
- VEN 93001 471-C7
W LEWIS ST
200 VEN 93001 471-B6
LEXINGTON CT
1400 CMRL 93010 524-E1
LEXINGTON DR
2300 VEN 93001 491-G2
2400 VEN 93003 491-G2
LEXINGTON WY
30900 AGRH 91301 557-F6
30900 WLKV 91361 557-F6
LEXINGTON HILLS LN
13000 VeCo 93012 496-F5
LEYTE ST
- PHME 93041 552-E4
LIBBEY AV
700 OJAI 93023 441-H6
LIBERTY CV
2600 PHME 93041 552-C3
LIBERTY BELL RD
- MRPK 93021 496-D2
LIBERTY CANYON RD
3900 AGRH 91301 558-E7
4000 Ago 91301 558-E7
LIBRARY VIEW RD
23600 VeCo 93021 497-B3
LICHO WY
- OXN 93030 522-J4
LICIA PL
2700 SIMI 93065 478-B7
2700 SIMI 93065 498-B1
LIDO BLVD
2500 PHME 93041 552-D2
2700 OXN 93035 552-E2
2700 OXN 93041 552-E2
LIDO CT
300 CMRL 93010 524-D3
LIDO DR
2600 PHME 93041 552-D2
2700 OXN 93035 552-D2
2700 OXN 93041 552-D2
LIGGETT ST
22000 Chat 91311 499-J6
LIGHTHOUSE LN
700 OXN 93030 522-F7
LIGHTHOUSE WY
500 PHME 93041 552-F7
LILAC LN
200 SPLA 93060 464-A5
7800 VeCo 93063 499-F3
10200 SIMI 93063 499-F3
LILAC WK
2500 OXN 93030 522-D4
LILAC WY
- VEN 93004 473-A7
LILLA PL
7500 LA 91304 529-E4
LILLIAN DR
400 PHME 93041 552-F5
LILY CT
3400 VeCo 91320 525-F7
LILY PL
200 VEN 93004 473-A7
LILYWOOD LN
1800 OXN 93030 522-H3
LIMCO RD
600 VeCo 93015 457-A6
LIME AV
1600 OXN 93033 553-B5
LIME CANYON RD
23600 VeCo 93040 367-D7
LIMEROCK TR
8600 LA 91304 529-E1
LIMONEIRA AV
- VeCo 93003 492-D2
- VEN 93003 492-D2
LINCOLN CT
- SIMI 93065 497-D5
1800 OXN 93033 553-A4
1900 OXN 93033 552-J5
LINCOLN DR
- VEN 93001 491-E1
LINDA CT
1500 SIMI 93065 497-J3
LINDA FLORA DR
12000 VeCo 93023 451-A2
LINDALE AV
2000 SIMI 93065 498-C2
LINDA VISTA AV
200 VEN 93001 491-E1
LINDAWOOD ST
800 THO 91320 556-C1
LINDBERGH DR
1800 OXN 93033 553-A1
LINDEN CIR
800 THO 91360 526-F7
LINDEN DR
400 OXN 93033 552-F2
N LINDEN DR
- VEN 93004 472-H7
S LINDEN DR
- VEN 93004 472-J7
LINDENGROVE ST
200 THO 91361 557-A4
LINDERO CANYON RD
100 THO 91362 557-G3
100 WLKV 91362 557-G3
200 VeCo 91377 557-G3
200 VeCo 91362 557-G3
800 VeCo 91362 527-G7
800 VeCo 91377 527-G7
5400 WLKV 91361 557-E5
W LINDERO CANYON RD
5300 WLKV 91362 557-C7
5400 WLKV 91361 557-C7
LINDSAY LN
100 VeCo 93060 463-H7
100 VeCo 93060 473-H1
LINDSAY PL
1000 OXN 93033 552-J4
LINFIELD DR
300 VEN 93003 492-A3
LINGDOLY RANCH RD
- VeCo 93060 463-E4
LINKS VIEW DR
- SIMI 93065 497-C6
LINLEY LN
7500 LA 91304 529-E4
LINVILLE CT
6400 MRPK 93021 477-A6
LION ST
300 OJAI 93023 441-H6
LION CANYON FIRE RD
23600 VeCo 93023 451-H3
23600 VeCo 93023 452-C3
LIONS CIR
- SIMI 93065 477-C7
LIONS GATE DR
600 OXN 93030 522-D4
LIRIO AV
1400 VeCo 93004 493-B2
LISA CT
700 VeCo 91320 525-G7
N LITA PL
2500 SIMI 93063 498-E1
LITTLE CREEK CIR
2300 THO 91320 555-J2
LITTLE FARMS RD
1500 OXN 93030 522-E5
LITTLE FAWN CT
1400 THO 91362 527-F6
LITTLE FEATHER AV
23600 SIMI 93063 479-A6
LITTLEFIELD CT
2500 THO 91362 527-D3
LITTLE HOLLOW PL
4000 MRPK 93021 496-D3
LITTLE OAK LN
6000 WdHl 91367 529-C7
LITTLE SYCAMORE CANYON RD
100 VeCo 90265 586-D4
100 LACo 90265 586-D4
LIVELY CIR
- VeCo 93023 452-D1
LIVEOAK AV
7300 VeCo 93060 453-B7
7300 VeCo 93060 463-B1
LIVE OAK CT
26800 CALB 91301 558-G7
LIVE OAK DR
- VEN 93001 491-E2
LIVE OAK RD
1500 THO 91320 556-A2
LIVE OAK ST
2500 THO 91362 557-A2
LIVE OAK TER
22600 Chat 91311 499-H5
LIVE OAK TR
6700 VeCo 93063 499-D4
LIVERMORE AV
100 VEN 93004 492-F1
LIVERPOOL CT
5500 VeCo 91377 527-J6
LIVORNO CT
30800 WLKV 91362 557-G6
LIZ CT
7400 LA 91304 529-E4
LLAMA CT
1200 VEN 93003 492-E4
LLANERCH LN
600 SIMI 93065 497-D5
LLEVARANCHO RD
2100 SIMI 93065 497-D2
LLOYD CT
- THO 91320 555-F2
LLOYD BUTLER RD
23600 VeCo 93030 493-D3
23600 VeCo 93066 493-D3
LLOYD TURN-OFF
- VeCo 93001 471-C4
LOBELIA AV
1500 VEN 93004 493-A2
LOBELIA DR
1900 OXN 93030 522-F1
LOCKE AV
1100 SIMI 93065 497-H4
LOCKFORD CT
3600 THO 91360 526-H1
LOCKHART LN
600 FILM 93015 456-A5
LOCKHURST DR
6000 WdHl 91367 529-E7
6300 CanP 91307 529-E7
LOCKWOOD CT
3400 SIMI 93063 498-D1
LOCKWOOD ST
700 OXN 93030 523-A3
1700 OXN 93030 522-J3
LOCKWOOD VALLEY RD
900 VeCo 367-A1
23600 VeCo 366-H2
LOCUST AV
- VeCo 91377 558-A2
LODESTONE CT
900 THO 91320 555-G5
LODGEWOOD ST
2800 THO 91320 555-G3
LODGEWOOD WY
900 OXN 93030 522-E3
LOEWE LN
900 VEN 93003 492-A4
LOFTUS CANYON RD
- VeCo 93066 465-A7
- VeCo 93066 474-J1
23600 VeCo 93066 465-J5
23600 VeCo 93066 464-J7
LOGAN AV
800 VEN 93004 492-G3
LOGWOOD RD
5800 WLKV 91362 557-G4
LOIRE CT
30800 WLKV 91362 557-F5
N LOIS AV
600 THO 91320 525-G7
600 VeCo 91320 525-G7
LOIS LN
1100 CMRL 93010 524-C4
LOISE ST
300 SPLA 93060 464-A7
LOLA WY
- OXN 93030 522-J4
LOMA DR
- CMRL 93010 494-F7
- VeCo 93010 494-F7
800 VeCo 93023 451-D1
1400 CMRL 93010 524-F1
LOMA LN
1000 VeCo 93063 499-B4
LOMA VERDE MTWY
- Cstc 91384 458-F1
- VeCo 93040 367-E7
- VeCo 93040 458-F1
LOMA VISTA PL
600 SPLA 93060 464-A4
LOMA VISTA RD
2600 VEN 93003 491-G2
4300 VEN 93003 492-C1
7500 VEN 93004 492-F1
10100 VeCo 93004 472-H7
10100 VEN 93004 472-H6
10900 VEN 93004 472-H6
LOMBARD ST
100 OXN 93030 523-A4
200 THO 91360 556-F1
LOMITA AV
600 VeCo 93023 441-C7
N LOMITA AV
100 VeCo 93023 441-E6
S LOMITA AV
100 VeCo 93023 441-E7
LOMITA ST
2300 CMRL 93010 524-E3
LONDELIUS ST
21900 LA 91304 529-J1
LONDON CIR
700 THO 91360 526-G7
LONDON GROVE CT
12100 MRPK 93021 496-D3
LONE OAK DR
400 THO 91362 556-J1
400 THO 91362 557-A1
400 THO 91362 526-J7
LONESTAR WY
2000 THO 91362 556-J1
2000 THO 91362 557-A1
LONE TREE CT
2400 THO 91362 526-J4
LONG CT
- THO 91360 556-G1
LONGBRANCH RD
100 SIMI 93065 497-F5
LONG CANYON DR
100 VeCo 93004 492-G1
100 VEN 93004 492-G1
LONG CANYON RD
1300 VeCo 93004 472-F5
23600 SIMI 93065 497-J6
23600 SIMI 93065 527-F1
LONGFELLOW CT
100 THO 91360 526-E3
LONGFELLOW ST
100 THO 91360 526-E3
LONGFELLOW WY
5100 OXN 93033 552-H5
S LONGFORD AV
600 THO 91320 555-F4
LONGHORN LN
100 OJAI 93023 441-H7
100 OJAI 93023 451-H1
LONG RIDGE CT
1500 THO 91360 526-E6
LONGRIDGE CT
6300 VEN 93003 472-D6
LONG SHADOW CT
5000 THO 91362 527-F7
LONGVIEW DR
9200 VEN 93004 492-H3
LONGVIEW PL
300 THO 91360 526-E5
LONGWOOD CT
200 THO 91320 555-E2
LONSDALE ST
2100 CMRL 93010 524-E1
LOOKOUT DR
1100 OXN 93035 522-C7
1500 OXN 93035 552-C1
LOOKOUT ROCK TR
1000 VeCo 93063 499-C4
LOON DR
- VeCo 93041 583-G1
E LOOP DR
300 CMRL 93010 494-F6
300 VeCo 93010 494-F6
N LOOP DR
100 VeCo 93010 494-E6
W LOOP DR
- CMRL 93010 494-E6
- CMRL 93010 524-E1
- VeCo 93010 494-E6
LOOP LN
18000 VeCo 93060 464-D4
LOOP RD
3000 VEN 93003 492-E6
LOPACO CT
300 VeCo 93010 494-A7
LORA LN
100 FILM 93015 456-B6
LORAINE PL
2700 SIMI 93065 478-B7
2700 SIMI 93065 498-B1
LORD CREEK RD
600 VeCo 93015 455-D4
LORENA DR
- OXN 93030 522-J4
LORENZO DR
500 VeCo 91377 557-G1
LORETA CT
3300 CMRL 93010 524-G2
LORETO CIR
3800 THO 91320 555-E1
N LORETTA CIR
2500 SIMI 93065 498-B1
LORETTA DR
11900 MRPK 93021 496-C2
LORI CIR
3000 SIMI 93063 478-E7
LORI LN
- VeCo 93010 494-E6
LORRAINE LN
- MRPK 93021 496-F2
LOS ALAMOS DR
400 OJAI 93023 442-A6
LOS ALISOS CT
23600 CMRL 93010 524-C4
LOS ALTOS ST
- VeCo 93035 552-A3
LOS AMIGOS AV
- SIMI 93065 497-E3
LOS ANGELES AV
- VeCo 93012 554-D4
- VEN 93004 493-A1
- VeCo 93035 552-C6
1000 VeCo 93004 493-A1
1300 VeCo 93015 465-E3
LOS ANGELES AV Rt#-118
- MRPK 93021 496-A2
900 VeCo 93010 493-H4
900 VeCo 93010 494-A4
900 VeCo 93066 493-H4
900 VeCo 93066 494-A4
1200 VeCo 93004 493-B2
1600 VeCo 93030 493-B2
4500 VeCo 93066 495-A4
8000 VeCo 93021 495-H3
10700 VeCo 93021 496-A2
E LOS ANGELES AV
100 SIMI 93065 497-G2
500 MRPK 93021 476-G7
500 MRPK 93021 496-F1
1700 SIMI 93065 498-A2
3200 SIMI 93063 498-A2
5400 SIMI 93063 499-A2
W LOS ANGELES AV
500 SIMI 93065 477-B7
500 SIMI 93065 477-E1
11700 MRPK 93021 477-B7
11700 MRPK 93065 477-B7
11700 SIMI 93021 477-B7
15400 MRPK 93021 476-J6
LOS ARCOS CIR
2500 THO 91360 526-G3
LOS ARCOS DR
5300 VeCo 91377 557-H1
LOS CABOS LN
- VeCo 93001 471-C2
LOS CEDROS CIR
2800 VeCo 93012 496-C6
LOS COYOTES PL
6800 CMRL 93012 495-D6
LOS ENCINOS RD
2000 VeCo 93023 451-A4
LOS FELIZ DR
1600 THO 91362 556-J1
2000 THO 91362 557-A2
LOS FELIZ ST
100 VeCo 93035 552-A3
200 OXN 93035 552-B3
LOS FRESNOS CIR
2800 VeCo 93012 496-C6
LOS LLAJAS CANYON RD
5000 VeCo 93063 478-J5
LOS NOGALES AV
2700 CMRL 93010 524-F1
LOS NOGALES RD
3300 SIMI 93063 478-F6
LOS OLIVOS
2900 OXN 93030 523-B2
LOS PADRES CT
6600 VEN 93003 472-D6
LOS PADRES DR
- THO 91361 556-F2
LOS PINOS CIR
2700 VeCo 93012 496-C6
LOS PRIETOS CT
1300 OXN 93035 552-E1
LOS PUEBLOS DR
100 CMRL 93012 525-A3
600 CMRL 93012 524-J2
LOS ROBLES DR
1200 SPLA 93060 464-B3
LOS ROBLES RD
2700 THO 91362 557-A2
LOS ROBLES ST
100 VeCo 93035 552-A4
LOS ROSAS ST
23900 LA 91304 529-E2
LOS SANTOS CT
23600 CMRL 93010 524-C4
LOS SERENOS DR
200 FILM 93015 455-H6
LOST HILLS RD
4100 CALB 91302 558-G7
4100 CALB 91301 558-G7
4700 Ago 91301 558-F5
4700 LACo 91301 558-G7
LOST OAK CT
26900 CALB 91301 558-G7
LOST POINT LN
1200 OXN 93030 522-E6
LOST SPRINGS DR
3800 CALB 91301 558-G7
N LOS VIENTOS DR
- THO 91320 555-E1
500 THO 91320 525-F7
S LOS VIENTOS DR
- THO 91320 555-E1
LOTA LN
- AGRH 91301 558-C5
LOTUS AV
500 THO 91360 526-D5
LOU DR
4100 SIMI 93063 498-F3
LOUIS DR
400 VeCo 91320 525-F7
400 VeCo 91320 555-G1
LOUISE ST
3200 SIMI 93063 478-D7
LOUISIANA PL
200 OXN 93030 492-H7
LOVE CIR
1700 SIMI 93063 499-B2
LOVEDAY AV
1000 SIMI 93065 498-C4
LOWELL CT
2500 SIMI 93065 497-J1
LOWELL PL
300 OXN 93033 552-H4
LOWER LAKE RD
- VeCo 91361 556-F7
LOWERY ST
1300 SIMI 93065 497-J4
LOYOLA AV
- VEN 93003 492-C2
LOYOLA PL
6600 MRPK 93021 476-H6
LOYOLA ST
14300 MRPK 93021 476-G6
LUBBOCK CT
23600 SIMI 93063 478-G7
LUBBOCK DR
4400 SIMI 93063 478-G7
LUCADA ST
100 SPLA 93060 463-J7
400 SPLA 93060 473-J1
400 SPLA 93060 474-A1
LUCAS CT
- THO 91320 555-J1
3800 SIMI 93063 498-E2
LUCERNE CT
1300 VEN 93004 492-H3
LUCERNE ST
9500 VEN 93004 492-H3
LUCERO CT
1100 CMRL 93010 524-D2
LUCERO ST
- OXN 93030 523-A4
- THO 91320 526-F1
1100 CMRL 93010 524-C2
LUCIA CT
23600 MRPK 93021 496-C4
LUCILLE CIR
600 MRPK 93021 476-F7
LUCILLE CT
700 MRPK 93021 476-F7
LUCKY LN
1800 SIMI 93063 498-G3
LUCY CIR
400 SIMI 93065 498-D5
LUDGATE DR
5000 CALB 91301 558-F6
LUFF CT
2900 OXN 93035 552-C1
LUGANO WY
400 VeCo 91377 557-G3
LUIS DR
5400 AGRH 91301 557-H5
LUKENS LN
2500 SIMI 93065 498-B4
LULL ST
7600 LA 91304 529-F4
LUNA DR
2900 VEN 93003 491-G2
LUNAR CT
3400 OXN 93030 523-D4
LUNDY DR
1100 SIMI 93065 497-G4
LUPE AV
- THO 91320 555-H1
LUPIN ST
2000 SIMI 93065 498-C2
LUPINE LN
4600 VeCo 93023 442-F5
LUPINE WY
300 VEN 93001 491-E1
LUPITA ST
100 OXN 93030 522-H6
LURAY CIR
2500 VeCo 93065 478-C7
LUTHER AV
3200 THO 91360 526-E2
LUTHER CIR
6800 MRPK 93021 476-H6
LUXENBERG DR
9200 VeCo 93021 475-G5
LYDIA CIR
1700 SIMI 93065 498-A3
LYME BAY
4400 OXN 93035 552-A2
LYNDBROOK CT
31900 WLKV 91361 557-C6
LYNDHURST AV
1700 CMRL 93010 494-D7
1700 CMRL 93010 524-D1
E LYNDHURST AV
1500 CMRL 93010 524-D1
LYNETTE ST
3100 SIMI 93063 498-D1
LYNN CT
3100 VeCo 91320 525-G7
3100 VeCo 91320 555-G1
3400 VEN 93003 491-H2
LYNN DR
200 VEN 93003 491-H2
LYNN RD
400 THO 91360 526-D3
400 THO 91360 556-C2
500 VeCo 91360 526-D3
1500 THO 91320 556-A2
1900 VeCo 91320 556-C2
2500 THO 91320 555-H2
W LYNN RD
3800 THO 91320 555-E4
LYNNBROOK AV
300 VEN 93003 492-B1
LYNNMERE DR
500 THO 91360 526-B4
LYNN OAKS AV
100 THO 91320 556-C2
LYNN OAKS CT
200 THO 91320 556-C2
LYNNVIEW ST
2500 THO 91320 555-H3
LYNNWOOD DR
5100 CMRL 93012 525-A1
5200 CMRL 93012 524-J1
LYNWOOD ST
500 THO 91360 526-C5
2300 SIMI 93065 498-B1
LYON PL
6100 VeCo 93063 499-B4
LYONS CT
700 SIMI 93065 497-G4
LYONS ST
- PHME 93043 552-D3
LYSANDER AV
2000 SIMI 93065 497-F2

M

M CT
900 OXN 93030 522-E7
M ST
- VeCo 93042 583-D4
400 OXN 93030 522-E6
1100 OXN 93033 522-E7
1100 OXN 93033 552-E1
3200 PHME 93041 552-F3
N M ST
300 OXN 93030 522-E4
MAARTEN DR
6000 VeCo 93021 475-J7
6000 VeCo 93021 495-H1
MABREY CT
1400 THO 91360 526-H2
MACADAM CT
6000 AGRH 91301 558-A3
MACADEMIA LN
23600 SIMI 93065 497-E5
MACARTHUR PL
1800 OXN 93033 552-J2
1800 OXN 93033 553-A2
MACAW AV
1900 VEN 93003 492-E5
MACDONALD LN
2500 PHME 93041 552-D2
MACHADO ST
2700 SIMI 93065 498-C3
MACKAY AV
200 VEN 93004 492-F2
MACMILLAN AV
- VEN 93001 491-E2
MACODA LN
11800 Chat 91311 479-J7
MAD RD
- VeCo 93042 583-D4
MADERA AV
- VEN 93003 492-C2
MADERA CIR
2400 PHME 93041 552-E2
MADERA PL
3000 OXN 93033 553-B3
MADERA RD
1900 SIMI 93065 497-F4
2200 VeCo 93065 497-F4
2800 SIMI 93065 477-F7
MADISON ST
3900 VEN 93003 491-J3
MADONNA LN
- THO 91320 556-B2
MADRESELVA CT
300 CMRL 93012 525-A2
MADRID AV
100 THO 91320 555-J1
MADRINA PL
500 OXN 93030 522-H5
MADRONE ST
2000 SIMI 93065 498-B2
MAEGAN PL
100 THO 91362 556-H1
MAESTRO AV
7600 LA 91304 529-F3
MAESTRO PL
23400 LA 91304 529-F4
MAGDA CIR
2100 THO 91360 526-E4
MAGELLAN AV
500 OXN 93033 552-G6
MAGELLAN ST
- THO 91360 526-F1
MAGNOLIA AV
100 OXN 93030 522-E5
MAGNOLIA DR
- VeCo 93001 471-C2
1300 SPLA 93060 464-B2
MAGNOLIA ST
600 MRPK 93021 476-E7
600 MRPK 93021 496-E1
2000 SIMI 93065 498-B2
2700 CMRL 93012 524-F4
MAGPIE CT
- THO 91320 525-J5
MAHAN CT
15300 MRPK 93021 476-J5
MAHAN RD
- MRPK 93021 476-G3
MAHOGANY LN
23600 SIMI 93065 497-E5
MAHONEY AV
- VeCo 93022 451-A6
600 VeCo 93001 451-A6
MAIDSTONE LN
400 THO 91320 556-D1
MAIDU CT
23600 SIMI 93063 479-B7
MAIN RD
- VeCo 93041 583-H3
- VeCo 93042 583-G4
MAIN ST
100 FILM 93015 456-B6
100 VeCo 93040 457-F3
700 SPLA 93060 463-J7
E MAIN ST
- VEN 93001 491-C2
100 SPLA 93060 464-B6
1300 VeCo 93060 464-B6
2300 VEN 93003 491-H4
3900 VEN 93003 492-A4
N MAIN ST
- VeCo 93015 465-E1
- VeCo 93015 455-E7
S MAIN ST
100 VeCo 93015 465-E1
W MAIN ST
- VEN 93001 491-A1
100 SPLA 93060 463-J6
100 SPLA 93060 464-A6
MAINMAST DR
30500 AGRH 91301 557-G5
MAINMAST PL
5600 AGRH 91301 557-G5
MAINSAIL CIR
3800 WLKV 91361 557-B6
MAINSAIL CT
100 PHME 93041 552-E6
MAINSAIL LN
- OXN 93035 522-E7
MAJESTIC CT
- MRPK 93021 496-E2
MAJORCA CT
800 THO 91360 526-C3
MAJORCA DR
1900 OXN 93035 552-A1
MALAGA CT
600 THO 91320 525-F7
MALAT DR
600 VeCo 91320 525-G7
MALCOLM ST
2000 SIMI 93065 498-A3
MALDEN ST
22300 LA 91304 529-H1
MALIBU AV
100 VeCo 93035 552-B5
200 VEN 93004 492-E1
MALIBU HILLS RD
26700 CALB 91301 558-G7
26700 CALB 91302 558-G7
MALLARD AV
1500 VEN 93003 492-E4
2900 THO 91360 526-F3
MALLARD ST
400 FILM 93015 455-H6
MALLARD WY
100 OXN 93030 522-E5
100 VeCo 93030 522-E5
MALLATT WY
1000 CMRL 93010 524-C3
MALLORY CT
15300 MRPK 93021 477-A4
MALLORY WY
300 OJAI 93023 441-H6
MALO CT
700 SIMI 93065 497-G4
MALONE ST
- PHME 93043 552-D3
E MALTON AV
5800 SIMI 93063 499-A1
N MALTON AV
2100 SIMI 93063 499-B2
MAMMOTH ST
10100 VEN 93004 492-J3
10300 VEN 93004 493-A2
MANASSAS AV
1400 VEN 93003 492-B4
MANCHESTER CT
2500 THO 91362 527-B3
MANCINI CT
5600 VEN 93003 492-C4
MANDALAY CT
1400 CMRL 93010 524-D1
MANDALAY BEACH RD
500 OXN 93035 521-H6
1200 OXN 93035 551-J1
1900 OXN 93035 552-A2
MANDAN CT
2500 VEN 93001 471-C5
MANDAN PL
400 SIMI 93065 497-D2
MANDELL ST
22300 LA 91304 529-J2
MANDEVILLE PL
23600 VeCo 91377 528-A7
MANDRILL AV
2000 VEN 93003 492-F5
MANET LN
2400 SIMI 93063 499-B1
MANGO LN
6100 SIMI 93063 499-B3
MANLEY CT
25900 LACo 91302 558-J3
MANORGATE PL
3200 SIMI 93065 498-D5
MANOR RIDGE RD
600 SPLA 93060 464-A4
MANORVIEW CT
4200 MRPK 93021 496-B3
MANSFIELD LN
100 CMRL 93010 494-E7
100 VeCo 93010 494-E7
MANTON AV
6100 WdHl 91367 529-F7
MANUEL CANYON
23600 VeCo 93001 471-D1
MANZANILLO DR
5200 VeCo 93021 475-G7
5200 VeCo 93021 495-G1
MANZANITA AV
200 VEN 93001 491-E1
MANZANITA DR
600 FILM 93015 455-J5
1200 SPLA 93060 464-B3
2200 OXN 93033 552-F2
MANZANITA LN
- THO 91361 557-A3
200 THO 91361 557-A3
200 THO 91361 556-J3
MANZANITA ST
300 CMRL 93012 524-J3
300 CMRL 93012 525-A3
MAPLE CT
200 VEN 93003 491-H3
500 FILM 93015 455-J4
23600 SIMI 93063 499-B3
MAPLE RD
100 THO 91320 556-B2
200 VeCo 91320 556-B2
MAPLE ST
200 OXN 93033 552-G2
1200 SPLA 93060 464-B2
3500 VEN 93003 491-J3
MAPLECREST ST
11800 MRPK 93021 496-C4
MAPLEGROVE ST
6400 VeCo 91377 558-B2
MAPLEKNOLL PL
3400 THO 91362 527-A1
MAPLELEAF AV
100 THO 91320 555-J2
MAPLERIDGE CT
11400 MRPK 93021 496-B4
MAPLE VIEW CIR
5300 CMRL 93012 525-A2
MAPLEWOOD AV
700 THO 91320 555-G4
MAPLEWOOD CT
700 THO 91320 555-G4
MAPLEWOOD WY
800 PHME 93041 552-F5
MARA AV
- VEN 93004 492-F2
MARBLEHEAD AV
300 SIMI 93065 497-D7
MARCELLA ST
1700 SIMI 93065 498-C3
MARCELLO AV
100 THO 91320 556-C1
MARCH AV
7500 LA 91304 529-F3
MARCH ST
200 SPLA 93060 463-J6
200 SPLA 93060 464-A6
MARCO DR
1800 CMRL 93010 494-H7
1800 CMRL 93010 524-H1
N MARCO DR
2200 CMRL 93010 494-H7
2300 VeCo 93010 494-H7
MARCY CT
3300 SIMI 93063 498-D1
MARDIGRAS CT
700 CMRL 93010 524-D2
MARETO WY
700 VeCo 91377 557-H1
MARGARITA AV
400 CMRL 93012 525-A5
MARGATE PL
1500 THO 91361 556-H6
MARGO DR
700 SIMI 93065 497-G3
MARIA DR
6200 VeCo 93021 475-J5

MARIA LN

VENTURA COUNTY STREET INDEX - With ZIP Codes

MORELAND RD 639

STREET
Block City ZIP Pg-Grid

MARIA LN
- VeCo 93010 494-E6
MARIA WY
23600 OXN 93030 522-H4
MARIAN AV
1500 THO 91360 526-D5
1500 VeCo 91360 526-D5
MARIANO DR
1100 VeCo 93023 451-B1
MARIANO ST
1600 VeCo 93010 493-J5
MARICIO CIR
1900 THO 91360 526-F5
MARICOPA DR
5300 SIMI 93063 478-J7
5400 SIMI 93063 479-A7
MARICOPA HWY Rt#-33
1000 OJAI 93023 441-E6
1000 OJAI 93023 451-F1
1700 VeCo 93023 441-B2
10000 VeCo 93023 366-J6
10200 VeCo - 366-J6
E MARIE ST
2300 SIMI 93065 498-B1
MARIETTA CIR
2800 THO 91360 526-H3
MARIGOLD AV
1500 VEN 93004 493-A2
MARIGOLD CT
26600 CALB 91302 558-G7
MARIGOLD LN
1100 SPLA 93060 464-B3
MARIGOLD PL
1200 THO 91360 526-H2
MARILLA ST
22200 Chat 91311 499-H5
MARILYN CT
3000 THO 91320 555-G2
MARILYN ST
2200 SIMI 93065 498-B1
MARIMAR ST
- THO 91360 526-F5
MARIN LN
7800 VEN 93004 492-E1
MARIN RD
100 SPLA 93060 464-A6
MARIN ST
100 THO 91360 556-E1
MARIN WY
2100 OXN 93033 553-A2
MARINA CIR W
300 VeCo 93040 457-F4
MARINA VILLAGE
700 PHME 93041 552-B2
MARINE WY
1400 OXN 93035 551-J1
MARINER CIR
4000 WLKV 91361 557-C6
MARINER CV
2600 PHME 93041 552-C3
MARINER DR
1300 OXN 93033 522-H7
1300 OXN 93033 552-H1
MARINE VIEW DR
- CMRL 93010 494-B7
- VeCo 93010 494-B7
MARINO WY
2000 VEN 93003 492-E5
MARION ST
1000 THO 91320 525-H7
MARIPOSA CT
- LA 91304 529-E2
MARIPOSA DR
100 CMRL 93012 525-A3
200 THO 91320 555-E1
300 VEN 93001 491-E1
400 CMRL 93012 524-J3
1100 SPLA 93060 464-B2
2200 OXN 93030 522-E2
MARIPOSA PL
5100 CMRL 93012 525-A3
MARIPOSA ST
2000 OXN 93030 522-E3
MARISA PL
2400 SIMI 93065 498-A1
MARISOL DR
1600 VEN 93001 491-E2
MARJORI AV
100 THO 91320 556-C2
MARK CT
700 SIMI 93065 497-G4
5300 AGRH 91301 557-H5
MARK DR
400 SIMI 93065 497-G4
MARK LN
1500 SIMI 93063 499-B3
MARKER ST
100 CMRL 93010 524-D4
MARKET ST
100 PHME 93041 552-E6
300 FILM 93015 456-B6
3400 VEN 93003 491-H4
3800 VeCo 93040 457-E4
4200 VEN 93003 492-A5
4700 VeCo 93003 492-A5
MARKHAM AV
2100 THO 91360 526-F4
MARKS RD
3800 Ago 91301 558-F7

MARK TWAIN LN
600 VEN 93003 492-D3
MARLA AV
8300 LA 91304 529-E2
N MARLBORO LN
- VeCo 91307 528-J4
- VeCo 91307 529-A3
MARLBOROUGH CT
7600 LA 91304 529-F4
E MARLIES AV
5800 SIMI 93063 499-A1
N MARLIES AV
2100 SIMI 93063 499-A2
MARLIES ST
28900 AGRH 91301 558-A3
MARLIN PL
22200 CanP 91303 529-J5
22400 CanP 91307 529-H5
MARLIN WY
5000 OXN 93035 551-J1
5000 OXN 93035 552-A1
MARLOWE ST
1800 THO 91360 526-E5
MARMON AV
- THO 91362 557-B3
MARMOTA CT
7400 VEN 93003 492-F4
MARMOTA ST
7000 VEN 93003 492-E4
MARQUAND AV
7700 LA 91304 529-E3
MARQUETTE CIR
14800 MRPK 93021 476-H5
MARQUETTE ST
14700 MRPK 93021 476-J6
N MARQUETTE ST
6400 MRPK 93021 476-J6
MARQUIS CT
7000 VeCo 91377 528-B7
MARQUITA ST
100 OXN 93030 522-J6
N MARQUITA ST
100 OXN 93030 522-H5
MARSDEN CT
25900 LACo 91302 558-J3
MARSEILLE WY
30800 WLKV 91362 557-F5
MARSELLA DR
- OXN 93030 522-J4
MARSHA AV
6200 SIMI 93063 499-B3
MARSHALL AV
2100 SIMI 93063 498-G1
MARSHALL ST
3900 VEN 93003 491-J3
MARSH BROOK RD
2100 VeCo 91361 556-E7
MARSH RONDO
700 CMRL 93010 524-F2
MARTER AV
2200 SIMI 93065 498-A2
N MARTER CT
2200 SIMI 93065 498-A2
MARTHA DR
500 VeCo 91320 525-G7
3000 VEN 93003 491-G2
N MARTHA MORRISON DR
- SIMI 93065 497-D7
S MARTHA MORRISON DR
- SIMI 93065 497-D7
100 SIMI 93065 527-D1
MARTHAS VINEYARD CT
1100 VEN 93001 491-E5
MARTIN CT
6300 VEN 93003 492-D5
MARTIN ST
800 VeCo 93023 451-C3
MARTINDALE AV
200 OJAI 93023 442-A6
MARTINIQUE DR
2100 OXN 93035 552-A2
9500 VeCo 93021 475-H6
MARTINIQUE PL
400 THO 91320 525-F7
400 THO 91320 555-F1
MARTIN LUTHER KING JR DR
23600 OXN 93030 522-H4
23600 VeCo 93030 522-H4
MARTONA DR
4900 VeCo 91377 557-G1
MARTY CT
- THO 91320 555-G2
MARTZ ST
3600 SIMI 93063 478-E6
N MARVEL AV
2000 SIMI 93065 498-A2
MARVELLA CT
12400 VeCo 93012 496-G6
MARVIEW DR
1600 THO 91362 526-J5
1700 THO 91362 527-A5
MARVIN CT
- SIMI 93065 497-E3
MAR VISTA DR
2300 CMRL 93010 494-G6
2300 VeCo 93010 494-G6

MARY CT
2900 THO 91320 555-H2
MARYGOLD AV
2500 OXN 93033 552-H2
MARYMOUNT CT
400 VeCo 93003 492-B1
400 VEN 93003 492-B1
MARYMOUNT ST
14500 MRPK 93021 476-H5
MARYVILLE AV
400 VEN 93003 492-A1
MASCAGNI ST
4900 VEN 93003 492-A4
MASEFIELD CT
8000 LA 91304 529-E3
MASON CT
2600 THO 91362 527-A1
3500 THO 91362 526-J1
MASON RD
- LACo 90265 586-D7
MASSEY ST
300 THO 91360 526-E5
MASTERSON DR
600 THO 91360 526-G7
MASTHEAD DR
1100 OXN 93035 522-C7
1600 OXN 93035 552-C1
MATILIJA RD
200 VeCo - 366-H6
200 VeCo - 441-A1
200 VeCo 93023 366-H6
200 VeCo 93023 441-A1
MATILIJA RD N
200 VeCo - 441-A1
200 VeCo 93023 441-A1
MATILIJA RD S
- VeCo - 441-A2
700 VeCo 93023 441-A2
MATILIJA ST
100 OJAI 93023 441-H6
W MATILIJA ST
100 OJAI 93023 441-H7
MATTEO ST
4800 VeCo 91377 557-G2
MATTHEWS DR
1500 VEN 93004 492-J3
MAUI LN
1800 OXN 93033 552-J5
1800 OXN 93033 553-A1
MAULHARDT AV
500 OXN 93030 523-B4
MAULHARDT RD
4000 OXN 93033 553-B4
4000 VeCo 93033 553-B4
MAUREEN LN
4700 MRPK 93021 496-C1
MAURICE DR
3900 THO 91320 555-E3
MAURY AV
5900 WdHl 91367 529-C7
E MAVERICK LN
- VeCo 91307 528-G3
MAX CT
23600 SIMI 93065 498-A6
MAXANA DR
400 VeCo 93023 451-D1
MAXINE AV
- VeCo 93022 451-B7
800 OXN 93033 552-F5
800 PHME 93041 552-F5
MAXINE DR
- VeCo 93010 494-E7
MAY CT
2100 SIMI 93063 499-C2
MAYA LINDA
3300 CMRL 93012 524-G2
MAYALL ST
21900 Chat 91311 499-J4
MAYANS LN
200 VEN 93001 471-C5
MAYBROOK AV
2200 CMRL 93010 494-E7
MAYBROOK WY
1700 SIMI 93065 497-F2
MAYENNE CT
30800 WLKV 91362 557-F5
E MAYFAIR ST
1300 SIMI 93065 497-J1
MAYFIELD CT
200 THO 91320 555-E2
MAYFIELD ST
3500 THO 91320 555-E2
MAYFLOWER ST
- THO 91360 526-F6
E MAYLAND PL
1900 SIMI 93065 498-A5
MAYNARD AV
- THO 91320 555-F2
6800 CanP 91307 529-H4
7600 LA 91304 529-H2
MAYSVILLE CIR
1700 THO 91360 526-C5
MAYWIND LN
23600 SIMI 93065 497-A1
MAYWOOD CT
300 THO 91362 557-G2
MAYWOOD WY
2500 OXN 93033 552-G2
MCAFEE CT
- THO 91360 526-F2

MCANDREW RD
100 VeCo 93023 442-F6
MCBEAN RD
5800 VeCo 93066 495-B2
MCBETH CT
4500 MRPK 93021 496-F2
MCCAMPBELL ST
200 FILM 93015 455-J6
MCCLOUD AV
400 THO 91360 526-E7
MCCLOUD RD
8900 VEN 93004 492-H4
MCCOY PL
- SIMI 93065 497-F3
MCCREA RD
2600 THO 91362 527-A1
3500 THO 91362 526-J1
MCCULLOCH ST
2600 CMRL 93010 524-F2
MCDONALD DR
11900 VeCo 93023 451-A1
MC DONALD ST
2200 SIMI 93065 498-A2
MCEDDON PL
100 VEN 93001 491-D1
MCFADDEN AV
300 MRPK 93021 496-E1
E MCFARLANE ST
- VEN 93001 471-C6
W MCFARLANE ST
- VEN 93001 471-B6
MCGILL AV
300 VEN 93003 491-J2
MCGRATH ST
4400 VEN 93003 492-A5
MCGREGER RD
- VeCo 93015 466-J1
- VeCo 93021 466-J1
MCHUGH CT
900 VEN 93003 492-C4
MCKEE ST
- VeCo 93001 471-C2
200 OJAI 93023 441-H6
MCKEEHAN DR
700 PHME 93041 552-F4
MCKEVETT HTS
400 SPLA 93060 464-B5
MCKEVETT RD
800 SPLA 93060 464-B5
MCKINLEY AV
- OXN 93030 522-H6
N MCKINLEY AV
100 OXN 93030 522-H5
MCKINLEY DR
2300 VEN 93003 491-G2
MCKNIGHT RD
1200 VeCo 91320 556-B2
1200 THO 91320 556-B2
S MCKNIGHT RD
100 VeCo 91320 556-B2
MCLAREN AV
6200 WdHl 91367 529-H7
6800 CanP 91307 529-H5
7500 LA 91304 529-H3
MCLEOD RONDO
700 CMRL 93010 524-F2
MCLOUGHLIN AV
1300 OXN 93035 552-D1
MCMILLAN AV
100 OXN 93033 552-G3
MCNAB CT
200 FILM 93015 455-H6
MCNELL RD
100 VeCo 93023 442-E5
MCPHERSON WY
10900 VeCo 93001 450-H5
MCWANE BLVD
400 OXN 93033 552-H7
W MCWANE BLVD
500 OXN 93033 552-G7
MEAD AV
1000 SIMI 93065 497-J4
1200 VEN 93004 492-J2
MEADOW CT
11600 MRPK 93021 496-B2
MEADOW ST
4600 MRPK 93021 496-B2
MEADOW TR
2500 OXN 93030 522-E1
MEADOWBLUFF CT
5300 CMRL 93012 525-A1
MEADOW BROOK CT
1900 THO 91362 526-J3
1900 THO 91362 527-A3
MEADOWBROOK RD
1100 OJAI 93023 441-J5
MEADOWCREST ST
700 THO 91320 555-F4
MEADOW GATE ST
3900 THO 91362 557-C3
MEADOWGLADE DR
6000 VeCo 93021 475-G7
MEADOWGLEN CT
1500 THO 91320 556-A1
MEADOW GROVE LN
200 THO 91362 557-E3
MEADOW HAVEN DR
6300 AGRH 91301 558-A3
MEADOWLAND CT
2300 THO 91361 557-B5

MEADOWLARK DR
- FILM 93015 455-J6
MEADOW LARK LN
1200 OXN 93030 522-E2
MEADOWLARK LN
100 VeCo 91377 557-J3
MEADOWLARK ST
6800 VEN 93003 492-E4
MEADOW MIST CT
200 SIMI 93065 498-A6
MEADOWMIST WY
29500 AGRH 91301 557-J4
MEADOW OAK DR
3200 WLKV 91361 557-C7
MEADOWRIDGE CT
5200 CMRL 93012 524-J1
5200 CMRL 93012 525-A1
MEADOWRUN ST
500 THO 91360 526-G1
MEADOWSIDE DR
2500 THO 91362 527-A3
MEADOWSTONE DR
2900 SIMI 93063 478-C7
MEADOW VIEW CT
1900 THO 91362 526-J5
MEADOWVIEW CT
6700 VEN 93003 472-D6
MEADOW VIEW DR
5100 CMRL 93012 524-J2
5200 CMRL 93012 525-A2
MEADOW VISTA WY
5400 AGRH 91301 557-J5
MEADOWWOOD AV
2900 THO 91360 526-F3
MEANDER DR
1400 SIMI 93065 497-J7
MEDEABROOK PL
5600 AGRH 91301 557-J5
MEDEA CREEK LN
- VeCo 91377 558-A1
MEDEA VALLEY DR
5500 AGRH 91301 558-A5
MEDFIELD ST
28500 AGRH 91301 558-B5
MEDFORD PL
800 VEN 93004 492-G3
MEDFORD ST
8300 VEN 93004 492-G3
MEDICAL CENTER DR
7100 CanP 91307 529-G5
N MEDICINE BOW CT
200 THO 91362 557-B3
S MEDICINE BOW CT
100 THO 91362 557-B3
N MEDINA AV
2000 SIMI 93063 498-C2
MEEHAM WY
13800 MRPK 93021 496-F3
MEG CT
3300 SIMI 93063 478-D7
MEINERS RD
1800 VeCo 93023 441-E6
MELBA AV
6200 WdHl 91367 529-G7
6600 CanP 91307 529-F4
7500 LA 91304 529-F2
MELBOURNE CT
3600 THO 91320 555-F3
MELFORD CT
2200 VeCo 91361 556-E7
MELIA ST
500 VeCo 93010 524-C1
6200 SIMI 93063 499-B3
MELLISA CT
3900 SIMI 93063 478-E6
MELLOW LN
800 SIMI 93065 497-H6
MELODY LN
3000 SIMI 93063 478-E7
MELRAY ST
6400 MRPK 93021 477-A6
MELROSE DR
200 VeCo 93035 552-B4
MELVILLE LN
500 VEN 93003 492-D1
MELVIN CT
3400 VeCo 91320 525-F7
E MELVINA PL
800 SIMI 93065 498-A5
MEMORIAL PKWY
- THO 91360 526-E2
MEMPHIS CT
600 VEN 93004 492-H1
MENCKEN AV
7900 LA 91304 529-E3
MENDOCINO CT
10100 VEN 93004 472-H7
MENDOCINO LN
1500 THO 91320 526-A7
MENDOCINO PL
3000 OXN 93033 553-B3
MENLO ST
6300 SIMI 93063 499-C2
MENLO PARK AV
- VEN 93004 492-G2
MENOTTI LN
4700 VEN 93003 492-B7
MENTA LN
1500 CMRL 93010 524-A1

MERALDA AV
2400 SIMI 93063 499-A1
MERCANTILE ST
700 OXN 93030 522-H7
MERCED DR
800 CMRL 93010 494-F7
1800 VEN 93004 492-G4
MERCED PL
3000 OXN 93033 553-B3
MERCED ST
10500 VEN 93004 472-H7
MERCER AV
600 OJAI 93023 442-A6
600 VEN 93004 492-J1
MERCURY PL
3800 SIMI 93063 498-E2
MEREDITH AV
300 VEN 93003 491-J1
MEREDITH CT
23900 LA 91304 529-E3
MERIDIAN AV
4200 OXN 93035 552-A2
E MERRILL CT
3800 SIMI 93063 498-E2
MERRITT AV
300 CMRL 93010 524-F3
MESA AV
- THO 91320 556-A2
MESA CIR
7200 VEN 93003 472-D7
MESA DR
- VeCo 93010 494-E6
100 VeCo 93023 441-D7
800 FILM 93015 456-A5
7800 VeCo 93063 499-F4
MESA RD
100 WHil 91304 499-D6
MESA RIDGE AV
1600 THO 91362 527-G6
MESA SCHOOL RD
- VeCo 93010 493-H4
- VeCo 93066 493-H4
MESA VERDE AV
1400 VEN 93003 492-C5
MESA VERDE DR
12800 MRPK 93021 496-E2
MESCALLERO PL
6100 SIMI 93063 479-B6
MESQUITE ST
500 CMRL 93012 524-J3
MESSINA PL
600 VeCo 91377 557-G1
META ST
400 OXN 93030 522-G6
1000 VEN 93001 491-D2
METZ CT
1900 SIMI 93065 498-A4
MEYER RD
1100 VeCo 93023 441-C5
MIAMI LN
800 VEN 93004 492-J2
MICAELA DR
5400 AGRH 91301 557-H5
MICHAEL DR
2200 THO 91320 555-H1
2900 VeCo 91320 555-G1
MICHALE ST
22100 LA 91304 529-H1
MICHELLE CT
3300 SIMI 93063 478-D6
MICHELLE DR
28800 AGRH 91301 558-B4
MICOMA CT
5500 SIMI 93063 479-A7
MIDBURY HILL RD
- VeCo 91320 556-B2
MIDDLE CREST DR
5600 AGRH 91301 557-H4
MIDDLE FORK CIR
4700 THO 91362 557-D1
MIDDLEGATE RD
3900 WLKV 91361 557-D6
MIDDLE RANCH RD
- MRPK 93021 476-G4
- VeCo 93021 476-G4
MIDDLE RANGE FIRE RD
23600 MRPK - 467-D7
23600 MRPK - 477-E1
23600 MRPK 93021 466-J7
23600 MRPK 93021 467-A7
23600 MRPK 93021 476-G1
23600 MRPK 93021 477-E1
23600 VeCo - 467-D7
23600 VeCo - 477-E1
23600 VeCo - 478-A1
23600 VeCo 93021 476-G1
23600 VeCo 93063 478-D2
23600 VeCo 93021 466-J7
23600 VeCo 93021 467-A7
23600 VeCo 93021 477-E1
MIDDLESBURY RIDGE CIR
7000 CanP 91307 529-E5
MIDNIGHT MOON LN
23600 SIMI 93065 497-A1
MIDWAY DR
4500 PHME 93041 552-E5
MIGUEL LN
400 OXN 93030 522-H4

MILAN DR
1400 SIMI 93065 497-G3
MILANO PL
23600 MRPK 93021 496-C4
MILBURN ST
1900 CMRL 93010 524-E3
MILDRED ST
5200 SIMI 93063 498-J3
MILL CT
23600 SIMI 93065 497-F7
MILL DR
- VeCo 93001 471-C3
MILL PL
1000 SPLA 93060 464-B4
N MILL ST
100 SPLA 93060 464-B4
S MILL ST
100 SPLA 93060 464-B6
MILLARD ST
- MRPK 93021 496-E1
MILLBRAE CT
200 VEN 93004 492-G2
MILL CANYON RD
23600 VeCo 93001 460-G7
23600 VeCo 93001 470-H1
23600 VeCo 93001 471-A1
MILL CREEK CT
3500 THO 91360 526-H2
MILLCROFT CT
700 SIMI 93065 498-D5
MILLER CT
800 VEN 93003 492-C3
MILLER PL
100 SPLA 93060 464-C5
E MILLERTON RD
4400 MRPK 93021 496-E2
MILLIGAN DR
1000 CMRL 93010 524-G2
MILLIGAN BARRANCA RD
4000 VeCo 93066 494-C2
4600 VeCo 93066 474-C7
MILLPARK LN
23600 SIMI 93065 497-A2
MILLS RD
- PHME 93043 552-C3
N MILLS RD
- VEN 93003 491-H2
S MILLS RD
- VEN 93003 491-H3
MILLTRACE WY
- SIMI 93065 497-F3
MILL VALLEY RD
4300 MRPK 93021 496-F2
MILLVILLE CT
1900 THO 91360 526-D5
MILLWOOD CIR
9900 VEN 93004 492-J3
MILLWOOD ST
9800 VEN 93004 492-J3
MILNE CT
15800 MRPK 93021 477-A5
MILPAS ST
4200 CMRL 93012 524-H4
MILTON AV
700 VEN 93003 491-H4
MILTON ST
- VeCo 93022 451-B7
MIMOSA CT
5600 VeCo 91377 557-J2
MINDENVALE CT
400 SIMI 93065 527-D1
MINERAL WELLS DR
3000 SIMI 93063 478-G7
MINGUS DR
30800 WLKV 91362 557-F3
MINNA ST
3300 VeCo 93030 492-J7
MINNECOTA DR
4100 THO 91360 496-J7
MINOR ST
300 MRPK 93021 496-F1
MINSTREL AV
6900 CanP 91307 529-G4
7600 LA 91304 529-G3
MINT LN
400 VEN 93001 491-E1
MINT WY
2400 OXN 93030 522-F2
MINUET PL
400 VeCo 93022 451-B7
MINUTEMAN WY
30900 AGRH 91301 557-F6
30900 WLKV 91361 557-F6
MIPOLOMOL RD
8100 VeCo 90265 585-F5
MIRABELLA ST
23600 MRPK 93021 496-C4
MIRADA LN
4100 OXN 93033 553-C4
MIRA FLORES CT
300 CMRL 93012 525-A2
MIRAGE CT
700 THO 91320 555-G6
MIRA LOMA CIR
500 OXN 93030 522-E6
500 OXN 93035 522-E6
MIRAMAR CT
2900 OXN 93035 522-C7

MIRAMAR DR
1700 VEN 93001 491-E1
MIRAMAR PL
2400 OXN 93035 522-D7
MIRAMAR ST
- CMRL 93010 524-D4
MIRAMAR WK
2000 OXN 93035 552-D1
2100 OXN 93035 522-D7
MIRAMAR WY
3300 OXN 93035 522-B7
MIRAMONTE DR
200 OXN 93030 522-J2
MIRA MONTES
7800 VeCo 93063 499-F3
MIRA SOL DR
4700 MRPK 93021 496-B2
MIRROR LAKE AV
1900 VeCo 93023 451-C3
MISSILE WY
- PHME 93043 552-C5
W MISSION AV
- VEN 93001 491-B1
MISSION CIR
11300 Chat 91311 499-H1
MISSION DR
- CMRL 93010 494-D7
- CMRL 93010 524-D1
100 VeCo 93010 494-D6
MISSION PZ
- VEN 93001 491-B2
MISSION TER
900 VeCo 93010 494-D6
MISSION OAKS BLVD
3000 CMRL 93012 524-F3
5100 CMRL 93012 525-A2
6200 CMRL 93012 495-B7
MISSION ROCK RD
100 VeCo 93060 473-F3
MISSION VERDE DR
5400 CMRL 93012 525-A1
MISTLETOE RD
8000 VeCo 93060 453-J5
MISTRAL PL
2000 OXN 93035 522-D6
MISTY CT
5900 AGRH 91301 558-B4
MISTY CANYON AV
600 THO 91362 557-G1
MISTY CREEK RD
1600 THO 91362 527-G6
MISTY FALLS CT
300 SIMI 93065 497-E6
MISTY GROVE ST
12400 MRPK 93021 496-D4
MISTY HOLLOW CT
4100 MRPK 93021 496-D3
MISTY LAKE CT
500 SIMI 93065 497-E6
MISTYMEADOW ST
4300 MRPK 93021 496-D3
MISTY TRAILS PL
400 SIMI 93065 497-E6
MITCHELL RD
800 THO 91320 525-J7
MOBERLY CT
2300 THO 91360 526-B4
MOBIL AV
- CMRL 93010 524-E2
MOBIL LN
100 VeCo 93001 461-A3
MOBILE ST
22300 CanP 91303 529-J7
22600 CanP 91307 529-E7
MOBIL PIER RD
23600 VeCo 93001 459-E6
MOBY DICK LN
700 OXN 93030 522-E7
MOCKINGBIRD CT
- VeCo 91377 557-J2
MOCKINGBIRD LN
400 FILM 93015 455-H6
2100 OXN 93033 553-A4
MOCKINGBIRD ST
6200 VEN 93003 492-D4
MODELLO CANYON RD
23600 VeCo 93040 367-D7
23600 VeCo 93040 457-G1
MODENA PL
5500 AGRH 91301 557-G5
MODESTO AV
200 VEN 93004 492-E1
MODESTO AV S
1000 CMRL 93010 524-D2
MODOC CT
- VEN 93004 472-J7
MODOC DR
3300 OXN 93033 553-B3
MODOC ST
10500 VEN 93004 472-J7
MOFFATT CIR
700 SIMI 93065 497-J5
MOHAVE DR
5100 SIMI 93063 478-J7
MOHAWK AV
- THO 91362 557-A2
2800 VEN 93001 471-C5
MOHICAN LN
2300 VEN 93001 471-C6

MOHICAN ST
6100 SIMI 93063 479-B6
MOJAVE DR
1600 VEN 93004 492-H4
E MOLINE ST
4100 SIMI 93063 478-F6
MOLLISON DR
300 SIMI 93065 497-F6
MOLLY CT
2900 VeCo 91320 555-G1
MONACO CT
30800 WLKV 91362 557-G6
MONACO DR
2300 OXN 93035 552-B2
MONARCH CT
2400 SIMI 93063 498-H1
MONDEGO PL
700 THO 91360 526-C3
MONDOVI CT
23600 MRPK 93021 496-C4
MONET CT
1500 OXN 93033 552-J4
MONET DR
9900 VeCo 93021 475-J6
MONET PL
1000 OXN 93033 552-J4
MONICA CIR
100 THO 91320 555-G2
MONITA DR
1700 VEN 93001 491-E1
MONMOUTH DR
2100 VEN 93001 491-E4
MONMOUTH WY
600 VEN 93001 491-E4
MONO CT
4900 VEN 93003 492-A1
MONO ST
1900 OXN 93030 522-J3
MONROE AV
15300 MRPK 93021 476-J5
MONROE ST
3900 VEN 93003 491-J3
MONTAGNE WY
3100 THO 91362 526-J2
MONTAIR DR
23600 MRPK 93021 496-A1
MONTALVO DR
6000 VeCo 93003 492-D6
6000 VEN 93003 492-D6
MONTANA CIR
300 VeCo 93023 441-F6
MONTANA DR
1900 VEN 93003 492-C5
MONTANA RD
100 OJAI 93023 441-E7
100 VeCo 93023 441-E7
MONTAUK LN
1000 VEN 93001 491-E4
MONT BLANC DR
700 VEN 93001 491-D1
MONTCLAIR DR
700 SPLA 93060 464-A4
6200 VEN 93003 472-C7
MONTE CT
500 VeCo 93022 451-A6
MONTEBELLO AV
200 VEN 93004 492-F2
MONTEBELLO ST
1100 SPLA 93060 464-C6
MONTE CARLO DR
3000 THO 91362 527-A2
3100 THO 91362 526-J2
3600 VeCo 93035 522-C6
MONTE CARLO ST
3700 OXN 93035 522-B6
23600 VeCo 93035 522-B6
MONTECITO AV
23600 THO 91362 527-B5
MONTELEONE AV
800 VeCo 91377 557-H1
MONTENEGRO CIR
- THO 91320 555-F1
MONTEREY CT
3900 THO 91320 555-E1
MONTEREY DR
- VeCo 93022 451-D4
MONTEREY PL
23600 SPLA 93060 464-B4
MONTEREY ST
3000 OXN 93033 552-F3
MONTE SERENO DR
900 THO 91360 526-D6
MONTESSA DR
5800 CMRL 93012 525-B1
MONTE VIA
- VeCo 93022 451-A6
MONTE VISTA
- THO 91320 525-E6
MONTE VISTA AV
500 VEN 93003 472-D7
MONTE VISTA CT
6900 VEN 93003 472-D7
MONTE VISTA DR
800 SPLA 93060 464-B4
1700 CMRL 93010 524-D3
MONTE VISTA PL
400 SPLA 93060 464-A4
MONTGOMERY AV
100 VeCo 93030 492-J5
500 VEN 93004 492-G2

MONTGOMERY AV
1300 VeCo 93004 492-G4
MONTGOMERY CT
900 THO 91360 526-G5
8300 VEN 93004 492-G3
MONTGOMERY PL
700 VEN 93004 492-G3
MONTGOMERY RD
1400 THO 91360 526-G5
9200 Chat 91311 499-F7
MONTGOMERY ST
100 OJAI 93023 441-J5
S MONTGOMERY ST
100 OJAI 93023 441-H7
MONTGOMERY FIRE RD
23600 SIMI 93065 498-A7
23600 SIMI 93065 528-B1
23600 VeCo 93065 528-B1
MONTICELLO AV
3300 SIMI 93063 478-F6
MONTILLA CIR
800 THO 91360 526-C3
MONTROSE DR
2000 THO 91362 527-A6
MONTROSE ST
1700 OXN 93033 552-H1
MONTVIEW CT
2700 WLKV 91361 557-A7
MONUMENT ST
- SIMI 93063 498-H1
MOODY CT
- THO 91360 556-G1
MOON DR
5700 VEN 93003 492-C5
5900 VeCo 93003 492-C5
MOON BEAM AV
- THO 91362 557-A2
MOONCREST CT
3300 THO 91320 555-G2
MOONDANCE ST
400 THO 91360 526-D2
MOONFLOWER CIR
2800 THO 91360 526-H3
MOONLIGHT CT
3500 THO 91362 527-D3
MOONRIDGE AV
300 THO 91320 555-J2
400 VeCo 91320 555-J3
MOONSEED LN
23600 SIMI 93065 497-A2
MOONSHADOW CIR
1700 CMRL 93012 495-B7
1700 CMRL 93012 525-A1
MOONSHADOW ST
23600 SIMI 93063 478-J6
23600 SIMI 93063 479-A6
MOONSTONE WY
5000 OXN 93035 521-J7
MOORCROFT AV
6500 CanP 91303 529-J4
7600 LA 91304 529-J1
8800 LA 91304 499-J7
MOORCROFT PL
8700 LA 91304 529-J1
MOORE ST
1700 SIMI 93065 497-J4
1700 SIMI 93065 498-A4
MOORE CANYON RD
23600 CanP 91307 529-C7
23600 VeCo 91302 529-C7
23600 VeCo 91307 529-C7
MOORING WK
1100 OXN 93030 522-F7
MOORPARK AV
100 MRPK 93021 496-E2
100 VeCo 93035 552-B5
100 VeCo 93043 552-B5
MOORPARK AV Rt#-23
- MRPK 93021 476-E7
500 MRPK 93021 496-E1
N MOORPARK AV Rt#-23
- MRPK 93021 496-E1
MOORPARK CIR
- VeCo 93012 554-E4
MOORPARK RD
- THO 91360 556-E2
- THO 91361 556-E2
3200 VeCo 93021 496-H4
13100 VeCo 91360 496-H4
13100 VeCo 93012 496-G5
13100 THO 91360 496-H4
13100 THO 93012 496-G5
N MOORPARK RD
200 THO 91360 556-F1
500 THO 91360 526-F1
3100 THO 91360 496-G6
3100 THO 93012 496-G6
3100 VeCo 91360 496-G6
3100 VeCo 93012 496-G6
MORADO PL
- OXN 93030 522-H4
MORAGA CT
2400 SIMI 93065 498-A1
MORAINE WY
2500 OXN 93030 522-D4
MORANDA PKWY
100 PHME 93041 552-F6
MORELAND RD
- SIMI 93065 497-E2

VENTURA CO.

INDEX

STREET Block City ZIP	Pg-Grid
MORELIA CT	
600 THO 91360	526-C6
MORENA LN	
4100 VeCo 93033	553-C4
MORENO DR	
800 VeCo 93023	451-B1
1400 SIMI 93063	498-D3
1400 VeCo 93063	499-A1
E MORGAN RD	
- VeCo 91307	528-H4
MORGAN ST	
1700 VeCo 93023	451-C3
MORGAN CANYON RD	
VeCo 93066	464-D7
MORGAN HILL ST	
200 SIMI 93065	527-E1
MORLEY ST	
1600 SIMI 93065	498-A3
MORNING ARBOR WY	
1600 SIMI 93065	497-F2
MORNING GLORY ST	
2000 SIMI 93065	498-A2
MORNING RIDGE AV	
THO 91362	527-D2
MORNINGSIDE CT	
2800 THO 91362	526-J3
2800 THO 91362	527-A3
MORNINGSTAR AV	
23600 THO 91360	526-E2
MORNING VIEW CT	
1900 THO 91362	526-J1
MORNINGWOOD WY	
23600 SIMI 93063	497-A1
MOROCCO LN	
9300 WHI 91304	499-E7
MORONGO DR	
1600 CRML 93012	525-D1
1700 CRML 93012	495-D7
MORRIS DR	
500 FILM 93015	456-A4
MORRIS ST	
1300 OXN 93030	522-J5
MORRISON LN	
400 SPLA 93060	463-H6
MORRISON RANCH RD	
Ago 93001	558-F4
26400 CALB 91302	558-F4
26400 LACo 91302	558-F4
MORRO WY	
700 SIMI 93041	552-H3
MORRO BAY LN	
5600 VeCo 93033	492-C4
MORROW CIR	
1300 THO 91362	527-A6
MORSE AV	
800 VeCo 91J5	491-J5
MORVALE DR	
2900 VeCo 91362	586-D2
MOSES LN	
500 VEN 93003	492-D1
MOSS CT	
2100 THO 91362	526-J4
MOTOR WY	
14100 VeCo 90265	625-G2
MOTT CT	
11000 VeCo 93012	526-B1
MOTT PL	
23600 VeCo 93060	453-G2
MOULTRIE LN	
200 SPLA 93060	464-A7
200 SPLA 93060	463-J7
MOUND AV	
3500 VEN 93003	491-H2
MOUNTAIN CREEK DR	
3900 THO 91360	555-E3
MOUNTAIN GATE DR	
LACo 91302	558-E3
MOUNTAIN LION RD	
11900 VeCo 93063	479-A6
MOUNTAIN LOOKOUT RD	
VeCo 93066	474-C1
S MOUNTAIN LOOKOUT RD	
23600 VeCo 93066	474-H2
23600 VeCo 93066	475-A2
MOUNTAIN MEADOW DR	
4200 MRPK 93021	496-C3
MOUNTAIN OAK PL	
1000 THO 91360	556-C1
MOUNTAIN PARK CT	
4100 MRPK 93021	496-B3
MOUNTAIN SHADOW CT	
2900 THO 91360	526-B2
MOUNTAIN TRAIL AV	
3300 THO 91360	555-G4
MOUNTAIN TRAIL ST	
11900 MRPK 93021	496-B3
MOUNTAIN VIEW AV	
500 OXN 93030	522-H6
800 OJAI 93023	441-J5
900 OJAI 93023	442-A5
MOUNTAIN VIEW DR	
5500 CRML 93012	525-D3
MOUNTAIN VIEW RD	
1200 VeCo 93063	556-B3
MOUNTAIN VIEW ST	
VeCo 93022	451-B7
500 FILM 93015	456-B5
MOUNTAIN VISTA LN	
SIMI 93065	498-A6

STREET Block City ZIP	Pg-Grid
MOUNTCLEF BLVD	
2800 THO 91360	526-F3
MOUNT PINOS RD	
23600 VeCo	367-A1
MOUNT SINAI DR	
23600 SIMI 93063	479-B7
23600 SIMI 93063	499-A1
MOUNT WHITNEY CT	
800 VEN 93003	492-C2
MOWER CT	
900 THO 91362	526-J7
MOZART LN	
5000 VEN 93003	492-B4
MUD CREEK RD	
VeCo 93060	454-A5
MUGU RD	
1300 VeCo 93041	583-G2
1300 VeCo 93042	583-F4
MUIR ST	
1200 VeCo 93015	455-G4
5800 SIMI 93063	499-A2
N MUIRFIELD AV	
800 SIMI 93063	498-A5
MUIRFIELD DR	
1600 OXN 93030	522-E2
E MUIRWOOD CT	
2800 SIMI 93063	478-H7
N MUIRWOOD CT	
2700 SIMI 93063	478-H7
MULBERRY CIR	
3000 THO 91360	526-H2
MULBERRY DR	
VeCo 93001	471-C3
MULBERRY LN	
23600 MRPK 93021	496-C4
MULBERRY PL	
23600 SIMI 93065	499-B3
MULBERRY RIDGE CT	
5600 CRML 93012	525-B2
MULCAHEY DR	
1800 SIMI 93065	553-F7
MULHOLLAND HWY	
32400 LACo 90265	586-J5
34700 LACo 90265	625-J3
MULHOLLAND HWY Rt#-23	
33000 LACo 90265	586-G6
MUNDA DR	
1100 PHME 93041	552-E4
MUNGER DR	
500 SPLA 93060	463-H6
MUNNINGS WY	
2700 VeCo 91361	586-C1
MUNSON ST	
1800 CRML 93010	524-F1
1800 CRML 93010	494-F7
MUPU AV	
100 SPLA 93060	464-A5
MUPU ST	
- VeCo	453-J4
MURDOCH ST	
700 VEN 93003	492-D3
MUREAU RD	
25400 CALB 91302	558-J5
25400 LACo 91302	558-J5
MURPHY LN	
1800 OXN 93033	553-B4
MURRAY AV	
CRML 93010	524-D3
MURRE WY	
3800 OXN 93035	552-B4
MURRIETA ST	
5400 VEN 93003	492-B3
MUSTANG CT	
1700 VeCo 93023	451-C3
MUSTANG DR	
- OXN 93030	522-E7
N MUSTANG LN	
VeCo 91307	528-H4
MUTAU CT	
200 FILM 93015	455-J6
MUTAU FLAT RD	
VeCo	366-L2
VeCo	367-A3
MYRNA DR	
500 PHME 93041	552-F6
MYRNA-JOYCE DR	
800 PHME 93041	552-F5
800 PHME 93041	552-F5
800 PHME 93041	552-F5
MYRTLE CT	
5100 VeCo 91377	557-H1
MYRTLE ST	
OXN 93030	522-H1
100 OXN 93030	522-H1
MYSTIC LN	
7300 CanP 91307	529-E5

STREET Block City ZIP	Pg-Grid
N	
N ST	
400 OXN 93030	522-E5
1100 OXN 93030	522-E7
1100 OXN 93033	522-E1
NADINE CT	
THO 91320	555-G2
NADIR ST	
23600 LA 91304	529-E2

STREET Block City ZIP	Pg-Grid
NAHUA LN	
2300 VEN 93001	471-D6
NANCHARO RD	
2100 VeCo 93012	496-A7
2100 VeCo 93012	526-A1
NANCY CIR	
1800 THO 91362	526-J6
NANCY ST	
300 VeCo 93010	494-D7
NANDINA CIR	
2400 OXN 93030	522-G2
NANDINA CT	
2300 OXN 93030	522-F2
NANDINA PL	
300 OXN 93030	522-F2
NANTUCKET PKWY	
3600 OXN 93035	522-B6
NAPA CT	
23600 SIMI 93065	497-G7
NAPA ST	
3000 SIMI 93063	552-E3
22100 LA 91304	529-H1
NAPLES CT	
1300 SIMI 93065	497-F3
NAPLES DR	
2800 OXN 93035	522-C6
23600 OXN 93035	522-C6
NAPOLEON AV	
1800 OXN 93033	552-J2
1800 OXN 93033	553-J1
5500 VeCo 91377	527-H6
NAPOLI DR	
2000 OXN 93035	552-B2
NAPOLI PL	
23600 MRPK 93021	496-C4
NARANJA	
700 VeCo 93023	455-D5
NARDO ST	
10900 VeCo 93004	493-A2
NARROWS CT	
1700 OXN 93035	552-C1
NASH LN	
1800 OXN 93033	553-B4
NASHVILLE PL	
1900 OXN 93033	553-A5
NASSAU DR	
2100 OXN 93030	522-E2
NATALIE LN	
8300 LA 91304	529-F2
NATALIE PL	
1600 OXN 93030	522-D4
NATALIE WY	
VeCo 93010	494-E7
NATASHA CT	
23600 AGRH 91301	557-H5
NATHAN LN	
1300 VEN 93001	491-F5
NAUMAN RD	
5600 VeCo 93033	553-E5
NAUTICAL WY	
1200 OXN 93035	522-E7
NAUTILUS ST	
4900 OXN 93035	521-J7
4900 OXN 93035	551-J1
NAVAJO AV	
2700 VeCo 91362	557-A2
NAVAL AIR RD	
7800 VeCo 93041	583-G1
15100 VeCo 93041	553-F6
15100 VeCo 93042	553-F6
18500 VeCo 93042	553-F6
NAVARRO ST	
100 THO 91320	522-J6
NAVIGATOR DR	
1100 VEN 93003	491-G6
NAVIGATOR WY	
OXN 93030	522-E7
NAVY LN	
4900 OXN 93035	522-C7
NEAL CT	
1800 SIMI 93065	497-H4
NEAP CT	
3100 OXN 93035	522-C7
NEAP PL	
3000 OXN 93035	522-C7
NEATH ST	
8400 VEN 93004	492-G4
NEBULA ST	
2800 SIMI 93063	522-D4
NECTARINE ST	
200 OXN 93033	552-G2
NEDDY AV	
6100 WdHI 91367	529-D7
6400 CanP 91307	529-D7
NEEDLES ST	
22100 Chat 91311	499-J5
NEISH ST	
2300 VeCo 93010	494-D7
E NELDA ST	
5900 SIMI 93063	499-B2
NELLIE CT	
200 THO 91320	555-H1
NELLORA ST	
2300 VeCo 93010	524-F3
NELSON PL	
23600 SIMI 93063	552-J4
NEMESIS PL	
PHME 93043	552-C5
NEPTUNE PL	
2500 PHME 93041	552-E2

STREET Block City ZIP	Pg-Grid
NEPTUNE SQ	
5100 OXN 93035	521-J6
5100 OXN 93035	551-J1
NET CT	
2900 OXN 93035	522-C7
NET PL	
3100 OXN 93035	522-C7
NETTLEBROOK ST	
6200 VEN 93003	472-C7
NEVA CIR	
3400 THO 91360	555-G1
NEVADA AV	
VEN 93004	472-H6
3000 OXN 93033	553-A3
6100 WdHI 91367	529-J7
6500 CanP 91307	529-J6
7700 LA 91304	529-J1
8900 LA 91304	499-J7
9600 Chat 91311	499-J5
NEVELSON LN	
5900 SIMI 93063	499-B1
NEVIN AV	
1400 VEN 93004	492-G4
NEW ST	
100 SPLA 93060	464-C5
NEWARK WY	
1800 VEN 93004	492-J2
NEW BEDFORD CT	
2800 OXN 93035	522-C6
NEWBOLT LN	
500 VEN 93003	492-D1
NEWBURY RD	
VeCo 93320	556-B2
800 THO 91320	556-A1
1900 THO 91320	555-J1
NEWCASTLE ST	
400 THO 91361	556-F2
NEWCOMB DR	
300 VEN 93003	492-A3
NEWGATE RD	
6900 CanP 91307	529-E5
NEW HAVEN PL	
2200 OXN 93030	522-D7
NEWHAVEN ST	
4900 VeCo 91377	557-G1
NEW LOS ANGELES AV Rt#-118	
500 MRPK 93021	496-F1
NEWMAN ST	
1200 SIMI 93065	497-H4
NEWMAN RANCH RD	
23600 VeCo 93063	450-H7
23600 VeCo 93063	460-J1
NEWPORT AV	
200 VEN 93004	492-G2
NEWPORT CIR	
1300 THO 91360	526-F6
7000 CanP 91307	529-E5
NEWPORT WEIGH	
23600 OXN 93035	552-B4
NEWQUIST CT	
2200 CRML 93010	494-D7
NEWTOWN ST	
8400 VEN 93004	492-G4
NEY CT	
1000 SIMI 93065	497-H4
NICE CT	
4000 OXN 93035	552-B2
NICHOLAS ST	
2500 SIMI 93065	478-E7
NICOLE DR	
500 THO 91320	525-H7
NICOLLE ST	
5700 VEN 93003	492-C6
NIDIA WY	
OXN 93030	522-J4
NIELSEN ST	
VEN 93003	492-A3
NIGHTFALL PL	
23600 SIMI 93063	479-A6
NIGHTINGALE PL	
800 THO 91320	522-F2
NIGHTINGALE ST	
6300 VEN 93003	492-D6
11800 MRPK 93021	496-C2
NIGHT RAIN LN	
23600 SIMI 93063	497-A1
NIGHTSKY DR	
13200 VeCo 93012	496-F4
NIGHTWIND LN	
23600 SIMI 93063	497-A1
NIKE ZEUS RD	
23600 VeCo 93042	583-D5
NILES ST	
2700 SIMI 93065	498-C2
NILGAI PL	
7200 VEN 93003	492-F4
NIMITZ DR	
4200 OXN 93035	552-H4
NINA DR	
300 OXN 93030	522-J4
NITA AV	
6200 WdHI 91367	529-J7
6800 CanP 91303	529-J6
7600 LA 91304	529-J3
9600 Chat 91311	499-J5
NIVEO LN	
23600 SIMI 93063	478-F7
NOTRE DAME AV	
9200 Chat 91311	499-F7

STREET Block City ZIP	Pg-Grid
NIXON CT	
7300 VEN 93003	492-E1
NO 2 CANYON FIRE RD	
23600 MRPK	477-B3
23600 MRPK 93021	477-B3
23600 MRPK 93065	477-B3
NOB HILL LN	
6200 VEN 93003	472-C7
NOBLE RD	
1300 VeCo 93023	451-E2
NOBLETREE CT	
500 VeCo 91377	557-H1
NOEL CIR	
2600 SIMI 93063	498-B3
NOGALES AV	
5600 MRPK 93021	476-G7
NOGUERA AV	
9600 Chat 91311	450-E3
NOLAN CT	
2300 THO 91360	527-F3
NOME DR	
300 THO 91360	526-F3
NONCHALANT DR	
4700 SIMI 93063	497-H6
NOONTIDE WY	
23600 OXN 93035	522-E7
NOPAL WK	
300 OXN 93030	522-J5
NOPALITO ST	
4700 VEN 93004	492-J1
NORDHOFF RD	
3800 VeCo 93023	442-E7
3800 VeCo 93023	452-E1
NORDHOFF ST	
22000 Chat 91311	499-J7
NORDMAN DR	
1000 CRML 93010	524-E2
NORFIELD CT	
2200 VeCo 91361	556-E7
NORFLEET LN	
1800 SIMI 93065	497-D6
NORITE PL	
2600 VeCo 93030	522-D4
NORMA CT	
4900 VeCo 93010	494-E7
2100 OXN 93035	522-E2
NORMA ST	
2300 OXN 93030	522-E3
NORMA WY	
1400 SIMI 93063	499-B3
NORMAN A AV	
100 THO 91360	526-F6
NORMANDY TER	
6800 VeCo 91377	528-B7
NORSEMAN CT	
500 OXN 93030	522-E6
NORTH ST	
4500 VeCo 93066	464-A4
4500 VeCo 93066	495-A4
NORTHAM AV	
THO 91320	555-J1
NORTH AMERICAN CUT OFF	
23600 VeCo 93063	479-B7
NORTH BANK DR	
6700 VEN 93003	492-E6
NORTHBROOK DR	
2400 OXN 93030	522-E1
NORTHCREST CT	
3600 SIMI 93063	478-E7
NORTHDALE DR	
11600 MRPK 93021	496-C3
NORTHLAKE CIR	
2400 THO 91361	557-B5
NORTHLAND ST	
2800 THO 91320	555-E2
NORTHPARK ST	
2200 THO 91362	527-A4
E NORTHRIDGE AV	
4400 VeCo 93066	493-F2
NORTHSHORE LN	
1100 THO 91361	557-B5
NORTHSTAR CV	
2600 PHME 93041	552-C3
NORTHSTAR LN	
2400 SIMI 93065	522-E1
NORTH VALLEY DR	
500 THO 91362	557-C2
NORTH VIEW DR	
1400 THO 91360	527-D6
NORTHWOOD PKWY	
2900 THO 91360	526-H2
NORTHWOODS VIEW RD	
23800 CanP 91307	529-E5
NORTON AV	
6800 VEN 93003	492-E5
NORWALK AV	
10000 VEN 93004	492-H2
NORWAY DR	
4200 OXN 93030	471-C1
4200 OXN 93030	461-C7
NORWICH AV	
1400 THO 91360	526-F6
NORWICH LN	
1100 VEN 93001	491-B5
NORWOOD CT	
1100 VeCo 93004	492-J2

STREET Block City ZIP	Pg-Grid
NOTRE DAME AV	
9200 Chat 91311	499-F7
9200 Chat 91311	499-F6
NOTTINGHAM DR	
700 OXN 93030	522-E4
NOTTINGWOOD CIR	
1200 THO 91361	557-B5
NOVA CT	
4900 VEN 93003	492-A1
NOVA LN	
1300 VeCo 93023	451-E2
NOVARA WY	
500 VeCo 91377	557-H1
NOVATO DR	
1200 OXN 93035	522-D7
1300 OXN 93035	552-D1
NOVINA PL	
500 CRML 93012	524-J3
N NOWAK AV	
1800 THO 91360	526-E5
NOYES AV	
2700 THO 91360	526-F3
NUEVE CT	
300 CRML 93012	525-A3
NUEVO CANYON RD	
VeCo 93040	367-E9
VeCo 93040	458-C1
NUMBER TEN CANYON RD	
23600 VeCo 93040	367-E9
23600 VeCo 93040	458-D7
NUTCRACKER CT	
900 THO 91362	557-C1
NUTMEG CIR	
2600 SIMI 93065	498-C1
NUTWOOD CIR	
5700 SIMI 93063	499-A2
NYE RD	
8600 VeCo 93021	461-A3
NYELAND AV	
2200 VeCo 93036	523-C2
NYE RANCH FIRE RD	
23600 VeCo 93001	460-J2

STREET Block City ZIP	Pg-Grid
O	
OAHU LN	
4900 OXN 93033	552-J5
OAK	
2000 VeCo 93023	451-C3
OAK AV	
300 VeCo 93015	455-G4
OAK BEND	
VeCo 91377	527-J7
VeCo 91377	528-A7
OAK CT	
800 PHME 93041	552-F5
OAK DR	
4500 VeCo 93022	451-B6
4500 VeCo 93066	495-A4
5100 OXN 93033	552-G6
OAK LN	
100 THO 91362	556-H1
OAK RD	
1400 SIMI 93063	499-B3
OAK ST	
CRML 93010	524-E3
100 OJAI 93023	441-J6
100 OJAI 93015	465-E1
600 VeCo 93023	451-B7
600 VeCo 93022	461-B1
N OAK ST	
100 VEN 93001	491-C2
S OAK ST	
VEN 93001	491-C2
100 SPLA 93060	464-C5
NORTHPARK ST	
2200 THO 91362	527-A4
W OAK ST	
23600 VeCo 93023	441-H6
OAK BANK	
VeCo 91377	557-J1
OAK BLUFF DR	
900 MRPK 93021	476-E7
OAK BRANCH DR	
700 VeCo 91377	558-B1
OAK BROOK DR	
2700 THO 91362	526-J4
OAKBURY CT	
2500 THO 91360	526-D3
OAK CANYON RD	
1400 THO 91360	527-D6
OAKCLIFF DR	
11200 MRPK 93021	496-G3
OAKCOTTAGE CT	
1800 THO 91320	526-A7
OAK CREEK DR	
23600 SIMI 93065	556-E2
OAK CREEK LN	
10000 VeCo 93023	441-A7
OAK CREST DR	
31200 WLKV 91361	557-E6
OAK CREST DR	
1400 THO 91360	556-F1
OAKDALE CIR	
100 FILM 93015	455-J7
OAKDALE LN	
100 VeCo 93022	451-A7

STREET Block City ZIP	Pg-Grid
OAKDALE PL	
1000 SPLA 93060	464-B3
OAK VIEW DR	
THO 91362	557-G5
OAKFEN CT	
5500 AGRH 91301	557-G5
OAK FOREST DR	
6500 VeCo 91377	558-A1
OAK GLEN AV	
100 OJAI 93023	442-A7
OAK GLEN CT	
4000 MRPK 93021	496-E3
OAK GLEN DR	
200 THO 91320	555-E1
OAK GLEN ST	
4300 CALB 91302	558-H7
OAK GROVE CT	
700 VeCo 93023	451-A3
OAK GROVE PL	
1200 THO 91362	527-C7
OAK GROVE FIRE RD	
7400 VeCo 93012	525-D5
OAKHAMPTON ST	
400 THO 91361	556-F3
OAK HAVEN AV	
2200 SIMI 93063	498-J1
OAK HAVEN CT	
400 VeCo 91377	558-B1
OAKHILL CIR	
2100 OXN 93030	522-E2
OAK HILLS DR	
1300 CRML 93010	524-E1
10700 VeCo 93023	451-D6
OAK KNOLL RD	
2600 SIMI 93065	498-C1
OAK KNOLLS RD	
5600 VeCo 93063	499-A3
OAKLAWN DR	
100 VeCo 93022	461-A1
OAKLEAF AV	
500 VeCo 91377	558-B2
OAK LEAF DR	
100 THO 91360	526-E7
OAK MEADOW PL	
5900 VeCo 91377	558-A2
OAK MIRAGE PL	
11900 THO 91362	527-D7
OAKMONT CT	
800 SIMI 93065	497-G5
OAKMONT PL	
23900 LA 91304	529-E1
OAKMORE ST	
1200 OXN 93035	552-C2
OAKMOUND AV	
800 THO 91320	555-E4
OAK PARK LN	
4900 VeCo 91377	557-G7
4900 VeCo 91377	527-G7
OAK PATH CT	
700 VeCo 91377	558-B1
OAKPATH DR	
28800 AGRH 91301	558-A4
OAK PLACE DR	
1400 THO 91362	527-C6
OAK POINT DR	
600 VeCo 91377	558-A1
OAK RANCH CT	
31800 WLKV 91361	557-D7
OAKRIDGE CT	
9900 Chat 91311	499-H6
OAKRIDGE PL	
9500 Chat 91311	499-H6
OAKRIM DR	
30800 WLKV 91361	557-F4
OHARA CANYON RD	
1900 VeCo 93063	463-E4
OJAI AV	
23600 OXN 93035	552-B5
OAK SHADOW VIEW PL	
700 VeCo 91377	559-C5
OAKSHORE DR	
2400 THO 91362	557-B6
2600 WLKV 91361	557-B6
OAK SPRINGS DR	
6500 VeCo 91377	558-B1
W OJAI AV Rt#-150	
2000 THO 91361	557-A6
OAKSTAFF CT	
4900 VeCo 91377	527-G7
OAK TERRACE LN	
1800 THO 91320	526-A7
OAK TRAIL RD	
23600 SIMI 93065	527-F1
OAK TREE CT	
100 THO 91360	556-F1
OAK TREE LN	
10900 VeCo 93022	451-C4
10900 VeCo 93022	441-C4
N OAKCREST AV	
10900 VeCo 93022	451-B4
OAK VALLEY LN	
2500 THO 91362	527-C3
OAK VIEW AV	
VeCo 93022	451-A7
E OAK VIEW AV	
VeCo 93022	451-B7

STREET Block City ZIP	Pg-Grid
OAK VIEW CT	
23600 SIMI 93065	527-F1
OAJAI SANTA PAULA RD Rt#-150	
3100 VeCo 93023	442-D7
7000 VeCo 93023	452-E1
4800 VEN 93003	492-D7
OJAI VALLEY SCHOOL	
23600 VeCo	366-L7
23600 VeCo	366-L7
OKAPI LN	
1100 VEN 93003	492-E4
OLD BALCOM CANYON RD	
6200 VeCo 93066	475-D7
OLD BALDWIN RD	
1700 SIMI 93063	451-B3
OLD BURY PL	
1300 THO 91361	556-J6
VEN 93003	491-B1
OLD BUTTERFIELD CT	
23600 THO 91362	496-F7
OLD CARRIAGE CT	
29900 AGRH 91301	558-A4
OLDCASTLE PL	
1500 THO 91361	556-H6
OLD COACH DR	
3000 VeCo 93010	494-C6
OLD COLONY WY	
30900 AGRH 91301	557-F6
30900 WLKV 91361	557-F6
OLD CONEJO RD	
3000 THO 91320	525-E6
100 FILM 93015	455-J6
OLD CREEK RD	
1900 THO 91362	526-J4
1900 THO 91362	527-A4
OLIVEWOOD CT	
2200 THO 91362	527-A4
OLIVEWOOD DR	
1900 THO 91362	526-J4
2300 OXN 93030	522-J4
OLIVIA ST	
23600 OXN 93030	522-J4
OLIVO CT	
3800 CRML 93010	524-H2
OLOROSO CIR	
6000 SIMI 93063	499-B1
OLSEN RD	
1100 THO 91360	526-G1
900 THO	496-H7
1100 THO	497-A6
2100 SIMI 93063	497-A6
1600 VeCo 93063	461-B1
1600 VeCo 93063	451-C3
2200 VeCo 91362	527-A4
W OLSEN RD	
2100 VeCo 93063	525-E6
OLYMPIA AV	
800 VEN 93004	492-G4
OLYMPIC ST	
1300 SIMI 93065	498-D3
OLYMPUS LN	
23600 OXN 93035	522-C6
OMAHA AV	
2800 THO 91360	471-C4
OMAHA CT	
VeCo 93060	471-D5
OMEGA AV	
3000 SIMI 93063	478-E7
ONA CIR	
3100 OXN 93030	498-J3
ONDA DR	
1700 CRML 93012	524-D2
ONE GTE PL	
4200 THO 91362	557-C4
ONEIDA CT	
3000 OXN 93033	553-A3
ONEIDA PL	
1500 OXN 93030	522-D4
ONEIDA WY	
9500 VEN 93004	492-H3
ONEILL PL	
1800 OXN 93033	552-J2
1800 OXN 93033	553-A2
ONE LN	
2400 SIMI 93063	499-A1
ONONDAGA LN	
100 VEN 93001	471-C5
ONTARIO AV	
VeCo 93022	492-G3
ONTARIO ST	
900 OXN 93035	522-J4
1400 OXN 93035	522-E1
ONYX CIR	
3300 THO 91360	478-D7
OPAL AV	
2800 SIMI 93063	478-E7
OPAL CT	
1700 THO 91360	556-A1
8000 VeCo 93023	478-E7
OLGA ST	
1900 OXN 93030	522-J4
OLIN DR	
9200 Chat 91311	499-F7

STREET Block City ZIP	Pg-Grid
OLIVAS PARK DR	
1100 VEN 93001	491-H7
3300 VeCo 93001	491-H7
4500 VeCo 93001	492-B7
4500 VEN 93001	491-H7
4500 VeCo 93003	492-D7
N OLIVE RD	
23600 VeCo 93060	491-B2
OLIVE ST	
OXN 93022	522-H1
OXN 93022	451-B7
VEN 93023	453-A1
N OLIVE ST	
100 SPLA 93060	464-A5
VEN 93001	471-B7
S OLIVE ST	
3000 VEN 93001	491-B2
464-B6	464-B6
W OLIVE ST	
3000 VEN 93001	494-C6
OLIVEGROVE PL	
2500 THO 91362	527-D3
N OLIVE HILL RD	
5100 VeCo 93066	495-B1
5600 VeCo 93066	475-C7
OLIVER ST	
400 FILM 93015	455-J6
OLIVEWOOD CT	
1900 THO 91362	526-J4
OLIVEWOOD DR	
1900 THO 91362	526-J4
OPEN CIR	
2600 SIMI 93063	478-E7
OPHELIA CT	
2600 SIMI 93063	478-E7

STREET
Block City ZIP Pg-Grid

OPTAR LN
400 OXN 93030 522-H4
W ORACLE CT
1900 THO 91320 555-J2
1900 THO 91320 556-A2
ORANGE CIR
10600 VEN 93004 472-H7
ORANGE CT
3600 SIMI 93063 478-E7
ORANGE DR
- VeCo 93030 492-J7
300 VeCo 93030 522-J1
900 VeCo 93030 523-A1
3200 OXN 93030 523-C2
ORANGE LN
1200 VeCo 93010 494-F7
ORANGE MALL
5100 OXN 93033 552-H5
ORANGE RD
600 OJAI 93023 442-B6
600 VeCo 93023 442-B6
ORANGE ST
200 VeCo 93015 465-E1
ORANGE BLOSSOM LN
100 FILM 93015 455-J6
ORANGE GROVE AV
200 FILM 93015 456-A6
3600 OXN 93033 553-B4
ORANGEWOOD AV
600 THO 91320 555-G3
N ORANGEWOOD PL
2400 SIMI 93065 498-A1
ORCHARD DR
- VeCo 93001 471-C3
1300 VeCo 93023 451-D2
ORCHARD LN
700 VeCo 93060 473-C2
ORCHARD PL
100 OXN 93030 522-F1
ORCHARD ST
400 FILM 93015 456-A6
600 VeCo 93040 457-F3
1000 SPLA 93060 464-B4
1500 VeCo 93060 464-B4
ORCHARD VW
- CMRL 93010 524-D4
ORCHARD FARM RD
23600 VeCo 93060 473-D4
ORCHARDVIEW CT
4200 WLKV 91361 557-D6
ORCHID AV
1900 SIMI 93065 498-B2
ORCHID DR
1700 OXN 93033 553-A2
ORCHID PL
200 VEN 93004 473-C7
ORCUTT RD
200 VeCo 93060 464-E3
ORCUTT CANYON RD
200 VeCo 93060 454-E7
1000 VeCo 93060 464-E2
OREGON DR
2100 VEN 93003 492-C5
ORENA CT
400 CMRL 93010 524-B1
ORILLA WK
300 OXN 93030 522-H4
ORINDA CT
1600 THO 91362 526-J4
ORIOLE CIR
1100 FILM 93015 455-H6
ORIOLE DR
- VeCo 93041 583-H2
ORIOLE LN
4000 OXN 93033 553-B4
ORIOLE ST
200 OJAI 93023 442-A6
6200 VEN 93003 492-D4
ORION WY
900 OXN 93030 522-F1
ORLEANS CT
30800 WLKV 91362 557-F4
RLOP PL
2000 OXN 93035 522-E6
RO ST
400 VeCo 93022 451-A7
RR AV
1600 SIMI 93065 498-C3
RR RD
100 VeCo 93060 473-G3
RTEGA DR
- THO 91320 556-B1
RTEGA ST
- OXN 93030 523-B4
900 FILM 93015 455-J6
4600 VEN 93003 492-A6
RWELL LN
500 VEN 93003 492-D1
SA CT
1100 OXN 93035 522-E7
SAGE CIR
800 CMRL 93012 525-A2
SAGE LN
1100 VEN 93004 492-H3
SBORN RD
23600 VeCo 93060 453-D1
SO RD
700 VeCo 93023 441-C5
SPREY AV
- THO 91320 526-A5

STREET
Block City ZIP Pg-Grid

N OSPREY LN
1100 VEN 93003 492-F4
S OSPREY LN
1300 VEN 93003 492-F4
OSTRICH HILL RD
1100 OXN 93030 522-E1
OTERO CT
500 VeCo 93010 494-B7
E OTONO CIR
2200 THO 91362 527-A2
OTONO CT
300 CMRL 93012 525-A2
OTTAWA DR
100 VEN 93001 471-C4
OTTER CREEK LN
2400 OXN 93030 522-E1
OUTER DR
- SPLA 93060 464-A7
OUTLET CENTER DR
2000 OXN 93030 523-B3
OUTLOOK CIR
1300 THO 91362 527-C7
OUTLOOK CV
2600 PHME 93041 552-C3
OUTRIGGER AV
3100 VEN 93001 491-G5
OUTRIGGER WY
5100 OXN 93035 521-J7
OUTSAIL LN
2000 OXN 93035 522-D7
OVERFALL DR
30800 WLKV 91362 557-F4
OVERLAND DR
24500 LA 91304 529-C4
OVERLOOK DR
700 VEN 93001 491-C1
OVERLOOK RD
600 SIMI 93065 497-E6
OVERLY ST
6400 MRPK 93021 477-A6
OWEN ST
1000 VeCo 93015 465-H3
OWENS AV
1200 VEN 93004 492-G3
OWL CT
6900 VEN 93003 492-E4
OWLS COVE LN
23600 SIMI 93065 497-G2
OXFORD CIR
14400 MRPK 93021 476-G6
OXFORD DR
600 OXN 93030 522-E4
OXFORD ST
10400 VEN 93004 492-J1
11900 VeCo 93021 476-D3
OXLEY PL
4900 THO 91362 527-E6
OXNARD AV
100 VeCo 93035 552-B5
7000 VeCo 93001 459-C4
OXNARD BLVD
1000 OXN 93030 522-G3
OXNARD BLVD Rt#-1
100 OXN 93030 522-G1
1200 OXN 93030 552-H1
1200 OXN 93033 522-G7
1200 OXN 93033 552-H1
2600 OXN 93030 492-G7
OXNARD SHORES DR
5100 OXN 93035 521-J6
OYSTER PL
1100 OXN 93030 522-E7
OYSTER ST
900 VeCo 93001 491-F5
900 VEN 93001 491-F5

P

PACIFIC AV
100 VeCo 93015 457-D5
500 OXN 93030 522-J7
700 SIMI 93065 497-G3
1100 OXN 93033 522-J7
1300 OXN 93033 552-J1
3500 VeCo 93040 457-D5
N PACIFIC AV
- VEN 93001 491-E2
S PACIFIC AV
- VEN 93001 491-E2
PACIFIC CIR
400 THO 91320 555-G3
PACIFIC RD
- PHME 93041 552-D4
- PHME 93043 552-D4
2800 VeCo 93041 583-H4
3400 VeCo 93042 583-H4
18600 VeCo 93012 583-H4
PACIFICA DR
100 OXN 93033 553-C4
PACIFIC COAST FRWY Rt#-1
- OXN - 552-J2
- OXN - 553-C4
- VeCo - 553-C4
- VeCo - 583-H1
PACIFIC COAST HWY Rt#-1
2900 VeCo 93001 470-B3
4200 VeCo 93001 366-G9
4200 VeCo 93001 459-F6

STREET
Block City ZIP Pg-Grid

PACIFIC COAST HWY Rt#-1
4200 VeCo 93001 469-H1
9000 VeCo - 387-F4
9000 VeCo 90265 387-F4
9000 VeCo 90265 625-A3
9400 VeCo - 584-A6
12300 LACo 90265 625-F5
19900 VeCo 93012 583-J5
19900 VeCo 93012 584-A6
23600 VeCo 93001 490-G1
34000 MAL 90265 625-F5
PACIFIC COVE DR
500 PHME 93041 552-C2
N PACIFIC MILLING RD
6400 VeCo 93030 493-D2
6400 VeCo 93066 493-D2
13600 VeCo 93060 473-E7
13600 VeCo 93060 493-D2
S PACIFIC MILLING RD
100 VeCo 93030 492-H6
PACIFIC OAK DR
22400 Chat 91311 499-H5
PACIFIC RIDGE RD
6300 VeCo 93063 499-C4
PACIFIC VIEW LN
900 VEN 93001 491-D1
PACIFIC VIEW RD
10300 VeCo 90265 585-A7
10700 VeCo 90265 387-A4
10700 VeCo 90265 625-A1
PACKARD CIR
100 THO 91362 557-C4
PACKARD ST
23600 OXN 93033 553-B4
PACOS ST
- VEN 93001 471-B5
PADDINGTON PL
800 OXN 93030 522-E4
PADELFORD RD
900 FILM 93015 456-B4
PADOVA CT
30800 WLKV 91362 557-F5
PADRE LN
- CMRL 93012 524-H1
200 VeCo 93060 464-D3
N PADRE JUAN AV
100 VeCo 93023 441-D6
S PADRE JUAN AV
100 VeCo 93023 441-D7
PADRE JUAN CANYON RD
4000 VeCo 93001 470-A3
23600 VeCo 93001 460-C7
PADUA CIR
100 THO 91320 555-E1
PADUA LN
3700 THO 91320 555-E1
PAGENT CT
3200 THO 91360 526-F2
PAGENT ST
- THO 91360 526-F2
PAIGE AV
3000 SIMI 93063 478-E7
3100 VeCo 93063 478-E7
PAIGE LN
600 THO 91362 526-G7
900 THO 91362 526-H6
PAINE AV
300 VEN 93003 492-B3
PAINTED PONY CIR
23600 SIMI 93063 479-A6
PAINTED SKY ST
3800 MRPK 93021 496-E4
PAIUTE AV
11200 Chat 91311 499-J2
PAIUTE LN
200 VEN 93001 471-C5
PAJARO AV
- VEN 93004 472-J6
- VEN 93004 473-A7
PALA DR
400 VeCo 93023 441-D7
PALA MESA DR
6800 VeCo 91377 528-B7
PALERMO CT
23600 SIMI 93063 478-G6
PALI DR
1000 OXN 93033 552-J5
N PALM AV
100 SPLA 93060 464-A6
S PALM AV
100 SPLA 93060 464-A6
PALM CT
1400 THO 91360 526-H2
E PALM CT
300 SPLA 93060 464-A5
N PALM CT
300 SPLA 93060 464-A5
PALM DR
- CMRL 93010 524-E4
23600 FILM 93015 456-C6
W PALM DR
100 OXN 93030 522-E5
PALM LN
5100 OXN 93033 552-H5
PALM ST
200 FILM 93015 456-A6

STREET
Block City ZIP Pg-Grid

N PALM ST
- VEN 93001 491-C2
S PALM ST
- VEN 93001 491-C2
PALMA DR
1400 VEN 93003 492-A6
2900 VeCo 93003 492-A6
PALMER AV
900 CMRL 93010 524-E2
PALMETTO LN
400 THO 91320 556-D1
PALMGROVE AV
- THO 91320 556-C2
PALMWOOD CIR
2500 THO 91362 527-D3
PALO ALTO
2100 VeCo 93023 451-C3
PALO COMADO DR
5900 AGRH 91301 558-D4
PALO COMADO CANYON RD
5000 AGRH 91301 558-D6
PALO COMADO FIRE RD
- VeCo 91377 527-J4
- VeCo 91377 528-A4
- VeCo 93065 528-A4
23600 SIMI 93065 527-J4
23600 VeCo 93065 527-J4
PALOMA CT
30800 WLKV 91362 557-F5
PALOMA DR
3600 VEN 93003 491-H2
PALOMAR AV
600 MRPK 93021 496-D1
2100 VEN 93001 491-F2
PALOMAR CIR
5800 CMRL 93012 495-B7
PALOMAR RD
200 OJAI 93023 441-G5
500 VeCo 93023 441-G6
PALOMAR WY
800 OXN 93033 552-F3
PALOMARES AV
- VEN 93003 491-H2
PALOMINO CIR
4100 THO 91362 527-C7
6000 VeCo 93066 495-B3
PALOMINO DR
4300 VeCo 93066 495-B3
PALOMITAS CIR
4200 MRPK 93021 496-D2
PALOS CT W
2100 THO 91320 555-J2
PALO SOLA MTWY
23600 VeCo - 367-F9
PALO VERDE CIR
11200 VeCo 93012 496-B6
PAMELA CT
100 SPLA 93060 463-J7
1800 SIMI 93065 497-J2
1800 SIMI 93065 498-A2
PAMELA LN
100 SPLA 93060 463-H6
PAMELA ST
1900 OXN 93030 522-E3
PAMELA WOOD ST
700 THO 91320 556-C1
PAMPAS LN
- VEN 93001 491-B1
PAN CT
23600 THO 91320 556-B1
PANAL CT
1200 OXN 93030 522-H4
PANAMA DR
2200 PHME 93035 552-B4
2200 PHME 93043 552-B4
2200 VeCo 93035 552-B4
2600 VeCo 93043 552-B4
E PANAMINT CT
2800 THO 91362 557-C3
W PANAMINT CT
2700 THO 91362 557-B3
PANCHO RD
100 VeCo 93012 524-H7
400 CMRL 93012 524-H7
1600 VeCo 93012 554-H1
S PANCHO RD
400 CMRL 93012 524-H4
PANDA PL
2300 VeCo 93003 492-E5
PANORAMA CT
1300 THO 91360 526-H2
PANSY PL
- VEN 93004 473-C7
PANSY ST
- SIMI 93063 499-A2
PAPAGO TER
8400 LA 91304 529-D1
PAQUITA ST
1000 CMRL 93012 525-C6
PARADE AV
- SIMI 93063 498-H1
PARADISE CIR
300 VeCo 93010 494-F6
PARAKEET CT
1600 VEN 93003 492-F4
PAR FIVE CT
1900 THO 91362 527-D5
PAR FIVE DR
1800 THO 91362 527-C6

STREET
Block City ZIP Pg-Grid

PARIS CT
30800 WLKV 91362 557-F5
PARK AV
- VeCo 93022 451-B7
400 PHME 93041 552-F4
PARK DR
1400 VeCo 93023 451-B2
2000 VEN 93003 492-C5
PARK LN
- MRPK 93021 496-E2
PARK PL
2200 THO 91362 527-A4
PARK RD
100 OJAI 93023 441-J5
PARK ST
- PHME 93041 552-E4
200 OJAI 93023 441-H6
700 VeCo 93040 457-F3
1000 SPLA 93060 464-B4
1600 SIMI 93063 498-G3
PARK CENTER DR
2600 SIMI 93065 477-F7
2600 SIMI 93065 497-F1
N PARKDALE AV
2400 SIMI 93063 498-E1
PARKER AV
- THO 91360 556-F1
PARKER CT
2000 SIMI 93065 498-A2
N PARKER CT
2100 SIMI 93065 498-A2
PARKER LN
8400 VEN 93004 492-G4
PARKFRONT PL
400 SIMI 93065 497-E6
PARKHAVEN CT
200 FILM 93015 455-H7
PARKHEATH DR
28900 AGRH 91301 558-B5
PARKHILL CIR
6000 VEN 93003 472-C6
PARKHILL CT
1300 CMRL 93010 524-E1
PARK HILL RD
23600 SIMI 93065 497-F7
23600 SIMI 93065 527-F1
PARKHURST ST
1200 SIMI 93065 497-H4
PARKING LOT RD
23600 VeCo 93063 498-H7
PARK MEADOW CT
2500 SIMI 93065 497-H1
PARKMOR RD
5300 CALB 91302 558-H3
E PARK ROW AV
- VEN 93001 491-B1
W PARK ROW AV
- VEN 93001 491-B1
PARKSIDE CT
- VeCo 91377 527-J7
- VeCo 91377 528-A7
PARKSIDE DR
23600 SIMI 93065 527-F1
PARK SPRINGS CT
400 VeCo 91377 558-B1
PARK TERRACE DR
4300 WLKV 91361 557-E6
PARKVIEW AV
2300 THO 91362 527-A4
PARKVIEW CT
23600 SIMI 93065 527-F1
PARK VIEW DR
100 VeCo 91377 558-A2
PARKVIEW DR
2400 THO 91362 527-A3
8000 VeCo 93001 461-A4
PARKVILLE RD
5000 CALB 91301 558-G6
5100 Ago 91301 558-G6
PARKWAY DR
2300 CMRL 93010 494-E7
PARKWOOD CT
1900 THO 91362 526-J3
PARMA DR
4800 VeCo 91377 557-G1
PARMENTER CT
700 THO 91362 527-A7
PARRISH PL
- VeCo 93003 492-A3
- VEN 93003 492-A3
PARRON ST
3900 CMRL 93010 494-H7
PARROT CT
1600 VEN 93003 492-E4
PARSONS AV
300 VEN 93003 492-A2
PARSONS DR
900 PHME 93041 552-E4
PARTHENIA ST
22000 LA 91304 529-J1
PARTRIDGE CT
5100 THO 91362 527-F6
PARTRIDGE DR
800 OXN 93030 522-F1
1000 VEN 93003 492-D3
PARTRIDGE PL
1600 VEN 93003 492-D4
PASADENA AV
100 VeCo 93035 552-C6
100 VeCo 93043 552-C6

STREET
Block City ZIP Pg-Grid

PASADENA AV
700 VeCo 93015 465-F2
700 VeCo 93015 466-A2
PASEO ARROYO
800 CMRL 93010 524-B2
PASEO BARONA
1300 CMRL 93010 524-C1
PASEO BRISAS LINDAS
23600 OXN 93030 523-C6
PASEO CAMARILLO
200 CMRL 93010 524-C3
PASEO CASTILLE
1000 CMRL 93010 524-C1
PASEO DE CORTAGA
600 CMRL 93010 524-B3
PASEO DE INVIERNO
3500 THO 91360 526-B1
PASEO DE LA PAZ
23600 THO 91320 555-D4
PASEO DEL CAMPO
5200 CMRL 93012 524-J1
5300 CMRL 93012 525-A1
PASEO DE LEON
500 THO 91320 555-F3
PASEO DEL ROBLEDO
800 VeCo 91360 526-C6
PASEO DEL ROBLES CT
1100 OJAI 93023 442-A6
PASEO DEL VALLE
200 CMRL 93010 524-B3
PASEO DE NUBLADO
3500 THO 91360 526-D1
PASEO DE PETALOS
23600 CMRL 93010 523-G2
PASEO DE PLAYA
300 VEN 93001 491-C2
PASEO ELEGANTE
- OXN 93030 523-A5
PASEO ENCANTADA
5900 CMRL 93012 525-B5
PASEO ESMERALDA
500 THO 91320 526-A7
PASEO ESPLENDIDO
- CMRL 93010 524-A2
PASEO GIRASOL
23600 CMRL 93012 494-H7
PASEO GRANDE
400 THO 91320 526-C7
PASEO HACIENDA
- OXN 93030 523-A5
PASEO ISLA
- OXN 93030 523-A4
PASEO LA PERLA
500 THO 91320 526-A7
PASEO LAS NUBES
23600 OXN 93030 523-B4
PASEO LA VIDA
23600 OXN 93030 523-C7
PASEO LA VISTA
6100 WdHl 91367 529-C7
PASEO LINDO
- OXN 93030 523-A4
PASEO LOMA
23600 CMRL 93010 524-D4
PASEO LUNAR
4400 CMRL 93010 524-B3
PASEO MARAVILLA
23600 CMRL 93012 494-H7
23600 CMRL 93012 524-H1
PASEO MARGARITA
- OXN 93030 523-A5
5400 CMRL 93012 525-A5
PASEO MERCADO
2800 OXN 93030 523-B2
PASEO MONTECITO
600 THO 91320 525-F7
PASEO MONTELENA
4600 CMRL 93012 524-J2
PASEO NOCHE
1800 CMRL 93012 495-C7
PASEO NOGALES
- OXN 93030 523-A5
PASEO ORTEGA
- OXN 93030 523-B5
PASEO RICOSO
5200 CMRL 93012 525-A2
PASEO SABANERO
100 CMRL 93012 524-H3
PASEO SANTA BARBARA
23600 THO 91320 555-D4
PASEO SANTA CATARINA
23600 THO 91320 555-D4
PASEO SANTA CRUZ
23600 THO 91320 555-D4
PASEO SANTA FE
23600 THO 91320 555-D4
PASEO SANTA MONICA
23600 THO 91320 555-D4
PASEO SANTA ROSA
23600 THO 91320 555-D4
PASEO SERENATA
800 CMRL 93012 525-C5
PASEO TESORO
23600 OXN 93030 523-C7
PASEO TOSAMAR
800 CMRL 93012 525-B5
PASEO VERDE
500 VeCo 93010 494-A6

STREET
Block City ZIP Pg-Grid

PASEO VISTA
500 THO 91320 526-C7
PASEO YOLO
2600 CMRL 93010 494-F7
N PASO FLORES RD
5500 VeCo 93066 475-C7
5500 VeCo 93066 495-B1
PASO ROBLES
1500 CMRL 93012 524-J1
7700 VEN 93004 492-E1
PASQUAL AV
100 VEN 93004 472-J7
100 VEN 93004 473-A7
PASSAGEWAY PL
30300 AGRH 91301 557-G5
PASTEUR DR
5800 VEN 93003 492-C6
PAT AV
5900 WdHl 91367 529-D7
6200 CanP 91307 529-D7
PATHELEN AV
- VeCo 93022 451-B7
PATHFINDER AV
1300 THO 91362 527-G6
4700 VeCo 91362 527-G6
4700 VeCo 91377 527-G6
PATHWAY AV
- SIMI 93063 498-H1
PATINA CT
- CMRL 93010 493-H6
PATRICIA AV
1200 SIMI 93065 497-H2
1700 SIMI 93065 498-A3
PATRICIA CT
900 OJAI 93023 441-J5
PATRICIA ST
1000 OXN 93030 522-E3
1800 SIMI 93065 497-H3
PATRICK ST
3100 SIMI 93065 498-D3
PATRICK HENRY PL
3800 AGRH 91301 558-E7
PATRIOT PL
- VeCo 93041 583-H2
- VeCo 93042 583-H2
PATTERSON RD
2400 PHME 93043 552-D5
2500 PHME 93041 552-D5
2700 PHME 93035 552-D5
N PATTERSON RD
100 VeCo 93030 522-D4
500 OXN 93030 522-C2
S PATTERSON RD
400 OXN 93030 522-D7
500 VeCo 93035 522-D7
500 VeCo 93030 522-D7
600 OXN 93035 522-D7
1200 OXN 93035 552-D1
PATTON CT
1600 OXN 93030 522-J7
PATTY CT
3100 SIMI 93063 478-E6
PAUL DR
800 PHME 93041 552-F5
PAUL ST
1400 SIMI 93065 497-G3
PAULA CIR
2900 OXN 93033 552-H3
PAULA ST
2900 OXN 93033 552-H3
PAULINE ST
800 OJAI 93023 441-H6
PAULING DR
600 THO 91320 526-A7
PAVAROTTI DR
500 VeCo 91377 557-G2
PAVO CT
2000 THO 91362 556-H2
PAWNEE CT
2500 VEN 93001 471-C5
3100 SIMI 93063 478-J6
PAZ MORADA
1000 VEN 93003 472-D6
PEACEFUL CT
400 SIMI 93065 497-J6
PEACE PIPE CT
23600 SIMI 93063 479-A7
PEACH AV
200 VEN 93004 473-A7
300 VeCo 93004 473-A7
PEACH LN
1400 OXN 93033 553-B5
PEACH HILL RD
13000 MRPK 93021 496-F2
PEACH SLOPE RD
4200 MRPK 93021 496-E3
PEACHSPRING CT
4200 MRPK 93021 496-B2
PEACHWOOD PL
32700 WLKV 91361 586-J1
PEACOCK AV
2300 VEN 93003 492-D5
PEACOCK CT
3900 THO 91362 527-C6
PEACOCK RIDGE RD
3700 CALB 91301 558-F7
PEAK PL
2100 THO 91362 527-A2
PEAR AV
1200 OXN 93033 553-B4

STREET
Block City ZIP Pg-Grid

PEARL CIR
3300 SIMI 93063 478-D6
PEARL CT
200 PHME 93043 552-E4
PEARL ST
100 PHME 93041 552-E6
600 OJAI 93023 441-J7
7900 VEN 93004 492-F3
PEARL WY
1600 OXN 93035 552-B1
PEARSON RD
400 PHME 93041 552-F3
PEBBLE PL
3500 THO 91320 555-F2
PEBBLE BEACH DR
100 THO 91320 556-D1
PEBBLE BEACH TR
2100 OXN 93030 522-D2
PEBBLESTONE PL
3100 SIMI 93063 478-D7
PECAN AV
6600 MRPK 93021 476-J5
PECAN VALLEY PL
2000 SIMI 93065 497-C6
PECIOLO CT
1600 THO 91362 556-J1
PECK PL
100 SPLA 93060 463-H7
N PECK RD
200 SPLA 93060 463-H6
200 VeCo 93060 463-H6
S PECK RD
200 SPLA 93060 463-J7
200 SPLA 93060 473-J1
PEDERSON RD
600 THO 91360 526-G2
1500 THO 91362 526-J3
19400 THO 91362 527-A3
PEGASUS ST
800 VeCo 93023 451-C3
PEGGY CT
3100 SIMI 93063 478-E6
PEKING ST
- VEN 93001 491-B1
PELICAN AV
1600 VEN 93003 492-D4
PELICAN WY
3700 OXN 93035 552-B4
PELLBURNE CT
200 SIMI 93065 527-E1
PEMBRIDGE ST
3300 THO 91360 526-G2
PEMBROKE CT
1700 THO 91362 527-E6
PEMBROKE ST
5600 VEN 93003 492-B1
E PENA CT
3400 SIMI 93063 498-D2
PENA RANCH RD
23600 Cstc 91384 458-H1
23600 VeCo 93040 458-G4
PENELOPE PL
2300 VeCo 93012 496-B7
PENGUIN ST
6800 VEN 93003 492-E6
PENINSULA CT
2000 OXN 93035 552-B2
PENINSULA RD
2200 OXN 93035 552-B3
PENINSULA ST
800 VEN 93001 491-F5
N PENLAN AV
2100 SIMI 93063 499-B2
PENN ST
6400 MRPK 93021 476-J6
PENNEY DR
3000 SIMI 93063 478-D7
PENNGROVE ST
1900 SIMI 93065 498-A1
PENNSFIELD PL
400 THO 91360 526-F7
400 THO 91360 556-F1
PENOBSCOT DR
- LA 91304 529-D4
PENROD DR
30400 AGRH 91301 557-G5
PENROSE AV
4700 MRPK 93021 496-C2
PENROSE CT
2000 THO 91362 527-A5
PENTLAND WY
23900 CanP 91307 529-E5
PEONY ST
10500 VEN 93004 493-A2
PEOPLES AV
200 CMRL 93010 524-F3
PEORIA AV
1800 OXN 93033 553-A5
E PEORIA AV
4000 SIMI 93063 478-F6
N PEORIA AV
3000 SIMI 93063 478-F7
PEORIA PL
1900 OXN 93033 553-A5
PEPPER
2100 VeCo 93023 451-C3
PEPPER LN
- VEN 93001 491-B1
6400 VeCo 93066 495-B3

STREET
Block City ZIP Pg-Grid

PEPPER RD
- THO 91320 556-B2
N PEPPERDINE CIR
6400 MRPK 93021 476-H6
PEPPER MILL ST
4600 MRPK 93021 496-B2
PEPPERMINT PL
3100 THO 91320 555-G3
PEPPERMINT ST
3200 THO 91320 555-G3
PEPPER TREE CT
1800 THO 91362 526-J4
PEPPER TREE LN
400 VeCo 93022 451-B7
PEPPERTREE LN
900 VeCo 93064 498-F4
1200 SIMI 93063 498-F4
1200 VeCo 93063 498-F4
6000 VeCo 93063 499-B3
PEPPERTREE CANYON RD
700 VeCo 93060 472-J3
700 VeCo 93060 473-A4
PEPPERWOOD CT
300 THO 91360 526-F2
PEPPERWOOD DR
2800 CMRL 93010 494-E6
PERALTA DR
300 SPLA 93060 463-J7
300 SPLA 93060 464-A7
PERCY ST
400 OXN 93033 552-H4
PEREGRINE CIR
- VeCo 91377 558-B3
PERELLO RANCH RD
- VeCo 93030 493-B4
PERES LN
300 VeCo 93060 464-E3
PERICLES PL
1800 OXN 93033 553-A2
PERIMETER RD
- OXN 93033 583-A2
- OXN 93042 583-A2
- VeCo 93041 583-G1
- VeCo 93042 553-G7
- VeCo 93042 583-G1
PERIWINKLE CT
400 THO 91360 526-D3
PERIWINKLE WY
- WdHl 91367 529-J7
PERKIN AV
3100 VEN 93003 492-D7
PERKINS RD
5100 OXN 93033 552-G7
PERRY DR
- PHME 93041 552-D4
PERRY WY
4700 VeCo 93030 493-A5
PERSIMMON LN
1400 OXN 93033 553-B5
PERTH PL
600 OXN 93035 522-D6
PERTHSHIRE CIR
6900 CanP 91307 529-E6
PESARO ST
4900 VeCo 91377 557-G1
PESTO WY
5300 VeCo 91377 557-H2
PETER PL
23600 SIMI 93065 498-A5
PETERSON AV
6100 WdHl 91367 529-E7
6500 CanP 91307 529-E6
N PETIT AV
- VEN 93004 492-F1
300 VEN 93004 472-F7
S PETIT AV
- VEN 93004 492-G2
1500 VeCo 93004 492-H3
PETIT CIR
9500 VEN 93004 492-H3
PETIT CT
9400 VEN 93004 492-H2
PETIT DR
3700 OXN 93033 552-H4
PETIT RD
1800 VeCo 93060 465-C5
PETIT ST
2600 CMRL 93012 524-G3
PETIT RANCH RD
1700 VeCo 93060 465-D5
PETREL PL
1800 VEN 93003 492-D4
PETTICOAT LN
500 OXN 93030 522-F1
PHEASANT LN
6700 VeCo 91377 528-A7
N PHEASANT LN
1100 VEN 93003 492-F4
S PHEASANT LN
1300 VEN 93003 492-F4
PHEASANT HILL
2600 CMRL 93010 524-F2
PHEASANT RUN ST
3900 MRPK 93021 496-E4
PHELPS AV
1100 VEN 93004 492-J2
1200 VEN 93004 493-A2
PHELPS CT
1000 VEN 93004 492-J2

STREET
Block City ZIP Pg-Grid

PHILRICH CIR
2600 CALB 91302 558-J4
E PHIPPS AV
2500 SIMI 93065 498-C3
PHLEGER RD
4900 VeCo 93066 495-B1
PHLOX CT
400 THO 91360 526-D3
PHOENIX AV
700 VEN 93004 492-G3
PHOENIX CIR
- VeCo 93042 583-H2
PHOENIX DR
4400 OXN 93033 553-A5
PHYLLIS CT
- THO 91320 556-B1
E PHYLLIS ST
2400 SIMI 93065 498-B1
N PHYLLIS ST
2500 SIMI 93065 498-B1
PICADO DR
5000 CMRL 93012 524-J1
PICASO LN
2400 SIMI 93063 499-B1
PICCADILLY CIR
2800 THO 91362 527-B3
PICKFORD CT
700 THO 91320 555-G3
PICKWICK CT
900 THO 91360 526-G5
PICKWICK DR
2100 CMRL 93010 524-E2
PICO AV
1300 SIMI 93065 497-H3
PICO PL
3000 OXN 93033 552-J3
PIDDUCK RD
2600 VeCo 93033 553-C4
PIEDMONT DR
4800 VeCo 91377 557-G2
PIEDMONT ST
900 OXN 93035 522-E7
1400 OXN 93035 552-E1
PIER WK
3400 OXN 93035 522-C7
PIERCE CT
600 THO 91360 556-G1
2400 SIMI 93065 498-B4
PIERCE ST
7300 VEN 93003 492-E1
PIERCE ARROW AV
- THO 91362 557-B4
PIERPONT BLVD
2000 VEN 93001 491-E3
PIERSIDE LN
1500 CMRL 93010 524-D4
PILOT WY
900 OXN 93035 522-C7
PIMA LN
2300 VEN 93001 471-C6
PIMLICO DR
10600 MRPK 93021 476-A6
PINATA DR
23600 OXN 93030 522-J4
23600 VeCo 93030 522-J4
PINE LN
- VEN 93001 491-B1
PINE RD
7400 VeCo 93060 473-B3
PINE ST
1200 VeCo 93063 499-C4
1400 OXN 93030 552-H1
PINEBLUFF PL
32500 WLKV 91361 557-B7
PINECLIFF PL
400 SIMI 93065 497-G5
PINECONE CT
100 SIMI 93065 497-F6
PINE CREEK CT
- THO 91320 526-A6
PINECREST DR
- THO 91361 556-E3
PINECREST ST
2200 SIMI 93065 498-B2
PINEDALE RD
11600 MRPK 93021 496-C3
PINEGROVE RD
5600 VeCo 93060 454-A6
5800 VeCo 93060 453-J4
PINEHILL LN
400 SPLA 93060 464-A5
PINEHILL ST
1000 THO 91320 555-E5
PINE HOLLOW PL
4000 MRPK 93021 496-D3
PINEHURST DR
2200 OXN 93030 522-E2
PINEHURST PL
1000 CMRL 93010 524-C2
PINELAKE DR
8400 LA 91304 529-F2
PINEPLANK LN
23600 SIMI 93065 497-A1
PINE RIDGE CT
4400 MRPK 93021 496-E3
PINESONG LN
23600 SIMI 93065 497-A1
PINE TERRACE DR
2000 THO 91362 527-A4

VENTURA COUNTY STREET INDEX - With ZIP Codes

VENTURA CO. INDEX

STREET	Block	City	ZIP	Pg-Grid
PINETREE CIR	500	THO	91360	526-E7
PINE VALLEY PL	4500	THO	91362	527-D6
PINE VIEW DR	23600	SIMI	93001	498-D5
	23600	SIMI	93065	498-D5
PINEWOOD AV	-	AGRH	91301	558-B2
	600	THO	91377	558-B2
N PINEWOOD PL	2000	SIMI		498-A1
PINION ST	6300	VeCo	91377	558-B2
PINK CEDAR CT	23600	SIMI	93065	498-D4
PINKERTON RD	13300	VeCo	93060	473-F4
PINKERTON RANCH RD	500	PHME	93043	552-D5
PINO CT	1400	CRML	93010	524-A1
PINTO ST	1400	SIMI	93065	497-J3
PIONEER AV	3200	THO	91360	526-E2
PIRATE CV	2600	PHME	93041	552-C3
PIRIE RD	200	OJAI	93023	441-F7
PIROPO CT	600	VeCo	93010	494-B6
PIRU AV	2200	VeCo	93035	552-B5
PIRU SQ	600	VeCo	93040	457-F4
PIRU CANYON RD	-	VeCo		367-D7
	23600	VeCo	93040	367-D7
	23600	VeCo	93040	457-G3
	23600	VeCo	93040	458-A1
PISCES CT	28700	AGRH	91301	558-B3
PISCO LN	1000	OXN	93035	522-E7
PISTACHIO AV	-	VEN	93004	473-A6
E PITTMAN ST	5600	SIMI	93063	449-A1
PITTSFIELD LN	1000	VEN	93001	491-E4
PIUMA CT	23600	SIMI	93063	479-B7
PIUTE AV	2700	THO	91362	557-A2
PIVOT POINT WY	-	OXN	93035	522-E7
PIXTON ST	23600	VeCo	91361	556-F6
PLACER AV	100	VEN	93004	472-H7
PLACER CT	23600	VeCo		472-H7
PLACERITA DR	5200	SIMI	93063	478-J7
	5400	SIMI	93063	498-J1
PLACERVILLE CT	2600	SIMI	93063	478-J7
	2600	SIMI	93063	498-J1
PLACID AV	1100	VEN	93004	492-G3
PLACID CT	1500	SIMI	93065	497-J6
PLACITA BUENA ROSA	23600	CRML	93012	524-H3
PLACITA SAN DIMAS	2200	CRML	93010	494-H6
PLACITA SAN LEANDRO	2200	CRML	93010	494-H6
PLACITA SAN RUFINO	2200	CRML	93010	494-H6
PLAINFIELD PL	2100	OXN	93030	522-E2
PLAINVIEW ST	5600	VEN	93003	472-C7
N PLANETREE AV	700	SIMI	93065	498-B5
PLATA LN	26300	CALB	91302	558-H4
PLATFORM PL	2000	OXN	93035	522-D7
PLATO CT	2000	SIMI	93065	497-G2
PLATT AV	6100	WdHl	91367	529-F7
	6400	CanP	91307	529-F5
	7300	LA	91304	529-F3
PLATTE AV	1200	VEN	93004	492-G3
PLAYA CT	3200	OXN	93035	552-B4
	3200	VeCo	93035	552-B4
N PLAZA	-	VeCo	93035	552-A3
S PLAZA	3200	OXN	93035	552-A3
PLAZA MALL	300	OXN	93030	522-G6
PLAZA LA VISTA	100	CRML	93010	524-C4
PLEASANT AV	500	OJAI	93023	441-J5
	800	OJAI	93023	442-A5
	1000	VeCo	93023	442-A5
PLEASANT PL	-	VEN	93001	471-B6
PLEASANT ST	100	SPLA	93060	464-A5
PLEASANT WY	2400	THO	91362	557-A2
PLEASANT DALE PL	400	THO	91362	557-G1
PLEASANT GROVE CIR	2400	THO	91362	526-J4
PLEASANT OAKS PL	1500	THO	91362	526-J6
PLEASANT VALLEY RD	-	PHME	93043	552-D5
	-	CRML	93010	524-A5
	-	VeCo	93010	524-A5
	100	PHME	93041	552-D5
	400	CRML	93010	523-J5
	400	CRML	93010	523-J5
	800	OXN	93033	552-D5
	1200	VeCo	93033	523-F7
	1200	VeCo	93033	553-C3
	1800	OXN	93033	553-A4
	2200	VeCo	93012	524-H5
	2200	CRML	93012	524-H5
	23600	VeCo	93030	523-J5
PLEASANT VALLEY RD Rt#-34	2200	VeCo	93012	524-F5
	2200	CRML	93012	524-F5
E PLEASANT VALLEY RD	-	OXN	93033	552-J5
	800	VeCo	93033	552-J5
W PLEASANT VALLEY RD	-	OXN	93033	552-G5
PLEASANT VALLEY CANAL RD	-	PHME	93043	552-C5
PLUM AV	1200	SIMI	93065	498-B4
PLUM PL	200	OXN	93030	522-G1
PLUM ST	11300	VEN	93004	473-A7
PLUMAS AV	300	VEN	93004	472-H7
	400	VEN	93004	472-H7
PLUMBAGO ST	500	VeCo	93010	524-C1
PLUMERIA CIR	1500	THO	91360	526-H3
PLUM HOLLOW CIR	1600	THO	91362	527-D6
PLUMMER ST	22400	Chat	91311	499-H6
PLUM TREE CT	24400	CanP	91307	529-D5
PLYMOUTH CIR	1400	THO	91360	526-G6
POCANO CT	2900	THO	91362	527-A2
POCATELLO CT	2400	SIMI	93065	497-J1
POCOMOKE CT	2400	SIMI	93065	497-J1
POE LN	-	VEN	93001	492-D1
POEMA PL	11400	Chat	91311	499-J7
	14100	Chat	91311	499-J7
POGGI ST	600	CRML	93010	524-C2
POINDEXTER AV	100	MRPK	93021	496-C1
POINSETTIA AV	900	THO	91362	557-F1
POINSETTIA PL	700	VEN	93001	491-C2
POINSETTIA GARDENS DR	-	VEN	93003	473-B7
	-	VEN	93003	493-A1
POINTED OAK PL	5500	AGRH	91301	558-A5
POKE LN	2100	SIMI	93065	498-A1
POL RD	-	OXN	93033	553-F6
POLARIS DR	-	VeCo	93041	583-H2
POLARIS WY	700	PHME	93041	552-F3
	800	OXN	93033	552-F3
POLE CANYON	-	FILM	93015	456-C4
	-	VeCo	93015	456-C4
N POLI AV	100	VeCo	93023	441-D6
S POLI AV	100	VeCo	93023	441-D7
POLI ST	100	VEN	93001	491-C1
	2400	VEN	93003	491-G2
POLK ST	23600	VEN	93003	492-E2
POLLOCK LN	6800	VEN	93003	492-D3
POMELO DR	6900	CanP	91307	529-E5
	7400	LA	91304	529-E4
POMO DR	200	VEN	93001	471-C5
POMONA ST	4000	VEN	93003	492-A3
	4400	VEN	93003	492-A2
PONCE AV	6300	WdHl	91367	529-H7
	6400	CanP	91307	529-H4
	7600	LA	91304	529-H2
PONDERA CIR	7200	CanP	91307	529-E5
PONDEROSA CIR	2900	THO	91360	526-H3
PONDEROSA DR	-	CRML	93010	524-C2
	300	CRML	93010	523-J2
	3400	CRML	93010	494-G7
W PONDEROSA DR	100	CRML	93010	524-A4
PONDEROSA DR N	3600	CRML	93010	494-G7
	3600	VeCo	93010	494-G7
PONDEROSA LP	2200	OXN	93033	553-B5
PONDEROSA RD	-	VeCo	93066	494-H4
PONOMA ST	100	PHME	93041	552-E6
PONS CT	900	THO	91320	555-F4
PONTOON WY	3200	OXN	93035	522-E6
POPE AV	1700	SIMI	93065	498-C3
POPE LN	600	OJAI	93023	441-J7
POPLAR CT	23600	VeCo	93063	498-D4
POPLAR ST	200	OXN	93033	552-G2
W POPLAR ST	800	OXN	93033	552-F2
POPLAR CREST AV	-	THO	91360	556-C2
POPPY CT	2900	THO	91360	526-D2
POPPY LN	1100	SPLA	93060	464-B3
POPPY ST	1500	VEN	93003	493-A2
POPPYGLEN CT	11500	MRPK	93021	496-B2
POPPYSEED PL	3900	CALB	91302	558-H7
POPPY TREE PL	23600	SIMI	93065	498-D4
POPPYVIEW DR	6600	VeCo	91377	558-B7
	6600	VeCo	91377	558-A1
PORPOISE WY	4100	OXN	93035	552-B2
PORT CIR	1100	OXN	93035	522-C7
PORT DR	1300	OXN	93035	522-C7
	1300	OXN	93035	552-C1
PORTAL ST	23600	VEN	93022	451-B7
PORTER LN	2800	VEN	93003	491-G3
PORTHOLE CT	1100	OXN	93030	522-F7
PORT HUENEME RD	100	PHME	93041	552-E6
	800	PHME	93041	552-E6
PORTIA ST	5100	SIMI	93063	478-J7
PORTOFINO PL	-	THO	91360	526-D6
PORTOLA CT	5700	WLKV	93362	557-G6
PORTOLA LN	300	FILM	93015	455-H6
	2100	THO	91361	557-A5
PORTOLA RD	700	VEN	93003	492-B4
	1800	VeCo	93003	492-B5
PORTOLA WY	800	OXN	93030	522-F3
PORTSIDE PL	30500	AGRH	91301	557-G5
PORTSMOUTH CT	700	VeCo	93010	557-H1
PORTULACA PL	3900	THO	91320	556-B1
POSADA LILLIA PETALOS	23600	CRML	93010	523-F2
POSEY LN	23600	LA	91304	529-E4
POSITA RD	8000	VeCo	93066	475-E6
POST ST	400	CRML	93010	523-J4
	400	CRML	93010	524-A4
POTEAU ST	-	VeCo	93001	471-C3
POTOMAC AV	-	VEN	93004	492-H4
POTRERO RD	-	VeCo	93061	556-A5
	700	VeCo	93061	555-G5
	900	VeCo	93023	555-G5
	900	THO	91320	555-G5
	900	THO	91361	555-H6
W POTRERO RD	1600	VeCo	93012	554-C4
	1600	VeCo	93012	555-C5
	3900	VeCo	93003	555-D4
	3900	THO	91320	555-D4
POTTER AV	1900	SIMI	93065	498-A2
N POTTER AV	2000	SIMI	93065	498-A2
POWDERHORN CT	1000	VeCo	91377	528-B7
POWELL DR	100	VeCo	93015	457-C6
POWELL RD	6900	CRML	93012	525-C1
E PRADERA RD	11500	VeCo	93012	496-C7
PRAIRIE CT	3300	THO	91320	555-G6
PRAIRIE ST	22000	Chat	91311	499-J7
PRAIRIE DOG PL	1300	SIMI	93065	492-F4
PRAIRIEVIEW LN	5100	CRML	93012	524-J2
PRANCE CT	1800	SIMI	93065	498-A6
N PRATHER ST	2500	SIMI	93065	498-B3
PRATO CT	23600	MRPK	93021	496-C5
PREAKNESS PL	700	THO	91320	555-E4
PREBLE AV	2400	VEN	93003	491-F3
PRENTISS ST	-	THO	91360	526-E4
PRESIDENTIAL DR	700	SIMI	93065	497-D5
	700	VeCo	93065	497-D5
PRESIDIO DR	3400	SIMI	93063	478-F5
	3400	VeCo	93063	478-G5
PRESILLA PL	2100	VeCo	93010	494-D7
PRESILLA RD	7500	VeCo	93012	495-D5
	10600	VeCo	93012	496-A5
PRESTON WY	300	SIMI	93065	497-D6
PRICE RD	4000	VeCo	93066	494-D3
	5100	VeCo	93066	474-D7
PRICE ST	400	FILM	93015	455-J6
PRIDE ST	1200	SIMI	93065	497-H6
PRIETO ST	1400	SPLA	93060	464-C4
PRIMA CT	1400	CRML	93010	524-D1
PRIMPTON CT	300	SIMI	93065	497-D7
PRIMROSE DR	5000	VeCo	93035	471-C1
	5200	VeCo	93035	461-C7
PRIMROSE ST	100	THO	91360	526-D3
PRINCE AL	1900	VEN	93001	491-E3
PRINCE RD	6000	VeCo	93063	499-B3
PRINCESSA DR	23600	OXN	93030	522-J5
PRINCETON AV	-	OXN	93030	522-H2
	200	OXN	93030	492-A3
	6500	MRPK	93021	476-H6
PRINCETON RD	1000	THO	91362	527-A2
	1800	VeCo	93063	492-B5
PRINCETON ST	300	SPLA	93060	463-J7
PRINCEVILLE LN	2200	OXN	93030	522-E2
PRINCIPE PL	10400	VeCo	93012	495-J7
PRINGLE CT	-	THO	91320	556-B1
PROMENADE	-	VEN	93001	491-B3
PROMENADE ST	-	SIMI	93065	498-H1
PROMONTORY PL	29400	AGRH	91301	557-J5
PROPANE RD	23600	VeCo	93015	456-F7
PROSPECT ST	2100	VeCo	93022	451-A7
E PROSPECT ST	-	VEN	93001	491-B1
W PROSPECT ST	-	VEN	93001	491-B1
PROSPECTOR PL	900	THO	91320	555-G4
PROVENCE PL	3100	THO	91362	526-J2
PROVIDENCE AV	600	VEN	93004	492-H2
PROVIDENT RD	27300	AGRH	91301	558-E7
PROVO LN	600	VEN	93004	492-J2
PUCCINI RD	4900	VEN	93003	492-B7
N PUEBLO AV	100	VeCo	93023	441-E6
S PUEBLO AV	100	VeCo	93023	441-D7
PUEBLO DR	500	THO	91360	526-H7
PUEBLO ST	9500	VEN	93004	492-H2
	22100	Chat	91311	499-H2
PUEBLO VISTA	6900	CRML	93012	525-C1
PUESTA DEL SOL	100	VeCo	91360	526-C7
	10500	VeCo	93023	451-B4
	10900	VeCo	93023	451-B4
PULLMAN AV	2000	SIMI	93063	499-A2
PURCELL LN	100	VEN	93004	492-A7
PURDUE AV	100	VEN	93003	492-A2
PURDUE ST	100	OXN	93030	522-H2
E PURDUE ST	14300	MRPK	93021	476-G6
PYLE RD	-	VeCo	93015	465-C2
PYRAMID AV	1500	VEN	93004	492-J3
PYRITE PL	2500	OXN	93030	522-D4

Q

STREET	Block	City	ZIP	Pg-Grid
Q ST	1500	VEN	93004	493-A2
QUAIL CT	300	SPLA	93060	464-C6
	1200	FILM	93015	455-H6
QUAIL ST	700	VeCo	93023	451-C1
	6400	VeCo	93003	492-D5
N QUAIL CANYON RD	3300	THO	91320	526-C2
QUAILCREEK CT	11600	MRPK	93021	496-C3
QUAIL OAKS DR	400	OJAI	93023	441-G6
QUAIL PASS RD	3300	SIMI	93065	527-D1
QUAILRIDGE DR	5300	CRML	93012	525-A1
QUAIL RUN DR	29100	AGRH	91301	558-A5
	29400	AGRH	91301	557-H5
QUAIL RUN WY	900	OXN	93030	522-F1
QUAILS TR	100	THO	91361	555-F2
QUAILSPRING CT	4200	MRPK	93021	496-B2
QUAIL SUMMIT	13200	MRPK	93021	496-E3
QUAIL VIEW CT	700	VeCo	91377	558-B1
QUAILWOOD ST	3900	MRPK	93021	496-C4
QUAINT ST	28600	AGRH	91301	558-B3
QUARTER HORSE LN	900	VeCo	93017	558-A1
QUARTERS A DR	-	PHME	93041	552-E6
N QUARZO CIR	3300	THO	91362	527-A2
QUASAR CT	23600	SIMI	93065	497-H4
QUEENS CT	6800	MRPK	93021	476-H6
QUEENS ST	23600	VEN	93003	492-B3
QUEENS WY	2700	THO	91362	527-B3
	23900	AGRH	91301	557-J4
	23900	SIMI	93065	498-A6
QUEENSBURY ST	300	THO	91362	526-E5
QUEENS GARDEN CT	23600	VeCo	93001	586-E1
QUEENS GARDEN DR	23600	VeCo	93015	586-E1
QUEENSLAND CT	2100	THO	91360	526-B4
QUIET CT	200	SIMI	93065	497-J6
QUIET HILLS CT	8200	LA	91304	529-E3
QUIMBY AV	7400	CanP	91307	529-G4
	7600	LA	91304	529-G4
QUIMISA DR	23600	VEN	93065	477-C7
QUINCY AV	3400	SIMI	93063	478-F6
QUINCY ST	8100	VEN	93004	492-F2
QUINTA VISTA DR	-	THO	91362	557-A2
QUITO CT	6900	CRML	93012	525-D1
	6900	CRML	93012	495-D7

R

STREET	Block	City	ZIP	Pg-Grid
R ST	1500	VEN	93004	493-A2
RABBIT CREEK LN	4200	THO	91320	555-E3
RACCOON CT	7200	VEN	93003	492-F4
RACHAEL AV	3400	SIMI	93063	478-F6
RACHEL DR	1100	OXN	93030	522-E4
RACINE ST	2700	SIMI	93065	498-C1
RACQUET CLUB LN	500	THO	91360	526-D7
RADCLIFF ST	5100	VEN	93003	492-B2
RADCLIFFE RD	800	THO	91360	526-G2
RADFORD CT	2500	SIMI	93063	498-D1
RADNOR AV	1500	VEN	93004	492-G4
RAEMERE ST	2100	CRML	93010	524-E3
RAFFERTY RD	4800	VeCo	93060	454-A7
RAFT LN	500	OXN	93035	522-D7
RAIDERS WY	1200	OXN	93033	552-J3
RAILROAD AV	800	SPLA	93060	464-B5
RAINBOW DR	100	OXN	93033	552-C3
	100	VEN	93004	492-G4
	8500	VEN	93004	492-G4
RAINBOW CREEK CT	3300	THO	91320	555-G6
N RAINBOW CREST DR	5500	AGRH	91301	557-G5
W RAINBOW CREST DR	29800	AGRH	91301	557-H5
RAINBOW HILL RD	5700	AGRH	91301	557-G3
RAINBOW VIEW DR	30300	AGRH	91301	557-G4
RAINCLOUD CT	3500	THO	91362	526-J1
RAINDANCE ST	300	THO	91360	526-D2
RAINEY RD	1200	VeCo	93063	499-A4
RAINFIELD AV	23600	THO	91362	527-B5
RAINIER ST	5400	VEN	93003	492-B1
RAINS CT	100	OJAI	93023	441-J5
	15300	MRPK	93021	476-J5
RAINTREE CT	800	THO	91361	557-A4
RAIN WOOD ST	5200	SIMI	93063	498-J2
RALEIGH PL	800	THO	91360	526-G2
RALLEY CT	2100	THO	91362	527-A2
RALPH WY	700	SPLA	93060	464-C3
RALSTON AV	2000	SIMI	93063	498-H1
RALSTON ST	4700	VeCo	93003	492-D4
	7300	VeCo	93003	492-E4
RAMA PL	6800	CRML	93012	524-J1
RAMBLE RIDGE DR	-	THO	91320	556-F2
RAMBLING RD	1700	SIMI	93065	497-H6
	1600	SIMI	93065	498-A6
RAMELLI AV	1100	VeCo	93004	492-E4
	1100	VEN	93003	492-F5
RAMELLI RANCH RD	23600	VeCo		366-G2
	23600	VeCo	93001	366-G8
	23600	VeCo	93001	459-H1
RAMONA DR	1100	THO	91320	556-A1
	1300	VeCo	93010	494-A6
	1400	VeCo	93010	493-J6
RAMONA PL	-	VeCo	93010	493-J7
	-	VeCo	93010	523-J1
E RAMONA ST	2100	SIMI	93065	498-C2
W RAMONA ST	-	VEN	93001	471-B7
RAMONA CANYON RD	-	VeCo	93040	458-D1
RAMROD CT	3500	THO	91320	555-F4
RAMSGATE CIR	1800	THO	91360	526-C5
N RAMUDA LN	21300	VeCo	91307	529-A5
RANCH RD	-	VeCo	93001	461-A4
	12400	VeCo	93060	473-C2
	23600	VeCo	93001	366-G9
	23600	VeCo	93001	459-D4
	23600	VeCo	93001	450-J2
RANCH CREEK CT	23600	SIMI	93065	497-G7
E RANCHERO RD	-	VeCo	93107	528-J4
	500	VeCo	93022	451-C6
RANCHGROVE DR	2400	WLKV	91361	586-J1
RANCH HOUSE RD	900	THO	91361	557-A5
RANCHITA LN	4100	OXN	93033	553-C4
RANCHO CT	1100	VeCo	93023	441-F6
RANCHO DR	100	OJAI	93023	441-E7
	100	OJAI	93023	441-E7
	300	THO	91362	526-H1
	2500	CRML	93010	524-E3
RANCHO LN	1300	THO	91362	556-H1
RANCHO RD	-	THO	91362	556-H1
	300	THO	91362	526-H1
	23600	THO	91362	556-H1
	23600	VeCo	93012	556-H7
S RANCHO RD	-	THO	91361	556-H2
RANCHO ADOLFO CT	100	CRML	93012	524-H2
RANCHO ADOLFO DR	-	CRML	93012	524-H2
RANCHO CALLEGUAS DR	100	CRML	93012	524-J2
RANCHO CONEJO BLVD	600	THO	91320	526-A5
	1000	THO	91320	526-B4
	23600	THO	91320	555-J1
RANCHO DOS RIOS	23600	VeCo	93012	451-F3
RANCHO DOS VIENTOS DR	-	THO	91362	555-B3
RANCHO FILOSO	400	SPLA	93060	463-H5
	400	VeCo	93060	463-H5
RANCHO LA VISTA RD	1500	VeCo	93023	451-E2
RANCHO VISTA CT	13300	VeCo	93012	496-E6
RANCHO VISTA LN	500	VeCo	93060	472-J5
RANCH VIEW PL	700	THO	91362	527-A7
RANCHWOOD ST	3200	THO	91320	555-G4
RAND ST	6400	MRPK	93021	476-J6
RANDI AV	6200	WdHl	91367	529-J7
	6400	CanP	91307	529-J7
RANDIWOOD LN	6600	LACo	91307	529-C6
RANDY DR	100	VeCo	93023	441-J5
RANGELY CT	200	SIMI	93065	497-F6
RANGER CT	3000	THO	91320	526-D2
RANSOM RD	13800	MRPK	93021	496-F4
RASPBERRY PL	1100	OXN	93030	522-G1
RATEL PL	7000	VEN	93003	491-J3
RATTLESNAKE RD	-	LACo	90265	586-G7
RAVELLO CT	-	THO	91362	527-C3
RAVEN LN	4000	OXN	93033	553-B5
RAVEN ST	1300	VEN	93003	492-C4
RAVENCREST CT	200	THO	91362	555-G2
RAVENNA ST	2100	SIMI	93065	498-C2
RAVENSBURY ST	500	SIMI	91361	556-G6
RAVENS POINT CT	23600	SIMI	93065	498-C5
RAVENWOOD AV	800	THO	91361	555-E4
RAVOLI DR	2000	VEN	93035	552-B1
RAWHIDE PL	900	THO	91320	555-G5
RAYBURN ST	1800	THO	91362	527-D5
RAYEN ST	22000	LA	91304	529-J1
	22300	WHII	91304	529-J1
RAYLENE CT	6200	SIMI	93063	499-C2
RAYMOND ST	200	VEN	93023	441-G6
E RAYMOND ST	170	SIMI	93065	498-A3
RAYSHIRE ST	1900	THO	91362	526-J7
	1900	THO	91362	527-A7
RAYTHEON RD	4100	VeCo	93033	553-F6
REA WY	200	VEN	93001	491-A2
READ RD	4500	THO	91360	496-J5
	4500	THO	91360	496-J5
	4900	THO	91362	496-J5
	4900	VeCo	93033	553-F6
READING DR	4400	OXN	93033	553-A5
REAGAN CT	100	VEN	93003	492-E1
REAL CANYON RD	700	VeCo	93063	457-E3
REATA AV	-	VEN	93004	473-A6
REBECCA ST	2000	SIMI	93063	498-F2
REBURTA LN	3500	SIMI	93063	478-E7
RECODO WY	5800	CRML	93012	525-B1
RED BARN RD	11000	VeCo	93012	496-A7
RED BLUFF CT	23600	SIMI	93063	479-A6
RED BLUFF DR	26000	CALB	91302	558-J4
REDCOAT LN	4200	WLKV	91361	557-F6
REDDINGTON CT	100	CRML	93010	524-D1
	100	AGRH	91301	494-D7
REDFIELD AV	300	SIMI	93022	451-C4
RED HILL RD	500	OJAI	93023	441-J5
RED LAKES PL	400	SIMI	93065	497-C5
	400	VeCo	93065	497-C5
REDMAN CT	2000	SIMI	93063	498-J2
REDMESA DR	10900	Chat	91311	499-J2
RED MOUNTAIN EAST FIRE RD	23600	VeCo	93060	460-G8
RED MOUNTAIN FIRE RD	23600	VeCo	93060	460-B2
RED OAK AV	100	THO	91320	556-D2
RED OAK PL	1000	CRML	93010	524-C2
REDONDO AV	2700	VeCo	93012	496-C6
REDONDO CIR	2700	VeCo	93012	496-C7
REDONDO ST	7600	VeCo	93004	492-E1
RED PINE DR	23600	SIMI	93065	498-D4
RED ROBIN PL	-	THO	91320	526-A5
RED ROCK CT	5100	THO	91362	527-F6
RED SAIL CIR	1300	THO	91361	557-B6
REDWING LN	1200	OXN	93030	522-E1
REDWOOD AV	7000	VEN	93003	491-J3
REDWOOD CIR	-	VEN	93001	491-J3
	1500	THO	91360	526-H3
REDWOOD DR	1000	VeCo	93063	499-C4
REDWOOD LN	100	SPLA	93060	464-A5
REDWOOD ST	200	OXN	93033	552-E2
	1500	OXN	93035	552-E1
REED WY	400	PHME	93041	552-D2
REEDER AV	2500	CRML	93012	495-B6
REEDLEY ST	14700	MRPK	93021	476-H6
REEF CIR	600	PHME	93041	552-F7
REEF ST	2900	VEN	93001	491-F5
REEF WY	5100	OXN	93035	521-J7
	11800	VeCo	90265	625-F5
REEVES RD	3200	VeCo	93023	442-G6
REFSING DR	3800	OXN	93033	552-G4
REFSING ST	4700	OXN	93033	552-G5
REGAL AV	100	THO	91320	555-J2
REGAL OAK CT	23200	Chat	91311	499-F7
REGAN CIR	170	SIMI	93065	498-A3
REGATTA PL	3300	OXN	93035	522-C7
REGENT AV	3200	THO	91360	526-E2
REGENT CT	700	SPLA	93060	464-A4
REGENT ST	1500	CRML	93010	524-D2
REGENTS CT	4400	WLKV	91361	557-D6
REGINA AV	2700	THO	91362	526-E3
REGIS DR	-	VeCo	93041	583-C1
REGULUS DR	100	VeCo	93041	583-C1
REIMER PETIT RD	1600	VeCo	93001	465-C5
N REINO RD	-	THO	91362	555-F1
	-	THO	91320	555-F7
S REINO RD	-	THO	91362	555-F3
REMINGTON AV	600	SIMI	93065	492-D3
REMINGTON PL	11000	VeCo	93012	555-G4
REMONT CIR	1600	VeCo	91377	527-H6
RENAISSANCE PL	-	WLKV	91362	557-F6
RENATA PL	26000	CALB	91302	558-J4
RENE ST	-	VeCo	93030	493-A7
RENEE DR	6500	VeCo	93066	475-A6
REPOSO DR	300	CRML	93010	524-D1
	300	AGRH	91301	494-D7
RESEDA CT	3500	CRML	93010	494-G7
RESERVOIR DR	2600	SIMI	93065	478-C1
	2600	SIMI	93065	498-C1
	2800	SIMI	93065	478-C7
	3000	VeCo	93065	478-C7
	3000	SIMI	93065	478-C7
RESTFUL CT	1700	SIMI	93065	497-J6
	1700	SIMI	93065	498-A6
RETIRO DR	1700	SIMI	93065	497-J6
REVELLO ST	23600	MRPK	93021	496-C1
REVERE CT	-	VEN	93004	472-H6
REX ST	1000	CRML	93010	524-C2
REXFORD PL	1100	THO	91360	526-F6
REXFORD ST	3400	VEN	93003	491-H4
REYES ADOBE RD	4900	AGRH	91301	557-G3
REYNOLDS CT	-	THO	91362	526-H7
RHAME TER	10	SPLA	93060	464-A5
RHAPSODY DR	4800	VeCo	91377	557-G2
RHEINLAND CT	23600	SIMI	93065	498-A5
RHODA ST	2000	SIMI	93065	498-A3
RHODES CT	200	FILM	93015	455-H6
RHONA CT	5300	AGRH	91301	557-H5
RHONDA AV	1900	OXN	93030	522-E3
RHONDA ST	1800	OXN	93030	522-E3
RIALTO ST	700	OXN	93035	522-E7
	1400	OXN	93035	552-E1
RIATA CT	2400	VeCo	93012	496-D6
RIAVE CT	2400	CRML	93012	495-B6
RICE AV	300	OXN	93033	523-B5
	800	OXN	93033	523-B5
	800	OXN	93033	523-B7
	1300	VEN	93003	553-B3
RICE RD	3200	VeCo	93023	441-C2
N RICE RD	-	VeCo	93023	441-C2
S RICE RD	100	VeCo	93023	441-C7
	100	VeCo	93023	451-C2
RICE ST	5300	VeCo	93066	459-A5
RICE CANYON RD	23600	VeCo	93023	441-B5
RICHARD RD	400	SPLA	93060	463-H6
RICHARD ST	1000	VEN	93004	492-J2
RICHARDSON AV	900	SIMI	93065	497-G5
RICHARDSON CANYON RD	-	VeCo	93066	464-D7
	-	VeCo	93066	474-E1
RICHFORD LN	400	VEN	93022	451-A7
RICHGROVE CT	31900	WLKV	91361	557-C6
RICHMOND AV	600	SIMI	93065	464-C4
	25900	LACo	91302	558-J3
RICHMOND CT	100	SPLA	93060	464-B4
RICKEY CT	3100	THO	91362	527-C7
RIDDEN ST	3400	CRML	93010	494-F3
RIDGE DR	12200	VeCo	93012	496-D6
RIDGEBROOK DR	5700	AGRH	91301	557-H5
RIDGEBROOK PL	2100	THO	91362	527-A3
RIDGECREST CT	6900	VeCo	93066	472-D7
RIDGE CREST DR	500	SIMI	93063	463-H6
RIDGECREST LN	6500	VeCo	93066	475-A6
RIDGECREST PL	900	THO	91362	527-C7
RIDGEFORD DR	3200	WLKV	91361	557-D7
RIDGEGATE LN	1700	SIMI	93065	497-E2
RIDGE LINE DR	400	VeCo	93012	451-C2
RIDGEMONT CT	3000	SIMI	93065	478-C7
RIDGEMOOR DR	5200	VeCo	93021	475-H7
	5200	SIMI	93021	495-J1
RIDGETON LN	-	SIMI	93065	498-C5
RIDGE VIEW CT	900	VeCo	93065	494-B5
RIDGE VIEW DR	2200	SIMI	93065	497-H1
RIDGE VIEW ST	2200	SIMI	93065	497-J1
RIDGE VIEW ST	4200	THO	91362	524-H4
RIDGEWAY CT	4800	THO	91362	527-F1
RIDGEWAY DR	29500	AGRH	91301	557-J3
RIDGEWAY PL	1600	MRPK	93012	496-B3
RIDGEWOOD DR	1600	SIMI	93012	496-A5
RIDLEY CIR	100	SPLA	93060	464-A5
RIENTE ST	23600	SIMI	93065	498-A5
RIESS RD	2000	SIMI	93065	498-A3
RIFLEMAN DR	200	FILM	93015	455-H6
RIGEL DR	5300	AGRH	91301	557-H5

STREET
Block City ZIP Pg-Grid

RIGGER RD
30500 AGRH 91301 557-G5
RIGGING PL
1100 OXN 93030 522-F7
RIKKARD DR
2400 THO 91362 527-A2
RILEY LN
500 VEN 93003 492-D1
RIM CREST CIR
2300 THO 91361 557-B4
RIM CREST DR
2200 THO 91361 557-B4
RIMROCK RD
200 VeCo 91361 556-G2
RINCON CT
300 SPLA 93060 463-J6
RINCON DR
- VeCo 93012 554-E3
RINCON RD Rt#-150
6600 StBC 93013 459-A1
6600 VeCo 93013 366-G9
6600 VeCo 93013 459-A1
RINCON ST
100 OJAI 93023 441-H6
100 VEN 93001 491-E2
1200 SIMI 93065 498-B4
RINCON WY
400 OXN 93033 552-G3
RINCON BEACH PARK DR
- VeCo 93001 459-G7
- VeCo 93001 469-G1
RING CIR
3200 SIMI 93063 478-D7
RINGWOOD ST
2700 SIMI 93063 478-H7
RINGWOOD ST
4900 SIMI 93063 478-H7
RIODOSA TR
5500 VeCo 91377 557-J1
RIO GRANDE CIR
500 THO 91360 526-D3
RIO HATO CT
3500 CMRL 93010 494-G7
RIO LINDO ST
400 OXN 93030 522-H2
RIOPELLE CT
900 THO 91320 555-F4
RIO SCHOOL LN
- VeCo 93030 522-H1
RIO VIA
200 VeCo 93022 451-B6
RIO VISTA CT
1300 SIMI 93065 497-H1
RIPLEY ST
- CMRL 93010 524-A2
RIPLEY WY
1700 OXN 93033 552-J3
RIPPLE DR
900 OXN 93035 522-C7
RIPPLE CREEK LN
13000 VeCo 93012 496-F5
RISING STAR AV
23600 SIMI 93063 479-A6
ISTA DR
5700 AGRH 91301 557-J4
IVA CT
23600 MRPK 93021 496-C4
IVAS LN
1100 OXN 93035 522-E7
IVENDELL CIR
1800 THO 91320 556-A2
IVER DR
3900 VeCo 93001 471-C3
IVER ST
100 FILM 93015 456-A6
500 VeCo 93040 457-F4
700 FILM 93015 455-H7
IVERA ST
800 SIMI 93065 497-G4
IVERBIRCH DR
2000 SIMI 93063 498-J2
IVER FARM DR
3700 WLKV 91361 557-C7
IVERFIELD CT
200 SIMI 93065 497-F6
IVERGLEN ST
4200 MRPK 93021 496-D3
IVERGROVE CT
1900 MRPK 93021 496-C3
IVERGROVE ST
2100 MRPK 93021 496-D3
IVER HILLS CT
500 SIMI 93065 497-G6
IVERMORE ST
3400 CMRL 93010 494-G7
IVER RIDGE RD
2200 OXN 93030 522-E2
IVERROCK CIR
400 THO 91362 557-G1
IVERRUN LN
3200 VeCo 93012 496-E4
IVERSIDE AV
700 VeCo 93015 465-H2
700 VeCo 93015 466-A2
IVERSIDE RD
- VeCo 93022 451-A6
IVERSIDE ST
700 VEN 93001 471-B7

RIVERSTONE LN
600 VeCo 91377 527-G7
RIVER WOOD CT
23600 SIMI 93063 499-B3
RIVOL RD
7000 CanP 91307 529-D5
RIXTAR RD
23600 SIMI 93065 497-F7
ROADRUNNER AV
- THO 91320 525-J5
- THO 91320 526-A5
ROADRUNNER DR
6800 VEN 93003 492-E4
ROADRUNNER PL
- THO 91320 525-J5
ROADSIDE DR
28300 AGRH 91301 558-B6
29300 AGRH 91301 557-J6
ROAN ST
1400 SIMI 93065 497-J3
ROB CT
2800 THO 91362 527-A3
ROBBINS CT
- SIMI 93065 497-E3
ROBERT AV
100 OXN 93033 552-G3
W ROBERT AV
200 OXN 93030 522-F4
ROBERTS AV
200 MRPK 93021 496-E1
ROBERTSON RD
23600 VeCo 93063 499-D4
ROBERTSON WY
- THO 91320 556-B1
ROBIN AV
1100 VEN 93003 492-D4
1100 VEN 93009 492-D4
2100 OXN 93033 553-A4
ROBIN CT
400 FILM 93015 455-H6
ROBIN ST
1100 OJAI 93023 442-A6
ROBIN HILL ST
3500 THO 91360 526-G2
ROBINWOOD LN
4300 MRPK 93021 496-F3
ROBLE LN
23600 OXN 93030 522-H3
ROBLES LN
5300 AGRH 91301 557-H5
ROBYN WY
1100 CMRL 93010 524-C3
ROCA AV
2600 THO 91360 526-C3
ROCA RD
23600 VeCo 93063 528-H2
ROCHELLE PL
2600 SIMI 93063 478-D7
2600 SIMI 93063 498-D1
ROCHESTER CT
600 VEN 93004 492-H1
ROCK ST
2700 SIMI 93065 498-C3
ROCKAWAY RD
- VeCo 93022 451-A5
ROCK CASTLE CT
5300 VeCo 91377 527-G6
ROCK CREEK RD
5600 AGRH 91301 558-A4
N ROCKDALE AV
2000 SIMI 93063 499-B1
ROCKEDGE DR
300 VeCo 91377 558-A1
ROCKET ST
- VeCo 93042 583-D4
ROCKETDYNE RD
23700 LA 91304 499-D7
23900 WHIl 91304 499-D7
24900 VeCo 93063 499-B7
ROCKFIELD ST
4800 THO 91362 557-G1
4900 VeCo 91362 557-G1
5000 VeCo 91377 557-H1
ROCKFORD CT
4700 VEN 93003 492-A2
ROCKGATE PL
3000 SIMI 93063 478-E7
ROCKHILL DR
23500 Chat 91311 499-F7
ROCKINGHAM DR
1300 SIMI 93063 499-C4
ROCKING HORSE DR
1700 SIMI 93065 497-J6
1700 SIMI 93065 498-A7
ROCKLITE RD
- VEN 93001 471-C6
ROCKLYN ST
2000 CMRL 93010 524-E1
ROCKMAN WY
400 PHME 93041 552-D2
ROCKRIDGE PL
2800 THO 91360 526-E3
ROCKRIDGE TER
7100 CanP 91307 529-E5
ROCKROSE LN
100 VeCo 91377 557-J2
ROCK SPRING ST
- THO 91320 526-A6
ROCK TREE DR
5500 AGRH 91301 558-A5

ROCK VISTA DR
29000 AGRH 91301 558-A5
ROCKY RD
1200 VeCo 93063 499-D4
ROCKY MESA PL
9200 WHIl 91304 499-D7
ROCKY MOUNTAIN
- VeCo 93001 461-B6
ROCKY PEAK FIRE RD
24000 WHIl 91304 529-D2
- Chat 91311 479-E3
- StvR 91381 479-E3
23600 SIMI 93063 499-F1
23600 VeCo 93063 479-D4
23600 VeCo 93063 499-F1
ROCKY POINT CT
2600 THO 91362 527-D3
ROCKYRIVER CT
1600 SIMI 93065 498-E3
ROCKYRIVER ST
3700 SIMI 93065 498-E3
ROD AV
6000 WdHI 91367 529-C7
RODAX ST
22700 LA 91304 529-H2
RODEO CT
2000 THO 91362 556-H2
RODEO DR
200 VeCo 93022 451-C5
W RODERICK AV
- OXN 93030 522-F4
RODGERS ST
200 VEN 93003 492-B3
RODNEY ST
2600 THO 91320 525-H7
ROGER RD
800 SPLA 93060 464-C3
12400 VeCo 93060 473-E6
ROGUE RIVER CIR
1800 VEN 93004 492-G4
ROHNER AV
2000 SIMI 93063 499-C2
ROHNER CT
2200 SIMI 93063 499-C1
ROLAND WY
5400 OXN 93033 552-F6
ROLDAN AV
1100 SIMI 93065 498-A4
ROLLING KNOLL RD
4400 MRPK 93021 496-F3
ROLLING MEADOWS CT
500 THO 91320 526-B7
ROLLING OAKS DR
100 THO 91361 556-F2
500 VeCo 91361 556-G2
ROLLING RIDGE DR
29900 AGRH 91301 557-H4
ROLLINGS AV
2800 THO 91360 526-H2
ROLLINS RD
9300 Chat 91311 499-F6
ROMAN AV
1700 CMRL 93010 494-G7
1700 CMRL 93010 524-G1
ROMANO DR
800 VeCo 93023 451-C1
ROMANY DR
4000 OXN 93035 552-B2
ROMAR ST
22000 Chat 91311 499-J4
ROMBERG LN
800 VEN 93003 492-B7
RONALD REAGAN FRWY Rt#-118
- Chat - 499-E2
- MRPK - 476-H7
- MRPK - 477-B6
- MRPK - 496-G1
- SIMI - 477-B6
- SIMI - 497-G1
- SIMI - 498-F1
- SIMI - 499-E2
- VeCo - 477-B6
RONDELL ST
4100 AGRH 91301 558-E7
RONEL CT
400 THO 91320 556-C1
ROOSEVELT AV
100 OXN 93030 522-H6
200 VEN 93003 492-E1
N ROOSEVELT AV
100 OXN 93030 522-H5
ROOSEVELT BLVD
2300 VeCo 93035 552-B5
ROOSEVELT CT
- SIMI 93065 497-D5
- VEN 93003 492-E1
RORY LN
1600 SIMI 93063 499-B3
RORY WY
5900 SIMI 93063 499-B3
ROSA LN
100 THO 91320 555-H2
W ROSA ST
200 OXN 93033 552-G5
ROSADA CT
900 VeCo 93010 494-B5
ROSAL LN
10900 VeCo 93004 493-B1
ROSALIE ST
3500 SIMI 93063 498-D2

ROSALINDA DR
23600 OXN 93030 522-J5
ROSARIO CT
500 THO 91362 526-H7
ROSARIO DR
400 THO 91362 526-H7
ROSCOE BLVD
22000 LA 91304 529-D2
24000 WHIl 91304 529-D2
ROSE AV
100 OXN 93030 522-J7
500 VeCo 93030 522-J7
1100 OXN 93033 522-J7
1100 OXN 93033 552-J2
1100 VeCo 93033 522-J7
1300 VeCo 93033 552-J2
2800 VeCo 93030 523-A1
3300 VeCo 93030 493-C5
N ROSE AV
100 OXN 93030 522-J3
2600 OXN 93030 523-A2
2600 VeCo 93030 523-A2
ROSE LN
2300 VeCo 93012 496-B7
ROSE ST
1200 VeCo 93063 499-B4
E ROSE ST
200 OXN 93033 552-G5
ROSEBAY ST
2000 THO 91361 557-A5
ROSEBUD DR
500 OXN 93030 522-F1
ROSECRANS ST
2100 SIMI 93065 498-A4
ROSECREEK DR
11400 MRPK 93021 496-B3
ROSEDALE CT
13100 VeCo 93012 496-E6
ROSEHEDGE LN
200 VeCo 91377 557-J2
ROSEHILL CIR
3200 THO 91360 526-F2
ROSELAND AV
8200 VeCo 93021 476-E2
ROSELAWN AV
1300 THO 91362 527-A6
ROSEMARY ST
2100 SIMI 93065 498-A4
ROSEMONT CT
4700 VEN 93003 492-A2
ROSETTE ST
2700 SIMI 93065 498-C5
ROSETTI LN
500 VEN 93003 492-D1
ROSE VALLEY RD
- VeCo - 366-K5
ROSEWATER PL
23600 OXN 93035 522-C6
ROSEWOOD AV
100 CMRL 93010 524-C3
ROSEWOOD CT
1800 OXN 93030 522-F3
1900 THO 91362 526-J3
1900 THO 91362 527-A3
ROSEWOOD DR
900 OXN 93030 522-F3
ROSEWOOD ST
200 VEN 93001 471-B7
ROSITA DR
1500 SIMI 93065 497-F3
ROSITA RD
8900 VeCo 93012 495-G7
10600 VeCo 93012 496-A7
ROSS CIR
1700 SIMI 93065 498-C3
ROSSINI LN
4600 VEN 93003 492-A4
ROSSMORE DR
200 VeCo 93035 552-B5
ROSWELL CT
700 VEN 93004 492-G2
ROSWELL ST
8300 VEN 93004 492-G3
ROTELLA ST
1000 THO 91320 555-F4
ROTH CT
2600 THO 91320 525-H6
ROTHKO LN
6000 SIMI 93063 499-B1
ROULETTE CIR
1700 THO 91362 526-J2
ROUNDHOUSE RD
- PHME 93043 552-D2
ROUND MOUNTAIN RD
- VeCo 93012 554-D4
ROUNDTREE PL
4800 THO 91362 557-F1
ROUNDUP CIR
3000 THO 91360 526-C2
N ROUNDUP RD
- VeCo 91307 528-J5
- VeCo 91307 529-A5
ROUSSEAU ST
- PHME 93041 552-E4
ROWELL AV
9200 Chat 91311 499-F6
9200 Chat 91311 499-F7
ROWLAND AV
2100 SIMI 93063 498-G1

E ROWLAND AV
1600 CMRL 93010 524-D1
N ROWLAND AV
300 CMRL 93010 524-E2
ROXBURY PL
1100 THO 91360 526-F6
ROXBURY ST
4100 SIMI 93063 478-F5
ROXY ST
2400 SIMI 93065 478-B7
ROYAL AV
- SIMI 93065 497-G3
1600 SIMI 93065 498-D3
3200 SIMI 93063 498-E3
ROYAL GLEN RD
3900 WLKV 91361 557-C6
ROYAL HILLS CT
23600 SIMI 93065 478-B7
ROYAL LONDON CT
23600 VeCo 91361 556-F5
ROYAL OAK PL
1100 SPLA 93060 464-B3
ROYAL OAKS DR
3000 THO 91362 557-A3
ROYAL RIDGE CT
5000 THO 91362 527-F6
ROYAL SAINT GEORGE DR
1600 THO 91362 527-D6
ROYAL VISTA CT
5000 THO 91362 557-E1
ROYCE CT
1400 CMRL 93010 524-D1
ROYCETON CT
32000 WLKV 91361 557-C6
ROYER AV
6200 WdHI 91367 529-G7
6400 CanP 91307 529-G5
7500 LA 91304 529-G2
ROYMOR DR
26100 CALB 91302 558-H4
RUBENS PL
600 OXN 93033 552-H4
RUBICON AV
1100 VEN 93004 492-J2
RUBICON CT
10000 VEN 93004 492-J3
RUBIO AV
100 CMRL 93010 524-D4
RUBY AV
800 VEN 93004 492-F3
RUBY DR
200 THO 91320 525-H6
2500 OXN 93030 522-D4
RUDDER AV
2500 PHME 93041 552-C2
RUDMAN DR
600 VeCo 91320 525-G7
RUDNICK AV
6600 CanP 91303 529-J6
7600 LA 91304 529-J1
9500 Chat 91311 499-J5
RUDOLPH DR
300 VeCo 91320 556-B3
RUGBY AV
1100 VEN 93004 492-G3
RUGBY CIR
1500 THO 91360 526-F5
RUGBY RD
1100 VeCo 93023 442-F5
RUNKLE FIRE RD
23600 VeCo 93063 528-E1
RUNKLE HAUL RD
- VeCo 93063 498-D7
RUNNING TRAILS AV
23600 SIMI 93063 478-J6
RUNNYMEDE ST
22000 CanP 91303 529-J4
22700 CanP 91307 529-G4
RUNWAY ST
4400 SIMI 93063 498-G3
RUSH CIR
2000 THO 91362 526-J6
2000 THO 91362 527-A6
RUSH HAVEN WY
1700 SIMI 93065 497-F3
RUSHING CREEK PL
500 THO 91360 526-G1
RUSHMORE ST
5400 VEN 93003 472-B7
RUSKIN AV
2100 THO 91360 526-G4
RUSS CT
3800 SIMI 93063 478-E6
RUSSELL CT
6800 VEN 93003 492-E3
RUSSELL RANCH RD
31300 WLKV 91362 557-E5
RUSSEL TEMPLE RD
300 VeCo 93060 455-B6
RUSSETWOOD LN
23600 SIMI 93065 497-A2
RUSTIC GLEN DR
2700 THO 91362 526-J3
RUSTIC HILLS DR
23600 SIMI 93065 527-F1
RUSTIC OAK DR
31500 WLKV 91361 557-D6
RUSTIC PARK CT
2100 THO 91362 527-A4

RUSTIC VIEW CT
4200 MRPK 93021 496-B2
RUSTLING OAKS DR
5900 AGRH 91301 558-A3
RUTGER CIR
14400 MRPK 93021 476-G6
RUTGERS CT
700 THO 91360 526-G5
RUTGERS DR
1800 THO 91360 526-G5
RUTH AV
200 MRPK 93021 496-E1
RUTH DR
600 VeCo 91320 525-G7
RUTHERFORD HILL DR
- LA 91304 529-D4
RUTHWOOD DR
5400 CALB 91302 558-H3
RUTLAND PL
2300 THO 91362 527-A2
RYDER CUP DR
1600 THO 91362 527-D6
RYNERSON CT
2600 SIMI 93065 478-B7

S

S ST
1500 VEN 93004 493-A2
S & D RD
- VeCo 93015 455-G5
S S & J RD
23600 VeCo 93015 456-J7
S & J RANCH RD
23600 VeCo 93015 456-J5
23600 VeCo 93015 457-A5
SABET CT
1800 CMRL 93010 494-G7
SABINA CIR
1500 SIMI 93063 499-A3
SABINA ST
8900 VEN 93004 492-H4
SABLE ST
7500 VEN 93003 492-F5
SABRA AV
- VeCo 91377 558-A2
SABRINA ST
1300 OXN 93030 522-J3
SACRAMENTO DR
300 VEN 93004 472-H6
SADDLE AV
2600 OXN 93030 522-G1
2600 OXN 93030 492-G7
SADDLE LN
200 OJAI 93023 441-J7
200 OJAI 93023 451-H1
SADDLE TR
200 VeCo 91361 556-G2
SADDLEBACK CIR
1100 CMRL 93012 525-B2
SADDLEBACK CT
3000 THO 91360 526-C2
SADDLEBACK TR
1100 CMRL 93012 525-B1
SADDLEBACK WY
5900 CMRL 93012 525-B1
N SADDLEBOW RD
- VeCo 91307 528-G3
SADDLEBROOK DR
29000 AGRH 91301 558-A4
SADDLE CREST LN
4200 WLKV 91361 557-E6
SADDLEHORN PL
900 THO 91320 555-G5
SADDLE MOUNTAIN DR
32300 WLKV 91361 557-C7
SADDLERIDGE CT
12600 VeCo 93012 496-D6
SADDLERIDGE LN
- CALB 91302 558-H4
SADDLE TREE DR
31500 WLKV 91361 557-D7
SADRING AV
7800 LA 91304 529-F3
SAFFRON CIR
3000 THO 91360 526-H2
SAGAMORE LN
1200 VEN 93001 491-E5
E SAGE LN
- VeCo 91307 528-J3
- VeCo 91307 529-A4
SAGE ST
11300 VEN 93004 473-A6
23600 SIMI 93065 497-F7
SAGEBRUSH PL
800 THO 91320 555-G5
SAGEWOOD DR
11500 MRPK 93021 496-C3
SAILBOAT CIR
5300 AGRH 91301 557-G6
SAILFISH WY
2600 OXN 93035 552-A2
SAILOR AV
2700 VEN 93001 491-F5
SAILVIEW LN
32100 WLKV 91361 557-C6
SAILWIND CT
400 SIMI 93065 497-E6
SAINT ANDREWS CT
1900 OXN 93030 522-D3

SAINT ANDREWS PL
1700 THO 91362 527-E5
SAINT CHARLES CT
- THO 91320 556-B1
SAINT CHARLES DR
200 THO 91360 526-E7
SAINT CHARLES PL
- THO 91360 526-E7
SAINT CLAIR AV
2100 SIMI 93063 499-B2
E SAINT CLAIR CT
2200 SIMI 93063 499-B2
SAINT CLAIR ST
10100 VEN 93004 493-A2
SAINT CROIX CT
4800 VeCo 91377 557-G2
SAINT EDENS CIR
24200 CanP 91307 529-D5
SAINT JAMES CT
- THO 91320 556-B1
SAINT JEAN CT
30800 WLKV 91362 557-F5
SAINT JOHN CT
- THO 91320 556-B1
SAINT LAURENT DR
5800 AGRH 91301 557-G3
SAINT LAWRENCE DR
1700 VEN 93004 492-G4
SAINT MARYS DR
100 OXN 93030 522-H2
SAINT PAULS DR
- VEN 93003 491-H2
SAINT STEPHEN CT
- THO 91320 556-B1
SAINT THOMAS DR
100 VeCo 93023 441-E7
4800 VeCo 91377 557-G2
SAINT VINCENT DR
300 VeCo 91377 557-G2
SAIPAN
- PHME 93041 552-E5
SALAS ST
500 SPLA 93060 463-J6
SALE AV
6100 WdHI 91367 529-H7
6400 CanP 91307 529-H4
7600 LA 91304 529-H2
SALEM AV
300 VeCo 93030 492-J7
700 VeCo 93030 493-A7
700 VeCo 93030 523-A1
SALERNO DR
5500 WLKV 91362 557-F5
SALINAS CT
5400 SIMI 93063 498-J1
5400 SIMI 93063 499-A1
SALISBURY RD
7000 CanP 91307 529-D5
SALLY ST
2300 SIMI 93065 478-B7
SALMON RIVER CIR
3400 THO 91362 557-C2
SALSA ST
- PHME 93043 552-D3
SALT CANYON RD
- Nwhl 91382 458-J7
SALT CREEK RD
23600 Nwhl 91382 458-J6
23600 Valc 91355 458-J6
23600 VeCo - 367-E9
23600 VeCo 93040 367-E9
23600 VeCo 93040 458-J6
SALTINO WY
4800 VeCo 91377 557-G2
SALT MARSH RD
- VeCo 93060 453-E5
SAMANTHA CT
2600 SIMI 93063 498-D1
SAMRA DR
8300 LA 91304 529-G2
N SAMSON AV
2000 SIMI 93063 498-E2
SAMUEL AV
2900 OXN 93033 552-G3
SAMUEL DR
3800 OXN 93033 552-G4
SAN ANDRES CIR
600 THO 91360 526-C3
SAN ANGELO AV
2900 SIMI 93063 478-H6
SAN ANTONIO ST
- THO 91320 555-E2
400 OJAI 93023 441-H7
SAN ARDO CT
6100 CMRL 93012 495-B7
SAN BENITO AV
- VEN 93004 492-F1
SAN BENITO ST
1900 OXN 93033 553-A2
SAN BERNARDINO AV
- VEN 93004 492-F1
SAN CARLOS DR
600 THO 91320 526-A7
SAN CAYETANO RD
1000 VeCo - 367-B7
1000 VeCo - 455-E1
1000 VeCo 93015 367-B7
1000 VeCo 93015 455-E1
SAN CAYETANO ST
900 VeCo 93015 465-F4

SANCHEZ DR
2100 CMRL 93010 494-H7
SAN CLEMENTE AL
1800 VEN 93001 491-E2
SAN CLEMENTE AV
100 VeCo 93035 552-B4
SAN CLEMENTE CT
3700 THO 91320 555-F1
SAN CLEMENTE ST
- VEN 93001 491-F3
300 SPLA 93060 463-J6
SAN CLEMENTE WY
900 VeCo 93010 494-D6
SAN COMO CT
1000 CMRL 93012 525-C6
SAN COMO LN
6300 CMRL 93012 525-C6
SAND CT
900 VEN 93001 491-F4
SANDALWOOD DR
6400 SIMI 93063 499-C3
SANDALWOOD PL
100 FILM 93015 456-B6
1700 THO 91362 526-J3
SANDALWOOD ST
23300 CanP 91307 529-E4
SANDBERG AV
2100 OXN 93033 553-A3
SANDBERG LN
800 VEN 93003 492-D3
SANDBERG ST
- THO 91320 526-E3
SAND CANYON RD
2700 SIMI 93065 478-A6
2700 SIMI 93065 498-A1
4200 VeCo 93066 495-C1
4700 VeCo 93066 475-D7
SANDCROFT ST
23600 VeCo 91361 556-G6
SANDERLING ST
2000 VEN 93003 492-D5
SANDHURST AV
2700 THO 91362 527-A3
SAN DIEGO AV
300 VEN 93004 492-F1
SANDIMAN ST
5400 SIMI 93063 498-J2
5500 SIMI 93063 499-A2
SAN DIMAS AV
5900 CMRL 93012 525-B5
SAN DOVAL PL
600 THO 91360 526-C3
SANDPIPER CIR
800 THO 91361 557-A5
SANDPIPER CT
900 VEN 93001 491-F5
3600 WLKV 91361 557-B7
SANDPIPER WY
5100 OXN 93035 521-J7
SANDPOINT LN
1100 VEN 93004 492-H3
SANDRA CT
- THO 91320 555-G2
SANDSPIT AV
2900 VEN 93001 491-F4
SANDSTONE
2900 SIMI 93063 478-D7
SANDTRAP DR
30400 AGRH 91301 557-G4
SANDY AV
600 SIMI 93065 498-C5
SANDY CIR
500 VeCo 93030 492-J5
SANDY HOLLOW CT
4100 MRPK 93021 496-D3
SAN FELICE CT
23600 MRPK 93021 496-C5
SAN FELIPE AV
3700 THO 91320 555-E1
SAN FERNANDO AV
100 VeCo 93035 552-C6
6800 VeCo 93001 459-C4
SANFORD ST
1800 OXN 93033 553-A5
1800 OXN 93033 552-J5
2000 VeCo 93033 553-A5
SAN FRANCESCA DR
5200 CMRL 93012 525-A2
SAN FRANCISCO AV
300 VEN 93004 472-F7
300 VEN 93004 492-F1
SAN GABRIEL AV
1700 VEN 93004 492-H4
SAN GABRIEL ST
1400 OJAI 93023 442-A6
3700 SIMI 93063 498-E1
SAN GORGONIO AV
1800 OXN 93030 522-J5
1800 OXN 93030 523-A5
SAN GUILLERMO RD
- VeCo - 366-L3
SANITATION RD
4900 CMRL 93012 524-J6
4900 CMRL 93012 525-A6
SAN JACINTO AV
2600 SIMI 93063 498-E1
SAN JACINTO ST
100 OXN 93030 523-A5
SAN JOAQUIN AV
1700 VEN 93004 492-H4

SAN JOAQUIN ST
5400 SIMI 93063 478-J7
5400 SIMI 93063 479-A7
SANJON RD
300 VEN 93001 491-D3
SAN JON BARRANCA RD
500 VeCo 93001 471-F5
500 VEN 93001 471-F7
500 VEN 93001 491-F1
SAN JOSE ST
2000 OXN 93030 523-A5
22000 Chat 91311 499-J4
SAN JUAN
100 FILM 93015 456-C6
SAN JUAN AV
3500 OXN 93033 552-H4
SAN JUAN ST
500 SPLA 93060 463-H6
SAN LUCAS AV
- THO 91320 555-E2
SAN LUIS AV
- VeCo 93012 554-E4
SAN LUIS ST
2000 OXN 93030 523-A5
3200 VEN 93003 491-H3
4000 THO 91320 555-E1
SAN MARCOS CT
3700 THO 91320 555-E1
SAN MARCOS ST
2200 VEN 93001 491-F3
2200 VEN 93003 491-F3
SAN MARINO AV
- VEN 93003 491-H2
SAN MARINO ST
1700 OXN 93033 552-G2
SAN MARINO OIL COMPANY RD
1300 VeCo 93015 465-J4
1300 VeCo 93015 466-A4
SAN MARTIN PL
600 THO 91360 526-C3
SAN MARTINEZ GRANDE CYN RD
28500 Cstc 91384 458-G1
N SAN MATEO AV
- VEN 93004 492-F1
300 VEN 93004 472-F7
S SAN MATEO AV
- VEN 93004 492-F2
SAN MATEO PL
1800 OXN 93033 553-A2
SAN MIGUEL AL
- VEN 93001 491-E2
SAN MIGUEL AV
- VeCo 93035 552-B4
SAN MIGUEL CIR
400 PHME 93041 552-E6
2600 THO 91360 526-C3
SAN MIGUEL DR
- VeCo 93010 494-D7
SAN MIGUEL WY
400 SPLA 93060 463-H5
SAN NICHOLAS ST
1600 VEN 93001 491-E2
2300 VEN 93003 491-E2
SAN NICOLAS AV
- VeCo 93035 552-B5
300 SPLA 93060 463-J5
SAN NICOLAS CIR
100 PHME 93041 552-E6
SAN NICOLAS CT
3700 THO 91320 555-E1
SAN ONOFRE DR
1700 CMRL 93012 495-B7
1700 CMRL 93012 525-C1
SAN PABLO ST
3300 VEN 93003 491-H2
SAN PEDRO ST
400 PHME 93041 552-E5
600 VEN 93001 491-E3
SAN RAFAEL AV
6200 CMRL 93012 525-C1
SAN RAFAEL ST
1400 OJAI 93023 442-A6
SAN RAFAEL WY
1200 CMRL 93012 525-C1
SAN RAMON WY
1200 OJAI 93023 442-A6
SAN REMO DR
1300 SIMI 93063 499-C3
SAN ROQUE AV
- VEN 93003 491-H2
SAN SEBASTIAN CT
- VeCo 93012 496-D7
SAN SEBASTIAN DR
1900 OXN 93035 552-A1
SAN SIMEON AV
3500 OXN 93033 552-J4
SAN SIMEON CT
1300 VEN 93003 492-C4
SAN SIMEON DR
800 THO 91320 526-A7
4200 OXN 93033 552-J4
SANTA ANA AV
100 VeCo 93035 552-A4
SANTA ANA BLVD
- VeCo 93022 451-A6
800 VeCo 93001 450-J6
800 VeCo 93022 450-J6

SANTA ANA RD
7700 VeCo 93001 460-J1
8300 VeCo 93001 461-A2
10400 VeCo 93001 450-E3
11000 VeCo 93001 451-A6
SANTA ANA ST
100 OJAI 93023 441-H7
SANTA ANA WY
- VeCo 93022 451-B6
SANTA ANITA CT
2100 CMRL 93010 494-D7
2100 VeCo 93010 494-D7
SANTA ANNA ST
100 SPLA 93060 464-A7
W SANTA ANNA ST
200 SPLA 93060 463-J7
200 SPLA 93060 464-A7
SANTA BARBARA AV
- VeCo 93012 554-D3
6700 VeCo 93001 459-C5
SANTA BARBARA CIR
400 THO 91320 555-F1
SANTA BARBARA ST
1600 VEN 93001 491-E2
E SANTA BARBARA ST
100 SPLA 93060 464-A6
W SANTA BARBARA ST
100 SPLA 93060 463-H7
100 SPLA 93060 464-A6
SANTA BELLA PL
23600 THO 91362 527-B4
SANTA CLARA AV
100 FILM 93015 456-A6
700 FILM 93015 455-J6
3000 OXN 93030 523-C2
3300 VeCo 93030 523-C2
3800 VeCo 93010 493-D7
3800 VeCo 93030 493-D7
SANTA CLARA ST
1200 SPLA 93060 464-C6
E SANTA CLARA ST
- VEN 93001 491-C2
W SANTA CLARA ST
- VEN 93001 491-B2
SANTA CREG LP
23600 SPLA 93060 473-J2
SANTA CRUZ AV
- VeCo 93035 552-B4
SANTA CRUZ CIR
400 PHME 93041 552-E6
SANTA CRUZ CT
3700 SIMI 93063 478-E7
SANTA CRUZ ST
500 SPLA 93060 464-A7
600 SPLA 93060 463-J7
700 SPLA 93060 473-J1
N SANTA CRUZ ST
- VEN 93001 491-E2
S SANTA CRUZ ST
- VEN 93001 491-E3
SANTA CRUZ WY
900 VeCo 93010 494-D6
SANTA FE AV
900 VEN 93004 492-H2
SANTA FELICIA CANYON FIRE RD
23600 VeCo 93040 367-E7
SANTA LUCIA AV
1800 OXN 93030 522-J5
1800 OXN 93030 523-A5
SANTA LUCIA ST
3700 SIMI 93063 478-E7
SANTA MARGARITA RD
8900 VEN 93004 492-H4
SANTA MARIA ST
700 SPLA 93060 473-J1
6200 VeCo 93063 499-B4
9300 VEN 93004 499-G2
E SANTA MARIA ST
100 SPLA 93060 464-C6
W SANTA MARIA ST
100 SPLA 93060 463-J7
100 SPLA 93060 464-A7
600 SPLA 93060 473-J1
SANTA MONICA AV
100 VeCo 93035 552-C6
SANTA MONICA CT
3800 THO 91320 555-E1
SANTA MONICA DR
200 VeCo 93035 552-B4
SANTA PAULA AV
- VeCo 93012 554-E4
100 VeCo 93035 552-B5
100 VeCo 93043 552-B5
7000 VeCo 93001 459-C4
SANTA PAULA FRWY Rt#-126
- SPLA - 463-J7
- SPLA - 464-D5
- SPLA - 473-F4
- VeCo - 473-F4
- VeCo - 492-D3
- VEN - 472-J7
- VEN - 473-B6
- VEN - 491-J4
- VEN - 492-D3
SANTA PAULA ST
700 VeCo 93015 465-G3
14600 VeCo 93060 463-G7
14900 VeCo 93060 473-E2

VENTURA CO.

INDEX

STREET Block City ZIP Pg-Grid

E SANTA PAULA ST
100 SPLA 93060 464-A5
W SANTA PAULA ST
100 SPLA 93060 463-J6
100 SPLA 93060 464-A6
SANTA PAULA CANYON RD
23600 VeCo 93040 458-A3
SANTA PAULA OJAI RD Rt#-150
4300 VeCo 93060 464-A1
4400 VeCo 93060 454-A7
4600 VeCo 93060 453-H4
12300 VeCo 93023 453-H4
SANTA ROSA AV
100 VeCo 93035 552-B5
SANTA ROSA DR
4100 VeCo 93021 496-A3
SANTA ROSA LP
400 SPLA 93060 473-J1
SANTA ROSA RD
4600 CMRL 93012 524-J3
5000 CMRL 93012 525-B2
6900 VeCo 93012 525-G1
7200 CMRL 93012 495-E7
7200 VeCo 93012 495-E7
10600 VeCo 93012 496-D7
N SANTA ROSA ST
- VEN 93001 491-E2
S SANTA ROSA ST
- VEN 93001 491-E2
SANTA SUSANA TR
8600 VeCo 93063 499-C4
SANTA SUSANA FIRE RD
23600 VeCo 93063 499-E4
SANTA SUSANA PASS RD
6600 SIMI 93063 499-G2
6700 VeCo 93063 499-D4
7600 Chat 91311 499-G2
SANTA TOMAS PL
3900 THO 91320 555-E1
SANTA YNEZ AV
2200 SIMI 93063 478-E7
2300 SIMI 93063 498-F1
SANTA YNEZ ST
1600 VEN 93001 491-E2
SANTEE CT
10000 VEN 93004 492-J3
SAN TELMO CIR
500 THO 91320 525-E7
500 THO 91320 555-E1
SANTI ST
23600 THO 91320 556-C1
SANTIAGO CT
2300 OXN 93030 523-B4
SANTIAGO ST
2900 THO 91362 557-C3
SANTINA ST
23600 Chat 91311 499-F7
SANTO DR
4900 VeCo 91377 557-G1
SANTO DOMINGO
- CMRL 93012 494-H7
- CMRL 93012 524-H1
SAN TROPEZ CIR
1700 OXN 93035 552-A1
SAN TROPEZ PL
23600 MRPK 93021 496-C4
SAN VINCENT CT
3600 THO 91320 555-F1
SAN VINCENT PL
3600 THO 91320 555-F1
SAN VINCENTE CIR
200 THO 91320 555-F1
SAN YSIDRO CT
1200 VEN 93003 472-D6
SAN YSIDRO ST
2200 CMRL 93010 494-G7
2300 VeCo 93010 494-G7
SAPPANWOOD AV
1400 THO 91320 526-A6
SAPPHIRE AV
500 VEN 93004 492-F3
2800 SIMI 93063 478-D7
SAPPHIRE CIR
900 VEN 93004 492-F3
SAPPHIRE DRAGON ST
1300 THO 91320 525-J5
1300 THO 91320 526-A5
SAPRA ST
1800 THO 91362 526-J5
1800 THO 91362 527-A5
SARA DR
23600 OXN 93030 522-J5
SARAH AV
200 MRPK 93021 496-E1
SARAH CT
2900 VeCo 91320 555-G1
SARALYN DR
9100 Chat 91311 499-E7
SARA LYNN RD
100 Chat 91311 499-E6
SARANAC ST
10200 VEN 93004 492-J2
SARATOGA AV
1100 VEN 93003 492-B4
SARATOGA ST
- FILM 93015 456-A5
700 OXN 93035 522-E7
1600 OXN 93035 552-E1
SARELDA RD
23800 WHil 91304 499-E7
SARGENT AV
2000 SIMI 93063 498-D2
SARGENT LN
6600 VEN 93003 492-D3
SARITA DR
100 OXN 93030 522-J6
SARNO CT
23600 MRPK 93021 496-C4
SASHA CT
2600 SIMI 93063 498-D1
2700 SIMI 93063 478-D7
SASPARILLA ST
6600 SIMI 93063 499-D2
SASSAFRAS WY
1300 VeCo 91377 527-H7
SATICOY AV
400 VeCo 93004 492-H1
400 VEN 93004 492-J1
1200 VEN 93004 493-A2
N SATICOY AV
100 VEN 93004 472-H7
100 VeCo 93004 472-H7
S SATICOY AV
- VeCo 93004 472-H7
- VEN 93004 472-H7
- VeCo 93004 492-H1
SATICOY ST
1000 SPLA 93060 464-C4
22000 CanP 91303 529-G4
22200 CanP 91307 529-G4
22800 LA 91304 529-F4
SATINWOOD AV
100 VeCo 91377 558-B2
SATURN AV
1200 CMRL 93010 524-F1
SAUL PL
300 VEN 93004 472-H6
SAUSALITO AV
6500 CanP 91307 529-J5
7600 LA 91304 529-J2
SAUSALITO DR
700 CMRL 93010 524-C1
SAVANNAH AV
1700 VEN 93004 492-H4
SAVIERS RD
1100 OXN 93033 522-G7
1100 OXN 93033 552-G3
SAVONA WY
500 VeCo 91377 557-G1
SAVOY CT
400 VeCo 91377 557-H2
SAWTELLE AV
100 VeCo 93035 552-C6
100 PHME 93041 552-C6
SAWTELLE CT
23600 SIMI 93065 497-F7
S SAWTOOTH CT
100 THO 91362 557-B2
SAWYER AV
1200 SIMI 93065 498-B4
SAXE CT
2100 THO 91360 526-F4
SAXON PL
1000 THO 91360 526-F6
SAY RD
1100 SPLA 93060 464-B3
SCANDIA AV
900 VEN 93004 492-J2
SCANNO DR
400 VeCo 91377 557-G2
SCARAB FIRE RD
23600 VeCo - 477-H3
23600 VeCo - 478-A2
23600 VeCo 93065 477-H3
SCARBOROUGH ST
200 THO 91361 556-F3
SCARBOROUGH PEAK DR
6900 CanP 91307 529-D5
SCARLET OAK AV
1200 THO 91360 526-H2
SCATTERWOOD LN
23600 SIMI 93065 497-G3
SCENIC DR
2200 SIMI 93065 497-E2
SCENICPARK ST
2200 THO 91362 527-A4
SCENIC WAY DR
800 VEN 93003 472-D6
SCHOENBORN ST
22200 LA 91304 529-E2
SCHOOL ST
2800 SIMI 93065 498-C2
SCHOOL CANYON RD
- VeCo 93001 471-C5
- VEN 93001 471-C5
SCHOOLCRAFT ST
22000 CanP 91303 529-J5
22300 CanP 91307 529-F6
SCHOOLHOUSE CIR
1600 THO 91362 527-C6
SCHOONER DR
1000 VeCo 93001 491-G6
1000 VEN 93001 491-G6
SCHOONER WK
3400 OXN 93035 522-B7
SCHUMAN PL
23600 VEN 93003 492-B7
SCHUMANN RD
23100 Chat 91311 499-G7
SCIENCE DR
- MRPK 93021 496-F1
SCIOTO CIR
1000 SIMI 93065 497-C5
SCOFIELD AV
3400 SIMI 93063 478-F6
SCOTER AV
2300 VEN 93003 492-E5
SCOTT AV
1800 VEN 93004 492-H4
SCOTT DR
3100 SIMI 93063 478-F6
SCOTT PL
2500 THO 91360 526-E4
SCOTT ST
100 PHME 93041 552-E6
SCOTTSDALE ST
9800 VEN 93004 492-H2
SCOTTYS TER
3100 SIMI 93063 478-F6
SCRIPPS CT
4700 VEN 93003 492-A1
SEABISCUIT PL
6000 MRPK 93021 476-A7
SEABORG AV
2800 VEN 93003 492-C7
2800 VeCo 93003 492-C7
SEABREEZE CT
1700 THO 91320 526-A5
SEABREEZE ST
- THO 91320 525-J5
- THO 91320 526-A5
SEABREEZE WY
5100 OXN 93035 521-J7
SEABURY CT
- THO 91320 555-J1
SEACLIFF CT
5700 VEN 93003 492-C4
SEACOVE CT
2500 PHME 93041 552-C2
SEACREST CT
23600 THO 91362 527-B2
SEADRIFT CT
2500 PHME 93041 552-C2
SEA ESTA DR
500 VEN 93003 491-J4
SEA ESTA PL
500 VEN 93003 491-J4
SEAFARER ST
1200 VEN 93001 491-F5
SEAFOAM CT
2500 PHME 93041 552-C2
SEAFOAM WY
2600 OXN 93035 552-A2
SEAGULL AV
2300 VEN 93003 492-E5
SEAHAWK ST
5900 VEN 93003 492-D5
6000 VeCo 93003 492-D5
SEAHORSE AV
2400 VEN 93001 491-F4
SEAHORSE CT
900 VEN 93001 491-F4
SEAHORSE WY
5000 OXN 93035 521-J7
SEAL CT
1100 VEN 93001 491-G5
SEALANE WY
4900 OXN 93035 521-J7
5100 OXN 93035 551-J1
SEAMIST CT
2500 PHME 93041 552-C2
SEAPORT DR
1100 OXN 93030 522-E7
SEASHELL AV
3100 VEN 93001 491-G5
SEASHORE CT
2500 PHME 93041 552-B2
SEASIDE CT
900 VEN 93001 491-F5
SEASIDE DR
2500 PHME 93041 552-C2
2700 OXN 93035 552-C2
2700 PHME 93035 552-C2
SEASPRAY WY
100 PHME 93041 552-E6
SEAVIEW AV
2900 VEN 93001 491-G5
SEAVIEW DR
5300 OXN 93035 521-H6
SEAVIEW ST
100 PHME 93041 552-E6
N SEAWARD AV
- VEN 93001 491-F2
- VEN 93003 491-F2
S SEAWARD AV
- VEN 93001 491-F3
- VEN 93003 491-F3
SEAWIND WY
600 PHME 93041 552-F7
SEBRING AV
2000 SIMI 93065 498-C2
SEBRING CT
2000 SIMI 93065 498-C2
SECKER DR
23600 WHil 91304 499-D6
SECO CT
2000 THO 91362 556-H2
SEDAN AV
6600 CanP 91307 529-G4
7600 LA 91304 529-G2
SEDGEWICK CT
7500 LA 91304 529-D4
SEDGEWORTH CT
600 SIMI 93065 527-C1
SEDGEWORTH PL
200 SIMI 93065 527-D1
SEELY PL
1100 SIMI 93065 497-H5
SEINE CT
5400 WLKV 91362 557-F5
SEITZ CT
15300 MRPK 93021 476-J5
15300 MRPK 93021 477-A5
SELBY CIR
1800 CMRL 93010 494-H7
SELF DEFENSE RD
- PHME 93043 552-C5
SEMINARY RD
4700 CMRL 93012 494-J6
SEMINOLE CIR
4800 SIMI 93063 478-H6
SEMINOLE LN
2300 VEN 93001 471-C6
SEMPLE ST
3500 SIMI 93063 498-E2
SEMRAD RD
6900 CanP 91307 529-E5
SENAN ST
3700 CMRL 93010 494-G7
SENECA PL
5100 SIMI 93063 478-J7
5400 SIMI 93063 479-A6
SENECA ST
- VEN 93001 471-C5
SENTINEL CIR
900 VEN 93003 472-C7
SEPTO ST
22000 Chat 91311 499-J5
SEQUAN CT
1400 CMRL 93010 524-D2
SEQUOIA AV
- VeCo 93003 492-D2
1400 SIMI 93063 498-D2
1400 SIMI 93065 498-D4
1400 VeCo 93063 498-D4
2400 SIMI 93063 478-D7
SEQUOIA CT
200 THO 91360 526-E7
SEQUOIA DR
1200 OXN 93033 553-B5
SEQUOIA ST
700 OXN 93033 552-H3
SERAPE PL
- CMRL 93010 494-F7
SERENA LN
4100 OXN 93033 553-C4
SERENA ST
5800 SIMI 93063 499-B1
SERENIDAD PL
- VeCo 93022 451-C5
SERENO AV
2600 VEN 93003 491-F4
SERENTO CIR
400 THO 91360 526-D3
SERRA DR
- FILM 93015 456-C6
SERRANO RD
11600 VeCo 90265 585-C5
SERRANO CANYON RD
- VeCo - 584-H7
- VeCo - 585-A6
SERVICE AREA RD
23600 VeCo 93063 498-J7
23600 VeCo 93063 499-A7
SESPE AV
- FILM 93015 456-A6
700 FILM 93015 455-H6
SESPE DR
1800 VEN 93004 492-H4
SESPE PL
700 FILM 93015 455-J6
700 FILM 93015 456-A6
SESPE ST
800 VeCo 93015 465-G2
S SESPE ST
1700 VeCo 93015 465-G4
SESPE LAND & WATER
100 FILM 93015 456-C6
100 VeCo 93015 456-C6
SESPE RIVER RD
- VeCo - 366-K6
- VeCo - 367-A5
SETON HALL AV
200 VEN 93003 492-A1
500 VEN 93003 492-A1
SEVENOAKS CT
4400 WLKV 91361 557-D6
SEVILLA ST
1300 CMRL 93010 524-D4
SEVILLE CT
3500 THO 91320 525-F7
SEXTANT AV
2500 PHME 93041 552-C2
SEXTON CANYON RD
2900 VeCo 93003 472-A4
2900 VeCo 93003 492-C1
2900 VEN 93003 472-B6
2900 VEN 93003 492-C1
SEYBOLT AV
1000 CMRL 93010 524-C2
SEYMOUR CREEK RD
- VeCo - 366-L1
- VeCo - 367-A1
SHAD CT
3100 SIMI 93063 478-E6
SHADE TREE LN
7000 CanP 91307 529-D5
SHADOW LN
23600 SIMI 93065 527-E1
SHADOWBEND WY
23600 SIMI 93065 497-F3
SHADOW BROOK LN
2900 THO 91361 557-C5
SHADOW CANYON PL
4800 THO 91362 557-F1
SHADOWGLEN CT
1400 THO 91361 556-J5
SHADOW HILL CIR
2900 THO 91360 526-B2
SHADOW HILLS RD
- CALB 91301 558-G7
SHADOW LAKE DR
500 THO 91360 526-D7
SHADOW MESA CIR
2900 THO 91360 526-B2
SHADOW OAK DR
10400 Chat 91311 499-J4
SHADOW OAKS PL
1400 THO 91362 526-J5
SHADOW RIDGE CT
7100 CanP 91307 529-D5
SHADOW SPRING PL
2200 THO 91361 557-B4
SHADOW VALLEY CIR
22200 Chat 91311 499-J1
SHADY LN
1100 FILM 93015 455-J4
N SHADY LN
100 OJAI 93023 442-A6
S SHADY LN
100 OJAI 93023 442-A7
SHADY BROOK CT
2400 THO 91362 527-A4
SHADY BROOK DR
1600 THO 91362 526-J4
1900 THO 91362 527-A4
SHADYCREEK DR
6000 AGRH 91301 558-A3
SHADY GROVE LN
100 THO 91361 556-F2
SHADY GROVE PL
25800 LACo 91302 558-J3
SHADY HILLS CT
200 SIMI 93065 497-E6
SHADY KNOLL CT
- MRPK 93021 496-F4
SHADY OAK LN
5500 SIMI 93063 499-A1
SHADY OAKS DR
400 THO 91320 526-A7
SHADY POINT DR
4100 MRPK 93021 496-F3
SHADYRIDGE DR
11100 MRPK 93021 496-B4
SHAKESPEARE PL
6900 MRPK 93021 477-A5
SHAKESPEARE WY
6500 VEN 93003 492-D1
SHALIMAR ST
2500 CMRL 93010 524-F1
SHALLOWS DR
800 OXN 93035 522-B7
SHAMROCK CT
100 THO 91320 556-A1
SHAMROCK DR
- VEN 93003 491-H2
400 VeCo 93003 491-H2
SHANNON AV
1700 VEN 93004 492-H4
SHANNON DR
2800 SIMI 93063 478-E7
SHARON DR
600 CMRL 93010 524-F2
SHARON LN
200 PHME 93041 552-D2
900 VEN 93001 491-E4
SHARP RD
2700 SIMI 93065 478-C6
2700 VeCo 93065 478-C6
SHASTA AV
- MRPK 93021 496-D1
400 OXN 93033 552-G4
SHASTA DR
100 OXN 93033 553-B5
600 SPLA 93060 463-H6
SHASTA PL
6000 CMRL 93012 525-B1
SHASTA ST
8100 VEN 93004 492-F3
SHASTA WY
2200 SIMI 93065 497-G2
SHAVER CT
900 SIMI 93065 497-F5
900 VeCo 93065 497-F5
SHAVER ST
8100 VEN 93004 492-F3
SHAW CT
1900 THO 91362 527-A6
SHAW WY
6500 VEN 93003 492-D3
SHAWNEE DR
- Chat 91311 499-J1
SHAWNEE LN
2300 VEN 93001 471-C6
SHAWNESS CT
1700 THO 91362 527-E6
SHEARWATER ST
6300 VEN 93003 492-D5
SHEFFIELD LN
200 FILM 93015 455-J6
SHEFFIELD PL
800 THO 91360 526-F7
SHEFFIELD ST
700 SPLA 93060 463-H6
SHEKELL RD
8000 VeCo 93021 476-A2
SHELBURN LN
1100 VEN 93001 491-E4
SHELBURNE LN
1000 SIMI 93065 497-D6
SHELBY LN
2000 SIMI 93065 498-A2
SHELDON DR
3600 VEN 93003 491-H2
SHELL RD
200 VeCo 93001 471-B4
400 SPLA 93060 473-J1
2200 VeCo 93060 473-J2
E SHELL RD
- VeCo 93001 471-C4
W SHELL RD
- VeCo 93001 471-C4
SHELLCREEK PL
2800 WLKV 91361 557-A7
SHELLEY CIR
6900 VEN 93003 492-E3
SHELL HARTMAN RD
- VeCo 93001 471-D3
SHELTER WOOD CT
2800 THO 91362 526-J3
SHELTONDALE AV
6200 WdHl 91367 529-D6
6300 CanP 91307 529-D6
SHENANDOAH AV
3200 SIMI 93063 498-D3
SHENANDOAH ST
400 THO 91360 526-D3
4700 VEN 93003 492-B4
SHEPHERD DR E
3100 CMRL 93010 524-F1
SHEPPARD RD
100 SPLA 93060 463-H7
SHERBORNE ST
2100 CMRL 93010 524-E1
SHERGRA PL
3300 SIMI 93063 498-D1
SHERI DR
3100 SIMI 93063 478-E6
SHERIDAN CT
2000 SIMI 93065 498-A2
SHERIDAN WY
400 VEN 93001 491-B1
500 VEN 93001 471-B7
SHERMAN AV
200 MRPK 93021 496-E1
SHERMAN PL
23100 CanP 91307 529-G5
SHERMAN ST
2000 SIMI 93065 498-A2
SHERMAN WY
22000 CanP 91303 529-G5
22300 CanP 91307 529-F5
SHERWIN AV
2600 VEN 93003 492-E6
SHERWOOD CT
300 THO 91361 556-F2
SHERWOOD DR
2400 VEN 93001 491-F2
SHERWOOD RD NW
800 VeCo 93023 451-C3
SHERWOOD WY
500 OXN 93033 552-G5
SHETLAND PL
1500 THO 91362 527-D6
SHIELDS CT
2700 THO 91360 526-E3
SHIELLS DR
600 FILM 93015 456-A5
SHIELLS CANYON
- VeCo 93015 466-E2
- VeCo 93021 466-E2
SHILOH WY
5200 VEN 93003 492-B4
SHIPPEE LN
1100 VeCo 93023 442-D5
SHIPSIDE RD
- PHME 93043 552-D5
SHIRLEY DR
2800 THO 91320 525-H7
2900 VeCo 91320 525-H7
SHIRLEY ST
1700 CMRL 93010 524-D4
SHOAL CREEK CT
2100 SIMI 93065 497-C6
SHOEMAKER LN
1900 THO 91320 525-J7
1900 THO 91320 526-A7
SHOKAT DR
700 VeCo 93023 450-J2
700 VeCo 93023 451-A2
SHOOTINGSTAR LN
23600 SIMI 93065 497-A1
SHOPPING LN
4200 SIMI 93063 498-F2
SHORE DR
1000 VEN 93001 491-E4
SHORELINE DR
- VEN 93001 491-B3
SHORELINE ST
1500 CMRL 93010 524-D2
SHORELINE WY
5000 OXN 93035 551-J1
5000 OXN 93035 552-A1
SHOREVIEW CIR
2800 THO 91361 557-C6
SHOREVIEW DR
400 PHME 93041 552-E6
3300 WLKV 91361 557-C7
SHORT ST
- VeCo 93042 583-E4
- VeCo 93022 451-B7
SHOSHONE AV
11300 Chat 91311 499-J1
SHOSHONE ST
- VEN 93001 471-C6
5500 SIMI 93063 479-A7
SHOUP AV
6100 WdHl 91367 529-J7
6400 CanP 91307 529-J4
7600 LA 91304 529-J4
9300 Chat 91311 499-J6
SHREVE AV
2200 SIMI 93063 499-C1
SHREWSBURY CIR
24300 CanP 91307 529-D5
SHROPSHIRE CT
4100 WLKV 91361 557-D6
SHRUBWOOD CIR
2600 SIMI 93065 498-C1
2700 SIMI 93065 478-C7
SHUNK RD
1700 SIMI 93063 499-B2
E SIBLEY ST
6400 SIMI 93063 499-C2
SIDEWINDER DR
- VeCo 93041 583-H3
SIDLEE ST
- THO 91360 526-F5
E SIDLEE ST
- THO 91360 526-F4
W SIDLEE ST
- THO 91360 526-E4
SIDNEY LN
500 VEN 93003 492-D1
SIDONIA AV
700 VEN 93003 491-H4
SIENA CT
23600 MRPK 93021 496-C5
SIENNA LN
1000 SIMI 93065 478-A7
1000 SIMI 93065 498-A1
SIENNA WY
5500 WLKV 91362 557-F5
SIERRA AV
100 MRPK 93021 496-D1
SIERRA CT
1200 VeCo 93023 451-B1
SIERRA DR
300 VEN 93003 491-H2
E SIERRA DR
3300 THO 91362 557-C3
W SIERRA DR
2700 THO 91362 557-B2
SIERRA PL
1900 OXN 93033 553-A3
SIERRA RD
100 OJAI 93023 441-G7
200 VeCo 93023 441-G7
SIERRA WY
2100 OXN 93033 553-B2
SIERRA HEIGHTS CT
400 THO 91320 555-G3
SIERRA MADRE CT
3700 SIMI 93063 478-E7
SIERRA MADRE DR
1500 CMRL 93010 524-F1
SIERRA MESA DR
1800 CMRL 93010 494-C7
1800 CMRL 93010 524-C1
SIERRA PASS PL
11200 Chat 91311 499-J2
SIERRA VISTA AV
200 FILM 93015 455-H6
SIESTA AV
100 THO 91360 526-E4
SIESTA CIR
2300 THO 91360 526-E4
SIESTA WY
3400 VeCo 93033 553-D5
SIGNAL ST
100 OJAI 93023 441-H6
S SIGNAL ST
100 OJAI 93023 441-H7
SIKORSKY ST
6000 VEN 93003 492-D6
SILAS AV
100 THO 91320 555-H2
100 VeCo 91320 555-H2
SILAS LN
200 THO 91320 555-H2
SILENTBROOK WY
1600 SIMI 93065 497-G3
SILKFIELD CT
- VeCo 91361 556-D7
SILK OAK AV
2800 THO 91362 527-C3
SILVERADO DR
1700 THO 91360 496-J7
SILVER CLOUD ST
700 THO 91360 526-C2
SILVER CREEK RD
28900 Ago 91301 558-B7
SILVER CREEK ST
12900 MRPK 93021 496-E3
SILVERCREST ST
11800 MRPK 93021 496-C4
SILVER FERN CT
400 SIMI 93065 497-E6
SILVER LAKE CT
400 SIMI 93065 497-E6
SILVER MAPLE CIR
3100 THO 91360 526-H2
SILVER MOSS CT
400 SIMI 93065 497-E6
SILVER SPRING DR
2100 THO 91361 557-A4
SILVER SPUR CT
1000 VeCo 93023 451-C3
3200 THO 91360 526-C2
SILVER SPUR LN
- VeCo 91307 529-A5
SILVER SPUR ST
1700 VeCo 93023 451-C3
SILVER VALLEY AV
5600 AGRH 91301 557-J5
SILVERWHEEL PL
500 THO 91320 555-H3
SILVERWOOD ST
1300 SIMI 93065 497-H5
SIMI AV
100 VeCo 93035 552-B5
SIMI ST
1200 VeCo 93015 465-H3
SIMI HILLS LN
2600 SIMI 93063 478-H7
SIMI VILLAGE DR
100 SIMI 93065 497-F3
SIMON WY
- VeCo 93030 492-J7
500 VeCo 93030 493-A7
700 VeCo 93030 523-A1
SIMPSON DR
4300 OXN 93033 553-A4
SIMPSON ST
200 VEN 93001 491-C1
E SIMPSON ST
- VEN 93001 491-B1
W SIMPSON ST
- VEN 93001 491-B1
200 VEN 93001 471-B7
SIMSBURY CT
1900 THO 91360 526-C5
SINALOA RD
300 SIMI 93065 497-G5
600 VeCo 93065 497-G5
SINALOA VILLA
400 SIMI 93065 497-G3
SINGLETREE LN
6700 VeCo 91377 528-A7
SIOUX AV
2800 VEN 93001 471-C5
SIOUX CT
3000 SIMI 93063 478-J7
SIOUX DR
22000 Chat 91311 499-J1
SIR GEORGE CT
700 MRPK 93021 476-F7
SIRIUS CIR
2600 THO 91360 526-F3
SIRIUS ST
2100 THO 91360 526-E3
SISAR RD
12000 VeCo - 366-L7
12000 VeCo 93023 366-L7
13000 VeCo 93023 453-C1
SI SE PUEDA
10200 VEN 93004 492-J3
10200 VEN 93004 493-A3
SISKIN CT
400 SIMI 93065 497-D2
SISKIN PL
400 SIMI 93065 497-D2
SISKIYOU ST
8100 VEN 93004 472-F7
8100 VEN 93004 492-F1
SITKA AV
1500 SIMI 93063 498-D3
SITTING BULL PL
6000 SIMI 93063 479-A7
SIX OAK CT
2400 SIMI 93063 499-A1
SKAGWAY ST
3400 SIMI 93063 498-D2
SKEEL DR
800 CMRL 93010 524-C2
SKELTON CANYON CIR
3800 THO 91362 557-C1
SKIDMORE CT
4500 MRPK 93021 496-F2
SKINNER CT
2100 THO 91362 556-H2
SKUNK RANCH RD
23600 OJAI 93023 451-H1
23600 VeCo 93023 451-H1
SKY CT
3100 SIMI 93063 478-E6
SKYBROOK CT
4200 MRPK 93021 496-B2
SKYCREST CT
800 VEN 93003 472-C7
SKYFLOWER LN
23600 SIMI 93065 497-A1
SKYGLEN CT
4400 MRPK 93021 496-D2
SKY HIGH DR
300 VeCo 93001 460-J4
N SKYLARK CT
4300 MRPK 93021 496-E3
SKYLINE DR
700 SPLA 93060 463-H6
23600 VeCo 93063 498-J7
23600 VeCo 93063 528-H1
N SKYLINE DR
100 THO 91362 557-A2
S SKYLINE DR
- THO 91362 557-A3
100 THO 91361 557-A3
100 THO 91361 556-J3
SKYLINE RD
500 VEN 93003 492-B1
600 VEN 93003 472-B7
8900 VeCo 93021 476-C1
SKYRIDGE CT
1600 THO 91320 556-A2
SKY RIDGE LN
5300 VeCo 91377 527-G7
SKYVIEW TER
6200 VEN 93003 472-C7
SKYVIEW WY
5700 AGRH 91301 558-A4
SKYWALKER DR
4000 VeCo 93066 493-F3
SKYWAY DR
200 CMRL 93010 523-J5
200 CMRL 93010 524-A5
SLATER TER
9200 Chat 91311 499-F7
SLEEPY HOLLOW ST
2900 SIMI 93065 498-D4
SLEEPY WIND ST
12900 MRPK 93021 496-E3
SLICERS CIR
5600 AGRH 91301 557-G5
SMETANA CT
600 VEN 93003 492-B7
SMETANA ST
600 VEN 93003 492-B7
SMITH RD
6500 SIMI 93063 499-C3
23100 Chat 91311 499-G7
SMITH ST
200 OXN 93033 552-G5
5100 VEN 93003 492-B1
SMITH CANYON RD
900 VeCo 93015 457-F7
900 VeCo 93040 457-F7
SMOKETREE AV
- VeCo 91377 558-A2
SMOKETREE WY
23600 SIMI 93065 527-E1
SMOKEWOOD CT
1900 THO 91362 526-J3
1900 THO 91362 527-A3
SMOKEY RIDGE AV
1800 THO 91362 527-G6
SNIPE AV
1200 VEN 93003 492-C4
SNIPE WK
600 OXN 93035 522-E6
SNOW AV
1900 OXN 93030 522-J3
SNOW CT
1000 VEN 93001 471-B7
SNOWBERRY CT
2000 SIMI 93065 498-J2
SNOW CREEK AV
5200 SIMI 93063 498-J2
SNOWPEAK DR
32400 WLKV 91361 557-B7
SOBRE COLINAS PL
400 CMRL 93012 524-J3
SOCORRO WY
1700 OXN 93030 522-J4
1700 OXN 93030 523-A4
SOCRATES AV
2000 SIMI 93065 497-F2
SOFTWIND WY
5400 AGRH 91301 557-J5
5400 AGRH 91301 558-A5
SOJKA DR
2800 SIMI 93065 498-C1
3000 SIMI 93063 498-C1
SOLANO DR
2000 CMRL 93012 495-D7
SOLANO ST
7800 VEN 93004 492-F1
SOLANO WY
2200 OXN 93033 553-B3
SOLANO VERDE DR
7000 VeCo 93066 475-A3
SOLAR DR
1800 OXN 93030 523-B3
SOLIMAR BEACH RD
2800 VeCo 93001 470-D4
SOLWAY CT
2300 THO 91362 527-A3
SOMERSET CIR
200 THO 91360 526-E6
SOMIS RD Rt#-34
2400 CMRL 93010 494-J6
2400 VeCo 93010 494-J6
2600 VeCo 93010 495-A5
2600 VeCo 93066 495-A5
SOMIS ST
- VeCo 93012 554-E4
SONATA WY
23600 SIMI 93065 527-D1
SONIA DR
- OXN 93030 522-J4
SONOMA CT
400 VEN 93004 492-E1
2100 THO 91362 526-J4
SONOMA LN
100 SPLA 93060 464-A6
SONOMA PL
22000 Chat 91311 499-J6
SONOMA ST
7800 VEN 93004 492-E1
SONOMA WY
500 OXN 93033 552-F5
SONORA CT
6700 VEN 93003 472-D6
SONORA DR
300 CMRL 93010 524-D4
SOPHIA CT
1500 OXN 93030 522-E4
SOPHIA DR
1600 OXN 93030 522-E3
SOPHOMORE CT
15700 MRPK 93021 477-A5
SORA ST
6500 VEN 93003 492-D4
SORORITY LN
23800 WHil 91304 499-E7
SORREL ST
1400 SIMI 93065 497-H3
1800 CMRL 93010 524-D
SORRELWOOD CT
800 THO 91361 557-A4
SORTINO CT
23600 MRPK 93021 496-C4
SOSNA CT
15300 MRPK 93021 476-J5
SOULE PARK DR
1100 OJAI 93023 442-A
1100 OJAI 93023 452-A
SOUSA RD
5100 VEN 93003 492-B
SOUTH DR
6400 VEN 93003 492-D
N SOUTH BANK RD
3800 VeCo 93030 492-J5
SOUTHBY DR
7500 LA 91304 529-D
SOUTHCREST PL
- SIMI 93065 497-E
SOUTHERN HILLS DR
2200 OXN 93030 522-E
SOUTHERN HILLS PL
1700 THO 91362 527-E
SOUTHHAMPTON RD
3800 MRPK 93021 496-F
SOUTH MOUNTAIN RD
400 SPLA 93060 464-D
2100 VeCo 93015 465-A
12300 VeCo 93060 465-A
16500 VeCo 93060 474-A
16700 VeCo 93066 474-A
17900 VeCo 93060 464-G
17900 VeCo 93066 464-G
20000 VeCo 93066 465-A
SOUTHPORT DR
1100 THO 91361 557-A
SOUTHRIDGE DR
300 VeCo 91377 558-A
SOUTH RIM ST
5000 THO 91362 527-F
SOUTHSHORE PL
32500 WLKV 91361 557-B
SOUTHVIEW CIR
6100 VEN 93003 472-C
SOUTHWICK ST
600 SPLA 93060 463-H
SOUTHWIND CIR
1300 THO 91361 557-B
SPALDING DR
100 VeCo 93015 465-D
SPALDING ST
600 THO 91360 526-G
SPANISH GATE DR
3700 THO 91320 525-F

STREET
Block City ZIP Pg-Grid

SPANISH MOSS PL
- CMRL 93010 524-A2
SPANISH OAK LN
5400 VeCo 91377 557-J1
SPARKMAN AV
1200 CMRL 93010 524-D1
SPARKS CT
1900 SIMI 93065 498-A4
SPARROW DR
- VeCo 93041 583-G2
SPARROW ST
6000 VEN 93003 492-C4
SPARROWHAWK LN
100 VeCo 91377 557-J3
SPARTA CT
2100 SIMI 93065 497-F2
SPECK LN
2100 THO 91320 555-J2
2100 THO 91320 556-A2
SPECTRUM CIR
500 OXN 93030 523-D5
SPENCE ST
1600 SIMI 93065 497-J2
SPENCER CT
25900 LACo 91302 558-J3
SPENSER LN
700 VEN 93003 492-D2
SPERRY AV
1700 VeCo 93003 492-C6
1700 VEN 93003 492-C6
SPICEWOOD CT
23600 SIMI 93063 498-E4
SPINDLEWOOD AV
200 CMRL 93012 524-H4
SPINDLEWOOD CT
4300 CMRL 93012 524-H4
SPINDRIFT CT
5300 CMRL 93012 525-A1
SPINNAKER AV
2400 PHME 93041 552-C2
SPINNAKER DR
1100 VEN 93001 491-F7
SPINWOOD LN
23600 SIMI 93065 497-A2
SPIRES ST
23200 LA 91304 529-F3
SPIRITLAKE CT
23600 SIMI 93063 479-A6
SPLIT ROCK LN
5300 VeCo 91377 527-G7
S P MILLING RD
500 VeCo 93001 471-A7
500 VEN 93001 471-A7
500 VEN 93001 491-A1
SPRING CT
7200 CanP 91307 529-F5
SPRING RD
100 MRPK 93021 496-F2
SPRING ST
100 VeCo 93001 461-C7
500 VeCo 93022 451-B7
600 VeCo 93022 461-B1
7600 VeCo 93021 476-D4
SPRING BREEZE CT
700 SIMI 93065 497-E6
SPRINGBROOK CT
23600 THO 91362 527-B2
SPRINGBROOK ST
23600 THO 91362 527-B2
SPRING CANYON PL
3000 THO 91320 555-G4
SPRING CREEK CT
12500 MRPK 93021 496-D3
SPRING CREEK RD
12300 MRPK 93021 496-D3
SPRINGDALE CT
- THO 91360 526-F2
SPRINGFIELD AV
600 VEN 93004 492-G2
E SPRINGFIELD ST
4200 SIMI 93063 478-F6
N SPRINGFIELD ST
3000 SIMI 93063 478-F7
SPRING FOREST LN
4000 THO 91362 557-D1
SPRINGGATE LN
1700 SIMI 93065 497-F3
SPRINGHAVEN AV
- THO 91320 556-A1
SPRING HILL CT
4800 THO 91362 557-F1
SPRING MEADOW AV
3200 THO 91360 526-F2
SPRINGMIST LN
23600 SIMI 93065 497-A1
SPRINGTIME LN
3900 MRPK 93021 496-E4
SPRINGVILLE RD
500 CMRL 93010 524-D5
3200 OXN 93030 523-E3
3200 VeCo 93030 523-E3
SPRING WOOD ST
600 THO 91320 556-C2
SPRUCE CIR
23600 SIMI 93065 497-F7
SPRUCE DR
100 OXN 93033 552-H5
SPRUCE ST
200 OXN 93033 552-F3

SPRUCE HILL CT
800 THO 91320 556-C2
SPRUCE MEADOW PL
400 THO 91362 557-D2
SPRUCEWOOD AV
300 VeCo 91377 558-A1
SPUR DR
100 OXN 93030 522-G1
SPURWOOD LN
23600 SIMI 93065 497-A2
SPYGLASS LN
500 THO 91320 556-D1
SPYGLASS TR
1800 OXN 93030 522-D3
SPYGLASS TR W
2400 OXN 93030 522-D2
SPYGLASS WY
1400 CMRL 93012 525-A1
SQUAW FLAT RD
- VeCo - 367-C5
- VeCo 93015 367-C5
SQUIRES DR
4500 OXN 93033 552-H5
SQUIRREL LN
1600 VEN 93003 492-E4
STABEN CT
100 SPLA 93060 464-A6
STABER RD
- VeCo - 555-H7
- VeCo 91361 585-J1
- VeCo 91361 586-A1
23600 VeCo 91361 555-H7
STACY DR
2800 SIMI 93063 478-E7
STACY LN
2000 CMRL 93012 495-B7
STADIUM AV
- VEN 93003 492-A2
STAFFORD RD
2200 VeCo 91361 556-F7
W STAFFORD RD
2200 VeCo 91361 556-D7
2200 VeCo 91361 586-D1
E STAGECOACH RD
- VeCo 91307 528-J3
- VeCo 91307 529-A4
STAGG ST
22100 LA 91304 529-D3
STALLION CT
1000 VeCo 93010 494-C6
N STALLION RD
- VeCo 91307 528-J4
STANFORD AV
- OXN 93030 522-G2
STANFORD DR
900 SIMI 93065 498-A4
STANFORD ST
200 SPLA 93060 464-B6
5500 VEN 93003 492-B2
23600 OXN 93030 522-G2
E STANFORD ST
14600 MRPK 93021 476-H6
STANHOPE CT
23600 VeCo 91361 556-F6
STANISLAUS AV
- VEN 93004 492-F1
2700 SIMI 93063 478-J7
2700 SIMI 93063 498-J1
STANLEY AV
- VEN 93001 471-B6
STANLEY CT
15300 MRPK 93021 476-J5
STANLEY PARK RD
- VeCo - 366-G8
- VeCo 93013 366-G8
STANTON CT
3600 SIMI 93063 478-E7
STANWOOD RD
23600 SIMI 93065 497-G7
STARBRIGHT CT
600 SIMI 93065 527-C2
STARDUST DR
100 SIMI 93065 497-E2
STARFIRE AV
3100 THO 91360 526-D2
STARFISH DR
4500 OXN 93035 552-A2
STARFISH LN
11800 VeCo 90265 625-F4
STARGAZE PL
400 SIMI 93065 497-E2
STARKLAND AV
8300 LA 91304 529-E2
STARLIGHT LN
24500 CanP 91307 529-D4
STARLING AV
2900 THO 91360 526-F3
STARPINE WY
1600 SIMI 93065 497-A2
STARR LN
2600 SIMI 93063 478-J7
2600 SIMI 93063 498-J1
STARSHINE ST
3500 THO 91360 526-H2
STARSTONE CT
100 SIMI 93065 497-J6
STARWOOD CT
1200 THO 91362 527-G7
STATHAM BLVD
1700 OXN 93033 552-J1

STATHAM PKWY
900 OXN 93033 552-H2
STAUNTON ST
400 CMRL 93010 524-F2
STEARMAN ST
500 CMRL 93010 524-A5
STEARNS ST
1700 SIMI 93063 498-J1
2600 SIMI 93063 478-J7
N STECKEL DR
100 SPLA 93060 463-J6
400 VeCo 93060 463-J6
S STECKEL DR
100 SPLA 93060 463-J6
200 SPLA 93060 464-A7
STEFFEN LN
800 VeCo 93063 499-B4
STEINBECK ST
6800 VEN 93003 492-D1
STELL DR
3800 SIMI 93063 478-F6
STELLAR DR
1100 OXN 93033 522-J7
1100 OXN 93033 552-J1
STEPHANIE WY
6000 SIMI 93063 499-B3
STEPHEN LN
8300 LA 91304 529-F2
STEPHENS ST
500 FILM 93015 456-A5
STEPHLY RD
1300 VeCo 93015 367-B7
1300 VeCo 93015 455-H1
STERLING AV
800 VEN 93004 492-F3
STERLING DR
1200 THO 91360 526-F6
STERLING CENTER DR
5300 WLKV 91361 557-E6
STERLING HILLS DR
- CMRL 93010 493-H6
STERLING OAKS CT
1300 VeCo 91377 527-G7
STERLINGVIEW DR
4100 MRPK 93021 496-B3
STERN CT
1000 OXN 93035 522-D7
STERN LN
900 OXN 93035 522-D7
STETSON CT
600 THO 91360 526-D4
STEVENS CIR
6900 VEN 93003 492-E3
STEVENS WY
9000 LA 91304 499-E7
9000 WHil 91304 499-E7
STILES AV
3100 CMRL 93010 524-F1
STILLWATER CT
10300 VEN 93004 492-J2
STILMAN CT
2100 SIMI 93063 498-J2
STINSON ST
500 CMRL 93010 524-A5
2100 SIMI 93065 498-A4
N STIRRUP LN
- VeCo 91307 529-B3
STOCK AV
1500 VEN 93004 493-A2
STOCKBRIDGE LN
100 VeCo 93023 441-E7
STOCKTON AV
- VEN 93004 492-F1
STOCKTON RD
7900 VeCo 93021 475-H3
7900 VeCo 93066 475-E7
STODDARD AV
1400 THO 91360 526-D5
E STOKE CT
6100 SIMI 93063 499-B1
STONE PL
8000 VEN 93004 492-F3
STONE ST
900 VeCo 93015 455-G4
7800 VEN 93004 492-F3
STONEBROOK ST
100 SIMI 93065 497-F6
STONE CREEK DR
1200 OXN 93030 522-E1
STONECREST DR
5700 AGRH 91301 557-H4
STONECROFT CT
2000 THO 91361 557-A5
STONEGATE DR
24500 LA 91304 529-D4
STONEGATE RD
1000 SPLA 93060 464-A2
STONEHAVEN LN
300 VeCo 91377 557-J2
STONEHEDGE DR
500 FILM 93015 456-A5
STONEHILL CIR
1900 THO 91360 526-C4
STONEMAN ST
1800 SIMI 93065 478-A7
STONE MEADOW DR
1300 CMRL 93010 524-E1
STONE MOUNTAIN LN
5200 THO 91362 527-G6

STONEPINE CT
1400 THO 91360 526-H2
STONERIVER CT
3400 THO 91360 557-C2
STONESGATE ST
1700 THO 91361 556-J5
1800 THO 91361 557-A5
STONESHEAD CT
1000 THO 91361 556-J5
STONETREE ST
4200 CMRL 93012 524-H4
STONEWALL CIR
1200 THO 91361 557-B5
STONEWOOD ST
2900 SIMI 93063 478-C7
STONEYBROOK LN
1100 THO 91361 557-C5
STONEYGLEN CT
4400 MRPK 93021 496-D3
STONEY PEAK CT
500 SIMI 93065 497-D2
STONEY RUN LN
23600 SIMI 93065 497-A2
STONEYVIEW LN
6400 SIMI 93063 499-C3
STORAGE RD
- VeCo 93042 583-F5
STORK ST
6400 VEN 93003 492-D5
STORM CLOUD ST
3200 THO 91360 526-C2
STORMCROFT CT
2300 THO 91361 557-B5
STOW ST
1500 SIMI 93063 499-A1
STRANDWAY CT
1600 THO 91361 556-J6
STRATFORD AV
200 VEN 93003 492-B2
STRATFORD ST
- THO 91360 526-F5
STRATHEARN PL
- SIMI 93065 497-E2
STRATHERN ST
22000 LA 91304 529-E3
STRATHMORE DR
3100 VEN 93003 491-H4
STRAUSS DR
500 THO 91320 525-H7
500 THO 91320 555-H1
800 VEN 93003 492-B7
STRAVINSKY LN
1000 VEN 93003 492-A7
STRAWBERRY LN
500 OXN 93030 522-F1
STRAWBERRY HILL DR
29600 AGRH 91301 557-J5
STRAWBERRY HILL RD
1300 THO 91360 526-G6
STRICKLAND DR
4700 VeCo 93030 493-A4
STRONG CT
400 VeCo 93003 491-J1
400 VEN 93003 491-J1
STROUBE ST
- VeCo 93030 522-H1
100 OXN 93030 522-H1
100 VeCo 93030 492-H7
100 OXN 93030 492-H7
1000 VeCo 93030 523-A2
STUART CIR
900 THO 91362 526-J6
STUART CT
400 OJAI 93023 451-F1
STUART LN
600 VEN 93003 492-D2
STUDENT ST
4600 VEN 93003 492-A3
STUDIO RD
7100 VeCo 93063 499-E5
STUMP RD
100 VeCo 93015 466-B2
STURGIS RD
2200 OXN 93030 523-B5
3400 VeCo 93030 523-E5
STYLES ST
22500 WdHl 91367 529-F7
SUBIDA CIR
3100 VeCo 93012 496-D6
SUBROCK CIR
- VeCo 93041 583-H3
SUDARIO CT
1000 VeCo 93010 494-C6
SUE WY
200 VeCo 93030 493-A4
N SUEDE AV
2000 SIMI 93063 499-B2
SUENO CT
1000 VeCo 93010 494-B5
SUE SUE LN
200 CMRL 93010 524-C4
SUFFOLK AV
1200 THO 91360 526-F6
SUFFOLK CT
4700 VEN 93003 492-A1
SUGAR MAPLE CT
4400 MRPK 93021 496-E3
SUGARPINE CT
500 THO 91320 556-D2

SULLIVAN ST
4500 VEN 93003 492-A4
SULPHUR CANYON
23600 VeCo 93001 451-H7
23600 VeCo 93001 461-J1
SULPHUR CASCADE
23600 VeCo 93060 453-G2
SULPHUR MOUNTAIN RD
- VeCo 93001 461-B2
6000 VeCo 93060 453-D3
6700 VeCo 93023 452-J2
6700 VeCo 93060 453-A4
9300 VeCo 93023 451-H6
12200 VeCo 93023 461-C2
SULPHUR SPRINGS ST
4600 SIMI 93063 478-G7
SUMAC DR
2000 VeCo 93023 451-C4
SUMAC LN
11000 VeCo 93012 526-A1
11300 VeCo 93012 496-B7
SUMMER ST
100 OJAI 93023 441-H6
12600 MRPK 93021 496-D3
SUMMER CLOUD DR
1700 THO 91362 526-J2
1700 THO 91362 527-A2
SUMMERFIELD ST
- THO 91360 526-F3
1400 CMRL 93012 525-A1
3000 CMRL 93012 495-A7
SUMMERGLEN CT
4400 MRPK 93021 496-C2
SUMMERHILL CT
6600 VeCo 91377 528-A7
SUMMER PARK CT
2200 THO 91362 527-A4
SUMMERSHADE LN
4000 MRPK 93021 496-F3
SUMMERSHORE LN
3600 WLKV 91361 557-C7
SUMMERTIME AV
23600 SIMI 93065 497-E3
SUMMER TREE CT
23600 SIMI 93065 498-A5
SUMMER VIEW CIR
10600 VeCo 93012 495-J7
10600 VeCo 93012 496-A7
SUMMERWOOD AV
- SIMI 93063 498-H1
SUMMIT AV
4700 SIMI 93063 478-H5
SUMMIT CIR
2900 VeCo 93012 496-E6
SUMMIT DR
400 VEN 93001 491-C1
23500 WHil 91304 499-E6
SUMMIT TR
100 VeCo 93023 453-C1
SUMMIT KNOLL CT
400 VeCo 91377 558-B1
N SUMMIT RIDGE CIR
22300 Chat 91311 499-H6
S SUMMIT RIDGE CIR
22300 Chat 91311 499-H6
SUMMIT RIDGE CT
3900 THO 91362 557-C1
SUMMIT VIEW DR
4900 THO 91362 557-E1
SUMMIT VUE DR
- WdHl 91367 529-J7
SUMMIT VUE DR E
- WdHl 91367 529-J7
SUMMIT VUE DR N
- WdHl 91367 529-J7
SUMTER CT
1800 THO 91360 526-D5
SUNBEAM LN
23600 SIMI 93065 497-A2
SUN BONNET ST
300 SIMI 93065 527-D2
SUNBURST PL
3000 THO 91360 526-H2
SUN CIRCLE CT
300 SIMI 93065 497-E7
SUNDANCE ST
300 THO 91360 526-D2
SUNDANCE WY
1400 CMRL 93012 525-A1
SUNDOWN RD
100 VeCo 91361 556-G2
SUNER CIR
2000 CMRL 93010 494-H7
SUNFIELD CT
300 THO 91362 557-F2
SUNFISH WY
500 PHME 93041 552-F7
SUNFLOWER ST
2900 THO 91360 526-D3
10500 VEN 93004 493-A2
SUNGLOW AV
3200 SIMI 93063 478-F6
SUNGROVE DR
700 CMRL 93010 524-C2
SUNKIST CIR
1800 OXN 93033 552-H1
SUNKIST DR
1900 OXN 93033 552-H1
SUNKIST ST
400 PHME 93041 552-E3

N SUNLAND AV
7000 VeCo 93001 459-C4
SUNLIGHT ST
23600 SIMI 93063 478-J6
SUNLOFT LN
23600 SIMI 93065 497-A1
SUNNY LN
13300 VeCo 93012 496-E6
SUNNY ST
300 SPLA 93060 464-A7
SUNNY BROOK CT
400 VeCo 91377 558-B1
SUNNYCREST AV
1000 VEN 93003 472-C6
SUNNYCREST DR
6000 VeCo 91377 558-A1
SUNNYDALE AV
1500 SIMI 93065 497-J5
1700 SIMI 93065 498-A6
SUNNYDALE CT
1600 SIMI 93065 497-J5
SUNNYGLEN AV
1100 OJAI 93023 442-A6
SUNNYGLEN DR
12300 MRPK 93021 496-D3
SUNNYHILL CT
6300 VEN 93003 472-C7
SUNNYHILL ST
4400 THO 91362 527-D7
SUNNY POINT ST
23600 THO 91362 527-A2
SUNNYRIDGE DR
30000 AGRH 91301 557-H4
SUNNYSLOPE PL
13300 MRPK 93021 496-E4
SUNNYVISTA AV
- VeCo 91377 558-A3
SUNNY WAY DR
- VEN 93001 471-B7
SUNOAK PL
300 THO 91320 556-A2
SUN RANCH CT
22100 Chat 91311 499-J2
SUNRIDGE DR
1500 VEN 93003 492-D4
SUNRISE CT
1400 CMRL 93010 524-D1
7000 VEN 93003 472-D7
SUNRISE DR
2100 SIMI 93065 497-E2
SUNRISEMEADOW CIR
12800 MRPK 93021 496-E2
SUNROCK CT
200 SIMI 93065 527-E1
SUNSET
10800 VeCo 93021 496-A4
SUNSET AV
100 VeCo 93022 461-B1
300 VeCo 93022 451-A7
23600 SIMI 93063 478-J6
SUNSET CT
100 VeCo 93022 451-C6
SUNSET DR
- THO 91362 557-A3
100 THO 91361 557-A3
200 VeCo 93035 552-B4
1700 VEN 93001 491-F1
5200 OXN 93035 521-H6
SUNSET LN
3300 OXN 93035 552-A3
3300 VeCo 93035 552-A2
SUNSET PL
800 OJAI 93023 441-J6
23600 SIMI 93063 479-A6
SUNSET ST
- VeCo 93022 451-B6
SUNSET HILLS BLVD
1000 THO 91360 526-H1
1700 THO 91362 526-H1
1900 THO 91362 527-A2
SUNSET KNOLLS DR
3500 THO 91362 526-J1
SUNSETMEADOW CT
4400 MRPK 93021 496-D3
SUNSET OAK CIR
1000 THO 91320 556-C2
SUNSET RIDGE CT
6800 CanP 91307 529-D6
SUNSETRIDGE RD
3800 MRPK 93021 496-B4
SUNSET VIEW CT
6100 VEN 93003 472-C7
SUNSHINE CT
1800 THO 91362 526-J2
SUNSTONE ST
4800 THO 91362 557-G1
SUN TREE LN
1600 SIMI 93063 498-J2
SUNVALE AV
500 VEN 93003 491-H4
SUN VALLEY CT
5400 AGRH 91301 557-J5
SUNWOOD LN
1000 VeCo 91377 528-A7
SUPERIOR AV
1100 VEN 93004 492-F3
SURFRIDER AV
2600 VEN 93001 491-F5
SURFRIDER WY
5100 OXN 93035 521-J7

SURFSIDE DR
500 OXN 93035 521-H6
600 PHME 93041 552-E6
W SURFSIDE ST
6900 VeCo 93001 459-C4
SURREY CIR
- OXN 93030 492-F7
- OXN 93030 522-F1
SURREY CT
2000 THO 91360 526-D4
SURREY WY
100 FILM 93015 456-A7
SURVEYOR AV
1600 SIMI 93063 498-F3
SUSAN AV
200 MRPK 93021 496-E1
10500 VeCo 93022 451-C6
SUSAN DR
1500 THO 91320 556-A2
SUSSEX CIR
800 THO 91360 526-G6
SUTTER AV
1100 SIMI 93065 497-H3
1700 SIMI 93065 498-A3
SUTTER DR
3300 OXN 93033 553-B3
SUTTER PL
1900 OXN 93033 553-A3
SUTTER ST
6000 VEN 93003 492-C1
SUTTON AV
2700 THO 91360 526-E3
SUTTON CREST TR
- VeCo 91377 527-J7
SUZANNE CT
100 THO 91320 556-B1
SWALLOW ST
6300 VEN 93003 492-D4
SWAN ST
6500 VEN 93003 492-D5
SWANFIELD CT
- VeCo 91361 556-E7
SWANSEA AV
1100 VEN 93004 492-H3
SWANSEA PL
1600 THO 91361 556-J6
SWEET BRIAR PL
1500 THO 91362 526-J3
SWEET BRIAR ST
4300 VEN 93003 491-J2
4300 VEN 93003 492-A2
SWEET CLOVER ST
3200 THO 91362 527-D3
SWEETLAND ST
2000 OXN 93033 553-A5
SWEETLEAF LN
23600 SIMI 93065 497-A2
SWEETWATER AV
1100 CMRL 93010 524-F1
SWEETWATER LN
9800 VEN 93004 492-H3
SWEETWOOD ST
3500 SIMI 93063 498-D1
N SWEETWOOD ST
2400 SIMI 93063 498-D1
SWIFT AV
1200 VEN 93003 492-D4
SWIFT PL
15800 MRPK 93021 477-A5
N SWINDON AV
2000 SIMI 93063 499-C2
SWISS PINE PL
23600 SIMI 93063 498-D4
SWITZAR LN
500 THO 91360 526-G7
SYCAMORE
100 OJAI 93023 442-A6
2100 VeCo 93023 451-C4
SYCAMORE DR
- VeCo 93001 461-A4
600 PHME 93041 552-F5
700 OXN 93033 552-F5
1000 SIMI 93065 498-C2
2600 SIMI 93065 478-C7
SYCAMORE LN
- VeCo 93023 441-E6
SYCAMORE RD
600 VeCo 93022 451-A5
1400 VeCo 93015 455-F4
3600 VeCo 93015 465-B2
3800 VeCo 93060 465-B2
SYCAMORE ST
- OXN 93030 522-H1
- VeCo 93030 522-H1
300 SPLA 93060 464-C4
3200 OXN 93033 552-H3
SYCAMORE CANYON RD
- VeCo - 387-A4
- VeCo - 555-C7
- VeCo - 584-H7
- VeCo - 585-A2
- VeCo 90265 387-A4
- VeCo 93012 555-C7
SYCAMORE GROVE ST
100 SIMI 93065 527-E1
100 SIMI 93065 497-E7
SYCAMORE RIDGE ST
100 SIMI 93065 497-D7
200 SIMI 93065 527-D1

SYLVAN DR
6100 VeCo 93063 499-B3
SYLVAN ST
22200 WdHl 91367 529-E7
SYMPHONY LN
4800 VeCo 91377 557-G2
SYRACUSE DR
4300 OXN 93033 553-A5
SYRINGA ST
400 THO 91360 526-D3

T

T ST
1500 VEN 93004 493-A3
TABOR CIR
800 VeCo 93010 494-F6
TACKABERRY CT
29000 AGRH 91301 558-A3
TACOMA ST
8700 VEN 93004 492-G3
TAFFRAIL CT
900 OXN 93035 522-B7
TAFFRAIL DR
1000 OXN 93035 522-C7
TAFFRAIL LN
2400 OXN 93035 522-B7
TAFT AV
100 VEN 93003 492-E2
TAHITI WY
600 OXN 93035 522-B6
TAHOE DR
8600 VEN 93004 492-G4
TAHOE LN
2200 OXN 93033 553-B5
TAHOE PL
6000 CMRL 93012 525-B1
TAHQUITZ CT
- CMRL 93012 524-H2
TAHQUITZ DR
- CMRL 93012 524-H2
TALAL CT
1800 VeCo 93012 526-B1
TALBERT AV
400 SIMI 93065 498-C4
TALLOWBERRY LN
23600 SIMI 93065 497-A1
TALMADGE RD
4700 MRPK 93021 496-C2
TALOS AV
- VeCo 93041 583-H3
TALOS RD
- PHME 93043 552-C5
TALUD TER
200 CMRL 93012 524-H2
TALUS ST
2800 OXN 93030 522-D3
TAM CT
2000 SIMI 93063 499-B2
TAMARAC ST
600 OXN 93033 552-H3
TAMARACK ST
1900 THO 91361 556-J4
1900 THO 91361 557-A4
TAMARIN AV
1700 VEN 93003 492-F4
TAMARIND ST
6000 VeCo 91377 558-A3
TAMARIX ST
1300 VeCo 93010 524-C1
1400 CMRL 93010 524-C1
TAMLEI AV
800 THO 91362 526-J7
TAM O SHANTER DR
4500 THO 91362 527-D6
TAMPA WY
10100 VEN 93004 492-J2
TANAGER ST
6400 VEN 93003 492-D4
TANBARK CT
1500 THO 91361 557-A6
TANGELO PL
6000 SIMI 93063 499-B3
TANGERINE PL
400 OXN 93033 552-G3
TANGLBRUSH LN
23600 SIMI 93065 497-A2
TANGLEWOOD CT
100 THO 91360 526-F2
TANGLEWOOD DR
2600 CMRL 93010 494-F6
TANISHA CT
23600 SIMI 93065 478-C7
TANNER RIDGE AV
400 THO 91362 557-G1
TANOAK LN
900 VeCo 91377 557-G1
TAORMINA LN
200 OJAI 93023 451-E1
TAPIES CT
900 THO 91320 555-F4
TAPIR CIR
1600 VEN 93003 492-E4
TAPLEY CT
1900 SIMI 93063 499-C2
TAPLEY ST
6500 SIMI 93063 499-C2
TAPO ST
3500 SIMI 93063 478-G7
3500 VeCo 93063 478-G7

TAPO ST
13500 SIMI 93063 498-G2
TAPO CANYON RD
- VeCo - 367-E9
1400 SIMI 93063 498-F2
2600 SIMI 93063 478-F7
3400 VeCo 93063 478-F6
4800 VeCo - 478-F3
23600 VeCo 93040 367-E9
23600 VeCo 93040 458-E6
TARA ST
600 THO 91320 525-H7
TARANTO WY
4800 VeCo 91377 557-G2
TARKIO ST
100 THO 91360 526-E4
TARLOW AV
- VEN 93003 492-A3
TARRYTOWN LN
3900 AGRH 91301 558-E7
TARSIER LN
7200 VEN 93003 492-F4
TARTAR DR
- VeCo 93041 583-H3
TARTAR RD
- PHME 93043 552-C5
TATU ST
3200 SIMI 93063 479-A6
TAXCO CT
1600 CMRL 93010 524-D4
W TAXCO CT
- SIMI 93065 497-F4
TAYLOR CT
- THO 91360 556-G1
- THO 91362 556-G1
TAYLOR ST
3800 VEN 93003 491-H2
TAYLOR RANCH RD
500 VeCo 93001 470-J4
500 VeCo 93001 471-A5
500 VeCo 93001 490-J1
500 VeCo 93001 491-A1
500 VEN 93001 490-J1
TEAGUE DR
600 SPLA 93060 464-B4
TEAGUE PL
23600 VeCo 93060 453-G2
TEAKWOOD CT
800 THO 91320 556-C2
TEAKWOOD ST
200 OXN 93033 552-F3
800 PHME 93041 552-F3
TEAL AV
1200 VEN 93003 492-D4
TEAL CT
2900 THO 91360 526-F3
TEAL CLUB RD
1500 OXN 93030 522-B5
1500 VeCo 93030 522-B5
TEARDROP CT
- THO 91320 555-F2
TEASDALE ST
- THO 91360 526-F4
TECH CIR
5400 MRPK 93021 496-D1
TECOLOTE CT
4200 MRPK 93021 496-E3
TECOPA SPRINGS LN
- SIMI 93063 479-A6
TEHAMA ST
1400 OXN 93035 552-E1
TEITSORT DR
- FILM 93015 456-A4
TEJEDA AV
12100 MRPK 93021 496-D1
TEJON CT
1600 CMRL 93010 524-D1
2800 SIMI 93063 479-A7
TELEGRAPH PL
- VEN 93003 491-J2
TELEGRAPH RD
11300 VEN 93004 473-A6
11300 VEN 93060 472-H7
11300 VEN 93060 473-A6
11300 VeCo 93060 473-A6
11500 VEN 93004 472-H7
11900 VeCo 93004 472-H7
13400 VEN 93004 492-G1
16300 VEN 93003 492-D2
16900 VEN 93003 492-D2
21200 VEN 93003 491-H3
TELEGRAPH RD
Rt#-126
- VeCo 93015 456-E6
900 VeCo 93015 457-E5
1400 VeCo 93040 457-G4
2200 VeCo 93040 458-B5
2700 VeCo 93015 465-C1
17900 VeCo 93060 464-F3
18400 SPLA 93060 464-F3
20100 VeCo 93060 465-A2
E TELEGRAPH RD
17000 VeCo 93060 464-D5
17200 SPLA 93060 464-D5
W TELEGRAPH RD
800 SPLA 93060 473-G1
800 VeCo 93060 463-H7
800 VeCo 93060 473-G1
900 SPLA 93060 463-H7
11000 VeCo 93004 473-B5

W TELEGRAPH RD
11000 VEN 93004 473-B5
TELEPHONE RD
4500 VeCo 93003 492-A7
4500 VEN 93003 492-B4
5800 VEN 93009 492-B4
7300 VEN 93004 492-H3
10500 VeCo 93004 493-A1
10500 VEN 93004 493-A1
TELEPHONE RELAY RD
23600 VeCo 93001 471-E7
TELLER RD
2200 THO 91320 525-H7
TELOMA DR
100 VEN 93003 492-B1
TELON CT
100 SIMI 93065 497-F6
TELSA ST
600 VeCo 93023 451-C3
TELSTAR DR
1100 OXN 93030 522-J7
1100 OXN 93033 522-J7
TEMESCAL ST
300 VeCo 93040 457-F4
TEMPE CT
4000 SIMI 93063 478-F6
TEMPE WY
32300 WLKV 91361 557-C7
TEMPLE AV
500 CMRL 93010 524-F1
700 VEN 93004 492-J1
1800 CMRL 93010 494-E6
TEMPLETON ST
- VeCo 93003 492-A4
- VEN 93003 492-A4
TENNEYSON DR
5700 AGRH 91301 557-J4
TENNYSON CT
2500 THO 91360 526-D3
TENNYSON LN
700 VEN 93003 492-D3
TENNYSON ST
100 THO 91360 526-D3
TERESA ST
23600 OXN 93030 522-J4
TERN CT
1500 VEN 93003 492-E4
TERNEZ DR
3800 VeCo 93021 496-A4
10400 VeCo 93021 495-J4
TERRA BELLA CT
5700 CMRL 93012 495-B7
TERRA BELLA LN
2200 CMRL 93012 495-A7
TERRACE AV
4200 OXN 93033 552-J5
TERRACE DR
200 SIMI 93065 497-E2
1800 VEN 93001 491-E1
3500 OXN 93033 552-J4
TERRACE HILL CIR
4900 THO 91362 557-G1
TERRACEMEADOW CT
4400 MRPK 93021 496-E3
TERRACERIDGE RD
3900 MRPK 93021 496-B4
TERRACE VIEW PL
400 PHME 93041 552-E6
TERRACINA DR
900 SPLA 93060 464-B4
TERRA GLEN WY
23600 SIMI 93065 497-A1
TERRAMAR WY
5000 OXN 93035 521-J7
TERRIER DR
- PHME 93043 552-C5
TERRIER ST
- VeCo 93041 583-H3
TERRY DR
4900 VEN 93003 492-A1
TERRY RD
- VeCo 93012 554-C5
TESORO ST
23600 OXN 93030 522-J4
23600 VeCo 93030 522-J4
TEST AREA RD
23600 VeCo 93063 498-H7
23600 VeCo 93063 528-G1
TETLOW AV
1700 SIMI 93063 499-C2
TETON LN
4700 VEN 93003 492-B4
TEWA CT
1600 VeCo 93023 451-E4
TEXANIA TER
- LA 91304 529-D2
TEXAS AV
2700 SIMI 93063 478-H7
3600 VeCo 93063 478-H7
TEXICO RD
23600 VeCo 93015 456-B5
THACHER RD
3000 VeCo 93023 442-E4
THACHER SCHOOL RD
5000 VeCo 93023 442-G4
THACKERAY CT
6800 VEN 93003 492-E3
THAMES ST
100 THO 91360 526-E5

STREET
Block City ZIP Pg-Grid

THAYER LN
700 PHME 93041 552-F3
THELMA LN
11000 VeCo 93012 496-A7
THERESA DR
2900 THO 91320 555-G1
2900 VeCo 91320 555-G1
THERESA ST
2600 THO 91320 555-H1
THICKET PL
2700 SIMI 93065 478-C7
THILLE ST
- VeCo 93003 492-A4
4600 VEN 93003 492-C3
7800 VEN 93004 492-F3
THIONNET PL
15300 MRPK 93021 476-J5
THISTLEGATE RD
900 VeCo 91377 528-A7
900 VeCo 91377 558-A1
THISTLEWOOD ST
3000 THO 91360 526-F2
THOMAS AV
100 OXN 93033 552-G3
THOMAS CT
4200 SIMI 93063 478-F5
THOMAS DR
300 SPLA 93060 464-A7
THOMAS LN
1000 VEN 93003 492-A7
E THOMAS ST
500 VeCo 93022 451-C6
THOMASVILLE CT
13000 MRPK 93021 496-E4
THOMPSON AV
9400 Chat 91311 499-F6
E THOMPSON BLVD
- VEN 93001 491-C2
2300 VEN 93003 491-E2
W THOMPSON BLVD
- VEN 93001 491-B2
THOMPSON LN
200 Chat 91311 499-F6
500 VeCo 93063 499-F6
1400 SIMI 93065 497-J3
9200 Chat 91311 499-F7
THOMPSON RD
300 Chat 91311 499-F6
9200 Chat 91311 499-F6
9200 Chat 91311 499-F6
THOREAU CIR
100 THO 91360 526-F6
THOREAU LN
500 VEN 93003 492-D1
THORNCROFT CT
1300 THO 91361 556-J5
THORNHILL AV
1400 THO 91361 556-J5
N THORNWOOD ST
800 SIMI 93065 498-A5
THORPE CIR
300 THO 91360 526-E5
THORSBY RD
2100 VeCo 91361 556-F7
THOUSAND OAKS BLVD
25800 LACo 91302 558-H4
26000 CALB 91302 558-H4
28700 AGRH 91301 558-A4
29400 AGRH 91301 557-G4
E THOUSAND OAKS BLVD
- THO 91360 556-F1
800 THO 91362 556-F1
2400 THO 91362 557-A3
30700 WLKV 91362 557-E4
30800 WLKV 91301 557-E4
W THOUSAND OAKS BLVD
- THO 91360 556-E1
THRASHER CT
1500 VEN 93003 492-F4
THREE OAK CT
2400 SIMI 93063 499-A1
THREE SPRINGS DR
2600 WLKV 91361 557-A7
THRUSH AV
1500 VEN 93003 492-E4
2200 OXN 93033 553-A4
THUNDERBIRD DR
2300 THO 91362 556-J2
2300 THO 91362 557-A2
THUNDERHEAD ST
2900 THO 91360 526-D2
TIARA DR
1800 VeCo 93023 451-D3
TIARA ST
8100 VEN 93004 492-F3
TIBER ST
8800 VEN 93004 492-H4
TIBURON CT
1600 THO 91362 526-J4
TICO AV
200 OJAI 93023 441-H6
TICO RD
400 VeCo 93023 441-D7
600 VeCo 93023 451-D2
N TICO RD
100 OJAI 93023 441-G6
TIERRA DR
1200 THO 91362 526-H7
TIERRA BUENA CT
23600 CMRL 93010 524-C4
TIERRA LINDA CT
700 CMRL 93010 524-C1
TIERRA REJADA RD
100 SIMI 93065 497-A3
500 VeCo 93021 497-A3
500 VeCo 93065 497-A3
2000 MRPK 93021 496-C2
9900 VeCo 93021 496-G4
TIFFANEY LN
2700 SIMI 93063 478-D7
TIFFANY CT
1600 CMRL 93010 494-D7
1600 CMRL 93010 524-D1
TIGHE LN
700 FILM 93015 456-A5
TIKI DR
1300 OXN 93033 552-J5
TIKI WK
1800 OXN 93033 552-J2
1800 OXN 93033 553-A1
TILBURY CT
2000 THO 91360 526-D4
TILLER AV
2500 PHME 93041 552-C2
2600 OXN 93035 552-C2
2600 PHME 93035 552-C2
TILLER DR
3600 OXN 93035 522-B7
TIMBER RD
- THO 91320 556-B2
- VeCo 91320 556-B2
TIMBER CANYON RD
1900 VeCo 93060 454-H4
3400 VeCo 93060 464-H2
TIMBERCREEK TR
800 OXN 93030 522-F1
TIMBERDALE RD
4200 MRPK 93021 496-C3
TIMBERHILL CT
1800 SIMI 93063 498-E2
TIMBERLANE AV
2100 SIMI 93063 499-A2
TIMBERLANE CT
2200 OXN 93030 522-E2
TIMBERLANE ST
6200 AGRH 91301 558-A3
TIMBERRIDGE CT
32400 WLKV 91361 557-B7
TIMBERRIDGE RD
3800 MRPK 93021 496-B4
TIMBERVIEW CT
3800 MRPK 93021 496-C4
TIMBERWOOD AV
400 THO 91360 526-D3
TINAS RUN
- VeCo 91320 555-D5
TINIAN
- PHME 93041 552-E5
TINKERMAN ST
5500 SIMI 93063 499-A2
TINSLEY MOUNTAIN RD
23600 VeCo 93060 453-F3
TIOGA DR
300 VEN 93001 491-C1
TIOGA PL
700 THO 91320 526-B7
22200 LA 91304 529-J1
TIPPERARY LN
1800 THO 91320 556-A1
TIRRE CT
300 SPLA 93060 464-A7
TITAN PL
1300 OXN 93033 522-J7
TITANIA PL
2600 SIMI 93063 478-J7
TIVOLI LN
1100 SIMI 93065 497-H1
TOBAGA WY
300 VeCo 91377 557-G2
N TOBY PL
2300 SIMI 93065 498-B1
TODD CT
300 OXN 93030 523-B5
TODD LN
100 SPLA 93060 473-H1
400 VeCo 93060 473-H2
TODD RD
100 VeCo 93060 473-E3
900 SPLA 93060 473-E3
TODD VIEW CT
8600 LA 91304 529-C1
TOLAND RD
100 VeCo 93060 454-J7
100 VeCo 93060 455-A6
100 VeCo 93060 464-J1
TOLAND PARK RD
- VeCo 93060 454-J7
- VeCo 93060 464-J1
TOLEDO CT
3500 THO 91320 525-F7
TOLTECS CT
2500 VEN 93001 471-C5
TOMAHAWK DR
- PHME 93043 552-C5
- VeCo 93042 583-H2
TOMAHAWK TER
8400 LA 91304 529-D1
TONALE WY
400 VeCo 91377 557-G1
TONGA ST
11500 VeCo 90265 625-F5
TONGAREVA ST
11400 VeCo 90265 625-F5
TONOPAH CT
23600 SIMI 93063 479-A6
TONY AV
6100 WdHl 91367 529-E7
6400 CanP 91307 529-E6
TOP CIR
4800 SIMI 93063 478-H5
TOPA LN
100 VeCo 93023 453-C1
TOPANGA CANYON BLVD Rt#-27
9500 Chat 91311 499-J6
TOPANGA CANYON PL
9500 Chat 91311 499-J6
TOPA TOPA CT
700 VEN 93003 472-B7
TOPA TOPA DR
100 OJAI 93023 441-H7
5400 VEN 93003 472-B7
E TOPA TOPA ST
100 OJAI 93023 441-H7
W TOPA TOPA ST
100 OJAI 93023 441-H7
TOPA VIEW TR
1400 VeCo 91320 556-B3
TOPAZ AV
1700 VEN 93004 492-G4
2800 SIMI 93063 478-D7
TOPAZ CT
900 OJAI 93023 441-J5
2400 OXN 93030 522-D3
TOPEKA AV
600 VEN 93004 492-H2
TOPSAIL CIR
2300 THO 91361 557-B6
TOPSAIL CT
900 OXN 93035 522-B7
TORINO ST
23600 MRPK 93021 496-C3
E TORRANCE ST
2100 SIMI 93065 498-A4
TORREPINES PL
30000 AGRH 91301 557-H5
TORREY RD
100 VeCo 93015 457-F5
100 VeCo 93040 457-F5
TORREY CANYON RD
- VeCo - 467-F1
- VeCo 93040 467-F1
900 VeCo 93015 457-F7
900 VeCo 93015 467-F1
TORREY PINE CT
1500 THO 91360 526-H2
TORREY PINES CT
2200 OXN 93033 553-B5
TORY WY
10100 VEN 93004 492-J2
TOSCOSA CT
- VeCo 91377 527-J7
TOTH PL
5700 AGRH 91301 558-C5
TOTTENHAM CT
1500 VeCo 91377 527-H6
TOUCAN WY
6900 VEN 93003 492-E4
TOULOUSE CIR
3100 THO 91362 526-J2
TOURMALINE DR
1000 THO 91320 525-H7
TOWER CT
- CMRL 93010 493-H7
TOWER DR
2500 VeCo 93023 442-C7
TOWER SQ
1300 VEN 93003 491-J4
TOWHEE CT
1400 VEN 93003 492-E4
TOWN CENTER DR
1000 OXN 93030 492-G7
TOWNLEY CIR
1700 SIMI 93063 499-A3
TOWNS CT
300 SPLA 93060 463-H6
TOWNSGATE RD
2100 THO 91361 557-B4
TOWNSHIP AV
2900 SIMI 93063 478-D6
2900 VeCo 93063 478-D6
TRABAJO DR
1000 OXN 93030 523-E3
TRABUCO OAK DR
23600 SIMI 93063 498-D4
TRACT 13 RD
- PHME 93043 552-C6
TRACT 14 RD
- PHME 93043 552-C3
N TRACY AV
2000 SIMI 93063 498-E2
TRACY CT
100 THO 91320 555-G2
TRAFALGER PL
1500 THO 91361 556-H6
TRAIL CREEK DR
29900 AGRH 91301 557-H5
TRAILCREST DR
4000 MRPK 93021 496-F4
TRAILROCK CT
700 SIMI 93065 527-C1
TRAILS END DR
23600 Chat 91311 499-F6
TRAILSIDE CT
200 THO 91320 556-C1
TRAILVIEW CT
3400 THO 91360 526-H2
TRAILWAY LN
29200 AGRH 91301 558-A5
29400 AGRH 91301 557-J5
TRANA CIR
26000 CALB 91302 558-J3
TRANCAS CANYON RD
- LACo 90265 586-H7
TRANCAS LAKES DR
- LACo 90265 586-H6
TRANQUIL LN
300 VeCo 91377 558-A1
600 SIMI 93065 497-G5
TRANQUILA CIR
100 CMRL 93012 524-H2
TRANQUILA DR
- CMRL 93012 524-H2
TRANSOM WY
600 OXN 93035 522-E6
TRANSPORT ST
3700 VEN 93003 491-J5
4100 VEN 93003 492-A5
TRAPANI CT
23600 MRPK 93021 496-C5
TRAVIS AV
2900 SIMI 93063 478-H6
TREADWELL AV
1000 SIMI 93065 498-B4
TREE FERN CT
- CMRL 93010 524-A2
TREE HOLLOW CT
400 SIMI 93065 527-E1
TREE HOLLOW GN
29300 AGRH 91301 558-A5
TREELINE RD
- PHME 93043 552-C3
TREE RANCH RD
12300 VeCo 93023 453-B1
TREE TOP LN
500 THO 91360 526-D6
TREEVIEW CT
11500 MRPK 93021 496-B2
TREFOIL AV
6400 VeCo 91377 558-B1
N TREMONT AV
2000 SIMI 93063 499-C2
E TREMONT CIR
6600 SIMI 93063 499-C2
TRENLEY CT
2600 SIMI 93063 498-E1
TRENT LN
300 SPLA 93060 463-H6
TRENTHAM RD
1900 VeCo 91361 556-H7
TRENTON LN
9700 VEN 93004 492-H2
TRENTWOOD DR
23600 VeCo 91361 556-E7
TREVI PL
400 VeCo 91377 557-G2
TREVINO TER
800 OXN 93033 552-H5
TRIANGLE ST
- THO 91360 526-F5
TRICKLNG BROOK CT
200 SIMI 93065 498-A6
TRIGGER PL
9700 Chat 91311 499-H5
E TRIGGER RD
- VeCo 91307 528-H4
TRIGGER ST
22700 Chat 91311 499-G6
TRILLIUM ST
2800 THO 91360 526-D3
TRINIDAD WY
800 OXN 93033 552-H3
TRINITY DR
3100 VEN 93003 491-G4
TRINITY PL
2400 OXN 93033 553-A2
TRINWAY AV
2100 SIMI 93065 498-C2
TRITON ST
2500 PHME 93041 552-D2
2800 OXN 93041 552-D2
TRIUNFO CANYON RD
100 THO 91361 557-B4
7000 WLKV 91361 557-A5
TRIUNFO RIDGE FIRE TR
- LACo 90265 586-D4
- VeCo 90265 586-D4
TROJAN CT
6700 MRPK 93021 476-H6
TROLLOPE CT
15700 MRPK 93021 477-A5
TROUSDALE ST
5300 VeCo 91377 527-H7
TROWBRIDGE CT
3900 WLKV 91361 557-D6
TRUCKEE DR
8300 VEN 93004 492-G4
TRUCK HAUL RD
100 VeCo 93030 492-H6
TRUENO AV
600 VeCo 93010 494-B5
TRUETT CIR
2000 THO 91360 526-D5
TRUMAN AV
- VEN 93004 492-E1
TRUMAN ST
2500 CMRL 93010 524-F1
TRUSTY LN
1300 VeCo 93023 451-B2
TUBA ST
22100 Chat 91311 499-J4
TUBBS ST
1600 THO 91362 526-J7
TUCKER ST
11900 VeCo 93021 476-D3
TUCSON ST
4100 SIMI 93063 478-F6
TUCSON WY
10100 VEN 93004 492-J2
TUDOR CIR
700 THO 91360 526-G6
TUDOR LN
1000 FILM 93015 455-J6
TUJUNGA AV
100 VeCo 93035 552-B5
TULANE AV
200 VEN 93003 491-J2
N TULANE AV
6700 MRPK 93021 476-G6
TULARE LN
28400 AGRH 91301 558-C6
TULARE PL
2400 OXN 93033 553-A2
TULARE ST
10100 VEN 93004 492-J2
TULIP AV
- SIMI 93063 499-A2
TULIP CT
200 VEN 93004 473-A7
TULSA CIR
10400 VEN 93004 492-J1
TULSA DR
4700 OXN 93033 553-A5
4700 VeCo 93033 553-A5
TULSA ST
22000 Chat 91311 499-J3
TUMBLEWEED AV
2600 SIMI 93065 478-C7
2600 SIMI 93065 498-C1
TUOLUMNE AV
100 VEN 93004 472-H7
N TUOLUMNE AV
500 THO 91360 526-D7
TUPELO WOOD CT
800 THO 91320 556-C2
TURFWAY RD
6100 MRPK 93021 476-A6
TURIN ST
400 VeCo 91377 557-G1
TURLOCK AV
1300 VEN 93004 492-H3
TURNBURY ST
1200 SIMI 93065 497-D7
TURQUOISE CIR
2500 THO 91320 525-H6
TUSCANA CT
23600 MRPK 93021 496-C4
TUSCANY DR
- VeCo 91377 557-G2
TUSCARORA AV
2300 VEN 93001 471-D6
TUTTLE AV
900 SIMI 93065 497-G5
TUXEDO RW
- OXN 93030 492-F7
TUXFORD PL
3300 THO 91360 526-G2
TWILIGHT CANYON TR
- VeCo 93063 499-E3
TWILIGHT GLEN LN
23600 SIMI 93065 497-A1
TWILIGHT RIDGE CIR
1600 THO 91362 527-F6
TWILLIN CT
700 SIMI 93065 497-D6
TWIN CIRCLE LN
6400 SIMI 93063 499-C3
TWIN FALLS CT
200 THO 91320 556-A1
TWINFOOT CT
1000 THO 91361 557-B5
TWINING LN
200 SIMI 93065 497-E6
TWIN LAKE RDG
3400 WLKV 91361 557-B7
TWIN OAK DR
1200 OXN 93030 522-E1
TWIN OAKS CT
400 THO 91362 557-A1
TWIN PEAKS ST
1300 SIMI 93065 497-D7
TWIN RIVER CIR
1800 VEN 93004 492-G4
TWIN SPRINGS AV
6300 VeCo 91377 558-A1
TWISTED OAK DR
- CanP 91307 529-C7
23600 SIMI 93065 527-F1
TWO OAK CT
2400 SIMI 93063 499-A1
TYLER AV
200 VEN 93003 492-E1
TYLER CT
- VEN 93003 492-E1
2900 SIMI 93063 478-G7
TYNEBOURNE CT
31800 WLKV 91361 557-D6

U

U ST
1500 VEN 93004 493-A3
UKIAH ST
200 PHME 93041 552-E2
1300 OXN 93035 552-E1
2000 OXN 93041 552-E1
ULVERSTON ST
4900 VeCo 91377 557-H1
ULYSSES ST
100 SIMI 93065 497-F2
UNDERPASS ST
2600 OXN 93030 522-G1
UNICORN CIR
7200 VEN 93003 492-E4
UNIDOS AV
12400 MRPK 93021 496-D2
UNION PL
2100 SIMI 93065 497-F2
UNITED RD
3900 AGRH 91301 558-F7
UNIVERSE CIR
1500 OXN 93033 552-J1
UNIVERSITY AV
- VEN 93003 492-A2
UNIVERSITY DR
1900 VeCo 93012 554-E2
6900 MRPK 93021 477-A5
UNIVERSITY PL
200 SPLA 93060 464-B6
UPLAND RD
4500 CMRL 93010 494-J7
4500 VeCo 93010 494-J7
4600 CMRL 93012 494-J7
5100 CMRL 93012 495-A7
6600 CMRL 93012 525-D1
UPPER BAY DR
700 OXN 93030 522-F1
UPPER LAKE RD
- VeCo 91361 586-F1
- VeCo 91361 556-F7
UPPER RANCH RD
1400 THO 91362 527-C5
UPPINGHAM DR
700 THO 91360 526-G2
URANIUM DR
2400 OXN 93030 522-D3
URBANA AV
- THO 91320 555-H1
URSULA DR
23600 OXN 93030 522-J4
UTE LN
200 VEN 93001 471-C6
UTICA AV
700 VEN 93004 492-H2

V

V ST
1500 VEN 93004 492-J2
1500 VEN 93004 493-A3
VALARIE AV
3200 SIMI 93063 478-E6
VALDEZ AL
- VEN 93001 491-B2
VALE PL
4000 THO 91362 527-C7
VALECROFT AV
900 THO 91361 556-J5
VALENCIA AV
2700 SIMI 93063 478-E7
2700 SIMI 93063 498-E1
VALENCIA CIR
2600 THO 91360 526-B3
VALENCIA CT
2600 SIMI 93063 498-E1
VALENCIA DR
1000 VeCo 93010 494-F6
VALENCIA PL
1400 OXN 93035 522-E7
VALENTINA DR
23600 OXN 93030 522-J5
VALENTINE RD
4400 VEN 93003 492-B4
5400 VeCo 93003 492-B5
VALERIO ST
22000 CanP 91303 529-H4
22300 CanP 91307 529-F4
23200 LA 91304 529-F4
VALERO CIR
4900 VeCo 91377 557-G2
VALEWOOD CIR
3200 THO 91360 526-F2
VALJEAN AV
1200 SIMI 93065 498-C4
VALLECITO DR
800 VEN 93001 491-D1
VALLEJO AV
800 SIMI 93065 498-A4
VALLE LINDO DR
700 CMRL 93010 524-C2
VALLERIO AV
100 OJAI 93023 441-F7
200 OJAI 93023 451-F1
VALLEY CIR
8300 LA 91304 529-E2
VALLEY RD
- VeCo 93022 451-A7
700 MRPK 93021 476-F7
23600 VeCo 91361 556-A6
VALLEY CIRCLE BLVD
6000 WdHl 91367 529-D6
6300 CanP 91307 529-D5
6600 LACo 91307 529-D5
7100 LA 91304 529-E2
8600 LA 91304 499-G7
9000 Chat 91311 499-H5
9200 Chat 91311 499-G7
VALLEY CIRCLE TER
6300 CanP 91307 529-D7
VALLEY CREST
3600 VeCo 93021 495-H3
VALLEY CREST RD
300 SIMI 93065 497-E5
VALLEY FAIR ST
4000 SIMI 93063 498-F2
VALLEYFIELD AV
2100 THO 91360 526-A4
VALLEY FLORES DR
7800 LA 91304 529-E1
VALLEY GATE RD
- SIMI 93065 497-F6
VALLEY HEIGHTS DR
28900 AGRH 91301 558-A5
VALLEY HIGH AV
800 THO 91362 527-A6
1200 THO 91362 527-A6
VALLEY MEADOW CT
2300 VeCo 93022 451-C4
2300 VeCo 93023 451-C4
VALLEY MEADOW DR
2100 VeCo 93022 451-C4
2100 VeCo 93023 451-C4
VALLEY OAK LN
600 THO 91320 556-D2
VALLEY PARK DR
1400 OXN 93033 552-G1
W VALLEY RIDGE ST
- VeCo 93023 451-B4
VALLEY SPRING DR
4000 THO 91362 527-C7
VALLEY TERRACE DR
23600 SIMI 93065 478-B7
VALLEY VIEW DR
- VeCo 93022 451-B6
VALLEY VIEW RD
1400 OJAI 93023 441-H4
1400 VeCo 93023 441-H4
1400 VeCo 93023 442-A4
VALLEYVIEW WY
500 VEN 93003 492-B1
VALLEY VISTA
800 FILM 93015 456-A5
VALLEY VISTA DR
1000 VeCo 93010 494-B6
13500 CMRL 93010 494-A7
18100 CMRL 93010 524-A1
18100 VeCo 93010 524-A1
VALMORE AV
300 VEN 93003 491-G4
VAL VERDE DR
8400 LA 91304 529-D1
8500 WHll 91304 529-D1
VAN BUREN ST
7300 VEN 93003 492-E2
7400 VEN 93004 492-E2
VANCOUVER AV
2600 VEN 93003 491-G3
VANDERBILT CT
4500 VEN 93003 492-A1
VANDERBILT DR
200 OXN 93030 522-H2
VAN DYKE ST
- THO 91360 526-E4
VANESSA ST
2000 SIMI 93063 498-F2
VANETTA ST
2000 VeCo 93033 553-A5
VANGUARD DR
1100 OXN 93033 522-J7
1100 OXN 93033 552-J1
2300 CMRL 93010 494-E7
VANITA PL
2100 VeCo 93010 494-D7
VAN NESS AV
300 OXN 93033 552-F5
VAN NUYS AV
100 VeCo 93035 552-C6
VANOWEN ST
21900 CanP 91303 529-G6
22200 CanP 91307 529-D6
24400 LACo 91307 529-D6
VAQUERO DR
1400 SIMI 93065 497-F3
VARSITY CT
- VEN 93003 492-A2
VARSITY ST
4200 VEN 93003 491-J3
4300 VEN 93003 492-A2
15000 MRPK 93021 476-J6
N VASSAR CIR
6400 MRPK 93021 476-H6
VASSAR ST
4300 VEN 93003 491-J1
4300 VEN 93003 492-A1
VAUGHN ST
23600 Chat 91311 499-G6
VEDDER MTWY
- VeCo 90265 586-C3
VEGA WY
800 VeCo 93023 451-C2
VEGAS DR
200 OXN 93030 522-J6
VEJAR DR
4900 AGRH 91301 558-B6
VELA CT
100 SPLA 93060 463-J6
VELARDE DR
600 THO 91360 526-C3
VELMA CT
2600 SIMI 93065 478-C7
VENADO AV E
100 THO 91320 556-C1
VENDELL RD
27400 AGRH 91301 558-E7
VENETIAN DR
5200 OXN 93035 521-J6
VENEZIA LN
- THO 91362 527-B3
VENICE RD
- PHME 93043 552-C6
VENICE ST
1300 SIMI 93065 497-G3
VENTANA CT
100 THO 91360 526-F1
VENTAVO DR
9400 VeCo 93012 495-J3
9400 VeCo 93021 495-J3
VENTOSO AV
6200 CMRL 93012 525-C1
VENTU PARK RD
400 THO 91320 526-A6
N VENTU PARK RD
- THO 91320 556-B1
400 THO 91320 526-B7
S VENTU PARK RD
- VeCo 91320 556-B2
- THO 91320 556-B2
VENTU PARK FIRE RD
1100 VeCo 91320 556-A3
2100 THO 91320 556-A3
2100 THO 91320 555-H3
2100 THO 91320 555-H3
23600 VeCo 91361 556-A3
VENTURA AV
100 VeCo 93035 552-C6
700 SIMI 93065 497-G3
2800 VEN 93001 471-C1
2800 VEN 93001 471-C4
5500 VEN 93001 461-B6
5900 VEN 93001 461-B6
VENTURA AV Rt#-33
- VeCo 93022 451-B5
4400 VeCo 93001 461-A2
4400 VeCo 93022 461-A2
11200 VeCo 93023 461-D2
11800 OJAI 93023 451-F1
N VENTURA AV
- VEN 93001 491-B1
600 VEN 93001 471-C6
2500 VEN 93001 471-C6
S VENTURA AV
- VEN 93001 491-B2
VENTURA BLVD
- OXN 93030 522-H1
100 VeCo 93030 522-H1
800 CMRL 93010 523-F3
1000 VeCo 93010 523-F3
1100 OXN 93030 523-A2
1200 VeCo 93030 523-C3
1200 CMRL 93010 523-F3
1500 CMRL 93010 524-D3
2300 VEN 93003 492-D6
2300 VeCo 93003 492-D6
E VENTURA BLVD
- CMRL 93010 524-B3
W VENTURA BLVD
- CMRL 93010 523-J3
- CMRL 93010 524-A3
VENTURA FRWY U.S.-101
- Ago - 558-D6
- AGRH - 557-G6
- AGRH - 558-D6
- CALB - 558-D6
- CMRL - 523-A3
- CMRL - 524-A3
- CMRL - 525-C5
- LACo - 558-D6
- OXN - 492-F7
- OXN - 522-H2
- OXN - 523-A3
- THO - 525-C5
- THO - 526-D7
VENTURA FRWY U.S.-101
- THO - 555-J1
- THO - 556-E1
- THO - 557-B4
- VeCo - 366-F9
- VeCo - 459-A3
- VeCo - 469-J1
- VeCo - 470-B3
- VeCo - 490-H1
- VeCo - 492-F7
- VeCo - 523-A3
- VeCo - 525-C5
- VeCo - 556-E1
- VEN - 490-H1
- VEN - 491-F4
- VEN - 492-F7
- WLKV - 557-B4
VENTURA RD
100 OXN 93030 522-E4
100 PHME 93041 552-E6
900 OXN 93035 522-E7
1100 OXN 93033 522-E7
1100 OXN 93033 552-E2
1200 OXN 93035 552-E2
2000 OXN 93041 552-E2
2800 OXN 93030 492-F7
2800 VeCo 93030 492-F7
3300 VEN 93003 492-E7
N VENTURA RD
100 OXN 93030 522-E1
100 PHME 93041 552-E5
2100 PHME 93043 552-E5
2400 OXN 93033 552-E5
2500 VeCo 93030 492-F7
2500 OXN 93030 522-E1
2700 OXN 93043 552-E5
2800 PHME 93033 552-E5
S VENTURA RD
- OXN 93030 522-E6
2300 OXN 93033 552-E1
2300 PHME 93033 552-E1
16600 OXN 93033 522-E6
VENTURA ST
- VeCo 93012 554-D3
100 OJAI 93023 441-H6
100 SPLA 93060 464-A6
800 VeCo 93015 465-H3
VENTURA ST Rt#-126
100 FILM 93015 456-A6
400 FILM 93015 455-F7
1100 VeCo 93015 455-F7
E VENTURA ST Rt#-126
- FILM 93015 456-C6
400 VeCo 93015 456-C6
S VENTURA ST
100 OJAI 93023 441-H7
100 OJAI 93023 451-H1
100 VeCo 93023 451-H1
VENTURA WY
100 Chat 91311 499-F7
9200 Chat 91311 499-F7
VENUS AV
600 SPLA 93060 463-J6
VENUS CT
2700 THO 91360 526-F3
VENUS ST
- THO 91360 526-F3
VENWOOD AV
800 VEN 93001 471-B7
N VERA CT
2000 SIMI 93063 499-B2
E VERA ST
6000 SIMI 93063 499-B2
VERACRUZ LN
2000 OXN 93030 522-G3
VERA CRUZ ST
- SIMI 93065 497-E3
VERANO DR
300 VeCo 93023 441-F7
VERBENA ST
10500 VEN 93004 493-A2
VERCELLY CT
5600 WLKV 91362 557-G6
N VERDA CT
2400 SIMI 93065 498-B1
VERDEMONT CIR
1200 SIMI 93065 497-H5
VERDE OAK DR
100 VeCo 93022 461-A1
VERDE RIDGE LN
1000 THO 91361 556-H6
VERDE VISTA DR
- THO 91360 526-F1
VERDI RD
100 VEN 93003 492-B4
VERDUGO WY
4900 CMRL 93012 524-J3
5100 CMRL 93012 525-A4
W VERDULERA ST
600 CMRL 93010 523-H3
N VERNA AV
600 VeCo 91320 525-G7
VERNON PL
300 SPLA 93060 464-A7
VERNON WY
300 SPLA 93060 464-A7
VERONA CT
5500 WLKV 91362 557-G6
VERSAILLE CT
3100 THO 91362 526-J2
VETS CT
30600 AGRH 91301 557-G3
VEVA WY
26100 CALB 91302 558-H4
VIA ACIANDO
23600 CMRL 93012 494-H7
VIA ACORDE
1400 CMRL 93010 494-D7
VIA ACOSTA
1100 THO 91320 555-B4
VIA ADORNA
1000 THO 91320 555-D4
VIA ALBA
6900 CMRL 93012 495-D7
6900 CMRL 93012 525-D1
VIA ALCAZAR
1100 CMRL 93010 494-C7
E VIA ALEGRE
5900 SIMI 93063 499-B2
VIA ALISTA
1000 THO 91320 555-C4
VIA ALLEGRA
23600 CMRL 93010 523-F2
VIA ALONDRA
500 CMRL 93012 524-G2
VIA AMISTOSA
27800 AGRH 91301 558-D6
VIA ANDREA
4800 THO 91320 555-C4
VIA ANITA
900 THO 91320 555-C4
VIA ARACENA
1400 CMRL 93010 523-J1
VIA ARANDANA
23600 CMRL 93012 494-H7
VIA ARROYO
200 VEN 93003 472-C5
500 VEN 93003 492-D1
VIA ARROYO CIR
6400 VEN 93003 472-C6
VIA AZUL
- THO 91320 555-D2
VIA BAJA
6100 VEN 93003 492-D1
6700 VEN 93003 472-D7
VIA BAJADA
1500 THO 91360 526-J1
VIA BARON
900 THO 91320 555-C4
VIA BENSA
4800 VeCo 91377 557-G1
E VIA BREVE
5900 SIMI 93063 499-B2
VIA BRISAS
23600 OXN 93030 523-B4
VIA CALDERON
5000 CMRL 93012 524-J3
5100 CMRL 93012 525-A3
VIA CANADA
4500 THO 91320 555-D4
VIA CANDELLA
900 THO 91320 555-B4
VIA CANTILENA
100 CMRL 93012 524-H3
VIA CAPOTE
23600 THO 91320 555-B3
VIA CARILLO
1100 THO 91320 555-D4
VIA CARRANZA
1100 CMRL 93012 524-J2
1100 CMRL 93012 525-A2
VIA CARRO
600 THO 91320 555-C3
VIA CIELITO
500 VEN 93003 472-C6
500 VEN 93003 492-C1
VIA COLINAS
- THO 91362 557-E4
- WLKV 91362 557-E5
VIA CON DIOS
900 VeCo 93010 494-B6
VIA CORZA
2600 CMRL 93010 494-F7
VIA COZUMEL
6200 CMRL 93012 525-C5
VIA CRISTAL
100 CMRL 93012 524-J3
100 CMRL 93012 525-A3
VIA CRISTINA
23600 THO 91320 555-B3
VIA CUPERTINO
4600 CMRL 93012 524-J2
VIA DE CERRO
800 VeCo 93010 494-A6
VIA DE COSTA
3500 THO 91360 526-D1
VIA DEL CABALLO
200 VeCo 91377 558-A1
200 VeCo 91377 557-J2
VIA DEL NOGAL
2700 CMRL 93010 494-F7
VIA DEL NORTE
23600 OXN 93030 522-J2
VIA DEL PRADO
200 SPLA 93060 473-E1
VIA DEL RANCHO
4500 THO 91320 555-D3

STREET
Block City ZIP Pg-Grid

VIA DEL REY
- THO 91320 555-D2
VIA DEL SUELO
2500 CMRL 93010 494-F7
VIA DE TIERRA
600 THO 91320 555-D3
VIA DOLORES
23600 THO 91320 555-B2
VIA DON LUIS
4600 THO 91320 555-D4
VIA DULCE
- CMRL 93012 524-H1
VIA EL MOLINO
23600 THO 91320 555-B1
VIA EL TORO
23600 THO 91320 555-C2
VIA ENCANTO
- THO 91320 555-D2
VIA ESPINOSA
23600 THO 91320 555-B2
VIA ESTRADA
23600 OXN 93030 523-A2
VIA FUSTERO
400 VeCo 93040 457-F4
VIA GABILAN
3900 CMRL 93012 524-H4
VIA GALO
23600 THO 91320 555-B3
VIA GOLETA
1000 THO 91320 555-D4
VIA GRANDE
4500 THO 91320 555-D3
VIA HELENA
23600 THO 91320 555-B3
VIA HERALDO
900 THO 91320 555-C4
VIA HISPANO
23600 THO 91320 555-C4
VIA IMPRESSO
900 THO 91320 555-C4
VIA JACARA
23600 CMRL 93012 524-H2
VIA JACINTO
23600 THO 91320 555-B3
VIA JUAREZ
23600 THO 91320 555-C3
VIA LA CIMA
23600 THO 91320 555-B1
VIA LA PAZ
500 VEN 93003 492-D1
VIA LA PRIMAVERA
3500 THO 91360 526-C1
VIA LAS BRISAS
23600 THO 91320 555-D3
VIA LA SILVA
1500 CMRL 93010 524-C1
VIA LATINA DR
900 CMRL 93012 525-B1
VIA LEAL
2500 CMRL 93010 494-F7
VIA LINDA
23600 THO 91320 555-C3
VIA LISBOA
3900 CMRL 93012 524-H4
VIA LOMA ST
2000 CMRL 93012 495-B7
VIA LORENTE
800 CMRL 93012 525-B5
VIA LOS ALTOS
23600 THO 91320 555-B1
VIA MADERA
600 THO 91320 555-D3
VIA MANTILLA
2400 CMRL 93010 494-H6
VIA MARINA AV
3100 OXN 93035 522-C7
VIA MARINA CT
2900 OXN 93035 522-D7
VIA MARISMA
3900 CMRL 93012 524-H4
VIA MARQUESA
500 CMRL 93012 524-H2
VIA MEDANOS
4200 CMRL 93012 524-H3
VIA MERIDA
- THO 91362 557-D4
VIA MERLA
23600 THO 91320 555-B3
VIA MESITA
23600 THO 91320 555-C2
VIA MIRA FLORES
23600 THO 91320 555-A3
VIA MONTANEZ
500 CMRL 93012 525-C5
VIA MONTECITO
1700 CMRL 93012 525-D1
1700 CMRL 93012 495-C7
VIA MONTOYA
1100 CMRL 93010 524-F2
VIA NICOLA
23600 THO 91320 555-B3
VIA NOGAL
2300 CMRL 93010 494-H7
VIA NOVELLA
500 VeCo 91377 557-J1
VIA OLAS
23600 THO 91320 555-B2
VIA OLIVERA
23600 CMRL 93012 524-H3
VIA ONDULANDO
500 VEN 93003 472-D7
VIA PACHECO
600 CMRL 93012 524-J2
VIA PACIFICA
1000 SPLA 93060 463-H7
23600 THO 91320 555-B2
VIA PACIFICA WK
3500 OXN 93035 522-B7
VIA PALERMO
900 THO 91320 555-C4
VIA PALOMA
3900 CMRL 93012 524-H3
VIA PARQUE
1500 THO 91360 526-J1
VIA PASADA
1000 SPLA 93060 473-E1
VIA PASITO
6100 VEN 93003 472-D7
VIA PATRICIA
23600 THO 91320 555-B2
VIA PESCADOR
3500 CMRL 93012 524-G2
VIA PETIRROJO
23600 THO 91320 525-J5
VIA PISA
23600 THO 91320 555-B2
VIA PLAZA
500 VEN 93003 492-D1
VIA QUINTO
23600 THO 91320 555-B2
VIA RAFAEL
1100 THO 91320 555-C4
VIA RICARDO
23600 THO 91320 555-B2
VIA RINCON
23600 THO 91320 555-B2
VIA RIO
23600 THO 91320 555-D2
VIA RIVERA
900 THO 91320 555-D4
VIA ROBLE EXT
23600 VeCo 93040 458-F6
VIA ROCAS
5400 WLKV 91362 557-E5
VIA RODEO
500 FILM 93015 455-J5
4500 THO 91320 555-D3
VIA ROSAL
- CMRL 93012 524-H4
VIA ROTA
900 CMRL 93012 525-B5
VIA SANDRA
23600 THO 91320 555-B2
VIA SAN JOSE
1000 THO 91320 555-C4
VIA SAN LUCAS
23600 THO 91320 555-B1
VIA SAN MARTIN
23600 THO 91320 555-C2
VIA SANTANA
23600 THO 91320 555-C1
VIA SECOYA
23600 CMRL 93012 494-J7
VIA SILVESTRE
23600 CMRL 93012 525-A2
VIA SINTRA
3900 CMRL 93012 524-H4
VIA SOLANA
100 SPLA 93060 463-H7
VIA SORRENTO
1000 THO 91320 555-B4
VIA TECA
23600 THO 91320 555-B2
VIA TERRADO
500 CMRL 93010 523-H1
VIA TERRASOL
2000 CMRL 93010 494-B7
2000 VeCo 93010 494-B7
VIA TOMAS
2300 CMRL 93010 494-F7
VIA VELA
2700 CMRL 93010 494-F7
VIA VENETO
1900 VeCo 93010 493-J7
1900 VeCo 93010 494-A7
VIA VERDE
3800 THO 91360 526-J1
VIA VISTA
23600 THO 91320 555-C3
VIA VISTOSA
23600 THO 91320 555-C1
VIA ZAMORA
400 CMRL 93010 523-J2
VIA ZURITA CT
2400 VeCo 93012 496-D6
VICKI CT
3400 SIMI 93065 478-D6
VICKIVIEW DR
6600 LACo 91307 529-C6
VICKSBURG LN
1400 VEN 93003 492-B4
VICKY AV
6500 CanP 91307 529-H5
7600 LA 91304 529-H4
VICTOR HERBERT DR
- VEN 93003 492-A7
VICTORIA AV
- VeCo 93003 492-C7
- VEN 93003 492-C7
100 OXN 93030 522-B3
100 VeCo 93030 522-B3
500 OXN 93035 522-B7
1300 OXN 93035 552-B3
1800 PHME 93035 552-B3
1800 VeCo 93003 552-B3
2000 PHME 93041 552-B3
4000 VeCo 93035 552-B3
N VICTORIA AV
- VEN 93003 492-C1
600 VeCo 93003 472-C7
600 VeCo 93003 492-C1
600 VEN 93003 472-C7
S VICTORIA AV
- VEN 93003 492-C2
700 VEN 93009 492-C3
2000 VeCo 93003 492-C3
VICTORIA ST
2400 SIMI 93065 498-B3
VICTORY BLVD
22000 WdHl 91367 529-C7
22000 CanP 91303 529-F7
22200 CanP 91307 529-C7
23600 VeCo 91302 529-C7
VIEJO DR
300 CMRL 93010 524-D3
VIENTOS RD
400 VeCo 93010 494-B7
VIEW DR
100 SPLA 93060 464-A5
2100 SIMI 93065 497-E2
VIEWCREST CT
5900 VEN 93003 472-C7
VIEWCREST DR
600 VeCo 93003 472-C7
600 VEN 93003 472-C7
VIEWLAKE LN
32000 WLKV 91361 557-C7
VIEW LINE DR
- SIMI 93065 477-F7
VIEW MESA ST
12900 MRPK 93021 496-E4
VIEW PARK CT
400 VeCo 91377 558-B1
VIEW POINT CIR
6100 VEN 93003 472-C5
VIEW POINTE DR
3200 WLKV 91361 557-C7
VIKING DR
1900 CMRL 93010 494-E7
VILLA ADOBE
600 CMRL 93012 524-J1
VILLA CAMPESINA AV
12400 MRPK 93021 496-D2
VILLAGE CT
1200 SIMI 93065 497-H4
1700 THO 91362 527-A5
VILLAGE GN
900 THO 91361 557-C5
VILLAGE PKWY
2100 SIMI 93065 497-E2
VILLAGE RD
200 PHME 93041 552-E6
VILLAGE SQ
200 FILM 93015 455-J6
VILLAGE 1
- CMRL 93012 525-A3
VILLAGE 2
100 CMRL 93012 525-A3
VILLAGE 3
200 CMRL 93012 525-A3
VILLAGE 4
100 CMRL 93012 525-A3
VILLAGE 5
300 CMRL 93012 525-A2
VILLAGE 6
- CMRL 93012 525-A3
VILLAGE 7
5600 CMRL 93012 525-A2
VILLAGE 8
- CMRL 93012 525-B2
VILLAGE 9
5700 CMRL 93012 525-B2
VILLAGE 11
500 CMRL 93012 525-B2
VILLAGE 13
5800 CMRL 93012 525-B2
VILLAGE 14
400 CMRL 93012 525-B2
VILLAGE 15
500 CMRL 93012 525-B2
VILLAGE 16
- CMRL 93012 525-A3
VILLAGE 17
5600 CMRL 93012 525-B3
VILLAGE 18
- CMRL 93012 525-A3
VILLAGE 19
- CMRL 93012 525-B3
VILLAGE 20
- CMRL 93012 525-B3
VILLAGE 22
5700 CMRL 93012 525-B3
VILLAGE 23
- CMRL 93012 525-B3
VILLAGE 24
5700 CMRL 93012 525-B3
VILLAGE 25
- CMRL 93012 525-B2
VILLAGE 26
5800 CMRL 93012 525-B3
VILLAGE 28
- CMRL 93012 525-B3
VILLAGE 29
6000 CMRL 93012 525-B2
VILLAGE 30
6000 CMRL 93012 525-C2
VILLAGE 31
6100 CMRL 93012 525-C2
VILLAGE 32
6000 CMRL 93012 525-C2
VILLAGE 33
6200 CMRL 93012 525-C2
VILLAGE 34
6200 CMRL 93012 525-C2
VILLAGE 35
6300 CMRL 93012 525-C2
VILLAGE 37
900 CMRL 93012 525-C1
VILLAGE 38
- CMRL 93012 525-C2
VILLAGE 39
900 CMRL 93012 525-C1
VILLAGE 40
6500 CMRL 93012 525-C2
VILLAGE 41
100 CMRL 93012 525-C1
VILLAGE 42
- CMRL 93012 525-D1
VILLAGE 44
1000 CMRL 93012 525-D1
VILLAGE BROOK RD
31800 WLKV 91361 557-D6
VILLAGE CENTER RD
31600 WLKV 91361 557-D6
VILLAGE SCHOOL RD
31600 WLKV 91361 557-D6
VILLAGEVIEW CT
11700 MRPK 93021 496-B2
VILLA MALLORCA PL
5200 CMRL 93012 525-A2
VILLAMONTE CT
4300 CMRL 93010 494-H7
VILLANOVA AV
- OXN 93030 522-H2
300 VEN 93003 492-B1
VILLANOVA RD
100 VeCo 93023 451-D3
E VILLANOVA RD
100 VeCo 93023 451-E2
800 OJAI 93023 451-E2
VINA DEL MAR
2100 OXN 93035 552-A2
E VINCE ST
- VEN 93001 471-C7
W VINCE ST
- VEN 93001 471-B7
VINCENNES ST
22000 Chat 91311 499-J6
VINCENTE AV
3800 CMRL 93010 494-G7
VINE PL
400 OXN 93033 552-G3
VINE ST
500 VeCo 93022 451-B7
500 VeCo 93022 461-B1
VINEWOOD
13300 MRPK 93021 496-F3
VINEYARD AV
100 OXN 93030 522-D2
VINEYARD AV Rt#-232
500 OXN 93030 522-G2
2600 VeCo 93030 522-G2
2800 OXN 93030 492-J7
2800 VeCo 93030 492-J7
3700 VeCo 93030 493-A5
VINTAGE ST
22000 Chat 91311 499-J5
VINTON CT
700 THO 91360 556-G1
VIOLET WY
500 OXN 93030 522-F1
VIOLETA ST
11000 VeCo 93004 493-A1
VIRGINIA DR
- VeCo 91320 555-H1
- VEN 93003 491-G2
VIRGINIA TER
100 SPLA 93060 464-A5
VIRGINIA COLONY PL
5500 MRPK 93021 476-H7
VIRGO CT
200 THO 91360 526-E2
VISALIA CT
100 VEN 93004 492-F2
VISALIA ST
1300 OXN 93035 552-E1
8200 VEN 93004 492-F2
VISTA CIR
2600 CMRL 93010 524-F1
VISTA CT
1300 CMRL 93010 524-F1
VISTA LP
2600 OXN 93030 492-F7
2600 OXN 93030 522-F1
VISTA RD
5900 VeCo 93063 499-B4
VISTA ST
2600 CMRL 93010 524-F1
VISTA ALCEDO
1800 CMRL 93012 495-D7
1800 CMRL 93012 525-D1
VISTA ANACAPA RD
9000 VeCo 93021 475-F5
VISTA ARRIAGO
800 CMRL 93012 525-C5
VISTA ARROYO DR
2500 VeCo 93012 496-E6
VISTA BONITA
100 THO 91320 525-E6
VISTA CONEJO
- THO 91320 525-E6
VISTA COTO VERDE
1100 CMRL 93010 494-C7
VISTA CREEK CIR
23600 SIMI 93065 497-D7
VISTA DEL CAMPO
800 VeCo 93010 494-A6
VISTA DEL CIMA
1100 VeCo 93010 494-B6
VISTA DEL MAR AV
1100 CMRL 93010 494-B7
1100 VeCo 93010 494-B7
VISTA DEL MAR DR
900 VEN 93001 491-E3
VISTA DEL MAR PL
1000 VEN 93001 491-D3
VISTA DEL MONTE
23600 FILM 93015 456-C6
VISTA DEL RINCON DR
6800 VeCo 93001 459-D5
VISTA DEL SOL
300 CMRL 93010 524-B3
VISTA DEL VALLE RD
4400 MRPK 93021 496-F2
VISTA DE VENTURA
500 VEN 93003 492-B1
VISTA DORADO LN
400 VeCo 91377 557-J2
VISTA GRANDE
2600 VeCo 93012 496-E6
VISTA GRANDE DR
23600 SPLA 93060 464-B4
VISTA HERMOSA DR
400 OJAI 93023 441-G5
VISTA HERMOSA ST
1100 SIMI 93065 497-E4
VISTA LAGO DR
- SIMI 93065 497-F4
- VeCo 93065 497-F4
VISTA LEVANA DR
13300 MRPK 93021 496-F2
VISTAMEADOW CT
4400 MRPK 93021 496-D3
VISTA MERCADO
3300 CMRL 93012 524-G2
VISTA MONTANA
400 VeCo 93010 494-A6
VISTA OAKS WY
1400 THO 91361 556-H6
VISTA PALACIO
700 CMRL 93012 524-H2
E VISTAPARK DR
13000 MRPK 93021 496-E2
VISTA POINTE PL
23600 SPLA 93060 464-B4
VISTA RIDGE LN
900 THO 91362 557-D1
VISTA WOOD CIR
2400 THO 91362 527-B4
VIVIAN CIR
800 THO 91320 526-C7
VIVIANA DR
- OXN 93030 522-J4
VOLCANO CT
2600 OXN 93030 522-D3
VOLTAIRE DR
3000 OXN 93033 552-J3
VOLTAIRE WY
10400 VeCo 93012 495-J6
10400 VeCo 93012 496-A6
VORALE AV
400 SIMI 93065 497-G3
VOSE ST
22500 CanP 91307 529-G5
VOYAGER AV
1600 SIMI 93063 498-E3
VOYAGER PL
1000 OXN 93033 522-H7

W

W ST
1500 VEN 93004 492-J3
1500 VEN 93004 493-A3
WABASH ST
8200 VEN 93004 492-G3
WACO DR
2900 SIMI 93063 478-G6
WACO ST
8700 VEN 93004 492-G2
WADE CIR
1600 SIMI 93065 497-J5
WADES RD
600 VeCo 93015 455-J1
600 VeCo 93015 456-A1
WAGNER RD
5100 VEN 93003 492-B4
WAGNER WY
5300 VeCo 91377 527-H6
N WAGON LN
- VeCo 91307 528-J3
WAGON WHEEL RD
900 OXN 93030 492-F7
1300 OXN 93030 522-G1
WAITE ST
100 OJAI 93023 441-J6
WAKEFIELD AV
1500 THO 91360 526-F5
E WAKEFORD AV
100 SPLA 93060 464-A6
W WAKEFORD AV
100 SPLA 93060 463-J6
100 SPLA 93060 464-A6
WAKE FOREST AV
- VEN 93003 492-C2
N WAKE FOREST AV
- VEN 93003 492-B2
WALDEMAR DR
23600 VeCo 91361 556-D7
WALDEN ST
100 SPLA 93060 463-H6
1900 OXN 93033 553-A5
WALDO AV
2100 SIMI 93065 498-C2
WALES DR
900 OXN 93035 522-E7
WALES ST
- THO 91360 526-F6
WALFORD CT
30200 AGRH 91301 557-H4
WALKER AV
400 CMRL 93010 524-F2
WALKER LN
- FILM 93015 456-A5
WALKER ST
4700 VEN 93003 492-B5
WALKER CUP CIR
1700 THO 91362 527-D6
WALKING HORSE LN
31500 WLKV 91361 557-E6
WALL ST
100 VEN 93001 491-B1
WALLABY CT
7400 VEN 93003 492-F4
WALLABY ST
7100 VEN 93003 492-E4
WALLACE ST
1500 SIMI 93065 497-J4
1700 SIMI 93065 498-A4
WALLBRIDGE WY
400 VeCo 93023 441-D7
WALLINGTON CT
31900 WLKV 91361 557-C6
WALNUT AV
4000 VeCo 93066 494-A3
WALNUT CT
700 THO 91320 556-C2
WALNUT DR
- VeCo 93030 492-J7
300 VEN 93003 492-A1
500 VeCo 93030 522-J1
700 VeCo 93030 523-A1
WALNUT ST
200 VEN 93001 491-B2
300 SPLA 93060 464-B5
600 MRPK 93021 476-E7
600 MRPK 93021 496-E1
3400 VeCo 93063 478-E6
3400 SIMI 93063 478-E6
WALNUT CANYON RD Rt#-23
800 MRPK 93021 476-E7
1000 VeCo 93021 476-E4
WALNUT CREEK RD
3900 MRPK 93021 496-D3
WALNUT RIDGE DR
5600 AGRH 91301 557-J5
WALSH RD
1100 VeCo 93063 499-G4
WALTER AV
100 THO 91320 555-F2
WALTER CIR
3600 THO 91320 555-F2
WALTER ST
600 VEN 93003 491-J5
WALTHAM CIR
1100 SIMI 93065 497-H4
WALTHAM RD
1000 SIMI 93065 497-H4
WALWORTH CT
1500 VeCo 91377 527-H6
WANDA AV
2600 SIMI 93065 498-B1
2600 SIMI 93065 478-B7
WANKEL WY
2300 OXN 93030 523-B3
WARBLE CT
- THO 91320 525-J5
100 THO 91320 526-A5
WARBLER AV
2300 VEN 93003 492-E5
WARD AV
2100 SIMI 93065 497-G2
WARD WY
1700 VeCo 93023 451-A3
WAREHOUSE AV
500 OXN 93030 522-H7
WARFIELD CIR
1700 SIMI 93063 499-A3
WARING PL
28400 AGRH 91301 558-C6
WARMSPRINGS AV
1300 THO 91320 526-A6
E WARNER ST
- VEN 93001 471-C7
W WARNER ST
- VEN 93001 471-B7
WARREN AV
100 SPLA 93060 464-A6
WARREN CIR
700 MRPK 93021 476-F7
WARRENDALE ST
1400 SIMI 93065 497-D7
WARRING CANYON RD
700 VeCo 93040 457-E2
WARRINGTON WY
1000 OJAI 93023 451-F1
WARWICK AV
400 THO 91360 526-F6
400 THO 91360 556-F1
W WASATCH CT
2700 THO 91362 557-C3
WASHBURN ST
- SIMI 93065 497-E3
WASHINGTON DR
1900 VEN 93003 492-C5
WATERBURY LN
900 VEN 93001 491-E4
WATERBY ST
2100 THO 91361 557-A5
WATERFALL LN
23600 SIMI 93065 478-C7
WATERFORD LN
900 FILM 93015 455-H7
WATERGATE CT
31900 WLKV 91361 557-C6
WATERGATE RD
2700 THO 91361 557-B5
32000 WLKV 91361 557-C6
WATEROAK LN
500 VeCo 91377 557-J1
WATERS RD
7800 VeCo 93021 475-G3
WATERSIDE CIR
23600 THO 91362 527-B4
WATERSIDE LN
32000 WLKV 91361 557-C7
WATERTOWN CT
2100 THO 91360 526-B4
WATERTREE CT
6200 AGRH 91301 558-A3
WATKINS WY
- VeCo 93022 451-B6
WATSON AV
600 SIMI 93065 498-C5
WATT DR
700 OXN 93030 552-H1
WATTS TREE FARM
12200 VeCo 93023 366-L7
WATTS TREE FARM RD
100 VeCo 93023 366-L7
100 VeCo 93023 453-B1
N WAUKEGAN AV
3000 SIMI 93063 478-F7
WAUNETA ST
3000 THO 91320 555-G2
WAVECREST WY
5000 OXN 93035 521-J7
WAVERLY AV
2600 CMRL 93010 524-F2
WAVERLY CT
500 OXN 93030 522-D4
2700 CMRL 93010 524-F2
WAVERLY DR
200 SIMI 93065 497-E2
WAVERLY HEIGHTS DR
600 THO 91360 526-G5
WAXWING AV
2300 VEN 93003 492-E5
WAYNE CIR
2300 SIMI 93065 498-A1
WAYSIDE CIR
1000 VeCo 93010 494-F6
WAYVIEW CT
6300 VEN 93003 472-D7
WEATHERFORD CT
3200 SIMI 93063 478-G6
WEATHERLY CIR
3800 WLKV 91361 557-B7
E WEAVER ST
600 SIMI 93065 497-G5
WEBB RD
23700 Chat 91311 499-E6
WEBER CIR
800 VEN 93003 492-A4
WEBER CT
4500 VEN 93003 492-A4
WEBSTER DR
4700 OXN 93033 553-A5
WEBSTER ST
5900 VEN 93003 492-C3
WEDGEWOOD CIR
100 THO 91360 526-F3
WEEPING WILLOW DR
3900 MRPK 93021 496-F4
29400 AGRH 91301 557-J4
WEINBERG ST
22400 Chat 91311 499-H4
WELAND
23600 VeCo 93015 456-F6
WELBY WY
2400 CanP 91307 529-D6
22100 CanP 91303 529-H6
24500 LACo 91307 529-C6
WELCOME CT
2300 SIMI 93063 499-B1
WELDON CANYON
23600 VeCo 93001 461-C5
WELLBROOK DR
32700 WLKV 91361 557-A7
32700 WLKV 91361 556-J7
WELLER CT
600 SIMI 93065 497-G4
WELLESLEY CT
700 THO 91360 526-G5
WELLESLEY DR
1700 THO 91360 526-G5
WELLINGTON CT
25900 LACo 91302 558-J3
WELLINGTON PL
1500 THO 91361 556-J6
WELLINGTON ST
8500 VEN 93004 492-G4
WELLS LN
200 WHil 91304 499-D6
WELLS RD
23600 VeCo 90265 585-G7
23600 VeCo 90265 625-G1
WELLS RD Rt#-118
700 VEN 93004 472-J7
700 VEN 93004 473-A7
800 VEN 93004 493-A1
900 VeCo 93004 493-A1
N WELLS RD
- VEN 93004 472-J6
- VeCo 93004 472-J6
- VEN 93060 472-J6
200 VeCo 93060 472-J6
S WELLS RD
- VEN 93004 472-J7
S WELLS RD Rt#-118
300 VEN 93004 472-J7
WELLSTON CT
3500 SIMI 93063 478-F5
WELSH CT
1400 SIMI 93065 497-E3
WEMBLY AV
5500 VeCo 91377 527-H6
WENDELL ST
2700 CMRL 93010 524-F1
N WENDY DR
100 VeCo 91320 555-G1
400 VeCo 91320 525-G7
600 THO 91320 525-G7
S WENDY DR
- THO 91320 555-G3
WENDY LN
400 SPLA 93060 464-A5
WENDY PL
2000 PHME 93041 552-D1
WESHAM ST
8400 VEN 93004 492-G4
WESLEY AV
200 VEN 93003 491-J3
WESLEYAN AV
300 VEN 93003 491-J1
WEST DR
1200 VEN 93003 492-D4
WEST RD
- PHME 93043 552-B4
WEST ST
3500 VeCo 93066 495-A5
WESTAR DR
1100 OXN 93033 552-J1
WESTBEND RD
600 THO 91362 557-D1
800 THO 91362 527-D7
WESTBLUFF PL
23600 SIMI 93065 497-E4
WESTBURY CT
- THO 91360 526-F6
WESTBURY ST
100 THO 91360 526-F6
WESTCHESTER CT
1900 OXN 93030 522-D3
WESTCHESTER LN
600 THO 91320 556-D1
WESTCLIFF DR
7300 LA 91304 529-D4
WESTCREEK LN
900 THO 91362 557-G1
900 VeCo 91362 557-G1
1000 THO 91362 527-G7
WESTDALE RD
4200 MRPK 93021 496-B3
WESTFIELD CT
600 VEN 93004 492-H2
WEST FORK HALL CANYON RD
2800 VeCo 93001 471-G4
WESTGATE RD
13200 MRPK 93021 496-E3
WESTHAM CIR
2700 THO 91362 527-A3
WESTHILLS CT
2600 SIMI 93065 477-E7
2600 SIMI 93065 497-E1
WESTINGHOUSE ST
4400 VEN 93003 492-A5
WESTLAKE BLVD
700 THO 91361 556-J6
WESTLAKE BLVD Rt#-23
100 LACo 90265 586-H4
400 WLKV 90265 586-H4
400 WLKV 91361 586-H4
800 LACo 91361 586-H4
1200 THO 91361 586-H4
N WESTLAKE BLVD
- THO 91362 557-C3
1000 THO 91362 527-B4
S WESTLAKE BLVD
- THO 91362 557-C4
S WESTLAKE BLVD Rt#-23
100 THO 91362 557-B5
100 THO 91361 557-B5
600 THO 91361 556-J7
800 THO 91361 586-H1
WESTLAKE EDISON RD
100 THO 91361 556-G4
100 VeCo 91361 556-G4
WESTLAND AV
23600 THO 91362 527-A1
WESTMINSTER AV
100 VEN 93003 492-B3
WESTMINSTER ST
500 THO 91360 526-G7
WESTMONT DR
12500 MRPK 93021 496-D3
WESTMONT ST
4400 VEN 93003 492-A3
WEST MOUNTAIN RD
20000 VeCo 93066 473-E7
20000 VeCo 93066 493-E1
WESTON CIR
1700 CMRL 93010 494-F7
1700 CMRL 93010 524-F1
WESTON CT
300 SPLA 93060 463-J6
WESTOVER PL
700 THO 91320 555-G3
WEST POINT ST
5000 VEN 93003 492-B1
WESTPORT ST
12900 MRPK 93021 496-E4
WESTRANCH PL
23600 SIMI 93065 497-E4
WESTRIDGE CIR
2900 THO 91360 526-C3
WESTRIDGE DR
1000 VEN 93003 472-D6
WEST SHORE LN
1300 THO 91361 557-A6
WEST VAIL DR
23100 CanP 91307 529-F5
WESTVIEW CT
4800 THO 91362 557-F1
WESTWIND CIR
1300 THO 91361 557-B6
WESTWOOD DR
2100 CMRL 93010 494-E7
E WESTWOOD ST
6300 MRPK 93021 476-G6
N WESTWOOD ST
700 MRPK 93021 476-G6
WETSTONE CT
2000 THO 91362 527-A4
WETSTONE DR
2100 THO 91362 527-A4
E WEXFORD CIR
1700 SIMI 93065 497-J5
1700 SIMI 93065 498-A5
WEYLAND CT
2600 SIMI 93065 478-B7
WEYMOUTH LN
1200 VEN 93001 491-F5
WHALEBOAT PL
30700 AGRH 91301 557-G5
WHALERS LN
11900 VeCo 90265 625-F5
WHEATFIELD CIR
2600 SIMI 93063 498-D1
2600 SIMI 93063 478-D7
WHEATON CT
14600 MRPK 93021 476-H6
WHEATON DR
4500 VEN 93003 492-A3
WHEELER CANYON RD
2500 VeCo 93060 473-B1
2600 VeCo 93060 463-A3
7300 VeCo 93060 453-B6
WHEELHOUSE AV
2400 PHME 93041 552-C2
WHEELHOUSE LN
5800 AGRH 91301 557-G4
WHEELWRIGHT LN
1900 THO 91320 525-J7
1900 THO 91320 526-A7
WHIM DR
30800 WLKV 91362 557-F4
WHIPPLE RD
100 VeCo 93060 464-D5
WHIPPOORWILL ST
6300 VEN 93003 492-D6
WHISPERING HILLS AV
23600 THO 91320 555-E4
WHISPERING OAKS PL
600 THO 91320 556-D1
WHISPERING PINES
4900 THO 91362 557-G1
WHISTLER WY
6500 VEN 93003 492-D1
WHITCOMB AV
1000 SIMI 93065 498-B4
WHITE ST
6300 SIMI 93063 499-C2
WHITE BIRCH CIR
3100 THO 91360 526-H2
WHITECAP CT
200 PHME 93041 552-E6
WHITE CAP DR
400 VEN 93003 491-H1
WHITECAP ST
5000 OXN 93035 521-J7
WHITE CEDAR PL
3100 THO 91362 527-C3
WHITECHAPEL PL
2400 THO 91362 527-B2
WHITECLIFF RD
900 THO 91360 526-G7
WHITE CLOUD CIR
5100 THO 91362 527-G7
WHITE DOVE CIR
1300 THO 91362 527-G7
WHITE FEATHER CT
1300 THO 91320 526-A6
WHITEGATE RD
400 THO 91320 555-H3
400 VeCo 91320 555-H3
E WHITEHALL CT
1900 SIMI 93065 498-A5
WHITEHALL LN
- CanP 91307 529-D5
WHITEHALL PL
1500 THO 91361 556-J6
WHITEHEAD PL
23600 VEN 93003 492-C6
WHITE OAK CIR
500 OJAI 93023 441-J5
WHITE OAK LN
600 THO 91320 556-D2
WHITE PINE CT
1300 VeCo 91377 527-G7
WHITE RIDGE PL
2700 THO 91362 527-B3
WHITE RIVER PL
3400 WLKV 91361 557-B7
WHITE SAGE RD
23600 MRPK 93021 496-G1
WHITESAIL CIR
4000 WLKV 91361 557-B6
WHITESIDE PL
200 THO 91362 557-A2
WHITE STALLION RD
- VeCo 91320 555-H4
- VeCo 91361 555-H4
WHITE SWAN CT
500 SIMI 93065 497-E6
WHITETAIL AV
23600 SIMI 93063 479-A6
WHITEWATER LN
11800 VeCo 90265 625-F5
WHITE WING CT
2600 VeCo 93012 496-A7
E WHITEWOOD ST
6500 SIMI 93063 499-C2
WHITFORD AV
23600 VeCo 91361 556-G6
WHITINGHAM CT
29300 AGRH 91301 558-A3
WHITMAN CT
500 THO 91360 526-G2
6800 VEN 93003 492-E3
WHITNEY AV
100 MRPK 93021 496-D1
WHITNEY CIR
100 OXN 93033 553-C3
WHITTIER CT
4300 VEN 93003 492-A3
WHITTIER ST
4400 VEN 93003 492-A3
WHITWORTH ST
100 THO 91360 526-E4
WICHITA FALLS AV
3200 SIMI 93063 478-H6
WICKLOW CT
1600 THO 91361 556-J5
WICKS RD
- MRPK 93021 476-E7
WIGGIN ST
4800 VeCo 91377 557-G1
WILBUR CT
500 THO 91360 526-G7
WILBUR RD
- THO 91360 556-E1
E WILBUR RD
- THO 91360 526-F7
W WILBUR RD
- THO 91360 526-F7
100 THO 91360 556-F1
WILCOX ST
2100 CMRL 93010 524-E2
WILDCAT AV
2300 VEN 93003 492-E5

STREET Block City ZIP Pg-Grid

WILD CLOVER WY
300 SIMI 93065 527-D1
WILDCREEK CIR
700 THO 91360 526-C2
WILDEN DR
- VeCo 93010 494-D7
WILDER ST
1200 THO 91362 527-A6
WILDFLOWER CT
11500 MRPK 93021 496-B2
WILD HORSE CT
3000 THO 91360 526-C2
WILDLIFE DR
- SIMI 93065 497-E5
W WILDOAK ST
- VeCo 93023 451-B4
WILDON RD
23600 CMRL 93010 524-C4
WILD ROSE ST
2500 THO 91361 557-B5
WILD SAGE CT
3900 THO 91362 527-C6
WILDWEST CIR
13800 MRPK 93021 496-F3
WILDWOOD AV
300 THO 91360 526-B1
WILDWOOD PL
22200 Chat 91311 499-J2
WILEMAN ST
800 FILM 93015 455-J6
WILEY CANYON RD
23600 VeCo - 467-B1
23600 VeCo 93015 467-B1
23600 VeCo 93021 467-B6
WILL AV
300 VeCo 93030 492-J7
700 VeCo 93030 493-A7
WILLAMETTE ST
10000 VEN 93004 492-J3
WILLARD RD
- VeCo 93060 464-F4
W WILLEY ST
- VeCo 93023 451-B4
WILLIAM CT
600 SIMI 93065 497-G4
WILLIAM DR
3300 VeCo 91320 555-F1
WILLIAMS DR
1900 OXN 93030 523-A3
WILLIAMS LN
1600 SIMI 93063 499-B3
WILLIAMS PL
700 OJAI 93023 441-J6
WILLIAMS ST
1800 SIMI 93065 497-H3
WILLIAMS WY
5900 SIMI 93063 499-B3
WILLIAMS CANYON RD
500 VeCo 93060 472-H5
500 VEN 93060 472-H5
WILLIAMS RANCH RD
12600 MRPK 93021 496-D3
WILLIS AV
200 CMRL 93010 523-J4
200 CMRL 93010 524-A4
WILLIS CANYON RD
- VeCo 93023 366-H7
- VeCo 93023 441-A6
WILLOUGHBY RD
- VeCo 93060 453-A6
23600 VeCo 93060 452-H7
WILLOW CT
2600 SIMI 93063 498-E1
WILLOW LN
100 SPLA 93060 464-A5
2400 THO 91361 556-J2
2400 THO 91361 557-A3
WILLOW ST
400 OXN 93033 552-G3
E WILLOW ST
400 OJAI 93023 441-J7
WILLOWBROOK DR
100 PHME 93041 552-F6
WILLOWBROOK LN
1400 SIMI 93065 497-H3
WILLOW CANYON ST
- THO 91362 527-C2
WILLOW CREEK CT
2200 OXN 93030 522-D1
WILLOW CREEK LN
3900 MRPK 93021 496-G3
WILLOW FOREST DR
12300 MRPK 93021 496-C3
WILLOW GLEN CIR
23600 SIMI 93065 527-F1
WILLOW GLEN ST
4300 CALB 91302 558-H7
WILLOWGREEN CT
1900 THO 91361 557-A5
WILLOW GROVE CT
12400 MRPK 93021 496-D3
WILLOW HAVEN CT
- THO 91362 527-C2
WILLOW HILL DR
12200 MRPK 93021 496-C3
WILLOWICK DR
3500 VEN 93003 491-H2
WILLOWOOD CT
11500 MRPK 93021 496-B2

WILLOWPARK CT
2200 THO 91362 527-A4
WILLOW SPRINGS DR
12200 MRPK 93021 496-C3
WILLOW TREE CT
1900 THO 91362 526-J4
1900 THO 91362 527-A4
WILLOWTREE DR
5700 AGRH 91301 557-H4
WILLOW VIEW DR
5300 CMRL 93012 525-A2
WILLSBROOK CT
1200 THO 91361 556-J5
1200 THO 91361 557-A5
E WILMOT ST
3200 SIMI 93063 498-D2
WILSHIRE PL
400 THO 91320 555-H3
WILSON AV
100 OXN 93030 522-H6
WILSON DR
800 VeCo 93015 455-D5
1000 SIMI 93065 498-C4
WILSON ST
2500 VeCo 93015 465-E1
23600 VEN 93003 492-E2
WILTON ST
1600 SIMI 93065 497-J2
WIMBLEDON CIR
1300 THO 91361 557-A5
WINCHESTER DR
300 OXN 93030 522-G1
6200 VeCo 93021 475-J6
WINCHESTER WY
5400 CMRL 93012 525-A1
WINDBREEZE AV
23600 THO 91362 527-B2
WINDBROOK CT
1900 THO 91361 557-A7
WINDCREST CT
2700 OXN 93030 492-F7
2700 OXN 93030 522-F1
WINDFLOWER CIR
3200 THO 91360 526-H2
WINDHARP LN
23600 SIMI 93065 497-A2
WINDHAVEN DR
4800 THO 91362 557-E2
WINDING LN
3000 THO 91361 557-C5
WINDINGWAY DR
800 VEN 93001 491-D1
WINDMILL LN
1000 VeCo 91377 528-B7
1000 VeCo 91377 558-A1
WINDMIST AV
23600 THO 91362 527-B2
WINDOM ST
22800 CanP 91307 529-G4
23200 LA 91304 529-F4
WINDOVER RD
8400 VeCo 93021 476-D3
WINDRIDGE AV
- THO 91362 527-C2
WINDRIFT CT
3000 THO 91360 526-F2
WIND RIVER CIR
400 THO 91362 557-B2
WINDROSE CT
23600 THO 91320 556-C1
WINDROSE DR
100 THO 91320 556-C1
WINDSONG LN
29600 AGRH 91301 557-J5
WINDSONG ST
2900 THO 91360 526-F2
WINDSOR CT
2200 CMRL 93010 494-D7
WINDSOR DR
1000 THO 91360 526-G6
WINDSWEPT PL
500 SIMI 93065 497-D7
500 SIMI 93065 527-D1
WINDTREE AV
100 THO 91320 556-C1
WINDWARD CIR
2300 THO 91361 557-B6
WINDWARD WY
1000 OXN 93035 522-D7
WINDWILLOW WY
1500 SIMI 93065 497-D6
WINDY MOUNTAIN AV
5000 THO 91362 527-F7
WINFIELD ST
900 THO 91320 555-E4
WINFORD AV
1100 VEN 93004 492-G3
WING RD
200 Chat 91311 499-F6
WINGED FOOT CT
2200 OXN 93030 522-D2
WINIFRED ST
2000 SIMI 93063 498-G2
WINNCASTLE ST
500 SIMI 93065 527-D2
WINONA CT
6400 VeCo 91377 558-A1
WINROCK WY
23600 SIMI 93065 497-A1

WINSIDE CT
4800 THO 91362 557-G2
WINSTON CT
1000 THO 91361 557-B5
WINTER AV
12600 MRPK 93021 496-E4
WINTERBERRY AV
5200 SIMI 93063 498-J2
WINTERBROOK CT
3100 THO 91360 526-F2
WINTERDEW AV
23600 SIMI 93065 497-D2
WINTERGREEN LN
13200 MRPK 93021 496-E4
WINTERSET PL
1800 SIMI 93065 497-D2
WINTERWOOD CT
4000 MRPK 93021 496-C3
WINTHROP CT
2500 SIMI 93065 497-J1
WINTHROP LN
1000 VEN 93001 491-E4
WISCASSET DR
- LA 91304 529-D4
WISDOM CT
3200 SIMI 93063 478-D6
WISHARD AV
600 SIMI 93065 497-J5
WISTERIA LN
900 SPLA 93060 473-J1
WISTERIA ST
2000 SIMI 93065 498-B2
WISTERIA WY
- VEN 93004 473-C7
WITHERSPOON DR
900 THO 91360 526-G2
WOLF CREEK CT
23600 SIMI 93063 479-A6
WOLFF RD
100 VeCo 93030 523-E7
500 VeCo 93033 523-E7
500 VeCo 93033 553-E1
WOLFF ST
100 OXN 93033 522-F7
WOLSEY CT
4500 WLKV 91361 557-C5
WOLVERINE ST
7000 VEN 93003 492-E5
WOLVERTON AV
1300 CMRL 93010 524-F1
1700 CMRL 93010 494-F7
WOLVERTON ST
9000 VEN 93004 492-H3
WOOD RD
- CMRL 93010 523-H3
400 VeCo 93010 523-H3
1000 VeCo 93012 523-H7
1100 VeCo 93012 553-H3
1100 VeCo 93033 523-H7
1100 VeCo 93033 553-H3
6400 VeCo 93012 583-G1
6400 VeCo 93033 583-G1
6800 VeCo 93041 583-G1
WOOD ST
1900 VEN 93003 492-A5
WOODBINE CT
3000 THO 91360 526-D3
WOODBLUFF CT
23600 THO 91362 527-A2
WOODBRIAR PL
30100 AGRH 91301 557-H4
WOODBRIDGE LN
- SIMI 93063 498-H1
WOODBROOK DR
29500 AGRH 91301 557-J4
WOODBURN AV
2000 THO 91361 557-A7
2600 WLKV 91361 557-A7
WOODBURY ST
5300 VEN 93003 492-B3
WOODCREEK CT
29000 AGRH 91301 558-A3
WOODCREEK RD
600 CMRL 93012 525-A1
1700 CMRL 93012 495-A7
WOODCREST PL
6500 VeCo 91377 558-B2
WOODCUTTER LN
1900 THO 91320 525-J7
1900 THO 91320 526-A7
WOODED VISTA
24600 CanP 91307 529-C7
WOODFERN CIR
3100 THO 91360 526-H2
WOODFLOWER ST
- THO 91362 527-B2
WOODGATE CT
1000 CMRL 93010 524-C2
WOODGLADE LN
24500 CanP 91307 529-C5
WOODGLEN DR
4300 MRPK 93021 496-E3
5800 AGRH 91301 557-H4
WOODGLEN ST
1800 SIMI 93065 478-A7
WOODGREEN CT
2900 THO 91362 527-B2
WOODGROVE RD
800 FILM 93015 456-A5

WOODHALL AV
7600 LA 91304 529-F3
WOODHAVEN ST
3500 SIMI 93063 498-D1
N WOODHAVEN ST
2400 SIMI 93063 498-E1
WOODHILL DR
11200 MRPK 93021 496-B3
WOODLAKE AV
6100 WdHl 91367 529-G7
6400 CanP 91307 529-G5
7500 LA 91304 529-G2
WOODLAKE MNR
3900 MRPK 93021 496-F4
WOODLAND AV
700 VeCo 93023 451-B3
WOODLAND DR
1000 SPLA 93060 464-B3
WOODLAND RD
23600 SIMI 93065 497-G7
WOODLAND ST
1400 OXN 93035 552-E1
5900 VEN 93003 492-C2
6200 VeCo 93003 492-C2
WOODLAND GROVE CT
1300 THO 91362 527-E7
WOODLAND VIEW DR
6000 WdHl 91367 529-C7
WOODLANE CT
4100 THO 91362 527-C6
WOODLAWN DR
500 THO 91360 526-D7
WOODLEY AV
- THO 91362 527-C2
WOODLOCH LN
23600 SIMI 93065 497-A2
WOODLOW CT
1300 THO 91361 557-A6
WOOD OPAL WY
2400 OXN 93030 522-D3
WOODPECKER AV
2300 VEN 93003 492-E5
N WOOD RANCH PKWY
300 SIMI 93065 497-D5
S WOOD RANCH PKWY
- SIMI 93065 527-E1
200 SIMI 93065 497-E7
WOODRIDGE AV
1100 THO 91362 527-A6
WOODROW AV
2300 SIMI 93065 498-B1
2600 SIMI 93065 478-C7
WOODROW CT
2600 SIMI 93065 498-B1
WOODSCENT LN
23600 SIMI 93065 497-A2
WOODSIDE DR
1600 THO 91362 526-J3
WOODSIDE PL
1100 OXN 93030 522-F1
WOODSTEAD WY
100 SIMI 93065 497-F3
WOODSTOCK LN
900 VEN 93001 491-E4
WOODSTONE CT
3100 THO 91360 526-C2
WOODSTONE PL
7100 CanP 91307 529-C5
WOODVALE CT
7000 CanP 91307 529-F5
WOODVIEW CT
3200 THO 91362 527-C3
WOODWIND CT
2000 SIMI 93063 498-J2
WOODWORTH AV
- THO 91362 527-C2
WOOLEY RD
100 OXN 93030 522-C7
100 OXN 93033 522-C7
1600 OXN 93035 522-C7
1800 VeCo 93030 522-C7
1800 VeCo 93030 523-A7
1800 VeCo 93033 522-C7
1800 VeCo 93033 523-A7
3800 VeCo 93035 522-A7
4800 OXN 93035 521-J7
E WOOLEY RD
- OXN 93030 522-H7
1000 OXN 93033 522-G7
WOOLSEY CANYON RD
23700 LA 91304 499-D7
23900 WHil 91304 499-D7
24900 VeCo 93063 499-B7
WOOSTER ST
4300 VEN 93003 491-J2
4300 VEN 93003 492-A2
WORDSWORTH CT
2600 THO 91362 527-B3
WORDSWORTH WY
6500 VEN 93003 492-D3
WORKMAN AV
2100 SIMI 93063 498-G2
WORMWOOD ST
- VeCo 93023 451-B4
WORTH WY
5200 CMRL 93012 495-A7
5200 VeCo 93012 495-B5
N WRANGLER LN
- VeCo 91307 529-B3

WRANGLER RD
- SIMI 93065 497-J7
WREN CT
6900 VEN 93003 492-E4
WRIGHT RD
200 VeCo 93030 522-H1
2500 VeCo 93010 493-F6
WYANDOTTE ST
22000 CanP 91303 529-J5
22700 CanP 91307 529-G5
WYCHOFF AV
1600 SIMI 93063 499-A3
WYETH LN
500 VEN 93003 492-D1
WYNN CT
300 THO 91362 557-A1
WYNNEFIELD AV
1300 THO 91362 527-C6
WYSTERIA DR
6100 VeCo 93063 499-B4

X

XANADU WY
300 SIMI 93065 527-D1
XAVIER AV
100 VEN 93003 492-B2

Y

YAGER WY
3300 WLKV 91361 557-B7
YALE AV
100 VEN 93003 492-B3
6400 MRPK 93021 476-H6
YALE CT
100 SPLA 93060 464-A6
400 OXN 93030 522-H2
YALE PL
500 OXN 93033 552-H4
YALE ST
200 SPLA 93060 464-A6
1100 OXN 93033 552-J4
YANA CT
23600 SIMI 93063 479-B7
YANKEE DR
4000 AGRH 91301 558-E7
YARDARM AV
2500 PHME 93041 552-B2
YARDLEY PL
3200 SIMI 93063 478-D6
YARNELL AV
3200 SIMI 93063 478-F6
YARNELL PL
800 OXN 93033 552-H1
YARNTON CT
23600 VeCo 91361 556-F6
YEARLING CT
800 CMRL 93010 524-C2
YEARLING PL
2600 OXN 93030 492-F7
2600 OXN 93030 522-F1
YEATS LN
600 VEN 93003 492-D1
YELLOW HILL RD
13900 LACo 90265 625-G4
13900 VeCo 90265 625-F2
YELLOWSTONE AV
200 THO 91320 556-D2
YELLOWSTONE DR
100 OXN 93033 553-C3
YELLOW THROAT PL
- THO 91320 525-J5
- THO 91320 526-A5
YELLOWWOOD DR
2600 WLKV 91361 557-A7
YERBA BUENA RD
8400 VeCo 90265 586-A3
9800 VeCo 90265 585-H4
12600 VeCo 90265 625-F2
YERBA SECA AV
6200 AGRH 91301 558-B3
YEW DR
2300 THO 91320 555-J1
YOKUTS CT
23600 SIMI 93063 479-A7
YOLANDA ST
1900 CMRL 93010 524-D2
YOLO ST
10600 VEN 93004 472-H7
YORBA LINDA PL
400 CMRL 93012 524-J1
YORK PL
1000 THO 91362 527-A7
YORK ST
1100 OXN 93033 552-J4
YORKFIELD CT
4400 WLKV 91361 557-D6
YORKSHIRE AV
800 THO 91360 526-G7
YOSEMITE
100 OXN 93033 553-C3
YOSEMITE AV
1500 SIMI 93063 499-A2
2600 SIMI 93063 479-A6
5000 SIMI 93063 478-J6
YOSEMITE CT
- VEN 93003 492-C2
YOSEMITE DR
100 OXN 93033 553-B5

YOUMANS DR
200 VEN 93003 492-B3
YOUNAN DR
- Chat 91311 479-H7
- Chat 91311 499-H1
YOUNG AV
1900 THO 91360 526-E4
YOUNG RD
2100 VeCo 93015 455-D5
YSRELLA AV
1500 SIMI 93065 498-A3
YUBA CT
8100 VEN 93004 492-F1
YUBA DR
2800 SIMI 93063 479-A7
YUCCA CT
3700 OXN 93033 552-H4
YUCCA DR
500 FILM 93015 455-J5
1800 VeCo 93012 495-J7
1800 VeCo 93012 525-J1
YUCCA LN
- THO 91362 557-A3
YUCCA ST
- OXN 93033 552-H4
800 PHME 93041 552-H4
W YUCCA ST
100 OXN 93033 552-G3
YUCCA WY
2300 VeCo 93012 495-J7
YUKON AV
4200 SIMI 93063 478-F7
YUKON TR
8400 LA 91304 529-C2
YUKONITE PL
1000 OXN 93030 522-D4
YUMA CT
2400 VEN 93001 471-C5
YUMA ST
4100 SIMI 93063 478-F6
YUROK CT
23600 SIMI 93063 479-A7

Z

ZACHARY ST
300 MRPK 93021 496-F1
ZALTANA ST
22500 Chat 91311 499-H1
N ZANJA LN
- VeCo 91307 528-H5
ZAPATA CT
2800 SIMI 93063 478-G7
ZELDA WY
9200 Chat 91311 499-G7
ZELZAH AV
6800 VeCo 93001 459-C4
ZENITH AV
3600 THO 91360 526-G1
ZENO DR
400 VeCo 91377 557-G3
ZEPHYR CT
2300 VEN 93001 491-E4
ZIMMAN LN
2600 SIMI 93063 478-J7
2600 SIMI 93063 498-J1
ZINNIA CT
600 THO 91360 526-D2
ZION AV
400 OXN 93033 552-G4
ZION WY
1300 VEN 93003 492-B4
ZIRCON AV
1600 OXN 93030 522-D3
ZOCALO CIR
4400 THO 91360 496-J7
ZOLA AV
500 VEN 93003 492-D1
ZUNI CT
2400 VEN 93001 471-C5
ZUNIGA RIDGE PL
1700 THO 91362 556-J2

#

1ST AV
- PHME 93043 552-C2
1ST ST
- MRPK 93021 496-E1
100 SIMI 93065 497-H2
200 THO 91320 556-B2
300 FILM 93015 456-A6
700 FILM 93015 455-J6
E 1ST ST
200 OXN 93030 522-H5
W 1ST ST
100 OXN 93030 522-F5
2ND ST
- MRPK 93021 496-E1
100 FILM 93015 456-A5
100 PHME 93041 552-E5
200 THO 91320 556-B2
700 FILM 93015 455-J5
1400 SIMI 93065 497-H3
E 2ND ST
200 OXN 93030 522-H5
W 2ND ST
100 OXN 93030 522-F5
3RD ST
- VeCo 93042 583-G2

3RD ST
- MRPK 93021 496-E1
100 FILM 93015 456-A5
100 OXN 93030 522-E6
100 PHME 93041 552-E5
200 THO 91320 556-B1
700 FILM 93015 455-J5
1400 SIMI 93065 497-G3
23600 VeCo 93063 498-G7
E 3RD ST
100 OXN 93030 522-H6
W 3RD ST
100 OXN 93030 522-F6
3 M DR
2600 CMRL 93012 524-F4
4TH AV
- PHME 93043 552-D2
4TH PL
400 PHME 93041 552-E5
4TH ST
- VeCo 93042 583-G2
- FILM 93015 456-A5
- OXN 93030 522-F6
600 FILM 93015 455-J5
1000 SIMI 93065 497-G3
N 4TH ST
100 SPLA 93060 464-A6
S 4TH ST
100 SPLA 93060 464-B6
5TH PL
1000 PHME 93041 552-E4
5TH ST
- VeCo 93042 583-G2
100 PHME 93041 552-E4
700 FILM 93015 455-J5
1600 SIMI 93065 497-G3
1700 VeCo 93015 455-E6
5TH ST Rt#-34
100 OXN 93030 522-H6
1800 VeCo 93030 522-H6
1800 VeCo 93030 523-A6
1800 OXN 93030 523-A6
2600 OXN 93033 523-A6
2600 VeCo 93033 523-D6
E 5TH ST Rt#-34
- VeCo 93012 523-H6
- VeCo 93012 524-C6
N 5TH ST
200 SPLA 93060 464-A5
S 5TH ST
300 SPLA 93060 464-B6
W 5TH ST
100 OXN 93030 522-F6
2900 VeCo 93030 522-A6
3800 OXN 93030 521-J6
3800 OXN 93035 521-J6
3800 VeCo 93030 521-J6
6TH PL
1000 PHME 93041 552-F4
6TH ST
- VeCo 93042 583-G2
100 OXN 93030 522-F6
600 FILM 93015 455-J4
600 FILM 93015 456-A4
600 VeCo 93015 456-A4
1000 PHME 93041 552-F4
E 6TH ST
- OXN 93030 522-G6
N 6TH ST
200 SPLA 93060 464-A5
7TH PL
1200 PHME 93041 552-F4
7TH ST
- VeCo 93042 583-F2
100 OXN 93030 522-F6
600 FILM 93015 455-J4
600 FILM 93015 456-A4
1000 PHME 93041 552-F4
1600 OXN 93035 522-E6
1700 VeCo 93015 455-F6
N 7TH ST
100 SPLA 93060 464-B5
S 7TH ST
100 SPLA 93060 464-B6
8TH AV
- PHME 93043 552-D2
8TH CIR
1600 PHME 93041 552-F3
8TH PL
1400 PHME 93041 552-F4
8TH ST
- OXN 93035 522-E7
- VeCo 93042 583-G3
- FILM 93015 455-J4
100 OXN 93030 522-G7
1400 PHME 93041 552-F4
5900 VEN 93003 492-C5
N 8TH ST
100 SPLA 93060 464-B5
S 8TH ST
100 SPLA 93060 464-B6
9TH AV NW
1100 VeCo 93023 451-C2
9TH ST
- VeCo 93042 583-G2
100 OXN 93030 522-G7
200 SPLA 93060 464-B5
1500 OXN 93035 522-E7
10TH AV
- PHME 93043 552-D3

10TH ST
- VeCo 93042 583-F3
23600 VeCo 93063 498-G7
23600 VeCo 93063 528-G1
N 10TH ST
300 SPLA 93060 464-B4
N 10TH ST Rt#-150
100 SPLA 93060 464-B5
S 10TH ST Rt#-150
100 SPLA 93060 464-C6
11TH AV
- PHME 93043 552-D3
11TH ST
600 VeCo 93042 583-F3
700 VeCo 93041 583-F3
23600 VeCo 93063 528-G1
N 11TH ST
100 SPLA 93060 464-C5
S 11TH ST
100 SPLA 93060 464-C5
12TH ST
- VeCo 93042 583-G4
23600 VeCo 93063 528-G1
N 12TH ST
100 SPLA 93060 464-C4
S 12TH ST
100 SPLA 93060 464-C5
13TH ST
- VeCo 93042 583-F4
N 13TH ST
100 SPLA 93060 464-C4
S 13TH ST
200 SPLA 93060 464-C5
14TH ST
- VeCo 93042 583-E3
300 SPLA 93060 464-C4
15TH AV
- PHME 93043 552-E3
15TH ST
- VeCo 93042 583-E4
16TH ST
- VeCo 93042 583-D4
16 DE SEPTIEMBRE
1500 VEN 93004 492-J3
1500 VEN 93004 493-A3
17TH ST
- VeCo 93042 583-D4
23600 VeCo 93063 528-F1
18TH ST
- VeCo 93042 583-D5
23600 VeCo 93063 528-G1
19TH AV
- PHME 93043 552-E3
19TH ST
- VeCo 93042 583-E6
20TH AV
- PHME 93043 552-E3
20TH ST
- VeCo 93042 583-F6
23600 VeCo 93063 528-F1
21ST AV
- PHME 93043 552-D3
22ND ST
23600 VeCo 93063 528-F1
24TH AV
- PHME 93043 552-E3
24TH ST
23600 VeCo 93063 528-F1
25TH AV
- PHME 93043 552-E3
27TH AV
- PHME 93043 552-E3
28TH AV
- PHME 93043 552-D3
29TH AV
- PHME 93043 552-E4
32ND AV
- PHME 93041 552-D4
- PHME 93043 552-C4
33RD AV
- PHME 93041 552-E4
34TH AV
- PHME 93041 552-D4
35TH AV
- PHME 93043 552-D4
36TH AV
- PHME 93041 552-E4
41ST ST
- PHME 93041 552-E5
- PHME 93043 552-E5
NW 144TH ST
400 OJAI 93023 451-G1
NW 171ST ST
1300 VeCo 93023 451-D2
N 188TH ST
700 OJAI 93023 451-H1
N 201ST ST
2000 VeCo 93023 451-C3
Rt#-N1 LAS VIRGENES RD
3700 CALB 91302 558-H7
4800 LACo 91302 558-H7
Rt#-1 OLD RINCON HWY
2900 VeCo 93001 470-F6
4200 VeCo 93001 366-G9
4200 VeCo 93001 459-F7
4200 VeCo 93001 469-H1
23600 VeCo 93001 490-G1

Rt#-1 OXNARD BLVD
100 OXN 93030 522-G1
1200 OXN 93030 552-H1
1200 OXN 93033 522-G7
1200 OXN 93033 552-H1
2600 OXN 93030 492-G7
Rt#-1 PACIFIC COAST FRWY
- OXN - 552-J2
- OXN - 553-C4
- VeCo - 553-C4
- VeCo - 583-H1
Rt#-1 PACIFIC COAST HWY
2900 VeCo 93001 470-B3
4200 VeCo 93001 366-G9
4200 VeCo 93001 459-F6
4200 VeCo 93001 469-H1
9000 VeCo - 387-F4
9000 VeCo 90265 387-F4
9000 VeCo 90265 625-A3
9400 VeCo - 584-A6
12300 LACo 90265 625-F5
19900 VeCo 93012 583-J5
19900 VeCo 93012 584-A6
23600 VeCo 93001 490-G1
34000 MAL 90265 625-F5
Rt#-N9 KANAN RD
4100 Ago 91301 558-A7
4100 AGRH 91301 558-A7
Rt#-23 A ST
- FILM 93015 456-A6
- FILM 93015 466-A1
Rt#-23 BELLEVUE AV
700 VeCo 93015 465-J3
700 VeCo 93015 466-A3
Rt#-23 BROADWAY
14900 VeCo 93021 476-D4
Rt#-23 CHAMBERSBURG RD
300 FILM 93015 466-A2
300 VeCo 93015 466-A2
Rt#-23 DECKER RD
1400 LACo 90265 586-F7
Rt#-23 FRWY
- MRPK - 496-G1
- THO - 496-J7
- THO - 497-A5
- THO - 526-J1
- THO - 556-H2
- VeCo - 496-H3
- VeCo - 497-A4
Rt#-23 GRIMES CANYON RD
1300 VeCo 93015 465-J4
4800 VeCo 93015 466-A5
4800 VeCo 93021 466-A5
8000 VeCo 93021 476-B2
Rt#-23 MOORPARK AV
- MRPK 93021 476-E7
500 MRPK 93021 496-E1
Rt#-23 N MOORPARK AV
- MRPK 93021 496-E1
Rt#-23 MULHOLLAND HWY
33000 LACo 90265 586-G6
Rt#-23 WALNUT CANYON RD
800 MRPK 93021 476-E7
1000 VeCo 93021 476-E4
Rt#-23 WESTLAKE BLVD
100 LACo 90265 586-H4
400 WLKV 90265 586-H4
400 WLKV 91361 586-H4
800 LACo 91361 586-H4
1200 THO 91361 586-H4
Rt#-23 S WESTLAKE BLVD
100 THO 91362 557-B5
100 THO 91361 557-B5
600 THO 91361 556-J7
800 THO 91361 586-H1
Rt#-27 TOPANGA CANYON BLVD
9500 Chat 91311 499-J6
Rt#-33 HIGHWAY
- VeCo - 366-H3
- VeCo 93023 366-J6
- VeCo 93252 366-G1
Rt#-33 MARICOPA HWY
1000 OJAI 93023 441-E6
1000 OJAI 93023 451-F1
1700 VeCo 93023 441-B2
10000 VeCo 93023 366-J6
10200 VeCo - 366-J6
Rt#-33 OJAI DR
- VeCo 93022 451-B6
Rt#-33 OJAI FRWY
- VeCo - 461-B6
- VeCo - 471-C3
- VEN - 471-B7
- VEN - 491-A1
Rt#-33 VENTURA AV
- VeCo 93022 451-B5
4400 VeCo 93001 461-A2
4400 VeCo 93022 461-A2
11200 VeCo 93023 451-D2
11800 OJAI 93023 451-F1

Rt#-34 5TH ST
100 OXN 93030 522-H6
1800 VeCo 93030 522-H6
1800 VeCo 93030 523-A6
1800 OXN 93030 523-A6
2600 OXN 93033 523-A6
2600 VeCo 93033 523-D6
Rt#-34 E 5TH ST
- VeCo 93012 523-H6
- VeCo 93012 524-C6
Rt#-34 N LEWIS RD
- CMRL 93010 524-G2
1700 CMRL 93010 494-H7
Rt#-34 S LEWIS RD
- CMRL 93010 524-F4
200 CMRL 93012 524-F4
Rt#-34 PLEASANT VALLEY RD
2200 VeCo 93012 524-F5
2200 CMRL 93012 524-F5
Rt#-34 SOMIS RD
2400 CMRL 93010 494-J6
2400 VeCo 93010 494-J6
2600 VeCo 93010 495-A5
2600 VeCo 93066 495-A5
Rt#-118 LOS ANGELES AV
- MRPK 93021 496-A2
900 VeCo 93010 493-H4
900 VeCo 93010 494-A4
900 VeCo 93066 493-H4
900 VeCo 93066 494-A4
1200 VeCo 93004 493-B2
1600 VeCo 93030 493-B2
4500 VeCo 93066 495-A4
8000 VeCo 93021 495-H3
10700 VeCo 93021 496-A2
Rt#-118 NEW LOS ANGELES AV
500 MRPK 93021 496-F1
Rt#-118 RONALD REAGAN FRWY
- Chat - 499-E2
- MRPK - 476-H7
- MRPK - 477-B6
- MRPK - 496-G1
- SIMI - 477-B6
- SIMI - 497-G1
- SIMI - 498-F1
- SIMI - 499-E2
- VeCo - 477-B6
Rt#-118 WELLS RD
700 VEN 93004 472-J7
700 VEN 93004 473-A7
800 VEN 93004 493-A1
900 VeCo 93004 493-A1
Rt#-118 S WELLS RD
300 VEN 93004 472-J7
Rt#-126 HENRY MAYO DR
31100 Cstc 91384 458-H5
31800 VeCo 93040 458-H5
Rt#-126 KOREAN WAR VET MEM HY
2600 VeCo 93015 455-E7
2700 VeCo 93015 465-B2
17900 VeCo 93060 464-F3
18400 SPLA 93060 464-F3
20100 VeCo 93060 465-B2
Rt#-126 OLD TELEGRAPH RD
2600 VeCo 93015 455-E7
2700 VeCo 93015 465-E1
Rt#-126 SANTA PAULA FRWY
- SPLA - 463-J7
- SPLA - 464-D5
- SPLA - 473-F4
- VeCo - 473-B6
- VeCo - 473-F4
- VeCo - 492-D3
- VEN - 472-J7
- VEN - 473-B6
- VEN - 491-J4
- VEN - 492-D3
Rt#-126 TELEGRAPH RD
- VeCo 93015 456-E6
900 VeCo 93015 457-E5
1400 VeCo 93040 457-G4
2200 VeCo 93040 458-B5
2700 VeCo 93015 465-C1
17900 VeCo 93060 464-F3
18400 SPLA 93060 464-F3
20100 VeCo 93060 465-A2
Rt#-126 VENTURA ST
100 FILM 93015 456-A6
400 FILM 93015 455-F7
1100 VeCo 93015 455-F7
Rt#-126 E VENTURA ST
- FILM 93015 456-C6
400 VeCo 93015 456-C6
Rt#-150 N 10TH ST
100 SPLA 93060 464-B5
Rt#-150 S 10TH ST
100 SPLA 93060 464-C6
Rt#-150 BALDWIN AV
200 VEN 93004 492-F2

STREET Block	City	ZIP	Pg-Grid	STREET Block	City	ZIP	Pg-Grid	STREET Block	City	ZIP	Pg-Grid	STREET Block	City	ZIP	Pg-Grid	STREET Block	City	ZIP	Pg-Grid	STREET Block	City	ZIP	Pg-Grid	STREET Block	City	ZIP	Pg-Grid	STREET Block	City	ZIP	Pg-Grid	STREET Block	City	ZIP	Pg-Grid

Rt#-150 BALDWIN RD

Block	City	ZIP	Pg-Grid
-	VeCo	93001	450-H3
-	VeCo	93023	450-H3
600	VeCo	93023	451-A3

Rt#-150 CASITAS PASS RD

Block	City	ZIP	Pg-Grid
2000	VeCo	93001	450-D5
3500	VeCo	93001	460-B1
4000	VeCo	93001	366-G8
4000	VeCo	93001	459-G1
5800	VeCo	-	366-G8
6100	VeCo	93013	366-G8
7100	StBC	93013	459-G1

Rt#-150 E OJAI AV

Block	City	ZIP	Pg-Grid
200	OJAI	93023	441-H7
1100	OJAI	93023	442-B7
1700	VeCo	93023	442-B7

Rt#-150 W OJAI AV

Block	City	ZIP	Pg-Grid
100	OJAI	93023	441-G7
1000	OJAI	93023	451-G1

Rt#-150 N OJAI RD

Block	City	ZIP	Pg-Grid
100	SPLA	93060	464-B3
300	VeCo	93060	464-B3

Rt#-150 OJAI SANTA PAULA RD

Block	City	ZIP	Pg-Grid
3100	VeCo	93023	442-D7
7000	VeCo	93023	452-E1
11900	VeCo	93023	453-A1

Rt#-150 RINCON RD

Block	City	ZIP	Pg-Grid
6600	StBC	93013	459-A1
6600	VeCo	93013	366-G9
6600	VeCo	93013	459-A1

Rt#-150 SANTA PAULA OJAI RD

Block	City	ZIP	Pg-Grid
4300	VeCo	93060	464-A1
4400	VeCo	93060	454-A7
4600	VeCo	93060	453-H4
12300	VeCo	93023	453-H4

Rt#-192 CASITAS PASS RD

Block	City	ZIP	Pg-Grid
6800	StBC	93013	459-A1

Rt#-232 VINEYARD AV

Block	City	ZIP	Pg-Grid
500	OXN	93030	522-G2
2600	VeCo	93030	522-G2
2800	OXN	93030	492-J7
2800	VeCo	93030	492-J7
3700	VeCo	93030	493-A5

U.S.-101 EL CAMINO REAL

Block	City	ZIP	Pg-Grid
-	VeCo	93001	366-E8
-	VeCo	93001	459-C5
-	VeCo	93001	469-H1
-	VeCo	93001	470-E5
-	VeCo	93001	490-H1
-	VeCo	93013	366-E8
-	VeCo	93013	459-C5
-	VEN	93001	490-H1
-	VEN	93001	491-G4
-	VEN	93003	491-G4

U.S.-101 VENTURA FRWY

Block	City	ZIP	Pg-Grid
-	Ago	-	558-D6
-	AGRH	-	557-G6
-	AGRH	-	558-D6
-	CALB	-	558-D6
-	CMRL	-	523-A3
-	CMRL	-	524-A3
-	CMRL	-	525-C5
-	LACo	-	558-D6
-	OXN	-	492-F7
-	OXN	-	522-H2
-	OXN	-	523-A3
-	THO	-	525-C5
-	THO	-	526-D7
-	THO	-	555-J1
-	THO	-	556-E1
-	THO	-	557-B4
-	VeCo	-	366-F9
-	VeCo	-	459-A3
-	VeCo	-	469-J1
-	VeCo	-	470-B3
-	VeCo	-	490-H1
-	VeCo	-	492-F7
-	VeCo	-	523-A3
-	VeCo	-	525-C5
-	VeCo	-	556-E1
-	VEN	-	490-H1
-	VEN	-	491-F4
-	VEN	-	492-F7
-	WLKV	-	557-B4
-	WLKV	-	557-G6

VENTURA CO.

INDEX

FEATURE NAME Address City, ZIP Code	PAGE-GRID

AIRPORTS

CAMARILLO — 523 - G4
275 PLEASANT VALLEY RD, CMRL, 93010
HELIPORT — 491 - F7
SPINNAKER DR, VEN, 93001
OXNARD — 522 - D5
2889 W 5TH ST, OXN, 93030
SANTA PAULA — 464 - B6
822 E SANTA MARIA ST, SPLA, 93060

BEACHES & HARBORS

CHANNEL ISLANDS BEACH PK — 552 - B4
VICTORIA AV & LAKE SHORE DR, OXN, 93035
COUNTY LINE BEACH — 625 - E5
VeCo, 90265
EMMA WOOD ST BCH — 490 - H1
SOUTH END OF HWY 1, VeCo, 93001
HOLLYWOOD BEACH — 552 - A4
OCEAN DR, VeCo, 93035
LEO CARRILLO ST BCH — 625 - F5
35000 PACIFIC COAST HWY, LACo, 90265
MANDALAY ST BCH — 521 - G4
GONZALES RD & HARBOR BLVD, OXN, 93035
MARINA COVE BEACH — 491 - F7
W END OF SPINNAKER DR, VEN, 93001
MCGRATH ST BCH — 521 - G2
211 HARBOR BLVD, OXN, 93035
NICHOLAS CANYON CO BCH — 625 - J6
NICHOLAS BEACH RD, MAL, 90265
OXNARD BEACH PK — 551 - J1
HARBOR BLVD, OXN, 93035
SAN BUENAVENTURA ST BCH — 491 - D3
E HARBOR BLVD, VEN, 93001
SILVER STRAND BEACH — 552 - C6
SAN NICOLAS AV & OCEAN DR, VeCo, 93035

BED & BREAKFAST

BELLA MAGGIORE INN — 491 - C2
67 S CALIFORNIA ST, VEN, 93001
THE FERN OAKS INN — 464 - B3
1025 OJAI RD, SPLA, 93060

BUILDINGS

FOR DOWNTOWN BUILDINGS SEE PAGE- — -
viii
ASSOC FOR RETARDED CITIZENS- — 554 - F1
VENTURA CO
1732 LEWIS RD, VeCo, 93012
BOY SCOUTS COUNTY HEADQUARTERS — 524 - B3
509 E DAILY DR, CMRL, 93010
COLONIA MULTI-SERVICE CTR — 522 - J5
COLONIA RD, OXN, 93030

BUILDINGS - GOVERNMENTAL

BRANDEIS-BARDIN INSTITUTE — 498 - F4
1101 PEPPERTREE LN, VeCo, 93064
COUNTY ADMIN BLDG — 492 - C3
800 S VICTORIA AV, VEN, 93009
CRIMINAL JUSTICE COMPLEX — 492 - C3
S VICTORIA AV, VEN, 93009
EAST COUNTY COURTHOUSE — 478 - E7
3855 ALAMO ST, SIMI, 93063
VENTURA COUNTY COURTHOUSE — 492 - C3
800 S VICTORIA AV, VEN, 93009
VENTURA COUNTY HONOR FARM — 451 - B3
S RICE RD, VeCo, 93023
VENTURA COUNTY JAIL — 473 - F5
600 TODD RD, VeCo, 93060

CEMETERIES

ASSUMPTION CEM — 497 - H4
1150 FITZGERALD RD, SIMI, 93065
BARDSDALE CEM — 465 - G4
1698 S SESPE ST, VeCo, 93015
CONEJO MTN MEM PK — 555 - A1
HOWARD RD, VeCo, 93012
F & AM CEM — 553 - B4
PLEASANT VALLEY RD & ETTING RD, OXN, 93033
IVY LAWN CEM — 492 - C6
5400 VALENTINE RD, VeCo, 93003
JAPANESE CEM — 553 - A4
PLEASANT VALLEY RD & ETTING RD, OXN, 93033
NORDHOFF CEM — 441 - F7
CUYAMA RD, OJAI, 93023
OAKWOOD MEM PK — 499 - H5
22601 LASSEN ST, Chat, 91311
PIRU CEM — 457 - D4
CENTER ST, VeCo, 93040

SANTA CLARA CEM — 522 - F2
2370 H ST, OXN, 93030
SANTA PAULA CEM — 463 - J5
380 CEMETERY RD, SPLA, 93060
SIMI CEM — 497 - J3
THOMPSON LN, SIMI, 93065
VALLEY OAKS MEM PK — 557 - F5
5600 LINDERO CANYON RD, WLKV, 91362

CHAMBERS OF COMMERCE

AGOURA HILLS — 558 - B4
5935 KANAN RD, AGRH, 91301
CAMARILLO — 524 - B3
632 N LAS POSAS RD, CMRL, 93010
CHANNEL ISLANDS NATL PK HDQTRS — 491 - F6
1901 SPINNAKER DR, VEN, 93001
CONEJO VALLEY — 526 - D7
625 W HILLCREST DR, THO, 91360
FILLMORE — 456 - A6
330 CENTRAL AV, FILM, 93015
HISPANIC CHAMBER OF VENTURA COUNTY — 522 - G6
721 S A ST, OXN, 93030
MOORPARK — 496 - E1
225 LOS ANGELES AV, MRPK, 93021
OJAI — 441 - H7
150 W OJAI AV, OJAI, 93023
OXNARD — 522 - G6
400 S A ST, OXN, 93030
PORT HUENEME — 552 - E6
220 MARKET ST, PHME, 93041
SANTA PAULA — 464 - B5
200 N 10TH ST, SPLA, 93060
SIMI VALLEY — 497 - F1
40 COCHRAN ST, SIMI, 93065
THOUSAND OAKS/WESTLAKE VILLAGE — 557 - A4
600 HAMPSHIRE RD, THO, 91361
VENTURA — 491 - F4
785 S SEAWARD AV, VEN, 93001
VENTURA VISITORS BUREAU — 491 - C2
89 S CALIFORNIA ST, VEN, 93001
WESTLAKE VILLAGE — 557 - F4
30847 THOUSAND OAKS BLVD, WLKV, 91362

CITY HALLS

AGOURA HILLS — 557 - H6
30101 AGOURA CT, AGRH, 91301
CALABASAS — 558 - H5
26135 MUREAU RD, CALB, 91302
CAMARILLO — 524 - D2
601 N CARMEN DR, CMRL, 93010
FILLMORE — 456 - A6
250 CENTRAL AV, FILM, 93015
MOORPARK — 476 - E7
799 MOORPARK AV, MRPK, 93021
OJAI — 441 - H7
401 S VENTURA ST, OJAI, 93023
OXNARD — 522 - G6
305 W 3RD ST, OXN, 93030
PORT HUENEME — 552 - E6
250 N VENTURA RD, PHME, 93041
SANTA PAULA — 464 - C6
970 VENTURA ST, SPLA, 93060
SIMI VALLEY — 478 - F7
2929 TAPO CANYON RD, SIMI, 93063
THOUSAND OAKS — 556 - J2
2100 E THOUSAND OAKS BLVD, THO, 91362
VENTURA — 491 - C1
501 POLI ST, VEN, 93001
WESTLAKE VILLAGE — 557 - E6
4373 PARK TERRACE DR, WLKV, 91361

COLLEGES & UNIVERSITIES

AQUINAS, THOMAS COLLEGE — 453 - H2
10000 N SANTA PAULA OJAI RD, VeCo, 93060
CALIFORNIA LUTHERAN UNIV — 526 - E2
60 W OLSEN RD, THO, 91360
CSU CHANNEL ISLANDS — 554 - E3
1878 S LEWIS RD, VeCo, 93012
CSU NORTHRIDGE AT CHANNEL ISLANDS — 554 - E3
1878 S LEWIS RD, VeCo, 93012
MOORPARK COLLEGE — 477 - A5
7075 CAMPUS RD, MRPK, 93021
OXNARD COLLEGE — 553 - A4
4000 ROSE AV, OXN, 93033
SAINT JOHNS SEMINARY COLLEGE — 494 - J7
5012 SEMINARY RD, CMRL, 93012
VENTURA COLLEGE — 492 - A2
4667 TELEGRAPH RD, VEN, 93003

DEPARTMENT OF MOTOR VEHICLES

OXNARD — 552 - G4
4050 SAVIERS RD, OXN, 93033

SANTA PAULA — 464 - A7
250 W HARVARD BLVD, SPLA, 93060
SIMI VALLEY — 478 - E7
3855 ALAMO ST, SIMI, 93063
THOUSAND OAKS — 526 - J4
1810 E AVD D LOS ARBOLES, THO, 91362
VENTURA — 492 - A5
4260 MARKET ST, VEN, 93003

ENTERTAINMENT & SPORTS

CIVIC ARTS PLAZA — 556 - J2
THOUSAND OAKS BLVD, THO, 91362
SEASIDE PK & VENTURA CO FAIRGROUNDS — 491 - B2
HARBOR BLVD & FIGUEROA ST, VEN, 93001

GOLF COURSES

BUENAVENTURA GC — 492 - C7
5882 OLIVAS PARK DR, VEN, 93003
CAMARILLO SPRINGS GC — 525 - A5
791 CAMARILLO SPRINGS RD, CMRL, 93012
CBC PORT HUENEME GC — 552 - D2
1ST AV, PHME, 93043
ELKINS RANCH GC — 466 - A3
1386 CHAMBERSBURG RD, VeCo, 93015
LAS POSAS CC — 494 - A5
955 FAIRWAY DR, VeCo, 93010
LINDERO CC — 557 - G4
5719 LAKE LINDERO DR, AGRH, 91301
LOS ROBLES GC — 556 - E1
299 MOORPARK RD, THO, 91361
MALIBU CC — 586 - J6
901 ENCINAL CANYON RD, LACo, 90265
MTN VIEW GC — 474 - B1
16799 SOUTH MOUNTAIN RD, VeCo, 93060
NORTH RANCH CC — 527 - D7
4761 VALLEY SPRING DR, THO, 91362
OJAI VALLEY INN AND SPA — 451 - G1
905 COUNTRY CLUB DR, OJAI, 93023
OLIVAS PK GC — 491 - H7
3750 OLIVAS PARK DR, VEN, 93001
POINT MUGU GC — 583 - F2
NAWS,BUILDING 153, VeCo, 93042
RIVER RIDGE GC — 522 - D1
2401 VINEYARD AV, OXN, 93030
SATICOY CC — 493 - F3
4450 N CLUBHOUSE DR, VeCo, 93066
SATICOY REGL GC — 493 - A1
1025 WELLS RD, VEN, 93004
SHERWOOD CC — 586 - E1
320 W STAFFORD RD, VeCo, 93361
SIMI HILLS GC — 478 - H6
5031 ALAMO ST, SIMI, 93063
SINALOA GC — 497 - F4
980 MADERA RD, SIMI, 93065
SOULE PK GC — 442 - A7
1033 E OJAI AV, OJAI, 93023
SPANISH HILLS GOLF & CC — 523 - H1
999 CRESTVIEW AV, CMRL, 93010
SUNSET HILLS CC — 496 - H7
4155 ERBES RD, THO, 91360
WESTLAKE GC — 557 - D5
4812 S LAKEVIEW CANYON RD, WLKV, 91361
WOOD RANCH GC — 497 - D6
301 N WOOD RANCH PKWY, SIMI, 93065

HOSPITALS

COLUMBIA LOS ROBLES HOSP & MED CTR — 526 - E4
215 W JANSS RD, THO, 91360
COLUMBIA-WEST HILLS MED CTR — 529 - G4
7300 MEDICAL CENTER DR, CanP, 91307
COM MEM HOSP OF SAN BUENAVENTURA — 491 - G2
147 N BRENT ST, VEN, 93003
OJAI VALLEY COMM HOSP — 441 - F7
1306 MARICOPA HWY, OJAI, 93023
SAINT JOHNS PLEASANT VALLEY HOSP — 494 - G7
2309 ANTONIO AV, CMRL, 93010
SAINT JOHNS REGL MED CTR — 523 - A3
1600 N ROSE AV, OXN, 93030
SANTA PAULA MEM HOSP — 464 - B4
825 N 10TH ST, SPLA, 93060
SIMI VALLEY HOSP & HEALTH CARE SERV — 478 - B7
2975 SYCAMORE DR, SIMI, 93065
VENTURA COUNTY MED CTR — 491 - H2
3291 LOMA VISTA RD, VEN, 93003

HOTELS & MOTELS

CASA SIRENA MARINA RESORT — 552 - B3
3605 PENINSULA RD, OXN, 93035
CLARION HOTEL — 497 - F3
1775 MADERA RD, SIMI, 93065
COLONY HARBORTOWN MARINA RESORT — 491 - G6
1050 SCHOONER DR, VEN, 93001

COUNTRY INN AT CAMARILLO — 523 - F2
1405 DEL NORTE RD, CMRL, 93010
COUNTRY INN AT PORT HUENEME — 552 - E6
350 PORT HUENEME RD, PHME, 93041
COUNTRY INN AT VENTURA — 491 - C1
298 CHESTNUT ST, VEN, 93001
COURTYARD MARRIOTT — 524 - J3
4994 VERDUGO WY, CMRL, 93012
DAYS INN — 556 - B1
1320 NEWBURY RD, THO, 91320
DEL NORTE INN — 523 - G2
4444 CENTRAL AV, CMRL, 93010
DOUBLETREE HOTEL — 491 - E3
2055 E HARBOR BLVD, VEN, 93001
HOLIDAY INN — 556 - B1
495 N VENTU PARK RD, THO, 91320
HOLIDAY INN BEACH RESORT — 491 - C2
450 E HARBOR BLVD, VEN, 93001
HOLIDAY INN SIMI VALLEY — 498 - A1
2550 ERRINGER RD, SIMI, 93065
HYATT WESTLAKE PLAZA — 557 - C4
880 S WESTLAKE BLVD, THO, 91361
LA QUINTA INN — 492 - C6
5818 VALENTINE RD, VeCo, 93003
MANDALAY BEACH RESORT — 552 - A2
2101 MANDALAY BEACH RD, OXN, 93035
OJAI VALLEY INN — 451 - G1
824 COUNTRY CLUB RD, OJAI, 93023
OXNARD HILTON INN — 522 - H2
600 ESPLANADE DR, OXN, 93030
RADISSON AGOURA HILLS — 557 - H6
30100 AGOURA RD, AGRH, 91301
RADISSON-SIMI VALLEY — 497 - G1
999 ENCHANTED WY, SIMI, 93065
RADISSON SUITE HOTEL AT RIVER RIDGE — 522 - E1
2101 W VINEYARD AV, OXN, 93030
RAMADA CLOCKTOWER INN — 491 - B2
181 E SANTA CLARA ST, VEN, 93001

LIBRARIES

AVENUE — 471 - B7
807 N VENTURA AV, VEN, 93001
BLANCHARD — 464 - B5
119 N 8TH ST, SPLA, 93060
CALABASAS — 558 - J5
26135 MUREAU RD, CALB, 91302
CAMARILLO — 524 - F1
3100 PONDEROSA DR, CMRL, 93010
DOHENY MEM — 494 - J6
ST JOHNS SEMINARY COLLEGE, CMRL, 93012
EL RIO — 522 - H1
2820 JOURDAN ST, VeCo, 93030
FILLMORE — 456 - A5
502 2ND ST, FILM, 93015
FOSTER, E P — 491 - C2
651 E MAIN ST, VEN, 93001
HIST MUS — 491 - B2
100 E MAIN ST, VEN, 93001
LAS VIRGENES — 558 - A6
29130 ROADSIDE DR, AGRH, 91301
MEINERS OAKS — 441 - E6
114 N PADRE JUAN AV, VeCo, 93023
MOORPARK — 476 - E7
699 MOORPARK AV, MRPK, 93021
NEWBURY PK — 555 - J1
2331 BORCHARD RD, THO, 91320
OAK PK — 558 - A1
899 KANAN RD, VeCo, 91377
OAK VIEW — 451 - B7
469 N VENTURA AV, VeCo, 93022
OJAI — 441 - H7
111 E OJAI AV, OJAI, 93023
OXNARD — 522 - G6
251 S A ST, OXN, 93030
OXNARD CTR BRANCH — 552 - G4
200 E BARD RD, OXN, 93033
PIRU — 457 - F4
3811 CENTER ST, VeCo, 93040
PLATT — 529 - F7
23600 VICTORY BLVD, WdHI, 91367
PRUETER, RAY — 552 - E5
510 PARK AV, PHME, 93041
SATICOY — 493 - B1
11426 VIOLETA ST, VeCo, 93004
SIMI VALLEY — 478 - F7
2969 TAPO CANYON RD, SIMI, 93063
SOMIS — 495 - A5
BELL ST, VeCo, 93066
THOUSAND OAKS — 526 - H5
1401 E JANSS RD, THO, 91362
WESTLAKE VILLAGE — 557 - E6
4371 PARK TERRACE DR, WLKV, 91361
WRIGHT, H P — 492 - A2
57 DAY RD, VEN, 93003

FEATURE NAME — PAGE-GRID
Address City, ZIP Code

MILITARY INSTALLATIONS

CALIFORNIA AIR NATL GUARD 553 - F7
4146 NAVAL AIR RD, VeCo, 93033
NATL GUARD ARMORY 491 - J4
1270 ARUNDELL AV, VEN, 93003
POINT MUGU NAVAL AIR WEAPONS STA 583 - E4
NAVAL AIR RD & WOOD RD, VeCo, 93042
US COAST GUARD STA 552 - B4
VICTORIA AV & PELICAN WY, OXN, 93035
US NAVAL CONSTRUCTION BATTALION CTR 552 - D4
N VENTURA RD & PLEASANT VLY RD, PHME, 93043

MUSEUMS

ALBINGER ARCHAEOLOGICAL MUS 491 - B2
113 E MAIN ST, VEN, 93001
CARNEGIE ART MUS 522 - G6
424 S C ST, OXN, 93030
CEC SEABEE MUS 552 - E3
CUTTING RD & DODSON ST, PHME, 93043
COMSTOCK, A J FIRE MUS 491 - B2
FIGUEROA ST, VEN, 93001
COUNTY HIST AND ART MUSE 491 - B2
100 E MAIN ST, VEN, 93001
FILLMORE HIST MUS 456 - A6
350 MAIN ST, FILM, 93015
RONALD REAGAN PRESIDENTIAL LIB 497 - C4
40 PRESIDENTIAL DR, VeCo, 93065
SANTA PAULA UNION OIL MUESEUM 464 - C5
1001 E MAIN ST, SPLA, 93060
STAGECOACH INN MUS 556 - B2
51 N VENTU PARK RD, THO, 91320
STRATHEARN MUS 497 - E2
137 STRATHEARN PL, SIMI, 93065
VENTURA COUNTY MARITIME MUS 552 - B2
2731 S VICTORIA AV, OXN, 93035

OPEN SPACE PRESERVES

CHATSWORTH NATURE-PRESERVE/RESERVOIR 499 - E7
BOX CANYON RD & LAKE MANOR DR, LA, 91304
MCCREA WILDLIFE REFUGE 496 - H7
N MOORPARK RD, THO, 91360
POINT MUGU GAME RESERVE 583 - D1
VeCo, 93033
SANTA CLARA RIVER ESTUARY NATURAL-RESER 521 - F2
211 HARBOR BLVD, OXN, 93035
SESPE CONDOR PRESERVE 367 - B6
VeCo
VENTURA COUNTY GAME RESERVE 583 - B3
VeCo, 93033

PARK & RIDE

ARMY NATL GUARD 491 - J4
1270 ARUNDELL AV, VEN, 93003
CAMARILLO METROLINK PK & RID 524 - F3
30 N LEWIS RD, CMRL, 93010
COCHRAN ST 498 - D1
3041 COCHRAN ST, SIMI, 93065
ERRINGER 498 - A1
ERRINGER RD & RT# 118, SIMI, 93065
FALLBROOK MALL 529 - H6
FALLBROOK AV & CRISWELL ST, CanP, 91307
HIGH ST & SPRING RD 496 - E1
HIGH ST, MRPK, 93021
JANSS 526 - H5
ROUTE 23 AT E JANSS RD, THO, 91362
KANAN RD (NW LOT) 558 - A5
CANWOOD ST & KANAN RD, AGRH, 91301
KANAN RD (SE LOT) 558 - A6
KANAN RD & 101 FRWY, AGRH, 91301
KANAN RD (SW LOT) 558 - A6
KANAN RD & ROADSIDE DR, AGRH, 91301
KMART 473 - J1
HWY 126 & S PECK RD, VeCo, 93060
KMART-THOUSAND OAKS 557 - A3
349 HAMPSHIRE RD, THO, 91361
LAS POSAS RD 524 - B3
E VENTURA BL & S LOS POSAS RD, CMRL, 93010
LOCKWOOD ST 523 - B3
LOCKWOOD ST, OXN, 93030
OAK VIEW COMM CTR 451 - B6
18 VALLEY RD, VeCo, 93022
OJAI 441 - J7
MONTGOMERY ST & OJAI AV, OJAI, 93023
OXNARD METROLINK 522 - G6
201 E 4TH ST, OXN, 93030
PLEASANT VALLEY RD 524 - J4
PLEASANT VALLEY RD & RT#-101, CMRL, 93012
RANCHO RD 556 - H2
RANCHO RD & RTES 23 & 101, THO, 91361
ROUTE 118 498 - C1
SYCAMORE DR & RT# 118, SIMI, 93065
SAINT PETER CLAVER 499 - A1
5649 E PITTMAN ST, SIMI, 93063
SIMI VALLEY 498 - F1
COCHRAN ST & VANESSA ST, SIMI, 93063
SIMI VALLEY 498 - J1
ROUTE 118 & STEARNS ST, SIMI, 93063
TAPO CANYON 498 - F1
TAPO CANYON RD & RT# 118, SIMI, 93063

PARKS & RECREATION

ADOLFO PK, CMRL 524 - G1
ANGELES NATL FOREST, VeCo 367 - D6
ARNEILL RANCH PK, CMRL 524 - E1
ARROYO PK, SIMI 497 - F2
ARROYO SIMI COMM PK, SIMI 498 - E3
ARROYO VERDE PK, VEN 472 - A7
ARROYO VISTA COMM PK, MRPK 496 - D2
ARROYSTOW PK, SIMI 499 - A3
ARUNDELL LINEAR PK, VEN 491 - H4
ATHERWOOD PK, SIMI 478 - B7
BANYAN PK, THO 555 - F4
BARD, RICHARD BUBBLING SPRINGS PK, 552 - F4
BARRANCA VISTA PK, VEN 492 - E4
BECK PK, OXN 552 - G2
BELAIRE LINEAR PK, VEN 492 - H3
BELL CANYON PK, CanP 529 - C5
BENNETT PK, WLKV 557 - D6
BERYLWOOD PK, SIMI 498 - B2
BEYER PK, THO 557 - A1
BIRCH VIEW PK, CMRL 525 - A2
BOAT LAUNCH RAMP & PK, OXN 552 - B2
BOLKER PK, PHME 552 - D2
BORCHARD OAK PK, OXN 522 - H3
BORCHARD PK, THO 555 - F1
BRISTOL BAY LINEAR PK, VEN 492 - E6
BROCK LINEAR PK, VEN 471 - D6
BUBBLING SPRINGS LINEAR PK, PHME 552 - F6
CABRILLO PK, OXN 522 - D4
CAMARILLO GROVE COUNTY PK, VeCo 525 - D5
CAMINO REAL PK, VEN 491 - J3
CAMP COMFORT PK, VeCo 451 - G3
CAMPUS CANYON PK, MRPK 476 - J5
CAMPUS PK, MRPK 476 - H6
CANADA PK, THO 496 - J7
CANYON OAKS PK, WLKV 557 - F3
CARTY PK, OXN 552 - G4
CASTLE PEAK PK, LA 529 - D4
CENTRAL PK, FILM 456 - A6
CHANNEL ISLANDS NATL PK, VeCo 386 - G5
CHANNEL VIEW PK, OXN 552 - B4
CHAPPARAL PK, VeCo 558 - A2
CHARTER OAK PK, CMRL 494 - E7
CHASE PK, LA 529 - H2
CHATSWORTH OAKS PK, Chat 499 - G6
CHATSWORTH PK NORTH, Chat 499 - J3
CHATSWORTH PK SOUTH, Chat 499 - H3
CHUMASH PK, AGRH 558 - B5
CHUMASH PK, SIMI 479 - B7
CHUMASH PK, VEN 492 - G2
CITRUS GROVE PK, SIMI 498 - A2
COHASSET MELBA PK, CanP 529 - F4
COLLEGE ESTATES PK, OXN 552 - J3
COLLEGE PK, OXN 553 - A3
COLONIA PK, OXN 522 - H5
COMM CTR PK, CMRL 524 - D2
COMM CTR PK EAST, OXN 522 - F7
COMM CTR PK WEST, OXN 522 - F6
CONEJO COMM PK, THO 526 - D6
CONEJO CREEK EQUESTRIAN PK, THO 526 - H5
CONEJO CREEK PK, THO 526 - H6
CONNELLY PK, OXN 522 - E2
CONSTITUTION PK, CMRL 524 - C2
CORRIGANVILLE REGL PK, SIMI 499 - D3
COUNTRY TRAIL PK, MRPK 496 - B4
COUNTY SQUARE LINEAR PK, VEN 492 - C3
CRESTVIEW PK, CMRL 524 - A2
CYPRESS PK, THO 555 - E3
DARRAH VOLUNTEER PK, SIMI 498 - E3
DEL SOL PK, OXN 522 - J5
DENNISON PK, VeCo 452 - E1
DEWAR PK, PHME 552 - E6
DIZDAR PK, CMRL 524 - E3
DOS CAMINOS PK, CMRL 494 - G7
DOS VIENTOS NEIGHBORHOOD PK, THO 555 - C4
DURLEY PK, OXN 552 - F1
EAGLE VIEW PK, VeCo 527 - H6
EASTWOOD MEM PK, OXN 522 - F4
EASTWOOD PK, VEN 491 - B2
EBELL PK, SPLA 464 - B6
EL ESCORPION PK, CanP 529 - C5
EL PARQUE DE LA PAZ, THO 557 - A2
ENCANTO PK, CMRL 525 - A3
ESTELLA PK, THO 556 - J1
EVENSTAR PK, THO 557 - A5
FARIA COUNTY PK, VeCo 469 - J3
FIORE PLAYFIELD, THO 526 - J4
FOOTHILL PK, SIMI 499 - D2
FOOTHILL PK, CMRL 494 - D7
FOREST COVE PK, AGRH 557 - H5
FORT WILDWOOD PK, THO 526 - D3
FOSTER PK, VeCo 460 - J6
FREEDOM PK, CMRL 523 - J5
FREMONT PK, OXN 522 - F4
FRONTIER PK, SIMI 498 - A3
GATES CANYON PK, LACo 558 - J3
GLEN WOOD PK, THO 526 - G6
GLENWOOD PK, MRPK 496 - C2
GRANT PK, VEN 491 - C1
GRAPE ARBOR PK, CALB 558 - G6
GRIFFIN, PAUL PK, MRPK 477 - A6
HAPPY CAMP CANYON REGL PK, VeCo 476 - G2
HARDING PK, SPLA 464 - D5
HARRY LYON PK, VEN 471 - C6
HERITAGE PK, CMRL 525 - B1
HERTEL LINEAR PK, VEN 492 - F2
HICKORY PK, THO 555 - E4
HOBERT PK, VEN 492 - G1
HOBSON COUNTY PK, VeCo 469 - G1
HOUGHTON SCHREIBER PK, SIMI 478 - F6
HUNGRY VALLEY ST VEH REC AREA, 367 - C2
HUNTSINGER, FRITZ YOUTH SPORTS, 492 - J1
INDIAN SPRINGS PK, VeCo 557 - H1
JOHNSON CREEK PK, OXN 552 - H4
JUANAMARIA PK, VEN 492 - E1
JUNIPERO SERRA PK, VEN 492 - H4
KENNEY GROVE PK, VeCo 455 - F5
KNAPP RANCH PK, CanP 529 - C7
KNOLL PK, THO 525 - F7
KNOLLS PK, VeCo 499 - B3
LA JANELLE PK, PHME 552 - C6
LAKE CASITAS REC AREA, VeCo 450 - E5
LANG RANCH PK, THO 527 - C3
LAS PIEDRAS PK, SPLA 464 - C4
LAS POSAS EQUESTRIAN PK, VeCo 494 - A7
LATHROP PK, OXN 552 - H1
LAURELWOOD PK, CMRL 524 - E2
LAZY J RANCH PK, LA 529 - E3
LEMONWOOD PK, OXN 553 - A2
LEO CARRILLO ST BCH, LACo 625 - H4
LIBBEY PK, OJAI 441 - H7
LINCOLN PK, SIMI 497 - H4
LINEAR PK, VEN 492 - J3
LINEAR PK, VEN 492 - H2
LINEAR PK, VEN 492 - E1
LOKKER PK, CMRL 494 - C7
LOS PADRES NATL FOREST, VeCo 441 - C2
LYNN OAKS PK, THO 556 - C2
MAE BOYAR PK, VeCo 558 - A2
MAE BOYAR REC CTR, CanP 529 - E6
MARINA PK, VEN 491 - F5
MARINA WEST PK, OXN 552 - D1
MARION CANNON PK, VEN 492 - B4
MAYFAIR PK, SIMI 497 - J1
MEDEA CREEK PK, VeCo 558 - A1
MEM PK, VEN 491 - D2
MILL PK, SPLA 464 - B4
MISSION OAKS COMM PK, CMRL 525 - B1
MISSION PK, VEN 491 - B2
MISSION VERDE PK, CMRL 525 - A1
MONTE VISTA NATURE PK, MRPK 496 - G3
MORANDA, WALTER B PK, PHME 552 - F6
MORRISON PK, AGRH 557 - J4
MTN MEADOWS PK, MRPK 496 - D3
NEPTUNE SQUARE PK, OXN 551 - J1
NEWBURY PK, THO 555 - J1
NORTHBANK LINEAR PK, VEN 492 - J3
NORTH RANCH PK, THO 527 - C6
NORTH RANCH PLAYFIELD, THO 557 - G1
OAKBROOK NEIGHBORHOOD PK, THO 526 - J3
OAKBROOK PK, THO 527 - B4
OAKBROOK REGL PK, THO 527 - D4
OAK CANYON COMM PK, VeCo 527 - J7
OAK PK, SIMI 477 - C7
OBREGON PK, SPLA 463 - J6
OCEAN AVENUE PK, VEN 491 - E2
OLD AGOURA PK, AGRH 558 - D5
OLD MEADOWS PK, THO 526 - J5
ORCHARD PK, OXN 522 - G2
ORCUTT RANCH HORTICULTURAL CTR PK, 529 - F2
PEACH HILL PK, MRPK 496 - E3
PENINSULA PK, OXN 552 - B3
PEPPER TREE PLAYFIELD, THO 525 - E7
PLAZA PK, VEN 491 - C2
PLAZA PK, OXN 522 - G6
PLEASANT VALLEY PK, CMRL 524 - F1
PLEASANT VALLEY PK, OXN 552 - H4
POINDEXTER PK, MRPK 496 - D1
POINT MUGU STATE PK, VeCo 555 - E7
PORT HUENEME BEACH PK, PHME 552 - E7
POTRERO OPEN SPACE, THO 555 - F3
PROMENADE PK, VEN 491 - B2
QUITO PK, CMRL 495 - D7
RALSTON VILLAGE LINEAR PK, VEN 492 - C4
RANCHO CONEJO PLAY FIELD, THO 526 - B6
RANCHO MADERA COMM PK, SIMI 497 - D6
RANCHO SANTA SUSANA COMM PK, SIMI 498 - H2
RANCHO SIMI COMM PK, SIMI 497 - J3
RANCHO TAPO COMM PK, SIMI 478 - E7
RANCHO VENTURA LINEAR PK, VEN 492 - E4
REYES ADOBE PK, AGRH 557 - H5
REYNOLDS, BLANCHE PK, VEN 491 - G4
RIO LINDO PK, OXN 522 - H2
RIVERVIEW LINEAR PK, VEN 492 - G4
ROSCOE-VALLEY CIRCLE PK, LA 529 - D3
RUSSELL PK, THO 557 - B2
RUSSELL RANCH PK, WLKV 557 - F5
SANTA MONICA MTNS NATL REC AREA, 558 - D1
SANTA MONICA MTNS NATL REC AREA, 555 - E5
SANTA MONICA MTNS NATL REC AREA, 585 - J4
SANTA SUSANA PK, VeCo 499 - C4
SARZOTTI PK, OJAI 441 - J6
SATICOY PK, VeCo 493 - B1
SEA AIR PK, OXN 522 - D7
SEASIDE WILDERNESS PK, VEN 490 - J2
SEAVIEW PK, OXN 522 - C7
SEQUOIA PK, SIMI 498 - E2
SHADOW RANCH PK, CanP 529 - H6
SHIELLS PK, FILM 455 - H5
SIERRA LINDA PK, OXN 522 - F2
SIMI HILLS NEIGHBORHOOD PK, SIMI 478 - H7
SOULE PK, OJAI 442 - A7
SOUTHBANK PK, OXN 522 - F1
SOUTH SHORE HILLS PK, THO 557 - A6
SOUTHWEST COMM PK, OXN 522 - D6
SOUTH WINDS PK, OXN 552 - G6
SPRING MEADOW PK, THO 526 - F2
SPRINGVILLE PK, CMRL 523 - J2
STAGECOACH INN PK, THO 556 - B1
STARGAZE PK, SIMI 497 - D2
STATE OWNED LANDS, Ago 558 - F5
STATE OWNED LANDS, LACo 586 - G7
STECKEL PK, VeCo 453 - J5
SUBURBIA PK, THO 526 - E3
SUMAC PK, AGRH 558 - B4
SUNSET PK, THO 527 - A2
SYCAMORE DRIVE COMM CTR, SIMI 498 - C3
SYCAMORE PK, SIMI 498 - B5
TAPO CANYON PK, VeCo 478 - F2
TAXCO TRAILS PK, LA 529 - F3
TEAGUE PK, SPLA 463 - J7
THOMPSON PK, OXN 523 - A5
THOUSAND OAKS COMM PK, THO 526 - F3
THREE SPRINGS PK, WLKV 557 - B7
TIERRA REJADA PK, SIMI 497 - D1
TIERRA REJADA PK, MRPK 496 - C3
TOLAND PK, VeCo 464 - J1
TRAILSIDE PK, CMRL 525 - A2
TRIUNFO COMM PK, THO 556 - J4
VALLE LINDO PK, CMRL 524 - C2
VALLEY VIEW PK, VeCo 557 - H1
VERDE PK, SIMI 499 - B2
VETERANS MEM PK, SPLA 464 - B6
VIA MARINA PK, OXN 552 - C1
VIRGINIA COLONY PK, MRPK 476 - H7
WALNUT GROVE PK, THO 556 - C1
WARRING PK, VeCo 457 - F3
WAVERLY PK, THO 526 - H5
WENDY PK, THO 555 - G4
WEST HILLS REC CTR, CanP 529 - D5
WEST PK, VEN 491 - B1
WEST VILLAGE PK, OXN 522 - J4
WILDFLOWER PLAYFIELD, THO 526 - C3
WILDWOOD REGL PK, THO 526 - B2
WILLOWBROOK PK, SIMI 497 - H3
WILSON PK, OXN 522 - G5
WOOD CREEK PK, CMRL 525 - A1
WOODSIDE LINEAR PK, VEN 472 - J7
WOODSIDE PK, CMRL 524 - H4

POINTS OF INTEREST

BRANDEIS CAMP & SCH 494 - D7
579 ANACAPA DR, VeCo, 93010
CALIFORNIA BOTANIC GARDEN 526 - E6
GAINSBOROUGH RD & JEAUNINE DR, THO, 91360
CAMP BLOOMFIELD 585 - J7
MULHOLLAND HWY, VeCo, 90265
CHUMASH INDIAN INTERPRETIVE CTR 527 - D4
3290 LANG RANCH PKWY, THO, 91362
DRY GULCH RANCH 625 - G1
HASLER RD & DRY GULCH TR, VeCo, 90265
EGG CITY 476 - B2
SHEKELL RD, VeCo, 93021
LIGHTHOUSE 552 - D6
HUENEME RD, PHME, 93043
MATILIJA HOT SPRINGS 441 - A2
MATILIJA RD S, VeCo, 93023

FEATURE NAME Address City, ZIP Code	PAGE-GRID
SANTA MONICA MNTS NRA VIS CTR 401 W HILLCREST DR, THO, 91360	526 - E7
STATE FISH HATCHERY TELEGRAPH & FISH HATCHERY RD, VeCo, 93015	456 - D7

POINTS OF INTEREST - HISTORIC

FEATURE NAME Address City, ZIP Code	PAGE-GRID
DON ADOLFO CAMARILLO FAMILY HOME MISSION OAKS BL, CMRL, 93012	524 - H3
FATHER SERRA CROSS GRANT PARK, VEN, 93001	491 - B1
OLIVAS ADOBE 4200 OLIVAS PARK DR, VEN, 93001	491 - J7
ORTEGA ADOBE 215 W MAIN, VEN, 93001	491 - B2
SAN BUENAVENTURA MISSION 211 E MAIN ST, VEN, 93001	491 - C2
STRATHEARN, ROBERT P HIST PK & MU 137 STRATHEARN PL, SIMI, 93065	497 - E2
VENTURA COUNTY COURTHOUSE 501 POLI ST, VEN, 93001	491 - C1

SCHOOLS - OTHER

FEATURE NAME Address City, ZIP Code	PAGE-GRID
VENTURA SCH CALIF YOUTH AUTHORITY 3100 WRIGHT RD, VeCo, 93010	493 - F7

SCHOOLS - PRIVATE ELEMENTARY

FEATURE NAME Address City, ZIP Code	PAGE-GRID
ASCENSION LUTHERAN 1600 E HILLCREST DR, THO, 91362	556 - J1
BETHANY CHRISTIAN 200 W BETHANY CT, THO, 91360	526 - E5
CARDEN CONEJO 975 EVENSTAR AV, THO, 91361	557 - B5
CARDEN SCH OF CAMARILLO 1915 LAS POSAS RD, CMRL, 93010	524 - D1
COCHRAN BAPTIST 4910 COCHRAN ST, SIMI, 93063	498 - H1
COLLEGE HEIGHTS CHRISTIAN 6360 TELEPHONE RD, VEN, 93003	492 - D4
COMM CHRISTIAN 723 S D ST, OXN, 93030	522 - G7
CONEJO ADVENTIST 2645 W HILLCREST DR, THO, 91320	525 - J7
CORNERSTONE CHRISTIAN 1777 ARNEILL RD, CMRL, 93010	524 - E1
FAITH BAPTIST 7644 FARRALONE AV, LA, 91304	529 - J4
FIRST BAPTIST ACADEMY 1250 ERBES RD, THO, 91362	527 - A6
FIRST LUTHERAN 380 ARNEILL RD, CMRL, 93010	524 - E3
FRIENDS 3503 ARUNDELL CIR, VEN, 93003	491 - H5
GOOD SHEPHERD LUTHERAN 2949 ALAMO ST, SIMI, 93063	478 - C7
GRACE BRETHREN 1717 ARCANE ST, SIMI, 93065	497 - J4
GRACE LUTHERAN CHRISTIAN DAY 6190 TELEPHONE RD, VEN, 93003	492 - D4
HILLCREST CHRISTIAN 384 ERBES RD, THO, 91362	556 - J1
HOLY CROSS 183 E MAIN ST, VEN, 93001	491 - B2
HUENEME CHRISTIAN 312 N VENTURA RD, PHME, 93041	552 - E5
JOHN JENKINS CHRISTIAN ACADEMY 217 N 10TH ST, SPLA, 93060	464 - B5
LAUREL SPRINGS 1002 E OJAI AV, OJAI, 93023	442 - A6
LINDA VISTA JR ACADEMY 5050 PERRY WY, VeCo, 93030	493 - B4
LITTLE OAKS 101 N SKYLINE DR, THO, 91362	557 - A2
MARY LAW PRIVATE 2931 ALBANY DR, OXN, 93033	552 - H3
MONICA ROS 783 MCNELL RD, VeCo, 93023	442 - E5
MONTESSORI ARROYO 225 ULYSSES ST, SIMI, 93065	497 - F2
OAK GROVE-KRISHNAMURTI 220 W LOMITA AV, VeCo, 93023	451 - D1
OJAI VALLEY 723 EL PASEO RD, OJAI, 93023	441 - G7
OJAI VALLEY CHILDRENS HOUSE 806 W BALDWIN RD, VeCo, 93001	451 - A3
OUR LADY OF GUADALUPE 530 N JUANITA AV, OXN, 93030	522 - H5
OUR LADY OF MOUNT CARMEL 4141 BEYER BLVD, THO, 91362	557 - A2
OUR LADY OF THE ASSUMPTION 3169 TELEGRAPH RD, VEN, 93003	491 - G3
PHOENIX RANCH 1845 OAK RD, SIMI, 93063	499 - A2
PINECREST 449 WILBUR RD, THO, 91360	526 - G7
PINECREST 4974 COCHRAN ST, SIMI, 93063	498 - H1
PLEASANT VALLEY BAPTIST CHURCH 1101 PONDEROSA DR, CMRL, 93010	524 - C2
SACRED HEART 10770 HENDERSON RD, VEN, 93004	493 - A1
SAINT ANTHONY 2421 C ST, OXN, 93033	552 - G2
SAINT BERNARDINE OF SIENA 6061 VALLEY CIRCLE BLVD, WdHl, 91367	529 - D7
SAINT JOHN LUTHERAN 1500 N C ST, OXN, 93030	522 - G3
SAINT JUDE THE APOSTLE 32036 LINDERO CANYON RD, WLKV, 91361	557 - C7
SAINT MARY MAGDALEN 2534 VENTURA BLVD, CMRL, 93010	524 - F3
SAINT PASCHAL BAYLON 154 E JANSS RD, THO, 91360	526 - F5
SAINT PATRICK 1 CHURCH RD, THO, 91362	526 - J5
SAINT PAUL 3290 LOMA VISTA RD, VEN, 93003	491 - H2
SAINT ROSE OF LIMA 1325 ROYAL AV, SIMI, 93065	497 - H3
SAINT SEBASTIAN 325 E SANTA BARBARA ST, SPLA, 93060	464 - A5
SANTA CLARA 324 S E ST, OXN, 93030	522 - F6
SHEPHERD OF THE VALLEY LUTHERAN 23838 KITTRIDGE ST, CanP, 91307	529 - E6
TEMPLE CHRISTIAN 5415 RALSTON ST, VEN, 93003	492 - C4
VENTURA MISSIONARY CHRISTIAN 500 HIGH POINT DR, VEN, 93003	472 - E7
WEST VALLEY CHRISTIAN 22944 ENADIA WY, CanP, 91307	529 - G5

SCHOOLS - PRIVATE HIGH

FEATURE NAME Address City, ZIP Code	PAGE-GRID
CHAMINADE 7500 CHAMINADE AV, LA, 91304	529 - F4
CORNERSTONE CHRISTIAN 1777 ARNEILL RD, CMRL, 93010	524 - E1
FAITH BAPTIST 7644 FARRALONE AV, LA, 91304	529 - J4
GRACE BRETHREN JR-SR 1350 CHERRY AV, SIMI, 93065	498 - B3
HILLCREST CHRISTIAN 384 ERBES RD, THO, 91362	556 - J1
LA REINA 106 W JANSS RD, THO, 91360	526 - F5
LAUREL SPRINGS 1002 E OJAI AV, OJAI, 93023	442 - A6
NEWBURY PK ADVENTIST ACADEMY 180 ACADEMY DR, THO, 91320	525 - H6
OAK GROVE-KRISHNAMURTI 220 W LOMITA AV, VeCo, 93023	451 - D1
OJAI VALLEY 723 EL PASEO RD, OJAI, 93023	441 - G7
SAINT BONAVENTURE 3167 TELEGRAPH RD, VEN, 93003	491 - H3
SANTA CLARA 2121 SAVIERS RD, OXN, 93033	552 - G2
THACHER 5025 THACHER SCHOOL RD, VeCo, 93023	442 - F4
VILLANOVA PREP 12096 VENTURA AV, VeCo, 93023	451 - F2
WEST VALLEY CHRISTIAN 23834 HIGHLANDER RD, CanP, 91307	529 - E6

SCHOOLS - PRIVATE JUNIOR HIGH

FEATURE NAME Address City, ZIP Code	PAGE-GRID
FIRST BAPTIST ACADEMY 1250 ERBES RD, THO, 91362	527 - A6
WEST VALLEY CHRISTIAN 23834 HIGHLANDER RD, CanP, 91307	529 - E6

SCHOOLS - PUBLIC ELEMENTARY

FEATURE NAME Address City, ZIP Code	PAGE-GRID
ACACIA 55 NORMAN AV, THO, 91360	526 - F6
ARNAZ 400 SUNSET AV, VeCo, 93022	461 - A1
ARROYO WEST 4117 COUNTRY HILL RD, MRPK, 93021	496 - B3
ASPEN 1870 OBERLIN AV, THO, 91360	526 - E5
ATHERWOOD 2350 E GREENSWARD ST, SIMI, 93065	498 - B1
BANYAN 1120 KNOLLWOOD DR, THO, 91320	555 - F4
BARD, RICHARD 622 PLEASANT VALLEY RD, PHME, 93041	552 - F5
BEDELL, THELMA B 1305 LAUREL RD, SPLA, 93060	464 - B2
BEDFORD OPEN 1099 BEDFORD DR, CMRL, 93010	524 - D2
BERYLWOOD 2300 HEYWOOD ST, SIMI, 93065	498 - B3
BIG SPRINGS 3401 BIG SPRINGS AV, SIMI, 93063	478 - G5
BLANCHARD 115 N PECK RD, SPLA, 93060	463 - J7
BRIGGS 14438 W TELEGRAPH RD, VeCo, 93060	473 - F2
BROOKSIDE 165 N SATINWOOD AV, VeCo, 91377	558 - B2
CAMARILLO HEIGHTS 35 W CATALINA DR, VeCo, 93010	494 - D7
CAMPUS CANYON 15300 MONROE AV, MRPK, 93021	476 - J5
CAPISTRANO AVENUE 8118 CAPISTRANO AV, LA, 91304	529 - J3
CHATSWORTH PK 22005 DEVONSHIRE ST, Chat, 91311	499 - J4
CONEJO 280 CONEJO SCHOOL RD, THO, 91362	557 - A1
CRESTVIEW 900 CROSBY AV, SIMI, 93065	498 - B5
CURREN, BERNICE 1101 N F ST, OXN, 93030	522 - F4
CYPRESS 4200 W KIMBER DR, THO, 91320	555 - E3
DOS CAMINOS 3635 APPIAN WY, CMRL, 93010	494 - G7
DRIFFILL 910 S E ST, OXN, 93030	522 - G7
EL DESCANSO 1099 BEDFORD DR, CMRL, 93010	524 - D2
ELMHURST 5080 ELMHURST ST, VEN, 93003	492 - B3
ELM STREET 450 ELM ST, OXN, 93033	552 - H1
EL RANCHO STRUCTURED 550 TEMPLE AV, CMRL, 93010	524 - F2
EL RIO 2714 VINEYARD AV, VeCo, 93030	522 - H1
FLORY 240 FLORY AV, MRPK, 93021	496 - E1
FOSTER, E P 20 PLEASANT PL, VEN, 93001	471 - B7
GARDEN GROVE 2250 N TRACY AV, SIMI, 93063	498 - E2
GLEN CITY 141 S STECKEL DR, SPLA, 93060	463 - J6
GLENWOOD 1135 WINDSOR DR, THO, 91360	526 - G6
HAMLIN STREET 22627 HAMLIN ST, CanP, 91307	529 - H6
HARRINGTON, NORMA 2501 GISLER AV, OXN, 93033	552 - H2
HATHAWAY, JULIEN 405 DOLLIE ST, OXN, 93033	552 - H5
HAYCOX, ART 5400 PERKINS RD, OXN, 93033	552 - G6
HAYNES 6624 LOCKHURST DR, CanP, 91307	529 - E6
HOLLOW HILLS 828 GIBSON AV, SIMI, 93065	497 - J5
HOLLYWOOD BEACH 4000 SUNSET LN, VeCo, 93035	552 - A2
HUENEME 354 3RD ST, PHME, 93041	552 - E6
JUANAMARIA 100 S CROCKER AV, VEN, 93004	492 - F2
JUSTICE STREET 23350 JUSTICE ST, LA, 91304	529 - F3
JUSTIN 2245 N JUSTIN AV, SIMI, 93065	498 - A2
KAMALA 634 W KAMALA ST, OXN, 93033	552 - F2
KATHERINE 5455 KATHERINE ST, SIMI, 93063	499 - A3
KNOLLS 6334 KATHERINE RD, SIMI, 93063	499 - C3
LADERA 1211 CL ALMENDRO, THO, 91360	526 - H3
LAGUNA VISTA 5084 ETTING RD, VeCo, 93012	553 - H4
LANG RANCH 2450 WHITECHAPEL PL, THO, 91362	527 - B3
LARSEN, ANSGAR 550 THOMAS AV, OXN, 93033	552 - H3
LAS COLINAS 5750 FIELDCREST DR, CMRL, 93012	525 - B1
LAS POSAS 75 E CL LA GUERRA, CMRL, 93010	524 - B2
LEMONWOOD 2200 CARNEGIE CT, OXN, 93033	553 - A2
LINCOLN 1107 E SANTA CLARA ST, VEN, 93001	491 - D2
LINCOLN, ABRAHAM 1220 4TH ST, SIMI, 93065	497 - G4
LOCKHURST DRIVE 6170 LOCKHURST DR, WdHl, 91367	529 - E7
LOMA VISTA 300 LYNN DR, VEN, 93003	491 - H2
LOS NOGALES 1555 KENDALL AV, CMRL, 93010	524 - F1
LOS PRIMEROS STRUCTURED 2222 E VENTURA BLVD, CMRL, 93010	524 - E3
LUPIN HILL 26210 ADAMOR RD, CALB, 91302	558 - H3
MADERA 250 ROYAL AV, SIMI, 93065	497 - F4
MADRONA 612 CM MANZANAS, VeCo, 91360	526 - D6
MANZANITA 2626 MICHAEL DR, THO, 91320	555 - H1
MAPLE 3501 KIMBER DR, THO, 91320	555 - F2
MARINA WEST 2501 CAROB ST, OXN, 93035	552 - D1
MAR VISTA 2382 ETTING RD, OXN, 93033	553 - B4
MCAULIFFE, CHRISTA 3300 W VIA MARINA AV, OXN, 93035	522 - C7
MCKEVETT 955 PLEASANT ST, SPLA, 93060	464 - B5
MCKINNA, DENNIS 1611 J ST, OXN, 93033	552 - F1
MEADOWS 2000 LA GRANADA DR, THO, 91362	527 - A6
MEINERS OAKS 400 S LOMITA AV, VeCo, 93023	441 - E7
MESA 3901 MESA SCHOOL RD, VeCo, 93066	493 - H4
MIRA MONTE 1216 LOMA DR, VeCo, 93023	451 - D2
MONTALVO 2050 GRAND AV, VEN, 93003	492 - D5
MOUND 455 S HILL RD, VEN, 93003	492 - D3
MTN MEADOWS 4200 MOUNTAIN MEADOW DR, MRPK, 93021	496 - D3
MTN VIEW 2925 FLETCHER ST, SIMI, 93065	498 - C4
MUPU 4410 SANTA PAULA-OJAI RD, VeCo, 93060	464 - A1
NEVADA AVENUE 22120 CHASE ST, LA, 91304	529 - J2
OAK HILLS 1010 N KANAN RD, VeCo, 91377	557 - H1
OAK VIEW 555 MAHONEY AV, VeCo, 93022	451 - A6
OLIVELANDS 12465 FOOTHILL RD, VeCo, 93060	473 - B2
PARKVIEW 1416 6TH PL, PHME, 93041	552 - F4
PEACH HILL 13400 CHRISTIAN BARRETT DR, MRPK, 93021	496 - F3
PIERPONT 1254 MARTHAS VINEYARD CT, VEN, 93001	491 - F5
PIRU 3811 E CENTER ST, VeCo, 93040	457 - E4
PK OAKS 1335 CL BOUGANVILLA, THO, 91360	526 - H4
PK VIEW 1500 ALEXANDER ST, SIMI, 93065	497 - J2
POINSETTIA 350 N VICTORIA AV, VEN, 93003	492 - C1
POMELO DRIVE 7633 MARCH AV, LA, 91304	529 - E4
PORTOLA 1350 PARTRIDGE DR, VEN, 93003	492 - D4
RED OAK 4857 ROCKFIELD ST, VeCo, 91377	557 - H1
REYNOLDS, BLANCHE 450 VALMORE AV, VEN, 93003	491 - G4
RIO LINDO 2131 SNOW AV, OXN, 93030	522 - J3
RIO PLAZA 600 SIMON WY, VeCo, 93030	492 - J7
RIO REAL 1140 KENNEY ST, VeCo, 93030	522 - J2
RITCHEN, EMILIE 2200 CABRILLO WY, OXN, 93030	522 - E4
ROGERS, WILL 316 HOWARD ST, VEN, 93003	491 - F3
ROSE AVENUE 220 DRISKILL AV, OXN, 93030	523 - A6
SAN ANTONIO 650 CARNE RD, VeCo, 93023	442 - D6
SAN CAYETANO 514 MOUNTAIN VIEW ST, FILM, 93015	456 - B5
SANTA ROSA 13282 SANTA ROSA RD, VeCo, 93012	496 - F6
SANTA SUSANNA 4300 APRICOT RD, SIMI, 93063	498 - G1

FEATURE NAME — Address City, ZIP Code — **PAGE-GRID**

SATICOY — 760 JAZMIN AV, VEN, 93004 — 492 - J1
SERRA, JUNIPERO — 8880 HALIFAX ST, VEN, 93004 — 492 - H3
SESPE — 425 ORCHARD ST, FILM, 93015 — 456 - A6
SHERIDAN WAY — 573 SHERIDAN WY, VEN, 93001 — 491 - B1
SIERRA LINDA — 2201 JASMINE ST, OXN, 93030 — 522 - F2
SIMI — 2956 SCHOOL ST, SIMI, 93065 — 498 - C3
SOMIS — 5268 NORTH ST, VeCo, 93066 — 495 - A5
SUMAC — 6050 CALMFIELD AV, AGRH, 91301 — 558 - B3
SUMMIT — 12525 SANTA PAULA OJAI RD, VeCo, 93023 — 453 - C1
SUNKIST — 1400 TEAKWOOD ST, PHME, 93041 — 552 - E3
SYCAMORE — 2100 RAVENNA ST, SIMI, 93065 — 498 - C2
THE LITTLE RED SCH HOUSE — 20030 TELEGRAPH RD, VeCo, 93060 — 464 - J2
THILLE, GRACE S — 1144 VENTURA ST, SPLA, 93060 — 464 - C6
TIERRA LINDA — 1201 WOODCREEK RD, CMRL, 93012 — 525 - A1
TIERRA VISTA — 2001 SANFORD ST, OXN, 93033 — 553 - A5
TOPA TOPA — 916 MOUNTAIN VIEW AV, OJAI, 93023 — 441 - J5
TOWNSHIP — 4101 TOWNSHIP AV, SIMI, 93063 — 478 - F6
UNIV — 2801 ATLAS AV, THO, 91320 — 526 - F3
VALLE LINDO — 777 AILEEN ST, CMRL, 93010 — 524 - C2
VISTA FUNDAMENTAL — 2175 WISTERIA ST, SIMI, 93065 — 498 - B2
WALNUT — 581 DENA DR, VeCo, 91320 — 555 - G1
WEATHERSFIELD — 3151 DARLINGTON DR, THO, 91360 — 526 - G2
WEBSTER, BARBARA — 1150 SATICOY ST, SPLA, 93060 — 464 - C5
WELBY WAY-MAGNET SCH — 23456 WELBY WY, CanP, 91307 — 529 - F6
WESTLAKE — 1571 POTRERO RD, THO, 91361 — 556 - J6
WESTLAKE HILLS — 3333 MEDICINE BOW CT, THO, 91362 — 557 - B3
WHITE OAK — 2201 ALSCOT AV, SIMI, 93063 — 499 - C2
WHITE OAK — 31761 W VILLAGE SCHOOL RD, WLKV, 91361 — 557 - D6
WILDWOOD — 620 W VELARDE DR, THO, 91360 — 526 - D3
WILLIAMS, FRED — 4300 ANCHORAGE ST, OXN, 93033 — 552 - J4
WILLOW — 29026 LARO DR, AGRH, 91301 — 558 - A4
WOOD RANCH — 455 CIRCLE KNOLL DR, SIMI, 93065 — 527 - D1

SCHOOLS - PUBLIC HIGH

AGOURA — 28545 W DRIVER AV, AGRH, 91301 — 558 - B5
APOLLO — 3150 SCHOOL ST, SIMI, 93065 — 498 - D3
BUENA — 5670 TELEGRAPH RD, VEN, 93003 — 492 - C2
CAMARILLO, ADOLFO — 4660 MISSION OAKS BLVD, CMRL, 93012 — 524 - H3
CHANNEL ISLANDS — 1400 RAIDERS WY, OXN, 93033 — 552 - J3
CHAPARRAL — 114 N MONTGOMERY AV, OJAI, 93023 — 441 - J6
CONEJO VALLEY — 1872 NEWBURY RD, THO, 91320 — 556 - A1
FILLMORE — 555 CENTRAL AV, FILM, 93015 — 456 - A5
FRONTIER — 280 SKYWAY DR, CMRL, 93010 — 524 - A5
HUENEME — 500 W BARD RD, OXN, 93033 — 552 - G4
INDIAN HILLS — 4345 N LAS VIRGENES RD, CALB, 91302 — 558 - H7
MOORPARK — 4500 TIERRA REJADA RD, MRPK, 93021 — 496 - C3
MOORPARK COMM CONT. — 5700 CONDOR DR, MRPK, 93021 — 476 - H7
NEWBURY PK — 456 N REINO RD, THO, 91320 — 525 - F7
NORDHOFF — 1401 MARICOPA HWY, OJAI, 93023 — 441 - E7

OAK PK — 899 KANAN RD, VeCo, 91377 — 558 - A1
OAK VIEW — 5701 E CONIFER ST, VeCo, 91377 — 558 - A2
OXNARD — 3400 GONZALES RD, VeCo, 93030 — 522 - C3
PACIFIC — 501 COLLEGE DR, VEN, 93003 — 491 - J3
RENAISSANCE — 404 N 6TH ST, SPLA, 93060 — 464 - A5
RIO MESA — 545 CENTRAL AV, VeCo, 93030 — 493 - B5
ROYAL — 1402 ROYAL AV, SIMI, 93065 — 497 - J3
SANTA PAULA — 404 N 6TH ST, SPLA, 93060 — 464 - A5
SANTA SUSANA — 3570 E COCHRAN ST, SIMI, 93063 — 498 - E1
SIMI VALLEY — 5400 COCHRAN ST, SIMI, 93063 — 499 - A1
SIMI VALLEY ADULT SCH — 3192 LOS ANGELES AV, SIMI, 93063 — 498 - D3
THOUSAND OAKS — 2323 MOORPARK RD, THO, 91360 — 526 - F4
VENTURA — 2155 E MAIN ST, VEN, 93001 — 491 - F2
WESTLAKE — 100 N LAKEVIEW CANYON RD, THO, 91362 — 557 - D3

SCHOOLS - PUBLIC INTERMEDIATE

FRANK — 701 N JUANITA AV, OXN, 93030 — 522 - H4
FREMONT, JOHN CHARLES — 1130 N M ST, OXN, 93030 — 522 - F4
HAYDOCK, RICHARD B — 647 W HILL ST, OXN, 93033 — 522 - F7
LOS ALTOS — 700 TEMPLE AV, CMRL, 93010 — 524 - F2
MONTE VISTA — 888 LANTANA ST, CMRL, 93010 — 524 - C2
REDWOOD — 233 W GAINSBOROUGH RD, THO, 91360 — 526 - E6
SEQUOIA — 2855 BORCHARD RD, THO, 91320 — 555 - H1

SCHOOLS - PUBLIC JUNIOR HIGH

BLACKSTOCK, CHARLES — 701 BARD RD, OXN, 93033 — 552 - H4
FILLMORE — 615 SHIELLS DR, FILM, 93015 — 456 - A5
GREEN, E O — 3739 C ST, OXN, 93033 — 552 - G4
MATILIJA — 703 EL PASEO RD, OJAI, 93023 — 441 - G7
MESA — 3901 MESA SCHOOL RD, VeCo, 93066 — 493 - H4
OCEAN VIEW — 4300 OLDS RD, OXN, 93033 — 553 - B4
RIO DEL VALLE — 3100 ROSE AV, VeCo, 93030 — 523 - A1

SCHOOLS - PUBLIC MIDDLE

ANACAPA — 100 S MILLS RD, VEN, 93003 — 491 - H3
BALBOA — 247 S HILL RD, VEN, 93003 — 492 - D2
CABRILLO — 1426 E SANTA CLARA ST, VEN, 93001 — 491 - E2
CHAPARRAL — 280 POINDEXTER AV, MRPK, 93021 — 496 - D1
COLINA — 1500 HILLCREST DR, THO, 91362 — 556 - J1
COLUMBUS — 22250 ELKWOOD ST, LA, 91304 — 529 - J3
DE ANZA — 2060 CAMERON ST, VEN, 93001 — 471 - C6
HILLSIDE — 2222 FITZGERALD RD, SIMI, 93065 — 498 - A4
ISBELL — 221 S 4TH ST, SPLA, 93060 — 464 - B6
LINDERO CANYON — 5844 LARBOARD LN, AGRH, 91301 — 557 - G4
LOS CERRITOS — 2100 AVD DE LAS FLORES, THO, 91362 — 556 - A1
MEDEA CREEK — 1002 DOUBLETREE RD, VeCo, 91377 — 558 - A1
MESA VERDE — 14000 PEACH HILL RD, MRPK, 93021 — 496 - G3
SINALOA — 601 ROYAL AV, SIMI, 93065 — 497 - G3
SOMIS — 5268 NORTH ST, VeCo, 93066 — 495 - A5
VALLEY VIEW — 3347 TAPO ST, SIMI, 93063 — 478 - G6

WRIGHT, ARTHUR E — 4029 N LAS VIRGENES RD, CALB, 91302 — 558 - H7

SHOPPING CENTERS - COMMUNITY

AGOURA MEADOWS CTR — THOUSAND OAKS BL & KANAN RD, AGRH, 91301 — 558 - A5
BEACHPORT CTR — 301 PORT HUENEME RD, PHME, 93041 — 552 - E6
BELWOOD CTR — ALAMO ST & TAPO ST, SIMI, 93063 — 478 - G7
BORCHARD CTR — S BORCHARD DR & E THOMPSON BL, VEN, 93003 — 491 - G3
CAMARILLO TOWN CTR — W VENTURA BLVD & LOS POSAS RD, CMRL, 93010 — 524 - A3
CAMARILLO VILLAGE SQUARE — LAS POSAS RD & ARNEILL RD, CMRL, 93010 — 524 - E1
CARMEN PLAZA — LANTANA ST & DAILY DR, CMRL, 93010 — 524 - C3
CARRIAGE SQUARE — OXNARD BL & GONZALES RD, OXN, 93030 — 522 - G3
CENTERPOINT PLAZA — LOS ANGELES AV & BLACKSTOCK AV, SIMI, 93063 — 498 - D2
CENTRAL CTR — TELEPHONE RD & S PETIT AV, VEN, 93004 — 492 - H3
CENTRAL PLAZA — ARNEILL RD & PONDEROSA DR, CMRL, 93010 — 524 - E2
CHANNEL ISLANDS CTR — VICTORIA AV & W HEMLOCK ST, OXN, 93035 — 552 - B1
CONEJO VALLEY PLAZA — N MOORPARK RD & E JANSS RD, THO, 91360 — 526 - G6
CROSSROADS VILLAGE CTR — 501 S VENTURA RD, OXN, 93035 — 522 - E6
DONLON PLAZA — E MAIN ST & DONLON ST, VEN, 93003 — 492 - A4
DOS CAMINOS PLAZA — LAS POSAS RD & PONDEROSA DR, CMRL, 93010 — 494 - G7
FREMONT SQUARE — N VENTURA RD, OXN, 93030 — 522 - E4
GATEWAY VILLAGE CTR — JOHNSON DR & NORTH BANK DR, VEN, 93003 — 492 - E6
HARBOR LANDING & MARINE EMPORIUM — HARBOR BLVD, OXN, 93035 — 552 - A2
HUENEME BAY CTR — E CHANNEL ISLDS BL & S VENTURA, PHME, 93041 — 552 - E2
LAS POSAS PLAZA — N LAS POSAS RD & PONDEROSA DR, CMRL, 93010 — 524 - B2
LUCKY & LONGS CTR — NEWBURY RD & MICHAEL DR, THO, 91320 — 555 - J1
MANDALAY VILLAGE MARKETPLACE — CHANNEL ISLDS BL & WHEELHOUSE, PHME, 93041 — 552 - C2
MISSION OAKS CTR — SANTA ROSA RD & ADOLFO RD, CMRL, 93012 — 524 - J3
MISSION OAKS PLAZA — MISSION OAKS BL & WOODCREEK RD, CMRL, 93012 — 525 - A1
MISSION PLAZA CTR — W MAIN ST & N VENTURA AV, VEN, 93001 — 491 - B1
MOORPARK PLAZA — NEW LOS ANGELES AV & SPRING RD, MRPK, 93021 — 496 - F2
MTN GATE PLAZA — 1135 E LOS ANGELES AV, SIMI, 93065 — 497 - H2
NEWBURY PK CTR — NEWBURY RD & GIANT OAK AV, THO, 91320 — 556 - A1
NORTH RANCH MALL — 3663 THOUSAND OAKS BLVD, THO, 91362 — 557 - C3
NORTHRANCH PLAZA — KANAN RD & LINDERO CYN, THO, 91362 — 527 - G7
OLIVEIRA PLAZA — VICTORIA AV & CHANNEL ISLDS BL, PHME, 93041 — 552 - B2
PARDEE PLAZA — SANTA ROSA RD & VERDUGO WY, CMRL, 93012 — 524 - J3
PASEO CAMARILLO — PASEO CAMARILLO & LANTANA ST, CMRL, 93010 — 524 - C3
PK OAKS CTR — N MOORPARK RD & E JANSS RD, THO, 91360 — 526 - G5
PLATT VILLAGE — PLATT AV & VICTORY BLVD, CanP, 91307 — 529 - F7
PLEASANT VALLEY CTR — W PLEASANT VLY RD & SAVIERS RD, OXN, 93033 — 552 - G5
PONDEROSA CTR — ARNEILL RD, CMRL, 93010 — 524 - E3
PONDEROSA NORTH — PONDEROSA DR & ARNEILL RD, CMRL, 93010 — 524 - E2
PRIME OUTLETS AT OXNARD — LOCKWOOD ST & OUTLET CENTER DR, OXN, 93030 — 523 - B3
SANTA PAULA CTR — 570 W MAIN ST, SPLA, 93060 — 463 - J7
SANTA ROSA PLAZA — SANTA ROSA RD, CMRL, 93012 — 525 - B2
SHOPPING AT THE ROSE — GONZALES RD & N ROSE AV, OXN, 93030 — 522 - J3
SIMI VALLEY PLAZA — 1357 E LOS ANGELES AV, SIMI, 93065 — 497 - H2
SINALOA PLAZA — E LOS ANGELES AV & SINALOA RD, SIMI, 93065 — 497 - G2
STONE GATE — LOS ANGELES AV & YOSEMITE AV, SIMI, 93063 — 499 - A2

SYCAMORE PLAZA — SYCAMORE DR & COCHRAN ST, SIMI, 93065 — 498 - C1
TAPO OAKS CTR — COCHRAN ST & TAPO CANYON RD, SIMI, 93063 — 498 - E1
TAPO PLAZA — COCHRAN ST & TAPO ST, SIMI, 93063 — 498 - G1
THE EVERGREENS — THOUSAND OAKS BL & AUBURN CT, THO, 91362 — 557 - B3
THE MARKETPLACE — VENTURA BL & PASEO MERCADO, OXN, 93030 — 523 - A2
THE PROMENADE — WESTLAKE BLVD & THOUSAND OAKS, THO, 91362 — 557 - C4
TWIN OAKS AGOURA CTR — KANAN RD & THOUSAND OAKS BL, AGRH, 91301 — 558 - A4
VENTURA HARBOR VILLAGE — 1559 SPINNAKER DR, VEN, 93001 — 491 - F7
VICTORIA VILLAGE CTR — S VICTORIA AV & RALSTON ST, VEN, 93003 — 492 - C4
WESTLAKE CTR — 960 S WESTLAKE BLVD, THO, 91361 — 557 - C5
WHIZIN CTR — AGOURA RD & CORNELL RD, AGRH, 91301 — 558 - B6

SHOPPING CENTERS - REGIONAL

CAMARILLO PREMIUM OUTLETS — 740 E VENTURA BLVD, CMRL, 93010 — 524 - C3
CENTERPOINT MALL — SAVIERS RD & W CHANNEL ISLANDS, OXN, 93033 — 552 - G2
ESPLANADE CTR — 195 ESPLANADE DR, OXN, 93030 — 522 - G1
FALLBROOK MALL — 6633 FALLBROOK AV, CanP, 91307 — 529 - G6
JANSS MARKETPLACE — 215 N MOORPARK RD, THO, 91360 — 556 - E1
LINCOLN OAKS VILLAGE — W HILLCREST DR & WILBUR RD, THO, 91360 — 556 - E1
PACIFIC VIEW MALL — 3301 E MAIN ST, VEN, 93003 — 491 - H4
SYCAMORE SQUARE — 2845 COCHRAN ST, SIMI, 93065 — 498 - C1
TELEPHONE ROAD PLAZA — TELEPHONE RD & VALENTINE RD, VEN, 93003 — 492 - A4
THE OAKS — 222 W HILLCREST DR, THO, 91360 — 556 - D1

TRANSPORTATION

AMTRAK/METROLINK STA — 5050 LOS ANGELES AV, SIMI, 93063 — 498 - H2
AMTRAK STA-VENTURA — E HARBOR BL & FIGUEROA ST, VEN, 93001 — 491 - B2
GREYHOUND BUS STA — 2799 THOUSAND OAKS BLVD E, THO, 91362 — 557 - A2
GREYHOUND STA-VENTURA — 291 E THOMPSON BLVD, VEN, 93001 — 491 - C2
METROLINK CAMARILLO STA — 30 N LEWIS RD, CMRL, 93010 — 524 - F3
METROLINK-MOORPARK STA — 300 HIGH ST, MRPK, 93021 — 496 - F1
METROLINK OXNARD STA — 201 E 4TH ST, OXN, 93030 — 522 - G6
OXNARD TRANSPORTATION CTR — 201 E 4TH ST, OXN, 93030 — 522 - G6

WINERIES

LEEWARD — 2784 JOHNSON DR, VEN, 93003 — 492 - E6
OLD CREEK RANCH — 10024 E OLD CREEK RD, VeCo, 93001 — 461 - C1

VENTURA CO.   INDEX

PRODUCT INFORMATION LIST

THOMAS GUIDES®
NOW INCLUDING ZIP CODES AND BOUNDARIES FOR 2001 EDITIONS

CALIFORNIA

Alameda County
Alameda / Contra Costa Counties
Alameda / Santa Clara Counties
Central Valley Cities
    (Coverage includes all urban areas from Stockton to Bakersfield)
Contra Costa County
Fresno / Madera Counties *(NEW - available 12/2000)*
Golden Gate
    (Marin, San Francisco, San Mateo, and Santa Clara Counties)
Kern County *(NEW - available 10/2000)*
Los Angeles County
* Los Angeles / Orange Counties
* Los Angeles / Ventura Counties
Marin County
Metropolitan Monterey Bay
Napa / Sonoma Counties
Orange County
Orange / Los Angeles Counties
Riverside County
Riverside / Orange Counties
Riverside / San Diego Counties
Sacramento County
    (Coverage includes portions of Placer & El Dorado Counties)
* Sacramento / Solano Counties
San Bernardino County
San Bernardino / Riverside Counties
* San Diego County including portions of Imperial County
San Diego / Orange Counties
San Francisco County
San Francisco / Alameda / Contra Costa Counties
San Francisco / San Mateo Counties
San Mateo County
Santa Barbara and San Luis Obispo Counties
* Santa Barbara and San Luis Obispo / Ventura Counties
Santa Clara County
Santa Clara / San Mateo Counties
Solano County including portions of Napa & Yolo Counties
Ventura County

*Thomas Guide & Thomas Guide *DigitalEdition*™ Combo Packs

ARIZONA - NEVADA - OREGON - WASHINGTON

* Clark County, NV
Metropolitan Phoenix Area, AZ *(NEW - available 7/2000)*
Metropolitan Tucson Area, AZ *(NEW - available 9/2000)*
* Portland Metro Area, OR
    (Coverage includes Clackamas, Columbia, Multnomah, Washington
    & Yamhill Counties and Greater Vancouver Area)
King County, WA
King / Pierce Counties, WA
King / Snohomish Counties, WA
Pierce County, WA
Snohomish County, WA

WASHINGTON, D.C. & VICINITY

Anne Arundel County, MD
Frederick County, MD
Howard County, MD
Loudoun County, VA
Montgomery County, MD
Northern Virginia & the Beltway
Prince George's County, VA
Prince William County, VA

ROAD ATLAS & DRIVER'S GUIDES

California Road Atlas & Driver's Guide
Pacific Northwest Road Atlas & Driver's Guide

METROPOLITAN THOMAS GUIDES®

CALIFORNIA

* Metropolitan Bay Area
    (Coverage includes Metro areas of Alameda, Contra Costa, Marin,
    San Francisco, San Mateo, and Santa Clara Counties)
* Metropolitan Inland Empire
    (Coverage includes Metro areas of San Bernardino, Riverside,
    Eastern Los Angeles, and Northeastern Orange Counties)

WASHINGTON

* Metropolitan Puget Sound
    (Coverage includes Metro areas of King, Pierce, and Snohomish
    Counties)

METROPOLITAN BALTIMORE & METROPOLITAN WASHINGTON, D. C.

* Metropolitan Baltimore, MD
* Metropolitan Washington DC includes Montgomery & Prince George's
    Counties, MD, and Northern Virginia

THOMAS GUIDE *DIGITALEDITION*™ (CD-ROM)

Tool Box *(NEW)* - Tool Box is a companion to any Thomas Guide *DigitalEdition*™ CD-ROM. It allows you to customize your maps and e-mail them to others with a full set of drawing tools, address locator, GPS interface, and query tools.

CALIFORNIA

State of California *(NEW)*

SOUTHERN CALIFORNIA

Los Angeles / Orange Counties
Los Angeles / Ventura Counties
Metropolitan Inland Empire
    (Coverage includes all of San Bernardino and Riverside,
    Eastern Los Angeles and Northeastern Orange Counties)
Santa Barbara / Ventura Counties

NORTHERN CALIFORNIA

Bay Area
    (Coverage includes Alameda, Contra Costa, Marin,
    San Francisco, San Mateo, and Santa Clara Counties)
Sacramento / Solano Counties

ARIZONA

Phoenix / Tucson, AZ *(NEW - available 9/2000)*

OREGON - WASHINGTON

Portland Metro Area, OR
Metropolitan Puget Sound, WA
    (Coverage includes all of King, Pierce, and Snohomish Counties)

NEVADA

Clark County

THOMAS GUIDE & *DIGITALEDITION*™ COMBO PACKS

Our Thomas Guide and Thomas Guide *DigitalEdition*™ sold together in one convenient package. Call for more information.

EXPRESS MAPS & EXPRESS WALL MAPS™

Affordable, high quality custom maps designed to your specifications. You select the coverage, choose black & white or full-color, optional ZIP & Census overlays. Lamination & mounting additional. Call for more information.

**For more information, or to order, please contact Customer Service at 1-800-899-6277 or
e-mail us at cust-serv@thomas.com or visit our web site at www.thomas.com**
Our Secure On-line Store is Now Open!

Information subject to change without notice